Fodor's

NEW ENGLAND

Welcome to New England

Whether you're skiing, hiking, or simply taking in a magnificent view, New England's distinctive sights and landscapes make it a classic American destination. Vermont's and New Hampshire's blazing fall foliage, Connecticut's Colonial towns, and Maine's rocky coast are just a few regional icons, as are the Gilded Age mansions in Newport, Rhode Island, and the stirring Revolutionary-era sites in Massachusetts. As you plan your trip, please confirm that places are still open and let us know when we need to make updates by writing to us at editors@fodors.com.

TOP REASONS TO GO

★ **Fall Foliage:** Scenic drives and walks reveal America's best festival of colors.

★ **History:** The Freedom Trail, Mystic Seaport, and more preserve a fascinating past.

★ **Small Towns:** A perfect day includes strolling a town green and locavore dining.

★ **The Coast:** Towering lighthouses and pristine beaches, plus whale-watching and sailing.

★ **Outdoor Fun:** Top draws are Acadia National Park, Cape Cod, and the Appalachian Trail.

★ **Regional Food:** Maine lobster and blueberries, Vermont maple syrup and cheese.

Contents

Fodor's Features

MAPS

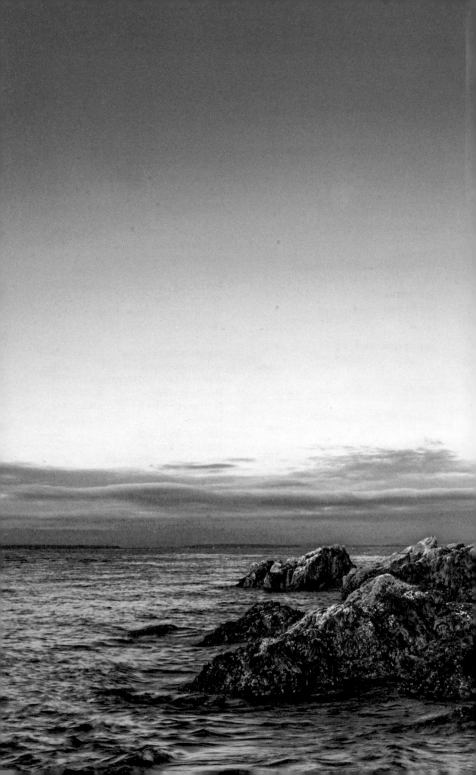

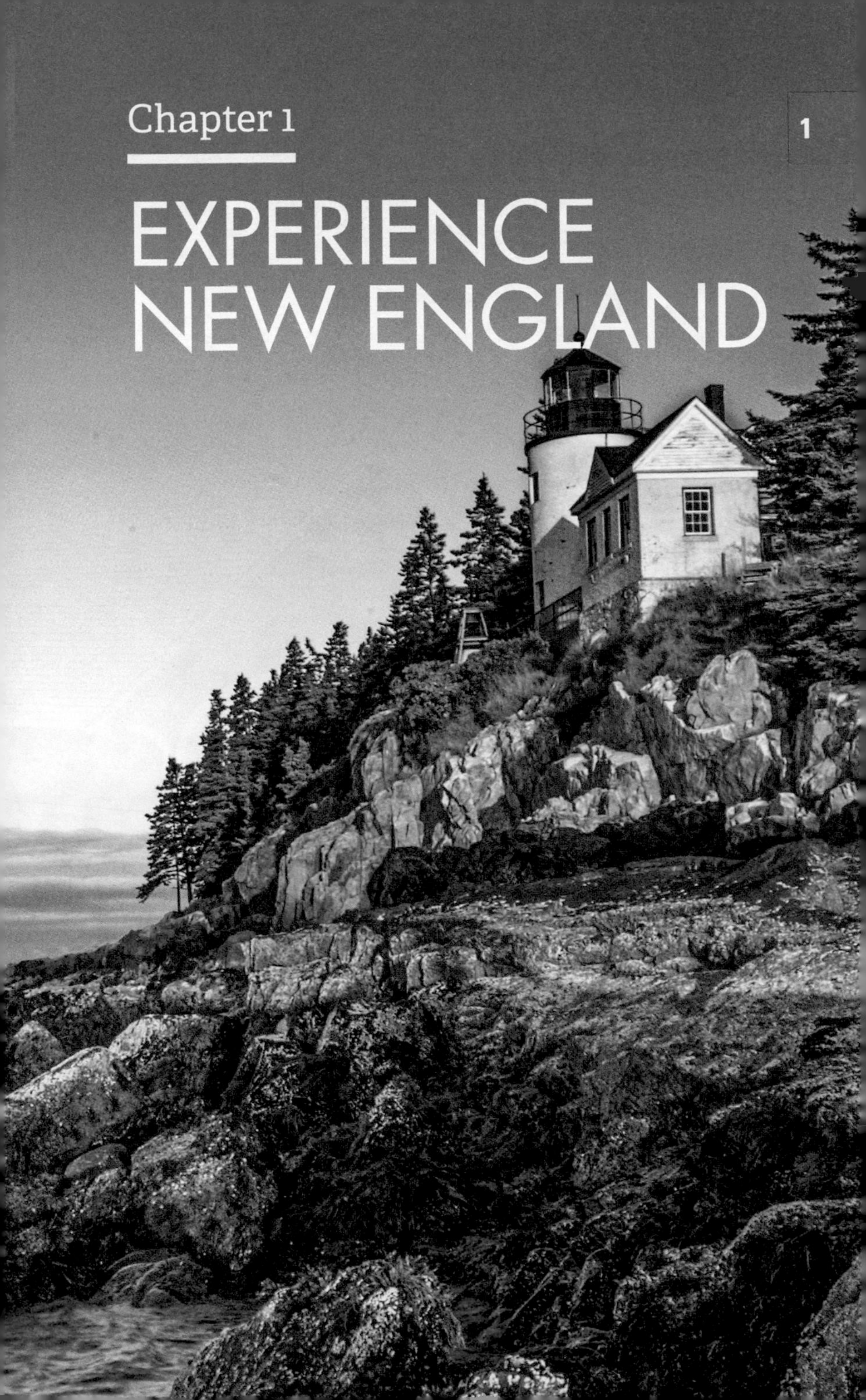

Chapter 1

EXPERIENCE NEW ENGLAND

26 ULTIMATE EXPERIENCES

New England offers terrific experiences that should be on every traveler's list. Here are Fodor's top picks for a memorable trip.

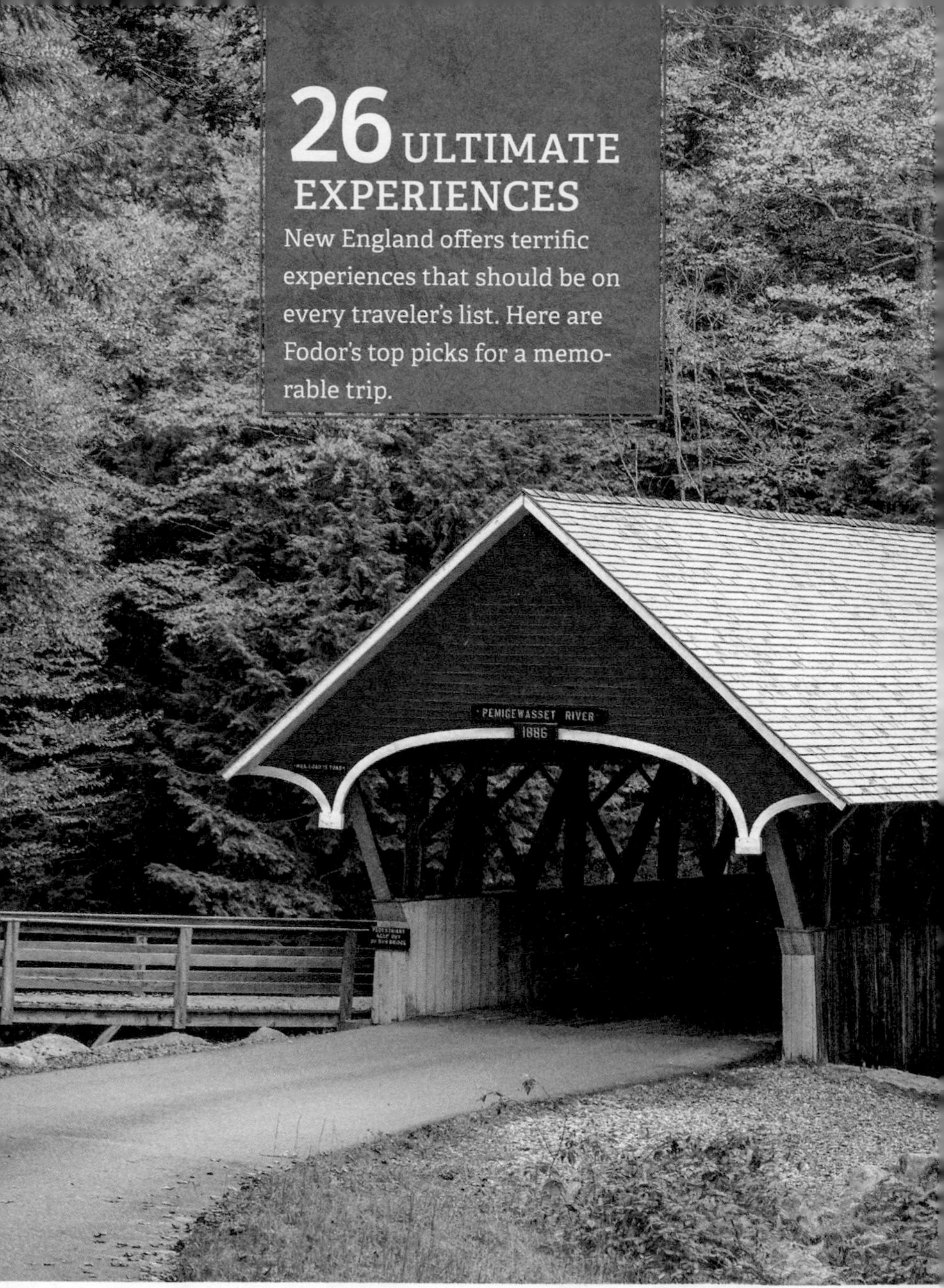

1 Count Covered Bridges

There are 54 of these American symbols still in use in New Hampshire. In fact, the Cornish-Windsor Bridge (1866) is New England's only covered bridge that connects two states, the country's longest wooden bridge, and the world's longest two-span covered bridge. (Ch. 10)

2 Drive Down to "P-town"

Provincetown (on the tip of Cape Cod) is full of inns, restaurants, shops, galleries, and nightlife. It's also one of the world's foremost LGBTQ vacation destinations. (Ch. 5)

3 Boating on Lake Champlain

The 107-mile-long lake is hugely popular for recreation—you can rent numerous types of vessels, take lessons, or, cruise aboard Spirit of Ethan Allen. (Ch. 9)

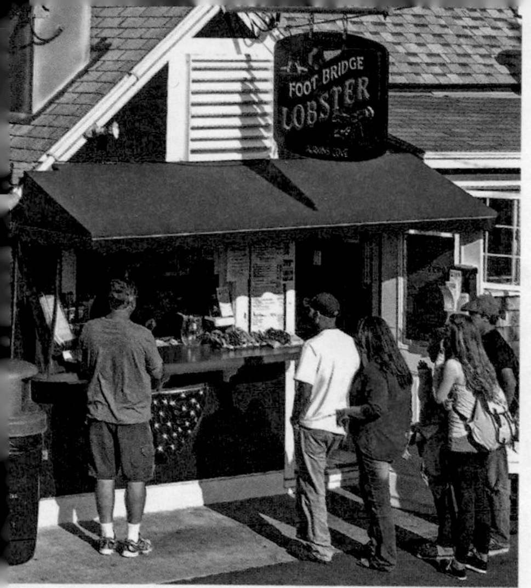

4 Have a Maine Lobster

A trip to Maine isn't complete without a meal featuring the official state crustacean. Whether it's a classic lobster dinner, a bowl of lobster stew, or a lobster roll, bring your appetite. (Ch. 12)

5 Visit the Ocean State

Known as "The Ocean State" for a reason, Rhode Island's south coast is replete with long strips of powdery white sand facing great swells of the Atlantic Ocean beckoning you to dive in. (Ch. 8)

6 Hike Mt. Monadnock

At 3,165 feet, Mt. Monadnock looms over southwestern New Hampshire. The only way to reach the summit is by foot, and the miles of trails attract well over 120,000 hikers each year. (Ch. 10)

7 Climb Aboard a Whaler at Mystic Seaport

More than 60 buildings fill this re-created 19th-century village, and a number of historic vessels including the Charles W. Morgan, the last of the wooden whaling ships. (Ch. 7)

8 Explore Acadia National Park

At New England's only national park, drive or bike the 27-mile Park Loop Road, climb the 1,530-foot summit of Cadillac Mountain, or explore miles of trails and carriage roads. (Ch. 13)

9 Dinosaurs in Connecticut

Check out Yale Peabody Museum's "Great Hall of Dinosaurs" before heading north to Rocky Hill and Dinosaur State Park—one of North America's largest dinosaur track sites. (Ch. 7)

10 Ferry Over to Block Island

Just 12 miles off Rhode Island's south coast, this laid-back island has 17 miles of sandy beaches, the 200-foot-high Mohegan Bluffs, the tranquil Great Salt Pond, and the charming town of New Shoreham. (Ch. 8)

11 Boating on Lake Winnipesaukee

At 182 miles around, you won't run out of space or adventures at New Hampshire's largest lake. Boats rentals are available to explore more than 250 islands, and there are numerous waterfront restaurants. (Ch. 10)

12 Vintage Steam Trains

The 12-mile round-trip journey along the picturesque Connecticut River will delight the whole family—particularly because the train's 1920s-era coaches are pulled by a vintage steam locomotive. (Ch. 7)

13 The Beautiful Berkshires

The "far west" of Massachusetts is green, mountainous, and scattered with interesting towns and villages tucked into pretty valleys. There are outdoor activities, artist enclaves, and excellent leaf-peeping. (Ch. 6)

14 Visit a Working Farm

Several Vermont farmers welcome visitors for a day, overnight, or a few days. Guests can help with chores like collecting eggs, milking cows, feeding sheep, picking veggies, or baking bread. (Ch. 9)

15 Historic and Hip Portland

Old Port has eclectic restaurants, boutiques, and high-end apartments, while the Arts District has the Portland Museum of Art. The Eastern Promenade has a 2-mile paved trail at the water's edge. (Ch. 12)

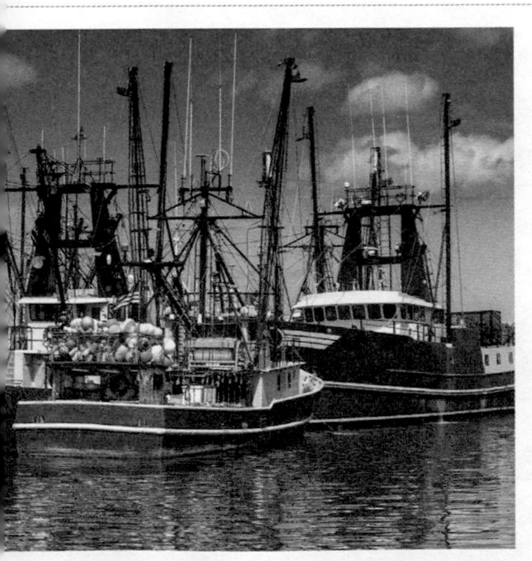

16 Whaling (and Lizzie Borden)

New Bedford was the world's most important whaling port in the 1800s. Visit the town's whaling museum, then tour the Lizzie Borden Bed & Breakfast—the "creep factor" is real. (Ch. 4)

17 Try Your Luck at a Mega-casino

Foxwoods and Mohegan Sun are 15 minutes apart in southeastern Connecticut. Both have slot machines, gaming tables, restaurants, shops, hotels, and a full schedule of events. (Ch. 7)

18 Ski Vermont

Snuggled in and around Vermont's Green Mountains are nearly two-dozen major ski resorts, including Sugarbush, Snow, Stratton, and Stowe. (Ch. 9)

19 Take a Walk Around Providence

Enjoy restaurants, beautiful Colonial homes, picturesque universities, the magnificent RISD Museum of Art, and, if your timing is right, the WaterFire celebration along the riverfront. (Ch. 8)

20 See How "the Other Half" Lived in Newport

America's wealthiest families summered here in the 19th century. Many of the mansions have been beautifully preserved and are open to the public for tours. (Ch. 8)

21 Cruise on a Windjammer

Pretty Camden Harbor and nearby Rockland are home ports for a fleet of owner-operated schooners that take guests on voyages around Maine's rugged coast, peninsulas, and islands. (Ch. 12)

22 Go Back in Time

Massachusetts has two living-history experiences worth exploring: Colonial and Native American life at Plimoth Patuxet Museums, and rural New England life at Old Sturbridge Village. (Ch. 4, 6)

23 Walk Boston's Freedom Trail

Boston's Freedom Trail is a 2½-mile-long marked path that links 16 historical landmarks, starting at the Boston Common and ending at the Bunker Hill Monument and USS Constitution. (Ch. 4)

24 Vermont Sugar Shacks

There are about 1,500 sugarhouses in Vermont. These shacks produce about 2.5 million gallons of syrup annually, or about half of all maple syrup consumed in the United States. (Ch. 9)

25 Wend Your Way Through the White Mountains

Mt. Washington (6,288 feet) is the highest peak in New Hampshire and the northeastern U.S. There are great views, but it's cold and windy even in midsummer. (Ch. 10)

26 Treat Yo'self at Ben & Jerry's

At the Ben & Jerry's Factory in Waterbury, take the half-hour guided factory tour to watch ice cream being made, then mosey over to the Scoop Shop for a treat. (Ch. 9)

WHAT'S WHERE

1 Boston. Massachusetts's capital is also New England's hub, where soaring skyscrapers cast shadows on Colonial graveyards.

2 Cape Cod, Nantucket, and Martha's Vineyard. Great beaches, delicious seafood, and artsy shopping districts fill scenic Cape Cod, chic Martha's Vineyard, and old-monied Nantucket.

3 The Berkshires and Western Massachusetts. The mountainous Berkshires live up to the storybook image of rural New England while supporting a thriving arts scene. To the east, the Pioneer Valley is home to a string of historic settlements.

4 Connecticut. The bustling southwest contrasts with the Quiet Corner in the northeast, known for its antique shops. Small villages line the southeastern coast, within reach of two casinos. The Connecticut River Valley and Litchfield Hills boast grand inns, rolling farmlands, and state parks.

5 Rhode Island. New England's smallest state has great sailing and glitzy mansions in

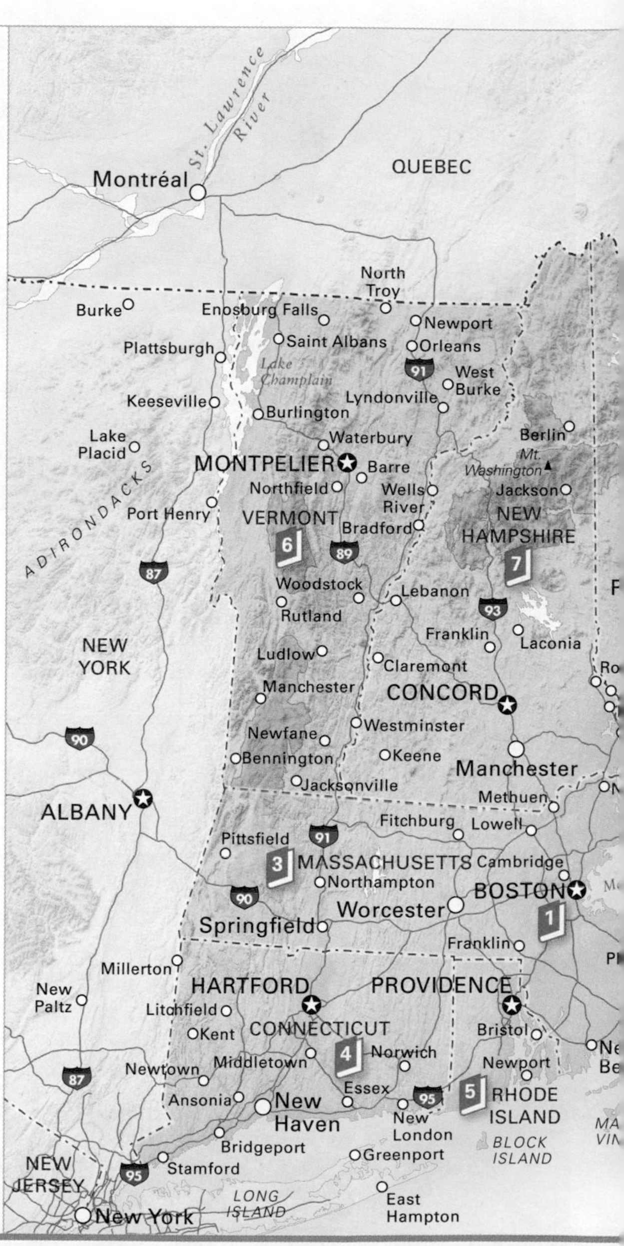

Newport. South County has quiet beaches and fertile countryside; scenic Block Island is a short ferry ride away.

6 Vermont. Vermont has farms, freshly starched towns and small cities, quiet country lanes, and bustling ski resorts.

7 New Hampshire. Portsmouth is the star of the state's 18-mile coastline. The Lakes Region is a popular summertime escape, and the White Mountains' dramatic vistas attract photographers and adventurous hikers farther north.

8 Inland Maine. The largest New England state's rugged interior—including the Western Lakes and vast North Woods regions—attracts skiers, hikers, campers, anglers, and other outdoors enthusiasts.

9 The Maine Coast. Classic villages, rocky shorelines, and picturesque Main Streets abound. Portland is a foodie town; Bar Harbor is the gateway town for Acadia National Park.

10 Acadia National Park. Majestic mountains meet the coast at New England's only national park; highlights include Cadillac Mountain and Jordan Pond.

New England's Best Seafood Shacks

BITE INTO MAINE, CAPE ELIZABETH, ME
Since 2008, this spot's been serving high-quality lobster rolls—locally sourced, never-frozen—no matter the season. The traditional lobster roll is one of the best, but the contemporary twists make the trip worth it, and the LBT (Lobster Bacon and Tomato) sandwich is sheer heaven.

ABBOTT'S LOBSTER IN THE ROUGH, NOANK, CT
Nestled on the banks of the storied Mystic River, Abbott's Lobster in the Rough has been serving delicious seafood dishes since 1947. Plan enough time to appreciate the view while enjoying the stuffed clams and pitch-perfect lobster rolls. And remember, the shack is BYOB.

CAPTAIN SCOTT'S LOBSTER DOCK, NEW LONDON, CT
Often touted as New London's best kept secret, Captain Scott's is a little off the beaten path, but it's worth it for the tasty Rhode Island Clam Chowder and piping hot clam fritters, not to mention a thick lobster bisque that will leave you swooning.

AUNT CARRIE'S, NARRAGANSETT, RI
Local lore states that this modest clam shack is where New Englanders first came up with the brilliant idea of frying fresh clams into cakes in the early 1920s. Since then, this joint has been serving up seafood, including traditional Rhode Island shore dinners—clam chowder, steamers, clam cakes, coleslaw, fried flounder, French fries, and sometimes a lobster.

THE LOBSTER SHACK, OGUNQUIT, ME
A fixture since 1947 in Ogunquit's bustling Perkins Cove, this cozy weathered shingle lobster pound is just across from the oft-photographed footbridge. Choose from a ¼- to a whopping 1-pound lobster roll, or try the delicious roll with handpicked Maine crab meat.

FIVE ISLANDS LOBSTER, GEORGETOWN, ME
Located on a lively working wharf overlooking Sheepscot Bay, this seafood spot welcomes hungry folks with its delicious seafood and stunning views. The family-friendly atmosphere extends to the menu, which also has options for diners not entirely keen on seafood.

ARNOLD'S LOBSTER & CLAM BAR, EASTHAM, MA
This legendary spot serves up generous portions of traditional fried and fresh seafood dishes along with hearty baked potatoes, a raw bar, and fresh salads. There's a kid-friendly menu, on-site minigolf, and an ice-cream stand.

CLAM BOX OF IPSWICH, IPSWICH, MA
Since 1938, this unmistakable saltbox shack—red-and-white-striped awnings and unique architectural shape—has been a go-to spot for locals and visitors alike. The fried clams are an institution, but you also can't go wrong with one of their seafood rolls or homemade coleslaw.

FLO'S CLAM SHACK AND DRIVE-IN, PORTSMOUTH, RI
The original Flo's Clam Shack got its start in 1936 when the owner set up shop in a chicken coop and began serving its signature fresh, juicy fried clams. Flo's has been wiped out by five massive hurricanes since then but somehow manages to keep on trucking, serving up the same heavenly seafood that keeps locals and visitors coming back.

BOB LOBSTER, NEWBURYPORT, MA
A trip to Plum Island isn't complete unless you grab a bite to eat at this local favorite, which got its start as a local seafood market. The menu always includes homemade seafood pies, creamy seafood chowders loaded with fresh meat, and to-die-for lobster mac-n-cheese.

Buy Local: Best New England Souvenirs

JAMS AND PRESERVES
Pick up strawberry preserves, apple butter, cranberry sauce, or blueberry jam at farmers' markets or country stores like Old Wethersfield (CT), Brown & Hopkins (RI), Wayside (MA), Old Country Store & Museum (NH), East Boothbay (ME), or the Vermont Country Store.

MOCCASINS
Maine shoemakers craft some of the best moccasins, and Quoddy, known for its custom, made-to-order moccasins, deck shoes, and boots, is one of the best. Reach out when you're Down East or back home; the wait for shoes is worth it. Ditto with Wassookeag, another great Maine maker of bespoke footwear.

CANVAS BAGS
Nothing says durability like canvas; nothing says coastal New England like sailing. Portland-based Sea Bags has creative, rope-handled totes made from recycled sails. Port Canvas in Kennebunkport, Maine, also hand-crafts sporty, customizable canvas totes and duffels—perfect for carrying souvenirs.

ANTIQUES AND COLLECTIBLES
Collectibles and antiques abound from cities like Boston (Charles Street), Providence (Wickenden Street), and Portland (Old Port District) to towns like Woodbury and Middlebury, CT; Chester, VT; Essex, MA; Littleton, NH; and Wells, ME. In May, July, and September, there's Massachusetts's Brimfield Antiques & Collectibles Show.

MAPLE SYRUP
Each spring, sugarhouses tap their maple trees and boil the resultant sap down into syrup. Although it takes about 40 gallons of sap to make 1 gallon of syrup, locally made varieties are readily available—Grades A and B and in light, medium, and dark (for baking only) shades of amber. The best-known states are New Hampshire and Vermont; the latter has a strict grading system.

TOYS

Vermont Teddy Bears are guaranteed for life; there's even a hospital for Teddy emergencies! Vermont's Real Good Toys makes finely crafted dollhouses and miniature accessories. New Hampshire's Annalee Dolls are distinctive, cute, and collectible—especially the holiday ones.

YARN AND KNITWEAR

The wares of independent spinners and knitters can be found throughout the region. Noteworthy companies include Bartlettyarns, Inc., which has been in Maine since 1821; Rhode Island's North Light Fibers; New Hampshire's Harrisville Designs, and Maine's Swans Island Company.

FLANNEL WOOLENS

New England's textile industry declined in the 1920s and '30s, but Vermont's Johnson Woolen Mills is still going strong. The warm, soft, and often boldly checked flannel shirts, jackets, capes, wraps, scarves, and hats sold in its factory store and elsewhere are splurge-worthy classics.

CRAFT BEER AND CIDER

New England has a long brewing history, but it's the region's newer, trendier operations that are most interesting like New Hampshire's Schilling Beer Co. and Vermont's Hill Farmstead Brewery. There's a small brewery (or cidery) in almost every city and small town. Notable cideries include Maine's Urban Farm Fermentory and Vermont's family-friendly Cold Hollow.

LOBSTER

Seafood markets, lobster pounds, and even some independent lobstermen sell lobster to-go. As soon as you buy them, you have 48 hours (max) to cook them, and lobsters must be kept sedated (i.e., lightly chilled) but alive, with claws rubber-banded, until then. Another option: ask about shipping or look into online pack-and-ship retailers like The Lobster Guy and Get Maine Lobster.

New England's Most Picturesque Towns

WOODSTOCK, VT
This quintessential Vermont town is ridiculously, wonderfully picturesque—classic covered bridges, local cheese makers, cider mills, working farms and orchards, sugar shacks, meandering brick streets, and a town center that is straight out of a Norman Rockwell painting.

KENT, CT
Located in the northwest corner of Connecticut, the historic town of Kent is a lively mix of art galleries, shops, and restaurants. There are also great outdoor destinations like Kent Falls State Park, home to the state's tallest waterfall, and the Appalachian Trail's longest river walk.

SIASCONSET, MA
This tiny Nantucket town gives visitors exactly what they want—sweeping panoramas of the Atlantic and Sankaty Head Light, rows of classic New England saltbox houses, delightfully overflowing gardens chock-full of beach peas and roses enclosed in white picket fences, and scenic coastal walks.

BRISTOL, RI
Tucked between Providence and Newport, this handsome seafaring town famous for having the nation's oldest 4th of July celebration offers breathtaking scenery and well-preserved, historic architecture, comprising picture-perfect Colonial, 19th-century, and Gilded Age buildings.

EASTPORT, ME
Most of Maine's visitors don't make it past the Mid-Coast, but Down East Maine is more than worth the hike, if only to pay a visit to Eastport, a picturesque seaside town with historic architecture situated on pristine Moose Island. A world apart, Eastport prides itself on its fishing and lobstering industries, excellent local arts scene, and vibrant Indigenous community.

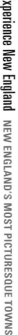

DAMARISCOTTA, ME
Just north of Wiscasset, this often overlooked village is surrounded by salt marsh preserves and oyster beds. The village's historic brick architecture and quaint but vibrant Main Street overlook the harbor where the annual and delightfully oddball Pumpkinfest and Regatta takes place.

NEWBURYPORT, MA
First settled by Europeans in 1635, this seaside town has immaculate redbrick streets and a vibrant working harbor that delivers that quintessential, New England feel. Classic seafood shacks, charming taverns with old-world flair, and a bevy of upscale specialty boutiques add to the charm.

CAMDEN, ME
With its brick architecture and Victorian mansions, Maine doesn't get any more picturesque than this village. Situated in the heart of the Mid-Coast, the charming town with its restaurants, galleries, and boutiques is surrounded by a working harbor that's dotted with windjammers.

ESSEX, CT
On the southwestern bank of the beautiful Connecticut River lies Essex, a quaint New England town scattered with cozy inns and taverns and historical architecture that are best explored on foot. With a picture-perfect harbor, a historic working steam train, and a delightfully eclectic cluster of buildings, Essex has a lot to offer in the way of small town charm.

JACKSON, NH
With a village green reached via a covered bridge and a slew of charming country inns, farm-to-table eateries, and ruggedly scenic trails for hiking and cross-country skiing, this peaceful hamlet lies in the heart of the White Mountains.

New England's Best Beaches

FOOTBRIDGE BEACH, OGUNQUIT, ME
This spot offers excellent swimming, beachcombing, and bodysurfing opportunities, as well as a boat launch for kayaks, small boats, and standup paddleboards. Typically less crowded than neighboring Ogunquit Beach, it's reached by crossing a footbridge that runs over the Ogunquit River.

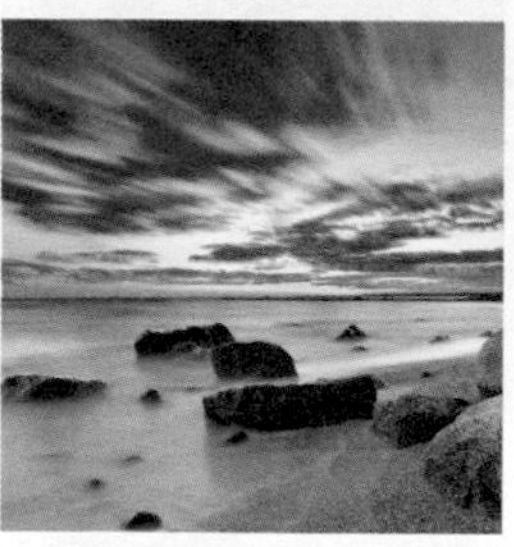

HAMMONASSET BEACH, MADISON, CT
At about 2 miles long, Connecticut's largest beach beckons day-trippers and campers to its shore for superb birding, swimming, and sandy strolls on the charming wooden boardwalk. There are also picnic spots, bike trails, great fishing, and the Meigs Point Nature Center.

EAST BEACH, MARTHA'S VINEYARD, MA
Between Cape Pogue Wildlife Refuge and Wasque Reservation on Chappaquiddick Island, East Beach—also known as Leland Beach—is popular for surf fishing. The half-mile beach is also excellent for birding, swimming, and peaceful sunset walks, but there's an entrance fee.

GOOSE ROCKS BEACH, KENNEBUNKPORT, ME
A wildly popular beach in warmer months and equally as beautiful in the off-season, Goose Rocks Beach is treasured for its long stretch of clean sand and close proximity to town. Parking can be tough in the high season and permits are required, but it's well worth the headache to get up early and snatch a spot for a glorious day in the sun at this picture-perfect beach.

WALLIS SANDS STATE BEACH, RYE, NH
This family-friendly swimmers' beach near Portsmouth has bright white sand, a picnic area, a store, and beautiful views of the Isles of Shoals.

EAST MATUNUCK STATE BEACH, SOUTH KINGSTOWN, RI
With well over 100 acres of sandy shoreline, this popular beach on Block Island Sound has everything you need for a perfect seaside outing with the whole family, including a beach pavilion with changing rooms, a concession stand, and a lifeguard tower.

SAND BAR STATE PARK, MILTON, VT
Vermont isn't known for its beaches, but its plethora of lakes means that there are actually quite a few beaches worth checking out. This 2,000-foot-long beach on Lake Champlain remains shallow well out from shore, making it a perfect spot for families with young kids.

Sand Beach, Acadia, ME

NAUSET LIGHT BEACH, EASTHAM, MA

Adjacent to Cape Cod National Seashore's Coast Guard Beach, this long, sandy beach is backed by tall dunes, frilly grass, and heathland. The trail to the Three Sisters lighthouses takes you through a pitch-pine forest. Parking fills up fast in the summer, so get here early or you may have to swim elsewhere.

SAND BEACH, ACADIA, ME

What this sandy beach lacks for in size is well compensated by its commanding view of the mountains and craggy shores that draw millions of people to Mount Desert Island each year. Several trail heads dot the beach and lead up the surrounding cliffs, where you'll be rewarded with spectacular panoramas of the shore and beach below.

RACE POINT BEACH, PROVINCETOWN, MA

Designated by President Kennedy as part of Cape Cod National Seashore in 1961, this sandy beach is known for its strong currents, which makes it great for surfers and serious swimmers. Its location on the Seashore's extreme northern side also makes it great for sunbathing.

MT. SUNAPEE STATE PARK, NEWBURY, NH

One of the prettiest and most relaxing of New Hampshire's many noteworthy freshwater beaches, this family-welcoming stretch of sand in the shadows of one of the state's favorite ski mountains is lovely for swimming, or renting kayaks, canoes, and standup paddleboards.

NORTH BEACH, BURLINGTON, VT

Lake Champlain's largest beach is also the only one with lifeguards during the summer. There's a grassy picnic area, a snack bar, and a playground, as well as kayak, canoe, and standup paddleboard rentals.

New England's Best Historical Sites

PORTLAND HEAD LIGHT, CAPE ELIZABETH, ME
Built in 1791, this 80-foot lighthouse is one of New England's most picturesque in any season. The keeper's quarters (operational 1891–1989) house a seasonally open museum and gift shop; surrounding Fort William Park, site of an army fort between 1872 and 1964, is open year-round.

MAINE MARITIME MUSEUM, BATH, ME
The museum's permanent exhibits cover it all from Bath Iron Works's role in building the nation's navy to a collection of more than 100 small wooden water crafts. In warmer months, board the 1906 schooner, the *Mary E.*, for sails with docents.

STRAWBERY BANKE, PORTSMOUTH, NH
Located in Portsmouth's historic district, the seasonal, 10-acre living-history complex has docents in period garb portraying merchants, artisans, and everyday folk, and more than 40 structures dating from the 17th to 20th centuries.

FREEDOM TRAIL, BOSTON, MA
The iconic, red-lined, 2½-mile trail features 16 historical sites, including the Old South Meeting House, where the Sons of Liberty organized their Tea Party, and Old North Church, where those two fateful lanterns were hung. Across the Charles River in Charlestown are the USS *Constitution* (aka Old Ironsides) and the Bunker Hill Monument.

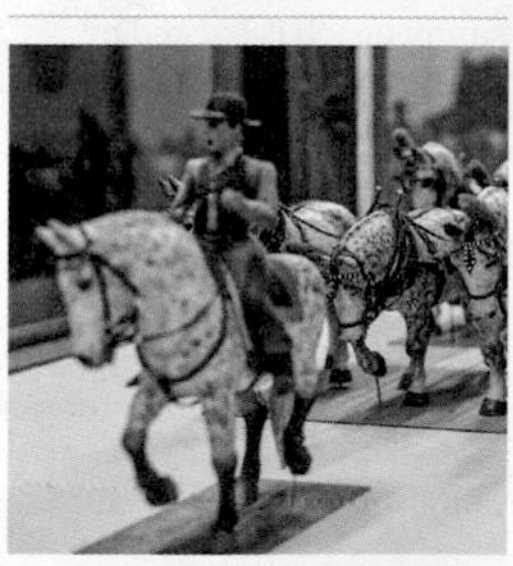

SHELBURNE MUSEUM, SHELBURNE, VT
Nothing says "Vermont" like a big red barn, and the museum has two really big, really red barns that house American fine, folk, and decorative art as well as vintage toys, hats, decoys, and firearms. There's a vintage carousel, miniature circus-parade figurines in the Circus Building, and more than 200 horse-drawn vehicles. There's even an old Lake Champlain steamship.

MYSTIC SEAPORT MUSEUM, MYSTIC, CT

The year-round Seaport Village contains sloops, schooners, tugboats, and other historic vessels that are open for tours, sails, and hands-on maritime experiences. Exhibits have intriguing seafaring themes and there's a planetarium. Don't miss the *Charles W. Morgan*, an 1841 whaling ship.

MARK TWAIN HOUSE AND MUSEUM, HARTFORD, CT

Twain penned classics such as *The Adventures of Tom Sawyer* and *A Connecticut Yankee in King Arthur's Court* here, and exhibits showcase the writer's storied life. If you have the time, plan a visit to the neighboring Harriet Beecher Stowe Center (combination tickets are available).

PLIMOTH PATUXET MUSEUMS, PLYMOUTH, MA

Reenactors portraying actual 1620s Plymouth Colony settlers tend to 17th-century village life, while a Patuxet homesite interprets the indigenous Wampanoag culture that has thrived here for centuries. The *Mayflower II* is a replica of the ship that carried the Pilgrims to the New World.

CLIFF WALK, NEWPORT, RI

The 3½-mile trail is hair-raising in spots, and the amazing views along either side are distracting, so wander with care. There are 10 mansions open to the public for touring, including the Italian Palazzo–style The Breakers; Rosecliff, modeled on a Versailles garden retreat; and The Elms, a French Chateau–style confection.

LEXINGTON AND CONCORD, MA

These two towns embody the American spirit. Minute Man National Historic Park, site of the first official Revolutionary War battle, is bookended by visitor centers in Lincoln, just outside Lexington, and Concord. In Concord, visit the Ralph Waldo Emerson House, Thoreau Farm, Walden Pond, or Orchard House, where Louisa May Alcott wrote *Little Women*.

Best Outdoor Activities

SKI VERMONT AND NEW HAMPSHIRE

Not far from the U.S.-Canadian border, some of New England's best ski slopes (and top-notch resorts) can be found in Vermont's Green Mountains (Jay Peak and Stowe) and New Hampshire's White Mountains (Bretton Woods and Cannon Mountain).

GO SAILING IN NEWPORT

One of the world's prime sailing capitals, Rhode Island's most famous port city is filled to the brim with rigs, including the America's Cup fleet. Numerous boats can be chartered for day trips or longer journeys, or you can try your hand at sailing a boat yourself.

FLY-FISHING ON THE HOUSATONIC RIVER

This pristine river rich with trout and bass curves through northwestern Connecticut's verdant Litchfield Hills, delighting both ardent and novice fly-fishing enthusiasts. In the quaint town of Cornwall, Housatonic River Outfitters offers lessons and guided fishing adventures.

PADDLE LAKE CHAMPLAIN

Best accessed from Burlington, you can rent a standup paddleboard or kayak to explore the lake while surrounded by majestic mountains covered in thick forests. Far from the crowds, you'll feel like nature is putting on a show just for you, especially during the Green Mountain State's stunning fall foliage season.

HIT THE LINKS IN MAINE AND NEW HAMPSHIRE

Coastal Maine and New Hampshire's mountains have some stunning, beautifully maintained golf courses that reward players with great challenges and magnificent scenery. The course at Rockport's Samoset Resort ranks among the best in the coastal New England, while Crotched Mountain in the Monadnocks and Waukewan near Lake Winnipesaukee are top courses in New Hampshire.

HIKE THE APPALACHIAN TRAIL

This is a bucket list item for hardcore trekkers, but tackling the entire length of America's most notorious hiking trail is a commitment. You can always explore some of its most scenic stretches, however, many of them set along the 161-mile leg through New Hampshire. Featuring more miles above treeline than any other state, this is one of the route's most challenging and rewarding sections, with steep inclines leading to stunning alpine tundra and breathtaking views.

Go on a Leaf Peeping Cycle Tour along the Stowe Bike Path, VT.

BOATING ON THE ALLAGASH WILDERNESS WATERWAY

The 92-mile-long series of rivers, streams, ponds, and lakes that comprises this northern Maine waterway ribbon their way through the delicate, tundralike landscape of the Northern Woods. The waterway remains fairly rustic with limited resources along the route, which seems to be one of the major reasons it attracts fans of canoeing and kayaking.

BIKING THE CAPE COD RAIL TRAIL

Passing through six Cape Cod towns, the Cape Cod Rail Trail covers 22 miles of paved trails. The reliably level terrain allows feasibly attainable long-distance excursions along the coastal landscape in a single day for all levels. During the winter months, exchange your wheels for skis to enjoy some of the Cape's best cross-country skiing.

TAKE A LEAF-PEEPING CYCLE TOUR

With its many nature preserves, green spaces, and hiking trails, Vermont shines in every season, but autumn may be its finest. You'd be hard-pressed to find a lovelier stroll through an autumnal Vermont landscape than in the charming village of Stowe, which is home to the Stowe Recreation Path, a paved, 5½-mile greenway that leads you to picture-perfect village and mountain views.

EXPLORE ACADIA NATIONAL PARK

Boasting around 160 miles of pristine coastal hiking trails and meandering carriage roads peppered with charming stone bridges, America's oldest national park east of the Mississippi River offers bountiful opportunities to experience Maine's raw, natural beauty.

New England with Kids

Throughout New England, there are kid-friendly hotels, restaurants, museums, beaches, parks, planetariums, and lighthouses. Favorite family vacation spots include Boston, Cape Cod, New Hampshire's White Mountains and Lakes Region, Mystic and southeastern Connecticut, and coastal Maine.

CAR SEATS

Each New England state has specific requirements regarding age and weight requirements for children in car seats and for whether you can smoke in a car with children as passengers. If you will need a car seat, make sure your rental-car agency has one or bring your own. Many airlines won't charge if you check your car seat, or there are numerous travel options like the Mifold or BubbleBum.

LODGING

New England has many family-oriented resorts with lively children's programs. Farms that accept guests can be great fun for children. Rental houses and apartments abound, particularly around ski areas and beaches. In the off-season, these can be especially economical, because most have kitchens—reducing your dependency on restaurant dining.

Most hotels in New England allow children under a certain age to stay in their parents' room at no extra charge, but others charge for them as extra adults; be sure to find out the cutoff age. Bed-and-breakfasts and historic inns are not always suitable for kids, and many flat-out refuse to accommodate them.

Most lodgings that welcome infants and small children will provide a crib or cot, but remember to provide notice so that one will be available for you. Many family resorts make special accommodations for small children during meals.

MASSACHUSETTS

Children's Museum, Boston. Make bubbles, climb through a maze, and while away the hours in this fun museum just for tykes in downtown Boston. A special play area for those under three lets them run around in a safe environment. There are seasonal festivals throughout the year.

Magic Wings Butterfly Conservatory & Gardens, Deerfield. Around 4,000 free-flying native and tropical butterflies are the star attraction here, contained within an 8,000-square-foot glassed enclosure that keeps the temperature upward of 80°F year-round. Relax around the Japanese koi pond on one of numerous benches and watch the kids chase the colorful creatures as they flit about. Or walk outside to the Iron Butterfly Outdoor Gardens, where flowers attract still more butterflies.

Massachusetts Audubon Wellfleet Bay Wildlife Sanctuary, South Wellfleet. With its numerous programs and its beautiful salt-marsh surroundings, this is a favorite stop for Cape vacationers year-round. Five miles of nature trails weave throughout the sanctuary's 1,100 acres of marsh, beach, and woods. If you're careful and quiet, you may be able to get close to sunbathing seals or birds like the great blue heron. Naturalists are on hand for guided walks and lectures.

Plimoth Patuxet Museums, Plymouth. Want to know what life was like for both Indigenous inhabitants and colonists from Europe in early America? A visit to these living-history museums is like stepping into a time machine and zooming back to the year 1627. Guides dress in period costume and share stories from the era.

CONNECTICUT

Connecticut Science Center, Hartford. With unique, high-quality, and highly interactive exhibits, this science center is a must. It's geared toward older kids, but there is a kids space for the under-seven set. There's also a 3D theater.

Dinosaur State Park, Rocky Hill. Dinosaur lovers can explore a 200-million year-old fossil trackway, take in interactive exhibits, and even cast a dinosaur footprint to take home.

Mystic Aquarium and Seaport Museum, Mystic. This aquarium is one of only a few North American facilities to feature endangered Steller sea lions; it's also home to New England's only beluga whale. You'll also see African penguins, harbor seals, graceful sea horses, Pacific octopuses, and sand tiger sharks—kids can even touch a cownose ray. Nearby Mystic Seaport is another great attraction for families.

RHODE ISLAND

Block Island. Hop on the ferry at Port Judith and head to Block Island for an easy and scenic bike ride or just to spend the day at one of its many gorgeous, and often uncrowded, beaches.

Providence Children's Museum. Aimed at children up to around age 10, PCM explores arts, culture, history, and science. Exhibits are based on the developmental needs of children and embrace a wide range of learning styles.

Roger Williams Park Zoo, Providence. Home to more than 150 species of animals from around the world, Roger Williams Park has more than 40 acres to explore. One highlight is Marco Polo's Adventure Trek, with takins, moon bears, snow leopards, red crowned cranes, and red pandas. Look for interactive educational programs.

VERMONT

ECHO, Leahy Center for Lake Champlain, Burlington. Lots of activities and hands-on exhibits make learning about the geology and ecology of Lake Champlain an engaging experience.

Montshire Museum of Science, Norwich. This interactive museum uses more than 150 hands-on exhibits to explore nature and technology. The building sits amid 110 acres of nature trails and woodlands, where live animals roam freely.

Shelburne Farms, Shelburne. This working dairy farm is also an educational and cultural resource center. Visitors can watch artisans make the farm's famous cheddar cheese from the milk of more than 100 purebred and registered Brown Swiss cows. A children's farmyard and walking trails round out the experience.

NEW HAMPSHIRE

Lost River Gorge and Whale's Tale Waterpark, Lincoln and North Woodstock. Kids can scramble through boulder caves in Lost River Gorge, and float on inner tubes and bodysurf in a giant wave pool at one of New England's biggest water parks. More family fun is nearby at Franconia Notch State Park.

Lake Winnipesaukee, Weirs Beach. The largest lake in the state, Lake Winnipesaukee provides plenty of family-friendly fun. Base yourself in the Laconia community of Weirs Beach, where kids can swim, play arcade games, cruise the lake, take a scenic railroad along the shoreline, and even see a drive-in movie.

SEE Science Center, Manchester. For kids who love LEGO, the models of old Manchester and the millyard are sure to impress. There are also rotating exhibits and science demonstrations.

MAINE

Acadia National Park, Mount Desert Island. Head out on a whale- and puffin-watching trip from Bar Harbor, drive up scenic Cadillac Mountain, swim at Echo Lake Beach, hike one of the many easy trails, and don't forget to sample some wild blueberry pie.

Coastal Maine Botanical Gardens, Boothbay. The "children's garden" is a wonderland of stone sculptures, rope bridges, small teahouse-like structures with grass roofs, and even a hedge maze. Children and adults alike adore the separate woodland fairy area.

Maine Narrow Gauge Railroad Museum, Portland. For train fans, check out the scenic rides on these narrow-gauge trains. In the winter, they have Polar Express theme trips.

New England Today

THE PEOPLE

The idea of the self-reliant, thrifty, and often stoic New England Yankee has taken on almost mythic proportions in American folklore, but in some parts of New England—especially in rural Maine, New Hampshire, and Vermont—there still is some truth to this image. It makes sense—you need to be independent if you farm an isolated field, live in the middle of a remote forest, or work a fishing boat miles off the coast. As in any part of the country, there are stark differences between the city mice and the country mice of New England. Both, however, are usually knowledgeable and fiercely proud of the region, its rugged beauty, and its contributions to the nation.

NEW ENGLAND AND COVID-19

New England—like the rest of the world—was gravely impacted by COVID-19. Most of the restaurants, hotels, shops, bars, and cultural institutions that were forced to close have resumed normal services by the time of this writing. But if you're planning a visit, be sure to call ahead to verify hours and to make sure the property is open.

CONNECTICUT

Connecticut has long been a melting pot, attracting immigrants who landed in New York or Boston and then sought work outside the city or simply yearned for life in the "country." Longtime Connecticut Yankees, celebrated authors and artists, and successful businesspeople blend easily with continuing generations of immigrants. Their hard work has contributed to the state having the nation's highest per-capita income (as of 2022). The founders saw "The Constitution State" as the model for our national government. Today's Connecticut voters generally vote Democratic for national offices but fluctuate between the parties for state and municipal officeholders, albeit with a decided blue lean over the past 20 years. Small manufacturers and defense contractors have been mainstays of Connecticut's economy since colonial days, supplying brass buttons for Revolutionary War and Civil War uniforms and Colt 45s to tame the Wild West. Today's workers build airplane engines, helicopters, and submarines. In between, bright minds came up with the cotton gin, the Erector Set, and the Frisbee.

MASSACHUSETTS

The Commonwealth of Massachusetts, New England's most populous state, is sometimes seen only through the lens of its capital city, Boston, which is home to the majority of the state's population. As a whole, the majority blue state is doing well. Since 2000, it's enjoyed the lowest unemployment rate in New England, and one that's better than the national average, though the cost of living, especially in Greater Boston, is among the highest in the nation. Boston-centric though it may be, the state does have its own very distinct regional identities, especially tourism-driven and ocean-minded Cape Cod and the islands and also the quieter, rural, and artsy western side of the state, which includes the Berkshires and the Pioneer Valley.

MAINE

In recent decades, Maine's Congressional delegation has hovered around 50–50—half Democrat and Republican, and half male and female, which somewhat resembles the makeup of the state. Voters legalized recreational marijuana in 2016, and the state now has nearly 100 retail pot shops. Since 2000, Somali immigration has generated both tensions and welcome cultural diversity in Lewiston and Portland. As paper mills shutter, farming is on the upswing, while the billion-dollar tourism industry struggles to find enough workers yet fuels rising real estate prices and rents in popular destinations.

NEW HAMPSHIRE

With its state motto of "Live Free or Die" and a long-running political reputation as one of the nation's swingiest—albeit *slightly* left of center—states, New Hampshire marches to its own drummer. The fifth smallest—and 10th least populous—state in America maintains a fierce libertarian streak, collects neither sales tax nor income tax, and each presidential year holds the country's first primary (at least as of this writing—Nevada has made a bid to hold its primary earlier in 2024). Like the rest of northern New England, ruggedly mountainous New Hampshire is characterized by a mostly rural, heavily wooded topography that gives way to more densely populated small cities and suburbs only in its southeastern corner. Relatively prosperous, with the eighth-highest median household income in the country, New Hampshire has also enjoyed slow but steady growth in recent years, lagging behind only Massachusetts in population growth since 2010 among New England's six states.

RHODE ISLAND

It may be one of the smallest states, but Rhode Island is the country's second most densely populated. Providence, the capital city, is a college town with a youthful vibe. To the north, descendants of French Canadian, Italian, and Irish workers who arrived during the birth of the American Industrial Revolution populate the cities and towns. Democrats have held sway over Rhode Island politics since the 1930s with a few notable exceptions. The revered Senator Claiborne Pell and John Chafee were Republicans, for example, as was Mayor "Buddy" Cianci of Providence, who was convicted on RICO charges and served four years in prison. Rhode Island was the birthplace of the American Industrial Revolution, and manufacturing has always been the predominant influence on the state's economy. Jewelry, silverware, machinery, and textiles have always been important local products, and Galilee continues to be a busy commercial fishing port.

VERMONT

Few states are more proud of its rugged, independent, and liberal spirit than Vermont. From Ethan Allen to Bernie Sanders, Vermonters have never been afraid to follow a different drumbeat and be outspoken about it. This is perhaps never more on display than in the state's long-standing protection of the environment that borders on obsession. It's one of only four states than ban billboards (Maine is the only other in New England), and strict regulations on land use and development makes many towns and villages appear as if pulled from Norman Rockwell paintings. During fall, the peak tourist season, the landscape literally takes your breath away with an array of fiery reds, golds, oranges, and bronze bursting from the hills and valleys. Cities are few and far between, with Burlington topping out at just 45,200 people, but a robust cultural and arts scene thrives throughout the state, thanks to the abundance of colleges, collectives, and individual artists that continually draw inspiration from the Vermont spirit and beauty. Locals and tourists do the same on the ski slopes, hiking trails, bike paths, and swimming holes, and there's plenty for all.

Indigenous Experiences

The area that now falls within the borders of New England's six states has been inhabited continuously by Indigenous tribes for at least 12,000 years. Among the tribes that have thrived here, the Abenaki, Penobscot, Passamaquoddy, Maliseet, Mi'qmaq, Wampanoag, Narragansett, Pequot, Mohegan, and Ojibwe have had an especially significant presence. These are some of the region's best places to learn about and interact with Indigenous culture.

CONNECTICUT

Institute for American Indian Studies, Washington. Walk through a re-created Algonquian Village and browse artwork in the on-site gallery of some of the nation's top Native American artists at this small but superb museum in the Litchfield Hills.

Mashantucket Pequot Museum and Research Center, Ledyard. Located near the tribally owned Foxwoods Casino, this is one of the world's foremost museums devoted to Indigenous culture.

MAINE

Abbe Museum, Bar Harbor. Stop by this outstanding Smithsonian-affiliated museum in downtown Bar Harbor to learn about Maine's rich Native American heritage.

Outdoor Heritage Museum, Oquossoc. Although devoted first and foremost to recreation in northern Maine's woodsy Rangeley Lakes region, this terrific museum also contains extensive holdings of Native American birch-bark canoes and other Indigenous artifacts.

MASSACHUSETTS

Aquinnah Cliffs, Martha's Vineyard. Located on the Wampanoag Reservation on one of the East Coast's most storied islands, this dramatic wall of red-clay cliffs is beautiful to walk along, and you can buy food and crafts from Native American vendors in the parking area.

Peabody Museum of Archaeology & Ethnology, Cambridge. On the regal campus of Harvard University, the Peabody contains one of the world's most important collections of artifacts related to Indigenous culture, with the Hall of the North American Indian a must-see.

Plimoth Patuxet Museums, Plymouth. Established as Plimoth Plantation with the aim of interpreting the lives of the European pilgrims who settled here in 1620, this renowned living history museum also preserves and interprets a Wampanoag homesite where visitors can learn about the Indigenous people who inhabited this land for many centuries before *The Mayflower* arrived.

NEW HAMPSHIRE

Mt. Kearsarge Indian Museum, Warner. At this excellent museum that's on the scenic road leading to the soaring mountain for which it's named, admire the impressive collection of traditional crafts, artwork, and historical exhibits from tribes throughout the United States.

Strawbery Banke Museum, Portsmouth. The outstanding "People of the Dawn" exhibit here at one of New England's premier living history museums tells the story of the Abenaki people, who have thrived in the region for more than 12,000 years.

RHODE ISLAND

Tomaquag Museum, Exeter. Devoted to Native history and culture, the museum contains crafts, artifacts, and photos related primarily to the Narragansett, Niantic, and Wampanoag tribes.

VERMONT

ECHO Leahy Center for Lake Champlain, Burlington. The museum's excellent "Indigenous Expressions" exhibit provides an in-depth look at the thousands of years of Native American history and community in Vermont.

Chapter 2

TRAVEL SMART

Updated by
Andrew Collins

★ CAPITALS
Hartford, CT; Augusta, ME; Boston, MA; Concord, NH; Providence, RI; Montpelier, VT

POPULATION
15,116,205

LANGUAGE
English

$ CURRENCY
U.S. Dollar

AREA CODES
CT: 203, 475, 860, 959; ME: 207; MA: 339, 351, 413, 508, 617, 774, 781, 857, 978; NH: 603; RI: 401; VT: 802

⚠ EMERGENCIES
911

DRIVING
On the right

ELECTRICITY
120–240 v/60 cycles; plugs have two or three rectangular prongs

TIME
Eastern Time (same as New York)

WEB RESOURCES
www.visitnewengland.com, newengland.com/category/travel

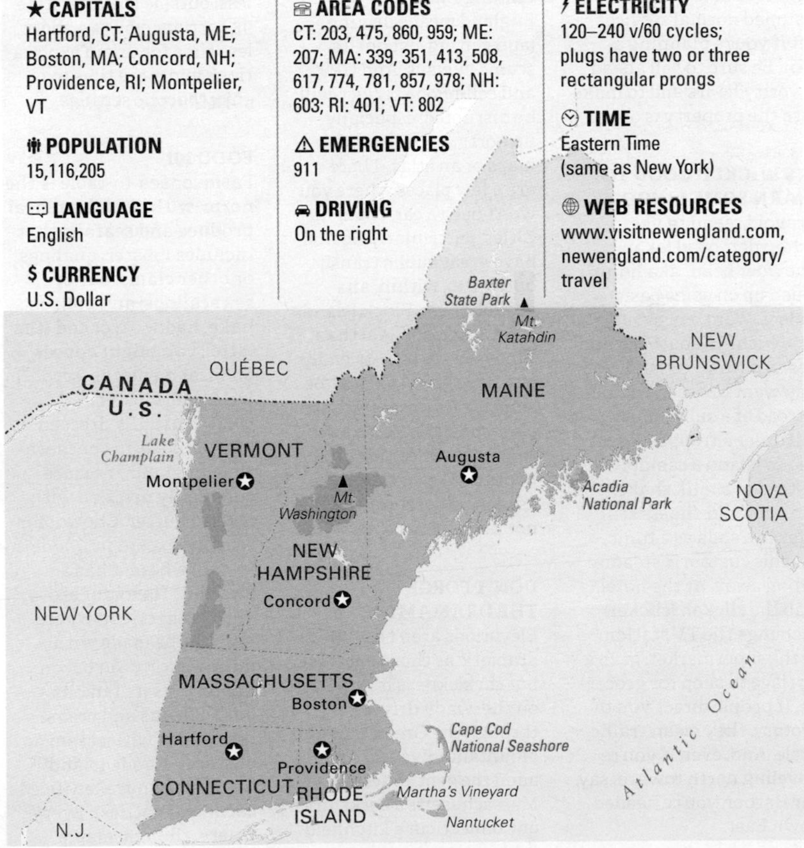

Know Before You Go

New England has its share of regional character, color, and flavor—not to mention a few geographical and seasonal challenges. Here are some tips that will enrich your trip and ease your travels.

COVID-19

New England—like the rest of the world—was gravely impacted by COVID-19. Most of the restaurants, hotels, shops, bars, and cultural institutions that were forced to close have resumed normal services, but if you're planning a visit, be sure to call ahead to verify hours and to make sure the property is open.

IT'S WICKED GOOD TO LEARN SOME LINGO

To avoid seeming like a chowdah-head (aka "chowder head" aka "idiot"), brush up on some basic dialect. Want a big, long sandwich? In southern and western New England, you may want to order a grinder instead of a sub. Some locals will order a frappe—or in Rhode Island a cabinet—instead of a milk shake, and a few old-timers still refer to a soda as a tonic, but this custom is steadily fading away. At the hotel, grab the clickah (clicker) to change the TV station. At the supermarket, grab a carriage to shop for groceries. If people direct you to a rotary, they mean traffic circle. And, even if you're traveling north toward, say, Bar Harbor, you're headed Down East.

YOU CAN'T ALWAYS GET THEAH FROM HEAH

As this famous regional saying implies, the shortest distance between two points isn't always a straight—or single—line. Finding the real New England means driving (and getting lost on) its scenic byways. And GPS and cell-phone service will be disrupted, especially up north, so pack road maps or an atlas. There are a few places where you won't need a car, though. Cities, particularly Boston, have great public transit options to, within, and around them. Block Island, Nantucket, and Martha's Vineyard are bike-friendly and have good taxi and/or shuttle services. In Acadia National Park, you'll have to trade your car for hiking boots, a bike, or a carriage (an actual horse and buggy, not a shopping cart).

DON'T FORGET THE DRAMAMINE

Elevations aren't as dramatic as those out west, but car sickness is possible on the windy drives through the Green or White Mountains. Even south, amid the gentler terrain of Massachusetts's Berkshires or Connecticut's Litchfield Hills, roads ribbon up, down, and around—just as they do along rugged, often precipitous stretches of Atlantic coast.

EVEN THE CITIES ARE RELATIVELY SMALL

Boston, the region's largest city, has just less than 700,000 residents; the next biggest, Worcester, Massachusetts, has about 211,000, which is about 18,000 more than Providence. Still, most cities have thriving cultural scenes; several are major university towns (New Haven, Providence, Burlington) and/or are steeped in history (Portland). Regardless, outside the Interstate 95 corridor, you can allow less time for urban explorations and more time to enjoy bucolic settings.

FOOD 101

Farm- or sea-to-table is the norm, with abundant local produce and seafood that includes lobster; quahogs or other clams; bay or sea scallops; and pollack, hake, haddock, or cod (the latter two might appear on local menus as "scrod"). In Maine, lobster-roll meat is usually dressed in mayonnaise; in southern New England, it's more commonly drizzled with melted butter. Chowder is creamy, except in Rhode Island, where it has a clear but flavorful broth, and Connecticut, where it might be made with milk and contain bacon. Boston has its famous baked beans and cream pies (made with cream or custard); Rhode Island has its johnnycakes (fried cornmeal patties). Everywhere, though, maple syrup adorns shaved ice (or snow!) and ice cream as well as pancakes; breakfast home fries are griddled and seasoned just so; and craft beer and cider pair well with boiled dinners and Yankee pot roast. Be sure to try a Moxie, an "energizing," regionally unique soft drink.

IN THE LAND OF THE COUNTRY INN, IT'S BEST TO BOOK AHEAD
Although there are abundant chain hotels and several large, notable Victorians—seaside and near the slopes—smaller inns, often historical and privately owned, are among the best lodgings. Although the growth of Airbnb has made it easier to find rooms in charming old homes, it's still prudent to book well ahead, especially during peak seasons, when there might also be a two- or three-night minimum. And "peak seasons" vary. Leaf-peeping season is roughly late September to mid-October in Maine, New Hampshire, and Vermont and mid- to late October in Connecticut, Massachusetts, and Rhode Island. In the southern ski areas, the season runs December through March; up north it might be November through April or even May.

THE ATLANTIC IS COLD UP HERE
Even in late August, ocean temperatures off Maine and New Hampshire only climb to the upper 50s or lower 60s—still limb-numbingly chilly. Wet suits (and water shoes for rockier shores) are musts. Temperatures are warmer near Boston and points south, where the Atlantic's summer highs are in the mid-60s to mid- to upper 70s. Obviously, the farther north you go, the shorter the beach season, with some properties reducing their hours or shuttering entirely between Labor Day and Memorial Day or July 4.

WHEN IT COMES TO PARKS, THE STATES HAVE 'EM
Although much of New England is woodsy, the entire region has only one national park (Acadia) and two national forests (Green Mountain and White Mountain). That said, there are plenty of opportunities to hike, canoe, kayak, mountain bike, camp, and otherwise embrace the outdoors in the plethora of park or recreation and wilderness areas overseen by each state.

SOME OF THE BUGS BITE
First, it's the black flies, whose bites leave red, itchy welts. May is the prime season, and it's particularly notorious in the three northern states. Then, in July, it's the deer flies. Summer also sees greenhead flies (aka saltmarsh greenheads) in some coastal areas. On hikes, use insect repellent and wear clothing that covers your arms and legs. And don't forget to check for ticks. The disease they're known to carry was named after a New England town: Lyme, Connecticut.

THE PEOPLE ARE WARM AND WELCOMING
The idea of the self-reliant, thrifty, and often stoic New England Yankee has taken on almost mythic proportions in American folklore, but in some parts of New England— especially in rural Maine, New Hampshire, and Vermont—there still is some truth to this image, which shouldn't come as a surprise. You need to be independent if you farm an isolated field, live in the middle of a vast forest, or work a fishing boat miles off the coast. As in any part of the country, there are stark differences between the city mice and the country mice of New England. Both, however, are usually knowledgeable and fiercely proud of the region, its rugged beauty, and its contributions to the nation.

SPORTS IS A RELIGION
This is Sox and Pats country. New England fans—with the exception of those in southwestern Connecticut, who are just as likely to root for New York teams—follow Massachusetts's sports teams as if they were their own. Boston is home to three of the region's four major sports teams—Red Sox baseball, Bruins hockey, and Celtics basketball. The New England Patriots (football) play nearby in the small suburb of Foxboro. The city is also home to the Boston Marathon, New England's largest sporting event and the world's oldest annual marathon.

Getting Here and Around

Boston, New England's largest and most cosmopolitan city, is also the region's major transportation and cultural center. Secondary hubs include Hartford, Connecticut, and Portland, Maine. Your best bet for exploring widely is to travel by car, as driving distances between most locations and attractions are short. Amtrak has frequent train service between New York and Boston, with stops in towns and cities in Connecticut (including Hartford) and Rhode Island (including Providence). Commuter rail service is available in Massachusetts, Connecticut, and Rhode Island. Public transportation is the best way to get around Boston, as driving and parking in the city can be a nightmare. Passenger ferry service is available to outlying islands, including lakes (some vessels accommodate vehicles).

See the Getting Here and Around section at the beginning of each chapter for more transportation information.

Air

Most travelers visiting New England use a major gateway, such as Boston, Providence, Hartford/Springfield, Manchester, or even New York City or Albany, and then rent a car to explore the region. The New England states form a fairly compact region, with few important destinations more than six hours apart by car. It's costly and generally impractical to fly within New England, the exceptions being the island resort destinations of Martha's Vineyard and Nantucket in Massachusetts and Block Island in Rhode Island, which have regular air service from Boston and a few regional airports.

Boston's Logan Airport is one of the nation's most important domestic and international airports, with direct flights arriving from all over North America and abroad. New England's other major airports receive few international flights (mostly from Canada) but offer many direct domestic flights from East Coast and Midwest destinations and, to a lesser extent, from the western United States. Some sample flying times to Boston are: 2½ hours from Chicago, 6½ hours from London, and 6 hours from Los Angeles. Times from other U.S. cities are similar, if slightly shorter, to Albany and Hartford, assuming you can find direct flights.

AIRPORTS

The main gateway to New England is Boston's Logan International Airport (BOS). Bradley International Airport (BDL), in Windsor Locks, Connecticut (12 miles north of Hartford), is convenient to Western Massachusetts and much of Connecticut. T.F. Green International Airport (PVD), just outside Providence, Rhode Island, and Manchester-Boston Regional Airport (MHT), in New Hampshire, are other major airports—and alternative approaches to Boston, which is a one-hour drive from each. Additional New England airports served by major carriers include Portland International Jetport (PWM) in Maine and Burlington International Airport (BTV) in Vermont.

Other convenient airports are Albany International Airport (ALB) in Albany, New York, near Western Massachusetts and Vermont; Westchester County Airport (HPN) in White Plains, New York, near Southern Connecticut; Bangor International Airport (BGR) in Bangor, Maine; and Cape Cod Gateway Airport (HYA) in Hyannis, Massachusetts. You can access Nantucket and Martha's Vineyard via ferries from Hyannis or fly directly to each island's airport.

FLIGHTS

The three major U.S. legacy airlines, along with Frontier, JetBlue, and Southwest, have scheduled flights to—with just some occasional exceptions—the airports in Albany, Boston, Hartford, Manchester, Portland, Providence, and Westchester County. Alaska, Allegiant, Boutique Air, Hawaiian, Spirit, and Sun Country fly into Boston. Cape Air, a regional carrier, serves mostly smaller New England airports in Maine, New Hampshire, Vermont, and Massachusetts—including those on Cape Cod and the islands. New England Airlines serves Block Island with regularly scheduled flights to and from Westerly, Rhode Island.

Travel Times from Boston to:	By Air	By Car
Acadia National Park (ME)	1 hour	5 hours
Burlington, VT	No direct flight	3½ hours
Hartford, CT	No direct flight	1¾ hours
New York, NY	¾–1 hour	4 hours
Portland, ME	No direct flight	2 hours
Providence, RI	No direct flight	1 hour
Provincetown, MA	½ hour	2¼ hours

Boat

Several ferry companies offer service to Martha's Vineyard and Nantucket from Cape Cod and elsewhere. Other ferry routes in New England connect Boston with Provincetown, Providence with Newport, Newport and Point Judith with Block Island, and Connecticut with Block Island and New York's Long Island. In Maine, ferries provide access to islands off the coast of Portland in Casco Bay and from Bar Harbor to Yarmouth, Nova Scotia. And ferries also cross Lake Champlain between Vermont and upstate New York. With the exception of the Lake Champlain ferries—which are first-come, first-served—reservations are advisable for cars.

Bus

With extremely low fares, FlixBus buses equipped with Wi-Fi and electrical outlets connect Boston, Providence, Hartford, and New Haven with New York, Washington, D.C., and other Mid-Atlantic cities. Megabus also offers low fares, and its buses (also with Wi-Fi) serve New York City and many other points on the East Coast.

Once in New England, regional bus service is relatively extensive, especially in southern New England, but although it's often useful for getting between key points, it's generally impractical if you're exploring rural areas. That said, it can be a handy and affordable means of getting around, as buses travel many routes that trains do not, including to Logan and other key airports. Concord Coach buses connect Boston with several cities in New Hampshire and Maine; the company also operates a route between New York City and Portland. Dartmouth Coach runs buses from both Boston and New York City to Hanover and Lebanon, in New Hampshire's Upper Valley. C&J buses (with Wi-Fi) serve Dover (near Durham) and Portsmouth, New Hampshire, Ogunquit, Maine, and Newburyport, Massachusetts; C&J also provides service to New York City. Both Concord and C&J leave from Boston's South Station, which is connected to the Amtrak rail station, and from Logan Airport.

Getting Here and Around

 Car

New England is best explored by car. Inland, especially in northwestern Connecticut, western Massachusetts, Vermont, New Hampshire, and Maine, public transportation options are limited; a car is essential. Coastal areas can get congested in summer, especially the roads to and from Cape Cod. Cars are a nuisance in Boston; street parking can be hard to find and hotel parking often costs a fortune. It can also be hard to find public parking in Providence and near the beach in many resort towns along the coast. Interstate 95 enters New England at the New York border, follows the Connecticut shoreline, and then heads north to Providence, Boston, and Portland before ending at the Canadian border in Calais, Maine. Interstate 90, the Massachusetts Turnpike, is a toll road that goes across the state from the New York border (near Albany) to Boston. If you rent a car at Logan International Airport, allow plenty of time to return it—as much as an hour to be on the safe side. Other major highways traverse the region, including Interstate 84 (across Connecticut and part of Massachusetts), Interstate 91 (north New Haven through Massachusetts and Vermont to Canada), Interstate 93 (north from Boston through New Hampshire to Canada), and Interstate 89 (north from Concord, New Hampshire through Vermont to Canada).

GASOLINE

Gas stations are easy to find along major highways and in most communities throughout the region, but beware that in rural parts of northern New England, it's possible even on numbered routes to go 30 miles or more between stations—it's best to keep your tank at least a quarter full at all times in these areas. Gas prices are relatively similar across New England, though a bit lower in the northern states, and often highest in city centers or remote small towns. Virtually all have self-serve pumps that accept credit or debit cards.

PARKING

In Boston and other large cities, finding a parking space on the street can be time-consuming and nerve-wracking. Your best bet is to park in a garage, but rates in Boston can top $50 and run $20 to $35 in other New England cities. You can often find the best deals on apps like SpotHero and ParkWhiz. In smaller cities, street parking is usually simpler, though parking garages are still convenient and, for the most part, reasonably priced. Pay attention to signs: some cities allow only residents to park on certain streets or limit street parking in winter to allow for snow removal. In most small towns, parking is not a problem—though some beach and lake parking areas are reserved for those with resident stickers.

CAR RENTAL

A car is the most practical way to get around New England. Major airports serving the region all have on-site car-rental agencies. A few train or bus stations have one or two car-rental agencies on-site, as well.

In general, rates throughout New England have increased since the onset of the pandemic. Prices at Boston's Logan Airport vary greatly according to supply and demand but generally begin at around $50 per day and $300 per week for an economy car with air-conditioning, automatic transmission, and unlimited mileage. The same car might go for around $40 per day and $220 per week at a smaller airport, such as Providence's or Hartford's. These rates do not include state tax on car rentals, which varies depending on the airport but generally runs 12%–15%. You can often save greatly, as much as $150 to $200 a week, by renting away from the airport, even factoring in the cost of an Uber or Lyft ride there and back.

Most agencies won't rent to drivers under the age of 21, and several major agencies won't rent to anyone under 25 or over the age of 75. When picking up a rental car, non-U.S. residents need a voucher for any prepaid reservation made in their home country, a passport, a driver's license, and a travel policy that covers each driver. Logan Airport is spread out and usually congested; if returning a rental vehicle there, allow plenty of time to do so before heading to your flight.

Train

Amtrak offers frequent daily service along its Northeast Corridor route from Washington, D.C., Philadelphia, and New York to Boston, with stops in Connecticut and Rhode Island. Amtrak's high-speed Acela trains link Boston and Washington, with stops at New York, Philadelphia, and other cities along the way. The *Downeaster* connects Boston and Brunswick, Maine, with stops in coastal New Hampshire and Portland.

Other Amtrak services include the *Vermonter* between Washington, D.C., and St. Albans, Vermont (via New York City); the *Ethan Allen Express* between New York City and Burlington, Vermont (with stops in Rutland, VT and Albany, NY); and the *Lake Shore Limited* between Boston and Chicago, which stops at Pittsfield, Springfield, Worcester, and Framingham in Massachusetts.

Several commuter services are handy for travelers. The Massachusetts Bay Transportation Authority (MBTA) operates within Boston and connects the city with outlying areas on the north and south shores of the state. Metro-North Railroad's New Haven Line offers service from New York City along the Connecticut coast up to New Haven, with spur lines north to New Canaan, Danbury, and Waterbury. Also in Connecticut, Shore Line East serves coastal towns between New Haven and New London.

When to Go

All six New England states are year-round destinations. Winter is popular with skiers, summer draws beach lovers, and fall delights those who love the bursts of autumnal color. Spring can also be a great time, with sugar shacks transforming maple sap into all sorts of tasty things.

TIP→ You'll probably want to avoid rural areas during mud season (April to early May) and black fly season (May to early June).

Memorial Day sets off the great migration to the beaches and the mountains, and summer begins in earnest on July 4. Those who want to drive to Cape Cod in July or August, beware: on Friday and Sunday, weekenders clog the overburdened U.S. 6. The same applies to the Maine Coast and its feeder roads, Interstate 95 and U.S. 1.

In the fall, a rainbow of reds, oranges, yellows, purples, and other vibrant hues emerges. The first scarlet and gold colors appear in mid-September in northern areas; "peak" color occurs at different times from year to year. Generally, it's best to visit the northern reaches in late September and early October and move south as October progresses.

Essentials

Dining

Although certain ingredients and preparations are common to the region as a whole, New England's cuisine varies greatly from place to place. Mostly coastal urban centers like Boston, Providence, New Haven, Portsmouth, and Portland—and upscale resort areas such as the Berkshires, Martha's Vineyard, and Nantucket—have stellar restaurants, many of them with culinary luminaries at the helm and a reputation for creative—and occasionally daring—menus.

Many small-town restaurants in quiet parts of New England increasingly feature globally influenced recipes and also source significantly from local farms, fisheries, and other purveyors. Menus in upscale and tourism-driven communities often note which Vermont dairy or Berkshires farm a particular goat cheese or heirloom tomato came from. Options for international food have also improved greatly in recent years, especially when it comes to Italian, French, Japanese, Indian, and Thai eateries. There are also plenty of old-school diners, cafés, and rustic taverns serving burgers and other comfort food—some serve breakfast all day.

RESERVATIONS AND DRESS

It's a good idea to make a reservation when you can. We specifically mention them only when reservations are essential—there's no other way you'll ever get a table—or when they are not accepted. For popular restaurants or during the high season, book as far ahead as you can and reconfirm as soon as you arrive. Large parties should always call ahead to check the reservations policy. We mention dress only when men are required to wear a jacket or a jacket and tie, which is rarely in New England.

WINE, BEER, AND SPIRITS

New England is no stranger to craft brewing. The granddaddy of New England's independent breweries is the Boston Beer Company, maker of Samuel Adams, but these days ardent beer lovers consider Sam Adams to be almost too mainstream to be interesting, especially given that virtually every New England town with at least a half-dozen restaurants now has a craft brewery, and some of the best beer in the region is produced by tiny operations that sell their beer only on-site. Artisan cider has also become increasingly popular, with Middlebury, Vermont's Green Mountain Cidery—the maker of Woodchuck Hard Cider—one of the region's stars.

New England has gradually begun to earn some respect as a wine-producing region. Cabernet Franc, Vidal, Riesling, and other grape varieties capable of withstanding the region's harsher winters and relatively shorter growing season compared to California and other leading areas have been the basis of promising enterprises such as Rhode Island's Sakonnet Vineyards and Connecticut's Hopkins Vineyard (part of the Connecticut Wine Trail). Even Vermont and New Hampshire have gotten into the act with the Snow Farm Vineyard in the Lake Champlain Islands, Boyden Valley Winery in the Green Mountains, and Seven Birches in the White Mountains.

Although a patchwork of state and local regulations affect the hours and locations of places that sell alcoholic beverages (e.g., Massachusetts bans "happy hour"), New England licensing laws are fairly liberal. State-owned or-franchised stores sell hard liquor in New Hampshire, Maine, and Vermont. New Hampshire offers some the region's lowest prices due to the absence of a sales tax; look for state-run liquor "supermarkets" on interstates in the southern part of the state—it's technically illegal to take untaxed liquor across state lines, but this law is virtually never enforced except in cases of drivers transporting huge quantities.

Health and Safety

Lyme disease, so named for its having been first reported in the town of Lyme, Connecticut, is a potentially debilitating disease carried by deer ticks. They thrive in dry, brush-covered areas, particularly in coastal areas. Always use insect repellent: the potential for outbreaks of Lyme disease makes it imperative that you protect yourself from ticks from early spring through summer and into fall. To prevent bites, wear light-color clothing and tuck pant legs into socks. Look for black ticks about the size of a pinhead around hairlines and the warmest parts of the body. If you have been bitten, consult a physician—especially if you see the telltale bull's-eye bite pattern. Flulike symptoms often accompany a Lyme infection. Early treatment is imperative.

New England's most annoying insect pests are black flies and mosquitoes. The former are a phenomenon of late spring and early summer and are generally a problem only in densely wooded areas of the far north. Mosquitoes, however, are a nuisance just about everywhere from spring through early autumn. The best protection against both pests is repellent containing DEET; if you're camping in the woods during black fly season, you'll also want to use fine mesh screening in eating and sleeping areas and even wear mesh headgear. One pest particular to coastal areas, especially salt marshes, is the greenhead fly, which has a nasty bite and is hard to kill. It is best repelled by a liberal application of Avon Skin So Soft or a similar product.

Coastal waters attract seafood lovers who enjoy harvesting their own clams, mussels, and even lobsters; permits are required, and casual harvesting of lobsters is strictly forbidden. Amateur clammers should be aware that New England shellfish beds are periodically visited by red tides, during which microorganisms can render shellfish poisonous. To keep abreast of the situation, inquire when you apply for a license (usually at town halls or police stations) and pay attention to red tide postings as you travel.

Rural New England is one of the country's safest regions. In cities—Boston, in particular—observe the usual precautions: avoid out-of-the-way or poorly lighted areas at night; keep handbags close to your body and don't let them out of your sight; and be on your guard in subways and on buses, not only during the deserted wee hours but also during crowded rush hours, when pickpockets may be at work. Keep your valuables in the hotel or room safe. When using an ATM, choose busy, well-lighted places, such as bank lobbies.

If planning to leave a car overnight to make use of off-road trails or camping facilities, use designated parking areas and don't leave any valuables in sight; cars left at trailhead parking lots are sometimes a target for theft or vandalism.

Lodging

New England is very much the domain of distinctive, independently owned country inns and bed-and-breakfasts, as well as a number of restored or well-kept old-fashioned cottage compounds and motels. In addition to often having distinct charms and scenic locations, these one-of-a-kind properties also provide a glimpse of local life. In ski areas and some coastal resort towns, you'll also find condo resorts offering a full slate of dining and recreational amenities.

Reservations are always a good idea, and are essential, as far in advance as possible on weekends and during peak seasons in summer and winter resort areas, in college towns in September and at graduation time in spring, and in areas renowned for autumn foliage. Most hotels and motels will hold your reservation until 6 pm; call ahead if you plan to arrive late.

Hotels are no-smoking by law in most of New England; best to call ahead if you require a smoking room. All lodgings listed have private baths unless otherwise noted.

Hotel prices are the lowest cost of a standard double room in high season.

VACATION RENTALS

You are most likely to find a house, apartment, or condo rental in areas of New England where ownership of second homes is common, such as beach resorts and ski country. Both Airbnb and VRBO have a large presence throughout New England, and many resort communities also have local rental agencies.

BED-AND-BREAKFASTS AND INNS

In many less touristy areas, bed-and-breakfasts offer an affordable, homey experience and sometimes quite lavish breakfasts that will fill you up for the better part of the day. Inns are similar but usually bigger, with 10 or more rooms, and rates that may or may not include breakfast. Often but not always, inns are a bit fancier and pricier than a typical bed-and-breakfast and have more amenities, such as restaurants, bars, pools, and even spas or tennis courts.

HOTELS

Major hotel and motel chains are amply represented in New England, especially in the cities, but don't overlook the many small, independent motels—these mom-and-pop operations often offer cheerful, convenient accommodations and great rates.

Packing

The principal rule of weather in New England is that there are no rules. A cold, foggy spring morning often warms to a bright, 60°F afternoon. A summer breeze can suddenly turn chilly, and rain often appears with little warning. Thus, the best advice on how to dress is to layer your clothing. Even in summer, you should bring long pants, a sweater or two, and a light jacket, for evenings are often chilly, and sea spray can make things cool. Showers are frequent, so pack a waterproof windbreaker or raincoat and umbrella. A hat, sunscreen, and insect repellent are also essential.

Casual sportswear—walking shoes and jeans or khakis—will take you almost everywhere, but swimsuits and bare feet will not. Shirts and shoes are required attire at even the most casual venues. Dress in restaurants is generally casual, except at some of the distinguished restaurants in Boston, Newport, Maine coastal towns (such as Kennebunkport), a few inns in the Berkshires, and in Litchfield and Fairfield counties in Connecticut, where sportier attire is expected. Upscale resorts, at the very least, will require men to wear long pants and collared shirts at dinner, and jeans are often frowned upon.

Best Tours

BIKE TOURS

Backroads. This internationally respected company offers luxurious multiday cycling tours along the Maine Coast, in Vermont's mountains, and across Martha's Vineyard and Nantucket. ☎ *800/462–2848* 🌐 *www.backroads.com* *From $3,100.*

VBT Bicycling and Walking Vacations. This global guide company leads bike tours in Vermont (around Burlington and Montpelier) as well as Maine (Acadia National Park) and Massachusetts (Cape Cod and Provincetown). E-bikes are available, as are self-guided tour options. ☎ *800/245–3868* 🌐 *www.vbt.com* *From $2,000.*

GENERAL INTEREST TOURS

Adventures by Disney. The 8-day, 7-night itinerary starts in Burlington, Vermont, with stops in Stowe, Vermont, and New Hampshire's White Mountains before ending in Bar Harbor, Maine. The trip includes two guides, most meals, admission fees, and first-rate accommodations, as well as a Lake Champlain cruise, kayaking on the Maine coast, a hike in the White Mountains, and a guided tour of Acadia National Park. ☎ *800/543–0865* 🌐 *www.adventuresbydisney.com.*

American Queen Voyages. This specialized cruise company offers itineraries on intimate (about 200-passenger) ships up and down the New England coast, calling in Newport, Bar Harbor, Boston, Provincetown, Portland, and other historic communities, and often continuing into Maritime Canada and Quebec. ☎ *833/583–1632* 🌐 *www.aqvoyages.com* *From $3,000.*

New England Vacation Tours. This versatile company conducts everything from packages that include flights and tours in luxury coaches to ones that involve cruises and sightseeing excursions on land. All transportation is covered, and every detail is attended to. You can also work with the helpful staff to create a completely customized itinerary to take you wherever your heart desires. ☎ *800/742–7669* 🌐 *www.newenglandvacationtours.com* *From $574.*

Northeast Unlimited Tours. As the name indicates, Northeast Unlimited's range of itineraries includes New England. The eight-day Taste of New England tour, for example, hits all the highlights from Boston to Maine, but you'll also find shorter trips, such as a four-day Cape Cod Getaway and five-day Maine Lobster Festival excursion. ☎ *800/759–6820* 🌐 *www.newenglandtours.com* *Call for prices.*

Wolfe Tours & Adventures. Wolfe specializes in tours for groups, including families. New England tours include Boston, Newport, the White Mountains, Vermont farms, maritime adventures, Cape Cod, and more. ☎ *978/255–1645* 🌐 *www.wolfetours.com* *Call for prices.*

Great Itineraries

Whether it's your first trip to New England or you vacation here every year, these itineraries will help you explore charming seaside towns and bustling cities, eat at cutting-edge restaurants and the best seafood shacks, and experience both popular spots and hidden gems. Mix and match the itineraries, or use them as a jumping-off point for your own adventure.

Cape Cod Beaches and Villages, 7 Days

Cape Cod can be all things to all visitors, with quiet villages and lively resorts, gentle bay-side wavelets and crashing surf. A car is the best way to meander along Massachusetts's beach-lined, arm-shape peninsula, but in busy town centers—such as Falmouth, Hyannis, Chatham, and Provincetown—you can get around quite easily on foot. Keep in mind that Cape-bound traffic is particularly bad on Friday late afternoon–evening and Saturday morning–afternoon (most house rentals are Saturday to Saturday), and traffic in the other direction is rough on Sunday, especially in the afternoon. Cross as early in the day as possible or wait until well after rush hour. For most visitors, time at the beach is key, but there is plenty to do and see once you've had enough sun and surf or if the weather doesn't cooperate. And about those beaches: be prepared to pay for day passes—most beach parking lots charge a sometimes-hefty fee.

Fly in: Logan International Airport (BOS), Boston

Fly out: Logan International Airport (BOS), Boston

DAY 1: HYANNIS

The best way to spend a week on the Cape is to pick a central location and use it as a launching point to explore. Begin by crossing the Bourne Bridge and head east on U.S. 6 toward Hyannis: make this centrally located, larger town your headquarters.

The crowded Mid Cape is a hive of activity, and its heart is **Hyannis.** Here you can cruise around the harbor or go on a deep-sea fishing trip. There are shops and restaurants along Main Street and plenty of kid-friendly amusements. Fans of John F. Kennedy shouldn't miss the museum in his honor. End the day with a concert at the **Cape Cod Melody Tent** (open seasonally) or the Cotuit Center for the Arts.

Logistics: 72 miles; via I–90 W, I–93 S, Rte. 3 S, U.S. 6 E, and Rte. 132 S; 1½ hours from Logan airport.

DAY 2: FALMOUTH

For your first excursion, wander along Route 28 until you reach **Falmouth** in the Upper Cape. Here you can stroll around the village green, duck into some of the historic houses, and stop at the Waquoit Bay National Estuarine Research Reserve for a walk along the barrier beach. Take some time to check out the village of **Woods Hole,** a center for international marine research, and the year-round ferry port for Martha's Vineyard. A small aquarium has regional sea-life exhibits and touch tanks. If you have extra time, head north to the lovely old town of **Sandwich,** known for the **Sandwich Glass Museum,** and the beautiful grounds and collection of antique cars at **Heritage Museums and Gardens.**

Logistics: 21 miles; via Rte. 28 N; 48 minutes, starting in Hyannis.

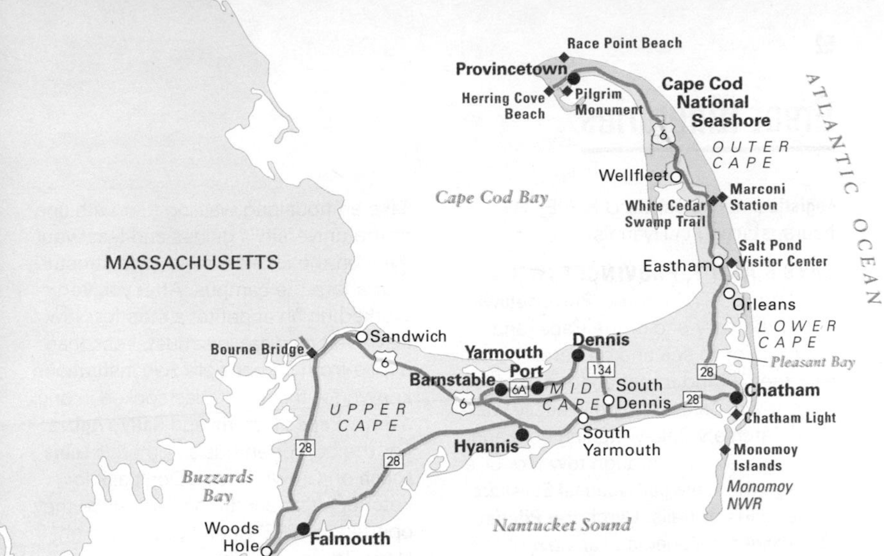

DAY 3: BARNSTABLE, YARMOUTH PORT, DENNIS

Spend your day exploring the northern reaches of the Mid Cape with a drive along scenic Route 6A, which passes through the charming, slow-paced villages of **Barnstable, Yarmouth Port,** and **Dennis.** There are beaches and salt marshes, antiques shops and galleries, and old cemeteries along this route. Yarmouth Port's **Bass Hole Boardwalk** makes for a particularly beautiful stroll. In Dennis there are historic houses to tour, and the **Cape Cod Museum of Art** merits a stop. End the day by climbing 30-foot Scargo Tower to watch the sun set. At night you can catch a film at the Cape Cinema, on the grounds of the **Cape Playhouse.**

If you're traveling with kids, spend some time in the southern sections of Yarmouth and Dennis, where Route 28 passes by countless amusement centers and miniature-golf courses.

Logistics: 9 miles; via Rte. 6A E; 20 minutes, starting in Hyannis.

DAY 4: CHATHAM

Chatham, with its handsome Main Street, is a perfect destination for strolling, shopping, and dining. A trip to the nearby **Monomoy Islands** is a must for bird-watchers and nature lovers. Back in town visit the many inviting galleries and restaurants, stop by the **Atwood House Museum,** and drive over to take in the view from **Chatham Light.**

Logistics: 19½ miles; via U.S. 6 E; 35 minutes, starting in Hyannis.

DAY 5: CAPE COD NATIONAL SEASHORE

On Day 5, leave your Hyannis hub and head for the farther reaches of Cape Cod. Take U.S. 6 east, before making a slight detour onto the less commercial end of Route 28. On the way north toward Orleans you'll drive past sailboat-speckled views of Pleasant Bay.

Stop in Eastham at the Cape Cod National Seashore's **Salt Pond Visitor Center.** Take time to stroll along one of the beaches—there are more than 40 miles of pristine sand from which to choose—or bike on the many picturesque trails. Head slightly farther north to historic **Marconi Station,** which was the landing point for the transatlantic telegraph early in the 20th century, or park your car in **Wellfleet**'s historic downtown area, where you'll find a bounty of intriguing shops and galleries. It's also worth walking the short but stunning White Cedar Swamp Trail. Continue on to Provincetown to spend two nights at the tip of the Cape.

Great Itineraries

Logistics: 47 miles; via U.S. 6 E; 1¼ hours, starting in Hyannis.

DAYS 6 AND 7: PROVINCETOWN
Bustling, LGBTQ-popular **Provincetown** sits at the very end of the Cape, and there's a lot to see and do here. You can park the car and forget about it until you leave town, as everything is easily walkable. Catch a whale-watching boat and take a trolley tour through town, or bike through the **Cape Cod National Seashore** on its miles of trails. Climb the **Pilgrim Monument** for a spectacular view of the area—on an exceptionally clear day you can see the Boston skyline. Visit museums, shops, and art galleries, or spend the afternoon swimming and sunning on the beaches at **Herring Cove** or **Race Point.**

Logistics: 116 miles; via U.S. 6W, Rte. 3 N and I–93 N; 2½ hours, starting in Provincetown and ending in Boston.

New Haven, Providence, and Boston in 5 days

These three cities offer some of the best dining in the Northeast, and each makes a case for having the finest Italian cuisine in the region, leaving you to judge whose cuisine reigns supreme. In addition, history buffs can get their fill while exploring New England's Colonial and maritime past.

Fly in: Bradley International Airport (BDA), Hartford

Fly out: Logan International Airport (BOS), Boston

DAY 1: NEW HAVEN
Start your journey in **New Haven,** Connecticut. The Constitution State's second-largest city is home to **Yale University,** named for British shipping merchant Elihu Yale. Take an hour-long walking tour with one of the university's guides and feast your eyes on the iconic Gothic-style structures that adorn the campus. After you've worked up an appetite, a stop for New Haven–style pizza is a must. Less than a mile from campus are two institutions known for thin-crust pies cooked in brick ovens: **Pepe's Pizzeria** and **Sally's Apizza.** For the burger enthusiast, there's **Louis' Lunch** on Crown Street. Don't ask for ketchup; it's been taboo here since they opened in 1895. Spend your first night in New Haven.

Logistics: 53 miles; via I–91 S; 1 hour staring at Bradley airport.

DAY 2: NEW HAVEN TO PROVIDENCE
On your second day, get an early start, and head north on Interstate 95 toward Providence, Rhode Island. There are plenty of small towns bursting with New England's maritime history along Connecticut's shoreline. Stop in Niantic, New London, or **Stonington** and explore the region's rich seafaring history. If you're planning on making one stop on the way to Rhode Island, the seaside village of **Mystic** is worth at least a half day to explore the seaport or to take a boat out on the water. **Mystic Seaport,** with its nearly 500 ships and more than 60 preserved historic buildings, will transport you back to 19th-century New England. For those looking to try their luck at a game of chance, take a slight detour north on Interstate 395 to either of Connecticut's two casinos, **Foxwoods Resort Casino** or **Mohegan Sun.** Overnight in Providence or in any of the seaside towns along the way.

Logistics: 103 miles; via I–95 N; 1 hour 45 minutes, starting in New Haven.

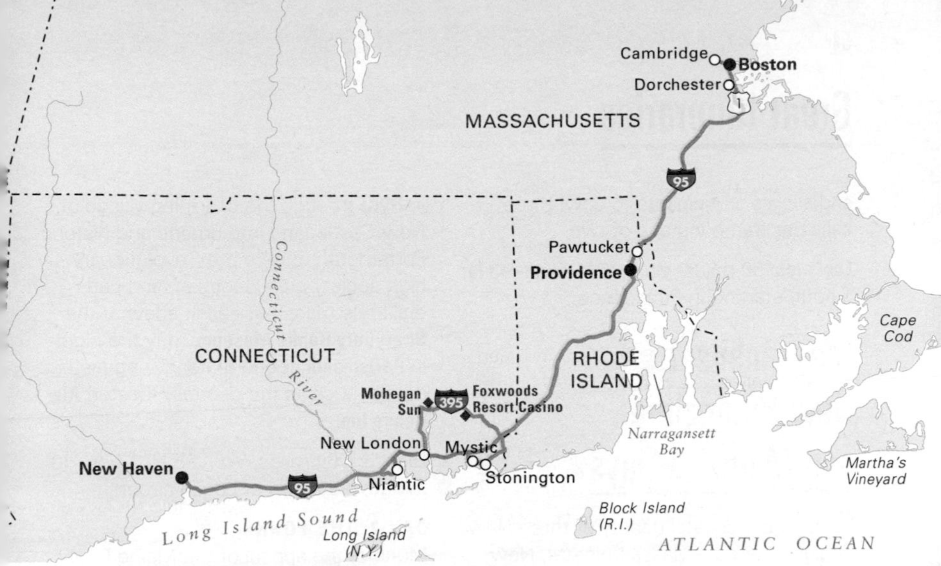

DAY 3: PROVIDENCE

Rhode Island's capital holds treasures like **Benefit Street,** with its Federal-era homes, and the **RISD Museum of Art** at the Rhode Island School of Design. Be sure to savor a knockout Italian meal on Atwells Avenue in **Federal Hill—Pane e Vino** is a popular choice. For dessert, it's hard to top the cannoli at **Scialo Bros. Bakery.** If you're visiting in early June, sample authentic eats from all over Italy, while live music fills the streets, during the Federal Hill Stroll. During the warmer months, typically late May–early November, Providence hosts **WaterFire,** a public celebration of art and performance. The festival's 100 bonfires on the rivers of downtown Providence attracts tens of thousands of viewers each year for the popular event. Spend the night in a downtown Providence hotel for easy access to sights and restaurants.

DAYS 4 AND 5: BOSTON

A short drive north on Interstate 95 will bring you to **Boston,** New England's cultural and commercial hub. To savor Boston's centuries-old ties to the sea, take a half-day stroll past **Faneuil Hall** and **Quincy Market** or a boat tour of the harbor (you can even head out on a whale-watching tour from here). In Boston, famous buildings such as Faneuil Hall are not merely civic landmarks, but national icons. From the **Boston Common,** the 2.5-mile **Freedom Trail** links treasures of America's struggle for independence, such as the **USS *Constitution*** (better known as "Old Ironsides") and **Old North Church** (of "one if by land, two if by sea" fame). Be sure to walk the gas-lighted streets of **Beacon Hill,** too. Boston's **North End** is the oldest residential neighborhood in the city, and has great dining options like **Antico Forno,** which offers pizza baked in a wood-burning brick oven.

The following day, either explore the massive **Museum of Fine Arts** and the grand boulevards and shops of **Back Bay,** or visit colorful **Cambridge,** home of **Harvard University** and the **Massachusetts Institute of Technology (MIT).** Lively **Harvard Square** is a perfect place to do some people-watching or catch a street performance; the **All Star Sandwich Bar** is an excellent choice for lunch. For an experience unique to the Boston area, head a few miles south of the city along U.S. 1 to Dorchester's **Boston Bowl** to cap off your trip with candlepin bowling. Here, at all hours of the night, Bay Staters play a smaller version of 10-pin bowling that uses balls weighing less than 3 pounds and allows participants to bowl three balls per frame instead of two.

Logistics: 50 miles; via I–95 N and I–93 N; 1 hour, starting in Providence.

Massachusetts, New Hampshire, and Maine, 7 Days

Revel in the coastal beauty of three New England states—Massachusetts, New Hampshire, and Maine—on the path from the region's largest city, Boston, to its highest peak, Mt. Washington. An assortment of New England's treasures are at your fingertips as you negotiate the ins and outs of the jagged northeastern coastline, before ascending the heights of the White Mountains.

Fly in: Logan International Airport (BOS), Boston

Fly out: Logan International Airport (BOS), Boston

DAY 1: THE NORTH SHORE AND NEW HAMPSHIRE COAST

After flying into Boston, pick up a rental car and head for the North Shore of Massachusetts. In **Salem,** the **Peabody Essex Museum** and the **Salem Maritime National Historic Site** chronicle the evolution of the country's early shipping fortunes. Spend some time exploring more of the North Shore, including the old fishing port of **Gloucester,** and **Rockport,** a great place to find that seascape rendered in oils. **Newburyport,** with its Federal-style ship-owners' homes, is home to the **Parker River National Wildlife Refuge,** beloved by birders and beach walkers.

New Hampshire fronts the Atlantic for a scant 18 miles, but it's a pretty drive up the coast to quiet **Odiorne Point State Park** in Rye, through the charming village of New Castle, and into urbane and historic Portsmouth, where pre-Revolutionary high society built Georgian- and Federal-style mansions—visit a few at the **Strawbery Banke Museum.** Stay the night in **Portsmouth** at one of its inviting historic hotels, such as the centrally located **Ale House Inn.**

Logistics: 64 miles; via I–95 N; 1 hour 10 minutes, starting at Logan airport.

DAY 2: THE YORKS

Much of the appeal of the Maine Coast lies in geographical contrast—from its long stretches of swimming and walking beaches in the south to the rugged, rocky cliffs in the north. As the shoreline physically evolves, each town along the way reveals a slightly different character, starting with **York.**

In **York Village** take a leisurely stroll through the buildings of the **Museums of Old York** getting a glimpse of 18th-century life in this gentrified town. Spend time wandering between shops or walking nature trails and beaches around York Harbor. There are several grand lodging options here, most with views of the harbor. If you prefer a livelier pace, continue on to **York Beach,** a haven for families with plenty of entertainment venues. After taking in the view of **Nubble Light,** stop at Fox's Lobster House for a seaside lunch or dinner.

Logistics: 10 miles; via I–95 N; 15 minutes, starting in Portsmouth.

DAY 3: OGUNQUIT AND THE KENNEBUNKS

For well over a century, **Ogunquit** has been a favorite vacation spot for those looking to combine the natural beauty of the ocean with the sophistication of fine art galleries and restaurants. Take a morning walk along the Marginal Way to see the waves crashing against the

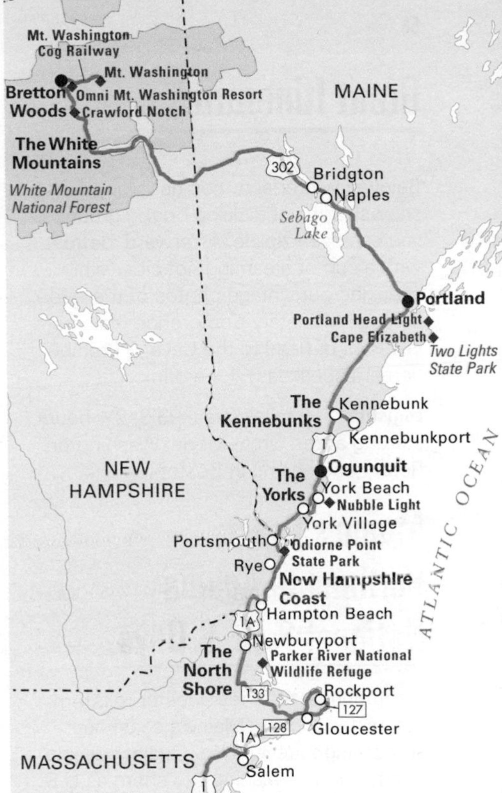

rocks. In **Perkins Cove,** have lunch, stroll the shopping areas, or sign on with a lobster-boat cruise to learn about Maine's most important fishery—the state's lobster industry satisfies more than 80% of the nation's appetite.

Head north to the Kennebunks, allowing at least two hours to wander through the shops and historic homes of Dock Square in **Kennebunkport.** This is an ideal place to rent a bike and ramble around backstreets, head out Ocean Avenue past large mansions, or ride to one of several beaches to relax awhile. Spend your third night in Kennebunkport.

Logistics: 22 miles; via I-95 N and Rte. 9 E; 30 minutes, starting in York.

DAYS 4 AND 5: PORTLAND

There's enough to keep you happily busy for several days in **Portland,** Maine's largest city. Explore its historic neighborhoods, shop and eat at the many hip, indie boutiques and restaurants in **Old Port** and elsewhere in town, and visit one of several excellent museums. A brief side trip to **Cape Elizabeth** takes you to **Portland Head Light,** Maine's first lighthouse, which was commissioned by George Washington in 1787. The lighthouse is on the grounds of Fort Williams Park and is an excellent place for a picnic; be sure to spend some time wandering the ample grounds. There are also excellent walking trails (and views) at nearby Two Lights State Park. If you want to take a boat tour while in Portland, get a ticket for Casco Bay Lines and see some of the islands that dot the bay. Spend two nights in Portland.

Logistics: 28 miles; via I–95 N; 40 minutes, starting in Kennebunkport.

DAY 6: BRETTON WOODS

Wake up early and drive to **Bretton Woods,** New Hampshire, where you'll spend nights six and seven. It's about a three-hour drive from Portland, much of it along windy, scenic roads. Drive northwest along U.S. 302 toward Sebago Lake, a popular water-sports area in the summer, and continue on toward the time-honored New England towns of Naples and Bridgton. Just 15 miles from the border of New Hampshire, and nearing Crawford Notch, U.S. 302 begins to thread through New Hampshire's **White Mountains,** passing beneath brooding **Mt. Washington** before arriving in Bretton Woods.

Logistics: 98 miles; via Rte. 113 N and U.S. 302 W; 3 hours, starting from Portland.

DAY 7: THE WHITE MOUNTAINS

In Bretton Woods, the **Mount Washington Cog Railway** chugs to the summit, and the **Omni Mount Washington Resort** recalls the glory days of White Mountain resorts.

Beloved winter activities here include snowshoeing and skiing on the grounds; you can even zipline. Afterward, defrost with a cup of steaming hot cider while checking out vintage photos of the International Monetary Conference (held here in 1944), or head to the Cave, a Prohibition-era speakeasy, for a drink.

Logistics: 159 miles; via I–93 S; 2½ hours, starting at the Omni Mount Washington Resort and ending in Boston.

Maine's Coast: Portland to Acadia National Park, 6 Days

Lighthouses, beaches, lobster rolls, and water sports—Maine's coast has something for everyone. Quaint seaside villages and towns line the shore as U.S. 1 winds its way toward the easternmost swath of land in the United States at Quoddy Head State Park. Galleries and funky old shops are a major draw, so keep an eye out for roadside retailers crammed with gems. New England's only national park, Acadia, is a highlight of the tour, drawing more than 4 million visitors per year.

Fly in: Portland International Jetport (PWM), Portland, Maine

Fly out: Portland International Jetport (PWM), Portland, Maine

DAY 1: PORTLAND TO BRUNSWICK

Use Maine's maritime capital as your jumping-off point to head farther up the Maine Coast, or, as Mainers call it, "Down East." Plan to spend half of your first day in Portland, then head to Brunswick for the night.

Portland shows off its restored waterfront at the **Old Port.** From there, before you depart, you can grab a bite at either of two classic Maine eateries: **Gilbert's Chowder House** or **Becky's Diner,** or check out what's new in this city's buzzy restaurant scene. For a peek at the freshest catch of the day, wander over to the **Harbor Fish Market,** a Portland institution since 1968, and gaze upon Maine lobsters and other delectable seafood. Two lighthouses on nearby **Cape Elizabeth, Two Lights** and **Portland Head,** still stand vigil.

Following U.S. 1, travel northeast along the ragged, island-strewn coast of Down East Maine and make your first stop at the retail outlets of **Freeport,** home of **L.L. Bean.** About 3 million people visit the massive flagship store every year, where you can find everything from outerwear to camping equipment. Just 10 miles north of Freeport on U.S. 1, **Brunswick** is home to the campus of **Bowdoin College,** the superb **Bowdoin College Museum of Art,** and also features a superb coastline for kayaking. Plan for dinner and an overnight in Bath.

Logistics: 30 miles; via U.S. 1 N; 30 minutes from Portland airport.

DAY 2: BATH

In **Bath,** Maine's shipbuilding capital, tour the **Maine Maritime Museum,** stopping for lunch on the waterfront. Check out the boutiques and antiques shops, or take in the plenitude of beautiful homes. From here it's a 30-minute detour down Route 127 to Georgetown Island and Reid State Park, where you will find a quiet beach lining Sheepscot Bay—and maybe even a sand dollar or two to take home, if you arrive at low tide. For a stunning vista, make your way to Griffith Head.

Drive north and reconnect with U.S. 1. Continue through the towns of **Wiscasset** and **Damariscotta,** where you may find yourself pulling over to stop at the outdoor flea markets and intriguing antiques

shops that line the road. Another hour from here is **Rockland,** where you'll spend your second night.

Logistics: 52 miles; via U.S. 1 N; 1 hour 15 minutes, starting in Brunswick.

DAY 3: ROCKLAND, CAMDEN, AND CASTINE

From Rockland, spend the day cruising on a majestic schooner or reserve a tee time at Samoset Resort's championship golf course, which overlooks the Rockland Harbor. If you're an art lover, save some time for Rockland's **Farnsworth Art Museum,** the **Wyeth Center,** and the **Center for Maine Contemporary Art.**

In **Camden** and **Castine,** exquisite inns occupy homes built from inland Maine's gold and timber. Camden is an ideal place to stay overnight as you make your way closer to Acadia National Park; it is a beautiful seaside town with hundreds of boats bobbing in the harbor, immaculately kept antique homes, streets lined with interesting stores, and restaurants serving sophisticated fare at every turn. The modest hills (by Maine standards, anyway) of nearby Mt. Battie offer good hiking and a great spot from which to picnic and view the surrounding area. It is also one of the hubs for the beloved and historic windjammer fleet—there is no better way to see the area than from the deck of one of these graceful beauties.

Logistics: 62 miles; via U.S. 1 N and Rte. 166 S; 1½ hours, starting in Rockland.

DAYS 4 AND 5: MOUNT DESERT ISLAND AND ACADIA NATIONAL PARK

On Day 4, head out early for **Bar Harbor** and plan to spend two nights here, using the bustling village as jumping-off point for the park—Bar Harbor is less than 5 miles from the entrance to **Mount Desert Island** 's 27-mile Park Loop Road. Spend at least a day exploring **Acadia National Park,** New England's only national park and one of its most popular tourist destinations. Enjoy the island's natural beauty by kayaking its coast, biking the 45-mile, historic, unpaved, carriage-road system, and driving to the summit of **Cadillac Mountain** for a stunning panorama.

Logistics: 52 miles; via Rte. 166 N, U.S. 1 N and Rte. 3 E; 1¼ hours, starting in Castine.

Great Itineraries

DAY 6: BAR HARBOR TO QUODDY HEAD STATE PARK

About 100 miles farther along U.S. 1 and "Way Down East" is Quoddy Head State Park in Lubec, Maine. Here, on the easternmost tip of land in the United States, sits the **West Quoddy Head Light,** one of 60 lighthouses that dot Maine's rugged coastline. Depending on the time of year (and your willingness to get up very early), you may be lucky enough to catch the East Coast's first sunrise here.

Logistics: 103 miles; via U.S. 1 N; 2½ hours, starting in Bar Harbor. From the park, it's 3 hours to back to Portland International Jetport.

Connecticut Wineries and Rhode Island Mansions, 5 Days

Travel through the Lower Connecticut River Valley as you meander toward the eastern section of the state's Wine Trail. While you sample varietals from the area's best wineries, get a taste of New England's literary and maritime history along the way. Stay overnight in seaside Mystic, another highlight, and then finish your tour by gawking at Newport's grand mansions and strolling the gorgeous Cliff Walk.

Fly in: Bradley International Airport (BGR), Hartford

Fly out: T. F. Green Airport (PVD), Warwick

DAY 1: HARTFORD

Start your journey in **Hartford,** Connecticut. The **Mark Twain House and Museum,** which Samuel Clemens and his wife built in the city's Victorian neighborhood of Nook Farm, is adjacent to the **Harriet Beecher Stowe Center,** which is also worth a visit. Downtown, you can visit the Nutmeg State's ornate **State Capitol** and the **Wadsworth Atheneum Museum of Art,** which houses fine Impressionist and Hudson River School paintings. Sports fans, take note: the **Naismith Memorial Basketball Hall of Fame** is only a quick detour up Interstate 91, in **Springfield,** Massachusetts, where Dr. James Naismith invented basketball in 1891. Spend your first night in Hartford.

DAY 2: CONNECTICUT RIVER VALLEY AND SOUTHEASTERN SHORE

Just a half-hour southeast of Hartford along Route 2 is your first wine stop, Priam Vineyards, in Colchester. Sample any of the boutique wines before bearing south on Route 149 to explore the centuries-old river towns of **East Haddam,** Chester, and **Essex.** In East Haddam, stop at Gillette Castle State Park—with its medieval-style stone mansion built for actor William Gillette—before crossing the Connecticut River on the historic (since 1769), eight-car Hadlyme-Chester ferry (April–November). In Essex, take a ride on the **Essex Steam Train**—the 12-mile excursion showcases the area's well-preserved countryside. (You can also return to Essex via riverboat.)

Continue on to **Mystic,** where the days of wooden ships and whaling adventures live on at **Mystic Seaport.** This world-class museum offers a peek into the past with restored vessels, historic buildings, figureheads, ship carvings, and much more. Spend your second night in Mystic.

Logistics: 60 miles; via Rte. 2 E; 1 hour, starting in Hartford (not including stops).

DAY 3: CONNECTICUT WINE TRAIL

A patchwork of six wineries—the heart of the eastern section of the **Connecticut Wine Trail**—sits in the southeastern

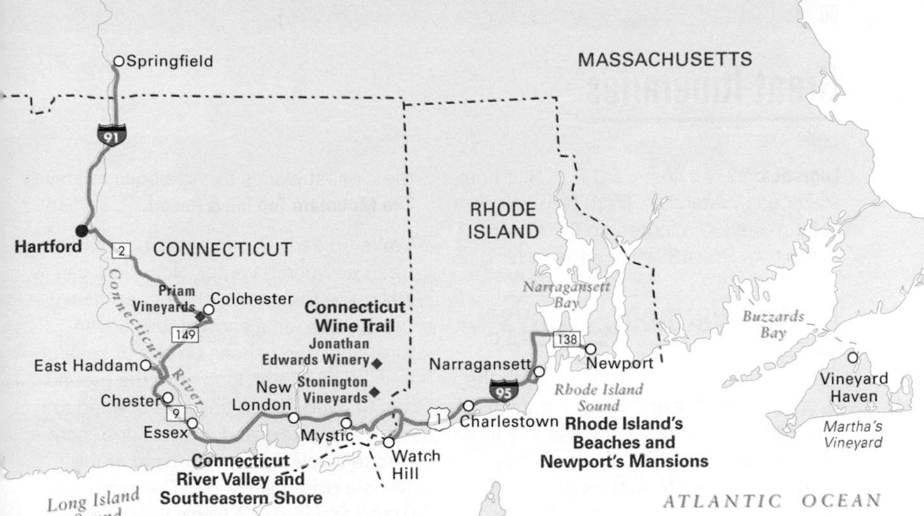

corner of the state. Taste through the portfolio at each of the picturesque vineyards until you find the perfect bottle to take home; many wineries offer self-guided walks through peaceful vineyards, allowing you to roam on your own. **Stonington Vineyards** has daily guided tours, and Jonathan Edwards Winery, farther inland in North Stonington, is a serene setting for picnics. Cap off the day by crossing the state line into Rhode Island and spend the night in **Watch Hill.** You can wander the grounds of the **Watch Hill Lighthouse;** in its museum, open midweek afternoons in summer, you can see the original Fresnel lens, a binnacle, mariners' sea chests, and historical documents and photos about the lighthouse and the area.

Logistics: 13½ miles; via U.S. 1 N; 25 minutes, starting in Mystic (not including stops).

DAYS 4 AND 5: RHODE ISLAND'S BEACHES AND NEWPORT'S MANSIONS

En route to Newport along U.S. 1 from **Watch Hill,** sandy beaches dot the coast from Misquamicut and Weekapaug to **Charlestown** and **Narragansett.** If it's summer and the weather is fine, spend the afternoon at the beach before continuing on to Newport. Despite its Colonial downtown and seaside parks, to most people **Newport** means mansions—the most opulent enclave of private homes ever built in the United States. Turn-of-the-20th-century "summer cottages" such as the **Breakers** and **Marble House** are must-sees. Embark on the scenic **Cliff Walk** for remarkable views of these great houses on one side and the Atlantic Ocean on the other. Newport's downtown is excellent for window-shopping, and there are plenty of places to enjoy fresh seafood.

Newport is known to many as the sailing capital of the East Coast, and you may get the best feel for it from the deck of a schooner cruising its famous harbor. Tours generally last around 90 minutes, and some offer beverages and snacks. Tennis enthusiasts can visit the **International Tennis Hall of Fame,** which, along with exhibits focusing on the legends of the game, has a unique interior designed by architect Stanford White. You can easily spend a few days exploring Newport.

Logistics: 39½ miles; via U.S. 1 N; 1 hour, starting in Watch Hill. From Newport, it is 26 miles (30 minutes) to T. F. Green Airport via Rte. 138 W and Rte. 4 N.

Best of Vermont, 7 Days

Following roads that weave through the Green Mountains and charming towns, this 200-mile journey is ideal at any time of year and covers Vermont from the bottom of the state to the top.

Fly in: Bradley International Airport (BDL), Hartford

Fly out: Burlington International Airport (BTV), Burlington

DAY 1: BRATTLEBORO

Artsy **Brattleboro** is the perfect place to begin a tour of Vermont, and it's worth taking a day to do some shopping and exploring. Catch a movie at the art deco **Latchis Theatre,** browse in a bookstore, or simply grab a cup of joe and people-watch. For dinner, make a reservation well in advance at tiny **T.J. Buckley's,** one of the best restaurants in the region. Spend your first night in Brattleboro.

Logistics: 78 miles; via I–91 N; 1 hour and 15 minutes from Bradley airport.

DAYS 2-4: KILLINGTON

Depart Brattleboro heading west on Route 9 and link up with Route 100 in Wilmington. As you travel north along the eastern edge of **Green Mountain National Forest,** you'll pass a plethora of panoramic overlooks and delightful ski towns. Stop to snap a photo, or take a moment to peruse the selection at a funky general store, as you make your way toward gigantic Killington Peak. Spend the next three nights in **Killington,** the largest ski resort in Vermont, and an outdoor playground year-round. A tip for skiers: one of the closest places to the slopes to stay is **The Mountain Top Inn & Resort.**

Wake up early to carve the mountain's fresh powder in winter. Nonskiers can still enjoy the snow, whether at the tubing park, on a snowmobile adventure, or in snowshoes on one of several trails. In summer, long after the ground has thawed, those trails are opened to mountain bikers and hikers. For a more leisurely activity, try your hand at the 18-hole disc-golf course. The excellent Grand Spa is also a lovely way to spend the day.

Logistics: 94 miles; via Rte. 9 W, Rte. 100 N, 2½ hours, starting in Brattleboro.

DAY 5: KILLINGTON TO BURLINGTON

Continue on Route 100 north until you reach Hancock, then head west on Route 125. Welcome to the land of poet Robert Frost, who spent almost 40 years living in Vermont, summering in the nearby tiny mountain town of Ripton, where he wrote numerous poems. Plaques along the 1.2-mile **Robert Frost Interpretive Trail,** a quiet woodland walk that takes about 30 minutes, display commemorative quotes from his poems, including his classic, "The Road Not Taken." After your stroll, head north on U.S. 7 until you hit Burlington.

Burlington, Vermont's largest city and home to the **University of Vermont,** is located on the eastern shore of Lake Champlain. Bustling in the summer and fall, the **Burlington Farmers Market** is filled with everything from organic meats and cheeses to freshly cut flowers and maple syrup. Spend the night in Burlington. In the evening, check out **Nectar's,** where the band Phish played their first bar gig, or wander into any of the many other pubs and cafés that attract local musicians.

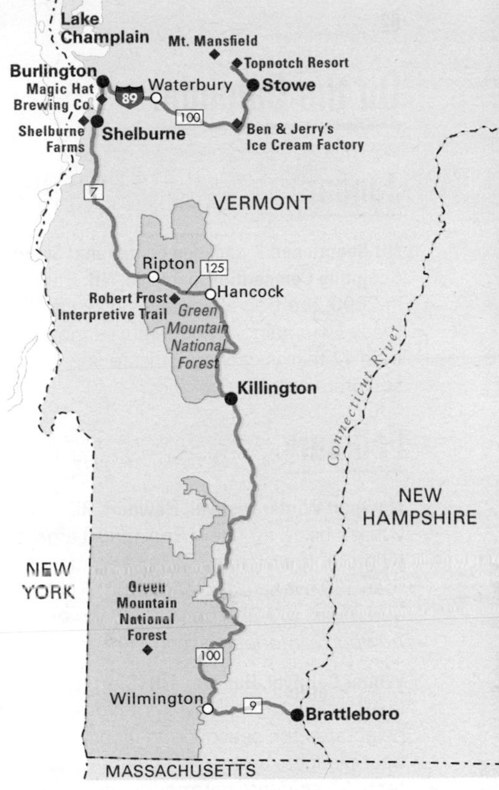

Logistics: 84 miles; via Rte. 100 N, Rte. 125 W, and U.S. 7 N; 2½ hours, starting in Killington.

DAY 6: SHELBURNE AND LAKE CHAMPLAIN

On your second day in Burlington, you can take a day trip south to Shelburne and family-friendly **Shelburne Farms.** Watch the process of making cheese from start to finish, or wander the gorgeous 1,400-acre estate designed by Frederick Law Olmsted, co-designer of New York's Central Park. The grounds overlook beautiful **Lake Champlain** and make the perfect setting for a picnic. In winter Shelburne Farms offers sleigh rides and other themed activities. If you're visiting in early August, don't miss the **Vermont Cheesemakers Festival,** showcasing more than 200 varieties of cheese crafted by 40 local purveyors. If you can't get enough, you can opt to spend the night here.

Logistics: 6.5 miles via U.S. 7 to Shelburne Farms; 30 minutes round-trip.

DAY 7: STOWE

A 30-minute drive down Interstate 89 from Burlington reunites you with Route 100 in the town of Waterbury. Head north in the direction of Stowe, and in under 2 miles you can make the obligatory pit stop at **Ben & Jerry's Ice Cream Factory.** The factory tour offers a lively behind-the-scenes look at how their ice cream is made; at the end of the tour, you get to taste limited-release creations only available at the factory before voting on your favorites.

Next, set out for the village of **Stowe.** Its proximity to Mt. Mansfield (Vermont's highest peak at 4,395 feet) has made Stowe a popular ski destination since the 1930s. If there's snow on the ground, hit the slopes, hitch a ride on a one-horse open sleigh, or simply put your feet up by the fire and enjoy a Heady Topper (an unfiltered, hoppy, American Double IPA beloved by beer aficionados the world over). In warmer weather, pop into the cute shops and art galleries that line the town's main street and sample some of the finest cheddar cheese and maple syrup that Vermont has to offer. Rejuvenate yourself at **Topnotch Resort,** which offers more than 100 different treatments. Spend your final night here.

Logistics: 36 miles; via I–89 S and Rte. 100 N; 45 minutes, starting in Burlington. From Stowe to the Burlington airport: 33 miles; via Rte. 100 and I–89 N; 41 minutes.

On the Calendar

January

NH Sanctioned & Jackson Invitational Snow Sculpting Competition, Jackson, NH. Started in 2000, the free event takes place at Black Mountain Ski and features more than 12 teams carving intricate snow sculptures. 🌐 *jacksonnh.com*

February

Newport Winter Festival, Newport, RI. What's billed as "New England's Largest Winter Extravaganza" features more than 150 events that range from food and music to a chili cook-off. 🌐 *www.newportwinterfestival.com*

Winter Carnival, Hanover, NH. Started in 1911, Dartmouth's winter festival celebrates the season with races, polar bear plunges, and snow sculpture contests. 🌐 *students.dartmouth.edu/collis/events/winter-carnival*

March

Connecticut Spring Antiques Show, Hartford, CT. Started in 1973, this is the premier gathering for collectors of early American furniture and decorative arts. 🌐 *www.ctspringshow.com*

April

Vermont Maple Festival, St. Albans, VT. This weekend is all about syrup. There's a pancake breakfast, a carnival and parade, and, of course, plenty of yummy maple treats. 🌐 *www.facebook.com/VermontMapleFestival*

May

Brimfield Antique and Collectible Shows, Brimfield, MA. Since the 1950s, Brimfield has welcomed thousands of visitors for a weeklong antiques and flea market extravaganza every May, July, and September. 🌐 *www.brimfieldantiquefleamarket.com*

WaterFire, Providence, RI. Late May through early November, more than 80 bonfires are lit on the city's three rivers on select weekends. 🌐 *waterfire.org*

June

Elephant's Trunk Country Flea Market, New Milford, CT. Open Sunday from late March through mid-December, Elephant's Trunk features antiques, up-cyclers, farm stands, food stalls, and vendors of all kinds. 🌐 *www.etflea.com*

Festival of Historic Homes, Providence, RI. Hosted by the Providence Preservation Society, this series of home tours highlights the city's historic neighborhoods, architecture, and history. 🌐 *www.providencehousetour.com*

Jacob's Pillow Dance Festival, Beckett, MA. This acclaimed festival, held mid-June through August, features more than 350 free performances, talks, tours, exhibits, community events, and classes. 🌐 *www.jacobspillow.org*

Rhode Island Pride, Providence, RI. One of New England's largest LGBTQ Pride festivals includes a unique illuminated Night Parade through downtown Providence. Other key Pride celebrations take place in Boston, Burlington, New Haven, Northampton, Portland, Portsmouth, and Provincetown. 🌐 *prideri.org*

July

Harborfest, Boston, MA. Boston's yearly festivities centered around Independence Day include the hugely popular Chowderfest cook-off as well as a parade and fireworks show. 🌐 *www.bostonharborfest.com*

Sailfest, New London, CT. A weekend of fireworks, music, boat cruises, and more than 200 vendors draw visitors to Connecticut's southeastern shore. 🌐 *sailfest.org*

August

League of New Hampshire Craftsmen's Fair, Newbury, NH. More than 350 talented artisans show their diverse wares at the nation's oldest juried crafts festival, held since 1940 over nine days at Mt. Sunapee Resort. 🌐 *www.nhcrafts.org*

Maine Lobster Festival, Rockland, ME. Stuff your face with lobster tails and claws during this "lobstravaganza" that puts almost 20,000 pounds of delicious crustacean at your finger tips. 🌐 *www.mainelobsterfestival.com*

Vermont Cheesemakers Festival, Shelburne, VT. Artisanal cheeses and local beer and wine highlight this daylong festival that features samples of more than 200 cheese varieties from 40 artisan cheese makers. 🌐 *vtcheesefest.com*

September

The Big E, West Springfield, MA. Also known as the Eastern States Exposition, this is the eastern seaboard's largest agricultural fair. 🌐 *www.thebige.com*

October

Fryeburg Fair, Fryeburg, ME. Established in 1851, this festive aggie fair includes horse, ox, and tractor pulling; animal, craft, and art exhibits; sheepdog trials; cooking contests; flower shows; a farm equipment museum; and food, food, food. 🌐 *www.fryeburgfair.org*

New Hampshire Pumpkin Festival, Laconia, NH. This family-friendly gathering tries to outdo itself each October by featuring the most lighted pumpkins. 🌐 *www.nhpumpkinfestival.com*

Salem Haunted Happenings, Salem, MA. The monthlong celebrations range from ghost tours and psychic readings to family-friendly events and art exhibits. 🌐 *www.hauntedhappenings.org*

Wellfleet OysterFest, Wellfleet, MA. This deliciously entertaining weekend celebrates the town's famous mollusk with food, art, and music. 🌐 *www.wellfleetspat.org*

November

America's Hometown Thanksgiving Celebration, Plymouth, MA. Celebrated the weekend before Thanksgiving in the holiday's birthplace, this event focuses on history, Americana, Pilgrims, and Native Americans. 🌐 *usathanksgiving.com*

December

Winter Wassail Weekend, Woodstock, VT. The annual fete features a parade with holiday-costume clad horses and riders, live music, house tours, kids' activities, and a Wassail Feast. 🌐 *www.woodstockvt.com*

Contacts

Air

AIRPORTS Albany International Airport. ✉ *Albany* ☎ *518/242–2222* 🌐 *www.albanyairport.com.* **Cape Cod Gateway Airport.** ✉ *Hyannis* ☎ *508/775–2020* 🌐 *www.flyhya.com.* **Bradley International Airport.** ✉ *Windsor Locks* ☎ *860/292–2000* 🌐 *www.bradleyairport.com.* **Burlington International Airport.** ✉ *South Burlington* ☎ *802/863–2874* 🌐 *www.btv.aero.* **Logan International Airport.** ✉ *Boston* ☎ *800/235–6426* 🌐 *www.massport.com* Ⓜ *Blue, Silver.* **Martha's Vineyard Airport.** ✉ *West Tisbury* ☎ *508/693–7022* 🌐 *www.mvyairport.com.* **Nantucket Memorial Airport.** ✉ *Nantucket* ☎ *508/325–5300* 🌐 *www.nantucketairport.com.* **Provincetown Municipal Airport.** ✉ *Provincetown* ☎ *508/487–0241* 🌐 *www.provincetown-ma.gov.* **T. F. Green International Airport.** ✉ *Warwick* ☎ *401/691–2000* 🌐 *www.flyri.com.* **Westchester County Airport.** ✉ *White Plains* ☎ *914/995–4860* 🌐 *airport.westchestergov.com.* **Bangor International Airport.** ☎ *207/992–4600* 🌐 *www.flybangor.com.* **Manchester-Boston Regional Airport.** ☎ *603/624–6556* 🌐 *www.flymanchester.com.* **Portland International Jetport.** ☎ *207/774–7301* 🌐 *www.portlandjetport.org.*

AIRLINE CONTACTS Cape Air. ☎ *800/227–3247* 🌐 *www.capeair.com.* **New England Airlines.** ☎ *800/243–2460* 🌐 *www.blockislandsairline.com.*

Train

Massachusetts Bay Transportation Authority. (*MBTA*). ☎ *617/222–3200* 🌐 *www.mbta.com.* **Metro-North Railroad.** ☎ *877/690–5114 from Connecticut* 🌐 *www.mta.info/mnr.* **Shore Line East.** ☎ *877/287–4337* 🌐 *www.shorelineeast.com.* **Amtrak.** ☎ *800/872–7245* 🌐 *www.amtrak.com.*

Visitor Information

Connecticut Office of Tourism. ☎ *888/288–4748* 🌐 *www.ctvisit.com.* **Greater Boston Convention & Visitors Bureau.** ☎ *888/733–2678* 🌐 *www.bostonusa.com.* **Maine Office of Tourism.** ☎ *888/624–6345* 🌐 *www.visitmaine.com.* **Massachusetts Office of Travel and Tourism.** ☎ *800/227–6277, 617/973–8500* 🌐 *www.visitma.com.* **New Hampshire Division of Travel and Tourism Development.** ☎ *800/386–4664* 🌐 *www.visitnh.gov.* **Yankee Magazine.** 🌐 *www.newengland.com.* **Rhode Island Tourism Division.** ☎ *800/556–2484* 🌐 *www.visitrhodeisland.com.* **Vermont Department of Tourism and Marketing.** ☎ *800/837–6668* 🌐 *www.vermontvacation.com.* **Visit New England.** 🌐 *www.visitnewengland.com.*

Chapter 3

BEST FALL FOLIAGE DRIVES AND ROAD TRIPS

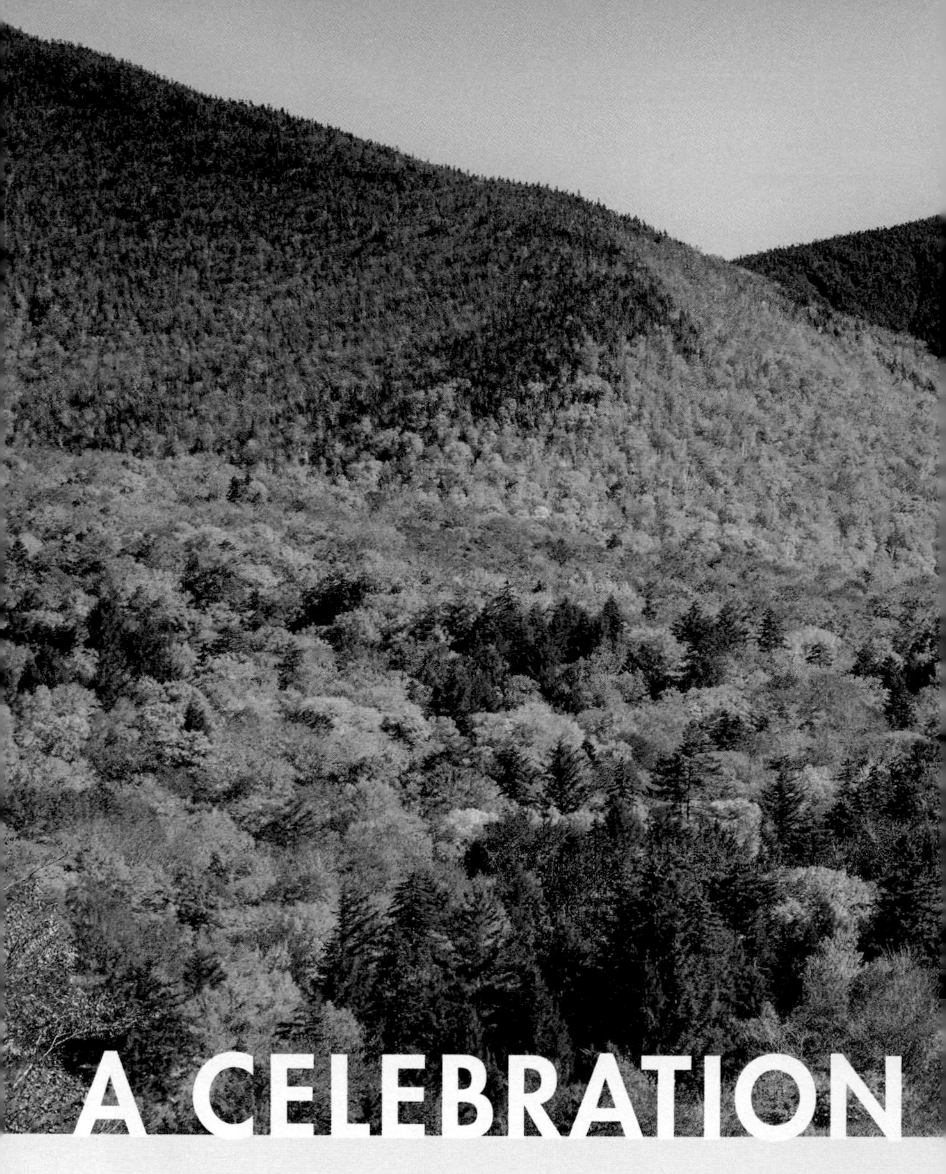

A CELEBRATION

Picture this: one scarlet maple offset by the stark white spire of a country church, a whole hillside of brilliant foliage foregrounded by a vintage barn, or perhaps a covered bridge straddling a cobalt river. Such iconic scenes have launched a thousand Instagram posts and turned New England into the ultimate fall destination for leaf peepers.

OF COLOR

Above, Vermont's Green Mountains are multicolored in the fall (and often white in winter).

Mother Nature, of course, puts on an annual autumn performance elsewhere, but this one is a showstopper. Like the landscape, the mix of deciduous (leaf-shedding) trees is remarkably varied here and creates a broader than usual palette. New England's abundant evergreens lend contrast, making the display even more vivid. Every September and October, leaf peepers arrive to cruise along country lanes, join outdoor adventures, or simply stroll on town greens.

Did you know the brilliant shades actually lurk in the leaves all year long? Leaves contain three pigments. The green chlorophyll, so dominant in summer that it obscures the red anthocyanins and orangey-yellow carotenoids, decreases in fall and reveals a crayon box of color.

PREDICTING THE PEAK

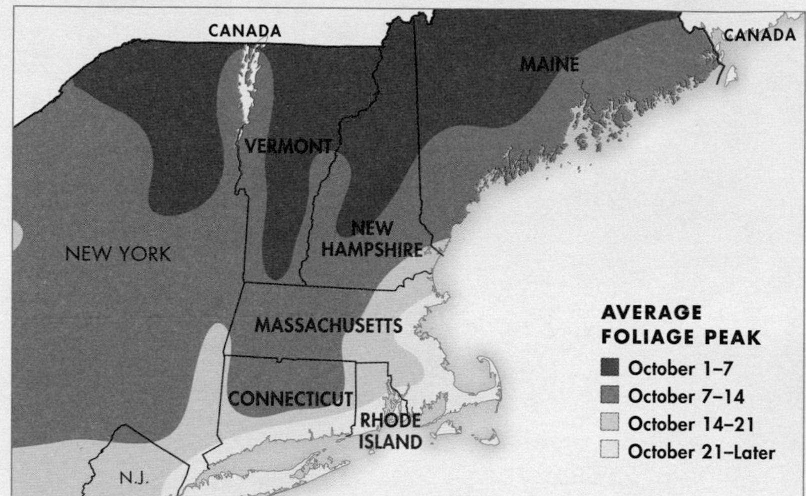

LOCATION

Pinning down precisely when colors will appear remains an inexact science, although location plays a major role. Typically, the transformation begins in the highest and northernmost parts of New England in mid-September, then moves steadily into lower altitudes and southern sectors throughout October.

For trip planning, think in terms of regions rather than states. In Maine (a huge state that runs north–south) leaf color can peak anytime from the fourth week of September to the third week of October, depending on the locale.

WEATHER

Early September weather is another deciding factor. From the foliage aficionado's perspective, the ideal scenario is calm, temperate days capped by nights that are cool but still above freezing. If the weather is too warm, it delays the onset of the season. If it's too dry or windy, the leaves shrivel up or blow off.

COLOR CHECK RESOURCES

Curious about current conditions? In season, most states maintain websites reporting on foliage conditions. Weather Channel has peak viewing maps and Foliage Network uses a network of spotters to chart changes.

- **Connecticut:** *www.ct.gov/dep*
- **Foliage Network:** *www.foliagenetwork.com*
- **Maine:** *www.mainefoliage.com*
- **Massachusetts:** *www.massvacation.com*
- **New Hampshire:** *www.visitnh.gov*
- **Rhode Island:** *www.visitrhodeisland.com*
- **Vermont:** *www.vermontvacation.com*
- **Weather Channel:** *www.weather.com*

TOP TREES FOR COLOR

A AMERICAN BEECH. This tree's smooth, steel-gray trunk is crowned with gold, copper, and bronze-tinted leaves in autumn, giving it a metallic sheen. Though the elliptical leaves sometimes hang on all winter, its "fruit" goes fast because beechnuts are a popular snack for birds, squirrels, and even bears.

B NORTHERN RED OAK. The upside of oaks is that they retain their fall shading until late in the season—the downside is that, for most species, that color is a boring brown. Happily, the northern red isn't like other members of the oak family. Its elongated, flame-shaped leaves turn fiery crimson and incandescent orange.

C QUAKING ASPEN. Eyes and ears both prove useful when identifying this aspen. Look for small, ovate leaves that usually become almost flaxen. Or listen for the leaves' quake: a sound, audible in even a gentle breeze, which the U.S. Forest Service likens to that made by "thousands of fluttering butterfly wings."

D SUGAR MAPLE. The leaf of the largest North American maple species is so lovely that Canada put it on its national flag. Each generally has five multi-pointed lobes—plus enough anthocyanin to produce a deep red color. The tree itself produces plentiful sap and is the cornerstone of New England's syrup industry.

E WHITE ASH. This tall tree typically grows to between 65 to 100 feet. Baseball enthusiasts admire the wood (which is used to craft bats); while foliage fans admire the compound leaves, each consisting of five to nine slightly serrated, tapering leaflets. They range in hue from burgundy and purple to amber.

F WHITE BIRCH. A papery, light, bright bark makes this slender hardwood easily recognizable. Centuries ago, Native Americans used birch wood to make everything from canoes to medicinal teas. Today's photographers know the bark also makes great pictures since it provides a sharp contrast to the tree's vibrant yellow leaves.

FANTASTIC FALL ITINERARY

The Berkshires

Fall is the perfect time to visit New England—country roads wind through dense forests exploding into reds, oranges, yellows, and purples. For inspiration, here is an itinerary for the truly ambitious that links the most stunning foliage areas; choose a section to explore more closely. Like autumn itself, this route works its way south from northern Vermont into Connecticut, with one or two days in each area.

VERMONT

NORTHWEST VERMONT

In Burlington, the elms will be turning colors on the University of Vermont campus. You can ride the ferry across Lake Champlain for great views of Vermont's Green Mountains and New York's Adirondacks. After visiting the resort town of Stowe, detour off Route 100 beneath the cliffs of Smugglers' Notch. The north country's palette unfolds in Newport, where the blue waters of Lake Memphremagog reflect the foliage.

NORTHEAST KINGDOM

After a side trip along Lake Willoughby, explore St. Johnsbury, where the Fairbanks Museum and St. Johnsbury Athenaeum reveal Victorian tastes in art and natural-history collecting. In Peacham, stock up for a picnic at the Peacham Store.

NEW HAMPSHIRE

WHITE MOUNTAINS AND LAKES REGION

Interstate 93 narrows as it winds through craggy Franconia Notch. Get off the interstate for the sinuous Kancamagus Highway portion of Route 112 that passes through the mountains to Conway. In Center Harbor, in the Lakes Region, you can ride the *MS Mount Washington* for views of the Lake Winnipesaukee shoreline, or ascend to Moultonborough's Castle in the Clouds for a falcon's-eye look at the colors.

MT. MONADNOCK

In Hanover, stroll around the Dartmouth College campus, then head south around Lake Sunapee. Several trails climb Mt. Monadnock, near Peterborough, and colorful vistas extend as far as Boston.

⇨ For local drives perfect for an afternoon, also see our Fall Foliage Drive Spotlights on Western Massachusetts, Connecticut, Rhode Island, Vermont, New Hampshire, and Inland Maine.

THE MOOSE IS LOOSE!

Take "Moose Crossing" signs seriously because things won't end well if you hit an animal that stands six feet tall and weighs 1,200 pounds. Some 40,000 reside in northern New England. To search out these ungainly creatures in the wild, consider an organized moose safari in northern New Hampshire or Maine.

MASSACHUSETTS

THE MOHAWK TRAIL

In Shelburne Falls, the Bridge of Flowers displays the last of autumn's blossoms. Follow the Mohawk Trail section of Route 2 as it ascends into the Berkshire Hills—and stop to take in the view at the hairpin turn just east of North Adams (or drive up Mt. Greylock, the tallest peak in Massachusetts, for more stunning vistas). In Williamstown, the Clark Art Institute has gorgeous grounds and houses a collection of impressionist works.

THE BERKSHIRES

The scenery around Lenox, Stockbridge, and Great Barrington has long attracted the talented and the wealthy. Near U.S. 7, you can visit the homes of novelist Edith Wharton (the Mount, in Lenox), sculptor Daniel Chester French (Chesterwood, in Stockbridge), and diplomat Joseph Choate (Naumkeag, in Stockbridge).

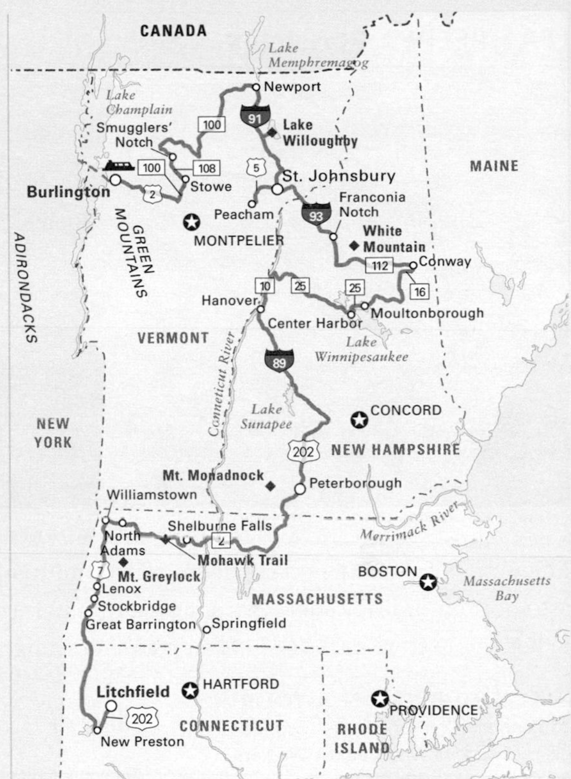

CONNECTICUT

THE LITCHFIELD HILLS

This area of Connecticut combines the feel of upcountry New England with exclusive urban polish. The wooded shores of Lake Waramaug are home to the striking Hopkins Inn and Hopkins Vineyard. Litchfield has a perfect village green—a quintessential New England town center.

FOLIAGE PHOTO HINT

Don't just snap the big panoramic views. Look for single, brilliantly colored trees with interesting elements nearby, like a weathered gray stone wall or a freshly painted white church. These images are often more evocative than big blobs of color or panoramic shots.

LEAF PEEPER PLANNER

Hot-air balloons and ski-lift rides give a different perspective on fall's color.

Enjoying fall doesn't necessarily require a multistate road trip. If you are short on time (or energy), a simple autumnal stroll might be just the ticket: many state parks even offer free short ranger-led rambles.

HIKE AND BIKE ON A TOUR

You can sign on for foliage-focused hiking holidays with **Country Walkers** (☎ *855/445–5603* 🌐 *www.country-walkers.com*) and **Boundless Journeys** (☎ *800/941–8010* 🌐 *www.boundless-journeys.com*); or cycling ones with **Discovery Bike Tours** (☎ *800/257–2226* 🌐 *www.discoverybiketours.com*) and **VBT Bicycling Vacations** (☎ *855/202–2251* 🌐 *www.vbt.com*). Individual state tourism boards list similar operators elsewhere.

SOAR ABOVE THE CROWDS

New Hampshire's Cannon Mountain (☎ *603/823–8800* 🌐 *www.cannonmt.com*) is only one of several New England ski resorts that provides gondola or aerial tram rides during foliage season. Area hot-air balloon operators, like **Above Reality Hot Air Balloon Rides** (☎ *802/373–4007* 🌐 *www.balloonvermont.com*), help you take it in from the top.

ROOM AT THE INN?

Accommodations fill quickly in autumn. Vermont's top lodgings sell out months in advance for the first two weeks in October. So book early and expect a two-night minimum stay requirement. If you can't find a quaint inn, try basing yourself at an Airbnb or off-season ski resort. Also, be prepared for some sticker shock; if you can travel midweek, you'll often save quite a bit.

RIDE THE RAILS OR THE CURRENT

Board the **Essex Steam Train** for a ride through the Connecticut countryside (☎ *800/377–3987* 🌐 *www.essexsteam-train.com*) or float through northern Rhode Island on the **Blackstone Valley Explorer** riverboat (☎ *401/724–2200* 🌐 *www.rivertourblackstone.com*).

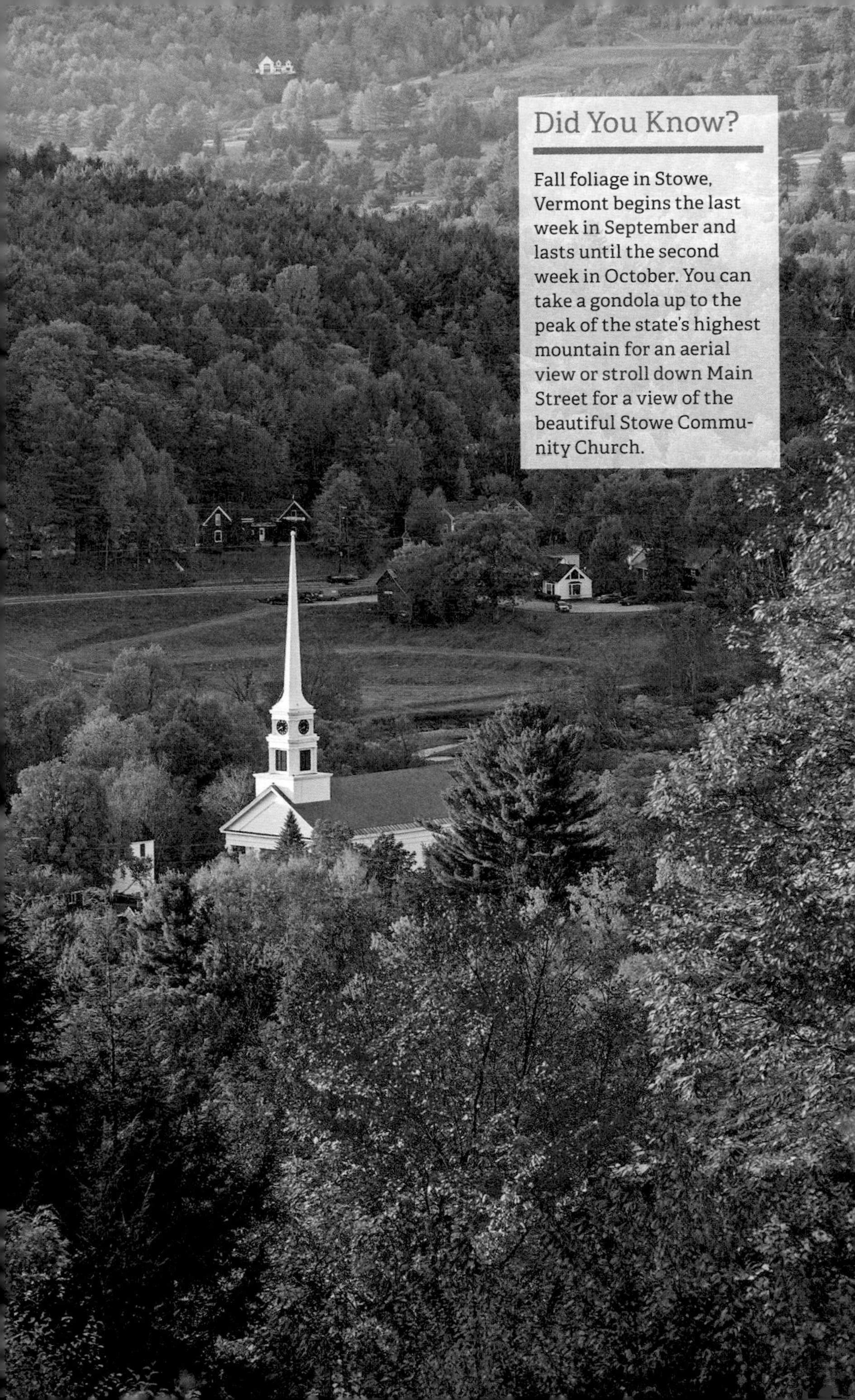
Did You Know?
Fall foliage in Stowe, Vermont begins the last week in September and lasts until the second week in October. You can take a gondola up to the peak of the state's highest mountain for an aerial view or stroll down Main Street for a view of the beautiful Stowe Community Church.

MASSACHUSETTS FALL FOLIAGE DRIVE

When fall foliage season arrives, the Berkshires are the place to appreciate the autumnal grandeur. Winding roads lined with dramatic trees ablaze—notably maples, birches, and beeches—pass alongside meadows, pasture, farmland, mountains, rivers, and lakes.

Begin in North Adams, a city transformed by art, and spend some time at the Massachusetts Museum of Contemporary Art (MASS MoCA). Just west of downtown off Route 2, the Notch Road leads into the **Mt. Greylock State Reservation,** ambling upward to the summit. At 3,491 feet, it's the state's highest point and affords expansive views of the countryside. Hike any of the many trails throughout the park, picnic at the peak, or stay for a meal at the rustic **Bascom Lodge.** Continue your descent on the Notch Road to Rockwell Road to exit the park and join Route 7 South.

BEST TIME TO GO

Peak leaf viewing generally happens in mid-October. Trees growing near water tend to have more vibrant colors that peak a bit sooner. The state regularly updates fall foliage information by phone and online (☎800/632–8038 🌐www.massvacation.com).

PLANNING YOUR TIME

This scenic loop is only about 35 miles, but you could easily spend the day leisurely exploring the circuit.

Follow Route 7 South into the small town center of Lanesborough, where you'll turn left onto Summer Street. Horse farms and wide-open pastures make up the landscape, with distant mountain peaks hovering grandly in the background. If you want to pick your own apples, take a 1½-mile detour off Summer Street and stop at **Lakeview Orchard.**

Summer Street continues to tiny Berkshire Village, where you'll pick up Route 8 heading back toward North Adams. Running parallel to Route 8 from Lanesborough to Adams, is the paved **Ashuwillticook Rail Trail** for biking and walking. Right in the midst of two mountain ranges, the trail abuts wetlands, mixed woodland (including beech, birch, and maple trees), the Hoosac River, and the Cheshire Reservoir. In Cheshire, **Whitney's Farm Market** is busy on fall weekends with pony rides, pumpkin picking, a corn maze, and hayrides; plus it sells baked goods like the pumpkin whoopie pie.

Continuing on Route 8, you'll start to leave farm country as you make your way back to North Adams. Once a part of its much larger neighbor, the town of Adams still has active mills and the **Susan B. Anthony Birthplace Museum.** The 1817 Federal home of her birth has been fully restored.

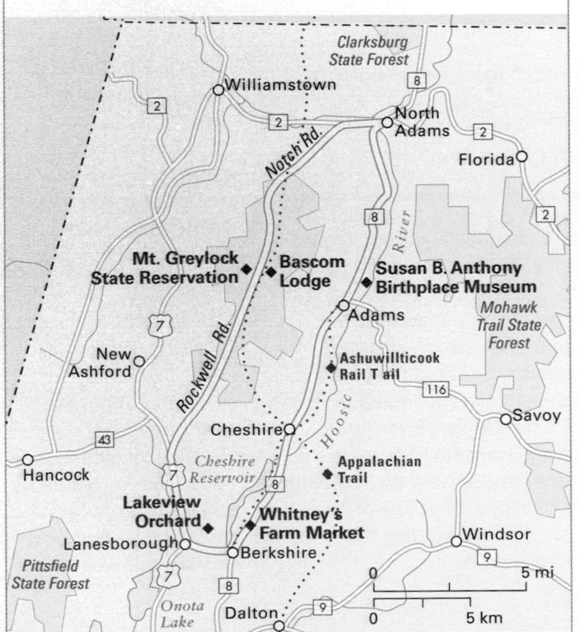

NEED A BREAK?

Bascom Lodge Built in the 1930s, this mountaintop lodge retains its rustic charm with comfortable, no-frills lodging and a restaurant in a stunning setting. ✉ *Mt. Greylock State Reservation, Adams* ☎ *413/743–1591* 🌐 *www.bascomlodge.net* ⏲ *Closed Nov.–May.*

Lakeview Orchard Here you can pick your own bushel of apples (and other fall fruit) and sip on freshly pressed cider. The friendly farmers also sell homemade pies and pastries, but make sure to sample their singular (and superb) cider doughnuts. ✉ *94 Old Cheshire Rd., Lanesborough* ☎ *413/448–6009* 🌐 *www.lakevieworchard.com.*

Whitney's Farm Market Whitney's Farm has a large market with baked goods and a deli; you can also pick your own seasonal fruit. The fun Pumpkin Fest takes place on weekends, mid-September–October. ✉ *1775 S. State Rd., Cheshire* ☎ *413/442–4749* 🌐 *www.whitneysfarm.com.*

CONNECTICUT FALL FOLIAGE DRIVE

Tucked into the heart of Litchfield County, the crossroads village of New Preston perches above a 20-foot waterfall on the Aspetuck River. Just north of here, you'll find Lake Waramaug nestled in the rolling foothills and, to the east, Mt. Tom—both areas ablaze with rich color every fall.

Start in **New Milford** and stroll along historic Main Street. Here you'll find one of the longest town greens in the state, as well as many shops, galleries, and restaurants within a short walk. Hop in the car and drive south on Main Street, then turn left to head north on wooded Route 202. Continue north on Route 202 to the junction of Route 45, and follow signs for Lake Waramaug. If you prefer to hike or bike, the **New Milford River Trail** extends about 5 miles along the Housatonic River, from Gaylordsville (northwest of the New Milford town green) north to the village of Kent. It's a beautiful walk or ride along a wide gravel trail, with short side routes down to the water, and especially lovely in autumn.

BEST TIME TO GO

Peak foliage occurs early October–early November. In season, the website (🌐 portal.ct.gov/DEEP/Forestry/Foliage) includes daily updates on leaf color. Hope for a wet spring, warm fall days, and cool (but not too cool) fall nights for the most dramatic display.

PLANNING YOUR TIME

It's less than 30 miles from New Milford to the center of Litchfield, but with stops at the New Milford River Trail, Lake Waramaug, and Mt. Tom you could easily spend most of the day enjoying the scenery.

Route 45 will bring you through the tiny village center of New Preston; stop here for a bit of shopping at **Dawn Hill Antiques.** Continue on 45 north to Lake Waramaug. The 8-mile drive around the lake is stunning in autumn with the foliage of fiery red maples, rusty brown oaks, and yellow birches reflected in the water. The beach area of **Lake Waramaug State Park,** about halfway around the lake, is a great place for a picnic, or even a quick dip on a warm fall day. **Hopkins Vineyard** is open daily; head to its Hayloft Wine Bar to enjoy a glass of wine and the spectacular lake views.

After completing a loop of Lake Waramaug, head back to Route 202 North toward Litchfield. Another excellent leaf-peeping locale is **Mt. Tom State Park,** about 4 miles or so from the junction of Routes 45 and 202. Here you can hike the mile-long trail to the summit and climb to the top of a stone tower that provides a 360-degree view of the countryside's colors—the vibrant reds of the sugar maples are always among the most dazzling. After your hike, continue north on Route 202, ending your journey in the quintessential New England town of Litchfield. Peruse the shops and galleries in the town center and end the day with a dinner at the chic **West Street Grill.**

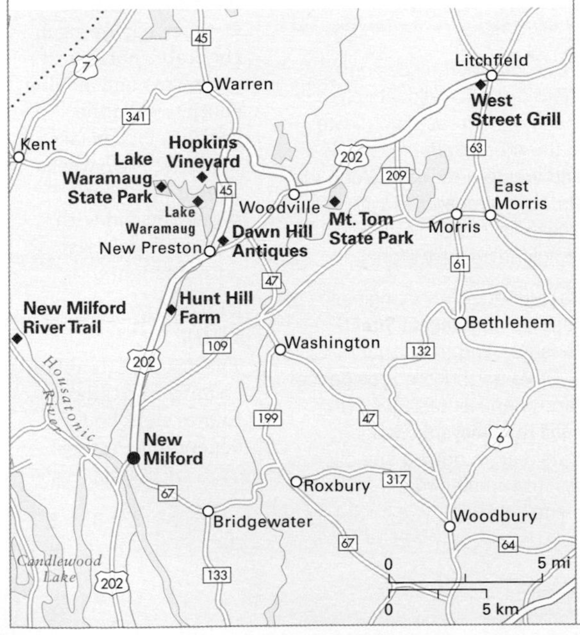

NEED A BREAK?

Dawn Hill Antiques This shop is filled with mainly Swedish antiques selected by the owners on their regular trips to Europe. ✉ *11 Main St., New Preston* ☎ *860/868–0066* 🌐 *dawnhillantiques.com.*

Hopkins Vineyard This winery produces more than 13 different wines, from sparkling to dessert. Tastings are available, and a wine bar in the hayloft with views of the lake serves a fine cheese-and-pâté board. ✉ *25 Hopkins Rd., off N. Shore Rd., New Preston* ☎ *860/868–7954* 🌐 *www.hopkinsvineyard.com* 🎫 *Tours $20.*

West Street Grill This sophisticated dining room on the town green is the place to see and be seen. It's the perfect spot for a casual lunch or formal dinner. ✉ *43 West St., Litchfield* ☎ *860/567–3885* 🌐 *www.weststreetgrill.com.*

RHODE ISLAND FALL FOLIAGE DRIVE

The Rhode Island State Tree is the red maple, whose leaves turn to shades of gold, purple, and scarlet in fall.

This tiny state is also home to such diverse species as scarlet oak, white oak, northern red oak, yellow birch, gray birch, ash, and black cherry. Pine forests dominate the southern woodlands, so the most dramatic leaf peeping is in the northern and western regions. Along the way, you'll find dense forests, rolling meadows with centuries-old stone walls, an occasional orchard or pumpkin patch, and archetypal New England country stores.

This tour through the state's quieter corners begins in **Providence,** where you can stroll along **Benefit Street,** admiring its architectural treasures and trees that burst up through brick sidewalks. Drive north from Providence on 95 to Route 146 North, and then Route 295 North to Route 114 North to **Diamond Hill Vineyards,** whose grapevines and apple trees yield an intriguing selection of wines, including some sweet varieties made from fruits and berries grown on-site—perfect on a cool October day.

BEST TIME TO GO

Foliage usually peaks in the second and third weeks of October, beginning in the state's northwestern corner and moving south toward the coast. Color can last more than two weeks in years without big storms but with plenty of cool, crisp autumn nights.

PLANNING YOUR TIME

The drive totals about 80 miles and takes four to eight hours, depending on stops.

To get from the Vineyard to Route 116, you have to double back south on Route 114. Once on Route 116, drive west about 12 miles to Greenville, turning west on U.S. 44 for 7 miles to the hamlet of Chepachet, where Colonial and Victorian buildings contain antique shops and quirky stores. Don't miss **Brown & Hopkins Country Store,** one of the country's oldest continuously operating general stores—complete with a nostalgia-inducing candy counter—or the **Tavern on Main,** a restaurant in a rambling 18th-century building that some say is haunted.

Follow U.S. 44 west 5 miles to the burst of changing colors in **Pulaski State Park and Memorial Recreation Area.** Turn left onto Route 94 and follow this for about 13 miles to Route 102, then continue southeast another 20 miles to Exeter. This mostly undeveloped route from Chepachet to Exeter is lined with red maple, white oak, beech, elm, and poplar trees.

From Route 102, continue east to Wickford, a Colonial seaport whose pretty harbor opens to Narragansett Bay. The town's oak- and beech-shaded lanes are perfect for a late-afternoon stroll among the galleries and boutiques.

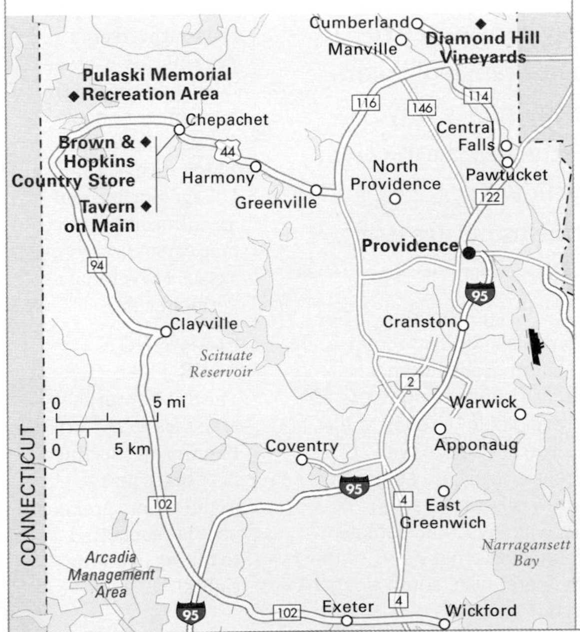

NEED A BREAK?

Brown & Hopkins Country Store Opened in 1809, this store carries candles, reproduction antiques, penny candy, and handmade soaps. ✉ *1179 Putnam Pike, Chepachet* ☎ *401/568–4830* 🌐 *shopbrownandhopkins.com.*

Diamond Hill Vineyards This winery produces Pinot Noir from grapes grown on-site, as well as wines made from local apples, blueberries, and other fruit. ✉ *3145 Diamond Hill Rd., Cumberland* ☎ *401/333–2751* 🌐 *www.diamondhillvineyards.com* 🎟 *Free.*

Pulaski State Park and Recreational Area The 100-acre recreation area has fishing, picnic spots, easy hiking trails, and the 13-acre Peck Pond. ✉ *151 Pulaski Rd., Chepachet* ☎ *401/723–7892* 🌐 *www.riparks.com.*

Tavern on Main Try the Rhode Island Veal Parmesan (topped with chunky sweet Italian sausage sauce and mozzarella) or the Biggest Lobster Roll served on a grilled sub roll. ✉ *1157 Putnam Pike, Chepachet* ☎ *401/710–9788* 🌐 *www.tavernonmainri.com.*

VERMONT FALL FOLIAGE DRIVE

Nearly 80% of Vermont is forested, with cities few and far between. The state's interior is a rural playground for leaf peepers, and it's widely considered to exhibit the most intense range of colors anywhere on the continent. Its tiny towns and hamlets—the few distractions from the dark reds, yellows, oranges, and russets—are as pristine as nature itself.

Begin this drive in Manchester Village, along the old-fashioned, well-to-do homes lining Main Street, and continue south to Arlington, North Bennington, and Old Bennington. Stop just a mile south along Route 7A at **Hildene.** The 412 acres of explorable grounds at the estate of Abraham Lincoln's son are ablaze with color, and the views over the Battenkill Valley are as good as any you can find. Drive south another mile along 7A to the **Equinox Valley Nursery,** where you can sample delicious apple cider and doughnuts amid views of the arresting countryside. A few more miles south along 7A is the small town of Arlington.

BEST TIME TO GO

Late September and early October are the times to go, with the southern area peaking about a week later than the north. Remember to book hotels in advance. The state has a Fall Foliage Hotline and an online interactive map (☎ 802/828–3239 🌐 www.foliage-vermont.com).

PLANNING YOUR TIME

The drive from Manchester to Bennington outlined here takes just 30 minutes, but a relaxed pace is best suited to taking in all the sights.

From Route 7A in Arlington you can take two adventurous and stunning detours. One is pure foliage: follow Route 313 west a few miles to the New York State border for more beautiful views. Or head east 1 mile to East Arlington, where there's a delightful chocolate emporium. (You can continue even farther east from this spot to Kelly Stand Road leading into the Green Mountains—a little-known route that can't be beat.) Back on 7A South in Arlington, stop at the delightful **Arlington Dairy Bar** for a Vermont creemee.

Farther south in Shaftsbury is **Clear Brook Farm,** a brilliant place for fresh produce and pumpkins. Robert Frost spent much of his life in South Shaftsbury, and you can learn about his life at his former home, the **Stone House.** From South Shaftsbury take Route 67 through North Bennington and continue on to Route 67A in Old Bennington. Ride the elevator up the 306-foot-high **Bennington Battle Monument** to survey the season's progress across four states. Back down from the clouds, walk a few serene blocks to the cemetery of the **Old First Church,** where Robert Frost is buried, and contemplate his autumnal poem, "Nothing Gold Can Stay."

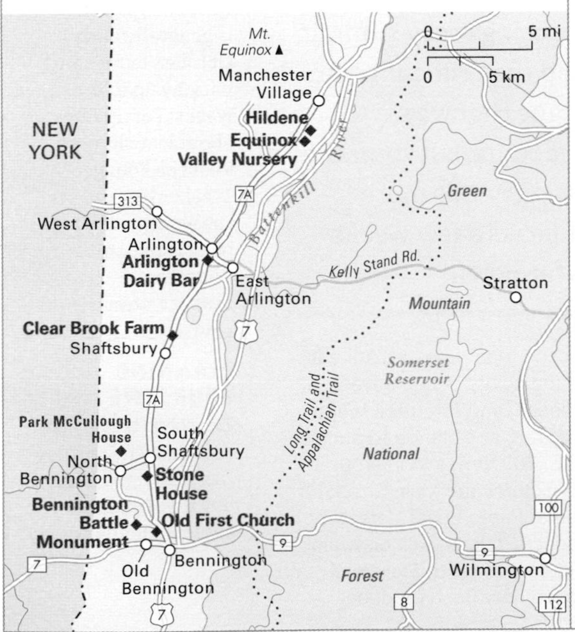

NEED A BREAK?

Arlington Dairy Bar Along 7A waits a big red dairy barn surrounded on all sides by Vermont's color-changing landscape. There are few greater ways to enjoy fall foliage than leaning on the hood of your car with a double scoop of local pumpkin and maple walnut ice cream, or a chocolate-dipped Vermont creemee. ✉ *3158 Rte. 7A, Arlington* ☎ *802/375–2546* 🌐 *www.facebook.com/ArlingtonDairyBar.*

Clear Brook Farm This 25-acre certified organic farm sells its own produce, in addition to plants, baked goods, and other seasonal treats. ✉ *47 Hidden Valley Rd., Manchester* ☎ *802/442–4273* 🌐 *www.clearbrook-farm.com.*

Equinox Valley Nursery This nursery carries fresh produce, seasonal snacks, and cider doughnuts. There's family-friendly fall activities—a corn maze, hayrides, and pumpkin carving—as well as the property's 300-odd scarecrows. ✉ *1158 Main St., Manchester* ☎ *802/362–2610* 🌐 *www.equinoxvalleynursery.com* 🎟 *Free.*

NEW HAMPSHIRE FALL FOLIAGE DRIVE

Quaint villages graced with green commons, white town halls, and covered bridges: southwestern New Hampshire is dominated by the imposing rocky summit of Mt. Monadnock and the brilliant colors of autumn. Kancamagus Highway is another classic foliage route, but for more solitude and less traffic, try this more accessible route that peaks a few weeks later than the state's far north.

The Granite State is the second-most-forested state in the nation; by mid-October the colors of the leaves of its maple, birch, elm, oak, beech, and ash trees range from green to gold, purple to red, and orange to auburn. Routes 12, 101, 124, and U.S. 202 form a loop around **Mt. Monadnock.** Start on the picturesque Main Street in Keene with a stop for coffee at Prime Roast Café; for New Hampshire–made products, take a walk on Main Street or detour west on Route 9 to reach **Stonewall Farm**, a lovely spot for a stroll or buy fresh produce.

BEST TIME TO GO

The best time to view foliage in southern New Hampshire is generally early October, but it can vary by up to four weeks. For updates about leaf changes, visit the Foliage Tracker page on the website of **Visit New Hampshire** (☎603/271-2665 🌐www.visitnh.gov).

PLANNING YOUR TIME

Expect to travel about 55 miles. The journey can take up to a full day if you stop to explore along the way.

From Keene, travel east on Route 101 through Dublin. In **Peterborough**, browse the local boutiques as well as the superb **Mariposa Museum,** which exhibits a colorful collection of costumes and musical instruments from every corner of the globe. If you need a bite to eat before continuing on your journey or later for dinner, stop by **Harlow's Pub,** a convivial spot in Peterborough's scenic downtown.

Then turn south on U.S. 202 toward Jaffrey Village. Just west on Route 124, in historic Jaffrey Center, be sure to visit the **Meeting House Cemetery,** where author Willa Cather is buried. One side trip, 4 miles south on U.S. 202, leads to the majestic **Cathedral of the Pines** in Rindge, one of the best places in the region for foliage viewing because evergreens offset the brilliant shades of red.

Heading west on Route 124, you can take Dublin Road to the main entrance of **Monadnock State Park** or continue along to the Old Toll Road parking area for one of the most popular routes up the mountain, the **Old Halfway House Trail.** All the hiking trails have great views, including the area's many lakes. Continuing on U.S. 124, head southwest on Fitzwilliam Road to Fitzwilliam. If you have time, pop into **Bloomin' Antiques** to browse their selection of fine art and unusual antiques.

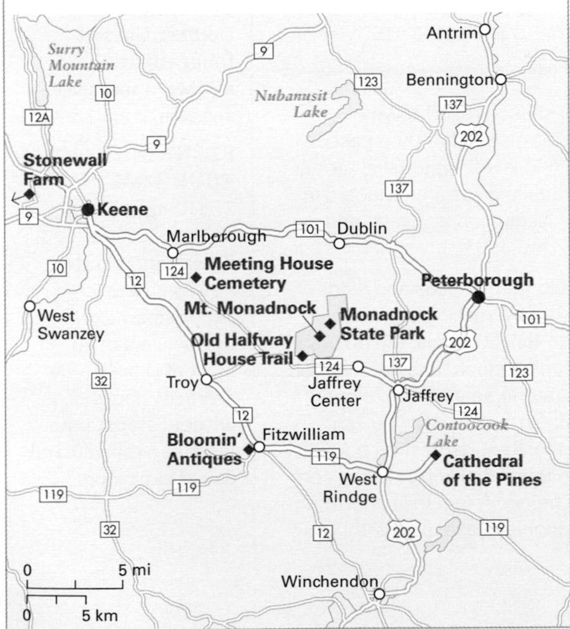

NEED A BREAK?

Bloomin' Antiques Fine art and unusual antiques. ✉ *3 Templeton Tpke., Fitzwilliam* ☎ *800/386–4664* 🌐 *bloominantiques.com.*

Harlow's Pub Open for lunch, dinner, and Sunday brunch, this friendly tavern with a patio overlooking Peterborough's scenic village center serves creative comfort fare and local craft beer. ✉ *3 School St., Peterborough* ☎ *603/924–6365* 🌐 *www.harlowspub.com.*

Stonewall Farm A working dairy farm with a dramatic setting amid fields and forests, Stonewall is open daily and presents an active schedule of events, including maple sugaring and seasonal horse-drawn hayrides. Walking and snowshoeing trails lace the property, and a farm shop sells organic produce, gourmet snacks, and the farm's own luscious Frisky Cow Gelato. Young children love the discovery room, and the interactive greenhouse is geared for all ages. ✉ *242 Chesterfield Rd., Keene* ☎ *603/357–7278* 🌐 *www.stonewallfarm.org.*

INLAND MAINE FALL FOLIAGE DRIVE

Swaths of pine, spruce, and fir trees offset the red, orange, and yellow of maples and birches along this popular foliage drive through western Maine's mountains.

Wending its way to the four-season resort town of Rangeley, near its northern terminus, the route passes stunning overlooks, forest-lined lakes, waterfalls, hiking trails, and a state park. Mountain vistas are reflected in the many (often connected) lakes, ponds, rivers, and streams.

Route 17 heads north past old homesteads and fields along the Swift River Valley before making a mountainous switchback ascent to **Height of Land,** the drive's literal pinnacle. The must-stop overlook here has off-road parking, interpretive panels, stone seating, and a short path to the **Appalachian Trail.** On a clear day, you can look west to mountains on the New Hampshire border. **Mooselookmeguntic Lake** and **Upper Richardson Lake** seem to float amid the forestland below. A few miles north of here is an overlook for Rangeley Lake, also with interpretive panels.

BEST TIME TO GO

Fall color usually peaks in the first or second week of October. Get fall foliage updates at 🌐www.mainefoliage.com.

PLANNING YOUR TIME

The Rangeley Lakes National Scenic Byway and a state byway (🌐www.exploremaine.org/byways) make up most of this 58-mile drive (1½ hours without stops), but plan for a relaxed, full day of exploring.

In tiny, welcoming Oquossoc, where Routes 17 and 4 meet, enjoy a burger or wood-fired pizza with one of the many Maine craft brews on tap at **Portage Tap House.** The hamlet is also home to the **Outdoor Heritage Museum,** where you can learn why visitors have come here to fish, hunt, and enjoy the outdoors since the mid-1800s. The trailhead for **Bald Mountain,** a popular hike, is just outside the village.

Rangeley, 7 miles east on Route 4, has restaurants, inns, a waterfront park, and outdoorsy shops. The countryside sweeps into view along public hiking trails at the 175-acre **Wilhelm Reich Museum.** There's also hiking at Rangeley Lakes Trail Center on Saddleback Mountain.

The road to **Rangeley Lake State Park** is accessible from both Routes 4 and 17, as is the **Appalachian Trail.** Overhanging foliage frames waterfalls at the scenic rest areas at each end of the drive: at Coos Canyon on Route 17 en route to Height of Land, and at Smalls Falls on Route 4 near Madrid, the terminus. Both spots have swimming holes, several falls, and paths with views of their drops. Coos Canyon is along the Swift River, a destination for recreational gold panning. You can rent or buy panning equipment at **Coos Canyon Rock and Gift,** across from its namesake. The seasonal shop also sells premade sandwiches, ice cream, and snacks.

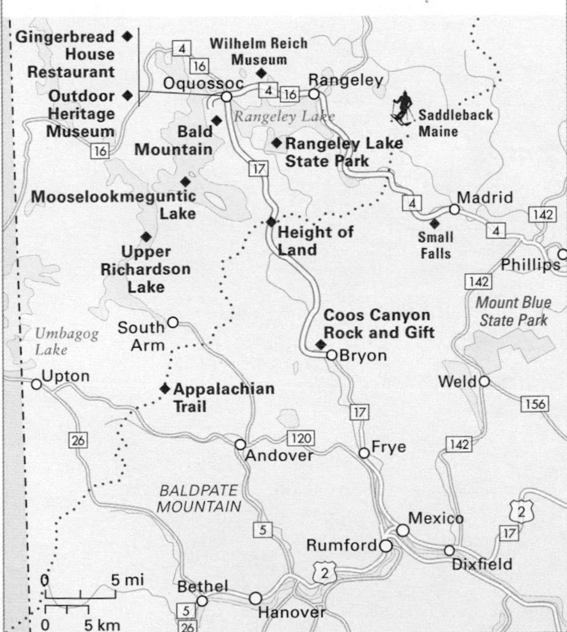

NEED A BREAK?

Coos Canyon Rock and Gift Along with prospecting equipment, the seasonal shop sells souvenirs, to-go foods, and ice cream. ✉ *472 Swift River Rd. (Rte. 17), Byron* ☎ *207/364–4900* 🌐 *www.coscanyonrockandgift.com.*

Rangeley Lakes Heritage Trust The trust protects 14,000 acres of land in the Rangeley Lakes area. Both online and at its Rangeley office, the trust has maps and descriptions of its 35 miles of recreational trails and access roads, along with information about fishing, hunting, snowmobiling, picnicking, and other outdoor activities. ✉ *2424 Main St., Rangeley* ☎ *207/864–7311* 🌐 *www.rlht.org.*

Wilhelm Reich Museum This seasonal museum showcases the life and work of controversial physician-scientist Wilhelm Reich (1897–1957). Open year-round, the 175-acre property has great trails and an observatory with magnificent views. ✉ *19 Orgonon Circle, off Rte. 4, Rangeley* ☎ *207/864–3443* 🌐 *www.wilhelmreichmuseum.org* 🎟 *Museum $10, grounds free.*

Did You Know?

Boston Public Garden's iconic boats have a secret. Creater Robert Paget first crafted the swans to hide the foot-propelled paddle wheel mechanism and cover the boat captain. Launched in 1877, the swans still ply the garden's lagoon.

Chapter 4

BOSTON AND ENVIRONS

4

Updated by
Cheryl Fenton, Leigh Harrington, Kim Foley MacKinnon

Sights ★★★★★ | Restaurants ★★★★★ | Hotels ★★★★★ | Shopping ★★★★★ | Nightlife ★★★★★

WELCOME TO BOSTON AND ENVIRONS

TOP REASONS TO GO

★ **Freedom's Ring:** Walk through America's early history on the 2½-mile Freedom Trail that snakes through town.

★ **Ivy-Draped Campus:** Hang in Harvard Square like a collegian or hit the university's museums: the Sackler (ancient art), the Botanical Museum, the Peabody (archaeology), and the Natural History Museum.

★ **Posh Purchases:** Strap on some stilettos and join the quest for fashionable finds on Newbury Street, Boston's answer to Manhattan's 5th Avenue.

★ **Sacred Ground:** Root for (or boo) the Red Sox at baseball's most hallowed shrine, Fenway Park.

★ **Tea Time:** Interact with the city's history at the Boston Tea Party Ships & Museum: greet reenactors and explore replicas of the ships at the actual spot where the tea met the sea.

1 Beacon Hill, Boston Common, and the West End. Historic Beacon Hill is bordered by Boston Common, which is the start of the Freedom Trail. The West End has the Museum of Science and the TD Garden.

2 Government Center and the North End. This area has Faneuil Hall and Quincy Market, while the North End is home to Boston's Little Italy.

3 Charlestown. Home to the USS *Constitution*and Bunker Hill Monument.

4 Downtown and the Waterfront. Downtown has many Freedom Trail sights. There's also the Theater District, the country's third-largest Chinatown, the residential Leather District, the Financial District, and the Waterfront.

5 The Seaport District. Across from the Waterfront with Boston's convention center, the Institute of Contemporary Art, and swanky restaurants and hotels.

6 Back Bay and South End. Back Bay has Newbury Street, the Boston Public Library, and Trinity Church. South End has shopping, Victorian row houses, and a large LGBTQ community.

7 Fenway and Kenmore Square. Fenway Park, the Museum of Fine Arts, and the Isabella Stewart Gardner Museum.

8 Cambridge. The collegiate home of Harvard and MIT.

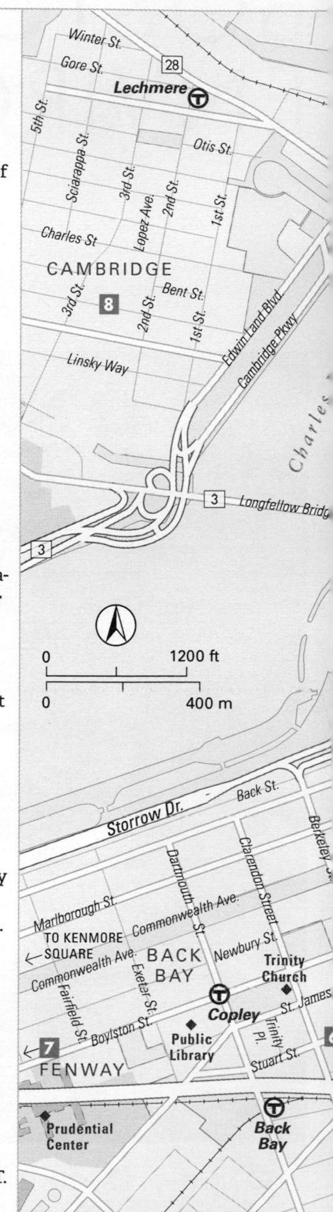

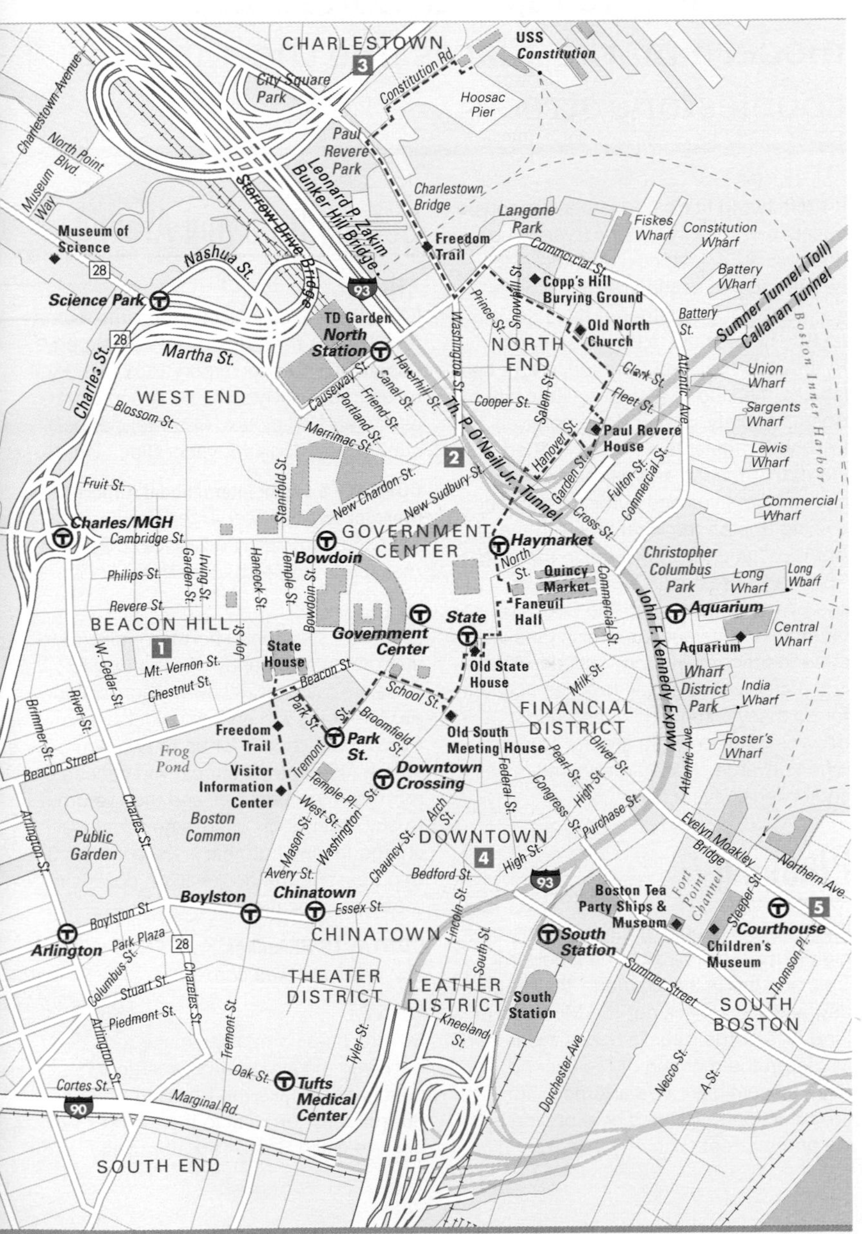
CHARLESTOWN
3
City Square Park
Constitution Rd.
USS Constitution
Hoosac Pier
Charlestown Avenue
North Point Blvd.
Museum Way
Paul Revere Park
Leonard P. Zakim Bunker Hill Bridge
Storrow Drive Bridge
Charlestown Bridge
Langone Park
Fiskes Wharf
Constitution Wharf
Museum of Science
28
Nashua St.
Freedom Trail
Commercial St.
Battery Wharf
93
Science Park
Copp's Hill Burying Ground
Snowhill St.
Prince St.
Battery St.
TD Garden
North Station
Washington St.
NORTH END
Old North Church
Sumner Tunnel (Toll)
Callahan Tunnel
Boston Inner Harbor
Martha St.
Charles St.
Causeway St.
Canal St.
Haverhill St.
Clark St.
Union Wharf
WEST END
Friend St.
Portland St.
Th. P. O'Neill Jr. Tunnel
Cooper St.
Salem St.
Fleet St.
Atlantic Ave.
Sargents Wharf
Blossom St.
Merrimac St.
Paul Revere House
2
Hanover St.
Garden St.
Lewis Wharf
Fruit St.
Staniford St.
New Chardon St.
New Sudbury St.
Fulton St.
Commercial St.
Commercial Wharf
Cross St.
Charles/MGH
Cambridge St.
GOVERNMENT CENTER
Haymarket
Bowdoin
North St.
Quincy Market
Christopher Columbus Park
Long Wharf
Philips St.
Irving St.
Garden St.
Hancock St.
Temple St.
Bowdoin St.
Faneuil Hall
Commercial St.
John F. Kennedy Expwy
Aquarium
Revere St.
BEACON HILL
Joy St.
Government Center
State
Central Wharf
1
W. Cedar St.
State House
Old State House
Aquarium
Mt. Vernon St.
Beacon St.
Wharf District Park
Chestnut St.
School St.
Milk St.
India Wharf
River St.
Brimmer St.
FINANCIAL DISTRICT
Freedom Trail
Park St.
Broomfield St.
Old South Meeting House
Oliver St.
Foster's Wharf
Frog Pond
Tremont St.
Park St.
Pearl St.
Beacon Street
Visitor Information Center
Downtown Crossing
Federal St.
Congress St.
High St.
Atlantic Ave.
Temple Pl.
Purchase St.
West St.
Washington St.
Arch St.
Boston Common
Mason St.
Evelyn Moakley Bridge
Arlington St.
Public Garden
Charles St.
DOWNTOWN
Chauncy St.
High St.
Northern Ave.
4
Avery St.
Bedford St.
Fort Point Channel
Chinatown
93
Boston Tea Party Ships & Museum
Sleeper St.
Boylston
Essex St.
Lincoln St.
5
Boylston St.
Courthouse
Children's Museum
Arlington
Park Plaza
CHINATOWN
South St.
South Station
28
Columbus St.
Thomson Pl.
Stuart St.
Charles St.
THEATER DISTRICT
LEATHER DISTRICT
South Station
Summer Street
SOUTH BOSTON
Piedmont St.
Kneeland St.
Arlington St.
Tremont St.
Tyler St.
Dorchester Ave.
Necco St.
A St.
Cortes St.
Oak St.
Tufts Medical Center
90
Marginal Rd.
SOUTH END

There's history and culture around every bend in Boston—skyscrapers nestle next to historic hotels, while modern marketplaces line the antique cobblestone streets.

It's difficult to fit Boston into a stereotype because of the city's many layers. The deepest is the historical one, the place where musket-bearing revolutionaries vowed to hang together or hang separately. The next tier, a dense spread of Brahmin fortune and fortitude, might be labeled the Hub. It was this elite caste of Boston society, descended from wealthy English Protestants who first settled the state, that funded and patronized the city's universities and cultural institutions, gaining Boston the label "the Athens of America" and felt only pride in the slogan "Banned in Boston." Over that layer lies Beantown, home to the Red Sox faithful and the raucous Bruins fans who crowded the old Boston "*Gah*-den"; this is the city whose ethnic loyalties account for its many distinct neighborhoods. Crowning these layers are the students who converge on the area's universities and colleges every fall.

Planning

If you have a couple of days, hit Boston's highlights—Beacon Hill, the Freedom Trail, and the Public Garden—the first day, and then check out the Museum of Fine Arts or the Isabella Stewart Gardner Museum the morning of the second day. Reserve day two's afternoon for an excursion to Harvard or shopping on Newbury Street.

Getting Here and Around

AIR

More than 40 airlines offer nonstop flights to 120 cities from Boston's major airport, Logan International Airport (BOS). Barely 2 miles from Downtown, the airport can be easily reached by taxi, water taxi, or bus/subway via MBTA's Silver or Blue Line.

CONTACTS Logan International Airport (Boston). ✉ *I–90 East to Ted Williams Tunnel, Boston* ☎ *800/235–6426* 🌐 *www.massport.com/logan-airport* Ⓜ *Airport.*

BIKE

Bluebikes, Boston's short-term bike rental program, is a handy and fun way for travelers to cover relatively short distances. Members are able to unlock a bike from a dock, ride it for up to two hours at a time (45 minutes a trip if you choose a monthly membership), and then return it to any other dock. There's no additional charge for any ride that lasts less than 30 minutes, and the docks are in dozens of metro area locations.

CONTACTS Bluebikes. ☎ *855/948–2929* 🌐 *www.bluebikes.com.*

BOAT

Several boat companies make runs between the airport and Downtown destinations. Take the free Shuttle Bus 66 from any terminal to the airport's ferry dock to catch Boston's water taxis.

MBTA commuter boat service operates weekdays between several Downtown harbor destinations, Charlestown, and quite a few locations on the South Shore. One-way fares range from $3.70 to $9.75 depending on destination; schedules change seasonally, so call ahead.

CONTACTS Boston Harbor Cruises. ☎ *617/227–4321* 🌐 *www.bostonharborcruises.com.* **MBTA Harbor Express.** ☎ *617/222–6999, 617/222–3200* 🌐 *www.mbta.com/schedules/ferry.* **Rowes Wharf Water Transport.** ✉ *Boston* ☎ *617/406–8584* 🌐 *www.roweswharfwatertransport.co.*

CAR

In a place where roads often evolved from cow paths, driving is no simple task. A surfeit of one way streets and inconsistent signage add to the confusion. Street parking is hard to come by, as much of it is resident-permit-only. Your own car is helpful if you're taking side trips, but for exploring the city it will only be a burden.

PEDICAB

Pedicabs, human-powered three-wheeled bicycle rickshaws that hold two adults easily and three with difficulty, are popular in spring and summer around Boston and Cambridge. There are no fixed fares, since the bikers work for tips; pay your biker (cash only) what you think the ride was worth, though be ready for a sour look if you pay much less than $10 a mile or so. Try to agree on a fee ahead of time. Most pedicabs also offer tours, with minimum fixed fees.

CONTACT Boston Pedicab. ✉ *Boston* ☎ *617/266–2005* 🌐 *www.bostonpedicab.com.*

PUBLIC TRANSIT

The "T," as the subway system is affectionately nicknamed, is the cornerstone of a far-reaching public transit network that also includes aboveground trains, buses, and ferries. Its five color-coded lines will put you within a block of virtually anywhere. Subways operate from 5 am to 1 am (schedules vary by line). The same goes for buses, which crisscross the city and suburbia.

To pay, there are two stored-value options: a plastic CharlieCard or paper CharlieTicket, both of which are reusable and reloadable with cash or credit or debit cards. A standard adult subway fare is $2.40 with cash or a CharlieCard. For buses it's $1.70 with cash or a CharlieCard. For most visitors, the best deal will be the unlimited one-day ($12.75) or one-week ($22.50) pass. For details on schedules, routes, and rates, visit the MBTA (Massachusetts Bay Transportation Authority) website.

CONTACT MBTA. ☎ *800/392–6100, 617/222–3200, 617/222–5146 TTY* 🌐 *www.mbta.com.*

TAXI

Cabs are available 24/7. Rides within the city cost $2.60 for the first 1/7 mile and 40¢ for each 1/7 mile thereafter (tolls, where applicable, are extra).

TRAIN

Boston is served by Amtrak at North Station, South Station, and Back Bay Station. North Station is the terminus for Amtrak's *Downeaster* service from Boston to New Hampshire and Maine. South Station and Back Bay Station, nearby, accommodate frequent Northeast Corridor departures to and arrivals from New York, Philadelphia, and Washington, D.C. Amtrak's Acela train cuts the travel time between Boston and New York to 3½ hours. South Station and Back Bay Station are the two stops in Boston for Amtrak's *Lake Shore Limited,* which travels daily between Boston and Chicago by way of Albany, Buffalo, and Cleveland.

Dining

In a city synonymous with tradition, Boston chefs have spent recent years rewriting culinary history. The stuffy, wood-paneled formality is gone; the endless renditions of *chowdah,* lobster, and cod have retired; and the assumption that true foodies better hop the next Amtrak to New York is also—thankfully—a thing of the past. Small, upscale neighborhood spots that use local New England ingredients—fresh fish and shellfish, locally grown fruits and vegetables, handmade cheeses, and humanely raised heritage game and meats—to delicious effect have taken their place. Traditional eats can still be found (Beantown Pub remains the best place for baked beans), but many diners now gravitate toward innovative food in understated environs. Whether you're looking for casual French, down-home Southern cooking, some of the country's best sushi, or Vietnamese banh mi sandwiches, Boston restaurants are ready to deliver.

Restaurant and hotel reviews have been shortened. For full information, visit Fodors.com.

What It Costs in U.S. Dollars

$	$$	$$$	$$$$
RESTAURANTS			
under $18	$18–$24	$25–$35	over $35
UNDER $200			
under $200	$200–$299	$300–$399	over $399

Lodging

Because of its status as a major college town, Boston students dictate the flow of hotel traffic. Commencement weekends in May and June book months in advance; prices can be triple the off-season rate, with minimum stays of two to four nights. Those returning students invade their city again for move-in months of August and September. Leaf-peepers arrive in early October, and fall conventions bring waves of business travelers, especially in the Seaport District. Events such as the Boston Marathon in April and the Head of the Charles in October are busy times for large hotels and small inns alike.

The hotel tax in Boston adds 14.95% to your bill; some hotels also tack on energy, service, or occupancy surcharges. Though it's not an absolute necessity, many visitors prefer to bring a car, but then parking is another expense to consider. Almost all lodgings have parking, and most charge for the privilege—anywhere from $15 per day for self-garaging to $35 for valet. When looking for a hotel, don't write off the pricier establishments immediately. Price categories are determined by "rack rates"—the list price of a hotel room, which is usually discounted. Specials abound, particularly in Downtown on weekends. With so many new rooms in Boston, pricing is very competitive, so always check out the hotel website in advance for current special offers.

Nightlife

Whether it's cheering on local sports at a watering hole, rocking out at an underground club, applauding a symphonic performance, or chilling with cocktails in an elegant lounge, Boston has a nightlife vibe to suit all types and moods. Consider it a Cinderella city, set aglow with energy that for some ends all too soon. With the T (subway and bus) making its final runs between midnight and 1 am, most nightspots follow accordingly, closing their doors typically by 2 am. Though night owls may be disappointed by the meager late-night options, except in Chinatown, visitors find plenty of possibilities for stepping out on the early side. The martini set may stroll Newbury and Boylston streets in the Back Bay or Downtown, selecting from swank restaurants, lounges, and clubs. Coffee and tea drinkers can find numerous cafés in Cambridge and Somerville, particularly Harvard and Davis squares. Microbrew enthusiasts find viable options at sports bars, pop-up beer gardens, and craft breweries, especially on the Rose Kennedy Greenway, along the water, near campuses and sports arenas. The thriving "lounge" scene in Downtown's cooler hybrid bar-restaurant-clubs provides a mellower, more mature alternative to the collegiate indie spots, and DJs spin the late night dance parties into a frenzy with house music at crowded clubs like The Grand in the Seaport. Tourists crowd Faneuil Hall for its pubs, comedy spots, and dance scenes. The South and North Ends cater to the "dinner-and-drinks" set. Several casual indie rock and music clubs abound with plenty of local bands on stage and cold beer behind the bar in Allston, Somerville, and Cambridge.

Performing Arts

Boston's cultural attractions are a bracing mix of old-world aesthetics and new-world experimentation. At the classical end of the spectrum, revered institutions like the Museum of Fine Arts, the Boston Symphony Orchestra and Boston Pops, and the Isabella Stewart Gardner Museum offer refined experiences. For less reverential attitudes toward the arts, the Institute of Contemporary Art (ICA) features edgy electronic concerts, and graffiti and multimedia exhibitions. Museums like the MFA, the Gardner, and the ICA also host special shows and festivals in strikingly handsome performance spaces.

Shopping

Shopping in Boston in many ways mirrors the city itself: a mix of classic and cutting-edge, the high-end and the handmade, and international and local sensibilities. There is a strong network of idiosyncratic gift stores, handicrafts shops, galleries, and a growing number of savvy, independent fashion boutiques. Boston's shops and department stores lie concentrated in the area bounded by Quincy Market, the Back Bay, and Downtown, with plenty of bargains in the Downtown Crossing area. The South End's gentrification creates its own kind of consumerist milieus, from housewares shops to avant-garde art galleries. In Cambridge you can find many shops around Harvard and Central squares, with independent boutiques migrating west along Massachusetts Avenue ("Mass Ave.") toward Porter Square and beyond. There's no state sales tax on clothing. However, there's a 6.25% sales tax on clothes priced higher than $175 per item; the tax is levied on the amount in excess of $175.

Most major shopping neighborhoods are easily accessible on the T: Boston's Charles Street and Downtown Crossing and Cambridge's Harvard, Central, and Porter squares are on the Red Line; Copley Place, Faneuil Hall, and Newbury Street are on the Green Line; the South End is an easy trip on the Orange Line.

Tours

Bites of Boston Food Tours

GUIDED TOURS | This popular outfitter offers culinary strolls with stops at some of Boston's most esteemed restaurants, with its South End excursion among the most popular. Occasional tours of Chinatown and Allston are also sometimes offered. ✉ *Boston* ☎ *617/702–2483* 🌐 *www.bitesofbostonfoodtours.com* 🎟 *From $82.*

★ **Urban Adventours**

SPECIAL-INTEREST TOURS | This bike shop in downtown Boston conducts guided tours of the city, Cambridge, and surrounding towns. For example, the 15-mile Emerald Necklace tour takes in the city's string of lush parks and parkways. ☎ *617/670–0637* 🌐 *www.urbanadventours.com* 🎫 *From $60.*

Visitor Information

Contact the city and state tourism offices for details about seasonal events, discount passes, trip planning, and attraction information. The National Park Service has a Boston office for Boston's historic sites that provides maps and directions. The Welcome Center and Boston Common Visitor Information Center offer general information. The Cambridge Tourism Office's information booth is in Harvard Square, near the main entrance to the Harvard T stop.

Boston.com, home of the *Boston Globe* online, has news and feature articles, ample travel information, and links to towns throughout Massachusetts. Revolutionary Spaces (formerly the Bostonian Society) answers some frequently asked questions about Beantown history on its website. The iBoston page has wonderful photographs of architecturally and historically important buildings. *The Improper Bostonian* and *WickedLocal* provide a more relaxed (and irreverent) take on Boston news and information.

CONTACTS Boston Common Visitor Information Center. ☎ *617/536–4100* 🌐 *www.bostonusa.com/visit/planyourtrip/resources/vic.* **Greater Boston Convention & Visitors Bureau.** ✉ *2 Copley Pl. Suite 105, Back Bay* ☎ *888/733–2678, 617/536–4100* 🌐 *www.bostonusa.com.* **National Parks Service Visitor Center.** ✉ *Faneuil Hall, Downtown* ☎ *617/242–5601* 🌐 *www.nps.gov/bost.*

When to Go

Summer brings reliable sunshine, sailboats to Boston Harbor, concerts to the Esplanade, and café tables to assorted sidewalks. If you're dreaming of a classic shore vacation, summer is prime.

Weather-wise, late spring and fall are the optimal times to visit Boston. Aside from mild temperatures, the former offers blooming gardens throughout the city and the latter sees the surrounding countryside ablaze with brilliantly colored foliage. At both times expect crowds.

Autumn attracts hordes of leaf peepers, and more than 250,000 students flood into the area each September, then pull out in May and June. Hotels and restaurants fill up quickly on move-in, move-out, and graduation weekends.

Winters are cold and windy.

Beacon Hill, Boston Common, and the West End

Beacon Hill is Boston at its most Bostonian. Redbrick row houses dressed with black shutters and the occasional violet-hued windowpane filter into view, and narrow streets return you to the 19th century just as surely as if you had stumbled into a time machine. Across Beacon Street from Beacon Hill, the wide expanse of Boston Common has provided green space for locals since 1634.

One of Boston's less-traveled neighborhoods, the West End features primarily recent construction—the brick tenements housing myriad ethnic groups and the tangled web of streets of the old West End were razed in the 1960s in the name of urban renewal. A few structures survived, namely Massachusetts General Hospital and the former Suffolk County

Jail, which now houses The Liberty, a luxury hotel. This is where the TD Garden holds court, hosting Bruins and Celtics games, and where you'll find the innovative Museum of Science. And, on the skyline one can spy the Leonard P. Zakim Bunker Hill Memorial Bridge, a majestic and modern piece of transportation architecture.

Sights

★ Acorn Street

STREET | Often called the city's most photographed passageway, Acorn Street offers its visitors an iconic image of "historic Boston." Short, steep, and narrow, the cobblestone street may be Boston's roughest ride, so leave your car behind. Brick row houses—once the homes of 19th-century artisans and tradespeople—line one side, and on the other, doors lead to Mt. Vernon's hidden gardens. Find American flags, creative door knockers, window boxes, and gas lights aplenty. ✉ *Between W. Cedar and Willow Sts., Beacon Hill* Ⓜ *Park, Charles MGH.*

★ Boston Common

CITY PARK | **FAMILY** | Nothing is more central to the city than Boston Common, the oldest public park in the United States. Dating from 1634, the Common started as 50 acres where freemen could graze their cattle. (Cows were banned in 1830.) Don't confuse the Common with its sister park, the Public Garden, where the Swan Boats glide. Around the park, visit-worthy sites include Brewer Fountain Plaza, the start of the Freedom Trail, the Boston Common Visitor Information Center, the Soldiers and Sailors Monument, the Frog Pond, the Central Burying Ground, and the newly restored Robert Gould Shaw 54th Regiment Memorial. ■ **TIP→ This is Freedom Trail stop 1.** ✉ *Bounded by Beacon, Charles, Tremont, and Park Sts., Beacon Hill* 🌐 *www.boston.gov/parks/boston-common* Ⓜ *Park, Boylston.*

Did You Know?

Beacon Hill's north slope played a key part in African American history. A community of free Blacks lived here in the 1800s; many worshipped at the African Meeting House, established in 1805 and still standing. It came to be known as the "Black Faneuil Hall" for the fervent antislavery activism that started within its walls.

★ Charles Street

STREET | You won't see any glaring neon signs, in keeping with the historic character of the area, but Charles Street more than makes up for the general lack of commercial development on Beacon Hill with a plethora of clothing, antiques, and gift boutiques, plus cafés. Once the home of Oliver Wendell Holmes and the publisher James T. Fields (of the famed Bostonian firm of Ticknor and Fields), Charles Street sparkles at dusk from gas-fueled lamps, making it a romantic place for an evening stroll. ✉ *Between Beacon and Cambridge Sts., Beacon Hill* Ⓜ *Charles/MGH.*

Massachusetts State House

GOVERNMENT BUILDING | **FAMILY** | On July 4, 1795, the surviving fathers of the Revolution were on hand to enshrine the ideals of their new Commonwealth in a graceful seat of government designed by Charles Bulfinch. Governor Samuel Adams and Paul Revere laid the cornerstone; Revere would later roll the copper sheathing for the dome. Inside the building, visitors can check out Doric Hall, with its statuary and portraits; the Hall of Flags, where an exhibit shows the battle flags from all the wars in which Massachusetts regiments have participated; the Great Hall, an open space used for state functions that houses 351 flags from the cities and towns of Massachusetts; the governor's office;

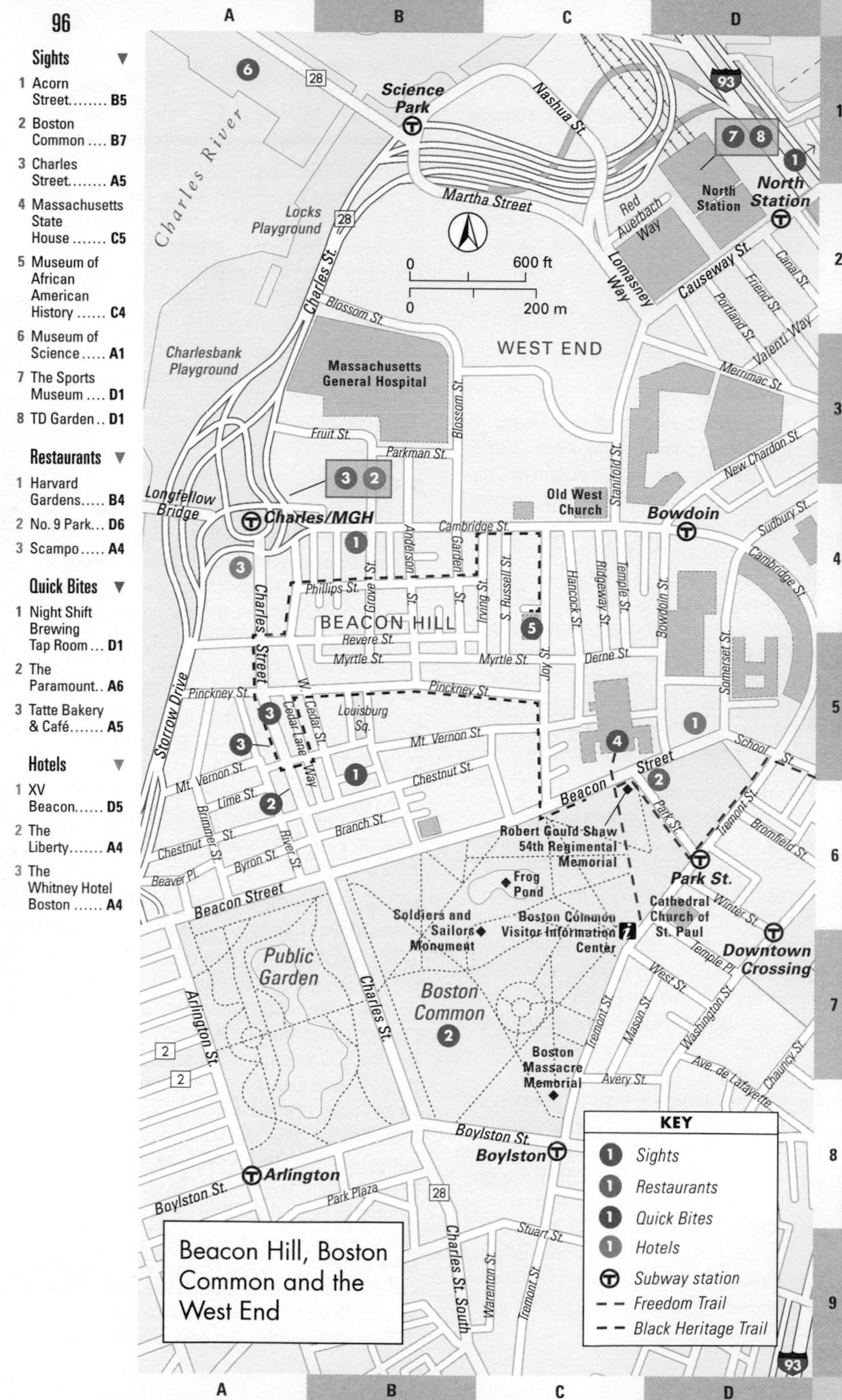
Sights
1 Acorn Street........ B5
2 Boston Common B7
3 Charles Street........ A5
4 Massachusetts State House C5
5 Museum of African American History C4
6 Museum of Science..... A1
7 The Sports Museum D1
8 TD Garden.. D1
Restaurants
1 Harvard Gardens..... B4
2 No. 9 Park... D6
3 Scampo..... A4
Quick Bites
1 Night Shift Brewing Tap Room ... D1
2 The Paramount.. A6
3 Tatte Bakery & Café....... A5
Hotels
1 XV Beacon...... D5
2 The Liberty....... A4
3 The Whitney Hotel Boston A4
A
B
C
D
1
2
3
4
5
6
7
8
9
Science Park
Nashua St.
North Station
Charles River
Locks Playground
Martha Street
Red Auerbach Way
Lomasney Way
Causeway St.
Canal St.
Friend St.
Portland St.
Valenti Way
Charles St.
Blossom St.
0
600 ft
200 m
WEST END
Charlesbank Playground
Massachusetts General Hospital
Merrimac St.
Fruit St.
Parkman St.
New Chardon St.
Staniford St.
Longfellow Bridge
Charles/MGH
Old West Church
Bowdoin
Sudbury St.
Cambridge St.
Anderson St.
Garden St.
Grove St.
Irving St.
S. Russell St.
Hancock St.
Ridgeway St.
Temple St.
Bowdoin St.
Phillips St.
BEACON HILL
Revere St.
Myrtle St.
Derne St.
Joy St.
Somerset St.
Charles Street
Storrow Drive
Pinckney St.
W. Cedar St.
Cedar Lane Way
Louisburg Sq.
Mt. Vernon St.
Chestnut St.
School St.
Beacon Street
Park St.
Tremont St.
Bromfield St.
Lime St.
Brimmer St.
River St.
Branch St.
Byron St.
Beaver Pl.
Robert Gould Shaw 54th Regimental Memorial
Frog Pond
Park St.
Winter St.
Cathedral Church of St. Paul
Soldiers and Sailors Monument
Boston Common Visitor Information Center
Downtown Crossing
Temple Pl.
West St.
Public Garden
Boston Common
Arlington St.
Mason St.
Washington St.
Ave. de Lafayette
Chauncy St.
Boston Massacre Memorial
Avery St.
Boylston St.
Boylston
Arlington
Park Plaza
Stuart St.
Charles St. South
Warrenton St.
KEY
Sights
Restaurants
Quick Bites
Hotels
Subway station
Freedom Trail
Black Heritage Trail
Beacon Hill, Boston Common and the West End

and the chambers of the House and Senate. Free guided tours are available; call for reservations. **TIP→ This is Freedom Trail stop 2.** *24 Beacon St., Beacon Hill 617/727–3676 www.sec.state.ma.us/trs/trsidx.htm Closed weekends M Park.*

Museum of African American History

HISTORY MUSEUM | FAMILY | The Museum of African American History was established in 1964 to recognize Boston's African American community, from slavery through the abolitionist movement. The Abiel Smith School, the first public school in the nation built specifically for Black children, now serves as the museum's main building, filled with exhibits. Just around the corner, the African Meeting House was built in 1806 entirely by Black labor; in 1832, William Lloyd Garrison formed the New England Anti-Slavery Society here, and in 2011 the building completed a $9.5-million restoration. *46 Joy St., Beacon Hill 617/725–0022 maah.org $10 Closed to walk-in visitors. Must reserve a ticket online to visit. M Park.*

★ Museum of Science

SCIENCE MUSEUM | FAMILY | From its perch above the Charles River, the Museum of Science sits half in Cambridge and half in Boston. This unique trait is the first of many at this 70-plus-year-old institution that's focused on science, technology, and hands-on learning. Diverse permanent exhibits explore dinosaurs, the electromagnetic spectrum, modern conservation, math, motion, nanotechnology, the natural world, space travel, and more. The Theater of Electricity hosts explosive daily lightening shows. Add-ons to admission include: the multisensory 4-D Theater, the Charles Hayden Planetarium, and the newly renovated Mugar Omni Theater with IMAX programming. *Science Park, 1 Museum of Science Driveway, Old West End 617/723–2500 www.mos.org $29 Timed tickets required; reserve in advance. M Science Park.*

The Sports Museum

SPORTS VENUE | FAMILY | The fifth and sixth levels of the TD Garden house The Sports Museum, where displays of memorabilia and photographs showcase New England–based amateur and pro sports history and legends. Test your sports knowledge with interactive games, see how you stand up to life-size statues of heroes Carl Yastrzemski and Larry Bird, and take an hour-long tour of the museum. *100 Legends Way, West End Use TD Garden's The Hub on Causeway grand entrance for access 617/212–6814 www.sportsmuseum.org $20 Closed during games and TD Garden events; check up-to-date calendar on website. M North Station.*

TD Garden

SPORTS VENUE | FAMILY | This mammoth, modern facility opened in 1995 to the chagrin of diehard local sports fans who occasionally still grieve the crusty, old Boston Garden. Today, the home arena of the Boston Celtics (basketball) and Boston Bruins (hockey) seats nearly 20,000 patrons and also hosts headlining musical acts, Disney on Ice, wrestling events, and Boston's famed Beanpot tourney. *100 Legends Way, Old West End Use The Hub on Causeway grand entrance for access to TD Garden 617/624–1000 www.tdgarden.com Closed during ticketed events M North Station.*

Restaurants

Harvard Gardens

$ | AMERICAN | A Beacon Hill legend, this was the first bar in the city to get its liquor license after the repeal of Prohibition. It opened in 1930, and was owned by the same family until the 1990s. **Known for:** a killer, house-made Bloody Mary mixed with the bar's own peppercorn vodka; a Reuben sandwich stuffed with corned beef that's made in-house; casual, comfortable vibe that's a little bit different from a typical Beacon Hill experience.

Average main: $17 316 Cambridge St., Beacon Hill 617/523–2727 www.harvardgardens.com Charles/MGH.

★ No. 9 Park

$$$$ | **EUROPEAN** | Welcome to the first and now flagship restaurant in acclaimed chef Barbara Lynch's empire. Even after 25 years, No. 9 Park continues to win rave reviews for Lynch's stellar, unique interpretation of fine French and Italian cuisine. **Known for:** a chef's six-course, wine-paired tasting menu; polished service; Lynch's memorably rich, prune-stuffed gnocchi. *Average main: $48 9 Park St., Beacon Hill 617/742–9991 www.no9park.com Park.*

★ Scampo

$$$$ | **ITALIAN** | The Italian word "scampo" translates to "escape" in English, and that's what this restaurant at The Liberty hotel—the former site of the Charles Street Jail—is: an escape into chef-owner Lydia Shire's delectable, buttery take on Italian-American cuisine. Everything is made from scratch, down to the bread, and including a dozen different exceptional pastas and nearly as many crusty pizzas. **Known for:** unique meal specials on the weekends; tandoori-oven–cooked, crusty pizzas (the lamb is a classic) and breads; eclectic vibe. *Average main: $41 The Liberty Hotel, 215 Charles St., Old West End 617/536–2100 www.scampoboston.com Charles/MGH.*

Coffee and Quick Bites

Night Shift Brewing Tap Room

$ | **AMERICAN** | More than just a tap room, this place satisfies a variety of different needs, although beer is at the forefront; there are more than two dozen beers on tap—as well as a couple hard seltzers and some nonalcoholic varieties. The lunch and dinner menu has items made from scratch like salads, sandwiches, flatbreads, and main dishes. **Known for:** brews its own beers; roasts its own coffee beans; tasty food. *Average main: $17 1 Lovejoy Wharf, Old West End 617/294–4233 www.nightshift-brewing.com North Station.*

★ The Paramount

$ | **AMERICAN** | **FAMILY** | Don't be surprised to see a queue at this neighborhood hot spot, no matter the time of day. Regulars happily line up for waffles topped with fresh fruit, caramel and banana french toast, huge salads, and hefty sandwiches, all made to order as you do from the counter. **Known for:** long, but quick-moving, lines; decadent, all-day breakfast items; Old Bay–seasoned home fries. *Average main: $12 44 Charles St., Beacon Hill 617/720–1152 www.paramountboston.com Charles/MGH.*

★ Tatte Bakery & Café

$ | **ISRAELI** | This upscale bakery and café with several locations in Boston takes pastries to the next level. From tea cakes to the Jerusalem bagel, expect hearty baked goods with an air of elegance and influenced by the owner's Israeli heritage. **Known for:** traditional North African shakshuka; signature nut tarts that are as pretty as they are tasty; convivial atmosphere. *Average main: $12 70 Charles St., Beacon Hill 617/723–5555 www.tattebakery.com Charles/MGH.*

Hotels

★ XV Beacon

$$$$ | **HOTEL** | The 1903 Beau-Arts exterior of this intimate, luxury boutique hotel is a study in sophistication and elegance. **Pros:** rooftop deck with amazing city views; complimentary Lexus car service; dogs of any size welcome for no fee. **Cons:** some rooms are small; can be expensive on weekends during peak months; no view from classic rooms. *Rooms from: $900 15 Beacon St., Beacon Hill 617/670–1500 www.xvbeacon.com 63 rooms No Meals Park.*

★ The Liberty
$$$$ | **HOTEL** | Few places in town can rival the soaring lobby—ringed by several layers of revamped metal catwalks—of the chic Liberty, formerly Boston's Charles Street Jail. **Pros:** Lydia Shire's popular restaurant Scampo; exclusive daily events, including art exhibits, live music, and yoga sessions; proximity to the Esplanade and Beacon Hill. **Cons:** loud in-house nightlife; very small fitness center; parking is expensive. [$] *Rooms from: $450* ✉ *215 Charles St., Old West End* ☎ *617/224–4000* 🌐 *www.liberty-hotel.com* *298 rooms* 🍽 *No Meals* Ⓜ *Charles/MGH.*

★ The Whitney Hotel Boston
$$$$ | **HOTEL** | This luxury boutique hotel fits right in with its Beacon Hill surroundings, views of which you can enjoy while you relax in-room in a plush Frette bathrobe with a cup of Nespresso coffee. **Pros:** excellent location within walking distance of the Back Bay, the West End, and Downtown; excellent restaurant on-site, Peregrine; complimentary bicycles. **Cons:** high valet fee; high noise levels from traffic in Storrow Drive–facing rooms; long wait for the valet. [$] *Rooms from: $600* ✉ *170 Charles St., Beacon Hill* ☎ *617/367–1866* 🌐 *www.whitneyhotelboston.com* *65 rooms* 🍽 *No Meals* Ⓜ *Charles/MGH.*

Government Center and the North End

This is a section of town Bostonians love to hate. While it's not Boston's prettiest locale (it's home to some of the city's bleakest architecture), it does have plenty of feathers in its tricorn cap, including City Hall Plaza (the site of feisty political rallies, summer concerts, and festivals), the country's oldest pushcart market (cobble-stoned Quincy Market), and the site where speeches were held encouraging independence from Great Britain (18th-century Faneuil Hall).

The warren of small streets on the northeast side of Government Center is the North End, Boston's Little Italy. In the 17th century, the North End *was* Boston, as much of the rest of the peninsula was still underwater or had yet to be cleared. Here the town grew rich for a century and a half before the birth of American independence. The quarter's dwindling ethnic character lingers along Salem or Hanover Street, where you can still hear people speaking with Abruzzese accents.

Sights

Copp's Hill Burying Ground
CEMETERY | An ancient and melancholy air hovers like a fine mist over this Colonial-era burial ground. The North End graveyard incorporates four cemeteries established between 1660 and 1819. Near the Charter Street gate is the tomb of the Mather family, the dynasty of church divines (Cotton and Increase were the most famous sons) who held sway in Boston during the heyday of the old theocracy. Also buried here is Robert Newman, who crept into the steeple of Old North Church to hang the lanterns warning of the British attack the night of Paul Revere's ride. Look for the tombstone of Captain Daniel Malcolm; it's pockmarked with musket-ball fire from British soldiers, who used the stones for target practice. Across the street is 44 Hull (Boston's historic Skinny House), the city's narrowest house, measuring at just a mere 10 feet wide, which recently fetched a selling price of $1.5 million. **■ TIP→ This is Freedom Trail stop 14.** ✉ *Intersection of Hull St. and Snowhill Rd., North End* ☎ *617/635–7361* 🌐 *www.cityofboston.gov/parks/hbgi/CoppsHill.asp* Ⓜ *North Station.*

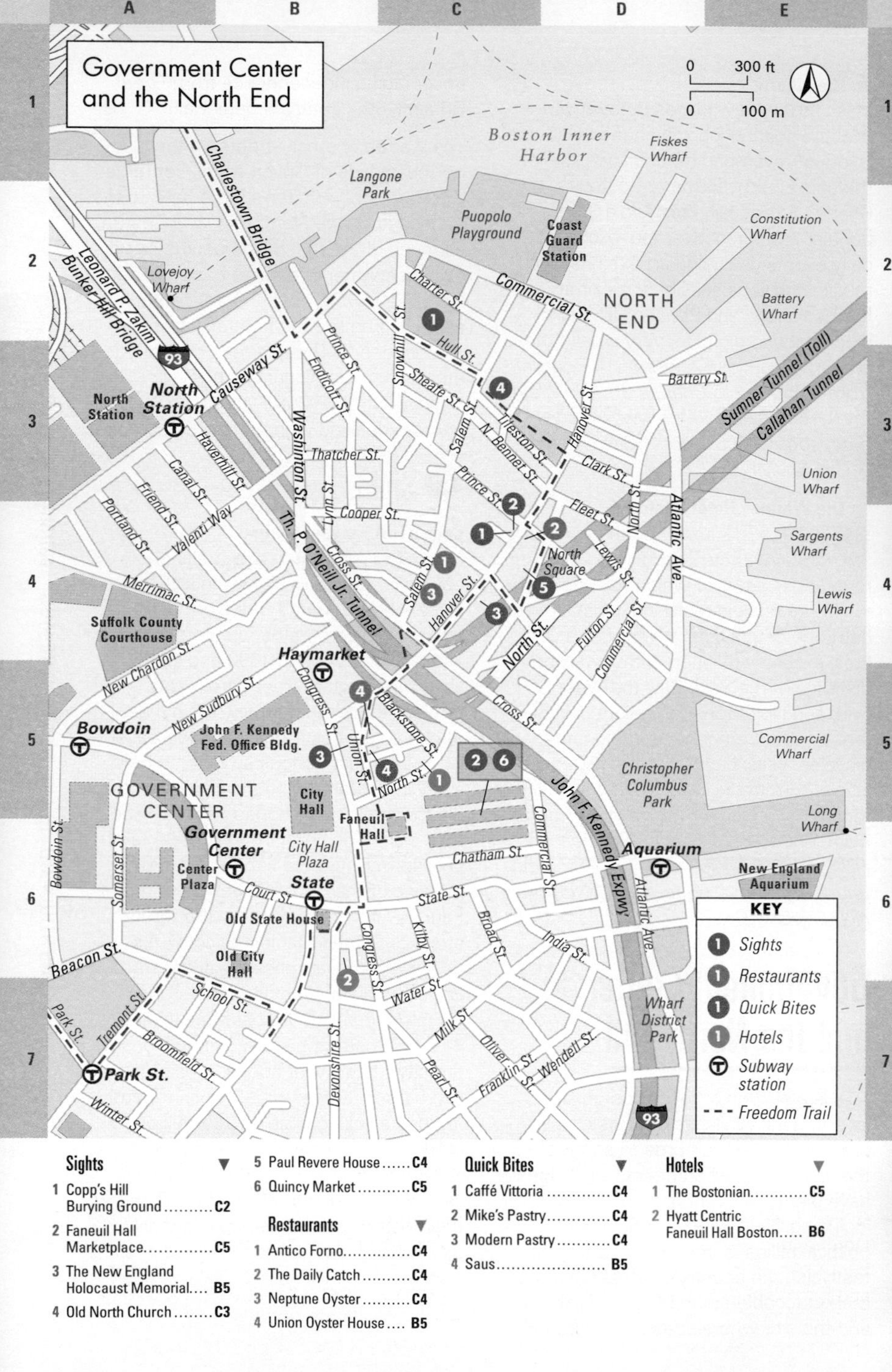

Sights

1 Copp's Hill Burying Ground C2

2 Faneuil Hall Marketplace.............. C5

3 The New England Holocaust Memorial.... B5

4 Old North Church C3

5 Paul Revere House...... C4

6 Quincy Market C5

Restaurants

1 Antico Forno............. C4

2 The Daily Catch C4

3 Neptune Oyster C4

4 Union Oyster House B5

Quick Bites

1 Caffé Vittoria C4

2 Mike's Pastry............. C4

3 Modern Pastry C4

4 Saus...................... B5

Hotels

1 The Bostonian............ C5

2 Hyatt Centric Faneuil Hall Boston..... B6

★ Faneuil Hall Marketplace

HISTORIC SIGHT | FAMILY | Faneuil Hall (pronounced *Fan*-yoo'uhl or *Fan*-yuhl) was erected in 1742, the gift of wealthy merchant Peter Faneuil, who wanted the hall to serve as both a place for town meetings and a public market. It burned in 1761 and was immediately reconstructed according to the original plan of its designer, the Scottish portrait painter John Smibert (who lies in the Granary Burying Ground). In 1763 the political leader James Otis helped inaugurate the era that culminated in American independence when he dedicated the rebuilt hall to the cause of liberty.

In 1772 Samuel Adams stood here and first suggested that Massachusetts and the other colonies organize a Committee of Correspondence to maintain semiclandestine lines of communication in the face of hardening British repression. In later years the hall again lived up to Otis's dedication when the abolitionists Wendell Phillips and Charles Sumner pleaded for support from its podium. The tradition continues to this day: in presidential-election years the hall is the site of debates between contenders in the Massachusetts primary.

Faneuil Hall was substantially enlarged and remodeled in 1805 according to a Greek Revival design of the noted architect Charles Bulfinch; this is the building you see today. Its purposes remain the same: the balconied Great Hall is available to citizens' groups on presentation of a request signed by a required number of responsible parties; it also plays host to regular concerts.

Inside Faneuil Hall are dozens of paintings of famous Americans, including the mural *Webster's Reply to Hayne* and Gilbert Stuart's portrait of Washington at Dorchester Heights. Park rangers give informational talks about the history and importance of Faneuil Hall every half hour. There are interactive displays about Boston sights, and National Park Service rangers at the visitor center on the first floor can provide maps and other information.

On the building's top floors are the headquarters and museum and library of the Ancient and Honorable Artillery Company of Massachusetts, which is free to visit (but a donation is welcome). Founded in 1638, it's the oldest militia in the Western Hemisphere, and the third-oldest in the world, after the Swiss Guard and the Honourable Artillery Company of London. The museum is open Wednesday through Friday from 11 am to 3 pm.

When such men as Andrew Jackson and Daniel Webster debated the future of the Republic here, the fragrances of bacon and snuff—sold by merchants in Quincy Market across the road—greeted their noses. Today the aroma of coffee wafts through the hall from a snack bar. The shops at ground level sell New England bric-a-brac. **■ TIP→ This is Freedom Trail stop 11.** ✉ *Faneuil Hall Sq., Government Center* ☎ *617/523–1300* 🌐 *www.nps.gov/bost/learn/historyculture/fh.htm* 🎫 *Free* Ⓜ *Government Center, Aquarium, State.*

★ Old North Church

HISTORIC SIGHT | At one end of the Paul Revere Mall is a church famous not only for being the oldest standing church building in Boston (built in 1723) but also for housing the two lanterns that glimmered from its steeple on the night of April 18, 1775. This is Christ, or Old North, Church, where Paul Revere and the young sexton Robert Newman managed that night to signal the departure by water of the British regulars to Lexington and Concord. Newman, carrying the lanterns, ascended the steeple, while Revere began his clandestine trip by boat across the Charles. Visitors are welcome to drop in for a self-guided tour or a 15-minute guided crypt tour. **■ TIP→ This is Freedom Trail stop 13.** ✉ *193 Salem St., North End* ☎ *617/858–8231* 🌐 *www.old-north.com* 🎫 *$5, additional $5 for crypt tour* Ⓜ *Haymarket, North Station.*

The New England Holocaust Memorial

MONUMENT | Located at the north end of Union Park, the Holocaust Memorial is the work of Stanley Saitowitz, whose design was selected through an international competition; the finished memorial was dedicated in 1995. During the day the six 50-foot-high glass-and-steel towers seem at odds with the 18th-century streetscape of Blackstone Square behind it; at night, they glow like ghosts while manufactured steam from grates in the granite base makes for a particularly haunting scene. Recollections by Holocaust survivors are set into the glass-and-granite walls; the upper levels of the towers are etched with 6 million numbers in random sequence, symbolizing the Jewish victims of the Nazi horror. ✉ *Union St. near Hanover St., Government Center* ☎ *617/457–8750* 🌐 *www.nehm.org* Ⓜ *Haymarket, Government Center, State.*

Paul Revere House

HISTORIC HOME | **FAMILY** | Originally on the site was the parsonage of the Second Church of Boston, home to the Rev. Increase Mather, the Second Church's minister. Mather's house burned in the great fire of 1676, and the house that Revere was to occupy was built on its location about four years later, nearly 100 years before Revere's 1775 midnight ride through Middlesex County. Revere owned it from 1770 until 1800, although he lived there for only 10 years and rented it out for the next two decades. Pre-1900 photographs show it as a shabby warren of storefronts and apartments. The clapboard sheathing is a replacement, but 90% of the framework is original; note the Elizabethan-style overhang and leaded windowpanes. A few Revere furnishings are on display here, and just gazing at his silverwork—much more of which is displayed at the Museum of Fine Arts—brings the man alive. Special events are scheduled throughout the year, many designed with children in mind, such as role play by characters dressed in period costume serving apple-cider cake and other Colonial-era goodies, a silversmith practicing his trade, a dulcimer player entertaining a crowd, or a military-reenactment group in full period regalia.

The immediate neighborhood also has Revere associations. The little cobblestone park in North Square is named after Rachel Revere, his second wife, and the adjacent brick Pierce-Hichborn House once belonged to relatives of Revere. The garden connecting the Revere House and the Pierce-Hichborn House is planted with flowers and medicinal herbs favored in Revere's day, but is sadly closed for tours. ■ **TIP→ This is Freedom Trail stop 12.** ✉ *19 North Sq., North End* ☎ *617/523–2338* 🌐 *www.paulreverehouse.org* 💵 *$6* ⏲ *Closed Mon. Jan.–Mar.* Ⓜ *Haymarket, Aquarium, Government Center.*

★ Quincy Market

MARKET | **FAMILY** | The market consists of three block-long annexes: Quincy Market, North Market, and South Market. The structures were designed in 1826 to alleviate the cramped conditions of Faneuil Hall and clean up the refuse that collected in Town Dock, the pond behind it. The central structure has kept its traditional market-stall layout, but the stalls now purvey international and specialty foods: sushi, frozen yogurt, bagels, calzones, sausage-on-a-stick, Chinese noodles, barbecue, and baklava, plus all the boutique chocolate-chip cookies your heart desires. Along the arcades on either side of the Central Market are vendors selling sweatshirts, photographs of Boston, and arts and crafts—some schlocky, some not—alongside a couple of patioed bars and restaurants. The North and South Markets house a mixture of chain stores and specialty boutiques. ✉ *Bordered by Clinton, Commercial, and Chatham Sts., Government Center* ☎ *617/523–1300* 🌐 *www.quincy-market.com* Ⓜ *Government Center, Aquarium, State.*

Restaurants

★ Antico Forno

$$$ | **ITALIAN** | Many of the menu choices here come from the eponymous wood-burning brick oven, which turns out surprisingly delicate thin-crust pizzas simply topped with tomato and buffalo mozzarella or complicated combos like pistachio pesto, fresh mozzarella, and sausage. While the name, which translates to "old oven," gives the pizzas top billing, Antico excels at a variety of Italian country dishes that harken back to the Old Country, like veal parmigiana, *osso buco* with pork shank, chicken saltimbocca, and handmade pastas; the specialty, gnocchi, is rich and creamy but light. **Known for:** wood-fired, brick-oven pizza; Italian country classics; casual, jovial atmosphere. *Average main: $28 ✉ 93 Salem St., North End ☎ 617/723–6733 ⊕ www.anticofornoboston.com Ⓜ Haymarket.*

★ The Daily Catch

$$ | **SEAFOOD** | You've just got to love this newly renovated shoebox-size place—for the noise, the intimacy, the complete absence of pretense, and, above all, the Sicilian-style seafood, which proved so popular, it spawned two other locations (one in Brookline and another in Boston's Seaport area). With garlic and olive oil forming the foundation for almost every dish, this cheerful, bustling spot specializes in calamari, black squid-ink pastas, and linguine with clam sauce, all served in the skillets in which they were cooked, hot from the stove. **Known for:** garlic-rich preparations; luscious seafood skillet pastas; intimate, elbow-to-elbow dining. *Average main: $24 ✉ 323 Hanover St., North End ☎ 617/523–8567 ⊕ thedailycatch.com ▭ No credit cards Ⓜ Haymarket.*

★ Neptune Oyster

$$$ | **SEAFOOD** | This *piccolo* oyster bar, the first of its kind in the neighborhood, has only 22 chairs, but the long marble bar adorned with mirrors has extra seating for 15 more patrons, who can watch the oyster shuckers deftly undo handfuls of more than a dozen different kinds of bivalves to savor as an appetizer or on a Neptune plateau, a gleaming tower of oysters and other raw-bar items piled over ice that you can order from the slip of paper they pass out listing each day's crustacean options. Daily specials run the gamut, from lobster spaghetti to scarlet prawns to sea urchin bucatini. **Known for:** casual setting; Italian-style seafood; generously packed lobster roll. *Average main: $34 ✉ 63 Salem St., North End ☎ 617/742–3474 ⊕ www.neptuneoyster.com Ⓜ Haymarket.*

Union Oyster House

$$$ | **SEAFOOD** | Opening its door in 1826 and earning a place on the National Historic Landmark list, the Union Oyster House is Boston's oldest restaurant. Dine like Daniel Webster (alongside his nightly hangover-heavy tumbler of brandy and water) and order oysters on the half shell at the ground-floor raw bar in the oldest part of the restaurant. **Known for:** oldest Boston restaurant; long waits on weekends; oysters. *Average main: $34 ✉ 41 Union St., Government Center ☎ 617/227–2750 ⊕ www.unionoysterhouse.com Ⓜ Haymarket.*

Coffee and Quick Bites

★ Caffé Vittoria

$ | **ITALIAN** | **FAMILY** | Established in 1929, Caffé Vittoria—Boston's oldest Italian café—is rightfully known as Boston's most traditional Italian café, which is one of the reasons the place is packed with locals. With gleaming brass, marble tabletops, four levels of seating, three bars that serve aperitifs, one of the city's best selections of grappa, and one massive, ancient espresso maker, this old-fashioned café will make you want to lose yourself in these surroundings. **Known for:** specialty coffee drinks; grapa; gelato. *Average main: $10 290–296 Hanover St., North End 617/227–7606 www.caffevittoria.com No credit cards.*

Mike's Pastry

$ | **BAKERY** | Every local knows the white box with the blue and white string as a to-go treasure chest of Italian delicacies. Known for their cannoli (they're the self-proclaimed "home of" the tubular treat), Mike's has been bringing the best in pastries and cookies to the North End (and presidential patrons like Bill Clinton) since 1946. **Known for:** cannoli; long lines; cases of Italian cookies. *Average main: $9 300 Hanover St., North End 617/742–3050 www.mikespastry.com.*

Modern Pastry

$ | **ITALIAN** | The North End's other favorite cannoli king, Modern is a hit with the locals. Using Old World recipes that were relied on for more than 150 years, their crusts are flaky, their fillings rich, and they have a selection of torrone nougat confections, cookies, French horns, and Napoleons. **Known for:** dainty cannoli; deliciously moist cakes; handmade Italian candies. *Average main: $8 257 Hanover St., North End 617/523–3783 www.modernpastry.com No credit cards.*

Saus

$ | **CAFÉ** | With 15 unique sauces on the menu, including homemade hot beer mustard, truffle ketchup, cheddar ale, smoky chipotle mayo, and gravy, Saus believes in the power of condiments, which accompany its made-from-scratch sandwiches. The hand-cut fries are house-aged and twice fried, and they're known for their hand-rolled beer-brined pork bratwurst. **Known for:** beer-brined sausages; large variety of dipping sauces; tiny space. *Average main: $9 33 Union St., Government Center 617/248–8835 www.sausboston.com Government Center.*

Mike's vs. Modern

Welcome to Boston's long-standing cannoli war. Mike's Pastry and Modern Pastry are widely considered the North End's two best cannoli spots, but locals can't seem to agree on which is better, splitting their strong allegiance right down the center. Modern's cannoli are smaller and more delicate than Mike's, while Mike's are crunchier, sweeter, and boast more flavors (18 to be exact). Which will you choose?

Hotels

The Bostonian

$$$ | **HOTEL** | **FAMILY** | Near historic Faneuil Hall, The Bostonian has guest rooms featuring Frette linens, pillow-top mattresses, and 40-inch TVs—many also have French doors with step-out balconies showcasing city views and the popular North End. Warmed up with red wall coverings, the lobby provides sofas and arm chairs, perfect for relaxing with a book chosen from one of the floor-to-ceiling bookshelves. **Pros:** updated fitness center; great location for sightseeing; on-site restaurant. **Cons:** some rooms get street noise; Faneuil Hall can get clogged with tourists; self parking is expensive. *Rooms from: $320 Faneuil Hall Marketplace, 26 North St., Downtown 617/523–3600, 866/866–8086 www.millenniumhotels.com 204 rooms No Meals Haymarket, Aquarium.*

Hyatt Centric Faneuil Hall Boston

$$$ | HOTEL | Across the street from Faneuil Hall, this coveted spot from the trusted brand is literally steps away from dozens upon dozens of Boston landmarks, parks, and restaurants. **Pros:** unbeatable location; city views; outstanding on-site restaurant. **Cons:** small rooms; noise from street can be heard at lower floors; parking is expensive. *Rooms from: $399 ✉ 54–68 Devonshire St, Government Center ☎ 617/720–1234 ⊕ www.hyatt.com 163 rooms ☞ Pet friendly Ⓜ Government Center.*

Nightlife

The Black Rose

PUBS | Hung with 20 bright county banners, decorated with pictures of Ireland and portraits of Samuel Beckett, Lady Gregory, and James Joyce, The Rose draws as many tourists as Ireland-loving locals. Friendly Irish bartenders serve up pints, blarney, and far more Irish whiskeys (28) than Scotches (12). Nightly shows by traditional Irish and contemporary musicians confirm its abiding Gaelic good cheer, or *craic*. Dine on Guinness beef stew and fish-and-chips—all served by staffers with authentic brogues. *✉ 160 State St., Government Center ☎ 617/742–2286 ⊕ www.blackroseboston.com Ⓜ Aquarium, State.*

Shopping

★ Boston Public Market

MARKET | Open year-round, the indoor Boston Public Market offers a great place to grab a sandwich, sample local foods, and even pick up a tasty souvenir. The New England–centric marketplace has 30 vendors, selling everything from fresh herbs and fruit to meat and seafood, as well as plenty of food stalls. Everything sold at the market is produced or originated in New England, including nonperishables like wool and carved wooden bowls. There's also a food demonstration kitchen, where visitors might be able to catch a live cooking class (with samples). Since it's all about staying with the season, the exciting thing about visiting the BPM is that no two days are the same. The Kids' Nook is a designated area for kids to gather and play, with activities throughout the week. *✉ 100 Hanover St., Government Center ⊕ bostonpublicmarket.org Ⓜ Haymarket/Government Center.*

Charlestown

Boston started here. Charlestown was a thriving settlement a year before Colonials headed across the Charles River at William Blaxton's invitation to found the city proper. Today the district's attractions include two of the most visible—and vertical—monuments in Boston: the Bunker Hill Monument, which commemorates the grisly battle that became a symbol of patriotic resistance against the British, and the USS *Constitution,* whose masts continue to tower over the waterfront where she was built more than 200 years ago.

Sights

★ Bunker Hill Monument

MONUMENT | Two misunderstandings surround this famous monument. First, the Battle of Bunker Hill was actually fought on Breed's Hill, which is where the monument sits today. (The real Bunker Hill is about ½ mile to the north of the monument.) In truth, Bunker was the originally planned locale for the battle, and for that reason its name stuck. Second, although the battle is generally considered a colonial success, the Americans lost. It was a Pyrrhic victory for the British Redcoats, who sacrificed nearly half of their 2,200 men; American casualties numbered 400 to 600. One thing is true: the Battle of Bunker Hill put the British on notice that they were up against a formidable opponent. According to history books, this is also the location of the famous war cry,

"Don't fire until you see the whites of their eyes," uttered by American colonel William Prescott or General Israel Putnam (there's still debate on who gave the actual command).

The monument's zenith is reached by a flight of 294 tightly spiraled steps, a space that's unfortunately still undergoing renovation and is closed to climbers. With an opening day on the horizon, take note: there's no elevator, but the views from the observatory are worth the effort of the arduous climb. Due to high numbers, all visitors who wish to climb must first obtain a pass from the Bunker Hill Museum at 43 Monument Square. Climbing passes are free, but limited in number and can be either reserved up to two weeks in advance or on a first-come, first-served basis. The museum's artifacts and exhibits tell the story of the battle, while a detailed diorama shows the action in miniature. **■TIP➔ This is Freedom Trail stop 16.** ✉ *Monument Sq., Charlestown* ☎ *617/242–5641* 🌐 *www.nps.gov/bost/historyculture/bhm.htm* 🎟 *Free* Ⓜ *Community College.*

★ USS Constitution

MILITARY SIGHT | FAMILY | Affectionately known as "Old Ironsides," the USS *Constitution* rides proudly at anchor in her berth at the Charlestown Navy Yard. The oldest commissioned ship in the U.S. fleet is a battlewagon of the old school, of the days of "wooden ships and iron men"—when she and her crew of 200 succeeded at the perilous task of asserting the sovereignty of an improbable new nation. Every July 4, she's towed out for a celebratory turnabout in Boston Harbor, where her keel was laid in 1797. **■TIP➔ This is Freedom Trail stop 15.** ✉ *Charlestown Navy Yard, 55 Constitution Rd., Charlestown* ☎ *617/242–7511* 🌐 *ussconstitutionmuseum.org* 🎟 *Free* Ⓜ *North Station.*

★ USS Constitution Museum

HISTORY MUSEUM | FAMILY | With nearly 2,000 artifacts and more than 10,000 archival records pertaining to the USS *Constitution* on display, exhibits spark excitement about maritime culture and naval service. All ages enjoy "All Hands on Deck: A Sailor's Life in 1812," complete with opportunities to scrub decks, scramble aloft to furl a sail, eat a meal of salted meat and ship's biscuit, and crawl into a hammock. History buffs get a stem-to-stern look at the ship's history, from its creation to battles. ✉ *Charlestown* ✣ *Adjacent to USS Constitution, Charlestown Navy Yard* ☎ *617/426–1812* 🌐 *www.ussconstitutionmuseum.org* 🎟 *Suggested donation from $5* Ⓜ *North Station; MBTA Bus 93 from the Haymarket or Sullivan Square Station to Charlestown Navy Yard stop; or Boston Harbor Cruise water shuttle from Long Wharf (near the New England Aquarium) to Pier 4.*

Restaurants

Warren Tavern

$$ | **AMERICAN** | Built in 1780 and reportedly one of the country's oldest taverns, this restored Colonial neighborhood pub in the quaint and historic gaslight district was once frequented by George Washington and Paul Revere. After a blustery walk through the Navy Yard, grab a seat by the fireplace and warm yourself with hearty chowder, lobster mac, or short rib shepherd's pie and a Sam Adams draft. **Known for:** historical atmosphere; beer selection; short rib shepherd's pie. $ *Average main: $21* ✉ *2 Pleasant St., Charlestown* ☎ *617/241–8142* 🌐 *www.warrentavern.com* Ⓜ *Community College.*

The Old South Meeting House is Boston's second-oldest church building; it's also where the spark was lit for the infamous Boston Tea Party.

Downtown and the Waterfront

Boston's commercial and financial districts—the area commonly called Downtown—are in a maze of streets that seem to have been laid out with little logic; they are village lanes now lined with modern 40-story office towers. Just as the Great Fire of 1872 swept the old Financial District clear, the Downtown construction in more recent times has obliterated many of the buildings where 19th-century Boston businessmen sat in front of their rolltop desks. Yet historic sites remain tucked among the skyscrapers; a number of them have been linked together to make up a fascinating section of the Freedom Trail.

The country's third-largest Chinatown, after those in San Francisco and Manhattan, is also home to many Asian cultures, from Thai to Taiwanese, Korean to Cambodian. Today, Beach Street serves as the neighborhood's main street. Just west of Chinatown, the majority of Boston's historic stages reside in the Theater District, which means the area is a hot spot for ballet, opera, Broadway tours, and stand-up comedy. And, to the east of Chinatown, a very small enclave known as the Leather District features a few destination standouts, including the city's best sushi restaurant and South Station.

Along the Waterfront, you'll encounter the bustling harbor: private vessels, luxury yachts, harbor cruises, ferries, and more. Long Wharf, Central Wharf with the New England Aquarium, and Rowes Wharf are the three most prominent. Other attractions in this neighborhood include Boston HarborWalk, the Rose Kennedy Greenway, and the lesser-known gem just offshore, the Boston Harbor Islands. Many upscale hotels and restaurants make the most of the expansive water views.

Downtown, Waterfront and the Seaport District
KEY
Sights
Restaurants
Quick Bites
Hotels
Subway station
Freedom Trail
BEACON HILL
FINANCIAL DISTRICT
DOWNTOWN
LEATHER DISTRICT
CHINATOWN
SOUTH BOSTON
Boston Common
Frog Pond
Government Center
State
Aquarium
Park St.
Downtown Crossing
Chinatown
Boylston
South Station
Courthouse
State House
Old City Hall
U.S. Custom House
Boston Opera House
Federal Reserve Tower
U.S Federal Courthouse
Central Wharf
India Wharf
Wharf District Park
Rowes Wharf
Foster's Wharf
Fort Point Channel
John F. Fitzgerald Kennedy Expwy. (Tunnel)
93
0 600 ft
0 200 m
Sights
1 Benjamin Franklin Statue/ Boston Latin School...... C1
2 Boston Children's Museum F3
3 Boston Harbor Islands National Recreation Area F1
4 Boston Harborwalk....... F3
5 Boston Massacre Site ... D1
6 Boston Tea Party Ships & Museum................ F3
7 Institute of Contemporary Art/Boston................ H3
8 King's Chapel.............. C1
9 New England Aquarium F1
10 Old South Meeting House C1
11 Old State House.......... D1
12 Rose Kennedy Greenway................. E1
Restaurants
1 Bostonia Public House... E1
2 haley.henry C1
3 Hei La Moon.............. C3
4 o ya....................... D3
5 Row 34 .... F3
6 Sportello F3
7 Woods Hill Pier 4......... H3
Quick Bites
1 Gracenote Coffee C3
2 James Hook & Co......... F2
3 Thinking Cup B2
Hotels
1 The Langham, Boston.... D2
2 Moxy A3
3 Omni Boston Hotel at the Seaport E3

Sights

Benjamin Franklin Statue/Boston Latin School

PUBLIC ART | FAMILY | This stop on the Freedom Trail, in front of Old City Hall, commemorates the noted revolutionary, statesman, and inventor. His likeness also marks the original location of the Boston Latin School, the country's oldest public school (founded in 1635). Franklin attended Boston Latin with three other signers of the Declaration of Independence—Samuel Adams, John Hancock, and Robert Treat Paine—but he has the dubious distinction of being the only one of the four not to graduate. **■ TIP→ This is Freedom Trail stop 6.** ✉ *45 School St., Downtown* ☎ *617/635–3911* 🌐 *www.thefreedomtrail.org* Ⓜ *Park.*

Boston Harbor Islands National Recreation Area

ISLAND | FAMILY | Comprising 34 tiny islands and peninsulas, this is one of the city's best hidden gems—and it's literally out of sight. Stretching from South Boston (Castle Island) to the coastlines of South Shore towns Hingham and Hull, each island is different, but most feature abundant nature with miles of lightly traveled trails, shoreline, sea life, and wild plants. The focal point is 39-acre Georges Island and its partially restored pre–Civil War Fort Warren that once held Confederate prisoners. Pets and alcohol are not allowed on the Harbor Islands. **■ TIP→ Ferries shuttle visitors from Boston to Georges and Spectacle Islands daily during summer months. Plan to spend a whole day exploring!** ✉ *Boston Harbor Islands National and State Park Welcome Center, 191 W. Atlantic Ave., Waterfront* ☎ *617/223–8666* 🌐 *www.bostonharborislands.org* ⏲ *Closed mid-Oct.–mid-May* Ⓜ *Aquarium.*

Boston Massacre Site

MONUMENT | FAMILY | A circle of cobblestones in front of the Old State House commemorates the Boston Massacre, which happened about 20 feet away. To recap: it was on the snowy evening of March 5, 1770, that nine British soldiers fired in panic upon a taunting mob of more than 75 colonists who were upset over British occupation and taxation. Five townsmen died. In the legal action that followed, the defense of the accused soldiers was undertaken by John Adams and Josiah Quincy, both of whom vehemently opposed British oppression but were devoted to the principle of a fair trial. All but two of the nine regulars charged were acquitted; the others were branded on the hand for the crime of manslaughter. Paul Revere lost little time in capturing the "massacre" in a dramatic engraving that soon became one of the Revolution's most potent images of propaganda. **■ TIP→ This is Freedom Trail stop 10.** ✉ *206 Washington St., Downtown* 🌐 *www.thefreedomtrail.org* Ⓜ *State.*

★ King's Chapel

HISTORIC SIGHT | FAMILY | Both somber and dramatic, King's Chapel looms large. Its distinctive shape wasn't achieved entirely by design; for lack of funds, it was never topped with a steeple. The first chapel on this site was erected in 1688 for the establishment of an Anglican place of worship, and it took five years to build the solid Quincy-granite structure seen today. As construction proceeded, the old church continued to stand within the rising walls of the new, the plan being to remove and carry it away piece by piece when the outer stone chapel was completed. The builders then went to work on the interior, which remains essentially as they finished it in 1754; it's a masterpiece of proportion and Georgian calm (in fact, its acoustics make the use of a microphone unnecessary for Sunday sermons). The pulpit, built in 1717, is the oldest pulpit in continuous use on the same site in the United States. To the right of the main entrance is a special pew once reserved for condemned prisoners, who were trotted in to hear a sermon before being hanged on the Common. The chapel's bell is Paul Revere's largest and, in his judgment, his sweetest sounding. For a behind-the-scenes look at the bell or crypt, take a guided tour. You won't be disappointed. ■ **TIP→ This is Freedom Trail stop 5.** ✉ *58 Tremont St., Downtown* ☎ *617/523–1749* 🌐 *www.kings-chapel.org* 🎫 *$5* Ⓜ *Park, State, Government Center.*

★ New England Aquarium

AQUARIUM | **FAMILY** | As interesting and exciting as it is educational, this aquarium is a must for those who are curious about what lives in and around the sea. Seals bark and swim in the outdoor tank. Inside the main facility, more than 30,000 animals of 800 different species frolic in simulated habitats. Penguins, hands-on creature touch tanks, and sea lions, are a few star exhibits. The real showstopper, though, is the four-story, 200,000-gallon ocean-reef tank. Ramps winding around the tank lead to the top level and allow you to view the inhabitants from many vantage points. Don't miss the five-times-a-day feedings; each lasts nearly an hour and takes divers 24 feet into the tank. ✉ *1 Central Wharf, Waterfront* ☎ *617/973–5200* 🌐 *www.neaq.org* 🎫 *$32; $10 IMAX; $65 whale watch* Ⓜ *Aquarium.*

★ Old South Meeting House

NOTABLE BUILDING | **FAMILY** | This is the second-oldest church building in Boston (although the building is no longer used for religious services), and were it not for Longfellow's celebration of Old North in "Paul Revere's Ride," it might well be the most famous. Today, visitors can learn about its history through exhibits and audio programs. Some of the fiercest of the town meetings that led to the Revolution were held here, culminating in the gathering of December 16, 1773, which was called by Samuel Adams to confront the crisis of three ships, laden with dutiable tea, anchored at Griffin's Wharf. The activists wanted the tea returned to England, but the governor would not permit it—and the rest is history. The Voices of Protest exhibit celebrates Old South as a forum for free speech from Revolutionary days to the present. ■ **TIP→ This is Freedom Trail stop 8.** ✉ *310 Washington St., Downtown* ☎ *617/720–1713* 🌐 *www.revolutionaryspaces.org* 🎫 *$15 (includes dual admission to Old State House)* Ⓜ *State, Downtown Crossing.*

★ Old State House

NOTABLE BUILDING | **FAMILY** | This Colonial-era landmark has one of the most recognizable facades in Boston, with its gable adorned by a brightly gilded lion and silver unicorn, symbols of British imperial power. This was the seat of the Colonial government from 1713 until the Revolution, and after the evacuation of the British from Boston in 1776 it served the independent Commonwealth until its replacement on Beacon Hill was completed in 1798. The Declaration of Independence was first read in public in Boston from its balcony. John Hancock was inaugurated here as the first governor under the new state constitution. Today, it's an interactive museum with exhibits, artifacts, and 18th-century artwork, and tells the stories of Revolutionary Bostonians through costumed guides. ■ **TIP→ This is Freedom Trail stop 9.** ✉ *206 Washington St., Downtown* ☎ *617/720–1713* 🌐 *www.revolutionaryspaces.org* 🎫 *$15 (includes dual admission to Old South Meeting House)* Ⓜ *State, Government Center.*

Rose Kennedy Greenway

CITY PARK | **FAMILY** | This one linear mile of winding parks marks the path the highway once took through the city (à la the Big Dig). A walk through shows off a wide variety of flora and fauna from the North End to Chinatown. Lawn furniture and games, seasonal farmers' and artists' markets, art installations, water features, live performances, free Wi-Fi, a beer garden, and more make it a lively spot, especially in warmer months. There's a one-of-a-kind, hand-carved carousel; and the food truck scene has grown into a bustling lunchtime destination.

⊠ *Waterfront* ✣ *Between New Sudbury St. in North End and Beach St. in Chinatown; along Atlantic Ave.* 🌐 *www.rosekennedygreenway.org* Ⓜ *State, Haymarket, Chinatown, Aquarium.*

 Restaurants

Bostonia Public House

$$$ | **AMERICAN** | **FAMILY** | Airy and classic in atmosphere, this modern restaurant focuses on two things: food and local history (it is, after all, situated in a historic 1902 building). The menu features elevated takes on comfort food; at lunch expect more sandwiches. **Known for:** fantastic weekend brunch; long bar with lots of seating; live music in the evenings. $ *Average main: $30* ⊠ *131 State St., Downtown* ☎ *617/948–9800* 🌐 *www.bostoniapublichouse.com* Ⓜ *Aquarium.*

★ haley.henry

$$$ | **WINE BAR** | Charcuterie, tinned fish, ceviche: You can eat well at this excellent Downtown wine bar that's small in size but big in reputation. Definitely make a reservation before showing up; it can be busy, even on a Wednesday night. **Known for:** wine from small, independent producers; staff knows their stuff; incredible service. $ *Average main: $35* ⊠ *45 Province St., Downtown* ☎ *617/208–6000* 🌐 *www.haleyhenry.com* 🕒 *Closed Sun.–Mon.* Ⓜ *Downtown Crossing, Boylston.*

★ Hei La Moon

$ | **CHINESE** | **FAMILY** | This Cantonese dim sum palace occupies two floors; its contemporary space is decked out with golden chandeliers and ultra-violet decor. Carts of dim sum delicacies are the star attraction here, but diners can also find a menu of Chinese dishes, including eight styles of soup, hot-pot dinners, moo shi, kung pao, lo mein, and egg foo yong. **Known for:** dim sum; inexpensive prices; hot pot. $ *Average main: $10* ⊠ *83 Essex St., Chinatown* ☎ *617/338–8813* 🌐 *www.heilamoon.com* Ⓜ *South Station.*

★ o ya

$$$$ | **SUSHI** | Despite o ya's tucked-away location and hidden door, the place isn't exactly a secret: critics from the *New York Times, Bon Appétit,* and *Food & Wine* have all named this improvisational sushi spot among the best in the country. The chef-owner plates a 20-course nightly omakase dinner with sushi and cooked preparations. **Known for:** delicate, beautiful, sophisticated sushi; expensive prices; advance reservations a must. $ *Average main: $250* ⊠ *9 East St., Chinatown* ☎ *617/654–9900* 🌐 *o-ya.restaurant/o-ya-boston* 🕒 *Closed Sun.–Mon.* Ⓜ *South Station.*

Coffee and Quick Bites

★ Gracenote Coffee

$ | **CAFÉ** | Gracenote roasts top-shelf coffee beans using its own unique process here in Massachusetts, and then serves it in a teeny Leather District storefront just across the border from Chinatown. The flavor is well worth the slightly out-of-the-way jaunt to this hipster haven for pour-overs and espresso drinks that are the focus of the menu. **Known for:** unmatched coffee; extensive variety of milk alternatives; really friendly baristas. $ *Average main: $6* ⊠ *108 Lincoln St., Chinatown* 🌐 *www.gracenotecoffee.com* Ⓜ *South Station.*

James Hook & Co.

$$$ | **SEAFOOD** | **FAMILY** | This Waterfront seafood shanty leaves all its frills for its lobster-loaded rolls; they're served with mayo or with butter, in a bun, and wrapped with foil so you can sit for a minute or eat it on the go. Other specialties include lobster mac and cheese, whole boiled lobster, stuffed clams, and the shrimp and corn chowder. **Known for:** lobster rolls on the go; whole-cooked lobsters; rustic vibe and no-frills seating. $ *Average main: $31* ⊠ *440 Atlantic Ave., Waterfront* ☎ *617/423–5501* 🌐 *www.jameshooklobster.com* Ⓜ *South Station.*

Thinking Cup

$ | **CAFÉ** | Across from Boston Common, Thinking Cup caters to a mixed crowd of area professionals and students from nearby Emerson College. Rarely is the coffeehouse not packed with caffeine addicts looking for their next fix of Stumptown coffee, whether it's in the form of a single origin pour-over or a macchiato. **Known for:** signature lattes: the hazelnut is made with roasted hazelnut paste, and the honey-cinnamon with a house-made syrup; awesome sandwiches, especially the Jittery Hen, made with coffee-braised chicken; no Wi-Fi access. *$ Average main: $10 ✉ 165 Tremont St., Downtown ☎ 617/482–5555 🌐 www.thinkingcup.com Ⓜ Boylston, Park.*

Hotels

★ The Langham, Boston

$$$$ | **HOTEL** | One of Boston's most luxurious hotels just got more so: an extensive renovation to the 1922 Renaissance Revival building has both preserved its heritage as the former Federal Reserve Bank of Boston and elevated it into a contemporary luxury retreat. **Pros:** concierge who specializes in Boston's universities; glass-enclosed, heated indoor pool; lavish rooms. **Cons:** a bit of a walk to public transportation; far from Seaport District and Fenway neighborhoods; cost is prohibitive to some. *$ Rooms from: $600 ✉ 250 Franklin St., Downtown ☎ 617/451–1900 🌐 www.boston.langhamhotels.com 312 rooms No Meals Ⓜ South Station.*

Moxy

$$ | **HOTEL** | One of Boston's newest hotels under the Marriott umbrella features a sleek exterior and artful flair (say, like custom murals by well-known street artists), and come nightfall, there's a boisterous, rave-like nightlife scene. **Pros:** 24th-floor rooftop lounge for guest-only use; floor-to-ceiling windows in every room; Bar Moxy work-fun space featuring board games, free Wi-Fi, coffee, cocktails, and food. **Cons:** not good for families; lots of street noise; small rooms. *$ Rooms from: $299 ✉ 240 Tremont St., Theater District ☎ 617/793–4200 🌐 www.marriott.com/hotels/travel/bosox-moxy-boston-downtown 340 rooms No Meals Ⓜ Boylston, Chinatown.*

Seaport District

What's the appeal of the Seaport District? Bostonians have only been able to answer that question recently. As the neighborhood becomes developed and its former life as a parking lot wasteland fades from peoples' minds, locals have realized its gorgeous potential, something the Moakley Courthouse, the Institute of Contemporary Art/Boston, and restaurateur-chef Barbara Lynch recognized more than a decade back.

Of all of Boston's neighborhoods, the Seaport is the least "Bostonian" in appearance. In fact, with all its skyscrapers and shiny glass, the Seaport could have been plucked straight out of New York. It's new, it's fresh, it's young.

Sights

★ Boston Children's Museum

OTHER MUSEUM | **FAMILY** | The country's second-oldest children's museum has always been ahead of the curve with creative hands-on exhibits, cultural diversity, and problem-solving. Some of the most popular stops are also the simplest, like the bubble-making machinery and the two-story climbing maze. At the Japanese House, you're invited to take off your shoes and step inside a Kyoto silk merchant's home. Children can dig, climb, and build at the Construction Zone, and in the toddler PlaySpace, children under three can run free in a safe environment. There's also a full schedule of special exhibits, festivals, and performances. *✉ 308 Congress*

St., Fort Point Channel ☎ *617/426–6500* 🌐 *www.bostonchildrensmuseum.org* 🎫 *$20* Ⓜ *South Station.*

Boston Harborwalk

TRAIL | For the last 30-plus years, a number of agencies and organizations have been collaborating to create a waterfront walking path along Boston's shoreline—currently, it stretches 43 miles. Boston's Seaport District boasts a hearty portion of the Harborwalk, which winds from the Fort Point Channel, around Fan Pier, up Seaport Boulevard, and out and around the Black Falcon Cruise Terminal. Along the way, pedestrians can see art exhibits, stationary viewfinders, open green spaces, and incredible Boston Harbor views. Marked signs point the way, and maps can be found online. ✉ *Seaport* ✣ *Congress St. Bridge by Children's Museum* 🌐 *www.bostonharborwalk.org* Ⓜ *South Station.*

★ **Boston Tea Party Ships & Museum**

OTHER ATTRACTION | **FAMILY** | Situated at the Congress Street Bridge near the site of Griffin's Wharf, this lively museum offers an interactive look at the past in a place as close as possible to the actual spot where the Boston Tea Party took place on December 16, 1773. Actors in period costumes greet patrons, assign them real-life Colonial personas, and then ask a few people to heave boxes of tea into the water from aboard historical reproductions of the ships forcibly boarded and unloaded the night Boston Harbor became a teapot. There are 3-D holograms, talking portraits, and even the Robinson Half Tea Chest, one of two original tea chests known to exist. **■ TIP→ Abigail's Tea Room (you don't need a museum ticket for entry) features a tea tasting of five tea blends that would have been aboard the ships.** ✉ *Congress St. Bridge, Fort Point Channel* 🌐 *www.bostonteapartyship.com* 🎫 *$32* Ⓜ *South Station.*

★ **Institute of Contemporary Art/Boston**

ART MUSEUM | The ICA mounts temporary exhibits by the contemporary art world's brightest talents, as well as curated pieces from its permanent collection, all of which are as cutting edge as the breathtaking, cantilevered edifice jutting out over Boston Harbor that houses them. The ICA's fourth floor is where most happens: incredible art and stunning water views. The Poss Family Mediatheque serves as a great resting spot for families. Live programming, from film festivals to outdoor live music concerts take place regularly. Don't miss the ICA Store on the ground level, where you can pick up an inventive trinket of your own. ✉ *25 Harbor Shore Dr., Seaport* ☎ *617/478–3100* 🌐 *www.icaboston.org* 🎫 *$15* ⏲ *Closed Mon.* Ⓜ *Courthouse.*

Restaurants

★ **Row 34**

$$$ | **SEAFOOD** | Emphasizing oysters and local craft beers, this contemporary seafood restaurant has a boisterous energy contained only by its soaring ceilings. A neighborhood crowd comes for the excellent menu devoted to raw things, fried seafood, a variety of "rolls," and fish-based entrées. **Known for:** local oysters fresh from restaurant's own oyster farm; seafood—carnivores and vegetarians should head elsewhere; excellent selection of American craft beer. 💲 *Average main: $31* ✉ *383 Congress St., Seaport* ☎ *617/553–5900* 🌐 *www.row34.com* Ⓜ *World Trade Center.*

Sportello

$$ | **ITALIAN** | One of the city's most widely awarded chefs, Barbara Lynch serves rustic, hearty Italian food with her team in a casual setting, where diners sit and eat at one long, winding counter. Fare like burrata, lamb meatballs, foccacia, braised rabbit, and bolognese are plentiful and tasty, if on the pricey side of things. **Known for:** pasta made in-house daily, by hand; casual, modern vibe; top-quality ingredients. $ *Average main: $22 ✉ 348 Congress St., Fort Point Channel ☎ 617/737–1234 ⊕ www.sportelloboston.com ⊙ Closed Mon. and Tues. M South Station.*

★ **Woods Hill Pier 4**

$$$$ | MODERN AMERICAN | Featuring floor-to-ceiling windows and sweeping 270-degree views of the Boston Harbor waterfront, this sophisticated and lively restaurant serves up midsized plates that are meant to be shared—two to three per person. The well-curated menu features meat and produce from the owner's 360-acre New Hampshire farm, as well as handmade pasta and sustainably sourced seafood. **Known for:** panoramic views of Boston Harbor; pasture-raised, sustainable, and organic farm-to-table ingredients; a killer Sunday brunch. $ *Average main: $45 ✉ 300 Pier 4 Blvd., Seaport ☎ 617/981–4577 ⊕ www.woodshillpier4.com ⊙ Closed Mon. M Courthouse.*

★ **Omni Boston Hotel at the Seaport**

$$$ | HOTEL | Opened in 2021, this Omni hotel debuts a chic, modern counterpoint to its grande dame Downtown property, Omni Parker House. **Pros:** year-round, outdoor, heated pool with bar area; seven food and drink options on-site; brand-new accommodations. **Cons:** far from Back Bay and Beacon Hill shopping; tight restrictions on pet policy. $ *Rooms from: $350 ✉ 450 Summer St., Seaport ☎ 617/476–6664 ⊕ www.omnihotels.com 1,054 rooms No Meals M World Trade Center, Silver Line Way.*

★ **Drink**

COCKTAIL LOUNGES | Barbara Lynch handles this elegant den as only a chef of world-wide acclaim would—like a restaurant. Behind the bar, tenders use herbs, infusions, and elixirs to custom-create a top-shelf libation for your palate; that is, there is no drink list. There are low, beamed ceilings and a wooden bar that snakes through the space, maximizing room for a discerning cocktail crowd. A limited menu features snacks and things, including a legendary burger. Drink is one of the best bars in Boston, and it's hugely popular, so you'll likely wait in line to get in, but once you do, there's room to breathe. *✉ 348 Congress St., Fort Point Channel ☎ 617/695–1806 ⊕ www.drinkfortpoint.com M South Station.*

The Back Bay and South End

The Back Bay is a mix of the historic and the new, happily coexisting in one of the city's loveliest areas, with everything from landmarks, like Trinity Church, and green spaces, such as the Esplanade, to a multitude of hip bars and fine-dining restaurants.

Adjacent to the Back Bay, the South End nonetheless has its own identity, with stunning Victorian row houses, art galleries galore, Boston's largest gay community, and plenty of unique shops and restaurants of every type.

★ **Boston Public Garden**

GARDEN | FAMILY | America's oldest botanical garden, the Public Garden is replete with gorgeous formal plantings. Keep in mind that the Boston Public Garden and Boston Common (not Commons!) are two separate entities with different histories and purposes and a distinct boundary between them at Charles Street. The central feature of the Public Garden is its irregularly shaped pond, intended to appear, from any vantage point along its banks, much larger than its nearly 4 acres. The pond has been famous since 1877 for its

The Swan Boats have been an iconic part of Boston Public Garden since 1877.

foot-pedal-powered (by a captain) Swan Boats (🌐 *swanboats.com*), which make leisurely cruises during warm months. The dominant work among the park's statuary is Thomas Ball's equestrian George Washington (1869), which faces the head of Commonwealth Avenue at the Arlington Street gate, but follow the children quack-quacking along the pathway between the pond and the park entrance at Charles and Beacon Streets to the *Make Way for Ducklings* bronzes sculpted by Nancy Schön, a tribute to the 1941 classic children's story by Robert McCloskey. ✉ *Bound by Arlington, Boylston, Charles, and Beacon Sts., Back Bay* ☎ *617/522–1966 Swan Boats* 🌐 *friendsofthepublicgarden.org* 🎟 *Swan Boats $4* Ⓜ *Arlington.*

★ Boston Public Library

LIBRARY | **FAMILY** | This venerable institution is a handsome temple to reading and a valuable research library, but you don't need a library card to enjoy the magnificent art. The library offers free art and architecture tours daily. The corridor leading from the annex opens onto the Renaissance-style courtyard—an exact copy of the one in Rome's Palazzo della Cancelleria. A covered arcade furnished with chairs rings a fountain; you can bring books or lunch into the courtyard, which is open all the hours the library is open, and escape the bustle of the city. Beyond the courtyard is the main entrance hall of the 1895 building, with its immense stone lions by Louis St. Gaudens, vaulted ceiling, and marble staircase. The corridor at the top of the stairs leads to Bates Hall, one of Boston's most sumptuous interior spaces. This is the main reference reading room, 218 feet long with a barrel vault ceiling 50 feet high. ✉ *700 Boylston St., at Copley Sq., Back Bay* ☎ *617/536–5400* 🌐 *www.bpl.org* Ⓜ *Copley.*

Esplanade

PROMENADE | **FAMILY** | Near the corner of Beacon and Arlington Streets, the recently redone Arthur Fiedler Footbridge crosses Storrow Drive to the 3-mile-long Esplanade and the Hatch Memorial Shell. The free concerts here in summer include

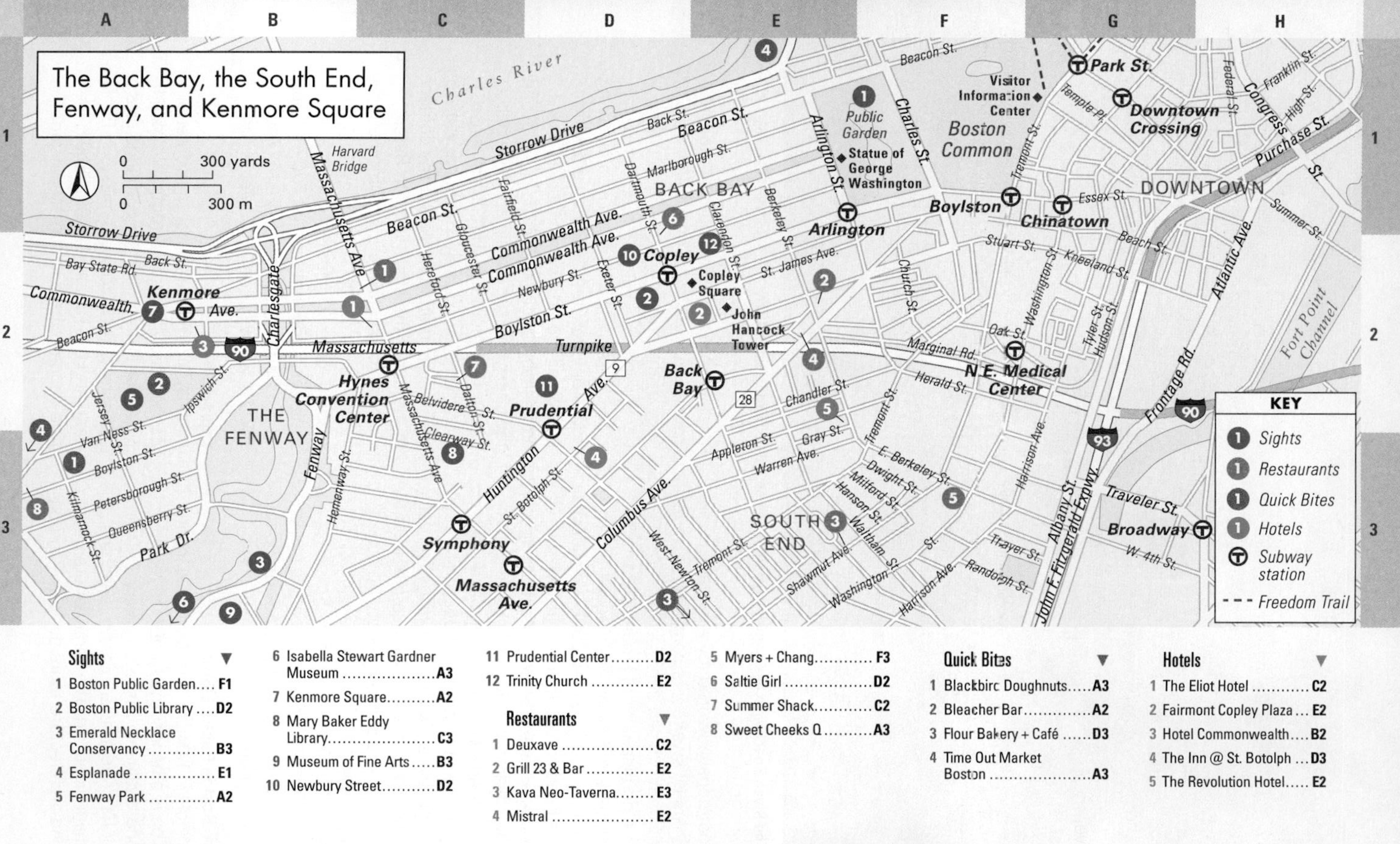

The Back Bay, the South End, Fenway, and Kenmore Square
0 300 yards
0 300 m
KEY
Sights
Restaurants
Quick Bites
Hotels
Subway station
Freedom Trail
Charles River
Harvard Bridge
Storrow Drive
Beacon St.
Back St.
Marlborough St.
Commonwealth Ave.
Newbury St.
Boylston St.
Massachusetts Ave
Massachusetts Turnpike
BACK BAY
THE FENWAY
SOUTH END
DOWNTOWN
Boston Common
Public Garden
Statue of George Washington
Visitor Information Center
Copley Square
John Hancock Tower
Kenmore
Hynes Convention Center
Prudential
Symphony
Massachusetts Ave.
Copley
Back Bay
Arlington
Boylston
Chinatown
Park St.
Downtown Crossing
N.E. Medical Center
Broadway
Columbus Ave.
Huntington Ave.
Fort Point Channel
Sights
1 Boston Public Garden.... F1
2 Boston Public Library D2
3 Emerald Necklace Conservancy B3
4 Esplanade E1
5 Fenway Park A2
6 Isabella Stewart Gardner Museum A3
7 Kenmore Square.......... A2
8 Mary Baker Eddy Library...................... C3
9 Museum of Fine Arts B3
10 Newbury Street........... D2
11 Prudential Center......... D2
12 Trinity Church E2
Restaurants
1 Deuxave C2
2 Grill 23 & Bar E2
3 Kava Neo-Taverna........ E3
4 Mistral E2
5 Myers + Chang............ F3
6 Saltie Girl D2
7 Summer Shack............ C2
8 Sweet Cheeks Q A3
Quick Bites
1 Blackbird Doughnuts..... A3
2 Bleacher Bar............... A2
3 Flour Bakery + Café D3
4 Time Out Market Boston A3
Hotels
1 The Eliot Hotel C2
2 Fairmont Copley Plaza ... E2
3 Hotel Commonwealth.... B2
4 The Inn @ St. Botolph ... D3
5 The Revolution Hotel..... E2

the Boston Pops' immensely popular televised July 4 performance. For shows like this, Bostonians haul lawn chairs and blankets to the lawn in front of the shell; bring a takeout lunch from a nearby restaurant, find an empty spot—no mean feat, so come early—and you'll feel right at home. An impressive stone bust of the late maestro Arthur Fiedler watches over the walkers, joggers, picnickers, and sunbathers who fill the Esplanade's paths on pleasant days. Here, too, is the turn-of-the-20th-century Union Boat Club Boathouse, headquarters for the country's oldest private rowing club. You can also access the park by crossing the Frances Appleton Pedestrian Bridge linking the Beacon Hill neighborhood to the Esplanade. ✉ *Back Bay* 🌐 *www.esplanadeassociation.org.*

Mary Baker Eddy Library

LIBRARY | FAMILY | One of the largest single collections by and about an American woman is housed at this library, located on the Christian Science Plaza. The library also includes two floors of exhibits, which celebrate the power of ideas and provide context to the life and achievements of Mary Baker Eddy (1821–1910).

The library is also home to the fascinating Mapparium, a huge stained-glass globe whose 30-foot interior can be traversed on a footbridge, where you can experience a unique sound-and-light show while viewing an accurate representation of the world from 1935. The Hall of Ideas showcases quotes from the world's greatest thinkers, which travel around the room and through a virtual fountain. In the Quest Gallery, explore how Mary Baker Eddy founded a church and a college, and at the age of 87, launched the *Christian Science Monitor* newspaper. ✉ *210 Massachusetts Ave., Back Bay* ☎ *617/450–7000* 🌐 *www.marybakereddylibrary.org* 🎫 *Hall of Ideas and 3rd-fl. library free, exhibits $6* Ⓜ *Prudential.*

Newbury Street

STREET | Eight-block-long Newbury Street has been compared to New York's 5th Avenue, and certainly this is the city's poshest shopping area, with branches of Chanel, Tiffany & Co., Valentino, Max Mara, Longchamp, and other top names in fashion. But here the pricey boutiques are more intimate than grand, and people live above the trendy restaurants and ubiquitous hair salons, giving the place a neighborhood feel. Toward the Massachusetts Avenue end, cafés proliferate and the stores get funkier, ending with Newbury Comics and Urban Outfitters. ✉ *From Arlington St. to Massachusetts Ave., Back Bay* 🌐 *www.newburystboston.com* Ⓜ *Hynes, Copley.*

Prudential Center

STORE/MALL | FAMILY | The 52-story Prudential Tower, or "the Pru," dominates the acreage between Boylston Street and Huntington Avenue. Its enclosed shopping mall anchored by Saks Fifth Avenue is home to over 60 stores and restaurants and is connected by a glass bridge to the more upscale Copley Place. The popular food emporium, Eataly, located in the Pru, offers a great spot for a quick bite or DIY fixings for an Italian feast. As for the Prudential Tower itself, the architectural historian Bainbridge Bunting made an acute observation when he called it "an apparition so vast in size that it appears to float above the surrounding district without being related to it." Later modifications to the Boylston Street frontage of the Prudential Center effected a better union of the complex with the urban space around it, but the tower itself floats on, vast as ever. In 2023, the top three floors of the Pru will welcome a new re-imagination of the famed SkyWalk, an incredible vantage point to view all of Boston with 360 degrees of observation from above. ✉ *800 Boylston St., Back Bay* ☎ *800/746–7778* 🌐 *www.prudentialcenter.com* Ⓜ *Prudential Center, Copley Station.*

★ Trinity Church

CHURCH | In his 1877 masterpiece, architect Henry Hobson Richardson brought his Romanesque Revival style to maturity; all the aesthetic elements for which he was famous come together magnificently—bold polychromatic masonry, careful arrangement of masses, sumptuously carved interior woodwork—in this crowning centerpiece of Copley Square. A full appreciation of its architecture requires an understanding of the logistical problems of building it here. The Back Bay is a reclaimed wetland with a high water table. Bedrock, or at least stable glacial till, lies far beneath wet clay. Like all older Back Bay buildings, Trinity Church sits on submerged wooden pilings. But its central tower weighs 9,500 tons, and most of the 4,500 pilings beneath the building are under that tremendous central mass. The pilings are checked regularly for sinkage by means of a hatch in the basement. For a nice respite, try to catch one of the Friday organ concerts beginning at 12:15. Free drop-in guided tours are held throughout the week. *206 Clarendon St., Back Bay 617/536–0944 trinitychurchboston.org Entrance free, guided and self-guided tours Tues.–Fri., $10 Closed Mon. Copley.*

Restaurants

★ Deuxave

$$$ | **MODERN AMERICAN** | At the corner of two avenues (Commonwealth and Massachusetts), which is how this restaurant got its name *(deux* is French for "two"), you'll find this snazzy, dark-wood enclave serving sophisticated dishes like spice-crusted ahi tuna and braised pork belly, pan-seared Atlantic halibut, and organic chicken with parsnip and foie gras agnolotti. Make sure to pair your meal with a bottle from the thoughtfully crafted and surprisingly affordable wine list served by an attentive staff. **Known for:** modern French food; nine-hour French onion soup; reasonably priced wine list. *Average main: $35 371 Commonwealth Ave., Back Bay 617/517–5915 www.deuxave.com No credit cards Hynes.*

★ Grill 23 & Bar

$$$$ | **STEAKHOUSE** | Pinstripe suits, dark paneling, Persian rugs, and waiters in white jackets give this single-location steak house a posh tone, and the kitchen places a premium on seasonal, organic ingredients and sustainable and humanely raised meats; the divine coconut cake is worth saving room for dessert. Two bars, a big, buzzing one overlooking Berkeley Street and a quieter, smaller one on the second floor by the cozy fireplace, serve excellent drinks, specialty Scotches, and bar bites, along with the full menu. **Known for:** locally owned steak house; Brandt family beef; party-dress vibe. *Average main: $40 161 Berkeley St., Back Bay 617/542–2255 grill23.com No lunch Back Bay/South End.*

★ Kava Neo-Taverna

$$$ | **GREEK** | This sweet little whitewashed taverna serves authentic Greek cuisine, with many ingredients imported directly from the Mediterranean, such as the feta, fish, and octopus. Order some crisp white wine off the hard-to-find Greek wines and liquors list to sip with a parade of home-style dishes, from tasty meze plates to entrées like grilled lamb chops. **Known for:** authentic Greek favorites; taverna feel; high-quality ingredients. *Average main: $27 315 Shawmut Ave., South End 617/356–1100 www.kavaneotaverna.com No lunch weekdays.*

★ Mistral

$$$$ | **FRENCH** | Since 1997, Boston's fashionable set has flocked to this long-popular South End restaurant with polished service and upscale yet unpretentious French-Mediterranean cuisine. While seasonal tweaks do occur, fail-safe favorites like Burgundy-style escargot, parfait of

Hudson Valley foie gras, tuna tartare, duck with cranberries, and Dover Sole Meunière are part of a menu that rarely changes—but no one's complaining. **Known for:** sophisticated Mediterranean cuisine; superb service; white-cloth, country French decor. Ⓢ *Average main: $42* ✉ *223 Columbus Ave., South End* ☎ *617/867–9300* 🌐 *mistralbistro.com* ⏲ *No lunch* Ⓜ *Back Bay.*

★ Myers + Chang

$$ | **CHINESE** | Pink and orange dragon decals cover the windows of this all-day Chinese café, where Joanne Chang (of Flour bakery fame) taps her familial cooking roots to create shareable platters of creative dumplings, wok-charred udon noodles, and stir-fries brimming with fresh ingredients and plenty of hot chili peppers, garlic, fresh herbs, crushed peanuts, and lime. The staff is young and fun, and the crowd generally follows suit. **Known for:** Asian soul food; fabulous cocktails; great service. Ⓢ *Average main: $22* ✉ *1145 Washington St., South End* ☎ *617/542–5200* 🌐 *www.myersandchang.com* Ⓜ *Back Bay.*

★ Saltie Girl

$$$ | **SEAFOOD** | Step into this Back Bay raw bar specializing in snappy cocktails and luscious preparations of all things seafood and you'll fall hook, line, and sinker for everything on the menu, including platters of fresh-shucked oysters on crushed ice, torched salmon belly with charred avocado, smoked fish that would make a New York deli owner proud, seafood-topped toasts, and a butter-drenched warm lobster roll overflowing with fresh meat. Rounding out the menu are tins of domestic and imported gourmet shellfish and fish (including caviar) served in all their oily goodness with bread, butter, smoked salt, lemon, and sweet pepper jam. **Known for:** creative seafood dishes; large tinned seafood selection; hip crowd. Ⓢ *Average main: $25* ✉ *279 Dartmouth St., Back Bay* ☎ *617/267–0691* 🌐 *saltiegirl.com.*

Summer Shack

$$$ | **SEAFOOD** | **FAMILY** | Boston uberchef Jasper White's casual New England seafood restaurant is a boisterous, bright, fun eatery next to the Prudential Center (he also has one in Cambridge and at Mohegan Sun in Connecticut), where creamy clam chowder and fried Ipswich clams share menu space with golden crab cakes and cedar-planked, maple-lemon–glazed salmon. In addition to a handful of chicken and meat dishes for those not into seafood, White features some of the most succulent lobsters in the city (he has a patented process for cooking them). **Known for:** fresh seafood; succulent lobster; fun, casual atmosphere. Ⓢ *Average main: $28* ✉ *50 Dalton St., Back Bay* ☎ *617/867–9955* 🌐 *www.summershackrestaurant.com* Ⓜ *Hynes.*

Hotels

★ The Eliot Hotel

$$ | **HOTEL** | One of the city's best small hotels, located on posh Commonwealth Avenue, expertly merges the old blue-blood Boston aesthetic with modern flair (like contemporary rugs mingling with crystal chandeliers); everyone from well-heeled Sox fans to traveling CEOs to tony college parents have noticed. **Pros:** top-notch restaurant; beautiful rooms; great location near Fenway and Newbury Street. **Cons:** can be pricey; some complain of elevator noise; parking is expensive. Ⓢ *Rooms from: $235* ✉ *370 Commonwealth Ave., Back Bay* ☎ *617/267–1607, 800/443–5468* 🌐 *www.eliothotel.com* *95 rooms* 🍽 *No Meals* Ⓜ *Hynes.*

★ Fairmont Copley Plaza

$$$ | **HOTEL** | **FAMILY** | Since 1912, this decadent, unabashedly romantic hotel has welcomed guests in style, immediately impressing as they enter under the huge black awning, flanked by golden lion statues, into the lobby decked out in Italian marble, stunning coffered ceilings, and gorgeous crystal chandeliers. **Pros:**

prime Back Bay location, centrally located in Copley Square; luxurious gym; 24-hour daily in-room dining. **Cons:** small bathrooms; valet parking is expensive; due to the historical nature, room sizes vary greatly. *Rooms from: $350 138 St. James Ave., Back Bay 617/267–5300, 866/540–4417 www.fairmont.com/copley-plaza-boston 383 rooms No Meals Copley, Back Bay.*

★ The Inn @ St. Botolph

$$ | **B&B/INN** | **FAMILY** | The posh yet homey 16-room Inn @ St. Botolph follows an edgy hotel model—no front desk, no restaurant, no keys, and no valet (there is, however, an office on-site that is staffed 24/7). **Pros:** short walk from the South End, Copley Square, and the Back Bay; free Wi-Fi; self-service laundry on-site. **Cons:** limited DIY parking nearby; no traditional front desk check-in services; may be too "off the beaten path" for some. *Rooms from: $279 99 St. Botolph St., Back Bay 617/236–8099 www.innatstbotolph.com 16 rooms Free Breakfast Prudential.*

The Revolution Hotel

$$ | **HOTEL** | An affordable option in a sea of sky-high rates, this art-filled hotel is an intriguing mix of luxurious touches—like pillow-top beds and a Peloton bike in the gym—and more downscale amenities, like shared bathrooms and tiny rooms. **Pros:** whimsical original artwork; inexpensive; on-site restaurant. **Cons:** inconvenient parking; small rooms; some rooms have shared bathrooms. *Rooms from: $200 40 Berkeley St., South End 617/848–9200 therevolutionhotel.com 177 rooms No Meals Back Bay.*

Coffee and Quick Bites

★ Flour Bakery + Café

$ | **AMERICAN** | **FAMILY** | When folks need coffee, a great sandwich, or an irresistible sweet, like a pecan sticky bun, lemon tart, or double chocolate cookie—or just a place to sit and chat—they pay a visit to one of owner Joanne Chang's 10 Flour bakeries, including this one in the South End. A communal table in the middle acts as a gathering spot, around which diners enjoy morning pastries, homemade soups, hearty bean and grain salads, and specialty sandwiches, which change seasonally. **Known for:** scrumptious sweets; delicious salads and sandwiches; laid-back setting. *Average main: $11 1595 Washington St., South End 617/267–4300 www.flourbakery.com Massachusetts Ave.*

Nightlife

★ Darryl's Corner Bar & Kitchen

BARS | This longtime neighborhood soul-food and jazz hangout still looks spiffy, and features real Southern cooking and live bands nearly nightly at light cover charges. Come for favorites like mac and cheese or glorified chicken and waffles, and on Sunday there is an all-you-can-eat blues brunch starting at 11 am. *604 Columbus Ave., South End 617/536–1100 www.dcbkboston.com Massachusetts Ave.*

Franklin Café

BARS | A neighborhood institution, the Franklin's renowned for creative cocktails, local microbrews, fine wines, and modern American food. There's no sign: just look for the white martini logo (or folks waiting for a dinner table) to know you're there. A full menu is served until 1:30 am every single night of the week, and the bar is open until 2 am. *278 Shawmut*

Ave., South End ☎ *617/350–0010* 🌐 *www.franklincafe.com* Ⓜ *Back Bay.*

★ OAK Long Bar + Kitchen

BARS | This stunning flagship bar in the 1912 Fairmont Copley Plaza hotel is a see-and-be-seen hot spot, with the original sky-high coffered ceilings, catbird views over Copley Square, and top-notch bartenders. Inside, coveted barstools are filled with an upscale crowd, while outside in warm weather, patrons can sit at outdoor tables while perusing a menu of signature martinis, single malts, shareable platters, and desserts. People-watch and enjoy a panorama that encompasses the Boston Public Library and Trinity Church in this historic spot. ✉ *Fairmont Copley Plaza, 138 St. James Ave., Back Bay* ☎ *617/267–5300* 🌐 *oaklongbarkitchen.com* Ⓜ *Copley.*

Fenway and Kenmore Square

The Back Bay Fens marshland gave this neighborhood its name, but two iconic institutions give it its character: Fenway Park, which in 2004 saw the triumphant reversal of an 86-year drought for Boston's beloved Red Sox, and the Isabella Stewart Gardner Museum, the legacy of a high-living Brahmin who attended a concert at Symphony Hall in 1912 wearing a headband that read "Oh, You Red Sox." Not far from the Gardner is another major cultural magnet: the Museum of Fine Arts. Kenmore Square, a favorite haunt for Boston University students, adds a bit of youthful flavor to the mix.

Sights

★ Emerald Necklace Conservancy

CITY PARK | **FAMILY** | The six large public parks known as Boston's Emerald Necklace stretch seven miles from the Back Bay Fens to Franklin Park in Dorchester, and include Arnold Arboretum, Jamaica Pond, Olmsted Park, and the Riverway. The linear parks, designed by master landscape architect Frederick Law Olmsted more than 100 years ago, remain a well-groomed urban masterpiece. ✉ *125 The Fenway, The Fenway* ☎ *617/522–2700* 🌐 *www.emeraldnecklace.org.*

★ Fenway Park

SPORTS VENUE | **FAMILY** | Fenway Park is Major League Baseball's oldest ballpark and has seen some stuff since its 1912 opening. For one, it's the home field for the Boston Red Sox, which overcame the "Curse of the Bambino" to win World Series championships in 2004, 2007, 2013, and 2018. Ticket-holding Sox fans can browse display cases mounted inside Fenway Park before and during a ballgame; these shed light on and show off memorabilia from particular players and eras of the club team's history. Fenway offers hour-long behind-the-scenes guided walking tours of the park; there are also specialized tour options. ✉ *4 Jersey St., Gate D, Kenmore Square* ☎ *617/226–6666 tours* 🌐 *www.mlb.com/redsox/ballpark/tours* 🎫 *$21* Ⓜ *Kenmore, Fenway.*

★ Isabella Stewart Gardner Museum

ART MUSEUM | A spirited society woman, Isabella Stewart built a Venetian palazzo to hold her collected art in one of Boston's newest neighborhoods in the 1860s. Her will stipulated that the building remain exactly as she left it—paintings, furniture, down to the smallest object in a hall cabinet—and so it has remained. The palazzo includes such masterpieces as Titian's *Europa,* Giotto's *Presentation of Christ in the Temple,* Piero della Francesca's *Hercules,* and John Singer Sargent's *El Jaleo.* Spanish leather panels, Renaissance hooded fireplaces, and Gothic tapestries accent salons; eight balconies adorn the majestic Venetian courtyard. There's a Raphael Room, Spanish Cloister, Gothic Room, Chinese Loggia, and a magnificent Tapestry Room for concerts.

On March 18, 1990, thieves disguised as police officers stole 12 works, including Vermeer's *The Concert*. None of the art has been recovered, and because Mrs. Gardner's will prohibited substituting other works, empty expanses of wall identify spots where the paintings once hung. ✉ *25 Evans Way, The Fenway* ☎ *617/566–1401* 🌐 *www.gardnermuseum.org* 🎫 *$20* 🕑 *Closed Tues.* Ⓜ *Museum.*

Kenmore Square

PLAZA/SQUARE | Two blocks north of Fenway Park is Kenmore Square, where you'll find shops, restaurants, and the city's emblematic sign advertising Citgo gasoline. The red, white, and blue neon sign from 1965 is so thoroughly identified with the area that historic preservationists fought, successfully, to save it. The old Kenmore Square punk clubs have given way to a block-long development of pricey stores and restaurants, as well as brick sidewalks, gaslight-style street lamps, and tree plantings. In the shadow of Fenway Park between Brookline and Ipswich is Lansdowne Street, a nightlife magnet for the trendy, who have their pick of dance clubs and pregame bars. The urban campus of Boston University begins farther west on Commonwealth Avenue, in blocks thick with dorms, shops, and restaurants. ✉ *Convergence of Beacon St., Commonwealth Ave., and Brookline Ave., The Fenway* Ⓜ *Kenmore.*

★ **Museum of Fine Arts**

ART MUSEUM | **FAMILY** | The MFA's collection of approximately 450,000 objects was built from a core of paintings and sculpture from the Boston Athenæum, historical portraits from the city of Boston, and donations by area universities. The MFA has more than 70 works by John Singleton Copley; major paintings by Winslow Homer, John Singer Sargent, Fitz Henry Lane, and Edward Hopper; and a wealth of American works ranging from native New England folk art and Colonial portraiture to New York abstract expressionism of the 1950s and 1960s. More than 30 galleries contain the MFA's European painting and sculpture collection, dating from the 11th century to the 20th. Contemporary art has a dynamic home in the MFA's dramatic I. M. Pei–designed building. ✉ *465 Huntington Ave., The Fenway* ☎ *617/267–9300* 🌐 *www.mfa.org* 🎫 *$27* 🕑 *Closed Tues. and Wed.* Ⓜ *Museum.*

Restaurants

★ **Sweet Cheeks Q**

$$ | **SOUTHERN** | Red Sox fans, foodies, and Fenway residents flock to this meat-lover's mecca, where Texas-style barbecue is the name of the game. Hefty slabs of dry-rubbed heritage pork, great northern beef brisket, and plump chickens cook low and slow in a jumbo black smoker, then come to the table heaped on a tray lined with butcher paper, along with homemade sweet pickles, shaved onion, and your choice of "hot scoops" (collard greens, mac and cheese) or "cold scoops" (coleslaw, potato salad). **Known for:** finger-licking barbecue; scrumptious sides; jeans and T-shirt atmosphere. Ⓢ *Average main: $22* ✉ *1381 Boylston St., The Fenway* ☎ *617/266–1300* 🌐 *www.sweetcheeksq.com* 🕑 *Closed Mon. No lunch Tues.–Fri.* Ⓜ *Fenway.*

Coffee and Quick Bites

Blackbird Doughnuts

$ | **AMERICAN** | Creative, delicious, and irresistible, the sweet treats from Blackbird Doughnuts have a cult following—even rock star Adele praised them when in town for a concert. One of several outposts in the city, the Fenway location is tiny and it's a good idea to get there early before your fave flavor sells out. **Known for:** fan favorite Boston Cream; creative, unusual flavors; turn your doughnut into an ice cream sandwich with soft-serve. Ⓢ *Average main: $4* ✉ *20 Kilmarnock St., The Fenway* ☎ *617/482–9000* 🌐 *www.blackbirddoughnuts.com/fenway* Ⓜ *Fenway.*

Bleacher Bar

$ | **AMERICAN** | This Fenway restaurant is famous for its enormous garage window which looks into Fenway Park, especially cool on game days, but it's also a fun place to relax with friends, nosh on nachos or fries, and catch all sorts of sporting events on the TV. **Known for:** sneaky way to see a Red Sox game; beers and burgers; sports fans. *Average main: $17 ✉ 82A Lansdowne St., The Fenway ☎ 617/262–2424 🌐 www.bleacherbarboston.com Ⓜ Kenmore.*

Time Out Market Boston

$$ | **INTERNATIONAL** | A food hall curated by the media company known for its magazines and books, Time Out Market Boston features more than a dozen eateries run by some of Boston's most acclaimed chefs, plus two bars, a demo cooking area, and communal seating. The 25,200-square-foot space is a fun place to sample everything from sweet treats at Union Square Donuts to meatballs at chef Michael Schlow's, by one of the city's most acclaimed chefs. **Known for:** variety of eateries; fun vibe; located in historic building. *Average main: $18 ✉ 401 Park Dr., The Fenway ☎ 978/393–8088 🌐 www.timeoutmarket.com/boston Ⓜ Fenway.*

Hotels

★ Hotel Commonwealth

$$$$ | **HOTEL** | Luxury and service without pretense make this hip spot a solid choice. **Pros:** down bedding; perfect locale for Red Sox fans; free Wi-Fi. **Cons:** area is absolutely mobbed during Sox games; small gym; pricey rates. *Rooms from: $500 ✉ 500 Commonwealth Ave., Kenmore Square ☎ 617/933–5000, 866/784–4000 🌐 www.hotelcommonwealth.com 245 rooms No Meals Ⓜ Kenmore.*

Cambridge

Boston's Left Bank—an uber-liberal academic enclave—is a must-visit if you're spending more than a day or two in the Boston area. Cambridge is packed with world-class cultural institutions, quirky shops, restaurants galore, and tons of people-watching.

Sights

★ Harvard Art Museums

ART MUSEUM | This is Harvard University's oldest museum, and in late 2014, it became the combined collections of the Busch-Reisinger, Fogg, and Arthur M. Sackler Museums. All three were united under one glorious, mostly glass roof, under the umbrella name Harvard Art Museums. Housed in a facility designed by award-winning architect Renzo Piano, the 204,000-square-foot museum is spread over seven levels, allowing more of Harvard's 250,000-piece art collection, featuring European and American art from the Middle Ages to the present day, to be seen in one place. Highlights include American and European paintings, sculptures, and decorative arts from the Fogg Museum; Asian art, Buddhist cave-temple sculptures, and Chinese bronzes from the Arthur M. Sackler collection; and works by German expressionists, materials related to the Bauhaus, and postwar contemporary art from German-speaking Europe from the Busch-Reisinger Museum.

In addition to the gallery spaces, there's a 300-seat theater, Jenny's Cafe, a museum shop, and the Calderwood Courtyard, plus conservation and research labs. *✉ 32 Quincy St., Harvard Square ☎ 617/495–9400 🌐 www.harvardartmuseums.org $20; free Sun. Ⓜ Harvard.*

Harvard University's Radcliffe Quad is surrounded by undergrad housing; it's about a 12-minute walk, or half a mile, from Harvard Square.

★ Harvard Museum of Natural History

SCIENCE MUSEUM | FAMILY | The Harvard Museum of Natural History (which exhibits specimens from the Museum of Comparative Zoology, the Harvard University Herbaria, and the Mineralogical and Geological Museum) reminds us nature is the original masterpiece. Cases are packed with zoological specimens, from tiny hummingbirds and deer mice to rare Indian rhinoceroses and one of the largest Amazon pirarucu ever caught. View fossils and skeletons alongside marvelous minerals, including a 1,600-pound amethyst geode. Harvard's world-famous Blaschka *Glass Flowers* collection is a creative approach to flora, with more than 4,300 hand-blown glass plant models. The museum combines historic exhibits drawn from the university's vast collections with new and changing multimedia exhibitions, such as *In Search of Thoreau's Flowers: An Exploration of Change and Loss* and *Lily Simonson: Painting the Deep,* plus a renovated Earth & Planetary Sciences gallery. ✉ *26 Oxford St., Harvard Square* ☎ *617/495–3045* 🌐 *www.hmnh.harvard.edu* 🎟 *$15; ticket includes admission to adjacent Peabody Museum* Ⓜ *Harvard.*

★ Harvard Square

PLAZA/SQUARE | FAMILY | Tides of students, tourists, and politically charged proponents are all part of the nonstop pedestrian flow at this most celebrated of Cambridge crossroads. Harvard Square is where Massachusetts Avenue, coming from Boston, turns and widens into a triangle broad enough to accommodate a brick peninsula (above the T station). The restored 1928 kiosk in the center of the square once served as the entrance to the MBTA station, and is now home to lively street musicians and artists selling their paintings and photos on blankets. Harvard Yard, with its lecture halls, residential houses, libraries, and museums, is one long border of the square; the other three are composed of clusters of banks, retailers, and restaurants. ✉ *Harvard Square* 🌐 *www.harvardsquare.com* Ⓜ *Harvard.*

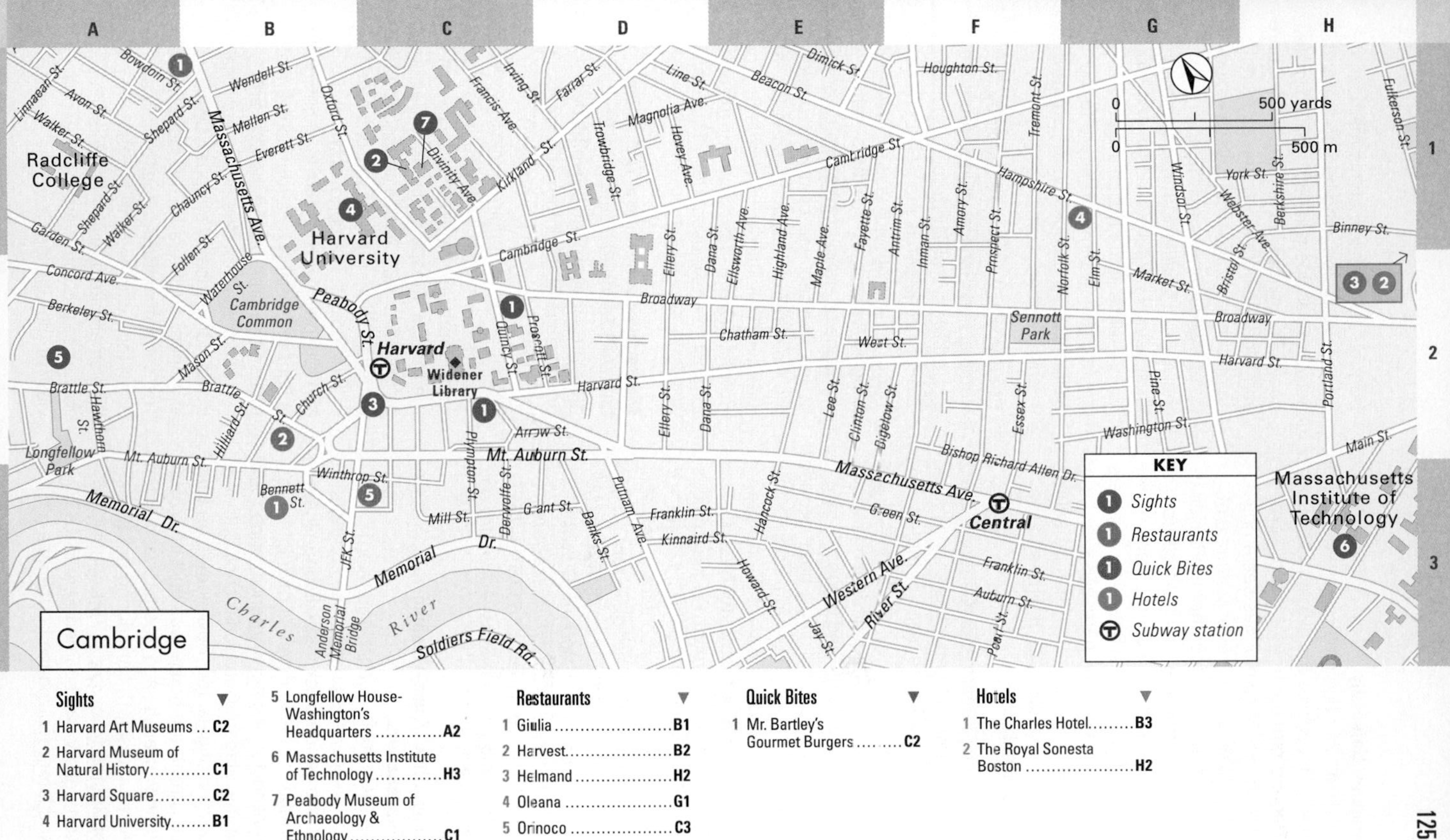

Sights ▼

1 Harvard Art Museums ... **C2**
2 Harvard Museum of Natural History............ **C1**
3 Harvard Square........... **C2**
4 Harvard University........ **B1**
5 Longfellow House-Washington's Headquarters **A2**
6 Massachusetts Institute of Technology **H3**
7 Peabody Museum of Archaeology & Ethnology **C1**

Restaurants ▼

1 Giulia **B1**
2 Harvest..................... **B2**
3 Helmand **H2**
4 Oleana **G1**
5 Orinoco **C3**

Quick Bites ▼

1 Mr. Bartley's Gourmet Burgers **C2**

Hotels ▼

1 The Charles Hotel......... **B3**
2 The Royal Sonesta Boston **H2**

Harvard University

COLLEGE | Although the college dates from the 17th century, the oldest buildings in Harvard Yard are from the 18th century (though you'll sometimes see archaeologists digging here for evidence of older structures). Together the buildings chronicle American architecture from the colonial era to the present. Many of Harvard's cultural and scholarly facilities are important sights in themselves, but most campus buildings, other than museums and concert halls, are off-limits to the general public.

The Harvard Information Center, in the Smith Campus Center, has a small exhibit space, distributes maps of the university area, and offers free student-led tours of Harvard Yard. The tour doesn't include visits to museums, and it doesn't take you into campus buildings, but it provides a fine orientation. The information center is open year-round (except during spring recess and other semester breaks). From the end of June through August, guides offer tours every half hour; however, it's best to call ahead to confirm times. You can also download a mobile tour on your smartphone. ✉ *Bounded by Massachusetts Ave. and Mt. Auburn, Holyoke, and Dunster Sts., 1350 Massachusetts Ave., Harvard Square* ☎ *617/495–1573 Information Center* 🌐 *www.harvard.edu* Ⓜ *Harvard.*

Longfellow House–Washington's Headquarters

HISTORIC HOME | Henry Wadsworth Longfellow, the poet whose stirring tales of the village blacksmith, Evangeline, Hiawatha, and Paul Revere's midnight ride thrilled 19th-century America, once lived in this elegant Georgian mansion. One of several original Tory Row homes on Brattle Street, the house was built in 1759 by John Vassall Jr., and George Washington lived (and slept!) here during the Siege of Boston from July 1775 to April 1776. Longfellow first boarded here in 1837 and later received the house as a gift from his father-in-law on his marriage to Frances Appleton, who burned to death here in an accident in 1861. For 45 years Longfellow wrote his famous verses here and filled the house with the exuberant spirit of his literary circle, which included Ralph Waldo Emerson, Nathaniel Hawthorne, and Charles Sumner, an abolitionist senator. Longfellow died in 1882, but his presence in the house lives on—from the Longfellow family furniture to the wallpaper to the books on the shelves (many the poet's own).

The home is preserved and run by the National Park Service; guided tours are offered Memorial Day through October. The formal garden is the perfect place to relax; the grounds are open year-round. Longfellow Park, across the street, is the place to stand to take photos of the house. The park was created to preserve the view immortalized in the poet's "To the River Charles." ✉ *105 Brattle St., Tory Row* ☎ *617/876–4491* 🌐 *www.nps.gov/long* 🎟 *Free* 🕑 *Closed Tues.–Thurs. and Nov.–Apr.* Ⓜ *Harvard.*

Massachusetts Institute of Technology

COLLEGE | Founded in 1861, MIT mints graduates that are the sharp blades on the edge of the information revolution. Architecture is important here, and although the original buildings were obviously designed by and for scientists, many represent pioneering designs of their times. Kresge Auditorium, designed by Eero Saarinen, with a curving roof and unusual thrust, rests on three, instead of four, points. The nondenominational MIT Chapel, a circular Saarinen design, is lighted primarily by a roof oculus that focuses natural light on the altar and by reflections from the water in a small surrounding moat; it's topped by an aluminum sculpture by Theodore Roszak. The serpentine Baker House, now a dormitory, was designed in 1947 by the Finnish architect Alvar Aalto in such a way as to provide every room with a view of the Charles River. The latest addition is the Green Center, punctuated by the splash of color that is Sol LeWitt's 5,500-square-foot mosaic floor.

The East Campus also has outstanding modern architecture and sculpture, including the stark high-rise Green Building by I. M. Pei. Just outside is Alexander Calder's giant stabile (a stationary mobile) *The Big Sail.* Another Pei work on the East Campus is the Wiesner Building, designed in 1985. Architect Frank Gehry made his mark on the campus with the cockeyed, improbable Ray and Maria Stata Center, a complex of buildings on Vassar Street. East Campus's Great Dome, which looms over neoclassical Killian Court, has often been the target of student "hacks" and has at various times supported a telephone booth with a ringing phone, a life-size statue of a cow, and a campus police cruiser.

MIT maintains a welcome center located at 292 Main Street in Kendall Square, where you can pick up campus maps, grab some water, and charge your phone weekdays 9 to 6. ✉ *77 Massachusetts Ave., Kendall Square* ☎ *617/253–4795* 🌐 *www.mit.edu* Ⓜ *Kendall/MIT.*

Peabody Museum of Archaeology and Ethnology
HISTORY MUSEUM | With one of the world's outstanding anthropological collections, the Peabody Museum is among the oldest anthropology museums in the world. Its collections focus on Native American and Central and South American cultures and are comprised of more than 1.2 million objects. The Hall of the North American Indian is particularly outstanding, with art, textiles, and models of traditional dwellings from across the continent. The Mesoamerican room juxtaposes ancient relief carvings and weavings with contemporary works from the Maya and other peoples. Of special note is the museum's only surviving collection of objects acquired from Native American people during the Lewis and Clark expedition. ✉ *11 Divinity Ave., Harvard Square* ☎ *617/496–1027* 🌐 *www.peabody.harvard.edu* 🎟 *$15, includes admission to the adjacent Harvard Museum of Natural History* Ⓜ *Harvard.*

Restaurants

★ Giulia
$$$ | ITALIAN | With exposed-brick walls and soft lighting, the heart and soul of this charming Italian restaurant is its communal pasta table at which chef Michael Pagliarini spends hours hand-rolling superlative pastas for dishes like buckwheat *pizzoccheri* and pasta *alla Bolognese.* Plates such as house-made lamb sausage, monkfish piccata, warm semolina cakes, grilled barramundi, and Sardinian flatbread are original, generous, and, of course delicious. Known for its romantic nature, it's the perfect place for lovers to linger over a chocolate terrine and cappuccino. **Known for:** excellent Italian food; silky pastas; warm, softly lit space. $ *Average main: $30* ✉ *1682 Massachusetts Ave., Harvard Square* ☎ *617/441–2800* 🌐 *www.giuliarestaurant.com* ⏲ *Closed Sun.*

★ Harvest
$$$$ | AMERICAN | Once a favorite of former Cambridge resident Julia Child, this sophisticated shrine to New England cuisine has been a perennial go-to spot for Harvard students when their parents are in town since 1975. The seasonal menu could feature Cape scallop crudo, fresh pasta with braised veal and pesto, or fresh Cape lobster with lemon hollandaise. **Known for:** elegant New England cuisine; expansive wine list; pretty patio dining area. $ *Average main: $40* ✉ *44 Brattle St., on walkway, Brattle Street* ☎ *617/868–2255* 🌐 *harvestcambridge.com* Ⓜ *Harvard.*

★ Helmand
$$$ | AFGHAN | The area's first Afghan restaurant, named after the country's most important river, welcomes you into its cozy Kendall Square confines with

Afghan rugs, a wood-burning oven, and exotic, yet extremely approachable food that reflects the motherland's location halfway between the Middle East and India. Standouts, beyond the chewy warm bread, include magical names from a faraway land like *aushak* (leek-stuffed ravioli over yogurt with beef ragu and mint), *chapendaz* (marinated grilled beef tenderloin served with cumin-spiced hot pepper–tomato puree), and a vegetarian baked pumpkin platter. **Known for:** excellent Afghan fare; enveloping atmosphere; incredible breads. 💲 *Average main: $28* ✉ *143 1st St., Kendall Square* ☎ *617/492–4646* 🌐 *helmandrestaurant.com* Ⓜ *Lechmere.*

★ Oleana

$$$ | MEDITERRANEAN | With two restaurants (including Sofra in Cambridge) and two cookbooks to her name, chef-owner Ana Sortun continues to bewitch area diners with her intricately spiced eastern Mediterranean mezes (small plates) made with fresh-picked produce from her husband's nearby Siena Farms. Oleana's menu changes often, but look for the hot, crispy-fried mussels starter and Sultan's Delight (tamarind-glazed beef with smoky eggplant puree) along with large plates of Iskender lamb kebab and lemon chicken. **Known for:** eastern Mediterranean menu; mouthwatering small plates; deft use of spices. 💲 *Average main: $27* ✉ *134 Hampshire St., Central Square* ☎ *617/661–0505* 🌐 *www.oleanarestaurant.com* Ⓜ *Central.*

★ Orinoco

$ | LATIN AMERICAN | Don't miss this red clapboard, Pan–Latin American restaurant located down an alleyway in Harvard Square. Owner Andres Branger's dream to bring bountiful plates of super-fresh family fare from his home country of Venezuela to Cambridge (as well as Brookline Village and the South End) rewards diners with delectable, palm-size *arepas* (crispy, hot, corn-flour pockets stuffed with beans, cheese, chicken, or pork), *pabellon criollo* (moist shredded beef with stewed beans, rice, and plantains), and red chili adobo–marinated, charred *pollo* (chicken). **Known for:** Venezuelan specialties; generous portions; great value. 💲 *Average main: $10* ✉ *56 JFK St., Harvard Square* ☎ *617/354–6900* 🌐 *www.orinocokitchen.com* ⏲ *Closed Mon.*

Coffee and Quick Bites

Mr. Bartley's Gourmet Burgers

$ | AMERICAN | FAMILY | It may be perfect cuisine for the student metabolism: a huge variety of variously garnished thick burgers with sassy names (many of them after celebrities, like the Marcus Smart, the POTUS Biden, or the Megan Thee Stallion), deliciously crispy regular and sweet-potato fries, award-winning onion rings, and toppings like an egg or mac and cheese. There's also a competent veggie burger, along with comforting dinner fare like baked meat loaf, fried chicken, and franks and beans. **Known for:** creative burgers; thick frappes; loud atmosphere. 💲 *Average main: $17* ✉ *1246 Massachusetts Ave., Harvard Square* ☎ *617/354–6559* 🌐 *www.mrbartley.com* ⏲ *Closed Sun. and Mon.* Ⓜ *Harvard.*

Hotels

★ The Charles Hotel

$$$ | HOTEL | FAMILY | It used to be that The Charles was *the* place to stay in Cambridge, and while other luxury hotels have since arrived to give it a little healthy competition, this Harvard Square staple is standing strong. **Pros:** two blocks from the T Red Line to Boston; on-site dining options; on-site 4,000-square-foot Corbu Spa & Salon. **Cons:** great location comes at a price; restricted pool hours for children; coffee pots and tea kettles are available by request only. 💲 *Rooms from:*

$399 ✉ *1 Bennett St., Harvard Square* ☎ *617/864–1200, 800/882–1818* 🌐 *www.charleshotel.com* *294 rooms* *No Meals* Ⓜ *Harvard.*

★ **The Royal Sonesta Boston**

$$$ | HOTEL | FAMILY | Right next to the Charles River, the certified-green Sonesta has one of the best city skylines and sunset views in Boston. **Pros:** walk to the Museum of Science and the T to Downtown Boston; pet-friendly; nice pool and fitness center with Peloton. **Cons:** pay parking; river-view guest rooms have much better view than Cambridge-view rooms; no air-conditioning in rooms. 💲 *Rooms from: $379* ✉ *40 Edwin Land Blvd., off Memorial Dr., Kendall Square* ☎ *617/806–4200, 800/766–3782* 🌐 *www.sonesta.com/boston* *400 rooms* *No Meals* Ⓜ *Lechmere.*

Activities

★ **Head of the Charles Regatta**

BOATING | In mid-October about 400,000 spectators turn out to cheer the more than 11,000 male and female athletes who come from all over the world to compete in the annual Head of the Charles Regatta, which in 2014 marked its 50th anniversary. Crowds line the banks of the Charles River with blankets and beer (although the police disapprove of the latter), cheering on their favorite teams and generally using the weekend as an excuse to party. Limited free parking is available, but the chances of finding an open space close to the race route are slim; take public transportation if you can. During the event, free shuttles run between the start and end point of the race route on both sides of the river. ✉ *Banks of the Charles River, Harvard Square* ☎ *617/868–6200* 🌐 *www.hocr.org* Ⓜ *Harvard, Central.*

Shopping

★ **The Harvard Coop**

BOOKS | What began in 1882 as a nonprofit service for students and faculty is now managed by Barnes & Noble College, a separate entity that manages college campus bookstores. Housed in the same location since 1906 and affectionately called The Coop (pronounced "coop," not "co-op"), the store sells books and textbooks (many discounted), school supplies, clothes, and accessories plastered with the Harvard emblem, as well as basic housewares geared toward dorm dwellers. If you need a public restroom, you'll find it here. And if you're looking for MIT swag, they have a location on that campus as well. ✉ *1400 Massachusetts Ave., Harvard Square* ☎ *617/499–2000* 🌐 *store.thecoop.com* Ⓜ *Harvard.*

Side Trips from Boston

History lies thick on the ground in the towns surrounding Boston—from Pilgrims to pirates, witches to whalers, the American Revolution to the Industrial Revolution. The sights outside the city are at least as interesting as those on Boston's Freedom Trail, especially in **Lexington**. When you're ready to trade history lessons for beach fun, Cape Cod to the south and the North Shore to the northeast entice sand-and-sun seekers.

Rich in more than history, the areas surrounding Boston also allow visitors to retrace the steps of famous writers, bask in the outdoors, and browse shops in funky artist communities. The haunts of literary luminaries of every generation lurk throughout Massachusetts. Head to **Concord** to visit the place where Henry David Thoreau wrote his prophetic *Walden* and where Louisa May Alcott's *Little Women* brightened a grim time during the Civil War. Relive Nathaniel Hawthorne's vision of Puritan-era **Salem**.

The seaside towns of Massachusetts were built before the Revolution, during the heyday of American shipping. On the North Shore, **Gloucester** is the country's oldest seaport and **Rockport** has artists' studios and seafood spots. South of Boston, you'll find **Plymouth** and the *Mayflower II*.

In a more contemporary vein, Boston and its suburbs have become a major destination for food and wine lovers, and the state's extensive system of parks, protected forests, beaches, and nature preserves satisfies everyone from the avid hiker to the beach bum.

Lexington

16 miles northwest of Boston.

Incensed against the British, American Colonials burst into action in Lexington in April 1775. On April 18, patriot leader Paul Revere alerted the town that British soldiers were approaching. The next day, as the British advance troops arrived in Lexington on their march toward Concord, the Minutemen were waiting to confront the redcoats in what became the first skirmish of the Revolutionary War.

These first military encounters of the American Revolution are very much a part of present-day Lexington, a modern suburban town that sprawls out from the historic sites near its center. Although the downtown area is generally lively, with ice-cream and coffee shops, boutiques, and a great little movie theater, the town becomes especially animated each Patriots' Day (April 19 but celebrated on the third Monday in April), when costume-clad groups re-create the Minutemen's battle maneuvers and Paul Revere rides again.

To learn more about the city and the 1775 clash, stop by the **Lexington Visitor Center.**

GETTING HERE AND AROUND

Massachusetts Bay Transportation Authority (MBTA) operates bus service in the greater Boston area and serves Lexington.

TOURS

CONTACTS Liberty Ride Trolley Tour. ✉ *1605 Massachusetts Ave., Lexington* ☎ *781/862–1450* 🌐 *www.tourlexington.us/liberty-ride-trolley-tours.*

VISITOR INFORMATION

CONTACTS Lexington Visitors Center. ✉ *1605 Massachusetts Ave., Lexington* ☎ *781/862–1450* 🌐 *www.lexingtonchamber.org.*

 Sights

Buckman Tavern

HISTORIC SIGHT | While waiting for the arrival of the British on the morning of April 19, 1775, the minutemen gathered at this 1690 tavern. A half-hour tour takes in the tavern's seven rooms, which have been restored to the way they looked in the 1770s. Among the items on display is an old front door with a hole made by a British musket ball. ✉ *1 Bedford St., Lexington* ☎ *781/862–3763* 🌐 *www.lexingtonhistory.org* 🎫 *$12* ⏲ *Closed Mon.–Fri. Dec.–Feb.*

Hancock-Clarke House

HISTORIC SIGHT | On April 18, 1775, Paul Revere came here to warn patriots John Hancock and Sam Adams (who were staying at the house while attending the Provincial Congress in nearby Concord) of the advance of British troops. Hancock and Adams, on whose heads the British king had put a price, fled to avoid capture. The house, a parsonage built in 1698, is a 10-minute walk from Lexington Common. Inside is the *Treasures of the Revolution* exhibit, and outside, a Colonial herb garden. ✉ *36 Hancock*

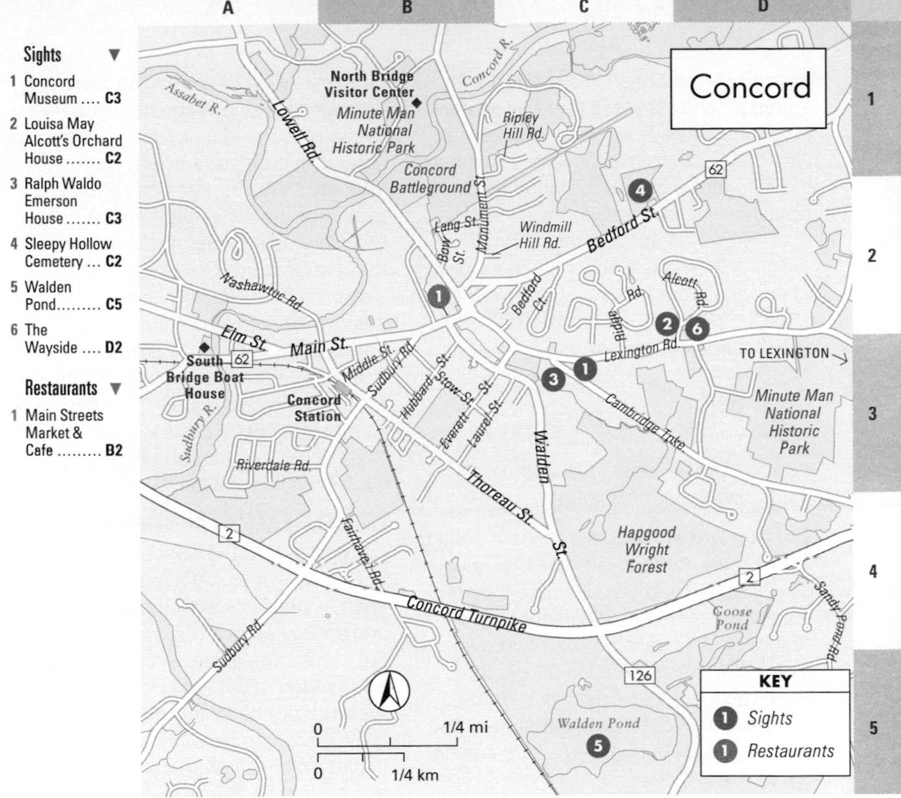

St., Lexington ☎ *781/862–3763* 🌐 *www.lexingtonhistory.org* 🎫 *$12* ⏲ *Closed Mon.–Fri. Apr.–Memorial Day.*

Lexington Green National Historic Landmark

MILITARY SIGHT | It was on this 2-acre triangle of land, commonly referred to as simply the "Battle Green," on April 19, 1775, that the first confrontation between British soldiers, who were marching from Boston toward Concord, and the Colonial militia known as the minutemen took place. The minutemen—so called because they were able to prepare themselves at a moment's notice—were led by Captain John Parker, whose role in the American Revolution is commemorated in Henry Hudson Kitson's renowned 1900 *Minuteman* statue. Facing downtown Lexington at the tip of the Battle Green, the statue is on a traffic island, making for a difficult photo op. ✉ *Junction of Massachusetts Ave. and Bedford St., Lexington* 🌐 *www.lexingtonma.gov/battle-green* 🎫 *Free.*

Minute Man National Historical Park

NATIONAL PARK | **FAMILY** | West of Lexington's center stretches this 1,000-acre park that also extends into nearby Lincoln and Concord. Begin your park visit at the Minute Man Visitor Center in Lexington to see the free multimedia presentation, "The Road to Revolution," a captivating introduction to the events of April 1775. Staffed by costumed park volunteers, the Whittemore House has a hands-on *Try on 1775!* exhibit where kids can wear Colonial clothing and gather ingredients for a meal.

Continuing along Highway 2A toward Concord, you pass the point where Revere's midnight ride ended with his capture by the British; it's marked with a boulder and plaque, as well as an enclosure with wayside exhibits. You can also visit the 1732 Hartwell Tavern, a restored drover's (driver's) tavern staffed by park employees in period costume; they frequently demonstrate musket firing and militia drills and talk about life in Colonial Massachusetts. ✉ *Rte. 2A, ¼ mile west of Rte. 128, Lexington* ☎ *978/369–6993* 🌐 *www.nps.gov/mima.*

Concord

About 10 miles west of Lexington, 21 miles northwest of Boston.

The Concord of today is a modern suburb with a busy center filled with arty shops, places to eat, and (recalling the literary history made here) old bookstores. Autumn lovers, take note: Concord is a great place to start a fall foliage tour. From Boston, head west along Route 2 to Concord, and then continue on to find harvest stands and apple picking around Harvard and Stow.

GETTING HERE AND AROUND

The MBTA runs buses to Concord. On the MBTA Commuter Rail, Concord is a 40-minute ride on the Fitchburg Line, which departs from Boston's North Station.

CONTACTS MBTA. ☎ *617/222–3200, 800/392–6100* 🌐 *www.mbta.com.*

VISITOR INFORMATION

CONTACTS Concord Visitor Center. ✉ *58 Main St., Concord* ☎ *978/318–3061* 🌐 *concordma.gov/1920/Visitor-Center.*

Sights

Concord Museum

HISTORY MUSEUM | FAMILY | The original contents of Emerson's private study, as well as the world's largest collection of Thoreau artifacts, reside in this 1930 Colonial Revival building just east of the town center. The museum provides a good overview of the town's history, from its original Native American settlement to the present. Highlights include Native American artifacts, furnishings from Thoreau's Walden Pond cabin (there's a replica of the cabin itself on the museum's lawn), and one of the two lanterns hung at Boston's Old North Church to signal that the British were coming by sea. Those with kids should stop by the Family Station to get kid-friendly guides, scavenger hunts, and drawing sets. ✉ *200 Lexington Rd., GPS address is 53 Cambridge Tpke., Concord* ☎ *978/369–9763* 🌐 *www.concordmuseum.org* 🎫 *$15* 🕒 *Closed Mon.*

Louisa May Alcott's Orchard House

HISTORIC HOME | The dark brown exterior of Louisa May Alcott's family home sharply contrasts with the light, wit, and energy so much in evidence within. Named for the apple orchard that once surrounded it, Orchard House was the Alcott family home from 1857 to 1877. Here Louisa wrote *Little Women,* based in part on her life with her three sisters; and her father, Bronson, founded the Concord School of Philosophy—the building remains behind the house. Because Orchard House had just one owner after the Alcotts left, and because it became a museum in 1911, more than 80% of the original furnishings remain, including the semicircular shelf-desk where Louisa wrote *Little Women.* The only way to visit the house is by guided tour; reservations are recommended. ✉ *399 Lexington Rd., Concord* ☎ *978/369–4118* 🌐 *www.louisamayalcott.org* 🎫 *$12.*

Ralph Waldo Emerson House

HISTORIC HOME | The 19th-century essayist and poet Ralph Waldo Emerson lived briefly in the Old Manse in 1834–35, then moved to this home, where he lived until his death in 1882. Here he wrote *Essays.* Except for artifacts from Emerson's study, now at the nearby Concord Museum, the Emerson House furnishings have been preserved as the writer left them, down to his hat resting on the newel post. You must join one of the half-hour-long tours to see the interior. ✉ *28 Cambridge Tpke., at Lexington Rd., Concord* ☎ *978/369–2236* 🌐 *ralphwaldoemersonhouse.org* 🎫 *$12* 🕒 *Closed Mon.–Wed. and Nov.–late-Apr.* ☞ *Call ahead for tour-scheduling information.*

Sleepy Hollow Cemetery

CEMETERY | This garden cemetery on the National Registry of Historic Places served as a place of inspiration and a final resting place for American literary greats like Louisa May Alcott, Ralph Waldo Emerson, Henry David Thoreau, and Nathaniel Hawthorne. Each Memorial Day Alcott's grave is decorated in commemoration of her death. ✉ *Bedford St. (Rte. 62), 24 Court La. and Bedford St., Concord* ✥ *1 block east of Monument Sq. in Concord* ☎ *978/318–3233* 🌐 *www.friendsofsleepyhollow.org.*

★ Walden Pond

STATE/PROVINCIAL PARK | For lovers of Early American literature, a trip to Concord isn't complete without a pilgrimage to Henry David Thoreau's most famous residence. Here, in 1845, at age 28, Thoreau moved into a one-room cabin—built for $28.12—on the shore of this 100-foot-deep kettle hole formed by the retreat of an ancient glacier. Living alone for the next two years, Thoreau discovered the benefits of solitude and the beauties of nature. *Walden,* published in 1854, is a mixture of philosophy, nature writing, and proto-ecology.

The site of the original house is staked out in stone. A full-size, authentically furnished replica of the cabin stands about a half mile from the original site, near the Walden Pond State Reservation parking lot. During the summer, don't be shocked if you aren't allowed entrance: Walden Pond has a visitor capacity. Get there early or visit later in the day for the best chance of getting in. ✉ *915 Walden St. (Rte. 126), Concord* ✥ *To get to Walden Pond State Reservation from Concord Center—a trip of only 1½ miles—take Concord's Main St. a block west from Monument Sq., turn left onto Walden St., and head for the intersection of Rtes. 2 and 126. Cross over Rte. 2 onto Hwy. 126, heading south for ½ mile* ☎ *978/369–3254* 🌐 *www.mass.gov/locations/walden-pond-state-reservation* 🎫 *Free, but parking is $8 for vehicles with Massachusetts plates, $30 for vehicles with non-Massachusetts plates* ☞ *No dogs allowed.*

The Wayside

HISTORIC HOME | Nathaniel Hawthorne lived at the Old Manse in 1842–45, working on stories and sketches; he then moved to Salem (where he wrote *The Scarlet Letter*) and later to Lenox (*The House of the Seven Gables*). In 1852 he returned to Concord, bought this rambling structure called The Wayside, and lived here until his death in 1864. The home certainly appealed to literary types: the subsequent owner of The Wayside, Margaret Sidney, wrote the children's book *Five Little Peppers and How They Grew* (1881), and before Hawthorne moved in, the Alcotts lived here, from 1845 to 1848. Notably, The Wayside is a site on the National Underground Railroad Network to Freedom program, as the Alcotts helped at least one enslaved person on his way to Canada and freedom. An exhibit center, in the former barn, provides information about the Wayside authors and links them to major events in American history. Hawthorne's tower-study, with his stand-up writing desk, is substantially as he left it. ✉ *455 Lexington Rd., Concord* ☎ *978/318–7863* 🌐 *www.nps.gov/mima/learn/historyculture/thewayside.htm* 🎫 *$7* 🕒 *Closed in winter.*

Restaurants

Main Streets Market & Cafe

$$ | **AMERICAN** | Cyclists, families, and sightseers pack into this brick building, which was used to store munitions during the Revolutionary War. Wood floors and blackboard menus add a touch of nostalgia, but the extensive menu includes many classic dishes, including mac and cheese, fish and chips, and steamed mussels. **Known for:** open early for breakfast; dog-friendly patio; full bar. *Average main: $18* ✉ *42 Main St., Concord* ☎ *978/369–9948* 🌐 *www.mainstreetsmarketandcafe.com* ⏲ *No dinner Sun.–Wed.*

Salem

16 miles northeast of Boston, 4 miles west of Marblehead.

Known for years as the Witch City, Salem is redefining itself. Though numerous witch-related attractions and shops still draw tourists, there's much more to the city. First, a bit on its bewitched past...

The witchcraft hysteria emerged from the trials of 1692, when several Salem-area girls fell ill and accused some of the townspeople of casting spells on them. More than 150 men and women were charged with practicing witchcraft, a crime punishable by death. After the trials later that year, 19 people were hanged and one man was crushed to death.

Though the witch trials might have built Salem's infamy, it'd be a mistake to ignore the town's rich maritime and creative traditions, which played integral roles in the country's evolution. Frigates out of Salem opened the Far East trade routes and generated the wealth that created America's first millionaires. Among its native talents are writer Nathaniel Hawthorne, the intellectual Peabody sisters, navigator Nathaniel Bowditch, and architect Samuel McIntire. This creative spirit is today celebrated in Salem's internationally recognized museums, waterfront shops and restaurants, galleries, and wide common.

To learn more on the area, stop by the **Regional Visitor's Center.** Innovatively designed in the Old Salem Armory, the center has exhibits, a 27-minute film, maps, and a gift shop.

VISITOR INFORMATION

CONTACTS Destination Salem. ✉ *81 Washington St., Suite 204, Salem* ☎ *978/741–3252, 877/725–3662* 🌐 *www.salem.org.* **Salem Armory Visitor Center.** ✉ *2 New Liberty St., Salem* ☎ *978/740–1650* 🌐 *www.nps.gov/ner/sama.*

Sights

The House of the Seven Gables

HISTORIC HOME | Immortalized in Nathaniel Hawthorne's classic novel, this site is itself a historic treasure. Built in 1668 and also known as the Turner-Ingersoll Mansion, the house includes the famous secret staircase, a re-creation of Hepzibah's scent shop from *The House of Seven Gables*, and some of the finest Georgian interiors in the country. Also on the property is the small house where Hawthorne was born in 1804; built in 1750, it was moved from its original location a few blocks away. To visit the house, you must join a guided tour. ✉ *115 Derby St., Salem* ☎ *978/744–0991* 🌐 *www.7gables.org* 🎫 *$20 for house tour and grounds; $10 for grounds only.*

★ **Peabody Essex Museum**

ART MUSEUM | Salem's world-class museum celebrates superlative works from around the globe and across time, including American art and architecture, Asian export art, photography, and maritime art and history, as well as Native American, Oceanic, and African art. With a collection of 1.8 million works, housed in a contemplative blend of modern design, PEM represents a diverse range of styles; exhibits include pieces ranging

Located in downtown Salem, the Peabody Essex Museum which was founded in 1799, is the country's oldest continuously operating museum.

from American decorative and seamen's art to an interactive Art & Nature Center and photography. While there, be sure to tour the Yin Yu Tang house. This fabulous 200-year-old house dates to the Qing Dynasty (1644–1911) of China. The museum brought it over from China in sections and reassembled it here. ✉ *East India Sq., Salem* ☎ *978/745–9500, 866/745–1876* 🌐 *www.pem.org* 🎫 *$20* 🕒 *Closed Tues. and Wed.*

Salem Maritime National Historic Site

HISTORIC SIGHT | Near Derby Wharf, this 9¼-acre site focuses on Salem's heritage as a major seaport with a thriving overseas trade. It includes the 1762 home of Elias Derby, America's first millionaire; the 1819 Custom House, made famous in Nathaniel Hawthorne's *The Scarlet Letter*; and a replica of the *Friendship*, a 171-foot, three-masted 1797 merchant vessel. There's also an active lighthouse dating from 1871, as well as the nation's last surviving 18th-century wharves. There is also the 1770 Pedrick Store House, moved from nearby Marblehead and reassembled right on Derby Wharf; the two-story structure once played a vital role in the lucrative merchant seaside trade. The grounds are open 24/7, but buildings open on a seasonal schedule. ✉ *193 Derby St., Salem* ☎ *978/740–1650 visitor center* 🌐 *www.nps.gov/sama/index.htm.*

Salem Witch Museum

HISTORY MUSEUM | An informative and fascinating introduction to Salem's witchcraft hysteria, this museum offers a look at 1692 with 13 life-size stage sets featuring narration of what life was like at that time, plus a 15-minute guided tour through the exhibit *Witches: Evolving Perceptions*, which describes witch hunts through the years. Tickets are sold online exclusively. In winter, the museum might not open in bad weather. Call ahead. ✉ *19½ Washington Sq. N, Salem* ☎ *978/744–1692* 🌐 *www.salemwitchmuseum.com* 🎫 *$16.50.*

Restaurants

Finz Seafood & Grill

$$$ | **SEAFOOD** | This contemporary seafood restaurant on Salem Harbor treats patrons to prime canal views. There is an extensive sushi and sashimi menu, plus lots of other seafood favorites, including sesame-crusted tuna and steamed lobster. **Known for:** outdoor seating; classic New England seafood; large sushi menu. *Average main: $30* ✉ *76 Wharf St., Salem* ☎ *978/744–8485* 🌐 *www.hipfinz.com.*

Hotels

★ **Amelia Payson House**

$$$ | **B&B/INN** | Built in 1845, this Greek Revival house is a comfortable bed-and-breakfast near all the historic attractions. **Pros:** fireplaces in each room; outdoor lounge with a fire pit; on-site parking. **Cons:** no children under 12; hard to get reservations; might be too quaint for some. *Rooms from: $250* ✉ *16 Winter St., Salem* ☎ *978/744–8304* 🌐 *www.ameliapaysonhouse.com* *3 rooms* *Free Breakfast.*

The Hawthorne Hotel

$$ | **HOTEL** | Elegantly restored, this full-service historic hotel celebrates the town's most famous writer and is within walking distance of the town common, museums, and waterfront. **Pros:** lovely, historic lobby; free parking available behind hotel; free Wi-Fi. **Cons:** many rooms are small; two-night minimum June through October; pricey pet policy. *Rooms from: $199* ✉ *18 Washington Sq. W, Salem* ☎ *978/744–4080, 800/729–7829* 🌐 *www.hawthornehotel.com* *93 rooms* *No Meals* ☞ *$50 charge per room per night for pets.*

Performing Arts

Cry Innocent: The People Versus Bridget Bishop

THEATER | This show, the longest continuously running play north of Boston, transports audience members to Bridget Bishop's witchcraft hearing of 1692. After hearing historical testimonies, the audience cross-examines the witnesses and decides whether to send Bridget to trial or not. Actors respond in character, revealing much about the Puritan frame of mind. Each show is different and allows audience members to play their "part" in history. ✉ *Old Town Hall, 32 Derby Sq., Salem* ☎ *978/810–2588* 🌐 *www.historyalivesalem.com* *$25.*

Gloucester

37 miles northeast of Boston, 4 miles southwest of Rockport on Rte. 127

On Gloucester's fine seaside promenade is a famous statue of a man steering a ship's wheel, his eyes searching the horizon. The statue, which honors those who go down to the sea in ships, was commissioned by the town citizens in celebration of Gloucester's 300th anniversary in 1923. The oldest seaport in the nation (with some of the North Shore's best beaches) is still a major fishing port. Sebastian Junger's 1997 book *A Perfect Storm* was an account of the fate of the *Andrea Gail*, a Gloucester fishing boat caught in the storm of the century in October 1991. In 2000 the book was made into a movie, filmed on location in Gloucester.

VISITOR INFORMATION

CONTACTS Cape Ann Chamber of Commerce. ✉ *33 Commercial St., Gloucester* ☎ *978/283–1601* 🌐 *www.capeannchamber.com.*

Sights

Cape Ann Museum

HISTORY MUSEUM | The Cape Ann Museum celebrates the art, history, and culture of Cape Ann. The museum's collection includes fine art from the 19th century to the present alongside artifacts from the fishing, maritime, and granite-quarrying industries, as well as textiles, furniture, a library-archives, and three historic houses. ✉ *27 Pleasant St., Gloucester* ☎ *978/283–0455* 🌐 *www.capeannmuseum.org* 🎫 *$14* 🕒 *Closed Mon.*

Hammond Castle Museum

CASTLE/PALACE | Inventor John Hays Hammond Jr., credited with more than 500 patents, including remote control via radio waves, built this structure in 1926 to resemble a "medieval" stone castle. The museum contains medieval-style furnishings and paintings, and the Great Hall houses an impressive 8,200-pipe organ. From the castle you can see Norman's Woe, the rock made famous by Longfellow in his poem "The Wreck of the Hesperus." In July and August, unique "Spiritualism Tours" are an additional option on Thursday night (for an extra fee), with discussion of topics like the Ouija board, spirit photography, séances, and the science behind Spiritualism. Note: the museum is not wheelchair accessible. Parts of the grounds are free to visit. ✉ *80 Hesperus Ave., south side of Gloucester off Rte. 127, Gloucester* ☎ *978/283–2080* 🌐 *www.hammondcastle.org* 🎫 *$20* 🕒 *Closed Jan. and Mon.–Thurs. in April, Nov., and Dec.*

Rocky Neck

NEIGHBORHOOD | On a peninsula within Gloucester's working harbor, the town's creative side thrives in this neighborhood, one of the oldest continuously working artists' colonies in the United States. Its alumni include Winslow Homer, Maurice Prendergast, Jane Peterson, and Cecilia Beaux. While some venues stay open year-round, expect many to be closed in winter. ✉ *6 Wonson St., Gloucester* ☎ *978/515–7004* 🌐 *www.rockyneckartcolony.org.*

Beaches

Gloucester has some of the best beaches on the North Shore. From Memorial Day through mid-September, parking costs $25 on weekdays and $30 on weekends, when the lots often fill by 10 am.

Good Harbor Beach

BEACH | FAMILY | This beach has calm, waveless waters and soft sand, and is surrounded by grassy dunes, making it perfect any time of year. In summer (June, July, and August), it is lifeguard patrolled and wheelchair accessible, and there is a snack bar if you don't feel like packing in food. The restrooms and showers are also accessible, and you can pick up beach toys at the concessions. On weekdays parking is plentiful, but the lot fills by 10 am on weekends. In June, green flies can be bothersome. **Amenities:** food and drink; lifeguards; parking (fee); showers; toilets. **Best for:** swimming; walking. ✉ *Gloucester* ✢ *Clearly signposted from Rte. 127A* 🌐 *gloucester-ma.gov* 🎫 *Parking $20–$35 per car; reserve online at gloucesterweb.yodelpass.com/beaches.*

★ Wingaersheek Beach

BEACH | With white sand and dunes, Wingaersheek Beach is a well-protected cove with both a beach side and a boat side. The white Annisquam lighthouse is in the bay. The beach is known for its miles of white sand and calm waters. Make a required parking reservation online after Memorial Day through summer. The parking lot is accessible and beach wheelchairs are available on request. **Amenities:** food and drink; parking (fee); toilets. **Best for:** swimming; walking. ✉ *232 Atlantic St., Gloucester* ✢ *Take Rte. 128 N to Exit 13* 🌐 *gloucester-ma.gov* 🎫 *Limited* *parking, from $30 per car; reserve online at gloucesterweb.yodelpass.com/beaches.*

Restaurants

Passports

$$$ | **ECLECTIC** | **FAMILY** | In the heart of downtown Gloucester, Passports serves a modern take on classic New England seafood. Whether you sit at the bar or a table, you'll be served delicious complimentary popovers to start. **Known for:** lively atmosphere; house haddock; great, central location. *Average main: $25* *110 Main St., Gloucester* *978/281–3680* *passportsrestaurant.com.*

Hotels

Cape Ann's Marina Resort

$$$ | **RESORT** | **FAMILY** | This year-round hotel less than a mile from downtown Gloucester comes alive in summer with an on-site restaurant and deep-sea fishing excursions. **Pros:** free Wi-Fi; full marina; indoor pool and Jacuzzi with poolside bar. **Cons:** hotel surrounded by parking lots; price hike during summer; bar area can be loud in summer. *Rooms from: $250* *75 Essex Ave., Gloucester* *978/283–2116, 800/626–7660* *www.capeannmarina.com* *30 rooms* *No Meals.*

★ Castle Manor Inn

$ | **B&B/INN** | With original woodwork and cozy fireplaces, this restored 1900 Victorian inn perfectly captures the Cape Ann aesthetic. **Pros:** discount parking passes to the local beaches; historic; close to Gloucester's beaches. **Cons:** closes for the winter; roads in the area can be winding and confusing; may be too intimate for some travelers. *Rooms from: $175* *141 Essex Ave., Gloucester* *978/515–7386* *www.castlemanorinn.com* *10 rooms* *No Meals.*

Rockport

41 miles northeast of Boston, 4 miles northeast of Gloucester on Rte. 127.

Rockport, at the very tip of Cape Ann, derives its name from the local granite formations. Many Boston-area structures are made of stone cut from its long-gone quarries. Today the town is a tourist center with a well-marked, centralized downtown that is easy to navigate and access on foot. Unlike typical tourist-trap landmarks, Rockport's shops sell quality arts, clothing, and gifts, and its restaurants serve seafood or home-baked cookies rather than fast food. Walk past shops and colorful clapboard houses to the end of Bearskin Neck for an impressive view of the Atlantic Ocean and the old, weather-beaten lobster shack known as Motif No. 1 because of its popularity as a subject for amateur painters and photographers.

VISITOR INFORMATION

CONTACTS Rockport Visitor Center. *Upper Main St. (Rte. 127), Rockport* *978/546–9372* *www.rockportusa.com.*

Restaurants

Brackett's Oceanview Restaurant

$$ | **SEAFOOD** | Enormous windows in this quiet, homey restaurant offer excellent views across Sandy Bay, along with plenty of chowder, fish cakes, lobster, and other seafood dishes. While the restaurant is only open seasonally, next door is Brackett's café, Brother's Brew Coffee Shop, which is open year-round and serves breakfast. **Known for:** local seafood; every table has a waterfront view; great downtown location. *Average main: $24* *25 Main St., Rockport* *978/546–2797* *www.bracketts.com* *Closed Columbus Day–mid-Apr.*

Plymouth

40 miles south of Boston.

On December 26, 1620, 102 weary men, women, and children disembarked from the *Mayflower* to found the first permanent European settlement north of Virginia. Today Plymouth is characterized by narrow streets, clapboard mansions, shops, antiques stores, and a scenic waterfront. To mark Thanksgiving, the town holds a parade, historic-house tours, and other activities. Historic statues dot the town, including depictions of William Bradford, Pilgrim leader and governor of Plymouth Colony for more than 30 years, on Water Street; a Pilgrim maiden in Brewster Gardens; and Massasoit, the Wampanoag chief who helped the Pilgrims survive, on Carver Street.

VISITOR INFORMATION

CONTACTS Plymouth Visitor Information Center. ✉ *130 Water St., at Rte. 44, Plymouth* ☎ *508/747–7525* 🌐 *www.seeplymouth.com.*

Sights

Mayflower II

HISTORIC SIGHT | FAMILY | This seaworthy replica of the 1620 *Mayflower* was built in England through research and a bit of guesswork, then sailed across the Atlantic in 1957. As you explore the interior and exterior of the ship, which was extensively refurbished in time for Plymouth's 400th anniversary in 2020, sailors in modern dress answer your questions about both the reproduction and the original ship, while costumed guides provide a 17th-century perspective. This attraction is part of the Plimoth Patuxet Museums system. Plymouth Rock is also nearby. ✉ *State Pier, Plymouth* ☎ *508/746–1622* 🌐 *www.plimoth.org* 🎫 *$15; combination tickets for other sites available* 🕓 *Closed late-Nov.–late-Mar.*

National Monument to the Forefathers

MONUMENT | Said to be the largest freestanding granite statue in the United States, this allegorical monument stands high on an 11-acre hilltop site. Designed by Hammatt Billings of Boston in 1854 and dedicated in 1889, it depicts Faith, surrounded by Liberty, Morality, Justice, Law, and Education, and includes scenes from the Pilgrims' early days in Plymouth. ✉ *72 Allerton St., Plymouth* 🌐 *www.seeplymouth.com/things-to-do/national-monument-forefathers.*

Pilgrim Hall Museum

HISTORY MUSEUM | FAMILY | From the waterfront sights, it's a short walk to one of the country's oldest public museums. Established in 1824, Pilgrim Hall Museum transports you back to the time of the Pilgrims' landing with objects carried by those weary travelers to the New World. Historic items on display include a carved chest, a remarkably well-preserved wicker cradle, Myles Standish's sword, and John Alden's Bible. In addition, the museum presents the story of the Wampanoag, the native people who lived here 10,000 years before the arrival of the Pilgrims, and who still live here today. ✉ *75 Court St. (Rte. 3A), Plymouth* ☎ *508/746–1620* 🌐 *www.pilgrimhall.org* 🎫 *$15* 🕓 *Closed Mon. and Tues. and Jan.–Mar.*

★ Plimoth Patuxet Museums

MUSEUM VILLAGE | FAMILY | Against the backdrop of the Atlantic Ocean, and 3 miles south of downtown Plymouth, this living museum shares the rich, interwoven story of the Plymouth Colony and the Wampanoag homeland through engaging daily programs and special events. A 1620s Pilgrim village has been carefully re-created, from the thatch roofs, cramped quarters, and open fireplaces to the long-horned livestock. Throw away your preconception of white collars and funny hats; through ongoing research, the Plimoth staff has developed a portrait of the Pilgrims that's more complex than the dour folk in school textbooks. Listen to the accents of the "residents," who never break out of character. Feel free to engage them in conversation about their life. Don't worry, 21st-century museum educators are on hand to help answer any questions you have as well. On the Wampanoag homesite, meet native people speaking from a modern perspective on the traditions, lifeways, and culture of Eastern Woodlands Indigenous people. Note that there's not a lot of shade here in summer. ✉ *137 Warren Ave. (Rte. 3A), Plymouth* ☎ *508/746–1622* 🌐 *www.plimoth.org* 🎟 *$32; combination tickets available for other sites* ⏲ *Closed late Nov.–late Mar.*

Plymouth Rock

HISTORIC SIGHT | This landmark rock, just a few dozen yards from the *Mayflower II,* is popularly believed to have been the Pilgrims' stepping-stone when they left the ship. Given the stone's unimpressive appearance—it's little more than a boulder—and dubious authenticity (as explained on a nearby plaque), the grand canopy overhead seems a trifle ostentatious. Still, more than a million people a year come to visit this world-famous symbol of courage and faith. ■ **TIP→ The views of Plymouth Harbor alone are worth the visit.** ✉ *Water St., Plymouth* ☎ *508/747–5360* 🌐 *www.mass.gov/locations/pilgrim-memorial-state-park.*

Restaurants

The Blue-Eyed Crab

$$$ | CARIBBEAN | FAMILY | Grab a seat on the outside deck overlooking the water at this friendly, somewhat funky (plastic fish dangling from the ceiling), Caribbean-inspired eatery. Enjoy fruity cocktails on the patio, or hang out in the colorful dining room. **Known for:** views of the water; funky decor; tropical cocktails. $ *Average main: $27* ✉ *170 Water St., Plymouth* ☎ *508/747–6776* 🌐 *www.blue-eyedcrab.com.*

Chapter 5

CAPE COD, MARTHA'S VINEYARD, AND NANTUCKET

Updated by
Diane Bair

Sights	Restaurants	Hotels	Shopping	Nightlife
★★★☆☆	★★★★☆	★★★★☆	★★★★☆	★★☆☆☆

WELCOME TO CAPE COD, MARTHA'S VINEYARD, AND NANTUCKET

TOP REASONS TO GO

★ **Beaches:** With high sand dunes, gorgeous sunsets, and never-ending seascapes, Cape Cod's picturesque beaches are the ultimate reason to visit.

★ **Visiting Lighthouses:** Lighthouses rise along Cape Cod's coast like architectural exclamation points. Highlights include Eastham's beautiful Nauset Light and Chatham and Nobska Lights for their spectacular views.

★ **Biking the Trails:** Martha's Vineyard and Nantucket have dedicated bike paths, but the 25-mile, relatively flat Cape Cod Rail Trail from South Dennis to south Wellfleet (with a spur out to Chatham) is the definitive route.

★ **Setting Sail:** Area tour operators offer everything from sunset schooner cruises and charter fishing expeditions to whale-watching adventures.

★ **Browsing the Galleries:** The Cape was a prominent art colony in the 19th century, and today it has a number of galleries.

1 **Sandwich.** Heritage and Sandwich Glass museums.

2 **Falmouth.** The family-friendly Old Silver Beach.

3 **Hyannis.** The Cape's unofficial capital.

4 **Barnstable.** The seven villages of Barnstable boast family favorites like Craigville Beach and Four Seas Ice Cream.

5 **Yarmouth.** South and West Yarmouth, and Yarmouthport.

6 **Dennis.** Museums and B&Bs.

7 **Brewster.** Rich in conservation lands and state parks.

8 **Harwich.** Boats of all shapes and sizes anchor in the harbors.

9 **Chatham.** A quietly posh seaside resort.

10 **Orleans.** Beautiful homes and beaches.

11 **Eastham.** A town full of hidden treasures.

12 **Wellfleet and South Wellfleet.** World-renowned for its oysters.

13 **Truro.** High dunes, estuaries, and vineyards.

14 **Provincetown.** Fun-loving town at the Cape's tip.

15 **Martha's Vineyard.** 7 miles off the Cape's southwest tip.

16 **Nantucket.** 30 miles off the coast of Hyannis.

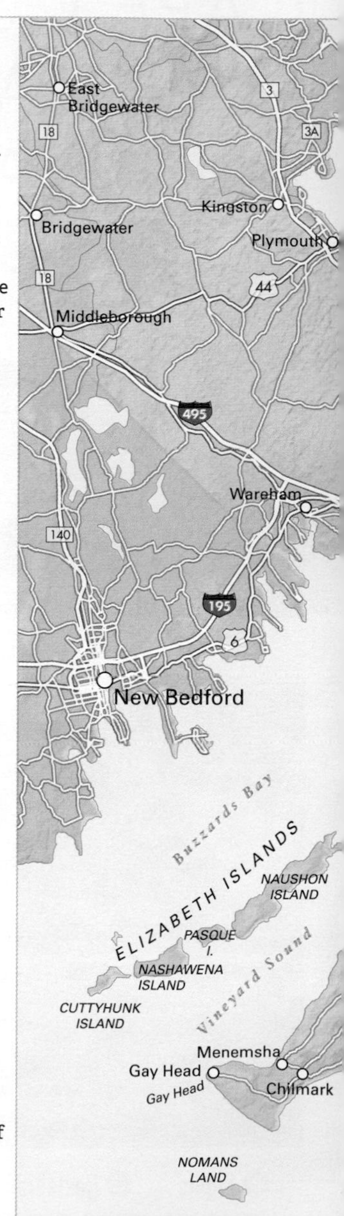

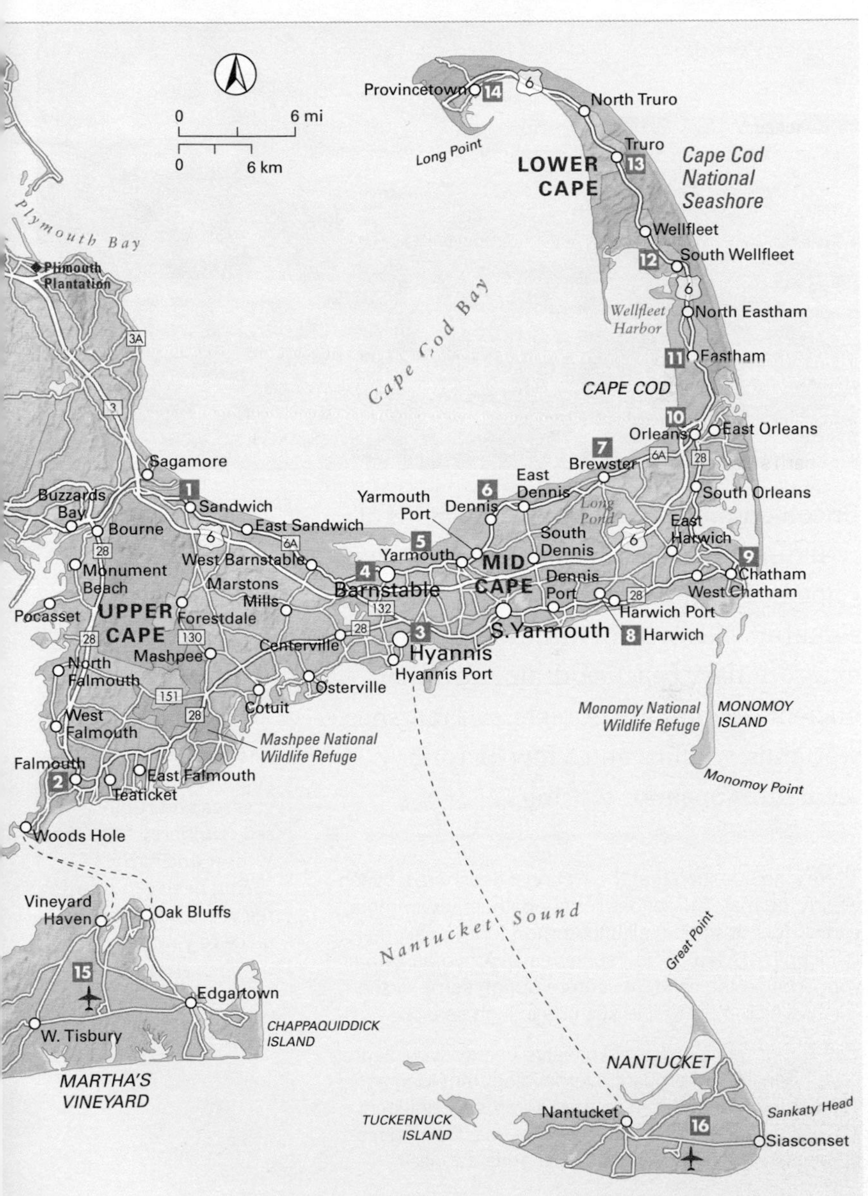
0
6 mi
0
6 km
Provincetown
14
Long Point
North Truro
Truro
13
LOWER CAPE
Cape Cod National Seashore
Wellfleet
12
South Wellfleet
Wellfleet Harbor
North Eastham
11
Eastham
CAPE COD
10
Orleans
East Orleans
7
Brewster
6A
28
South Orleans
Plymouth Bay
Plimouth Plantation
3A
3
Cape Cod Bay
Sagamore
1
Sandwich
Buzzards Bay
Bourne
28
6
East Sandwich
6A
West Barnstable
Monument Beach
Pocasset
UPPER CAPE
Forestdale
130
28
Marstons Mills
Mashpee
North Falmouth
151
28
West Falmouth
Falmouth
2
Teaticket
East Falmouth
Mashpee National Wildlife Refuge
Cotuit
Osterville
Centerville
28
132
4
Barnstable
3
Hyannis
Hyannis Port
Yarmouth Port
5
Yarmouth
6
Dennis
East Dennis
MID CAPE
South Dennis
Long Pond
Dennis Port
S.Yarmouth
East Harwich
9
Chatham
West Chatham
28
Harwich Port
8
Harwich
Monomoy National Wildlife Refuge
MONOMOY ISLAND
Monomoy Point
Woods Hole
Vineyard Haven
Oak Bluffs
15
Edgartown
W. Tisbury
CHAPPAQUIDDICK ISLAND
MARTHA'S VINEYARD
Nantucket Sound
Great Point
NANTUCKET
Nantucket
16
Sankaty Head
Siasconset
TUCKERNUCK ISLAND

CAPE COD NATIONAL SEASHORE

The national seashore can be explored with Art's Dune Tours.

Encompassing more than 44,000 acres of coastline from Chatham to Provincetown, Cape Cod National Seashore is the Cape's signature site. Within its borders, there are extraordinary beaches, dramatic dunes, ancient swamps and forests, salt marshes, wetlands, wildlife, and a few historic structures open for touring

There's no question that the National Seashore's beaches are the main attractions for sunbathers, swimmers, and surfers. It's not at all uncommon for the parking lots to fill up by 11 am on hot, sunny days. Arrive early to find your spot on the sand, or venture out on some of the less-traveled trails to find solitude in high season.

Without protection, such expansive beauty would surely have been lost to rampant overdevelopment long ago. Thankfully, John F. Kennedy marked off a magnificent 40-mile swath of the Massachusetts coast during his presidency, protecting it for future generations.

BEST TIME

Swimming at **Cape Cod National Seashore** (☎508/255–3421 🌐 www.nps.gov/caco) is best in summer, but in the fall, the park becomes utterly sublime with golden salt-marsh grasses and ruby-red cranberry bogs. Winter and early spring nearly guarantee you'll have the place to yourself.

BEST WAYS TO EXPLORE

TAKE A WALK

There are 11 self-guided trails that begin at various points throughout the park, leading through shaded swamps, alongside marshes, and through meadows, forest, and dunes. Most of the terrain is flat and sometimes sandy.

RIDE A BIKE

Three well-maintained bicycle trails run through the park. In Eastham, the short Nauset Trail heads from the Salt Pond Visitor Center through the woods to Coast Guard Beach. Truro's Head, off the Meadow Trail, edges a large salt meadow that's great for birding. The park's most dramatic and physically demanding trail is the Province Lands Trail, with more than 7 miles of steep hills and hairpin curves through forest and sand dunes. Mountain bikers can make their own trails on the miles of well-maintained fire roads.

SEE THE SIGHTS

Several historic homes and sites are open for touring, and there are a few notable overlooks accessible by car. Climb the steep steps of lighthouses in Eastham and Truro or see rescue reenactments at Provincetown's Old Harbor Life-Saving Station. Scenic overlooks include Eastham's exquisite Fort Hill area; Wellfleet's Marconi Station Site, where the first transatlantic wireless message was sent in 1903; Truro's Pilgrim Heights; and Provincetown's scenic 2-mile Race Point Road.

TOUR WITH A RANGER

Available from mid-May–October, mostly free ranger-guided activities include full-moon dune hikes, a beach campfire, a paddling trip, or a photography workshop.

Bikes can go on designated bike trails, paved roads, and unpaved fire roads.

SHIFTING SANDS

Forged by massive moving glaciers more than 20,000 years ago, Cape Cod's landscape is still in perpetual motion, continually shaped by the powerful forces of sand, wind, and water. The Cape's land is slowly giving way to rising ocean levels and erosion, losing an average of nearly 4 feet of outer beach per year. Many a home or structure has succumbed to the unrelenting ocean over the years; some—like Truro's Highland Light and Eastham's Nauset Light—have been moved to safety. Eventually Cape Cod will likely be lost to the sea, but not for thousands of years.

You'll see many signs on beaches and trails asking walkers to keep off the dunes. Take heed, for much of the fragile landscape of the outer Cape is held together by its dune formations and the vegetation that grows within them.

Even if you haven't visited Cape Cod and the islands, you can likely—and accurately—imagine "sand dunes and salty air, quaint little villages here and there." As that 1950s Patti Page song promises, "you're sure to fall in love with old Cape Cod."

Cape Codders are fiercely protective of the environment. Despite some occasionally rampant development, planners have been careful to preserve nature and encourage responsible, eco-conscious building. Nearly 30% of the Cape's 412 square miles is protected from development, and another 35% has not yet been developed (on Nantucket and Martha's Vineyard, percentages of protected land are far higher). Opportunities for sports and recreation abound, as the region is rife with biking and hiking trails, serene beaches, and waterways for boating and fishing.

The area is also rich in history. Many don't realize that the Pilgrims landed here first: in November 1620, the lost and travel-weary sailors dropped anchor in what is now Provincetown Harbor and spent five weeks here, scouring the area for food and possible settlement. Were it not for the aid of the resident Native Americans, the strangers would barely have survived. Even so, they set sail again for fairer lands, ending up across Cape Cod Bay in Plymouth.

Virtually every period style of residential American architecture is well represented on Cape Cod, including—of course—that seminal form named for the region, the Cape Cod–style house. These low, 1½-story domiciles with clapboard or shingle siding—more traditionally the latter in these parts—and gable roofs have been a fixture throughout Cape Cod since the late 17th century. You'll also find grand Georgian and Federal mansions from the Colonial era, as well as handsome Greek Revival, Italianate, and Second Empire houses that date to Victorian times. Many of the most prominent residences were built for ship captains and sea merchants. In recent decades, the region has seen an influx of angular, glassy, contemporary homes, many with soaring windows and skylights, and massive wraparound porches that take advantage of their enviable sea views.

MAJOR REGIONS

The Cape is divided into four major areas and is shaped roughly like an arm bent at the elbow: the **Upper Cape** (the shoulder); the **Mid Cape** (the upper arm); the **Lower Cape** (the bicep and forearm); and the **Outer Cape** (the wrist and hand). Each of the Cape's 15 towns are further broken up into smaller villages.

Upper Cape (closest to the bridges) has the oldest towns like **Sandwich** and **Falmouth**, plus fine beaches and fascinating little museums. **Mid Cape** has sophisticated Colonial-era hamlets but also motels and miniature golf courses. There's **Barnstable, Dennis,** and **Yarmouth**, as well as **Hyannis**, the Cape's unofficial capital. **Lower Cape** consists of **Brewster, Chatham, Harwich,** and **Orleans**. Here you'll find casual clam shacks, lovely lighthouses, funky art galleries, and stellar natural attractions. **Eastham, Wellfleet, Truro**, and **Provincetown** populate the narrow forearm of the **Outer Cape**, which is famous for sand dunes, crashing surf, and scrubby pines.

The islands, **Martha's Vineyard** and **Nantucket,** lie to the south. Martha's Vineyard is about 7 miles off the Cape's southwest tip, while Nantucket is some 30 miles south of Hyannis. Both are connected to the Cape by ferries, and both also have air service.

Planning

The region can be enjoyed for a few days or a few weeks, depending on the nature of your trip. As the towns are all quite distinct on Cape Cod, it's best to organize your trip based on your interests: an outdoors enthusiast would want to head to the National Seashore region, for example; those who prefer shopping and amusements would do better in the Mid Cape area. As one Fodors.com forum member noted, the Cape is generally "not something to see... instead, people go to spend a few days or weeks, relax, go to the beach... that sort of thing." A day trip to Nantucket to wander the historic downtown is manageable; several days is best to appreciate Martha's Vineyard's diversity.

Getting Here and Around

AIR

The major air gateways are Boston Logan International Airport (BOS) and Rhode Island T. F. Green International Airport (PVD) in Providence. Most major airlines fly to Boston; several fly to Providence; even fewer fly directly to the Cape and the islands, and many of those flights are seasonal. Smaller municipal airports are in Barnstable, Martha's Vineyard, Nantucket, and Provincetown.

CAR

Cape Cod is easily reached from Boston via Route 3 and from Providence via Interstate 195. Once you cross Cape Cod Canal, you can follow U.S. 6. Without any traffic, it takes about an hour to 90 minutes to reach the canal from either Boston or Providence. Allow an extra 30–60 minutes' travel time in peak periods.

Parking, in general, can be a challenge in summer, especially in congested downtowns and at popular beaches. If you can walk, bike, carpool, or cab it somewhere, do so. But unless you are planning to focus your attention on a single community, you'll probably need a car on the Cape. Authorities on both Nantucket and Martha's Vineyard strongly encourage visitors to leave their cars on the mainland: taking a vehicle onto the island ferries is expensive and requires reservations. On-island car rental is another option. But both islands have inexpensive and efficient shuttle bus systems that make it doable to go car-free. Renting bicycles to get to the beach is also a popular strategy.

FERRY

Martha's Vineyard and Nantucket are easily reached by passenger ferries (traditional and high-speed boats) from several Cape towns; farther afield you can get a seasonal ferry from Plymouth, MA; New Bedford, MA; Highlands, NJ; and Manhattan. Ferries to Provincetown embark from Boston and Plymouth. Some services run year-round, while others are seasonal. Even parking for the ferries must be reserved during the busy season, but passenger reservations are rarely necessary. Trip times vary from as little as 45 minutes to about two hours and run $9.50–$50 one-way; bicycles can be taken aboard many ferries for $8, while cars cost $59–$125 one-way (reservations required and very limited).

In season, ferries connect Boston and Plymouth with Provincetown. Bay State Cruise Company offers standard and high-speed ferry services between Commonwealth Pier in Boston and MacMillan Wharf in Provincetown. High-speed service runs a few times daily (mid-May–September, $108-$118 round-trip); the ride takes 90 minutes. Standard service runs Saturday only in July ($70 round-trip); the ride takes three hours. Boston Harbor Cruises runs a fast ferry from Long Wharf in Boston (mid-May–mid-October, $108 round-trip). From the State Pier in Plymouth, Captain John Boats operates a 90-minute ferry daily (mid-June to mid-September, $75 round-trip for same-day travel, $90 round-trip for travel on two different days). Seastreak runs seasonal ferries from Highlands, NJ, and Manhattan to Martha's Vineyard and Nantucket. The long but luxurious ride (just over five hours to MV from NYC) costs $175–$210 one-way (bikes $20); the ferry to Nantucket stops first on Martha's Vineyard, adding an hour to the trip ($175–$210). Seastreak also has service from New Bedford to each island; it's a 55-minute ride ($45) to Martha's Vineyard. The trip to Nantucket is about 90 minutes ($55).

PROVINCETOWN FERRIES Bay State Cruise Company. ✉ *Commonwealth Pier, 200 Seaport Blvd., Boston* ☎ *877/783–3779, 617/748–1428* 🌐 *baystatecruisecompany.com.* **Boston Harbor Cruises.** ✉ *Long Wharf, 1 Seaport La., Boston* ☎ *877/733–9425, 617/227–4321* 🌐 *www.bostonharborcruises.com.* **Captain John Boats.** ✉ *10 Town Wharf, Plymouth* ☎ *508/342-5569* 🌐 *www.captjohn.com.* Fast ferry from Plymouth to Provincetown

NANTUCKET FERRIES Freedom Cruise Line. ✉ *Saquatucket Harbor, 702 Main St., Harwich* ☎ *508/432–8999* 🌐 *www.nantucketislandferry.com.*

TRAIN

The seasonal *Cape Flyer* passenger train only runs on weekends (Friday-Sunday) from Boston's South Station, Memorial Day-Labor Day. The 2½-hour trip makes stops in Braintree, Brockton, Middleborough, Wareham Village, Buzzards Bay, Bourne, and Hyannis. Round-trip fare from Boston is $40; bring your bike for no extra fee. Kids 11 and under ride free with an adult.

CONTACT Cape Flyer. ✉ *Hyannis Transportation Center, 215 Iyannough Rd., Barnstable* ☎ *508/775–8504* 🌐 *www.capeflyer.com.*

Hotels

B&Bs are king in the Cape, so you can bed down in a former sea captain's home or even a converted church. However, there are also a few larger resorts and even a handful of chain hotels. You'll want to make reservations for inns well in advance for peak summer periods. Smoking is prohibited in all Massachusetts hotels.

Many travelers to the Cape and the islands rent a house if they're going to stay for a week or longer. There are a slew of properties available through Airbnb and VRBO, and many local real-estate agencies deal with rentals. Be sure to book a property well in advance of your trip: prime properties are often rented out to the same people year after year. Expect rentals on both Martha's Vineyard and Nantucket to be significantly higher than those on the Cape, simply because there are fewer options.

Hotel reviews have been shortened. For full information, visit Fodors.com.

What It Costs in U.S. Dollars

	$	$$	$$$	$$$$
RESTAURANTS				
	under $18	$18–$24	$25–$35	over $35
HOTELS				
	under $200	$200–$299	$300–$399	over $399

Restaurants

Cape Cod kitchens have long been closely associated with seafood: the waters off the Cape and the islands yield a bounty of lobsters, clams, oysters, scallops, and myriad fish that make their way onto local menus. In addition to the region's strong Portuguese influence, globally inspired and contemporary fare commonly turn up among restaurant offerings. Also gaining in popularity is the use of locally, and often organically, raised produce, meat, and dairy.

Note that ordering an expensive lobster dinner may push your meal into a higher price category than this guide's price range shows for the restaurant. You can indulge in fresh local seafood and clambakes at seat-yourself shanties for a lower price than at their fine-dining counterparts.

Restaurant reviews have been shortened. For full information, visit Fodors.com.

When to Go

The Cape and the islands teem with activity during high season: roughly late June to Labor Day. If you're dreaming of a classic beach vacation, this is prime time. However, along with the dream come daunting crowds and high costs. Fall has begun to rival summer in popularity, at least on weekends through late October, when the weather is temperate and the scenery remarkable. The region enjoys fairly moderate weather most of the year, with highs typically in the upper 70s and 80s in summer, and in the upper 30s and lower 40s in winter.

FESTIVALS AND EVENTS

Cape Cod Hydrangea Festival. A ten-day Cape-wide festival in mid-July that celebrates the region's signature blooms. 🌐 www.facebook.com/CapeCodHydrangeaFest

Visitor Information

Numerous towns on the Cape have weekly beach and lawn concerts, pancake breakfasts, art shows, and more. The Cape Week Section of the Cape Cod Times (🌐 www.capecodtimes.com) is a great source for information to help plan your days, as is the Cape Cod Chamber of Commerce (🌐 www.capecodchamber.org).

Sandwich

3 miles east of Sagamore Bridge, 11 miles west of Barnstable.

The oldest town on Cape Cod, Sandwich was established in 1637 by some of the Plymouth Pilgrims and incorporated on March 6, 1638. Today, it is a well-preserved, quintessential New England village with a white-columned town hall, a grist mill, and streets lined with 18th- and 19th-century houses.

GETTING HERE AND AROUND

Sandwich, 3 miles east of Sagamore Bridge, is accessible via Route 6A and Route 130. Driving east on Route 6A east brings you to the Sagamore and Bourne bridges; going west will take you all the way to Orleans. Route 130 heads southwest to Falmouth. The center of town is easily explored on foot, but a car is necessary to reach nearby attractions.

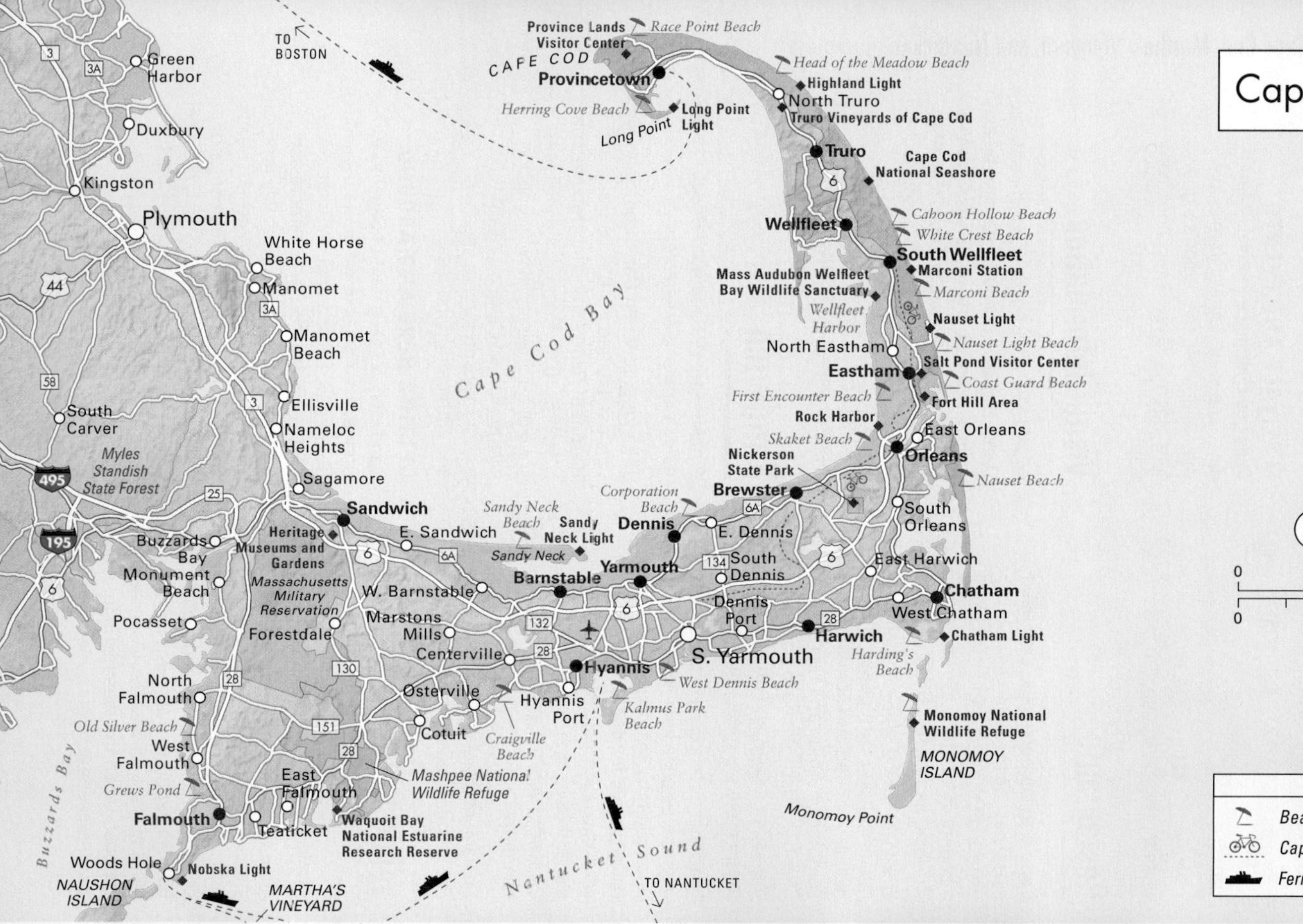

Cape Cod
TO BOSTON
Green Harbor
Duxbury
Kingston
Plymouth
White Horse Beach
Manomet
Manomet Beach
Ellisville
Nameloc Heights
Sagamore
South Carver
Myles Standish State Forest
Sandwich
Heritage Museums and Gardens
Buzzards Bay
Monument Beach
Pocasset
Massachusetts Military Reservation
Forestdale
North Falmouth
Old Silver Beach
West Falmouth
Grews Pond
Falmouth
Woods Hole
Nobska Light
NAUSHON ISLAND
MARTHA'S VINEYARD
Buzzards Bay
East Falmouth
Teaticket
Waquoit Bay National Estuarine Research Reserve
Mashpee National Wildlife Refuge
Cotuit
Osterville
Craigville Beach
Hyannis Port
Centerville
Marstons Mills
W. Barnstable
E. Sandwich
Sandy Neck Beach
Sandy Neck
Sandy Neck Light
Barnstable
Hyannis
Yarmouth
Dennis
Corporation Beach
Kalmus Park Beach
West Dennis Beach
S. Yarmouth
Dennis Port
South Dennis
E. Dennis
Brewster
Nickerson State Park
Harwich
Harding's Beach
East Harwich
Chatham
West Chatham
Chatham Light
Monomoy National Wildlife Refuge
MONOMOY ISLAND
Monomoy Point
Nantucket Sound
TO NANTUCKET
South Orleans
Orleans
East Orleans
Nauset Beach
Skaket Beach
Rock Harbor
Fort Hill Area
First Encounter Beach
Eastham
Coast Guard Beach
Salt Pond Visitor Center
Nauset Light Beach
Nauset Light
North Eastham
Wellfleet Harbor
Marconi Beach
Mass Audubon Wellfleet Bay Wildlife Sanctuary
Marconi Station
South Wellfleet
White Crest Beach
Cahoon Hollow Beach
Wellfleet
Cape Cod National Seashore
Truro
Truro Vineyards of Cape Cod
North Truro
Highland Light
Head of the Meadow Beach
Race Point Beach
Province Lands Visitor Center
CAPE COD
Provincetown
Herring Cove Beach
Long Point Light
Long Point
Cape Cod Bay
0 8 mi
0 8 km
KEY
Beaches
Cape Cod Bike Trail
Ferry

VISITOR INFORMATION

CONTACTS Sandwich Chamber of Commerce. ✉ *520 Rte. 130, Sandwich Center* ☎ *508/681–0918* 🌐 *www.sandwichchamber.com.*

★ Heritage Museums and Gardens

GARDEN | FAMILY | These 100 beautifully landscaped acres overlooking the upper end of Shawme Pond are one of the region's top draws. Paths crisscross the grounds, which include gardens planted with hostas, heather, herbs, and fruit trees. Rhododendrons are in full glory mid-May–mid-June, and daylilies reach their peak mid-July–early August. In 1967, pharmaceuticals magnate Josiah K. Lilly III purchased the estate and turned it into a nonprofit museum. One highlight is the reproduction Shaker Round Barn, which showcases classic and historic cars—including a 1919 Pierce-Arrow, a 1915 Stutz Bearcat, a 1911 Stanley Steamer, and a 1930 yellow-and-green Duesenberg owned by movie star Gary Cooper. The art museum has an extraordinary collection of New England folk art, including paintings, weather vanes, Nantucket baskets, and scrimshaw. Both adults and children can enjoy riding on a Coney Island–style carousel dating to the early 20th century. Other features include Hidden Hollow, an outdoor activity center for families with children.

A shuttle bus, equipped with a wheelchair lift and space to stow baby strollers, transports visitors on certain days. The center of the complex is about ¾ mile on foot from the in-town end of Shawme Pond. ✉ *67 Grove St., Sandwich Center* ☎ *508/888–3300* 🌐 *www.heritagemuseumsandgardens.org* 🎟 *$21* ⏲ *Closed mid-Oct to late Apr.*

Sandwich Glass Museum

ART MUSEUM | Shimmering glass was manufactured here nearly two centuries ago, and the Sandwich Glass Museum shows you what the factory looked like in its heyday. There's an "ingredient room" showcasing a wide spectrum of glass colors, along with the minerals added to the sand to obtain them, and an outstanding collection of blown and pressed glass in many shapes and hues. Large lamps, vases, and pitchers are impressive, as are the hundreds of candlesticks on display. There are glassblowing demonstrations daily on the hour from 10 to 4. The extensive gift shop sells some handsome reproductions, including many made by local and national artisans. The glass museum is part of the Sandwich Historical Society. ✉ *129 Main St., Sandwich Center* ☎ *508/888–0251* 🌐 *www.sandwichglassmuseum.org* 🎟 *$12* ⏲ *Closed Jan.; Mon. and Tues. Feb. and Mar.*

Restaurants

Dunbar House Tea Room & Wine Bar

$$ | BRITISH | Settle in for a proper afternoon tea, with tiered trays of finger sandwiches and diminutive desserts, at this English-style tea room set in a 1920s vintage carriage house overlooking Shawme Pond. A full tea service is offered all day, along with an à la carte lunch service and Sunday brunch (think lobster eggs Benedict and duck confit hash) and desserts are baked in-house. **Known for:** long menu of teas and tisanes; monthly wine dinners; vegetarian, gluten-free, and child-friendly tea service options. 💲 *Average main: $18* ✉ *1 Water St., Sandwich Center* ☎ *508/833–2485* 🌐 *www.thedunbarhouse.com* ⏲ *Closed Wed. No dinner.*

Fishermen's View

$$$ | SEAFOOD | Owned by two commercial fishermen (who happen to be brothers), this casually upscale seafood spot (attached to a seafood market) offers indoor and outdoor waterside dining at Cape Cod Canal. The menu offers a nice break from the usual fried seafood baskets, so diners opt for fresh oysters, sushi, and steamed lobster and crab buckets. **Known for:** boat-to-table dining; award-winning clam chowder; live music in season. *Average main: $34 20 Freezer Rd., Sandwich 508/591-0088 www.fishermensview.com.*

Coffee and Quick Bites

Twin Acres Ice Cream Shoppe

$ | **AMERICAN** | **FAMILY** | Pop into this popular spot for an ice-cream cone, sausage roll, or a milk shake and enjoy it on the 2 acres of landscaped grounds dotted with gardens. **Known for:** 70-plus ice-cream flavors; Italian sausage roll; vegan, dairy-free, and sugar-free options. *Average main: $6 21 Rte. 6A, Sandwich 508/888–0566 www.twinacresicecreamshoppe.com Closed Oct.–mid-Mar.*

Hotels

Belfry Inn & Bistro

$$ | **B&B/INN** | This sophisticated complex comprises a 1901 former church (the Abbey), an ornate wood-frame 1882 Victorian (the Painted Lady), and an 1827 Federal-style house (the Village House), and the theme in each is a nod to the buildings' respective histories—the Painted Lady's charmingly appointed guest rooms, for example, are named after former inhabitants. **Pros:** great in-town location; bright, beautiful, and spacious rooms; dramatic architecture. **Cons:** some steep stairs; not suited for families; some rooms can be on the smaller side. *Rooms from: $249 6 Jarves St., Sandwich Center 508/888–8550, 800/844–4542 www.belfryinn.com 19 rooms Free Breakfast.*

Isaiah Jones Homestead Bed & Breakfast

$$ | **B&B/INN** | Expect extraordinary service in an equally stellar setting—graceful lines and high ceilings, period antiques and stained glass—at this venerable Victorian. **Pros:** easy walk to town center; beautiful grounds; elegant surroundings. **Cons:** some steep stairs; some bathrooms are small; close quarters might not be for everyone. *Rooms from: $249 165 Main St., Sandwich Center 508/888–9115 www.isaiah-jones.com 7 rooms Free Breakfast.*

Shopping

Downtown Sandwich has a sprinkling of specialty shops, as well as several good antiques co-ops, boutiques, and galleries. Along Route 6A, you'll find more of the same, just spread out along the miles.

★ Titcomb's Bookshop

BOOKS | You'll find used, rare, and new books here, including a large collection of Americana. There's also an extensive selection of children's books. Look for frequent author events and book signings. *432 Rte. 6A, East Sandwich 508/888–2331 www.titcombsbookshop.com.*

Falmouth

15 miles south of Bourne Bridge, 20 miles south of Sandwich.

Falmouth, the Cape's second-largest town, was settled in 1660. Today it is largely suburban, with a mix of old and new developments and a sizable year-round population. Many residents commute to other towns on the Cape, to southeastern Massachusetts, and even to Boston. The town has a quaint downtown area, with a typically old New England village green and a shop-lined Main Street. South of town center, Falmouth faces Nantucket Sound and has several often-crowded beaches popular with families. To the east, the Falmouth Heights neighborhood mixes inns, B&Bs, and private homes, nestled close together on residential streets leading to the sea. Bustling Grand Avenue, the main drag in Falmouth Heights, hugs the shore and the beach.

The village of Woods Hole, part of Falmouth, is home to several major scientific institutions, including the National Marine Fisheries Service, the Marine Biological Laboratory (MBL), and the Woods Hole Oceanographic Institution. It's also a departure point for ferries to Martha's Vineyard.

GETTING HERE AND AROUND

Heading from the Bourne Bridge toward Falmouth, County Road and Route 28A are prettier alternatives to Route 28, and Sippewisset Road meanders near Buzzards Bay between West Falmouth and Woods Hole. If you're coming from Falmouth to Woods Hole, either ride your bicycle down the straight and flat Shining Sea Trail or take the Cape Cod Regional Transit Authority's WHOOSH trolley. In summer, the basically one-street village overflows with thousands of visiting scientists, students, and tourists heading to the islands. Parking, limited to a relatively small number of metered spots on the street, can be nearly impossible.

CONTACTS Cape Cod Regional Transit Authority. ☎ *800/352–7155* 🌐 *www.capecodrta.org.*

Sights

Nobska Light

LIGHTHOUSE | This imposing lighthouse has spectacular views from its base of the nearby Elizabeth Islands and of Martha's Vineyard, across Vineyard Sound. The 42-foot cast-iron tower, lined with brick, was built in 1876 with a stationary light. It shines red to indicate dangerous waters or white for safe passage. Friends of Nobska Light, a nonprofit group, has been carefully restoring the structure, converting the lighthouse keeper's house into a museum. The grounds are open daily from dawn to dusk for sightseeing, though parking is very limited. Best to arrive by bike along the scenic bike path. **■ TIP→ Tours depend on both weather and volunteer availability. Call ahead to inquire.** ✉ *233 Nobska Rd., Woods Hole* 🌐 *www.friendsofnobska.org* 🎫 *Free.*

Ocean Science Exhibit Center

SCIENCE MUSEUM | **FAMILY** | Here visitors can get a glimpse of the extraordinary scientific marine research that goes on within the Woods Hole Oceanographic Institute. Climb inside a replica of *Alvin,* the submersible that dove thousands of feet deep to explore the wreck of the *Titanic.* Other exhibits show footage of the rich life at vast depths of the ocean, and how climate change is impacting coral reefs. Scientists give informative lectures on a regular basis in July and August. ✉ *15 School St., Woods Hole* ☎ *508/289–2252* 🌐 *www.whoi.edu/main/ocean-science-exhibit-center* 🎫 *$5 suggested donation* ⏲ *Closed Jan.-mid-Apr.*

Waquoit Bay National Estuarine Research Reserve

NATURE PRESERVE | **FAMILY** | Encompassing 3,000 acres of estuaries, woodlands, salt marshes, and barrier beaches, this research reserve is a good place for walking, fishing, and birding. In July and August, there are nature programs for families, including an outdoor lecture series on Tuesday evening. On the grounds, check out the Wampanoag wetu (summer dwelling); indoors, a Discovery Room offers nature exhibits for kids. South Cape Beach State Park is part of the reserve; you can lie out on the sand or join one of the interpretive walks. Flat Pond Trail runs through several different habitats, including fresh- and saltwater marshes. You can reach Washburn Island on your own by boat; it offers 330 acres of pine barrens and trails, and swimming. ✉ *149 Rte. 28, Waquoit Village* ✣ *3 miles west of Mashpee rotary* ☎ *508/457–0495* 🌐 *www.waquoitbayreserve.org* 🎫 *Free; $15 daily parking fee for beach.*

★ Woods Hole Science Aquarium

AQUARIUM | FAMILY | This impressive facility displays numerous large tanks and many more smaller ones filled with regional fish and shellfish. Rooms are small, but they are crammed with stuff to see. Magnifying glasses and a dissecting scope help you examine marine life. Several hands-on pools hold banded lobsters, crabs, snails, starfish, and other creatures. The stars of the show are two harbor seals, on view in the outdoor pool near the entrance; watch their feedings, most days, at 11 and 4. ✉ *166 Water St., Woods Hole* ☎ *508/495–2001* 🌐 *www.fisheries.noaa.gov/new-england-mid-atlantic/outreach-and-education/woods-hole-science-aquarium* 🎫 *Free* ⏲ *Closed Sun.–Mon.*

Beaches

Old Silver Beach

BEACH | FAMILY | This long, beautiful crescent of soft white sand is anchored by the Sea Crest Beach Resort at one end. It's especially good for small children because a sandbar keeps it shallow at the southern end and creates tidal pools full of crabs. Very popular, this beach has its share of crowds on nice, sunny days. **Amenities:** food and drink; lifeguards; parking (fee); showers; toilets. **Best for:** swimming; walking. ✉ *296 Quaker Rd., North Falmouth* 🌐 *www.falmouthmass.us* 🎫 *$30 daily parking.*

Restaurants

★ C Salt Wine Bar & Grille

$$$ | AMERICAN | With an open kitchen that turns out some excellent and artful dishes, especially seafood, this tiny place keeps its tables full and its guests happy (reservations strongly recommended). Fine service by a friendly and knowledgeable staff adds greatly to the overall atmosphere. **Known for:** raw oyster selection; notable wine list; excellent service. $ *Average main: $32* ✉ *75 Davis Straits (Rte. 28), Falmouth* ☎ *774/763–2954* 🌐 *www.csaltfalmouth.com.*

Jim's Clam Shack

$$ | SEAFOOD | Fried clams are crisp and fresh at this basic seafood joint right on Falmouth Harbor; the meaty lobster roll and the fish-and-chips platter are good choices, too. Place your order at the counter, and then take your tray to the picnic tables on the roof deck for the best views. **Known for:** fried clams; summer crowds; waterfront perch. $ *Average main: $22* ✉ *227 Clinton Ave., Falmouth Harbor* ☎ *508/540–7758* ⏲ *Closed early Sept.–mid-May.*

★ La Cucina Sul Mare

$$$ | ITALIAN | Northern Italian and Mediterranean cooking distinguish this upscale, popular place. Make sure to come hungry—portions of classic favorites here are huge. **Known for:** chicken or veal Parmesan; boisterous atmosphere; attentive service. $ *Average main: $28* ✉ *237 Main St., Falmouth Center* ☎ *508/548–5600* 🌐 *www.lacucinasulmare.com.*

Coffee and Quick Bites

Bean & Cod

$ | SANDWICHES | This specialty food shop sells cheeses, breads, soups, great sandwiches, including lobster rolls, and picnic fixings, along with coffees and teas. **Known for:** daily soup specials; great sandwiches; delicious coffee. $ *Average main: $10* ✉ *145 Main St., Falmouth Center* ☎ *508/548–8840* 🌐 *www.beanandcod.com* ⏲ *Closed Sun.–Mon. No dinner.*

Pie in the Sky Bakery & Cafe

$ | BAKERY | Crowds line up for tasty treats at this beloved year-round bakery, in business since 1982, which serves up a lot more than pie, though that is not to be missed. Sticky buns and scones fly out of the kitchen at breakfast, while daily soup specials, wraps, and salads are popular at lunch. **Known**

for: made-from-scratch baked goods; delicious quiches; popovers. *Average main: $11.50* ✉ *10 Water St., Woods Hole* ☎ *508/540–5475* 🌐 *www.piecoffee.com.*

Hotels

AutoCamp Cape Cod

$ | **RESORT** | **FAMILY** | At AutoCamp's first East Coast glamping location guests choose among three types of accommodation—safari-style canvas tents, pod suites, or 31-foot Airstreams with kitchenettes. **Pros:** lots of greenery; proximity to the ocean and Shining Sea Bikeway; complimentary yoga and stargazing. **Cons:** some hills to navigate; no bathrooms in tents; signs of construction. *Rooms from: $184* ✉ *836 Palmer Ave., Falmouth* ☎ *855/203–1518* 🌐 *www.autocamp.com* *Tents are closed from Apr.–Oct.* *108 units* *No Meals.*

The Captain's Manor Inn

$$$ | **B&B/INN** | With its expansive landscaped grounds ringed by a wrought-iron fence, this elegant 1849 Italianate inn with a wraparound porch and grand foyer resembles a private estate. **Pros:** easy walk to town center; elegant setting; ample grounds make you feel worlds away from the hustle and bustle. **Cons:** not for those with small children; long stairway to second-floor rooms; not for those traveling on a budget. *Rooms from: $335* ✉ *27 W. Main St., Falmouth Center* ☎ *508/388–7336* 🌐 *www.captainsmanorinn.com* *7 rooms* *Free Breakfast.*

Coonamessett Inn

$$$ | **B&B/INN** | At this delightful inn, a Lark Hotel property, five buildings of one- and two-bedroom suites ring a landscaped lawn that leads to a scenic wooded pond. **Pros:** lush grounds; high marks for restaurant's food; large rooms. **Cons:** constant weddings; some complain the continental breakfast is too small; no room service. *Rooms from: $303* ✉ *311 Gifford St., at Jones Rd., Falmouth* ☎ *508/548–2300* 🌐 *www.thecoonamessett.com* *29 rooms* *Free Breakfast.*

★ Inn on the Sound

$$ | **B&B/INN** | At this understated and serene but stylish inn, perched on a bluff overlooking Vineyard Sound, common areas include an art-laden living room with a boulder fireplace and water views, oversize windows, and modern white couches; a bistrolike breakfast room; and a porch with more stunning water views. **Pros:** grand water views; elegant setting; easy walk to beach. **Cons:** not an in-town location; not for those with small children; no pets. *Rooms from: $299* ✉ *313 Grand Ave., Falmouth Heights* ☎ *508/457–9666* 🌐 *www.innonthesound.com* *12 rooms* *Free Breakfast.*

Woods Hole Passage

$$ | **B&B/INN** | **FAMILY** | A century-old carriage house and barn have been converted into a romantic showcase with more than 2 acres that include beautiful gardens; when you want to explore outside the grounds, hop on the town trolley, which runs right by the inn. **Pros:** family-friendly; easy walk to beach; extremely helpful innkeepers; Martha's Vineyard ferry is five minutes away. **Cons:** not an in-town location; some steep stairs; two-night minimum stay on weekends in summer and fall. *Rooms from: $259* ✉ *186 Woods Hole Rd., Woods Hole* ☎ *508/548–9575* 🌐 *www.woodsholepassage.com* *5 rooms* *No Meals.*

Activities

BASEBALL

The Cape Cod Baseball League, begun in 1885, is an invitational league of college players that counts Carlton Fisk, Ron Darling, Mo Vaughn, Nomar Garciaparra, and the late Thurman Munson as alumni. Considered the country's best summer league, it's scouted by every major-league team. The 10 teams of the Cape Cod Baseball League play a 44-game season mid-June–mid-August; attendance is free.

Falmouth Commodores

BASEBALL & SOFTBALL | FAMILY | The Falmouth Commodores of the collegiate Cape Cod Baseball League play their home games at Guv Fuller Field, mid-June–mid-August. Players and coaches lead youth baseball clinics in June and July. ✉ *790 Main St., Falmouth Center* 🌐 *www.falmouthcommodores.com* 🎟 *Free.*

BIKING

★ Shining Sea Bikeway

BIKING | The wonderful Shining Sea Bikeway is almost 11 miles of paved bike path through four of Falmouth's villages, running from Woods Hole to North Falmouth. It follows the shore of Buzzards Bay, providing water views, and dips into oak and pine woods; a detour onto Church Street takes you to Nobska Light. A brochure is available at the trailheads. If you're taking your bike to Martha's Vineyard, park in one of Falmouth's Steamship Authority lots and ride to the ferry. Free shuttles from Falmouth to the Woods Hole ferry dock have bike carriers. There's also a parking area near Depot Avenue, on County Road at the other end. ✉ *Falmouth.*

Shopping

Falmouth Village has an easily walkable and attractive Main Street, lined with specialty shops—you won't find major chain stores here—and an assortment of good restaurants. The pretty Marine Park is home to many events, including an impressive Thursday afternoon Farmers' Market held late-May–early-October, noon to 5.

Hyannis

23 miles east of the Bourne Bridge, 21 miles northeast of Falmouth.

Best known for its association with the Kennedy clan, the Hyannis area was also a vacation site for President Ulysses S. Grant in 1874 and later for President Grover Cleveland. A bustling year-round hub of activity, Hyannis has the Cape's largest concentration of businesses, shops, malls, hotels and motels, restaurants, and entertainment venues.

GETTING HERE AND AROUND

There's plenty of public parking around town, on both sides of Main Street as well as in several public parking lots. The island ferry companies have designated parking lots ($15–$20 daily fee in summer season) with free shuttles to the docks. Hyannis is the Cape's transit hub and is served by a number of bus routes.

CONTACTS Hyannis Transportation Center. ✉ *215 Iyanough Rd., Barnstable* ☎ *508/775-8504* 🌐 *www.capecodrta.org.*

VISITOR INFORMATION

CONTACTS Hyannis Chamber of Commerce. ✉ *Hyannis* ☎ *508/775–7778* 🌐 *www.hyannis.com.*

Sights

Cape Cod Maritime Museum

NAUTICAL SIGHT | FAMILY | This waterfront museum stands as testament and tribute to the bustle of the harbor that it overlooks. Changing maritime art exhibits, classes on boatbuilding and other nautical arts, and an active boatbuilding shop all highlight the importance of the sea, in past and present alike. Take a harbor sail on the historic replica Crosby Catboat *Sarah*, and learn "dead reckoning"—real navigation without the aid of modern technology. ✉ *135 South St., Hyannis Harbor* ☎ *508/775–1723* 🌐 *www.capecodmaritimemuseum.org* 🎫 *$10* 🕑 *Closed Sun.-Tues.*

John F. Kennedy Hyannis Museum

HISTORY MUSEUM | In Main Street's Old Town Hall, this museum explores JFK's Cape years (1934–63) through enlarged and annotated photographs culled from the archives of the JFK Library near Boston, as well as a seven-minute video narrated by Walter Cronkite. Changing exhibits focus on various members of the family at different stages of their life and career. Events include lectures, book signings, a summer author series, and speaking engagements by those with close connections to the family, both past and present. Guided walking tours of Hyannis include stops at ancient cemeteries and public art to reflect on local history. ✉ *397 Main St., Hyannis* ☎ *508/790–3077* 🌐 *www.jfkhyannismuseum.org* 🎫 *$13* 🕑 *Closed Sun.–Wed. Dec.–mid-Apr.*

Beaches

Kalmus Park Beach

BEACH | **FAMILY** | This wide, sandy beach has an area set aside for windsurfers and a sheltered area that's good for kids. It's a great spot for watching boats go in and out of the harbor. **Amenities:** food and drink; lifeguards; parking (fee); showers; toilets. **Best for:** swimming; walking; windsurfing. ✉ *End of Ocean St., Hyannis Harbor* 🌐 *www.hyannis.com* 🎫 *Parking $25.*

Restaurants

★ Brazilian Grill

$$$$ | **BRAZILIAN** | At this all-you-can-eat churrascaria, waiters continually circulate through the dining room offering more than a dozen grilled meats—beef, pork, chicken, sausage, and the beloved Brazilian chicken hearts on large, swordlike skewers. The massive buffet is laden with soups, salads, and side dishes, including plantains, rice, and beans (vegetarians could happily eat from the buffet). **Known for:** grilled meats, Brazilian style; loud and festive atmosphere; homemade flan. 💲 *Average main: $43* ✉ *680 Main St., West End* ☎ *508/771–0109* 🌐 *www.braziliangrillrestaurants.com.*

★ Naked Oyster Bistro & Raw Bar

$$$ | **ECLECTIC** | More than 1,000 oysters are eaten here on an average summer weekend, a good deal of them procured near daily from the restaurant's own oyster farm in nearby Barnstable. You'll always find close to two dozen raw and "dressed" oyster dishes; there's also a nice range of nonoyster entrées, salads, and appetizers. **Known for:** oyster stew; locally sourced ingredients; lively atmosphere. 💲 *Average main: $34* ✉ *410 Main St., Hyannis* ☎ *508/778–6500* 🌐 *www.nakedoyster.com* 🕑 *Closed Sun. mid-Oct.–mid-Apr.*

Coffee and Quick Bites

Chez Antoine Café

$ | **BELGIAN** | Owner/baker Antoine Vera has brought the French and Belgian boulangerie experience to Hyannis with this charming cafe, located just steps from the Village Green. Order fair-trade coffee, tea, and a wonderful pastry—or perhaps a prosciutto and cheese sandwich—and enjoy conversation with a friend at one of the indoor or outdoor bistro tables. **Known for:** croque monsieurs; almond croissants and melt-in-your-mouth macarons; crispy, golden baguettes. 💲 *Average main: $3.50* ✉ *357 Main St., Hyannis* ☎ *774/470–2180* 🌐 *www.orderchezantoine.com.*

Katie's Ice Cream

$ | **AMERICAN** | Making small batch ice cream and pastries in-house daily, Katie's has a huge following for its delicious flavors, like the popular Cape Cod Mud, a concoction of coffee ice cream, chocolate, house-made fudge, roasted almonds, and chopped chocolate sandwich cookies. Try to figure out the secret recipe of the Cape Cod Sand ice cream, a hit since 2002, when it was developed by Katie's younger brother Gene, but don't expect anyone to give it away. **Known for:** creative flavors, like lavender honeycomb and ginger lemon cookie; friendly staff; offers both soft serve and hard-packed ice cream. *Average main: $5 568 Main St., Hyannis 508/771–6889 katiesicecreamcapecod.com Closed early Oct.-mid-Apr.*

Hotels

★ Anchor-In

$$$ | HOTEL | Most rooms at this small motel on the north end of Hyannis Harbor have harbor views and small balconies overlooking the water; its simple street-side appearance belies its spacious and immaculate accommodations, extensive grounds, and nice touches like afternoon treats and complimentary use of bicycles. **Pros:** easy walk to downtown and island ferries; great harbor views; well-appointed rooms. **Cons:** no elevator—second-floor rooms accessed via stairs; not for the budget-minded; crowded area. *Rooms from: $349 1 South St., Hyannis Harbor 508/775–0357 www.anchorin.com 42 rooms Free Breakfast.*

Sea Street Inn

$$$ | B&B/INN | Outside, this 1895 sea captain's home looks like many other historic houses on the Cape; inside is a surprisingly upscale boutique B&B appointed with reclaimed barn wood, leather furnishings, and two gallery rooms filled with fine art photography. **Pros:** adults-only; indulgent four-course breakfasts; easy walk to Main Street shops and dining and Keyes Memorial Beach. **Cons:** the five guest rooms fill up quickly; no kids or pets; fairly small spaces. *Rooms from: $328 328 Sea St., Hyannis 508/360–6389 www.seastreetinn.com Closed mid-Nov.-Apr. 5 rooms Free Breakfast.*

Performing Arts

Cape Cod Melody Tent

CONCERTS | FAMILY | In 1950, actress Gertrude Lawrence and her husband, producer-manager Richard Aldrich, opened the Cape Cod Melody Tent to showcase Broadway musicals and concerts. Today, it's the region's top venue for pop concerts and comedy shows. Performers who have played here in the round include the Indigo Girls, Lyle Lovett, ZZ Top, Diana Krall, and the Beach Boys. Comedians including Nate Bargatze and Amy Schumer are also headliners. *21 W. Main St., West End 508/775–5630 www.melodytent.org.*

Activities

BASEBALL

Hyannis Harbor Hawks

BASEBALL & SOFTBALL | FAMILY | The Hyannis Harbor Hawks of the collegiate Cape Cod Baseball League play home games at McKeon Park mid-June–mid-August. Interested 5- to 17-year-olds can sign up with the Youth Baseball Academy. *McKeon Park, 120 High School Rd., Hyannis 508/420–0962 www.harborhawks.org.*

Shopping

Main Street in downtown Hyannis has gradually become one of the top shopping destinations on the Cape, buzzing with a funky mix of mostly independent boutiques and gift emporia. Among the specialty stores is a vintage clothing shop, a sprawling Army-Navy surplus store, a popcorn shop and not one but two chocolatiers. You'll also discover numerous restaurants along this walkable stretch, including several cafés that offer everything from Thai cuisine to Peruvian-Italian fusion. Heading through the villages of Barnstable along Route 6A, you'll find no shortage of intriguing art galleries and rustic antiques shops.

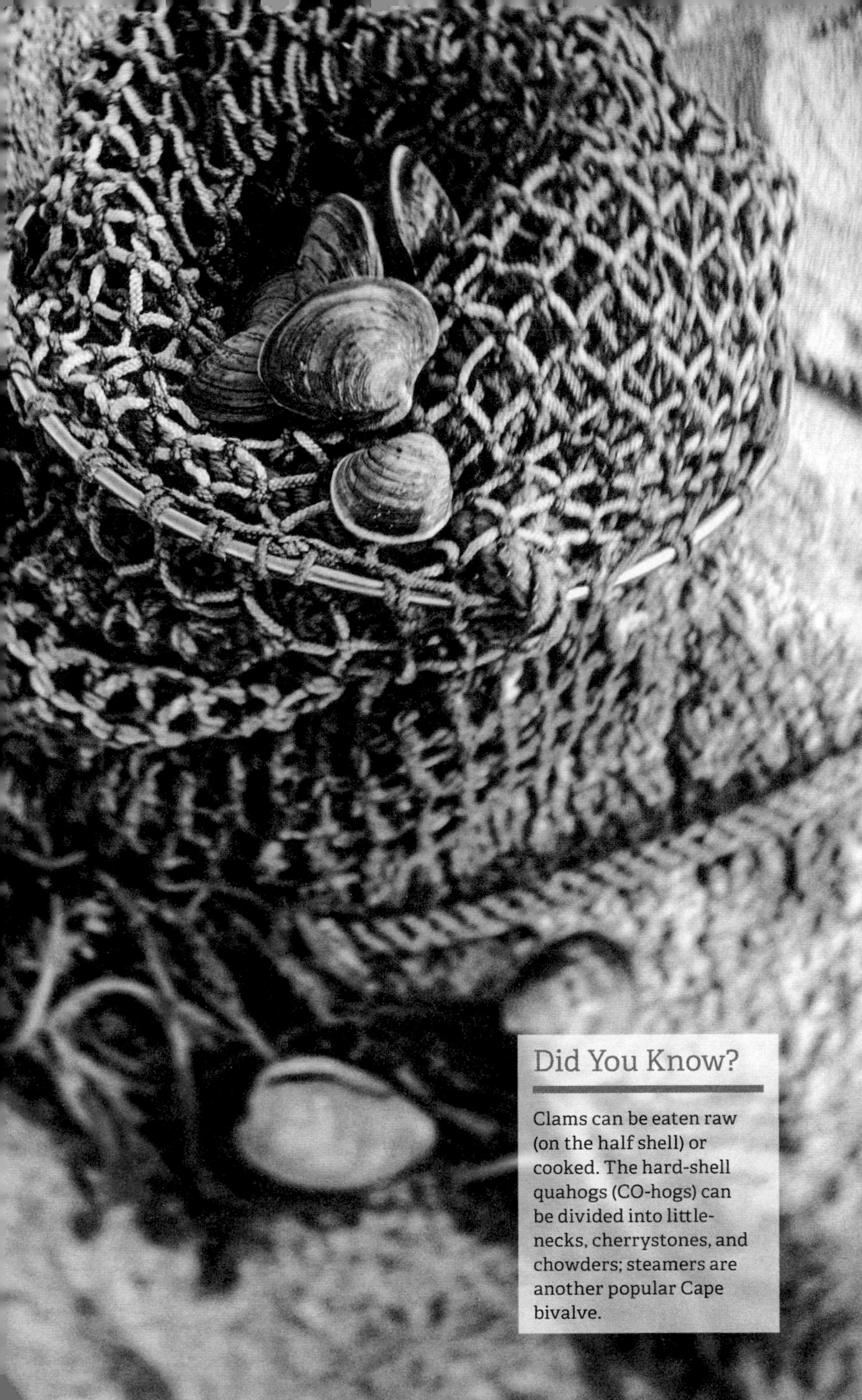

Did You Know?

Clams can be eaten raw (on the half shell) or cooked. The hard-shell quahogs (CO-hogs) can be divided into littlenecks, cherrystones, and chowders; steamers are another popular Cape bivalve.

HyArts Artist Shanties

ART GALLERIES | Located in two areas on Ocean Street (51 and 180), on a boardwalk that parallels the Hyannis Harbor and at Bismark Park, several artist shanties host a rotating slate of Cape Cod-based artists. Work ranges from photography and paintings to handmade jewelry, ceramics, and wood carving. Hours vary for artists, so check the website for details. ✉ *Hyannis Harbor, 51 Ocean St., Hyannis Harbor* ☎ *508/862–4990* 🌐 *arts-barnstable.com/hyarts-shanties.*

Kandy Korner

CANDY | **FAMILY** | Fudge, chocolate, caramel corn, ice cream, and taffy are some of the sweet reasons to visit this family-run shop, open all year (no ice cream in winter). The front of the store is devoted to display cases of fine chocolates and glass jars filled with old-fashioned "penny" candy. In the back are gifts galore: sea glass ornaments, Cape-made soap, lobster-printed onesies, and other items with a beach vacation theme. Take a selfie out front with the big stuffed bear, propped on a bench. ✉ *474 Main St., Downtown* ☎ *508/771-5313* 🌐 *www.kandykorner.com.*

Soho Arts Co.

SOUVENIRS | Main Street is chock-a-block with gift shops and T-shirt stores, but if you're looking for a special memento of your time on the Cape, head to this little shop. Shelves and display cases overflow with a well-curated selection of jewelry, home goods, gifts, art (including cool pieces made from beach rocks), and more; many pieces are made regionally or locally. ✉ *342 Main St., Downtown* ☎ *508/771–7646* 🌐 *www.sohocompany.net.*

Barnstable

With nearly 50,000 year-round residents, Barnstable is the largest of the Cape's 15 towns, and the second oldest. Founded in 1639, you can get a feel for the town's age with all of the lovely and large old homes on and near Main Street (Route 6A) in Barnstable Village. The village is one of the seven that make up the town of Barnstable: the other villages, each with their own charms, are Centerville, Cotuit, Hyannis, Osterville, Marstons Mills, and West Barnstable.

GETTING HERE AND AROUND

Most people drive to Barnstable via Route 6 or Route 6A. The Cape Cod Regional Transit Authority operates the Barnstable Villager, a small bus that travels from the village of Barnstable to Hyannis. Service is daily late June–Labor Day; buses run about every hour.

Beaches

Sandy Neck Beach

BEACH | **FAMILY** | Sandy Neck Beach stretches some 6 miles across a peninsula that ends at Sandy Neck Light. The beach is one of the Cape's most beautiful—dunes, sand, and bay spread endlessly east, west, and north. The marsh used to be harvested for salt hay; now it's a haven for birds, which are out and about in the greatest numbers in morning and evening. The lighthouse, standing a few feet from the eroding shoreline at the tip of the neck, has been out of commission since 1952. It was built in 1857 to replace an 1827 light, and it used to run on acetylene gas. As you travel east along Route 6A from Sandwich, Sandy Neck Road is just before the Barnstable line, although the beach itself is in West Barnstable. **Amenities:** food and drink; lifeguards; parking (fee); showers; toilets. **Best for:**

sunset; swimming; walking. ✉ *425 Sandy Neck Rd., West Barnstable* 🌐 *www.town.barnstable.ma.us/sandyneckpark/default.aspx* *Parking $25.*

Restaurants

Crisp

$$ | **ITALIAN** | It's notoriously difficult to snag a table here in the summertime, but it's worth the wait as their wood-fired flatbreads are positively toothsome, made with organic four, local sea salt, and tasty toppings like braised beef short rib, butternut squash, and linguica sourced from a Massachusetts farm. Pasta dishes are a good option, too, and salads are fresh and creative, not an afterthought. **Known for:** locally sourced ingredients; indoor and outdoor seating; fire pits. *Average main: $22* ✉ *791 Main St., Osterville* ☎ *508/681–0922* 🌐 *www.crispflatbread.com.*

Coffee and Quick Bites

Four Seas Ice Cream

$ | **DESSERTS** | **FAMILY** | Lining up for an ice cream cone or frappe at Four Seas, a former blacksmith shop near Craigville Beach, has been a rite of summer on the Cape since 1934; it made the ice cream for Caroline Kennedy's wedding (the flavor: fresh peach) and has won a bazillion 'best' awards. They also sell lobster salad rolls, hot dogs, and other sandwiches. **Known for:** local institution since 1934; penuche pecan, a flavor they dreamed up; homemade fresh peach, strawberry, or cantelope ice cream. *Average main: $5* ✉ *360 S. Main St., Centerville* ☎ *508/775–1394* 🌐 *www.fourseasicecream.com* *limited service Sept.–May.*

Hotels

Captain David Kelley House

$$ | **B&B/INN** | Entertaining innkeepers, tasty baked goods, and proximity to the beach are three good reasons to consider this gleaming circa 1835 Greek Revival-style inn, located in the Barnstable village of Centerville. **Pros:** three-course breakfasts; ten-minute walk to Craigville Beach and Nantucket Sound; friendly on-site innkeepers. **Cons:** not a waterfront property; residential location; rooms sell out quickly. *Rooms from: $229* ✉ *539 Main St., Centerville* ☎ *508/775–4707* 🌐 *www.captaindavidkelleyhouse.com* *6 rooms* *Free Breakfast.*

Yarmouth

Yarmouth Port 3 miles east of Barnstable Village, West Yarmouth 2 miles east of Hyannis.

Once known as Mattacheese, or "the planting lands," Yarmouth was settled in 1639 by farmers from the Plymouth Bay Colony. By then the Cape had begun a thriving maritime industry, and men turned to the sea to make their fortunes. Many impressive sea captains' houses—some now B&Bs—still line enchanting Route 6A and nearby side streets, and Yarmouth Port has some real old-time stores in town. West Yarmouth has a very different atmosphere, stretched along busy commercial Route 28 south of Yarmouth Port.

GETTING HERE AND AROUND

Route 6A is the main route to Yarmouth Port, and there are lovely streets heading north toward the water and through hidden residential areas filled with beautiful old homes. West Yarmouth lies in the midst of busy Route 28, between Hyannis and South Yarmouth. If you want to avoid this road entirely, a sensible option is to take speedy U.S. 6 to the exit nearest what you want to visit and then cut south across the interior. If you must travel the Route 28 area, take Buck Island Road, which runs north of and parallel to much of the busy route in West and South Yarmouth. Like West Yarmouth, South Yarmouth has a stretch of blight and overdevelopment on Route 28, but it also has some nice beaches that are good for families. In high season, avoid Route 28 if you aim to get anywhere quickly.

VISITOR INFORMATION

CONTACTS Yarmouth Chamber of Commerce. ✉ *West Yarmouth* ☎ *508/778–1008* 🌐 *www.yarmouthcapecod.com.*

Sights

Bass Hole Boardwalk

PROMENADE | FAMILY | Taking in one of Yarmouth Port's most beautiful areas, Bass Hole Boardwalk extends over a swampy creek, crosses salt marshes, and winds around vegetated wetlands and upland woods. Gray's Beach is a little crescent of sand with still water that's good for kids inside the roped-in swimming area. At the end of the boardwalk, benches provide a place to relax and look out over abundant marsh life and, across the creek, the beautiful, sandy shores of Dennis's Chapin Beach. At low tide you can walk out on the flats for almost a mile. ✉ *Center St., near Gray's Beach parking lot, Yarmouth Port* 🌐 *www.yarmouth.ma.us/678/Bass-Hole-Beach.*

Edward Gorey House

ART MUSEUM | Explore the eccentric doodles and offbeat humor of the late acclaimed artist and illustrator. Regularly changing exhibitions, arranged in the downstairs rooms of Gorey's former home, include drawings of his oddball characters and reveal the mysterious psyche of the sometimes dark but always playful illustrator. ✉ *8 Strawberry La., Yarmouth Port* ☎ *508/362–3909* 🌐 *www.edwardgoreyhouse.org* 🎫 *$8* ⏲ *Closed Jan.–early-Apr.*

Restaurants

★ Inaho

$$$ | JAPANESE | Yuji Watanabe, chef-owner of the Cape's best Japanese restaurant, makes early-morning journeys to Boston's fish markets to shop for the freshest local catch, and the resulting selection of sushi and sashimi is vast and artful. The serene and simple Japanese garden out back has a traditional koi pond. **Known for:** chef's tasting menu; moody lighting; seafood tempura. $ *Average main: $34* ✉ *157 Main St., Yarmouth Port* ☎ *508/362–5522* ⏲ *Closed Sun.-Tues. No lunch.*

Skipper Chowder House

$$$ | SEAFOOD | Award-winning clam chowder and crave-worthy hot-buttered lobster rolls draw seafood lovers to this Cape Cod mainstay, wooing diners since 1936. If there's a long wait (and there will be) at this spot across the street from the beach, eat dessert first; there's an ice-cream shack adjoining the restaurant. **Known for:** three types of lobster rolls; views of Nantucket Sound; fried seafood plates. $ *Average main: $28* ✉ *152 S. Shore Rd., South Yarmouth* ☎ *508/394–7406* 🌐 *www.skipperrestaurant.com.* ⏲ *Closed mid-Oct.–mid-Apr.*

Hotels

Bayside Resort

$$$ | HOTEL | FAMILY | A bit more upscale than most properties along Route 28, the Bayside overlooks pristine salt marshes and Lewis Bay, and although it's not right on the water, there's a small beach and a large outdoor pool with a tiki bar (there's also an indoor pool). **Pros:** ideal for families with children; close to attractions of busy Route 28; views of the water. **Cons:** no beach swimming; some traffic noise; public areas can be noisy. $ *Rooms from: $329* ✉ *225 Rte. 28, West Yarmouth*

☎ *508/775–5669* 🌐 *www.baysideresort.com* 🛏 *128 rooms* 🍽 *Free Breakfast.*

★ Capt. Farris House

$$ | B&B/INN | A short hop off congested Route 28 sits this imposing 1845 Greek Revival home where thoughtful amenities abound, from the soft bathrobes, beach supplies, and fresh flowers in each room to a selection of complimentary cordials. **Pros:** beautiful grounds; ideal location for exploring Mid Cape area; close to area restaurants and attractions. **Cons:** no elevator; not close to the beach; not for those with children under age 14. $ *Rooms from: $275* ✉ *308 Old Main St., Bass River Village* ☎ *508/760–2818* 🌐 *www.captainfarris.com* 🛏 *10 rooms* 🍽 *Free Breakfast.*

★ The Inn at Cape Cod

$$$ | B&B/INN | A stately 19th-century Greek Revival building with imposing columns, the inn has one of the most dramatic facades of any house on the Cape; it sits near nature trails and has its own fine gardens, patios, and tree-shaded lawns. **Pros:** elegant lodging; mini-fridge in every guest room; serene surroundings. **Cons:** no water views or direct beach access; some steep stairs; not for small children. $ *Rooms from: $349* ✉ *4 Summer St., Yarmouth Port* ☎ *508/375–0590,* 🌐 *www.innatcapecod.com* 🛏 *9 rooms* 🍽 *Free Breakfast.*

★ Liberty Hill Inn

$$ | B&B/INN | Smartly and traditionally furnished common areas—including the high-ceiling parlor, the formal dining room, and the wraparound porch—are a major draw to this dignified 1825 Greek Revival house. **Pros:** tasteful surroundings; good value for the area; extravagant homemade breakfast. **Cons:** some steep stairs; on a busy street; not a waterfront location. $ *Rooms from: $229* ✉ *77 Rte. 6A, Yarmouth Port* ☎ *508/362–3976* 🌐 *www.libertyhillinn.com* ⏲ *Closed in winter* 🛏 *9 rooms* 🍽 *Free Breakfast.*

Nightlife

Oliver's & Planck's Tavern

BARS | Fish tanks illuminate this friendly bar (with a pub menu), which hosts live music on most evenings. There's also a midweek trivia night. ✉ *960 Main St., off Rte. 6A, Yarmouth Port* ☎ *508/362–6062* 🌐 *oliversandplancks.com.*

Performing Arts

Cultural Center of Cape Cod

ARTS CENTERS | This lively center plays host to a full schedule of art openings and exhibits, workshops, readings, various performances, and great live music. ✉ *307 Old Main St., South Yarmouth* ☎ *508/394–7100* 🌐 *www.cultural-center.org* 🎟 *$10* ⏲ *Closed Sun.-Mon.*

Shopping

If you're heading along Route 6A, expect to see a multitude of art galleries, craft and antiques stores, specialty shops, and boutiques that adhere to the modest and subdued aesthetics demanded by the Historic Commission. Over on Route 28, though, there are no building codes or rules on good taste; there you'll find larger stores that can advertise their wares with flashy signage, selling souvenirs, T-shirts, gigantic inflatable beach toys, and other fun vacation goodies.

Just Picked

SOUVENIRS | This Cape Cod–focused shop features local artisans and crafters who fill its shelves with a wide variety of home, garden, food, and gift items. ✉ *13 Willow St., Yarmouth Port* ☎ *508/362–0207* 🌐 *justpickedgifts.com.*

BASEBALL

Yarmouth-Dennis Red Sox

BASEBALL & SOFTBALL | FAMILY | The Yarmouth-Dennis Red Sox of the collegiate Cape Cod Baseball League play home games at Dennis-Yarmouth High School's Red Wilson Field, mid-June–mid-August. Baseball clinics for girls and boys age five and up run throughout the season. ✉ *Dennis-Yarmouth High School, 210 Station Ave., South Yarmouth* ☎ *508/394–9387* 🌐 *ydredsox.com.*

Dennis

Dennis Village 4 miles east of Yarmouth Port, West Dennis 1 mile east of South Yarmouth.

The back streets of Dennis Village still retain the Colonial charm of their seafaring days. The town, which was incorporated in 1793, was named for the Reverend Josiah Dennis. There were 379 sea captains living here when fishing, salt making, and shipbuilding were the main industries. The elegant houses they constructed—now museums and B&Bs—still line the streets.

GETTING HERE AND AROUND

Route 6A is also known as Main Street as it passes through Dennis Village. If you're driving between West Dennis and Harwich, Lower County Road is a more scenic alternative to overdeveloped Route 28: it gives you occasional glimpses of the Atlantic between the cottages and beachfront hotels.

VISITOR INFORMATION

CONTACTS Dennis Chamber of Commerce. ✉ *West Dennis* ☎ *508/398–3568,* 🌐 *www.dennischamber.com.*

★ Cape Cod Museum of Art

ART MUSEUM | This multiple-gallery museum on the grounds of the Cape Playhouse has a permanent collection of more than 850 works by important Cape-associated artists such as Hans Hoffman, William Paxton, and Charles Hawthorne; Hawthorne was the founder of America's first artists' colony in 1899 in Provincetown. Rich in cultural programming, changing exhibits, special events, workshops, and classes are held throughout the year. ✉ *60 Hope La., Dennis* ☎ *508/385–4477* 🌐 *www.ccmoa.org* *$10* *Closed Mon.–Tues.*

Scargo Tower

VIEWPOINT | On a clear day, you'll have unbeatable views of Scargo Lake, Dennis Village's scattered houses below, Cape Cod Bay, and distant Provincetown from the top of this tower. A wooden tower built on this site in 1874 was one of the Cape's first tourist attractions; visitors would pay a nickel to climb to the top for the views. That tower burned down, and the present all-stone 30-foot tower was built in 1901 to replace it. Winding stairs bring you to the top; don't forget to read the unsightly but amusing graffiti on the way up. Expect crowds at sunrise and sunset. ✉ *Scargo Hill Rd., off Rte. 6A or Old Bass River Rd., South Dennis* *Free.*

Parking at all Dennis beaches is $30 per day in season for nonresidents.

Corporation Beach

BEACH | FAMILY | Once a privately owned packet landing, this is a beautiful crescent of white sand backed by low dunes on Cape Cod Bay. **Amenities:** snack bar; lifeguards; parking (fee); showers; toilets. **Best for:** sunset; swimming; walking. ✉ *250 Corporation Rd., Dennis* *Parking $30.*

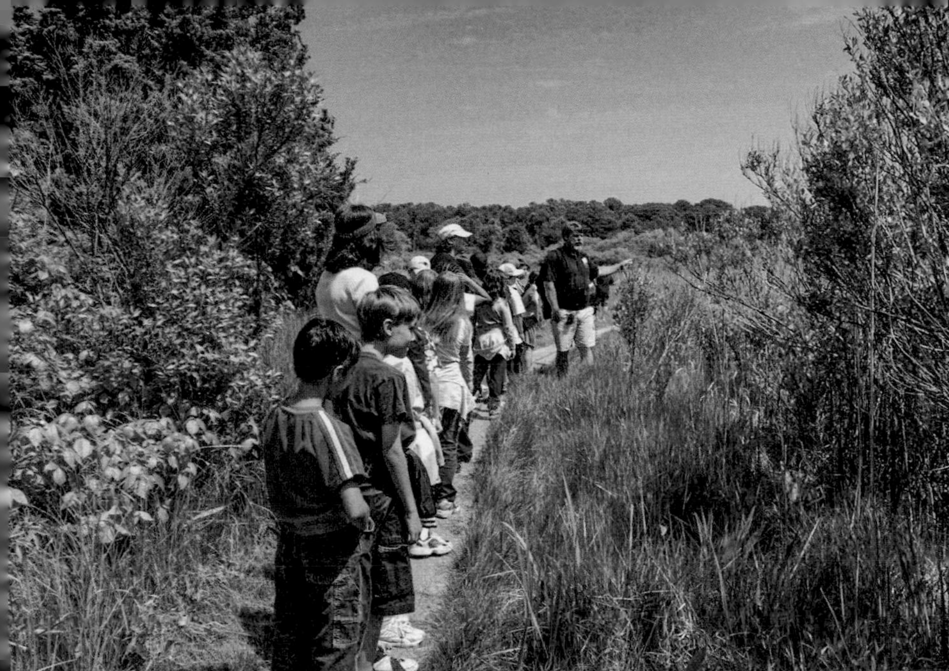

Learn more about the Cape's marshlands, forests, and ponds at the Cape Cod Museum of Natural History in neighboring Brewster.

West Dennis Beach

BEACH | FAMILY | This is one of the best beaches on the south shore (Nantucket Sound), with the crowds to prove it. A breakwater was started here in 1837 in an effort to protect the mouth of Bass River, but that was abandoned when a sandbar formed on the shore side. It's a long, wide, and popular sandy beach, stretching for 1½ miles, with marshland and the Bass River across from it. **Amenities:** food and drink; lifeguards; parking (fee); toilets. **Best for:** swimming; walking; windsurfing. ✉ *Lighthouse Rd., off Lower County Rd., West Dennis* 🎫 *Parking $30.*

Restaurants

FIN Cape Cod

$$$ | SEAFOOD | As the name suggests, seafood is the star here, from salmon to red snapper, halibut to tuna, and all very recently caught in Atlantic waters. Two floors of seating in an antique home make for an eclectic setting aglow with candlelight in the company of many satisfied diners. **Known for:** oyster chowder with smoked bacon; attentive and knowledgeable service; extensive wine list. $ *Average main: $34* ✉ *800 Main St., off Rt. 6A, Dennis* ☎ *508/385–2096* 🌐 *fincapecod.com* ⏲ *Closed Mon.*

Ocean House

$$$$ | ASIAN FUSION | This fine-dining hot-spot boasts exquisite views of Nantucket Sound, and the food is equally sublime—some consider it the best on the Cape. Seafood plays a starring role, with a Pan-Asian tilt, especially on the appetizer side; think tempura, sashimi, and ramen. **Known for:** Bento box; fabulous views; elegant surroundings. $ *Average main: $48* ✉ *425 Old Wharf Rd., Dennis Port* ☎ *508/394–0700* 🌐 *www.oceanhouserestaurant.com* ⏲ *Closed Nov.–Mar. No lunch.*

The Oyster Company

$$$ | SEAFOOD | Supplies pour in from the restaurant's own oyster farm in the bay, though oysters (and clams) from other towns are well represented and can be had a variety of ways—raw on the half shell is the best way to enjoy these superfresh bivalves. It's a fun place all around, with great food and a boisterous atmosphere. **Known for:** $1.50 oysters til 6:30; the "Red Sox" martini (among other fanciful martinis); locally sourced food. *Average main: $34 202 Depot St., Dennis Port 508/398–4600 www.theoystercompany.com.*

Scargo Café

$$$ | **AMERICAN** | With the Cape Playhouse right across the street, this upscale contemporary American restaurant is a favorite before- and after-show haunt. There's plenty of seafood on the eclectic menu, which includes seafood strudel with crab, shrimp, and scallops baked in a pastry crust and topped with Newburg sauce, but carnivores will delight in dishes like linguine Bolognese or the Mongolian pork chop with braised red cabbage. **Known for:** specialty cocktails like the Scargo Bloody Mary and the Crantucket Lemonade; seafood strudel with crab, shrimp, and scallops in a flaky pastry crust with Newburg sauce; Chesapeake Bay crab cakes with pineapple salsa fresca. *Average main: $34 799 Rte. 6A, Dennis 508/385–8200 www.scargocafe.com.*

Coffee and Quick Bites

Captain Frosty's

$$ | **SEAFOOD** | **FAMILY** | A great stop after the beach, this modest joint has a regular menu of seafood classics like fried clams and fish-and-chips supplemented by specials posted on the board and a counter where you order and take a number written on a french-fries box. There's seating inside as well as outside on a shady brick patio. **Known for:** classic fried seafood platters; soft-serve ice cream and frappes; good value. *Average main: $22 219 Rte. 6A, Dennis 508/385–8548 www.captainfrosty.com Closed Tues. Closed Nov.-Apr.*

Grumpy's

$ | **AMERICAN** | Open year-round, this friendly family-owned and operated restaurant serves up homey food for breakfast and lunch. Favorites from the extensive menu include traditional breakfast items like pancakes and eggs for breakfast, and fish-and-chips and a variety of sandwiches at lunch. **Known for:** daily blackboard specials; stuffed French toast; friendly vibe. *Average main: $13 1408 Main St., East Dennis 508/385–2911 for takeout www.grumpyscapecod.com No dinner.*

Hotels

★ Isaiah Hall B&B Inn

$$ | **B&B/INN** | Lilacs, pink roses and beautiful perennial gardens add a floral flourish this 1857 Greek Revival farmhouse located on a quiet residential road near the bay. **Pros:** beautiful grounds; walk to Corporation Beach; generous breakfast and cookies in the afternoon. **Cons:** not for those with children under seven; some very steep steps; some rooms are on the small side. *Rooms from: $235 152 Whig St., Dennis 508/385–9928 www.isaiahhallinn.com 12 rooms Free Breakfast.*

★ Pelham House Resort

$$ | **HOTEL** | A multi-million dollar renovation in 2022 has transformed this beachfront property into something special, with a new pool and outdoor bar, a gorgeous rooftop dining area, an oceanfront patio with year-round fire pits, and a bar, set within in a newly constructed building. **Pros:** ocean-view rooms; private beach; beautiful outdoor spaces. **Cons:** not close to town; property gets booked up with weddings; limited parking. *Rooms from: $299 14 Sea St., Dennis Port 508/398-6076 www.pelhamhouseresort.com 33 rooms.*

Performing Arts

★ Cape Playhouse

THEATER | FAMILY | For Broadway-style dramas, comedies, and musicals, attend a production at the Cape Playhouse, the country's oldest professional summer theater. In 1927 Raymond Moore, who had been working with a theatrical troupe in Provincetown, bought an 1838 Unitarian meetinghouse and converted it into a theater. The opening performance was *The Guardsman,* starring Basil Rathbone. Other stars who performed here in the early days—some in their professional stage debuts—include Bette Davis (who first worked here as an usher), Gregory Peck, Lana Turner, Ginger Rogers, Humphrey Bogart, Tallulah Bankhead, and Henry Fonda, who appeared with his then-unknown 20-year-old daughter, Jane. Mainstage productions run from June to September and they offer children's programming in July and August. The playhouse is situated on the property of the Cape Cod Center for the Arts in Dennis Village. The campus also includes the Cape Cod Museum of Art, the Cape Cinema, and a restaurant. ✉ *820 Rte. 6A, Dennis* ☎ *508/385–3911* 🌐 *www.capeplayhouse.com.*

Activities

BIKING

You can pick up the Cape's premier bike path, the more than 25-mile **Cape Cod Rail Trail**, at several points; continuing expansion has extended to South Yarmouth, with plans to reach farther west to Barnstable. Though it is possible, riding the entire trail in a single day doesn't do justice to its sights and side trips. Many cyclists, especially those with small kids, prefer the piecemeal method because they can relax and enjoy the sights—and not turn their legs to jelly in the process.

There is ample parking at the lot off Route 134 south of U.S. 6, near Theophilus Smith Road in South Dennis, and at the post office in South Wellfleet. Access points in Brewster are Long Pond Road, Underpass Road, and Nickerson State Park. There's also a spur off the trail that goes to Chatham.

A guidebook published by the Dennis Chamber of Commerce includes bike tours and maps. You can rent bikes from a number of places along the Cape Cod Rail Trail.

Brewster

7 miles northeast of Dennis, 20 miles east of Sandwich.

Brewster's location on Cape Cod Bay makes it a perfect place to learn about the region's ecology. The Cape Cod Museum of Natural History is here, and the area is rich in conservation lands, state parks, forests, freshwater ponds, and brackish marshes. When the tide is low in Cape Cod Bay, you can stroll the beaches and explore tidal pools up to 2 miles from the shore on the Brewster flats.

GETTING HERE AND AROUND

Brewster—6 miles north of Chatham and 5 miles west of Orleans—is spread along Route 6A. Take it slow through the town limits, not just in honor of the speed limit, but to appreciate the array of grand old homes, fanciful rose arbors, antiques shops, and countless historic details that make this one of the region's prettiest towns.

Sights

Brewster Store

STORE/MALL | FAMILY | Built in 1852 as a church, this local landmark has been a typical New England general store since 1866, with such essentials as daily newspapers, penny candy, groceries, and benches out front for conversation. It specializes in oil lamps and antique lanterns of all types. Next door, the

Brewster Scoop serves ice cream from Memorial Day–early September. Upstairs, memorabilia from antique toys to World War II bond posters is displayed. Downstairs there's a working antique nickelodeon; locals warm themselves by the old coal stove in colder months. ✉ *1935 Rte. 6A, Brewster* ☎ *508/896–3744* 🌐 *www.brewsterstore.com.*

★ Cape Cod Museum of Natural History

CHILDREN'S MUSEUM | FAMILY | A short drive west from the heart of Brewster, this spacious museum and its pristine grounds include a shop, a natural-history library, and exhibits such as a working beehive and an aquarium with live specimens from local waters. Walking trails wind through 80 acres of forest, marshland, and ponds, all rich in birds and other wildlife. A pollinator path lined with blooming plants leads to a seasonal (June-Sept.) Butterfly House. The exhibit hall upstairs has a wall display of aerial photographs documenting the process by which the famous Chatham sandbar was split in two. In summer there are guided field walks, nature programs, and art classes for preschoolers through ninth graders. ✉ *869 Rte. 6A, West Brewster* ☎ *508/896–3867* 🌐 *www.ccmnh.org* 🎫 *$15.*

Nickerson State Park

STATE/PROVINCIAL PARK | FAMILY | These 1,961 acres were once part of a vast estate belonging to Roland C. Nickerson, son of Samuel Nickerson, a Chatham native who founded the First National Bank of Chicago. Roland and his wife, Addie, lavishly entertained such visitors as President Grover Cleveland at their private beach and hunting lodge in English country-house style, with coachmen dressed in tails and top hats and a bugler announcing carriages entering the front gates. In 1934 Addie donated the land for the state park in memory of Roland and their son, who died during the 1918 flu epidemic. The park consists of acres of oak, pitch-pine, hemlock, and spruce forest speckled with seven freshwater kettle ponds formed by glaciers. Some ponds are stocked with trout for fishing. You can swim, canoe, sail, and kayak in the ponds, and bicycle along 8 miles of paved trails that connect to the Cape Cod Rail Trail. Bird-watchers seek out the thrushes, wrens, warblers, woodpeckers, finches, larks, cormorants, great blue herons, hawks, owls, and ospreys. Red foxes and white-tailed deer are occasionally spotted in the woods. The over 400 campsites are extremely popular: reservations are necessary. ✉ *3488 Rte. 6A, East Brewster* ☎ *508/896–3491* 🌐 *www.mass.gov/locations/nickerson-state-park* 🎫 *$30 parking Memorial Day–Oct.*

Restaurants

Brewster Fish House

$$$ | SEAFOOD | Gorgeously presented, impeccably fresh seafood is standard here: lunch and dinner selections range from just-off-the-boat scallops to tuna, local oysters, and octopus. It can be noisy and it's always crowded in summer, but it's worth the wait. **Known for:** artful seafood presentations; sophisticated atmosphere; locally sourced ingredients. [$] *Average main: $34* ✉ *2208 Rte. 6A, Brewster* ☎ *508/896–7867* 🌐 *www.brewsterfishhousecapecod.com* ⏲ *Closed Mon.-Wed. for lunch; closed Mon. and Tues. for dinner.*

JT's Seafood

$$ | SEAFOOD | FAMILY | Fresh and ample portions of fried seafood take center stage at this casual joint, which is very popular with families. Place your order at the counter and sit inside or out: be sure to save room for ice cream. **Known for:** fried clams; hot lobster rolls; fish tacos. [$] *Average main: $24* ✉ *2689 Rte. 6A, Brewster* ☎ *508/896–3355* 🌐 *www.jt-seafood.com* ⏲ *Closed mid-Sept.–mid-Apr.*

Hotels

★ Captain Freeman Inn

$$$ | **B&B/INN** | Named for the sea captain who had the home built in 1866, this gracious inn exudes mellowed elegance with original ornate plaster ceiling medallions and marble fireplaces, along with a fun modern touch—a heated saltwater pool, open year-round. **Pros:** authentic historic lodging with modern amenities; it's a short walk to Breakwater Beach on the bay, even shorter to the ice-cream shop next to the Brewster General Store; three-course breakfast and afternoon tea. **Cons:** not for those with children; not a waterfront location; most rooms upstairs. *Rooms from: $339 ✉ 15 Breakwater Rd., Brewster ☎ 508/896–7481 ⊕ www.captainfreemaninn.com 10 rooms Free Breakfast.*

★ Ocean Edge Resort & Golf Club

$$$$ | **RESORT** | **FAMILY** | The expansive Ocean Edge Resort & Golf Club, set on 429 acres of prime Cape Cod real estate, offers a host of amenities and perks, from a Jack Nicklaus–designed golf course and a private beach to several pools, tennis courts, and a gorgeous spa. **Pros:** five pools, two inside; access to private beach; great kids' activities. **Cons:** expensive; busy with weddings in summer; Arbor and Britterige Villas at The Villages do not have access to the private beach. *Rooms from: $500 ✉ 2907 Main St., Brewster ☎ 508/896–9000 ⊕ www.oceanedge.com 337 rooms No Meals.*

★ Old Sea Pines Inn

$ | **B&B/INN** | **FAMILY** | With its white-column portico and wraparound veranda overlooking a broad lawn, Old Sea Pines, which housed a women's "charm and personality" school in the early 1900s, resembles a vintage summer estate. **Pros:** welcomes families; beautiful grounds; reasonable rates. **Cons:** no TV in main building; steep stairway to upper floors; not for those looking for upscale design. *Rooms from: $155 ✉ 2553 Rte. 6A, Brewster ☎ 508/896–6114 ⊕ www.oldseapinesinn.com ⏲ Limited room availability Nov.–Apr. 24 rooms Free Breakfast.*

Performing Arts

MUSIC

Brewster Band Concerts

CONCERTS | **FAMILY** | Sunday evenings by the bay (July 4th through Labor Day) are filled with the sounds of the town-band concerts, held in the gazebo on the grounds of Drummer Boy Park. Bring your beach chairs, blankets, and a picnic for a lovely evening outing. The park is about ½ mile west of the Cape Cod Museum of Natural History, on the western side of Brewster. *✉ Drummer Boy Park, 773 Main St., West Brewster ⊕ thebrewsterband.weebly.com Free.*

THEATER

Cape Cod Repertory Theatre Co

THEATER | **FAMILY** | Several impressive productions, from original works to the classics, are staged every year in this indoor Arts and Crafts–style theater set way back in the woods. There are popular outdoor shows for kids offered on weekday mornings during the summer, as well as puppet shows. *✉ 3299 Rte. 6A, west of Nickerson State Park, East Brewster ☎ 508/896–1888 ⊕ www.caperep.org ⏲ Closed Dec.–Mar.*

BASEBALL

Brewster Whitecaps

BASEBALL & SOFTBALL | **FAMILY** | The Brewster Whitecaps of the collegiate Cape Cod Baseball League play home games mid-June–mid-August. Kids 5–13 can sign up for fun clinics led by the players. *✉ Stony Brook Elementary School, 384 Underpass Rd., Brewster ☎ 508/896–8500 ⊕ www.brewsterwhitecaps.com.*

Shopping

With Brewster's abundant historic and natural appeal, it's no surprise that shoppers will appreciate the bounty of antiques shops, art galleries, and specialty shops here.

★ Brewster Book Store

BOOKS | FAMILY | A special place, Brewster Book Store is filled to the rafters with all manner of books by local and international authors, with an extensive fiction selection and kids' section. Author signings and children's story times take place year-round. ✉ *2648 Rte. 6A, East Brewster* ☎ *508/896–6543* 🌐 *www.brewsterbookstore.com.*

Harwich

6 miles south of Brewster, 5 miles east of Dennis.

The Cape's famous cranberry industry took off in Harwich in 1844, when Alvin Cahoon was its principal grower; there are still working cranberry bogs throughout Harwich. Three naturally sheltered harbors on Nantucket Sound make the town, like its English namesake, popular with boaters, and you'll find dozens of elegant sailboats and elaborate yachts in Harwich's harbors, plus plenty of charter fishing boats. By land, the Harwich Conservation Trust has protected 600-plus acres and created more than ten miles of trails, making sure that the town retains its beautiful natural spaces.

GETTING HERE AND AROUND

The center of Harwich, 6 miles south of Brewster, is easily accessed off Exit 10 of U.S. 6. It sits at the crossroads of several roads that branch off to various towns. Route 39, which becomes Main Street in town, leads to Orleans; Bank Street, next to the Brooks Free Library, is the most direct route to Harwich Port.

VISITOR INFORMATION

CONTACTS Harwich Chamber of Commerce. ☎ *508/430–1165* 🌐 *www.harwichcc.com.*

Sights

Cape Cod Lavender Farm

FARM/RANCH | Cape Cod Lavender Farm consists of several thousand lavender plants, making it one of the largest such farms on the East Coast. Harvest time (best for visits) is usually around late-June–mid-July, when you'll see acres and acres of stunning purple waves, and they sell fresh bunches of lavender. The eleven-acre farm is surrounded by 60 acres of conservation land and walking trails. The farm sells soaps and bath salts, candles, potpourri, marmalade, lemonade, and many other lavender-infused goods. Keep your eyes peeled for its sign (on the right) as you're driving south on Route 124—it's easy to miss. ✉ *Corner of Rte. 124 and Weston Woods Rd., off U.S. 6, Exit 10, Harwich* ☎ *508/432–8397* 🌐 *www.capecodlavenderfarm.com* ⏲ *Closed Jan.–Feb.*

Restaurants

★ Buca's Tuscan Roadhouse

$$$ | ITALIAN | This romantic roadhouse near the Chatham border, adorned with tiny white lights, wine bottles, and warm-hue walls, might just transport you to Italy—and if it doesn't, the fantastic food certainly will. There are always excellent specials added to the menu; in the fall and winter, look for value-priced entrées, and in summer, their hot dog cart (in the parking lot) serves the best wieners on the Cape. **Known for:** Buca's bolognese with wild boar; chocolate Italian wedding cake; crowds: make reservations. [$] *Average main: $34* ✉ *4 Depot Rd., Harwich* ☎ *508/432–6900* 🌐 *www.bucastuscanroadhouse.com* ⏲ *No lunch.*

★ Cape Sea Grille
$$$$ | **AMERICAN** | This chef-owned gem with distant sea views uses what's locally available as the inspiration for an ever-changing and creative menu that's complemented by a vibrant, welcoming atmosphere. There are also generous wine, martini, and drink lists. **Known for:** inviting atmosphere; inventive seafood entrées; creative cocktails. *Average main: $39 31 Sea St., Harwich Port 508/432–4745 www.capeseagrille.com Closed Mon. and Tues.*

 Coffee and Quick Bites

Sundae School
$ | **AMERICAN** | **FAMILY** | Churning out ice cream in small batches since 1976, this popular place usually has lines out the door. The shop uses only the freshest ingredients, so flavors like banana or blueberry are made with the real deal, but you can always count on the classics like vanilla and chocolate. **Known for:** amazing hot fudge sundaes; creative flavors; friendly service. *Average main: $6 606 Main St., Harwich Port 508/430–2444 www.sundaeschool.com Closed Labor Day–Memorial Day.*

 Hotels

★ Wequassett Resort and Golf Club
$$$$ | **RESORT** | **FAMILY** | On 27 acres of shaded landscape partially surrounded by Pleasant Bay, 20 Cape-style cottages and an attractive hotel make up this traditionally elegant resort by the sea. **Pros:** attentive service; activities and programs for all ages; babysitting services and full children's program. **Cons:** rates are steep; not an in-town location; isolated area. *Rooms from: $1,000 2173 Orleans Rd. (Rte. 28), Harwich 508/432–5400 www.wequassett.com Closed Nov.–Mar. 120 rooms No Meals.*

Winstead Inn & Beach Resort
$$$$ | **B&B/INN** | With its graceful columns and welcoming front veranda, the regal Winstead Inn sits along a quiet street; many of the rooms have a view of the heated, outdoor saltwater pool, a real oasis with potted palms, fountains, and flowers. **Pros:** spacious, elegant rooms; pretty pool area; beach access. **Cons:** numerous stairs; not for those on a budget; beach guests can't use pool. *Rooms from: $400 116 Parallel St., Harwich 508/432–4444 www.winsteadinn.com Closed Nov.–Apr. 29 rooms Free Breakfast.*

 Activities

BASEBALL

Harwich Mariners
BASEBALL & SOFTBALL | **FAMILY** | The Harwich Mariners of the collegiate Cape Cod Baseball League play home games at Whitehouse Field on Oak Street mid-June–mid-August. The team leads a youth clinic for boys and girls ages 5-17. *Whitehouse Field, 75 Oak St., Harwich 508/432–2000 www.harwichmariners.org.*

 Shopping

Harwich Port has a busy little Main Street area lined with shops and restaurants, though the majority of Harwich is somewhat rural with little in the way of a dense shopping area. In East Harwich, on the way to Orleans, is a large commercial center with a large grocery store, drug stores, and other retail options.

Chatham

5 miles east of Harwich.

At the bent elbow of the Cape, with water nearly surrounding it, Chatham has all the charm of a quietly posh seaside resort, with plenty of shops but none of the crass commercialism that plagues some other towns on the Cape. The town has gray-shingle houses—many improbably large and grandiose—with tidy awnings and cheerful flower gardens, an attractive Main Street with crafts and antiques stores alongside dapper cafés, and a beloved candy store, Chatham Candy Manor. Although it can get crowded in high season—and even on weekends during shoulder seasons—Chatham remains a true New England village.

VISITOR INFORMATION

CONTACTS Chatham Chamber of Commerce. ✉ *Chatham* ☎ *508/945–5199* 🌐 *www.chathaminfo.com.*

Sights

Atwood House Museum

HISTORY MUSEUM | Built by sea captain Joseph C. Atwood in 1752, this museum has a gambrel roof, hand-hewn floor planks, an old kitchen with a wide hearth and a beehive oven. The New Gallery features a rotating slate of exhibits. The Joseph C. Lincoln Room has the manuscripts, first editions, and mementos of the Chatham writer; antique tools are displayed in an additional gallery. There's also a local commercial fishing gallery and an exhibit on the famous Pendleton wreck and rescue. In a remodeled freight shed are the stunning and provocative murals (1932–45) by Alice Stallknecht Wight portraying religious scenes in Chatham settings. On the grounds are an herb garden, the old turret and lens from the Chatham Light, a simple camp house rescued from eroding North Beach, and a Wampanoag wetu dwelling. ✉ *347 Stage Harbor Rd., West Chatham* ☎ *508/945–2493* 🌐 *www.chathamhistoricalsociety.org* 🎟 *$10* 🕒 *Closed Sun. and Mon. Closed Nov.–May (special events scheduled in off-season).*

Chatham Fish Pier

MARINA/PIER | **FAMILY** | Smells and sights are abundant at Chatham's most popular tourist destination; keep an eye out for the many lingering seals who are hoping for a free meal. The unloading of the boats is a big local event, drawing crowds who watch it all from an observation deck. From their fishing grounds 3–100 miles offshore, fishermen bring in haddock, cod, flounder, lobster, halibut, and pollack, which are packed in ice and shipped to New York and Boston or sold at the fish market here. Also here is *The Provider,* a monument to the town's fishing industry, showing a hand pulling a fish-filled net from the sea. ✉ *54 Barcliff Rd. Ext., North Chatham* 🌐 *www.chatham-ma.gov/chatham-fish-pier* 🎟 *Free.*

Chatham Lighthouse

LIGHTHOUSE | The view from this lighthouse—of the harbor, the sandbars, and the ocean beyond—justifies the crowds. The lighthouse is especially dramatic on a foggy night, as the beacon pierces the mist. Coin-operated telescopes allow a close look at the famous "Chatham Break," the result of a fierce 1987 nor'easter that blasted a channel through a barrier beach just off the coast. The U.S. Coast Guard auxiliary, which supervises the lighthouse, offers free tours May–October on most Wednesdays (1–3:30 p.m.; every other Wed. in spring and fall); otherwise, the interior is off-limits. There is free parking in front of the lighthouse—the 30-minute limit is strictly monitored. ✉ *Main St., near Bridge St., West Chatham* ☎ *508/945-3830* 🎟 *Free.*

★ Monomoy National Wildlife Refuge

WILDLIFE REFUGE | This 2,500-acre preserve includes the Monomoy Islands, a fragile 9-mile-long barrier-beach area south of Chatham. A haven for bird-watchers, the refuge is an important stop along the North Atlantic Flyway for migratory waterfowl and shorebirds—peak migration times are May and late July. It also provides nesting and resting grounds for 285 species, including gulls—great black-backed, herring, and laughing—and several tern species. White-tailed deer wander the islands, and harbor and gray seals frequent the shores in winter. The only structure on the islands is the South Monomoy Lighthouse, built in 1849. The visitor center offers maps and some guided walks in the summer (open June through Labor Day.) ✉ *Wikis Way, Morris Island, Chatham* ☎ *508/945–0594* 🌐 *www.fws.gov/refuge/Monomoy* 🎫 *Free.*

Beaches

Harding's Beach

BEACH | FAMILY | West of Chatham center, on the calmer and warmer waters of Nantucket Sound, Harding's Beach is very popular with families. It can get crowded, so plan to arrive earlier or later in the day. **Amenities:** food and drink; lifeguards; parking (fee); showers; toilets. **Best for:** swimming; walking; windsurfing. ✉ *Harding's Beach Rd., off Barn Hill Rd., West Chatham* 🌐 *www.chathaminfo.com/beaches* 🎫 *Parking $20.*

Restaurants

Del Mar Bar and Bistro

$$$ | ECLECTIC | Fanciful cocktails, an intriguing menu, live music, and daily blackboard specials make this a popular Chatham spot. There's also a changing tapas menu for quick bites at the bar. **Known for:** wood-fired meals; live jazz; intriguing specials. 💲 *Average main: $32* ✉ *907 Rte. 28, Chatham* ☎ *508/945–9988* 🌐 *www.delmarbistro.com* ⏲ *No lunch. Closed Sun. from mid-June–mid-Sept; closed Sun. and Mon. from mid-Sept.-mid-June.*

Hotels

Chatham Bars Inn

$$$$ | RESORT | One of the grande dames of Cape Cod's resort scene, this sprawling 25-acre oceanfront estate was built in 1914 as a private hunting lodge; now, more than 200 rooms are spread over 30-plus separate buildings and share a quarter-mile private beach. **Pros:** activities galore; children welcome; oceanfront location. **Cons:** not for the budget-conscious; some lodgings are far from the action; "Americana"-themed decor doesn't appeal to all tastes. 💲 *Rooms from: $725* ✉ *297 Shore Rd., Chatham* ☎ *508/945–0096, 800/527–4884* 🌐 *www.chathambarsinn.com* 🛏 *217 rooms* 🍽 *No Meals.*

★ **Chatham Gables Inn**

$$$ | B&B/INN | The embodiment of understated elegance, this 1839 former sea captain's home shines in the simple beauty of 19th-century craftsmanship in gleaming wide-plank floors, and graceful molding and wainscoting. **Pros:** exquisite historic lodging; 10-minute walk to town and beach; exceptional service. **Cons:** not a waterfront location; not for those traveling with small children; not an in-town location. 💲 *Rooms from: $325* ✉ *364 Old Harbor Rd., Chatham* ☎ *508/945–5859* 🌐 *www.chathamgablesinn.com* 🛏 *8 rooms* 🍽 *Free Breakfast.*

Nightlife

Chatham Squire

BARS | Boasting four bars (including a raw bar), this is a rollicking year-round local hangout, drawing a young crowd to the bar side and a mixed crowd of locals to the restaurant. There's live entertainment on weekends. ✉ *487 Main St., Chatham* ☎ *508/945–0942* 🌐 *www.thesquire.com.*

Performing Arts

Chatham Town-Band Concerts

CONCERTS | FAMILY | Chatham's summer town-band concerts—a tradition that began in the 1940s—begin at 8 pm on Friday and draw thousands of onlookers. As many as 500 fox-trot on the roped-off dance floor, and there are special dances for children and sing-alongs for all. ✉ *Kate Gould Park, Main St., Chatham* ☎ *508/945–5199* 🌐 *www.chathamband.com* 🎫 *Free.*

BASEBALL

Chatham Anglers

BASEBALL & SOFTBALL | FAMILY | Chatham Anglers baseball games are great free entertainment by the collegiate-level players in the Cape Cod Baseball League. Clinics for aspiring 6- to 17-year-olds are led by the team. ✉ *Veterans' Field, 1 Veterans Field Rd., near rotary, Chatham* ☎ *508/348-1607* 🌐 *www.chathamanglers.com* 🎫 *Free.*

Shopping

Main Street is a busy shopping area with a diverse range of merchandise, from the wallet-friendly to the pricier and more upscale. Here you'll find galleries, crafts, clothing stores, bookstores, and a few good antiques shops.

Chatham Candy Manor

CANDY | FAMILY | Shops don't get more adorable than this downtown candy store with the bright pink awning, winning sweet-toothed fans since 1955 for their slow-cooked, small-batch confections. Their version of a clambake is a too-cute assortment of chocolate sea creatures on a bed of chocolate rocks. Sea salt caramels, made with local sea salt, are a favorite, and they stay open year-round. ✉ *484 Main St., Chatham* ☎ *508/945-0825* 🌐 *www.candymanor.com.*

★ Yankee Ingenuity

JEWELRY & WATCHES | Here you'll find a varied selection of unique jewelry, gifts, whimsical folk art, and home decor—including many pieces created by local artisans—at reasonable prices (especially for Chatham). The gallery also showcases the award-winning landscape photography of the shop's owner, Jon Vaughan. ✉ *525 Main St., Chatham* ☎ *508/945–1288* 🌐 *www.yankee-ingenuity.com* 🕒 *Closed Mon.-Fri. in Jan. and Feb.*

Orleans

8 miles north of Chatham, 35 miles east of Sagamore Bridge.

Orleans has a long heritage of fishing and seafaring, and many beautifully preserved homes from the Colonial era still remain in the small village of East Orleans, home of the town's Historical Society and Museum. In other areas of town, such as down by Rock Harbor, more modestly grand homes stand near the water's edge.

GETTING HERE AND AROUND

Downtown Orleans, 8 miles north of Chatham, is a kind of extended triangle made by Route 28, Route 6A, and Main Street. Main Street crosses Route 28 as it makes its way east toward the lovely enclave of East Orleans and Nauset Beach. Heading west, Main Street blends into Rock Harbor Road, which makes its journey all the way to Cape Cod Bay. A bus connecting Hyannis and Orleans serves the Lower Cape region. Year-round transport on the Flex service goes from Harwich to Provincetown, serving the towns of Brewster, Orleans, Eastham, Wellfleet, and Truro along the way. For schedules, visit 🌐 www.capecodrta.org.

VISITOR INFORMATION

CONTACTS Orleans Chamber of Commerce. ✉ *Orleans* ☎ *508/255–1386* 🌐 *orleanscapecod.org.*

Rock Harbor

MARINA/PIER | FAMILY | This harbor was the site of a War of 1812 skirmish in which the Orleans militia kept a British warship from docking. In the 19th century Orleans had active saltworks, and a flourishing packet service between Rock Harbor and Boston developed. Today it's the base of charter fishing and party boats in season, as well as a small commercial fishing fleet.

The historic Coast Guard vessel CG36500, featured in the book and film, *The Finest Hours* and owned by the Orleans Historical Society, is berthed at Rock Harbor each summer. The 36-foot wooden lifeboat, the only operating vessel of its class on the East Coast, can be viewed from the dock; talks and tours are sometimes scheduled. Sunsets over the harbor are spectacular, and it's a great place to watch the boats float past. Parking is free.

Fronting the harbor, the magnificently adorned Church of the Transfiguration incorporates mosaics, frescoes, sculpted bronze, wood, stone, and glass to illustrate acts of God from Genesis to Revelation. Constructed of limestone, with a massive bell tower, the church is an architectural masterpiece. The church is typically open for tours (free) daily except Wednesday, when it closes for services. *Rock Harbor Rd., Orleans.*

Beaches

There is a daily parking fee for both beaches mid-June–Labor Day. Fees for parking on Saturday and Sunday begin on Memorial Day weekend. The increased presence of great white sharks in the area (they dine on the massive seal population) seems to be both a tourist boon and a concern. It's not unusual to hear the blare of lifeguard whistles followed by orders to exit the water until the coast is clear. Best tip: don't swim with the seals.

Nauset Beach

BEACH | FAMILY | This town-managed beach—not to be confused with Nauset Light Beach on the National Seashore—is a 10-mile sweep of sandy ocean beach with low dunes and large waves good for bodysurfing or board surfing. Despite its size, the massive parking lot often fills up on sunny days; arrive quite early or in the late afternoon if you want to claim a spot. The beach gets extremely crowded in summer; unless you walk a bit, expect to feel very close to your neighbors on the sand. **Amenities:** food and drink; lifeguards; parking (fee); showers; toilets. **Best for:** sunrise; surfing; swimming; walking. *Beach Rd., Nauset Heights 508/240–3780 orleanscapecod.org/beaches Parking $30 Memorial Day–Labor Day.*

Skaket Beach

BEACH | FAMILY | On Cape Cod Bay, Skaket Beach is a sandy stretch with calm, warm water good for children. When the tide is out, you can walk seemingly endlessly on the sandy flats. The parking lot fills up fast on hot July and August days; try to arrive before 10 or after 2. The many tide pools make this a favorite spot for families. Sunsets here draw a good crowd. **Amenities:** food and drink; lifeguards; parking (fee); showers; toilets. **Best for:** sunset; swimming; walking. *Skaket Beach Rd., Orleans 508/240–3775 orleanscapecod.org/beaches Parking $30 Memorial Day–Labor Day.*

Restaurants

Land Ho!

$$ | AMERICAN | Tried-and-true tavern fare is the rule at Orleans's flagship local restaurant. The scene is usually fun and boisterous; dozens of homemade wooden signs heralding local businesses hang from the rafters above the red-checker tablecloths. **Known for:** daily blackboard specials; thriving local bar scene; chowder. *Average main: $18 38 Cove Rd., Orleans 508/255–5165 www.land-ho.com.*

Mahoney's Atlantic Bar and Grill

$$$ | ECLECTIC | This always-hopping downtown spot serves commendable dinner fare and draws big crowds for cocktails and appetizers. The bar is long and comfortable, and is a good spot to dine if there are no tables available. **Known for:** seafood bouillabaisse; specialty cocktails; lively local hangout. *Average main: $30 28 Main St., Orleans 508/255–5505 www.mahoneysatlantic.com No lunch.*

Coffee and Quick Bites

Hole In One

$ | **BAKERY** | Fuel up for a beach day at this bustling family-owned breakfast and lunch spot, where options range from a kombucha and a cruller to a balsamic-drizzled veggie wrap and an iced chai latte. Guests order food at the downstairs level, confronted by an array of decadent baked goods (hand-cut donuts are a specialty), and take it to go or eat in the upstairs solarium or at a picnic table next to the parking lot. **Known for:** crab cake Benedict; apple fritter; homemade chai latte. *Average main: $13 ✉ 98 Route 6A, Orleans ☎ 508/255-3740 🌐 www.theholecapecod.com.*

Hotels

Ship's Knees Inn

$$$ | **B&B/INN** | Giving a generous nod to its name and its 19th-century heritage, this inn is full of nautical and historic touches: seaside artwork and furnishings, steeply pitched roof lines, wide-plank floors, antiques, and a good deal of painted furniture. **Pros:** short walk to beach; beautifully maintained property; outdoor features include pool, hammock, and fire pit. **Cons:** not for families with kids under age 12; feels a bit cluttered; Continental breakfast, not hot food. *Rooms from: $330 ✉ 186 Beach Rd., Orleans ☎ 508/255–1312 🌐 www.shipskneesinn.com ⏲ Closed mid-Oct.–Apr. 17 rooms, 1 apartment Free Breakfast.*

Activities

BASEBALL

Orleans Firebirds

BASEBALL & SOFTBALL | **FAMILY** | The Orleans Firebirds of the collegiate Cape Cod Baseball League play home games at Eldredge Park mid-June–July. Kids can sign up for daily clinics with the players. *✉ Eldredge Park, 84 Rte. 28 at Eldredge Pkwy., Orleans ☎ 508/255–0793 🌐 www.orleansfirebirds.com Free.*

BOATING AND FISHING

Many of Orleans's freshwater ponds offer good fishing for perch, pickerel, trout, and more. Anglers will need a license for both fresh and saltwater fishing. Pleasant Bay is popular for boating and paddling.

Arey's Pond Boat Yard

BOATING | There's a sailing school here offering individual and group lessons. The company also rents sailboats, kayaks, row boats, and standup paddleboards. *✉ 45 Arey's La., off Rte. 28, South Orleans ☎ 508/255–0994 🌐 www.areyspondboatyard.com.*

Goose Hummock Shop

FISHING | Fishing licenses and gear are available at the Goose Hummock Shop, which also rents powerboats, canoes, paddleboards, and kayaks. Lessons and tours are available. *✉ 15 Rte. 6A, Orleans ☎ 508/255–0455 🌐 www.goosehummockshops.com.*

Shopping

Orleans's Main Street, between Route 6A and Route 28, is lined with a number of specialty shops. It's a great area for browsing or taking a break on a park bench with coffee and a pastry.

Eastham

3 miles north of Orleans, 6 miles south of Wellfleet.

Often overlooked on the speedy drive up toward Provincetown on Route 6, Eastham is a town of hidden treasures. Unlike other towns on the Cape, it has no official town center or Main Street; the highway bisects it, and the town touches both Cape Cod Bay and the Atlantic. Amid the gas stations, convenience stores, restaurants, and large motel complexes, Eastham has a wealth of natural beauty. It is also the home of the Cape Cod National Seashore's Salt Pond Visitor Center.

GETTING HERE AND AROUND

Eastham's main drag is busy Route 6, which gives visitors no feel for the town's natural beauty. It's hard to get lost in Eastham, which is about 3 miles north of Orleans. You're never more than a few miles from the beach, where all side streets seem to lead. Take the time to meander and see what's off the highway on both the bay and ocean sides.

VISITOR INFORMATION

CONTACTS Eastham Chamber of Commerce. ✉ *Eastham* ☎ *508/240–7211* 🌐 *www.easthamchamber.com.*

Sights

★ Cape Cod National Seashore

NATIONAL PARK | FAMILY | The region's most expansive national treasure, Cape Cod National Seashore was established in 1961 by President John F. Kennedy, for whom Cape Cod was home and haven. The lands and waters of the Seashore comprise 44,000 acres of the Cape, extending from Chatham to Provincetown. The protected area includes 40 miles of pristine sandy beach; rolling dunes; swamps, marshes, and wetlands; and pitch-pine and scrub-oak forest. Self-guided nature trails, as well as biking and horse trails, wind through these landscapes. Hiking trails from Salt Pond Visitor Center lead to Nauset Marsh, Salt Pond, and the Buttonbush Trail, a quarter-mile nature path designed for people with low or no vision. A hike or bike ride to Coast Guard Beach leads to a turnout looking out over marsh and sea. A section of the cliff here was washed away in 1990, revealing the remains of a prehistoric dwelling. The National Seashore has two visitor centers, one in Eastham and one in Provincetown.

Salt Pond Visitor Center, open year-round at the southern end of the Seashore, reveals expansive views of the Salt Pond and Nauset Marsh. Activities offered (typically from May to October) include ranger-led walks, canoe and kayak tours, demonstrations, and lectures, as well as evening beach walks, campfire talks, and other programs. The centerpiece of the visitor center lobby is a large map showing Cape Cod's location in the Gulf of Maine, displaying the Cape's glacial history and the powerful natural forces that continue to shape it. The visitor center's museum explores the cultural themes represented on Cape Cod, including the Wampanoag, "The First People of the Light," plus European settlement, fishing, life-saving, lighthouses, communication technology and tourism. An air-conditioned auditorium shows films on geology, sea rescues, whaling, Henry David Thoreau, and Guglielmo Marconi. ✉ *Salt Pond Visitor Center, 50 Doane Rd., Eastham* ☎ *508/255–3421 for Salt Pond Visitor Center* 🌐 *www.nps.gov/caco* 🎫 *Free.*

★ Fort Hill Area

NATURE SIGHT | The road to the Cape Cod National Seashore's Fort Hill area ends at a parking area with a lovely view of old farmland traced with stone fences that rolls gently down to Nauset Marsh. The marsh winds around brilliant green grasses and makes its way to the ocean beyond; it is one of the more dramatic views on the Cape. Appreciated by bird-watchers and nature photographers, trails pass through wetlands and to Skiff Hill, an overlook with benches and informative plaques that quote Samuel de Champlain's account of the area from when he moored off Nauset Marsh in 1605. Also on Skiff Hill is Indian Rock, a large boulder moved to the hill from the marsh below. Once used by the local Nauset tribe of the Wampanoag as a sharpening stone, the rock is cut with deep grooves and smoothed in circles where ax heads were whetted. Trails are open from dawn to dusk. ✉ *50 Fort Hill Rd., off U.S. 6, Eastham* 🌐 *www.nps.gov/caco* 🎫 *Free.*

Nauset Light

LIGHTHOUSE | Moved 350 feet back from its perch at cliff's edge in 1996, this much-photographed red-and-white lighthouse tops the bluff where the Three Sisters Lighthouses once stood. (The Sisters themselves can be seen in a little landlocked park surrounded by trees; they're reached by paved walkways off Nauset Light Beach's parking lot.) How the lighthouses got there is a long story. In 1838 three brick lighthouses were built 150 feet apart on the bluffs in Eastham overlooking a particularly dangerous area of shoals (shifting underwater sandbars). In 1892, after the eroding cliff dropped the towers into the ocean, they were replaced with three wooden towers. In 1918, two were moved away, as was the third in 1923. Eventually the National Park Service acquired the Three Sisters and brought them together in the inland park, where they would be safe. Lectures on and guided tours of the lighthouses (free, donations accepted) are conducted Sunday early May–October, as well as Wednesday in July and August. ✉ *Ocean View Dr. and Cable Rd., Eastham* ☎ *508/240–2612* 🌐 *www.nausetlight.org* 🎟 *Free.*

Coast Guard Beach

BEACH | **FAMILY** | Considered one of the Cape's prettiest beaches, Coast Guard Beach, part of the National Seashore, is a long beach backed by low grass and heathland. A handsome former Coast Guard station is here, though it's not open to the public, and the beach has a very small parking lot (restricted to residents and vehicles displaying handicapped placards from mid-June to Labor Day), so the best bet is to head to the Salt Pond Visitor Center and follow signs to the Little Creek Staging Area parking lot. From there, take the free shuttle to the beach. Shuttles run frequently and can accommodate gear and bicycles. At high tide the size of the beach shrinks considerably, so watch your blanket. **Amenities:** lifeguards; parking (fee); showers; toilets. **Best for:** sunrise; surfing; swimming; walking. ✉ *Off Ocean View Dr., Eastham* 🌐 *www.nps.gov/caco/planyourvisit/coast-guard-beach-eastham.htm* 🎟 *Parking $25; the annual seashore pass grants access to all six national park beaches and costs the same as three days of parking.*

First Encounter Beach

BEACH | **FAMILY** | A great spot for watching sunsets over Cape Cod Bay, First Encounter Beach is rich in history. Near the parking lot, a bronze marker commemorates the first encounter between local Native Americans and passengers from the *Mayflower,* led by Captain Myles Standish, who explored the entire area for five weeks in 1620 before moving on to Plymouth. The beach is popular with families who favor its warmer, calmer waters and tide pools. **Amenities:** parking (fee); showers; toilets. **Best for:** sunset; swimming; walking; windsurfing. ✉ *1699 Samoset Rd., off Rte. 6, Eastham* 🌐 *www.eastham-ma.gov* 🎟 *Parking $30.*

★ Nauset Light Beach

BEACH | Adjacent to Coast Guard Beach, this sandy beach is backed by tall dunes, frilly grasses, and heathland. The trail to the Three Sisters lighthouses takes you through a pitch-pine forest. Parking here is extremely limited and fills up quickly in summer; plan to arrive early or you may have to go elsewhere. **Amenities:** lifeguards; parking (fee); showers; toilets. **Best for:** sunrise; surfing; swimming; walking. ✉ *Off Ocean View Dr., Eastham* 🌐 *www.nps.gov/caco/planyourvisit/nauset-light-beach.htm* 🎟 *Parking $25; the annual seashore pass grants access to all six national park beaches and costs the same as three days of parking.*

Restaurants

Arnold's Lobster & Clam Bar

$$ | **SEAFOOD** | **FAMILY** | You can't miss this hot spot on the side of Route 6: look for the riot of colorful flowers lining the road and the patient folks waiting in long lines for fried seafood and other fixings. Unusual for a clam shack like this is the full bar, offering beer, wine, mixed drinks, and the house specialty: margaritas. **Known for:** lobster rolls; ice cream from Richardson's Dairy Farm; fried clams. *Average main: $24 3580 Rte. 6, Eastham 508/255–2575 www.arnoldsrestaurant.com No credit cards Closed mid-Sept.–mid-May.*

Fairway Restaurant and Pizzeria
$$ | **ITALIAN** | **FAMILY** | The friendly, family-run Fairway specializes in Italian comfort food but also has a very popular breakfast. Attached to the Hole in One Bakery and Coffee Shop—a favorite among locals for exceptional hand-cut doughnuts and muffins—the Fairway puts a jar of crayons on every paper-covered table and sells its own brand of root beer. **Known for:** hearty pizza; homemade dessert; chicken Parmesan. *Average main: $24 4295 Rte. 6, Eastham 508/255–3893 www.fairwaycapecod.com No lunch.*

Hotels

★ **Fort Hill Bed and Breakfast**
$$$$ | **B&B/INN** | This enchanting, adults-only B&B is in an 1864 Greek Revival farmhouse nestled in the tranquil Fort Hill area—located within the National Seashore—which is minutes off busy U.S. 6, but steps away from quiet, secluded trails that wind through cedar forests, fields crisscrossed by old stone fences, and a red-maple swamp. **Pros:** pastoral setting; close to nature trails; private and elegant lodging. **Cons:** not for those traveling with children; need to make reservations far in advance; only three rooms. *Rooms from: $450 75 Fort Hill Rd., Eastham 508/240–2870 www.forthillbedandbreakfast.com Closed mid-Oct.–May 2 suites, 1 cottage Free Breakfast.*

★ **Whalewalk Inn & Spa**
$$$ | **B&B/INN** | Set amid 3 landscaped acres, this 1830 whaling master's home has wide-plank pine floors, fireplaces, and updated guest digs; decor styles range from from 'Cape Cod beach-cottage' to 'classic B&B' with color-coordinated wallpaper and window treatments. **Pros:** beautiful grounds; elegantly appointed rooms; on-site wellness center. **Cons:** not for those traveling with small children; no water views; not an in-town location. *Rooms from: $300 220 Bridge Rd., Eastham 508/255–0617 www.whalewalkinn.com Closed Dec.–Mar. 16 rooms Free Breakfast.*

Wellfleet and South Wellfleet

6 miles north of Eastham, 13 miles southeast of Provincetown.

Still globally famous for its succulent namesake oysters, Wellfleet is today a tranquil community; many artists and writers call it home. Less than 2 miles wide, it's one of the most attractively developed Cape resort towns, with a number of fine restaurants, historic houses, and art galleries, and a good old Main Street in the village proper.

GETTING HERE AND AROUND

Like many Cape Cod towns, Wellfleet is spread out on either side of U.S. 6. Wellfleet Village is on the bay side, about 3 miles north of the entrance to Marconi Beach. Main Street makes its way past several businesses. A left turn will take you toward the harbor along Commercial Street, which is full of shops and galleries. The center of Wellfleet is quite compact, so it's best to leave your car in one of the public parking areas and take off on foot.

For a scenic loop through a classic Cape landscape near Wellfleet's Atlantic beaches—with scrub and pines on the left, heathland meeting cliffs and ocean below on the right—take LeCount Hollow Road just north of the Marconi Station turnoff. All the beaches on this strip rest at the bottom of a tall grass-covered dune, which lends dramatic character to this outermost shore. Winter storms continue to drastically alter the dunescape; don't be surprised to find a precipitous descent to area beaches.

Some beaches are restricted in the busy summer season to locals and long-term renters; the Beach Sticker Office issues permits so you can visit (you need a proof-of-stay form).

VISITOR INFORMATION

For information about restricted beaches, call the Wellfleet Beach Sticker Office. You can also purchase weekly or seasonal stickers here if you are renting a house in town (you'll need a proof-of-stay form).

CONTACTS Wellfleet Beach Sticker Office. ⊠ *255 Commercial St., Wellfleet* ☎ *508/349–9818* 🌐 *www.wellfleet-ma.gov.* **Wellfleet Chamber of Commerce.** ☎ *508/349–2510* 🌐 *www.wellfleetchamber.com.*

Sights

Marconi Station

HISTORIC SIGHT | On the Atlantic side of the Cape is the site of the first transatlantic wireless station erected on the U.S. mainland. It was from here on January 18, 1903, that Italian radio and wireless-telegraphy pioneer Guglielmo Marconi sent the first American wireless message to Europe: "most cordial greetings and good wishes" from President Theodore Roosevelt to King Edward VII of England. There's a lookout deck that offers a vantage point of both the Atlantic and Cape Cod Bay. Off the parking lot, a 1½-mile trail and boardwalk lead through the Atlantic White Cedar Swamp, one of the most beautiful trails on the seashore; free maps and guides are available at the trailhead. Marconi Beach, south of the Marconi Station on Marconi Beach Road, is one of the National Seashore's lovely ocean beaches. ⊠ *Marconi Site Rd., South Wellfleet* ☎ *508/255–3421* 🌐 *www.nps.gov/caco* 🎟 *Free.*

★ Mass Audubon Wellfleet Bay Wildlife Sanctuary

WILDLIFE REFUGE | **FAMILY** | Encompassing nearly 1,000 acres, this reserve is home to more than 300 species of birds. A jewel of Mass Audubon's statewide network of wildlife sanctuaries, Wellfleet Bay is a superb place for walking, birding, and watching the sun set over the salt marsh and Cape Cod Bay. The Esther Underwood Johnson Nature Center contains six aquariums that offer an up-close look at marine life common to the region's tidal flats, marshes, and ponds. From the nature center you can hike five short nature trails, including a fascinating boardwalk trail that leads over a salt marsh to a small beach, or you can wander through the pollinator garden. ⊠ *291 U.S. 6, South Wellfleet* ☎ *508/349–2615* 🌐 *www.massaudubon.org/wellfleetbay* 🎟 *$8* 🕒 *Closed Mon. from Labor Day to Memorial Day.*

Beaches

Extensive storm-induced erosion has made the cliffs to most of Wellfleet's ocean beaches quite steep, so be prepared for an energetic trek up and down the dune slope. Only the Cape Cod National Seashore beach at Marconi has steps; some have handrails to aid in the descent.

Though this does not apply to the beaches listed in this section, access to several Wellfleet beaches requires a resident or temporary resident parking stickers (this includes saltwater and freshwater ponds) in season only, from the last week of June through Labor Day. To get a three-day ($65), weekly ($100), or season ($325) pass, visit the Beach Sticker Booth on the town pier with your car registration in hand and a proof-of-stay form,

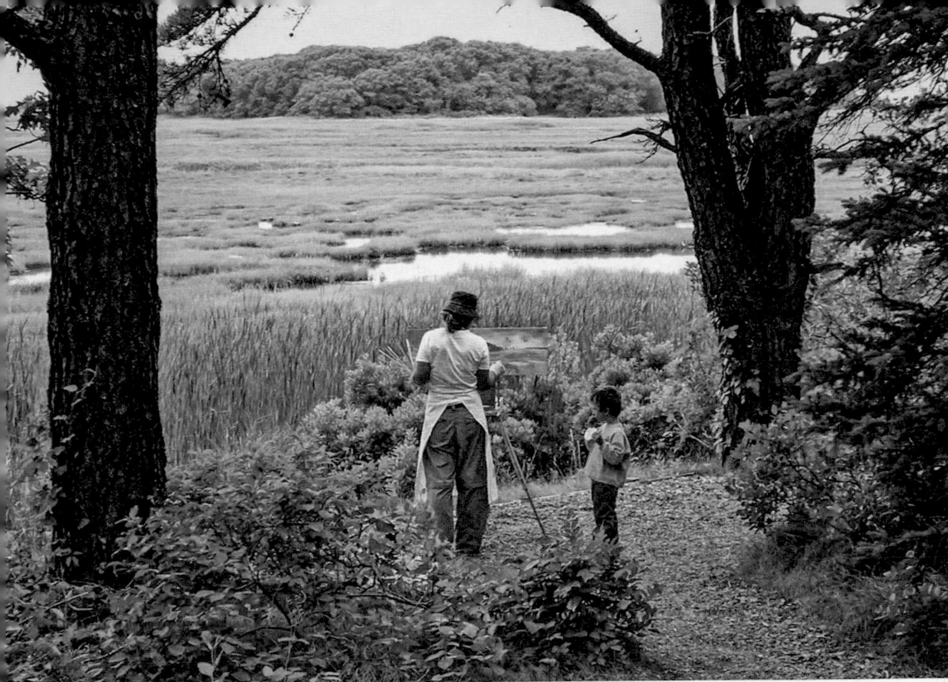

Artists and birders flock to the Wellfleet Bay Wildlife Sanctuary, protected by the Massachusetts Audubon Society.

available from rental agencies and hotels. For the rest of the year, anyone can visit these beaches for free.

■ **TIP→ Note that people arriving on foot or by bicycle, or after 5 pm, can visit the beaches at any time; the sticker is for parking only.**

Cahoon Hollow Beach

BEACH | The rustic restaurant and music club set on top of the dune are the main attractions at Cahoon Hollow Beach, which tends to draw younger crowds and plenty of families. It's a big Sunday-afternoon gathering place. The Beachcomber restaurant has paid parking, which is reimbursed when you buy something to eat or drink. Erosion has made getting to the beach a steep climb. **Amenities:** food and drink; lifeguards; parking (fee); toilets. **Best for:** surfing; swimming; walking; a casual bite to eat with ocean views. ✉ *1120 Cahoon Hollow Rd., Greater Wellfleet* ☎ *508/349–6055* 🌐 *www.thebeachcomber.com* 🎫 *Parking $30.*

★ Marconi Beach

BEACH | Part of the Cape Cod National Seashore, Marconi Beach is accessed via a very long and steep series of stairs leading down to the beach. It's also popular with both surfers and surf casters looking for striped bass or bluefish. Erosion from fierce storms has compromised beach access. **Amenities:** lifeguards; parking (fee); showers; toilets. **Best for:** sunrise; surfing; swimming; walking. ✉ *Marconi Beach Rd., off U.S. 6, South Wellfleet* 🌐 *www.nps.gov/caco* 🎫 *Parking $25; the annual seashore pass grants access to all six national park beaches and costs the same as three days of parking.*

Restaurants

Mac's on the Pier

$$ | **SEAFOOD** | **FAMILY** | Located at Wellfleet Harbor, this ambitious little spot serves some of the freshest seafood around. Sit along the pier and soak up the great water views while you chow down on a vast variety of local fish dishes, plus globe-trotting fare like burritos (with their house-made Scotch bonnet pepper sauce), a Caribbean seafood bowl, and tuna poke made with fresh local fish. **Known for:** gluten-free fried seafood; hot lobster roll; fish tacos. *Average main: $20 ✉ 265 Commercial St., Wellfleet Harbor ☎ 508/349–9611 🌐 www.macs-seafood.com ⏲ Closed Nov.–Apr.*

Moby Dick's

$$$ | SEAFOOD | FAMILY | A meal at this good-natured, rough-hewn fish shack with a hypernautical theme is an absolute Cape Cod tradition for some people. Bring your own libations, and if you need to kill time (the lines are sometimes daunting), stop inside Moby's Cargo, the bustling gift shop next door. **Known for:** the Nantucket Bucket—a pound of whole-belly Monomoy steamers, a pound of native mussels, and corn on the cob served in a bucket; lobster bisque; friendly international staff. *Average main: $25 ✉ 3225 Rte. 6, Greater Wellfleet ☎ 508/349–9795 🌐 www.mobydicks-restaurant.com ⏲ Closed Tues. Closed mid-Oct.–Apr.*

★ PB Boulangerie Bistro

$$ | FRENCH | Once a clam shack, this bistro has found new life and won legions of fans in this seaside town selling just-baked breads and succulent pastries—by early morning (even in off-season) the line snakes into the parking lot. There's outdoor and indoor seating for breakfast, lunch, and dinner; the latter is a three-course prix-fixe meal ($95) that changes with the seasons, featuring locally sourced produce that highlights the finer flavors of this French kitchen. **Known for:** delectable French pastries; fresh bread; authentic French experience. *Average main: $20 ✉ 15 LeCount Hollow Rd., South Wellfleet ☎ 508/349–1600 🌐 www.pbboulangeriebistro.com ⏲ Closed Mon. and Tues. Bistro closed in winter.*

PJ's Family Restaurant

$$$ | SEAFOOD | FAMILY | For more than 50 years, this family-run seafood and ice cream shack has been serving hungry vacationers. It's a go-to joint for a quick post-beach dinner (or pre-beach lunch) with a menu that goes beyond the usual deep-fried items: Options include broiled seafood plates, hot and cold lobster rolls, and 15 different salads. **Known for:** onion rings; lobster rolls; broiled scallops. *Average main: $28 ✉ 2616 Route 6, Greater Wellfleet ☎ 508/349–2126 🌐 www.pjscapecod.com ⏲ Closed Wed. Closed mid-Sept.–May.*

Hotels

Even'tide

$$ | HOTEL | FAMILY | Long a summer favorite, this peaceful motel is set back from the main road, surrounded by 5 acres of trees and lawns, which include a 60-foot indoor pool. **Pros:** short drive or bike ride to Wellfleet's beaches; suites are a bargain for families; direct access to Cape Cod Rail Trail. **Cons:** need a car to get downtown; motel-style rooms; no dining venues. *Rooms from: $200 ✉ 650 Rte. 6, South Wellfleet ☎ 508/349–3410, 800/368–0007 🌐 www.eventide-motel.com ⏲ Closed mid-Oct.–Apr. 31 rooms, 9 cottages No Meals ☞ 1-wk minimum for cottages in summer.*

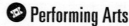

Performing Arts

FILM

★ Wellfleet Drive-In Theater

FILM | FAMILY | A classic Cape experience is the Wellfleet Drive-In Theater, located near the Eastham town line. Regulars spend the night in style: chairs, blankets, and picnic baskets. Films start at dusk nightly May–September, and there's also a standard indoor cinema with four screens, a miniature-golf course, and a bar and grill. It's also the home of the beloved Wellfleet Flea Market, held weekends late spring–mid-October. *✉ 51 U.S. 6, South Wellfleet ☎ 508/349–7176 🌐 www.wellfleetcinemas.com.*

What the Shark?

In 2018, Massachusetts had its first fatal shark attack since 1936—only the fourth recorded in the state's history—when a young man was killed in the waters off Wellfleet. Unfortunately, shark sightings have increased every year. One of the major factors is the increase in the protected seal population on the outer Cape—more seals, means more sharks coming to eat. People share the waters with these native inhabitants and our greatest defense is education and common sense.

Be Shark Smart

A good rule of thumb is, don't swim where there are seals. Avoid murky water and areas where there's evidence of fish feeding. Make sure you pay attention to all signs at the beaches and if the lifeguards say get out of the water, definitely listen. And, keep an eye out for the purple flag, because if it's flying, white sharks are in the area. Visit the Atlantic White Shark Conservancy's website 🌐 www.atlanticwhiteshark.org for more information.

THEATER

Wellfleet Harbor Actors Theater

THEATER | The well-regarded Wellfleet Harbor Actors Theater continues its tradition, since 1985, of producing provocative, often edgy, world premieres of American plays, satires, farces, and black comedies in its mid-May–late-September season. In July and August there are productions aimed for kids, held under a white tent. From October to April, opera lovers can watch performances from the Met, live in HD. ✉ *2357 U.S. 6, Greater Wellfleet* ☎ *508/349–9428* 🌐 *www.what.org.*

Activities

BOATING

Jack's Boat Rental

BOATING | Jack's rents canoes, kayaks, Sunfish sailboats, surfboards, SUPs, and large floating mats. Free delivery is available for rentals within Wellfleet; delivery is available for Provincetown and Brewster (fee.) Delivery is required for Sunfish sailboats due to size. With all rentals, the third day is free. ✉ *2616 Rte. 6, at Cahoon Hollow Rd., Greater Wellfleet* ☎ *508/349–9808* 🌐 *www.jacksboatrental.com* ⏲ *Closed late-Sept.-late May.*

Truro

13 miles north of Eastham, 9½ miles southeast of Provincetown.

Today Truro is a town of wind-swept dunes, expansive shorelines, and protected estuaries fringed by beach grass and rolling moors. It's a popular retreat for artists, writers, politicos, and those seeking a quiet escape. Edward Hopper summered here from 1930 to 1967, finding the Cape light ideal for his austere brand of realism. One of the largest towns on the Cape in terms of land area—about 43 miles—Truro is also the Cape's narrowest town. From a high perch you can see the Atlantic Ocean on one side and Cape Cod Bay on the other.

If you thought neighboring Wellfleet's downtown area was small, wait till you see (or don't see) Truro's. It consists of a post office, a town hall, and a shop or two—you'll know it by the sign that says "Downtown Truro" at a little plaza entrance. Truro also has a library, a firehouse, and a police station, but that's about all. The North Truro section contains most of the town's accommodations, either along U.S. 6 or fronting the bay along Route 6A, just south of the Provincetown border. Many people who live (about 2,400 year-round residents) or vacation in Truro choose it for its easygoing, quiet personality and lack of development. Its proximity to the excitement and commerce of Provincetown and Wellfleet is also a plus.

Settled in 1697, Truro has had several names during its long history. It was originally called Payomet or Pamet after the local Native Americans who inhabited the area before the pilgrims settled. In 1705 the name was changed to Dangerfield in response to all the sailing mishaps offshore. "Truroe" was the final choice, named for a Cornish town that homesick settlers thought it resembled; the final "e" was eventually dropped. Although sleepy and rural now, the town once bustled with activity related to the sea: whaling, shipbuilding, and cod fishing were the main industries.

GETTING HERE AND AROUND

Truro sits near the end of Cape Cod, just 2 miles north of Wellfleet. U.S. 6 is the way most people reach Truro, though the real beauty of the town lies farther afield on back roads that lead to either Cape Cod Bay or the Atlantic. The Cape is quite narrow here, so you will never find yourself hopelessly lost.

The Provincetown/North Truro Shuttle, run by the Cape Cod Regional Transit Authority, provides a much-needed transportation boost. Traveling along Route 6A, it stops wherever a passenger requests; it runs every 30 minutes and can haul bicycles.

Sights

Highland House Museum

HISTORY MUSEUM | Home to the Truro Historical Society, the 1907 Highland House was once a grand summer hotel in its time, boasting of many private rooms, meals, and even one shared indoor bathroom. Now a museum, each season a new exhibition highlights Truro's rich history; upstairs you can see how early settlers lived and the unique industries they created to survive. There is also a room dedicated to Edward and Jo Hopper and their art and lives in Truro. Throughout the summer, talks, live music events, and children's programs are offered. ✉ *6 Highland Light Rd., Truro* ☎ *508/487–3397* 🌐 *www.trurohistoricalsociety.org* 🎫 *$8* ⏲ *Closed Sun. and Mon. and closed Oct.–May.*

Highland Light

LIGHTHOUSE | Truly a breathtaking sight, this is the Cape's oldest lighthouse. The first light on this site, powered by 24 whale-oil lamps, began warning ships of Truro's treacherous sandbars in 1797—the dreaded Peaked Hills Bars, to the north, had claimed hundreds of ships. The current light, a 66-foot tower built in 1857, is powered by two 1,000-watt bulbs reflected by a huge Fresnel lens; its beacon is visible for more than 20 miles.

One of four active lighthouses on the Outer Cape, Highland Light has the distinction of being listed in the National Register of Historic Places. Henry David Thoreau used it as a stopover in his travels across the Cape's backside (as the Atlantic side is called). Twenty-five-minute tours of the lighthouse are given daily in summer; especially grand are the special full-moon tours. Children must be 48 inches tall to enter. ✉ *27 Highland Light Rd., Truro* ☎ *508/404-9117* 🌐 *www.highlandlighthouse.org* 🎫 *$4* ⏲ *Closed mid-Oct.–mid-May.*

★ Truro Vineyards of Cape Cod

WINERY | Owned and operated by the Roberts family, this vineyard has greatly stepped up production, and has begun experimenting with some new varieties. The vineyard makes several notable blends, both red and white. It also makes a red table wine that's flavored with cranberries and known for its unusual bottle, shaped like a lighthouse. There is also an aged rum, whiskey, and gin distillery on the property, South Hollow Spirits, which produces organic spirits; tours and tastings available. There are many excellent wine and food events scheduled throughout the summer. It's a great place to picnic, and there's a resident food truck on-site. ✉ *11 Shore Rd. Rte. 6A, Truro* ☎ *508/487–6200* 🌐 *www.turovineyardsofcapecod.com* 🎫 *Free.*

Beaches

Parking at some of Truro's town beaches is reserved for residents and renters in season, although anyone can walk or bicycle in. Truro has several accessible beaches stretched along Cape Cod Bay. All are beautiful and ideal for long, lazy days of watching boats go by and taking in views of Provincetown in the distance. On the ocean side, a few spectacular beaches are marked by massive dunes and bracing surf. Renters can purchase a weekly ($50) or seasonal ($225) beach sticker with a proof-of-stay form from the property owner.

Performing Arts

Payomet Performing Arts Center of Truro
ARTS CENTERS | FAMILY | From mid-June through late September, the Payomet Performing Arts Center of Truro presents a wide range of concerts, plays, films, music, and classes inside a big tent at Cape Cod National Seashore. Past performers have included Tom Rush, the Cowboy Junkies, and Ladysmith Black Mambazo. There's also a kids' circus camp, and Cirque by the Sea professional circus shows for families. ✉ *29 Old Dewline Rd., Truro* ☎ *508/349–2929* 🌐 *www.payomet.org.*

Provincetown

9 miles northwest of Wellfleet, 62 miles from Sagamore Bridge.

Many people know that the Pilgrims stopped here at the curved tip of Cape Cod before proceeding to Plymouth. Historical records suggest that an earlier visitor, Thorvald, brother of Viking Leif Erikson, came ashore here in AD 1004 to repair the keel of his boat and consequently named the area Kjalarness, or Cape of the Keel. In 1602, Bartholomew Gosnold came to Provincetown and named the area Cape Cod after the abundant codfish he found in the local waters.

Incorporated as a town in 1727, Provincetown was for many decades a bustling seaport, with fishing and whaling as its major industries. In the late 19th century, groups of Portuguese fishermen and whalers began to settle here, lending their expertise and culture to an already cosmopolitan town. Fishing is still an important source of income for many Provincetown locals, but today the town ranks among the world's leading whale-watching—rather than whale-hunting—outposts.

Artists began to arrive in the late 1890s to take advantage of the unusual Cape Cod light; in fact, Provincetown is the nation's oldest continuous art colony. By 1916, with five art schools flourishing here, painters' easels were nearly as common as shells on the beach. This bohemian community, along with the availability of inexpensive summer lodgings, attracted young rebels, as well as writers like John Reed (*Ten Days That Shook the World*) and Mary Heaton Vorse (*Footnote to Folly*), who in 1915 began the Cape's first significant theater group, the Provincetown Players. The young, then unknown Eugene O'Neill joined them in 1916, when his *Bound East for Cardiff* premiered in a tiny wharf-side East End fish house.

America's original gay resort, Provincetown today is as appealing to artists as it is to gay and lesbian—as well as straight—tourists. Massachusetts's legalization of same-sex marriage (the first state in the nation to do so) and a full calendar of events tailored to the LBGTQ population, has enhanced the town's reputation as the most visibly gay vacation community in America.

GETTING HERE AND AROUND

You're at the end of the line here, which means driving to Provincetown in the height of summer often means slogging through slow traffic. Congestion is heaviest around Wellfleet and it can be slow going. Driving the 3 miles of Provincetown's main downtown thoroughfare, Commercial Street, in season could take forever. No matter, there are plenty of pretty vistas on the way along U.S. 6 and Route 6A. Parking is not one of Provincetown's better amenities (there are two large, paid central parking lots if you can find a space), so bike and foot are the best and most popular ways to explore the downtown area. But Provincetown can also be reached by air (year-round via Cape Air from Boston) or ferry (multiple options from Boston in season).

The Provincetown/North Truro Shuttle, run by the Cape Cod Regional Transit Authority, provides a much-needed seasonal transportation boost in season. Once in Provincetown, the shuttle heads up Bradford Street, with stops at First Pilgrim Park and Herring Cove Beach, Province Lands Visitor Center, Race Point Beach, and the Provincetown Airport. A limited number of bikes are accommodated.

BUS CONTACTS Cape Cod Regional Transit Authority. ✉ *1 Transportation Ave., Provincetown* ☎ *508/775–8504* 🌐 *www.capecodrta.org.*

VISITOR INFORMATION

CONTACTS Provincetown Business Guild. ☎ *508/487–2313* 🌐 *www.ptown.org.* **Provincetown Chamber of Commerce.** ☎ *508/487–3424* 🌐 *www.ptownchamber.com.*

Sights

★ Commercial Street

STREET | Take a casual stroll by the many architectural styles—Greek Revival, Victorian, Second Empire, and Gothic, to name a few—used in the design of the impressive houses for wealthy sea captains and merchants. The center of town is where you'll find the crowds and the best people-watching, especially if you try to find an empty spot on the benches in front of the exquisitely renovated Town Hall. The East End has a number of nationally renowned galleries; the West End has a number of small inns with neat lawns and elaborate gardens. There is one-way vehicle traffic on this street, though pedestrians dominate the pavement, particularly in July and August. Commercial Street runs parallel to the water, so there is always a patch of sand close at hand, should you need a break. ✉ *Provincetown* 🌐 *ptowntourism.com.*

Pilgrim Monument and Provincetown Museum

MONUMENT | The first thing you'll see in Provincetown is this grandiose edifice, somewhat out of proportion to the rest of the low-rise town. The monument commemorates the Pilgrims' first landing in the New World and their signing of the Mayflower Compact (the first colonial rules of self-governance in what would become the United States) before they set off to explore the mainland. Climb the 116 steps and 60 short ramps of the 252-foot-high tower for a panoramic view—dunes on one side, harbor on the other, and the entire bay side of Cape Cod beyond. At the tower's base is a museum of Lower Cape and Provincetown history, with exhibits on whaling, shipwrecks, and scrimshaw. There are also arrowheads, tools, and images of the local Native American Wampanoag tribe, the town's first fire engine, a recreation of a 19th-century sea captain's parlor, a diorama of the Mayflower Compact being signed, and more. Admission includes both the museum and monument. ✉ *1 High Pole Hill Rd., Downtown Center* ☎ *508/487–1310* 🌐 *www.pilgrim-monument.org* 🎫 *$20.94* 🕐 *Closed Tues. and Wed.*

★ Province Lands Visitor Center

VISITOR CENTER | Part of the Cape Cod National Seashore, the Province Lands stretch from High Head in Truro to the tip of Provincetown and are scattered with ponds, cranberry bogs, and scrub. More than 7 miles of bike and walking trails lace through forests of stunted pines, beech, and oak and across desert-like expanses of rolling dunes. At the visitor center you'll find short films on local geology and exhibits on the life of the dunes and the shore. You can also pick up information on guided walks, birding trips, lectures, and other programs, as well as on the Province Lands' pristine beaches, Race Point and Herring Cove, and walking, biking, and horse trails. Don't miss the awe-inspiring panoramic view of the dunes and the surrounding ocean from the observation deck. This terrain provides optimal conditions for the deer tick, which can cause Lyme disease, so use extra caution. ✉ *171 Race Point Rd., east of U.S. 6, Greater Provincetown* ☎ *508/487–1256* 🌐 *www.nps.gov/caco* 🎫 *Free* 🕒 *Visitor center closed Nov.–Apr.*

★ Provincetown Art Association and Museum

ART MUSEUM | Founded in 1914 to collect and exhibit the works of artists with Provincetown connections, this facility has a 1,650-piece permanent collection, displayed in changing exhibitions that mix up-and-comers with established 20th-century figures like Milton Avery, Philip Evergood, William Gropper, Charles Hawthorne, Robert Motherwell, Claes Oldenburg, Man Ray, John Singer Sargent, Andy Warhol, and Agnes Weinrich. A stunning contemporary wing has greatly expanded the exhibit space. The museum store carries books of local interest, including works by or about area artists and authors, as well as posters, crafts, cards, and gift items. Art classes (single day and longer) offer the opportunity to study under such talents as Hilda Neily, Selina Trieff, and Doug Ritter. ✉ *460 Commercial St., East End* ☎ *508/487–1750* 🌐 *www.paam.org* 🎫 *$15* 🕒 *Closed Tues. Nov.–April.*

Beaches

Herring Cove Beach

BEACH | FAMILY | Herring Cove Beach is relatively calm and warm for a National Seashore beach, but it's not as pretty as some because its parking lot isn't hidden behind dunes. It's close to town, so in warm weather it's always crowded. The lot to the right of the bathhouse is a great place to watch the sunset. **■ TIP→ Daily parking is $25; the annual seashore pass grants access to all six national park beaches and costs $60. Amenities:** food and drink; lifeguards; parking (fee); toilets; showers. **Best for:** sunset; swimming; walking. ✉ *Provincetown* 🌐 *www.nps.gov/caco* 🎫 *From late June–Labor Day and weekends and holidays from Memorial Day to mid-Sept. $25 per vehicle, $15 per person.*

★ Race Point Beach

BEACH | FAMILY | Race Point Beach, one of the Cape Cod National Seashore beaches in Provincetown, has a wide swath of sand stretching far off into the distance around the point and Coast Guard station. Because of its position facing north, the beach gets sun all day long. Keep an eye out for whales offshore; it's also a popular fishing spot. **■ TIP→ Daily parking is $25; the annual seashore pass grants access to all six national park beaches for $60. Amenities:** lifeguards; parking (fee); showers; toilets. **Best for:** sunrise; sunset; surfing; swimming; walking. ✉ *Race Point Rd., east of U.S. 6, Provincetown* ☎ *508/487–1256* 🌐 *www.nps.gov/caco* 🎫 *From late June–Labor Day and weekends and holidays from Memorial Day to mid-Sept. $25 per vehicle, $15 per person.*

Restaurants

★ The Canteen

$ | AMERICAN | This casual spot specializes in classics like grilled cheese sandwiches, hand-cut fries, and local seafood in a lively spot. Order at the counter, then grab a seat inside or at one of the several outdoor seating options; there's also a large beer menu with New England offerings, a good selection of wines, and fun cocktails. **Known for:** hot or cold lobster rolls; raw bar; great atmosphere out back. *Average main: $13* *225 Commercial St., Downtown Center* *508/487–3800* *www.thecanteenptown.com.*

★ The Lobster Pot

$$$$ | **SEAFOOD** | Provincetown's Lobster Pot, a mainstay for more than 40 years, is fit to do battle with all the lobster shanties anywhere (and everywhere) else on the Cape; although it's often jammed with tourists, the crowds reflect the generally high quality, and the water views can't be beat. The hardworking kitchen turns out classic New England cooking: lobsters, generous and filling seafood platters, and some of the best chowder around. **Known for:** award-winning clam chowder; local icon; extensive menu. *Average main: $35* *321 Commercial St., Downtown Center* *508/487–0842* *www.ptownlobsterpot.com* *Closed in winter.*

★ The Mews Restaurant & Cafe

$$$$ | **AMERICAN** | This perennial favorite with magnificent harbor views focuses on local seafood and organic meat and produce with a cross-cultural flair (there's also a lighter bistro menu for smaller appetites). The view of the bay from the bar is nearly perfect, and the gentle lighting makes this a romantic spot to have a drink. **Known for:** waterfront setting; ambience; two levels of dining. *Average main: $35* *429 Commercial St., East End* *508/487–1500* *mewsptown.com* *Closed Sun. and Mon.*

Napi's

$$$ | **ECLECTIC** | The food and the interior share a penchant for unusual, striking juxtapositions—a classical sculpture in front of an abstract canvas, for instance, or an artful plate of boneless chicken and scallops in Thai peanut sauce arrayed on a bed of lo mein noodles. The art collection on display here is significant, and includes many noted Provincetown artists; the late Napi Van Dereck and his wife Helen collected gems for many, many years. **Known for:** seafood stew; free parking for patrons; ample vegetarian options. *Average main: $35* *7 Freeman St., Downtown Center* *508/487–1145* *www.napisptown.com* *Closed Mon.*

★ The Pointe

$$$ | **AMERICAN** | Inside the snazzy Crowne Pointe Inn, this intimate, casually handsome restaurant occupies the parlor and sunroom of a grand sea captain's mansion and serves finely crafted, healthful, modern American food with daily specials focused on local ingredients. There's a substantial wine list, with more than a 125 selections to choose from, as well as a large martini menu. **Known for:** superb service; cocktails in the lounge; truffle popcorn. *Average main: $30* *Crowne Pointe Inn, 82 Bradford St., Downtown Center* *508/487–2365* *www.provincetown-restaurant.com* *Closed Mon.–Wed. No lunch.*

Provincetown Brewing Co.

$$ | **AMERICAN** | This fun and funky establishment offers a range of craft beers and bar food in a convivial space. Relax with a Double Rainbow IPA or nonalcoholic kombucha on a comfy couch inside, or bring Fido and sit on the pet-friendly patio. **Known for:** friendly service; great brews; great sandwiches. *Average main: $16* *141 Bradford St., Downtown Center* *508/413–9076* *www.provincetownbrewingco.com.*

Hotels

★ The Brass Key Guesthouse

$$$$ | **B&B/INN** | One of the Cape's most luxurious small resorts, this meticulously kept year-round getaway comprises a beautifully restored main house—originally a sea captain's home built in 1828—and several other carefully groomed buildings and cottages all centered on a beautifully landscaped pool area. **Pros:** ultraposh

rooms; beautiful and secluded grounds; pool on-site. **Cons:** among the highest rates in town; not for those with children; significant minimum-stay requirements in summer. *Rooms from: $400 67 Bradford St., Downtown Center 508/487–9005, 800/842–9858 www.brasskey.com 43 rooms Free Breakfast*

Pets allowed in certain rooms.

★ Crowne Pointe Historic Inn and Spa

$$$$ | **B&B/INN** | Created meticulously from six different buildings, this inn hasn't a single detail left unattended—period furniture and antiques fill common areas and guest rooms; a queen-size bed is the smallest you'll find, dressed in 300-thread-count linens; treats are left on the pillow for nightly turndown service; and there's complimentary wine and cheese in the afternoon. **Pros:** great on-site amenities like the full-service Shui Spa; posh and luxurious room decor; professional and well-trained staff. **Cons:** among the highest rates in town in season; significant minimum-stay requirements in summer; no children allowed. *Rooms from: $340 82 Bradford St., Downtown Center 508/413–2213, 877/276–9631 www.crownepointe.com 40 rooms Free Breakfast.*

Salt House Inn

$$ | **B&B/INN** | Though one side of this aged beauty sits right on busy Conwell Street, the interior is all serenity, bathed in white, an ideal backdrop for the brilliant wood floors, statement furniture, and art pieces—think Colonial farmhouse with a decidedly modern and hip edge. **Pros:** in-town location, walk to everything; on-site concierge service is extremely helpful; on-site complimentary parking. **Cons:** some rooms are quite small; one room is extremely close to the road; some rooms with detached (but private) bathroom. *Rooms from: $275 6 Conwell St., Downtown Center 508/487–1911 www.salthouseinn.com Closed Nov.–Mar. 15 rooms Free Breakfast.*

★ White Porch Inn

$$$ | **B&B/INN** | This sterling, light-filled B&B offers a soothing respite from the bustle of town; opt for one of the carriage-house rooms for even more seclusion. **Pros:** wine hour on summer weekends; open year-round; enthusiastic and friendly staff. **Cons:** somewhat long walk to West End shopping and businesses; not for those with children; limited parking. *Rooms from: $299 7 Johnson St., Downtown Center 508/364–2549, 508/487–0592 www.whiteporchinn.com 10 rooms Free Breakfast.*

Nightlife

Provincetown is a party town. While the nightclub scene is decidedly gay, in most venues there is a clear "straight-friendly" welcome.

BARS

Atlantic House

DANCE CLUBS | Atlantic House, aka A-House, is the grandfather of the gay nightlife scene. With a dance club and two other bars, there's something for everyone here. *4 - 6 Masonic Pl., Downtown Center 508/487–3169 www.ahouse.com.*

Boatslip

DANCE CLUBS | The Tea Dance at the Boatslip is a real Provincetown tradition. From early May through October, the music starts at 4, and the crowds (mostly men) gather around the pool to start the night dancing, drinking, and merrymaking until 7. The music and cover charge vary (there is always a cover), but a real favorite is the Solid Gold Tea, spinning dance classics from the 1970s and '80s. *161 Commercial St., Provincetown 508/487–1669 www.boatslipresort.com.*

Paramount

DANCE CLUBS | Part of the Crown & Anchor complex of entertainment options, the Paramount is the hotel's main nightlife venue, offering poolside dancing to skilled DJs—including many names from the top international dance scene—on many nights. It's also host to cabaret performances and live theater. Next door is a video bar and a male-only leather bar, The Vault. Cover charges vary. ✉ *247 Commercial St., Downtown Center* ☎ *508/487–1430* 🌐 *www.onlyatthecrown.com/paramount.*

Performing Arts

During the busy summer season, hawkers in full-on drag (or wearing very little) compete with the din on Commercial Street to announce showtimes of the evening's performances. Pick your pleasure: dancing poolside at a few big nightclubs; watching talented drag performers strut their stuff; enjoying excellent live theater; strolling between art galleries; or sipping colorful cocktails at the water's edge. Much of the summer entertainment is first-class, drawing top Broadway and cabaret performers from New York City and beyond, offered at prices that would be a bargain back home.

THEATER

Post Office Cafe & Cabaret

MUSIC | Downstairs, it's a lively place for a meal (open for breakfast, lunch, and dinner), with tables facing Commercial Street that offer great people-watching. Upstairs, you can expect even jauntier—and often playfully raunchy—entertainment in the nightly cabaret offerings and popular drag shows on weekends. ✉ *303 Commercial St., Downtown Center* ☎ *508/487–0008* 🌐 *www.postofficecafe.net* ⏲ *Closed mid.-Dec.–Mar.*

The Provincetown Theater

THEATER | This year-round venue provides excellent theater, showcasing many new works, as well as more unusual fare. In addition, they host dance performances, readings by playwrights, and workshops. ✉ *238 Bradford St., East End* ☎ *508/487–7487* 🌐 *www.provincetowntheater.org.*

Activities

TOURS

★ Art's Dune Tours

FOUR-WHEELING | Art's Dune Tours has been taking eager passengers into the dunes of the Province Lands since 1946. A bumpy but controlled ride (about one hour) transports you through sometimes surreal sandy vistas peppered with beach grass, along a shoreline patrolled by seagulls and sandpipers. Head out at sunset for a stunning ride, available with or without a provided dinner and bonfire. Dune and water tours are further options. ✉ *4 Standish St., Downtown Center* ☎ *508/487–1950, 800/894–1951* 🌐 *www.artsdunetours.com* 🎟 *From $37; must call to reserve* ⏲ *Closed Nov.–Apr.*

WHALE-WATCHING

★ Dolphin Fleet

WILDLIFE-WATCHING | **FAMILY** | Tours are led by scientists from the Center for Coastal Studies in Provincetown, who provide commentary while collecting data on the whales they've been monitoring for years. They know many of them by name and will tell you about their habits and histories. These trips are most often exciting and incredibly thrilling, with close-up encounters. ■ **TIP→ Look for discount coupons in local free brochures and publications, as well as online.** ✉ *Chamber of Commerce Bldg., MacMillan Wharf, Downtown Center* ☎ *508/240–3636, 800/826–9300* 🌐 *www.whalewatch.com* 🎟 *$70.*

Shopping

Provincetown shopping can be artistic, sophisticated, whimsical, and even downright tawdry—a perfect reflection of the town's very character. There is also a wide selection of touristy schlock. You'll find exquisite original art galleries primarily on the east end but also next to taffy and fudge shops, high-end home decor and designer clothing boutiques next to tattoo parlors and T-shirt shops, and even boutiques specializing in alternative interests (think leather and adult novelties). Most shopping is concentrated along Commercial Street.

ART GALLERIES

★ Julie Heller Galleries

ART GALLERIES | Heller's two galleries—one on Commercial Street, and one on the beach on Gosnold Street—offer exhibitions of both historic and contemporary paintings and sculpture, featuring some of Provincetown's most influential and innovative artists. Included in the collection are Milton Avery, Oliver Chaffee, Nanno de Groot, Charles Hawthorne, Henry Hensche, Hans Hoffman, Blanche Lazzell, Ross Moffett, Robert Motherwell, Alvin Ross, and William Zorach, along with a roster of contemporary artists. ✉ *465 Commercial St., Downtown Center* ☎ *508/487–2169* 🌐 *www.juliehellergallery.com.*

The Schoolhouse Gallery

ART GALLERIES | This gallery, in an 1844 former school, shows the works of more than 50 local and national artists (modern and contemporary), as well as that of printmakers and photographers. ✉ *494 Commercial St., East End* ☎ *508/487–4800* 🌐 *galleryschoolhouse.com.*

SPECIALTY STORES

Marine Specialties

OTHER SPECIALTY STORE | Marine Specialties is full of treasures, knickknacks, and clothing. Here you can purchase some very reasonably priced casual- and military-style clothing, as well as seashells, marine supplies, stained-glass lamps, candles, rubber sharks (you get the idea), and prints of old advertisements. ✉ *235 Commercial St., Downtown Center* ☎ *508/487–1730* 🕓 *Closed Jan.–Mar.*

Tim's Used Books

BOOKS | Set back off the street at the end of a wooden walkway, this fantastic little slice of literary heaven is packed with volumes upon volumes—rooms of used-but-in-good-shape books, including some rare and out-of-print texts. It's a great place to lose track of time year-round. ✉ *242 Commercial St., Downtown Center* ☎ *508/487–0005.*

Martha's Vineyard

Far less developed than Cape Cod—thanks to the local conservation organizations—yet more cosmopolitan than neighboring Nantucket, Martha's Vineyard is an island with a double life. From Memorial Day through Labor Day, the quieter (some might say the real) Vineyard quickens into a vibrant, star-studded place.

The busy main port, Vineyard Haven, welcomes day-trippers fresh off ferries and private yachts to browse in its array of shops. Oak Bluffs, where pizza and ice-cream emporiums reign supreme, has the air of a Victorian boardwalk. Edgartown is flooded with seekers of chic who wander tiny streets that hold boutiques, stately whaling captains' homes, and charming inns.

Summer regulars have included a host of celebrities over the years, among them Oprah Winfrey, Carly Simon, Ted Danson, Spike Lee, and Diane Sawyer; former president Barack Obama and his family vacationed here nearly every summer of his two terms in the Oval Office and bought a vacation home on the island. If you're planning to stay overnight on a summer weekend, be sure to make reservations well in advance. Things stay busy on September and October weekends, a favorite time for weddings, but begin to slow down soon after. In many ways the Vineyard's off-season persona is even more appealing than its summer self, with more time to linger over pastoral and ocean vistas, free from the throngs of cars, bicycles, and mopeds.

GETTING ORIENTED

The island is roughly triangular, measuring about 20 miles east to west and 10 miles north to south. The west end of the Vineyard, known as Up-Island—from the nautical expression of going "up" in degrees of longitude as you sail west—is more rural and wild than the eastern Down-Island end, comprising Vineyard Haven, Oak Bluffs, and Edgartown.

Vineyard Haven (Tisbury). One of the island's busiest towns, Vineyard Haven receives ferry traffic all year long. A fairly compact downtown area keeps most shopping and dining options within easy reach.

Oak Bluffs. Once a Methodist campground, Oak Bluffs is a little less refined than the other towns. It has a vibrant vacation vibe, with lots of nightlife, dining, and shopping.

Edgartown. Dominated by the impeccably kept homes of 19th-century sea captains, Edgartown has a sense of sophistication. There's great history here, and several museums tell the story.

Chappaquiddick Island. Take the tiny ferry from Edgartown to explore Chappaquiddick Island's vast nature preserves. It's a favorite place for bird-watchers and anglers.

West Tisbury. There's beautiful farm country out this way, and the 1859 Grange Hall is still the center of action. During the warmer months, don't miss the bountiful West Tisbury Farmers' Market.

Menemsha. An active fishing harbor, Menemsha is known for its splendid sunsets. There are a few shops and galleries, and a couple of excellent take-out spots for the freshest of seafood.

Aquinnah. Formerly known as Gay Head, Aquinnah is famous for its grand and dramatic red clay cliffs, as well as the resident lighthouse.

AIR

Cape Air has regular, year-round flight service to the island from Hyannis, Boston, and Providence's T. F. Green Airport and seasonal service (starting mid-June) from White Plains, NY (including a bus transfer to and from Manhattan). JetBlue provides seasonal nonstop service from New York–JFK; Delta offers seasonal service from New York-LaGuardia, and American Airlines offers the route between Washington, DC and Martha's Vineyard seasonally as well.

BUS

Once on the island, the Martha's Vineyard Transit Authority (VTA) provides regular service to all six towns on the island, including stops at all ferry landings and the airport. The buses can accommodate three bicycles on an exterior rack on a first-come, first-served basis, and the island has an excellent network of well-maintained bike trails. The VTA also has free in-town shuttle-bus routes in Edgartown and Vineyard Haven (summer only). You can also get around by bicycle (rentals are available) and by taxi (an expensive option), Uber, and Lyft.

BUS CONTACTS Martha's Vineyard Transit Authority. *(VTA)* ☎ *508/693–9440* 🌐 *www.vineyardtransit.com.*

CAR

Although traffic can be bad during the season, it can be handy to have a car in order to see all of Martha's Vineyard and travel freely. Instead of bringing one over on the Steamship Authority ferry from Woods Hole (the only ferry service that transports cars—expensively), it's sometimes easier and more economical to rent one once you're on the island for a few days of exploring, particularly during the busy season when car reservations on the ferry are hard to come by. Don't expect a bargain for on-island rentals either; you'll pay about $200 per day for an SUV. The island does its best to discourage extra automobile traffic.

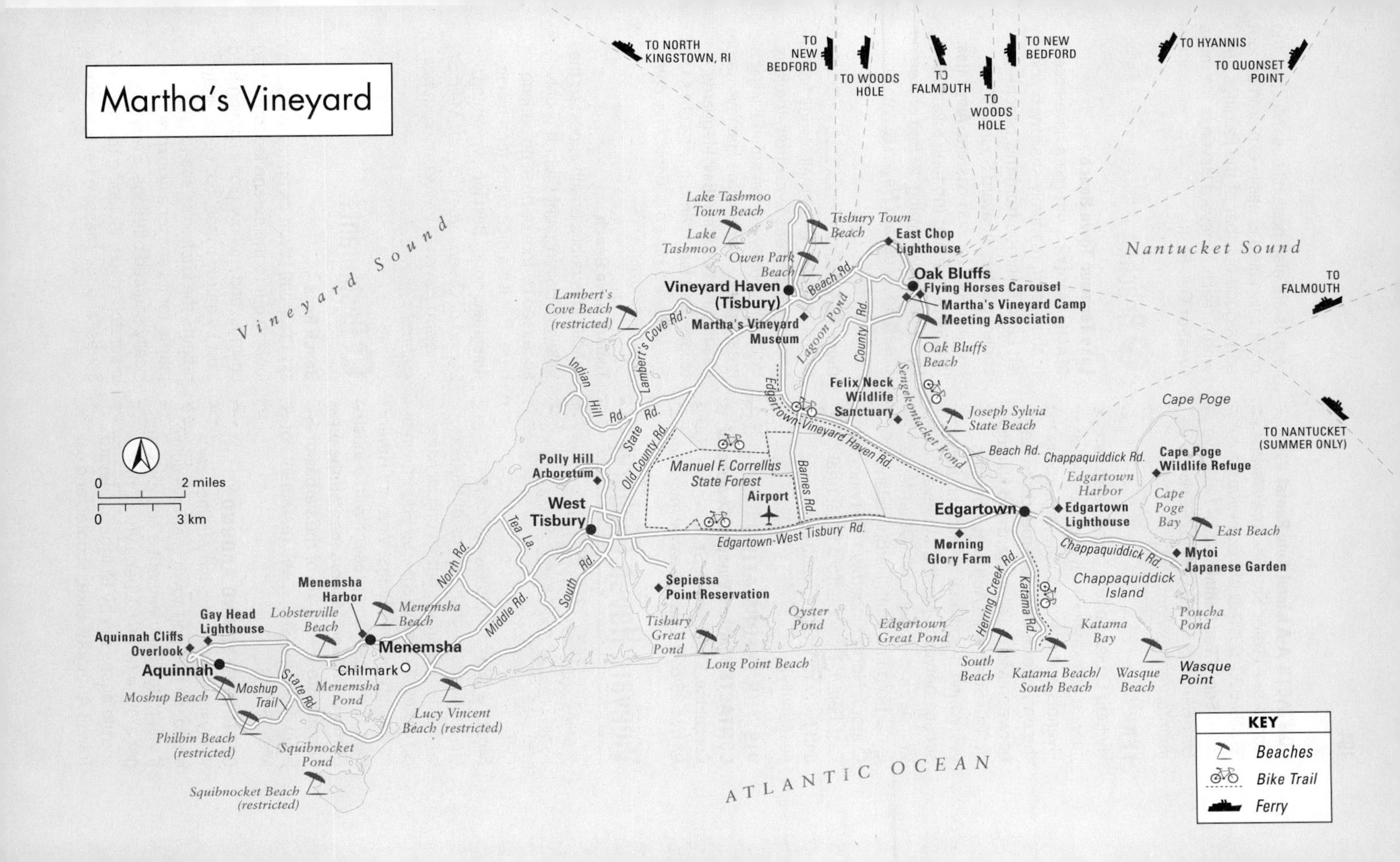

Martha's Vineyard

TO NORTH KINGSTOWN, RI
TO NEW BEDFORD
TO WOODS HOLE
TO FALMOUTH
TO WOODS HOLE
TO NEW BEDFORD
TO HYANNIS
TO QUONSET POINT
TO FALMOUTH
TO NANTUCKET (SUMMER ONLY)

Vineyard Sound
Nantucket Sound
ATLANTIC OCEAN

Lake Tashmoo Town Beach
Lake Tashmoo
Tisbury Town Beach
Owen Park Beach
East Chop Lighthouse
Oak Bluffs
Flying Horses Carousel
Martha's Vineyard Camp Meeting Association
Oak Bluffs Beach
Vineyard Haven (Tisbury)
Martha's Vineyard Museum
Beach Rd.
Lagoon Pond
County Rd.
Lambert's Cove Beach (restricted)
Lambert's Cove Rd.
Indian Hill Rd.
State Rd.
Old County Rd.
Edgartown-Vineyard Haven Rd.
Felix Neck Wildlife Sanctuary
Sengekontacket Pond
Joseph Sylvia State Beach
Beach Rd.
Cape Poge
Chappaquiddick Rd.
Cape Poge Wildlife Refuge
Edgartown Harbor
Cape Poge Bay
Edgartown Lighthouse
East Beach
Polly Hill Arboretum
Manuel F. Correllus State Forest
Barnes Rd.
Airport
West Tisbury
Tea La.
Edgartown-West Tisbury Rd.
Edgartown
Morning Glory Farm
Chappaquiddick Rd.
Mytoi Japanese Garden
Chappaquiddick Island
North Rd.
Middle Rd.
South Rd.
Sepiessa Point Reservation
Herring Creek Rd.
Katama Rd.
Menemsha Harbor
Menemsha Beach
Gay Head Lighthouse
Lobsterville Beach
Menemsha
Aquinnah Cliffs Overlook
Aquinnah
Chilmark
Moshup Trail
State Rd.
Menemsha Pond
Moshup Beach
Tisbury Great Pond
Oyster Pond
Long Point Beach
Edgartown Great Pond
Poucha Pond
Katama Bay
South Beach
Katama Beach/ South Beach
Wasque Beach
Wasque Point
Lucy Vincent Beach (restricted)
Philbin Beach (restricted)
Squibnocket Pond
Squibnocket Beach (restricted)

0 2 miles
0 3 km

KEY
Beaches
Bike Trail
Ferry

CONTACTS A-A Island Auto Rental. ✉ *5 Corners, 4 Water St., Vineyard Haven* ☎ *508/696–5300* 🌐 *www.mvautorental.com.* **Sun 'n' Fun Rentals.** ✉ *28 Lake Ave., Oak Bluffs* ☎ *508/693–5457* 🌐 *www.sunnfunrentals.com.*

FERRY

Hy-Line Cruises offers high-speed ferry service seasonally (May-Oct.) between Hyannis and Martha's Vineyard, and is the only line to offer year-round service between Martha's Vineyard and Nantucket. The Steamship Authority operates year-round, traditional steamship ferry service between Martha's Vineyard and Woods Hole (Cape Cod). Other ferries leave from Falmouth Harbor (Island Queen); North Kingstown, RI (Vineyard Fast Ferry); New Bedford (Seastreak); and New York City (Seastreak, seasonally).

VISITOR INFORMATION

CONTACTS Martha's Vineyard Chamber of Commerce. ✉ *24 Beach St., Vineyard Haven* ☎ *508/693–0085* 🌐 *www.mvy.com.*

Vineyard Haven (Tisbury)

7 miles southeast of Woods Hole, 3½ miles west of Oak Bluffs, 8 miles northwest of Edgartown.

Most people call this town Vineyard Haven because of the name of the port where ferries arrive, but its official name is Tisbury. Not as yacht-y as Edgartown or as touristy as Oak Bluffs, Vineyard Haven blends the past and present with a touch of the bohemian. Visitors step off the ferry right into the bustle of the harbor, one block from the shops and restaurants of Main Street.

GETTING HERE AND AROUND

Vineyard Haven sees ferry traffic year-round, so this port town is always active. If you're traveling without a car, you can get around by taxi, Uber, Lyft, or the shuttle buses run by Martha's Vineyard Transit Authority. Bike, scooter, and car rentals are also possibilities. Much of the downtown area is easily explored on foot, and a good number of the lodgings are within reach. Vineyard Haven is 3½ miles west of Oak Bluffs.

Beaches

Lake Tashmoo Town Beach

BEACH | FAMILY | Swimmers have access to the warm, relatively shallow, brackish Lake Tashmoo from this beach—or cooler, gentler Vineyard Sound. It's a favorite spot for surf casters. **Amenities:** lifeguards; parking (no fee); toilets. **Best for:** sunset; swimming. ✉ *End of Herring Creek Rd., Vineyard Haven* 🌐 *www.mvy.com/beaches.html.*

Owen Park Beach

BEACH | FAMILY | This small, sandy harbor beach is just steps away from the ferry terminal in Vineyard Haven, making it a great spot to catch some last rays before heading home. **Amenities:** lifeguards; toilets. **Best for:** swimming. ✉ *Off Main St., Vineyard Haven* 🌐 *www.mvy.com/beaches.html.*

Tisbury Town Beach

BEACH | This public beach is next to the Vineyard Haven Yacht Club. It is only accessed by foot or bike: no parking here. But it's a nice place for a picnic. **Amenities:** none. **Best for:** swimming. ✉ *End of Owen Little Way, off Main St., Vineyard Haven* 🌐 *www.mvy.com/beaches.html.*

Restaurants

Beach Road

$$$ | SEAFOOD | With its ample windows looking out to the serene lagoon, lofted ceilings, and mellow globe lighting held aloft by sturdy ropes, the decor aptly reflects the kitchen's "sea-to-table" theme for its seasonally inspired and locally sourced offerings. Everything is scratch-made, including the baked goods, and the massive bar is a popular spot for dining and cocktails. **Known for:** panzanella salad; intriguing small plates; elegant nautical-meets-farmhouse atmosphere. *Average main: $34* *79 Beach Rd., Vineyard Haven* *508/693–8582* *www.beachroadmv.com.*

Black Dog Tavern

$$$ | **AMERICAN** | **FAMILY** | This island landmark—part of a mini-complex that includes a general store and a kid's shop—lies just steps from the ferry terminal in Vineyard Haven. The dining room—roaring fireplace, dark-wood walls, maritime memorabilia, and a grand view of the water—makes everyone feel at home; there's additional seating on the patio when the weather allows. **Known for:** menu featuring local fish, chowders, and chops; long wait for breakfast in July and August; water views. *Average main: $32* *20 Beach St. Ext., Vineyard Haven* *508/693–9223* *www.theblackdog.com.*

Hotels

Mansion House

$$$$ | **HOTEL** | There has been a hostelry on this conveniently located Main Street site just above Vineyard Haven Harbor since 1794. **Pros:** on-site health club; steps from shopping and ferry; light-filled rooms. **Cons:** location can be a little noisy; pool and spa can be busy with nonhotel guests; limited parking. *Rooms from: $459* *9 Main St., Vineyard Haven* *509/693–2200, 800/332–4112* *www.mvmansionhouse.com* *40 rooms* *Free Breakfast.*

★ **Nobnocket Boutique Inn**

$$$ | **B&B/INN** | One of the best hotels in the Northeast, this stylish 1908 Arts & Crafts-style manor house marries "coastal grandma" chic with a personal touch. **Pros:** two acres of gardens and woodland; gourmet breakfast; bright contemporary design. **Cons:** not ideal for groups; limited parking; no pool. *Rooms from: $350* *60 Mt. Alworth Rd., Vineyard Haven* *508/696–0859* *www.nobnocket.com* *7 rooms* *Free Breakfast.*

Performing Arts

THEATER

Martha's Vineyard Playhouse

THEATER | **FAMILY** | Martha's Vineyard Playhouse operates year-round, producing professional productions showcasing diverse work and developing new plays through staged readings, workshops and world premieres on the intimate Patricia Neal stage. Music, poetry, art and drama classes are offered for adults and children in this historic theater in downtown Vineyard Haven. Each summer season, the theater stages vibrant Shakespeare productions and original plays for children in the outdoor Tisbury Amphitheater. *24 Church St., Vineyard Haven* *508/696–6300* *mvplayhouse.org/theater.*

Shopping

Vineyard Haven has a good concentration of shopping along Main Street, which is intersected with several shorter streets that also hold shops of interest. Conveniently, since many people arrive by ferry without their vehicles, the majority of shopping is easily accessible right from the ferry docks. You won't find any large-scale chain stores here—rather, a good variety of upscale clothing shops, galleries, and other independently owned businesses selling everything from kitchenware to luxury bath products.

Bunch of Grapes Bookstore

BOOKS | Bunch of Grapes Bookstore is an excellent independent shop, with eager and knowledgeable booksellers and a varied selection of new books for adults and children. It also sponsors book signings. *23 Main St., Vineyard Haven* *508/693–2291* *www.bunchofgrapes.com.*

Rainy Day

CRAFTS | FAMILY | As the name suggests, Rainy Day carries gifts and amusements perfect for one of the island's gloomy afternoons when you just need a warm, dry diversion. You'll find toys, crafts, cards, soaps, home accessories, gifts, and more. ✉ *66 Main St., Vineyard Haven* ☎ *508/693–1830* 🌐 *www.rainydaymv.com.*

Tuck and Holand

CRAFTS | Nationally renowned for creating distinctive, hand-sculpted metal weathervanes, Tuck and Holand has a studio gallery a 10-minute walk from downtown. Here you can examine Anthony Holand and the late Travis Tuck's otherworldly creations, including copper Martha's Vineyard wall maps, an 11-foot seahorse sculpture, and the signature custom weathervanes. ✉ *275 State Rd., Vineyard Haven* ☎ *508/693–3914* 🌐 *www.tuckandholand.com* ☞ *No appointment needed, but call to be sure Anthony is on site.*

Oak Bluffs

3½ miles east of Vineyard Haven.

Circuit Avenue is the bustling heart of the action in Oak Bluffs, with most of the town's shops, bars, and restaurants. Colorful gingerbread-trimmed guesthouses and food and souvenir joints enliven Oak Bluffs Harbor, once the setting for several grand hotels. This small town is more high-spirited than haute, more fun than refined.

■ TIP→ Look for the yellow tourist information booth at the bottom of Circuit Avenue. It's open May–mid-October and is staffed with helpful folks from the area.

GETTING HERE AND AROUND

Oak Bluff is the terminal for seasonal ferries. If you have a car, it's best to find a space and park it while you walk, bike, or take the buses operated by Martha's Vineyard Transit Authority.

Sights

East Chop Lighthouse

LIGHTHOUSE | One of five lighthouses on Martha's Vineyard, the 40-foot structure was built out of cast iron in 1876 to replace an 1828 tower (used as part of a semaphore system) that burned down. While the lighthouse is not currently open to the public, the views of Nantucket Sound from atop the 79-foot bluff are spectacular. ✉ *229 E. Chop Ave., Oak Bluffs* ☎ *508/627–4441* 🌐 *mvmuseum.org/visit/east-chop* 🎫 *$5.*

Flying Horses Carousel

AMUSEMENT RIDE | FAMILY | A National Historic Landmark, this is the nation's oldest continuously operating merry-go-round. Handcrafted in 1876—the horses have real horsehair and glass eyes—and brought from Coney Island in 1884, the ride gives children a taste of entertainment from an era before smartphones. Kids delight in trying to grab the brass ring for a free ride. ✉ *15 Lake Ave., Oak Bluffs* ☎ *508/693–9481* 🌐 *vineyardtrust.org/property/flying-horses-carousel* 🎫 *$4* 🕒 *Closed mid-Oct–mid-May.*

★ Martha's Vineyard Camp Meeting Association

HISTORIC DISTRICT | This 34-acre warren of streets is tightly packed with more than 300 gaily painted Carpenter Gothic Victorian cottages with wedding-cake trim; they date mainly to the 1860s and '70s, when visitors coming for Methodist revivalist services began to lease lots and build houses for summer use. As you wander through this fairy-tale setting, imagine it on a balmy summer evening, lighted by the warm glow of paper lanterns hung from every cottage porch. This describes the scene on Illumination Night at the end of the Camp Meeting season, which is attended these days by some fourth- and fifth-generation cottagers—and newcomers: some houses do change hands, and some are rented. Attendees mark the occasion as they have for more than a century, with lights, song, and open houses for families and friends. Ninety-minute tours of the area are conducted at 11 am on Tuesday and Thursday in July and August; the Friday night Sunset Concert Series on Tabernacle Green is always festive. ✉ *Off Circuit Ave., Oak Bluffs* ☎ *508/693–0525* 🌐 *www.mvcma.org* 🎟 *Tour $12.*

Beaches

Joseph A. Sylvia State Beach

BEACH | FAMILY | This 2-mile-long sandy beach has a view of Cape Cod across Nantucket Sound. Occasional food vendors and calm, warm waters make it a popular spot for families. Arrive early or late in high summer: the parking spots fill up quickly. It's best to bike, walk, or take the shuttle here. **Amenities:** parking (no fee). **Best for:** swimming. ✉ *Off Beach Rd., between Oak Bluffs and Edgartown, Oak Bluffs* 🌐 *www.mvy.com/beaches.html.*

Restaurants

Biscuits

$ | SOUTHERN | There will be a line, but this hole-in-the-wall breakfast joint is a great spot for grabbing a hand-held breakfast sandwich—say, a honey-chicken biscuit—en route to the ferry. If you're not in a rush, nab a table, and peruse the extensive menu featuring Southern favorites like shrimp and grits and chicken and waffles along with stuffed French toast and linguica hash. **Known for:** shrimp and grits; house-made biscuits; breakfast sandwiches. 💲 *Average main: $12* ✉ *20 Lake Ave., Oak Bluffs* ☎ *508/693–2033* 🌐 *www.mvbiscuits.com* 🕒 *Closed mid-Oct.–Apr. No dinner.*

Lookout Tavern

$$ | AMERICAN | Sometimes, you don't feel like a fifty-dollar, fancy-schmancy entrée—you just want a big, fat lobster roll and a beer, and that's what you'll get at Lookout Tavern. Dig into fresh lobsters from Katama Bay, eight kinds of tacos (beer-battered cod is the best), or sushi and sashimi. **Known for:** rum punch; great views of the busy harbor; lobster rolls (served with mayo or sautéed in butter) and lobster bisque. 💲 *Average main: $20* ✉ *8 Seaview Ave., Oak Bluffs* ☎ *508/696–9844* 🌐 *www.lookoutmv.com* 🕒 *Closed Jan.–Apr.*

Offshore Ale Company

$$ | AMERICAN | The island's first microbrewery restaurant is quite popular with locals and visitors alike, especially since it is open year-round. There are private wooden booths, a dart board in the corner, and live music year-round. **Known for:** rotating beers on tap; unique pizzas; fish-and-chips. 💲 *Average main: $22* ✉ *30 Kennebec Ave., Oak Bluffs* ☎ *508/693–2626* 🌐 *www.offshoreale.com* 🕒 *No lunch weekdays.*

Red Cat Kitchen

$$$$ | SEAFOOD | Standing at nearly 6½ feet tall and covered with colorful tattoos, chef-owner Ben Deforest turns out an extraordinary array of dishes—chorizo-stuffed local calamari, crab and wild mushroom risotto, or truffle arancini—from a tiny kitchen visible from the dining room. Regulars love the funky artwork, thundering tunes, and the irreverent spirit of the place, but no question here: it's the food that keeps them coming back. **Known for:** frequently changing (sometimes daily) seasonal-based menu; crispy Brussels sprouts; ample portions. 💲 *Average main: $42* ✉ *14 Kennebec Ave., Oak Bluffs* ☎ *508/696–6040* 🌐 *www.redcatkitchen.com* 🕒 *Closed Nov.–Mar.*

Sweet Life Café

$$$$ | AMERICAN | Housed in a charming Victorian house, this island favorite's warm hues, low lighting, and handsome antique furniture will make you feel like you've entered someone's home. The cooking is more sophisticated than home style, however: dishes are prepared in inventive ways and change often with the seasons. **Known for:** superb desserts; outdoor dining by candlelight in a shrub-enclosed garden; locally sourced food. *Average main: $37 63 Upper Circuit Ave., Oak Bluffs 508/696–0200 www.sweetlifemv.com Closed Mon. and Tues. and Jan.–Mar. No lunch.*

Coffee and Quick Bites

Back Door Donuts

$ | **DESSERTS** | Who needs saltwater taffy when you can have a freshly-baked apple fritter or gooey, buttermilk glazed donut? This is a donut shop with a secret: By day, it's a tucked-away bakery; at 7 pm, they open the back door and sell warm treats to in-the-know fans who line up for the privilege. **Known for:** early evening secret baked treats; apple fritters; buttermilk glazed donuts. *Average main: $3 1-11 Kennebec Ave., Oak Bluffs 508/693–3688 www.backdoordonuts.com Closed Tues.; back door portion of business closed from mid-Oct.–May.*

Hotels

Oak Bluffs Inn

$$$ | **B&B/INN** | This 1870s Victorian has charm to spare, and feels like staying at a relative's home—albeit a discerning one, who appreciates Frette linens and Aveda bath products. **Pros:** wraparound porch; within walking distance to ferry; complimentary snacks. **Cons:** some rooms have twin beds; decor is sort of a hodge-lodge; limited parking. *Rooms from: $350 64 Circuit Ave., Oak Bluffs 508/693–7171 www.oakbluffsinn.com Closed Nov.-Apr. 10 rooms Free Breakfast.*

Summercamp

$$$$ | **HOTEL** | **FAMILY** | Located at the edge of Oak Bluffs' crazy-colorful collection of cottages, this is the last of the town's grand old hotels (circa1879), reimagined with a playful summer camp theme. **Pros:** use of lockers for storing bags; convenient to ferry and town; great for families. **Cons:** some rooms are on the small side; some rooms have detached bathrooms; no bathtubs except in suites. *Rooms from: $589 70 Lake Ave., Oak Bluffs Harbor 800/638–9027 www.summercamphotel.com Closed Nov.–Mar. 95 rooms No Meals.*

Nightlife

Loft

BARS | This adults-only venue makes its home in the vast space above the MV Chowder Co. and has long historic roots. Today it's home to an over-21 hotspot for concerts, comedy, DJs, and events. The 400-seat club is one of the hosts of the MV summer concert series and draws national and regional live music acts to its stage. A game area offers pool tables, Ping-Pong, darts, foosball, video games, and a full bar. A full menu is available in the restaurant space below the club. *9 Oak Bluffs Ave., Oak Bluffs 508/696–3000 www.mvloft.com.*

The Ritz Cafe

BARS | Islanders, wash-a-shores, gay, straight, whatever—all are welcome at this unpretentious dive bar/rock club featuring live music year-round. There's been a bar at this spot on Circuit Avenue since 1944; these days, it draws a mixed crowd for live music, karaoke, pool-playing, and dancing—lots of dancing. There's live music nightly in season, and on weekends off season. *4 Circuit Ave., Oak Bluffs 508/693–9851 www.theritzmv.com.*

Activities

FISHING

Dick's Bait & Tackle

FISHING | You can buy fishing accessories and bait, and check out a current copy of the fishing regulations here. *108 New York Ave., Oak Bluffs 508/693–7669.*

Shopping

You'll find touristy shops selling T-shirts, souvenirs, taffy, and the like, mixed in with galleries featuring local art, funky clothing shops, and beach gear. The shopping zone starts right off the ferry dock and is mainly concentrated along busy Circuit Avenue.

Edgartown

6 miles southeast of Oak Bluffs.

Once a well-to-do whaling center, Edgartown remains the Vineyard's toniest town and has preserved parts of its elegant past. Sea captains' houses from the 18th and 19th centuries, with well-manicured gardens and lawns, line the streets.

A sparsely populated area with many nature preserves, Chappaquiddick Island, 1 mile southeast of Edgartown, makes for a pleasant day trip or bike ride on a sunny day. The "island" is actually connected to the Vineyard by a long sand spit that begins in South Beach in Katama. It's a spectacular 2¾-mile walk, or you can take the ferry, which departs about every five minutes.

On the island's Mytoi preserve, a boardwalk runs through part of the grounds, where you're apt to see box turtles and hear the sounds of songbirds. Elsewhere you can fish, sunbathe, or even dip into the surf; use caution, as the currents are strong.

GETTING HERE AND AROUND

Once you've reached Edgartown, a car isn't necessary. It's actually a hindrance, as parking spaces can be difficult to find in summer. The Martha's Vineyard Transit Authority operates a fleet of buses that can get you almost anywhere you want to go. The town runs a helpful visitor center on Church Street.

The best way to get around Chappaquiddick Island is by bike; bring one over on the ferry ($6 round-trip for bike and rider) and ride the few miles to Cape Pogue Wildlife Refuge. Sign up for a tour with the Trustees of Reservations for an in-depth look at the island's wonders.

Sights

Cape Poge Wildlife Refuge

WILDLIFE REFUGE | FAMILY | A collection of habitats where you can swim, walk, fish, or just sit and enjoy the surroundings, the Cape Poge Wildlife Refuge, on the easternmost shore of Chappaquiddick Island, encompasses more than 6 square miles of wilderness. Its dunes, woods, cedar thickets, moors, salt marshes, ponds, tidal flats, and barrier beach serve as an important migration stopover and nesting area for numerous sea- and shorebirds. You'll need an oversand permit to drive your own vehicle or you can call to inquire about guided tours. Admission paid at Cape Pogue, Wasque, or Mytoi provides visitor access to all three Trustees properties on Chappaquiddick Island for the day. ✉ *East end of Dike Rd., Chappaquiddick Island* ☎ *508/627–7689* 🌐 *www.thetrustees.org/places-to-visit/cape-cod-islands/cape-pogue.html* 🎫 *$5 from late May to mid-Oct; otherwise free. Always free for pedestrians.*

Edgartown Lighthouse

LIGHTHOUSE | FAMILY | Surrounded by a public beach, this cast-iron tower was floated by barge from Ipswich, Massachusetts, in 1939. It is still an active navigational aid. Renovations from 2005 to 2007 included the installation of a spiral staircase that visitors can ascend for great views. There's a touching memorial to children who have died, in the form of engraved granite cobblestones, surrounding the lighthouse. In 2001, the lighthouse was dedicated as the Children's Memorial. ✉ *121 N. Water St., Edgartown* ☎ *508/627–4441* 🌐 *mvmuseum.org/visit/edgartown* 🎫 *$5* 🕒 *Closed Labor Day-late June and Mon. Closed week days from Labor Day–mid-Oct.*

Felix Neck Wildlife Sanctuary

WILDLIFE REFUGE | FAMILY | The nearly 200-acre Mass Audubon preserve, 3 miles outside Edgartown toward Vineyard Haven, has 4 miles of hiking trails traversing marshland, fields, woods, seashore, and fresh and saltwater ponds. Naturalist-led events include hikes, stargazing, reptile or bird walks, and kayaking tours. ✉ *100 Felix Neck Rd., off Edgartown–Vineyard Haven Rd., Edgartown* ☎ *508/627–4850* 🌐 *www.massaudubon.org* 🎟 *$4.*

Martha's Vineyard Museum

HISTORY MUSEUM | Perched on 1 acre overlooking the Lagoon Pond and outer Vineyard Haven harbor, the museum is located in the formerly shuttered 1895 Marine Hospital, which the nonprofit organization purchased in 2011, renovated, and made its home in 2019. The expansive property includes 14 exhibition areas, a classroom, program room, research library, gift shop, and small café. Exhibits include "One Island, Many Stories," which explores the history of the island; "Challenges of the Sea," which gives an overview of island shipwrecks, navigation, and more; and "Flashes of Brilliance," with an 1854 Fresnel lens from the Gay Head Light. ✉ *151 Lagoon Pond Rd., Edgartown* ☎ *508/627–4441* 🌐 *mvmuseum.org* 🎟 *$18.*

★ Morning Glory Farm

FARM/RANCH | This farm store is full of incredible goodies, most made or grown on the premises, including fresh farm greens in the salads and vegetables in the soups, and homemade pies, breads, quiches, cookies, and cakes. A picnic table and grass to sit on while you eat make this an ideal place for a simple country lunch. ✉ *W. Tisbury Rd., Edgartown* ☎ *508/627–9003* 🌐 *www.morninggloryfarm.com* ⏲ *Closed late Dec.–early May.*

★ Mytoi

GARDEN | The Trustees of Reservations' 14-acre preserve is a serene, beautifully tended, Japanese-inspired garden with a creek-fed pool spanned by a bridge and rimmed with Japanese maples, azaleas, bamboo, and irises. A boardwalk runs through part of the grounds, where you're apt to see box turtles and hear the sounds of songbirds. There are few more enchanting spots on the island. Restrooms and fresh water are available. Note that admission paid at Mytoi, Cape Pogue, or Wasque provides visitor access to all three Chappaquiddick Island properties for the day. ✉ *56 Dike Bridge Rd., 3½ miles from Edgartown via Chappaquiddick Rd, Edgartown* ☎ *508/627-7689* 🌐 *www.thetrustees.org/places-to-visit/cape-cod-islands/mytoi.html* 🎟 *$5.*

Beaches

South Beach/Katama Beach

BEACH | This very popular and accessible 3–4 mile stretch of Atlantic-facing beach is backed by high dunes. The protected salt pond cove is good for families on one side, while big waves on the other side draw surfers. **Amenities:** toilets; lifeguards; parking (no fee). **Best for:** surfing; sunrise; walking. ✉ *Katama Rd., Edgartown* ✣ *4 miles south of Edgartown* 🌐 *www.mvy.com/beaches.html.*

Restaurants

Alchemy Bistro and Bar

$$$$ | EUROPEAN | Alchemy aims for a European-chic bistro-style scene and menu, missing only the patina of age—and French working-folks' prices—but you can expect quality and imagination. On balmy evenings, the half-dozen outdoor tables on the candlelit brick patio are highly coveted. **Known for:** specialty cocktails; swanky candle-lit ambience; surf and turf. 💲 *Average main: $48* ✉ *71 Main St., Edgartown* ☎ *508/627–9999* *www.alchemyedgartown.com* *Closed Sun. No lunch.*

★ Détente

$$$$ | EUROPEAN | A dark, intimate wine bar and restaurant with hardwood floors and richly colored banquette seating, Détente serves more than a dozen wines by the glass as well as numerous half bottles. Even if you're not much of an oenophile, it's worth a trip just for the innovative food, much of it from local farms and seafood purveyors. **Known for:** hip, sophisticated atmosphere; hand-rolled pasta; exquisite food preparations. *Average main: $38* *15 Winter St., Edgartown* *508/627–8810* *www.detentemv.com* *Closed Sun. and Mon. and Nov.–late Apr. No lunch.*

l'étoile

$$$$ | FRENCH | Michael Brisson has been at the helm of this creative French kitchen since the mid-1980s, yet his dedication to fresh, exquisitely prepared local food remains as fervent as ever. Changing with what's seasonally available, his menu many include sautéed Menemsha fluke or perhaps roasted Long Island duck breast; for lighter fare or to indulge in a fancy martini, head to the stunning copper bar with its sleek leather-backed chairs or the lovely terrace for alfresco dining. **Known for:** elegant surroundings; foie gras; excellent service. *Average main: $55* *The Sydney Martha's Vineyard, 22 N. Water St., Edgartown* *508/627–5187* *www.letoile.net* *Closed Wed. and Dec.–mid-May.*

19 Raw Oyster Bar

$$$$ | SEAFOOD | Nothing says 'summer on the island' like slurping local oysters outdoors on a patio, and head chef Joe Monteiro will make sure you have a shucking good time. They aim for a true oyster bar—something the Vineyard was lacking—and they nail it, right down to the reclaimed wood and industrial accents. **Known for:** tasty seafood dishes; fresh local oysters; charred octopus. *Average main: $39* *19 Church St., Edgartown* *774/224–0550* *www.19rawoysterbar.com* *Closed Nov.-Mar.*

Coffee and Quick Bites

Espresso Love

$ | CAFÉ | When you need a pick-me-up, pop into Espresso Love for a cappuccino and a homemade raspberry scone or blueberry muffin. If you prefer something cold, the staff also makes fruit smoothies. **Known for:** breakfast sandwiches; courtyard tables; make-your-own salad bowls. *Average main: $13* *17 Church St., Edgartown* *508/627–9211* *www.espressolove.com.*

Hotels

Charlotte Inn

$$$$ | B&B/INN | From the moment you walk up to the dark-wood Scottish barrister's desk to check in at this regal 1864 inn, you'll be surrounded by the trappings and customs of a bygone era—beautiful antique furnishings, objets d'art, and paintings fill the property. **Pros:** over-the-top lavish; quiet yet convenient location; beautifully landscaped. **Cons:** can feel overly formal; intimidating if you don't adore museum-quality antiques; not for those with children. *Rooms from: $700* *27 S. Summer St., Edgartown* *508/627–4751, 800/735–2478* *www.thecharlotteinn.com* *19 rooms* *No Meals.*

Edgartown Inn

$$$ | B&B/INN | The inside of the former home of whaling captain Thomas Worth still evokes its late-18th-century origins—but with the boutique Lark Hotels group now in charge, the updated decor is best described as farmhouse chic, with airy spaces and vintage notes. **Pros:** great value; rich in history—Nathaniel Hawthorne wrote much of his Twice-Told Tales here; close to shopping and dining. **Cons:** many rooms are accessed by stairs only; not for those with small children; pricey parking. *Rooms from: $371* *56 N. Water St., Edgartown* *508/939–4005*

🌐 *www.theedgartowninn.com* 🛏 *12 rooms* 🍽 *Free Breakfast.*

Harbor View Hotel and Resort
$$$$ | RESORT | FAMILY | After more than 130 years of pampering guests, including Steven Spielberg and the *Jaws* cast and crew in 1975, this historic hotel is a true island classic. **Pros:** great harbor views; on-site restaurants; excellent concierge service. **Cons:** a few blocks from commercial district; steep rates; lots of weddings. 💲 *Rooms from: $595* ✉ *131 N. Water St., Edgartown* ☎ *844/248–1167* 🌐 *www.harborviewhotel.com* 🛏 *108 rooms* 🍽 *No Meals.*

★ Hob Knob
$$$$ | B&B/INN | This 19th-century Gothic Revival boutique hotel blends the amenities and service of a luxury property with the ambience and charm of a small B&B with art and antiques that help capture the island's rural, seaside charm. **Pros:** full breakfast—organic and locally gathered—and lavish afternoon tea are included; on-site spa; a short walk from the harbor, it's on the main road into town—but far enough out to avoid crowds. **Cons:** steep rates; not overlooking harbor; not for those with small children. 💲 *Rooms from: $495* ✉ *128 Main St., Edgartown* ☎ *508/627–9510, 800/696–2723* 🌐 *www.hobknob.com* 🛏 *17 rooms* 🍽 *Free Breakfast.*

The Sydney
$$$ | HOTEL | This chic, seasonal hotel consists of a 19th-century whaling captain's home and an adjacent newer building, located in the heart of Edgartown. **Pros:** pretty courtyard with fire pit; knowledgable front desk staff; children welcome. **Cons:** many rooms have queen beds, not kings; limited paid parking; located on a busy street. 💲 *Rooms from: $399* ✉ *22 Winter St., Edgartown* ☎ *508/939–9299* 🌐 *www.larkhotels.com* 🕑 *Closed Nov.–Apr.* 🛏 *22 rooms* 🍽 *Free Breakfast.*

★ Winnetu Oceanside Resort
$$$$ | RESORT | FAMILY | A departure from most properties on the island, the contemporary Winnetu—styled after the grand multistory resorts of the Gilded Age—has successfully struck a fine balance in that it both encourages families and provides a contemporary seaside-resort experience for couples. **Pros:** a full slate of excellent children's programs offered late June–early September; resort arranges bicycling and kayaking trips, lighthouse tours, boat excursions to Nantucket Island, and other island activities; fantastic restaurant. **Cons:** not an in-town location; lots of kids in summer; books up quickly. 💲 *Rooms from: $495* ✉ *31 Dunes Rd., Edgartown* ☎ *866/335–1133, 508/310–1733* 🌐 *www.winnetu.com* 🕑 *Closed late Oct.–mid-Apr.* 🛏 *58 suites, 68 homes* 🍽 *No Meals.*

Shopping

Edgartown Books
BOOKS | This longtime island favorite, open year-round, carries a large selection of island-related titles, periodicals, and bestsellers, and the staff will be happy to make a summer reading recommendation. The children's section is very good. A wonderful little café behind the bookshop, called Behind the Bookstore, is open seasonally, serving breakfast, lunch, and dinner. ✉ *44 Main St., Edgartown* ☎ *508/627–8463* 🌐 *www.edgartownbooks.com* 🕑 *Closed Mon. from mid-Jan.–mid-May.*

West Tisbury

8 miles west of Edgartown, 6½ miles south of Vineyard Haven.

West Tisbury retains its rural vibe and maintains its agricultural tradition at several active horse and produce farms. The town center looks very much like a small New England village, complete with a white-steepled church.

Sights

Polly Hill Arboretum

GARDEN | FAMILY | The late horticulturist and part-time Vineyard resident Polly Hill tended some 2,000 species of plant and developed nearly 100 species herself on her old sheep farm in West Tisbury. On-site are azaleas, tree peonies, dogwoods, hollies, lilacs, magnolias, and more. Hill raised them from seeds without the use of a greenhouse, and her patience is the inspiration of the arboretum. Run as a nonprofit center, the arboretum also runs guided tours, a lecture series, and a visitor center and gift shop. It's a beautiful spot for a picnic. The grounds are open year-round. *809 State Rd., West Tisbury 508/693 9426 www.pollyhillarboretum.org $5 Visitor center closed mid-Oct.–mid-May.*

Sepiessa Point Reservation

NATURE PRESERVE | A paradise for bird-watchers, Sepiessa Point Reservation consists of 174 acres on splendid Tisbury Great Pond. There are expansive pond and ocean views, walking trails around coves and saltwater marshes, horse trails, swimming areas, and a boat launch. *Tiah's Cove Rd., West Tisbury 508/627–7141 www.mvlandbank.com Free.*

Restaurants

★ State Road Restaurant

$$$$ | AMERICAN | FAMILY | High ceilings, exposed beams, and a beautiful stone fireplace make for a warm and light-filled meal. The menu takes advantage of delightfully prepared local and organic products, creating memorable dishes. **Known for:** creative and large selection of plates ample for sharing and sampling; wonderful ambience; scallop chowder. *Average main: $39 688 State Rd., West Tisbury 508/693–8582 www.stateroadrestaurant.com Closed Mon. and Tues.*

Hotels

★ Lambert's Cove Inn, Farm & Restaurant

$$$$ | B&B/INN | A narrow road winds through pine woods and beside creeper-covered stone walls to this posh, handsomely designed farmhouse inn (1790) surrounded by extraordinary gardens and old stone walls set on 8 acres. **Pros:** guests receive free passes (and transport) to beautiful and private Lambert's Cove beach (there's also a pool); fantastic restaurant; serene grounds. **Cons:** need a car to explore island; far from the action; pricey. *Rooms from: $469 90 Manaquayak Rd., off Lambert's Cove Rd., West Tisbury 508/422-8051 www.lambertscoveinn.com 15 rooms Free Breakfast.*

Shopping

West Tisbury is truly a long and beautiful stretch of rural splendor. There is no distinct downtown area, though along the bucolic roadways you'll find a few one-of-a-kind retail gems worth a closer look.

Alley's General Store

GENERAL STORE | FAMILY | Step back in time with a visit to Alley's General Store, a local landmark since 1858, and the island's oldest retail business. Stock includes everything from groceries to gourmet cheeses, and toys for all ages, from stuffed animals for the kids to housewares for adults. Alley's is a treasure trove of the playful and practical items that define a country store. The coffee bar sells some of the best brew in town, and there's a post office inside. *1045 State Rd., West Tisbury 508/693–0088 vineyardtrust.org/property/alleys-general-store.*

Menemsha

1½ miles southwest of West Tisbury.

Seemingly unchanged for decades, this working port is a jumble of weathered fishing shacks, fishing and pleasure boats, drying nets, and lobster pots. The village is popular with cyclists who like to stop for ice cream or chowder. Menemsha is often busy with folks eager to see the sunset.

GETTING HERE AND AROUND

You can take a Martha's Vineyard Transit Authority bus here; there's frequent service in summer and more limited service the rest of the year. If you're exploring the area by bike, you can get between Menemsha and the Aquinnah Cliffs via the Menemsha Bike Ferry. It's a quick trip across the water (and a small fee applies), but it saves a lot of riding on the busy State Road.

Sights

Menemsha Harbor

BODY OF WATER | Where Menemsha Pond meets Vineyard Sound, this tiny seaside outpost has been an active fishing center for centuries. Well-weathered fishing boats, including some that have been in the same family for generations, tie up at the docks when not out to sea. Spectacular sunsets make this a very popular evening spot. Several fish markets offer the freshest catch of the day. There's also a beach here, with gentle waters that are welcoming to families. If the harbor looks familiar, it might be because several scenes from the movie *Jaws* were filmed here. ✉ *Basin Rd., Menemsha.*

Coffee and Quick Bites

★ Larsen's

$ | **SEAFOOD** | Basically a retail fish store, Larsen's has a raw take-out counter and will also boil lobsters for you. Dig into a plate of fresh littlenecks or cherrystones; oysters are not a bad alternative. **Known for:** made-to-order lobster roll; freshest seafood; friendly service. [$] *Average main: $14* ✉ *Dutcher's Dock, 56 Basin Rd., Menemsha* ☎ *508/645–2680* 🌐 *www.larsensfishmarket.com* ⏲ *Closed mid-Oct.–mid-May.*

Menemsha Galley

$ | **AMERICAN** | Line up at this charming family-owned spot, around for more than 70 years, for everything from chowder to fresh swordfish sandwiches to soft serve ice cream. Once you pick up your order, enjoy it sitting on the rocks at the harbor or head to the beach. **Known for:** Galley fries; reasonable prices; friendly staff. [$] *Average main: $12.50* ✉ *515 North Rd., Menemsha* ☎ *508/645–9819* ⏲ *Closed Columbus Day–mid-May.*

Aquinnah

6½ miles west of Menemsha, 10 miles southwest of West Tisbury, 17 miles southwest of Vineyard Haven.

Aquinnah, called Gay Head until the town voted to change its name in 1997, is an official Native American township. The Wampanoag tribe is the guardian of the 420 acres that constitute the Aquinnah Native American Reservation. Aquinnah (pronounced a- *kwih*-nah) is Wampanoag for "land under the hill." Count on good views of Menemsha and Nashaquitsa ponds, the woods, and the ocean beyond from Quitsa Pond Lookout on State Road. The town is best known for the red-hued Aquinnah Cliffs. This is the end of the world, or so it seems when you're standing on the edge of the cliff looking out over the ocean.

GETTING HERE AND AROUND

Aquinnah, 6½ miles west of Menemsha and 10 miles southwest of West Tisbury, gets lots of traffic, for good reason. You can drive here (and pray for a parking space) or ride the Martha's Vineyard Transit Authority buses, which offer frequent service in summer.

Sights

★ Aquinnah Cliffs

VIEWPOINT | A National Historic Landmark, the spectacular Aquinnah Cliffs are part of the Wampanoag Reservation land. These

Sacred to the Wampanoag Tribe, the red-hue Aquinnah Cliffs are a popular attraction on Martha's Vineyard.

dramatically striated walls of red clay are the island's major attraction, as evidenced by the tour bus–filled parking lot. Native American crafts and food shops line the short approach to the overlook, from which you can see the Elizabeth Islands to the northeast across Vineyard Sound and Nomans Land Island, a wildlife preserve, 3 miles off the Vineyard's southern coast. ✉ *State Rd., Aquinnah.*

Gay Head Lighthouse

LIGHTHOUSE | This brick lighthouse (also called the Aquinnah Lighthouse) was successfully moved back from its precarious perch atop the rapidly eroding cliffs in spring 2015. Bad weather may affect its hours. Parking can be limited here, but views are outstanding. ✉ *9 Aquinnah Circle, Aquinnah* ☎ *508/645–2300* 🌐 *www.gayheadlight.org* 🎟 *$6* 🕒 *Closed Columbus Day-Memorial Day.*

Hotels

Outermost Inn

$$$ | **B&B/INN** | This rambling, sun-filled inn by the Aquinnah Cliffs stands alone on acres of moorland, a 10-minute walk from the beach. **Pros:** spectacular setting; extremely popular restaurant, open to the public, serves a nightly prix-fixe dinner in summer; service. **Cons:** far from bigger towns on island; steep rates; not suitable for young kids. 💲 *Rooms from: $360* ✉ *81 Lighthouse Rd., Aquinnah* ☎ *508/645–3511* 🌐 *www.outermostinn.com* 🕒 *Closed mid-Oct.–mid-May* 🛏 *7 rooms* 🍽 *Free Breakfast.*

Nantucket

At the height of its prosperity in the early 19th century, the little island of Nantucket was the foremost whaling port in the world. Its harbor bustled with whaling ships and merchant vessels; chandleries, cooperages, and other shops crowded the wharves. Burly ship hands loaded

Diversity and acceptance, island-style 

Martha's Vineyard has a long history of embracing those who land on its shores, including people of color. "With an intolerance for slavery close to 100 years before the Civil War, the island initially became a refuge for people escaping the vicious business via maritime means," says Skip Finley, historian and author of "Historic Tales of Oak Bluffs" and "Whaling Captains of Color: America's First Meritocracy." The town of Oak Bluffs was a particular favorite of Black travelers, "who felt safe enough to transform it into the seasonal resort we know today," Finley notes. Scores of Black families began vacationing there in the 1800s; some opened businesses and erected colorful gingerbread cottages that continue to draw visitors. Inkwell Beach, a stretch of beach near the Oak Bluffs ferry, became a treasured gathering place. Over the years, Martha's Vineyard regulars have included African American luminaries galore, including a certain first family: Barack and Michelle Obama bought a seven-bedroom home on Martha's Vineyard, and add plenty of sparkle when they pop up at local restaurants and on the golf course. The hospitality of Oak Bluffs has been acknowledged by a permanent exhibit, "The Power of Place," in the Smithsonian's National Museum of African American History & Culture. To learn more, tour the 34 sites (and counting) along the African American Heritage Trail of Martha's Vineyard (mvafricanamericanheritagetrail.org).

barrels of whale oil onto wagons, which they wheeled along cobblestone streets to refineries and candle factories. Sea breezes carried the smoke and smells of booming industry through town as its inhabitants eagerly took care of business. Shipowners and sea captains built elegant mansions, which today remain remarkably unchanged, thanks to a very strict building code initiated in the 1950s. The entire town of Nantucket is now an official National Historic District encompassing more than 800 pre-1850 structures within 1 square mile.

Day-trippers usually take in the architecture and historical sites, dine at one of the many delightful restaurants, and browse in the pricey boutiques, most of which stay open mid-April–December. Signature items include Nantucket lightship baskets, originally crafted by sailors whiling away a long watch; artisans who continue the tradition now command prices of $800 and up, and antiques are exponentially more expensive.

GETTING ORIENTED

Nantucket is a boomerang-shaped island 26 miles southeast of Hyannis on Cape Cod, and 107 miles southeast of Boston. Its nearest neighbor to the west is the somewhat larger island of Martha's Vineyard; eastward, the nearest landfall would be the Azores off Portugal. The island has only one town, which also goes by the name of Nantucket. The only other community of note is tiny Siasconset, a cluster of shingled seaside manses and lovingly restored fishing shacks 8 miles west of town. A 3-mile main road directly south of town leads to Surfside Beach, among the island's most popular. Nantucket's small but busy airport is located east of Surfside.

Nantucket Town. As the ferry terminal—from Hyannis and, seasonally, Martha's Vineyard—Nantucket Town is the hub of all activity and the starting point for most visits. At the height of summer, its narrow cobblestone streets are in a constant state of near-gridlock. The town itself is easily walkable, and bikes are available for exploring.

Siasconset and Wauwinet. An allee of green lawns leads to the exclusive summer community of Siasconset (or 'Sconset, as locals say). Tucked away on either side of the village center are warrens of tiny, rose-covered cottages, some of them centuries old. About 5 miles northwest is the even tinier community of Wauwinet, which boasts the country's second-oldest yacht club.

GETTING HERE AND AROUND

Year-round flight service to Nantucket from Boston, Hyannis, New Bedford, MA and Martha's Vineyard is provided by Cape Air/Nantucket Airlines. JetBlue offers seasonal service to the island from Boston, Washington, D.C., Charlotte, NC, and New York City. American Airlines, United, and Delta also offer seasonal flights from select cities.

Arriving by ferry puts you in the center of town. Hy-Line Cruises offers year-round high-speed ferry service between Hyannis and Nantucket. The Steamship Authority operates year-round, traditional steamship service between Hyannis and Nantucket and seasonal (late March-Oct.) high-speed ferry service aboard *Iyannough* between Hyannis and Nantucket. Freedom Cruise Line offers seasonal service between Harwich Port and Nantucket. The only company that carries cars is Steamship Authority; car service is very expensive, and reservations must be made far in advance.

There is little need for a car here to explore; ample public transportation and smoothly paved bike paths can take you to the further reaches with ease. The Nantucket Regional Transit Authority (NRTA) runs shuttle buses from in town to most areas of the island. Service is generally available late May–mid-October. If you're still determined to rent a car while on Nantucket, book early—and expect to spend at least $95 a day during high season. If your car is low-slung, don't attempt the dirt roads. Some are deeply pocked with puddles, and some are virtual sandpits, challenging even to four-wheel-drive vehicles.

VISITOR INFORMATION

CONTACTS Nantucket Chamber of Commerce. ✉ *Nantucket* ☎ *508/228–1700* 🌐 *www.nantucketchamber.org.* **Nantucket Visitor Services and Information Bureau.** ✉ *Nantucket* ☎ *508/228–0925* 🌐 *www.nantucket-ma.gov.*

Town of Nantucket

30 miles southeast of Hyannis, 107 miles southeast of Boston.

After the Great Fire of 1846 leveled all its wooden buildings, Main Street was widened to prevent future flames from hopping across the street. The cobblestone thoroughfare has a harmonious symmetry: the Pacific Club anchors its foot, and the Pacific National Bank, another redbrick building, squares off the head. The cobblestones were brought to the island as ballast in returning ships and laid to prevent the wheels of carts heavily laden with whale oil from sinking into the dirt. At the center of Lower Main is an old horse trough, today overflowing with flowers. From here the street gently rises; at the bank it narrows to its pre-fire width and leaves the commercial district for an area of mansions that escaped the blaze.

TOURS

The self-guided Black Heritage Trail tour covers nine sites in and around town, including the African Meeting House, the Whaling Museum, and the Atheneum. A trail guide is available free of charge from the Friends of the African Meeting House on Nantucket, who also lead a "Walk the Black Heritage Trail" tour by appointment in season.

★ **Nantucket Historical Association** (*NHA*)
This association maintains an assortment of venerable properties in town. A $23

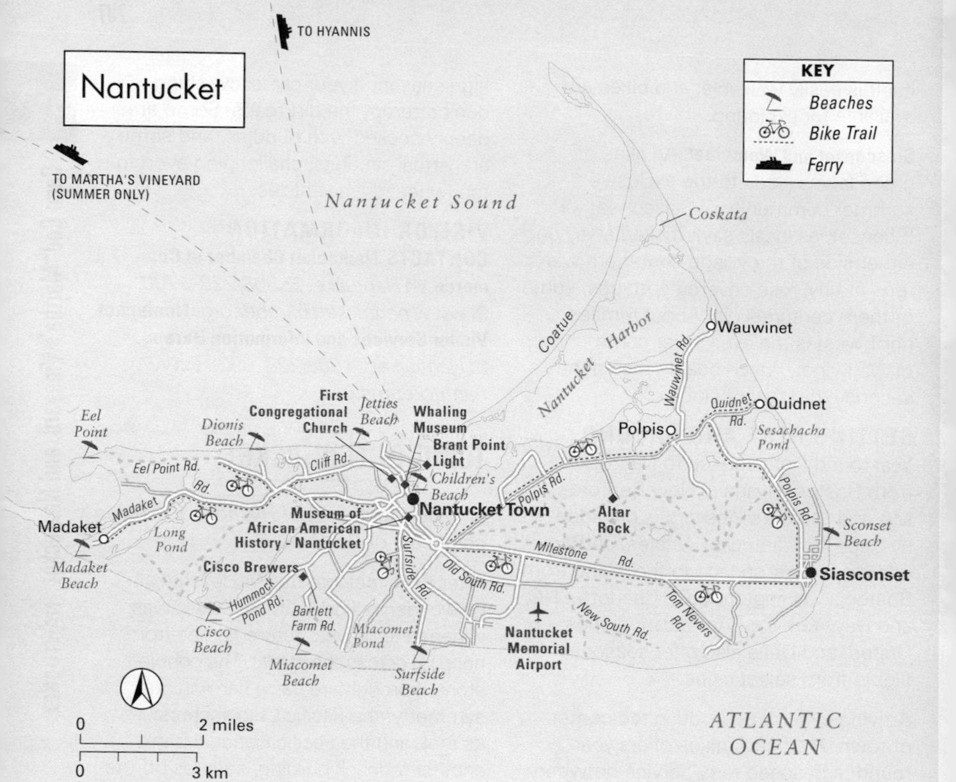

Nantucket

TO HYANNIS
TO MARTHA'S VINEYARD (SUMMER ONLY)
Nantucket Sound
KEY: Beaches; Bike Trail; Ferry
Coskata
Coatue
Nantucket Harbor
Wauwinet
Wauwinet Rd.
Quidnet
Quidnet Rd.
Sesachacha Pond
Polpis
Polpis Rd.
Eel Point
Dionis Beach
First Congregational Church
Jetties Beach
Whaling Museum
Brant Point Light
Children's Beach
Eel Point Rd.
Cliff Rd.
Madaket Rd.
Nantucket Town
Altar Rock
Madaket
Long Pond
Museum of African American History - Nantucket
Surfside Rd.
Milestone Rd.
Sconset Beach
Siasconset
Madaket Beach
Cisco Brewers
Old South Rd.
Hummock Pond Rd.
Bartlett Farm Rd.
Miacomet Pond
Nantucket Memorial Airport
New South Rd.
Tom Nevers Rd.
Cisco Beach
Miacomet Beach
Surfside Beach
ATLANTIC OCEAN
0 2 miles
0 3 km

pass gets you into all of the association's sites, including the glorious Whaling Museum and Hadwen House: historic properties including the Oldest House, Old Mill, Old Gaol, Greater Light are free for all visitors. Reserve in advance for two very popular walking tours, which depart daily late May–early September: a 60-minute Historic Downtown tour and a Historic Homes & Architecture tour. Both cost $20. ✉ *15 Broad St., Nantucket* ☎ *508/228–1894* 🌐 *www.nha.org.*

Sights

Brant Point Light

LIGHTHOUSE | The promontory where this 26-foot-tall, white-painted beauty stands offers views of the harbor and town. The point was once the site of the second-oldest lighthouse in the country (1746); the present, much-photographed light was built in 1901. There are no tours inside the lighthouse, but the grounds are open to the public. ✉ *End of Easton St., across footbridge, Nantucket* 🌐 *www.nps.gov/nr/travel/maritime/brn.htm.*

Cisco Brewers

BREWERY | The microconglomerate of Cisco Brewers, Nantucket Vineyard, and Triple Eight Distillery makes boutique beers, wine, and vodka on-site. Tours and tastings are available (fee) and there is regular live music starting in the late afternoon and sometimes food trucks. ✉ *5 Bartlett Farm Rd., Nantucket* ☎ *508/325–5929* 🌐 *www.ciscobrewers.com.*

First Congregational Church

VIEWPOINT | The tower of this church provides the best view of Nantucket—for those willing to climb its 94 steps. Rising 120 feet, the tower is capped by a weather vane depicting a whale catch. ✉ *62 Centre*

Each beach on Nantucket has a unique approach—sometimes getting there is half the fun.

St., Nantucket ☎ *508/228–0950* 🌐 *www.nantucketfcc.org* 🎫 *Tower tour $5.*

Museum of African American History - Nantucket

HISTORY MUSEUM | When the island abolished slavery in 1773, Nantucket became a destination for free blacks and escaping slaves. The African Meeting House was built in the 1820s as a schoolhouse, and it functioned as such until 1846, when the island's schools were integrated. A complete restoration has returned the site to its authentic 19th-century appearance. Next door is the late-18th-century Seneca Boston-Florence Higginbotham house, originally purchased by Seneca Boston, a former slave and weaver, and purchased by Florence Higginbotham in 1920. The museum offers a free self-guided Nantucket Black Heritage Trail map that includes 10 sites around the island. ✉ *29 York St., Nantucket* ☎ *508/228–9833* 🌐 *www.maah.org* 🎫 *$10.*

Nantucket Black Heritage Trail

TRAIL | Providing insight into Nantucket's African American history, the self-guided trail is divided into two parts, Downtown and New Guinea (an African American community in the 18th and 19th centuries). There are ten stops on the trail including the African Meeting House and the Seneca Boston Florence Higginbotham House. ✉ *Nantucket* ☎ *617/725–0022 ext. 440* 🌐 *www.maah.org.*

★ Whaling Museum

HISTORY MUSEUM | **FAMILY** | With exhibits that include a fully rigged whaleboat and a skeleton of a 46-foot sperm whale, this must-see museum—a complex that includes a restored 1846 spermaceti candle factory—offers a crash course in the island's colorful history. Items on display include harpoons and other whale-hunting implements; portraits of whaling captains and their wives (a few of whom went whaling as well); the South Seas curiosities they brought home; a large collection of sailors' crafts; a full-size tryworks once used to process whale oil; and the original 16-foot-high 1850 lens from Sankaty Head Lighthouse. The museum also offers a rotating gallery with a new exhibit each season, a fine art gallery, and a world-class scrimshaw collection. The Children's Discovery Room provides interactive-learning opportunities. Be sure to climb—or take the elevator—up to the observation deck for a view of the harbor. ✉ *13 Broad St., Nantucket* ☎ *508/228–1894* 🌐 *www.nha.org* 🎫 *$23, includes other historic sites* 🕒 *Closed Jan. Closed Sun. from Feb.-Apr.*

Beaches

Jetties Beach

BEACH | FAMILY | A short bike or shuttle-bus ride from town, Jetties Beach is popular with families because of its calm surf. It's also a good place to try out kayaks and sailboards. The shore is a lively scene, with a playground and volleyball nets on the beach and adjacent public tennis courts. There is a boardwalk to the beach (special wheelchairs are available). You'll have a good view of passing ferries—and an even better one if you clamber out on the jetty itself. (Careful, it's slippery.) **Amenities:** food and drink; lifeguards; parking (fee); showers; toilets; water sports. **Best for:** swimming; windsurfing. ✉ *4 Bathing Beach Rd., 1½ miles northwest of Straight Wharf, Nantucket* 🌐 *www.nantucket-ma.gov/Facilities/Facility/Details/Jetties-Beach-34.*

★ Surfside Beach

BEACH | Surfside Beach, accessible via the Surfside Bike Path (3 miles) or by shuttle bus, is the island's most popular surf beach. This wide strand of sand comes fully equipped with conveniences. It draws teens and young adults as well as families and is great for kite flying and, after 5 pm, surf casting. **Amenities:** food and drink; lifeguards; parking (fee); showers; toilets. **Best for:** surfing; swimming; walking. ✉ *Surfside Rd., South Shore* 🌐 *www.nantucket-ma.gov/facilities/facility/details/surfsidebeach-44.*

Restaurants

B-ack Yard BBQ

$$ | AMERICAN | This game-day favorite offers a rowdy, not rarified, atmosphere and big platters of smoked meats suitable for sharing. But, don't let the casual vibe fool you, as they pay great attention to the food, offering gluten-free versions of all side dishes (except cornbread), great mac-and-cheese, perfectly cooked meats, and their own delicious sauces. **Known for:** great place to watch the game; beef burnt ends; loaded pulled pork nachos. 💲 *Average main: $22* ✉ *20 Straight Wharf, Nantucket* ☎ *508/228–0227* 🌐 *www.ackbackyard.com* 🕒 *Closed Jan.–Feb.*

The Beet

$$ | FUSION | Eating your vegetables is a total pleasure at this tiny lunch and dinner spot, where gorgeous greens meet Latin and Asian flavors in a happy, healthy marriage. Oh, there's protein on the menu—including Korean BBQ quesadillas, Moo Shu-style duck, and pork Bao buns—but it's the green food that really shines. **Known for:** great to-go options; Latin and Asian inspired protein dishes; The Hulk veggie bowl, a triumph of charred Brussels spouts and crispy kale. 💲 *Average main: $25* ✉ *9 South Water St., Nantucket* ☎ *508/680–1857* 🌐 *www.thebeetnantucket.com* 🕒 *Closed Sun.*

Brotherhood of Thieves

$$ | AMERICAN | No, it's not really an 1840s whaling bar—though the atmospheric basement, which dates all the way back to 1972, presents an "olde tavern" vibe. The owners added three new dining concepts as well, including the upscale Notch Whiskey Bar, the surf-themed Cisco Kitchen & Bar, and a beer garden patio, but they haven't changed crowd favorites like curly fries and big, juicy burgers. **Known for:** juicy burgers; fish-and-chips; signature curly fries. 💲 *Average main: $24* ✉ *23 Broad St., Nantucket* ☎ *774/325–5812* 🌐 *www.brotherhoodofthieves.com* 🕒 *Closed Tues.*

Oran Mor Bistro

$$$$ | **INTERNATIONAL** | Climb the copper-clad stairs into this historic home, settle in at one of three dining rooms, and get ready to enjoy the island's freshest fish and produce, impeccably prepared. The menu changes with the seasons, but count on house-made pasta (available in half portions) and toothsome mains with an international tilt, like Moroccan fish tagine. **Known for:** seasonally influenced menu; vegetarian and vegan options; lobster gemelli. *Average main: $35 2 South Beach St., Nantucket 508/228–8655 www.oranmorbistro.com Closed Wed. and Thurs. Sept.–Nov. Closed Dec.–May. No lunch.*

★ **Straight Wharf**

$$$$ | **MODERN AMERICAN** | This loft-like restaurant with a harborside deck has enjoyed legendary status since the mid-1970s; these days, the focus is on re-interpreting summer classics that highlight local produce and fresh seafood. The two-course dinner menu ($78), served in the dining room, features such delectables as iced Nantucket oysters, perhaps followed by slow-poached salmon with a Brussels sprout and baby kale caesar. **Known for:** menu changes daily; locally sourced ingredients; outdoor seating with water view. *Average main: $78 6 Harbor Sq., Nantucket 508/228–4499 www.straightwharfrestaurant.com Closed Mon. and mid-Oct.–mid-May.*

 Hotels

Jared Coffin House

$$$$ | **B&B/INN** | The largest house in town when it was built in 1845, this three-story brick manse is still plenty impressive, and the property is actually comprised of two buildings, the Main House (closed off season) and the Jared Coffin House. **Pros:** knowledgeable concierge; in-town location; historical setting. **Cons:** some tiny rooms; street noise in front; no pets. *Rooms from: $515 29 Broad St., Nantucket 800/248–2405 www.jaredcoffinhouse.com 54 rooms Free Breakfast.*

Life House Nantucket

$$$$ | **HOTEL** | Located atop a hill on a quiet street about ten minutes from town, this old Victorian sea captain's home has a grandma's house-gone-trendy feel. **Pros:** pretty courtyard; wrap-around porch; quiet location, but not far from town. **Cons:** street parking only; no water views; an uphill walk to the inn. *Rooms from: $499 10 Cliff Rd., Nantucket 866/466–7534 www.lifehousehotels.com Closed Nov.–Apr. 14 rooms Free Breakfast.*

★ **The Nantucket Hotel and Resort**

$$$$ | **RESORT** | **FAMILY** | The original impressive 19th-century shell remains, though its interior is sleek, gleaming, and crisp, with a blend of calming neutrals and navy. **Pros:** immaculate and large rooms, many with kitchens; kid's camp included with stay (fee for evenings); full-service restaurant. **Cons:** can be noisy in summer; expensive; many children in summer. *Rooms from: $1,000 77 Easton St., Nantucket 508/228–4747, 866/807–6011 www.thenantuckethotel.com Closed Feb. 44 rooms, 3 cottages Free Breakfast.*

Ships Inn

$$$ | **B&B/INN** | This 1831 home exudes history: it was built for whaling captain Obed Starbuck on the site of the birthplace of abolitionist Lucretia Mott. **Pros:** large rooms; handsome decor; ideal in-town location. **Cons:** on busy street; not for those traveling with small children (under nine); no pets. *Rooms from: $300 13 Fair St., Nantucket 508/228–0040 www.shipsinnnantucket.com Closed late Oct.–late May 10 rooms Free Breakfast.*

★ Union Street Inn
$$$$ | B&B/INN | Ken Withrow worked in the hotel business, Deborah Withrow in high-end retail display, and guests get the best of both worlds in this 1770 house, a stone's throw from the bustle of Main Street. **Pros:** pampering by pros; several rooms have a wood-burning fireplace; impeccable design. **Cons:** bustle of town; some small rooms; not for those with children. *Rooms from: $589 ✉ 7 Union St., Nantucket ☎ 508/228–9222 🌐 www.unioninn.com ⏱ Closed Nov.–late Apr., except for Christmas stroll weekend in early Dec. 12 rooms 🍽 Free Breakfast.*

Nightlife

Chicken Box (*The Box*)
LIVE MUSIC | Live music—including some big-name bands—plays six nights a week in season, and weekends year-round, at this unpretentious roadhouse. *✉ 16 Dave St., Nantucket ☎ 508/228–9717 🌐 www.thechickenbox.com.*

Muse
LIVE MUSIC | This is a year-round venue hosting live bands, including the occasional big-name act. The crowd—the barnlike space can accommodate nearly 400—can get pretty wild. There's also an eatery serving great pizza, burgers, and other bar-type snacks. *✉ 44 Surfside Rd., Nantucket ☎ 508/228–6873 🌐 www.themusenantucket.com.*

Performing Arts

Dreamland
CULTURAL FESTIVALS | Originally built in 1832 as a Quaker meetinghouse, this gem has been fully restored and is now home to year-round entertainment and enrichment. Current movies are shown here, as well as live theater, comedy, and other performing arts. Theater workshops are available for all ages. *✉ 17 S. Water St., Nantucket ☎ 508/228–1784, 508/332–4822 🌐 www.nantucketdreamland.org.*

Activities

BIKING

The best way to tour Nantucket is by bicycle. Nearly 30 miles of paved bike paths wind through all types of terrain from one end of the island to the other: for details, consult the maps posted by the Town & County of Nantucket's website (🌐 www.nantucket-ma.gov). It is possible to bike around the entire island in a day; should you tire, however, you and your bike are welcome aboard the in-season Nantucket Regional Transit Authority (NRTA) buses. The main bike routes start within ½ mile of town, which can be dauntingly congested.

All routes are well marked and lead—eventually—to popular beaches. The paths are also perfect for runners and bladers—but not mopeds, which must remain on the road (to the frustration of impatient drivers). Note that Nantucket requires bike riders 12 and under to wear a helmet. Several shorter spurs connecting popular routes have been continuously added in the island's quest to make Nantucket even more bike-friendly.

■ TIP→ There are multiple bike rental outfits downtown, very close to the ferry terminal; most offer delivery to lodging per request.

The easy 2.2-mile **Surfside Bike Path** leads to Surfside, the island's premier ocean beach. A drinking fountain and rest stop are placed at about the halfway point. The **Milestone Bike Path,** a straight shot linking Nantucket Town and 'Sconset, is probably the most monotonous of the paths but can still be quite pleasant. (It's about 6 miles; paired with the scenic Polpis Road Path, it becomes a 16-mile island loop.) The **Old South Road Bike Path** spurs off from the Milestone Rotary and ends about 1½ miles later close to the airport. At 1.2 miles, the **Cliff Road Path,** on the north shore, is one of the easiest bike paths, but it's still quite scenic, with gentle hills. It intersects with the Eel Point and Madaket paths.

The **Eel Point/Dionis Beach Path** starts at the junction of Eel Point Road and Madaket Road and links the Cliff Road and Madaket bike paths to Dionis Beach; it's less than a mile long. The 9-mile **Polpis Road Path** skirts scenic bays and bogs as it wends its way toward 'Sconset; it intersects with Milestone Path east of the rotary. The **Madaket Path** starts at the intersection of Quaker and Upper Main Streets and follows Madaket Road out to Madaket Beach on the island's west end, about 6 miles from the edge of Nantucket Town. About a third of the way along, you could turn off onto Cliff Road Path or the Eel Point/Dionis Beach Path.

BOATING

Nantucket Community Sailing

BOATING | FAMILY | Renting sailboats, sailboards, and kayaks at Jetties Beach, NCS also offers youth and adult sailing classes and water-sport clinics for disabled athletes. Its Outrigger Canoe Club—a Polynesian tradition—heads out several evenings a week in season. ✉ *Jetties Beach, 4 Winter St., Nantucket* ☎ *508/228–6600* 🌐 *www.nantucketcommunitysailing.org.*

Shopping

Much of the appeal of Nantucket is its concentrated downtown area, all of it easily walkable—just watch your step along the lumpy historic cobblestones. Shoppers will find many high-end stores here, offering up elegant housewares, art, jewelry, upscale women and men's clothing, and many things that Nantucket holds dear: whale belts, "Nantucket Reds," Nantucket lightship baskets, and all things maritime and nautical. Despite being the slow season, the annual Christmas Stroll (🌐 christmasstroll.com) during the first weekend in December is still a popular time, when shops stay open late and offer refreshments, but it's more than just a holiday shopping event now. Hundreds of trees decorate downtown and carolers roam the streets in costume, belting out songs of cheer.

MARKETS

★ Bartlett's Farm

MARKET | Bartlett's Farm encompasses 100 acres overseen by eighth-generation Bartletts. Healthy, tasty prepared foods—within a minisupermarket—are added incentive to make the trek out. If you're not up it, however, a produce truck is parked on Main Street through the summer. ✉ *33 Bartlett Farm Rd., Nantucket* ☎ *508/228–9403* 🌐 *www.bartlettsfarm.com.*

Siasconset

7 miles east of Nantucket Town.

First a fishing outpost and then an artists' colony—Broadway actors favored it in the late 19th century—Siasconset (or 'Sconset, in local vernacular) is a charming cluster of rose-covered cottages linked by driveways of crushed clamshells; at the edges of town, the former fishing shacks give way to magnificent sea-view mansions. The small town center consists of a market, post office, café, lunchroom, and a combination liquor store–lending library.

Sights

Altar Rock

VIEWPOINT | A dirt track leads to the island's highest point, Altar Rock (101 feet), and the view is spectacular. The hill overlooks approximately 4,000 acres of rare coastal heathland laced with paths leading in every direction. ✉ *Altar Rock Rd., 3 miles west of Milestone Rd. rotary on Polpis Rd., Siasconset.*

Beaches

Sconset Beach

BEACH | Known for its wild surf and for its dunes, this beautiful spot is repeatedly blasted by winter erosion. Restaurants and restrooms are in the nearby village. **Amenities**: lifeguards. **Best for**: surfing; swimming; walking. ✉ *Milestone Rd., at the end, Siasconset.*

Coffee and Quick Bites

Handlebar Cafe

$ | CAFÉ | Opened by the founders of Nantucket Bike Tours, this cozy spot offers a welcome space to relax with a coffee or tea and check your email, or just read a book. If you need a snack, scones, muffins, and nuts can be ordered to go with your beverage of choice. **Known for:** "Cup of Sunshine" turmeric latte; nitro cold brew; open year-round. *$ Average main: $3* ✉ *15 Washington St., Nantucket* ☎ *508/825–5929* 🌐 *handlebar-cafe.myshopify.com.*

Hotels

★ The Wauwinet

$$$$ | RESORT | This resplendently updated 1875 resort straddles a "haulover" poised between ocean and bay (think beaches on both sides); it features cushy country-chic guest rooms (lavish with Pratesi linens) and a fine-dining restaurant, Topper's. **Pros:** the staff-to-guest ratio exceeds one-to-one; dual beaches; peaceful setting. **Cons:** not for those with small children; distance from town; pricey rates. *$ Rooms from: $825* ✉ *120 Wauwinet Rd., Wauwinet* ☎ *508/228–0145* 🌐 *www.wauwinet.com* ⏲ *Closed Nov.–mid-Apr.* 🛏 *32 rooms, 4 cottages.*

Activities

BIKING

'Sconset Bike Path

BIKING | This 6½-mile bike path starts at the rotary east of Nantucket Town and parallels Milestone Road, ending in 'Sconset. It is mostly level, with some gentle hills. Slightly longer (and dippier), the 9-mile **Polpis Road Path,** veering off to the northeast, is far more scenic and leads to the turnoff to Wauwinet. ✉ *Off Milestone Rd., Siasconset.*

Chapter 6

THE BERKSHIRES AND WESTERN MASSACHUSETTS

Updated by
Lindsey Hollenbaugh

Sights
★★★★☆

Restaurants
★★★★☆

Hotels
★★★★☆

Shopping
★★★☆☆

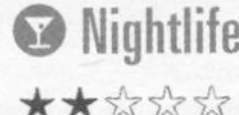
Nightlife
★★☆☆☆

WELCOME TO THE BERKSHIRES AND WESTERN MASSACHUSETTS

TOP REASONS TO GO

★ **The Countryside:** Rolling hills, dense stands of forest, open pastures, and scenic valleys greet your eye at every turn.

★ **The Food:** Experience farm-to-table cuisine where community-supported agriculture was first founded in the 1980s.

★ **Summer Festivals:** Watch renowned dance companies perform at Jacob's Pillow, or listen to the Boston Symphony Orchestra at Tanglewood in Lenox.

★ **Under-the-Radar Museums:** Western Massachusetts has an eclectic assortment of institutions, from the Eric Carle Museum of Picture Book Art to the Basketball Hall of Fame.

★ **Pioneer Valley College Towns:** Three academic centers—Amherst (University of Massachusetts, Amherst College, and Hampshire College), Northampton (Smith College), and South Hadley (Mount Holyoke College)—pulse with cultural activity and youthful energy.

1 North Adams. The ideal Berkshires getaway is home to the Massachusetts Museum of Contemporary Arts.

2 Williamstown. Built around the prestigious Williams College, this town has two noteworthy art museums and the renowned Williamstown Theatre Festival.

3 Hancock. A great location for year-round outdoor enthusiasts, it's also the closest town to the ski and snowboard resort, Jiminy Peak.

4 Pittsfield. This busy little city is called the heart of the Berkshires for its central location to dining, live theater, and family friendly festivals.

5 Lenox. The famed Tanglewood music festival takes up residence every summer.

6 Otis. Plenty of outdoor activities are available here year-round, but the popular Jacob's Pillow Dance Festival, in nearby Becket, draws the attention in the summer months.

7 Stockbridge. Such a quintessential New England town that even Norman Rockwell called home.

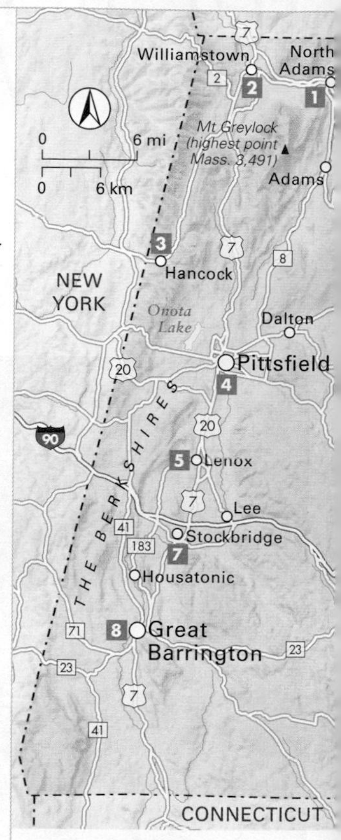

8 Great Barrington. A great place for delicious food and antiques hunting.

9 Springfield. The city's home to the Naismith Memorial Basketball Hall of Fame and the Springfield Museums, which includes the Amazing World of Dr. Seuss.

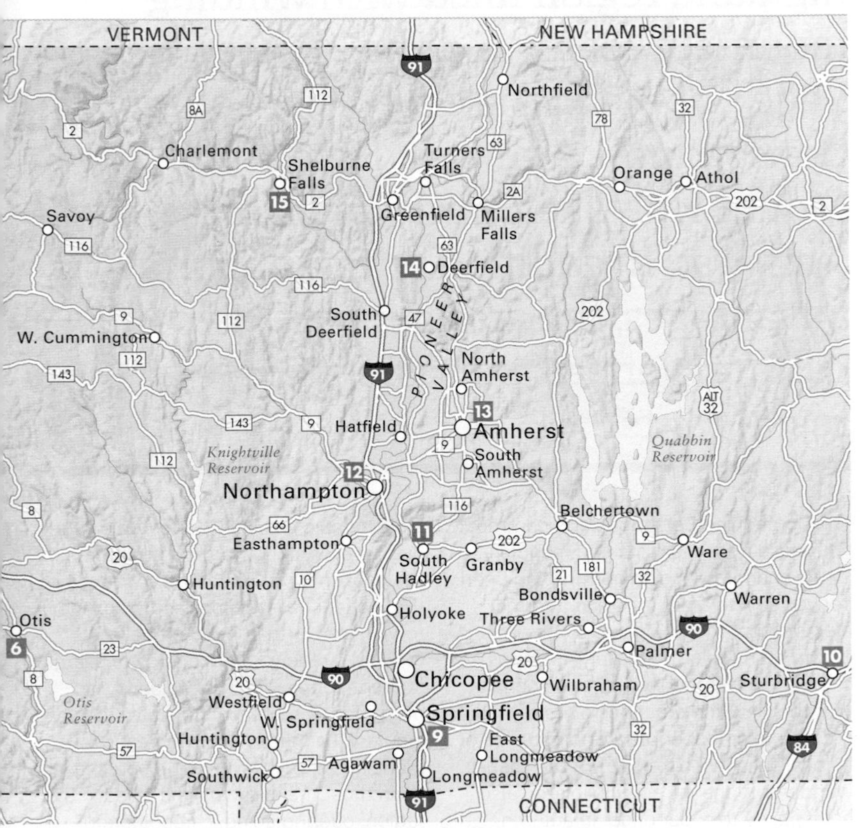

10 Sturbridge. A re-created early-19th-century village, Old Sturbridge Village is the area's premier attraction.

11 South Hadley. A quiet college town home to Mount Holyoke College.

12 Northampton. The cultural hub of Western Massachusetts is also home to Smith College.

13 Amherst. A mecca for world-renowned authors, poets, and artists, Amherst is also known for its trio of colleges: Amherst, Hampshire, and the University of Massachusetts.

14 Deerfield. The perfect New England village complete with a white-steepled church and perfectly maintained 18th-century homes.

15 Shelburne Falls. The community is filled with art galleries, shops, and farm stands.

The Bay State's most westerly portion consists of the Berkshires, a bucolic highland region filled with winding mountain roads, and the Pioneer Valley, home to the elite "Five College Consortium": Amherst, Hampshire, Mount Holyoke, Smith, and UMass Amherst. In addition to their natural advantages, the area supports dynamic cultural venues and risk-taking restaurants.

The burgeoning Berkshires arts community arose from the ruins of a manufacturing economy—aging mills having been converted into artist lofts and a former electric plant morphing into a contemporary art museum. Smaller museums can be found throughout the region, and you can view the creations of its myriad artists and craftspeople at their studios or in local galleries. Hikers, from the casual wanderer to the intrepid trailblazer, also have plenty to experience. In autumn, leaf peepers descend to explore this area renowned for fall foliage with vibrant oranges, yellows, and reds that typify the harvest season.

Though it might be presumptuous to proclaim a "renaissance," it can't be denied that the concentration of arts and culture in the Berkshires has reinvigorated the whole region. Along with this artistic explosion, a renewed focus on fresh, local food grown just up the road from many high-class restaurants helps turn this formerly depressed postindustrial area into a hot spot for farm-to-table cuisine with festivals celebrating everything from ice sculptures to the spoken word. The trend continues in the Pioneer Valley, especially in college towns like Northampton, propelled forward by the youthful energy of a large student population. The region is also beginning to embrace the state's newest industry: cannabis. Small recreational marijuana shops have begun popping up in most major towns and cities in the region, offering an educated, tasteful experience for those looking to partake. However, if it's not your thing, you won't even notice most of the shops with streamlined, discreet store fronts.

MAJOR REGIONS

Occupying the far western end of the state, **the Berkshires** are only about three hours by car from Boston or New York City, yet the region lives up to the storybook picture of rural New England: wooded hills, narrow winding roads, fall foliage, and quaint downtowns. Skiing is popular in winter—Hancock is the closest village to Jiminy Peak—and sugar-maple sap runs in the spring. Summer brings cultural events, like the renowned Tanglewood classical music festival in Lenox, the theater festival in Williamstown, and the Jacob's Pillow Dance Festival in Becket. Norman Rockwell called Stockbridge home, the Hancock Shaker Village is in Pittsfield, and North Adams has the Massachusetts Museum of Contemporary Arts. Great Barrington has great food, antiques shops, and the Mahaiwe Performing Arts Center.

Overshadowed somewhat by Boston to the east and the Berkshires to the west, **the Pioneer Valley** is home to historic settlements, unique museums, college towns, and natural treasures. Sturbridge's Old Sturbridge Village—a re-created early-19th-century village with restored buildings, reenactments, and activities—is the premier attraction here. The principal city here is Springfield, home to the Naismith Memorial Basketball Hall of Fame and the family-friendly Springfield Museums, but most of the area is quite rural—this is where the idyllic New England countryside of the imagination comes to life. College towns like South Hadley, Northampton, and Amherst serve as cultural hubs that have attracted former city dwellers who relish the ample natural scenery, sophisticated cultural venues, and lively dining and shopping. The picturesque towns of Deerfield and Shelburne Falls draw visitors for foliage and history tours.

Planning

Getting Here and Around

AIR

Most travelers arrive at Boston's Logan International Airport, the state's major airline hub. From Boston you can reach most parts of the Pioneer Valley in less than two hours by car, the Berkshires in about three.

Bradley International Airport in Windsor Locks, Connecticut, 18 miles south of Springfield, Massachusetts, on Interstate 91, serves the Pioneer Valley and the Berkshires. Another alternative—and actually closer to the area than Logan—is T. F. Green International Airport in Providence, Rhode Island.

CAR

Public transportation can be spotty in this region, with buses that don't run on Sunday or in the evening, so you'll almost certainly need a car. But you'll want one anyway so you can take leisurely drives to see the fall foliage. Be warned, though, that the winding mountain roads here are not for the fainthearted.

TRAIN

The Northeast Corridor and high-speed Acela services of Amtrak link Boston with the principal cities between it and Washington, D.C. Amtrak's *Lake Shore Limited,* which stops at Springfield, carries passengers from Chicago to Boston. For destinations north and west of Boston, trains depart from Boston's North Station. Amtrak's Berkshire Flyer line, connecting New York City to Pittsfield, runs weekends in the summer but that may increase as popularity increases.

Restaurants

On the menus at country inns, upscale restaurants, and even the coffee shop around the corner in the Berkshires and the Pioneer Valley, you will most likely learn what farm provided each ingredient, right down to the cheese platter or garnishes for cocktails. Chefs, restaurant owners, and local farmers have close, almost familial relationships in these parts, and the food is all the better for it.

Don't expect baked beans or slow-boiled meats of New England winters past when you visit. Instead, modern cafés and trendy restaurants now serve everything from fusion cuisine to pizza with inspired, seasonally appropriate toppings.

Perhaps most enticingly, an influx of multiculturalism to the Berkshires has resulted in a number of excellent international food options, especially in the Northern/Central region. In addition to the standard Chinese, Indian, and Thai, visitors can now partake of a wider range of cuisines—including Peruvian, Spanish, Colombian, and Malaysian.

Hotels

The signature accommodation outside Boston is the country inn; in the Berkshires, where magnificent mansions have been converted into luxury lodgings, these inns have reached a very grand scale indeed. Less extravagant and less expensive are bed-and-breakfast establishments, many in private homes. Make reservations for inns well ahead during peak periods (summer through winter in the Berkshires).

Campers can pitch their tents amid acres of pine forest dotted with rivers and lakes or in the shadows of the rolling Berkshire Hills. The camping season in Massachusetts generally runs late May–mid-October. For more about camping, contact the Massachusetts Department of Conservation and Recreation (☎617/626–1250 www.mass.gov/topics/parks-recreation).

■ TIP→ Hotel reviews have been shortened. For full information, visit Fodors.com.

What It Costs in U.S. Dollars

$	$$	$$$	$$$$
RESTAURANTS			
under $18	$18–$24	$25–$35	over $35
HOTELS			
under $200	$200–$299	$300–$399	over $399

Visitor Information

CONTACTS Berkshire Regional Transit Authority. ✉ *Pittsfield* ☎ *800/292–2782, 413/499–2782* 🌐 *www.berkshirerta.com.* **Massachusetts Department of Fish and Game.** ✉ *Boston* ☎ *617/626–1500* 🌐 *www.mass.gov/eea/agencies/dfg.* **1Berkshire.** ✉ *Pittsfield* ☎ *413/499–1600* 🌐 *www.berkshires.org.*

When to Go

The dazzling foliage and cool temperatures make fall the best time to visit Western Massachusetts, but the Berkshires and the Pioneer Valley are evolving into a year-round destination. Visit in spring, and witness the burst of color that signals winter's end. Summer is a time of festivals, adventure sports, and outdoor concerts. Many towns save their best for winter, when inns open their doors to carolers and shops serve eggnog. Though usually considered the off-season, it's the perfect time to try cross-country skiing or to spend a night by the fireplace, tucked under a quilt while catching up on books by Nathaniel Hawthorne or Henry David Thoreau.

North Adams

130 miles northwest of Boston, 73 miles northwest of Springfield, 20 miles south of Bennington, Vermont.

If you're looking for a Berkshires getaway that combines culture with outdoor fun and a cool place to stay, put North Adams on your short list. In addition to the Massachusetts Museum of Contemporary Arts (Mass MoCA), North Adams has a number of smaller art galleries, as well as a few mills and factory buildings that have been converted into artist studios. This city with a "small town" feel is always hosting festivals, downtown parades, and on most weekends,

The Ins and Outs of Cannabis

Travelers looking for a little extra relaxation may be interested in stopping by one of the region's newest recreational marijuana shops open to those 21 or older. While these aren't your parents' pot shops with lingering smells and tie-dye wall hangings (these days, dispensaries—as they prefer to be called—go for a more clean, almost clinical look with modern fixtures and elements of nature), you may still have to wait in a parking lot to get your fix. In order to meet state capacity guidelines, there's often a line snaking around parking lots filled with shoppers waiting to enter.

The Basics

How to pay: Due to federal marijuana laws, many national and state-chartered banks that are federally insured do not want to be involved with marijuana transactions. Therefore, many dispensaries ask for cash only, and a few may take debit cards. Your best bet? Always come prepared with cash.

Identification: You'll need a government-issued ID for age validation. Acceptable forms include a driver's license, passport, state ID card, or military ID. Make sure you check that expiration date—if your ID is expired it will not be accepted. You don't have to live in the state to purchase marijuana, but remember, products purchased in the Bay State are only legal here. If you cross state lines, you're on your own.

What to buy: Recreational marijuana customers may legally purchase up to 1 ounce of marijuana flower or 5 grams of marijuana concentrate per day. Shops now offer a variety of options—from edibles such as gummies and chocolate bars, to vaping products and prerolled joints. Western Mass sellers have built a reputation for being friendly, helpful, and more than willing to offer advice on what to purchase and at what concentrate. Don't be afraid to ask for recommendations.

Now what? Once you leave the store, you can't have an open container of any form of marijuana in the passenger area of your car while on the road or at a place where the public has access. It must be stored in a closed container in your trunk or a locked glove compartment. It also cannot be used in public areas, only in private where owners are OK with it. Check with your lodging for specific rules and regulations.

a farmers' market where locals shop, visit, and grab up in-season produce from their favorite farms. The 12.7-mile Ashuwillticook Rail Trail is accessible in nearby Adams, as is Mt. Greylock State Reservation, if you venture there on foot via one of the local trailheads.

GETTING HERE AND AROUND

Arrive at North Adams from Pittsfield in the south via Route 8, or from Williamstown in the west via Route 2. Once in town you can see everything on foot in good weather, with most of the action within a few blocks of Main Street. Natural Bridge State Park is the exception, but it's still a reasonable walk.

Sights

Down Street Art

PUBLIC ART | FAMILY | This public-arts project includes 31 galleries in downtown North Adams. From late June through September, DSA presents visual and performing arts events including exhibitions, video screenings, site-specific installations, and, on the last Thursday of the month, opening galas and performances. ✉ *51 Main St., North Adams* ☎ *413/662–5253.*

Hoosac Valley Train Rides

TRAIN/TRAIN STATION | Themed (fall foliage, Christmas) hour-long train rides make the 10-mile journey between Adams and North Adams in restored historic cars. All trains depart from (and return to) Adams Station. ✉ *Adams Visitor Center, 4 Hoosac St., Adams* ☎ *413/663–4189* 🌐 *www.berkshiretrains.org.*

★ Massachusetts Museum of Contemporary Arts (*Mass MoCA*)

FACTORY | FAMILY | Formerly the home of the Sprague Electrical Company, the nation's largest center for contemporary visual and performing arts is one of the finest such facilities in the world, a major draw for its art shows, large music festivals, dance presentations, and film screenings. Expansion in 2017 nearly doubled the amount of gallery space, bringing the total to a quarter million square feet, which includes the wall drawings of Sol LeWitt, an immersive light-based exhibit by James Turrell, and a large room in the main gallery that allows for massive exhibits that wouldn't fit anywhere else. A Kidspace, studios, cafés, shops, and festivals and other special events round out the offerings. ✉ *87 Marshall St., North Adams* ☎ *413/662–2111* 🌐 *www.massmoca.org* 🎫 *$20.*

Natural Bridge State Park

STATE/PROVINCIAL PARK | The 30-foot span that gives this 48-acre park its name crosses Hudson Brook, yielding appealing views of rocky chasms. The marble arch at the park's center rises in what functioned as a marble quarry from the early 1880s to the mid-1900s. Natural Bridge has picnic sites, hiking trails, and well-maintained restrooms. In winter the area is popular for cross-country skiing. Do check for trail closures due to maintenance before going. ✉ *McCauley Rd., off Rte. 8, North Adams* ☎ *413/663–6392* 🌐 *www.mass.gov/locations/natural-bridge-state-park.*

Susan B. Anthony Birthplace Museum

HISTORY MUSEUM | This museum celebrates the extraordinary life and legacy of Susan B. Anthony, who played a pivotal role in winning women the right to vote. In addition to viewing suffrage mementos, you can learn about the abolition and temperance movements, in which she also participated. Definitely worth a look is the collection of 19th-century postcards supporting these three campaigns. ✉ *67 East Rd., Adams* ☎ *413/743–7121* 🌐 *www.susanbanthonybirthplace.com* 🎫 *$10.*

Western Gateway Heritage State Park

OTHER ATTRACTION | FAMILY | The old Boston & Maine Railroad yard is the site of this park whose free museum has exhibits that trace the construction of the Hoosac Tunnel and the impact of train travel on the region. A scale model of North Adams in the 1950s is on display, and there's a short film that documents the intense labor required to construct the nearby Hoosac Tunnel; the tunnel is best viewed from a pedestrian bridge one block from the park where you can see the tracks as they disappear into the tunnel. ✉ *9 Furnace St., Bldg. 4, North Adams* ☎ *413/663–6312* 🌐 *www.mass.gov/locations/western-gateway-heritage-state-park* 🎫 *Free* 🕒 *Museum closed Tues. and Wed. Nov.–Apr.*

Restaurants

The Break Room at Greylock Works

$$ | **AMERICAN** | Fans of Berkshires' favorite head chef Brian Alberg won't want to miss his latest restaurant adventure located in a renovated cotton mill complex that offers indoor and outdoor seating with a relaxed, industrial feel. The menu is constantly changing to reflect the freshest in-season ingredients, and an acclaimed pastry chef is on staff so you'll never want to skip dessert or a stop for brunch; most dishes start as vegetarian but offer protein options for an additional price. **Known for:** rotating farm-to-table menu; delicious pastries; Saturday night summer dinners outdoors on the grill. *Average main: $26 508 State Rd., North Adams 413/346–4035 www.thebreakroomgw.com Closed Tues. and Wed. No lunch Mon.*

Grazie

$$ | **ITALIAN** | **FAMILY** | This cozy Italian restaurant serves up traditional Italian dishes with an American touch. The pasta and homemade meatballs come in large portions and the staff is friendly and attentive; you can order family-style meals to share with the table if that's more your style. **Known for:** generous portions; delicious sea scallop risotto; excellent service. *Average main: $28 26 Marshall St., North Adams 413/664–0044 www.graziena.com Closed Mon. and Tues. No lunch.*

Meng's Pan-Asian

$ | **ASIAN** | Formerly known as Sushi House, this pan-Asian restaurant on the main drag offers up Chinese, Thai, Korean, and Japanese classics in a comfortable atmosphere. From curries and *bibim bap* to sushi and bento boxes, Meng's extensive menu has something for everyone, at an affordable price. **Known for:** pad see you (Thai stir-fried noodles); cheap lunch specials; half-price-sushi Tuesday. *Average main: $13 45 Main St., North Adams 413/664–9388 Take-out available only.*

Coffee and Quick Bites

Jack's Hot Dog Stand

$ | **HOT DOG** | Not much has changed at this hole-in-the-wall including its single lunch counter lined with a small row of stools and its cash-only policy. Locals head here for inexpensive wieners and hamburgers, plain or topped with chili, cheese, or both, but don't expect to find a seat during lunch hour. **Known for:** a family-owned institution since 1917; onion rings and fries; hot-dog-eating contests. *Average main: $3 12 Eagle St., North Adams 413/664–9006 www.jackshotdogstand.com No credit cards Closed Sun.*

Trés Niños Taqueria

$ | **MEXICAN** | **FAMILY** | Taco lovers adored this local Mexican food truck so much, the owners had no choice but to open a dine-in option. This is a bare-bones establishment with friendly staff, quick service and delicious breakfast and lunch options; check their Facebook page for daily specials. **Known for:** stuffed burritos and rice bowls; tasty taco salad; taco kits to take home for when you don't want to cook. *Average main: $8 20 Marshall St., North Adams 413/346–4000 www.facebook.com/tresninosNA Closed Sun.*

Hotels

★ Porches Inn

$$ | **B&B/INN** | Around the corner from Mass MoCA and Main Street, these Victorian mill-workers' houses dating to the 1890s have been restored and are connected with one long porch and some interior hallways walled with exteriors of the old houses to become one of New England's quirkiest hotels. **Pros:** outdoor heated pool and hot tub; large guest rooms; packages that include museum admission. **Cons:** small breakfast room; no indoor pool; not much indoor public space. *Rooms from: $219 231*

River St., North Adams ☎ 413/664–0400 🌐 www.porches.com 🛏 47 rooms 🍽 Free Breakfast.

Topia Inn

$$ | B&B/INN | Innkeepers Nana Simopoulos and Caryn Heilman have transformed a derelict downtown building into an eco-friendly marvel, with solar panels and natural clay walls. **Pros:** artsy rooms; organic breakfasts; workshops on green cooking and cleaning. **Cons:** short on parking; next door to a bar; you can't bring your own nonorganic shampoos—it's a hotel rule. *$ Rooms from: $275 ✉ 10 Pleasant St., Adams ☎ 413/743–9600 🌐 www.topiainn.com 🛏 7 rooms 🍽 Free Breakfast.*

★ TOURISTS

$$ | HOTEL | This minimalist hotel has many oak-covered surfaces, a large fireplace in the rustic lobby, amazing views of Mt. Greylock from the patio deck and courtyard, and walking trails that lead guests to a suspension bridge, sound sculpture, and a restaurant. **Pros:** outdoor showers for every room; trendy Airport Room eatery attached for late-night snacks; some rooms have private balconies. **Cons:** no tubs in bathrooms; no phone in room; location is traffic heavy. *$ Rooms from: $290 ✉ 915 State Rd., North Adams ☎ 413/347-4995 🌐 www.touristswelcome.com 🛏 48 rooms 🍽 No Meals.*

Activities

KAYAKING

Berkshire Outfitters

KAYAKING | If you're itching to explore the Cheshire lakes by kayak, the Ashuwillticook Rail Trail by bike, or Mt. Greylock's summit on snowshoes, visit Berkshire Outfitters. Just 300 yards from the trail, this shop rents bicycles, kayaks, canoes, paddleboards, snowshoes, and cross-country skis. The knowledgeable staff are happy to dispense free trail maps and advice. *✉ 169 Grove St., Adams ☎ 413/743–5900 🌐 www.berkshireoutfitters.com.*

Williamstown

5 miles west of North Adams.

Williamstown is largely built around the prestigious Williams College, a smallish but verdant campus bisected by Route 2. Williams is one of the "Little Ivies," and indeed there are ivy-covered buildings, a Gothic-style chapel, marble columns, and various other architectural features. Although "downtown" consists of just a few streets, two noteworthy art museums can be found near the town center, and there are enough upscale shops and restaurants offering international cuisine. In summertime, theatergoers replace college students for the **Williamstown Theatre Festival**; if you're lucky, you may catch a famous actor at a local bar.

GETTING HERE AND AROUND

Williamstown encompasses the surrounding farms and rolling hills, but the town proper straddles Route 2. On the Williams College campus you can walk to Spring Street and Water Street, and anything else you want to see is probably just a short drive off Route 2 (or you can a hop onto the BRTA bus).

Sights

★ Clark Art Institute

ART MUSEUM | One of the nation's notable small art museums, the Clark has won numerous architectural awards for its 2014 redesign by Reed Hilderbrand and for the new Clark Center by Pritzker Prize–winning architect Tadao Ando. The polished concrete of the latter visually connects it to the landscape through glass windows and open spaces.

The museum has a large collection of Impressionist works, in particular many significant Renoir paintings.

Other strengths include English silver, European and American photography 1840–1920, and 17th- and 18th-century Flemish and Dutch masterworks. *✉ 225 South St., Williamstown ☎ 413/458–2303*

Winslow Homer's "West Point, Prout's Neck" is among the notable paintings at Williamstown's Clark Art Institute.

www.clarkart.edu *$20 (2-day ticket)* *Closed Mon. Sept.–June.*

Mt. Greylock State Reservation

MOUNTAIN | The centerpiece of this 10,327-acre reservation south of Williamstown is Mt. Greylock, the highest point in Massachusetts at 3,491 feet, and the fictional location of Pottermore's North American school of magic, Ilvermorny School of Witchcraft and Wizardry. The reservation has facilities for cycling, fishing, horseback riding, camping, and snowmobiling. Many treks—including a portion of the Appalachian Trail—start from the parking lot at the summit in Adams, an 8-mile drive from the mountain's base. *Visitor center, 30 Rockwell Rd., Lanesborough* *413/499–4262* *www.mass.gov/locations/mount-greylock-state-reservation.*

★ Williams College Museum of Art

ART MUSEUM | **FAMILY** | The collection at this fine museum spans a range of eras and cultures, with American and 20th-century art as two major focuses. The original octagonal structure facing Main Street was built as a library in 1846, and the painted wall above the stairs is by Sol LeWitt—actually the third mural to occupy the wall. Special events take place on the outdoor patio on Thursday night in summer. Get an inside look at Williams students' experience with Object Lab, a hybrid gallery-classroom curated by faculty to coincide with students' studies. *15 Lawrence Hall Dr., Williamstown* *413/597–2376* *wcma.williams.edu* *Free* *Closed Mon.*

Restaurants

★ Coyote Flaco

$ | **MEXICAN** | The best Mexican food in the Berkshires can be found at this unassuming spot where traditional cuisine meets local ingredients. The menu is small but every item is done well, and often served with side dishes in cute little tortilla cups. **Known for:** enchilada Oaxaca with mole sauce; delicious margaritas; nightly specials. *Average main: $16* *505 Cold Spring Rd., Williamstown* *413/458–4240* *www.*

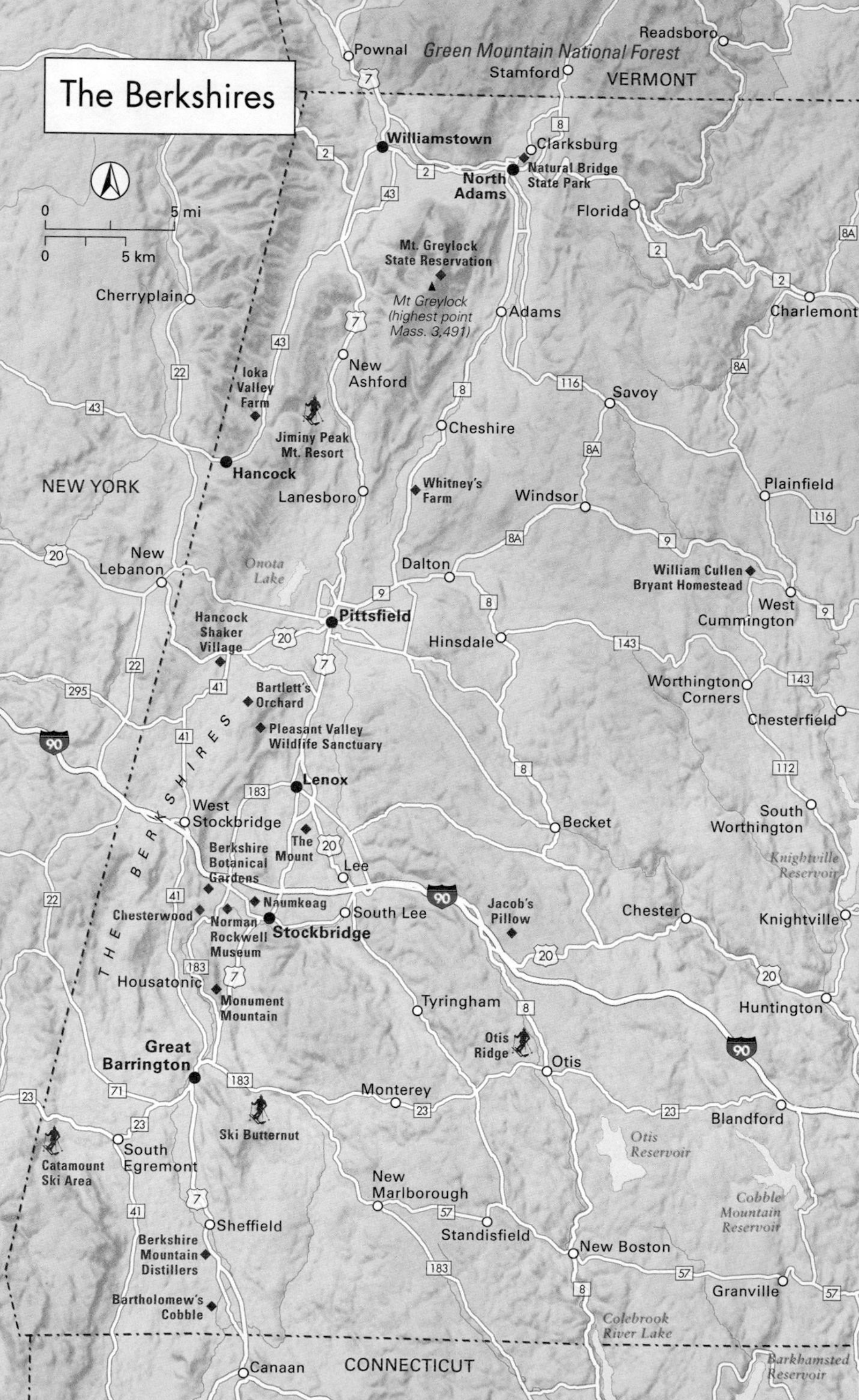

The Berkshires
0
5 mi
0
5 km
Green Mountain National Forest
VERMONT
NEW YORK
CONNECTICUT
THE BERKSHIRES
Pownal
Readsboro
Stamford
Williamstown
Clarksburg
Natural Bridge State Park
North Adams
Florida
Mt. Greylock State Reservation
Mt Greylock (highest point Mass. 3,491)
Adams
Charlemont
Cherryplain
New Ashford
Savoy
Ioka Valley Farm
Jiminy Peak Mt. Resort
Cheshire
Hancock
Lanesboro
Whitney's Farm
Windsor
Plainfield
New Lebanon
Onota Lake
Dalton
William Cullen Bryant Homestead
West Cummington
Pittsfield
Hancock Shaker Village
Hinsdale
Worthington Corners
Bartlett's Orchard
Pleasant Valley Wildlife Sanctuary
Chesterfield
Lenox
West Stockbridge
Becket
South Worthington
The Mount
Berkshire Botanical Gardens
Lee
Knightville Reservoir
Naumkeag
Chesterwood
Norman Rockwell Museum
Stockbridge
South Lee
Jacob's Pillow
Chester
Knightville
Housatonic
Monument Mountain
Tyringham
Huntington
Otis Ridge
Otis
Great Barrington
Monterey
Blandford
Ski Butternut
Catamount Ski Area
South Egremont
Otis Reservoir
New Marlborough
Cobble Mountain Reservoir
Sheffield
Standisfield
Berkshire Mountain Distillers
New Boston
Granville
Bartholomew's Cobble
Colebrook River Lake
Canaan
Barkhamsted Reservoir

facebook.com/coyoteflaco ⏲ *Closed Mon. and Tues. No lunch.*

Mezze Bistro & Bar

$$$ | **ECLECTIC** | With a beautiful hilltop location and dishes inspired by local ingredients, the bistro can get crowded in summer, when Williamstown Theatre Festival ticket holders try to squeeze in dinner before the curtain goes up. With an emphasis on local and seasonal ingredients, the menu is always in a state of flux, but it's bound to contain steak, duck, and a great burger. **Known for:** excellent cocktail, wine list; Garganelli pasta with beef ragu; smallish portions. *Average main: $27* ✉ *777 Cold Spring Rd., Williamstown* ☎ *413/458–0123* 🌐 *www.mezzerestaurant.com* ⏲ *No lunch. Closed Mon. and Tues.*

Coffee and Quick Bites

A-Frame Bakery

$ | **BAKERY** | The tiny A-frame at the intersection of U.S. 7 and Route 2 isn't much to look at, but the bakery within sells delectable goods that inspire loyalty in locals and visitors alike. The babka—especially the chocolate, though there's also a cinnamon edition—is second to none and must be ordered a day ahead. **Known for:** crumb cakes, scones, and muffins; many items need to be ordered a day in advance; buttercream frosting. *Average main: $3* ✉ *1194 Cold Spring Rd., Williamstown* ☎ *413/458–3600* 🌐 *www.facebook.com/AFrameBakery* *No credit cards* ⏲ *Closed Mon.–Wed.*

The Spring Street Market and Café

$ | **AMERICAN** | **FAMILY** | This Spring Street staple is equal parts market, bakery, and sandwich shop and is often filled with Williams College students grabbing lunch, a homemade cookie, or a few dorm room staples. The tight shop offers little space to stay and eat, but is filled to the brim with delicious-smelling pastries, desserts, and smiling students behind the cash register. **Known for:** friendly and welcoming atmosphere; stuffed, creative sandwiches; homemade cookies. *Average main: $9* ✉ *66 Spring St., Williamstown* ☎ *413/458–6192* 🌐 *www.thespringstreetmarketandcafe.com* ⏲ *Closed Mon.*

Tunnel City Coffee

$ | **CAFÉ** | After doing some shopping along Spring Street, stop in for a pick-me-up of freshly brewed drip coffee, espresso, or tea and one of the many delicious baked goods made on-site. During the summer, you're sure to bump into famous actors in between rehearsals stopping by for specialty coffee reminiscent of what they'd get in Manhattan. **Known for:** bean blends that can be enjoyed at home; fresh blueberry muffins; cold brew coffee. *Average main: $6* ✉ *100 Spring St., Williamstown* ☎ *413/458–5010* 🌐 *www.tunnelcitycoffee.com.*

Hotels

Guest House at Field Farm

$$ | **B&B/INN** | Built in 1948, this guesthouse contains a fine collection of art on loan from Williams College and the Whitney Museum, as well as lobby that wouldn't be out of place on a 1960s movie set. **Pros:** wonderful art collection; luxurious robes and towels; seasonal swimming pool. **Cons:** no TV in rooms; children under 12 not permitted; off the beaten path. *Rooms from: $269* ✉ *554 Sloan Rd.* ☎ *413/458–3135* 🌐 *www.guesthouseatfieldfarm.org* ⏲ *Closed Jan.–Mar.* *6 rooms* *Free Breakfast.*

★ River Bend Farm

$ | **B&B/INN** | Listed on the National Register of Historic Places, this 1770 Georgian Colonial is a rustic place to discover simpler times. **Pros:** free Wi-Fi; good breakfast; friendly innkeepers. **Cons:** uneven floors; shared bathrooms; no TVs; credit cards not accepted. *Rooms from: $150* ✉ *643 Simonds Rd., Williamstown* ☎ *413/458–3121* 🌐 *www.riverbendfarmbb.com* *No* *credit cards* ⏲ *Closed Nov.–Mar.* ⇌ *4 rooms* 🍽 *Free Breakfast.*

Performing Arts

Images Cinema

FILM | The Berkshires' premier (and, admittedly, only) year-round nonprofit independent film house showcases art-house films, documentaries, and the latest from Sundance on two screens. There are outdoor shows during the summer. ✉ *50 Spring St., Williamstown* ☎ *413/458–5612* 🌐 *www.imagescinema.org.*

★ Williamstown Theatre Festival

ARTS FESTIVALS | The festival, a past Tony Award winner for outstanding regional theater, is Williamstown's hottest summer ticket. From June through August, the long-running event presents well-known theatrical works featuring famous performers on the Main Stage and contemporary works on the Nikos Stage. ✉ *Williams College, '62 Center for Theatre and Dance, 1000 Main St., Williamstown* ☎ *413/458-3200* 🌐 *www.wtfestival.org.*

Shopping

★ Where'd You Get That?

TOYS | **FAMILY** | Jam-packed with toys, games, and more bizarre novelty items than you could possibly imagine, this store benefits from the enthusiasm of owners Ken and Michele Gietz. Grab an offbeat gift for a friend (and some of the interesting candies for yourself). ✉ *100 Spring St., Williamstown* ☎ *413/458–2206* 🌐 *www.wygt.com.*

Hancock

15 miles south of Williamstown.

Tiny Hancock, the village closest to the Jiminy Peak ski resort, really comes into its own in winter, though it's also a great base for outdoors enthusiasts year-round, with biking, hiking, and other options in summer.

GETTING HERE AND AROUND

You can take Route 43 from Williamstown, U.S. 7 north from Pittsfield to Bailey Road west in Lanesborough, or the BRTA bus from Lanesborough, with plenty of mountain views and trees along the way.

Sights

Ioka Valley Farm

FARM/RANCH | **FAMILY** | Bring the kids to this 600-acre farm whose family-friendly activities include games and tractor rides. Seasonal offerings range from pick-your-own pumpkins (mid-September–October) to cut-your-own Christmas trees (late November–late December) and a petting farm from late June through August. For a real treat, catch a weekend brunch (late February–early April) with homemade maple syrup atop pancakes, waffles, and French toast. ✉ *3475 Rte. 43, Hancock* ☎ *413/738–5915* 🌐 *www.iokavalleyfarm.com.*

Hotels

Country Inn at Jiminy Peak

$ | **RESORT** | **FAMILY** | Massive stone fireplaces in the lobby and lounge lend this hotel a ski-lodge atmosphere—suites in the building's rear overlook the slopes—and the condo-style suites (privately owned but put into a rental pool) can accommodate up to four people. **Pros:** lodging-and-skiing package deals; nice bathrooms; eat-in kitchenettes. **Cons:** remote location; outdoor pool is small; rooms have no character. [$] *Rooms from: $135* ✉ *37 Corey Rd., Hancock* ☎ *413/738–5500, 800/882–8859* 🌐 *www.jiminypeak.com* ⇌ *103 suites* 🍽 *No Meals.*

The Springs Motel

$ | **MOTEL** | Step back in time and sleep comfortably in one of the fun, retro rooms or plan a weekend away with a group of friends or family at the cabins that can sleep up to six Magnolia Network fans will recognize this newly renovated hotel's owner Lindsey Kurowski, who bought and renovated the roadside motel on the second season of her show *Inn the Works*. **Pros:** attentive hotel owner; outdoor bar and '60s-inspired pool; fun, quirky design features. **Cons:** no indoor pool; sits on a busy road; small with not many rooms. *Rooms from: $145 ✉ 94 Rte. 7, New Ashford ☎ 413/200–8464 ⊕ www.springsmotel.co 3 rooms, 2 cabins No Meals.*

Activities

SKIING

Jiminy Peak

SKIING & SNOWBOARDING | The only full-service ski and snowboard resort in the Berkshires, Jiminy Peak is also the largest in southern New England. This is mostly a cruising mountain. Trails are groomed daily, though some small moguls are left to build up along the slope sides. The steepest black-diamond runs are on the upper head walls; longer, outer runs make for good intermediate terrain. There's night skiing daily, and snowmaking capacity can cover 93% of skiable terrain. Jiminy has three terrain parks, as well as a weekends-only mountain coaster: a two-person cart that shoots down the mountain at speeds of up to 25 mph. During the summer, the resort transforms into an adventure park. **Facilities:** 45 trails; 170 acres; 1,150-foot vertical drop; 9 lifts. *✉ 37 Corey Rd., Hancock ☎ 413/738–5500, 888/454–6469 ⊕ www.jiminypeak.com Lift ticket: $109.*

Pittsfield

21 miles south of Williamstown, 11 miles southeast of Hancock.

Pittsfield is a workaday city without the quaint, rural demeanor of the comparatively small Colonial towns that surround it. There's a positive buzz in Pittsfield these days, though, thanks to a resurgence of sorts: the beautifully restored Colonial Theatre hosts 250 performances every year, and a number of new shops and restaurants have appeared along North Street. City-sponsored art walks and the addition of a new Amtrak line, *The Berkshire Flyer*, bringing New Yorkers directly into downtown every summer weekend are additional evidence of Pittsfield's comeback.

GETTING HERE AND AROUND

U.S. 7 (1st Street, in town), U.S. 20 (South Street), and Route 9 (East Street) all converge on Pittsfield. Trains and buses stop at the Intermodal Transportation Center, one block from North Street, along which you can walk to museums, interesting stores, and all sorts of restaurants. Buses service the mall and Allendale, but to get elsewhere you'll need to drive.

Sights

Arrowhead

HISTORIC HOME | Literary fans (and those particularly fond of *Moby-Dick*) will want to visit this historical 18th-century house where Herman Melville lived and wrote his most famous works. After viewing all the exhibits, take a walk around the meadow that boasts over 100 species of wildflowers, hike a trail, or just enjoy the majestic view of Mt. Greylock, the inspiration for Melville's white whale.

TIP→ Tours on the hour. *✉ 780 Holmes Rd., Pittsfield ☎ 413/442–1793 ⊕ www.mobydick.org $16 (guided tours included) Closed Nov.–May.*

Many of New England's back roads are lined with historic split-rail fences or stone walls.

Bartlett's Orchard

FARM/RANCH | The smell of freshly baked cider doughnuts greets you upon entering this orchard's market, which also sells cider and maple syrup. Seasonally you'll find many apple varieties bagged for purchase, but it's more fun to head into the orchard and pick your own. ✉ *575 Swamp Rd., Richmond* ☎ *413/698–2559* 🌐 *www.bartlettsorchard.com.*

Berkshire Museum

HISTORY MUSEUM | **FAMILY** | Opened in 1903, this "universal" museum has a little bit of everything: paintings from the Hudson River School, local artifacts, and natural history specimens both animal and mineral. The Hall of Innovation showcases Berkshires innovators whose creations range from special effects for *Star Wars* to the paper used for U.S. currency. Don't miss the Egyptian mummy, or the aquarium with a touch tank in the basement. ✉ *39 South St., Pittsfield* ☎ *413/443–7171* 🌐 *www.berkshiremuseum.org* 🎫 *$15.*

Hancock Shaker Village

MUSEUM VILLAGE | America's third Shaker community, Hancock was founded in the 1790s. At its peak in the 1840s, the village had almost 300 inhabitants who made their living farming, selling seeds and herbs, making medicines, and producing crafts. The religious community officially closed in 1960, but visitors today can still see demonstrations of blacksmithing, woodworking, and more. Many examples of Shaker ingenuity are on display: the Round Stone Barn and the Laundry and Machine Shop are two of the most interesting buildings. The Shaker focus on sustainability has been maintained in the form of water turbines, sustainable gardens, and a solar array. There's also a farm (with a wonderful barn), some period gardens, a museum shop with reproduction Shaker furniture, a picnic area, and a café. Visit in April to catch the baby animals at the farm, or in September for the country fair. Reserve early if you want a spot at the Shaker-inspired suppers in October. ✉ *34 Lebanon Mountain Rd., off U.S. 20 at Rte. 41,*

Pittsfield ☎ 413/443–0188, 800/817–1137 🌐 www.hancockshakervillage.org 🎟 $20.

Whitney's Farm

FARM/RANCH | **FAMILY** | In addition to offering pick-your-own blueberries, tomatoes, and pumpkins on a seasonal basis, Whitney's sells fresh produce, herbs, and dairy products. A deli and a bakery are also on-site, as well as an outdoor playground and greenhouse. ✉ *1775 S. State Rd., Cheshire* ☎ *413/442–4749* 🌐 *www.whitneysfarm.com.*

Restaurants

★ District Kitchen & Bar

$$ | **MODERN AMERICAN** | Delicious food and good wine keep this small restaurant packed most nights. This gem can almost be missed just off busy North Street, but couples looking for an intimate date-night or professionals grabbing after-work drinks have made it a hot spot. **Known for:** delicious burgers; house fries with aioli sauce you won't want to share; small rotating seasonal menu. Ⓢ *Average main: $24* ✉ *40 West St., Pittsfield* ☎ *413/442–0303* 🌐 *district.kitchen.*

La Fogata

$$ | **SOUTH AMERICAN** | The open kitchen looks almost like a lunch counter at this no-frills corner restaurant known for good, honest Colombian food, where it's hard to go wrong unless you're a vegetarian. Served with chimichurri and plantains, all the meats are delicious, from the thin, perfectly seasoned chicken to the pork rind that bacon aspires to be. **Known for:** Latin American soft drinks; South American food market in corner; "Picada La Fogata" giant meat platter. Ⓢ *Average main: $20* ✉ *770 Tyler St., Pittsfield* ☎ *413/443–6969* ⏲ *Closed Mon.*

Coffee and Quick Bites

Ayelada

$ | **AMERICAN** | **FAMILY** | FroYo lovers won't want to miss this locally crafted frozen yogurt made with ingredients from nearby farms, right down to the milk. Enjoy the tart, yet refreshing, Original flavor, or one of the rotating special flavors like Peach Pie or S'Mores. **Known for:** rotating flavors; vegan options; toppings bar complete with fruit, candies, and cereals. Ⓢ *Average main: $7* ✉ *505 East St., Pittsfield* ☎ *413/344–4126* 🌐 *www.ayelada.com.*

Dottie's Coffee Lounge

$ | **AMERICAN** | The raised seating area by the windows somehow adds a touch of class to this quintessential coffee shop where the art crowd hangs out. In addition to fine coffee, friendly baristas serve soups and sandwiches, as well as Sunday brunch alongside live music. **Known for:** tasty baked goods; peanut butter lattes; artsy events. Ⓢ *Average main: $8* ✉ *444 North St., Pittsfield* ☎ *413/443–1792* 🌐 *www.dottiescoffeelounge.com* ⏲ *No food Sat.*

Hotels

★ Hotel on North

$$ | **HOTEL** | This restored building in the center of town mixes original brickwork and hardwood with tasteful modern decor to provide spacious accommodations and common spaces, including a large horseshoe bar. **Pros:** on-site restaurant with oyster bar; spacious bathrooms; flat-screen TVs and Wi-Fi in rooms. **Cons:** creaky floors; exposed brick may not appeal to everyone; Central Pittsfield location is not picturesque. Ⓢ *Rooms from: $209* ✉ *297 North St., Pittsfield* ☎ *413/358–4741* 🌐 *hotelonnorth.com* 🛏 *45 rooms* 🍽 *No Meals.*

Performing Arts

★ Barrington Stage Company

THEATER | In the summer, this theater company keeps two stages bustling with creative activity. The Main Stage hosts major musical productions and big names, while a smaller black box theater showcases new works-in-progress. Cabaret nights and a winter 10-minute play festival round out the yearly offerings. *Boyd-Quinson Mainstage, 30 Union St., Pittsfield* *413/236–8888* *barringtonstageco.org.*

Colonial Theatre

MUSIC | Back in the day, stars such as Helen Hayes and Al Jolson appeared at this 780-seat 1903 theater; now restored, it hosts live music, theater and popular traveling shows. A second stage, the Garage, hosts $5 comedy nights and programs for children. *111 South St., Pittsfield* *413/997–4444* *www.berkshiretheatregroup.org.*

Activities

HIKING

Ashuwillticook Rail Trail

TRAIL | FAMILY | Passing through the Hoosac River Valley, the paved 12.7-mile Ashuwillticook (pronounced *Ash*-oo-will-ti-cook) trail links Adams with Pittsfield. The trail follows an old railroad, passing through rugged woodland and alongside Cheshire Reservoir. Walkers, joggers, cyclists, in-line skaters, and cross-country skiers all enjoy this route. *3 Hoosac St., Adams* *413/499-7003* *www.mass.gov/eea/agencies/dcr/massparks/region-west/ashuwillticook-rail-trail.html* *Free.*

SKIING

Bousquet Ski Area

SKIING & SNOWBOARDING | FAMILY | This hometown favorite recently got a major facelift with complete renovations to the trails and ski lodge. On the tamer side of Berkshire ski options, Bousquet has 23 trails if you count merging slopes separately. Experts will probably wish to go elsewhere: Bousquet has a few steeper pitches, but it's focused mainly on good beginner and intermediate runs. **Facilities:** 23 trails; 200 acres; 750-foot vertical drop; 5 lifts. Snow tubing is also available. *101 Dan Fox Dr., off U.S. 7, Pittsfield* *413/442–8985* *bousquet-mountain.com* *From $71.*

ZIPLINING

Ramblewild

ZIP LINING | FAMILY | One of the Northeast's largest tree-to-tree adventure parks, Ramblewild has eight trails with over a hundred physical challenges that range in difficulty—including climbing, swinging, leaping, ziplining, and even a "skayak"—throughout 11 acres of forest. Privately guided hikes and climbing tours are also available on the 1,400-acre property. *110 Brodie Mountain Rd., Lanesborough* *413/499–9914* *www.ramblewild.com* *$100.*

Shopping

Museum Facsimiles Outlet Store

SOUVENIRS | This store has the perfect mix of artsy home decor and interesting artwork that will check off anyone on your shopping list. Book lovers will love the signature book-spine artwork and hand-stamped stationery. An added plus, all purchases come with free gift wrapping. *31 South St., Pittsfield* *413/499–1818* *museumfacsimiles.com.*

Lenox

10 miles south of Pittsfield, 130 miles west of Boston.

The famed Tanglewood music festival has been a fixture in upscale Lenox for decades, and it's one of the reasons the town remains fiercely popular in summer. Booking a room here or in any of the nearby communities can set you back dearly during musical or theatrical events. Many of the town's most impressive homes are downtown; others you can only see by setting off on the curving back roads that thread the region. In the center of the village, a few blocks of shabby-chic Colonial buildings contain shops and eateries. Five miles south of Lenox is **Lee,** famous for its harder-than-average marble, quarried in 19th century for use in the cottages of the Vanderbilts and their ilk. Today the bustling downtown area has a mix of touristy and workaday shops and restaurants.

GETTING HERE AND AROUND

Just off Interstate 90, Lenox is south of Pittsfield. During the summer Tanglewood season, traffic in Lenox and environs often moves at a slow pace.

ESSENTIALS

VISITOR INFORMATION Lenox Chamber of Commerce. ✉ *4 Housatonic St., Lenox* ☎ *413/637–3646* 🌐 *www.lenox.org.*

Sights

Frelinghuysen Morris House & Studio
HISTORIC HOME | This modernist property on a 46-acre site exhibits the works of American abstract artists Suzy Frelinghuysen and George L. K. Morris, as well as those of their contemporaries, including Pablo Picasso, Georges Braque, and Juan Gris. In addition to the paintings, frescoes, and sculptures on display, a 57-minute documentary on Frelinghuysen and Morris plays on a continuous loop. Tours are offered on the hour—just be aware that it's a long walk to the house. Painting demonstrations and workshops occasionally take place. ✉ *92 Hawthorne St., Lenox* ☎ *413/637–9790* 🌐 *www.frelinghuysen.org* 🎫 *$20* ⏲ *Closed Nov.–mid-June.*

★ Jacob's Pillow Dance Festival
OTHER ATTRACTION | For 10 weeks every summer, the tiny town of Becket, 14 miles southeast of Lenox, becomes a hub of the dance world. The Jacob's Pillow Dance Festival showcases world-renowned performers of ballet, modern, and international dance. Before the main events, works in progress and even some of the final productions are staged outdoors, often free of charge. ✉ *358 George Carter Rd., at U.S. 20, Becket* ☎ *413/243–9919* 🌐 *www.jacobspillow.org.*

★ The Mount
HISTORIC HOME | This 1902 mansion with myriad classical influences was the summer home of novelist Edith Wharton. The 42-room house and 3 acres of formal gardens were designed by Wharton, who is considered by many to have set the standard for 20th-century interior decoration. In designing the Mount, she followed the principles set forth in her book *The Decoration of Houses* (1897), creating a calm and well-ordered home. To date, nearly $15 million has been spent on an ongoing restoration project. Summer is a fine time to enjoy the informal café and occasional free concerts on the terrace. Guided tours take place during regular hours, the private "ghost tour" after hours, and noteworthy authors make regular visits to discuss their latest books. ✉ *2 Plunkett St., Lenox* ☎ *413/551–5111* 🌐 *www.edithwharton.org* 🎫 *$20* ☞ *The grounds are free and open daily from dawn to dusk.*

Pleasant Valley Wildlife Sanctuary
FOREST | FAMILY | Beaver ponds, hardwood forests, and sun-dappled meadows abound at this preserve run by the Massachusetts Audubon Society. Recent wildlife sightings are noted on whiteboards at the entrance and the visitor center, so you'll know what to watch for on the 7 miles of trails. These include loops that range in difficulty from a half-hour stroll around a pond to a three-hour mountain hike. Trails are also open in winter for snowshoeing. At the visitor center there's a nature play area for children. ✉ *472 W. Mountain Rd., Lenox* ☎ *413/637–0320* 🌐 *www.massaudubon.org* 🎫 *$5* ☞ *No pets allowed.*

Ventfort Hall Mansion and Gilded Age Museum
HISTORIC HOME | Built in 1893, Ventfort Hall was the summer "cottage" of Sarah Morgan, the sister of financier J. P. Morgan. Lively tours offer a peek into the lifestyles of Lenox's superrich "cottage class." The museum's temporary exhibits explore the role of Lenox and the Berkshires as the era's definitive mountain retreat. Victorian high tea served during guest lectures and workshops is among the highlights. ✉ *104 Walker St., Lenox* ☎ *413/637–3206* 🌐 *www.gildedage.org* 🎫 *$18* ☞ *Self-guided audio tour is available.*

The Wit Gallery
ART GALLERY | If you walked past this gallery, you'd inevitably end up ducking in for a closer inspection of the stunning glassworks in the windows. The expertly curated selection inside has more to offer, however, including everything from wooden sculptures to cold-cast metal faces, almost every piece demanding attention. ✉ *27 Church St., Lenox* ☎ *413/637–8808* 🌐 *www.thewitgallery.com* 🎫 *Free.*

Restaurants

★ Alpamayo
$$ | PERUVIAN | Don't let the no-frills decor fool you; what this family-owned restaurant lacks in style it more than makes up for in bold flavors, especially at dinner. Enjoy a menu of fresh and flavorful Peruvian favorites ranging from ceviche to plantains, and don't forget to grab a caramel custard for dessert. **Known for:** chicha morada (incredible purple corn drink); lomo saltado (steak strips sauteed with tomatoes, onions, and fries); Peruvian corn on the cob. $ *Average main: $19* ✉ *60 Main St., Lee* ☎ *413/243–6000* 🌐 *www.alpamayorestaurant.com* ⏲ *Closed Mon.*

Antojitos Oaxaca
$$ | MEXICAN | FAMILY | It's not often you get authentic food from the Oaxaca region in southern Mexico served inside an old train station, but that's what you get at Antojitos. The owners of this establishment moved into the former Sullivan Station restaurant, bringing with them Oaxacan-style tamales, tacos, sopes, and huaraches. **Known for:** indoor and outdoor dining options; fresh ingredients; homemade guacamole. $ *Average main: $19* ✉ *109 Railroad St., Lee* ☎ *413/394–5895* 🌐 *antojitosoaxaca.com* ⏲ *Closed Wed.*

Bistro Zinc
$$$ | FRENCH | Pastel-yellow walls, tall windows, a pressed-metal ceiling, and small-tile floors set an inviting tone at this stylishly modern French bistro with a long zinc-top bar from which it gets its name. The kitchen turns out expertly prepared and refreshingly simple classics, from steak frites to coq au vin. **Known for:** French onion soup; duck confit rolls; trendy nightlife at the bar. $ *Average main: $26* ✉ *56 Church St., Lenox* ☎ *413/637–8800* 🌐 *www.bistrozinc.com.*

Firefly Gastropub and Catering Co.
$$$ | MODERN AMERICAN | This upscale pub with a few modern dining rooms and porch seating is the perfect place to grab dinner if you're looking for something casual. The menu isn't large, but offers reliably good, but slightly fussy, pub standards. **Known for:** excellent burgers (including a veggie option); not a lot of seating; live music Friday and Saturday. $ *Average main: $25* ✉ *71 Church St., Lenox* ☎ *413/637–2700* 🌐 *www.firefly-lenox.com* ⏲ *Closed Sun. No lunch.*

Pizzeria Boema
$$ | AMERICAN | FAMILY | Good luck finding a seat at this popular pizza spot in the middle of the summer, where locals and tourists can't get enough of its gourmet wood-fired pizza. Vegan and gluten-free diners will rejoice at the special dietary

offerings just for them, but be prepared to pay a premium price for these pies. **Known for:** small portions; busy in the summer season; vegan, gluten-free pizza options. *$ Average main: $19 ✉ 84 Main St., Lenox ☎ 413/881-4936 🌐 pizzeriaboema.com.*

Coffee and Quick Bites

★ Chocolate Springs Cafe

$ | **BAKERY** | Escape into chocolate bliss here, where even the aromas are intoxicating. This award-winning chocolatier offers wedges of decadent cakes, ice creams, and sorbets, and dazzling chocolates all made on-site. **Known for:** decadent hot chocolate; truffles, truffles, truffles; perfect, prepackaged gift boxes for any occasion. *$ Average main: $6 ✉ Lenox Commons, 55 Pittsfield/Lenox Rd., Lenox ☎ 413/637–9820 🌐 www.chocolatesprings.com.*

Starving Artist Creperie and Cafe

$ | **BISTRO** | **FAMILY** | If you can find a parking spot along the busy main road through Lee, you'll want to stop and grab a sweet or savory crepe from this casual breakfast and lunch spot. Menu choices include delicious flavor pairings like a spicy Reuben crepe or lemon lavender crepe. **Known for:** flavorful, innovative crepes; coffees, smoothies, and a killer mango mimosa; busy on weekends, but service is quick. *$ Average main: $15 ✉ 40 Main St., Lee ☎ 413/394–5046 🌐 starvingartistcreperie.com ⏲ Closed Tues. and Wed.*

Hotels

Brook Farm Inn

$$ | **B&B/INN** | Tucked away in a wooded glen a short distance from Tanglewood, this cozy 1880s inn often has classical music playing in the fireplace-lighted library; the breakfast room, overlooking the glen, serves afternoon tea with homemade scones on weekends. **Pros:** massage room; delicious breakfasts; close proximity to Tanglewood. **Cons:** books up fast; feels old-fashioned; surrounding area busy during Tanglewood season. *$ Rooms from: $200 ✉ 15 Hawthorne St., Lenox ☎ 413/637–3013, 800/285–7638 🌐 www.brookfarm.com 🛏 15 rooms 🍽 Free Breakfast.*

Chambery Inn

$ | **B&B/INN** | A converted 19th-century country schoolhouse houses these unique accommodations in downtown Lee where the cavernous guest rooms—some big enough for two queen beds—maintain their schoolhouse roots with blackboards still hanging on their walls. **Pros:** good value; spacious suites; restaurants within walking distance. **Cons:** limited choices for breakfast; walls are a bit thin; no common space. *$ Rooms from: $196 ✉ 199 Main St., Lee ☎ 413/243–2221 🌐 www.chamberyinn.com 🛏 10 rooms 🍽 Free Breakfast.*

★ Devonfield Inn

$$$ | **B&B/INN** | Occupying a grand Federal house from 1800, the Devonfield sits atop a birch-shaded hillside overlooking 32 acres of rolling meadows, and offers elegant but not ostentatious guest rooms that deftly blend Colonial style (four-poster beds, working fireplaces, some Oriental rugs) and modern convenience (Wi-Fi, flat-screen TVs, and in some cases whirlpool tubs). **Pros:** heated pool; separate cottage available; beautiful lawns and tennis court. **Cons:** not ideal for children; not many rooms; breakfast menu is not very large. *$ Rooms from: $389 ✉ 85 Stockbridge Rd., Lee ☎ 413/243–3298, 800/664–0880 🌐 www.devonfield.com 🛏 14 rooms 🍽 Free Breakfast.*

Gateways Inn and Restaurant

$$$ | **B&B/INN** | Once the 1912 summer cottage of Harley Procter (as in, Procter & Gamble), this beautifully updated country inn has guest rooms and suites in various configurations and styles; most have working fireplaces, detailed moldings, and plush carpeting. **Pros:** well-appointed rooms; great location in the heart of

Lenox; late-night nibbles in the piano bar. **Cons:** lots of stairs; weddings sometimes take over the lobby; some rooms are small. *Rooms from: $380* *51 Walker St., Lenox* *413/637–2532* *www.gatewaysinn.com* *12 rooms* *Free Breakfast.*

Miraval Berkshires

$$$$ | **RESORT** | This 380-acre resort underwent a $130 million renovation and name change, transforming the former Cranwell Resort into a more polished, high-end Miraval property. **Pros:** golfing with a view; variety of packages, classes that include hikes off site; delicious, healthy dining options. **Cons:** extra cost for some classes and spa treatments; small portion sizes; expensive to stay and difficult to find pricing. *Rooms from: $800* *55 Lee Rd., Rte. 20, Lenox* *800/232–3969* *www.miravalberkshires.com* *146 rooms* *All-Inclusive.*

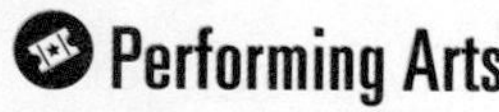

Shakespeare and Company

THEATER | The works of William Shakespeare and other writers are performed between five theaters. The Tina Packer Playhouse and Elayne P. Bernstein Theatre are both indoors, so you can enjoy productions throughout much of the year. Outdoor theaters include the The New Spruce Theatre, Roman Garden Theatre, and the Rose Footprint Theatre, the latter of which reflects the dimensions of the Rose, Shakespeare's first performance space in London. *70 Kemble St., Lenox* *413/637–3353* *www.shakespeare.org.*

★ Tanglewood

CONCERTS | **FAMILY** | The 200-acre summer home of the Boston Symphony Orchestra, Tanglewood attracts thousands every summer to concerts by world-famous musicians. The 5,000-seat main shed hosts larger concerts; the more intimate Seiji Ozawa Hall seats around 1,200 and is used for chamber music and solo performances. The hall is named for the renowned conductor, for years the BSO's music director, a job now held by the Latvian-born Andris Nelsons. Among the most rewarding ways to experience Tanglewood is to purchase lawn tickets, arrive early with blankets or lawn chairs, and enjoy a picnic under the stars. Except for the occasional big-name concert, lawn tickets cost only $21–$23. Inside the shed, tickets vary in price, with most of the good seats costing $50–$120. You can hear the same music for much less by attending an open rehearsal. *297 West St., off Rte. 183, Lenox* *617/266–1492, 888/266–1492* *www.bso.org/tanglewood.*

SPAS

Canyon Ranch

SPAS | Set in Bellefontaine Mansion, an 1897 replica of Le Petit Trianon in Versailles, the Berkshires' outpost of the Arizona resort couldn't be more elegantly old-fashioned. Looks can be deceiving, though: housed within is a state-of-the-art fitness center with the latest classes and the best equipment, a staff of chefs cooking up healthful cuisine, and, of course, a holistic spa. Treatments range from Eastern-inspired therapies like ayurvedic treatments to the Canyon Ranch's signature full-body massages—hot stones optional. If you're looking to get away from it all, this is the place to enjoy a spa day in between hiking and paddling through the Berkshire countryside. *165 Kemble St., Lenox* *800/742–9000, 413/637–4400* *www.canyonranch.com.*

Shopping

Hoadley Gallery

ART GALLERIES | One of New England's foremost crafts centers, the gallery shows and sells American arts and crafts, with a strong focus on pottery, jewelry, and textiles. *21 Church St., Lenox* *413/637–2814* *www.hoadleygallery.com.*

Purple Plume

WOMEN'S CLOTHING | Carefully curated artsy tops, scarves, and jewelry fill this store bursting with color and fun fashion finds. The boutique also specializes in graphic prints and fabrics, flowing tops, and statement necklaces. It's the perfect stop before your next local gallery opening. ✉ *35 Church St., Lenox* ☎ *413/637–3442* 🌐 *www.thepurpleplume.com.*

Stockbridge

20 miles northwest of Otis, 7 miles south of Lenox.

The quintessence of small-town New England charm, Stockbridge is untainted by large-scale development. It is also the blueprint for small-town America as represented on the covers of the *Saturday Evening Post* by painter Norman Rockwell, the official state artist of Massachusetts. From 1953 until his death in 1978, Rockwell lived in Stockbridge and painted the simple charm of its buildings and residents. James Taylor sang about the town in his hit "Sweet Baby James," as did balladeer Arlo Guthrie in his famous Thanksgiving anthem "Alice's Restaurant," in which he tells what ensued when he tossed some garbage out the back of his Volkswagen bus down a Stockbridge hillside.

Indeed, Stockbridge is the stuff of legend. Travelers have been checking into the Red Lion Inn on Main Street since the 18th century, and Stockbridge has only slightly altered in appearance since that time. The 18th- and 19th-century buildings surrounding the inn contain engaging shops and eateries. The rest of Stockbridge is best appreciated on a country drive or bike ride along its hilly, narrow lanes.

GETTING HERE AND AROUND

Stockbridge is accessible from West Stockbridge or Lee, both of which are exits off the Massachusetts Turnpike (Interstate 90). Once here, you can easily walk around the village and drive around the larger area.

ESSENTIALS

VISITOR INFORMATION Stockbridge Chamber of Commerce. ✉ *Stockbridge* ☎ *413/298–5200* 🌐 *www.stockbridgechamber.org.*

Sights

★ Berkshire Botanical Gardens

GARDEN | **FAMILY** | The gardens' 15 acres contain extensive plantings of exotic and native flora—some 2,500 varieties in all—plus greenhouses, ponds, nature trails, and a small gallery. A guided tour, included with admission, leaves daily at 11 am, or grab a self-guided tour at your leisure. October's Harvest Festival is by far the biggest of the facility's annual events. ✉ *5 W. Stockbridge Rd., Stockbridge* ☎ *413/298–3926* 🌐 *www.berkshirebotanical.org* 🎫 *$18* 🕒 *Closed Nov.–Apr.*

Chesterwood

HISTORIC HOME | For 33 years, this was the summer home of the sculptor Daniel Chester French (1850–1931), who created *The Minute Man* in Concord and the Lincoln Memorial's famous seated statue of the president in Washington, D.C. Occasional tours are given of the house, which is maintained in the style of the 1920s, but the real prize is the studio, where you can view the casts and models French used to create the Lincoln Memorial. The beautifully landscaped 122-acre grounds make for an enchanting stroll or bucolic picnic. ✉ *4 Williamsville Rd., off Rte. 183, Stockbridge* ☎ *413/298–2023* 🌐 *www.chesterwood.org* 🎫 *$20* 🕒 *Closed Oct.–May.*

★ Schantz Galleries

ART GALLERY | Jim Schantz's gallery is small and tucked behind a bank, but it displays some of the finest glasswork in the world. With items from nearly five dozen contemporary artists—including Dale Chihuly and Lino Tagliapietra—the

Norman Rockwell: Illustrating America

I was showing the America I knew and observed to others who might not have noticed. My fundamental purpose is to interpret the typical American. I am a storyteller.

—Norman Rockwell

If you've ever seen old copies of the *Saturday Evening Post*, no doubt you're familiar with American artist Norman Rockwell. He created 321 covers for the well-regarded magazine, and the *Post* always sold more copies when one of Rockwell's drawings was on the front page. The accomplished artist also illustrated Boy Scouts of America calendars, Christmas cards, children's books, and even a few stamps for the U.S. Postal Service—in 1994 a stamp bearing his image came out in his honor. His illustrations tended to fit the theme of Americana, family, or patriotism.

Born in New York City in 1894, the talented designer had a knack for art early on but strengthened his talent with instruction at the National Academy of Design and the Art Students League. He was only 22 when he sold his first cover to the *Post*. He married three times and had three sons by his second wife. He died in 1978 in Stockbridge, Massachusetts, where he had lived since 1953.

Famous Rockwell works include his *Triple Self-Portrait* and the *Four Freedoms*, illustrations done during World War II. The latter series of oil paintings represents freedom of speech, freedom of worship, freedom from want, and freedom from fear. In a poetic turn, in 1977, President Gerald R. Ford bestowed on Rockwell the Presidential Medal of Freedom, the highest civilian honor a U.S. citizen can be given. Ford praised Rockwell for his "vivid and affectionate portraits of our country."

museum-quality collection is truly stunning. Call ahead because hours are limited during the winter. ✉ *3 Elm St., Stockbridge* ☎ *413/298–3044* 🌐 *www.schantzgalleries.com.*

★ Naumkeag

HISTORIC HOME | FAMILY | The Berkshire cottage of Joseph Choate (1832–1917), an influential New York City lawyer and the ambassador to Great Britain during President William McKinley's administration, provides a glimpse into the Gilded Age lifestyle. The 44-room gabled mansion, designed by Stanford White and completed in 1887, sits atop Prospect Hill. Its many original furnishings and artworks span three centuries; the collection of Chinese porcelain is particularly noteworthy. The meticulously kept 8 acres of formal gardens, a three-decade project of Choate's daughter, Mabel, and landscape designer Fletcher Steele, alone make this site worth a visit. Creative use of the property now includes a Winter Lights display, with over 200,000 twinkling LED lights; a Halloween-inspired pumpkin trail and haunted house; live music nights with picnics; and a springtime Daffodil Festival. ✉ *5 Prospect Hill Rd., Stockbridge* ☎ *413/298–8138* 🌐 *thetrustees.org/place/naumkeag* 🎫 *$20.*

Norman Rockwell Museum

ART MUSEUM | FAMILY | This charming museum traces the career of one of America's most beloved illustrators, beginning with his first *Saturday Evening Post* cover in 1916. The crown jewel of the 570 Rockwell illustrations is the famed Four Freedoms gallery, although various works—including his *Post* covers and self-portraits—are equally charming. The museum also mounts exhibits of work by other artists. Rockwell's studio was moved to the museum grounds and is complete in every detail. Stroll the 36-acre site, picnic on the grounds, or relax at the outdoor café (late May–mid-October). There's a children's version of the audio tour and a scavenger hunt. ✉ *9 Rte. 183, Stockbridge* ☎ *413/298–4100* 🌐 *www.nrm.org* 🎟 *$20* ⏲ *Closed Wed.*

Restaurants

Truc Orient Express
$$ | VIETNAMESE | Mixed in among shops filled with arts and crafts, this family-owned business has been serving up authentic Vietnamese food for more than 30 years. *Bánh xèo* (rice pancakes) figure prominently on the menu, among other classics, but there's some adventurous fare, too. **Known for:** ca chien (whole fried flounder in a pungent fish sauce); bánh xèo; Vietnamese crafts store in entryway. $ *Average main: $21* ✉ *3 Harris St., West Stockbridge* ☎ *413/232–4204* ⏲ *Closed Mon.–Thurs. No lunch.*

Coffee and Quick Bites

The Lost Lamb
$ | FRENCH | FAMILY | Enjoy a small slice of Paris at this French-Berkshire fusion pâtisserie run by Pastry Chef Claire Raposo. There's often a line out the door to get one of Raposo's Pain au Chocolats, *macarons*, or specialty cupcakes, but if you don't have a sweet tooth, there are also baguette sandwiches. **Known for:** delicious and beautiful pastry creations; French macarons; friendly service. $ *Average main: $5* ✉ *31 Main St., Stockbridge* ☎ *413/298–7156* 🌐 *www.thelostlambpatisserie.com* ⏲ *Closed Mon. and Tues.*

No. Six Depot Roastery & Cafe
$ | CAFÉ | This small-batch roastery and café also serves as an art gallery and community hangout. Stop in for expertly poured slow drip coffee or cold brew made with their own coffee bean blend soaked in cold water for 18 hours. **Known for:** rich, bold cold brew; expert Americano, latte and espresso pours; cool community vibe. $ *Average main: $8* ✉ *6 Depot St., West Stockbridge* ☎ *413/232–0205* 🌐 *www.sixdepotcafe.com.*

Hotels

★ The Inn at Stockbridge
$$$ | B&B/INN | Antique furnishings accent the guest rooms of this comfortable 1906 Georgian Revival inn, where each of the spacious and airy rooms has a decorative theme, such as Kashmir, Provence, or the Berkshires. **Pros:** heated pool; some rooms have gas fireplaces or whirlpool tubs; lovely furniture. **Cons:** noise from highway (most noticeable in suites); not within walking distance of town; pool is outdoors. $ *Rooms from: $320* ✉ *30 East St., Stockbridge* ☎ *413/298–3337* 🌐 *www.stockbridgeinn.com* *16 rooms* *Free Breakfast.*

The Red Lion Inn
$$$ | B&B/INN | An inn since 1773, the Red Lion has hosted presidents, senators, and other celebrities, in the large and historic main building filled with antiques and small guest rooms. **Pros:** inviting lobby with fireplace; rocking chairs on porch; quaintly romantic. **Cons:** overpriced dining; minuscule fitness center; no mobile reception. $ *Rooms from: $300* ✉ *30 Main St., Stockbridge* ☎ *413/298–5545* 🌐 *www.redlioninn.com* *150 rooms* *No Meals.*

Performing Arts

Berkshire Theatre Group
THEATER | This theater company has presented plays since 1929. Those on the Main Stage tend to be better-known works with established actors. A smaller theater mounts more experimental works, and some festival productions, including family-friendly shows and the

holiday staple "A Christmas Carol" take place at the Colonial Theatre in Pittsfield. ✉ *6 East St., Stockbridge* ☎ *413/997-4444* 🌐 *www.berkshiretheatregroup.org.*

Activities

Kripalu Center

SPAS | You'll see many people sitting peacefully on the grounds as you approach this health and yoga retreat proficient at helping patrons achieve a heightened state of grace. Meals always include gluten-free items in addition to more standard fare. A great spot to pick up new yoga gear, vegan cookbooks, or self-help books. ✉ *57 Interlaken Rd., Stockbridge* ☎ *413/448-3152* 🌐 *www.kripalu.org.*

Shopping

Williams and Sons Country Store

SOUVENIRS | **FAMILY** | Well-worn wooden floors and old-time music provide an authentic feel that pairs well with the country-store staples for sale here: toys, maple goodies, jams, and an abundance of candy.

■ TIP→ Don't confuse Williams and Sons with the sparse "general store" down the street. ✉ *38 Main St., Stockbridge* ☎ *413/298–3016* 🌐 *stockbridgecountrystore.com.*

Great Barrington

7 miles southwest of Stockbridge, 13 miles north of Canaan, Connecticut.

The largest town in South County became, in 1781, the first place in the United States to free a slave under due process of law and was also the birthplace, in 1868, of W. E. B. DuBois, the civil rights leader, author, and educator. The many ex–New Yorkers who live in Great Barrington expect great food and service, and the restaurants here accordingly deliver complex, delicious fare. The town is also a favorite of antiques hunters, as are the nearby villages of South Egremont and Sheffield. On U.S. 7 alone, dozens of antiques shops await your discerning eye.

GETTING HERE AND AROUND

The nearest international airports are Bradley International Airport in Windsor Locks, Connecticut, and Albany International Airport in Albany, New York, but you are better off driving in on U.S. 7 from either Stockbridge or Canaan, Connecticut. Great Barrington is also on the BRTA bus line from Stockbridge. There's plenty of parking in town, most of which is walkable as well.

ESSENTIALS

VISITOR INFORMATION Southern Berkshire Chamber of Commerce. ✉ *Great Barrington* ☎ *413/528–4284* 🌐 *southernberkshirechamber.com.*

Sights

Bartholomew's Cobble

TRAIL | **FAMILY** | This rock garden beside the Housatonic River (the Native American name means "river beyond the mountains") is a National Natural Landmark, with 5 miles of hiking trails passing through fields of wildflowers. The 277-acre site has a visitor center and a museum, as well as the state's largest cottonwood trees. ✉ *105 Weatogue Rd., Sheffield* ☎ *413/229–8600* 🌐 *www.thetrustees.org* 🎟 *$5.*

★ Berkshire Mountain Distillers

DISTILLERY | The sweet scent of the country's premier craft gin permeates the Berkshires' first legal distillery since Prohibition. The retail store, open every afternoon, sells Greylock Gin, a multiple gold-medal winner, and Ethereal Gin, whose ingredients are reimagined every season, among other spirits. Take a self-guided distillery tour and try a complimentary tasting. During the summer, there's live music in the outdoor pavilion where you can sip on craft cocktails. ✉ *356 S. Main St., Sheffield* ☎ *413/229–0219* 🌐 *www.berkshiremountaindistillers.com.*

Blueberry Hill Farm
FARM/RANCH | FAMILY | Organic blueberries are ripe for the picking here on midsummer weekends starting in late July. Bring your own container. ✉ *358 East St., Mount Washington* ↔ *About 10 miles southwest of Great Barrington* ☎ *413/528–1479* 🌐 *www.austinfarm.com* ⏲ *Closed Sun.–Thurs.*

Howden Farm
FARM/RANCH | About 4 miles south of the town center, you can pick raspberries from Labor Day to mid-October and pumpkins late September–October. Locals have snatched up the farm's famous sweet corn for decades. ✉ *303 Rannapo Rd., off Rte. 7A, Sheffield* ☎ *413/229–8481.*

Monument Mountain
MOUNTAIN | FAMILY | For great views with minimal effort, hike Monument Mountain, famous as a spot for literary inspiration. Nathaniel Hawthorne and Herman Melville trekked it on August 5, 1850, seeking shelter in a cave during a thunderstorm. There they discussed ideas that would become part of a novel called *Moby-Dick.* While poet William Cullen Bryant stayed in the area, he penned a lyrical poem, "Monument Mountain," about a lovesick Mohican maiden who jumped to her death from the cliffs. Most hikers find the 2½-mile loop an easy stroll. ✉ *Trailhead at parking lot on west side of U.S. 7, 3 miles north of Rte. 183, Great Barrington* ☎ *413/298–3239* 🌐 *www.thetrustees.org.*

Taft Farms
FARM/RANCH | FAMILY | Raspberries ripen here early July–August, and you can pick your own pumpkin September and October. Grab a roast turkey (or other) sandwich, served on freshly baked bread, for a fine homemade lunch. If you have time to linger, check out the small turtle pond in the plant nursery, and see the animal area replete with goats, chickens, llamas, and more. ✉ *119 Park St. N, Great Barrington* ☎ *413/528–1515* 🌐 *taftfarmsgb.com.*

Vault Gallery
BANK | Housed inside a former bank, this small art gallery based on French salon galleries includes the vault room with the original safe door intact. While the building itself is impressive, the gallery also features artwork by owner Marilyn Kalish in a variety of media, as well as some work by other artists and a small collection of antiques. ✉ *322 Main St., Great Barrington* ☎ *413/854–7744* 🌐 *vaultgallery.net.*

Restaurants

Aroma Bar and Grill
$ | INDIAN | Popular with college students for its reasonable prices, this restaurant serves up delicious food all day with especially good deals at lunch and the Sunday brunch buffets. The cooks do well with everything from tandoori chicken and other standards to the full Raja Thali dinner special, all served with a trio of flavorful chutneys. **Known for:** stuffed naan; moist minced-lamb seekh kebab; takeout available. *$ Average main: $16* ✉ *485 Main St., Great Barrington* ☎ *413/528–3116* 🌐 *aromabarandgrill.com.*

Baba Louie's Sourdough Pizza Co
$ | PIZZA | Specialty pizzas at this trattoria go far beyond the usual toppings, from roasted sweet potatoes and fennel to pineapple and coconut: combinations are weird, but tasty. Baba Louie's fires up sourdough ground wheat, spelt-berry, and even gluten-free crusts in their often crowded, rustic interior. **Known for:** excellent thin-crust pizza; Hannah Jo special (mozz, ricotta, shrimp, pineapple, green chili sauce); smallish dining area and portions. *$ Average main: $14* ✉ *42/44 Railroad St., Great Barrington*

☎ *413/528–8100* 🌐 *www.babalouiespizza.com* 🕓 *Closed Tues. and Wed.*

Bizen

$$ | **JAPANESE** | Expect crowds—and, on busy nights, a wait—at this Railroad Street mainstay where dining room tables wrap around three sides of the large central sushi bar that offers an extensive menu of very fresh fish. Besides the sushi menu, dishes range from *robata* (charcoal grill) to katsu and tempura. **Known for:** harumaki (deep-fried lobster and fish in rice paper); una jyu (grilled river eel in a sweet sauce); tea ceremonies and 10-course tasting menus by reservation. *$ Average main: $22* ✉ *17 Railroad St., Great Barrington* ☎ *413/528–4343* 🌐 *www.bizensushi.com.*

Coffee and Quick Bites

★ **The Bistro Box**

$ | **AMERICAN** | **FAMILY** | Just a short drive from the busy downtown you'll find this seasonal road-side food shack that always has a line of locals waiting to order the famous Box Burger with hand-cut parmesan and truffle oil fries. Fresh lobster and crab rolls, fish tacos, and pulled pork sandwiches with rhubarb barbecue sauce are the last thing you'd expect to find at this eclectic spot along a busy road out of town. **Known for:** delicious burgers and hand-cut fries; freshly squeezed lemonade and fruit slushies; Spring Fries made with ramp pesto, wild mushrooms, goat cheese, and a balsamic reduction. *$ Average main: $15* ✉ *937 Main St., Great Barrington* ☎ *413/717–5958* 🌐 *www.thebistrobox.rocks* 🕓 *Closed Wed. and Nov.–Apr.*

SoCo Creamery

$ | **AMERICAN** | **FAMILY** | Micro-batched and hand-crafted ice cream makes this small shop tucked in a side street a must stop for any ice-cream lover. Be adventurous and try one-of-a-kind flavors like Blueberry Honey Lavender or Mission Figs, made with figs hand-shucked by the makers. **Known for:** using local ingredients; Madagascar Vanilla, which is better than any vanilla ice cream you've ever tasted; new, surprise flavors every few months. *$ Average main: $6* ✉ *5 Railroad St., Great Barrington* ☎ *413/644-9866* 🌐 *www.sococreamery.com.*

Hotels

The Barrington

$$$ | **B&B/INN** | As a third-floor bed-and-breakfast above retail frontage, the Barrington may lack the exterior aesthetic appeal of its Berkshire peers, but it more than compensates for this by its central Main Street location and spacious, eclectically furnished guest rooms. **Pros:** flat-screens and Wi-Fi; conscientious innkeepers; handicapped-accessible suite with piano. **Cons:** no guest lobby; dismal exterior and hallway; pricey for the setting. *$ Rooms from: $325* ✉ *281 Main St., 3rd fl., Great Barrington* ☎ *413/528–6159* 🌐 *www.thebarringtongb.com* *6 rooms* *Free Breakfast.*

Performing Arts

Mahaiwe Performing Arts Center

ARTS CENTERS | Catch a performance by Arlo Guthrie or the Paul Taylor Dance Company at the center's stunning 1905 theater. The year-round schedule includes theater, music, dance, comedy, and film. ✉ *14 Castle St., Great Barrington* ☎ *413/528–0100* 🌐 *www.mahaiwe.org.*

Activities

HIKING

A 90-mile swath of the Appalachian Trail cuts through the Berkshires. You'll also find hundreds of miles of trails elsewhere throughout the area's forests and parks.

Appalachian Trail

HIKING & WALKING | You can walk part of the Appalachian Trail on a moderately strenuous stretch that leads to Ice Gulch, a gorge so deep and cold that there is often ice in it, even in summer. Follow the Ice Gulch ridge to the shelter and a large, flat rock from which you can enjoy a panoramic view of the valley. The hike takes about 45 minutes one-way. ✉ *Trailhead on Lake Buel Rd., about 100 feet northwest of Deerwood Park Dr., Great Barrington* 🌐 *www.appalachiantrail.org.*

SKIING

Catamount Ski Area

SKIING & SNOWBOARDING | FAMILY | Skiers seeking a family experience often end up here. Although it's not the biggest mountain in the area, Catamount can be less crowded than other options when it's not a holiday weekend, and the terrain is varied. The Sidewinder, an intermediate cruising trail, is more than 1 mile from top to bottom. Just watch out for ice on the tougher trails. There's also night skiing and snowboarding, plus three terrain parks for snowboarders and others. During the summer, the aerial adventure park has guests traveling between treetops. **Facilities:** 43 trails; 130 acres; 1,000-foot vertical drop; 9 lifts. ✉ *78 Catamount Rd., South Egremont* ☎ *413/528–1262, 413/528–1262 for snow conditions* 🌐 *www.catamountski.com* 🎟 *Lift ticket: $100* ☞ *Order tickets online in advance and lift tickets will be cheaper.*

Ski Butternut

SKIING & SNOWBOARDING | With a variety of trails and slopes, including a 1½-mile run, Ski Butternut is good for skiers of all ability levels. There are a few beginner and advanced trails, and more than half the mountain is mellow intermediate terrain. For snowboarders there are top-to-bottom terrain parks and a beginner park, and eight lanes are available for snow tubing. Eleven lifts, including four carpet lifts and the longest quad in the Berkshires, keep traffic spread out. **Facilities:** 22 trails; 110 acres; 1,000-foot vertical drop; 10 lifts. ✉ *380 State Rd., Great Barrington* ☎ *413/528–2000* 🌐 *www.skibutternut.com* 🎟 *Lift ticket: $80 weekends.*

Shopping

ANTIQUES

The Great Barrington area, including the small towns of Sheffield and South Egremont, has the Berkshires' greatest concentration of antiques stores. Some shops are open sporadically, and many are closed on Tuesday.

Elise Abrams Antiques

ANTIQUES & COLLECTIBLES | The owner of this store selling dining-related antique porcelain, glassware, and tabletop accessories is an expert in the field. The prices match the high quality of her selections. ✉ *11 Stockbridge Rd., near Rte. 183, Great Barrington* ☎ *413/528–3201* 🌐 *www.eliseabramsantiques.com* 🕒 *Closed Sun.-Wed.*

Great Barrington Antiques Center

ANTIQUES & COLLECTIBLES | The feeling is "indoor flea market" in this space, where 30-plus dealers sell oriental rugs, vintage furniture, and smaller decorative pieces. ✉ *964 S. Main St., Great Barrington* ☎ *413/644–8848* 🌐 *www.greatbarringtonantiquescenter.com.*

FOOD

Bizalion's Fine Food

FOOD | This French specialty-food shop carries imported cheeses, cured meats, and the finest olive oils from carefully sourced producers, who also sell their wares to fancy restaurants in New York City and Martha's Vineyard. Bizalion doubles as an informal eatery; on the small menu are some appealing sandwiches, including one with arugula, pine nuts, prosciutto, goat cheese, and olive oil on toasted bread. ✉ *684 Main St., Great Barrington* ☎ *413/644–9988* 🌐 *www.bizalions.com* 🕒 *Closed Sun. and Mon.*

Boardman's Farm Stand

MARKET | Known for its sweet corn, Boardman's makes a fine quick stop to pick up fresh fruits and vegetables, from pumpkins and peppers to peaches and nectarines. ✉ *64 Hewins St., off Maple Ave., southeast from U.S. 7, Sheffield* ☎ *413/770-3064.*

Robin's Candy

CANDY | FAMILY | You'll feel like a kid in a candy shop, no matter what your age, in this store packed with hard-to-find sweets that you haven't seen since childhood. Owner Robin Helfand searches out and buys up vintage candy and keeps a stock of jelly beans in just about every flavor imaginable. ✉ *288 Main St., Great Barrington* ☎ *413/528–8477* 🌐 *www.robinscandy.com.*

HOME DECOR

★ Asia Barong

ANTIQUES & COLLECTIBLES | The eye-catching sculptures visible from the roadside only hint at the vast spectacle inside what bills itself as America's largest Asian art store—customers include the Smithsonian and the Hell's Angels Clubhouse. Carvings of every conceivable material (from wood to whalebone), size (from half an inch to 8 feet tall), and subject matter (albeit heavy on the gods and dragons) can be found here (or made to order and shipped). The sheer volume of art outstrips many museums, but you can still buy a traditional sarong or a gift from the $5 shelves. Humorous signs throughout the store add a touch of character. ✉ *199 Stockbridge Rd., Great Barrington* ☎ *413/528–5091* 🌐 *www.asiabarong.com.*

Springfield

90 miles west of Boston, 30 miles north of Hartford, Connecticut.

Springfield is the busy hub of the Pioneer Valley. Known as the birthplace of basketball—the game was devised here in 1891 as a gym instructor's last-ditch attempt to keep a group of unruly teenagers occupied in winter—the city also has a cluster of fine museums and family attractions.

GETTING HERE AND AROUND

Springfield is roughly the center of Massachusetts, accessible by bus, train, and Interstates 90 and 91. Parts of Springfield are walkable, but you're better off driving or using the local PVTA buses.

ESSENTIALS

VISITOR INFORMATION Greater Springfield Convention & Visitors Bureau. ✉ *Springfield* ☎ *413/787–1548* 🌐 *explorewesternmass.com.*

Sights

The Amazing World of Dr. Seuss Museum

ART MUSEUM | FAMILY | Opened in 2017, this museum offers a look into the Springfield childhood of Theodor Geisel (aka Dr. Seuss) with a wide range of interactive exhibits and wall drawings, all among rooms so colorful that the museum is like walking into a Dr. Seuss book. Part art gallery, part hands-on children's museum, the second floor re-creates Geisel's studio and living room (with the furniture and art materials he actually used); you'll see never before publicly displayed artwork. ✉ *21 Edwards St., Springfield* ☎ *413/425–9289* 🌐 *springfieldmuseums.org* 🎫 *$25* 🕓 *Closed Mon.*

George Walter Vincent Smith Art Museum

ART MUSEUM | The museum houses a fascinating private art collection that includes a salon gallery with 19th-century American paintings by Frederic Church and Albert Bierstadt, as well as a Japanese antiquities room filled with armor, textiles, porcelain, and carved jade. Lovers of architecture will appreciate the Italian palazzo-style building, built in 1896, with fully restored original Tiffany stained glass windows—the windows are rare examples of Tiffany work commissioned for a museum building. ✉ *Chestnut St., Springfield* ☎ *413/425–9289* 🌐 *springfieldmuseums.org/about/*

smith-art-museum 🎫 *$25* ☞ *Ticket price includes 5 museums.*

The Lyman and Merrie Wood Museum of Springfield History

HISTORY MUSEUM | Learn about the town's manufacturing heritage, including bikes and memorabilia from the former Indian Motorcycle Company, which was headquartered in Springfield. The Firearms Collection includes more than 1,600 firearms, with the largest collection of Smith & Wesson guns in the world. Board game lovers will enjoy the Hasbro GameLand exhibit, which honors Milton Bradley, who after moving to Springfield in 1856, created "The Checkered Game of Life." ✉ *21 Edwards St., Springfield* ☎ *413/425–9289* 🌐 *springfieldmuseums.org/about/museum-of-springfield-history* 🎫 *$25* ☞ *Ticket price includes 5 museums.*

The Michele and Donald D'Amour Museum of Fine Arts

ART MUSEUM | This small gem of a museum houses a comprehensive collection of American, Asian, and European paintings, prints, watercolors, and sculpture. The Currier & Ives (active 1834–1907) Collection is the largest holdings of lithographs in the nation. ✉ *21 Edwards St., Springfield* ☎ *413/425–9289* 🌐 *springfieldmuseums.org/about/museum-of-fine-arts* 🎫 *$25* ☞ *Ticket price includes 5 museums.*

★ Naismith Memorial Basketball Hall of Fame

SPORTS VENUE | **FAMILY** | This 80,000-square-foot facility—named for Canadian phys-ed instructor Dr. James Naismith, who invented the game of basketball in 1891 during his five years at Springfield's YMCA Training Center—showcases plenty of jerseys, memorabilia, and video highlights. High-profile players such as Michael Jordan and Kareem Abdul-Jabbar of the NBA and Nancy Lieberman of the WNBA are among the nearly 300 enshrinees, but the hall celebrates the accomplishments of players, coaches, and others at all levels of the sport. In addition to displays chronicling basketball history, the hall has a soaring domed arena where you can practice jumpers, walls of inspirational quotes you can view, dozens of interactive exhibits, and video footage and interviews with former players. The hall is easy to find: look for the 15-story spire with an illuminated basketball on top. ✉ *1000 Hall of Fame Ave, Springfield* ☎ *413/781–6500, 877/446–6752* 🌐 *www.hoophall.com* 🎫 *$28.*

Six Flags New England

AMUSEMENT PARK/CARNIVAL | **FAMILY** | With more than 160 rides and shows, this massive attraction is the region's largest theme and water park. You can visit Looney Tunes town and climb aboard DC Superhero rides such as Batman: The Dark Knight and Superman: The Ride, which is more than 20 stories tall and has a top speed of 77 mph. New rides are added frequently, like the Wicked Cyclone, a hybrid wooden structure with a steel track, and the Fireball, a seven-story loop coaster. Visit in autumn to catch Fright Fest haunted events and attractions. ✉ *1623 Main St., Agawam* ☎ *413/786–9300* 🌐 *www.sixflags.com/newengland* 🎫 *$50.*

The Springfield Science Museum

SCIENCE MUSEUM | **FAMILY** | Scientists young and old will enjoy taking in a show at the oldest operating planetarium in the United States. There are also dinosaur exhibits, an extensive collection of stuffed and mounted animals, and an African Hall through which you can take an interactive tour of that continent's flora and fauna. There's also a small aquarium, where you'll see fishes from tropical reefs around the world as well as frogs, turtles, snakes, and spiders from the rain forests. ✉ *21 Edwards St., Springfield* ☎ *413/425–9289* 🌐 *springfieldmuseums.org/about/springfield-science-museum* 🎫 *$25* ☞ *Includes admission to 5 museums.*

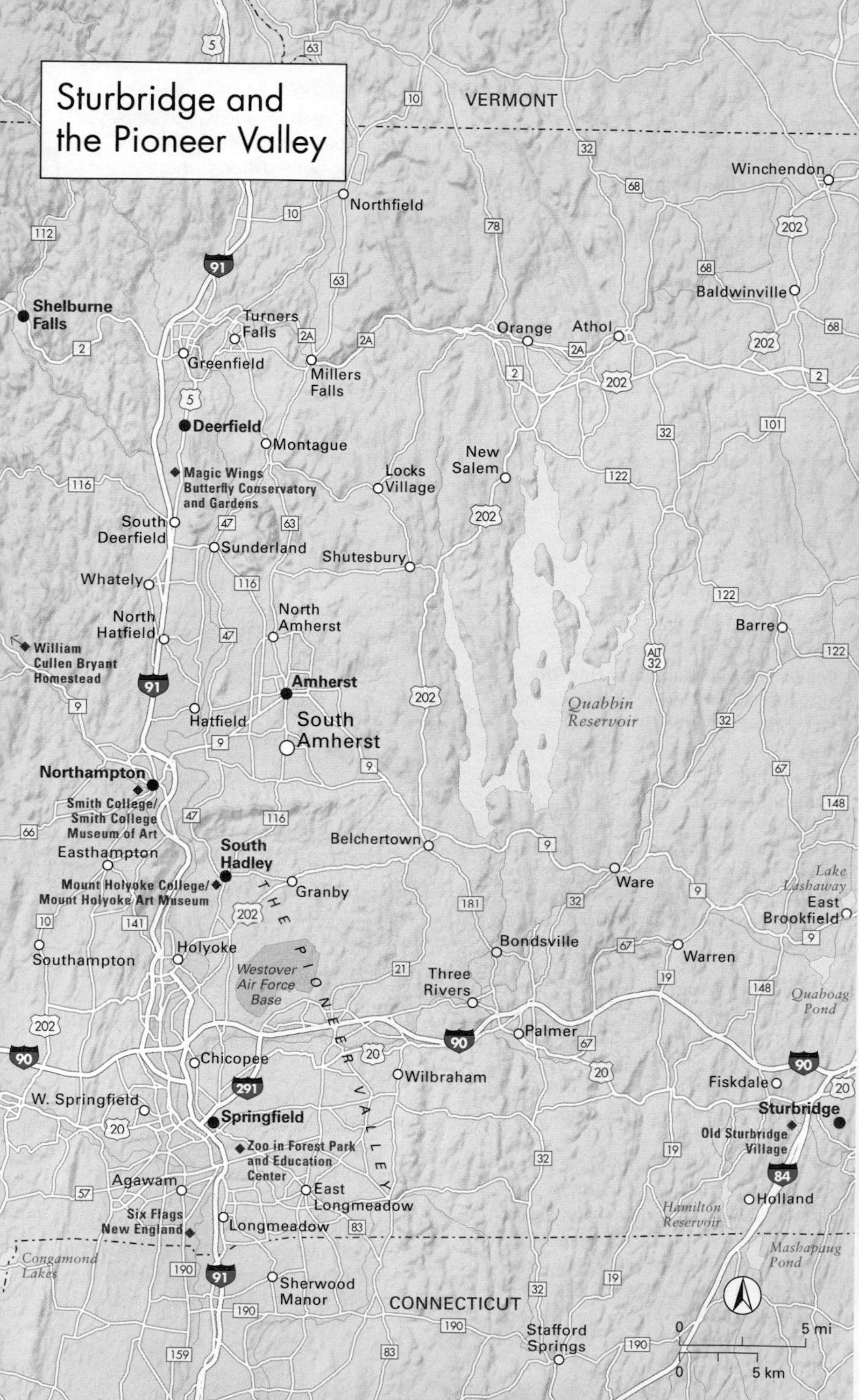
Sturbridge and the Pioneer Valley
VERMONT
CONNECTICUT
Winchendon
Northfield
Baldwinville
Shelburne Falls
Turners Falls
Greenfield
Millers Falls
Orange
Athol
Deerfield
Montague
Magic Wings Butterfly Conservatory and Gardens
New Salem
Locks Village
South Deerfield
Sunderland
Shutesbury
Whately
North Hatfield
North Amherst
William Cullen Bryant Homestead
Barre
Amherst
South Amherst
Hatfield
Quabbin Reservoir
Northampton
Smith College/ Smith College Museum of Art
Easthampton
Belchertown
South Hadley
Mount Holyoke College/ Mount Holyoke Art Museum
Granby
Ware
Lake Lashaway
East Brookfield
Southampton
Holyoke
Bondsville
Warren
Westover Air Force Base
Three Rivers
Quaboag Pond
Palmer
THE PIONEER VALLEY
Chicopee
Wilbraham
Fiskdale
W. Springfield
Springfield
Sturbridge
Old Sturbridge Village
Zoo in Forest Park and Education Center
Agawam
East Longmeadow
Holland
Six Flags New England
Longmeadow
Hamilton Reservoir
Congamond Lakes
Mashapaug Pond
Sherwood Manor
Stafford Springs
0
5 mi
5 km

Zoo in Forest Park and Education Center
CITY PARK | FAMILY | At this leafy, 735-acre retreat, hiking paths wind through the trees, paddleboats navigate Porter Lake, and hungry ducks float on a small pond. The zoo, where Theodor Geisel—better known as Dr. Seuss—found inspiration for his children's books, is home to nearly 200 animals, from camels and bobcats to lemurs and wallabies. It's manageable in size, and spotting animals in the exhibits is fairly easy, which makes this an especially good stop for families with small children. Another plus: you can purchase small cones of food from the gift shop to feed many of the animals. Leave time to explore the park after you finish the zoo. ✉ *293 Sumner Ave., Springfield* ☎ *413/733–2251* 🌐 *www.forestparkzoo.org* 🎫 *$10* 🕑 *Closed Mon.–Fri.*

Restaurants

Pho Saigon
$ | VIETNAMESE | A little out of the way, this understated eatery serves authentic Vietnamese cuisine at wallet-pleasing prices. Whether you enjoy the eponymous made-from-scratch soups, fried dishes with meat, or plentiful vegetarian options, the menu has you covered. **Known for:** variety of authentic homemade pho; bánh xèo; getting your car towed if you park in the lot across the street. 💲 *Average main: $15* ✉ *400 Dickinson St., Springfield* ☎ *413/781–4488* 🌐 *www.phosaigonspringfield.com* 🕑 *Closed Tues. and Wed.*

Red Rose
$$ | ITALIAN | FAMILY | Featuring massive chandeliers, an open kitchen, and a large dining area, this half-century-old family restaurant is a big, brassy eatery where everyone from canoodling couples to huge parties can feel right at home. The menu features the usual gamut of Italian favorites such as the exquisite eggplant dishes, as well as a variety of pizzas made from a half-century-old recipe. **Known for:** eggplant Parmigiana; primavera pizza; heaping platters of pasta. 💲 *Average main: $20* ✉ *1060 Main St., Springfield* ☎ *413/739–8510* 🌐 *www.redrosepizzeria.com* 🕑 *Closed Mon., Tues.*

★ **The Student Prince & The Fort**
$$ | GERMAN | Impressive beer-stein and corkscrew collections at the bar and darkwood paneling lend this restaurant the feel of a convivial hunting lodge, which the antlers and stained-glass windows in the side dining room accentuate. The menu is decidedly meat-centric—beef, chicken, veal, lamb, pork, and delectable homemade sausages—focused on German dishes with some must-have sauerkraut. **Known for:** incredible homemade sauerkraut; various German sausages; impressive decor. 💲 *Average main: $21* ✉ *8 Fort St., Springfield* ☎ *413/734–7475* 🌐 *www.studentprince.com.*

Coffee and Quick Bites

Donut Dip
$ | AMERICAN | FAMILY | This family-run business has been making doughnuts since 1957. Doughnut purists go there for the Old Fashioned Sour Cream, Apple Cider, and Honey Dip, but if you're feeling more adventurous there's plenty to choose from in the jelly, frosting, and sprinkles department, including a decadent bacon-topped creation. **Known for:** Old Fashioned Sour Cream doughnuts; friendly service—if you don't see a doughnut you want, ask for it; freshly brewed coffee. 💲 *Average main: $5* ✉ *1305 Riverdale St., Springfield* ☎ *413/733–9604* 🌐 *donutdip.com.*

La Fiorentina Pastry Shop
$ | BAKERY | Springfield's South End is home to a lively Little Italy, including this full bakery that has doled out a wide variety of heavenly pastries (and coffee) since the 1940s. **Known for:** chocolate-covered cannoli; breakfast menu; attached deli. 💲 *Average main: $3* ✉ *883 Main St., Springfield* ☎ *413/732–3151* 🌐 *www.lafiorentinapastry.com.*

★ Naomi's Inn

$$ | **B&B/INN** | This elegantly restored house in a residential neighborhood is long on charm, due in no small part to the comfortable and character-filled suites, which are individually decorated—the Louis XIV suite has 19th-century armoires and a down-filled sofa, while the Global Fusion suite has a four-poster bed and a loveseat. **Pros:** Bluetooth, bidets, and big-screen TVs with Netflix in rooms; luxe linens and other fabrics; warm and knowledgeable hosts. **Cons:** near a hospital, so you may hear sirens; smallish kitchen; no pool. *Rooms from: $210 ✉ 20 Springfield St., Springfield ☎ 413/433–6019 🌐 www.naomisinn.net ⇨ 8 suites 🍴 Free Breakfast.*

Sturbridge

35 miles east of Springfield.

Sturbridge is a bit farther toward the coast than the rest of the Pioneer Valley, and off the beaten path lies a rural area that exemplifies old New England. Nowhere is this more true than in Old Sturbridge Village, a re-created early-19th-century village with restored buildings and reenactments, which serves as the central attraction of the town. This is a large enough draw that many inns and hotels are available within walking distance of Old Sturbridge Village, but most of the more appealing dining options, such as The Duck, will require a drive.

GETTING HERE AND AROUND

From Springfield, take Interstate 90 East (or the slower Route 20 East if you're allergic to toll roads). Old Sturbridge Village is centrally located just off Route 20, as are most places you'll want to eat or stay (if they're not right on Route 20, known as Sturbridge's Main Street).

ESSENTIALS

VISITOR INFORMATION Sturbridge Area Tourist Association. *✉ Sturbridge ☎ 800/628–8379, 508/347–2761 🌐 www.sturbridgetownships.com.*

★ Old Sturbridge Village

MUSEUM VILLAGE | A re-creation of a New England village circa 1790–1840, this site contains more than 40 historic buildings moved here from other towns. There are several industrial buildings, including a working sawmill, and guides in period costumes demonstrate home-based crafts like spinning, weaving, and shoemaking. In season, take an informative stagecoach ride, or cruise the Quinebaug River while learning about river life in 19th-century New England and catching glimpses of ducks, geese, turtles, and other local wildlife. Other popular seasonal events include Christmas by Candlelight weekends in December, and the Redcoats and Rebels reenactment brigade during the first week of August. An associated inn is available for those looking to spend multiple days immersed. *✉ 1 Old Sturbridge Village Rd., Sturbridge ☎ 508/347–3362, 800/733–1830 🌐 www.osv.org 🎫 $28 ⏲ Closed Mon. and Tues.*

B.T.'s Smokehouse

$ | **BARBECUE** | Walk up to the counter and order perfectly cooked barbecued meat by the pint or tray at this no-frills barbecue joint. There aren't many tables: grab one while someone else in your group orders. **Known for:** friendly staff; pulled pork and beef brisket; constantly busy. *Average main: $15 ✉ 392 Main St., Sturbridge ☎ 508/347–3188 🌐 btsmokehouse.com ⏲ Closed Mon.*

The Duck

$$ | **MODERN AMERICAN** | In a Greek Revival–style building known as the Whistling Swan lie two restaurants; the more

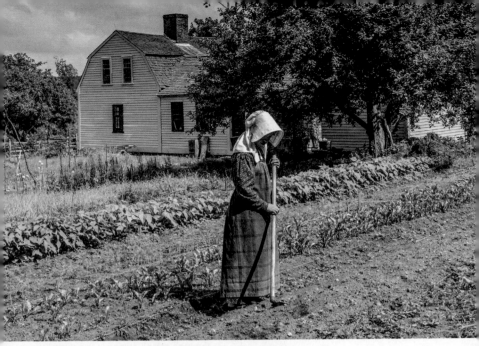

Costumed historians are part of the 19th-century Old Sturbridge Village.

notable one is on the second floor in an unpretentious space resembling a barn hayloft. The Duck offers up generous portions of everything from salad to braised lamb as well as various dishes, which, naturally, incorporate duck. **Known for:** duck confit poutine; lobster deviled duck eggs; bar and sister Italian restaurant (Avellino) downstairs. *Average main: $24* *502 Main St., 2nd fl., Sturbridge* *508/347–2321* *www.theducksturbridge.com* *Closed Sun. and Mon.*

Coffee and Quick Bites

Whoopie-Doo & Cupcakes too

$ | **BAKERY** | **FAMILY** | This small bakery is big on cupcake creativity. Beyond your basic vanilla or chocolate, this spot offers flavors like Root Beer Float, Strawberry Crunch, and the occasional Unicorn Poop, which is a fun, colorful sprinkle concoction. **Known for:** creative cupcakes with towering buttercream toppings; delicious bagels; whoopie pies. *Average main: $5* *179 Main St., Sturbridge* *774/241–3370* *www.whoopiedoocupcakes.com* *Closed Mon. and Tues.*

Hotels

The Publick House

$ | **B&B/INN** | Step back in time at this rambling 1771 inn, whose 60-acre property sits on the town green encompassing five buildings including the neighboring Chamberlain House and the Country Motor Lodge. **Pros:** Colonial ambience and architecture; historical significance; flat-screen TVs. **Cons:** slanted hallway floor; thin walls, loud pipes; rooms outside main inn less appealing. *Rooms from: $189* *277 Main St., Sturbridge* *508/347–3313, 800/782–5425* *www.publickhouse.com* *100 rooms* *No Meals.*

Sturbridge Host

$ | **HOTEL** | Across the street from Old Sturbridge Village and beside a pleasant lake that some room balconies overlook, this hotel has luxuriously appointed bedrooms in Colonial style, reproduction furnishings, and updated baths with granite tops. **Pros:** lakefront property with picnic tables and paddleboat rentals; quiet setting; indoor courtyard with pool and restaurants. **Cons:** often hosts conferences; smell of the pool's chlorine through whole building; inner courtyard can be noisy. *Rooms from: $159* *366 Main St., Sturbridge* *508/347–7393* *www.sturbridgehosthotel.com* *232 rooms* *No Meals.*

South Hadley

12 miles north of Springfield.

A quiet college town with a cluster of Main Street cafés and stores, South Hadley is surrounded by rolling hills and farmland. It's best known for the Mount Holyoke College Art Museum, one of the region's finest cultural facilities.

GETTING HERE AND AROUND

With Bradley International Airport and the Springfield Amtrak station to the south, South Hadley is easy to access. By car, it's east of Interstate 91 and north of U.S. 202 at the intersection of Route 47 and Route 116. You can walk around the Mount Holyoke campus, but you'll need to drive to get most anywhere else.

 Sights

Mount Holyoke College

COLLEGE | Founded in 1837, Mount Holyoke was the first women's college in the United States. Among its alumnae are poet Emily Dickinson and playwright Wendy Wasserstein. The handsome wooded campus, encompassing two lakes and lovely walking or riding trails, was landscaped by Frederick Law Olmsted, the co-designer of Manhattan's Central Park. *50 College St., South Hadley* *413/538–2000* *www.mtholyoke.edu.*

Mount Holyoke College Art Museum

ART MUSEUM | The 24,000 works in the college's collection include Asian, European, and American paintings, as well as sculpture and contemporary art from around the world. The coins and numismatics exhibit is definitely worth a look. On summer Wednesdays and Sundays, the Skinner Museum, a church packed full of the eclectic collection of a wealthy mill owner, is open. *Lower Lake Rd., South Hadley* *3 blocks north of Morgan St.* *413/538–2245* *artmuseum.mtholyoke.edu* *Free* *Closed Mon.*

 Restaurants

Food 101 Bar & Bistro

$$$ | **ECLECTIC** | There's nothing basic about this popular restaurant across from the Mount Holyoke campus, and the atmosphere—from the fancy plating to the nice lighting—almost justifies the high prices, which is why this little spot is a magnet for foodies, yuppies, and college students on their parents' tabs. Dishes—everything from seafood to steak—are complicated but mostly successful. **Known for:** pricey, yet elegant; French fries with wasabi mayo; filet mignon. *Average main: $30* *19 College St., South Hadley* *413/535–3101* *www.food101bistro.com* *Closed Mon. No lunch.*

IYA Sushi and Noodle Kitchen

$ | **JAPANESE** | With puns on the menu and the staff's shirts, this sushi and noodle bar serves up fun in addition to ramen, bao, and a wide variety of sushi. The atmosphere is upscale casual and would be even more pleasant if it weren't always busy, but that's the price you pay for good food. **Known for:** amusing food puns located everywhere; big bowls of rich-brothed ramen; poke bowls. *Average main: $13* *Village Commons, 15 College St., South Hadley* *413/532–8000* *iyasushi.com.*

Coffee and Quick Bites

Flayvors of Cook Farm

$ | AMERICAN | FAMILY | The main advantage of stopping for the delicious homemade ice cream at this family farm is that you can see the dairy cows from the dining tables—and even pet them, if you're brave. Sandwiches and mac and cheese are available as well, if for some reason, you're not in the mood for ice cream. **Known for:** very locally sourced dairy; proximity to cows; asparagus ice cream. *Average main: $5 Cook Farm, 129 S. Maple St., Hadley 413/584–2224 www.flayvors.com.*

Shopping

The Odyssey Bookshop

BOOKS | In addition to stocking 50,000 new and used titles, Odyssey has readings and book signings by locally (and sometimes nationally) known authors. There's a special event more nights than not. *9 College St., South Hadley 413/534–7307 www.odysseybks.com.*

Northampton

10 miles northeast of South Hadley.

The cultural center of Western Massachusetts is without a doubt the city of Northampton (nicknamed "Noho"), whose vibrant downtown is packed with interesting restaurants, lively clubs, and offbeat boutiques. The city attracts artsy types, academics, activists, members of the LGBTQ community, and just about anyone else seeking the culture and sophistication of a big metropolis but the conviviality and easy pace of a small town.

GETTING HERE AND AROUND

Amtrak's *Vermonter* train, which travels between Washington, D.C., and St. Albans, Vermont, stops in Northampton. The city is also served by buses from nearby Springfield's train station, although most people arrive by car on Interstate 91. Downtown is crossed by Routes 5, 9, and 10, and walking to most downtown locations is not only possible, but an excellent way to spend an afternoon. Local PVTA buses are also available. If you're arriving by car, your best bet is to park in the garage attached to Thorne's Marketplace, which is the center of this mostly walkable city.

ESSENTIALS

VISITOR INFORMATION Greater Northampton Chamber of Commerce. *Northampton 413/584–1900 www.explorenorthampton.com.*

Sights

★ R. Michelson Galleries

ART GALLERY | FAMILY | In an unassuming former bank lies a large multifloor gallery filled with the works of many artists, but the collection's crown jewel is the room filled with the work from dozens of children's book illustrators. Originals by everyone from Maurice Sendak to Mo Willems are featured, as well as a Dr. Seuss area that includes a few sculptures along with his illustrations. *132 Main St., Northampton 413/586–3964 www.rmichelson.com.*

Smith College

COLLEGE | The nation's largest liberal arts college for women opened its doors in 1875, funded by a bequest from Sophia Smith, a local heiress. Renowned for its School of Social Work, Smith has a long list of distinguished alumnae, among them activist Gloria Steinem, chef Julia Child, and writer Margaret Mitchell. One of New England's most serene campuses, Smith is a leading center of political and cultural activity. The on-campus **Lyman Plant House** is worth a visit. The flourishing **Botanic Garden of Smith College** covers the entire 150-acre campus.

✉ *College La., Northampton* ☎ *413/584–2700* 🌐 *www.smith.edu.*

Smith College Museum of Art

ART MUSEUM | A floor of galleries with natural light, an enclosed courtyard, and artist-designed restrooms and benches make up this museum, whose permanent collection's highlights include pivotal paintings by Mary Cassatt, Paul Cézanne, Edgar Degas, Georgia O'Keeffe, Auguste Rodin, and Georges Seurat. More recent acquisitions include African, Asian, and Islamic art. ✉ *Brown Fine Arts Center, 20 Elm St., at Bedford Terr., Northampton* ☎ *413/585–2760* 🌐 *www.smith.edu/artmuseum* 🎟 *$5 (free 2nd Fri. of month 4–8)* ⏲ *Closed Mon.*

William Cullen Bryant Homestead

HISTORIC HOME | About 20 miles northwest of Northampton, in the scenic hills west of the Pioneer Valley, is the country estate of the 19th-century poet and author William Cullen Bryant. The 195-acre grounds overlooking the Westfield River Valley are a great venue for bird-watching, cross-country skiing, and picnics. Experience one of the many literary-themed events held throughout the year on the property. ✉ *207 Bryant Rd., Cummington* ☎ *413/532-1631* 🌐 *thetrustees.org/place/william-cullen-bryant-homestead* 🎟 *Free.*

Restaurants

Bombay Royale

$$ | **INDIAN** | The deep-blue walls and spacious interior lend a calming vibe to this Indian restaurant, whose extensive menu ranges from South Indian to Indo-Chinese dishes. Whether you're in the mood for chicken, lamb, or something vegan, you'll have a dozen good options in your chosen category. **Known for:** lunch buffets; giant masala dosa; spotty service. $ *Average main: $20* ✉ *1 Roundhouse Plaza, Suite 4, Northampton* ☎ *413/341–3537* 🌐 *www.bombayroyale.com* ⏲ *Closed Mon.*

Caminito Steakhouse

$$$ | **ARGENTINE** | Caminito's red-and-black interior offers casual elegance in spades. The menu is small, but the flavor is not, so you can count on excellent results whether you order your steak raw as tartare, baked into empanadas, or simply as a large individual cut. **Known for:** filet mignon; empanadas with rotating fillings; live Spanish guitar music at a reasonable volume. $ *Average main: $30* ✉ *7 Old South St., Northampton* ☎ *413/387–6387* 🌐 *caminitosteakhouse.com* ⏲ *Closed Mon. and Tues. No lunch.*

Northampton Brewery

$$ | **AMERICAN** | In a rambling building in Brewster Court, this noisy and often-packed pub has extensive outdoor seating on a deck. The kitchen turns out sandwiches and comfort food, including stuffed peppers and burgers with blue cheese and caramelized onions. **Known for:** flaky-light catfish bites; humanely sourced meat; beer-battered appetizers. $ *Average main: $18* ✉ *11 Brewster Ct., near Hampton Ave., Northampton* ☎ *413/584–9903* 🌐 *www.northampton-brewery.com* ⏲ *Closed Wed.*

Osaka

$$ | **JAPANESE** | The hillside enclosed porch overlooking the center of town makes Osaka the most recognizable restaurant in Northampton, as well as one of the best dining spots. Whether you're in the mood for sushi, a bento box lunch, or a full hibachi dinner, Osaka serves up traditional Japanese favorites in a welcoming atmosphere. **Known for:** kobe beef sushi; entertaining hibachi chefs; bento box lunches. $ *Average main: $20* ✉ *7 Old South St., Northampton* ☎ *413/587–9548* 🌐 *www.osakarestaurantgroup.com.*

Coffee and Quick Bites

★ Herrell's Ice Cream

$ | **CAFÉ** | On the lower level of Thornes Marketplace, Herrell's is known for not only having some of the state's best ice cream, but also for being the first ice-cream shop to mix in brand-name candies with its ice cream. Flavors often rotate, but an up-to-the-minute list is available online. **Known for:** homemade small-batch hot fudge; malted vanilla and chocolate pudding flavors; dairy-free and sugar-free flavors. *$ Average main: $5* *8 Old South St., Northampton* *413/586–9700* *www.herrells.com* *No credit cards.*

The Roost

$ | CAFÉ | The Noho coffee scene is filled with small spots for college students to refuel and tourists to take a break, but none have the same vintage-meets-industrial charm of The Roost. Grab a house-drip coffee with a breakfast sandwich or one of their bakery items. **Known for:** industrial coffeehouse vibe with exposed brick and subway tiles; theme nights that include bingo, board games; inventive vegan options. *$ Average main: $8* *1 Market St., Northampton* *413/587–2625* *roostnorthampton.square.site.*

Hotels

Hotel Northampton

$$ | HOTEL | Commanding a huge presence in downtown Northampton with its formidable glass-paned front, this 1927 hotel is a magnet for visiting professors and parents, although location—shops and restaurants are right outside the door—is the main thing the historic property has going for it. **Pros:** on-site tavern and restaurant are favorite hangouts of visitors and locals; top location in town; flat-screen TVs. **Cons:** small rooms; drain pipes are loud; surge pricing. *$ Rooms from: $250* *36 King St., Northampton* *413/584–3100, 800/547–3529* *www.hotelnorthampton.com* *106 rooms* *No Meals.*

Nightlife

Bishop's Lounge

BARS | This hip little third-floor bar and lounge has a small outside patio. Depending on the night, the lineup here might include live music, DJ sets, stand-up comedy, or even karaoke. There's sometimes a small cover charge, sometimes not. *41 Strong Ave., 3rd fl., Northampton* *413/586–8900.*

Fitzwilly's

BARS | A reliable bar for a night out, Fitzwilly's draws a friendly mix of locals and tourists for drinks and tasty pub fare. (Try the Gorgonzola garlic bread.) *23 Main St., Northampton* *413/584–8666* *www.fitzwillys.com.*

Activities

Norwottuck Rail Trail

BIKING | FAMILY | Part of the Connecticut River Greenway State Park, this paved 11-mile path links Northampton with Belchertown by way of Amherst. Great for biking, rollerblading, jogging, and cross-country skiing, it runs along the old Boston & Maine Railroad route. Free trail maps are available on the Mass.gov website. *446 Damon Rd., at Rte. 9, Northampton* *413/586–8706* *www.mass.gov.*

Shopping

★ Thornes Marketplace

MALL | A quintessential stop on any Northampton visit—and not just because the market's centrally located garage is your best bet for convenient parking—Thornes contains an eclectic lineup of shops ranging from Glimpse of Tibet for Tibetan handicrafts to Herrell's Ice Cream and Captain Candy for sweets and desserts. Also here are Booklink Booksellers, Cedar Chest, a yoga studio, a chair-massage parlor, and clothing and jewelry stores. *150 Main St., Northampton* *413/584–5582* *www.thornesmarketplace.com.*

Williamsburg General Store

GENERAL STORE | This Pioneer Valley landmark has an in-store bakery in addition to the usual candy, spices, jams, maple confections, kitchen items, and other gifts you might expect. Try a "Wrapple": a hand pie made with apples from local orchards. ✉ *12 Main St., Northampton* ☎ *413/268–3036* 🌐 *www.wgstore.com.*

Amherst

8 miles northeast of Northampton.

One of New England's most visited spots, Amherst is known for its scores of world-renowned authors, poets, and artists. The above-average intelligence quotient of its population is no accident, as Amherst is home to a trio of colleges: Amherst, Hampshire, and the University of Massachusetts. Art galleries, book and music stores, and several downtown cultural venues tickle the intellectual fancy of the college-age crowd, the locals, and the profs.

GETTING HERE AND AROUND

The closest airport is Bradley International in Connecticut. Amtrak's *Vermonter* train stops in nearby Northampton. From there you can take a PVTA bus into town, where the buses are also a good way to get around. If driving, reduce hassle by bringing change for the parking kiosks.

ESSENTIALS

VISITOR INFORMATION Amherst Area Chamber of Commerce. ✉ *Amherst* ☎ *413/253–0700* 🌐 *www.amherstarea.com.*

Sights

Emily Dickinson Museum

HISTORIC HOME | The famed Amherst poet lived and wrote in this brick Federal-style home. Admission is by guided tour only, and to say that the tour guides are knowledgeable would be a massive understatement; the highlight of the tour is the sunlit bedroom where the poet wrote many of her works. Next door is **The Evergreens,** the imposing Italianate Victorian mansion in which Emily's brother Austin and his family resided for more than 50 years. ✉ *280 Main St., Amherst* ☎ *413/542–8161* 🌐 *www.emilydickinsonmuseum.org* 🎫 *$16* ⏲ *Closed Mon.* ✍ *Timed tickets required.*

★ Eric Carle Museum of Picture Book Art

ART MUSEUM | FAMILY | If you have kids in tow—or if you just love children's book illustrations—"the Carle" is a must-see. This light-filled museum celebrates and preserves not only the works of renowned children's book author Eric Carle, who penned *The Very Hungry Caterpillar,* but also original picture-book art by Maurice Sendak, William Steig, Chris Van Allsburg, and many others. Puppet shows and storytelling events are among the museum's ongoing programs. Children are invited to create their own works of art in the studio or read classics or discover new authors in the library. ✉ *125 W. Bay Rd., Amherst* ☎ *413/559–6300* 🌐 *www.picturebookart.org* 🎫 *$9* ⏲ *Closed Mon. and Tues.*

Yiddish Book Center

ARCHIVE | Founded in 1980, this nonprofit organization received a National Medal for Museum and Library Service for its role in preserving the Yiddish language and Jewish culture. The award recognized the center's rescue of more than a million Yiddish books that might otherwise have been lost. Housed in a cool, contemporary structure that mimics a traditional Eastern European shtetl, or village, the collection comprises more than 100,000 volumes. Special programs take place throughout the year. The biggest is Yidstock, a mid-July festival celebrating klezmer and other Jewish music. ✉ *Hampshire College, 1021 West St., Amherst* ☎ *413/256–4900* 🌐 *www.yiddishbookcenter.org* 🎫 *$8* ⏲ *Closed Sat.*

Restaurants

Bub's Bar-B-Q

$ | BARBECUE | You can smell the sweet and tangy homemade barbecue sauce even before you enter this down-home rib joint where awards and positive newspaper reviews line the walls and a stuffed pig carries your order to the kitchen. Everything from hush puppies to pulled pork is expertly done, and the dinners all come with a large and sumptuous buffet of sides. **Known for:** free jukebox; hot bar and cold bar; copious outdoor seating. *$ Average main: $14 ✉ 676 Amherst Rd., Sunderland ☎ 413/548–9630 ⊕ www.bubsbbq.com ⊙ Closed Mon. and Tues.*

Mission Cantina

$ | **MEXICAN** | Diners pack this loud and colorful cantina daily to enjoy Mexican food at reasonable prices. What the small menu lacks in variety, it makes up for in reliability; everything from the crispy fish tacos to the carnitas enchiladas is worth trying. **Known for:** long waits during prime dinner hours; delicious (but not free) chips and salsa; offbeat margaritas with interesting fruits and flavors. *$ Average main: $15 ✉ 485 West St., Amherst ☎ 413/230–3580 ⊕ www.themissioncantinaamherst.com ⊙ No lunch weekdays.*

Coffee and Quick Bites

Amherst Coffee + Bar

$ | **CAFÉ** | Grab a coffee or a cocktail before the movies at this hip café-by-morning, bar-by-night spot that shares an address with the Amherst Cinema building. **Known for:** great scotch menu; friendly service; impressive latte art. *$ Average main: $7 ✉ 28 Amity St., Amherst ☎ 413/256–8987 ⊕ amherstcoffee.com.*

Hotels

Allen House Inn

$ | **B&B/INN** | Meticulous attention to detail distinguishes this late-19th-century inn, which has been gloriously restored to reflect Victorian aesthetics—colorful wall coverings, plentiful antiques, lace curtains, and hand-stenciled details—though the guest-room beds topped with goose-down comforters are the finest that modernity has to offer. **Pros:** charm and elegance; great linens; free parking. **Cons:** dark and cluttered with ornate furnishings; tiny baths; easy to drive past. *$ Rooms from: $175 ✉ 599 Main St., Amherst ☎ 413/253–5000 ⊕ www.allenhouse.com 14 rooms Free Breakfast.*

Inn on Boltwood

$$ | **B&B/INN** | On the town common of downtown Amherst, this rambling 1926 inn owned by Amherst College is a favorite among visiting parents and professors for its variety of rooms, from smallish doubles to larger suites. **Pros:** great location on the town common; various weekend packages including a farmers' market special; spacious lobby and rooms. **Cons:** some baths are closet-size; many wedding, school, and graduation celebrations are held here. *$ Rooms from: $285 ✉ 30 Boltwood Ave., Amherst ☎ 413/256-8200 ⊕ www.lordjefferyinn.com 49 rooms No Meals.*

Shopping

Atkins Farms Country Market

MARKET | An institution in the Pioneer Valley, this market sells produce, baked goods, and specialty foods—try a cider doughnut to sample the best of all three. *✉ 1150 West St., Amherst ☎ 413/253–9528 ⊕ www.atkinsfarms.com.*

Deerfield

10 miles northwest of Amherst.

In Deerfield a horse pulling a carriage clip-clops past perfectly maintained 18th-century homes, neighbors tip their hats to strangers, kids play ball in fields by the river, and the bell of the impossibly beautiful brick church peals from a white steeple. This is the perfect New England village, though not without a past darkened by tragedy. Its original Native American inhabitants, the Pocumtucks, were all but wiped out by deadly epidemics and a war with the

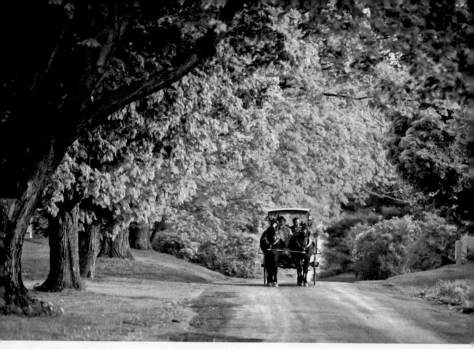

Historic Deerfield is one of many places in the region to experience America's past through living history.

Mohawks. English pioneers eagerly settled into this frontier outpost in the 1660s and '70s, but two bloody massacres at the hands of Native Americans and the French prompted them to abandon it until 1707, when construction began on the buildings that remain today.

GETTING HERE AND AROUND

You can take the train to Springfield, but the most direct public transportation to Deerfield is a Peter Pan bus. If you're driving, take Route 10 from the south or Route 2 from the west. Aside from walking around Historic Deerfield, however, you won't get far without a car.

Sights

★ Historic Deerfield

HISTORIC HOME | With 52 buildings on 93 acres, Historic Deerfield provides a vivid glimpse into 18th- and 19th-century America. Along the tree-lined main street are 12 museum houses, built between 1720 and 1850, some with original doorways. Four are open to the public on self-guided tours, and the remainder can be seen on guided tours that begin on the hour. The **Frary House** displays arts and crafts from the 1900s; the attached Barnard Tavern was the main meeting place for Deerfield's villagers. Other houses depict 18th-century life, including everything from kitchens to adult cradles for those who had fallen victim to tuberculosis. Also of note is a one-room schoolhouse, an old burial ground, and the **Flynt Center of Early New England Life,** which contains needlework, textiles, and clothing dating back to the 1600s. The visitor center is located at Hall Tavern, 80 Old Main Street. Plan to spend at least one full day at Historic Deerfield. ✉ *Old Main St., Deerfield* ☎ *413/775–7214* 🌐 *www.historic-deerfield.org* 🎫 *$18* 🕓 *Closed Mon. and Tues.*

Magic Wings Butterfly Conservatory and Gardens

GARDEN | **FAMILY** | This glass conservatory glitters with more than 4,000 butterflies. Kids love the butterfly nursery, where newborns first take flight. Outside is a three-season garden filled with plants that attract local species. There's also a snack bar and gift shop. ✉ *281 Greenfield Rd., South Deerfield* ☎ *413/665–2805* 🌐 *www.magicwings.com* 🎟 *$16* 🕓 *Closed Mon.*

Memorial Hall Museum

HISTORY MUSEUM | Located in the middle of Historic Deerfield, this stand-alone three-story museum displays Native American artifacts, as well as quilts, furnishings, and crafts from the early settlers. Highlights include the farm equipment, period rooms, children's room, and the military room with rifles and Revolutionary War jackets. ✉ *8 Memorial St., Deerfield* ☎ *413/774–3768* 🌐 *memorialhalldeerfield.org* 🎟 *Free.*

Coffee and Quick Bites

Richardson's Candy Kitchen

$ | **CAFÉ** | The name is no joke: the back half of this store is a kitchen where you can see delectable chocolates being made. A short drive from Historic Deerfield, Richardson's sells luscious cream-filled chocolates, truffles, and other handmade confections, not to mention ice cream. **Known for:** melt-in-your-mouth Almond Acorns; selection of sugar-free chocolates; chocolate-covered strawberries. [$] *Average main: $5* ✉ *500 Greenfield Rd., Deerfield* ☎ *413/772–0443* 🌐 *www.richardsonscandy.com* 💳 *No credit cards.*

Hotels

For visitors to Historic Deerfield, there aren't many options if you want to stay in town.

Shopping

★ The Montague Bookmill

BOOKS | This old mill complex along the Saw Mill River—since converted into a quintet of businesses—exudes old New England. The Bookmill is a quirky secondhand bookshop whose comfortable chairs make it easy to curl up with a book. The good-humored staffers at the adjoining Lady Killigrew café serve beer, coffee, and bagels; there's free Wi-Fi, too. The fantastic waterfall views from the deck of Alvah Stone, which serves lunch and dinner, justify its slightly elevated prices. From Friday to Sunday, you can visit Turn It Up for music and movies, and Wednesday through Monday the Sawmill River Arts crafts gallery offers items by local artists. The complex is incredibly picturesque, if not entirely wheelchair accessible. ✉ *440 Greenfield Rd., Montague* ✥ *¼ mile past village green over small bridge* ☎ *413/367–9206* 🌐 *www.montaguebookmill.com.*

Shelburne Falls

18 miles northwest of Deerfield.

A tour of New England's fall foliage wouldn't be complete without a trek across the famed Mohawk Trail, a 63-mile section of Route 2 that runs past Shelburne Falls. The community, separated from neighboring Buckland by the Deerfield River, is filled with little art galleries and interesting shops on Bridge Street. The surrounding area is filled with orchards, farm stands, and sugar houses.

GETTING HERE AND AROUND

Shelburne Falls lies on Route 2, otherwise known as the Mohawk Trail, useful not only for driving through town, but for setting off to the Berkshires as well.

Sights

Bridge of Flowers

GARDEN | From April to October, an arched, 400-foot trolley bridge is transformed into this promenade bursting with color and a wide variety of flowers. ✉ *Water St., Shelburne Falls* ☎ *413/625–2544* 🌐 *www.bridgeofflowersmass.org.*

Shelburne Falls Trolley Museum

TRANSPORTATION | Take a ride on an old-fashioned trolley from 1896 at this tribute to the old Colrain Street Railway Combine No. 10, which was the first car on the Shelburne line in the early 20th century. A car barn and rails host other trolleys being restored, including a PCC, the last trolley built in Massachusetts. ✉ *14 Depot St., Shelburne Falls* ☎ *413/625–9443* 🌐 *www.sftm.org* 🎟 *All-day trolley pass $4.*

Restaurants

Hearty Eats

$ | **VEGETARIAN** | You don't have to be vegetarian to appreciate the fresh, local, organic offerings at this tiny community-focused café. Sharing an entrance with an arts co-op, the café itself lacks ambience, but does offer up a tasty variety of healthy options that exclude any meat except fish. **Known for:** wide vegetarian selection; falafel and fried-fish bites; fresh juices. 💲 *Average main: $10* ✉ *24 Bridge St., Shelburne Falls* ☎ *413/625–6460* 🌐 *heartyeats.org.*

West End Pub

$$ | **AMERICAN** | Overlooking the Bridge of Flowers and Deerfield River, this quaint upscale pub filled with plants and local artwork is a charming place to catch lunch. Tables on the enclosed porch offer a nice view while you enjoy a hearty burger or fancy salad. **Known for:** grass-fed Black Angus beef burgers from local farms; gluten-free rolls and pasta; tough to access bathroom. 💲 *Average main: $18* ✉ *16 State St., Shelburne Falls* ☎ *413/625–6216* 🌐 *westendpubinfo.com* ⏲ *Closed Sun.–Tues.*

Coffee and Quick Bites

Mocha Maya's Coffee House

$ | **CAFÉ** | Locals come here for the cool vibe, live music, and great coffee. Local art, which is often for sale, decorates the rich red walls, completing the artsy vibe. **Known for:** live music; craft/micro-brewed beers; fun blended drinks like frozen hot chocolate. 💲 *Average main: $5* ✉ *47 Bridge St., Shelburne Falls* ☎ *413/625–6292* 🌐 *www.mochamayas.com.*

Activities

RAFTING

Zoar Outdoor

WHITE-WATER RAFTING | **FAMILY** | White-water rafting, canoeing, and kayaking in the Class II–III rapids of the Deerfield River are popular summer activities. From April to October, Zoar Outdoor conducts kid-friendly rafting trips along 10 miles of challenging rapids, as well as floats along gentler sections of the river. Zipline tours and rock climbing are also offered in season. ✉ *7 Main St., off Rte. 2, Charlemont* ☎ *413/339-4010* 🌐 *www.zoaroutdoor.com.*

Shopping

Salmon Falls Gallery

ART GALLERIES | The showroom features sculpture, pottery, and glass by more than 100 artisans, including hand-blown pieces by Josh Simpson. ✉ *1 Ashfield St., Suite 9, Shelburne Falls* ☎ *413/625–9833* 🌐 *www.salmonfallsgallery.com.*

Sidehill Farm

MARKET | This farm sells yogurt, raw milk, and cheese, as well as beef, from grass-fed cows. Vegetables and fruits are generally available throughout the year. ✉ *58 Forget Rd., Hawley* ☎ *413/339–0033* 🌐 *www.sidehillfarm.net.*

Chapter 7

CONNECTICUT

Updated by
Jane Zarem

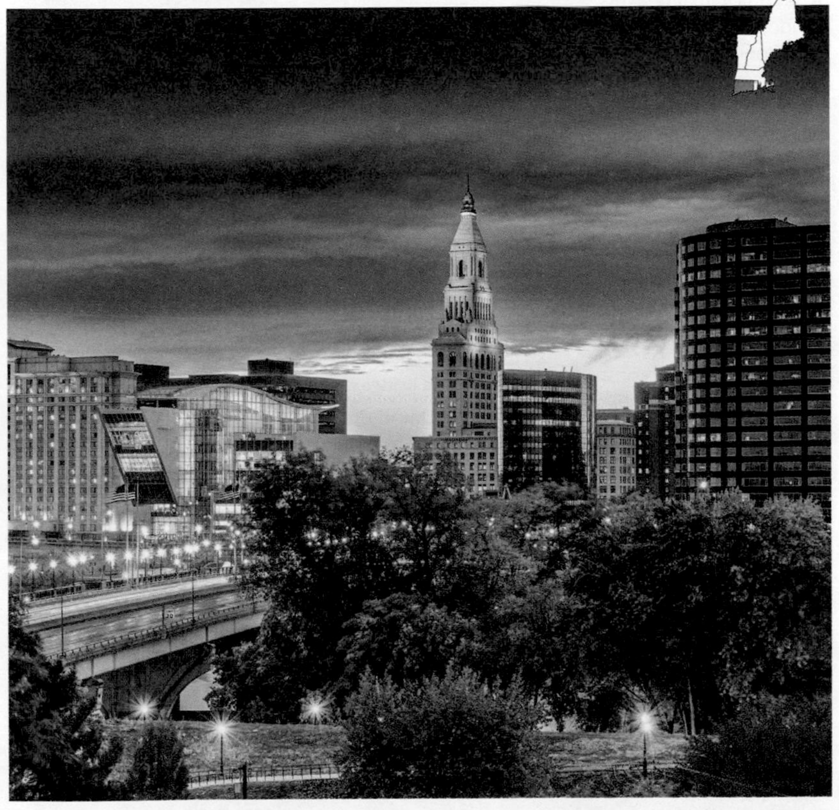

Sights ★★★★★ | Restaurants ★★★★☆ | Hotels ★★★☆☆ | Shopping ★★★☆☆ | Nightlife ★★☆☆☆

WELCOME TO CONNECTICUT

TOP REASONS TO GO

★ **Country Driving:** Meander along the winding roads of Litchfield County through charming towns and villages like Kent, Salisbury, Washington, and Litchfield itself.

★ **Maritime History:** New London, Groton, Mystic, and Stonington have interesting nautical attractions related to Connecticut's rich seafaring history.

★ **Urban Exploring:** Anchored by Yale, downtown New Haven buzzes with hip restaurants, smart boutiques, fascinating museums, and acclaimed theaters.

★ **Literary Giants:** In one historic Hartford neighborhood, you can explore the homes—and legacies—of Mark Twain and Harriet Beecher Stowe; in New London, visit Eugene O'Neill's summer cottage.

★ **Antiques Hunting:** You'll find fine antiques shops, galleries, and auction houses in cities and towns all around the state, but Woodbury and Putnam are two towns that particularly stand out.

1 **Greenwich.** An upscale downtown and a nature center.

2 **Stamford.** Restaurants, nightlife, shopping, and Amtrak.

3 **Norwalk.** Shopping, dining, and the Maritime Aquarium.

4 **Ridgefield.** Pretty main street and a great art museum.

5 **Westport.** A magnet for artists and musicians and Sherwood Island State Park.

6 **New Milford.** Shops, galleries, and dining around the town green.

7 **New Preston.** Boating on Lake Waramaug and wine tasting nearby.

8 **Kent.** Numerous art galleries and Kent Falls State Park.

9 **Cornwall.** Lovely vistas and a covered bridge.

10 **Norfolk.** One of the Northeast's best-preserved villages.

11 **Litchfield.** A classic New England downtown with shops and restaurants.

12 **Washington.** One of Connecticut's best-preserved Colonial towns.

13 **Woodbury.** Numerous antique shops for browsing.

14 **Hartford.** The capital with arts and culture.

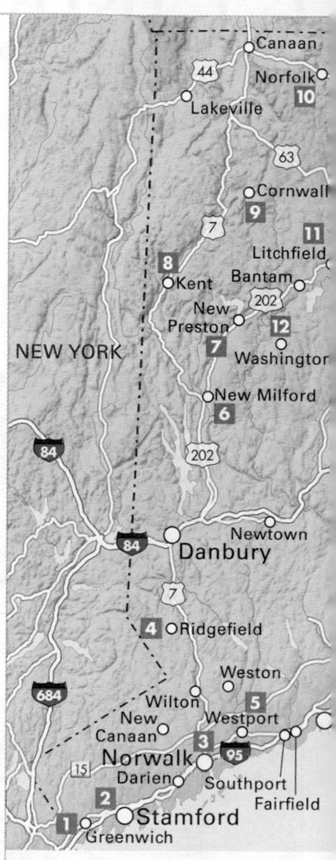

15 **Farmington.** A classic river town with a preserved main street.

16 **Middletown.** Home to Wesleyan University and Dinosaur State Park.

17 **New Haven.** Yale, its museums, and famous New Haven pizza.

18 **Madison.** Ice cream shops, boutiques, and Hammonasset Beach State Park.

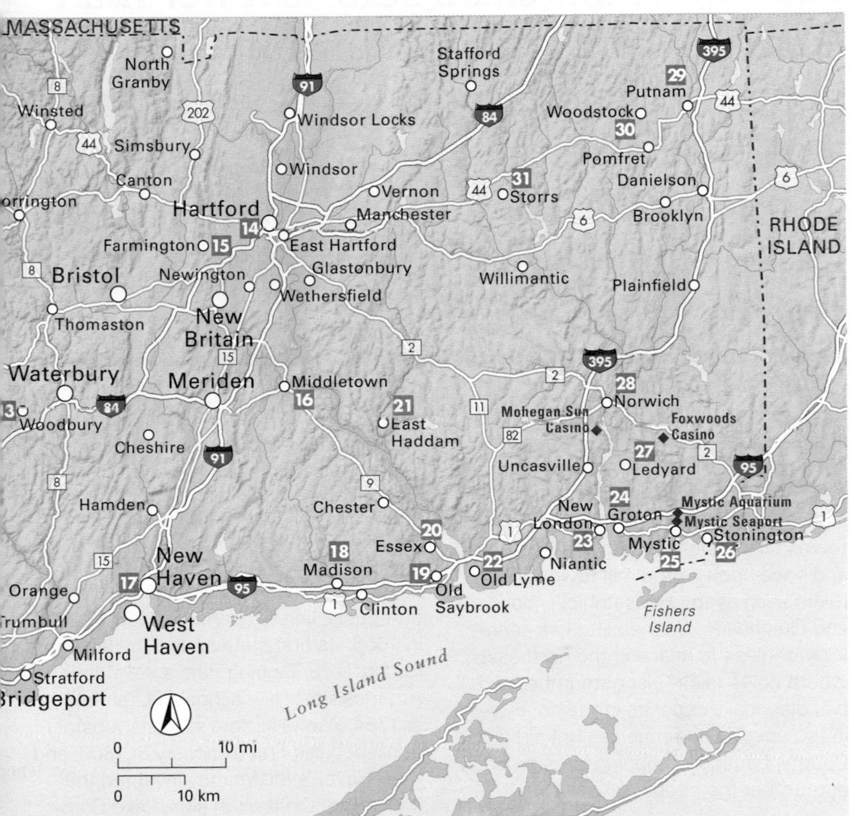

19 Old Saybrook. A picturesque downtown, The Kate, and the waterfront.

20 Essex. A quaint river town and home to the Essex Steam Train.

21 East Haddam. Charming town, Gillette Castle, and Goodspeed Opera House.

22 Old Lyme. An artists' haven with a lovely shoreline.

23 New London. Home to the U.S. Coast Guard Academy and Ocean Beach Park.

24 Groton. Location of the U.S. Naval Submarine Base and submarine museum.

25 Mystic. Mystic Seaport and Aquarium, and lively village.

26 Stonington. Historic and pretty fishing village.

27 Ledyard. Foxwoods casino.

28 Norwich. Mill town with beautiful homes; Mohegan Sun is nearby.

29 Putnam. Hub of the Quiet Corner's antique trade.

30 Woodstock. Tranquility and pastoral environment.

31 Storrs. Home to UConn's main campus.

You can travel from just about any point in Connecticut to any other in less than two hours; this small state is fewer than 60 miles from top to bottom and only about 100 miles across. Yet, it would take weeks (or a lifetime!) to ramble all of Connecticut's "back roads," explore all of its small towns and quaint villages, and enjoy all of its unique attractions.

Along Connecticut's 253 miles of shoreline, salty sea air wafts across beach communities—like Madison, Old Lyme, New London, and Stonington—while a patchwork of forested hills and tiny towns fill the state's northwestern corner and once-upon-a-time mill towns line rivers such as the Housatonic, Moodus, and Quinebaug. Connecticut has seemingly endless farmland in the northeast, where cows might just outnumber people; diagonally opposite in the southwest, in the upscale communities of Fairfield County, boutique shopping bags probably outnumber the people.

Just as diverse as the landscape are the state's residents, who number more than 3.6 million. Many "Connecticut Yankees" can trace their roots to the 1600s, when Connecticut was settled as one of the 13 original colonies; but the state motto is "He who transplanted still sustains." And so the face of the Nutmegger today is both the family from Naples making pizza in New Haven and the farmer in Norfolk whose land dates back five generations, the grandmother in New Britain who makes the state's best pierogi and the ladies who lunch in Westport, the celebrity nestled in the Litchfield Hills and the Bridgeport entrepreneur trying to close the gap between Connecticut's struggling cities and its affluent suburbs.

Qualities that all Connecticut Yankees seem to have in common, historically, is inventiveness, intellect, and the desire to have a little fun. For example: the nation's first public library opened in New Haven in 1656; its first state house, in Hartford in 1776. Tapping Reeve developed America's first law school in Litchfield in 1784, West Hartford's Noah Webster published the first dictionary in 1806; and New Haven's Eli Whitney invented the cotton gin. On the fun side, Lake Compounce in Bristol was the country's first amusement park; Bethel's P. T. Barnum staged the first three-ring circus; Bridgeport's Edwin Land invented the Polaroid camera; New Haven's Charles Goodyear made vulcanized rubber; and the hamburger, the lollipop, the can opener, the Frisbee, the whiffle ball, FM radio, the portable typewriter, the.45 Colt revolver, even the lobster roll—and, of course, the nuclear submarine—were all invented in Connecticut. And don't forget: The Fundamental Orders of Connecticut, established in 1639, was the first written constitution in North America and the archetype of the U. S. Constitution.

Today, thanks to the state's rich history, cultural environment, and abundant natural beauty (including 92 state parks and 30 state forests), tourism has become one of Connecticut's leading industries.

MAJOR REGIONS

Southwestern Connecticut, otherwise known as Fairfield County, is a rich swirl of vintage New England and suburban New York—a region that consistently reports one of the highest costs of living and most expensive homes of any area in the country. Venture beyond the wealthy communities of **Greenwich** and **Westport**, and you'll discover cities struggling through various stages of renewal: **Stamford, Norwalk, Bridgeport**, and **Danbury**. These four have some of the region's best cultural and shopping opportunities.

The **Litchfield Hills** present some of Connecticut's most enchanting scenery. Two highways, Interstate 84 and Route 8, form the southern and eastern boundaries of the region; New York, to the west, and Massachusetts, to the north. Rolling farmlands abut thick forests, and trails—including a section of the Appalachian Trail—traverse state parks and forests. Two rivers, the Housatonic and the Farmington, and two large lakes, Bantam and Waramaug, attract anglers, canoers, hikers, and campers. **New Preston** is a good base when visiting Waramaug. Sweeping town greens and stately homes anchor **Litchfield** and **New Milford**; **Kent** and **Woodbury** draw avid antiquers; **Washington** and **Norfolk** provide a glimpse of New England village life as it might have been two centuries ago; and **Cornwall** is known for its fantastic vistas and covered bridge.

Less touristy than the coast, **Hartford** and the **Connecticut River Valley** embrace the busy capital city and, heading south along both sides of the river, a swath of quaint towns, villages, and hamlets—such as **Farmington**, **Wethersfield**, **East Haddam**, and **Essex**—and one small city, **Middletown**. Visitors are attracted to the area's antique shops, scenic drives, romantic restaurants, and country inns.

As you drive northeast along Interstate 95 or south along Interstate 91 from Hartford to culturally rich **New Haven** and the **Southeastern Coast,** you can first wander through Yale's campus, including its amazing art museums and the Peabody Museum of Natural History, before enjoying a classic New Haven pizzeria. Continuing east along Connecticut's jagged coastline, which stretches to the Rhode Island border, you'll weave your way through the quiet town of **Old Saybrook,** the relatively undisturbed beaches in **Madison,** and the artists' haven of **Old Lyme**. The cities of **New London** and **Groton** are on either side of the Thames River; **Mystic**, home to the Mystic Seaport, and the historic fishing village of **Stonington** are not far beyond. In Uncasville, near the mill town of **Norwich**, the Mohegan Tribe runs the Mohegan Sun casino; near the towns of **Ledyard** and North Stonington, the Mashantucket Pequot Reservation owns and operates the Foxwoods Casino and the Mashantucket Pequot Museum & Research Center. Along with gaming, those two properties have noteworthy hotels, marquee restaurants, and events galore.

Few visitors to Connecticut experience the old-fashioned ways of **The Quiet Corner,** a vast patch of sparsely populated, mostly rural towns that seem a world away from the rest of the state. In **Putnam**, a small mill town on the Quinebaug River, the formerly industrial town center has been transformed into a year-round antique mart. In nearby **Woodstock**, where authentic Colonial homesteads still abound, the scenic drive along route 169 has been named a National Scenic Byway. Nearby, the University of Connecticut's main campus occupies nearly all of the tiny village of **Storrs**.

Planning

The Nutmeg State—also known as The Constitution State and The Land of Steady Habits—is a confluence of different worlds, where farm country meets country homes and fans of the New York Yankees and Boston Red Sox can (quasi-) peacefully coexist. To get a true sense of Connecticut's variety, head for the scenic Litchfield Hills, where you can hike along marked trails, stroll on historic town greens, and relax at trendy cafés. If you have a bit more time, head south to explore the state's wealthy southwestern panhandle and then over to New Haven, with its cultural attractions. If you have five days or a week, add the capital city of Hartford, the villages of the Connecticut River Valley, and the maritime sights in laid-back cities and towns along the southeastern shoreline.

Restaurants

Southern New England is enjoying a gastronomic revolution. Preparation and ingredients reflect the culinary trends of nearby Manhattan and Boston; indeed, the quality and diversity of many Connecticut restaurants rival those of sophisticated metropolitan areas. Although traditional favorites remain—New England clam chowder, buttery lobster rolls, and fish-and-chips—you may also find that sliced duck is wrapped in phyllo, served with a ginger-plum sauce (the orange glaze decidedly absent) and that everything from lavender to fresh figs is used to season and complement dishes. Dining is also increasingly international: You'll find Indian, Vietnamese, Thai, Malaysian, South American, and Japanese restaurants—even Spanish tapas bars—along with the usual Chinese and Italian options in both cities and suburbs. The farm-to-table movement influences what appears on your plate in many establishments, with conscientious chefs partnering up with local producers to provide the best seasonal ingredients. The one drawback of this turn toward sophistication is that finding a dinner entrée for less than $10 is difficult.

Restaurant reviews have been shortened. For full information, visit Fodors.com.

Getting Here and Around

AIR

People visiting Connecticut from afar can fly into New York City, Boston, or Providence—or directly into Hartford or smaller regional airports in New Haven or Westchester County (NY).

AIRPORT CONTACTS Bradley International Airport. ✉ *11 Schoephoester Rd., Windsor Locks* ☎ *860/292–2000* 🌐 *www.bradleyairport.com.* **Tweed New Haven Airport.** ✉ *155 Burr St., New Haven* ☎ *203/466–8833* 🌐 *www.flytweed.com.*

CAR

Interstates are the quickest routes to or between many points in Connecticut, but those highways can be quite congested. From New York City, Interstate 95 hugs the Connecticut shoreline into Rhode Island; for the Litchfield Hills and Hartford, head north on Interstate 684, then east on Interstate 84. From central New England, Interstate 91 intersects Interstate 84 in Hartford and, farther south, Interstate 95 in New Haven. From Boston, take Interstate 95 south through Providence or take the Massachusetts Turnpike west to Interstate 84. Interstate 395 runs north–south between southeastern Connecticut and Massachusetts.

Often more pleasant because of no truck traffic, the historic Merritt Parkway (Route 15) winds its way between Greenwich and Stratford before blending into the Wilbur Cross Parkway, which continues on to Middletown and intersects with Interstate 91; U.S. 7 and Route 8 are north-south highways between Interstate 95 and the Litchfield Hills; Route

9 heads south from Hartford through the Connecticut River Valley to Essex and Old Saybrook; and scenic Route 169 meanders through the Quiet Corner.

FERRY

The seasonal Block Island Express is available to passengers (and bicycles) between New London and Rhode Island's Block Island, with daily service mid-June–Labor Day; weekends only Memorial Day–mid-June and September. Crossing time is 80–90 minutes, depending on the weather and the vessel. Cross Sound Ferry operates year-round passenger and vehicle ferry service between New London and Orient Point, New York, at the tip of Long Island's North Fork. The high-speed passenger ferry can make the trip in 40 minutes; the auto ferry takes twice that time.

The year-round Bridgeport & Port Jefferson Steamboat Co. transports passengers and vehicles between Bridgeport and Port Jefferson, Long Island.

FERRY CONTACTS Block Island Express. ✉ *2 Ferry St., New London* ☎ *860/444–4624* 🌐 *www.goblockisland.com.* **Bridgeport & Port Jefferson Steamboat Co..** ✉ *1 Ferry Access Rd., Bridgeport* ☎ *888/443–3779* 🌐 *88844ferry.com.* **Cross Sound Ferry.** ✉ *2 Ferry St., New London* ☎ *860/443–5281* 🌐 *www.longislandferry.com.*

TRAIN

Amtrak trains between New York City and Boston stop in Stamford, Bridgeport, and New Haven before heading either north through Hartford or east through New London. Metro-North runs along the coastline between New York City and New Haven, stopping at several towns in Fairfield County (including Greenwich, Stamford, Darien, South Norwalk, Westport, and Fairfield). Shore Line East is a commuter line that runs between New Haven and New London, stopping at several towns in between (Branford, Guilford, Madison, Clinton, Westbrook, and Old Saybrook).

TRAIN CONTACTS Amtrak. ☎ *800/872–7245* 🌐 *www.amtrak.com.* **Metro-North Railroad.** ☎ *877/690–5116* 🌐 *www.new.mta.info.* **Shore Line East.** ☎ *877/287–4337* 🌐 *www.shorelineeast.com.*

Hotels

Connecticut has plenty of chain hotels and low-budget motels, along with many inns, resorts, bed-and-breakfasts, and country hotels that are more typical of New England. You'll pay dearly for rooms on the coast in summer, when the beaches beckon, and in the hills in autumn, when the changing leaves attract thousands of visitors. Rates are lowest in winter, but so are the temperatures; spring is always lovely and also a good season for bargain seekers.

Hotel reviews have been shortened. For full information, visit Fodors.com.

What It Costs in U.S. Dollars

$	$$	$$$	$$$$
RESTAURANTS			
under $18	$18–$24	$25–$35	over $35
HOTELS			
under $200	$200–$299	$300–$399	over $399

Tours

Connecticut Beer Trail

SELF-GUIDED TOURS | You'll find more than125 microbreweries throughout the state—from Stamford to Stonington, Woodbury to Woodstock. Many have a tasting room or brewpub where visitors can discover fresh, handcrafted, locally brewed beers. Connecticut Brewers Guild has put together a passport, where you can earn prizes for visiting multiple breweries within a year. ✉ *Connecticut Brewers Guild, 470 James St., New*

Haven ☎ *203/293–8622* 🌐 *www.connecticut.beer/ctbeertrail.*

Connecticut Freedom Trail

DRIVING TOURS | FAMILY | The state's African American heritage and struggle for freedom is documented and celebrated on the trail, which includes more than 130 historic monuments, vessels, cemeteries, museums, and more across 50 towns. ✉ *State Historic Preservation Office, One Constitution Plaza, 2nd fl., Hartford* ☎ *860/256–2800* 🌐 *www.ctfreedomtrail.org.*

Taste of New Haven

GUIDED TOURS | Colin Caplan and his guides take you on foodie adventures—walking, bike, and party bike tours—in and around New Haven, which boasts a burgeoning restaurant scene and, of course, the famous New Haven pizza! ✉ *New Haven* ☎ *888/975–8664* 🌐 *tasteofnewhaven.com.*

Visitor Information

VISITOR CONTACTS Connecticut Office of Tourism. ✉ *Hartford* ☎ *888/288–4748* 🌐 *www.ctvisit.com.*

When to Go

Connecticut is an all-season destination, but fall and spring are particularly appealing times to visit. An autumn drive along the state's back roads or the Merritt Parkway, a National Scenic Byway, is a memorable experience when spots of yellow, orange, and red leaves dot the landscape. In winter, you can ski in the northwest hills. Then, the state blooms in springtime, when town greens are filled with daffodils and tulips and dogwoods and flowering fruit trees punctuate the rich green countryside. The prime time for attractions, however, is summer, when travelers have the most options but also plenty of company—especially at beaches along the shore.

■ TIP→ Beaches in towns along the shoreline charge nonresidents $40 per vehicle per day for parking ($50 on weekends). A state park (Sherwood Island, Hammonasset Beach, Rocky Neck) is a better choice for a day at the beach—same sand, same water, less expensive.

Greenwich

35 miles northeast of New York City, 82 miles southwest of Hartford.

Leafy woodlands, rolling hills, elegant homes, beautiful views overlooking sparkling Long Island Sound, and a picture-perfect downtown area filled with chic boutiques and trendsetting restaurants: Welcome to Greenwich. It's easy to see why this ritzy enclave has become a haven for the rich and famous. Soak up some art and science at the Bruce Museum, then head to Greenwich Avenue for excellent (expensive) shopping and dining.

GETTING HERE AND AROUND

If you're traveling north from New York City, Greenwich will be the first town in Connecticut once you cross the state line. Greenwich is easily accessible from either Interstate 95 or the Merritt Parkway if you're coming by car; Metro-North commuter trains also service Greenwich.

Sights

★ Bruce Museum of Arts and Science

SCIENCE MUSEUM | FAMILY | The owner of this 19th-century home, wealthy textile merchant Robert Moffat Bruce, bequeathed it to the town of Greenwich in 1908 with the stipulation that it be used "as a natural history, historical, and art museum." Today this diversity remains, reflected in the museum's changing exhibitions—more than a dozen new ones each year—highlighting fine and decorative arts, natural history, and anthropology. On permanent display is a spectacular mineral collection. Kids especially enjoy the touchable meteorite and glow-in-the-dark minerals, as well as the fossilized dinosaur tracks. The gift shop is terrific, too! ✉ *1 Museum Dr., Greenwich* ✣ *Off I–95, Exit 3* ☎ *203/869–0376* 🌐 *brucemuseum.org* 🎫 *$10 (free Tues.)* ⏲ *Closed Mon.*

Bush-Holley House

ART MUSEUM | In the 1890s, visitors from New York's Art Students League journeyed to the Cos Cob section of Greenwich to take classes taught by American Impressionist John Henry Twachtman at a boarding house for artists and writers run by Josephine and Constant Holley. Thus, the Cos Cob Art Colony was born and flourished until 1920. Today, the circa-1730 house is known as the Bush-Holley House, which displays a wonderful collection of 19th- and 20th-century art by Twachtman, along with rotating art, history, and cultural exhibitions. The collection also includes personal papers, photographs, and records that reflect the long history of Greenwich and its inhabitants, from farmers to Gilded Age barons, politicians, artists and writers, and shopkeepers. ✉ *47 Strickland Rd., Greenwich* ☎ *203/869–6899* 🌐 *www.greenwichhistory.org* 🎫 *$10, includes guided tour* ⏲ *Closed Mon. and Tues.*

Greenwich Audubon Center

NATURE PRESERVE | **FAMILY** | Opened in 1943 as the National Audubon Society's first educational nature center, the sanctuaries and trails are the best location in the area for bird-watching. During the Fall Festival and Hawk Watch each September, you can spot large numbers of hawks and other migrating raptors. Other events include early morning bird walks, summer and winter bird counts, birding classes, and field trips. The center is filled with interactive exhibits, galleries, classrooms, a wildlife observation room, and a deck with sweeping views of wildlife activity. Outside are 7 miles of hiking trails passing through 285 acres of woodland, wetland, and meadow. ✉ *613 Riversville Rd., Greenwich* ☎ *203/869–5272* 🌐 *greenwich.audubon.org* 🎫 *$6* ⏲ *Center closed Mon.-Wed.*

Restaurants

Elm Street Oyster House

$$$ | **SEAFOOD** | Locals come here for outstanding oysters and the freshest fish in town; expect an especially lively crowd on weekends. Menu standouts include the fresh oysters, of course, along with classic lobster rolls, and fish tacos. **Known for:** seafood, seafood, seafood—and a cheeseburger or steak for landlubbers; colorful artwork adds cheer to the rather cramped dining room; friendly, efficient service—but you're never rushed. 💲 *Average main: $34* ✉ *11 W. Elm St., Greenwich* ☎ *203/629–5795* 🌐 *www.elmstreetoysterhouse.com.*

The Ginger Man

$$ | **AMERICAN** | **FAMILY** | Come for lunch when shopping along Greenwich Avenue, brunch on Sunday, dinner anytime, or just liquid refreshment, as The Ginger Man has a long, friendly bar and casual seating up front, a cozy dining room with a fireplace in back, and formal dining upstairs via a grand curved staircase. Whether you order a burger and fries, fish-and-chips, or a NY strip with roasted fingerlings, you won't leave hungry—or thirsty. **Known for:** burgers famously served on an English muffin; relaxing, local atmosphere; more than 50 beers, half on tap. 💲 *Average main: $24* ✉ *64 Greenwich Ave., Greenwich* ☎ *203/861–6400* 🌐 *gingermanct.com.*

Le Fat Poodle

$$$$ | **BISTRO** | A modern take on a classic (and classy) French bistro, you'll find the usual French standards on the menu like steak frites, along with international dishes such as Madras lamb curry, Peking duck, and San Francisco cioppino. As for decor, you'll find potted palms, ceiling fans, a partially open kitchen, and floor-to-ceiling windows in the bright,

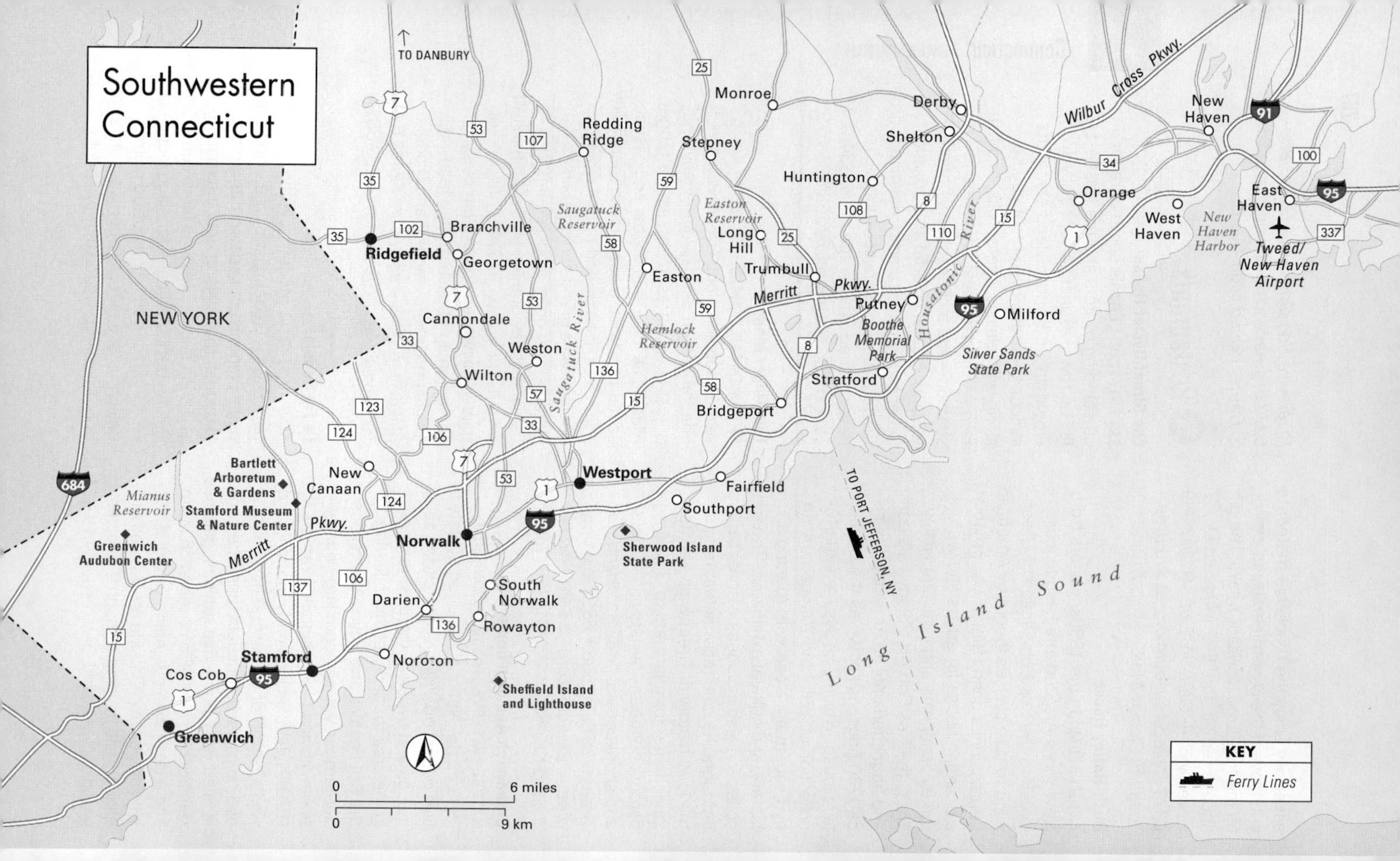
Southwestern Connecticut
TO DANBURY
NEW YORK
Ridgefield
Branchville
Georgetown
Redding Ridge
Saugatuck Reservoir
Cannondale
Weston
Wilton
Saugatuck River
Easton
Hemlock Reservoir
Stepney
Monroe
Easton Reservoir
Long Hill
Trumbull
Huntington
Derby
Shelton
Wilbur Cross Pkwy.
New Haven
Orange
West Haven
East Haven
New Haven Harbor
Tweed/New Haven Airport
Merritt Pkwy.
Putney
Housatonic River
Milford
Boothe Memorial Park
Silver Sands State Park
Stratford
Bridgeport
Fairfield
Southport
Westport
Sherwood Island State Park
TO PORT JEFFERSON, NY
Long Island Sound
Bartlett Arboretum & Gardens
Stamford Museum & Nature Center
Mianus Reservoir
Greenwich Audubon Center
New Canaan
Norwalk
South Norwalk
Rowayton
Darien
Noroton
Stamford
Cos Cob
Greenwich
Sheffield Island and Lighthouse
0
6 miles
0
9 km
KEY
Ferry Lines

airy dining room. **Known for:** professional service; vegetarian and gluten-free options; terrace dining in warm weather. *Average main: $35 20 Arcadia Rd., Old Greenwich 203/717–1515 www.lefatpoodle.com.*

Hotels

★ Delamar Greenwich Harbor Hotel

$$$ | **HOTEL** | This luxury waterfront hotel just blocks from downtown Greenwich resembles a villa on the Italian Riviera. **Pros:** the Champagne welcome sets a luxe tone; easy walk (or free shuttle) to downtown restaurants, shopping, and train; nearby beach passes/harbor cruises (additional cost). **Cons:** fairly pricey; fee added to your bill to cover tips; dogs are welcome in first floor rooms—just so you know. *Rooms from: $322 500 Steamboat Rd., Greenwich 203/661–9800 www.delamar.com/greenwich-harbor 82 rooms Free Breakfast.*

Stamford

6 miles northeast of Greenwich, 40 miles southwest of New Haven.

While business is often what brings people to Stamford, what keeps them coming are the restaurants, nightclubs, and shops along Atlantic and lower Summer Streets. Weekenders have plenty of options beyond the downtown canyons: beaches, boating on the Sound, and nature trails are only minutes away.

GETTING HERE AND AROUND

Stamford is easily accessible from both Interstate 95 and the Merritt Parkway. It is also a major rail hub for Metro-North commuter trains and Amtrak, whose high-speed Acela trains stop here en route between Boston and Washington, D.C.

Sights

Bartlett Arboretum & Gardens

GARDEN | **FAMILY** | This 93-acre natural sanctuary is home to 13 gardens with more than 2,000 varieties of annuals, perennials, wildflowers, and trees. There's a greenhouse, marked ecology trails (dogs are welcome), a pretty pond, and a boardwalk through a red maple swamp. Brilliant, bold colors make the wildflower garden stunning in spring. *151 Brookdale Rd., off High Ridge Rd., Stamford 203/487–5264 www.bartlettarboretum.org Free.*

Stamford Museum & Nature Center

MUSEUM VILLAGE | **FAMILY** | Oxen, sheep, pigs, and other animals roam this 118-acre New England farmstead. Once the estate of Henri Bendel, the property includes a Tudor Revival stone mansion housing exhibits on natural history, art, and Americana. Nature trails wind through 80 acres of woods—perfect for a daytime hike year round or on a summer evening. Special experiences include maple sugaring in February, a farm market on summer Sundays, and apple cidering on fall weekends. *39 Scofieldtown Rd. (Museum), 151 Scofieldtown Rd. (Farmhouse), Stamford 203/977–6521 www.stamfordmuseum.org $14.*

Restaurants

★ The Capital Grille

$$$$ | **STEAKHOUSE** | This swanky and splurge-worthy steak house serves up impeccable steaks and chops, along with a host of other well-crafted entrées, in the dimly lit dining room with an old-school gentleman's club feel. Though dry-aged, hand-carved steaks are the specialty, Capital Grille also excels at seafood: pan-seared scallops, Maine lobster, and sushi-grade seared sesame tuna are equally delicious choices. **Known for:** the steaks, of course, prepared exactly as you like; creamed spinach, truffle fries, lobster mac 'n' cheese—lots of sides to

share; perfect for a special occasion (or when you're really hungry). *Average main: $50* ✉ *Stamford Town Center, 230 Tressor Blvd., Stamford* ☎ *203/967–0000* 🌐 *www.thecapitalgrille.com* ⊙ *No lunch weekends.*

Prime Stamford

$$$$ | **STEAKHOUSE** | Enjoy a full view of the waterfront while partaking of USDA Prime dry-aged steak, chops, or seafood with classic steakhouse sides and enhancements such as horseradish cream, Bearnaise, blue cheese, or Bordelaise sauce. Start with a selection from the raw bar, wagyu meatballs, octopus carpaccio, or caramelized figs, among other options—and end with a "movie theater" sundae. **Known for:** no kids under 6; glass wine room with more than 750 labels; outdoor dining in summer. *Average main: $50* ✉ *78 Southfield Ave., Stamford* ☎ *203/817–0700* 🌐 *stamford.restaurantprime.com.*

Hotels

The Lloyd

$$ | **HOTEL** | Named for John Lloyd, a prominent 18th-century shipping magnate and businessman from Stamford, The Lloyd is a luxury boutique hotel that offers personalized, "curated" service to travelers looking for a convenient, comfortable place to stay. **Pros:** walk to businesses, shopping, restaurants, theaters; 24-hour fitness center; free shuttle service (within 5 miles). **Cons:** no full restaurant, but breakfast and light "bar bites" are available; some rooms are quite small; self-park in adjacent public lot when valet lot is full. *Rooms from: $214* ✉ *909 Washington Blvd., Stamford* ☎ *203/363–7900* 🌐 *thelloydstamford.com* *94 rooms* *No Meals.*

Stamford Marriott Hotel & Spa

$$ | **HOTEL** | **FAMILY** | Business travelers in particular appreciate the 16-floor hotel's up-to-date facilities and convenience to trains and airport shuttles. **Pros:** an easy walk to downtown restaurants and Stamford Mall; complimentary shuttle to nearby train station; weekend travelers enjoy lower prices. **Cons:** rooms are ready for updating, which apparently is planned; hotel restaurants are good but pricey; parking garage is expensive. *Rooms from: $249* ✉ *243 Tresser Blvd., Stamford* ☎ *203/357–9555, 888/236–2427* 🌐 *www.marriott.com* *506 rooms* *No Meals.*

Performing Arts

MUSIC

★ Orchestra LUMOS

MUSIC | The orchestra (formerly Stamford Symphony) performs mainly at The Palace Theatre, but selected musicians also perform at smaller venues in Stamford and nearby towns. ✉ *The Palace Theatre, 61 Atlantic St., Stamford* ☎ *203/325–1407 x10 for tickets, 203/325–4466 Palace Theatre box office* 🌐 *orchestralumos.org.*

THEATER

The Palace Theatre

THEATER | **FAMILY** | Plays, comedy shows, concerts, ballet, kids' shows, and film festivals are presented at the 1,600-seat Palace, originally a vaudeville house, which is now owned and operated by Stamford Center for the Arts. ✉ *61 Atlantic St., Stamford* ☎ *203/325–4466 box office* 🌐 *www.palacestamford.org.*

Norwalk

10 miles northeast of Stamford, 45 miles northeast of New York City.

In the 19th century, Norwalk was a major New England port and manufacturing center that produced hats, pottery, clocks, watches, shingle nails, and paper. The city later fell into neglect and remained so for much of the 20th century. In the 1980s and '90s, however, Norwalk's coastal business district was the focus of major redevelopment. Much of South Norwalk has since turned into a hot spot for trendy shopping, culture, and dining—much of it along Washington Street. Known as SoNo, it's *the* place to be if you're young, single, and living it up in Fairfield County.

GETTING HERE AND AROUND

If you are traveling by car, Norwalk is easily reached by Interstate 95 or the Merritt Parkway. Metro-North commuter trains also make two stops here. Exit at the South Norwalk station to put yourself within walking distance of SoNo shops, restaurants, and bars.

Sights

The Lockwood-Mathews Mansion Museum
HISTORIC HOME | This ornate tribute to Victorian decorating, built in 1864 as the summer home of financier and railroad tycoon LeGrand Lockwood, remains one the oldest (and finest) surviving Second Empire–style country homes in the United States. It's hard not to be impressed by its octagonal skylighted rotunda and more than 50 rooms of gilt, frescoes, marble, intricate woodwork, and etched glass. Movie buffs will be interested in knowing that the mansion was used as the location of the Stepford Men's Association in *The Stepford Wives*—the original (1975) film. ✉ *295 West Ave., Norwalk* ☎ *203/838–9799* 🌐 *www.lockwoodmathewsmansion.com* 🎫 *From $10* ⏲ *Closed Mon.–Tues.*

★ **The Maritime Aquarium at Norwalk**
AQUARIUM | **FAMILY** | This 5-acre waterfront center, the cornerstone of the city's SoNo district, explores the marine life and maritime culture of Long Island Sound. The aquarium's more than 20 habitats include some 1,000 creatures indigenous to the Sound, including sting rays, sea turtles, harbor seals, river otters, and jellyfish. You can see toothy bluefish and sand tiger sharks in the 110,000-gallon Ocean Beyond the Sound aquarium. The Maritime Aquarium also operates an Environmental Education Center, leads marine-mammal cruises aboard *R/V Spirit of the Sound,* and has the state's largest IMAX theater. ✉ *10 N. Water St., Norwalk* ☎ *203/852–0700* 🌐 *www.maritimeaquarium.org* 🎫 *$30.*

Sheffield Island and Lighthouse
LIGHTHOUSE | **FAMILY** | Sheffield Island is a prime spot for a picnic and some bird-watching; the lighthouse, built in 1868, has 10 rooms on four levels that you can explore. A ferry departs from the Sheffield Island Dock on N. Water Street for the 3-hour excursion, including 1.5 hours on the island. Clambakes are held Tuesday evenings June–August. ✉ *Sheffield Island Dock, 4 N. Water St. at Washington St., Norwalk* ☎ *800/838–9444* 🌐 *www.seaport.org* 🎫 *$40* ⏲ *Closed Oct.–Memorial Day; closed weekdays, May, June, and Sept.* ✍ *Reservations recommended.*

Stepping Stones Museum for Children
CHILDREN'S MUSEUM | **FAMILY** | The Color-Coaster, a 27-foot-high kinetic structure in constant motion, is the centerpiece of this hands-on museum with exhibits organized by age. Visit the Energy Lab, where youngsters learn about wind, water, and solar power while splashing around the extensive water play area. The Light Gallery has colorful LED displays; Studio K has a green screen and video feed for real-time "newscasting"; and for babies and toddlers, Tot Town is a safe place where they can play with toys and puzzles, "cook" in a play kitchen, and learn about animals on Old MacDonald's Farm. ✉ *Mathews Park, 303 West Ave., Norwalk* ☎ *203/899–0606* 🌐 *www.steppingstonesmuseum.org* 🎫 *$16.*

Restaurants

★ **Match**
$$$ | **MODERN AMERICAN** | A SoNo fixture since 1999, Match's high ceilings, exposed brick, and industrial fixtures provide a sleek, urban look. Indulge in one of

Norwalk's Maritime Aquarium is a great way to come eye-to-eye with animals found in Long Island Sound, like sea turtles and harbor seals.

the signature wood-fired pizzas straight out of the oven or savor the light-as-air gnocchi tossed in brandy-truffle cream, blackened swordfish, or steak frites. **Known for:** something delicious at every price point; creative wood-oven pizzettes, including bacon-potato-egg, shrimp fra diablo, and "forest"; "New School" raw bar, featuring Norwalk oysters. 💲 *Average main: $30* ✉ *98 Washington St., Norwalk* ☎ *203/852–1088* 🌐 *www.matchsono.com* ⏲ *Closed Mon.-Tues.; no lunch.*

Hotels

Hotel Zero Degrees Norwalk

$$ | HOTEL | FAMILY | This ultramodern boutique lodging is a great addition to an area choked with chain hotels. **Pros:** on-site fitness center; tasty Tuscan cuisine at the in-house Siena Ristorante Italiano; self-parking. **Cons:** noise from the nearby train tracks; weeknight prices can jump 30%–40%; complimentary breakfast choices are limited. 💲 *Rooms from: $201* ✉ *353 Main Ave., Norwalk* ☎ *203/750–9800* 🌐 *www.hotelzerodegrees.com/hotels/norwalk* 🛏 *96 rooms* 🍴 *Free Breakfast.*

Nightlife

★ Barcelona Wine Bar

WINE BARS | Savor wines primarily from Spain—tinto, rosado, or blanco, with more than 40 available by the glass—while nibbling on charcuterie, cheese, or a selection of tapas. ✉ *The Wayside, 515 West Ave., Norwalk* ☎ *203/854–5600* 🌐 *www.barcelonawinebar.com.*

Ridgefield

15 miles north of Norwalk, 43 miles west of New Haven.

In Ridgefield, you'll find an outstanding contemporary art museum nestled in a classic New England town within an hour of Manhattan. Main Street, a large leafy boulevard, has a number of small businesses; otherwise, "downtown" is largely a residential sweep of lawns and majestic homes. Ridgefield is snug against the Connecticut/New York border; to reach the state line, you drive along Peaceable Street—which pretty much sums up Ridgefield.

GETTING HERE AND AROUND

From Interstate 95 or the Merritt Parkway, head north on U.S. 7 to Route 33 to reach Ridgefield; Metro-North will take you to the Branchville station in Ridgefield, but you'll need a car from there.

Sights

★ The Aldrich Contemporary Art Museum

ART MUSEUM | Cutting-edge art is not necessarily what you'd expect to find in a stately, 18th-century structure that, by turns, served as a general store, a post office, and, for 35 years, a church. Nicknamed "Old Hundred," this historic building is just part of the vast facility, which includes a 17,000-square-foot exhibition space that puts its own twist on traditional New England architecture. The white-clapboard-and-granite structure houses 12 galleries, a screening room, a sound gallery, a 22-foot-high project space for large installations, a 100-seat performance space, and an education center. Outside is a 2-acre sculpture garden. *258 Main St., Ridgefield* *203/438–4519* *thealdrich.org* *$12; every third Saturday, admission is free* *Closed Tues.*

Restaurants

Luc's Café

$$$ | **BISTRO** | A cozy French bistro set inside a stone building with low ceilings and closely spaced tables, Luc's takes full advantage of its handy location in Ridgefield's iconic downtown. The place charms patrons with carefully prepared food—salade niçoise, croque monsieur, or the classic steak au poivre with a velvety Roquefort sauce and crispy frites—and low-key, friendly service. **Known for:** nonstop service from 11 am until closing; special plat du jour offered daily; all dishes prepared à la minute. *Average main: $28* *3 Big Shop La., Ridgefield* *203/894–8522* *www.lucscafe.com* *Closed Sun.*

Coffee and Quick Bites

Heibeck's Stand

$ | **FAST FOOD** | **FAMILY** | Just south of the Ridgefield town line on U.S. 7, you'll see a huge ice-cream cone on the roadside marking Heibeck's Stand, where you can choose a made-to-order burger or hot dog with a variety of toppings or a sandwich, Philly cheesesteak, lobster roll, taco, salad—even a house-marinated portobello mushroom "burger." Best of all is the ice cream, which is rich, creamy, and deee-licious—in midsummer, try the fresh peach ice cream. **Known for:** the ice cream; patio dining in the back; easy in, easy out, easy parking. *Average main: $16* *951 Danbury Rd., U.S. 7, Wilton* *203/917–9313* *www.heibecksstand.com* *Closed early Oct.–mid-Apr. Closed Mon.*

Sycamore Drive-In

$ | **DINER** | **FAMILY** | Heading north from Fairfield County toward the Litchfield Hills along rural Route 53, definitely stop at the Sycamore Drive-In in Bethel for a burger, fries, milkshake, and authentic 1950s atmosphere. During the summer, Saturday "Cruise Nights" (5-8 pm) see classic cars and "hot rods" fill the parking lot (more parking across the street) and rock 'n' roll music fills the air. **Known for:** the "Dagwood Burger" with everything on it; eat inside or in your car; Saturday "Cruise Night." *Average main: $15* *282 Greenwood Ave., corner of Rte. 53, Bethel* *203/748–2716* *www.sycamoredrivein.com.*

Performing Arts

★ The Ridgefield Playhouse

THEATER | **FAMILY** | This historic, fully renovated, country playhouse presents national and local musicians, comedians, magicians, theatrical performances, classic and new films, and insightful lectures. Stars ranging from Gordon Lightfoot to Lyle Lovett, Dana Carvey to Amy Schumer, and performances such as Puccini's *Madama Butterfly* and Shakespeare's *Henry V* have been headliners over the years. ✉ *80 East Ridge, Ridgefield* ☎ *203/438–5795* 🌐 *ridgefield-playhouse.org.*

Westport

47 miles northeast of New York City.

Westport, an artists' community since the turn of the 20th century and the epitome of suburbia, continues to attract creative types despite an influx of commuters and corporations over the years.

GETTING HERE AND AROUND

You can reach Westport by car via Interstate 95 (Exit 17 will take you closer to the center of town and main shopping areas) or the Merritt Parkway. Metro-North also has two stops here: Westport (closer to town) and Greens Farms (farther east toward Fairfield).

★ Sherwood Island State Park

STATE/PROVINCIAL PARK | FAMILY | Summer visitors congregate at this state park, Connecticut's first, which has a 1½-mile sweep of sandy beach, two picnic areas at the water's edge, sports fields, and several food stands (open seasonally). The on-site nature center offers various programs from bird-watching to nature walks. ✉ *Sherwood Island Connector, Westport* ✣ *Off I–95, Exit 18* ☎ *203/226–6983* 🌐 *www.ct.gov/deep/sherwoodisland* 🎟 *Memorial Day–Labor Day: $15 per vehicle weekdays, $22 weekends* ⏲ *Nature Center: closed Mon. and Tues., Labor Day–Memorial Day* ☞ *No alcohol, no pets.*

Hudson Malone

$$$ | **STEAKHOUSE** | Mainly a chophouse, where you might choose a 40-ounce Tomahawk steak, 10-ounce filet mignon, double-cut pork chop with a choice of sauce or herbed butter; but the rather extensive menu also includes grilled fish, burgers, and several small plates. **Known for:** emphasis on local, natural, sustainable, and organic products; long list of cocktails, wines, and beers; popular bar. [$] *Average main: $28* ✉ *323 Main St., Westport* ☎ *203/635–7400* 🌐 *www.hudsonmalone.com.*

Spotted Horse Tavern

$$$ | **MODERN AMERICAN** | The theme for this neighborhood favorite is horse, of course; the atmosphere reflects the historic building (circa 1808), and the menu offers old-fashioned comfort foods with modern flourishes. The grilled pork chop has a whole-grain mustard glaze, chicken Milanese includes a side of lemon yogurt sauce, steak frites comes with Parmesan fries—and items on the Pony Menu will delight the kids. **Known for:** street-side alfresco dining in warm months; busy bar; convenient downtown location. [$] *Average main: $25* ✉ *26 Church La., Westport* ☎ *203/557–9393* 🌐 *spottedhorsect.com.*

Tarantino Restaurant

$$$ | **ITALIAN** | One of several area restaurants operated by the Marchetti-Tarantino family over the past four decades, Maria Marchetti still makes all of the restaurant's homemade pasta and ravioli. You'll also find traditional Italian fish (il pesce) meat (la carne), and poultry (il pollo) dishes on the menu, along with a full roster of antipasti. **Known for:** friendly atmosphere; tasty, reasonable, and consistent; nice local vibe. [$] *Average main: $35* ✉ *30 Railroad Pl., Westport* ☎ *203/454–3188* 🌐 *www.tarantinorestaurant.com* ⏲ *Closed Sun., no lunch Sat.*

Performing Arts

The Levitt Pavilion for the Performing Arts
CONCERTS | FAMILY | Enjoy an excellent series of mostly free outdoor summer concerts here that range from jazz to classical, folk to blues, and one night each week focused especially on children. (You must reserve or buy a ticket online.) Bring a blanket or beach chair—and a picnic, if you like, but snacks and drinks are also available. ✉ *40 Jesup Rd., Westport* ☎ *203/221–2153 concert hotline, 203/602–4122 box office* 🌐 *www.levittpavilion.com* *Mostly free* ⏲ *Closed late Aug.–late May.*

Westport Country Playhouse
THEATER | Long associated with local benefactors Joanne Woodward and the late Paul Newman, the venerable and intimate Westport Country Playhouse presents high-quality performances from April through November and special family programs from December through March. ✉ *25 Powers Ct., Westport* ☎ *203/227–4177* 🌐 *www.westportplayhouse.org* *Varies.*

New Milford

56 miles west of Hartford, 37 miles north of Norwalk.

If you're approaching the Litchfield Hills from the south, New Milford is a practical starting point to begin a visit. It was also a starting point for a young cobbler (and later a lawyer) named Roger Sherman, who opened the town's first shop in 1743 at the corner of Main and Church streets. A Declaration of Independence signatory, Sherman also helped draft the Articles of Confederation and the Constitution. You'll find shops, galleries, and eateries all within a short stroll of the New Milford town green.

GETTING HERE AND AROUND

New Milford is best visited by car. From Danbury and points south, take U.S. 7 to U.S. 202 to reach the town.

Sights

★ Elephant's Trunk Flea Market
MARKET | FAMILY | In the same spot since 1976, this outdoor flea market has grown from a dozen or so vendors to more than 500 on a typical Sunday, along with food trucks offering everything from a snack to full meals. You'll never know what usual and unusual treasures you'll find spread out on the field, as every Sunday brings out a different collection of vendors selling all manner of antiques, collectibles, housewares, and merchandise, along with, simply, "things." Serious buyers arrive by 5:30 am and pay $20 admission for the privilege; other "early birds" prepay $10 online to enter at 7 am; the rest of us are happy to browse from 8 am to 2 pm and pay just $3. ✉ *490 Danbury Rd., U.S. 7/U.S. 202, New Milford* ☎ *860/355–1448* 🌐 *www.etflea.com* *From $3* ⏲ *Closed Mon.–Sat. and mid-Dec.–late Mar.*

Restaurants

The Cookhouse
$$ | BARBECUE | FAMILY | Stop here for some of the best "slow-smoked" barbecue in Connecticut or for one of the comfort-food staples on the extensive menu. You'll love the barbecued baby back ribs, half-chicken, brisket, and pulled pork—or try chicken-fried steak, cookhouse meat loaf, or fried catfish—all with your choice of sides. **Known for:** something to please everyone in the family; Wednesday night's all-you-can-eat BBQ for $25; wide selection of draft beers. *Average main: $24* ✉ *31 Danbury Rd., New Milford* ☎ *860/355–4111* 🌐 *www.thecookhouse.com* ⏲ *Closed Mon.*

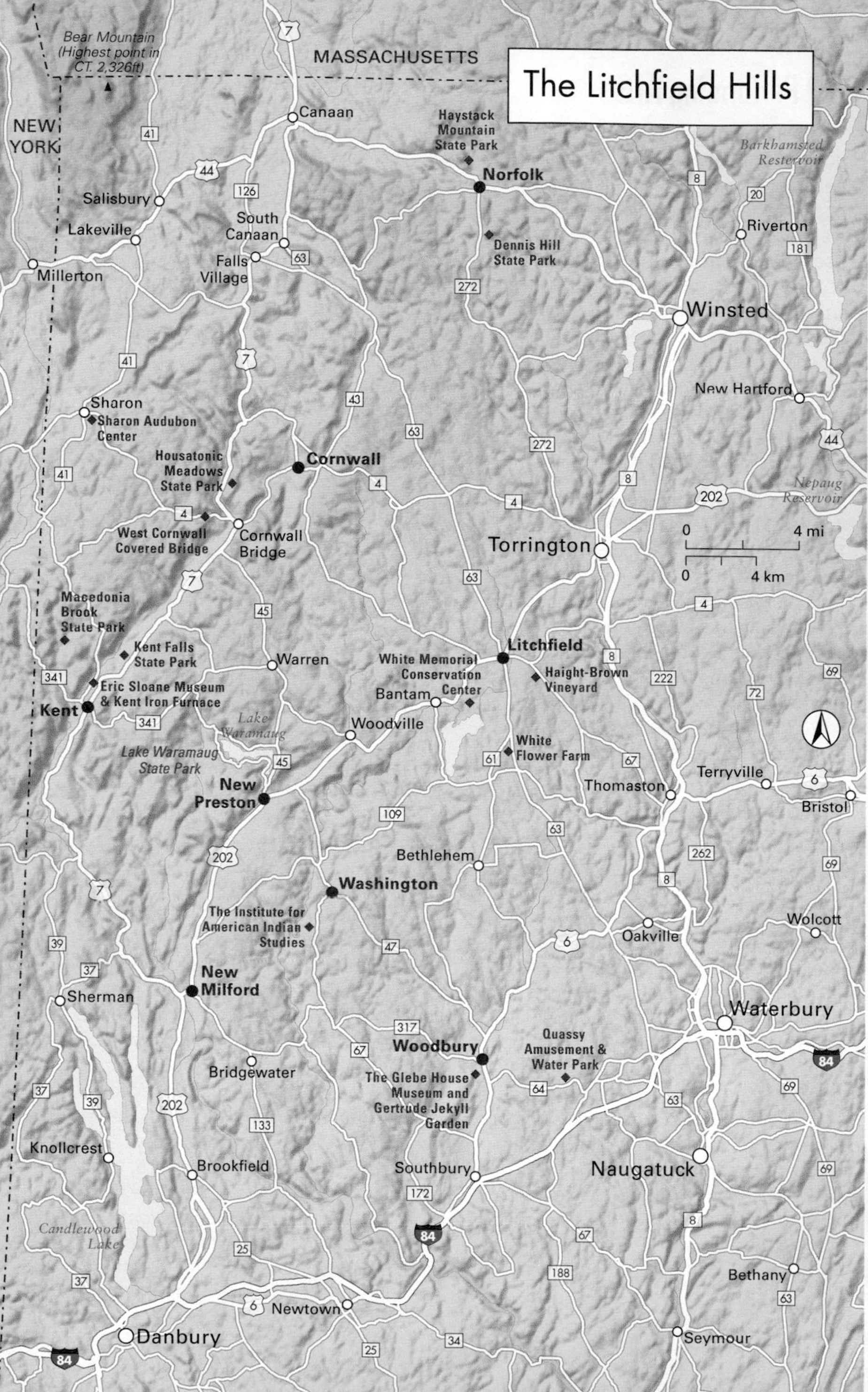

The Litchfield Hills
MASSACHUSETTS
NEW YORK
Bear Mountain (Highest point in CT. 2,326ft)
Canaan
Haystack Mountain State Park
Norfolk
Barkhamsted Reservoir
Riverton
Salisbury
Lakeville
South Canaan
Falls Village
Millerton
Dennis Hill State Park
Winsted
New Hartford
Sharon
Sharon Audubon Center
Housatonic Meadows State Park
Cornwall
Nepaug Reservoir
West Cornwall Covered Bridge
Cornwall Bridge
Torrington
0 4 mi
0 4 km
Macedonia Brook State Park
Kent Falls State Park
Warren
Litchfield
White Memorial Conservation Center
Haight-Brown Vineyard
Eric Sloane Museum & Kent Iron Furnace
Bantam
Kent
Lake Waramaug
Woodville
Lake Waramaug State Park
White Flower Farm
New Preston
Thomaston
Terryville
Bristol
Bethlehem
Washington
The Institute for American Indian Studies
Wolcott
Oakville
New Milford
Sherman
Waterbury
Quassy Amusement & Water Park
Woodbury
Bridgewater
The Glebe House Museum and Gertrude Jekyll Garden
Knollcrest
Brookfield
Southbury
Naugatuck
Candlewood Lake
Bethany
Newtown
Danbury
Seymour

Hotels

★ The Homestead Inn

$ | **B&B/INN** | **FAMILY** | High on a hill overlooking New Milford's town green, this Victorian masterpiece opened as an inn in 1928. **Pros:** open year-round; close to shops and restaurants; substantial, delicious, homemade breakfasts. **Cons:** adults only in main house; free breakfast only for main house guests; some bathrooms are tiny, with sinks in the bedroom. *Rooms from: $180 ✉ 5 Elm St., New Milford ☎ 860/354–4080 🌐 www.homesteadct.com 16 rooms Free Breakfast.*

New Preston

8 miles north of New Milford.

The crossroads village of New Preston, perched above a 40-foot waterfall on the Aspetuck River, has a little town center that's packed with antiques shops specializing in everything from 18th-century furnishings to contemporary art.

Lake Waramaug, north of New Preston on Route 45, is named for Chief Waramaug, one of the most revered figures in Connecticut's Native American history. You can drive around the 8-mile perimeter of the lake, but you'll definitely want to stop and enjoy the view—especially in autumn.

GETTING HERE AND AROUND

To reach New Preston, drive north from New Milford along U.S. 202 for about 8 miles or south along Route 45 from U.S. 7 at Cornwall Bridge for about 12 miles—both lovely drives.

Sights

Hopkins Vineyard

WINERY | This 35-acre vineyard overlooking Lake Waramaug produces more than 14 varieties of wine—from sparkling to dessert. A weathered red barn houses a gift shop and a tasting room, where knowledgeable staff explain the various wines and wine-making techniques. A wine bar in the Hayloft, with views of the lake, serves a fine cheese and pâté board. There's also a picnic area. *✉ 25 Hopkins Rd., New Preston ☎ 860/868–7954 🌐 www.hopkinsvineyard.com Tasting, $8.50 Closed Mon.–Tues. Jan.–Apr.*

Lake Waramaug State Park

STATE/PROVINCIAL PARK | **FAMILY** | The 95-acre parkland surrounding idyllic Lake Waramaug, one of Connecticut's largest and most picturesque natural lakes, is a great place for swimming, boating, fishing, and picnicking. The park has 76 campsites in wooded and open settings (with bathrooms and showers available) that are available from Memorial Day through Labor Day; canoes and kayaks can be rented on-site in summer, too. *✉ 30 Lake Waramaug Rd., New Preston ☎ 860/868–0220 🌐 portal.ct.gov/DEEP/State-Parks/Parks/Lake-Waramaug-State-Park Parking fee ($10 weekday, $15 weekend) for nonresidents; free for Connecticut residents.*

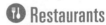

Restaurants

The Hopkins Inn Restaurant

$$$ | **SWISS** | This 19th-century country inn overlooking Lake Waramaug is a lovely place for breakfast, alfresco lunch, midafternoon tea, or a European-inspired dinner. The menu includes features French escargot, Austrian Wiener schnitzel, Swiss *rösti* potatoes, and Italian veal piccata—as well as American favorites like broiled Atlantic salmon. **Known for:** beautiful setting overlooking Lake Waramaug; gluten-free and children's menus, too; associated inn and winery. *Average main: $27 ✉ 22 Hopkins Rd., Warren ☎ 860/868–7295 🌐 www.thehopkinsinn.com Closed Jan.-Mar.; Mon.; no lunch Sun.*

★ The White Horse

$$ | **AMERICAN** | **FAMILY** | Locals, leaf peepers, and folks just passing through stop at The White Horse, a country pub and restaurant that draws its varied menu from British pub, American comfort, and French bistro favorites. Dine on the deck, on the patio, or along the river in the warm months—or inside in front of the fire during the winter chill. **Known for:** historical artifacts throughout and a London-style taxi named Audrey; produce grown on its own farm, "The Back Forty"; vegan, gluten-free, and vegetarian menus, too. *Average main: $23 ✉ 258 New Milford Tpke. (Rte. 202), New Preston ☎ 860/868–1496 ⊕ www.whitehorsecountrypub.com.*

Cornwall

12 miles northeast of Kent.

Connecticut's Cornwalls can get confusing: there's Cornwall, Cornwall Bridge, West Cornwall, Cornwall Hollow, East Cornwall, and North Cornwall. Northwestern Connecticut is known for its winding country roads and stunning vistas of forested hills and mountains, all of which are evident in the Cornwalls—along with a covered bridge that spans the Housatonic River.

GETTING HERE AND AROUND

Head north from Kent on U.S. 7 to reach the various Cornwalls.

Sights

Cornwall Bridge Pottery

FACTORY | Visitors are welcome to watch potters as they work, producing a variety of items that are fired in an on-site, 35-foot-long, wood-fired tube kiln. A selection of items—including seconds—are available for purchase in the workshop. A larger store, located farther north in West Cornwall (415 Sharon-Goshen Turnpike), offers the wood-fired pots along with complementary items made by local glassmakers, woodworkers, and metalsmiths. ✉ *Workshop, 69 Kent Rd. S (U.S. 7), Cornwall Bridge* ☎ *860/672–6545* ⊕ *cbpots.com* ⏲ *Store closed weekdays.*

Housatonic Meadows State Park

STATE/PROVINCIAL PARK | The park is marked by its tall pine trees near the Housatonic River and has terrific riverside campsites (seasonal). Fly-fishers consider this 2-mile stretch of the river among the best places in New England to test their skills catching trout and bass (license required).

■ TIP → This is a family-friendly park: no alcohol allowed. ✉ *90 U.S. 7 N, Sharon* ☎ *860/927–3238* ⊕ *portal.ct.gov/DEEP/State-Parks/Parks/Housatonic-Meadows-State-Park* *Free.*

Sharon Audubon Center

NATURE SIGHT | **FAMILY** | With 11 miles of hiking trails, this 1,147-acre property—a mixture of forests, meadows, wetlands, ponds, and streams—provides myriad hiking opportunities. The visitor center shares its space with small hawks, an owl, and other animals in the live-animal display in the Natural History Exhibit Room; in the Children's Adventure Center, kids learn about the importance of water quality and watersheds, crawl through a tunnel to a beaver lodge, and look for various fish and other sea life in the large aquarium. ✉ *325 Cornwall Bridge Rd., Sharon* ☎ *860/364–0520* ⊕ *sharon.audubon.org* *Visitor center free, $5 suggested donation for aviaries and trails* ⏲ *Visitor center closed Mon.*

West Cornwall Covered Bridge

BRIDGE | A romantic reminder of the past, this single-lane bridge over the Housatonic River is on Route 128, just east of U.S. 7, in West Cornwall. The 172-feet-long and 15-feet-wide lattice truss bridge was built in 1841 and still carries vehicular traffic. The design incorporates strut techniques that were later copied by bridge builders around the country. ✉ *Junction of U.S. 7 and Rte. 128, West Cornwall* 🌐 *cornwallct.org/explore-cornwall-ct/cornwall-ct-covered-bridge/.*

Hotels

Cornwall Inn

$ | B&B/INN | FAMILY | This 19th-century inn, with four bedrooms and a two-bedroom suite, combines country charm with contemporary elegance; eight rustic guest rooms in the adjacent lodge are slightly more private and have cedar-post beds. **Pros:** tranquil setting and lovely grounds; seasonal swimming pool and year-round hot tub; kids and pets welcome. **Cons:** a bit far from neighboring towns; allergy alert: the main inn is pet-free; rooms are fairly small and bathrooms are quite small. *Rooms from: $169* ✉ *270 Kent Rd. S, Cornwall* ☎ *860/672–6884* 🌐 *www.cornwallinn.com* *13 rooms* *Free Breakfast.*

Activities

BOATING AND RAFTING

Clarke Outdoors

CANOEING & ROWING | FAMILY | This outfitter rents canoes, kayaks, paddleboards, and rafts—and operates 10-mile and 6-mile canoe or raft trips downstream from Falls Village to Housatonic Meadows State Park. The water is a mix of flat water and easy white water, suitable for novices. **■ TIP→ Rafts, which are more stable than canoes, are recommended for parties with young children or weak swimmers.** ✉ *163 U.S. 7, West Cornwall* ✣ *1 mile south of covered bridge* ☎ *860/672–6365* 🌐 *www.clarkeoutdoors.com.*

FISHING

Housatonic River Outfitters

FISHING | This outfitter operates a full-service fly shop, leads guided (wade) fishing trips, conducts classes in fly-fishing, and offers a good selection of vintage and antique gear. **■ TIP→ CT fishing license required and can be purchased online.** ✉ *24 Kent Rd., Cornwall Bridge* ☎ *860/672–1010* 🌐 *www.dryflies.com.*

SKIING

Mohawk Mountain

SKIING & SNOWBOARDING | FAMILY | Mohawk Mountain has plenty of intermediate terrain, some trails for beginners, and steeper ones for advanced skiers. A small area is devoted to snowboarders and another to snow tubing. Trails are serviced by five triple lifts and three magic carpets; 16 trails are lighted for night skiing. The base lodge has a cafeteria and a retail shop; halfway up the slope the Pine Lodge Restaurant offers full-service dining, a roaring fire in a natural stone fireplace, and an outdoor patio. Facilities: 26 trails; 112 skiable acres; 650-foot vertical drop; 8 lifts; snowmaking (which was actually invented here) available on 100% of terrain. ✉ *46 Great Hollow Rd., off Rte. 4, Cornwall* ☎ *860/672–6100* 🌐 *www.mohawkmtn.com* *Day lift tickets $40 midweek, $75 weekends/holidays.*

Kent

14 miles northwest of New Milford.

Kent was once known for its ironworks; today, it boasts a pretty village full of shops and art galleries—some nationally renowned—as well as an eponymous prep school, the scenic and functional Bull's Covered Bridge (one of three in Connecticut), and the Schaghticoke Indian Reservation. During the Revolutionary War, 100 Schaghticokes helped defend the colonies by communicating army intelligence from the hilltops of Litchfield Hills to Long Island Sound by way of shouts and drumbeats.

GETTING HERE AND AROUND

To reach Kent by car, travel 14 miles north from New Milford on U.S. 7.

Sights

Bulls Bridge

BRIDGE | One of three covered bridges in Connecticut, Bulls Bridge is open to cars. ✉ *71 Bull's Bridge Rd., just off Rte. 7, Kent.*

Eric Sloane Museum & Kent Iron Furnace

HISTORY MUSEUM | Hardware-store buffs and vintage-tool aficionados will feel right at home at this museum. Artist and author Eric Sloane (1905–1985) was fascinated by Early American woodworking tools, and his collection showcases examples of American craftsmanship from the 17th to 19th centuries. The museum contains a re-creation of Sloane's last studio and also encompasses the ruins of a 19th-century iron furnace. Sloane's illustrated books and prints, which celebrate vanishing aspects of Americana, are available for sale here. ✉ *31 Kent–Cornwall Rd. (U.S. 7), 1 mile north of Rte. 341 intersection, Kent* ☎ *860/927–2150* 🌐 *portal.ct.gov/ECD-EricSloaneMuseum* 🎫 *$10* 🕒 *Closed Nov.–April, weekdays.*

Kent Falls State Park

STATE/PROVINCIAL PARK | Heading north from Kent toward Cornwall, you'll pass the entrance to 295-acre Kent Falls State Park, where you can walk across a covered bridge, hike a short way to one of the prettiest waterfalls in the state, and picnic in the green meadows at the base of the falls. ✉ *462 Kent-Cornwall Rd. (U.S. 7), Kent* ☎ *860/927–3238* 🌐 *portal.ct.gov/DEEP/State-Parks/Parks/Kent-Falls-State-Park* 🎫 *Parking for nonresidents Memorial Day–Oct. weekends $15, weekdays $10, free for Connecticut residents.*

Macedonia Brook State Park

STATE/PROVINCIAL PARK | Early-season trout fishing (license required) is superb at 2,300-acre Macedonia Brook State Park, where you can also hike and cross-country ski. The Blue Trail crosses several peaks, and you can see as far as the Catskills and Taconics in neighboring New York State. The expansive mountain views are amazing year-round; the leaves are magnificent in the fall. ✉ *159 Macedonia Brook Rd., off Rte. 341, Kent* ☎ *860/927–3238* 🌐 *portal.ct.gov/DEEP/State-Parks/Parks/Macedonia-Brook-State-Park* 🎫 *Free.*

Coffee and Quick Bites

Kent Coffee and Chocolate Company

$ | ICE CREAM | FAMILY | This shop sells delicious homemade chocolates, old-time favorite candies, and baked goods like muffins and coffee cake. There's also an extensive menu of coffees, teas, and smoothies. **Known for:** great coffee; breakfast options like smoothies, bagels, and granola parfaits; options for most dietary restrictions. 💲 *Average main: $5* ✉ *45 N. Main St., Kent* ☎ *860/927–1445* 🌐 *www.kentcoffee.com.*

Hotels

Fife 'n Drum Inn

$$ | B&B/INN | If you like to shop, eat, and rest your head in a cozy, simple place, you can do all three at this pet-friendly, family-owned inn. **Pros:** quaint inn in quaint town; walk to local shops and galleries; "family" rooms have a twin-size day bed. **Cons:**"front desk" in the next-door restaurant; book early for fall foliage season; two-night minimum May–October weekends. 💲 *Rooms from: $205* ✉ *53 Main St., Kent* ☎ *860/927–3509* 🌐 *www.fifendrum.com* 🕒 *Restaurant closed Tues.* 🛏 *15 rooms* 🍽 *No Meals.*

Activities

Appalachian Trail

HIKING & WALKING | The 2,190-mile Appalachian Trail, which stretches through 14 states from Georgia to Maine, is the longest hiking-only footpath in the world. About 52 miles of the trail pass through the northwestern tip of Connecticut. Just off Route 341, the nearly 5-mile-long, well-maintained River Walk from Kent to Cornwall Bridge meanders along the Housatonic River—one of the longest sections of the trail that, mile after mile, follows a river. ✉ *Kent* 🌐 *appalachiantrail.org/explore/explore-by-state/connecticut/.*

Norfolk

23 miles northeast of Cornwall, 41 miles west of Hartford, 60 miles north of New Haven.

Thanks to having the coolest temperatures in Connecticut and a rather rocky terrain, Norfolk has resisted development and stands as one of the best-preserved villages in the Northeast. Notable industrialists have been summering here for two centuries, and many enormous homesteads still exist. The striking town green, at the junction of Route 272 and U.S. 44, has a fountain designed by Augustus Saint-Gaudens (executed in 1889 by Stanford White) at its southern corner. The fountain is a memorial to Joseph Battell, who turned Norfolk into a major trading center in the mid-19th century.

GETTING HERE AND AROUND

To reach Norfolk by car, use either U.S. 7 or U.S. 8 and U.S. 44.

Sights

Dennis Hill State Park

STATE/PROVINCIAL PARK | FAMILY | Dr. Frederick Shepard Dennis, the former owner of these 240 acres and a noted New York surgeon, lavishly entertained his guests—among them President William Howard Taft and several Connecticut governors—in the stone pavilion at the summit of the estate. From its 1,627-foot height, you have a panoramic view of Haystack Mountain and parts of New Hampshire to the north and, on a clear day, New Haven Harbor about 60 miles south. Picnic on the park's grounds or hike one of its many trails. Autumn foliage here is spectacular! ✉ *Rte. 272, Norfolk* ☎ *860/482–1817* 🌐 *portal.ct.gov/DEEP/State-Parks/Parks/Dennis-Hill-State-Park* 🎫 *Free.*

Hotels

Blackberry River Inn

$ | B&B/INN | Set upon 27 acres in Connecticut's Berkshire Mountains, this historic (1763) home turned inn has two rooms and two suites in the Main House and a dozen simpler—but still lovely—rooms in the adjacent Carriage House, plus a full home-cooked breakfast is served in a sunny breakfast room every morning. **Pros:** swimming pool open in summer; wood-burning fireplaces in most Main House rooms; raised waffles (made with yeast) and real maple syrup at breakfast. **Cons:** two-night minimum on weekends; no room TV in Main House rooms; beware of wildlife (an occasional bear). 💲 *Rooms from: $169* ✉ *538 Greenwoods Rd. W (U.S. 44 W), Norfolk* ☎ *860/542–5100* 🌐 *www.blackberryriverinn.com* 🛏 *17 rooms* 🍽 *Free Breakfast.*

Performing Arts

★ Infinity Music Hall & Bistro

CONCERTS | Built in 1883, this modernized 300-seat music hall with a world-class sound system hosts more than 200 shows a year by local performers as well as nationally known folk, soft rock, and jazz groups. The intimate setting puts you close to the stage. Before the performance, have drinks, snacks, or a meal at the on-site GoodWorks Smokehouse. ✉ *20 Greenwoods Rd. W (U.S. 44), Norfolk* ☎ *866/666–6306, 860/560–7757* 🌐 *www.infinityhall.com.*

Norfolk Chamber Music Festival

FESTIVALS | Held at the Music Shed on the 70-acre Ellen Battell Stoeckel Estate, Norfolk Chamber Music Festival—under the auspices of the Yale Summer School of Music—presents world-renowned artists and ensembles on summer evenings in July and August. Stroll the 70-acre grounds or visit the art gallery, too. ✉ *Ellen Battell Stoeckel Estate, 20 Litchfield Rd., Norfolk* ☎ *860/542–3000* 🌐 *music.yale.edu/norfolk* 🕑 *Closed Sept.–Jun.*

Litchfield

60 miles northeast of Norwalk, 34 miles west of Hartford, 40 miles northwest of New Haven.

Everything in Litchfield, the most noteworthy town in the Litchfield Hills, seems to exist on a larger scale than in neighboring villages, especially the impressive Litchfield Green and the white Colonial and Greek Revival homes that line the broad, tree-lined streets. Harriet Beecher Stowe, author of *Uncle Tom's Cabin,* and her brother, abolitionist preacher Henry Ward Beecher, were born and raised in Litchfield; many other famous Americans earned law degrees at the Litchfield Law School. Today, lovely but expensive boutiques and restaurants line the downtown area.

GETTING HERE AND AROUND

To reach Litchfield by car from points north or south, the most direct route is U.S. 8 to Route 118 west.

Sights

Haight-Brown Vineyard

WINERY | A founding member of the Connecticut Wine Trail, the state's oldest winery opened its doors in 1975. You can stop in for tastings with or without a snack—or bring your own picnic. Enjoy live music as you sip on Saturday evenings. ✉ *29 Chestnut Hill Rd., off Rte. 118, Litchfield* ☎ *860/361–6969* 🌐 *haightbrownwine.com* 🎫 *Tasting $3.75 per 3 oz. sample* 🕑 *Closed Mon.-Wed.*

Litchfield History Museum

HISTORY MUSEUM | In this well-regarded museum, seven neatly organized galleries highlight family life and work during the 50 years following the American Revolution. The extensive reference library has information about the town's historic buildings, including the Sheldon Tavern where George Washington slept on several occasions and the Litchfield Female Academy where, in the late 1700s, Sarah Pierce taught girls not only sewing and deportment but also mathematics and history. ✉ *7 South St., at Rtes. 63, 118, and U.S. 202, Litchfield* ☎ *860/567–4501* 🌐 *www.litchfieldhistoricalsociety.org* 🎫 *Free* 🕑 *Closed Mon. and Dec.–mid-Apr.*

Tapping Reeve House and Litchfield Law School

HISTORY MUSEUM | In 1774, Judge Tapping Reeve enrolled his first student, Aaron Burr, in what became the first law school in the country. (Before Judge Reeve opened his school, students studied the law as apprentices, not in formal classes.) This school is dedicated to Reeve's achievement and to the notable students who passed through its halls, including three U.S. Supreme Court justices. There are multimedia exhibits, an excellent introductory film, and restored facilities. ✉ *82 South St., Litchfield* ☎ *860/567–4501* 🌐 *www.litchfieldhistoricalsociety.org* 🎫 *Free* 🕑 *Closed Mon. and Dec.–Apr.*

★ White Memorial Conservation Center

NATURE PRESERVE | **FAMILY** | This 4,000-acre nature preserve houses top-notch natural-history exhibits. You'll find 30 bird-watching platforms, two self-guided nature trails, several boardwalks, boating facilities, and 40 miles of hiking, cross-country skiing, and horseback-riding trails. The Nature Museum has displays depicting the natural diversity found throughout the preserve, dioramas, live animals, a beehive, a digital microscope, and other unique exhibits of interest to kids of all ages (especially the scavenger hunt). ✉ *80 Whitehall Rd., off U.S. 202, Litchfield* ☎ *860/567–0857* 🌐 *www.whitememorialcc.org* 🎫 *Grounds free, museum $6* ⊙ *Closed Mon.*

 Restaurants

The Village Restaurant

$$ | **AMERICAN** | Beloved among visitors and locals alike, this storefront eatery in a redbrick town house serves tasty, unfussy food—inexpensive pub grub in one room, updated contemporary American cuisine in the other. Whether you order a cheeseburger or horseradish-and-Parmesan-crusted salmon, you're bound to be pleased. **Known for:** really good food at reasonable prices; all-day dining; weekday happy hours. $ *Average main: $23* ✉ *25 West St., Litchfield* ☎ *860/567–8307* 🌐 *www.village-litchfield.com* ⊙ *Closed Tues.*

West Street Grill

$$$ | **MODERN AMERICAN** | This sophisticated dining room on the town green is *the* place to see and be seen. Dinner selections might include free-range chicken with potato purée, braised short ribs with Cabernet demi-glace, or Scottish grilled salmon with ratatouille. **Known for:** sidewalk café tables in warm weather; perfect for a casual lunch or formal dinner; house-made ice creams and sorbets. $ *Average main: $34* ✉ *43 West St., Litchfield* ☎ *860/567–3885* 🌐 *www.weststreetgrill.com* ⊙ *Closed Mon.-Wed.*

The Litchfield Inn

$$ | **B&B/INN** | This Colonial-style inn offers standard guest rooms with modern decor, along with 12 uniquely decorated theme rooms. **Pros:** on-site restaurant and lounge; bridal suite with a fireplace; particularly comfy beds. **Cons:** you'll want a car to get around the area; uneven service; more like a small hotel than a country inn. $ *Rooms from: $231* ✉ *432 Bantam Rd., Litchfield* ☎ *860/567–4503* 🌐 *www.litchfieldinnct.com* *32 rooms* 🍽 *Free Breakfast.*

★ Winvian Farm

$$$$ | **RESORT** | This private, 113-acre hideaway a few miles south of Litchfield consists of 18 imaginative and luxuriously outfitted cottages, each with a distinctive, often amusing, theme—like the Helicopter Cottage, built around a genuine, 1968-vintage Sikorsky helicopter (the fuselage has been fitted with a wet bar). **Pros:** whimsical and superplush accommodations; quiet getaway... very quiet; stunning setting. **Cons:** superpricey; size and amenities differ for each cottage; two-night stay required on weekends. $ *Rooms from: $799* ✉ *155 Alain White Rd., Morris* ☎ *860/567–9600* 🌐 *www.winvian.com* *19 suites* 🍽 *Free Breakfast.*

 Activities

HIKING

Mt. Tom State Park

HIKING & WALKING | Hike the mile-long trail to the stone lookout tower atop Mt. Tom and enjoy expansive views—or take a swim in the pond below and picnic on the beach. ✉ *U.S. 202, Litchfield* ✣ *7 miles southwest of Litchfield* ☎ *860/868–2592 (Labor Day–Memorial Day), 860/567–8870 (Memorial Day–Labor Day)* 🌐 *portal.ct.gov/DEEP/State-Parks/Parks/Mount-Tom-State-Park* 🎫 *Parking free for residents, $15 on weekends for nonresidents.*

HORSEBACK RIDING

Lee's Riding Stable

HORSEBACK RIDING | **FAMILY** | Ride a well-behaved steed through Litchfield's rolling hills and countryside. Adults and kids age seven and up are welcome to join a guided, hour-long trail ride. Youngsters enjoy a pony ride around the ring. Private or semiprivate lessons are also available. Or you can just enjoy a delightful afternoon at Windfield Morgan Farm, where Lee's Riding Stable is located. ✉ *57 E. Litchfield Rd., Litchfield*

☎ *860/567–0785* 🌐 *www.windfieldmorganfarm.com* 🎫 *Trail rides, $50 per hr; pony rides, from $20.*

Washington

14 miles southwest of Litchfield.

The beautiful buildings of The Gunnery, a private prep school, mingle with stately homes and churches in Washington, one of Connecticut's best-preserved Colonial towns. Mayflower Inn & Spa, south of The Gunnery on Route 47, attracts an exclusive clientele. The town was settled in 1734; in 1779, it became the country's first town to be named for the country's first president.

GETTING HERE AND AROUND

Washington is accessible only by car. Route 47 runs through the rural town, connecting it with New Preston to the north and Woodbury to the south.

The Institute for American Indian Studies

HISTORY MUSEUM | FAMILY | The exhibits in this small but excellent and thoughtfully arranged collection detail the history and continuing presence of 10,000 years of Native American life in New England, specifically in "Quinnetukut." Highlights include 15 acres of nature trails, a simulated archaeological site, and an authentically constructed 16th-century Algonkian Village with wigwams, a longhouse, a rock shelter, and more. A gift shop presents the work of some of the country's best Native American artists. ✉ *38 Curtis Rd., off Rte. 199, Washington* ☎ *860/868–0518* 🌐 *www.iaismuseum.org* 🎫 *$12* 🕒 *Closed Mon. and Tues.*

G. W. Tavern

$$ | AMERICAN | This cozy tavern, once an 1850s-era Colonial home overlooking the Shepaug River, is a nod to George Washington, who passed through the little village back in the day. The chef prepares traditional New England favorites like oven-roasted cod, chicken potpie, and meat loaf, as well as seasonal specialties like soft shell crabs in spring and game throughout the winter. **Known for:** "George's cherry pie" for dessert; relax by the floor-to-ceiling fireplace with a glass of wine or draught beer; outdoor riverside dining in summertime. $ *Average main: $22* ✉ *20 Bee Brook Rd., Washington* ☎ *860/868–6633* 🌐 *www.gwtavern.com* 🕒 *Closed Tues. and Wed.*

★ Mayflower Inn & Spa

$$$$ | RESORT | Running streams, rambling stone walls, and rare-specimen trees fill the country manor–style inn's 58 acres of rolling countryside. **Pros:** special activities for kids, some free and some for a fee; accessible rooms available; hiking, biking, and nature walks at the back door. **Cons:** very pricey; $42.50 per day resort fee added to all rates; some rooms undergoing well-needed refurbishment. $ *Rooms from: $827* ✉ *118 Woodbury Rd., Rte. 47, Washington* ☎ *866/217–0869, 860/868–9466* 🌐 *aubergeresorts.com/mayflower* *35 rooms* *No Meals.*

Woodbury

10 miles southeast of Washington.

Woodbury may have more antique shops than all other towns in the Litchfield Hills combined. Some of the best-preserved examples of Colonial architecture in New England can be found here, as well, including five magnificent churches and the Greek Revival King Solomon's Lodge No. 7 Masonic Temple (1838).

GETTING HERE AND AROUND

To reach Woodbury by car from Washington, take Route 47 south; from elsewhere, take Interstate 84 to U.S. 6 north.

Sights

The Glebe House Museum and Gertrude Jekyll Garden

GARDEN | This property in the center of town includes the large, antiques-filled, gambrel-roof Georgian Colonial home of Dr. Samuel Seabury—who, in 1783, was elected the first Episcopal bishop in the United States. The house, built in 1740, and its outstanding furniture collection comprise one of the earliest and most authentic house museums in the region. The garden was designed in the 1920s by renowned British horticulturist Gertrude Jekyll. Though small, it's a classic, old-fashioned, English-style garden and the only one of the three Jekyll-designed gardens in the United States that are still in existence. ✉ *49 Hollow Rd., Woodbury* ☎ *203/263–2855* 🌐 *www.glebehouse-museum.org* 🎫 *$7* ⏲ *Museum closed Mon.–Thurs. and mid-Oct.–Apr.*

Quassy Amusement & Water Park

AMUSEMENT PARK/CARNIVAL | **FAMILY** | Families have been enjoying the rides here for more than a century. There are kiddie rides, family rides that mom and dad even enjoy, and thrill rides—more than two-dozen rides altogether—plus Splash Away Bay Water Park. The custom-designed Wooden Warrior roller coaster is rated one of the top 25 in the world. ✉ *Lake Quassapaug, 2132 Middlebury Rd. (Rte. 64), Woodbury* ✣ *4 miles southeast of Woodbury via U.S. 6 and Rte. 64* ☎ *800/367–7275, 203/758–2913* 🌐 *www.quassy.com* 🎫 *$35* ⏲ *Closed Oct.–Apr.*

Restaurants

★ Good News Restaurant & Bar

$$$ | **AMERICAN** | Since Carole Peck—a well-known name throughout New England (and beyond)—opened her spot here in 1992, foodies have been flocking to Woodbury to sample her superb cuisine. The emphasis is on healthy, innovative, and surprisingly well-priced fare like wok-seared Gulf shrimp with new potatoes, grilled green beans, and a garlic aioli. **Known for:** "star" chef cooks up creative cuisine; farm-to-table dishes feature local, seasonal ingredients; decor includes original artwork by local artists. $ *Average main: $25* ✉ *Sherman Village Plaza, 694 Main St. S, Woodbury* ☎ *203/266–4663* 🌐 *goodnewsrestaurantandbar.com* ⏲ *Closed Mon. and Tues.*

Coffee and Quick Bites

★ Ferris Acres Creamery

$ | **ICE CREAM** | **FAMILY** | This popular creamery, located on a massive family-owned and-operated dairy farm since 1864, creates its own made-on-the-farm frozen desserts (that's *ice cream*!) daily. Choose from more than 30 "regular" flavors, like coffee almond fudge and maple walnut, and as many "special" flavors, like Caramalt and Sunset on the Peach (with a raspberry swirl). **Known for:** fun flavor names like Ali-Oop, Bad Habit, Elvis Dream, and Route 302 Chocolate Moo; bucolic scene with 50 dairy cows roaming the adjacent pastures; about as close as you can get to homemade ice cream without making it yourself. $ *Average main: $8* ✉ *144 Sugar St., Newtown* ✣ *About 15 miles and scenic ½-hr drive southwest of Woodbury* ☎ *203/426–8803* 🌐 *www.ferrisacrescreamery.com.*

Hotels

Evergreen Inn Bed + Breakfast

$$ | B&B/INN | A short drive from Woodbury's antiques shops and restaurants, this Federal Colonial house (circa 1818) offers a bounty of pleasing comforts—from high-quality antique furnishings and soft bedding with lots of pillows to floral gardens and a stone-and-granite pool surrounded by a private hedge. **Pros:** delicious, made-from-scratch full breakfast; beautifully kept grounds and garden; 24-hour self-serve snack bar with coffee/wine/beer. **Cons:** only five rooms, so reserve in advance; on a fairly busy road; you won't want to leave. *$ Rooms from: $229 ✉ 782 Main St. N (Rte. 6), Southbury ✣ 3 miles south of Woodbury ☎ 203/586–1876 🌐 www.evergreeninnsouthbury.com ⇆ 5 rooms ꟾ⊙ꟾ Free Breakfast.*

Shopping

Mill House Antiques

ANTIQUES & COLLECTIBLES | The Mill House carries high-end formal and country English and French furniture and decor. *✉ 1068 Main St. N, Woodbury ☎ 203/263–3446 🌐 www.millhouseantiquesandgardens.com.*

Hartford

39 miles north of New Haven, 52 miles northwest of New London, 78 miles northeast of Stamford.

Midway along the inland route between New York City and Boston, Hartford is Connecticut's capital city and the "Insurance Capital of the World." Founded in 1635 on the banks of the Connecticut River, Hartford was once home to authors Mark Twain and Harriet Beecher Stowe, inventors Samuel and Elizabeth Colt, landscape architect Frederick Law Olmsted, and Ella Grasso, the first woman to be elected a state governor. Today Hartford boasts a revitalized downtown core featuring a bustling convention center and a top-notch science museum, the Connecticut Science Center. The city is once again on the verge of discovery.

GETTING HERE AND AROUND

Hartford is located in the middle of the state, at the intersection of two main highways: Interstate 91, which runs north from New Haven, across central Massachusetts and along the entire length of Vermont to the Canadian border; and Interstate 84, which runs generally east–west from the small town of Union at Connecticut's northeast border with Massachusetts, through Hartford and Danbury to the New York border. Amtrak serves Hartford on its Northeast Regional line. Bradley International Airport in Windsor Locks, 15 minutes north of Hartford, offers nonstop flights to more than 30 destinations in the United States, Canada, Ireland, and the Caribbean.

Sights

Bushnell Park

CITY PARK | FAMILY | Fanning out from the State Capitol building, this city park is the oldest publicly funded park in the United States. Conceived by Rev. Horace Bushnell in the early 1850s, the park was designed by Swiss-born landscape architect and botanist Jacob Weidenmann. Some 1,100 trees and shrubs (157 different varieties) were planted, creating an urban arboretum. Kids love the Bushnell Park Carousel (open weekends, June–August), with its 48 intricately hand-carved horses and booming Wurlitzer band organ, built in 1914 by the Artistic Carousel Company of Brooklyn, New York, and installed in the park in 1974. A welcome oasis of green in a busy city, the park has a pond and about 750 trees, including a first-generation offspring of the state's historic Charter Oak (the state tree) and four enormous state champion trees. *✉ 99 Trinity St., Hartford*

☎ *860/232–6710* 🌐 *www.bushnellpark.org* 🎫 *Free; $2 carousel ride.*

Butler-McCook House & Garden
HISTORIC HOME | Built in 1782, this was home to four generations of Butlers and McCooks until it became a museum in 1971. Today, it houses Hartford's oldest intact collection of art and antiques, including Connecticut-crafted furnishings, family possessions, and Victorian-era toys that show the evolution of American tastes over nearly 200 years. The beautifully restored Victorian garden was originally designed by Jacob Weidenmann. ■ **TIP→ Open for guided tours by reservation at least 7 days in advance.** ✉ *396 Main St., Hartford* ☎ *860/522–1806* 🌐 *www.ctlandmarks.org* 🎫 *$12* ⏲ *Closed Jan.–Apr.* ✍ *Reservations required.*

The Children's Museum
CHILDREN'S MUSEUM | **FAMILY** | A life-size walk-through replica of a 60-foot sperm whale greets patrons at this museum. Located in West Hartford, the museum also has a wildlife sanctuary and a planetarium with real-life images of outer space beamed in from NASA, as well as a hands-on puzzle exhibit that introduces kids to various scientific and mathematical concepts and optical illusions. ✉ *950 Trout Brook Dr., 5 miles west of downtown, West Hartford* ☎ *860/231–2824* 🌐 *www.thechildrensmuseumct.org* 🎫 *$15* ⏲ *Closed Mon. Sept.–June.*

★ **Connecticut Science Center**
SCIENCE MUSEUM | **FAMILY** | This strikingly modern building, designed by world-renowned architect César Pelli, houses 40,000 square feet of exhibit space under a wavelike roof that appears to float over the structure. Among the more than 165 hands-on exhibits, youngsters, teens, and adults alike can dive into a black hole and examine the moon's craters in the Exploring Space exhibit, race mini-sailboats and magnetic trains at Forces in Motion, and discover hidden athletic talents in the Sports Lab. Kid Space is perfect for ages three to six, and everyone enjoys mingling with free-flying butterflies in the Butterfly Encounter. Complete your visit by taking in a movie in the 3-D digital theater. ✉ *250 Columbus Blvd., Hartford* ☎ *860/724–3623* 🌐 *www.ctsciencecenter.org* 🎫 *$25.95* ⏲ *Closed Mon. Labor Day–Memorial Day.*

Harriet Beecher Stowe Center
HISTORIC HOME | Abolitionist and author Harriet Beecher Stowe (1811–96) spent her final years at this 1871 Victorian Gothic cottage, now a popular stop on the Connecticut Freedom Trail. The center was built around the cottage in tribute to the author of the antislavery novel, *Uncle Tom's Cabin*. Stowe's personal writing table and effects are housed inside. ✉ *77 Forest St., Hartford* ☎ *860/522–9258* 🌐 *www.harrietbeecherstowecenter.org* 🎫 *$20* ⏲ *Closed Tues.–Wed.*

★ **Mark Twain House & Museum**
HISTORIC HOME | Built in 1874, this was the home of Samuel Langhorne Clemens (better known as Mark Twain) until 1891. In the time he and his family lived in this 25-room Victorian "Stick Style" mansion, Twain published seven major novels, including *The Adventures of Tom Sawyer*, *The Adventures of Huckleberry Finn*, and *The Prince and the Pauper*. The home has one of only two Louis Comfort Tiffany–designed domestic interiors open to the public. A contemporary museum on the grounds presents an up-close look at the author and screens an outstanding documentary on his life introduced by Ken Burns. ■ **TIP→ Tour size is limited; book online before your visit.** ✉ *351 Farmington Ave., at Woodland St., Hartford* ☎ *860/247–0998* 🌐 *marktwainhouse.org* 🎫 *$24.*

Old State House
HISTORIC SIGHT | This Federal-style building with an elaborate cupola and roof balustrade was designed in the early 1700s by Charles Bulfinch, architect of the U.S. Capitol. It served as Connecticut's state capitol until a new building opened in 1879, when it became Hartford's city hall

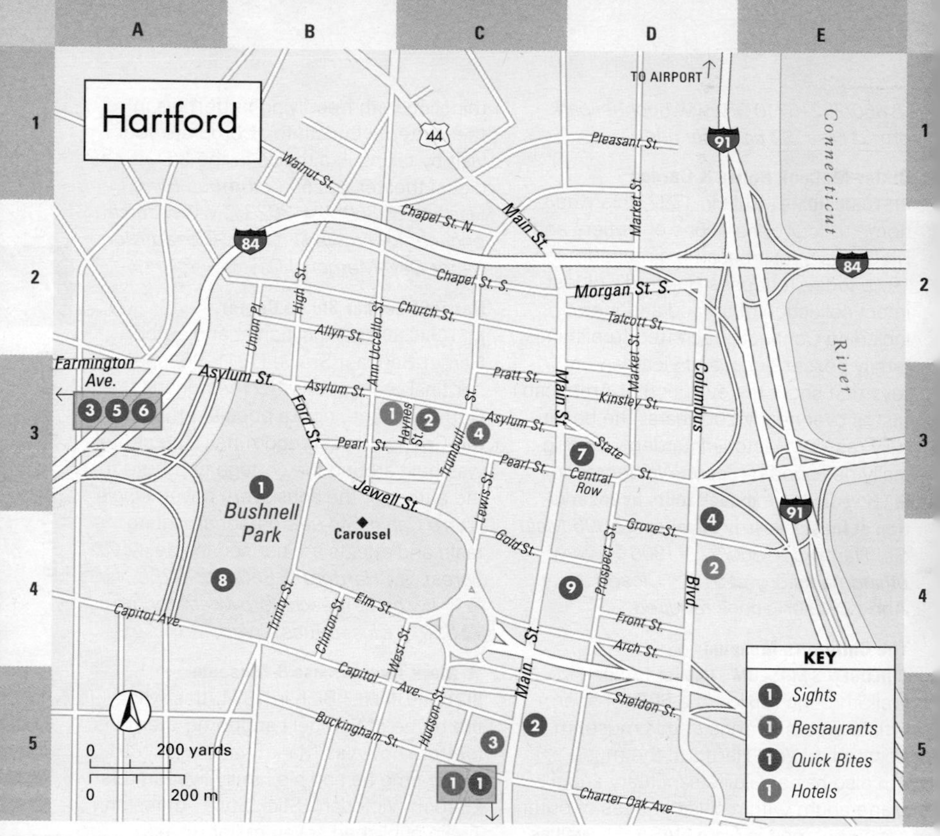

Sights

1 Bushnell Park B3
2 Butler-McCook House & Garden C5
3 The Children's Museum A3
4 Connecticut Science Center D4
5 Harriet Beecher Stowe Center........... A3
6 Mark Twain House & Museum.............. A3
7 Old State House......... D3
8 State Capitol............. B4
9 Wadsworth Atheneum Museum of Art.......... D4

Restaurants

1 First and Last Tavern C5
2 Max Downtown.......... C3
3 Peppercorn's Grill........ C5
4 Trumbull Kitchen......... C3

Quick Bites

1 Mozzicato De Pasquale's Bakery & Pastry Shop C5

Hotels

1 Goodwin Hotel C3
2 Hartford Marriott Downtown.............. D4

Connecticut's Victorian Gothic Capitol building overlooks Hartford's Bushnell Park.

until 1915. In the 1820 Senate Chamber, where everyone from John Adams and Abraham Lincoln to Jimmy Carter and George H. W. Bush has spoken, you can view a portrait of George Washington by Gilbert Stuart; and in the Courtroom, you can find out about the trial of the *Amistad* Africans in the very place it began. In summer, enjoy concerts and a farmers' market (which dates back to the 1600s). ✉ *800 Main St., Hartford* ☎ *860/522–6766* 🌐 *www.cga.ct.gov/osh* 🎫 *$8* 🕙 *Closed Sun. and Mon. and mornings.*

★ State Capitol

GOVERNMENT BUILDING | FAMILY | The gold-domed State Capitol building, built in 1878 overlooking Bushnell Park, houses the state's executive offices and legislative chamber, as well as historical memorabilia. Walk past the statue Nathan Hale, the official state hero, to the Hall of Flags to see historic battle flags carried by Connecticut troops in wars from the Civil War through the Korean Conflict—along with a camp bed used by Marquis de Lafayette when he came to Hartford to meet with George Washington during the Revolutionary War. When the General Assembly is in session (January–early June in odd-numbered years; February–early May in even-numbered years), visitors can observe the proceedings from the public galleries. **■ TIP→ The League of Women Voters provides free guided tours each morning by reservation.** ✉ *210 Capitol Ave., Hartford* ☎ *860/240–0222* 🌐 *www.cga.ct.gov/capitoltours* 🎫 *Free* 🕙 *Closed weekends.*

★ Wadsworth Atheneum Museum of Art

ART MUSEUM | The nation's oldest public art museum—and the first American museum to acquire works by Salvador Dalí and Italian Renaissance artist Caravaggio—houses more than 50,000 artworks and artifacts spanning 5,000 years, along with 7,000 items documenting African American history and culture in partnership with the Amistad Foundation. Particularly impressive are the museum's Baroque, Impressionist, and Hudson River School collections. ✉ *600 Main*

St., Hartford ☎ 860/278–2670 🌐 www.thewadsworth.org 🎟 $15 ⏲ Closed Mon.–Wed.

Restaurants

First and Last Tavern

$$ | **ITALIAN** | What looks to be a simple neighborhood spot south of downtown is actually one of the state's most hallowed Italian restaurants and pizza parlors, serving superb thin-crust pies and much, much more since 1936. The old-fashioned wooden bar is jammed most evenings with suburbia-bound daily-grinders; the main dining room, which is just as noisy, has a brick wall covered with celebrity photos. **Known for:** brick-oven pizzas and great bread; sauce like Mom used to make (if she's Italian!); take-out available. *$ Average main: $20 ✉ 939 Maple Ave., Hartford ☎ 860/956–6000 🌐 www.firstandlasttavern.com ⏲ Closed Mon. No lunch Sun.*

★ Max Downtown

$$$$ | **STEAKHOUSE** | With its contemporary design, extensive martini list, and sophisticated cuisine, this chop house is a favorite among the city's well-heeled—as well as a popular after-work spot. Creative entrées include filet mignon Oscar, sesame-crusted tuna, organic Scottish salmon, and a range of perfectly prepared steaks: New York (boneless) or Kansas City (bone-in) strip, cowboy cut ribeye, and tomahawk. **Known for:** whiskey bar with more than 200 selections from around the world; simply but exquisitely prepared fish; tavern menu with sandwiches and small plates. *$ Average main: $45 ✉ 185 Asylum St., Hartford ☎ 860/522–2530 🌐 maxdowntown.com ⏲ Closed Sun. No lunch Sat.*

Peppercorn's Grill

$$$ | **ITALIAN** | This mainstay of Hartford's restaurant scene (beginning in 1898) presents contemporary "farm-to-chef" Italian cuisine in a lively but cozy setting. Enjoy homemade potato gnocchi, ravioli al'arancia (orange), slow-roasted osso buco, or a simply grilled veal chop—but save room for the warm Valrhona chocolate cake or homemade gelato or sorbet. **Known for:** consistently good food and service; good choice pre-theater or pre-sports event; Tuesday through Friday happy hours. *$ Average main: $30 ✉ 357 Main St., Hartford ☎ 860/547–1714 🌐 www.peppercornsgrill.com ⏲ Closed Mon. No lunch Sat.–Thurs.*

Trumbull Kitchen

$$$ | **ECLECTIC** | **FAMILY** | Upbeat, hip, and casual, Trumbull Kitchen is the place to see and be seen. A loft-style dining area with leather-clad walls overlooks the action below where an eclectic menu features selections like seared Point Judith scallops, pan-seared salmon, brick-pressed chicken, and truffled onion burger, or a "stone pie" (pizza). **Known for:** the place to see and be seen; something for everyone, even the kids; convenient to the XL Center and nearby theaters. *$ Average main: $27 ✉ 150 Trumbull St., Hartford ☎ 860/493–7412 🌐 www.maxrestaurantgroup.com/trumbull ⏲ No lunch Sun.*

Coffee and Quick Bites

Mozzicato De Pasquale's Bakery & Pastry Shop

$ | **BAKERY** | **FAMILY** | Located on Franklin Avenue in Hartford's Little Italy neighborhood, this shop serves delectable Italian pastries in the bakery and espresso, cappuccino, and gelato in The Caffé. **Known for:** cookie platters to take home or gift; authentic Italian atmosphere; full liquor bar, too. *$ Average main: $10 ✉ 329 Franklin Ave., Hartford ☎ 860/296–0426 🌐 www.mozzicatobakery.com.*

Hotels

★ Goodwin Hotel

$$$ | **HOTEL** | This 1881 Hartford landmark, with its classic terra-cotta façade, was reborn in 2017 from a mere architectural

relic to a stylish boutique hotel with historic charm and modern amenities, and easy access to sights, entertainment, and transportation. **Pros:** easy access to sights, entertainment, and transportation; on-site bar/restaurant; the only boutique hotel in Hartford. **Cons:** no room service; street or valet parking only; some rooms are interior-facing and rather dark. *Rooms from: $359 ✉ 1 Haynes St., Hartford ☎ 860/246–1881 ⊕ goodwinhartford.com 124 rooms No Meals.*

Hartford Marriott Downtown

$$$ | HOTEL | FAMILY | This convenient, upscale hotel is connected to the Connecticut Convention Center and within walking distance of the Connecticut Science Center, Wadsworth Atheneum, Old State House, and other attractions. **Pros:** lots of restaurants nearby; Starbucks café in the lobby; accessible rooms available. **Cons:** standard accommodations, nothing outstanding; pay for parking (nearby or valet); room service items are prepackaged and ready-to-eat—not cooked to order. *Rooms from: $325 ✉ 200 Columbus Blvd., Hartford ☎ 860/249–8000, 866/249–8181 ⊕ www.marriott.com 409 rooms No Meals.*

Nightlife

Arch Street Tavern

LIVE MUSIC | This classic bar—in a former carriage factory, firehouse, and body shop—across from the Connecticut Convention Center in the city's Front Street Entertainment District, hosts local rock bands on Friday and Saturday nights. You can have a bite to eat, too. **■ TIP→ Free (validated) parking nearby.** *✉ 85 Arch St., Hartford ☎ 860/246–7610 ⊕ www.archstreettavern.com.*

Black-Eyed Sally's Southern Kitchen & Bar

BARS | For barbecue any day and live blues, jazz, rock, and roots music on weekends, head to laid-back Black-Eyed Sally's. *✉ 350 Asylum St., Hartford ☎ 860/278–7427 ⊕ www.blackeyedsallys.com ⊙ Closed Mon. and Tues.*

Performing Arts

MUSIC

★ Infinity Music Hall

CABARET | This intimate, acoustically excellent, 500-seat music hall—a sister venue to Infinity Hall in Norfolk, Connecticut—presents live music (folk, jazz, rock, alternative) and comedy shows throughout the year. The mezzanine level features cabaret-style seating and beverage service. *✉ 32 Front St., Hartford ☎ 860/560–7757, 866/666–6306 box office ⊕ www.infinityhall.com.*

THEATER

★ The Bushnell

CONCERTS | In addition to national tours of major Broadway shows, concerts, comedy acts, and family theater, The Bushnell is home to the Hartford Symphony Orchestra. **■ TIP→ The box office is open Monday through Friday, 10 am to 5 pm, and 2 hrs before curtain.** *✉ 166 Capitol Ave., Hartford ☎ 860/987–6000 administration, 860/987–5900 box office ⊕ www.bushnell.org.*

Hartford Stage

THEATER | Hartford Stage presents new and classic plays from around the world in an intimate (489-seat) setting. **■ TIP→ Box office is open Tuesday through Sunday, noon to 5 pm or curtain time. Discounted parking at adjacent garage.** *✉ 50 Church St., Hartford ☎ 860/527–5151 ⊕ www.hartfordstage.org.*

TheatreWorks

THEATER | This is the Hartford equivalent of Off-Broadway, where new and experimental dramas are presented. *✉ 233 Pearl St., Hartford ☎ 860/527–7838 ⊕ twhartford.org ⊙ Closed Mon.*

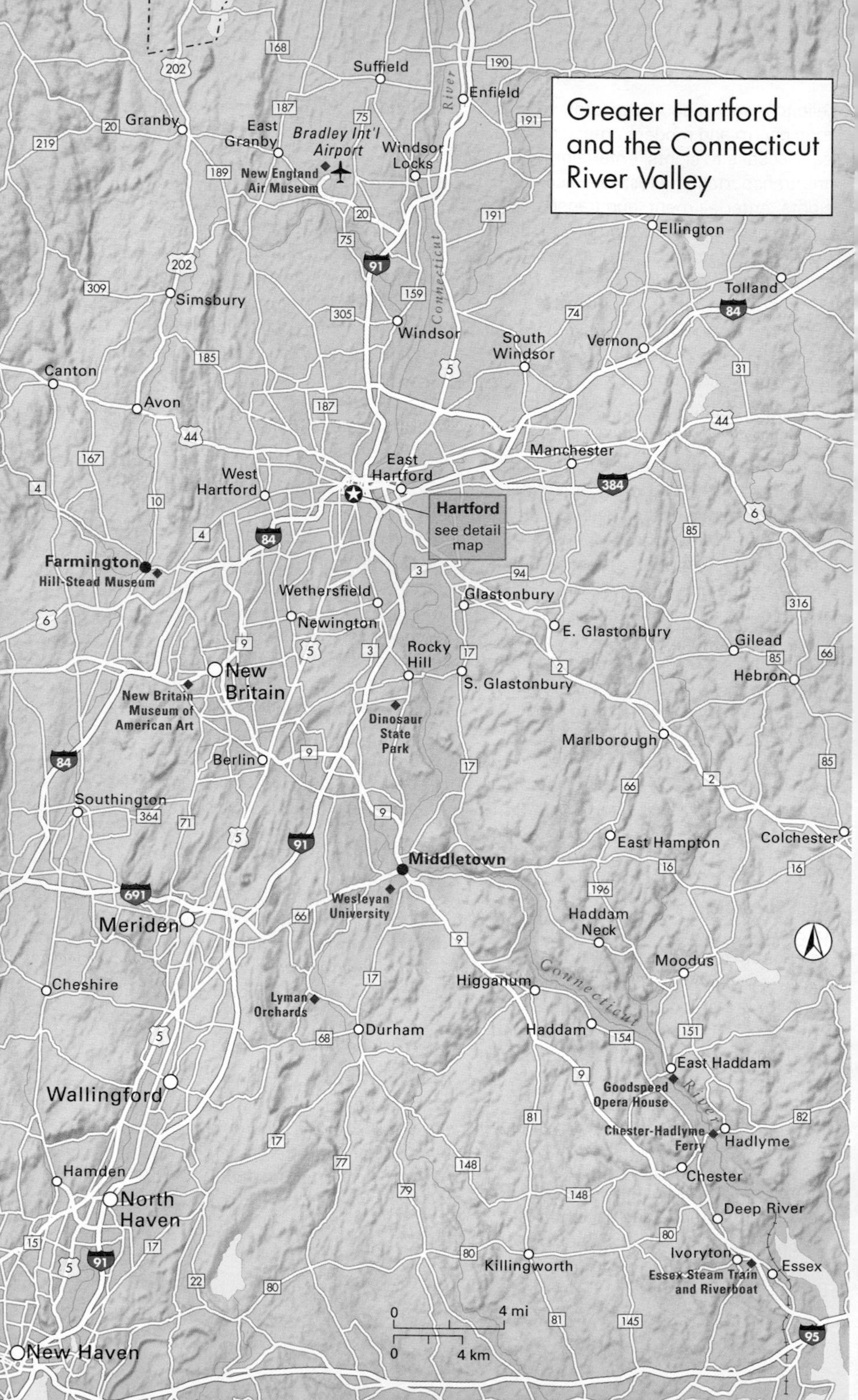

Greater Hartford and the Connecticut River Valley
Suffield
Enfield
Granby
East Granby
Bradley Int'l Airport
Windsor Locks
New England Air Museum
Ellington
Tolland
Simsbury
Windsor
South Windsor
Vernon
Canton
Avon
Manchester
East Hartford
West Hartford
Hartford
see detail map
Farmington
Hill-Stead Museum
Wethersfield
Newington
Glastonbury
E. Glastonbury
Rocky Hill
S. Glastonbury
Gilead
Hebron
New Britain
New Britain Museum of American Art
Dinosaur State Park
Marlborough
Berlin
Southington
East Hampton
Colchester
Middletown
Wesleyan University
Meriden
Haddam Neck
Moodus
Cheshire
Higganum
Lyman Orchards
Durham
Haddam
East Haddam
Goodspeed Opera House
Wallingford
Chester-Hadlyme Ferry
Hadlyme
Chester
Hamden
North Haven
Deep River
Ivoryton
Killingworth
Essex
Essex Steam Train and Riverboat
New Haven
Connecticut River
0
4 mi
0
4 km

Farmington

10 miles southwest of Hartford.

Farmington, incorporated in 1645, is a classic river town with a perfectly preserved main street. This bucolic and affluent suburb of Hartford oozes historical charm. Antiques shops are near the intersection of Routes 4 and 10, along with some fascinating historic homes that are now museums.

GETTING HERE AND AROUND

Farmington is most easily reachable by car. From Hartford, take Interstate 84 west to Route 4 west.

Sights

Hill-Stead Museum

HISTORIC HOME | Converted from a private home into a museum by its talented owner, turn-of-the-20th-century female architect (unusual at the time) Theodate Pope, the house has a superb collection of French Impressionist art displayed in situ, including Claude Monet's *Grainstacks* and Edouard Manet's *The Guitar Player* hanging in the drawing room. Poetry readings take place in the elaborate Beatrix Farrand–designed sunken garden every other week in summer. ✉ *35 Mountain Rd., Farmington* ☎ *860/677–4787* 🌐 *www.hillstead.org* 🎟 *$18 for tour, grounds free* ⏲ *Closed Mon.-Tues.*

Lake Compounce

AMUSEMENT PARK/CARNIVAL | **FAMILY** | Opened in 1846, the country's oldest amusement park is known to locals simply as "The Lake." Today's attractions include a lakefront beach, a water park, and a clipper ship with a 300-gallon bucket of water that gives unsuspecting guests a good dousing. There are also some pretty hair-raising rides, such as the Sky Coaster, Wildcat (New England's oldest roller coaster), Boulder Dash ("World's #1 wooden coaster"), and Zoomerang. ✉ *822 Lake Ave., off I–84, Bristol* ☎ *860/583–3300* 🌐 *www.lakecompounce.com* 🎟 *$60* ⏲ *Closed Labor Day–Memorial Day.*

★ New Britain Museum of American Art

ART MUSEUM | An important stop for art lovers, this 100-year-old museum's collection of more than 8,500 works, from 1740 to the present, focuses solely on American art. Among its treasures are paintings by John Singer Sargent, Winslow Homer, and Georgia O'Keeffe, as well as sculpture by Isamu Noguchi. Of particular note is the selection of Impressionist artists, including Mary Cassatt, William Merritt Chase, Childe Hassam, and John Henry Twachtman, as well as Thomas Hart Benton's five-panel mural *The Arts of Life in America.* The museum also has a café, a large shop, and a library of art books. ✉ *56 Lexington St., New Britain* ✥ *About 8 miles southeast of Farmington* ☎ *860/229–0257* 🌐 *www.nbmaa.org* 🎟 *$15 (free Sat. 10–noon)* ⏲ *Closed Mon. and Tues.*

★ New England Air Museum

OTHER MUSEUM | **FAMILY** | The more than 100 aircraft at this museum include gliders and helicopters, a World War II–era P-47 Thunderbolt, and a B-29 Superfortress, along with other vintage fighters and bombers—and an extensive collection of engines, instruments, parts, uniforms, and personal memorabilia. There's even a fighter-jet simulator. Next to Bradley International Airport, the museum also frequently holds open-cockpit days, allowing both young and old to play pilot. ✉ *36 Perimeter Rd., off Rte. 75, Windsor Locks* ✥ *16.3 miles north of Hartford via I-91* ☎ *860/623–3305* 🌐 *www.neam.org* 🎟 *$18* ⏲ *Closed Mon. Labor Day–Memorial Day.*

Middletown

16 miles south of Hartford, 27 miles northeast of New Haven.

Despite its Connecticut River setting, easy access to major highways, and historic architecture, Middletown is perhaps best known as the location of Wesleyan University. The town's High Street is an architecturally eclectic thoroughfare—Charles Dickens once called it "the most beautiful street I have seen in America." Wesleyan students add a youthful vigor to the town when school is in session.

GETTING HERE AND AROUND

Middletown is best reached by car. From Hartford, follow Interstate 91 south to Route 9 south; from New Haven, Interstate 91 north; from the southeast coast, Interstate 95 to Route 9 north.

Sights

Dinosaur State Park

NATURE SIGHT | **FAMILY** | In this park in Rocky Hill, about 9 miles north of downtown Middletown (halfway to Hartford), see 500 tracks left by the dinosaurs that roamed the area some 200 million years ago. The tracks are preserved under a giant geodesic dome—1,500 more are buried for preservation—making this one of the largest dinosaur-track sites in North America. You can even make plaster casts of tracks on a special area of the property. **■TIP→ To make a plaster cast, BYO 1/4 c. cooking oil, 10 lb. of Plaster-of-Paris, cloth rags/paper towels, and a 5 gal. bucket!** ✉ *400 West St., 1 mile east of I–91, Exit 23, Rocky Hill* ☎ *860/529–5816* 🌐 *www.dinosaurstatepark.org* 🎟 *$6* 🕓 *Closed Mon.*

★ Lyman Orchards

FARM/RANCH | **FAMILY** | Looking for a quintessential New England outing? The Lyman family first settled on a 37-acre plot just south of Middletown in 1741; today, it's an 1,100-acre orchard that's not to be missed. Get lost in the sunflower maze, then pick your own seasonal fruits—berries, peaches, pears, apples, and even pumpkins—from June to October. Or stop by the Apple Barrel Market, open all year long, to shop for farm-fresh pies, fruit baskets, jams and preserves, and gifts. ✉ *32 Reeds Gap Rd., Junction of Rtes. 147 and 157, Middlefield* ☎ *860/349–6000* 🌐 *www.lymanorchards.com.*

Restaurants

O'Rourke's Diner

$ | **AMERICAN** | **FAMILY** | This glass-and-steel classic is the place to go for top-notch diner fare, including creative specialties like the omelet stuffed with roasted portobello mushrooms, Brie, and asparagus. Arrive early for lunch, as the line often files right out the door and the place closes at 1 pm! **Known for:** steamed cheeseburgers—a favorite since 1941 but not available on weekends; Irish dishes, like bangers, colcannon, and Irish stew; breakfast served 6 am–1 pm. 💲 *Average main: $13* ✉ *728 Main St., Middletown* ☎ *860/346–6101* 🌐 *www.orourkesmiddletown.com* 🕓 *Closed Tues. No dinner.*

Hotels

Inn at Middletown

$$ | **HOTEL** | Rooms at this inn, in an 1800s-era National Guard Armory in the heart of downtown Middletown, mix Colonial-style furnishings with modern amenities; all have views of the Connecticut River. **Pros:** two blocks from Wesleyan campus; steps from downtown shopping; accessible rooms available with ADA-compliant amenities. **Cons:** a city location, no real grounds; rates rise when Wesleyan is in session; valet parking fee. 💲 *Rooms from: $255* ✉ *70 Main St., Middletown* ☎ *860/854–6300* 🌐 *www.innatmiddletown.com* 🛏 *100 rooms* 🍽 *No Meals.*

Connecticut's Historic Gardens

These extraordinary Connecticut gardens form Connecticut's Historic Gardens, a "trail" of natural beauties across the state. For more information on each of the gardens, visit www.cthistoricgardens.org.

Bellamy-Ferriday House & Garden, North Bethlehem. Highlights of this garden include an apple orchard and a circa-1915 formal parterre garden that blossoms with peonies, roses, and lilacs.

Butler-McCook House & Garden, Hartford. Landscape architect Jacob Weidenmann created a Victorian garden full of peonies, roses, and iris that serves as an amazing respite from downtown city life.

Florence Griswold Museum, Old Lyme. The gardens at the historic Florence Griswold Museum, once the home of a prominent Old Lyme family and later a haven for artists, have been restored to their 1910 appearance and feature masses of hollyhocks, iris, foxglove, day lilies, and heliotrope.

Glebe House Museum, Woodbury. Legendary British garden writer and designer Gertrude Jekyll designed only three gardens in the United States, and the one at the Glebe House Museum is the only one still in existence. It is a classic example of Jekyll's ideas about color harmony and plant combinations; a hedge of mixed shrubs encloses a mix of perennials.

Harriet Beecher Stowe Center, Hartford. The grounds at the Harriet Beecher Stowe Center feature Connecticut's largest magnolia tree, a pink dogwood that's more than 100 years old, and eight distinct gardens: an antique rose garden; a woodland garden; a wildflower meadow; a high-Victorian texture garden; a blue cottage garden; and formal color-coordinated gardens.

Hill-Stead Museum, Farmington. The centerpiece of the Hill-Stead Museum is a circa-1920 sunken garden enclosed in a yew hedge and surrounded by a wall of rough stone. At the center of the octagonal design is a summer-house with 36 flowerbeds and brick walkways radiating outward.

Promisek at Three Rivers Farm, Bridgewater. The prolific Beatrix Farrand designed the original garden at Promisek; restored in recent years, it now overflows with beds of annuals and perennials that include hollyhocks, peonies, and always-dashing delphiniums.

Roseland Cottage, Woodstock. At Roseland Cottage, the boxwood parterre garden includes 21 flowerbeds surrounded by boxwood hedges.

Thankful Arnold House Museum, Haddam. Gravel paths divide granite-edged Colonial Revival-style gardens filled with more than 50 varieties of herbs that Thankful Arnold likely used in the early 1800s for cooking, medicine, dyeing, fragrance, and other household uses.

Webb-Deane-Stevens Museum, Wethersfield. This Colonial Revival garden is filled with fragrant, old-fashioned flowers such as peonies, pinks, phlox, hollyhocks, and larkspur, as well as a profusion of roses.

Performing Arts

THEATER

Wesleyan University Center for the Arts

ARTS CENTERS | See modern dance or a provocative new play, hear top playwrights and actors discuss their craft, or take in an art exhibit or concert at this college arts center. ✉ *271 Washington Terr., Middletown* ☎ *860/685–3355* 🌐 *www.wesleyan.edu/cfa.*

New Haven

46 miles northeast of Greenwich, 40 miles south of Hartford.

Though the city is best known as the home of Yale University, New Haven's historic district dates back to the 17th century—and the city's distinctive shops, prestigious museums, and highly respected theaters are major draws. The restaurant scene also garners considerable acclaim, particularly the city's "apizza" legacy.

GETTING HERE AND AROUND

By car, New Haven is accessible from both Interstate 95 and Interstate 91. By rail, Amtrak's Northeast Regional and high-speed Acela trains stop here; New Haven is also the end of the Metro-North commuter line from New York City. Shore Line East train service connects New Haven with Old Saybrook, Madison, and New London. Tweed New Haven Airport has limited regional service for both scheduled commercial and private planes.

ESSENTIALS

VISITOR INFORMATION Visit New Haven. ✉ *5 Science Park, New Haven* ☎ *203/777–8550, 800/332–7829* 🌐 *www.visitnewhaven.com.*

Sights

Beinecke Rare Book and Manuscript Library

LIBRARY | The library's collection of literary papers, early manuscripts, and rare books include a Gutenberg Bible and original Audubon bird prints; the exhibition spaces on the ground floor and mezzanine are open to the public. The building that houses them is an attraction in its own right: the walls are made of marble cut so thin that the light shines through, making the interior a breathtaking sight on sunny days. Introductory tours for individuals are offered on Saturday afternoons; group tours are Yale-led and require advance registration at the Yale Visitor Information Center ✉ *121 Wall St., New Haven* ☎ *203/432–2977* 🌐 *beinecke.library.yale.edu* 🎫 *Free* ⏲ *Closed weekend mornings.*

★ IT Adventure Ropes Course

OTHER ATTRACTION | **FAMILY** | Oddly enough, you'll find the world's largest indoor adventure ropes course within Jordan's Furniture Store. The 60-foot-high courses have more than 100 activities, like walking across zigzag swinging beams rope ladders, bridges, moving planks, a 50-foot free-fall jump, four 200-foot-long ziplines, and more. At Little IT, toddlers and little kids can zip along, too. ✉ *Jordan's Furniture Store, 40 Sargent Dr., adjacent to I–95, New Haven* ☎ *203/812–9981* 🌐 *www.itatjordans.com* 🎫 *$30.*

New Haven Green

PLAZA/SQUARE | **FAMILY** | Bordered on its west side by the Yale campus, the New Haven Green is a fine example of early urban planning. Village elders set aside the 16-acre plot as a town common as early as 1638. Three early-19th-century churches—the Gothic Revival-style **Trinity Episcopal Church,** the Federal-style **Center Congregational Church,** and **United Church**—have contributed to its present appeal. For a year, from September 1839 to August 1840, survivors of the slave

Connecticut's Unusual Museums

Throughout the state, small, unusual museums (sometimes even quite odd ones) reflect the occupations, interests, and whims of Connecticut Yankees over time. Some of these museums have limited or fickle opening hours, so check before your visit.

American Clock & Watch Museum in Bristol is devoted entirely to clocks and watches—more than 5,500 timepieces are on display, including clocks dating back to 1680 and watches dating back to 1595. The best time to come? Noon, of course.

Also in Bristol, the **New England Carousel Museum** has one of the country's largest antique carousel collections, both full-size pieces and miniatures. Oddly enough, it's also home to the **Museum of Fire History**, which displays vintage equipment and memorabilia.

The Company of Fifers & Drummers in Ivoryton, whose mission is to perpetuate America's heritage in fife and drum music, maintains **The Museum of Fife & Drum**, which has artifacts dating back to the 1700s.

At Windsor's **Vintage Radio & Communications Museum of Connecticut**, exhibits explain how communications have changed over the years—from Morse code to satellites and everything in between. An offshoot of the museum, **Vintage Hi-Fi Museum** in West Hartford, displays mid-20th-century TVs, stereo sets, and other baby boomer artifacts.

In Terryville, the collection at the **Lock Museum of America** includes thousands of antique door locks, padlocks, safe locks, handcuffs, keys, and more—including a 4,000-year-old lock from Egypt and a treasure chest from the Spanish Armada.

Many of the buttons for soldier uniforms in the Revolutionary War, the War of 1812, both sides of the Civil War, and even recent wars were made in Connecticut. The **Waterbury Button Museum** has thousands of buttons—military and otherwise—on display.

At New Haven's **Eli Whitney Museum**, there are exhibits on the man, his cotton gin, and the dam built to power the historic building—plus exhibits on A. C. Gilbert, the inventor of the Erector set and maker of educational toys.

The **Connecticut Antique Machinery Association Museum** in Kent displays old-fashioned steam engines, agricultural equipment, combustion engines, a narrow-gauge railroad with a steam locomotive, and mining artifacts. The Hall of Geology and Paleontology adds dinosaur tracks and fossils.

Barker Character Comic & Cartoon Museum in Cheshire has 80,000 toys and collectibles on display—from Betty Boop to Popeye, Shirley Temple dolls to the Simpsons, Halloween costumes, and so much more.

The Glass House in New Canaan, built between 1949 and 1995 by architect Philip Johnson and now a National Trust Historic Site, has a permanent collection of 20th-century paintings and sculptures.

And for all things PEZ, head for the **PEZ Visitor Center** in Orange, which has the largest collection of PEZ memorabilia in the world—and, of course, a retail shop.

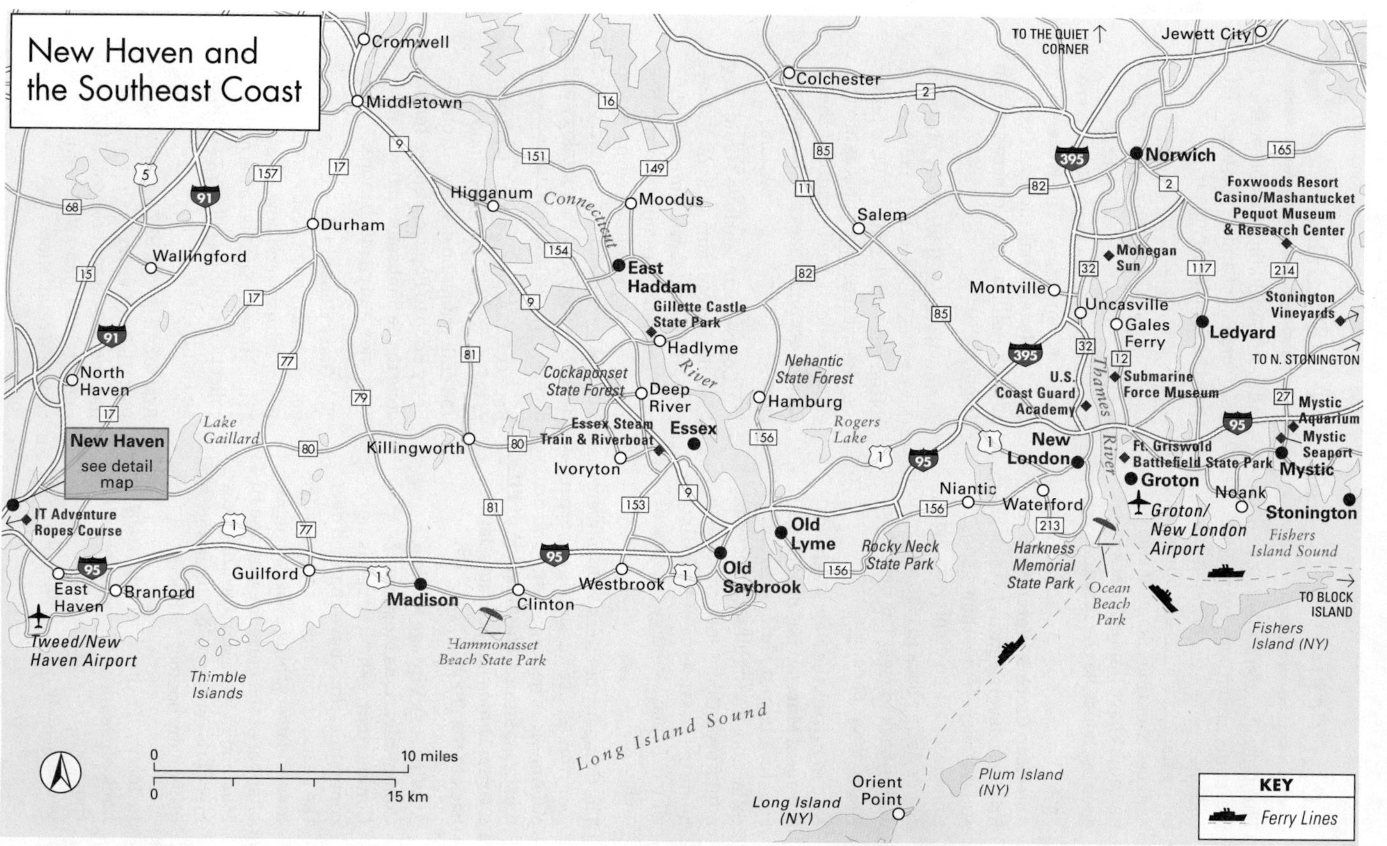
New Haven and the Southeast Coast
Cromwell
Middletown
Colchester
TO THE QUIET CORNER
Jewett City
Norwich
Foxwoods Resort Casino/Mashantucket Pequot Museum & Research Center
Higganum
Connecticut River
Moodus
Salem
Durham
Wallingford
East Haddam
Mohegan Sun
Montville
Uncasville
Gales Ferry
Ledyard
Stonington Vineyards
TO N. STONINGTON
Gillette Castle State Park
Hadlyme
North Haven
Cockaponset State Forest
Deep River
Nehantic State Forest
Hamburg
U.S. Coast Guard Academy
Thames River
Submarine Force Museum
Mystic Aquarium
Mystic Seaport
Lake Gaillard
New Haven see detail map
Killingworth
Essex Steam Train & Riverboat
Essex
Rogers Lake
New London
Ft. Griswold Battlefield State Park
Mystic
Ivoryton
Groton
Niantic
Waterford
Noank
Stonington
IT Adventure Ropes Course
Groton/ New London Airport
Old Lyme
Rocky Neck State Park
Harkness Memorial State Park
Fishers Island Sound
Guilford
Westbrook
Old Saybrook
East Haven
Branford
Madison
Clinton
Ocean Beach Park
TO BLOCK ISLAND
Tweed/New Haven Airport
Hammonasset Beach State Park
Fishers Island (NY)
Thimble Islands
Long Island Sound
0
10 miles
0
15 km
Orient Point
Plum Island (NY)
Long Island (NY)
KEY
Ferry Lines

Connecticut Lobster Rolls

Behold the lobster roll: Sweet, succulent, and sinfully rich, it's the ultimate buttery icon of a Connecticut summer. Many New Englanders prefer to chill out with a cold lobster salad in their bun, but Nutmeggers generally like their lobster rolls served hot and buttery.

The traditional Connecticut lobster roll, said to have been invented in the early 1930s at Perry's, a now-defunct seafood shack on the Boston Post Road in Milford, consists of nothing more than plump chunks of hot lobster meat and melted butter served on a butter-toasted "hot dog" roll; in other words, heaven on a bun. From seafood shanties along the shore to gourmet getaways farther inland, Connecticut is fairly swimming in eateries that offer these revered rolls. Here are three favorites:

Abbott's Lobster in the Rough, Noank. A lobster roll at Abbott's Lobster in the Rough is best enjoyed from a picnic table at the edge of Noank Harbor, watching boats bobbing at anchor.

Captain Scott's Lobster Dock, New London. Whether hot and buttery or cold and creamy, the lobster rolls at Captain Scott's Lobster Dock—on a spit of land overlooking Shaw's Cove—come on grilled-in-butter buns, either regular size or "foot-long."

Lenny and Joe's Fish Tale, Madison. At Lenny and Joe's Fish Tale, kids of all ages love to eat their lobster rolls outdoors by a hand-carved Dentzel carousel with flying horses (and a whale, frog, lion, seal, and more), which the restaurant operates early May–early October.

ship*Amistad* were incarcerated in a jail on the east side of the green and were brought out of jail to exercise there. An *Amistad* memorial now resides at the site of the former jail. Besides being a pleasant urban park, the Green is also the venue for festivals and events throughout the year. ✉ *250 Temple St., between Church, College, Elm, and Chapel Sts., New Haven* 🌐 *www.downtownnewhaven.com* 🎫 *Free.*

★ Yale Center for British Art

ART MUSEUM | Featuring the largest collection of British art outside Britain, the center surveys the development of English art, life, and thought from the Elizabethan period to the present. The skylighted galleries, one of architect Louis I. Kahn's final works, contain artwork by John Constable, William Hogarth, Thomas Gainsborough, Joshua Reynolds, and J. M. W. Turner, to name but a few. You'll also find rare books and paintings documenting English history. Explore on your own or take a free guided tour, offered Thursday and Saturday at 11 am and weekends at 2 pm. ✉ *1080 Chapel St., New Haven* ☎ *203/432–2800, 877/274–8278 in U.S.* 🌐 *britishart.yale.edu* 🎫 *Free* 🕐 *Closed Mon.*

★ Yale University

COLLEGE | **FAMILY** | New Haven's manufacturing history dates to the 19th century, but the city owes its fame to merchant Elihu Yale. In 1718, his contributions enabled the Collegiate School, founded in 1701 at Saybrook, to settle in New Haven and change its name to Yale College. In 1887, all of its schools were consolidated into Yale University. This is one of the nation's great institutions of higher learning, and its campus holds some handsome neo-Gothic buildings and noteworthy museums. Student guides

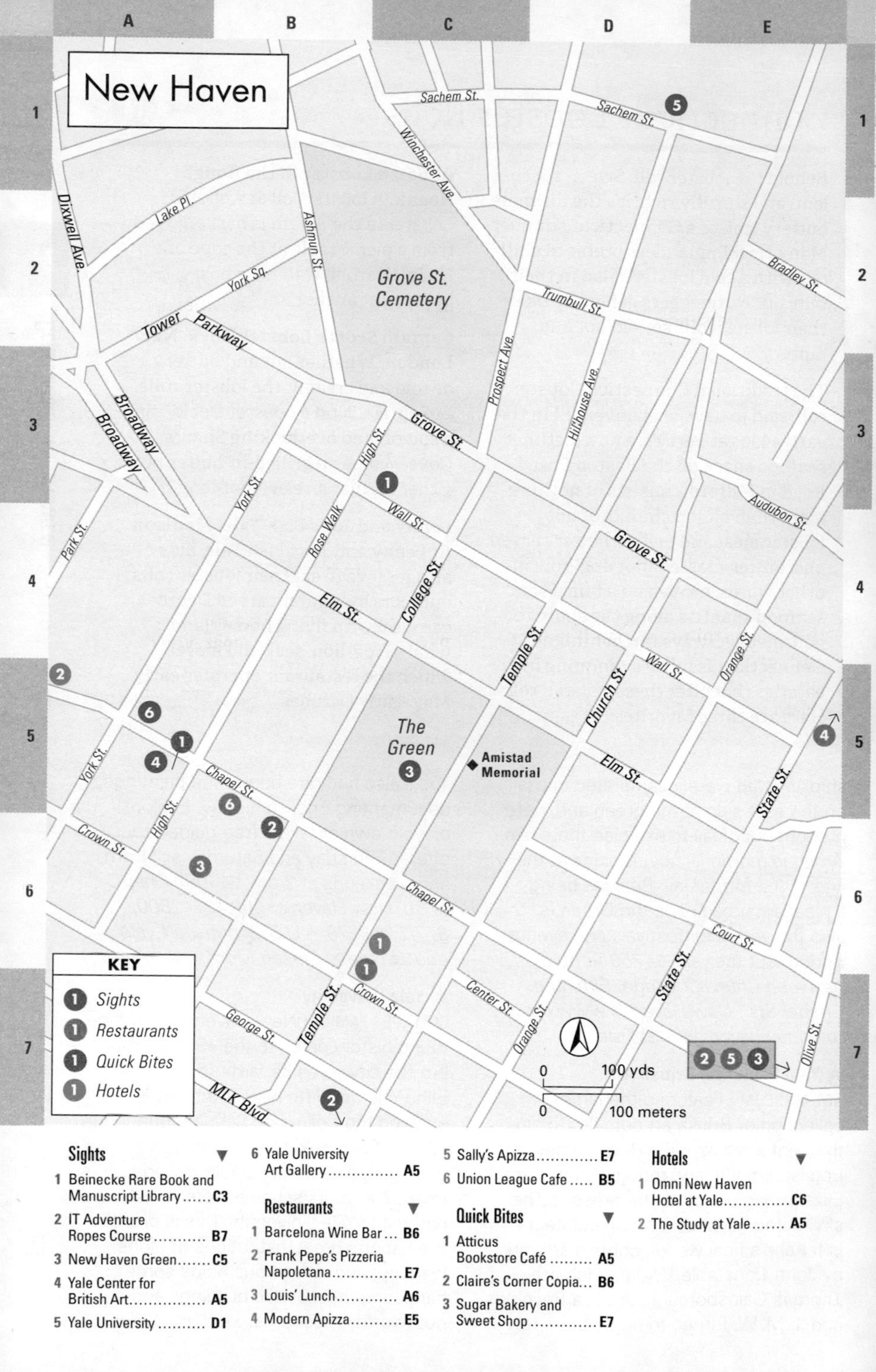
New Haven
A
B
C
D
E
1
2
3
4
5
6
7
Sachem St.
Winchester Ave.
Lake Pl.
Dixwell Ave.
Ashmun St.
York Sq.
Grove St. Cemetery
Trumbull St.
Bradley St.
Tower Parkway
Prospect Ave.
Hillhouse Ave.
Broadway
Grove St.
High St.
York St.
Wall St.
Audubon St.
Park St.
Rose Walk
College St.
Elm St.
Temple St.
Church St.
Orange St.
The Green
Amistad Memorial
Chapel St.
State St.
Crown St.
Court St.
Center St.
George St.
MLK Blvd
0
100 yds
100 meters
KEY
Sights
Restaurants
Quick Bites
Hotels
Sights
1 Beinecke Rare Book and Manuscript Library C3
2 IT Adventure Ropes Course B7
3 New Haven Green....... C5
4 Yale Center for British Art................ A5
5 Yale University D1
6 Yale University Art Gallery A5
Restaurants
1 Barcelona Wine Bar... B6
2 Frank Pepe's Pizzeria Napoletana............... E7
3 Louis' Lunch............. A6
4 Modern Apizza........... E5
5 Sally's Apizza............ E7
6 Union League Cafe B5
Quick Bites
1 Atticus Bookstore Café A5
2 Claire's Corner Copia... B6
3 Sugar Bakery and Sweet Shop E7
Hotels
1 Omni New Haven Hotel at Yale............. C6
2 The Study at Yale....... A5

New Haven Pizza 101

New Haven has been on the radar of pizza lovers for decades. The "apizza" (pronounced "ah-beetz" by locals) style, defined by its thin, chewy crust, is baked in a coal-fired brick oven, which results in a unique—and, some would argue, superior—pizza experience. For everything from the original tomato pie to white clam and other specialty pies, check out these three authentic New Haven pizzerias.

Frank Pepe Pizzeria Napoletana—known simply as Pepe's Pizza—is where it all began: In 1925, Frank Pepe opened his eponymous pizzeria and created what would become the iconic New Haven–style pizza. Eager customers line up for hours to get a taste of the famous thin-crust pies, in particular Frank Pepe's pièce de résistance—the white clam pizza. This masterful creation consists of olive oil, garlic, oregano, grated Parmesan cheese, and littleneck clams atop a thin crust.

Just two blocks from Pepe's on Wooster Street (New Haven's Little Italy), **Sally's Apizza** has been a rival of Frank Pepe's since 1938, when Pepe's nephew opened his own place. Now visitors to New Haven must pledge their allegiance to just one of these famed Wooster Street pizzerias, although no one will blame you if you decide to be a double agent.

If you don't want to get involved with that feud, there's always **Modern Apizza**, which differentiates itself by *not* being on Wooster Street. Serving its signature plain pies (with a layer of tomato sauce and a sprinkling of Parmesan cheese) since 1934, you can add mozzarella and other toppings if you want, including clams, bacon, hot cherry peppers, salami, and more.

conduct hour-long walking tours that include Connecticut Hall in the Old Campus, one of the oldest buildings in the state, which housed a number of illustrious students—including Nathan Hale, Noah Webster, and Eli Whitney. Tours start from the visitor center. ✉ *The Mead Visitor Center, 149 Elm St., New Haven* ☎ *203/432–2300* 🌐 *visitorcenter.yale.edu* 🎟 *Free* ✍ *Reservations required.*

★ Yale University Art Gallery

ART GALLERY | Since its founding in 1832, this art gallery has amassed more than 200,000 works from around the world, dating from ancient Egypt to the present day. Highlights include works by Vincent van Gogh, Edouard Manet, Claude Monet, Pablo Picasso, Winslow Homer, and Thomas Eakins, as well as Etruscan and Greek vases, Chinese ceramics and bronzes, early Italian paintings, and a collection of American decorative arts that is considered one of the world's finest. The gallery's landmark main building is also of note: Opened in 1953, it was renowned architect Louis I. Kahn's first major commission and the first modernist building on the neo-Gothic Yale campus. ✉ *1111 Chapel St., at York St., New Haven* ☎ *203/432–0600* 🌐 *artgallery.yale.edu* 🎟 *Free* ⏲ *Closed Mon.*

Restaurants

Barcelona Wine Bar

$$ | **SPANISH** | There's no need to take a transatlantic flight to Spain when you can feast on authentic Spanish cuisine right here in New Haven. There are "large plate" entrées and salads on the menu, but the tapas are the best bet—rich, tasty, and full of flavor. **Known for:** more than 30 tapas on the menu; charcuterie and cheese menu; 2,000-bottle wine cellar. $ *Average main: $24* ✉ *Omni New Haven Hotel, 155 Temple St., New Haven* ☎ *203/848–3000* 🌐 *www.barcelonawinebar.com* 🕘 *No lunch Mon.–Sat.*

★ Frank Pepe's Pizzeria Napoletana

$$ | PIZZA | FAMILY | Pepe's may serve the best pizza in the world, as so many people claim. Try the justifiably famous white-clam pie (especially good topped with bacon), but just thinking about the original tomato pie (with mozzarella) makes your mouth water. **Known for:** long line for a table—often an hour or more—but takeout is quicker; thin-crust pizza baked in a coal-fired brick oven; pies cut in odd-shaped pieces—great for kids. $ *Average main: $24* ✉ *157 Wooster St., New Haven* ☎ *203/865–5762* 🌐 *www.pepespizzeria.com* ▬ *No credit cards.*

Heirloom

$$$ | CONTEMPORARY | This isn't your typical hotel restaurant: Occupying half of The Study at Yale hotel lobby, this contemporary American eatery has a casually refined decor. The seasonal menu emphasizes the freshest locally sourced ingredients, with highlights like a warm local ricotta appetizer with thyme and truffle on a crostini, lamb cavatelli pasta, and Connecticut grass-fed beef burger. **Known for:** fresh, bright, and contemporary; innovative farm-to-table cuisine; enjoy a pre- or post-dinner cocktail at the bar. $ *Average main: $28* ✉ *The Study at Yale, 1157 Chapel St., New Haven* ☎ *203/503–3919* 🌐 *www.heirloomnewhaven.com.*

Louis' Lunch

$ | BURGER | This family-owned luncheonette, opened since 1895, is recognized as the birthplace of the "hamburger sandwich." Its first-rate burgers are cooked to order in an old-fashioned cast-iron grill (that dates back to 1898) and served with a slice of cheese, tomato, and onion (the only accepted garnishes) on two pieces of white toast. Add potato salad or chips and a slice of pie, and you're all set! **Known for:** no ketchup allowed; all-day (afternoon and evening) dining; open until 1 am Thursday–Saturday. $ *Average main: $12* ✉ *261 Crown St., New Haven* ☎ *203/562–5507* 🌐 *louislunch.com* ▬ *No credit cards* 🕘 *Closed Sun. and Mon., August.*

Modern Apizza

$ | PIZZA | FAMILY | It's not what Modern Apizza has that sets it apart from the rest but what its signature pie doesn't have: toppings. The pizzeria's "plain" pie is a thin crust with a layer of tomato sauce and just a sprinkling of Parmesan cheese. $ *Average main: $15* ✉ *874 State St., New Haven* ☎ *203/776–5306* 🌐 *modernapizza.com* 🕘 *Closed Mon.*

Sally's Apizza

$$ | PIZZA | FAMILY | This place has been a rival of Frank Pepe's since 1938, when Salvatore Consiglio, Pepe's nephew, decided to break away from his relatives and open his own place. The result of this family feud is two competing pizzerias and a divided city: those who believe Frank Pepe's serves the best pizza and those who are devoted to Sally's. **Known for:** plan to wait—for a table and then for your pizza; hand-tossed pies baked in a coal-fired brick oven; Sal's family sold out in 2017, but new owners vow to continue the tradition. $ *Average main: $20* ✉ *237 Wooster St., New Haven* ☎ *203/624–5271* 🌐 *www.sallysapizza.com* ▬ *No credit cards.*

★ Union League Cafe

$$$$ | BRASSERIE | In a gorgeous Beaux Arts dining room, this lively brasserie wins high marks for its updated French cuisine. The knowledgeable staff are happy to recommend wine pairings to complement whatever dishes you select—perhaps potato-crusted halibut with fennel compote and ratatouille, a grilled beef filet with fingerling potatoes, or the plat du jour. **Known for:** prices are steep but worth the splurge; elegant atmosphere and impeccable service; always great food and exemplary service. $ *Average main: $36* ✉ *1032 Chapel St., New Haven* ☎ *203/562–4299* 🌐 *www.unionleaguecafe.com* 🕘 *Closed Sun. and Mon. No lunch.*

Coffee and Quick Bites

★ Atticus Bookstore Café

$ | **CAFÉ** | Come to this independent bookstore, café, and bakery to buy a book, have lunch (or breakfast), or have breakfast (or lunch) *and* buy a book. "Nourishment for mind and body" is the approach here—in the style of a European neighborhood café. **Known for:** sandwiches, salads, soups, and a few "plates & bowls"; delicious homemade breads and pastries; congenial atmosphere all day long. *Average main: $12 1082 Chapel St., New Haven 203/776–4040 www.atticusbookstorecafe.com.*

Claire's Corner Copia

$ | **VEGETARIAN** | Claire's has been a New Haven institution since 1975, and it remains a popular destination for vegetarians and vegans. The large menu offers sandwiches, quesadillas, burritos, gluten-free dishes, kosher food, salads of every sort, and breakfast items (some served all day). **Known for:** organic, sustainable ingredients; no alcohol; try the signature Lithuanian coffee cake with or without frosting. *Average main: $12 1000 Chapel St., New Haven 203/562–3888 www.clairescornercopia.com Closed Tues.*

Sugar Bakery and Sweet Shop

$ | **BAKERY** | **FAMILY** | Stop in to try one of dozens of cupcake flavors or one of the special flavors featured each month—or you may like a cookie or a whole cake. With flavors like cannoli, cookie dough, and Boston Cream cupcakes, you're bound to find one (or more) to fuel your sugar high. **Known for:** past winner of Food Network's Cupcake Wars; buy a 6, 8, or 12 pack; vegan and gluten-free cupcakes available. *Average main: $4 424 Main St., East Haven 203/469–0815 www.thesugarbakery.com Closed Sun.*

Hotels

Omni New Haven Hotel at Yale

$$$ | **HOTEL** | **FAMILY** | This large hotel near the heart of New Haven is outfitted with all the modern amenities; some upper-floor guest rooms enjoy great views. **Pros:** inviting lobby with complimentary fruit-infused ice water or hot chocolate; nice gym and spa; walk to shops and restaurants. **Cons:** no pool; rooms a bit dated; view of rooftops from most rooms. *Rooms from: $339 155 Temple St., New Haven 203/772–6664 www.omnihotels.com/hotels/new-haven-yale 306 rooms No Meals.*

The Study at Yale

$$$ | **HOTEL** | With a pair of spectacles emblazoned on all hotel signature items and overflowing bookshelves in the hotel's lobby, The Study at Yale is chic lodging for the scholarly set. **Pros:** valet parking; excellent restaurant; great location in the middle of everything. **Cons:** small bathrooms; room refrigerator available only upon request; street noise may be an issue in front-facing rooms. *Rooms from: $329 1157 Chapel St., New Haven 203/503–3900 www.thestudyatyale.com 124 rooms No Meals.*

Nightlife

★ BAR

BREWPUBS | This spot is a cross between a dance club, a brick-oven pizzeria, and a brewpub. Come for live music and dancing Wednesday–Saturday; pizza and beer, anytime—but you must be age 21 or older. *254 Crown St., New Haven 203/495–8924 www.barnightclub.com No lunch Mon.–Thurs.*

Toad's Place of New Haven

LIVE MUSIC | Alternative and traditional rock, hip-hop, blues, and other types of bands play at Toad's Place, which has attracted college students and other "cool" clubbers since the 1970s. *300*

York St., New Haven ☎ *203/624–8623* 🌐 *www.toadsplace.com.*

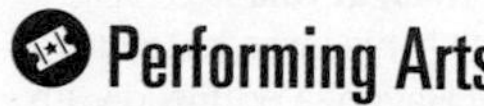

Performing Arts

THEATER

★ Long Wharf Theatre

THEATER | The well-regarded Long Wharf Theatre presents works by contemporary writers and revivals of otherwise neglected classics. The season runs August through May. ✉ *222 Sargent Dr., New Haven* ☎ *203/693–1486 box office* 🌐 *longwharf.org* ⏲ *Closed June–July.*

Shubert Theatre

ARTS CENTERS | Broadway musicals, dance performances, comedy, music concerts, and more are on the bill at the Shubert, a 1,600-seat theater that originally opened in 1914. ✉ *247 College St., New Haven* ☎ *203/624–1825 box office* 🌐 *www.shubert.com.*

Woolsey Hall

MUSIC | Built in 1901 to commemorate Yale's bicentennial, the 2,650-seat Woolsey Hall hosts performances by the New Haven Symphony Orchestra, Yale Symphony Orchestra, Yale Philharmonia, Yale Concert Band, and Yale Glee Club, as well as occasional guest recitals on the Newberry Memorial Organ. ✉ *500 College St., at Grove St., New Haven* ☎ *203/432–4158 box office* 🌐 *woolsey.yale.edu.*

Yale Repertory Theatre

THEATER | This theater stages both premieres and fresh interpretations of classics from October through May. ✉ *1120 Chapel St., New Haven* ☎ *203/432–1234 box office* 🌐 *www.yalerep.org.*

Yale School of Music

MUSIC | Most of the 200-plus performances in the impressive roster of concerts by the Yale School of Music—featuring students, faculty, and guest artists—take place in Sprague Memorial Hall, and many are free, Other venues include Woolsey Hall, Sudler Recital Hall, and Marquand Chapel—all on the Yale campus. ✉ *Sprague Memorial Hall, 98 Wall St., New Haven* ☎ *203/432–4158 box office* 🌐 *music.yale.edu.*

Madison

21 miles east of New Haven, 65 miles northeast of Greenwich.

Coastal Madison has an understated charm. Ice-cream parlors and dozens of locally owned boutiques prosper along U.S. 1, the town's main street. Stately Colonial homes line the town green, site of summer concerts and a farmers' market, while iconic cedar-shingled beach homes line the waterfront. The Madison shoreline, particularly the long stretch of soft white sand at Hammonasset Beach State Park, draws visitors year-round—although they bundle up in the dead of winter.

GETTING HERE AND AROUND

Madison is accessible by either car or train. Drive north from New Haven or south from New London on Interstate 95 or take the Shore Line East train from New Haven or New London to the Madison stop.

Beaches

★ Hammonasset Beach State Park

BEACH | **FAMILY** | The largest of the state's public beach parks, Hammonasset Beach State Park has 2 miles of white-sand beach, a top-notch nature center, excellent birding, and a hugely popular campground with more than 550 open sites. **Amenities:** food and drink; lifeguards; parking (fee); showers; toilets. **Best for:** swimming; walking. ✉ *1288 Boston Post Rd. (U.S. 1), Exit 62 off I–95, Madison* ☎ *203/245–2785 for park, 203/245–1817 for campground* 🌐 *portal.ct.gov/DEEP/State-Parks/Parks/Hammonasset-Beach-State-Park* 🎫 *CT residents free; nonresidents parking fee from $15.*

Restaurants

Lenny and Joe's Fish Tale
$$ | **SEAFOOD** | **FAMILY** | At Lenny and Joe's Fish Tale, kids of all ages love to eat their lobster rolls or fried seafood served indoors or, better yet, outdoors near a hand-carved Dentzel carousel with flying horses (and a whale, frog, lion, seal, and more), which the restaurant runs from early May through August (sometimes later) and donates all proceeds to charity. Most of the menu involves fish of one kind or another, but Lenny and Joe's also serves burgers, franks, and chicken sandwiches or dinners. *Average main: $24 ✉ 1301 Boston Post Rd. (U.S. 1), Madison ☎ 203/245–7289 🌐 www.ljfishtale.com.*

Coffee and Quick Bites

Ashley's Ice Cream
$ | **ICE CREAM** | **FAMILY** | Right in the town center, a hop and a skip from popular Hammonasset Beach State Park, Ashley's has flavors of homemade ice cream to tempt every tastebud. The business that began in New Haven in 1979 was named for the owner's champion Frisbee-catching dog, Ashley Whippet, who's favorite flavor was chocolate banana; if you're inclined to buy a pup-size treat—and even though Ashley Whippett loved it—chocolate is not recommended for dogs! **Known for:** more than 100 possible flavors and always adding more; ice-cream pies and cakes to go, too; more Ashley's are in New Haven, Hamden, Branford, and Guilford. *Average main: $6 ✉ 724 Boston Post Rd (U.S. 1), Madison ☎ 203/245–1113 🌐 www.ashleysicecream.net/madison.*

Hotels

Scranton Seahorse Inn
$ | **B&B/INN** | In the heart of Madison, this historic (1833) inn run by pastry chef Michael Hafford offers a restful retreat within walking distance of the beach and shops. **Pros:** fab food; gracious innkeeper; meticulous attention to detail. **Cons:** books up quickly; BYOB at dinner; rooms are small, but this is a historic home after all. *Rooms from: $199 ✉ 818 Boston Post Rd. (U.S. 1), Madison ☎ 203/245–0550 🌐 www.scrantonseahorseinn.com ⇆ 7 rooms 🍽 Free Breakfast.*

Old Saybrook

32 miles east of New Haven, 19 miles west of New London.

Old Saybrook, at the mouth of the Connecticut River, was one of the three original settlements of the Connecticut Colony (called Saybrook at the time) and an important 17th-century trading port. Today, Old Saybrook is a picturesque small town with more than 100 historic homes, a downtown that's an especially pleasing place for a stroll, and a shoreline that attracts boaters and others lured by the salt air of summer.

GETTING HERE AND AROUND

Drive north on Interstate 95 to Route 154 (Exit 67) and head south to Old Saybrook. The town is also served by Amtrak's Northeast Regional line and the Shore Line East commuter trains between New Haven and New London.

Sights

★ The Katharine Hepburn Cultural Arts Center
ARTS CENTER | The Kate, as the Center is generally known, is an intimate, 250-seat theater in the Old Saybrook Town Hall building on the historic town green. The Kate presents a full calendar of concerts, dance, drama, opera, comedy, films (including some classic Hepburn films), and children's theater. (Some performances are broadcast on PBS TV in the national series, "The Kate.") In addition to the performances and presentations,

a small museum displays memorabilia and reminiscences about Katharine Hepburn's life and career. She was a resident of Old Saybrook from 1912 (age five) until her death in 2003. *300 Main St., Old Saybrook* *860/510–0453 box office* *www.katharinehepburntheater.org* *Museum free* *Museum closed Sat.–Mon.*

Restaurants

Café Routier
$$$ | **CONTEMPORARY** | Grilled hanger steak, cioppino, and pan-roasted duck breast are among the favorites at this bistro, which specializes in New England favorites and seasonal dishes. Check out the Mood Lounge for excellent cocktails and smaller plates meant for sharing. **Known for:** ecclectic menu that changes seasonally; prompt but unobtrusive service; outdoor dining in nice weather. *Average main: $30* *1353 Boston Post Rd. (U.S. 1), 5 miles west of Old Saybrook, Westbrook* *860/399–8700* *www.caferoutier.com* *No lunch.*

The Essex
$$$$ | **MODERN AMERICAN** | In this tiny (13-seat) restaurant, the chef applies French techniques to both modern cuisine and old favorites. You might start with Niantic Bay oysters or Essex (New England) clam chowder, followed by steamed local halibut, chicken à la Normande, or steak frites; at the 6-seat Chef's Tasting Bar, guests opt for the five-course ($85) or seven-course ($105) tasting menu. **Known for:** locally sourced ingredients from farm and sea; extensive wine list; outdoor dining in warm weather but you may be out of luck if it rains. *Average main: $45* *247 Main St., Old Saybrook* *860/237–4189* *theessex.com* *Closed Mon. and Tues. No lunch.*

Hotels

Saybrook Point Resort & Marina
$$$ | **RESORT** | Guest rooms at the cushy Saybrook Point Inn are done up in 18th-century style, with reproductions of British furnishings and Impressionist art; many have fireplaces, making them especially cozy on cool evenings. **Pros:** tasteful room decor; excellent waterfront restaurant (open to the public); marina provides a picturesque setting. **Cons:** comparatively pricey; you'll need a car to get to local attractions; the water view from "water view" rooms varies considerably. *Rooms from: $374* *2 Bridge St., Old Saybrook* *860/395–2000* *www.saybrook.com* *100 rooms* *No Meals.*

Essex

33 miles east of New Haven, 37 miles southeast of Hartford, 20 miles west of New London.

Essex, hugging the west bank of the Connecticut River, is one of the most appealing small towns in the country—and still looks much as it did at the height of its shipbuilding prosperity in the mid-19th century. Essex's boat manufacturing was so important to the early United States that the British burned 28 ships here during the War of 1812. Gone are the days of steady trade with the West Indies, when the aroma of imported rum, molasses, and spices hung in the air. Now, whitewashed houses—many the former roosts of sea captains—line Main Street, where today's shops sell clothing, antiques, paintings and prints, and sweets.

GETTING HERE AND AROUND

The best way to reach Essex is by car; take Interstate 95 to Route 9 north (Exit 69).

Sights

★ Connecticut River Museum

HISTORY MUSEUM | FAMILY | Housed in an 1878 steamboat warehouse, this museum tells the story of the Connecticut River through maritime artifacts, interactive displays, and ship models. The riverfront museum even has a full-size working reproduction of the world's first submarine, the *American Turtle* (named for its appearance); the original was built by David Bushnell, from nearby Westbrook, in 1775 as a "secret weapon" to win the Revolutionary War. ✉ *Steamboat Dock, 67 Main St., Essex* ☎ *860/767–8269* 🌐 *www.ctrivermuseum.org* 🎟 *$12* ⏲ *Closed Mon.*

★ Essex Steam Train & Riverboat

TRAIN/TRAIN STATION | FAMILY | This excursion offers some of the best views of the Connecticut River Valley from a vintage steam locomotive pulled by 1920s-era coaches and an old-fashioned riverboat. The train, traveling along the Connecticut River through the lower valley, makes a 12-mile round-trip from Essex to Deep River Landing. Before returning by train to Essex, you have the option of boarding the *Becky Thatcher* riverboat and cruising along the river past Gillette Castle, Goodspeed Opera House, and fascinating deep-water coves and inlets. (The open promenade deck on the boat's third level offers the best views.) The train also hosts themed excursions such as the seasonal North Pole Express (from mid-November until Christmas). ✉ *Valley Railroad Company, 1 Railroad Ave., Essex* ☎ *860/767–0103, 800/377–3987* 🌐 *essexsteamtrain.com* 🎟 *Steam train from $25; steam train and riverboat from $40* ⏲ *Closed late Oct.–May.*

Restaurants

Oak Room at The Copper Beech Inn

$$$ | MODERN AMERICAN | Crystal sparkles, silver shines, and candles glow in Copper Beech Inn's main dining room—or you can dine more casually at the bar. Notable dishes have included a starter of jumbo lump crab cakes with remoulade dressing and entrées ranging from steak frites and honey-grilled chicken to grilled swordfish and blackened salmon. **Known for:** venerable country inn environment; many gluten-free selections; happy hour at the bar Tuesday-Friday. 💲 *Average main: $34* ✉ *Copper Beech Inn, 46 Main St., Ivoryton* ✣ *4 miles west of Essex* ☎ *860/767–0330* 🌐 *www.copperbeechinn.com* ⏲ *Closed Mon. No lunch.*

Scotch Plains Tavern

$$ | BISTRO | Share small plates, have a pub-style sandwich, or enjoy a full entrée at this iconic neighborhood tavern—there's something on the menu that will appeal to everyone; the Friday Night Prime Rib Special is a big draw. There's also a great selection of local craft beer and cider and a full wine list. **Known for:** patio dining by the fire pit in warmer weather; game room with pool and shuffleboard; live music Wednesday through Sunday. 💲 *Average main: $23* ✉ *124 Westbrook Rd., Essex* ☎ *860/662–4032* 🌐 *www.scotchplainstavern.com.*

Hotels

The Copper Beech Inn

$$ | B&B/INN | A magnificent copper beech tree shades this 1890 inn, set on 7 acres of Connecticut River Valley woodlands. **Pros:** perfect for a romantic weekend; excellent on-site dining; Carriage House rooms are a good deal. **Cons:** some rooms and baths are ready for a facelift; short drive from downtown Essex; rooms too near the bar-restaurant can be noisy. 💲 *Rooms from: $250* ✉ *46 Main*

The vintage Essex Steam Train makes a 12-mile roundtrip excursion through the Connecticut River Valley.

St., Ivoryton ✣ *4 miles west of Essex* ☎ *860/767–0330* 🌐 *www.copperbeech-inn.com* 🛏 *22 rooms* 🍴 *No Meals.*

The Griswold Inn

$$ | **B&B/INN** | Two-plus centuries of catering to changing tastes at what's billed as one of America's oldest continuously operating inns has resulted in a kaleidoscope of decor—some Colonial, a bit of Federal, a little Victorian—with just as many modern touches as necessary to meet present-day expectations. **Pros:** in the heart of historic downtown Essex; rich history—since opening in 1776; fun pub with live music every night. **Cons:** rooms above/near the Tap Room are noisy until 11 pm; no room TVs—head for the common room if you must; some rooms are quite small. 💲 *Rooms from: $235* ✉ *36 Main St., Essex* ☎ *860/767–1776* 🌐 *griswoldinn.com* 🛏 *33 rooms* 🍴 *Free Breakfast.*

East Haddam

15 miles north of Essex, 28 miles southeast of Hartford.

Farms, tanneries, and blacksmiths were the chief enterprises of 17th-century East Haddam, on the east bank of the Connecticut River. By the 20th century, residents (including actor William Gillette) were drawn to the area for its rural nature and riverside location. Now, fully into the 21st century, this lovely community retains its old-fashioned charm—mostly centered around the historic downtown.

GETTING HERE AND AROUND

The best way to reach East Haddam is by car. From Interstate 95 (Exit 69), take Route 9 north to Route 82 and then Route 149.

Sights

Chester-Hadlyme Ferry
TRANSPORTATION | FAMILY | This quaint ferry route has operated on the Connecticut River since 1769—originally a barge pushed by long poles, later using steam power, and now an open, self-propelled vessel. The crossing aboard *Selden III*, which accommodates 8 or 9 cars and 49 passengers, takes just five minutes but saves 12 miles of driving compared to taking the bridge. The bonus on the ferry ride: a beautiful view of Gillette's Castle, which overlooks the river. ✉ *Ferry Rd., Rte. 148, Chester* ☎ *860/662–0701* 🌐 *portal.ct.gov/DOT/Traveler/ferries/Chester-Hadlyme Ferry* 🎫 *$5 per vehicle* ⏲ *Closed Dec.-Mar.*

★ Gillette Castle State Park
STATE/PROVINCIAL PARK | FAMILY | The 122-acre park's main attraction is a rather outrageous, 24-room, oak-and-fieldstone hilltop castle—modeled after medieval fortresses of the Rhineland and built between 1914 and 1919 by the eccentric actor and playwright William Gillette. You can tour the castle (and its secret passages) and hike trails near the remains of a 3-mile private railroad, which chugged about the property until the owner's death in 1937. Gillette, who was born in Hartford, wrote two famous plays about the Civil War and was especially beloved for his play *Sherlock Holmes* (in which he performed the title role). In his will, he demanded that the castle not fall into the hands of "some blithering saphead who has no conception of where he is or with what surrounded." ✉ *67 River Rd., off Rte. 82, East Haddam* ☎ *860/526–2336* 🌐 *portal.ct.gov/DEEP/State-Parks/Parks/Gillette-Castle-State-Park* 🎫 *Park free, castle $6* ⏲ *Castle closed Labor Day—Memorial Day.*

★ Goodspeed Opera House
PERFORMANCE VENUE | This magnificent 1876 Victorian-gingerbread "wedding cake" theater on the Connecticut River—so called for its turrets, mansard roof, and grand filigree—is widely recognized for its role in the preservation and development of American musical theater. More than 20 Goodspeed productions have gone on to Broadway, including *Annie* and *Man of La Mancha*. Performances take place from May through December; one-hour Opera House tours are offered on the first Saturday of the month. ✉ *6 Main St., East Haddam* ☎ *860/873–8668* 🌐 *www.goodspeed.org* 🎫 *Tour $5.*

Hotels

The Boardman House
$$ | B&B/INN | Built around 1860 for wealthy silversmith Norman S. Boardman, this glamorous Second Empire–style mansion combines the charm of the gilded age with modern conveniences. **Pros:** style and sophistication in a sleepy riverside village; a short stroll to/from Goodspeed Opera House and riverside restaurants; perfect for a romantic getaway, anniversary, or honeymoon. **Cons:** two-night minimum stay on weekends; some traffic noise heard in front rooms; no breakfast served. [$] *Rooms from: $249* ✉ *8 Norwich Rd., Rte. 82, East Haddam* ☎ *860/873–9233* 🌐 *boardmanhouse.com* *5 rooms* *No Meals.*

Old Lyme

34 miles east of New Haven, 15 miles west of New London.

Old Lyme, on the eastern shore at the mouth of the Connecticut River (opposite Old Saybrook), is renowned among art lovers for its past as the home of the Lyme Art Colony—the most famous gathering of Impressionist painters in the United States beginning in 1899. Artists (and others) continue to be attracted to the area for its lovely countryside and shoreline, especially in the summer.

GETTING HERE AND AROUND

Old Lyme is best reached by car. Interstate 95 (at Exit 70) passes right through Old Lyme.

Sights

★ **Florence Griswold Museum**

ART MUSEUM | FAMILY | Central to Old Lyme's artistic reputation is this grand late-Georgian-style mansion, which served as a boardinghouse for members of the Lyme Art Colony in the first decades of the 20th century. When artists such as Willard Metcalf, Clark Voorhees, Childe Hassam, and Henry Ward Ranger flocked to the area to paint its varied landscape, Miss Florence Griswold offered both housing and artistic encouragement. The house has been restored to its 1910 appearance, when the colony was in full flower (clues to the house's layout and décor were gleaned from members' paintings). The museum's 10,000-square-foot Krieble Gallery, on the riverfront, hosts changing exhibitions of American art. Café Flo, on-site, serves lunch on the veranda or have a picnic on the lawn. *96 Lyme St., Old Lyme* *860/434–5542* *florencegriswoldmuseum.org* *$10* *Closed Mon.*

Coffee and Quick Bites

Hallmark Drive-In

$ | FAST FOOD | FAMILY | En route to or from the beach—or to or from anywhere, for that matter—stop at this seasonal roadside stand for a bite to eat (burgers, hot dogs, sandwiches, grinders, fish-and-chips) or just a summertime treat. Arguably the best ice cream around, whether in a cup, on a cone, or in a milk shake, root beer float, or sundae. **Known for:** the ice cream, of course; picnic area with a view of Long Island Sound; occasional live music in the evening. *Average main: $12* *113 Shore Rd. (Rte. 156), Old Lyme* *860/598–9680* *hallmarkdrivein.com* *Closed Labor Day–late Apr.*

Hotels

Old Lyme Inn

$$ | B&B/INN | This traditional country inn, constructed in 1865 on a 300-acre estate in this quiet town on the Connecticut coast, is right across from the Florence Griswold Room. **Pros:** Side Door Jazz Club, on-site, is an added bonus; Room 6 has the best view; contemporary New England fare served in the restaurant. **Cons:** 2-3 night minimum and higher rates for some holiday periods or events; wheelchair accessible property but only one "accessible" room; 14-day cancellation notice required; no refund for holiday periods. *Rooms from: $200* *85 Lyme St., Old Lyme* *860/434–2600* *oldlymeinn.com* *13 rooms* *Free Breakfast.*

New London

46 miles east of New Haven, 52 miles southeast of Hartford.

New London, on the western bank of the Thames River (pronounced *thaymes*, not *tems*), was founded in 1646 by John Winthrop Jr. The Pequot Indians called the area "Nameaug," and the Connecticut Colony's legislature wanted it renamed "Faire Harbour"; but the colonists prevailed and named it after their hometown. In the mid-1800s, New London was the second-largest whaling port in the world. Today, the U.S. Coast Guard Academy uses its campus on the Thames to educate and train its cadets. The prestigious Connecticut College is across the avenue from the Academy; Ocean Beach Park, an old-fashioned playland with a broad sandy beach and long wooden boardwalk, is a perfect place for the whole family to spend a hot summer day.

GETTING HERE AND AROUND

New London is accessible by car off Interstate 95 and can also be reached via Amtrak's high-speed Acela and Northeast Regional trains, as well as Shore Line East commuter trains from New Haven and towns in between.

Fort Trumbull State Park

HISTORIC SIGHT | FAMILY | Once the location of the U.S. Coast Guard Academy and later the U.S. Navy Underwater Sound Laboratory, the fort was originally built to defend New London Harbor from British attack. You'll now find a 19th-century stonework-and-masonry fort, an extensive visitor center focusing on military history, a top-rate fishing pier, a waterfront boardwalk with fantastic views, and a picnic area when you want to relax. ✉ *90 Walbach St., New London* ☎ *860/444–7591* 🌐 *portal.ct.gov/DEEP/State-Parks/Parks/Fort-Trumbull-State-Park* 🎫 *Grounds and parking free, visitor center $6.*

Lyman Allyn Art Museum

ART MUSEUM | Housed in a neoclassical granite building that overlooks the U.S. Coast Guard Academy and Long Island Sound, this museum was founded in 1932 with funds bequeathed by Harriet Upson Allyn in memory of her whaling merchant father, Captain Lyman Allyn (1797–1874). Inside is an impressive collection of more than 15,000 objects covering a span of 5,000 years. Works also include contemporary, modern, and Early American fine arts; American Impressionist paintings; Connecticut decorative arts; and European works from the 16th through 19th centuries. The 12 acres of surrounding grounds includes a sculpture trail. ✉ *625 Williams St., New London* ☎ *860/443–2545* 🌐 *www.lymanallyn.org* 🎫 *$12* 🕒 *Closed Mon.*

U.S. Coast Guard Academy

COLLEGE | The 100-acre cluster of redbrick buildings you see overlooking the Thames River makes up one of the four U.S. military academies. Visitors are welcome, and security is obviously tight, but being there when the Coast Guard training ship, the barque *Eagle,* is in port is a special treat. A small museum, located in Waesche Hall on the grounds, explores the Coast Guard's 230+ years of maritime service and includes some 200 ship models, as well as figureheads, paintings, uniforms, life-saving equipment, and cannon. ✉ *31 Mohegan Ave., New London* ☎ *860/444–8270 for public affairs, 860/444–8511 for the museum* 🌐 *www.uscga.edu* 🎫 *Free* 🕒 *Museum closed weekends.*

★ Ocean Beach Park

BEACH | FAMILY | Possibly the state's finest beach, the 50-acre park has a broad white-sand beach, an Olympic-size outdoor pool with a triple waterslide, an 18-hole miniature-golf course, an arcade, a half-mile-long boardwalk, kiddie rides, food concessions, a nature trail, and a picnic area. **Amenities:** food and drink; lifeguards; parking (fee); showers; toilets. **Best for:** partiers; swimming; walking. ✉ *98 Neptune Ave., at foot of Ocean Ave., New London* ☎ *860/447–3031* 🌐 *www.ocean-beach-park.com* 🎫 *Walk-in $8, parking and admission $25.*

Restaurants

Captain Scott's Lobster Dock

$$ | SEAFOOD | FAMILY | Don't be put off by the long line waiting to order classic fare like lobster rolls (hot or cold, small or large), steamers, fried clams, homemade clam fritters, "chowda"—plus foot-long hot dogs. This outdoor restaurant on Shaw's Cove—where you eat at picnic tables (BYOB) alongside the marina—is a great place to eat and a great place to spend time on a hot summer day. **Known for:** picturesque waterfront spot; everything made on-site and to order; Ed's hot fudge sundae. *Average main: $20 80 Hamilton St., off Howard St., New London 860/439–1741 www.captscottsnl.com Closed mid-Oct.–mid-Apr.*

Coffee and Quick Bites

Michael's Dairy

$ | ICE CREAM | FAMILY | The local go-to place for authentic, old-fashioned, New England-style ice cream, Michael's Dairy has been a fixture on the campus of Mitchell College since 1943. The 39 flavors (plus sherbet, sorbet, frozen yogurt) range from old favorites like butter crunch, orange pineapple, and black raspberry to more modern flavors like salted caramel chocolate pretzel, campfire s'mores, and birthday cake. **Known for:** a few tables and chairs inside and out; scoops, sundaes, milk shakes, floats—plus pints, quarts, and half-gallons; sugar-free and vegan offerings, too. *Average main: $6 629 Montauk Ave., New London 860/443–2464 www.michaelsdairynl.com Closed mid-Sept.–Memorial Day.*

Performing Arts

Garde Arts Center

ARTS CENTERS | National and international opera and dance performances, concerts, comedy, Broadway musicals, film festivals, and children's events are all on the bill at this arts center—a beautifully restored, 1,440-seat, art deco theater. *325 State St., New London 860/444–7373 www.gardearts.org.*

Groton

2 miles east of New London.

Across the river from New London, Groton is the location of Naval Submarine Base New London, the U.S. Navy's primary East Coast submarine base, and of the Electric Boat Division of General Dynamics, designer and manufacturer of nuclear submarines. Often referred to as the "Submarine Capital of the World," Groton is the birthplace of *Nautilus,* the nation's first nuclear submarine and a National Historic Landmark, which is now permanently berthed here at the Submarine Force Museum.

Sights

Fort Griswold Battlefield State Park

MILITARY SIGHT | FAMILY | It was here (legend has it), on the Groton side of the Thames River, that the infamous traitor Benedict Arnold stood watching the important port of New London (a supply center for the Continental Army and friendly port for Connecticut privateers) burn in 1781 during the Revolutionary War. Whether Arnold actually stood there is open to question; but the American defenders of Ft. Griswold were massacred by Arnold's British troops during the Battle of Groton Heights—and New London did burn according to his orders. The 134-foot-high Groton Monument, which you can climb for a sweeping view of the river and New London, is a memorial to the fallen. The adjacent Monument House Museum has historic displays; the Ebenezer Avery House, on the grounds and recently restored, is where the wounded were sheltered in 1781. *Park Ave. at Monument St., Groton 860/449–6877 seasonal, 860/444–7591 c/o Fort Trumbull State Park portal.ct.gov/DEEP/State-Parks/Parks/Fort-Griswold-Battlefield-State-Park Free.*

Mystic Seaport has a number of vessels that you can board and tour.

★ Submarine Force Museum

NAUTICAL SIGHT | FAMILY | The world's first nuclear-powered submarine, USS *Nautilus (SSN-571)*—and the first submarine to complete a submerged transit of the North Pole (in 1958)—was launched and commissioned in Groton in 1954. The *Nautilus* spent 25 active years as a showpiece of U.S. technological know-how and is now permanently docked at the Submarine Force Museum, a couple of miles upriver from where the sub was built. Visitors are welcome to climb aboard and explore. The museum, just outside the entrance to Naval Submarine Base New London, is a repository of thousands of artifacts, documents, and photographs detailing the history of the U.S. Submarine Force component of the U.S. Navy, along with educational and interactive exhibits. ✉ *1 Crystal Lake Rd., Groton* ☎ *800/343–0079* 🌐 *www.ussnautilus.org* 🎟 *Free* 🕒 *Closed Tues.*

Mystic

10 miles east of New London, 8 miles south of Ledyard.

Mystic, a village that lies half in the town of Groton and half in the town of Stonington, has devoted itself to recapturing the seafaring spirit of the 18th and 19th centuries. Some of the nation's fastest clipper ships were built here in the mid-19th century; today, the 37-acre Mystic Seaport is the state's most popular attraction. Downtown Mystic has an interesting collection of boutiques and galleries.

GETTING HERE AND AROUND

By car, take Interstate 95 to Route 27 south (Exit 90) to reach Mystic. Amtrak's Northeast Regional train service also stops here.

Sights

★ Mystic Aquarium

AQUARIUM | FAMILY | The famous Arctic Coast exhibit—which holds 750,000 gallons of water, measures 165 feet at its longest point by 85 feet at its widest point, and ranges from just inches to 16½ feet deep—is just a small part of this revered establishment and home to three graceful beluga whales and several species of seals and sea lions. You can also see African penguins, fascinating sea horses, Pacific octopuses, and sand tiger sharks. Don't miss feeding time at the Ray Touch Pool, where rays suction sand eels right out of your hand. The animals here go through 1,000 pounds of herring, capelin, and squid each day—Juno, a male beluga whale, is responsible for consuming 85 pounds of that himself. ✉ *55 Coogan Blvd., Mystic* ☎ *860/572–5955* ⊕ *www.mysticaquarium.org* 🎟 *from $29.*

★ Mystic Seaport Museum

MUSEUM VILLAGE | FAMILY | Mystic Seaport, the nation's leading maritime museum, encompasses 19 acres stretched along the Mystic River. The indoor and outdoor exhibits include a re-created New England coastal village, a working shipyard, and formal museum buildings with more than 1 million artifacts, including figureheads, models, tools, ship plans, scrimshaw, paintings, photos, and recordings. Along the narrow village streets and in some of the historic buildings, craftspeople demonstrate skills such as open-hearth cooking and weaving, interpreters bring the past to life, musicians sing sea chanteys, and special squads with maritime skills show how to properly set sails on a square-rigged ship. The museum's more than 500 vessels include the *Charles W. Morgan,* the last remaining wooden whaling ship afloat, and the 1882 training ship *Joseph Conrad*; you can climb aboard both for a look around or for sail-setting demonstrations and reenactments of whale hunts.

■ **TIP→ Children under three are admitted free.** ✉ *75 Greenmanville Ave. (Rte. 27), Mystic* ✣ *1 mile south of I–95* ☎ *860/572–0711* ⊕ *www.mysticseaport.org* 🎟 *$27.*

Setting Sail at Mystic Seaport

Kids can learn the ropes—literally—of what it takes to be a sailor during one of Mystic Seaport's many sailing classes and camps. Younger children and those who wish to stay ashore can sign up for courses on building boats (from construction to varnish), blacksmithing, wood carving, and open-hearth cooking. The Seaport's planetarium also offers instruction on navigating a ship by the stars. Prices for classes vary. Call Mystic Seaport (☎ 860/572–5331) or visit its website (⊕ www.mysticseaport.org) for details.

Restaurants

★ Abbott's Lobster in the Rough

$$ | SEAFOOD | FAMILY | If you want some of the freshest lobster, crab, mussels, or clams on the half shell (there are also non-seafood options), head down to this unassuming seaside lobster shack in sleepy Noank, a few miles southwest of Mystic. Most seating is outdoors or on the dock, where the views of Noank Harbor are magnificent. **Known for:** fresh seafood by the seaside in the fresh air; lobster dinner, lobster roll, lobster bisque—all delish; perfect coastal atmosphere. 💲 *Average main: $22* ✉ *117 Pearl St., Noank* ☎ *860/536–7719* ⊕ *www.abbottslobster.com* ⏲ *Closed Columbus Day–Apr. and Mon.–Thurs. early May and Sept.*

Oyster Club

$$$ | MODERN AMERICAN | In the Oyster Club's rustic, barnlike dining room, start your meal with a selection of oysters and clams from the raw bar or a cup of the raved-about quahog clam chowder—New England (creamy) or Rhode Island (clear) style—before moving along to either fresh-from-the-sea surf or prime turf for your entrée. In summer, the open-air Treehouse offers another lively spot to enjoy a casual meal or a drink—weather permitting. **Known for:** menu changes daily; ingredients sourced from local farms and waters; happy hour at the Treehouse summer afternoons. $ *Average main: $28* ✉ *13 Water St., Mystic* ☎ *860/415–9266* ⊕ *www.oysterclubct.com* ⏲ *Closed Tues. No lunch Mon.–Thurs.*

Coffee and Quick Bites

Mystic Drawbridge Ice Cream

$ | ICE CREAM | FAMILY | Sit inside or outside at this classic ice-cream parlor, right next to the Mystic River Drawbridge, and enjoy homemade ice cream and other soda fountain favorites—maybe a New York egg cream or an ice cream shake. This ice cream has half the air whipped into it compared to other "homemade" and mass-produced products, making it richer, creamier, and more flavorful. **Known for:** Drawbridge original flavors—Mystic Mud, Mystic Turtle, and Seaport Salty Swirl; espresso, pastries, and smoothies, too; close up view of the drawbridge opening and closing to allow boats to pass through. $ *Average main: $6* ✉ *2 W. Main St., Mystic* ☎ *860/572–7978* ⊕ *www.mysticdrawbridgeicecream.com.*

Hotels

Mystic Marriott Hotel & Spa

$ | HOTEL | FAMILY | This six-story, Georgian-style hotel has modern rooms accented with old-world touches, such as rich fabrics, gleaming wood furnishings, and elegant detailing. **Pros:** convenient to Mystic attractions; Starbucks coffee bar in the lobby; swim winter or summer in the indoor pool. **Cons:** on a busy road; often filled with conference or wedding guests; you might prefer an outdoor pool in summer. $ *Rooms from: $220* ✉ *625 North Rd. (Rte. 117), Groton* ⊕ *5 miles from both Mystic Seaport Museum and Mystic Aquarium* ☎ *860/446–2600* ⊕ *www.marriott.com* *285 rooms* *No Meals.*

The Whaler's Inn

$$$ | HOTEL | A perfect compromise between a chain motel and a country inn, this five-building complex with public rooms furnished with lovely antiques is one block from the Mystic River and downtown area. **Pros:** discounted tix to area attractions; complimentary afternoon treats and dining credit in on-site restaurant; EV charging stations. **Cons:** rooms in some buildings have less character; on the busy main street; pleasant hotel but not "luxurious". $ *Rooms from: $300* ✉ *20 E. Main St., Mystic* ☎ *860/536–1506* ⊕ *www.whalersinnmystic.com* *45 rooms* *No Meals.*

Stonington

7 miles southeast of Mystic, 57 miles east of New Haven.

Pretty Stonington Borough, the seaside "downtown" of the town of Stonington, pokes into Fishers Island Sound. A quiet fishing community clustered around white-spired churches, "the Borough," as it's called, is far less commercial than downtown Mystic. In the 19th century, though, it was a busy whaling, sealing, and transportation center. Historic buildings line the town green and border both sides of Water Street down to the imposing Old Lighthouse Museum and Stonington Point.

GETTING HERE AND AROUND

Stonington is a rather large town, but to travel by car to "The Borough," the small seaside town center, take Route 1 north from Mystic (you'll actually be heading eastward, but don't be concerned) to Route 1A.

Sights

The Old Lighthouse Museum

LIGHTHOUSE | FAMILY | This museum occupies a stone citadel with an attached lighthouse tower originally built in 1823 and rebuilt on higher ground 17 years later. Climb to the top of the tower for a spectacular view of Long Island Sound and three states. Six rooms of exhibits depict the maritime and agricultural history of the small coastal town. ✉ *7 Water St., Stonington* ☎ *860/535–1440* 🌐 *www.stoningtonhistory.org* 🎫 *$10* 🕑 *Closed Tues.-Wed. and mid-Oct..–Mar.*

Restaurants

★ Breakwater

$$$ | SEAFOOD | FAMILY | Enjoy fresh-caught New England seafood (and more) dockside at Breakwater, midway along Water Street in Stonington Borough. Dine inside or outside on the deck in warm weather; the roomy bar is a popular gathering place in winter months. **Known for:** takeout and boatside delivery; amazing sunsets; all-day dining. $ *Average main: $28* ✉ *66 Water St., Stonington* ☎ *860/415–8123* 🌐 *breakwaterstonington.com* 🕑 *Closed Mon.-Tues.*

Dog Watch Café

$$ | SEAFOOD | FAMILY | Seafood is the draw at this harborside restaurant—clam chowder, oysters or clams on the half-shell, "dogwiches," fish-and-chips, bouillabaisse, roasted cod, Stonington scallops, and more. Alternatively, choose a grilled chicken sandwich, flat-iron steak, burger, or soup and salad. **Known for:** great food, of course; lawn games and live music in the "Dog Pound"; the ice cream tent. $ *Average main: $24* ✉ *194 Water St., Stonington* ☎ *860/415–4510* 🌐 *www.dogwatchcafe.com.*

Hotels

★ The Inn at Stonington

$$ | B&B/INN | The views of Stonington Harbor and Fishers Island Sound are spectacular from this waterfront inn in the heart of Stonington Borough. **Pros:** seaside rooms face the harbor and Fishers Island Sound; walking distance to village shops and dining; intimate adult (and kids 14-plus) atmosphere. **Cons:** no on-site restaurant (but several nearby); minimum stay on summer weekend and holidays; strict seven-day notice for cancellations, no exceptions. $ *Rooms from: $285* ✉ *60 Water St., Stonington* ☎ *860/535–2000* 🌐 *innatstonington.com* 🛏 *19 rooms* 🍽 *Free Breakfast.*

Ledyard

10 miles northeast of New London and Groton, 50 miles southeast of Hartford.

In the woods of southeastern Connecticut, rural Ledyard has become best-known in recent years as the location of the Mashantucket Pequot Tribal Nation's vast Foxwoods Resort Casino and its excellent Mashantucket Pequot Museum & Research Center, through which the tribe is educating the public about its history and that of other Northeast Woodland tribes.

GETTING HERE AND AROUND

Driving is the only way to get to Ledyard; take Interstate 95 to Route 184 east (Exit 84). If you are only planning to visit Foxwoods, many bus companies run direct charter trips from New York City and elsewhere.

Sights

Foxwoods Resort Casino

CASINO | FAMILY | Owned and operated by the Mashantucket Pequot Tribal Nation on reservation lands near Ledyard, Foxwoods is the largest resort casino in North America. The enormous compound, which opened in 1992, draws 40,000-plus visitors daily to its seven casinos with more than 3,400 slot machines, 300 gaming tables, and a 3,600-seat bingo parlor. This 9-million-square-foot complex includes four luxury hotels, a 5,500-square-foot pool "sanctuary," two full-service spas, a retail concourse, numerous dining options, several theaters and other venues that attract national performers, a video arcade, extreme sports facilities, a bowling alley, children's activities, an 18-hole championship golf course, and—as counterpoint to all that action—marked trails through the surrounding woods. ✉ *350 Trolley Line Blvd., Ledyard* ☎ *800/369–9663* 🌐 *www.foxwoods.com.*

★ Mashantucket Pequot Museum & Research Center

INDIGENOUS SIGHT | FAMILY | Housed in a large complex 1 mile from Foxwoods, this museum brings to life in exquisite detail the history and culture of the Northeastern Woodland tribes in general and the Mashantucket Pequots in particular. Highlights include views of an 18,000-year-old glacial crevasse, a caribou hunt from 11,000 years ago, and a 17th-century fort. Perhaps most remarkable is a sprawling "immersion environment": a 16th-century village with more than 50 life-size figures and real smells and sounds. Audio devices provide detailed information about the sights. A full-service restaurant offers both Native and traditional American cuisine. A 185-foot stone-and-glass tower provides sweeping views of the surrounding countryside. ✉ *110 Pequot Tr., Ledyard* ☎ *860/396–6910* 🌐 *www.pequotmuseum.org* 🎟 *$22* 🕓 *Closed Sun.–Tues.*

Hotels

Stonecroft Country Inn

$$ | B&B/INN | The sunny, 19th-century Georgian Colonial–style house marks the center of Stonecroft: 6½ acres of green meadows, woodlands, and rambling stone walls. **Pros:** scenic and verdant grounds; cheerful service; pleasant drive to Mystic attractions. **Cons:** minimum 2-night stay required on weekends; no room TVs in 1807 House rooms; no kids under 12. $ *Rooms from: $235* ✉ *515 Pumpkin Hill Rd., Ledyard* ☎ *860/572–0771* 🌐 *stonecroft.com* *10 rooms* 🍽 *Free Breakfast.*

Norwich

15 miles north of New London, 40 miles southeast of Hartford.

Handsome restored Georgian and Victorian houses surround the historic town green in the city of Norwich, founded in 1659 on land that a handful of settlers purchased from Mohegan Sachem Uncas; more historic buildings can be found along the Thames River. The former mill town is hard at work on restoration and rehabilitation efforts.

GETTING HERE AND AROUND

To reach Norwich from the coast by car, take Interstate 95 to Interstate 395 north to Route 82 east.

Sights

Leffingwell House Museum

HISTORIC HOME | What began as a two-room home around 1675 evolved into a pre-Revolutionary War tavern; by 1776, it was the elegant home of a local patriot that has since been lovingly restored by the Society of the Founders of Norwich. The house is furnished with Early American artifacts, and interpreters explain the architecture of the house and the lifestyle of those who lived or frequented the home over the centuries. ✉ *348*

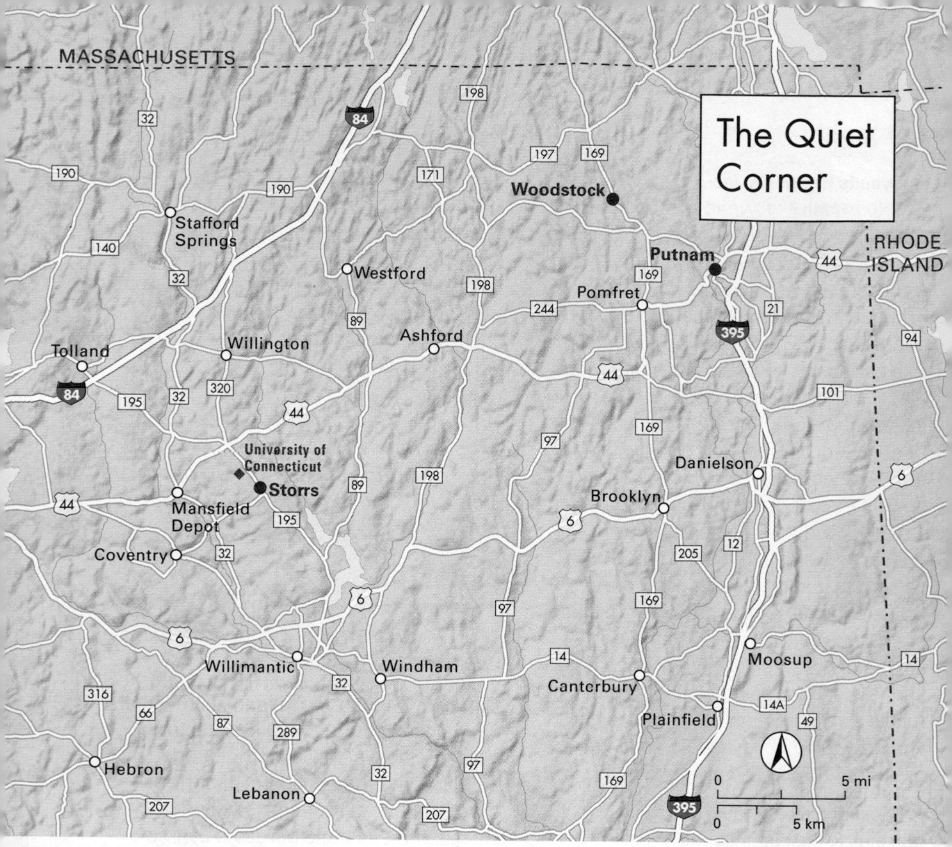

The Quiet Corner

Washington St., Norwich ☎ *860/889–9440* 🌐 *www.leffingwellhousemuseum.org* 🎫 *$8* ⏲ *Closed Mon.–Fri. and Nov.–Mar.*

Mohegan Sun

CASINO | FAMILY | The Mohegan Tribe of Connecticut, known as Wolf People, opened this casino just south of Norwich in 1996; today, it has more than 300,000 square feet of gaming space in three casino areas, totaling nearly 5,000 slot machines and more than 300 gaming tables. Also part of the complex: the Kids Quest/Cyber Quest family entertainment center, a shopping mall with 32 retail stores, 43 dining options, 19 bars and lounges, and two high-rise luxury hotels—each with a pool and a full-service spa. The 10,000-seat Mohegan Sun Arena, home to the WNBA's Connecticut Sun, draws major performances; bands play in the Wolf Den nearly every night; Comix Roadhouse presents comedy acts, as the name implies, and country music; and the 175,000-square-foot Earth Expo & Convention Center holds events. ✉ *1 Mohegan Sun Blvd., off I–395, Uncasville* ☎ *888/226–7711* 🌐 *mohegansun.com.*

Hotels

The Spa at Norwich Inn

$$ | HOTEL | On 42 rolling acres right by the Thames River and a stone's throw from Mohegan Sun, this Georgian-style inn is best known for its spa, which offers the full range of skin-care regimens, body treatments, and fitness classes. **Pros:** excellent spa treatments; expansive grounds; Kensington's Restaurant serves Connecticut-sourced, health-conscious fare. **Cons:** focused mainly on spa guests (who are often wandering around in their robes); few activities beyond the spa; Villa rooms need attention—choose the Main Inn. *Rooms from: $200* *607 W. Thames St. (Rte. 32), Norwich* *860/425–3500* *www.thespaatnorwichinn.com* *100 rooms* *No Meals.*

Putnam

50 miles east of Hartford, 34 miles north of Norwich.

Ambitious antiques dealers have reinvented Putnam, a mill town that was neglected after the Depression. Putnam's downtown Antiques Marketplace, a four-level emporium with space for 350 antiques and collectibles dealers, is the heart of the Quiet Corner's antiques trade.

GETTING HERE AND AROUND

By car from Hartford, take Interstate 384 and U.S. 44 east; from Norwich, follow Interstate 395 north to Route 12 north.

Restaurants

85 Main

$$$ | **MODERN AMERICAN** | **FAMILY** | This stylish bistro is *the* place to go for a break from antiquing. Typical lunchtime offerings include roasted corn and clam chowder, pesto chicken salad, and burgers with hand-cut fries; dinner could be maple-glazed sea scallops, steak frites, or butternut squash ravioli in brown butter. **Known for:** seafood and steaks worthy of a big city; raw bar and full sushi menu; outdoor patio for warm-weather dining. *Average main: $27* *85 Main St., Putnam* *860/928–1660* *85main.com.*

Woodstock

40 miles north of Norwich, 46 miles northeast of Hartford.

The landscape of this enchanting town that cozies up to the Massachusetts border is splendid in every season: the rolling hills seem to stretch for miles. Scenic roads lead past antiques shops, a country inn in the grand tradition, orchards, livestock grazing in grassy fields, and the fairgrounds of one of the state's oldest agricultural fairs held each Labor Day weekend.

GETTING HERE AND AROUND

By car from Hartford, follow Interstate 84 east to U.S. 44 east to Route 197 east; from Norwich, follow Interstate 395 north to U.S. 44 west and then Route 171 to Route 169 north.

Sights

Roseland Cottage

HISTORIC HOME | This pink board-and-batten Gothic Revival-style house was built in 1846 as a summer home for New York silk merchant, publisher, and abolitionist Henry C. Bowen and his wife, Lucy. The house and outbuildings (including a carriage barn with the nation's oldest indoor bowling alley) hold a prominent place in history, having hosted four U.S. presidents: Ulysses S. Grant, Rutherford B. Hayes, William Henry Harrison, and William McKinley. The parterre garden features 21 flower beds surrounded by 600 yards of boxwood hedge. *556 Rte. 169, Woodstock* *860/928–4074* *www.historicnewengland.org/property/roseland-cottage* *$15* *Closed Mon. and Tues. and mid-Oct.–May.*

Coffee and Quick Bites

We-Li-Kit Ice Cream

$ | **ICE CREAM** | **FAMILY** | When moseying around the Quiet Corner of Connecticut, stop by We-Li-Kit for a dish, cone, sundae, frappe, float, or banana split made with premium farmstead-fresh ice cream. Choose among dozens of flavors change with the seasons—then enjoy your treat, relax in the gardens, and visit the farm animals. **Known for:** hand-packed pints and quarts, ice-cream cakes, and custom flavors (in advance); New England clam chowder and clam cakes on Friday and weekends; maple syrup from the sugar house and farm-fresh USDA beef, too. *Average main: $6* *728 Hampton Rd. (Rte. 97), Pomfret Center* *About 10 miles (15 min.) south of Woodstock via Rte. 169 and Rte. 97* *860/974–1095* *www.welikit.com* *Closed Nov.–Mar.*

Hotels

The Inn at Woodstock Hill
$ | B&B/INN | Filled with antiques, this massive inn overlooking the countryside has guest rooms with four-poster beds, handsome fireplaces, pitched ceilings, and timber beams. **Pros:** beautiful grounds and gardens; pretty rooms; several pleasant sitting areas for afternoon tea. **Cons:** rooms are small; quite a hike up to third-floor rooms; expensive restaurant. *Rooms from: $155* *94 Plaine Hill Rd., Woodstock* *860/928–0528* *www.woodstockhill.com* *21 rooms* *Free Breakfast.*

Storrs

26 miles east of Hartford; 25 miles north of Norwich.

Storrs, an otherwise rural village in the town of Mansfield, is primarily occupied by the 4,100 acres (and some 19,000 students) of the main campus of the University of Connecticut. As a result, many cultural programs, sporting events, and other happenings take place here.

GETTING HERE AND AROUND

By car from Hartford, take Interstate 84 to US 44 east; from Norwich, follow Route 32 north.

Sights

Mansfield Drive-In
FILM | FAMILY | Spring through fall, one of the state's few remaining drive-in theaters (family-run since 1954) shows movies (double features) on its three big screens; there's a huge flea market held on the grounds every Sunday, rain or shine, from 8 am to 2 pm. You can bring leashed dogs to the movies—but no barking! *228 Stafford Rd., Mansfield* *860/423–4441 movies, 860/456–2578 flea market* *mansfielddrivein.com* *$13, carload Wednesdays $26 (whether 1–10 people)* *Closed mid-Oct.–March and Mon.-Thurs. Apr.–mid-June and Sept.–mid-Oct.*

University of Connecticut
COLLEGE | FAMILY | UConn's large, sprawling main campus offers lots for visitors to see and do. The William Benton Museum of Art's permanent collection includes centuries-old European and American paintings, drawings, prints, photographs, and sculptures, and the Jorgensen Center for the Performing Arts presents a series of 25–30 music, dance, and theater programs during the academic year. The Ballard Institute and Museum of Puppetry has more than 2,500 puppets on display (UConn is one of two colleges in the country that offer a puppetry degree); and, depending on the season, you might catch a Connecticut Huskies football game or watch the amazing women's basketball team play at home. *Storrs Rd., Rte. 195, Storrs* *860/486–2000* *uconn.edu.*

Coffee and Quick Bites

UConn Dairy Bar
$ | ICE CREAM | FAMILY | Stop by the UConn Dairy Bar in the UConn Department of Animal Science Creamery for the most delicious ice cream you've ever tasted. Students produce the 24 regular, two seasonal, and occasional limited-edition flavors. **Known for:** ice cream as a learning experience; shakes, floats, parfaits, plus sandwiches, salads and soups; farm-fresh eggs and creamery-made cheeses. *Average main: $5* *George White Bldg., 17 Manter Rd., Storrs* *860/486–1021* *dining.uconn.edu/uconn-dairy-bar* *Closed Mon. and Tues.*

Chapter 8

RHODE ISLAND

8

Updated by
Robert Curley

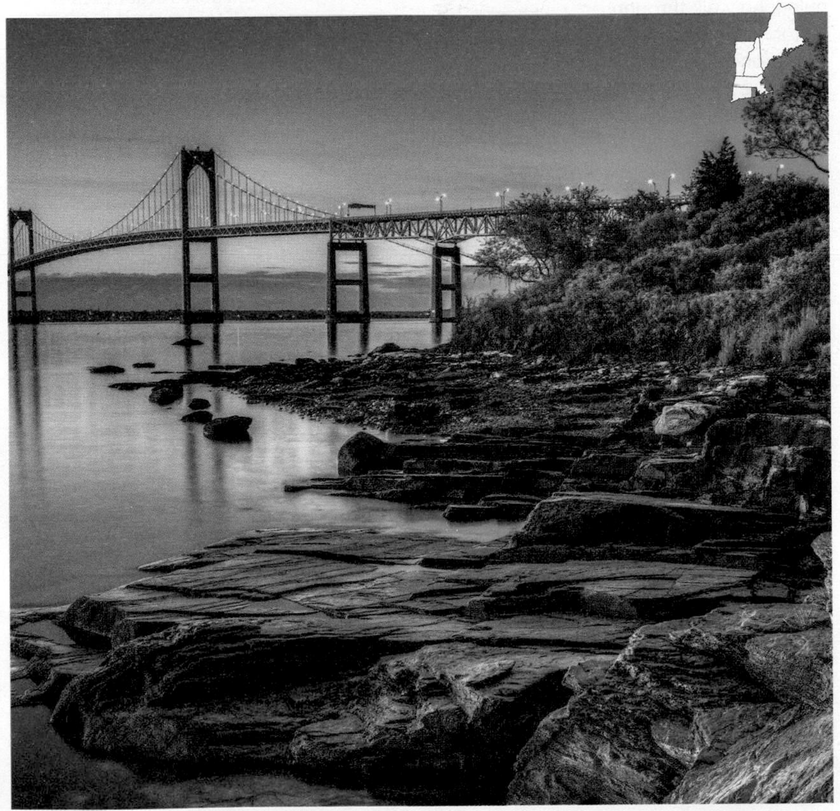

Sights ★★★★★

Restaurants ★★★★★

Hotels ★★★☆☆

Shopping ★★★★☆

Nightlife ★★☆☆☆

WELCOME TO RHODE ISLAND

TOP REASONS TO GO

★ **Mansions:** See how the social elite lived during Newport's Gilded Age on a tour of The Breakers, Cornelius Vanderbilt's opulent, 70-room "summer cottage."

★ **Historic Streets:** For a mile-long walk through history, follow Benefit Street on Providence's East Side and see ornate homes built by leading Colonial merchants.

★ **Nature:** Block Island is one of the most serene spots on the Eastern Seaboard—especially at Rodman's Hollow, where winding paths lead to the sea.

★ **Sand:** Take your pick of South County's numerous white-sand beaches—perhaps East Matunuck State Beach in South Kingstown.

★ **Food Enclave:** From food trucks to upscale dining, Providence has an exciting culinary scene fueled in large part by young chefs trained at Johnson & Wales University.

1 Westerly. Galleries, shops, restaurants, and more than 15 buildings on the National Historic Register provide this seaside town with tons of charm.

2 Watch Hill. With perfect beaches and luxurious lodgings, this seaside village is the ideal spot for a chic vacation.

3 Misquamicut. This family-friendly destination has old-school amusements, movies on the beach, and evening concerts.

4 Charlestown. A sheltered coastline makes it a great spot for swimming, sailing, bird-watching, and beachcombing.

5 North Kingstown and South Kingstown. The coastal village of Wickford oozes Colonial charm and the Gilbert Stuart birthplace and Smith's Castle. South Kingstown is home to the University of Rhode Island and the historic villages of Wakefield and Peace Dale.

6 Narragansett. Beautiful beaches and the Point Judith Lighthouse are highlights of this quiet beach town.

7 Block Island. This laid-back resort island is about an hour's ferry ride from Point Judith.

8 Jamestown. Located on Conanicut Island, Jamestown has beautiful parks and a quaint downtown.

9 Newport. One of the world's great sailing cities also hosts world-class music festivals, Gilded Age mansions, and the International Tennis Hall of Fame.

10 Middletown. Some of Newport's best beaches are actually in this neighboring town on Aquidneck Island.

11 Portsmouth. On Aquidneck Island with Newport, the community has polo matches and tastings at Greenvale Vineyards.

12 Bristol. Once a center for boatbuilding, Bristol is known for its long-running July 4 celebration.

13 Tiverton and Little Compton. East of Newport, this bucolic corner of the state is home to artists and farmers.

14 Providence. The capital of Rhode Island is also a vibrant college town with great food and a thriving arts community.

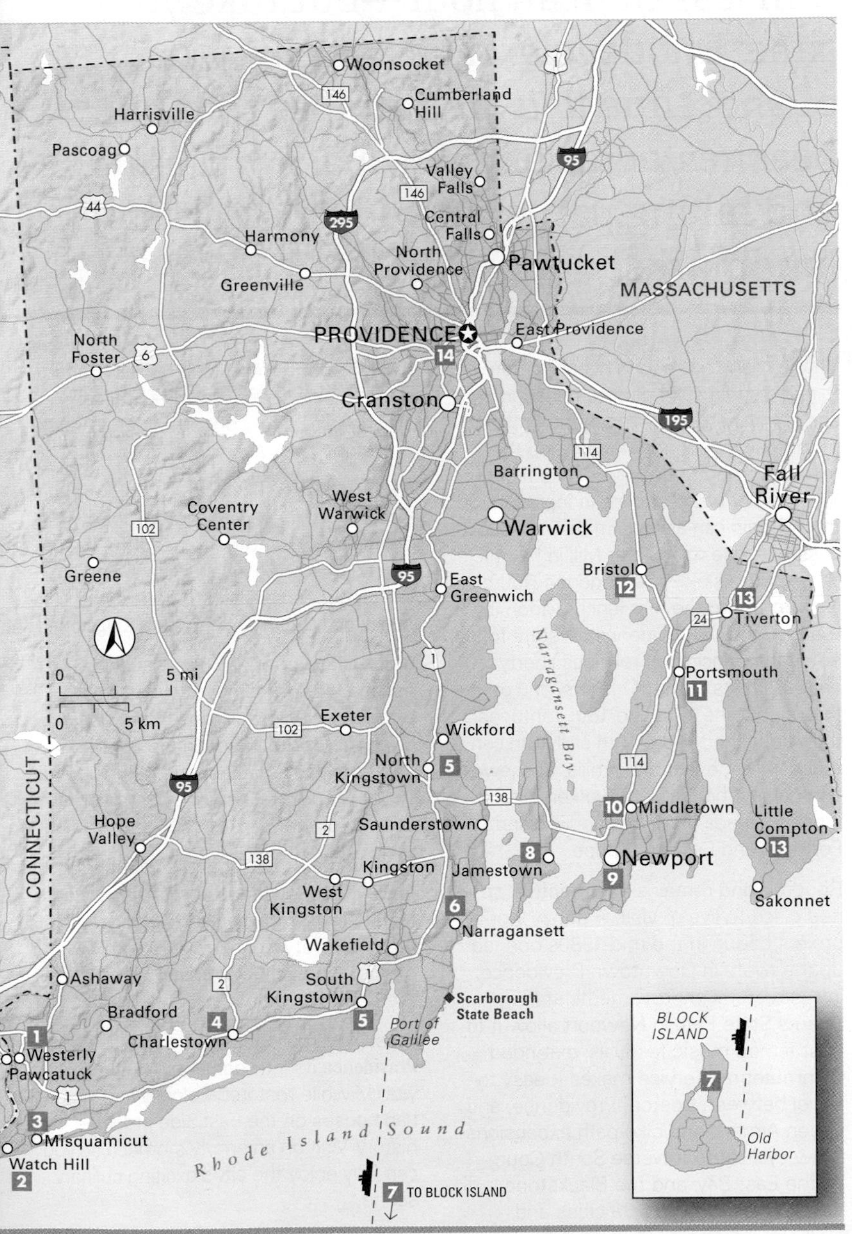

Woonsocket
Cumberland Hill
Harrisville
Pascoag
Valley Falls
Central Falls
Harmony
North Providence
Pawtucket
Greenville
MASSACHUSETTS
PROVIDENCE
East Providence
North Foster
Cranston
Barrington
Fall River
West Warwick
Coventry Center
Warwick
Greene
Bristol
East Greenwich
Tiverton
Narragansett Bay
Portsmouth
0 5 mi
0 5 km
Exeter
Wickford
North Kingstown
Middletown
Little Compton
Saunderstown
Hope Valley
Kingston
Jamestown
Newport
West Kingston
Sakonnet
Narragansett
CONNECTICUT
Wakefield
Ashaway
South Kingstown
Scarborough State Beach
Bradford
Charlestown
Port of Galilee
Westerly
Pawcatuck
BLOCK ISLAND
Misquamicut
Rhode Island Sound
Old Harbor
Watch Hill
TO BLOCK ISLAND

Consider the Ocean State's small size its biggest asset. You can drive across it in less than an hour—but take your time: Rhode Island has nearly 400 miles of shoreline to explore, more than 100 beaches, acres of open space with hiking and biking paths, and dozens of historic landmarks.

Rhode Island has a long history of forward thinking and a spirit of determination and innovation embodied in the bronze, 11-foot-tall Independent Man atop the marble-domed State House. The first of the 13 colonies to declare independence from Britain can also claim the first successful textile mill (Slater Mill in Pawtucket), America's oldest synagogue (Touro in Newport), and the first lunch wagon (by Walter Scott in Providence). A state founded on the principle of religious liberty drew Baptists, Jews, Quakers, and others throughout the 17th and 18th centuries, then flourished in the 19th and 20th centuries with the factories, mills, and jewelry companies that brought workers from French Canada, Italy, Ireland, England, Portugal, and Eastern Europe.

Rhode Island remains an attractive, spirited place to live or visit. A public works project begun in the mid-1980s opened up the rivers in Downtown Providence; infrastructural improvements at Ft. Adams State Park in Newport allow it to host famed music festivals; extended commuter rail service makes it easy to travel between Boston, Providence, and Green Airport; and bike-path expansions allow cyclists to traverse South County, the East Bay, and the Blackstone Valley. Rhode Island's 39 cities and towns—none more than 50 miles apart—offer natural beauty, inspired culinary artistry, and many opportunities to relax and enjoy their scenic vistas.

MAJOR REGIONS

Officially named Washington County, **South County** is home to beautiful beaches and charming locales like **Westerly, Watch Hill, Misquamicut, Charlestown, Narragansett, Wickford,** and **South Kingstown.**

Block Island offers a classic seaside escape in summer, even when the population swells. Relax on the beach, or at one of the Victorian inns or bed-and-breakfasts, peruse the galleries and shops, and have a seafood lunch or farm-to-table dinner.

Newport County, a longtime yachting enclave, consists of **Newport, Jamestown, Middletown, Portsmouth, Tiverton,** and **Little Compton**. Between Newport and Providence, the **East Bay's Bristol** hosts one of the country's oldest July 4 celebrations.

Prestigious colleges and universities give **Providence** its intellectual and cultural vitality, while restored Colonial and Victorian houses on the East Side preserve its history. Visit on an empty stomach so you can fully enjoy the city's exciting culinary scene.

Planning

By car, it's usually an hour or less from any one place in Rhode Island to another. Although distances are short, Rhode Island is the second-most-densely populated state (after New Jersey), so allow extra time for traffic congestion in and around Providence.

Most sights in Providence can be seen in two or three days. The Blackstone Valley makes a good day trip from Providence. Newport, though not even 12 square miles, offers enough to fill two days—and the same can be said for South County, with its superb beaches. If you have a full week, you can visit all four regions of the state, as well as Block Island.

Getting Here and Around

AIR

The state's main airport, Rhode Island T. F. Green International Airport (PVD), is in Warwick, just south of Providence; it's served by Air Canada, Allegiant, American, Breeze, Delta, Frontier, JetBlue, Southern Airways Express, Southwest, Sun Country, and United.

Smaller commercial airports, with limited carriers, are in Westerly and on Block Island; Newport has a general aviation airport.

Boston's Logan International Airport is an hour's drive from Providence.

AIR CONTACT Rhode Island T. F. Green International Airport. ✉ *2000 Post Rd., off I–95, Warwick* ☎ *401/691–2000* 🌐 *www.pvdairport.com.*

BUS

Rhode Island Public Transit Authority (RIPTA) offers low-cost bus service throughout the entire state—just $2 per ride or $6 per day within the city, to another town, or to the beach.

BUS CONTACT Rhode Island Public Transit Authority (RIPTA). ✉ *Kennedy Plaza Passenger Terminal, 1 Kennedy Plaza, Providence* ☎ *401/781–9400* 🌐 *www.ripta.com.*

CAR

New England's main highway, Interstate 95, cuts diagonally through Rhode Island, spanning 43 miles from Connecticut to Massachusetts, with multiple exits in Providence. Interstate 295 serves the western half of the state, splitting from I-95 in Warwick and running 27 miles northwest and then east, bypassing Providence before reconnecting to I-95 in Attleboro, Massachusetts.

Interstate 195 southeast from Providence leads to New Bedford, Massachusetts, and Cape Cod. Route 146 northwest from Providence passes through the Blackstone Valley en route to Worcester, Massachusetts, and Interstate 90 (Massachusetts Turnpike). U.S. 1 follows much of the Rhode Island coast heading east from Connecticut before turning north to Providence. Route 138 heads east from Interstate 95 or U.S. 1, crossing bridges over Narragansett Bay to reach Jamestown, Newport, Middletown, and Portsmouth. Route 114 leads south from East Providence down through the East Bay community of Bristol and then to Newport.

Once you're here, a car is your best way to get around the state. Parking is easy to find outside cities, though challenging and sometimes expensive in downtown Providence and Newport. Parts of Providence and Newport are easily walkable.

Activities

The Audubon Society of Rhode Island manages nearly 9,500 acres in more than a dozen wildlife refuges across the state, plus one nearby in Massachusetts. All trails are open free to the public, and visitors are welcome to hike from sunrise to sunset (unless posted otherwise).

Contact the Department of Environmental Management's Division of Licenses for boating and fishing information, regulations, and licenses. A three-day nonresident freshwater fishing license costs $16; a nonresident saltwater fishing license costs $10 and is good for a year. Licenses can be purchased online.

Audubon Society of Rhode Island
The society manages nearly 9,500 acres in more than a dozen wildlife refuges across the state, plus one nearby in Massachusetts. All trails are open free to the public, and visitors are welcome to hike from sunrise to sunset (unless posted otherwise). ✉ *12 Sanderson Rd., Smithfield* ☎ *401/949–5454* 🌐 *www.asri.org.*

Dining

The creative passion of award-winning chefs, many in their twenties and early thirties, fuels Rhode Island's vibrant restaurant scene. Abundant fresh seafood makes for outstanding variations on New England staples like fish-and-chips, clam chowder, and stuffed quahogs (hard clams)—all best savored at a beachside clam shack. Fresh-caught Block Island swordfish and calamari can't be beat. Then there's uniquely Rhode Island fare, such as the johnnycake (a thin corn pancake cooked on a griddle), coffee milk, Del's frozen lemonade, and Gray's Ice Cream. Authentic Italian-American restaurants can be found in Providence's Federal Hill neighborhood.

What It Costs in U.S. Dollars

$	$$	$$$	$$$$
RESTAURANTS			
under $18	$18–$24	$25–$35	over $35
HOTELS			
under $200	$200–$299	$300–$399	over $399

Lodging

Major chain hotels are certainly represented in Rhode Island, but boutique hotels, small bed-and-breakfasts, and historic inns provide a more intimate experience. Rates vary seasonally. In Newport, for example, a winter stay often costs less than half the summer price. Some inns in coastal towns are closed in winter.

Reviews have been shortened. For full information, visit Fodors.com.

Visitor Information

CONTACTS Providence Warwick Convention & Visitors Bureau. ✉ *Rhode Island Convention Center, 1 Sabin St., Providence* ☎ *401/2229604 Headquarters, 401/751–1177 Visitor Center* 🌐 *www.goprovidence.com.* **South County Tourism Council.** ✉ *4160 Old Post Road, Charlestown* ☎ *800/548–4662* 🌐 *www.southcountyri.com.* **Visit Rhode Island.** ☎ *800/556–2484* 🌐 *www.visitrhodeisland.com.*

When to Go

With its arts and music festivals and gorgeous beach days, summer is high season in Rhode Island and a great time to visit, but there are fun and exciting things to do here year-round. Newport's Jazz and Folk Festivals heat up the town in late July and early August, just after the Newport Music Festival for classical music fans in July. This is also the time to take the ferry to low-key, beach-ringed Block Island for a day trip or overnight stay.

The shoulder seasons (April and May and September and October) bring pleasant weather and more affordable accommodations. In late summer, the return of student life to Providence colleges and universities gives the capital city energy and a youthful vibe. October is a good time to catch fall foliage in the Blackstone Valley, around the University of Rhode Island in Kingston, or in picturesque Tiverton and Little Compton.

Late fall, winter, and early spring each have their own charms—such as skiing at Yawgoo Valley in Exeter, ice bumper cars at the Providence Rink, and restaurant weeks in Newport and Narragansett, when eateries offer special multicourse prix-fixe menus.

Westerly

95 miles southwest of Boston; 140 miles northeast of New York City.

The picturesque and thriving business district in this town of 23,000 people bordering Pawcatuck, Connecticut, has a lot going for it: art galleries, shops, and restaurants; a Victorian strolling park; and more than 15 structures on the National Register of Historic Places. Once a busy little railroad town in the late 19th century, Westerly is now a stop on the New York–Boston Amtrak corridor. The town was known in the past for its red granite, which was used in monuments around the country. It has since sprawled out along U.S. 1 and grown to encompass more than a dozen villages in a 30-square-mile area including Westerly itself (also called downtown Westerly), along with Watch Hill, Dunn's Corners, Misquamicut, Bradford, Shelter Harbor, and Weekapaug.

GETTING HERE AND AROUND

When traveling between New York City and Boston, Amtrak makes stops at Westerly, West Kingston, and Providence.

Sights

Westerly Library and Wilcox Park

CITY PARK | **FAMILY** | The library, in the heart of downtown Westerly, also serves neighboring Pawcatuck, Connecticut. The library's Hoxie Gallery holds art exhibitions. Adjacent to the library, Wilcox Park, a 14½-acre Victorian strolling park designed in 1898 by Warren Manning—an associate of Frederick Law Olmsted, co-creator of New York's Central Park—has a pond, a meadow, an arboretum, a perennials garden, sculptures, fountains, and monuments. *The Runaway Bunny,* a sculpture inspired by the children's book of the same name, is popular with the little ones. A garden market, arts festivals, concerts, and Shakespeare-in-the-park productions are held periodically. ✉ *44 Broad St., Westerly* ☎ *401/596–2877* 🌐 *www.westerlylibrary.org* 🎟 *Free* 🕓 *Library closed Sun.*

Restaurants

B&B Dockside

$ | **AMERICAN** | It's all about breakfast and burgers at this café overlooking the Pawcatuck River. Burgers rule the lunch menu, including the deliciously decadent Fat Elvis—with peanut butter, bacon, cheese, and caramelized bananas, it'll leave you saying, "Thank you, thankyouverymuch." **Known for:** great waterfront view; mouthwatering roast beef hash—for breakfast; friendly service, even when crowded. [$] *Average main: $10* ✉ *19 Margin St., Westerly* ☎ *401/315–2520* 🌐 *www.bnbdockside.com* 🕓 *Closed Tues. and Wed.*

Evie's

$$ | **SEAFOOD** | This restaurant defies its strip mall location with a bright interior design soaked in natural light and a high-fenced courtyard for warm-weather dining. Coast-inspired comfort food like fish and chips occupies the menu alongside fish tacos, short-rib grilled cheese, and a savory salmon gyro; oysters—on the half-shell or Rockefeller—are harvested in nearby Watch Hill. **Known for:** cocktails with house-made infusions; good selection of local beers on draft; more than a dozen wines by the glass. [$] *Average main: $22* ✉ *224 Post Rd., Westerly* ☎ *401/388–4201* 🌐 *eviesri.com.*

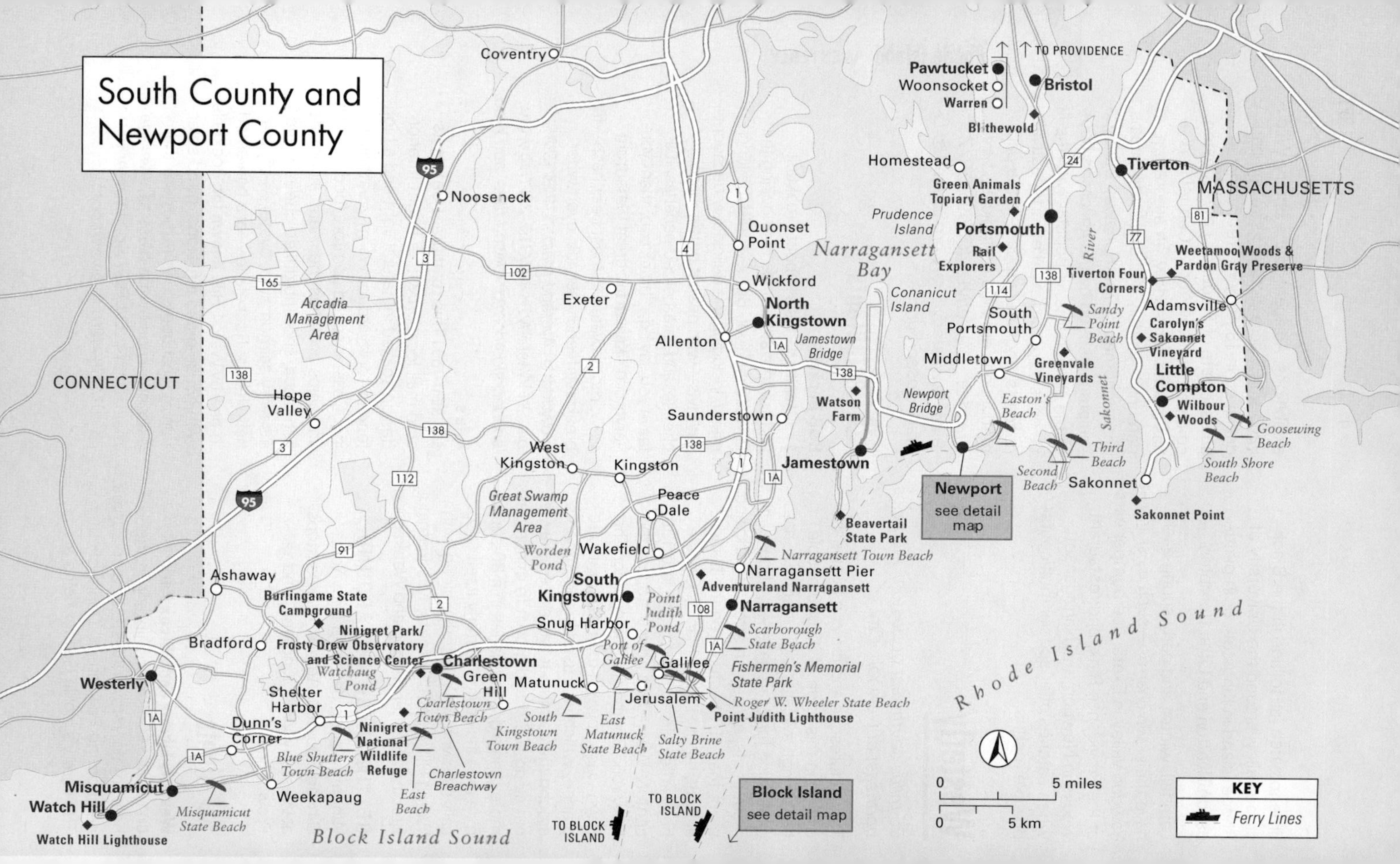

South County and Newport County
CONNECTICUT
MASSACHUSETTS
Coventry
Nooseneck
TO PROVIDENCE
Pawtucket
Woonsocket
Warren
Bristol
Blithewold
Homestead
Green Animals Topiary Garden
Prudence Island
Portsmouth
Rail Explorers
Tiverton
Quonset Point
Narragansett Bay
River
Weetamoo Woods & Pardon Gray Preserve
Tiverton Four Corners
Adamsville
Wickford
Exeter
Arcadia Management Area
North Kingstown
Conanicut Island
South Portsmouth
Sandy Point Beach
Carolyn's Sakonnet Vineyard
Allenton
Jamestown Bridge
Middletown
Greenvale Vineyards
Little Compton
Hope Valley
Watson Farm
Newport Bridge
Sakonnet
Easton's Beach
Wilbour Woods
Goosewing Beach
Saunderstown
Jamestown
Third Beach
South Shore Beach
West Kingston
Kingston
Second Beach
Sakonnet
Newport see detail map
Great Swamp Management Area
Peace Dale
Beavertail State Park
Sakonnet Point
Worden Pond
Wakefield
Narragansett Town Beach
Ashaway
South Kingstown
Narragansett Pier
Burlingame State Campground
Adventureland Narragansett
Point Judith Pond
Narragansett
Snug Harbor
Scarborough State Beach
Rhode Island Sound
Bradford
Ninigret Park/ Frosty Drew Observatory and Science Center
Port of Galilee
Galilee
Watchaug Pond
Charlestown
Fishermen's Memorial State Park
Westerly
Green Hill
Matunuck
Shelter Harbor
Jerusalem
Roger W. Wheeler State Beach
Charlestown Town Beach
Point Judith Lighthouse
Dunn's Corner
South Kingstown Town Beach
Ninigret National Wildlife Refuge
East Matunuck State Beach
Salty Brine State Beach
Blue Shutters Town Beach
Charlestown Breachway
Misquamicut
Weekapaug
Block Island see detail map
0 5 miles
0 5 km
KEY
Ferry Lines
Watch Hill
East Beach
TO BLOCK ISLAND
TO BLOCK ISLAND
Misquamicut State Beach
Watch Hill Lighthouse
Block Island Sound
95
95
1
1
1A
1A
1A
1A
1A
2
2
3
3
4
24
77
81
91
102
108
112
114
138
138
138
138
138
138
165

Hotels

Shelter Harbor Inn

$ | **B&B/INN** | With whimsically sumptuous decor styled by celebrity fashion designer Randolph Duke, this early-19th-century farmhouse inn and restaurant has 21st-century Instagrammability. **Pros:** quiet location with easy parking; on-site dining and spa services; ideal for off-season escapes. **Cons:** most rooms require a climb up stairs; nothing is within walking distance; two-night minimum on summer weekends. *$ Rooms from: $139 ✉ 10 Wagner Rd., off U.S. 1, Shelter Harbor ☎ 401/322–8883 🌐 www.shelterharborinnri.com ⇆ 23 rooms 🍽 No Meals.*

★ **Weekapaug Inn**

$$$$ | **RESORT** | Guest rooms at this lovingly restored Relais & Chateaux inn on Quonochontaug (Quonnie) Pond are furnished with luxury linens and the work of area artists. **Pros:** low-key luxury; guest pantry stocked with tasty treats; complimentary use of kayaks and canoes; meals made with locally sourced food. **Cons:** expensive; not directly oceanside; few off-season activities (after Labor Day). *$ Rooms from: $590 ✉ 25 Spray Rock Rd., Westerly ☎ 401/637–7600, 855/679–2995 🌐 www.weekapauginn.com ⇆ 33 rooms 🍽 No Meals.*

Nightlife

The Knickerbocker Music Center

LIVE MUSIC | The band Roomful of Blues was born at "The Knick," and national touring artists still gig at this club near the Westerly train station. The venue hosts R&B, jazz, and alt-country touring acts on its main stage and intimate Tap Room; local bands also perform, and there are occasional open-mike nights and dance lessons, too. *✉ 35 Railroad Ave., Westerly ☎ 401/315–5070 🌐 www.knickmusic.com.*

Watch Hill

6 miles south of downtown Westerly.

For generations, this seaside village has attracted movers and shakers looking for a low-key getaway. Watch Hill has nearly 2 miles of gorgeous beaches, including Napatree Point Conservation Area, a great spot to see shorebirds and raptors and take in the sunset. Stargazers might catch a glimpse of Taylor Swift or Conan O'Brien, both of whom have homes here. The heart of the town is Bay Street, a seasonal business district with boutiques selling upscale beachwear, fashions, home goods, jewelry, and souvenirs. There are also cafés and a historic carousel.

Sights

Flying Horse Carousel

AMUSEMENT RIDE | **FAMILY** | At the beach end of Bay Street twirls one of the oldest carousels in America, built by the Charles W. F. Dare Company of New York City and part of a traveling carnival that came to Watch Hill before 1883. The carved wooden horses with real horsehair manes and leather saddles are suspended from chains attached to the ceiling, creating the impression the horses are flying. Riders must be under 13. Grab the brass ring from one of the outside horses to win a free ride. *✉ 151 Bay St., Watch Hill ☎ 401/388–8136 🌐 www.merrygoroundbeach.com 🎟 $1 inside horse, $4 outside horse ⏲ Closed mid-Sept.–mid-May.*

Watch Hill Lighthouse

A tiny museum at this 1856 lighthouse contains the original Fresnel light, letters and journals from lighthouse keepers, documentation of famous local shipwrecks, and photographs of the hurricane of 1938 and 19th- and early-20th-century sailing vessels off Watch Hill. Parking is for the handicapped and senior citizens only; everyone else must walk down the peninsula along a private road off Larkin Road. ✉ *Lighthouse Rd., Watch Hill* 🌐 *www.watchhilllighthouse-keepers.org* 🎟 *Free* ⏲ *Museum closed mid-Sept.–June and Fri.–Mon.*

Restaurants

★ Olympia Tea Room

$$$ | AMERICAN | Overlooking the water since it first opened as an ice-cream parlor in 1916, the Olympia's varnished wood booths and a long marble counter echo the restaurant's rich history. The kitchen focuses on local and artisanal ingredients served with simple elegance and abundant flavor, including spicy flaked haddock and Milanese-style crispy chicken. **Known for:** bistro-style menu; sidewalk tables outside and antique booths inside; a fine selection of wines available by the glass. 💲 *Average main: $25* ✉ *74 Bay St., Watch Hill* ☎ *401/348–8211* 🌐 *www.olympiatearoom.com* ⏲ *Closed early Nov.–early Apr.*

Hotels

★ Ocean House

$$$$ | RESORT | High on bluffs overlooking Block Island Sound stands this extraordinary replica of the Victorian grande dame of the same name built here in 1868. **Pros:** exceptional service; beach with private cabanas; championship croquet lawn; spa with 25-meter lap pool. **Cons:** expensive during high season (and low season); three-night minimum on weekends; an uphill walk from Watch Hill's shopping and dining. 💲 *Rooms from: $1,020* ✉ *1 Bluff Ave., Watch Hill* ☎ *401/584–7000, 855/678–0364* 🌐 *www.oceanhouseri.com* 🛏 *67 rooms* 🍽 *No Meals.*

Misquamicut

2½ miles northeast of Watch Hill.

This family-oriented summer destination, stretching 7 miles from Watch Hill to Weekapaug, has an ocean-facing sandy beach the color of brown sugar. From hermit crab races to kiddie rides, the town's family-geared amusements provide countless diversions. You can also hop on a Jet Ski, pedal a hydrobike, or find a spot for sunbathing. Evenings bring concerts and movies on the beach, and there are shoreside festivals in the spring and fall.

The Native American name for this sandy strip of beachfront means "Red Fish," referring to the Atlantic salmon once common to the Pawcatuck River; the entire Westerly area, settled in 1661, previously bore this name.

Sights

Atlantic Beach Park

BEACH | FAMILY | The largest and busiest of the kid-oriented amusements along Misquamicut Beach, this century-old facility offers nostalgic fun for the entire family, including an antique (1915) carousel, bumper cars, a dragon roller coaster, ice-cream parlor, and a large arcade with games that spout tickets you can redeem for prizes. The Windjammer Surf Bar has live music in the summer and an oceanfront deck for drinks and snacks; unlike the amusement park, the bar is open year-round. ✉ *321 Atlantic Ave., Misquamicut* ☎ *401/322–0504* 🌐 *www.atlanticbeachpark.com* 🎟 *Free entry, $2 per ride; parking from $20* ⏲ *Closed late Oct.–Apr.; bar stays open on off-season weekends.*

Beaches

Misquamicut State Beach

BEACH | FAMILY | Part of the several-mile-long stretch of sandy beach that makes up Misquamicut, this ½-mile state-run portion is exceedingly popular. Expect the 2,100-space parking lot to fill up on sunny summer weekends. Bring your own chairs or blankets. **Amenities:** food and drink; lifeguards (seasonal); parking (fee); showers; toilets. **Best for:**

sunset; swimming; family fun. ✉ *257 Atlantic Ave., Misquamicut* ☎ *401/667–6200* 🌐 *www.riparks.com* 🎫 *Admission is free; parking is $20 for nonresidents.*

Restaurants

Maria's Seaside Cafe

$$$ | MEDITERRANEAN | This family-owned restaurant at the Hotel Maria serves Mediterranean cuisine, from casual (pizza, raw bar) to fancy (Cioppino, local pan-seared sea scallops). It's right across the street from the beach and a standout on a strip of ice-cream stands, take-out shacks, and motels that have seen better days. **Known for:** indoor-outdoor seating with heaters for cool summer nights; homemade pasta; lobster pizza. $ *Average main: $28* ✉ *132 Atlantic Ave., Misquamicut* ☎ *401/596–6886* 🌐 *www.mariasseasidecafe.com* ⏲ *Closed early Sept.–May.*

Hotels

Breezeway Resort

$$ | HOTEL | A great choice for families, this well-maintained 50-room boutique motel is less than a quarter-mile from the ocean. **Pros:** access to private stretch of Misquamicut Beach; complimentary bicycles for adults; away from the late-night hubbub near the beach. **Cons:** rooms are a bit cramped; can be noisy with so many kids; hotel prices, motel accommodations. $ *Rooms from: $282* ✉ *70 Winnapaug Rd., Misquamicut* ☎ *401/348–8953* 🌐 *www.breezewayresort.com* ⏲ *Closed late Oct.–early May* *50 rooms* 🍽 *Free Breakfast.*

Nightlife

Windjammer Surf Bar

DANCE CLUBS | This venerable beach bar hosts live entertainment six nights a week, late June–mid-September. Renovations following Superstorm Sandy included the addition of a function room that hosts weddings and other events. Children are welcome until 10 pm; after that patrons must be 21 or older. ✉ *321 Atlantic Ave., Misquamicut* ☎ *401/322–0504* 🌐 *www.windjammersurfbarri.com* ⏲ *Closed Mon.-Fri. mid-Sept.-late June.*

Charlestown

10 miles northeast of Misquamicut.

Charlestown's secluded coastline makes it a great spot for swimming, sailing, surfing, beachcombing, bird-watching, and boating. Approximately 20% of Charlestown is conservation and recreation land, including Burlingame State Park, Ninigret National Wildlife Refuge, Ninigret Park, and East Beach. The city regulates outdoor lighting to keep the night sky dark, so it's a fantastic place for stargazers of all ages, particularly at the Frosty Drew Observatory at Ninigret Park. Charlestown is also home to the Narragansett Indian Tribe Reservation, which every August holds the oldest recorded annual powwow in North America.

Sights

★ Frosty Drew Observatory and Science Center

OBSERVATORY | FAMILY | In Ninigret Park but independently operated by a non-profit, the observatory offers the state's best views of the night sky. Frosty Drew opens every Friday around sunset for stargazing and stays open until 10 pm or later if the skies are clear and visitors keep coming. It's also open on nights when meteor showers and other astronomical events are forecast. On cloudy nights, astronomers give presentations and offer tours. The place isn't heated, so dress for the season. ✉ *Ninigret Park, 61 Park La., off Old Post Rd., Charlestown* ☎ *401/859–1450* 🌐 *www.frostydrew.org/observatory* 🎫 *Free.*

Ninigret National Wildlife Refuge

WILDLIFE REFUGE | **FAMILY** | Spring brings opportunities to view the male American woodcock's mating ritual at this 858-acre refuge, but bird-watchers flock here year-round to commune with nature among 4 miles of hiking trails and diverse upland and wetland habitats, including grasslands, shrublands, wooded swamps, and freshwater ponds. There's an abandoned naval air station on Ninigret Pond, the state's largest coastal salt pond, and a fine place to watch the sunset. Wear blaze orange while hiking between November and January, when permitted hunters are allowed to cull white-tailed deer. Explore an impressive collection of wildlife and natural history displays at the Kettle Pond Visitor Center on the southbound side of U.S. 1 at 50 Bend Road. ✉ *Ninigret Entrance Rd., off U.S. 1, Charlestown* ☎ *401/364–9124* 🌐 *www.fws.gov/refuge/ninigret* 🎫 *Free.*

Beaches

Blue Shutters Town Beach

BEACH | With wonderful views of Block Island Sound, Blue Shutters is a popular escape for beachcombers and quietude seekers who don't mind paying a bit extra for soft sand, sea, and serenity. Beachgoers can see Block Island and Long Island from the shaded deck of the pavilion. Beach-accessible wheelchairs are available at no cost. **Amenities:** lifeguards; showers; toilets; parking (fee). **Best for:** walking; sunsets. ✉ *469 East Beach Rd., Charlestown* ☎ *401/364–1222* 🌐 *www.charlestownri.org* 🎫 *Nonresident parking $20 on weekdays, $40 on weekends.*

East Beach

BEACH | Across the street from Blue Shutters Town Beach, this tranquil and unspoiled barrier beach spans 3 narrow miles of shoreline that separates Ninigret Pond from the ocean, dead-ending at the Charlestown Breachway. East Beach stands in stark contrast to Narragansett's bustling Scarborough Beach, and it's a rare East Coast beach that permits beach camping and four-wheel drive vehicles on the sand. Parking is limited, and the lot fills up quickly. Be careful when swimming: the ocean side is known for riptides. **Amenities:** lifeguards; parking (fee); toilets. **Best for:** solitude; walking, camping. ✉ *East Beach Rd., off U.S. 1, Charlestown* ☎ *401/667-6200* 🌐 *www.riparks.com/Locations/LocationEastBeach.html* 🎫 *RI Resident parking $6; nonresident parking $12.*

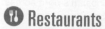

Restaurants

The Charlestown Rathskeller

$$ | **AMERICAN** | The hand-cut fries at this former speakeasy hidden in the woods are revered across southern New England, and steaks and burgers are big and cooked to perfection. Lawn games like horseshoes, bocce, and corn hole; an enormous stone fire pit; and the "Down Back" outdoor music stage make the grounds feel like the backyard of your dreams. **Known for:** the coldest beer in Rhode Island; schnitzels, stroganoff, and pretzels; live music and outdoor games. 💲 *Average main: $19* ✉ *489A Old Coach Rd., Charlestown* ☎ *401/792–1000* 🌐 *www.thecharlestownrathskeller.com* 🕒 *Closed Mon.*

Shopping

Fantastic Umbrella Factory

SOUVENIRS | **FAMILY** | With a hippie vibe, the kid- and couple–friendly Fantastic Umbrella Factory contains a handful of rustic shops built around a wild garden and bamboo forest. Unusual flowers, succulents, and other plants are for sale, along with interesting clothing and jewelry, CBD products, soy candles, creative pottery, Native American handcrafts, quirky gifts, and incense. For $3 you can buy a bag full of seeds to feed the fenced-in emus and roaming chickens. ✉ *4820 Old Post Rd., off U.S. 1, Charlestown* ☎ *401/364–1060* 🌐 *www.fantasticumbrellafactory.com.*

North Kingstown and South Kingstown

North Kingstown is 10 miles north of Narragansett Pier, 25 miles south of Providence; South Kingstown is 10 miles northeast of Charlestown.

North Kingstown is a community of villages founded in the 17th, 18th, and 19th centuries, including Saunderstown, Lafayette, Davisville, Hamilton, and Wickford, the latter a quaint Colonial village on a small harbor.

Quonset Point was once one of the biggest Navy bases in the world; a small military presence remains at the Quonset Airport, but most of the complex has been transformed into a commerce park and recreational facilities, including a 2.7 mile bike path and several small beaches on Narragansett Bay.

People often discover South Kingstown through the University of Rhode Island but return for its historic charm, arts-oriented community, great surfing beaches, and outdoor lifestyle. Almost a third of South Kingstown's 57 square miles is protected open space, allowing the town to maintain a rural character even as the population has doubled. There are two beaches, three rivers, several salt ponds, a 7-mile bike path, and numerous hiking trails, making it a great place for outdoor enthusiasts.

■ TIP→ Locals often refer not to South Kingstown but the names of its 14 distinct villages, including Wakefield, Peace Dale, Matunuck, Snug Harbor, West Kingston, and Kingston, home of the University of Rhode Island's main campus. Note that Kingston and West Kingston omit North Kingstown and South Kingstown's "w."

Sights

Kenyon's Grist Mill

FACTORY | On the banks of the Queen's River, this circa 1886 mill still grinds cornmeal for johnnycakes the old-fashioned way, with enormous granite millstones quarried in Westerly. You can arrange group tours lasting up to 90 minutes, or wait until the weekend and request an individual tour. Special tour weekends in the summer and fall are combined with kayaking and a clam cake and chowder festival, respectively. Products may be purchased in the mill shop during business hours. ✉ *21 Glen Rock Rd., West Kingston* ☎ *401/783–4054, 800/753–6966* 🌐 *www.kenyonsgristmill.com* 🎫 *Tour $6.*

Tomaquag Museum

INDIGENOUS SIGHT | Rhode Island's first and only museum devoted to Native history and culture contains crafts, historical items, and photos related primarily to the Narragansett, Niantic, Wampanoag, and other southeastern New England tribes. ✉ *390A Summit Rd., Exeter* ☎ *401/491–9063* 🌐 *www.tomaquagmuseum.org* 🎫 *$6* ⏲ *Closed Sun.; Mon.–Tues. and Thurs.–Fri. private tours only.*

Wickford Village

HISTORIC DISTRICT | Dating to 1709, Wickford began as a fishing village, later a modestly busy port, and today retains its colonial charms with street after street lined with preserved buildings dating from the 18th and 19th centuries, including a number of sea captain's homes. One of the oldest Episcopal churches in America, the circa 1707 Old Narragansett Church, was originally located about five miles away but moved to Wickford in 1800. Wickford Harbor is a popular haven for pleasure boaters, and the calm waters also attract kayakers and standup paddleboarders. Fresh fish can still be bought off the town dock at the end of Main Street, and a pair of petit bridges over tidal coves help define the pleasantly walkable shopping area on Brown Street. Several walking trails access undeveloped areas on the outskirts of town, and the town beach is a short walk or bike ride south along scenic route 1A. Wickford hosts Daffodil Days in the spring, the Wickford Art Festival in July, Wicked Week Halloween festivities late October, and the Festival of Lights in December. ✉ *Brown St., Wickford* 🌐 *wickfordvillage.org.*

Beaches

★ East Matunuck State Beach

BEACH | FAMILY | Vigorous waves, white sands, and views of Block Island on crystal-clear days account for the popularity of this 144-acre beach. Crabs, mussels, and starfish populate the rock reef that extends to the right of the strand, inspiring visitors to channel their inner marine biologist. A wind turbine provides power for the Daniel L. O'Brien Pavilion, named for a police officer killed in the line of duty while rescuing people stranded in this area during Hurricane Carol in 1954. Currents can be strong, so keep an eye on kids **Amenities:** food and drink; lifeguards; parking (fee); showers; toilets. **Best for:** swimming; walking. ✉ *950 Succotash Rd., South Kingstown* ☎ *401/789–8374* 🌐 *riparks.com/beach/east-matunuck.php* 🎫 *nonresident parking $12.*

South Kingstown Town Beach

BEACH | FAMILY | The ⅓-mile-long town beach—with a playground, a boardwalk, a volleyball court, and picnic tables—cannot be seen from the road and doesn't fill as quickly as the nearby state beaches. **Amenities:** lifeguards; parking (fee); toilets. **Best for:** sunset; swimming; walking. ✉ *719 Matunuck Beach Rd., South Kingstown* ☎ *401/789–9301* 🌐 *southkingstownri.com/575/Town-Beach-at-Matunuck* 🎫 *nonresidents from $15* 🕒 *Closed after Labor Day–late May.*

Restaurants

★ Matunuck Oyster Bar

$$$ | SEAFOOD | Shuckers are hard at work at the raw bar in this awesome waterside restaurant, an offshoot of the nearby Matunuck Oyster Farm. This year-round business committed to serving fresh, local produce, along with farm-raised and wild-caught seafood, draws a crowd—snag an outside table if you can. **Known for:** alfresco dining at sunset; mainly seafood menu but a handful of other choices; raw oysters raised right here are sweet, on the smaller side, and beginner-friendly. 💲 *Average main: $25* ✉ *629 Succotash Rd., South Kingstown* ☎ *401/783–4202 ext. 1* 🌐 *www.rhodyoysters.com.*

Mews Tavern

$ | AMERICAN | This cheery tavern has three bars and 69 beers on tap, but hungry folks flock here for burgers and tasty pizzas—like the Pink Panther, which is topped with chicken, prosciutto, and pasta in a house-made pink vodka sauce. Also on the menu are Mexican dishes, mac and cheese with local Whalers beer in the sauce, and other comfort foods. **Known for:** going strong since 1947; appetizers, snacks, full entrées, and more; rare, limited, and local beers with "no crap on tap." 💲 *Average main: $15* ✉ *456 Main St., Wakefield* ☎ *401/783–9370* 🌐 *www.mewstavern.com.*

Tavern by the Sea

$$ | SEAFOOD | Lunch or dinner on the deck or patio at this Wickford restaurant is an essential part of a visit to North Kingstown's most scenic village. Watch fish swim and ducks paddle into the cove as you dine on Greek-inspired pizzas and sandwiches, salads and seafood entrees, or shared plates of mussels, calamari served Rhode Island or Asian-style, and stuffed Quahog clams. **Known for:** outdoor bar; waterfront dining; excellent gyros and souvlaki. 💲 *Average main: $24* ✉ *16 West Main St., North Kingstown*

☎ 401/294–5771 ⊕ *tavernbythesea ri.com*
⏲ *Closed Mon. and Nov.-Apr.*

Hotels

Preserve Sporting Club & Residences
$$$$ | RESORT | Set amid 3,500 acres of rural land in South County, the upscale Preserve has a large variety of lodging options from hotel suites in the Hilltop Lodge to dozens of tiny houses, condos, and entire homes. **Pros:** accommodations to suit every need and taste; unique dining experiences; remarkable array of activities available to overnight guests. **Cons:** overnight guests take a backseat to the needs of club members; activities are very expensive; opportunities for unguided exploration are limited. $ *Rooms from: $495* ✉ *87 Kingstown Rd., Richmond* ✣ *about 17 miles southwest of North Kingston via via Rte. 2 S and Rte. 138 W* ☎ *855/593–8473* ⊕ *preservesportingclub.com* *18 suites* *No Meals.*

Nightlife

For an extensive calendar of South County events pick up the free *South County Life, So Rhode Island* magazine, or browse ⊕ www.independentri.com/calendar.

Ocean Mist
BARS | The Ocean Mist has a beachfront deck where you can watch surfers on the point and catch some rays while enjoying a beer, a burger, or breakfast. Bands, including rock, throwback pop, and reggae acts, perform nightly in summer and on Thursdays and weekends the rest of the year. The music is free on Sunday Funday, but get there early, it's popular. Considered one of Rhode Island's best hangouts, "the Mist," as it's called by locals, is that cool beach bar that every coastal area has—or wishes it had.
✉ *895 Matunuck Beach Rd., Matunuck*
☎ *401/782–3740* ⊕ *www.oceanmist.net.*

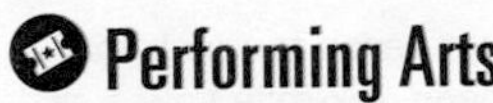

Performing Arts

★ **Theatre By The Sea**
THEATER | FAMILY | Since 1933, directors, choreographers, and performers have been coming from New York City to present a season of summer musicals, concerts, and events (including a children's festival) in an old 500-seat barn theater a quarter mile from the ocean. This is high-quality summer stock. Arrive early for dinner at the bistro on the property and to enjoy the stunning gardens. ✉ *364 Cards Pond Rd., Wakefield* ☎ *401/782–8587* ⊕ *www.theatrebythesea.com*
Varied ⏲ *Closed early Sept.–late May.*

Wickford Art Association
ARTS CENTERS | This gallery hosts juried arts shows and sponsors the Wickford Art Festival in July. The association's gallery at the North Kingstown Town Beach stages exhibitions by local artists and association members and offers painting classes. ✉ *36 Beach St., Wickford*
☎ *401/294–6840* ⊕ *www.wickfordart.org*
⏲ *Closed Mon.-Tues.*

Activities

BIKING

Quonset Bike Path
BIKING | This mostly flat, 2.7 mile (one way) out-and-back paved recreational path begins at Post Road and proceeds along the fringe of the Quonset Point commerce park to Calf Pasture Beach, where riders can dismount and enjoy a walk along Narragansett Bay before pedaling back. ✉ *Quonset Point, Newcomb Rd., North Kingstown* ☎ *401/294–2632*
⊕ *www.quonset.com.*

William C. O'Neill Bike Path
BIKING | FAMILY | This scenic 8-mile(ish) paved route, also known as the South County Bike Path, begins at Amtrak's Kingston train station in West Kingston and travels through farmlands, the Great Swamp, and downtown Peace Dale and Wakefield, ending close enough to

Narragansett Town Beach to reach the shore via local roads. A 2-mile spur trail leads to the Kingston campus of the University of Rhode Island. Public art, including a sanctioned graffiti tunnel, decorates the path. Where it crosses Main Street in Wakefield, a comfort station with restrooms is open during daylight hours. ✉ *1 Railroad Ave., South Kingstown* ☎ *401/789–9301* 🌐 *www.southcountybikepath.org.*

Shopping

Different Drummer

CRAFTS | This boutique shop has been a mainstay in Wickford Village since 1971, selling a wide variety of local crafts, stationary, glassware, pottery, and quirky gift items. It's a delight just to stroll around and admire the collection of unique and curious goods packing every shelf, and while you can spend hundreds on some one-of-a-kind items, the shop isn't so precious as to eschew a few $10 touristy trinkets, too. ✉ *7 West Main St., North Kingstown* ☎ *401/294-4867* 🌐 *www.differentdrummerri.com.*

Narragansett

6 miles east of South Kingstown, 30 miles south of Providence.

A summer resort destination during the Victorian era, Narragansett still has as its main landmark The Towers, the last remaining section of the 1886 Narragansett Pier Casino designed by McKim, Mead & White, which burned down in 1900. The town is much quieter now, but it has beautiful beaches and remains home to a large commercial fishing fleet. Take a scenic drive south from town on Ocean Road (Route 1A) to see the churning Atlantic and grand old shingle-style homes. You'll eventually wind up at Point Judith Lighthouse, which has been in continuous operation since the 19th century.

TOURS

Frances Fleet

BOAT TOURS | **FAMILY** | With four boats and expert captains who know just where the fish are biting and the whales are spouting, this tour company offers myriad on-water adventures. From June through early September, whale-watching excursions aboard the 105-foot *Lady Frances* take you through the impressive Block Island Wind Farm out to where you'll get a chance to spot finback whales and other species. Sightings are guaranteed, or you'll receive a voucher for a future sailing. The company also conducts a range of fishing trips, from beginner-friendly fluke chases to late night squid hunts. ✉ *Frances Fleet, 33 State St., Narragansett* ☎ *401/783–4988, 800/662–2824* 🌐 *www.francesfleet.com* 🎟 *From $65.*

Seven B's V

BOAT TOURS | Year-round, this tour service takes both novices and experienced anglers on memorable voyages. Even if you don't reel in a hefty cod or a googly eyed fluke, you'll learn about the species that inhabit these waters and appreciate your next fish dinner all the more. The 80-foot *Seven B's V* holds up to 113 passengers and departs daily, conditions permitting. ✉ *Port of Galilee Dock RR, 30 State St., Narragansett* ☎ *401/789–9250, 800/371–3474* 🌐 *www.sevenbs.com* 🎟 *from $55.*

Sights

Adventureland Narragansett

AMUSEMENT RIDE | **FAMILY** | Kids love the two kinds of bumper boats, nautical-theme miniature golf course, batting cages, carousel, go-kart track, and other carnival-like attractions, which all add up to great fun. ✉ *112 Point Judith Rd. (Rte. 108), Narragansett* ☎ *401/789–0030* 🌐 *www.adventurelandri.com* 🎟 *Admission is free; attractions from $4* ⏲ *Closed mid-Oct.–mid-Apr.*

Point Judith Lighthouse is just one of 21 such beacons in the Ocean State.

Point Judith Lighthouse

LIGHTHOUSE | From the Port of Galilee, it's a short drive to this 1857 lighthouse and a beautiful ocean view. Because the lighthouse is an active Coast Guard Station, only the grounds are open to the public. At times when the grounds are closed, head back out Ocean Road and watch for a tiny white sign on the left for the Fisherman's Memorial. A dirt road drive leads to this elevated park, from which you'll have a spectacular view of the 65-foot lighthouse, as well as to Camp Cronin, a secret beach and fishing area. ✉ *1460 Ocean Rd., Narragansett* ☎ *401/789–0444 U.S. Coast Guard Station Point Judith* 🎫 *Free.*

Port of Galilee

BEACH | **FAMILY** | This little corner of Narragansett is a working fishing village, where you can eat lobster on a deck overlooking the wharf, go for a swim at one of two state beaches, or watch fishermen unload their catch and sometimes even buy from them right on the docks. This is also the location of the mainland terminal for the ferry service to Block Island. ✉ *Great Island Rd., off Galilee Escape Rd., west from Rte. 108, Narragansett* ☎ *401/789–1044* 🌐 *www.narragansettri.gov/383/port-of-galilee.*

South County Museum

HISTORY MUSEUM | **FAMILY** | On part of Rhode Island's Civil War-era governor William Sprague's 19th-century estate, now a town park, this museum founded in 1933 holds 25,000 artifacts dating from pre-European settlement to the mid-20th century. Six exhibit buildings include a print shop, a blacksmith forge, a carpentry shop, and a carriage barn. A living-history farm has Romney sheep, Nubian goats, and a heritage flock of Rhode Island Red chickens, the state bird. Attending the annual chick-hatching is an Independence Day tradition for local families. ✉ *115 Strathmore St., Narragansett* ☎ *401/783–5400* 🌐 *www.southcountymuseum.org* 🎫 *$12* 🕒 *Closed mid-Oct. to mid-Apr., Sun.–Wed.*

Narragansett is the king of beaches in Rhode Island: the town has three state beaches and a town beach that's the focal point of the Narragansett Pier community.

Narragansett Town Beach

BEACH | **FAMILY** | This beloved and lively beach is perfect for surfing, sunbathing, people-watching, sandcastle making, crab hunting, and strolling its half-mile length; it also has seven ADA surf chairs, offered on a first-come, first-served basis. A sea wall (with free on-street parking) stretches along Ocean Road and attracts an eclectic crowd, including guitarists and motorcyclists. Covering approximately 19 acres, Narragansett Town Beach has a beautiful sandy beachfront, but it is the only beach in the state that you can't walk onto for free: the town charges (rather hefty) fees for admission (ages 12 and up) and parking. **Amenities:** food and drink; lifeguards; parking (fee); showers; toilets. **Best for:** surfing; swimming; nostalgic views. ✉ *39 Boston Neck Rd., Narragansett* ☎ *401/783–6430* 🌐 *www.narragansettri.gov/323/Narragansett-Town-Beach* 🎫 *$12; parking from $10.*

Roger W. Wheeler State Beach

BEACH | **FAMILY** | This breakwater-sheltered beach—which some locals still call Sand Hill Cove, even though the name changed decades ago—has calm, warm water and fine white sand that slopes gently into the water. It's a perennial favorite for parents with young children, thanks in part to the playground situated right in the sand. **Amenities:** food and drink; lifeguards; playground; parking (fee); showers; toilets. **Best for:** classic vibe; family time; swimming; walking. ✉ *100 Sand Hill Cove Rd., Narragansett* ☎ *401/789–8374* 🌐 *www.riparks.com/Locations/LocationRogerWheeler.html* 🎫 *Parking: from $12.*

Salty Brine State Beach

BEACH | Formerly known as Galilee State Beach, Salty Brine was renamed in 1990 for a Rhode Island radio legend. It's a small but popular destination, especially for foodies. Located near the state's largest commercial fishing port of Galilee, Salty Brine is permeated with the sights, sounds, and scents of Rhode Island's daily fishing culture. The 100-yard-long beach, near bustling seafood restaurants, provides the best seat in the state for viewing the steady parade of ferries, fishing boats, and charters moving in and out of the channel while noshing on a lobster roll or fried clams. People flock here for the annual Blessing of the Fleet parade of vessels on the last weekend in July. **Amenities:** food and drink; lifeguards; parking (fee); showers; toilets. **Best for:** saltwater fishing; sunset; swimming; walking. ✉ *254 Great Island Rd., Narragansett* ☎ *401/789–8374* 🌐 *www.riparks.com/Locations/LocationSaltyBrine.html* 🎫 *Parking: from $12.*

Scarborough State Beach

BEACH | **FAMILY** | With generally moderate surf, this 42-acre beach has stunning views of where the Narragansett Bay empties into the ocean—although the scent of the neighboring wastewater treatment plant can mar the experience. There's a concrete boardwalk with gazebos and an observation tower. A grassy section on the southern end of the beach is good for kite flying and picnicking, and a trail connects it to Black Point, a scenic fishing and hiking area along the rocky coastline. RIPTA buses service the beach, making it the easiest to access by transit. **Amenities:** food and drink; lifeguards; parking (fee); showers; toilets. **Best for:** surfing; swimming; walking; windsurfing. ✉ *870 Ocean Rd., Narragansett* ☎ *401/789–2324* 🌐 *riparks.com/beach/scarborough-north.php.*

Restaurants

★ Aunt Carrie's

$$$ | **SEAFOOD** | **FAMILY** | Family owned and operated for four generations, this iconic Point Judith indoor-outdoor dining spot has been a must for Rhode Islanders every summer since it opened in 1920. Its peerless, waterside location and unpretentious atmosphere are the main draws, along with favorites like steamers, fish-and-chips, and namesake Carrie Cooper's clam cakes, still made using the original recipe. **Known for:** complete shore dinners; delicious pies based on Carrie Cooper's recipes; picnic tables and an ice-cream stand across the street. *Average main: $25 ✉ 1240 Ocean Rd., Point Judith, Narragansett ☎ 401/783–7930 🌐 www.auntcarriesri.com ⏲ Closed Oct.–Mar.*

★ Coast Guard House

$$$ | **SEAFOOD** | Built in 1888 as a U.S. Life-Saving Service Station, this restaurant has been nearly destroyed twice by storms—by Hurricane Bob in 1991 and Superstorm Sandy in 2012. Regardless, the dining area has spectacular views of the ocean, the roof deck is a great hangout (try the frozen Dark 'n Stormy cocktail), and the patio is about as close to the sea as you could be without getting wet. **Known for:** raw bar and local seafood; alfresco drinks and dining on the deck; stunning view of Rhode Island Sound. *Average main: $27 ✉ 40 Ocean Rd., Narragansett ☎ 401/789–0700 🌐 www.thecoastguardhouse.com ⏲ Closed Mon.*

Crazy Burger Cafe & Juice Bar

$ | **ECLECTIC** | Vegetarians, vegans, and omnivores flock to this funky café not far from Narragansett Town Beach for smoothies, creative juice blends, and breakfast served until 4 pm daily. Signature burgers are categorized as "hoof, fin, and claw," but there are vegan options, too. **Known for:** extensive menu; often a wait to be seated; BYOB, but there is a corkage fee. *Average main: $14 ✉ 144 Boon St., Narragansett ☎ 401/783–1810 🌐 www.crazyburger.com.*

★ George's of Galilee

$$$ | **SEAFOOD** | Owned by the same family since 1948, this local landmark near Salty Brine State Beach has its own private patch of sand and beach blanket service in the summertime, along with a lively tiki bar. Try traditional Rhode Island favorites, including calamari, clam cakes, and "stuffies" (stuffed quahogs), as well as raw bar treats like oyster shooters. **Known for:** alfresco dining with spectacular waterfront views; summertime takeout clam shack and beach service; fish bowl cocktails. *Average main: $28 ✉ 250 Sand Hill Cove Rd., Port of Galilee, Narragansett ☎ 401/783–2306 🌐 www.georgesofgalilee.com.*

Spain of Narragansett

$$$ | **SPANISH** | This Spanish restaurant earns high marks for beautifully prepared and presented food and deft service; the paella is legendary. Arched architectural features and greenery help create a Mediterranean mood, and in summer you can dine on a patio anchored by a three-tier fountain and a massive brick fireplace. **Known for:** traditional seafood paella (for two); impressive wine list—plus sangria; well-run restaurant with upscale, professional service. *Average main: $26 ✉ 1144 Ocean Rd., Narragansett ☎ 401/783–9770 🌐 www.spainri.com ⏲ Closed Mon. and Tues. No lunch.*

Trio

$$ | **SEAFOOD** | Close to Narragansett Town Beach, this welcoming place emphasizes seafood, classic comfort food favorites like shaved steak sandwiches and shepherd's pie, and artisanal pizzas. The festive patio is where you'll want to be on a bright day, sipping summer flavors like watermelon, cucumber, and peach mixed into refreshingly creative cocktails. **Known for:** easy, free parking; more than 20 wines by the

glass; patio dining in summer. [$] *Average main: $22* ✉ *15 Kingstown Rd., Narragansett* ☎ *401/792–4333* 🌐 *www.trio-ri.com* ⏲ *No lunch weekdays.*

Hotels

★ The Break

$$$ | HOTEL | Narragansett's sole upscale boutique hotel has a laid-back boho surfer vibe—minus the feel of the cramped VW Vanagon—and on a clear day, you can see the Newport Bridge and Block Island from the Chair 5 rooftop bar and restaurant. **Pros:** complimentary gourmet small-plates breakfast; Chair 5, the restaurant named after a gathering spot at the town beach, serves locally sourced seasonal cuisine; spa services available. **Cons:** a hike to the beach; small signs, you might miss it the first drive by; two-night minimum on summer weekends. [$] *Rooms from: $379* ✉ *1208 Ocean Rd., Narragansett* ☎ *401/363–9800* 🌐 *www.thebreakhotel.com* *16 rooms* *Free Breakfast.*

The Shore House

$$ | HOTEL | Massive Victorian hotels once lined the sea wall in Narragansett Pier: the Shore House isn't quite that grand, but this boutique seafront inn is the first new hotel to open in town in many years, and it's a welcome addition. **Pros:** great location near beach and shopping; excellent on-site restaurant; some room with ocean views. **Cons:** no swimming pool; some rooms in a motel-like building; limited common areas for hotel guests. [$] *Rooms from: $199* ✉ *113 Ocean Rd., Narragansett* ☎ *855/652–0143* 🌐 *www.shorehouseri.com/* *31 rooms* *No Meals.*

Activities

BOATING

Narrow River Kayaks

BOATING | FAMILY | Narrow River Kayaks rents kayaks, canoes, and paddleboards for self-guided adventures on the tidal Narrow River and leads sunset tours, ECO tours, and full-moon paddles in the six-mile river's watershed and the John H. Chafee National Wildlife Refuge. Rent for as little as two hours or for multiple days. ✉ *94 Middlebridge Rd., Narragansett* ☎ *401/789–0334* 🌐 *www.narrowriverkayaks.com.*

SURFING

Narragansett Surf and Skate

SURFING | This shop rents surfboards, SUPs, and wet suits and offers individual and group skating, standup paddleboard, and surfing lessons—the latter led by East Coast surfing legend Peter Pan. Surf camps are offered in the spring, summer, and fall. ✉ *74 Narragansett Ave., Narragansett* ☎ *401/789–7890* 🌐 *narragansettsurfandskate.com.*

Block Island

Block Island, with its 1,400 year-round residents, is a laid-back community about 12 miles off Rhode Island's southern coast. The island has 17 miles of beaches that are all open to everyone. Despite the influx of summer visitors and thanks to the efforts of local conservationists, Block Island's beauty remains intact. More than 43% of the land is preserved, and the relatively small island's 365 freshwater ponds support some 150 bird species that migrate seasonally along the Atlantic Flyway.

Also known by its sole town's name, New Shoreham, Block Island is not all beaches and birds. Nightlife abounds in the summer at bars and restaurants, and it's casual—you can go anywhere in shorts and a T-shirt. The busiest season, when the population explodes to 15,000 to 20,000 per day, is May–mid-October. If you plan to stay overnight in the summer, make reservations well in advance: for weekends in July and August, booking in March is not too early. In the off-season, most restaurants, inns, stores, and visitor services close down, though some visitors brave the elements on Groundhog Day to join island residents who gather at a local pub for an informal census.

The island made national headlines when the Block Island Wind Farm, the first offshore wind farm in the nation, was built about 3 miles off the coast and, in December 2016, began supplying power to the island. The wind farm not only connected Block Island to the mainland electric power grid for the first time but also created a whole new industry for the island.

Cell service and Internet can be spotty here, especially when it is raining and the entire island seems to be trying to stream content simultaneously. GPS isn't terribly useful, because street addresses aren't commonly used.

GETTING HERE AND AROUND

AIR

New England Airlines operates frequent scheduled flights year-round between Westerly and Block Island State Airport.

Block Island State Airport. ✉ *4 Center Rd., New Shoreham* ☎ *401/466–5511* 🌐 *www.flyblockislandairport.com.* **New England Airlines.** ✉ *Westerly State Airport, 56 Airport Rd., Westerly* ☎ *401/596–2460, 800/243–2460* 🌐 *www.blockislandsairline.com.* **Westerly State Airport.** ✉ *56 Airport Rd., Westerly* ☎ *401/596–2357* 🌐 *https://www.flywesterlyairport.com/.*

CAR

A car isn't necessary on the island, but can be helpful if you're staying far from Old Harbor or visiting for a long time; there are no ride-share services like Uber or Lyft on the island. Bikes and mopeds are other fun options to get around the island.

Block Island Bike and Car Rental. ✉ *834 Ocean Ave., New Shoreham* ☎ *401/466–2297* 🌐 *www.blockislandbikeandcarrental.com.*

FERRY

There's year-round car-and-passenger ferry service to Block Island from the Port of Galilee, in the town of Narragansett in Rhode Island's South County. Seasonal passenger-only ferry service is available from Newport; New London, Connecticut; and Montauk, New York. Most ferry companies permit bicycles; the charge for bicycles runs $3.50–$10 each way.

The most heavily trafficked route is Block Island Ferry's car-passenger service and high-speed passenger service between Point Judith Terminal in Galilee, on the mainland, and Block Island's Old Harbor. By traditional ferry, the 55-minute trip costs about $12 one-way for passengers (rates fluctuate with oil prices) and $40 one-way for automobiles. Ferries run from one to three times per day in winter to eight or nine times per day in summer. Make car reservations well ahead by telephone. Arrive 45 minutes ahead in high season to allow time to find parking in the pay lots ($5–$15 per day) that surround the docks. From early June to mid-October daily (and Friday through Sunday until late November, plus daily Thanksgiving week), the high-speed service makes two to six 30-minute trips ($25.50 one-way) along the same route. There is no auto service on the high-speed ferry, but you can bring a bicycle ($4; electric bikes $10); passenger reservations are recommended.

Block Island Ferry also operates seasonal high-speed service from Newport's Perrotti Park to Old Harbor. The passengers-only ferry makes two trips a day, each way, from late June through Labor Day. One-way rates are about $25.50; online reservations are recommended. Approximate sailing time is 60 minutes.

From late May through Labor Day, passenger-only ferries operated by Block Island Express run between New London, Connecticut, and Old Harbor. The ferries depart from New London several times a day and take about 80

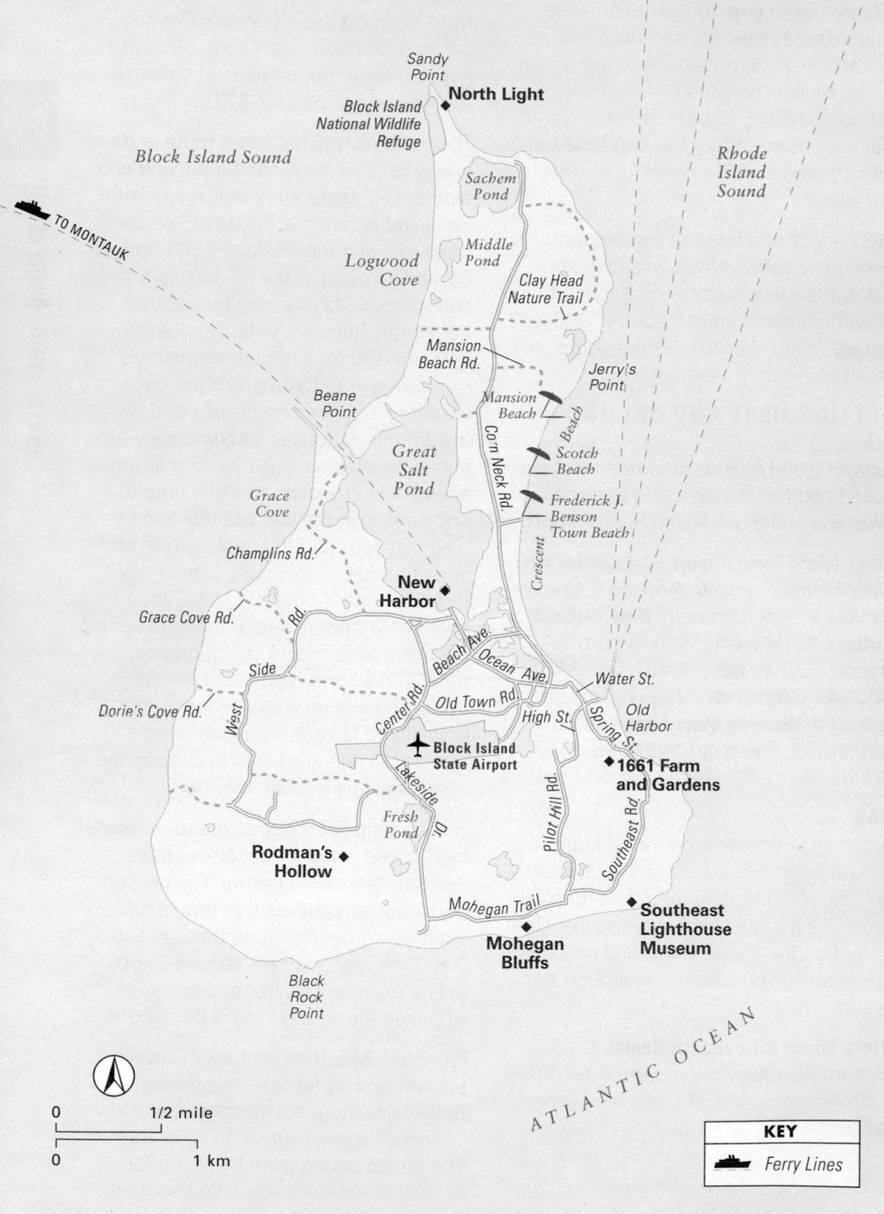
Block Island
TO NEW LONDON, CT
TO POINT JUDITH
TO NEWPORT
TO MONTAUK
Sandy Point
North Light
Block Island National Wildlife Refuge
Block Island Sound
Rhode Island Sound
Sachem Pond
Middle Pond
Logwood Cove
Clay Head Nature Trail
Mansion Beach Rd.
Jerry's Point
Mansion Beach
Beane Point
Crescent Beach
Scotch Beach
Great Salt Pond
Corn Neck Rd.
Frederick J. Benson Town Beach
Grace Cove
Champlins Rd.
New Harbor
Grace Cove Rd.
Beach Ave.
Ocean Ave.
Water St.
Side
West
Dorie's Cove Rd.
Center Rd.
Old Town Rd.
High St.
Old Harbor
Spring St.
Block Island State Airport
1661 Farm and Gardens
Lakeside Dr.
Pilot Hill Rd.
Southeast Rd.
Fresh Pond
Rodman's Hollow
Mohegan Trail
Southeast Lighthouse Museum
Mohegan Bluffs
Black Rock Point
ATLANTIC OCEAN
0
1/2 mile
0
1 km
KEY
Ferry Lines

minutes. Tickets are about $31.25 one-way; bikes cost $10. Reservations are recommended.

Viking Fleet runs high-speed passenger service from Montauk, Long Island, to New Harbor on Block Island from Memorial Day through Columbus Day. The boat departs from Montauk at 10 am and leaves Block Island at 2 pm, plus an additional trip on Sundays in July and August that departs from Block Island at noon and Montauk at 5 pm. The fare is $40 one-way; bicycles are allowed. Travel time is one hour and 15 minutes.

Taxi cabs typically gather at the ferry terminal as boats arrive.

Block Island Express. ✉ *2 Ferry St., New London* ☎ *401/466–2212, 860/444–4624* 🌐 *www.goblockisland.com.* **Block Island Ferry.** ✉ *304 Great Island Rd., Narragansett* ☎ *401/783–7996, 866/783–7996* 🌐 *www.blockislandferry.com.* **Viking Fleet.** ✉ *462 W. Lake Dr., Montauk* ☎ *631/668–5700* 🌐 *www.vikingfleet.com.*

VISITOR INFORMATION

CONTACTS Block Island Chamber of Commerce. ✉ *120 Water St., New Shoreham* ☎ *401/466–2474* 🌐 *www.blockislandchamber.com.* **Block Island Tourism Council.** ✉ *40 Center Road, New Shoreham* ☎ *401/466–2474* 🌐 *www.blockislandinfo.com.*

Sights

★ Mohegan Bluffs

BEACH | FAMILY | The dramatic 200-foot clay cliffs along Mohegan Trail, one of the island's top sights, offer a craggy beauty not found anywhere else in New England. On a clear day you can see all the way to Montauk Point on Long Island. The bluffs can be enjoyed from street level, but to access the beach below requires descending a steep set of 141 stairs that lead to the bottom. The cove to the west has a narrow strip of secluded sandy beach, with wave action that attracts surfers. Wear walking shoes, and don't attempt the descent unless you're in reasonably good shape, as you may have to scramble over rocks at the base of the stairs. Remember, you'll also have to climb back up! ✉ *Mohegan Bluffs Trailhead, 289 Spring St., New Shoreham.*

New Harbor

BUSINESS DISTRICT | The Great Salt Pond has a culture all its own, centered on the three marinas, several inns, a resort hotel, and the restaurants clustered along its southern shore that make up this commercial area about a 30-minute walk from Old Harbor. Up to 2,000 boats create a forest of masts on summer weekends, drawn by sail races and fishing tournaments. Over on the quiet north and east shores, clammers and windsurfers claim the tidal flats. The Montauk ferry docks at Champlin's, the largest of the marinas. ✉ *Great Salt Pond, New Shoreham.*

North Light

TRAIL | FAMILY | An 1867 granite lighthouse on the northern tip of Block Island (the fourth lighthouse on this site), North Light also serves as a maritime museum. The surrounding Block Island National Wildlife Refuge is home to American oystercatchers, piping plovers, and other rare migrating birds. From a parking lot at the end of Corn Neck Road, it's a ½-mile hike over sand to the lighthouse. Seals sun themselves on nearby Sandy Point in winter, and some even summer here. ✉ *Block Island National Wildlife Refuge, Corn Neck Rd., New Shoreham* ☎ *401/364–9124* 🌐 *www.fws.gov/refuge/block-island* 🎫 *Suggested donation.*

★ Rodman's Hollow

NATURE PRESERVE | FAMILY | This easy-to-find nature preserve is many people's first point of contact with the island's Greenway Trails system. The main trail runs south about 1 mile to clay bluffs with great ocean views, from which a winding path descends to the rocky beach below. Side trails cross the

230-acre tract, offering longer hikes and the allure of getting mildly lost. The striking, if muted, natural beauty makes it easy to understand why, 40 years ago, this was the property that first awoke the local land conservation movement, now close to achieving its goal of preserving half the island. Geology buffs will appreciate this fine example of a glacial outwash basin. Nature lovers may enjoy looking for the Block Island meadow vole (field mouse), the northern harrier (a threatened raptor species), and the American burying beetle (the equally imperiled state insect). A small parking lot sits just south of Cooneymus Road near a stone marker. ✉ *Cooneymus Rd., New Shoreham* 🌐 *www.nature.org/en-us/get-involved/how-to-help/places-we-protect/block-island/.*

1661 Farm and Gardens

FARM/RANCH | FAMILY | Animals you know and love and some you never knew existed—like the zedonk, a cross between a zebra and a donkey—are on display at this farm. Camels, llamas, kangaroos, and even fainting goats (whose legs stiffen when they get excited, causing them to keel over) will all gladly munch pellets out of your hand. Lemurs leap around their own enclosure, and a herd of gentle alpacas provides fibers for the adjacent North Light Fibers textile mill and shop. ✉ *Off Spring St., New Shoreham* ☎ *401/466–2421* 🌐 *www.blockislandresorts.com/exotic-farm-and-gardens* 🎫 *Free.*

Southeast Lighthouse Museum

LIGHTHOUSE | The small museum is housed inside an 1875 redbrick lighthouse with striking architectural details. The lighthouse, which was moved back 300 feet from the eroded clay cliffs of Mohegan Bluffs, is a National Historic Landmark. Tower tours are offered during the summer. ✉ *122 Mohegan Tr., New Shoreham* ☎ *401/466–5009* 🎫 *Museum $10; Tower tour $15; combination $20* 🕓 *Closed Mon.–Fri. in fall, closed Columbus Day–Memorial Day.*

Beaches

Block Island is ringed by 17 miles of ocean beaches, all open free to the public. Beaches on the eastern side of the island, in particular, have calm, warm waters that are ideal for swimming June–September.

★ Crescent Beach

BEACH | This 3-mile beach runs north from Old Harbor, and its white sands become wider and the crowds thinner the farther away from town you go. It is divided into smaller beaches with access points off Corn Neck Road. Farthest north is Mansion Beach: look for the sign, then follow the dirt road to the right. From the parking area, it's a short hike to reach what is easily one of New England's most beautiful beaches. In the morning, you might spot deer on the dunes; to the north, surfers can often be seen dotting Jerry's Point. Closer to Old Harbor, Scotch Beach, with its small parking lot directly off Corn Neck Road, attracts a lively crowd of young adults. Fred Benson Town Beach, in the middle, is where you'll find facilities. **Amenities:** food and drink; lifeguards; parking (no fee); showers; toilets. **Best for:** sunrise; sunset; swimming; walking. ✉ *Corn Neck Rd., New Shoreham.*

Restaurants

The Beachead

$$$ | SEAFOOD | FAMILY | The food—baked Atlantic cod, shrimp and pea pasta, lobster rolls—is consistently great, the price is right, and you won't feel like a tourist at this local favorite. Catch ocean breezes on the patio, or in stormy weather sit at the bar and watch breakers roll in 30 feet away. **Known for:** Block Island-caught lobster cooked four ways; children's menu; alfresco dining on the patio or porch. [$] *Average main: $28* ✉ *598 Corn*

Neck Rd., New Harbor, New Shoreham ☎ 401/466–2249 🌐 www.beacheadbi.com ⏲ Closed mid-Sept.–May.

★ Block Island Oyster Bar & Grill
$$$ | **AMERICAN** | Open up your meal with oysters Thermidor, Japanese style with miso, or grilled and topped with Parmesan cheese. Sip a fine vintage, relax, and pause to appreciate the sublime garden setting—complete with hopping rabbits nibbling at the landscaping—before diving into sea scallops served over lemon risotto or grilled sticky Thai shrimp. **Known for:** oyster bar; dining in gorgeous gardens; attentive service. $ *Average main: $30 ✉ Hotel Manisses, 251 Spring St., Old Harbor, New Shoreham ☎ 401/466–9898 hotel, 401/402–9225 dining reservations 🌐 www.hotelmanisses.com/dine ⏲ Closed Wed. and Oct.–late May.*

Eli's
$$$ | **AMERICAN** | Creative cuisine emerges from the kitchen of this intimate bistro—the fare changes seasonally but may include pan-seared sea scallops, brined chicken, and the mouthwatering Eli's burger with seasoned fries. Arrive before opening and join the queue for a table; if they're all taken, dining at the bar, accompanied by excellent craft cocktails, is a small compromise. **Known for:** Rhode Island–caught tuna; vegetarian menu; hugely popular with locals. $ *Average main: $35 ✉ 456 Chapel St., Old Harbor, New Shoreham ☎ 401/466–5230 🌐 www.elisblockisland.com ⏲ Closed Jan.–mid-Mar. No lunch.*

Poor People's Pub
$ | **AMERICAN** | The black 1961 Ford Galaxie parked out front is the landmark steering you to this fun indoor-outdoor restaurant, bar, and night spot in Old Harbor. Find a table on the porch or in the garden and dig into the house specialty, barbecued pulled pork mac & cheese, washed down with a margarita blended with a local blackberry and honey puree. **Known for:** big menu with everything from pub food to fine dining; porch and patio dining; live music, DJs and themed parties. $ *Average main: $16 ✉ 33 Ocean Ave., New Shoreham ☎ 401/446–8533 🌐 www.pppbi.com ⏲ Closed Nov.–mid Apr.*

Coffee and Quick Bites

Payne's Donuts
$ | **AMERICAN** | In a state that takes its doughnuts seriously, the best doughy orbs require an island jaunt. Now served from a humble food truck, Payne's "killer" doughnuts have been a summer morning tradition for generations. **Known for:** an inexpensive treat; worth the mile-long walk or bike ride from the ferry dock; limited beverages and other menu items. $ *Average main: $2 ✉ 216 Ocean Ave., New Shoreham ⏲ Closed Columbus Day–late June.*

Hotels

It's advisable to book accommodations well in advance, especially for weekends in July and August when many hotels require a two-night minimum. The Block Island Chamber of Commerce tracks last-minute availability at member properties. Many visitors rent homes for stays of a week or more. Blockislandreservations.com is a good resource for booking a room, but there are many direct rentals not listed on booking sites.

★ The Atlantic Inn
$$ | **HOTEL** | Perched on a hill amid floral gardens and undulating lawns, away from the hubbub of the Old Harbor area, this classic Victorian (1879) resort dazzles guests with its big windows, high ceilings, sweeping staircase, and mesmerizing views. **Pros:** spectacular hilltop location; beautiful veranda for whiling away the afternoon; grand decor; excellent Restaurant 1879 serves small and large plates. **Cons:** an uphill trek from the ferry dock; no handicap-accessible rooms; no TV in most rooms and slow Internet in the lobby only. $ *Rooms from:*

$250 ✉ 359 High St., Old Harbor, New Shoreham ☎ 401/466–5883, 800/224–7422 🌐 www.atlanticinn.com ⏲ Closed mid-Oct.–early May 🛏 23 rooms.

The Barrington Inn
$$ | **B&B/INN** | **FAMILY** | This 19th-century Victorian farmhouse, high on a hill overlooking Great Salt Pond, is now a quiet, refreshed, and bright B&B inn with water views from most rooms. **Pros:** commanding views; reasonably priced; close to beaches. **Cons:** three-night minimum on July and August weekends; extra nightly fee for children ages six and up; breakfast not included for weekly guests. 💲 *Rooms from: $200 ✉ 584 Beach Ave., New Harbor, New Shoreham ☎ 401/347–3646 🌐 www.barringtoninnbi.com ⏲ Closed Dec.–Apr. 🛏 9 units 🍽 Free Breakfast.*

Champlin's Hotel, Marina and Resort
$$$$ | **RESORT** | A rarity on Block Island, this full-service resort is outside of town, making it a quiet oasis from the summer bustle in New Harbor. **Pros:** newly renovated rooms are bright and comfortable; cafe opens early for breakfast and has seating on an outside deck; free bikes for use by hotel guests. **Cons:** remodeling hasn't yet touched some parts of property; no beach; ferry terminal and Old Harbor not within walking distance (about a 10-minute bike ride). 💲 *Rooms from: $575 ✉ 80 West Side Rd., Newport ☎ 800/762–4541, 401/466–7777 🌐 www.champlinsresort.com/ 🛏 46 rooms.*

★ Payne's Harbor View Inn
$$ | **B&B/INN** | This 2002 inn, designed to blend with the island's historic architecture, occupies a breezy hillside overlooking the Great Salt Pond and is just minutes from Crescent Beach. **Pros:** free parking; kayak and paddleboard rentals; handicap ramp and ADA accessible shower in Room 1. **Cons:** books up fast; no children under 12; about a mile from "town". 💲 *Rooms from: $235 ✉ 111 Beach Ave., corner of Ocean Ave., New Shoreham ⊕ New Harbor ☎ 401/466–5758 🌐 www.paynesharborviewinn.com ⏲ Closed mid-Oct.–late May 🛏 10 rooms 🍽 Free Breakfast.*

★ Spring House Hotel
$$$ | **HOTEL** | **FAMILY** | This charming old (1852) seaside inn—the island's oldest, largest, and most famous hotel—has rooms that suit today's expectations with a welcoming atmosphere and panoramic island or ocean views. **Pros:** stunning views from the breezy front porch; happily accommodates infants and children; farm-to-table, indoor-outdoor dining on-site from June–September. **Cons:** dining areas sometimes closed for private events; no elevator; about a 15-minute walk to the activity at Old Harbor. 💲 *Rooms from: $395 ✉ 52 Spring St., Old Harbor, New Shoreham ☎ 401/466–5844 🌐 www.springhouseblockisland.com ⏲ Closed Nov.–Apr. 🛏 50 rooms, 16 units 🍽 No Meals.*

 Nightlife

Nightlife, at least in season, is one of Block Island's highlights—and you have your pick of some two dozen places to grab a drink. Check the Block Island Chamber's online calendar for music and entertainment listings.

Ballard's Beach Resort
DANCE CLUBS | On its own private beach, Ballard's has oceanfront tiki bars, VIP cabana rentals, and a barnlike restaurant with a dance floor and live music. It tends to be livelier by day, although you can also arrange for a private beach bonfire at night. *✉ 42 Water St., Old Harbor, New Shoreham ☎ 401/466–2231, 844/405–3275 🌐 www.ballardsbi.com ⏲ Closed Oct.-May.*

Captain Nick's Rock n' Roll Bar
PIANO BARS | This place sets itself apart from the others by hosting June's Block Island Music Festival, a free roundup of soon-to-be-discovered bands from around the country. It has live music inside and out, a dog-friendly area, frozen

cocktails, and a suntanned crowd. Disco Monday has been an island tradition for more than two decades. ✉ *34 Ocean Ave., New Shoreham* ☎ *401/466–5670* 🌐 *www.captainnicksbi.com* ⏲ *Closed mid-Oct. to late May.*

Club Soda

BARS | Club Soda is a lively hangout with a 12x8-foot outdoor TV. Shoot pool or tuck into some tasty pub grub. Live music, trivia, karaoke, musical Bingo, and outdoor movies keep the weeknight scene lively. ✉ *35 Connecticut Ave., New Shoreham* ☎ *401/466–5397* 🌐 *www.clubsodabiri.com* ⏲ *Closed mid-Oct. to May 1.*

Mahogany Shoals

LIVE MUSIC | A tiny shack built over the water at Payne's Dock, Mahogany Shoals has a laid-back vibe and live music every night. The place has expanded, gracefully, with an outdoor bar and an upper-level deck. It remains the best spot on the island to enjoy a quiet drink, peer at beautiful yachts, and catch a breeze on even the hottest of nights. ✉ *Payne's Dock, 218 Ocean Ave., New Harbor, New Shoreham* ☎ *401/864-3832* 🌐 *paynes-dock.com* ⏲ *Closed Labor Day-Memorial Day.*

Yellow Kittens Tavern

LIVE MUSIC | Patrons here amuse themselves with darts, pinball, table tennis, and pool, to the sound of live bands or DJs on many summer nights. By day, order drinks and a big plate of nachos on Los Gatitos Deck overlooking the dunes at the southern end of Crescent Beach. ✉ *214 Corn Neck Rd., New Harbor, New Shoreham* ☎ *401/466–5855* 🌐 *www.yellowkittens.com* ⏲ *Closed Nov.-April.*

Activities

BIKING

The best way to explore Block Island is by bicycle ($20–$30 a day to rent) or moped (from $35 per hour, from $95 per day). Most rental places are open spring–fall and offer baby seats and tag-alongs for bikes and free helmets (required for those under 16). All rent bicycles in various styles and sizes, including mountain bikes, comfort cruisers, tandems, and children's bikes. The tourism office has a free bike tour map that organizes a dozen marked stops into a 7.5-mile loop ride.

Island Moped and Bike Rentals

BIKING | FAMILY | This shop has bikes (single and tandem) and scooters for hourly, daily, multiday, and weekly rentals. Pickup is free from anywhere on the island; discounts are available for groups of three or more. For $5 they'll also rent you a foldable beach chair that you can carry on your bike or moped. ✉ *41 Water St., Old Harbor* ☎ *401/466–2700* 🌐 *www.bimopeds.com.*

Old Harbor Bike Shop

BIKING | FAMILY | Descend from the Block Island Ferry and hop right on a bike at this shop, which rents cruisers, tandems, and baby seats, tag-alongs, and trailers, as well as mopeds, Jeeps, and cars. ✉ *1 Water St., south of ferry dock, New Shoreham* ☎ *401/466–2029* 🌐 *blockislandmoped.com.*

BOATING

Fort Island Kayaks & SUPs

KAYAKING | FAMILY | Kayaks and standup paddleboards (including pedalboards) are available for all ages and abilities and may be rented by the hour, half- or full-day, or week. A single kayak or SUP rents for about $100 per day. ✉ *Block Island Fishworks, 40 Ocean Ave., New Harbor, New Shoreham* ☎ *401/466–5392, 401/742-3992* 🌐 *www.sandypointco.com* ⏲ *Closed Nov.–Apr.*

★ Pond and Beyond Kayak

BOATING | FAMILY | Guided paddling ecotours around the Great Salt Pond are a specialty here, as are family and full moon kayak tours. Located on the Block Island Maritime Institute property, this outfitter also rents single and double kayaks and provides a brief introduction for those who want to explore for an hour or more on their own. Standup paddleboards also are available to rent. Call for reservations—online booking isn't an option. ✉ *216 Ocean Ave., corner West Side Rd., New Harbor, New Shoreham* ☎ *401/578–2773* 🌐 *www.pondandbeyondkayak.com* 🕐 *Closed mid-Oct.–late May.*

FISHING

Most of Rhode Island's record-setting fish have been caught off Block Island, including a 77.4-pound whopper caught in 2011. From almost any beach, skilled anglers can land tautog and bass. The Coast Guard channel is a good spot to hook porgy. Shellfishing licenses ($20 for 7 days) may be obtained at the harbormaster's building at the Boat Basin in New Harbor. Call 401-466-3204 for information.

Block Island Fishworks

FISHING | A tiny shop in New Harbor, Block Island Fishworks sells bait and tackle and rents rods and reels. It also offers guide services and charter fishing trips targeting stripers, blues, sea bass, bonito, albies, and fluke. A pair of boats can be chartered for half-, three-quarter, and full-day fishing trips; options include light tackle, fly fishing, and bottom-dweller fishing. ✉ *40 Ocean Ave., New Shoreham* ☎ *401/742–3992, 401/466–5392* 🌐 *www.sandypointco.com.*

HIKING

★ Clay Head Nature Trail

HIKING & WALKING | **FAMILY** | The outstanding Clay Head Nature Trail meanders past Clay Head Swamp and along 150-foot clay bluffs. Songbirds chirp and flowers bloom along the paths; stick close to the ocean for a stunning hike that ends at Sachem Pond or venture into the interior's intertwining paths for hours of wandering and blackberrying in an area called The Maze. The trailhead is recognizable by a simple white post marker on the east side of Corn Neck Road, about 2 miles north of Old Harbor. ✉ *Clay Head Trail, New Shoreham* 🌐 *www.nature.org.*

WATER SPORTS

Diamondblue Surf Shop

WATER SPORTS | This shop stocks surf gear and offers wet suit, boogie board, surfboard, and standup paddleboard rentals. Their instructors will get you up riding waves in a 1.5-hour surfing lesson. Discounted surfer clothing is on display on the front lawn; the pricier stuff is inside the shop. ✉ *442 Dodge St., corner Corn Neck Rd., New Harbor, New Shoreham* ☎ *401/466–3145* 🌐 *www.diamondbluebi.com.*

Shopping

ART GALLERIES

Jessie Edwards Studio

ART GALLERIES | This gallery specializes in the work of local and regional artists: photographs, sculptures, ceramics, and contemporary American paintings, often with coastal themes. Works from more than 30 artists are on display at the gallery overlooking Old Harbor from the second floor of the Post Office building. ✉ *Post Office Bldg., 32 Water St., 2nd fl., New Shoreham* ✣ *Old Harbor* ☎ *401/466–5314* 🌐 *www.jessieedwardsgallery.com* 🕐 *By appointment only Jan.-April.*

Malcolm Greenaway Gallery

ART GALLERIES | Malcolm Greenaway has taken magnificent photographs of Block Island places and scenes since moving here in 1974. In his Water Street gallery, he sells prints in various sizes—print only, matted, or matted and framed. Come in and meet the artist himself: he's usually around when the shop is open. ✉ *Water St., Old Harbor, New Shoreham* ☎ *401/466–5331, 800/840–5331* 🌐 *www.malcolmgreenaway.com.*

Spring Street Gallery

ART GALLERIES | The gallery, located in a renovated horse barn for nearly 40 years, exhibits paintings, photographs, pottery, and jewelry by island artists and artisans. The rustic gallery also serves as a community arts center, hosting artist openings, art classes, movie screenings, and lectures. ✉ *105 Spring St., Old Harbor, New Shoreham* ☎ *401/466–5374* 🌐 *www.springstreetgallery.org* ⏲ *Closed Mon.-Wed. in fall; closed Columbus Day-Memorial Day.*

JEWELRY

Golddiggers

JEWELRY & WATCHES | You can pick up handmade pendants, rings, earrings, and bracelets with maritime (and Block Island) themes at this jewelry store. ✉ *90 Chapel St., Old Harbor, New Shoreham* ☎ *401/466–2611* 🌐 *www.blockislandgolddiggers.com.*

Jamestown

31 miles south of Providence, 5 miles west of Newport.

Surrounded by Narragansett Bay's East and West passages, Conanicut Island comprises the town of Jamestown. About 9 miles long and 1 mile wide, the island is home to beautiful state parks, historic Beavertail Lighthouse, farmland, and a downtown village with a quaint mix of shops and restaurants.

Sights

Beavertail State Park

CITY PARK | FAMILY | Water conditions range from tranquil to harrowing at this park straddling the southern tip of Conanicut Island. In rough weather, waves crash dramatically (and dangerously) on the rocky point. On a clear, calm day, however, the park's craggy shoreline invites for sunning, hiking, and climbing. There are portable restrooms open daily, year-round. On several dates (July–October), the Beavertail Lighthouse Museum Association opens the 1856 Beavertail Lighthouse, the nation's third-oldest lighthouse, letting you climb the tower's 49 steps (and then a 7-foot ladder) to enjoy the magnificent panorama from the observation catwalk. A museum occupies the lighthouse keeper's former quarters; the lighthouse's last "beehive" Fresnel lens is on display. The old fog signal building has a saltwater aquarium with local species of fish. Both are open seasonally. ✉ *Beavertail Rd., Jamestown* ☎ *401/884–9834* 🌐 *www.riparks.com/parks/beavertail.php* 🎟 *Free.*

Jamestown Fire Department Memorial Museum

HISTORY MUSEUM | FAMILY | A working 1859 hand pumper and an 1894 horse-drawn steam pump are among the antique equipment at this informal firefighting equipment display in a garage that once housed the fire company. Inquire at the fire station next door if the place is locked; the town fire chief or whoever is on duty is usually happy to show visitors around. ✉ *50 Narragansett Ave., Jamestown* ☎ *401/423–0062* 🌐 *www.jamestownfd.com* 🎟 *Free.*

Jamestown Windmill

WINDMILL | This English-designed smock windmill built in 1787 ground corn for more than 100 years. One of the most photographed sights on the island, the structure, named for its resemblance to farmers' smocks of yore, still works. In summer and early fall, you can enter the three-story, octagonal structure and see the 18th-century technology. The windmill turns on the biennial Windmill Day, when the sails are attached to catch the breeze on Windmill Hill. ✉ *North Rd., north of Weeden La., Jamestown* ☎ *401/423–0784 summer, 401/423–7202 year-round* 🌐 *www.jamestownhistoricalsociety.org* 🎟 *Free* ⏲ *Closed mid-Oct.–mid-June and Mon.–Thurs.*

Watson Farm

FARM/RANCH | FAMILY | This Historic New England–operated farm on Narragansett Bay, in existence since 1789, is still a working farm. The farmers use sustainable practices to raise heritage-breed cows and sheep and to produce wool blankets for local markets. They also host educational programs; for example, during the annual Sheep Shearing Day in May you can visit the baby lambs, see the flock being shorn by local shearers, and watch spinning and weaving demonstrations. You can also stroll more than 2 miles of trails and view seasonal farm activities. ✉ *455 North Rd., Jamestown* ☎ *401/423–0005* 🌐 *www.historicnewengland.org/property/watson-farm* 🎟 *$10* ⏲ *Closed Oct.-May; Closed Sun.-Wed. and Fri., in June and Sept.; closed Sun., Wed., and Fri. in July and August.*

Restaurants

★ Beech

$$ | AMERICAN | With five indoor and outdoor dining areas, this casually elegant restaurant is the center of Jamestown nightlife in the summer, especially at its expansive open-air bar. A 150-year-old beech tree in the courtyard lends its name to the locally owned restaurant, which has retained key staff from the former Trattoria Simpatico at the same location and menu highlights include local calimari, a hot lobster roll, housemade pasta, and grilled seafood dishes. **Known for:** outdoor bar scene; photo-worthy decor and dishes; fresh seafood. [$] *Average main: $23* ✉ *13 Narragansett Ave., Jamestown* ☎ *401/560–4051* 🌐 *www.beechjt.com* ⏲ *No lunch.*

Hotels

East Bay Bed & Breakfast

$$ | B&B/INN | This 1892 Victorian is peaceful day and night, even though it's only a block from Jamestown's two main streets and ferry wharf. **Pros:** quick, easy access to Newport; large rooms; fine, Massachusetts-made Matouk bedding. **Cons:** small showers; only three parking spaces; no kids under 13. [$] *Rooms from: $225* ✉ *14 Union St., Jamestown* ☎ *401/423–0330, 800/243–1107* 🌐 *www.eastbaybnb.com* 🛏 *5 rooms* 🍽 *Free Breakfast.*

Newport

34 miles south of Providence, 72 miles south of Boston.

The Gilded Age mansions on Bellevue Avenue are the go-to attraction for many Newport visitors. These ornate, late-19th-century "cottages," designed for very wealthy New Yorkers, are almost obscenely grand. Their owners—Vanderbilts, Astors, Belmonts, and other budding aristocrats who made Newport their summer playground for a mere six- to eight weeks each year—helped establish the best young American architects and precipitated the arrival of the New York Yacht Club, which turned Newport into the sailing capital of the world.

Newport's music festivals are another draw: Bob Dylan famously went electric at the Newport Folk Festival; in recent years, the outdoor festival has featured up-and-coming and internationally known indie and folk bands. In its earlier days, the Newport Jazz Festival hosted the likes of Miles Davis and Frank Sinatra; today it remains a showcase of traditional and avant-garde jazz. The Newport Music Festival brings classical music to the mansions, many of the artists and ensembles making their American debuts.

History buffs are enthralled by the large collection of Colonial-era architecture—Trinity Episcopal Church, Touro Synagogue, and the Colony House among them—reveling in these monuments to Newport's past as a haven for seekers of religious freedom.

Pedestrian-friendly Newport has so much else to offer in such a relatively small geographical area—beaches, seafood restaurants, galleries, shopping, and cultural life. Summer can be extremely busy, but fall and spring are almost as nice and far less crowded, and winter by the sea can be magical and soul-soothing.

GETTING HERE AND AROUND

You'll need to cross at least one of four major bridges to reach Newport. The largest is the Claiborne Pell Newport Bridge, spanning Narragansett Bay's East Passage via Route 138 and linking the island community of Jamestown with Newport. The toll is $6 both ways for motorists. Newport anchors Aquidneck Island, also home to the towns of Middletown and Portsmouth. From the north end of Portsmouth, Route 24 takes you across the Sakonnet River Bridge to Tiverton. Follow Route 77 south through Tiverton to reach quiet Little Compton. From the northwestern end of Portsmouth, you cross the Mt. Hope Bridge to reach the charming towns of Bristol and Warren in Bristol County, home to the oldest continuously held Independence Day celebration in the country. The Jamestown Verrazzano Bridge connects Jamestown to North Kingstown over Narragansett Bay's West Passage.

CAR

In Newport several lots around town offer pay parking. The largest and most economical is the Gateway parking lot and garage at 23 America's Cup Avenue, where the rate is $2 for the first half-hour, $1.50 for each additional half-hour, from June–October. Parking is free November–April. Street parking can be difficult to find in summer.

FERRY

Visitors headed to Newport from the west can save themselves the hassle of parking in Newport, as well as the Newport Bridge toll, by parking their cars for free (if they're lucky to find street parking) in Jamestown and boarding the Jamestown Newport Ferry. Conanicut Marine Services operates this open-air passenger ferry from 1 East Ferry Wharf in Jamestown and offers a free shuttle service from a large paid parking area at 260 Conanicus Avenue. The ferry runs daily, early June–mid-October. The ferry links the village of Jamestown to Rose Island, Ft. Adams State Park, Perrotti Park, and Ann Street Pier. A $27 round-trip, hop-on/hop-off rate is good for all day, but one-way passage rates and bicycle/stroller rates are available. In the summer, ferry service starts at 9 am in Jamestown, and the last run leaves Newport around 9:30 pm. The ferry operates on an abbreviated schedule in spring and fall.

Oldport Marine Services operates a Newport Harbor shuttle service Monday–Thursday noon–6 and on Friday and weekends 11–7 ($12 hop on/off all day). The shuttle lands at Perrotti Park, Bowen's Wharf, Ann Street Pier, the Sail Newport dock, Ft. Adams, and Goat Island.

Seastreak operates seasonal ferry service (Memorial Day–Columbus Day) between Providence (India Point) and Newport (Perrotti Park). The fare is $12 each way, and parking is free at the Providence Ferry Terminal; a complimentary shuttle bus makes several trips between the ferry terminal and the train station, convention center, and downtown.

Jamestown Newport Ferry. ✉ *1 E. Ferry Wharf, Jamestown* ☎ *401/423–9900* 🌐 *www.jamestownnewportferry.com.* **Oldport Marine Services.** ✉ *1 Sayer's Wharf, Newport* ☎ *401/847–9109* 🌐 *www.oldportmarine.com.* **Seastreak New England.** ✉ *25 India St., Providence* ☎ *800/262–8743* 🌐 *www.seastreak.com.*

TAXI

Orange Cab of Newport connects Aquidneck Island towns with the West Kingston train station and T. F. Green Airport in Warwick.

Orange Cab of Newport. ✉ *312 Connell Hwy., Newport* ☎ *401/841–0030* 🌐 *www.newportcabs.com.*

FESTIVALS

★ Newport Classical

CONCERTS | A great way to experience one of the Newport mansions is at one of the 30 or so classical music concerts presented every July during the Newport Music Festival. Performances by world-class artists are scheduled at the Elms, the Breakers, and other venues. Selected works are chosen from 19th-century chamber music, vocal repertoire, Romantic-era piano literature, opera, and even Broadway and popular music. Every year features a free family concert. ✉ *Newport* ☎ *401/846–1133* 🌐 *newportclassical.org.*

★ Newport Folk Festival

CONCERTS | The Newport Folk Festival has been going strong since 1959, when it introduced musicians such as Joan Baez and the Kingston Trio. Held the last full weekend in July, the festival's acts now span folk, blues, country, bluegrass, folk rock, alt-country, indie folk, folk punk, even reggae. Lineups mix veteran performers like Brandi Carlisle, Joni Mitchell, Phil Lesh, and Grace Potter with younger stars like Hozier, Molly Tuttle, and Bonny Light Horseman. The festival is held rain or shine, and seating is general admission on a large, uncovered lawn. Purchase tickets early. ✉ *Ft. Adams State Park, 90 Ft. Adams Dr., Newport* 🌐 *www.newportfolk.org* 🎫 *From $106.*

Newport Jazz Festival

MUSIC | The grandfather of all jazz festivals, founded in 1954, takes place over three days at the end of July and/or beginning of August. The festival showcases both jazz veterans and up-and-coming artists, playing traditional and avant-garde styles. Performers in recent years have included Herbie Hancock, Wynton Marsalis, Dianne Reeves, Kendrick Scott, Norah Jones, and Diana Krall. The festival is held rain or shine, with open-air lawn seating. ✉ *Ft. Adams State Park, 90 Ft. Adams Dr., Newport* 🌐 *www.newportjazz.org* 🎫 *From $79.*

TOURS

More than a dozen companies run boat tours of Newport Harbor and Narragansett Bay. Outings usually run two hours and cost anywhere from $25 to $100 per person.

★ Classic Cruises of Newport

BOAT TOURS | **FAMILY** | You have your choice of two vessels at Classic Cruises of Newport: the 19th-century-style *Madeleine* is a 72-foot schooner that cruises around the harbor; the 1929 yacht *Rum Runner II*, built for two New Jersey mobsters to carry "hooch," evokes the days of smuggling along the coast. Choose from a variety of tours, including gorgeous sunset sails. ✉ *24 Bannister's Wharf, Newport* ☎ *401/847–0298* 🌐 *www.cruisenewport.com* 🎫 *From $35.*

Newport Historical Society

WALKING TOURS | Various guided walking tours focus on Newport's four centuries of American history. The 60-minute tours are available April–December, weather permitting, as well as during Winter Festival in February. Topics covered range from the Colonial period to the Gilded Age as well as Newport's neighborhoods and African American and women's history. ✉ *Newport Historical Society Museum & Shop, 127 Thames St., Newport* ☎ *401/841–8770* 🌐 *www.newporthistorytours.org* 🎫 *From $20.*

Sightsailing of Newport

BOAT TOURS | From May through early November, the 80-foot schooner *Aquidneck*, 46-foot sloop *Sightsailer*, and 34-foot sailboat *Starlight* depart Bowen's Wharf on 105-minute or longer public or private tours of Newport Harbor and Narragansett Bay. ✉ *32 Bowen's Wharf, Newport* ☎ *401/849–3333* 🌐 *www.sightsailing.com* 🎫 *From $33.*

★ Viking Tours of Newport

BUS TOURS | Viking offers 90-minute narrated trolley tours of Newport daily, June–October, and Friday and Saturday November–May. All tours include the

Newport Mansions but may also include a circuit of Ocean Drive and admission to individual mansions, not just a drive-by. ✉ *21 Long Wharf Mall, Newport* ☎ *401/847–6921* 🌐 *www.vikingtoursnewport.com* 🎫 *from $25.*

VISITOR INFORMATION

CONTACTS Discover Newport. ✉ *21 Long Wharf Mall, Newport* ☎ *401/849–8048, 800/326–6030* 🌐 *www.discovernewport.org.*

Downtown Newport and Historic Hill

Downtown Newport and, moving away from the water, the city's Historic Hill neighborhood are the city's Colonial heart. More than 200 pre-Revolutionary buildings, mostly private residences, remain on the streets running uphill from Newport Harbor; but you'll also encounter 19th-century landmarks such as St. Mary's Church, at the corner of Spring Street and Memorial Boulevard West, where John Fitzgerald Kennedy and Jacqueline Bouvier were married on September 12, 1953 (and now open for tours). The Point, an old Quaker neighborhood with streets named after trees, is immersive in its concentration of historic homes. The waterfront is beautiful, and there are many boutiques and restaurants on the very active wharfs that jut into the harbor. In summer, traffic is thick and narrow one-way streets can be frustrating to navigate; consider parking in a pay lot and exploring the area on foot.

Sights

Great Friends Meeting House

NOTABLE BUILDING | The oldest surviving house of worship in Rhode Island reflects the quiet reserve and steadfast faith of Colonial Quakers, who gathered here to discuss theology, peaceful alternatives to war, and the abolition of slavery. Built in 1699, the two-story structure has wide-plank floors, simple benches, a balcony, and a wood-beam ceiling. The Newport Historical Society can arrange group tours. ✉ *21 Farewell St., Newport* ☎ *401/846–0813* 🌐 *newporthistory.org* 🎫 *Tour $15.*

Hunter House

HISTORIC HOME | The oldest house owned and maintained by the Preservation Society of Newport County, constructed between 1748 and 1754, Hunter House served as the Revolutionary War headquarters of French admiral Charles Louis d'Arsac de Ternay after the home's Loyalist owner fled the city. Featuring a balustraded gambrel roof and heavy stud construction, it is an excellent example of early Georgian Colonial architecture. The carved pineapple over the doorway was a symbol of welcome throughout Colonial America. A collection of Colonial furniture includes pieces crafted by Newport's famed 18th-century Townsend-Goddard family of cabinetmakers and paintings by Cosmo Alexander, Gilbert Stuart, and Samuel King. The house is named for William Hunter, a U.S. Senator and President Andrew Jackson's chargé d'affaires to Brazil. ✉ *54 Washington St., Newport* ☎ *401/847–1000* 🌐 *www.newportmansions.org* 🎫 *$25* 🕒 *Closed mid-Oct.–mid-May.*

Museum of Newport History at Brick Market

HISTORY MUSEUM | FAMILY | The restored 1762 Brick Market building houses the Museum of Newport History, which explores the city's social and economic influences. Antiques such as the printing press of James Franklin (Ben's brother) inspire the imagination. Designed by Peter Harrison, who was responsible as well for Touro Synagogue and the Redwood Library, the building also served as a theater and a town hall. Today, besides the museum exhibits, there's a very nice gift shop that serves as a departure point for guided walking tours of Newport. ✉ *127 Thames St., Newport*

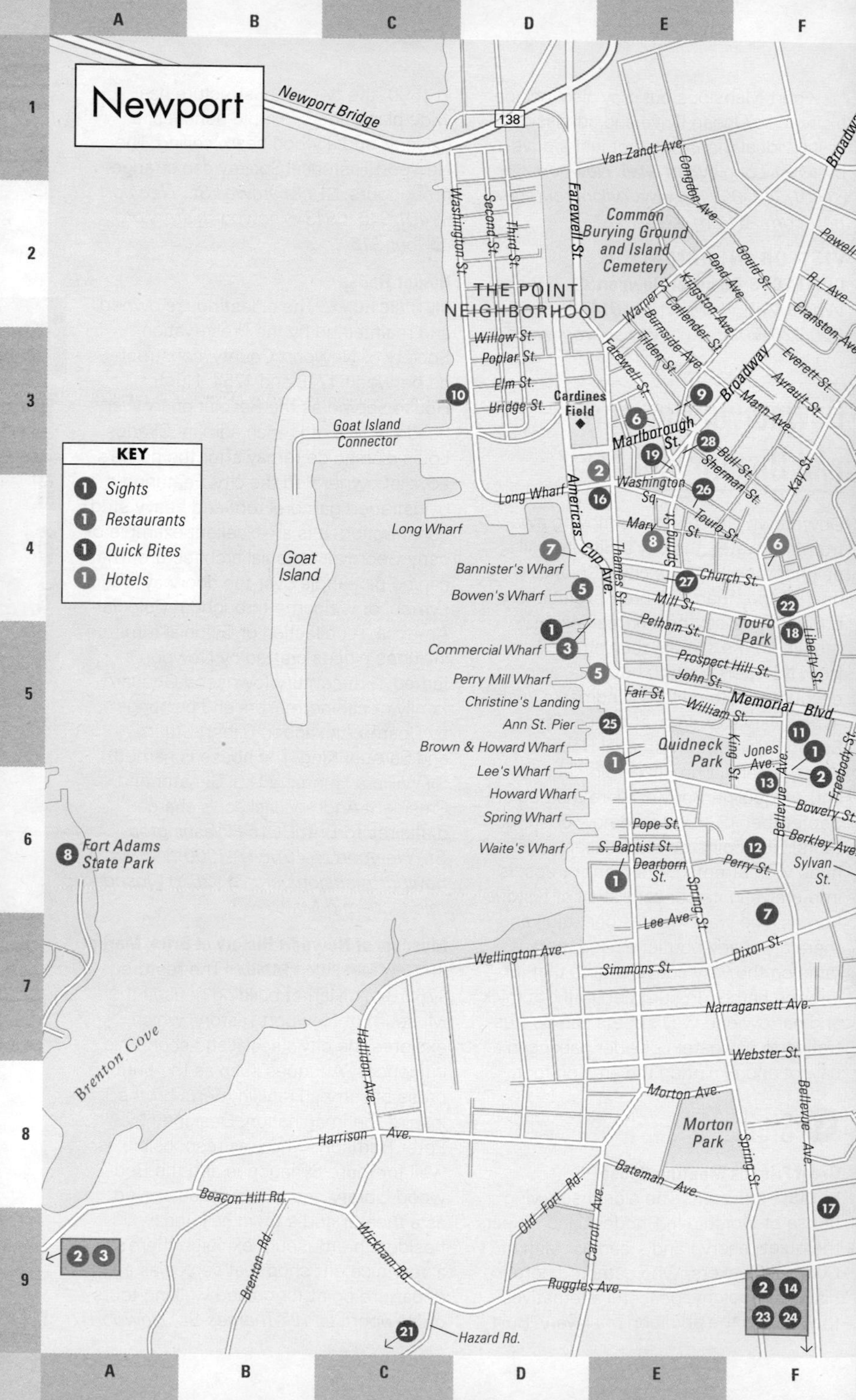

Newport
KEY
Sights
Restaurants
Quick Bites
Hotels
Newport Bridge
138
Van Zandt Ave.
Broadway
Congdon Ave.
Powell
Common Burying Ground and Island Cemetery
Washington St.
Second St.
Third St.
Farewell St.
Gould St.
Pond Ave.
Kingston Ave.
R.I. Ave.
Cranston Ave.
THE POINT NEIGHBORHOOD
Warner St.
Callender St.
Burnside Ave.
Tilden St.
Farewell St.
Willow St.
Poplar St.
Elm St.
Bridge St.
Cardines Field
Everett St.
Ayrault St.
Mann Ave.
Marlborough St.
Bull St.
Sherman St.
Kay St.
Goat Island Connector
Long Wharf
Washington Sq.
Americas Cup Ave.
Touro St.
Mary St.
Spring St.
Long Wharf
Goat Island
Bannister's Wharf
Bowen's Wharf
Thames St.
Church St.
Mill St.
Pelham St.
Touro Park
Liberty St.
Commercial Wharf
Prospect Hill St.
Perry Mill Wharf
John St.
Christine's Landing
Fair St.
Memorial Blvd.
William St.
Ann St. Pier
Quidneck Park
King St.
Jones Ave.
Bellevue Ave.
Freebody St.
Brown & Howard Wharf
Lee's Wharf
Howard Wharf
Bowery St.
Spring Wharf
Pope St.
Berkley Ave.
Fort Adams State Park
Waite's Wharf
S. Baptist St.
Dearborn St.
Perry St.
Sylvan St.
Lee Ave.
Spring St.
Dixon St.
Wellington Ave.
Simmons St.
Narragansett Ave.
Brenton Cove
Halidon Ave.
Webster St.
Morton Ave.
Bellevue Ave.
Morton Park
Harrison Ave.
Spring St.
Bateman Ave.
Beacon Hill Rd.
Old Fort Rd.
Carroll Ave.
Brenton Rd.
Wickham Rd.
Ruggles Ave.
Hazard Rd.

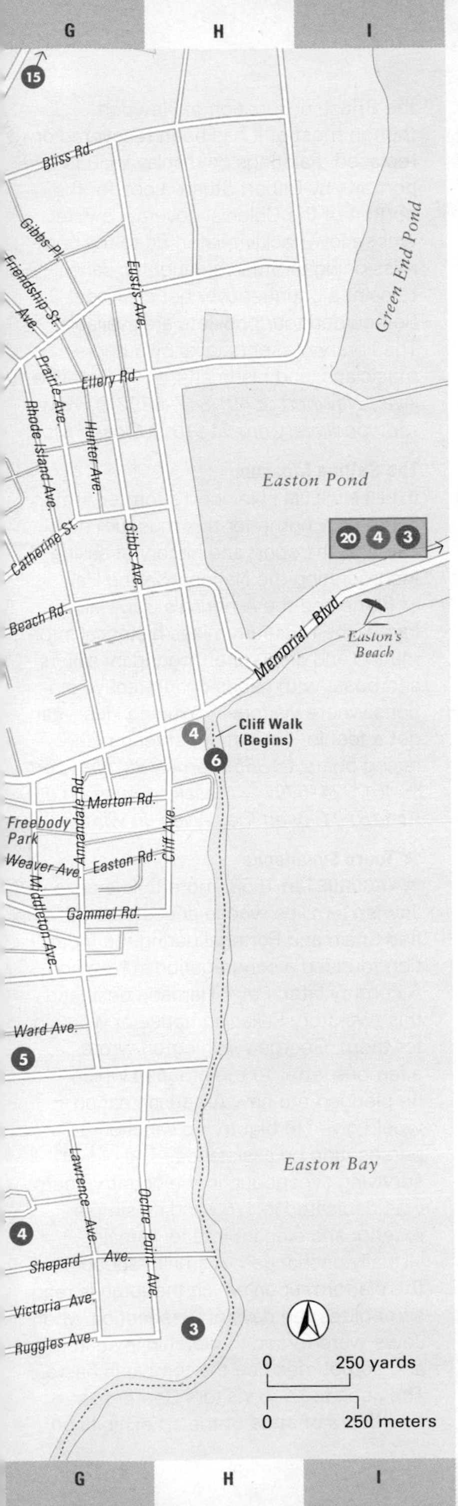

Sights

1 Audrain Automobile Museum F5
2 Belcourt of Newport F9
3 The Breakers H9
4 Chateau-sur-Mer G8
5 Chepstow G7
6 Cliff Walk H5
7 The Elms F6
8 Fort Adams State Park A6
9 Great Friends Meeting House E3
10 Hunter House C3
11 International Tennis Hall of Fame F5
12 Isaac Bell House F6
13 Kingscote F6
14 Marble House F9
15 Middletown G1
16 Museum of Newport History at Brick Market E4
17 National Museum of American Illustration ... F8
18 Newport Art Museum ... F5
19 Newport Colony House E3
20 Norman Bird Sanctuary I4
21 Ocean Drive C9
22 Redwood Library & Athenaeum F4
23 Rosecliff F9
24 Rough Point Museum ... F9
25 The Sailing Museum E5
26 Touro Synagogue E4
27 Trinity Episcopal Church E4
28 Wanton-Lyman-Hazard House E3

Restaurants

1 Bouchard Inn & Restaurant E6
2 Castle Hill Inn A9
3 Clarke Cooke House D4
4 Flo's Clam Shack I4
5 22 Bowen's Wine Bar & Grille D4
6 The White Horse Tavern E3

Quick Bites

1 Coffee Grinder D4
2 CRU Cafe F5
3 Mission I4

Hotels

1 Admiral Fitzroy Inn E5
2 The Brenton E3
3 Castle Hill Inn A9
4 The Chanler at Cliff Walk H5
5 Hammetts Hotel E5
6 Hydrangea House Inn ... F4
7 Newport Harbor Hotel and Marina D4
8 The Vanderbilt E4

☎ *401/841–8770* 🌐 *www.newporthistory.org* 🎫 *$5 suggested donation.*

Newport Art Museum

ART MUSEUM | Founded in 1912, the museum galleries today span two buildings: the Cushing/Morris Gallery and the 1864 Griswold House, a National Historic Landmark designed by Richard Morris Hunt. In the museum's permanent collection are works by Fitz Henry Lane, George Inness, William Trost Richards, John La Farge, Nancy Elizabeth Prophet, Gilbert Stuart, Winslow Homer, and Helena Sturtevant, as well as contemporary artists like Dale Chihuly, Howard Ben Tré, and Joseph Norman. ✉ *76 Bellevue Ave., Newport* ☎ *401/848–8200* 🌐 *www.newportartmuseum.org* 🎫 *$15* ⏲ *Closed Mon.*

Newport Colony House

HISTORIC SIGHT | Completed in 1739, this National Historic Landmark on Washington Square was the center of political activity in Colonial Newport. The Declaration of Independence was read from its steps on July 20, 1776, and British troops later used this structure as a barracks during their occupation of Newport. In 1781, George Washington met here with the French general Rochambeau, cementing an alliance that led to the American victory at Yorktown. Colony House served as Rhode Island's primary statehouse until 1901, when the new capitol building opened in Providence. The Newport Historical Society manages the Colony House and offers guided tours. ✉ *Washington Sq., Newport* ☎ *401/846–0813* 🌐 *newporthistory.org* 🎫 *$15.*

Redwood Library & Athenaeum

LIBRARY | In 1747, Abraham Redwood gave 500 pounds sterling to found a library of arts and sciences; three years later, this Georgian Palladian–style building (with its wood exterior and columns cleverly styled to look like stonework) opened with 751 titles. More than half of the original collection vanished during the British occupation of Newport, though most of it has been recovered or replaced. Paintings on display include five portraits by Gilbert Stuart. Look for the portrait of the Colonial governor's wife, whose low neckline later led to the commissioning of Stuart's daughter, Jane, to paint a bouquet over her cleavage. Self-guided tour booklets are available. The library presents talks by authors, musicians, and historians. ✉ *50 Bellevue Ave., Newport* ☎ *401/847–0292* 🌐 *www.redwoodlibrary.org* 🎫 *$10* ⏲ *Closed Mon.*

The Sailing Museum

OTHER MUSEUM | Newport's former Armory is the new home for this museum dedicated to the sport and history of sailing. Incorporating the National Sailing Hall of Fame and the America's Cup Hall of Fame, the museum mixes historical information and displays on legendary sailors and boats with hands-on interactive stations where visitors—including kids—can get a feel for navigating, steering, and racing boats. ✉ *365 Thames St., Newport* ☎ *401/324–5761* 🌐 *thesailingmuseum.org* 🎫 *$18* ⏲ *Closed Tues.-Wed. in winter.*

★ Touro Synagogue

SYNAGOGUE | In 1658, more than a dozen Jewish families whose ancestors had fled Spain and Portugal during the Inquisition founded a congregation in Newport. A century later, Peter Harrison designed this two-story Palladian house of worship for them. George Washington wrote a famous letter to the group in which he pledged the new American nation would give "to bigotry no sanction, to persecution no assistance." The oldest surviving synagogue in the country, Touro was dedicated in 1763 and its simple exterior and elegant interior remain virtually unchanged. A small trapdoor in the platform upon which the Torah is read symbolizes the days of persecution when Jews were forced to worship in secret–and sometimes flee the temple in haste. The John L. Loeb Visitors Center has two floors of state-of-the-art exhibits on early American Jewish life and Newport's history of religious freedom.

■ **TIP→ Tickets, available at the Loeb Visitors Center, are required for entry into the synagogue.** ✉ *Loeb Visitors Center, 52 Spring St., Newport* ☎ *401/847–4794* 🌐 *www.tourosynagogue.org* 🎫 *$12* ☞ *Closed Sat. May–Oct., Closed Mon.–Sat. Nov.–Apr. No tours on Jewish holidays.*

Trinity Episcopal Church
CHURCH | George Washington once sat in the distinguished visitor pew close to this church's distinctive three-tier wineglass pulpit. Completed in 1726, this structure is similar to Boston's Old North Church; both were inspired by the designs of Sir Christopher Wren. Trinity's 1733 London-made organ is believed to be the first big pipe organ in the 13 colonies. Among those buried in the churchyard's historic cemetery is French admiral d'Arsac de Ternay, commander of the allied French Navy in Newport, who was buried with special permission in 1780 as there were then no Roman Catholic cemeteries in New England. ✉ *1 Queen Anne Sq., Newport* ☎ *401/846–0660* 🌐 *www.trinitynewport.org* 🎫 *$5 donation* ⏲ *No tours during parish events and Mon.–Sat. in Nov.–late May.*

Wanton-Lyman-Hazard House
HISTORIC HOME | As Newport's oldest surviving house, built circa 1697, this residence provides a glimpse of the city's Colonial and Revolutionary history. The dark-red building was damaged during the city's Stamp Act riots of 1765. After the British Parliament levied a tax on most printed material, the Sons of Liberty stormed the house, which was then occupied by a prominent Loyalist. ✉ *17 Broadway, Newport* ☎ *401/846-0813* 🌐 *newporthistory.org* 🎫 *Tour $15.*

Restaurants

★ Clarke Cooke House
$$$ | AMERICAN | Drinks at a bar favored by the sailing crowd, intimate dinners by the fire, and relaxing lunches overlooking Newport Harbor are a few of the experiences possible at this multilevel complex. The first-floor Candy Store serves casual fare and has a sushi bar; the second-floor offers casual dining in the Bistro and cocktails in the Midway Bar; and the Summer Porch and 12 Metre Yacht Club Room on the third floor have elegant fine dining requiring proper dress. **Known for:** clam chowder—"best in the city"; "Snowball in Hell" ice-cream dessert; partying in the Boom Boom Room. 💲 *Average main: $32* ✉ *26 Bannister's Wharf, Newport* ☎ *401/849–2900* 🌐 *www.clarkecooke.com.*

Bouchard Inn & Restaurant
$$$ | FRENCH | Regional variations on French cuisine are the focus at this upscale yet laid-back establishment inside a gambrel-roof 1785 Colonial. Nightly specials are based on the fresh catch from Rhode Island waters, which may include scallops, swordfish, and cod. **Known for:** excellent dining, excellent service; extensive wine list; no children under age seven. 💲 *Average main: $35* ✉ *505 Thames St., Newport* ☎ *401/846–0123* 🌐 *www.bouchardnewport.com* ⏲ *Closed Tues. No lunch.*

★ 22 Bowen's Wine Bar & Grille
$$$$ | STEAKHOUSE | Excellent service, perfectly cooked steaks, and an extensive, award-winning wine list make dinner here a memorable experience. Although the restaurant is known for its steaks—and it's impossible to go wrong ordering one—you'll find plenty of choices if you're in the mood for something from the sea. **Known for:** steaks, chops, and fresh local seafood; choose one of eight sauces/butters to accompany your steak; abundant gluten-free options. 💲 *Average*

main: $40 ✉ *22 Bowen's Wharf, Newport* ☎ *401/841–8884* 🌐 *www.22bowens.com.*

The White Horse Tavern

$$$ | **AMERICAN** | The first tavern opened here in 1673—and ever since, the premises have served, in turn, as a tavern, boardinghouse, restaurant, and even a meetinghouse for Colonial Rhode Island's General Assembly. Today, the tavern provides an intimate fine-dining experience, the mood set by the low dark-beam ceilings, uneven plank floors, and four still-working fireplaces; an outside patio is a recent addition. **Known for:** oldest operating restaurant in the country; beef Wellington, fresh seafood, just-picked produce; extensive wine list. [$] *Average main: $34* ✉ *26 Marlborough St., Newport* ☎ *401/849–3600* 🌐 *www.whitehorsenewport.com.*

Coffee and Quick Bites

Coffee Grinder

$ | **CAFÉ** | Now located in Perry Mill, this tiny espresso bar has views of Newport's vibrant harbor and downtown. Pair a flavored latte and a pastry on a fog-bound early morning, and you'll feel the essence of the city as it awakens around you. **Known for:** coffee drinks made-to-order with real Italian espresso; savory scones and turnovers; outdoor patio is a perfect place to people watch. [$] *Average main: $8* ✉ *Perry Mill, 337 Thames St., Newport* ☎ *401/935–7676* 🌐 *www.coffeegrindernewport.com* ⏲ *No dinner.*

CRU Cafe

$ | **CAFÉ** | From Russell Morin, one of Newport's most exclusive caterers, comes this chalkboard-menu café where beautifully crafted light fare is served at surprisingly down-to-earth prices. Breakfast—try the egg- and tomato-topped avocado toast—is served all day, and creative salads and sandwiches are the makings of a perfect picnic to tote down the street and enjoy on an oceanview mansion lawn. **Known for:** hidden in a parking lot on tony Bellevue Avenue; elevated, farm-fresh cuisine; BYOB. [$] *Average main: $9* ✉ *1 Casino Terr., Newport* ☎ *401/314–0500* 🌐 *www.crucafenewport.com* ⏲ *No dinner.*

Hotels

Admiral Fitzroy Inn

$$$$ | **B&B/INN** | The restful retreat in the heart of Newport's bustling waterfront district was once a convent in a different location—the tidy 1854 Victorian building was dismantled in 1986 and rebuilt to its original size and style in its current location. **Pros:** elevator service to first three floors; close to shops, restaurants, and bars; complimentary parking; continental breakfast included. **Cons:** some noise from Thames Street in summer; walk up from third floor to rooftop rooms and deck; rooms are fairly small but it is a historic property. [$] *Rooms from: $436* ✉ *398 Thames St., Newport* ☎ *800/848–8780* 🌐 *www.admiralfitzroy.com* *18 rooms* *Free Breakfast.*

★ The Brenton

$$$$ | **HOTEL** | Inside and out, every detail of Newport's newest hotel is a thoughtful homage to its place on the waterfront and in the city's architectural progression including its residential-feeling rooms that feature linens and robes crafted by Matouk just 25 miles away in Fall River, Massachusetts. **Pros:** largest rooms in Newport; entirely pet-friendly; local inspiration and artisanship throughout the property. **Cons:** prime location comes at a price; pool and fitness center off-site at the adjacent Newport Marriott; parking is $40 per night. [$] *Rooms from: $750* ✉ *31 America's Cup Ave., Newport* ☎ *401/849–3100* 🌐 *www.brentonhotel.com* *57 rooms* *No Meals.*

Hammetts Hotel

$$$$ | **HOTEL** | Opened in the midst of 2020, this anchor of the newly built Hammetts Wharf complex is located in the heart of the Newport harborfront which

lends an energetic pulse to the property, though the rooms are quiet retreats. **Pros:** enormous windows with city or water views; chic outdoor deck reserved for guests; freestyle Italian cuisine (try the olive oil cake) at adjacent Giusto restaurant. **Cons:** rooms are somewhat bland and on the smaller side; only one elevator; tiny fitness room overlooks the city, not the water. *Rooms from: $699 4 Commercial Wharf, Newport 401/324–7500 www.hammettshotel.com 84 rooms No Meals.*

Hydrangea House Inn

$$$ | **B&B/INN** | This mid-19th-century inn exudes romance and every detail has been thought of in the decadent suites and guest rooms—some have fireplaces, whirlpool tubs, and steam showers. **Pros:** convenient central location; huge rooms and great bathrooms; highly personal service. **Cons:** slightly over-the-top decor; street-level rooms can be noisy at night; no kids 12 and under. *Rooms from: $395 16 Bellevue Ave., Newport 401/846–4435, 800/945–4667 www.hydrangeahouse.com 10 rooms Free Breakfast.*

★ Newport Harbor Hotel and Marina

$$$$ | **RESORT** | **FAMILY** | A former Navy base that's now connected by causeway to the downtown area, Goat Island is home to this resort (formerly known as Gurney's Newport) that comes complete with a walking path around the island, a marina full of yachts, a fitness center, and a picturesque lighthouse. **Pros:** unmatched harbor views; ADA accessible rooms available; quiet location. **Cons:** no shuttle service, and it's a 15-minute walk to downtown activities; awkward building layout and design; limited free parking. *Rooms from: $550 1 Goat Island, Newport 401/847–9000, 800/955–2558 www.newporthotel.com 257 rooms No Meals.*

The Vanderbilt

$$$$ | **HOTEL** | Built in 1909 by Alfred Gwynne Vanderbilt for his mistress, Agnes O'Brien Ruiz, this Auberge Resorts property aims to impress—and does, with its exclusive mansion feel, enormous (and recently renovated) guest rooms, and elegant dining in the conservatory and garden. **Pros:** full-service spa; indoor and outdoor pools; boozy popsicles and cocktails served on the hidden Garden Terrace. **Cons:** on a narrow street that's busy in summer; somewhat sterile decor; minimum stay requirements may apply. *Rooms from: $1,200 41 Mary St., Newport 401/846–6200, 833/242–8850 www.aubergeresorts.com/vanderbilt 33 rooms No Meals.*

Bellevue Avenue and Beyond

East of Newport Harbor and the historic part of town, you begin to discover stunning, opulent mansions along Bellevue Avenue and its ocean-leading side streets. These "summer cottages" were built by wealthy families in the late 1800s and early 1900s as seasonal residences. Public beaches are nearby, off the east end of Memorial Boulevard and in neighboring Middletown.

Sights

Audrain Automobile Museum

TRANSPORTATION | The museum showcases a revolving selection of impressive vehicles, curated from private collections of more than 350 rare, fully restored automobiles dating from 1899 to the present day. You might see super cars, mini- and micro-cars, pre–World War II specimens, or touring cars. Racing simulators allow visitors to take a few spins around the track. Auto enthusiasts

Continued on page 366

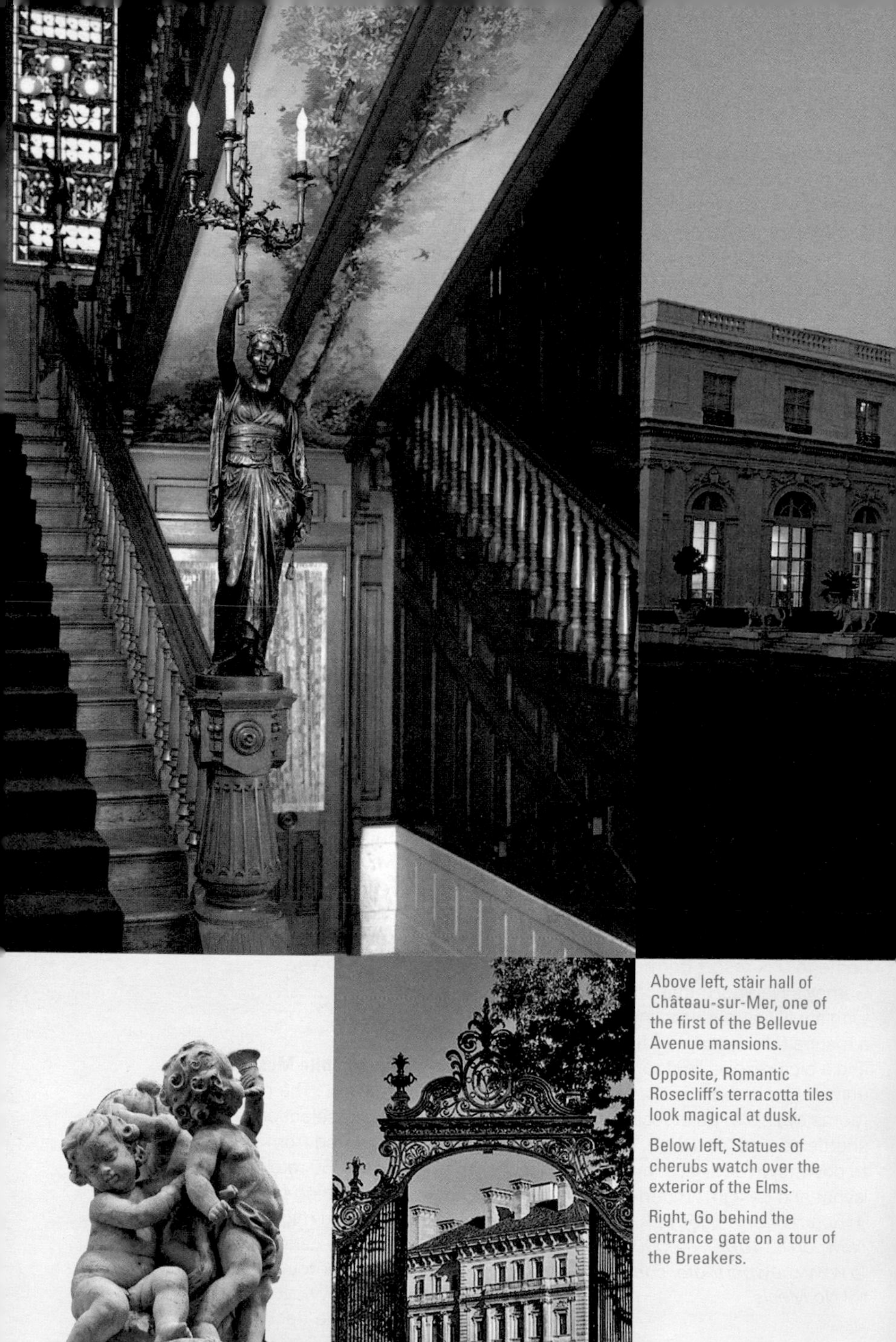

Above left, stair hall of Château-sur-Mer, one of the first of the Bellevue Avenue mansions.

Opposite, Romantic Rosecliff's terracotta tiles look magical at dusk.

Below left, Statues of cherubs watch over the exterior of the Elms.

Right, Go behind the entrance gate on a tour of the Breakers.

The Mansions of Newport

GILDED AGE GEMS

Would you call a home with 70 rooms a cottage? If not, you're obviously not Cornelius Vanderbilt II. The Breakers, the "summer cottage" of the 19th-century multimillionaire, is one of a dozen mansions in Newport that are now by far the city's top attractions. Many of the homes are open to the public for tours, giving you a peek into the lives of the privileged.

THE SOCIAL SCENE

The Breakers dining room, just one of the opulent mansion's 70 rooms.

To truly appreciate a visit to Newport's mansions, you need to understand the times and the players—those who built these opulent homes and summered here for six weeks a year.

Newport at the turn of the 20th century was where the socialites of Boston, New York, and Philadelphia came for the summer. They were among the richest people in America at the time—from railroad tycoons and coal barons to plantation owners.

The era during which they lived here, the late 1800s up through the 1920s, is often referred to as the Gilded Age, a term coined by Mark Twain and co-author Charles Dudley Warner in a book by the same name. It was a time when who you knew was everything.

Caroline Schermerhorn Astor was the queen of New York and Newport society; her list of the "Four Hundred" was the first social register. Three übersocialites were Alva Vanderbilt Belmont, Marion (Mamie) Fish, and Tessie Oelrichs. These ladies who seriously lunched threw most of *the* parties in Newport.

While the women gossiped, planned soirees, and dressed and redressed thoughout the summer days, the men were usually off yachting.

In terms of the deepest pockets, the two heavyweight families during Newport's Gilded Age were the Vanderbilts and the Astors.

Madeleine Force was only 19 when she married John Jacob Astor IV at the Beechwood mansion in 1911; he was 47.

LEADING FAMILIES

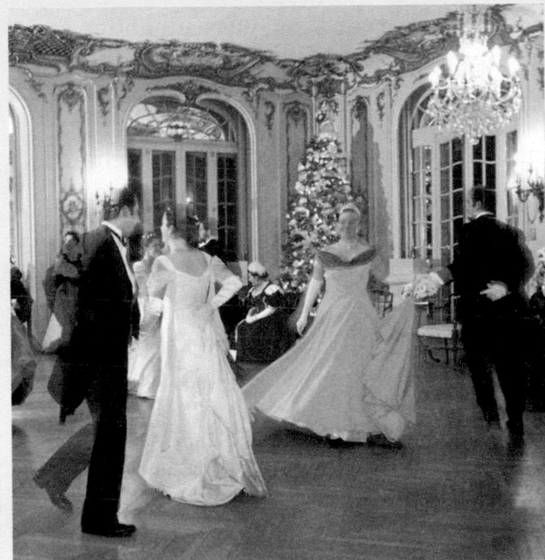

Work is underway to reinvent Beechwood.

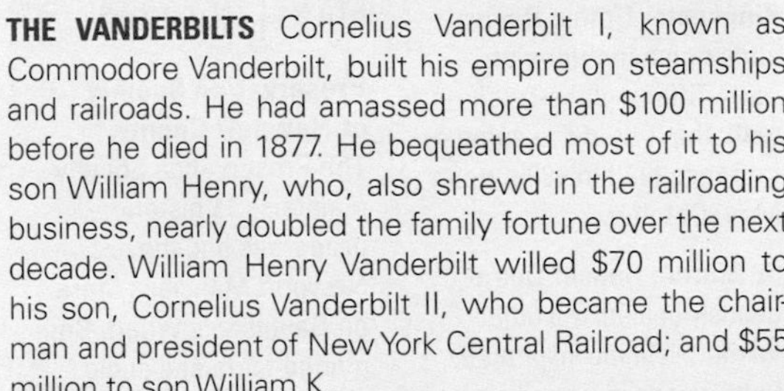

THE VANDERBILTS Cornelius Vanderbilt I, known as Commodore Vanderbilt, built his empire on steamships and railroads. He had amassed more than $100 million before he died in 1877. He bequeathed most of it to his son William Henry, who, also shrewd in the railroading business, nearly doubled the family fortune over the next decade. William Henry Vanderbilt willed $70 million to his son, Cornelius Vanderbilt II, who became the chairman and president of New York Central Railroad; and $55 million to son William K.

Vanderbilt, who also managed railroads for a while and saw his yacht, The Defender, win the America's Cup in 1895. One of Cornelius Vanderbilt II's sons, Alfred Gwynne Vanderbilt, died on the Lusitania, which sank three years after the Titanic. Visit: The Breakers, Marble House.

THE ASTORS Meanwhile, in the Astor camp, John Jacob Astor IV, who perished on the *Titanic*, had the riches his great-granddad had made in the fur trade as well as his own millions earned from successful real estate ventures, including New York City hotels such as the St. Regis and the Astoria (later the Waldorf–Astoria). His mother was Caroline Astor. Her mansion, Beechwood, is now owned by Oracle co-founder and chairman Larry Ellison.

Alva Vanderbilt Belmont

Cornelius Vanderbilt

John Jacob Astor IV

John Jacob Astor

WHICH MANSION SHOULD I VISIT?

Even though the Newport "summer cottages" were inhabited for only six weeks each year, it would take you almost that long to explore all the grand rooms and manicured grounds. Each mansion has its own style and unique features. Here are the characteristics of each to help you choose those you'd like to visit:

★ **The Breakers:** The most opulent; enormous Italian Renaissance mansion built by Cornelius Vanderbilt II; guided, audio, and family-geared audio tours are options; open all year.

Château-sur-Mer: The prettiest gardens and grounds; High Victorian–style mansion built in 1852; remodeled and redecorated in 1870s by Richard Morris Hunt; open most of the year.

Chepstow: Italianate villa with a fine collection of art; a bit less wow factor; open mid-May–mid-October.

★ **The Elms:** A French chatea-style home with 10 acres of stunningly restored grounds; guided Elms Servant Life Tour takes you into a hidden dormitory, roof, and basement; open all year.

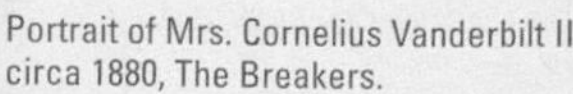

Portrait of Mrs. Cornelius Vanderbilt II circa 1880, The Breakers.

Belcourt: French Renaissance and Gothic are among the many architectural elements in this 1894 mansion; open most of the year.

Ochre Court: The French chalet style mansion is Salve Regina University's administration building; it's the second largest of the Newport mansions; open for summer tours.

Kingscote: Gothic Revival–style home includes an early Tiffany glass-brick wall; the first of the summer cottages built in 1839; open May–October.

★ **Marble House:** Outrageously opulent the other Vanderbilt home inspired by Petit Trianon in Versailles; tour at your own pace with digital audio tour; open summer and weekends in the winter.

Rosecliff: Romantic 1902 mansion; modeled after Grand Trianon in Versailles; open most of the year.

Rough Point: 1889 English manor–style mansion built by Frederick Vanderbilt, later owned and furnished by Doris Duke; small group or self-guided tours; open April–November.

Astors Beechwood: An Italianate villa, built in 1852-3 and extensively renovated in 1881. Current owner Larry Ellison plans to turn it into a museum for his art collection.

MANSION TOURS

Preservation Society of Newport County. The Preservation Society maintains 11 historic properties and the Newport Mansions Store on Bannister's Wharf. Both guided tours and audio tours are available; you can purchase a combination ticket to see multiple properties for a substantial discount. The hours and days the houses are open in fall and winter vary. ☎ *401/847–1000* 🌐 *www.newportmansions.org* 🎫 *A variety of admission packages are available. A ticket allowing entrance to any three mansions is $46.*

Consider viewing mansions from the Cliff Walk for a different perspective.

Marble House at night.

TOP EXPERIENCE

★ **Cliff Walk.** See the backyards of Newport's famous oceanfront Gilded Age mansions while strolling along this 3½-mile public access walkway. The designated National Recreation Trail stretches from Memorial Boulevard at the west end of Easton's Beach (also called First Beach) southerly to the east end of Bailey's Beach. Along the way you'll pass the Breakers, Rosecliff, and Marble House and its Chinese Tea House. The north half of the walk is paved but the trail turns to large flat boulders south of Ruggles Avenue. Be prepared for increasingly rough terrain not suitable for small children, strollers, or people with mobility problems. Park on either Memorial Boulevard or Narragansett Avenue.

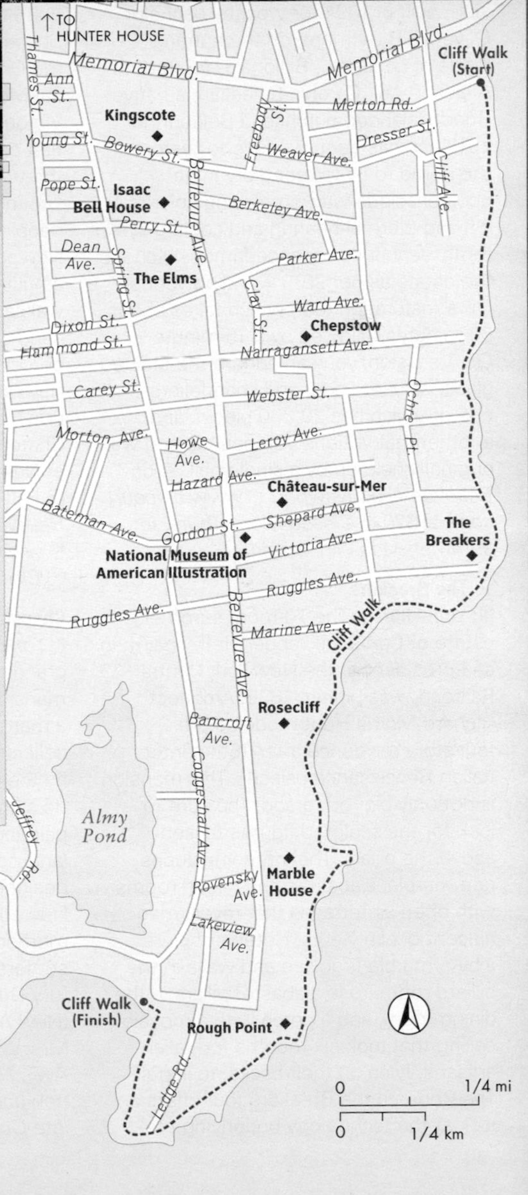

↑TO HUNTER HOUSE
Memorial Blvd.
Cliff Walk (Start)
Thames St.
Ann St.
Kingscote
Freebody St.
Merton Rd.
Young St.
Bowery St.
Weaver Ave.
Dresser St.
Cliff Ave.
Pope St.
Isaac Bell House
Bellevue Ave.
Berkeley Ave.
Perry St.
Dean Ave.
Spring St.
The Elms
Parker Ave.
Clay St.
Ward Ave.
Dixon St.
Chepstow
Hammond St.
Narragansett Ave.
Carey St.
Webster St.
Ochre Pt.
Morton Ave.
Howe Ave.
Leroy Ave.
Hazard Ave.
Château-sur-Mer
Bateman Ave.
Gordon St.
Shepard Ave.
The Breakers
National Museum of American Illustration
Victoria Ave.
Ruggles Ave.
Ruggles Ave.
Marine Ave.
Cliff Walk
Rosecliff
Bancroft Ave.
Coggeshall Ave.
Almy Pond
Jeffrey Rd.
Ocean Ave.
Rovensky Ave.
Marble House
Lakeview Ave.
Cliff Walk (Finish)
Rough Point
Ledge Rd.
Gooseberry Island
0 1/4 mi
0 1/4 km

will enjoy perusing past exhibitions on the museum's website. ✉ *222 Bellevue Ave., Newport* ☎ *401/856–4420* 🌐 *www.audrainautomuseum.org* 🎫 *$18.*

Belcourt of Newport

HISTORIC HOME | Richard Morris Hunt based his design for this 60-room mansion, built in 1894 for wealthy bachelor Oliver H. P. Belmont, on the hunting lodge of Louis XIII. Billionaire founder of Alex and Ani, Carolyn Rafaelian, a native Rhode Islander, purchased Belcourt in 2012 and has been working to restore the home to its former glory in an eco-conscious way, employing solar panels and thermal-heating-and-cooling systems. Jennifer Lawrence famously chose the estate as her 2019 wedding venue. On a restoration tour, which takes about 50 minutes followed by a 15-minute Q&A session, you can admire the stained glass, carved wood, and chandeliers—one of which has 20,000 pieces and another that weighs 460 pounds and was originally held up by a single nail. ✉ *657 Bellevue Ave., Newport* 🌐 *www.belcourt.com* 🎫 *$20* ⏲ *Closed Mon.–Thurs. in summer, Mon.–Fri. in winter.*

★ The Breakers

HISTORIC HOME | The 70-room summer estate of Cornelius Vanderbilt II, chairman and president of the New York Central Railroad, was built in 1895. Architect Richard Morris Hunt modeled the four-story residence after 16th-century Italian Renaissance palaces. This mansion is not only big, but grand—be sure to look for the sculpted figures tucked above the pillars. The interior includes rare marble, alabaster, and gilded rooms with open-air terraces that reveal magnificent ocean views. Noteworthy are a blue marble fireplace and walls in the billiard room, rose alabaster pillars in the dining room, and a porch with a mosaic ceiling that took six months for Italian artisans, lying on their backs, to install. The Beneath the Breakers tour offers a look at the technology underlying the home that was state-of-the-art in the late 19th century, including the electrical and plumbing systems used to keep the massive household running. ✉ *44 Ochre Point Ave., Newport* ☎ *401/847–1000* 🌐 *www.newportmansions.org* 🎫 *$29.*

★ Chateau-sur-Mer

HISTORIC HOME | Built in 1852 for William Shepard Wetmore, a merchant in the China Trade, the palatial Chateau-sur-Mer, a stunning example of High Victorian architecture, was Newport's first grand residence. In 1857, Wetmore threw an extravagant, unprecedented "country picnic" for more than 2,000 people, ushering in the Gilded Age in Newport. The house is a treasure trove of Victorian architecture, furniture, wallpapers, ceramics, and stenciling; see hand-carved Italian woodwork, Chinese porcelains, and Japanese and Egyptian Revival wallpapers. The grounds contain rare trees from as far away as Mongolia. Chateau-sur-Mer, along with several other Newport mansions, is among the stars of HBO's series, *The Gilded Age.* ✉ *474 Bellevue Ave., Newport* ☎ *401/847–1000* 🌐 *www.newportmansions.org* 🎫 *$25* ⏲ *Closed early Nov.–late Mar.*

Chepstow

HISTORIC HOME | Though only slightly less grand than some of the other Newport mansions, this Italianate-style villa with a mansard roof houses a remarkable collection of art and furniture gathered by the Morris family of New York City. Its significant 19th-century American paintings include Hudson River School landscapes. Built in 1860, the home was designed by George Champlin Mason, a Newport architect, for Edmund Schermerhorn, a descendent of one of the first settlers of New Netherland, the 17th-century Dutch colony centered on New York (New Amsterdam) and first cousin of Mrs. William Astor. ✉ *120 Narragansett Ave., Newport* ☎ *401/847–1000* 🌐 *www.newportmansions.org* 🎫 *$25* ⏲ *Closed late Oct.–mid-Apr.*

★ Cliff Walk

TRAIL | See the "backyards" of Newport's famous oceanfront Gilded Age mansions while strolling along this 3½-mile public walkway. The designated National Recreation Trail stretches from Memorial Boulevard at the western end of Easton's Beach (also called First Beach) south to the eastern end of Bailey's Beach. Along the way you'll pass Salve Regina University's Ochre Court, the Breakers, Forty Steps at Narragansett Avenue, Rosecliff, and Marble House and its Chinese Tea House. Park on either Memorial Boulevard or Narragansett Avenue. The trail is relatively flat and easily walkable between Memorial Boulevard and the Angelsea mansion; beyond that point, it's a mix of unpaved trail and scrambles over rocky cliffs. However, a partial collapse of the Cliff Walk between 40 Steps and Ochre Court in 2022 has necessitated a short street detour for the foreseeable future. Make sure you apply sunscreen, wear comfortable rubber-soled shoes, and bring your own water. ✉ *119 Memorial Blvd., Newport* ☎ *401/845–5300* 🌐 *www.cliffwalk.com* 🎟 *Free.*

★ The Elms

HISTORIC HOME | Architect Horace Trumbauer modeled this imposing 48-room French neoclassical home and its grounds after the Château d'Asnières near Paris. The Elms was built in 1901 for Edward Julius Berwind, a coal baron from Philadelphia and New York. It was one of the first Newport mansions to be fully electrified. At the foot of the 10-acre estate is a spectacular sunken garden, marble pavilions, and fountains. The Servant Life tour, which offers a glimpse into the lives of the Elms' staff members and the operation of facilities like the boiler room and kitchen, is one of the best of the mansion tours. ✉ *367 Bellevue Ave., Newport* ☎ *401/847–1000* 🌐 *www.newportmansions.org* 🎟 *$25* ⏲ *Closed mid-Oct.–mid-May.*

Fort Adams State Park

BEACH | **FAMILY** | The largest coastal fortress in the United States can be found at this park, which hosts Newport's annual folk and jazz festivals and sailing events like the Ocean Race. The nonprofit Ft. Adams Trust offers a varied schedule of guided tours of the fort, where soldiers lived from 1841 to 1950. Tours take in the fort's overlooks and underground tunnels, as well as its impressive walls. The views of Newport Harbor and Narragansett Bay are exquisite. The park also includes the Sail Newport marina, where boating lessons and rentals are available, and Eisenhower House, the summer White House of President Dwight D. Eisenhower. ✉ *80 Ft. Adams Dr., Newport* ☎ *401/841–0707* 🌐 *www.fortadams.org* 🎟 *Park free, guided tour $20, self-guided tour $10* ⏲ *Fort closed Jan., Feb. (except school vacation week), and Mon.–Fri. in Mar.*

★ International Tennis Hall of Fame

SPORTS VENUE | **FAMILY** | Tennis fans and lovers of history, art, and architecture will enjoy visiting the birthplace of U.S. championship tennis. The museum contains interactive exhibits, a holographic theater that simulates being in a room with Roger Federer, displays of clothing worn by the sport's biggest stars, video highlights of great matches, and memorabilia that includes the 1874 patent from England's Queen Victoria for the game of lawn tennis. The 7-acre site is home to the Bill Talbert Stadium with its manicured grass courts, the historic shingle-style Newport Casino—which opened in 1880 and was designed by architects McKim, Mead & White—and the recently restored Casino Theatre. The 13 grass tennis courts, one clay court, and an indoor tennis facility are open to the public for play. The grass-court Hall of Fame Tournament held each July attracts top male professional players and is a highlight of the Newport summer calendar. ✉ *194 Bellevue Ave., Newport* ☎ *401/849–3990* 🌐 *www.tennisfame.com* 🎟 *$18.*

Isaac Bell House

HISTORIC HOME | Revolutionary in design when it was completed in 1883, the shingle-style Isaac Bell House combines Old English and European architecture with Colonial American and exotic details, such as a sweeping open floor plan and bamboo-style porch columns. McKim, Mead & White of New York City designed the home for Isaac Bell, a wealthy cotton broker. ✉ *70 Perry St., at Bellevue Ave., Newport* ☎ *401/847–1000* 🌐 *www.newportmansions.org* 🎫 *$25* 🕓 *Closed late Oct.–mid-Apr.*

Kingscote

HISTORIC HOME | Among Newport's first summer cottages, this 1841 Gothic Revival mansion designed by Richard Upjohn was built for George Noble Jones, a Georgia plantation owner. The house is named for its second owners, the King family, one of whose members hired McKim, Mead & White to expand and redesign it. The dining room, one of the 1881 additions, contains a cork ceiling and one of the first installations of Tiffany glass windows. Furnishings reflect the King family's involvement in the China trade. ✉ *253 Bellevue Ave., Newport* ☎ *401/847–1000* 🌐 *www.newportmansions.org* 🎫 *$25* 🕓 *Closed late Oct.–mid-Apr.*

★ Marble House

HISTORIC HOME | One of the most opulent of the Newport mansions, Marble House contains 500,000 cubic feet of marble (valued at $7 million when the house was built from 1888 to 1892). William K. Vanderbilt, grandson of Commodore Cornelius Vanderbilt, gave Marble House to his wife, Alva, as a gift for her 39th birthday. The house was designed by architect Richard Morris Hunt, who took inspiration from the Petit Trianon at Versailles. The Vanderbilts divorced three years later, in 1895. Alva married Oliver H. P. Belmont and moved down the street to Belcourt. After Belmont's death, she reopened Marble House and had the Chinese Tea House built on the back lawn, where she hosted "Votes for Women" rallies. ✉ *596 Bellevue Ave., Newport* ☎ *401/847–1000* 🌐 *www.newportmansions.org* 🎫 *$25* 🕓 *Closed Mon.-Fri. in winter.*

Middletown

TOWN | Newport occupies a relatively small corner of southwestern Aquidneck Island, and a good number of 'Newport' attractions are actually located in neighboring Middletown. Second Beach and Third Beach, for example, are in Middletown, as is the Norman Bird Sanctuary, Sachuest Point National Wildlife Refuge, and Flo's Clam Shack. It's also well worth the short drive north from Newport to explore Middletown's Newport Vineyards (which also has a restaurant and brewery), the Revolutionary-era Prescott Farm, and the 100-acre Sweet Berry Farm, which has pick-your-own fruit in season and live music in the summer. ✉ *Middletown* 🌐 *www.middletownri.com.*

National Museum of American Illustration

HISTORIC HOME | This museum exhibits original work by Norman Rockwell, J. C. Leyendecker, Maxfield Parrish, N. C. Wyeth, and more than 150 others spanning the "Golden Age of American Illustration" (1895–1945). All 323 of Rockwell's printed *Saturday Evening Post* covers are on display. Vernon Court, the 1898 beaux-arts–style building is an adaptation of an 18th-century French château and was designed by the same architects responsible for the New York Public Library and other landmarks; Frederick Law Olmsted designed the grounds. ✉ *492 Bellevue Ave., Newport* ☎ *401/851–8949* 🌐 *www.americanillustration.org* 🎫 *$20* 🕓 *Closed mid-Sept.-late May.*

Norman Bird Sanctuary

WILDLIFE REFUGE | FAMILY | Stroll through the woods or hike to the top of Hanging Rock for a spectacular view at this 325-acre sanctuary for diverse wildlife including more than 300 species of birds. The sanctuary, located in nearby Middletown, has about 7 miles of trails traversing ridges, forests, thickets, fields, ponds, streams, salt marsh, and sandy beach. The raucous dawn chorus of birdsong in the spring is one of the great wildlife experiences in Rhode Island. ✉ *583 Third Beach Rd., Middletown* ☎ *401/846–2577* 🌐 *www.normanbirdsanctuary.org* 🎫 *$7.*

★ Ocean Drive

SCENIC DRIVE | FAMILY | Also called Ten-Mile Drive, this is a stunningly scenic route starting from the end of Thames Street and looping around the Newport shoreline by following Harrison Avenue and Ridge Road to Ocean Drive and Bellevue Ave., ending at Memorial Blvd. You'll pass by Fort Adams State Park and President Eisenhower's "summer White House"; Hammersmith Farm, Jacqueline Bouvier Kennedy Onassis' family home and the site of her wedding reception when she married John F. Kennedy in 1953; the 89-acre Brenton Point State Park, famous for kite-flying and the ruined remains of The Bells estate; and several small beaches.

Rosecliff

HISTORIC HOME | Newport's most romantic mansion was commissioned by Tessie Fair Oelrichs, who inherited a Nevada silver fortune from her father. Stanford White modeled the 1902 palace after the Grand Trianon at Versailles. Rosecliff has a heart-shape staircase and Newport's largest private ballroom. The mansion stayed in the Oelrichs family until 1941, went through several ownership changes, and then was purchased by Mr. and Mrs. J. Edgar Monroe of New Orleans in 1947. The Monroes were known for throwing big parties. Scenes from the films *The Great Gatsby* (1974), *True Lies* (1994), and *Amistad* (1997) were shot here. The property underwent renovations in 2023. ✉ *548 Bellevue Ave., Newport* ☎ *401/847–1000* 🌐 *www.newportmansions.org* 🎫 *$25* 🕑 *Closed Nov.–Apr.*

★ Rough Point Museum

HISTORIC HOME | Tobacco heiress, philanthropist, and preservationist Doris Duke furnished her 39,000-square-foot English manorial–style house at the southern end of Bellevue Avenue with family treasures, fine art and antiques purchased on her world travels. Highlights include paintings by Renoir, Van Dyck, and Gainsborough, numerous Chinese porcelains, Turkish carpets and Belgian tapestries, and a suite of Louis XVI chairs. Duke's two camels, Baby and Princess (who came with an airplane she had purchased from a Middle Eastern businessman), once summered here on the expansive grounds designed by landscape architect Frederick Law Olmsted. Duke bequeathed the oceanfront house with all of its contents to the Newport Restoration Foundation to operate as a museum after her death. Each year, the foundation assembles an exhibit devoted to Duke's lifestyle and interests, which is included with a guided tour. ✉ *680 Bellevue Ave., Newport* ☎ *401/847–8344* 🌐 *www.newportrestoration.org* 🎫 *$20* 🕑 *Closed Mon. and mid-Nov.–early Apr., except for Fri.-Sun. from Thanksgiving to New Year's.*

Beaches

Easton's Beach (*First Beach*)

BEACH | FAMILY | A ¾-mile-long surfing beach, Easton's has a boardwalk, vintage carousel, aquarium, and playground. Public facilities include restrooms, indoor and outdoor showers, an elevator, and beach wheelchairs for people with disabilities. The snack bar's twin lobster rolls are very popular (and a great deal). **Amenities:** food and drink; lifeguards; parking (fee); showers; toilets. **Best for:** swimming; walking. ✉ *175 Memorial Blvd., Newport* ☎ *401/845–5810* 🌐 *www.cityofnewport.com/visiting-newport/eastons-beach* 🎫 *Free; parking from $15/day.*

Sachuest Beach (*Second Beach*)
BEACH | Located just over the town line in Middletown and more commonly known as Second Beach, this mile-long sandy beach is known for its lively surf–the western end, aptly known as Surfer's End, attracts many surfers. Surfboard and standup paddleboard rentals are available. **Amenities:** food and drink; lifeguards; parking (fee); showers; toilets. **Best for:** surfing; swimming; walking; sunsets. ✉ *474 Sachuest Point Rd., Middletown* ☎ *401/842–6522* 🌐 *www.middletownri.com/349/Beaches* 🎫 *Free; parking from $20.*

Third Beach
BEACH | Located near the mouth of the Sakonnet River in Middletown, Third Beach is more peaceful than other nearby ocean beaches and a great spot for families and windsurfers. It has grills, picnic tables, and a shade structure near the boat ramp. You'll find gear rentals near the south end. **Amenities:** parking (fee); lifeguards. **Best for:** swimming; walking; windsurfing. ✉ *804 Third Beach Rd., Middletown* ☎ *401/842–6519* 🌐 *www.middletownri.com/349/Beaches.*

Restaurants

★ Castle Hill Inn
$$$$ | **AMERICAN** | No other restaurant in Newport can compete with the spectacular water views from the Sunset Room, one of four dining rooms inside the historic main inn. A perfect spot for a romantic dinner, Castle Hill Inn also serves lunch and dinner on The Lawn, allowing you to savor regional cuisine while watching sunlit clouds drift by. **Known for:** New England food done well; prix-fixe dinner menus; 800-bottle wine list. 💲 *Average main: $135* ✉ *590 Ocean Dr., Newport* ☎ *888/466–1355, 401/849–3800* 🌐 *www.castlehillinn.com* ⏲ *Closed Tues.–Wed.*

Flo's Clam Shack
$$ | **SEAFOOD** | **FAMILY** | With Bruce the shark out front and a weathered, kitschy vibe, this local institution across from Easton's Beach in Middletown is as casual as they come. Lobster rolls, fried seafood, baked fish, clam cakes, cold beer, and a great raw bar make for long lines in summer. **Known for:** the best fried clams—ever; raw bar and other dishes served at the upstairs bar; outdoor and upper deck seating available. 💲 *Average main: $19* ✉ *4 Wave Ave., Middletown* ☎ *401/847–8141* 🌐 *www.flosclamshacks.com* 💳 *No credit cards* ⏲ *Closed Nov.–early Mar.*

Coffee and Quick Bites

Mission
$ | **BURGER** | This casual eatery within walking distance of Easton Beach in Middletown has a simple "mission"—deliver great burgers, fries, and hot dogs to the hungry and thirsty shore crowds. A thick and juicy cheeseburger can be had for under $10; toppings are extra and include options like jalapenos or a fried egg. **Known for:** local beer pairings and Nitro coffee on draft; no-frills dining room; big burgers. 💲 *Average main: $9.50* ✉ *58 Aquidneck Ave., Middletown* ☎ *401/324–5811* 🌐 *www.missionnpt.com* ⏲ *Closed Mon.–Tues.*

Hotels

★ Castle Hill Inn
$$$$ | **HOTEL** | Built as a summer house in 1874 for Alexander Agassiz, a scientist and explorer, this luxurious and romantic getaway on a 40-acre peninsula has its own private beach, Farmaesthetics spa, and trails to the Castle Hill Lighthouse, as well as Adirondack chairs on the lawn that beckon you to relax and watch the passing boats. **Pros:** stunning views; excellent restaurant with an elaborate Sunday brunch with live jazz music; variety of rooms; home to the Retreat

at Castle Hill, a "wellness sanctuary" by Rhode Island's own Farmaesthetics. **Cons:** 3 miles from downtown Newport; very expensive; no children under 13 in mansion rooms. *Rooms from: $1,125 ✉ 590 Ocean Dr., Newport ☎ 401/849–3800, 888/466–1355 🌐 www.castlehillinn.com ⇆ 33 rooms 🍽 Free Breakfast.*

★ The Chanler at Cliff Walk

$$$$ | HOTEL | The custom-designed rooms at this 19th-century mansion on the Cliff Walk, now a landmark boutique hotel, represent some of the most unique and luxurious accommodations in Newport. **Pros:** celebrity-level exclusivity and privacy; panoramic water views from many rooms; excellent fine-dining restaurant, Cara; complimentary car service. **Cons:** no elevator; some rooms have steps to access bathroom; expensive. *Rooms from: $1,125 ✉ 117 Memorial Blvd., Newport ☎ 401/847–1300, 866/793–5664 🌐 www.thechanler.com ⇆ 20 rooms 🍽 No Meals.*

Nightlife

To sample Newport's lively nightlife, you need only stroll down Thames Street or the southern end of Broadway after dark.

Fastnet Pub

PUBS | Named for the Fastnet Lighthouse off the coast of Cork, Ireland, this pub hosts Irish jam sessions on Sunday evening, when guest musicians, singers, and dancers familiar with traditional Irish repertoire are invited to participate. Soccer matches bring out raucous crowds that fill the interior as well as the courtyard out back. Irish beers and ciders are on draft, and the food menu includes bangers and beans along with the usual fish and chips and burgers. *✉ 1 Broadway, Newport ☎ 401/845–9311 🌐 www.thefastnetpub.com.*

The Fifth Element

BARS | This chic bar and restaurant, a popular locals hangout, offers specialty cocktails and elevated pub fare amid a smattering of Asian and Mexican-inspired apps and entrees. Next door, the Outer Element is a cute little beer garden where you can toss back a 'Gansett (what locals call Narragansett beer) and ditch Newport's preppy side. *✉ 111 Broadway, Newport ☎ 401/619–2552 🌐 www.thefifthri.com.*

Newport Blues Café

LIVE MUSIC | Housed in a former bank building built in 1892, this café hosts live music, including touring blues acts and tribute bands, plus improv comedy nights. Wallflowers can watch the bands from the second floor, but the real action is on the dance floor in front of the stage. *✉ 286 Thames St., Newport ☎ 401/841–5510 🌐 www.newportblues.com.*

One Pelham East

LIVE MUSIC | An all-ages crowd heads here for eats, drinks, and live music seven days a week, including dueling pianos on Friday and Saturday nights at the Top of Pelham bar upstairs. *✉ 270 Thames St., Newport ☎ 401/847–9460 🌐 www.thepelham.com ⏲ Closed Mon.-Wed. in winter.*

Shopping

Many of Newport's shops and art and crafts galleries are on Thames Street, Spring Street, and at Bowen's and Bannister's Wharfs. The Brick Market area—between Thames Street and America's Cup Avenue—has more than 25 shops. Bellevue Avenue, just south of Memorial Boulevard near the International Tennis Hall of Fame, contains a strip of high-end fashion, skin care, and jewelry shops.

ANTIQUES

Aardvark Antiques

ANTIQUES & COLLECTIBLES | This 30,000-square-foot shop specializes in distinctive architectural salvage such as mantels, doors, stained glass, fountains, and garden statuary including items plucked from places like the Belcourt mansion. *✉ 9 J.T. Connell Hwy., Newport*

☎ 401/849–7233, 800/446–1052 🌐 *aardvarkantiques.com* ⏲ *Closed Sun. except by appointment.*

ART AND CRAFTS GALLERIES

Mariner Gallery

ART GALLERIES | Serious collector or casual art lover, you'll be mesmerized by the luminous maritime paintings exhibited within the 1772 Stephen DuBois House. Works by contemporary masters are strongly represented. Don't leave without making a voyage downstairs to the Constellation Room, a gallery space paneled in solid oak and modeled after the *USS Constellation*. ✉ *267 Spring St., Newport* ☎ *401/218–3309, 401/406–9531* 🌐 *www.marinergallery.com* ⏲ *Closed Mon.-Thurs.*

Spring Bull Gallery

ART GALLERIES | This Rhode Island artists' cooperative, a working studio gallery, changes its shows frequently. One wall is dedicated to its members, who are primarily painters. The gallery's name is a nod to its original location at the corner of Spring and Bull streets. The juried Fakes and Forgeries exhibit, now in its fourth decade, awards prizes for the best copies and reinterpretations of popular paintings. ✉ *55 Bellevue Ave., Newport* ☎ *401/849–9166* 🌐 *www.springbullgallery.com* ⏲ *Closed Tues.*

★ Thames Glass

ART GALLERIES | Through a window in the gallery at Thames Glass, you can watch Matthew Buechner and his team making blown-glass gifts. Sign up for a lesson to make an ornament, paperweight, or vase out of molten glass. ✉ *688 Thames St., Newport* ☎ *401/846–0576* 🌐 *www.thamesglass.com.*

SPAS

The Retreat at Castle Hill by Farmaesthetics

SPAS | Located at Castle Hill Inn, this "wellness sanctuary" operates in collaboration with Farmaesthetics, a Rhode Island-based line of 100% natural herbal skin-care products. Many of the ingredients are harvested from local seaside farms. Spa services include facials, therapeutic and acupressure massage, and pre- or post-treatment saltwater soaks. ✉ *Castle Hill Inn, 590 Ocean Dr., Newport* ☎ *401/849–3800* 🌐 *www.castlehillinn.com/boutique-spa.*

SpaFjör

SPAS | The outstanding SpaFjör, located in the Hotel Viking, offers custom-designed Balinese massage and body rituals and other globally inspired spa experiences—facials, bath rituals, and body wraps—that promote health and well-being but also provide a sense of complete relaxation. For a truly luxurious escape, pick a "journey": the three-hour Day of Bliss (massage, body wrap, and facial) or the 3½-hour Ultimate Escape (Balinese massage, facial, back and foot treatment, and bath ritual). ✉ *Hotel Viking, 1 Bellevue Ave., Newport* ☎ *401/847–3300* 🌐 *www.hotelviking.com/spa.*

Activities

BIKING

Downtown Newport has a bit too much traffic in the summer for carefree biking, but the 10-mile loop around Ocean Drive offers amazing coastal views.

Ten Speed Spokes

BIKING | FAMILY | This shop rents hybrid bikes for $50 per day, and e-bikes for $85 per day. You can also rent by the hour, week, or month (the latter hybrid bikes only). Helmets and locks are included in the rental price. ✉ *18 Elm St., Newport* ☎ *401/847–5609* 🌐 *www.tenspeedspokes.com* ⏲ *Closed Sun. and Mon. and Oct.–Apr.*

BOATING

Sail Newport

BOATING | Enjoy a one-hour "Try Sailing!" experience, take private lessons, or rent a 19- or 22-foot sailboat at Sail Newport, New England's largest public sailing center. The education center and marina are located at Fort Adams State Park.

Newport's naturally protected harbor has made the city a sailing capital.

✉ *Ft. Adams State Park, 72 Ft. Adams Dr., Newport* ☎ *401/846–1983* 🌐 *www.sailnewport.org* ⏲ *Closed Nov.–Memorial Day weekend.*

FISHING

Sara Star Charters

FISHING | Capt. Joe Aiello and his first mate, daughter Coral Rose, will take you on a half- or full-day inshore or offshore fishing trip where you can try to catch your dinner and have a good time. All gear is provided—you just relax and reel. Half-day charters start at $120 per person. ✉ *142 Long Wharf, Newport* ☎ *401/623–1121* 🌐 *www.sarastarcharters.com.*

Performing Arts

Pick up the free *Newport This Week*, or visit www.newportri.com or www.whatsupnewp.com for entertainment listings and news about featured events.

Firehouse Theater

THEATER | FAMILY | It's all about comedy here—local comics, improv, audience participation, even some geared to children. Management of the 75-seat theater tries to keep all shows PG-13, but there's no guarantee. It's BYOB; you can buy water and soda. ✉ *4 Equality Park Pl., Newport* ☎ *401/849–3473* 🌐 *www.firehousetheater.org.*

Newport Playhouse and Cabaret Restaurant

THEATER | The dinner theater offers a varied schedule of comedies and musical shows, and tickets include a hearty buffet with homemade meatballs, pasta, turkey, ham, and lots of veggies and sides. The adorably intimate theater puts you practically in the play, and after the show you'll see the performers again as they put on a musical/comedy cabaret show at the bar. ✉ *102 Connell Hwy., Newport* ☎ *401/848–7529* 🌐 *www.newportplayhouse.com* 🎟 *$67.95.*

Newport Off Season

Summer in Newport can be busy and pricey, but the more affordable off-season takes on a serene, romantic character. No crowds, lower lodging rates, easy and free parking, and midweek specials at restaurants all make the city an appealing destination. The twice-a-year Newport Restaurant Week, held in early November and late March or early April, offers special discounts on two-course lunches and three-course dinners, buy-one, get-one meals, and deals on gift cards at more than 70 participating restaurants.

Fall visitors will enjoy end-of-season sales up and down Thames Street. Although there may be no need to pack a bikini, brisk walks on the beach and Cliff Walk get the blood flowing. In the wintertime, holiday lights glimmer in the early dusk, and bundled-up folks duck into restaurants to warm themselves by the fire and enjoy a drink and a bite to eat.

Newport's holiday season is lovely. A light snowfall can peel back the years, and it isn't difficult to imagine the city 200 years ago. Bowen's Wharf, decked out in white lights, provides Newport with its version of the Rockefeller Center tree. "Christmas in Newport," a program that began in 1971, hosts a number of activities—tree lightings, Nativity scenes, a lighted boat parade, dances, concerts, and visits by Santa—for nearly every day of the December calendar. The Breakers, the Elms, and Marble House are dressed up in full holiday regalia beginning in mid-November. The Breakers, filled with evergreens and thousands of poinsettias, hosts live holiday music on Saturday evenings, and Rosecliff is an exquisite setting for performances of *The Nutcracker.*

Fun options with the kids are ice skating at the Newport Harbor Hotel's outdoor rink and, during February school break, the annual Newport Winter Festival, with concerts, ice-carving demos, the Mac & Cheese Smackdown, and a chili cook-off.

Portsmouth

9 miles north of Newport.

Largely a bedroom community for Newport, Portsmouth attracts visitors for polo matches, its fanciful topiary garden, and the Greenvale winery. The town also has an interesting history. A religious dissident named Anne Hutchinson (for whom New York's Hutchinson River Parkway is named) led a group of settlers to the Portsmouth area in 1638 after being banished from the Massachusetts Bay Colony. The town was also the site of the Battle of Rhode Island in August 1778, when American troops—including a locally recruited African American regiment—withdrew, leaving Aquidneck Island under British control.

Sights

Green Animals Topiary Garden

GARDEN | FAMILY | Fanciful animals, a sailing ship, and geometric shapes populate this large topiary garden on a Narragansett Bay-side Victorian estate that served as the summer residence of a Fall River, Massachusetts, textile mill owner. In addition to the whimsical topiaries, there are flower and herb gardens, orchards, and winding pathways. Picnicking among the shrubbery is encouraged. ✉ *380*

Spend an afternoon wandering among living sculptures at the Green Animals Topiary Garden in Portsmouth.

Cory's La., off Rte. 114, Portsmouth ☎ 401/847–1000 🌐 www.newportmansions.org 🎫 $20.

Greenvale Vineyards

WINERY | A restored stable on an eight-generations-old farm houses the tasting room of this small producer. All wines, including the semisweet Skipping Stone White with peach notes and the well-balanced Meritage red blend, are made from grapes grown and hand-harvested on the property. Tastings are offered most of the year, and outdoor tables overlooking neat rows of vines abound. On Saturday, May–early December, the winery hosts live jazz concerts. ✉ *582 Wapping Rd., Portsmouth ☎ 401/847–3777 🌐 www.greenvale.com 🎫 Tastings and tours from $15 🕒 Closed weekdays Jan.–mid-Feb.*

Rail Explorers

SCENIC DRIVE | **FAMILY** | The tracks for the Old Colony Railroad were laid in the 1860s; Rail Explorers' tandem and quad rail machines are newfangled contraptions that make it easy to glide six miles along Narragansett Bay as long as at least one member of your group is willing to pedal. Guide-led tours of either the Northern Ramble or Southern Circuit offer glimpses of shorebirds, coastal woodlands, and historic sites few travelers get the chance to see. ✉ *1 Alexander Rd., Portsmouth ☎ 877/833–8588 🌐 www.railexplorers.net 🎫 from $40 per person 🕒 Closed Nov.–mid-May.*

Activities

POLO

Newport International Polo Series

POLO | **FAMILY** | Head to America's oldest polo club for an action-packed afternoon. Teams from across the nation and around the world compete in Saturday matches during the Newport International Polo Series, June to September, at Glen Farm in Portsmouth. Spectators are invited to stomp divots at the half and mingle with players and pet the horses after the match. Dress spiffy and arrive early with your picnic lunch to get a choice tailgating spot. Food trucks and walk-up bars are also available, or have the Veuve Clicquot Cart deliver bubbly to your picnic spot. ✉ *Glen Farm, 250 Linden La., Portsmouth* ☎ *401/846–0200* 🌐 *www.nptpolo.com* 🎫 *From $20.*

Bristol

15 miles north of Newport, 17 miles southeast of Providence.

The home of the longest-running July 4 celebration—it began in 1785—Bristol shows off its patriotism with a red-white-and-blue center stripe down Hope Street, its charming business district, and flags flying from many homes and businesses. Midway between Newport and Providence—each a 30-minute drive away—Bristol sits on a 10-square-mile peninsula, shared with the town of Warren and located between Narragansett Bay to the west and Mt. Hope Bay to the east. Bristol was once a boatbuilding center; the Herreshoff Manufacturing Company built five consecutive America's Cup defenders between 1893 and 1920. Independence Park marks the southern end of the 14½-mile East Bay Bike Path, which crosses the access road for Colt State Park, a great spot for picnicking and kite flying.

Sights

Blithewold

GARDEN | **FAMILY** | Starting with a sea of daffodils in April, this 33-acre estate on Bristol Harbor blooms all the way to fall. Highlights include fragrant pink chestnut roses and one of the largest giant sequoia trees on the East Coast. The gardens are open year-round. The 45-room English-style manor house, opened seasonally, is filled with original antiques and artworks. ✉ *101 Ferry Rd. (Rte. 114), Bristol* ☎ *401/253–2707* 🌐 *www.blithewold.org* 🎫 *$15* ⏲ *Closed Mon. in summer and Mon.–Tues. in winter.*

Herreshoff Marine Museum/America's Cup Hall Of Fame

OTHER MUSEUM | This maritime museum, devoted to the sport of yachting, honors the Herreshoff Manufacturing Company, maker of yachts for five consecutive America's Cup defenses. The museum's several dozen boats range from an 8½-foot dinghy to the *Defiant,* a 75-foot successful America's Cup defender. Halsey Herreshoff, a four-time cup defender and the grandson of yacht designer and company co-founder Nathanael Greene Herreshoff, established the Hall of Fame in 1992 as an arm of the museum, which hosts talks on yacht design and restoration and operates a sailing school for both kids and adults. ✉ *1 Burnside St., Bristol* ☎ *401/253–5000* 🌐 *www.herreshoff.org* 🎫 *$15* ⏲ *Closed Mon.–Tues. in Oct.; Mon.–Wed., Nov. and Dec. Closed Jan.–Apr.*

Warren

TOWN | North of Bristol, Warren has the distinction of being the smallest town in the smallest county in the smallest state in the United States. The East Bay Bike Path travels through Warren's commercial district, so stop for a Del's frozen lemonade, browse the unmissable Imagine Gift Store, or catch a performance at the eclectic Galactic Theater. ✉ *Warren* 🌐 *www.discoverwarren.com.*

Restaurants

Beehive Café

$ | **AMERICAN** | This aptly named two-story café is abuzz with college students and foodies who appreciate the freshly baked bread, especially when it's used to make inventive sandwiches like roasted butternut squash with caramelized onions, Vermont cheddar, and tangy-sweet pesto. The extensive breakfast menu (served 12 hours a day) includes thick-cut French toast, cornbread hash, and granola made on-site. **Known for:** downtown location; cozy seating; patio and balcony dining in warm weather. 💲 *Average main: $14* ✉ *10 Franklin St., Bristol* ☎ *401/396–9994* 🌐 *www.thebeehivecafe.com.*

DeWolf Tavern

$$$ | ECLECTIC | An 1818 rum distillery houses this distinctive waterfront restaurant—look for the timber ceilings, African granite from slave ship ballast in the walls, and framed sections of early-19th-century graffiti-covered plaster. Chef Sai Viswanath reinvents traditional New England fare by combining it with Indian preparations to create dishes like lobster roasted in a 900°F tandoor oven and chicken empanadas served with a tamarind and mint chutney. **Known for:** buck-a-shuck oysters on Monday; alfresco dining on the back deck in summer; cozy dining upstairs by the fireplace in winter; breakfast on weekends. 💲 *Average main: $32* ✉ *259 Thames St., Bristol* ☎ *401/254–2005* 🌐 *www.dewolftavern.com.*

The Lobster Pot

$$$$ | SEAFOOD | Folks have been coming here since 1929 for lobster: as a salad roll, on pizza, or whole—but wait, there's also grilled swordfish, pan-seared cod, broiled scallops, bouillabaise, and steak or chicken, too. At lunch or dinner, start with a craft brew or cocktail, then build your own plate from the raw bar: jumbo shrimp, oysters, littleneck and cherrystone clams, or cold lobster cocktail. **Known for:** classic New England seafood; harborside location; patio dining in summer, cozy fireplace in winter. 💲 *Average main: $38* ✉ *119 Hope St., Bristol* ☎ *401/253–9100* 🌐 *www.lobsterpotri.com* ⏲ *Closed Mon. and Tues. in off-season.*

Roberto's

$$$ | ITALIAN | The East Bay's best Italian restaurant can compete with any establishment on Federal Hill with its house-made meatballs, classic veal and chicken preparations, and a thoughtful wine list. One wall of the elegant dining room is paneled with wine crates; breakfast and lunch are served at the affiliated Roberto's Cafe. **Known for:** cell-phone-free zone; reservations essential on summer weekends; alfresco dining in summer. 💲 *Average main: $25* ✉ *450 Hope St., Bristol* ☎ *401/254–9732* 🌐 *www.robertos-bristol.com/* ⏲ *No lunch.*

Hotels

Bristol Harbor Inn

$ | HOTEL | Ideally situated adjacent to DeWolf Tavern and just steps from the East Bay Bike Path, this waterfront boutique hotel has fresh, nautical styling and sunny guest rooms. **Pros:** reasonably priced for a waterfront hotel; convenient location; spa on-site; free parking. **Cons:** other than shops, restaurants, and marina, there are no exterior grounds; no breakfast or coffee available free to guests (although Empire Tea & Coffee is on-site); no room service. 💲 *Rooms from: $179* ✉ *Thames Landing, 259 Thames St., Bristol* ☎ *401/254–1444, 866/254–1444* 🌐 *www.bristolharborinn.com* *52 rooms* *No Meals.*

Activities

BIKING

East Bay Bike Path

BIKING | FAMILY | Affording majestic views of Narragansett Bay, the flat, paved, 14½-mile East Bay Bike Path connects Providence and Bristol's historic downtown. Along the way, riders, skaters, runners and walkers will pass through Riverside with its historic carousel, the towns of Barrington and Warren, Colt State Park, and Burr's Hill Park where the grave site of the great Wampanoag chief Massasoit is located. ✉ *Thames St., Bristol* ☎ *401/222-2450* 🌐 *www.dot.ri.gov/travel/bikeri/eastbay.php.*

Fishing boats rest off the coast of Rhode Island.

Tiverton and Little Compton

Tiverton, 8 miles south of Bristol; Little Compton, 12 miles south of Tiverton.

This southernmost corner of Rhode Island, home to artists and working farms, is a pleasant afternoon drive from Newport or Bristol. Consider a hike in Tiverton's Weetamoo Woods or Little Compton's Wilbour Woods. Or, wander Tiverton Four Corners to check out the village's artist studios and arts center and make a stop at Little Compton's Commons for history and johnnycakes.

GETTING HERE AND AROUND

From Route 24 at the Sakonnet River Bridge, take Route 77 south for about 5¾ miles to reach historic Tiverton Four Corners. Continuing south to Little Compton you'll pass rolling estates, lovely homes, farmland, woods, and a gentle shoreline. Turn north to explore Tiverton.

Sights

Carolyn's Sakonnet Vineyard

WINERY | White, rosé, red, and dessert wines are all in the portfolio of this winery founded in 1975 and reinvigorated since 2012 by second owner Carolyn Rafaelian of Alex and Ani jewelry fame. If you've ever wondered what a Rhode Island Red (not the chicken!) might taste like, here's your chance to find out. Several of the wines are award winners. In the winery's tasting room you can sample seven of them and keep the glass. ✉ *162 W. Main Rd., Little Compton* ☎ *401/635–8486* 🌐 *www.sakonnetwine.com* 🎫 *Tasting $14* 🕒 *Closed Tues.–Thurs.*

Little Compton Commons

PLAZA/SQUARE | This archetypal coastal New England town square is actually Rhode Island's only town common. More of a long triangle than a square, the common is anchored by the Georgian-style United Congregational Church. Among the headstones in the nearby cemetery, you'll find one for Elizabeth Pabodie, the eldest daughter of *Mayflower* Pilgrims John and Priscilla Alden. Surrounding the green are a rock wall and all the elements of a small community: town hall, community center, schools, library, general store, and restaurant. ✉ *1 Commons, Little Compton* 🌐 *www.littlecomptonri.org.*

Sakonnet Point

NATURE SIGHT | A scenic drive down Route 77 ends at this quiet southeastern tip of Rhode Island. People like to fish off the Army Corps of Engineers breakwater, or walk along it to enjoy views of the harbor. The 1884 Sakonnet Lighthouse on Little Cormorant Rock is picturesque, offshore, and not open to the public. Parking is limited in the area. ✉ *Sakonnet Point, 19 Bluff Head Ave., Little Compton.*

Tiverton Four Corners

BUSINESS DISTRICT | Historic Tiverton Four Corners has been a part of Tiverton's history since 1629 when Governor Bradford of the Plymouth Colony purchased the area (then called Pocasset) from the native inhabitants. The "four corners" intersection follows the original trails. Today, the Four Corners Arts Center, in the circa 1800 Soule-Seabury House, hosts an annual antiques show, as well as art festivals and exhibits, concerts and movement classes, and other special events. Gray's Ice Cream and the Groundswell Cafe & Bakery also are located here. ✉ *Rte. 179, at Rte. 77, Tiverton* 🌐 *www.tivertonfourcorners.com.*

Weetamoo Woods & Pardon Gray Preserve

FOREST | FAMILY | Weetamoo Woods takes its name from a formidable female sachem of the Pocasset Wampanoag tribe. There are more than 10 miles of walking trails within this 650-acre town-owned parcel and the adjacent 230-acre Pardon Gray Preserve, which encompass a coastal oak-holly forest, an Atlantic white cedar swamp, two grassland meadows, early-American cellar holes, and the remains of a mid-19th-century village sawmill. The main entrance to Weetamoo Woods, ¼-mile east of Tiverton Four Corners, has a parking area and a kiosk with maps. ✉ *East Rd., Tiverton* ☎ *401/625–1300* 🌐 *www.tivertonlandtrust.org.*

Wilbour Woods

FOREST | FAMILY | This 85-acre hollow with picnic tables and a waterfall is a good place for a casual hike along a marked 1.6-mile loop trail that passes through a rare maritime oak-holly forest and winds along and over Dundery Brook. The trail passes a boulder dedicated to Queen Awashonks, who ruled the local Saugkonnates tribe during the early Colonial period. ✉ *100 Swamp Rd., Little Compton* 🌐 *www.littlecomptonri.org.*

Restaurants

The Boat House

$$$ | SEAFOOD | This Tiverton restaurant masters the art of elegant waterfront dining with views of the Mount Hope Bridge and a menu that covers all of the New England seafood bases, from the raw bar and chowder to calamari and curried mussels. It's the kind of place meant for lingering over a long dinner, but not too pretentious to leave sandwiches off the menu. **Known for:** good mix of local favorites and classic dishes; energetic atmosphere in the dining room; great water views, including bridge lights at night. 💲 *Average main: $27* ✉ *227 Schooner Dr., Tiverton* ☎ *401/624–6300* 🌐 *www.boathousetiverton.com.*

The Commons Lunch

$ | AMERICAN | Not only are johnnycakes a unique Rhode Island food, but there are also regional variations within this small state on how to make these white corn pancakes. Located right on the Little Compton Commons, of course, the Commons is a leading purveyor of the thin and crispy East Bay variety, along with family-friendly meal-time options, and fried local seafood. **Known for:** Rhode Island johnnycakes; affordable food; local atmosphere. [$] *Average main: $10* ✉ *48 Commons St., Little Compton* ☎ *401/635–4388.*

Coffee and Quick Bites

Evelyn's Drive In

$ | **SEAFOOD** | This family-run roadside seafood shack draws summer visitors like moths to a streetlight. Lobster chow mein is an unusual specialty of the house, but the menu also includes more familiar fried seafood favorites along with burgers and other quick bites. **Known for:** outdoor dining; fried clams and lobster chop suey; homemade desserts. [$] *Average main: $16* ✉ *2335 Main Rd., Tiverton* ☎ *401/624–3100* 🌐 *www.evelynsdrivein.com* ⏲ *Closed Oct.–mid-May.*

★ **Gray's Ice Cream**

$ | **AMERICAN** | A summertime pilgrimage for people from every corner of the state, Gray's has been around since 1923 and sells more than 30 flavors of ice cream, all made on the premises. Coffee is the go-to flavor for many Rhode Islanders, but specialties such as Indian pudding and apple caramel spice have their adherents. **Known for:** cones, cups, cabinets (milk shakes without ice cream), and frappes (milk shakes with ice cream), frozen yogurt, sherbet, and sugar-free flavors, too; open 365 days year-round. [$] *Average main: $6* ✉ *16 East Rd., Tiverton* ☎ *401/624–4500* 🌐 *www.graysicecream.com.*

Providence

Big-city sophistication with small-city charm: Providence has the best of both worlds. A thriving arts community, prestigious Brown University and Rhode Island School of Design (RISD), an impressive restaurant scene bolstered by the College of Culinary Arts at local Johnson & Wales University, countless festivals and events, a revitalized Downtown, and on-water recreation all help the city live up to its nickname: the Creative Capital. Providence is a worthy stop on any New England tour.

The Moshassuck and Woonasquatucket Rivers merge just southeast of the Rhode Island State House to form the Providence River. Scenic Waterplace Park hosts WaterFire, a crowd-pleasing series of summer and fall evening bonfires on the rivers. This relatively recent tradition beloved by locals and visitors alike began in the 1990s, but Providence gives equal weight to its long history, celebrating everything from its wealth of Colonial architecture to its literary tradition. After all, H. P. Lovecraft, author of fantasy and horror fiction, was a son of Providence, and Edgar Allan Poe courted poet Sarah Helen Whitman here.

GETTING ORIENTED

The narrow Providence River acts as a natural boundary between two major neighborhoods in the heart of the city. Downtown, the business district, lies west of the river; the East Side, on the opposite shore, is where the city's history began. (Don't confuse Providence's East Side with East Providence, a separate city.) Federal Hill, historically an Italian neighborhood, pushes west of Downtown along Atwells Avenue; the up-and-coming West Side includes dining and shopping along Broadway and Westminster Street. The white-marble dome of the Rhode Island State House is visible just north of Downtown. On the East Side, South Main and Benefit Streets run parallel to the Providence River. The Brown University campus is in the East Side neighborhood called College Hill, at the top of which Thayer Street runs north–south. Farther north and east are mainly residential neighborhoods.

GETTING HERE AND AROUND

Rhode Island T. F. Green International Airport is 10 miles south of Providence in Warwick. By taxi, the ride between the airport and Downtown hotels takes about 20 minutes and costs around $35.

An Uber or LYFT ride will cost $15–$25, depending on your destination. The Massachusetts Bay Transportation Authority (MBTA) commuter rail service connects the airport and Downtown for $3.25, although service is limited.

At Kennedy Plaza you can board the local Rhode Island Public Transit Authority (RIPTA) buses. The Route 92 bus links Federal Hill to the East Side, and the Route 6 bus links Downtown to the Roger Williams Park Zoo. RIPTA fares are $2 per ride; an all-day pass is $6. Exact change is needed when boarding buses, or you'll get your change back in the form of a fare card. RIPTA buses also service T. F. Green International Airport from Providence via Route 20. RIPTA also operates a seasonal ferry service between Providence and Newport, with bus connections between the Providence Amtrak station and the ferry terminal at India Point Park.

Rhode Island Public Transit Authority. (*RIPTA*) ✉ *Kennedy Plaza Passenger Terminal, 1 Kennedy Plaza, Downtown* ☎ *401/781–9400* 🌐 *www.ripta.com.*

Overnight parking is not generally allowed on Providence streets. During the day it can be difficult to find curbside parking, especially Downtown and on Federal Hill and College Hill. There is a large parking garage at Providence Place mall with reasonable rates for short stays. Metered rates for street parking are 75 cents for 30 minutes or 25 cents for every 10 minutes.

The basic taxi rate in Providence is $3.50 for the first mile, and $0.30 for each succeeding tenth of a mile.

Amtrak trains between New York and Boston stop at Westerly, West Kingston, and Providence. From Boston, you can also take an MBTA commuter train to Providence, T.F. Green Airport, and Wickford Junction (North Kingstown).

Massachusetts Bay Transportation Authority. (*MBTA*) ☎ *617/222–3200* 🌐 *www.mbta.com.*

DINING

The hard part about dining in Providence is choosing among its many superb restaurants. If you're in the mood for Italian, take a stroll along Atwells Avenue on Federal Hill; Downtown is home to excellent fine-dining establishments; and the East Side has great neighborhood and upscale-casual restaurants, as well as an assortment of spots with a hip ambience and an international menu.

NIGHTLIFE

For events listings, consult the daily *Providence Journal* or the websites 🌐 www.providenceonline.com or 🌐 www.goprovidence.com. The monthly *Motif* or *Providence Monthly* are both available (free) in restaurants and shops.

SHOPPING

Providence has a handful of small but engaging shopping areas. In Fox Point, Wickenden Street has many antiques stores and several art galleries. Near Brown University, Thayer Street has a number of boutiques, though there has been an influx of chain stores. With its eclectic collection of specialty stores, Hope Street has branded itself as the East Side's "Main Street." Wayland Square, also on the East Side, is a historic neighborhood emerging as a destination for upscale home goods and clothing. Downtown's Westminster Street has morphed into a strip of independently owned fashion boutiques and design stores.

TOURS

Gallery Night Providence

SPECIAL-INTEREST TOURS | During Gallery Night, held on the third Thursday of the month March–November, many galleries and museums hold open houses and mount special exhibitions. Free two-hour Trolley Tours, some led by local celebrities, visit four or five galleries; tours depart at scheduled times, typically between 5:30 pm and 7 pm, from the Graduate Providence (one monthly tour departs from the WaterFire Arts Center). ✉ *Graduate Providence, 11 Dorrance St., Providence* ☎ *401/484–0726* 🌐 *www.gallerynight.org.*

Providence Preservation Society

SELF-GUIDED TOURS | The historical preservation society publishes about two dozen digital tours focusing on various aspects of Providence architecture, including pre-Revolutionary Providence, endangered properties, and neighborhood tours from Federal Hill to the Jewelry District. ✉ *24 Meeting St., at Benefit St., Providence* ☎ *401/831–7440* 🌐 *www.ppsri.org/tours* 🎫 *$3.*

Rhode Island Red Food Tours

SPECIAL-INTEREST TOURS | This Newport-based tour company offers food journeys (3–3½ hours) in Providence's Downcity Arts District, tasting and sipping your way through at least six eateries—from casual comfort food to fine-dining restaurants. Along the way you'll learn about the district's architecture and history. The tours are offered on Friday, Saturday, and Sunday, mid-April through November, starting at noon. It's a 1.7-mile walking tour, so wear comfortable shoes. ✉ *270 Bellevue Ave., Newport* ☎ *401/684–1110* 🌐 *www.rhodeislandredfoodtours.com* 🎫 *From $74.*

VISITOR INFORMATION

CONTACTS Providence Warwick Convention & Visitors Bureau. ✉ *10 Memorial Blvd., Providence* ☎ *401/456–0200* 🌐 *www.goprovidence.com.*

Downtown

Providence has 25 official neighborhoods and a handful of unofficial ones, each with its own identity. The Downtown neighborhood, sometimes referred to as Downcity, is the city's thriving artistic, financial, mercantile, transportation, and political core. Downtown comprises a very walkable area (it's flat!) roughly bordered by the Providence River on the east, Interstate 95 on the west, the Rhode Island State House to the north, and the Providence River Pedestrian Bridge in the south. You'll find theaters, hotels, shops, restaurants, and college buildings on Downtown's maze of streets, as well as the often-bustling Waterplace Park—a perfect place to watch the summer and autumn WaterFire displays.

Sights

★ BankNewport City Center

OTHER ATTRACTION | FAMILY | The 14,000-square-foot outdoor ice rink, right in the heart of downtown Providence, is twice the size of the one at New York City's Rockefeller Center. The facility is open for skating and ice bumper cars daily, late November–mid-March, and skate and helmet rentals are available. In summer, kids love driving the bumper cars, roller skating (and roller disco!), and bubble soccer (trying to score while wearing a giant bubble). The center also hosts movies, summer concerts, festivals, and other events. ✉ *2 Kennedy Plaza, Providence* ☎ *401/680–7390* 🌐 *www.theprovidencerink.com* 🎫 *From $7.*

★ Providence Children's Museum

CHILDREN'S MUSEUM | FAMILY | The vibrant, interactive, hands-on learning environments here are geared to children ages 1 to 11 and their families. Favorite exhibits and activities include Water Ways, ThinkSpace, Maker Studio, and Coming to Rhode Island, which encourages kids to imagine the experience of immigrating to the Ocean State. Littlewoods, for toddlers, has a tree house, bear cave, and a slide. Kids can also explore an outdoor climbing structure and imitate burrowing creatures in Underland. ✉ *100 South St., Jewelry District* ☎ *401/273–5437* 🌐 *www.providencechildrensmuseum.org* 🎫 *$14.*

Providence Pedestrian Bridge

BRIDGE | Officially the Michael S. Van Leesten Memorial Bridge (named for a prominent civil-rights advocate, business leader, and driver of economic advancement in Providence), this 450-foot-long footbridge spans the Providence River. Similar in style to New York's High Line, the bridge features performance spaces, public seating, and fantastic skyline views. Opened in 2019, the bridge is the final link creating a downtown loop walk that includes new parks on the East Side and the Jewelry District banks of the river, and extending north through downtown's Waterplace Park. ✉ *South Water St., Downtown* ✣ *at James St.*

Rhode Island State House

GOVERNMENT BUILDING | **FAMILY** | Designed by the noted architecture firm McKim, Mead & White and completed in 1904, Rhode Island's beautiful capitol building boasts the world's fourth-largest self-supported marble dome. The gilded Independent Man statue that tops the dome was struck by lightning at least 27 times before lightning rods were installed in 1975. Inside, visitors can see a full-length portrait of George Washington by Rhode Islander Gilbert Stuart, who also painted the portrait of Washington that appears on the $1 bill. On display in the Governor's State Room are the military accoutrements of Nathanael Greene, a Quaker who served as George Washington's second-in-command during the Revolutionary War. The State Library, on the north side of the building, has moon rocks and the state flag carried on board Apollo 11's first lunar landing mission in 1969 among its displays. The centerpiece of the State House's Charter Museum is Rhode Island's original 1663 Colonial Charter granted by King Charles II—the first charter signed by a monarch that guaranteed religious liberty. Guided tours lasting 50 minutes are offered at 10 am and 1 pm on weekdays, excluding holidays. You can also follow a self-guided tour. ✉ *82 Smith St., Downtown* ☎ *401/222–3983* 🌐 *www.sos.ri.gov/divisions/civics-and-education/ri-state-house* 🎫 *Free* ⏲ *Closed weekends.*

Waterplace Park

PLAZA/SQUARE | **FAMILY** | Venetian-style footbridges, cobblestone walkways, and an amphitheater encircling a tidal basin set the tone at this 4-acre tract along the Woonasquatucket River near where it joins the Moshassuck to form the Providence River. In summer and fall, it's the site of WaterFire, a multisensory installation featuring music, performances, and 80 wood-fired braziers permanently placed in the middle of the river and set afire between dusk and midnight on some nights. WaterFire attracts nearly 1 million visitors annually. Gondola and riverboat tours of the park and rivers are offered seasonally at during special events. ✉ *1 Finance Way, overlooking Woonasquatucket River, Downtown* ☎ *401/273–1155 for WaterFire information.*

 Restaurants

CAV

$$$ | **ECLECTIC** | Chandeliers hang from the ceiling, and African and Asian artwork adorns the walls (everything is for sale) at this restaurant-antiques store. The menu is extensive—seafood is particularly, but not exclusively, featured—the food is rich in flavor, and the ambience, occasionally augmented with live music, is full of personality. **Known for:** imaginative presentation of menu favorites; bistro menu Monday–Wednesday; brioche toast at weekend brunch. 💲 *Average main: $29* ✉ *14 Imperial Pl., Jewelry District* ☎ *401/751–9164* 🌐 *www.cavrestaurant.com.*

Durk's BBQ

$$ | **BARBECUE** | Rhode Island isn't top-of-mind when you think of great barbecue joints—this ain't Texas, Memphis, or the Carolinas, to be sure—but it's hard to find fault with Durk's succulent brisket, moist

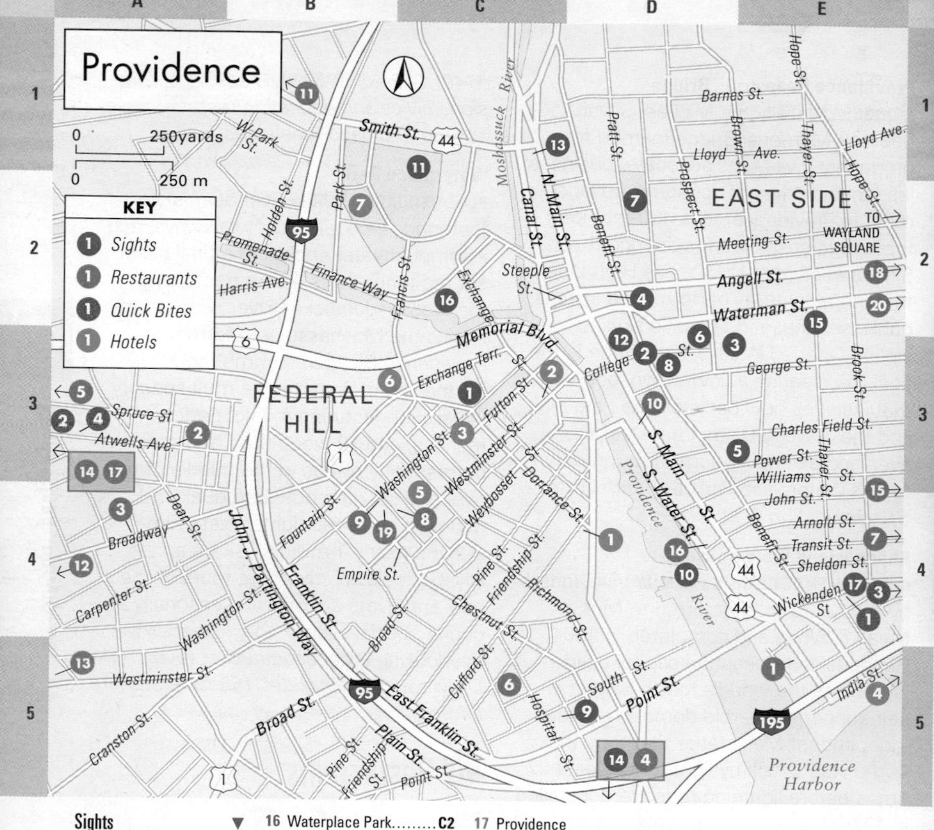

Sights

1 BankNewport City Center C3
2 Benefit Street D3
3 Brown University D3
4 First Baptist Church in America D2
5 John Brown House Museum E3
6 John Hay Library D3
7 Prospect Terrace D2
8 Providence Athenaeum D3
9 Providence Children's Museum D5
10 Providence Pedestrian Bridge D4
11 Rhode Island State House C1
12 RISD Museum D3
13 Roger Williams National Memorial C1
14 Roger Williams Park Zoo & Carousel Village D5
15 Thayer Street E2
16 Waterplace Park C2
17 Wickenden Street E4

Restaurants

1 Al Forno E5
2 Angelo's Civita Farnese A3
3 Broadway Bistro A4
4 Buttonwoods Brewery D5
5 Caserta Pizzeria A3
6 CAV C5
7 Chomp Kitchen & Drinks E4
8 Durk's BBQ C4
9 Gracie's B4
10 Hemenway's D3
11 Los Andes B1
12 Nick's on Broadway A4
13 Ogie's Trailer Park A5
14 Pane e Vino A3
15 Persimmon E3
16 Plant City D4
17 Providence Oyster Bar A3
18 Red Stripe E2
19 Rosalina B4
20 The Salted Slate E2

Quick Bites

1 Coffee Exchange E4
2 Costantino's Venda Ravioli A3
3 PVDonuts E4
4 Scialo Bros. Bakery A3

Hotels

1 Aloft Providence D4
2 The Beatrice C3
3 Graduate Providence C3
4 Hilton Garden Inn E5
5 Hotel Providence C4
6 Omni Providence B3
7 Renaissance Providence Downtown Hotel B2

Providence's annual WaterFire festival has more than 80 bonfires set upon the river.

pulled pork, and smoky ribs. Savory sides like skillet cornbread and mac & cheese provide the right flavor balance on the plate, and drinks draw heavily from the collected "whiskey wall" behind the bar—you can't go wrong with the barrel-aged Old Fashioned on draft. **Known for:** BBQ fresh out of "Stella" the smoker; extensive whiskey and bourbon collection; fun appetizers like corn dogs and pierogies. *Average main: $16* *33 Aborn St., Downtown* *401/563–8622* *durksbbq.com* *No lunch Mon.–Fri.*

★ Gracie's

$$$$ | MODERN AMERICAN | The city's best spot for a romantic meal is Table 21 in a private alcove at Gracie's, across the street from the Trinity Rep theater. Owner Ellen Gracyalny mixes sophistication with whimsy in the main dining room, and executive chef Matthew Varga sources many of his ingredients from a local Rhode Island farmer; Varga's tasting menus are a standard setter for fine dining in Providence. **Known for:** seasonally inspired menu; four-course prix-fixe and seven-course, wine-paired chef's tasting menus; personalized service. *Average main: $55* *194 Washington St., Downtown* *401/272–7811* *www.graciesprov.com* *Closed Mon.–Tues. No lunch.*

★ Rosalina

$$$ | ITALIAN | You'll find some of the best southern Italian food you've ever tasted at this cozy, family-run Italian restaurant tucked away on a Providence side street. The chef also serves up delicious grilled swordfish, whole branzino, and NY strip steak, but be sure to have the antipasto, fried dough with Pomodoro sauce, or eggplant parm appetizers—all great for sharing. **Known for:** focus on locally sourced foods; imported olive oil from family-owned groves in Kalamata, Greece; portions are generous so prepare to share. *Average main: $28* *50 Aborn St., Downtown* *401/270–7330* *www.eatatrosalina.com* *No lunch.*

Aloft Providence

$$ | **HOTEL** | The Jewelry District is Providence's hottest neighborhood, and in the heart of the action is the new Aloft hotel, with rooms that have a colorful pop-art design that nods to its proximity to the Rhode Island School of Design and both a trendy lobby cocktail bar, WXYZ, and a popular rooftop nightclub, Blu Violet. **Pros:** wide variety of nightlife options; clever room decor enhancing city views; located in the vibrant Innovation and Design District aka the Jewelry District. **Cons:** valet parking is $32 a day; food service limited to small bites at WXYZ; long-ish walk to some downtown attractions. *Rooms from: $249* ✉ *191 Dorrance St., Jewelry District* ☎ *401/252–0710* 🌐 *www.marriott.com* *175 rooms.*

The Beatrice

$$ | **HOTEL** | The historic four-story Exchange Bank Building is the perfect location for one of Providence's newest luxury boutique hotels, which has a cozy charm paired with stylish rooms and views of downtown streets. **Pros:** excellent downtown location; Bellini is one of the city's top restaurants; pet-friendly. **Cons:** Bellini Rooftop open only to club members and hotel guests; parking is $35-45 per night. *Rooms from: $299* ✉ *90 Westminster St., Downtown* ☎ *401/443–2960* 🌐 *www.thebeatrice.com* *47 rooms.*

Graduate Providence

$ | **HOTEL** | **FAMILY** | The city's beloved landmark since 1922, the former Providence Biltmore revels in nostalgia for its flapper heyday, but it has refreshed appeal for tourists thanks to a chic and studious makeover, with welcome additions like new restaurants and a spa. **Pros:** spacious suites with a literary vibe; great Downtown location; complimentary bikes; Poindexter Coffee and Reiners restauranrt are off the lobby. **Cons:** some bathrooms are cramped; street noise, especially in lower-floor rooms. *Rooms from: $188* ✉ *11 Dorrance St., Downtown* ☎ *401/421–0700* 🌐 *www.graduatehotels.com/providence* *294 rooms* *No Meals.*

Hotel Providence

$$ | **HOTEL** | In the heart of the city's Arts and Entertainment District, this intimate boutique hotel sets the standard for elegant decor and attentive service. **Pros:** convenient location for theatergoers; handicapped accessible rooms available; pet-friendly; restaurant, Backstage Kitchen + Bar, serves creative, well-prepared small plates, light meals, and full entrées. **Cons:** late risers may not appreciate the 8 am pealing of Grace Church's 16 bells; street noise also an issue; parking is $32 per night. *Rooms from: $229* ✉ *139 Mathewson St., Downtown* ☎ *401/861–8000, 800/861–8990* 🌐 *www.hotelprovidence.com* *96 rooms* *No Meals.*

★ Omni Providence

$$ | **HOTEL** | **FAMILY** | Towering over Downtown, the Omni is steps from restaurants, the Rhode Island Convention Center, the Amica Mutual Pavilion (formerly Dunkin' Donuts Center), and Waterplace Park, home of WaterFire. **Pros:** indoor pool; beautiful views of the city from upper floors; child- and pet-friendly. **Cons:** rooms are rather ordinary; in-room Wi-Fi costs extra if not a rewards member; breakfast is $11 and up; valet parking is $34. *Rooms from: $289* ✉ *1 W. Exchange St., Downtown* ☎ *401/598–8000, 888/444–6664* 🌐 *www.omnihotels.com/hotels/providence* *564 rooms* *No Meals.*

Renaissance Providence Downtown Hotel

$$$ | **HOTEL** | This luxury hotel occupies one of Providence's most mysterious addresses, a stately nine-story Neoclassical Revival building constructed as a Masonic temple between 1926 and 1928 but unoccupied for an inconceivable 79 years. **Pros:** convenient location next to Providence Place Mall; three meals per day served at on-site Public Kitchen &

The Independent Man sculpture atop the State House symbolizes Rhode Island's free-thinking spirit.

Bar; beautiful views of the Capitol. **Cons:** some rooms have small windows or no view; rooms on I–95 side can be noisy; valet parking is $32 per night. *Rooms from: $323 ✉ 5 Ave. of the Arts, Downtown ☎ 401/919–5000, 800/468–3571 🌐 www.marriott.com 272 rooms No Meals.*

Nightlife

BARS

The Eddy

BARS | The Eddy specializes in classic cocktails like a Manhattan, gin and tonic (on draft), or Gibson; creative concoctions like the rum-based "Kingston negroni-doli" or the rye-Calvados-montenegro "High Horse"; draft and bottled beers; and a few interesting wines. Add charcuterie, cheese, sliders, seafood, and good bread, and you have a great night out. *✉ 95 Eddy St., Downtown ☎ 401/831–3339 🌐 www.eddybar.com.*

Rooftop at the Providence G

BARS | On the rooftop of the Providence G residential building, the lively bar is open evenings year-round (it has a retractable glass rooftop and fire pits) for drinks, snacks, dinner, music, and general conviviality. Valet parking is complimentary. *✉ 100 Dorrance St., Downtown ☎ 401/632–4904 🌐 www.rooftopattheg.com.*

MUSIC CLUBS

The Boombox Karaoke

LIVE MUSIC | At Downtown's first and only karaoke lounge, have a drink, belt out a tune from a searchable app of more than 30,000 songs (updated each month), or book a private room for yourself and your friends. *✉ The Dean Hotel, 122 Fountain St., Downtown ☎ 401/861–0040 🌐 singboombox.com.*

The Strand Ballroom & Theatre

LIVE MUSIC | This 100-year-old, five-story theater (operated as Lupo's Heartbreak Hotel until the venue resumed its original name in late 2017), hosts nationally known musical acts: rock, blues, hip-hop,

Roger Williams

It was an unthinkable idea: total separation of church and state. Break the tie between them, and where would the government get its authority? The answer threatened the Puritan way of life. And that's why in the winter of 1636 the Massachusetts Bay Colony banished a certain preacher with radical opinions. Roger Williams fled south into the wilderness, with the goal of establishing a new colony founded on religious tolerance and fair dealings with native tribes, and arranged to buy land from the Narragansett sachems Canonicus and Miantonomi at the confluence of the Woonasquatucket and Moshassuck rivers. Word spread that this new settlement, which Williams named Providence, was a place where civil power rested in the hands of the people. Those persecuted for their beliefs flocked there, and it thereafter grew into a prosperous Colonial shipping port. What started out as a radical experiment became the basis of American democracy.

Americana, country, Latin, metal, funk—plus live comedy. ✉ *79 Washington St., Downtown* ☎ *401/618–8900* 🌐 *www.thestrandri.com.*

Performing Arts

Amica Mutual Pavilion

MUSIC | Formerly the Dunkin' Donuts Center, this 14,000-seat arena hosts major rock, R&B, country, and other musical acts, as well as Providence College basketball games and the American Hockey League's Providence Bruins. ✉ *1 LaSalle Sq., Downtown* ☎ *401/331–6700* 🌐 *www.amicamutualpavilion.com.*

Providence Performing Arts Center

ARTS CENTERS | The 3,100-seat center, which opened in 1928 as a Loew's State Theater, hosts concerts, national tours of hit Broadway shows, and other large-scale performances and events. Major renovations to this building, which is listed on the National Register of Historic Places, restored the stage, lobby, and arcade to their original splendor. The mighty Wurlitzer organ is a particular source of pride. ✉ *220 Weybosset St., Downtown* ☎ *401/421–2787* 🌐 *www.ppacri.org.*

Trinity Repertory Company

THEATER | A past Tony Award winner for outstanding regional theater company, this troupe presents classic plays, intimate musicals, and new works by young playwrights, as well as an annual version of *A Christmas Carol*—all in a renovated former vaudeville house. Shows are presented on two separate stages: the 500-seat Elizabeth and Malcolm Chace Theater and the recently-renovated 250-seat Sarah and Joseph Dowling, Jr. Theater. ✉ *201 Washington St., Downtown* ☎ *401/351–4242* 🌐 *www.trinityrep.com.*

The Vets

CONCERTS | This 1,900-seat auditorium has a proscenium stage and an exquisite interior; it hosts concerts, operas, and comedy and dance performances. From September to May, the Vets is the home of the Rhode Island Philharmonic Orchestra. ✉ *1 Ave. of the Arts, Downtown* ☎ *401/421–2787* 🌐 *www.thevetsri.com.*

Shopping

ANTIQUES AND HOME FURNISHINGS

Craftland

CRAFTS | Etsy fans will be delighted by the handmade wares at this colorful shop and gallery: jewelry, notecards, prints, silk-screened T-shirts, fashion accessories, bags, Rhode Island-themed trinkets, and other sparkly handmade objects by local artists are all for sale. You'll save money on every purchase, too, because there's no sales tax on art in Rhode Island. ✉ *212 Westminster St., Downtown* ☎ *401/272–4285* 🌐 *shop.craftlandshop.com/.*

HomeStyle

SOUVENIRS | Drop by HomeStyle along increasingly gentrified Westminster Street for eye-catching objets d'art, stylish housewares, and other innovative, extraordinary, or whimsical decorative items. ✉ *233 Westminster St., Downtown* ☎ *401/277–1159* 🌐 *www.homestyleri.com* ☞ *Validated parking at InTown Parking Lot on Weybosset St.*

CLOTHING

The Vault Collective

SECOND-HAND | This high-ceilinged, multidealer emporium is a standout in a city known for its vintage boutiques. Walk your wardrobe back in time with colorful finds, from mid-century designer dresses to throwback Patriots merch and rock concert tees. ✉ *235 Westminster St., Downtown* ☎ *401/250–2587* 🌐 *www.thevaultcollective.com.*

FOOD

★ Yoleni's

FOOD | There's a deli to the left and café seating to the right, but straight back in this bright corner shop you'll find all kinds of amazing Greek specialty products all packaged up and ready to go: olives, olive oil, honey, nuts, sauces, spreads and dips, pastas, legumes, herbs and spices, cookies and candy. Buy some for yourself, pick out a ready-made gift, or both. ✉ *292 Westminster St., Downtown* ☎ *401/500–1127* 🌐 *providence.yolenis.com/* ⏲ *Closed Mon.*

MALLS

The Arcade Providence

MALL | Built in 1828, America's oldest indoor shopping mall has a handful of restaurants on its first floor and one signature shop, the Lovecraft Arts & Sciences Council, for quirky gifts and books on the supernatural by Providence's own H. P. Lovecraft and other authors. The rest of the former retail space has been converted into microloft apartments. The Greek Revival building has entrances on both Westminster and Weybosset Streets. ✉ *65 Weybosset St., Downtown* ☎ *401/454–4568* 🌐 *www.arcadeprovidence.com.*

Providence Place

MALL | Macy's, Boscov's, and an Apple Store are among the anchor tenants at this large mall with 13 restaurants include the Cheesecake Factory and P. F. Chang's. Also here are Dave & Buster's and a 16-screen cinema and IMAX theater. Parking in the garage is free for the first two hours. ✉ *1 Providence Pl., at Francis and Hayes Sts., Downtown* ☎ *401/270–1012* 🌐 *www.providenceplace.com.*

East Side

Home to Brown University and the Rhode Island School of Design (RISD), the East Side is Providence's intellectual center and a beautiful residential neighborhood. The East Side neighborhood highlights include Benefit Street, dubbed the "mile of history" for its high concentration of Colonial architecture; RISD's top-quality art museum; and Thayer Street, a gentrified mix of shops, restaurants, and an art-house cinema popular with college students.

★ Benefit Street

STREET | **FAMILY** | The city's wealthiest lived along this Colonial thoroughfare, dubbed "the mile of history," during the 18th and early 19th centuries—and most of the original wood-frame structures have been beautifully restored as homes for today's families. Benefit Street passes by the campuses of Brown University and the Rhode Island School of Design. Of particular interest are the 1707 Stephen Hopkins House on the corner of Benefit Street and Hopkins Street, a former governor's home open for tours; the Providence Athenaeum at 251 Benefit St., a onetime haunt of Edgar Allan Poe; and the John Brown House museum on the Brown University campus. ✉ *Benefit St., East Side* 🌐 *www.rihs.org.*

Brown University

COLLEGE | Founded in 1764, this Ivy League institution is the nation's seventh-oldest college and offers degrees in 82 undergraduate concentrations, 33 master's programs, and 51 doctoral programs. On a stroll through the College Hill campus, you'll encounter Gothic and Beaux Arts structures, as well as the imposing Van Wickle Gate, which opens twice a year—in fall to welcome first-year students and spring to bid graduating seniors farewell. On the ground floor of Manning Hall, the Haffenreffer Museum of Anthropology exhibits artifacts from around the world. The David Winton Bell Gallery in the List Art Building hosts several major art exhibitions a year. Attending a Brown Bears Ivy League football game is an old-school experience, with games played at monumental Brown Stadium, which first welcomed fans in 1925. ✉ *Stephen Robert '62 Campus Center, 75 Waterman St., East Side* ☎ *401/863–1000* 🌐 *www.brown.edu.*

First Baptist Church in America

CHURCH | This historic house of worship was built in 1775 for a congregation originally established in 1638 by Roger Williams and his fellow Puritan dissenters. The writer H. P. Lovecraft attended Sunday school here briefly as a child. Architecture and design buffs will appreciate the 185-foot, glistening white steeple, erected in just 3½ days, as well as the auditorium's large crystal chandelier from Ireland, installed in 1792. Guided tours of the Meeting House are available on weekdays from 10 am to 2 pm and Sundays at the conclusion of worship services. Smartphone-enabled elf-guided tours are also an option and are available in multiple languages. ✉ *75 N. Main St., East Side* ☎ *401/454–3418* 🌐 *firstbaptistchurchinamerica.org* 🎟 *Guided tour $2, self-guided tour free.*

John Brown House Museum

HISTORIC HOME | Rhode Island's most famous 18th-century home was the stately residence of John Brown, a wealthy businessman, slave trader, politician, and China trade merchant. John Quincy Adams called the home, designed in late-Georgian, early-Federal style and the first mansion built in Providence, "the most magnificent and elegant private mansion that I have ever seen on this continent." An ardent patriot, Brown was a noteworthy participant in the defiant burning of the British customs ship *Gaspee* in 1772—which, Rhode Islanders will remind you, took place 18 months before the Boston Tea Party. Tours are by reservation. ✉ *52 Power St., East Side* ☎ *401/331–8575* 🌐 *www.rihs.org/locations/the-john-brown-house-museum* 🎟 *$10* 🕒 *Closed Sun.–Mon.*

John Hay Library

LIBRARY | Built in 1910 and named for Abraham Lincoln's secretary, "the Hay" houses Brown University Library's collections of rare books and manuscripts. World-class collections of Lincoln-related items, H. P. Lovecraft letters, Napoléon's death mask, Walt Whitman's personal copy of *Leaves of Grass*, and 6,000 toy soldiers are of particular interest. The

Providence in One Day

Begin at the **Rhode Island State House**, where the south portico looks over the city of Providence, the Providence River, and the head of Narragansett Bay. Cross the Moshassuck River to the East Side, drive up the hill a block, and stroll south along **Benefit Street** toward College Hill and Brown University. Touring possibilities in this neighborhood of abundant Colonial architecture are **Prospect Terrace**, a pocket park with a statue of Roger Williams and a gorgeous view of Downtown, the magnificent **John Brown House Museum** at the corner of Benefit and Power streets, the **Providence Athenaeum**, and the **RISD Museum.** You'll find plenty of great lunch options, as well as some cool shops, along **Wickenden Street**, at Benefit Street's southern end.

Head back along Benefit, South Main, or South Water Street and cross over the Steeple Street bridge toward Downtown, strolling along **Waterplace Park and Riverwalk**, the centerpiece of the city's revitalization. Complete the park loop along the Providence River by crossing the **Providence Pedestrian Bridge**. As dinnertime approaches, make your way west into the famed Italian-American neighborhood of **Federal Hill**, where you'll find dozens of restaurants and cafés.

library is open to the public, but you need a photo ID to enter. ✉ *20 Prospect St., East Side* ☎ *401/863–3723* 🌐 *library.brown.edu/hay* 🎫 *Free* 🕙 *Closed Sat. and Sun.*

Prospect Terrace

PUBLIC ART | FAMILY | This pocket park in College Hill offers one of the most scenic views of Downtown, particularly in the fall when the surrounding foliage plays spectacularly off the urban backdrop. Prospect Terrace's centerpiece is a statue of Roger Williams, Rhode Island's forward-thinking founder—who here seems to be groovin' to the 1980s song "Walk Like an Egyptian." In reality, however, he's buried under the statue. ✉ *Between Congdon and Pratt Sts., at Cushing St., East Side.*

Providence Athenaeum

LIBRARY | Philadelphia architect William Strickland designed this 1838 Greek Revival library building in which Edgar Allan Poe courted the poet (and avid reader) Sarah Helen Whitman; the collection here includes a Poe-signed periodical containing "Ulalume," a poem he published anonymously. An 1870s Manet print that illustrated Poe's "The Raven" hangs in the rare book room, which also contains two medieval illuminated manuscripts. Raven signs are posted at eight points of interest on a self-guided library tour. Among them is a special cabinet modeled after an Egyptian temple, which houses the library's multivolume imperial edition of *Description de l'Egypte* (1809–22), commissioned by Napoléon. ✉ *251 Benefit St., East Side* ☎ *401/421–6970* 🌐 *www.providenceathenaeum.org* 🎫 *Free* 🕙 *Closed Mon.*

★ RISD Museum

ART MUSEUM | This museum houses more than 100,000 objects ranging from ancient art to work by contemporary artists and designers from around the world. Highlights include Impressionist paintings, costumes, textiles, decorative arts, Gorham silver, Newport furniture, an ancient Egyptian mummy, and a 12th-century Buddha—the largest historic Japanese wooden sculpture in the United States. Artists represented include major figures in the history of visual art and culture, including Cézanne, Chanel, Copley, Degas, Hirst, Homer, LeWitt, Matisse, Manet, Picasso, Rothko, Sargent, Turner, Twombly, van Gogh, and Warhol—to name a few. Particularly significant are the displays of works by current and past RISD faculty and students. Stop by the museum's Café Pearl for a bite to eat. ✉ *20 N. Main St., East Side* ✣ *Additional entrance at 224 Benefit St.* ☎ *401/454–6500* 🌐 *www.risdmuseum.org* 🎫 *$17; free Thurs. and Fri. 5–7 pm and Sun. 10–5* 🕑 *Closed Mon.*

Roger Williams National Memorial

NATIONAL PARK | This 4½-acre park dedicated to Rhode Island's founder has a symbolic well to mark the site of the spring around which Roger Williams built Providence's original settlement in 1636. A visitor center has a five-minute film about the park's namesake. There's the park's flourishing pollinator garden, as well as a demonstration garden showing how Native Americans cultivated corn, beans, and squash, and how English colonists grew herbs (call ahead to see if it's open). The park has several picnic tables, public restrooms, and 20 free parking spaces (a two-hour parking limit is strictly enforced). ✉ *282 N. Main St., East Side* ☎ *401/521–7266* 🌐 *www.nps.gov/rowi* 🎫 *Free* 🕑 *Visitor Center closed Mon.–Wed.*

Thayer Street

STREET | Bustling Thayer Street bears a proud old New England name and is very much a part of campus life at Brown, RISD, and other local colleges. Gentrification has resulted in an influx of chain stores. In the blocks between Waterman and Bowen Streets, though, you'll still find fashion boutiques, shops selling funky gifts, the art deco–style Avon Cinema, and restaurants serving every kind of cuisine from Greek to Korean. ✉ *Thayer St., between Waterman and Bowen Sts., East Side* 🌐 *www.thayerstreetdistrict.com.*

Wickenden Street

STREET | Named for a Baptist minister who was one of Providence's first settlers, this main artery in the Fox Point district is home to antiques stores, art galleries, and trendy cafés. It also hosts the Coffee Exchange, one of the area's most popular gathering spots. Sidewalk sales are held in the spring and fall. Once home to mainly working-class Portuguese-Americans, the Wickenden Street area has become a popular area for off-campus student housing; Our Lady of the Rosary Church on adjacent Traverse Street still conducts some weekend Masses in Portuguese. ✉ *Wickenden St., East Side.*

Restaurants

★ Al Forno

$$$ | ITALIAN | When it opened in 1980, Al Forno put Providence on the national dining map as the originator of its distinctive grilled pizza. Still consistently good, the restaurant retains a loyal following for its thin-crust pizza, handmade pastas, and wood-grilled or roasted entrées. **Known for:** spicy roasted clams; wood-grilled pizza; upstairs tables, where the city's movers and shakers congregate. 💲 *Average main: $28* ✉ *577 S. Water St., East Side* ☎ *401/273–9760* 🌐 *www.alforno.com* 🕑 *Closed Sun. and Mon. No lunch.*

Chomp Kitchen & Drinks

$ | AMERICAN | A tiny Warren restaurant known for offbeat beers, hot chicken sandwiches, and a burger stacked 10 inches tall has blossomed into this second location with more expansive indoor-outdoor seating and an equally enticing menu of decidedly adult, made-from-scratch comfort grub. Pair zesty Mozambique chicken tenders that are definitely not your kids' chicken nuggets with frozen sangria on a summer's day. **Known for:** gourmet burgers including the piled-high Stack; rich, gooey mac and cheese you won't want to share; eclectic and revolving menu of rare, limited-edition craft beers. *Average main: $16* *117 Ives St., East Side* *401/537–7556* *www.chompri.com* *Closed Mon. and Tues. No lunch.*

Hemenway's
$$$ | SEAFOOD | In a city where culinary newcomers tend to garner all the attention, Hemenway's continues to be one of the state's best seafood restaurants. The high-ceiling dining room's huge windows look out on Providence's World War II Memorial; in warm weather, dine outside on the front patio. **Known for:** raw bar platters; fresh-caught lobster stuffed with scallops, shrimp, and crab; extensive wine cellar and craft-beer list. *Average main: $30* *121 S. Main St., East Side* *401/351–8570* *www.hemenwaysrestaurant.com.*

★ Persimmon
$$$ | MODERN AMERICAN | This intimate neighborhood bistro seats only 38 patrons, so reservations are essential on summer weekends. Neutral walls, white table linens, and simple but elegant china focus attention on the artfully composed dishes of chef and co-owner Champe Speidel, a four-time semifinalist for a James Beard Foundation Award. **Known for:** draft cocktails; in-house butcher shop; ever-changing menus. *Average main: $30* *99 Hope St., East Side* *401/432–7422* *www.persimmonri.com* *Closed Sun.–Tues. No lunch.*

Plant City
$ | VEGETARIAN | Even omnivores can get behind this chic vegan food hall, positioned near the waterfront and the city's new Providence River Pedestrian Bridge. On two floors and cascading outdoors, you'll find three restaurants, a bakery, a coffee bar, and a market offering familiar fare like tacos, pizza, lasagna—even burgers—all made exclusively from plants. **Known for:** world's first plant-based vegan food hall; gorgeous patio dining; grab-and-go options. *Average main: $17* *334 S. Water St., East Side* *401/429–2029* *www.plantcitypvd.com.*

Red Stripe
$$ | ECLECTIC | A giant fork hangs outside this neighborhood brasserie in Wayland Square, and the chefs do things big here—from the everything-but-the-kitchen-sink chopped salad to supersize sangrias. The menu is eclectic, but you'll find plenty of Italian- and French-inspired bistro items, including French onion soup, steak frites, rigatoni Bolognese, and mussels prepared six ways and served with hand-cut frites. **Known for:** large, varied menu with something to appeal to everyone; homemade bread is fabulous; lively atmosphere (i.e., noisy). *Average main: $21* *465 Angell St., East Side* *401/437–6950* *www.redstriperestaurants.com.*

The Salted Slate
$$$ | AMERICAN | Ben Lloyd, the chef-owner of this "agri-driven" American restaurant, is committed to honoring the origins of the food he prepares. He purchases humanely raised and harvested meat, poultry, and fish whole from local vendors, butchers them in-house, and uses every part from nose to tail—combined with eggs at breakfast, cheese and fries at lunch, and fresh vegetables at dinner. **Known for:** small-batch artisanal cheeses and house-cured charcuterie; innovative menus change frequently; best bacon you'll ever eat. *Average main: $25* *Wayland Sq., 186 Wayland Ave., East Side* *401/270–3737* *www.saltedslate.com* *Closed Mon.*

Coffee and Quick Bites

Coffee Exchange
$ | CAFÉ | One of the area's most popular gathering spots, the Coffee Exchange is the place to come for pastries, a coffee (hot or cold), and a chat. Family-run, the coffee shop has been an East Side landmark for nearly 40 years, adopting socially conscious sourcing long before that was common or trendy. **Known for:** serves international Fair Trade Organic coffees; coffee roasted daily; ships coffee

around the country. [$] *Average main: $3.75* ✉ *207 Wickenden St., Fox Point* ☎ *401/273–1198* 🌐 *www.thecoffeeexchange.com.*

PVDonuts

$ | BAKERY | FAMILY | Just as sneakerheads line up for hot releases, doughnutheads stake their places on the sidewalk outside this one-of-a-kind shop to try limited-edition flavors like S'mores or Chocolate Churro. There are filled and old-fashioned-style donuts to sample, but the stars of the monthly changing line-up are the light and fluffy, oversized brioche dough orbs. **Known for:** cereal-studded doughnuts and trademark creations like the Friendsgiving doughnut; vegan options; locally roasted coffee. [$] *Average main: $3.75* ✉ *79 Ives St., Providence* ☎ 🌐 *www.pvdonuts.com* ⏲ *Closed Mon. and Tues.*

Hotels

Hilton Garden Inn

$$ | HOTEL | The only hotel on Providence's East Side is uniquely situated at India Point, across the street from the waterfront park of the same name and with the entrance ramp for the East Bay Bike Path right out the back. **Pros:** convenient to ferry and Fox Point area; only hotel on the East Side, close to Brown and RISD; Garden Grille has indoor and outdoor dining with a view. **Cons:** a bit isolated, especially at night; more than a mile from downtown Providence; average hotel restaurant. [$] *Rooms from: $221* ✉ *220 India St., East Side* ☎ *401/272–5577* 🌐 *www.hilton.com* *136 rooms* *No Meals.*

Nightlife

Fish Co.

BARS | Marina and skyline views, a waterfront deck, live tunes, beer buckets, frozen concoctions, and the city's best clam cakes and chowder make this indoor-outdoor bar and grill on the Fox Point waterfront an ideal place to unwind or catch a game. The name is a nod to a time when the docks below were the domain of fishermen, not pleasure boaters. ✉ *15 Bridge St., Fox Point* ☎ *401/588–5158* 🌐 *www.fishcopvd.com* ⏲ *Closed Mon.*

Hot Club

GATHERING PLACES | You may recognize the Hot Club from the opening scenes of the movie *Something About Mary*. For more than 30 years, this place has been a favorite hangout for young professionals, university professors, and politicians. On summer afternoons until the wee hours of the morning, you'll find the hip set on the outdoor deck overlooking the Providence River. For cheap eats, try local favorites like the Saugy dog (hot dog) or a "stuffie" – a stuffed quahog clam that's a Rhode Island seafood staple. ✉ *25 Bridge St., East Side* ☎ *401/861–9007* 🌐 *www.hotclubprov.com.*

The Wild Colonial Tavern

BARS | East Side gentrification has not touched this (kind of) riverfront bar on South Main Street. Studiedly unpretentious, the Wild Colonial occupies the brick-lined basement of an old warehouse building; strain your eyes, and you might get a glimpse of the Providence River across the parking lot. Food choices are limited to the likes of cheese plates and hummus, but the bartenders take pride in the beer list and in pouring the best Guinness drafts in the city. If you're looking for a place to duck in for a reasonably priced beer or cocktail on Waterfire nights (or any night, really), this is it. ✉ *250 Smith St., East Side* ☎ *401/621–5644* 🌐 *wildcolonial.com.*

Performing Arts

FILM

Avon Cinema

FILM | This independent movie theater on Thayer Street, near Brown University, screens primarily art-house, independent, and foreign films. The College Hill theater's art deco styling dates back to its opening in 1938. ✉ *260 Thayer St., East Side* ☎ *401/421-2866* 🌐 *www.avon-cinema.com* 🎫 *$12.*

THEATER

The Players at Barker Playhouse

THEATER | Historic Benefit Street is an appropriate location for the oldest continuously running little theater in the U.S. The Players have been taking the stage every year since 1909 and at the Barker Playhouse since 1932—a pretty good run for an amateur theater group. The actors may not get paid, but performances are nothing short of professional: talent fairly leaps off the stage at the former church built in 1839. Past shows have included everything from Shakespeare to Christmas plays, original works by Providence playwrights to Stephen Sondheim musicals. ✉ *400 Benefit St., East Side* ☎ *401/273–0590* 🌐 *playersri.org* 🎫 *$30.*

Activities

East Bay Bike Path

BIKING | FAMILY | This mostly flat, 14½-mile bike path connects Providence's India Point Park with Independence Park in Bristol. Along the way, you pass six additional parks and enjoy views of coves and saltwater marshes. A half-mile detour on Crescent View Avenue in East Providence leads to the 1895 Charles Looff–designed Crescent Park Carousel. The route can be congested on fine-weather weekends. A newer on- and off-street route also connects the path to the 24-mile Blackstone River Bikeway; check out the George Redman Linear Park on the Washington Bridge over the Seekonk River, which is accessible from India Point Park. ✉ *India Point Park, India St., Fox Point* ☎ *401/667–6200* 🌐 *www.dot.ri.gov/travel/bikeri/eastbay.php.*

Shopping

ANTIQUES

Nostalgia Antiques and Collectables

ANTIQUES & COLLECTIBLES | Antiquers (and maybe yard-salers, too) could get lost for hours in this three-story shop that offers a collection of "curiosities, oddities, and treasures from another time" for sale. Fed by more than 200 dealers, the shelves here burst with every imaginable kind of antique items, including clothing, furniture, statuary, midcentury appliances, housewares, and vintage swag from local schools. ✉ *236 Wickenden St., Providence* ☎ *401/400-5810* 🌐 *www.nostalgiaprovidence.com.*

ART GALLERIES

Chazan Gallery at Wheeler

ART GALLERIES | This public gallery at Providence's private Wheeler School exhibits works from Rhode Island's extensive population of local artists, including past and current attendees of the nearby Rhode Island School of Design. Attached to Wheeler's library, the gallery features winners from about a half-dozen juried art shows it sponsors annually, in a variety of media. ✉ *228 Angell St., East Side* ☎ *401/528-2227* 🌐 *www.chazangallery.org.*

HANDICRAFTS AND HOME FURNISHINGS

Frog + Toad

HOUSEWARES | Clothing, housewares, fair-trade handicrafts, and novelty items can all be found at this small curiosity shop and gift boutique, which stocks one of the best collections of Rhode Island-made goods in the state. ✉ *795 Hope St., East Side* ☎ *401/831-3434* 🌐 *www.frogandtoadstore.com.*

Rhody Craft

SOUVENIRS | Whimsy and practicality converge at this shop devoted to goods lovingly conceived and handmade in little Rhody. Each item, whether something useful for your kitchen or baby or a decidedly frivolous indulgence, is curated to make you smile. ✉ *769 Hope St., East Side* ☎ *401/626–1833* 🌐 *www.rhodycraft.com.*

RISD Store

MUSEUM SHOP | This shop associated with RISD's art museum has a selection of inspired toys, totes, gifts, and jewelry, plus accessories by Rhode Island School of Design students and alumni, including designer Andrea Valentini's sustainable-fabric bags. ✉ *30 N. Main St., East Side* ☎ *401/454–6464* 🌐 *www.risdstore.com.*

Federal Hill

Federal Hill has been home to generations of Italian-American families. While the neighborhood may no longer be predominantly Italian-American, it remains infused with Italian charm and hospitality. The stripe down Atwells Avenue, the main thoroughfare, is painted in red, white, and green; and a huge pine cone (*La Pigna*), an Italian symbol of abundance and quality, hangs on an arch soaring over the street. Grocers sell pasta, pastries, and hard-to-find Italian groceries. To get the full experience, have a seat near the fountain in DePasquale Square, especially during the Feast of St. Joseph in March, the Federal Hill Stroll in early in June, the Federal Hill Summer Festival in late June, or the three-day Columbus Day Weekend Festival and parade in October. Federal Hill lies to the west of Downtown, separated by Interstate 95, and is bounded by Broadway to the south and Route 6 to the west and north. Some restaurants and shops are located on Broadway and Westminster Street, which are considered part of the city's West Side (or West End, depending on who you ask) neighborhood. For a look at what's on, check out www.federalhill-prov.com and www.wbna.org.

Restaurants

Angelo's Civita Farnese

$$ | ITALIAN | FAMILY | Locals come to this third-generation, family-owned restaurant in the heart of Federal Hill for the chicken or eggplant Parmesan, veal with peppers, and braciola like (your Italian) grandma used to make. The prices are reasonable; the atmosphere, warm and casual. **Known for:** family-friendly; familiar southern Italian menu; a landmark since 1924. 💲 *Average main: $17* ✉ *141 Atwells Ave., Federal Hill* ☎ *401/621–8171* 🌐 *www.angelosri.com* 🕓 *Closed Mon. and Tues.*

Broadway Bistro

$$ | AMERICAN | On the city's increasingly gentrified West Side (which fringes Federal Hill), this convivial bar and restaurant occupies a single-story redbrick storefront with a handful of sidewalk tables. A mix of students, artists, and neighborhood locals find their way here nightly for fair-priced, deftly prepared bistro chow and imaginative salads. **Known for:** cozy comfort food; casual, come-as-you-are vibe; quirky cocktails and good wine and beer selection. 💲 *Average main: $19* ✉ *205 Broadway, Federal Hill* ☎ *401/331–2450* 🌐 *www.broadwaybistrori.com* 🕓 *Closed Sun. and Mon. No lunch.*

Caserta Pizzeria

$ | PIZZA | Rhode Island's pizza universe has expanded in recent years—you can get a decent slice of New York, New Haven, or Detroit style—but the more things change the more they stay the same at Caserta, the landmark pizzeria on Federal Hill. Homemade sauce, fresh mozzarella, quality toppings, and a thick but crispy crust combine to create a unique Rhode Island-by-way-of-Sicily pie. **Known for:** busy location, better to order in advance even if you plan to dine in; Wimpy Skippy spinach pies; unique thick-crust pizza. 💲 *Average main: $11* ✉ *121 Spruce St., Federal Hill* ☎ *401/272–3618, 401/621–9190, 401/621–3618* 🌐 *casertapizzeria.com* 🕓 *Closed Mon.*

★ Nick's on Broadway

$$ | **MODERN AMERICAN** | For two decades Derek Wagner has earned a seat at the table among Rhode Island's top chefs by helming this amped-up diner on Providence's West Side (the namesake "Nick" was the owner of the original diner at the site). Breakfast features classic comfort food like pancakes and egg dishes composed with all-local ingredients, like eggs from Baffoni Farms and potatoes from Schartner Farms, and pasture-fed Blackbird Farm Black Angus beef shows up in the Bolognese sauce and slow-cooked BBQ, while all of the plated fish entrees at dinner were swimming in local waters a short time before. **Known for:** satisfying seasonal risottos; rosé and oyster pairings; opt for patio seating for an escape from the pace of the city. *$ Average main: $20 ✉ 500 Broadway, Federal Hill ☎ 401/421–0286, 401/421–0287 🌐 www.nicksonbroadway.com ⏲ Closed Mon. and Tues. No dinner Sun.*

Ogie's Trailer Park

$ | **AMERICAN** | Fun and kitschy Ogie's bar and restaurant fuses trailer-park chic and colorful (maybe even garish) 1950s-style decor. The "Granny Boo's Kitchen" menu emphasizes "gourmet comfort food," which translates into the likes of tater tots with white truffle oil, grilled peanut butter and jelly, and mac 'n' cheese croquettes. **Known for:** Rhody fried chicken, encrusted with Doritos; outdoor dining on front and back patios; drinks at the outdoor tiki bar in warm weather. *$ Average main: $13 ✉ 1155 Westminster St., Federal Hill ☎ 401/383–8200 🌐 www.ogiestrailerpark.com ⏲ No lunch Mon.–Fri.*

Pane e Vino

$$$ | **ITALIAN** | Portions are big in the Rhode Island comfort-food tradition at this southern Italian *ristorante* on Federal Hill; count on fresh ingredients presented in a simple, straightforward way. Share a pasta if you dare, but keep in mind that the veal chop could probably topple Fred Flintstone's footmobile; gluten-free dishes are also available. **Known for:** all your favorites, Italian style; dozens of regional Italian wines; $24 prix-fixe menu at dinner (except Friday and Saturday). *$ Average main: $25 ✉ 365 Atwells Ave., Federal Hill ☎ 401/223–2230 🌐 www.panevino.net ⏲ No lunch.*

Providence Oyster Bar

$$$ | **SEAFOOD** | In a neighborhood where Italian food dominates, this spirited seafood restaurant offers a refreshing alternative. Oysters—and clams, lobster, and shrimp—are the main attraction, of course, but landlubbers will enjoy a steak or rotisserie chicken. **Known for:** oysters—mostly local—on the raw bar; sushi creations like the surf-and-turf roll; splurge-worthy hot buttered lobster rolls. *$ Average main: $32 ✉ 283 Atwells Ave., Federal Hill ☎ 401/272–8866 🌐 www.providenceoysterbar.com ⏲ No lunch Mon.*

Coffee and Quick Bites

★ Costantino's Venda Ravioli

$$ | **ITALIAN** | **FAMILY** | The scents and flavors of Italy surround you at Costantino's as you peruse the amazing selection of homemade pastas and imported foods. The convivial banter between customers and employees adds to the atmosphere. *$ Average main: $21 ✉ 275 Atwells Ave., Federal Hill ☎ 401/421–9105 🌐 www.vendaravioli.com 💳 No credit cards.*

Scialo Bros. Bakery

$ | **BAKERY** | Get your Italian cookie or cannoli fix at this landmark bakery, which has been in business since 1916. The place almost closed for good due to retirement and COVID-19, but young new owners have puffed new energy into the place. **Known for:** Italian cookies, zeppoles, and cannoli; custom cakes; delicious window shopping. *$ Average main: $5 ✉ 257 Atwells Ave., Federal Hill ☎ 401/421–0986 🌐 www.facebook.com/scialobrosbakery 💳 No credit cards.*

Nightlife

BARS

Courtland Club

DANCE CLUBS | In a dimly lit space born as a bakery in the 1920s and converted to a social club at the tail end of World War II, this speakeasy is also a pizza joint and ice creamery. Pair your favorite boozy concoction with the POW (Pizza of the Week) and small-batch sorbet and ice-cream flavors like mint chocolate chip made with real mint. DJs spin music most nights, and the classic speakeasy vibe is a perfect match for live jazz on Sunday nights. ✉ *51 Courtland St., Federal Hill* ☎ *401/227–9300* 🌐 *www.courtlandclub.com* ⏲ *Closed Mon.-Tues.*

Greater Providence

In the southern end of Providence, you'll find the city's well-regarded Roger Williams Park and Zoo about 3½ miles south of Downtown.

Sights

★ Roger Williams Park Zoo & Carousel Village

ZOO | FAMILY | Plan a full day to take in this regal 435-acre Victorian park where you can picnic, see diverse plant life at the indoor-outdoor Botanical Center, rent a swan-shape paddleboat, ride a Victorian-style carousel, and stargaze in a planetarium. The 40-acre zoo—one of the nation's oldest—has African elephants, Masai giraffes, zebras, red pandas, snow leopards, moon bears, gibbons, tree kangaroos, and harbor seals in natural settings. Howler monkeys, Chilean flamingos, giant river otters, a giant anteater, toucans, and more inhabit the Rainforest exhibit, opened in summer 2018. In October, more than 5,000 creatively carved pumpkins are illuminated for the well-attended Jack-O-Lantern Spectacular, which can be viewed from a walking trail or zip line ride. In Carousel Village, a short walk from the zoo, kids love the classic horses and other creatures on the carousel, pony rides, and train excursions (all individually priced). ✉ *1000 Elmwood Ave., Elmwood, Providence* ☎ *401/785–9450 for museum, 401/785–3510 for zoo* 🌐 *www.rwpzoo.org* 🎟 *Zoo $19.95* ⏲ *zoo closed Tues.–Wed. in winter.*

Restaurants

Buttonwoods Brewery

$ | PIZZA | A brewery tucked into an industrial park near the railroad tracks doesn't seem super inviting, but the tasting room here is warm and friendly, and the beers have creativity by the barrel (IPAs, yes, but also wild ales, barleywines, and a revival of a historical varietal called Kentucky Common). If the adults need a drink after a day at the zoo, Buttonwoods is right in the neighborhood, and hungry kids can be placated with comfort food and pizza from the brewery's pop-up kitchen and a rotation list of visiting food trucks. **Known for:** fun events including cooking classes and trivia; attractive tasting room; creative beers. 💲 *Average main: $10* ✉ *530 Wellington Ave., Cranston* ☎ *401/563–8451* 🌐 *shop.buttonwoodsbrewery.com* ⏲ *Closed Mon. No lunch Tues.–Thurs.*

Los Andes

$$$ | LATIN AMERICAN | Los Andes is perennially at or near the top of every Rhode Island "best of" restaurant list. Credit the state's Latin American diaspora, Rhode Island's melting pot status, but mostly credit chef Cesin Curi for his masterful Latin fusion cuisine that draws upon the rich culinary traditions of Bolivia and Peru. **Known for:** Peruvian Pisco sour cocktails; creative ceviche and paella dishes; beautiful courtyard dining. 💲 *Average main: $32* ✉ *903 Chalkstone Ave., South Providence* ☎ *401/649–4911* 🌐 *losandesri.com* ⏲ *Closed Mon. and Tues. No lunch.*

Chapter 9

VERMONT

Updated by
Jordan Barry
and Jessica Kelly

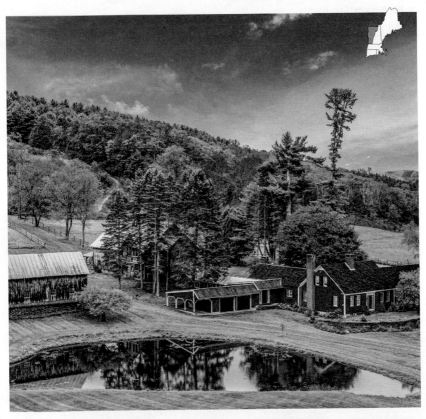

WELCOME TO VERMONT

TOP REASONS TO GO

★ **Small-Town Charm:** Vermont rolls out a seemingly never-ending supply of tiny towns replete with white-steepled churches, town greens, red barns, general stores, and bed-and-breakfasts.

★ **Ski Resorts:** The East's best skiing can be found in well-managed, modern facilities with great views and lots and lots of powdery, fresh snow.

★ **Fall Foliage:** Perhaps the most vivid colors in North America wave from the trees in September and October.

★ **Gorgeous Landscapes:** This sparsely populated, heavily forested state is an ideal place to find peace and quiet amid the mountains, valleys, and lakes.

★ **Vibrant Local Eats:** The rich soil, and an emphasis on the state's maker-artisan culture, has led to great dairies, orchards, vineyards, specialty stores, and farm-to-table restaurants. Even the world-famous beer scene is known to highlight state-grown hops and locally made malt.

1 **Brattleboro.** A hippie enclave with an artistic and activist disposition.

2 **Wilmington.** The hub of Mt. Snow Valley.

3 **Bennington.** The economic center of southwest Vermont.

4 **Arlington.** Once the home of painter Norman Rockwell.

5 **Manchester.** Sophisticated with upscale shopping.

6 **Dorset.** Home to two of the state's best and oldest general stores.

7 **Stratton.** It's all about Stratton Mountain Resort.

8 **Weston.** Home to the Vermont Country Store.

9 **Ludlow.** Okemo Mountain Resort's home.

10 **Grafton.** Both a town and a museum.

11 **Norwich.** One of the most picturesque towns.

12 **Quechee.** Restaurants and shops in old mills.

13 **Woodstock.** Upscale shops and the venerable Woodstock Inn.

14 **Killington.** The East Coast's largest ski resort.

15 **Rutland.** Slowly gaining traction as a foodie town.

16 **Brandon.** Artists Guild and the Basin Bluegrass Festival.

17 **Middlebury.** Restaurants, shops, and Middlebury College.

18 **Waitsfield and Warren.** The ski meccas of Mad River Glen and Sugarbush.

19 **Montpelier.** The state's capital.

20 **Stowe.** Quintessential eastern ski town.

21 **Jeffersonville.** The four-season Smugglers' Notch Resort.

22 **Burlington.** Vermont's most populous city with a lively food scene.

23 **Shelburne.** Shelburne Farms and Shelburne Museum.

24 **Lake Champlain Islands.** Numerous islands including Isle La Motte, North Hero, Grand Isle, and South Hero.

25 **Montgomery and Jay.** Small village near the Jay Peak ski resort and the Canadian border.

26 **Lake Willoughby.** Home to the world-renowned Bread and Puppet Theater museum.

27 **Greensboro.** Home to one of the world's best breweries.

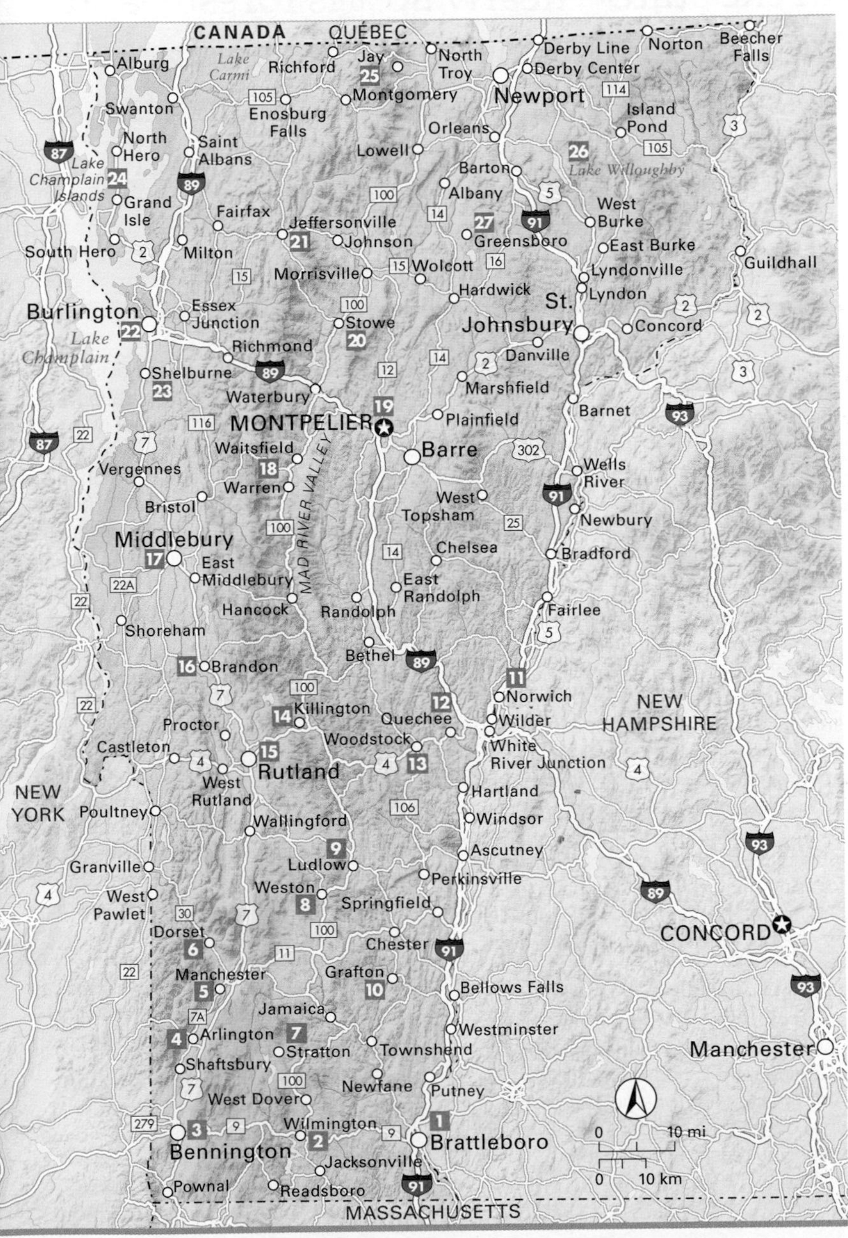
CANADA
QUÉBEC
Lake Carmi
Alburg
Richford
Jay
25
North Troy
Derby Line
Norton
Beecher Falls
Derby Center
Newport
Swanton
105
Enosburg Falls
Montgomery
114
Island Pond
3
North Hero
Saint Albans
87
Lake Champlain Islands
24
Orleans
Lowell
26
105
Lake Willoughby
89
Grand Isle
Barton
5
Albany
100
West Burke
Fairfax
Jeffersonville
14
27
91
21
Johnson
Greensboro
East Burke
South Hero
2
Milton
15
Wolcott
16
Guildhall
Lyndonville
15
Morrisville
Hardwick
Lyndon
Burlington
Essex Junction
100
St. Johnsbury
2
2
22
Lake Champlain
Stowe
20
Concord
Richmond
14
Danville
12
2
3
Shelburne
23
89
Marshfield
Waterbury
19
Barnet
93
116
MONTPELIER
Plainfield
22
7
Waitsfield
Barre
302
87
Vergennes
18
MAD RIVER VALLEY
Wells River
Warren
91
Bristol
West Topsham
Newbury
25
Middlebury
100
Chelsea
17
East Middlebury
14
Bradford
22A
East Randolph
Fairlee
22
Hancock
Randolph
Shoreham
5
Bethel
89
16
Brandon
11
100
7
Norwich
NEW HAMPSHIRE
22
12
Killington
14
Quechee
Wilder
Proctor
Woodstock
Castleton
15
White River Junction
4
13
4
4
West Rutland
Rutland
NEW YORK
Hartland
Poultney
106
Windsor
Wallingford
9
93
Ascutney
Ludlow
Granville
Perkinsville
4
West Pawlet
Weston
89
8
30
7
Springfield
Dorset
100
CONCORD
6
Chester
11
91
22
Manchester
Grafton
10
5
Bellows Falls
Jamaica
93
7A
4
Arlington
7
Westminster
Stratton
Townshend
Manchester
Shaftsbury
7
100
Newfane
Putney
West Dover
279
3
9
Wilmington
1
Brattleboro
0
10 mi
2
9
Bennington
Jacksonville
0
10 km
Pownal
Readsboro
91
MASSACHUSETTS

Vermont's a land of hidden treasures and unspoiled scenery. Wander anywhere in the state—nearly 80% is forest—and you'll find pristine countryside dotted with farms and framed by mountains. Tiny towns with picturesque church steeples, village greens, and covered bridges are perfect for exploring.

Sprawl has no place here. Highways are devoid of billboards by law, and on some roads cows still stop traffic twice a day en route to and from pasture. In spring, sap boils in sugarhouses, some built generations ago, while up the road a chef trained at the now-closed New England Culinary Institute in Montpelier might use the syrup to glaze a pork tenderloin.

It's the landscape, for the most part, that attracts people to Vermont. Rolling hills belie rugged terrain underneath the green canopy of forest growth. In summer, clear lakes and streams provide ample opportunities for swimming, boating, and fishing; hills attract hikers and mountain bikers. The more than 14,000 miles of roads, many of them only intermittently traveled by cars, are great for biking. In fall the leaves have their last hurrah, painting the mountainsides in vibrant yellow, gold, red, and orange. Vermont has the best ski resorts in the eastern United States, centered on the spine of the Green Mountains running north to south; and the traditional heart of skiing here is the town of Stowe. Almost anywhere you go, no matter what time of year, the Vermont countryside will make you reach for your camera.

Although Vermont may seem locked in time, technological sophistication appears where you least expect it: wireless Internet access in a 19th-century farmhouse-turned-inn and cell phone coverage from the state's highest peaks. Like an old farmhouse under renovation, though, the state's historic exterior is still the main attraction.

MAJOR REGIONS

Vermont can be divided into three regions: **Southern Vermont, Central Vermont,** and **Northern Vermont.**

Most people's introduction to the state is **Southern Vermont,** a relatively short drive from New York and Boston. As elsewhere across the state, you'll find unspoiled towns, romantic B&Bs, lush farms, and pristine forests. The area is flanked by **Bennington** on the west and **Brattleboro** on the east. There are charming towns like **Wilmington, Arlington, Manchester, Dorset, Weston, Grafton,** and **Townshend**, as well as ski destinations like **Stratton** and **Ludlow** (home to Okemo Resort).

Central Vermont is characterized by the rugged Green Mountains, which run north–south through the center of the state, and the gently rolling dairy lands east of Lake Champlain. It's home to the state's capital, **Montpelier,** the former mill towns of **Quechee** and **Middlebury**, artist enclaves like **Brandon**, and beautiful towns like **Norwich** and **Woodstock**, and plucky **Rutland.** Ski buffs flock to **Killington** and **Waitsfield** and **Warren** (for Mad River Glen and Sugarbush).

Northern Vermont is a place of contrasts. It's where you'll find the area known as the Northeast Kingdom, a refuge for nature lovers and those who love getting away from it all, as well as the state's largest city, **Burlington**, which has dramatic views of Lake Champlain and the Adirondacks, and it's neighboring Winooski. There's plenty of skiing in **Stowe, Jeffersonville** (Smugglers' Notch Resort), and **Jay** (Jay Peak) as well as outdoor adventures in **Lake Willoughby** and East Burke. And postcard-perfect scenery oozes in **Shelburne**, Charlotte, **Montgomery**, and the **Lake Champlain Islands**.

Planning

There are many ways to take advantage of Vermont's beauty: skiing or hiking its mountains, biking or driving its back roads, fishing or sailing its waters, shopping for local products, visiting museums and sights, or simply finding the perfect inn and never leaving the front porch.

Getting Here and Around

Distances are relatively short, yet the mountains and back roads will slow a traveler's pace. You can see a representative north–south cross section of Vermont in a few days; if you have up to a week, you can really hit the highlights.

AIR

American, Delta, JetBlue, Porter, and United fly into Burlington International Airport. Rutland State Airport has daily service to and from Boston on Cape Air.

CAR

Vermont is divided by a mountainous north–south middle, with a main highway on either side: scenic U.S. 7 on the western side and Interstate 91 (which begins in New Haven, Connecticut, and runs through Hartford, central Massachusetts, and along the Connecticut River in Vermont to the Canadian border) on the east. Interstate 89 runs from New Hampshire across central Vermont from White River Junction to Burlington and up to the Canadian border. For current road conditions, check New England 511's website.

New England 511
☎ *511* 🌐 *newengland511.org.*

FERRY

This company operates ferries on three routes between Vermont and New York: from Grand Isle, Vermont to Plattsburgh, New York; Burlington to Port Kent, New York; and Charlotte, Vermont to Essex, New York.

TRAIN

Amtrak has daytime service on the *Vermonter*, linking Washington, D.C. and New York City with Brattleboro, Bellows Falls, Windsor, White River Junction, Randolph, Montpelier, Waterbury, Essex Junction, and St. Albans.

Other Amtrak services include the *Ethan Allen Express*, which connects New York City with Castleton, Rutland, Middlebury, Vergennes, and Burlington.

Amtrak
☎ *800/872–7245* 🌐 *www.amtrak.com.*

Hotels

Vermont's relatively rare large chain hotels are mostly found in Burlington, Manchester, and Rutland; elsewhere it's primarily inns, B&Bs, and small motels. The inns and B&Bs, some of them quite luxurious, provide what many visitors consider the quintessential Vermont lodging experience. Most areas have traditional ski-base condos; at these you sacrifice charm for ski-and-stay deals and proximity to the lifts. Lodging rates are highest during foliage season, late September–mid-October, and lowest in late spring and November, although many properties close during these times. Winter is high season at ski resorts.

Hotel reviews have been shortened. For full reviews visit Fodors.com.

Creemee vs. Soft-Serve

A creemee is Vermont's answer to soft-serve ice cream. It often has a higher fat content than typical soft-serve—thanks in part to state specialties like local dairy and maple syrup—making it especially rich, silky and, well, creamy. (Hence the name.)

Restaurants

Everything that makes Vermont good and wholesome is distilled in its restaurants. Many of them belong to the **Vermont Fresh Network** (🌐 www.vermontfresh.net), a partnership that encourages chefs to create menus emphasizing Vermont's wonderful bounty; especially in summer and early fall, the produce and meats are impeccable.

Great chefs come to Vermont for the quality of life, and the Montpelier-based New England Culinary Institute was until recently a recruiting ground for new talent. Seasonal menus use local fresh herbs and vegetables along with native game. Look for imaginative approaches to New England foods like maple syrup (Vermont is the largest U.S. producer); dairy products (cheese in particular); native fruits and berries; heritage apples (explore the ever-growing cider scene); and regional game like venison, quail, and pheasant. Small-batch goods, from salsa to caramels, are made with Vermont ingredients. Beer has become yet another claim to fame in Vermont, thanks to more breweries per capita than any other state and recognition far and wide. Indeed, craft brewers as far away as Poland are now producing "Vermont-style" IPAs, and Hill Farmstead in Greensboro has been dubbed the best brewery in the world seven times by RateBeer, a brew-review website, since opening doors in 2010.

Your chances of finding a table for dinner vary with the season: lengthy waits are common in tourist centers at peak times—a reservation is always advisable.

Restaurant reviews have been shortened. For full reviews visit Fodors.com.

What It Costs in U.S. Dollars

	$	$$	$$$	$$$$
RESTAURANTS				
	under $18	$18–$24	$25–$35	over $35
HOTELS				
	under $200	$200–$299	$300–$399	over $399

Tours

Inn to Inn
SPECIAL-INTEREST TOURS | This company arranges guided and self-guided hiking, skiing, snowshoeing, and biking trips from inn to inn in Vermont. ✉ *52 Park St., Brandon* ☎ *802/247–3300* 🌐 *www.inntoinn.com* ⏲ *Closed Nov.–mid-May.*

VBT Bicycling and Walking Vacations
BICYCLE TOURS | This global guide company leads bike tours in Vermont as well as Maine and Massachusetts. The Vermont itineraries included a self-guided tour of the Middlebury countryside and the Lake Champlain coast and a guided tour of

Burlington, the Champlain Islands, and surrounding country villages. ✉ *Williston* ☎ *855/335–9225* 🌐 *www.vbt.com* 🎫 *From $1795.*

Visitor Information

CONTACTS Ski Vermont/Vermont Ski Areas Association. ✉ *Montpelier* ☎ *802/223–2439* 🌐 *www.skivermont.com.* **Vermont Department of Tourism and Marketing.** ✉ *Montpelier* ☎ *800/837–6668* 🌐 *www.vermontvacation.com.* **Vermont's Northeast Kingdom.** ☎ *802/626–8511* 🌐 *getnekedvt.com.*

When to Go

In summer Vermont is lush and green, and in winter the hills and towns are blanketed white with snow, inspiring skiers to challenge the peaks at Stowe and elsewhere. Fall, however, is always the most amazing time to come. If you have never seen the state's kaleidoscope of autumn colors, it's well worth braving the slow-moving traffic and shelling out a few extra bucks for lodging. The only time things really slow down is during "stick season" in November, when the leaves have fallen but there's no snow yet, and "mud season" in late spring, when even innkeepers counsel guests to come another time. Activities in the Champlain Islands essentially come to a halt in the winter, except for ice fishing and snowmobiling, and two of the biggest attractions, Shelburne Farms and the Shelburne Museum, are closed mid-October–April. Otherwise, Vermont is open for business year-round.

Brattleboro

60 miles south of White River Junction.

Brattleboro has drawn political activists and earnest counterculturists since the 1960s. The arts-oriented town and environs (population 12,000) remains politically and culturally active; after Burlington, this is Vermont's most offbeat locale.

GETTING HERE AND AROUND

Brattleboro is near the intersection of Route 9, the principal east–west highway also known as the Molly Stark Byway, and Interstate 91. For downtown, take Exit 2 from Interstate 91.

ESSENTIALS

VISITOR INFORMATION Brattleboro Area Chamber of Commerce. ✉ *Brattleboro* ☎ *802/254–4565, 877/254–4565* 🌐 *www.brattleborochamber.org.*

Sights

Brattleboro Museum and Art Center

ART MUSEUM | Downtown is the hub of Brattleboro's art scene, at the forefront of which is this museum in historic Union Station. It presents changing exhibitions of works by local, national, and international artists, and hosts lectures, readings, and musical performances. ✉ *10 Vernon St., Brattleboro* ☎ *802/257–0124* 🌐 *www.brattleboromuseum.org* 🎫 *$10 suggested donation* ⏲ *Closed Mon. and Tues.*

Putney

TOWN | Nine miles upriver, this town of fewer than 3,000 residents—the country cousin of bustling Brattleboro—is a haven for writers and fine-craft artists. There are many pottery studios to visit, the requisite general store, and a few orchards. Each November during the Putney Craft Tour, dozens of artisans open their studios and homes for live demonstrations and plenty of fun. ✉ *Putney.*

Restaurants

Cai's Dim Sum Catering

$ | CHINESE | The sourcing and gathering of local ingredients at the heart of chef-owner Cai Xi Silver's cooking is inspired by the food memories of her childhood in Chongqing, China. Her

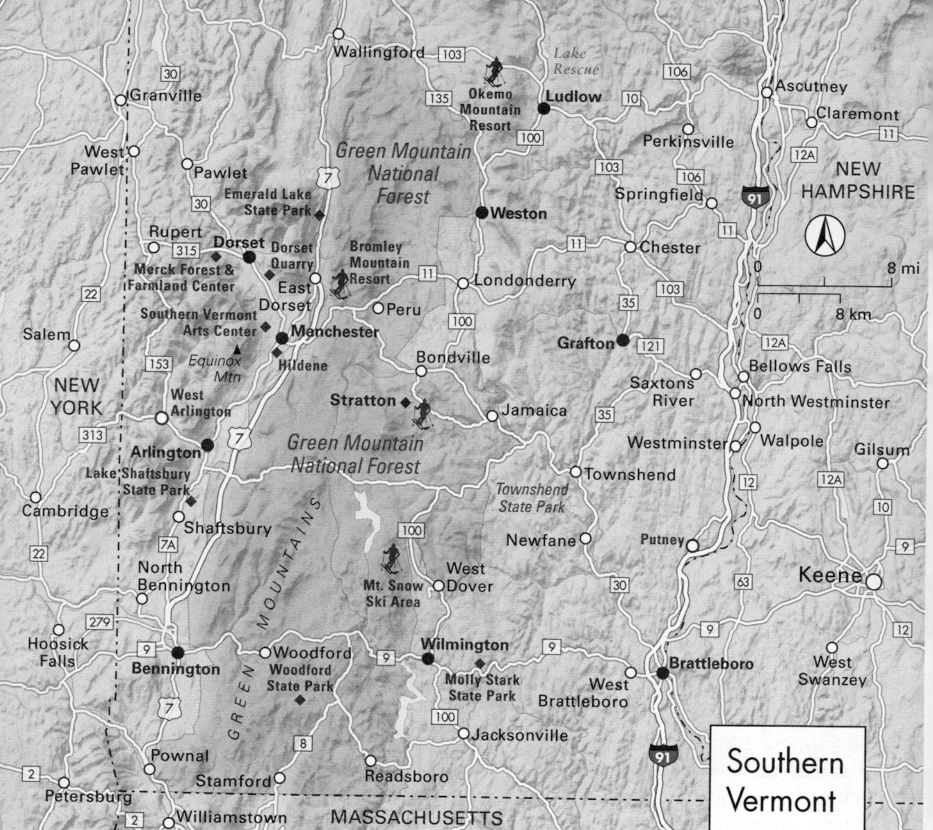

family's Sichuan and Shanghai influences come to life in a to-go menu that includes delicate steamed buns, perfect dumplings, and abundance boxes highlighting regional home cooking backed by Vermont ingredients. **Known for:** steamed buns; assorted seasonal dumplings; abundance boxes with local vegetables, rice, chicken, or tofu. $ *Average main: $15* ✉ *814 Western Ave., Brattleboro* ☎ *802/257–7898* 🌐 *dimsumvt.com* ⏲ *Closed Tues and for in-room dining; take-out/delivery only.*

★ Peter Havens

$$$ | **AMERICAN** | A longtime Brattleboro favorite helmed since 2012 by chef Zachary Corbin, this chic little bistro is known for impeccably presented cuisine that draws heavily on local sources. One room is painted a warm red, another in sage, and a changing lineup of contemporary paintings adorns the walls of both rooms. **Known for:** pan-roasted duck breast; cocktail and wine list; vanilla bean crème brûlée. $ *Average main: $30* ✉ *32 Elliot St., Brattleboro* ☎ *802/257–3333* 🌐 *www.peterhavens.com* ⏲ *Closed Mon. and Tues. No lunch Sun., Wed., and Thurs.*

Top of the Hill Grill

$ | **BARBECUE** | **FAMILY** | Don't let the diminutive size of this roadside smokehouse deceive you. The place produces big flavors locals line up for: hickory-smoked ribs, apple-smoked turkey, beef brisket, and pulled pork, to name a few. **Known for:** "burnt ends" (brisket burnt ends); excellent view of West River; outdoor deck. $ *Average main: $15* ✉ *632 Putney Rd., Brattleboro* ☎ *802/258–9178* 🌐 *www.topofthehillgrill.com* ⏲ *Closed Nov.–Mar.*

Whetstone Station Restaurant and Brewery

$ | **INTERNATIONAL** | One of Brattleboro's most happening hangouts is this nano-brewery and restaurant perched over the Connecticut River. The beer and classic American comfort food are good, but it's the view of the river and its forested banks that drops jaws. **Known for:** rooftop beer garden; "Big 'Stoner" imperial IPA; poutine and steak tips. *Average main: $16 ✉ 36 Bridge St., Brattleboro ☎ 802/490–2354 🌐 www.whetstonestation.com.*

Coffee and Quick Bites

★ Chelsea Royal Diner

$ | **DINER** | **FAMILY** | Built into a vintage 1938 Worcester diner, one of the few remaining in the country, the Chelsea Royal Diner serves all-day breakfast and Blue Plate specials from produce (eggs included) sourced from their backyard farm. Save room for homemade ice cream made with local milk and cream from the St. Albans Co-op Creamery—flavors range from VT Maple Cream to Blueberry, Pumpkin, and Mocha Malted Milk Ball. **Known for:** homemade ice cream and soft serve; all-day breakfast; Blue Plate Specials, like Friday Fish Fry and Sunday Yankee Pot Roast. *Average main: $13 ✉ 487 Marlboro Rd., Brattleboro ☎ 802/254–8399 🌐 www.chelsearoyaldiner.com.*

Mocha Joe's Cafe

$ | **CAFÉ** | The team at this spot for coffee and conversation takes great pride in sourcing direct-trade beans from places like Kenya, Ethiopia, and Guatemala, and pairs them with an assortment of cookies, cakes, and muffins. This is ground zero for Brattleboro's bohemian contingent and fellow travelers. **Known for:** socially conscious coffee; maple latte; trendy clientele. *Average main: $5 ✉ 82 Main St., at Elliot St., Brattleboro ☎ 802/257–7794 🌐 www.mochajoes.com.*

Hotels

★ The Inn on Putney Road

$$ | **B&B/INN** | Thoughtful and comforting details abound in this 1931 French-style manse such as the mini-refrigerator and basket stocked with complimentary soda, water, granola bars, and snacks, as well as gas fireplaces in several guest rooms. **Pros:** lovely breakfast room; nice blend of traditional and modern design; pottery by artist Steven Procter scattered throughout. **Cons:** tight parking; outside downtown; rooms in front sometimes suffer traffic noise. *Rooms from: $239 ✉ 192 Putney Rd., Brattleboro ☎ 802/536–4780 🌐 www.innonputneyroad.com 6 rooms Free Breakfast.*

Latchis Hotel

$ | **HOTEL** | Though not lavish, the guest rooms in this 1938 art deco building have the original sinks and tiling in the bathrooms, and many overlook Main Street, with New Hampshire's mountains in the background. **Pros:** heart-of-town location; lots of personality; reasonable rates. **Cons:** limited breakfast; sound-masking machines sometimes required; few parking spots. *Rooms from: $130 ✉ 50 Main St., Brattleboro ☎ 802/254–6300, 800/798–6301 🌐 www.latchishotel.com 33 rooms Free Breakfast.*

Performing Arts

Latchis Theatre

THEMED ENTERTAINMENT | This movie theater's architecture represents a singular blending of art deco and Greek Revival style, complete with statues, columns, and 1938 murals by Louis Jambor (1884–1955), a noted artist and children's book illustrator. The Latchis hosts art exhibits, streams live events, and has four screening rooms. For a sense of the theater's original grandeur, buy a ticket for whatever is showing on the big screen. Though the space may not be a state-of-the-art cinema, watching a film here is far more memorable than at any multiplex. ✉ *50 Main St., Brattleboro* ☎ *802/254–6300, 800/798–6301* 🌐 *www.latchis.com.*

Shopping

ART GALLERIES

Gallery Art Walk

ART GALLERIES | On this walk, you'll pass more than 30 galleries and other venues downtown and nearby that exhibit art; it takes place 5:30–8:30 pm on the first Friday evening of the month. ☎ *802/257–2616* 🌐 *www.gallerywalk.org.*

Gallery in the Woods

ART GALLERIES | This funky trilevel store sells art, jewelry, and light fixtures from around the world. Rotating shows take place in the upstairs and downstairs galleries. ✉ *145 Main St., Brattleboro* ☎ *802/257–4777* 🌐 *www.galleryinthewoods.com.*

Vermont Artisan Designs

ART GALLERIES | Artworks and functional items in ceramic, glass, wood, fiber, and other media created by more than 300 artists are on display at this gallery. ✉ *106 Main St., Brattleboro* ☎ *802/257–7044* 🌐 *www.vtart.com.*

Vermont Center for Photography

ART GALLERIES | The center exhibits works by American photographers. Opening receptions are held on the first Friday evening of the month. ✉ *49 Flat St., Brattleboro* ☎ *802/251–6051* 🌐 *www.vcphoto.org.*

BOOKS

Brattleboro Books

BOOKS | Bibliophiles will love hunting for buried treasure in this mini labyrinth of used books. ✉ *36 Elliot St., Brattleboro* ☎ *802/257–7777* 🌐 *www.brattleborobooks.com.*

Activities

BIKING

Brattleboro Bicycle Shop

BIKING | This shop rents hybrid bikes (call ahead to reserve one), does repair work, and sells maps and equipment. ✉ *165 Main St., Brattleboro* ☎ *802/254–8644, 800/272–8245* 🌐 *www.bratbike.com.*

CANOEING AND KAYAKING

Vermont Canoe Touring Center

CANOEING & ROWING | Canoes and kayaks are available for rent here. Payment is by cash or check only. ✉ *451 Putney Rd., Brattleboro* ☎ *802/257–5008* 🌐 *www.vermontcanoetouringcenter.com.*

HIKING

Fort Dummer State Park

HIKING & WALKING | You can hike and camp within the 217 acres of forest at this state park, the location of the first permanent European settlement in Vermont. That site is now submerged beneath the Connecticut River, but it is viewable from the northernmost scenic vista on Sunrise Trail. ✉ *517 Old Guilford Rd., Brattleboro* ☎ *802/254–2610* 🌐 *www.vtstateparks.com/fortdummer.html* 💵 *$5* ⏲ *Facilities closed early Sept.–late May.*

MULTISPORT OUTFITTERS

Burrows Specialized Sports

BIKING | This full-service sporting goods store rents and sells bicycles, snowboards, skis, and snowshoes, and has a repair shop. ✉ *105 Main St., Brattleboro* ☎ *802/254–9430* 🌐 *www.burrowssports.com.*

Sam's Outdoor Outfitters

LOCAL SPORTS | At this labyrinthine two-story sports emporium you can find outerwear, shoes, and gear for all seasons and activities. Grab a bag of free popcorn while you're shopping. ✉ *74 Main St., Brattleboro* ☎ *802/254–2933* 🌐 *www.samsoutfitters.com.*

Wilmington

18 miles west of Brattleboro.

The village of Wilmington, with its classic Main Street lined with 18th- and 19th-century buildings, anchors the Mt. Snow Valley. Most of the valley's lodging and dining establishments, however, can be found along Route 100, which travels 5 miles north to West Dover and Mt. Snow, where skiers flock on winter weekends. The area abounds with cultural activity from concerts to art exhibits year-round.

GETTING HERE AND AROUND

Wilmington is at the junction of Route 9 and Route 100. West Dover and Mount Snow are a few miles to the north along Route 100.

ESSENTIALS

VISITOR INFORMATION Southern Vermont Deerfield Valley Chamber of Commerce. *✉ Wilmington ☎ 802/464–8092, 877/887–6884 🌐 www.visitvermont.com.*

Who Was Molly Stark?

In the heart of Wilmington beside the Crafts Inn stands a sculpture in honor of Molly Stark, the wife of the Revolutionary War general John Stark. The general was said to have roused his troops in the Battle of Bennington, vowing victory over the British: "They are ours, or this night Molly Stark sleeps a widow!" He lived, and hence the victory path across Vermont (now Route 9) is called the Molly Stark Trail (or Byway).

Sights

Molly Stark State Park

STATE/PROVINCIAL PARK | FAMILY | The park is known for its great camping (there are two loops) and popular snowshoe trails, and there's a picnic pavilion. The Molly Stark Heritage Trail runs through this area, known as a scenic bypass. There is a 1.7-mile loop hike to the fire tower atop Mt. Olga that culminates in a 360-degree view of southern Vermont and northern Massachusetts. *✉ 705 Rte. 9 E, Wilmington ☎ 802/464–5460 🌐 www.vtstateparks.com/mollystark.html.*

Restaurants

Dot's Restaurant

$ | DINER | FAMILY | Under the classic red neon sign at the main corner in downtown Wilmington, Dot's remains a local landmark and a reminder of diners of yore. Residents and skiers pack the tables and counter for American comfort food classics, starting at 5:30 am with the Berry-Berry pancake breakfast, with four kinds of berries. **Known for:** convivial community hangout; river-view seating; Dot's "jailhouse" chili. *$ Average main: $10 ✉ 3 W. Main St., Wilmington ☎ 802/464–7284 🌐 www.facebook.com/DotsofVermont.*

La Casita Taqueria y Mas

$ | MEXICAN | FAMILY | Hidden away in the back of a parking lot behind The Anchor, La Casita is a favorite haunt for Mexican fare, including homemade bottled hot sauces, shatteringly crisp flautas, and loaded burritos. The drink menu is no slouch either, with a variety of local beers and seasonal margaritas on hand to wash down platters of tacos and sizzling fajitas. **Known for:** sizzling fajita platters; warm, friendly atmosphere; cooked-to-order carne asada. $ *Average main: $16* ✉ *14 S. Main St., Wilmington* ☎ *802/464–8500.*

The Village Roost

$ | **INTERNATIONAL** | This bigger-on-the-inside café and lunch joint comes with ample space, especially in the barn-chic back room that serves resting travelers, gaming locals, and conferring coworkers. Keeping them oiled is a menu of organic, non-GMO, locally sourced sandwiches, burgers, soups, and salads. **Known for:** large stone fireplace in the back; quality coffee and tea; hangout space. $ *Average main: $11* ✉ *20 W. Main St., Wilmington* ☎ *802/464–3344* 🌐 *www.villageroost.com* ⏲ *No dinner.*

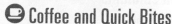

Coffee and Quick Bites

Butter Mountain Bakery

$ | **BAKERY** | Chewy homemade bagels, craggy loaves of sourdough, and brown butter maple cookies are just a handful of the offerings waiting at this tucked-away hidden gem, but remember to preorder as walk-ins aren't usually accommodated. Keep an eye out for seasonal specials like fresh fruit galettes and walnut-studded chocolate brownies—the menu is always changing. **Known for:** crusty loaves of sourdough; seasonal galettes, like strawberry-basil; snickerdoodle cookies. $ *Average main: $5* ✉ *1 School St., Wilmington* ☎ *802/780–0232* 🌐 *www.buttermountainbakery.com/* ⏲ *Closed Sun.–Thurs.*

1a Coffee Roasters

$ | **CAFÉ** | This great new addition to Vermont's coffee scene has some of the best cold brew in the state. Mainly solar-powered, it recently got a sustainability grant from Oatly, and serves its iced drinks in sleek glass jars; pastries come from nearby Starfire Bakery. **Known for:** great outdoor patio; cold brew coffee; solar-powered coffee roaster. $ *Average main: $5* ✉ *123 W Main St., Wilmington* ☎ *802/265–0284* 🌐 *www.1acoffee.com* ⏲ *Closed Mon.–Tues. No dinner.*

Hotels

Deerhill Inn

$ | **B&B/INN** | The restaurant at this quintessential New England inn is among the best in town. **Pros:** complimentary house-baked cookies; some rooms have whirlpool tubs; toiletries by L'Occitane. **Cons:** must drive to Mount Snow and town; traditional flowered wallpaper and upholstery in spots; two-night minimum required for weekends. $ *Rooms from: $165* ✉ *14 Valley View Rd., West Dover* ☎ *802/464–3100, 800/993–3379* 🌐 *www.deerhillinn.com* *13 rooms* *Free Breakfast.*

Grand Summit Hotel

$$$ | **RESORT** | **FAMILY** | Mount Snow's comfortable main hotel is an easy choice for skiers whose main priority is getting on the slopes as quickly as possible. **Pros:** easy ski access; lots of children's activities; fitness center. **Cons:** somewhat bland decor; can be busy and crowded; resort fee. $ *Rooms from: $380* ✉ *39 Mt. Snow Rd., West Dover* ☎ *800/451–4211* 🌐 *www.mountsnow.com* *196 rooms* *No Meals.*

Activities

Molly Stark State Park is home to some of the state's most popular snowshoe trails. Mount Olga Trail is a relatively easy 1.7-mile loop culminating in a 360-degree view of southern Vermont and northern Massachusetts.

SKIING

Mount Snow

SKIING & SNOWBOARDING | The closest major ski area to all of the Northeast's big cities, Mount Snow prides itself on its hundreds of snowmaking fan guns—more than any other resort in North America. There are four major downhill areas. The main mountain comprises

The poet Robert Frost is buried in Bennington at the Old First Church.

mostly intermediate runs, while the north face has the majority of expert runs. The south face, Sunbrook, has wide, sunny trails. It connects to Carinthia, which is dedicated to terrain parks and glade skiing. In summer, the 600-acre resort has an 18-hole golf course, 11.3 miles of lift-serviced mountain-bike trails, and an extensive network of hiking trails. In 2018, the resort debuted a brand-new, $22 million, 42,000-square-foot Carinthia Base Lodge, five times the size of the previous lodge. **Facilities:** 86 trails; 600 acres; 1,700-foot vertical drop; 20 lifts. ✉ *39 Mt. Snow Rd., West Dover* ☎ *802/464–3333, 802/464–2151 for snow conditions, 800/245–7669* 🌐 *www.mountsnow.com* 🎫 *Lift ticket: $149.*

Timber Creek
SKIING & SNOWBOARDING | North of Mount Snow, this appealingly small cross-country skiing and snowshoeing center has 4½ miles of groomed loops. You can rent equipment and take lessons here. ✉ *13 Tanglewood Rd., at Rte. 100, West Dover* ☎ *802/464–0999* 🌐 *www.timbercreekxc.com* 🎫 *$25.*

Bennington

21 miles west of Wilmington.

Bennington is the commercial focus of Vermont's southwest corner and home to Bennington College. It's really three towns in one: Downtown Bennington, Old Bennington, and North Bennington. Downtown has retained much of the industrial character it developed in the 19th century, when paper mills, gristmills, and potteries formed the city's economic base. The outskirts of town are commercial and not worth a stop, so make your way right into Downtown and Old Bennington to appreciate the area's true charm.

GETTING HERE AND AROUND

The heart of modern Bennington is the intersection of U.S. 7 and Route 9. Old Bennington is a couple of miles west on Route 9, at Monument Avenue. North Bennington is a few miles north on Route 67A.

ESSENTIALS

VISITOR INFORMATION Bennington Area Chamber of Commerce. ✉ *Bennington* ☎ *802/447–3311* 🌐 *www.bennington.com.*

Sights

Bennington Battle Monument

MONUMENT | FAMILY | This 306-foot stone obelisk with an elevator to the top commemorates General John Stark's Revolutionary War victory over the British, who attempted to capture Bennington's stockpile of supplies. Inside the monument you can learn all about the battle, which took place near Walloomsac Heights in New York State on August 16, 1777, and helped bring about the surrender of British commander "Gentleman Johnny" Burgoyne two months later. The top of the tower affords commanding views of the Massachusetts Berkshires, the New York Adirondacks, and the Vermont Green Mountains. ✉ *15 Monument Circle, Old Bennington* ☎ *802/447–0550* 🌐 *www.benningtonbattlemonument.com* 🎫 *$5* ⏲ *Closed Wed. and Nov.–Apr.*

Bennington College

COLLEGE | Contemporary stone sculpture and white-frame neo-Colonial dorms surrounded by acres of cornfields punctuate the green meadows of the placid campus of Bennington College. ✉ *1 College Dr., off U.S. 7, North Bennington* ☎ *802/442–5401* 🌐 *www.bennington.edu.*

★ Bennington Museum

HISTORY MUSEUM | The rich collections here feature military artifacts, early tools, dolls, and the Bennington Flag, one of the oldest of the Stars and Stripes in existence. Other areas of interest include early Bennington pottery, the Gilded Age in Vermont, mid-20th-century modernist painters who worked in or near Bennington, glass and metalwork by Lewis Comfort Tiffany, and photography, watercolors, and other works on paper. The highlight for many visitors, though, is the largest public collection of works by Grandma Moses (1860–1961), the popular self-taught artist who lived and painted in the area. ✉ *75 Main St., Old Bennington* ☎ *802/447–1571* 🌐 *www.benningtonmuseum.org* 🎫 *$12* ⏲ *Closed Jan.–Mar.*

Lake Shaftsbury State Park

STATE/PROVINCIAL PARK | FAMILY | You'll find a swimming beach, nature trails, boat and canoe rentals, and a snack bar at this pretty park. ✉ *262 Shaftsbury State Park Rd., 10½ miles north of Bennington, Bennington* ☎ *802/375–9978* 🌐 *www.vtstateparks.com/shaftsbury.html* ⏲ *Facilities closed early Sept.–mid-May.*

Old Bennington

HISTORIC DISTRICT | West of downtown, this National Register Historic District is well endowed with stately Colonial and Victorian mansions. The site of the Catamount Tavern, where Ethan Allen organized the Green Mountain Boys to capture Ft. Ticonderoga in 1775, is marked by a bronze statue of Vermont's indigenous mountain lion, now extinct. ✉ *Monument Ave., Old Bennington.*

The Old First Church

CEMETERY | In the graveyard of this church, the tombstone of the poet Robert Frost proclaims, "I had a lover's quarrel with the world." ✉ *1 Monument Circle, at Monument Ave., Old Bennington* ☎ *802/447–1223* 🌐 *www.oldfirstchurchbenn.org* 🎫 *Free.*

Park-McCullough House

HISTORIC HOME | The architecturally significant Park-McCullough House is a 35-room classic French Empire–style mansion, built in 1865 and furnished with period pieces. Several restored flower gardens grace the landscaped grounds, and a barn holds some antique carriages. Guided tours happen on the hour while the house is open. The grounds are open daily year-round. ✉ *1 Park St., at West St., North Bennington* ☎ *802/442–5441* 🌐 *www.parkmccullough.org* 🎫 *$15* ⏲ *Closed Oct.–May.*

Robert Frost Stone House Museum

HISTORIC HOME | Robert Frost came to Shaftsbury in 1920, he wrote, "to plant a new Garden of Eden with a thousand apple trees of some unforbidden variety." The museum, now part of Bennington College, tells the story of the poet's life and highlights the nine years (1920–29) he spent living in the house with his wife and four children. It was here that he penned "Stopping by Woods on a Snowy Evening" and published two books of poetry. You can wander 7 of the Frost family's original 80 acres. Among the apple boughs you just might find inspiration of your own. ✉ *121 Historic Rte. 7A, Shaftsbury* ☎ *802/447–6200* 🌐 *www.bennington.edu* 🎟 *$10* ⏲ *Closed Tues. and Wed.*

Woodford State Park

STATE/PROVINCIAL PARK | **FAMILY** | At 2,400 feet, this has the highest state campground in Vermont. Adams Reservoir is the dominant feature and focus of activities, with swimming, fishing, and boating, including canoes, kayaks, and paddleboards for rent. A nature trail also circles the reservoir. ✉ *142 State Park Rd., Bennington* ✣ *10 miles east of Bennington* ☎ *802/447–7169* 🌐 *www.vtstateparks.com/woodford.html* ⏲ *Facilities closed mid-Oct.–mid-May.*

Restaurants

Harvest Brewing

$ | **MEXICAN FUSION** | This nanobrewery in the heart of downtown Bennington is a haven of craft beers with English-style porters and inventive brews like Melon Grab fruited IPA. All of these beers become the perfect palate cleansers for good pub fare like loaded nachos and deep fried chimichangas. **Known for:** hazy IPAs; hearty Mexican-inspired pub fare; seasonal brews from smooth stouts to crisp lagers. $ *Average main: $8* ✉ *201 South St., Bennington* ☎ *802/430–9915* 🌐 *www.harvestbrewing.net.*

Madison Brewing Company

$$ | **BURGER** | Since opening in the 1990s as the area's first brewpub, this enclave of exposed brick and bubbling brewing tanks has become a watering hole for fresh IPAs and stacked burgers. A full bar and myriad pub fare offer plenty of reasons to elbow up to the wraparound bar. **Known for:** craft beer on draft; classic New England–style pub fare; gourmet burgers. $ *Average main: $21* ✉ *428 Main St., Bennington* ☎ *802/442–7397* 🌐 *www.madisonbrewingco.com.*

Village Garage Distillery

$ | **ECLECTIC** | An old highway equipment garage is now filled with a shiny copper still and barrels of aging spirits, visible through big windows from the attached tasting room; cocktails made with the distillery's gin, vodka, rye, and bourbon are twists on the classics, detailed in blueprint-like sketches on the menu. The food is surprisingly inventive for tasting room fare, including chicken and waffles, bowls of ramen, and a burger made from cattle fed the distillery's spent grain, served on a spent grain bun. **Known for:** local grain in the distillery; live music; Village Bonfire whiskey with smoked maple syrup. $ *Average main: $17* ✉ *107 Depot St., Bennington* ☎ *802/447–7663* 🌐 *villagegarage.com* ⏲ *Closed Mon.–Tues.*

Hotels

The Eddington House Inn

$ | **B&B/INN** | In the heart of North Bennington, just around the corner from three covered bridges and Bennington College, this impeccably maintained, 18th-century three-bedroom house is a great value. **Pros:** budget prices for a great B&B; "endless desserts" in dining room 24 hours a day; summer guest passes to Lake Paran. **Cons:** slightly off usual tourist track; only three rooms so it fills up fast; no front desk or after-hours reception. $ *Rooms from: $159* ✉ *21 Main St., North Bennington*

☎ 802/442–1511 ⊕ www.eddingtonhouseinn.com ⇐ 3 suites ǀ◎ǀ Free Breakfast.

★ Four Chimneys Inn

$ | **B&B/INN** | This exquisite, three-story, neo-Georgian (circa 1915) looks out over a substantial lawn and a wonderful old stone wall. **Pros:** walking distance to several Bennington sights; a complimentary full country breakfast; extremely well kept. **Cons:** dinner only offered for special events; no coffee or tea in rooms; a bit stuffy. *[$] Rooms from: $189 ✉ 21 West Rd., Old Bennington ☎ 802/447–3500 ⊕ www.fourchimneys.com ⇐ 11 rooms ǀ◎ǀ Free Breakfast.*

The Hardwood Hill

$ | **HOTEL** | Built in 1937, this fully renovated roadside motel has been given a distinct artsy, boutique upgrade by a foursome of new owners, three of whom are working artists, which translates into a sculpture garden out front, regular workshops by a resident artist, and performances on the red stage on the vast, hammock-dappled back lawn. **Pros:** excellent restaurant right next door; good value for cost; "arts package" includes tickets and discounts at local sights. **Cons:** must drive to town; rooms somewhat small; no restaurant or dining area. *[$] Rooms from: $99 ✉ 864 Harwood Hill Rd., Bennington ☎ 802/442–6278 ⊕ www.harwoodhillmotel.com ⇐ 17 rooms ǀ◎ǀ Free Breakfast.*

South Shire Inn

$$ | **B&B/INN** | Originally built for banker Louis A. Graves, this beautiful Victorian is a cozy and intimate bed and breakfast that looks like a regular house from the outside. **Pros:** set back from crowds; plenty of character; breakfast included. **Cons:** small-scale property; not within walking distance of much; no on-site restaurant. *[$] Rooms from: $200 ✉ 124 Elm St., Bennington ☎ 802/447–3839 ⊕ southshire.com ⇐ 9 rooms ǀ◎ǀ Free Breakfast.*

Billboardless Vermont

Did you know that there are no billboards in Vermont? The state banned them in 1967 (similar laws exist in Maine, Alaska, and Hawaii), and the last one came down in 1975, so when you look out your window, you see trees and other scenery—not advertisements.

Performing Arts

Basement Music Series

MUSIC | The Vermont Arts Exchange sponsors this fun and funky contemporary music series at the downtown Masonic Lodge. Some performances sell out, so it's wise to purchase tickets in advance. *✉ 504 Main St., Bennington ☎ 800/838–3006 for ticket hotline ⊕ www.vtartxchange.org/music.*

Oldcastle Theatre Company

MUSIC | This fine regional theater company focuses on American classics and crowd-pleasing musicals. The group's venue also hosts occasional concerts. *✉ 331 Main St., Bennington ☎ 802/447–0564 ⊕ www.oldcastletheatre.org ⏲ Closed Dec.–Mar.*

Shopping

The Apple Barn & Country Bake Shop

MARKET | **FAMILY** | Homemade baked goods, fresh cider, Vermont cheeses, maple syrup, and around a dozen varieties of apples are among the treats for sale here. There's berry picking in season, for a fun family stop, and on weekends you can watch the bakers make cider doughnuts. *✉ 604 Rte. 7S, 1½ miles south of downtown Bennington, Bennington ☎ 802/447–7780 ⊕ www.theapplebarn.com.*

Vermont Maple Syrup

Vermont is the country's largest producer of maple syrup. A visit to a maple farm is a great way to learn all about sugaring, the process of extracting maple tree sap and making syrup. Sap is stored in a sugar maple tree's roots in the winter, and in the spring when conditions are just right, the sap runs up and can be tapped. Sugaring season runs March to April, which is when all maple syrup in the state is produced.

One of the best parts of visiting a maple farm is getting to taste and compare the four grades of syrup. As the sugaring season goes on and days become warmer, the sap becomes progressively darker and stronger in flavor. Grades are defined by color, clarity, density, and flavor. Is one grade better than another? Nope, it's just a question of taste. Sap drawn early in the season produces the lightest color, and has the most delicate flavor: this is called golden. Amber has a mellow flavor. Dark is much more robust, and Very Dark is the most flavorful, making it often the favorite of first-time tasters.

When visiting a maple farm, make sure they make their own syrup, as opposed to just bottling or selling someone else's. You'll learn more about the entire process that way. **Vermont Maple Syrup** (☎802/858–9444; 🌐www.vermontmaple.org), a great resource, has a map of maple farms that host tours, a directory of producers open year-round, and a list of places from which you can order maple syrup by mail. You can also get the lowdown on events such as the annual Maple Open House Weekend, when sugarhouses throughout the state open their doors to visitors.

The Bennington Bookshop

BOOKS | The state's oldest independent bookstore sells the latest new releases and hosts weekly readings, signings, and lectures. ✉ *467 Main St., Bennington* ☎ *802/442–5059* 🌐 *www.bennington-bookshop.com.*

Now And Then Books

BOOKS | This labyrinthine second-story bookstore stocks nearly 45,000 secondhand volumes. ✉ *439 Main St., Bennington* ☎ *802/442–5566* 🌐 *www.nowandthenbooksvt.com.*

Activities

HIKING

Long Trail

HIKING & WALKING | Four miles east of Bennington, the Long Trail crosses Route 9 and runs south to the top of Harmon Hill. Allot two or three hours for this steep hike. ✉ *Bennington.*

Arlington

15 miles north of Bennington.

Smaller than Bennington and more down-to-earth than upper-crust Manchester to the north, Arlington exudes a certain Rockwellian folksiness, and it should: the illustrator Norman Rockwell lived here from 1939 to 1953, and many neighbors served as models for his portraits of small-town life.

GETTING HERE AND AROUND

Arlington is at the intersection of Route 313 and Route 7A. Take Route 313 West to reach West Arlington.

Sights

West Arlington

TOWN | Norman Rockwell once lived in this place with a quaint town green. If you follow Route 313 west from Arlington, you'll pass by the Wayside Country Store, a slightly rickety charmer where you can pick up sandwiches and chat with locals. The store carries everything from ammo and sporting goods to toys, teas, and maple syrup. Continue on, and cross West Arlington's red covered bridge, which leads to the town green. To loop back to Route 7A, take River Road along the south side of the Battenkill River, a scenic drive. ✉ *West Arlington.*

Coffee and Quick Bites

Arlington Dairy Bar

$ | **AMERICAN** | **FAMILY** | The big red barn with a sprawling lawn and walk-up ice cream window is a quintessential summer snack shack. It's where paper boats holding cheeseburgers, loaded hot dogs, and lobster rolls make way for soft-serve sundaes, stacked ice-cream cones, and root beer floats. **Known for:** nostalgic snack bar atmosphere; ice-cream cones and sundaes; cheeseburgers and hot dogs. $ *Average main: $5* ✉ *3158 Rte. 7A, Arlington* ☎ *802/375–2546.*

Wayside Country Store

$ | **AMERICAN** | **FAMILY** | The motto of Arlington's one-stop-shop says it all: "If we don't have it, you don't need it!" This charming country store is known for carrying anything from toilet paper to boxed cocoa mix and boasts a popular deli complete with build-your-own sandwiches, prepared foods, and house-made specials like freshly baked biscuits. **Known for:** locally made goods; deli wraps and sandwiches; specialty prepared foods, from stuffed peppers to roasted chicken legs. $ *Average main: $7* ✉ *3307 Rte. 313 W, Arlington* ☎ *802/375–2792.*

Hotels

The Arlington Inn & Spa

$ | **B&B/INN** | The Greek Revival columns of this 1847 home lend it an imposing presence in the middle of town, but the atmosphere within is friendly and old-fashioned. **Pros:** heart-of-town location; breakfast included for guests; on site massages available for guests. **Cons:** no dinner service; elegant but old-fashioned decor; no tea or coffee in rooms. $ *Rooms from: $199* ✉ *3904 Rte. 7A, Arlington* ☎ *802/375–6532* 🌐 *www.arlingtoninn.com* *17 rooms* *Free Breakfast.*

★ Hill Farm Inn

$$ | **B&B/INN** | **FAMILY** | Few hotels or inns in Vermont can match the sumptuous views of Mt. Equinox and surrounding hillscape of this former dairy farm built in 1830, whether seen from the large wraparound porch, the fire pit (where you can roast s'mores), or the outdoor hot tub. **Pros:** outdoor pool and hot tub; perfect Vermont wedding setting; Vermont Castings stoves in many rooms. **Cons:** books up on weekends with weddings; bringing alcohol not allowed; can be buggy in summer, like all Vermont. $ *Rooms from: $235* ✉ *458 Hill Farm Rd., off Rte. 7A, Sunderland* ☎ *802/375–2269* 🌐 *www.hillfarminn.com* *12 rooms* *Free Breakfast.*

West Mountain Inn

$$ | **B&B/INN** | **FAMILY** | This 1810 farmhouse sits on 150 mountainside acres with hiking trails and easy access to the Battenkill River, where you can canoe or go tubing; in winter, guests can sled down a former ski slope or borrow snowshoes or cross-country skis. **Pros:** atmospheric Colonial dining room; lots of activities; wood-panel dining room with fireplace. **Cons:** dining room not ideal for kids; dirt road to property uneven and pitted; tiny bathrooms in some rooms. $ *Rooms from: $205* ✉ *144 W. Mountain Inn Rd., at Rte. 313, Arlington*

☎ *802/375–6516* 🌐 *www.westmountain-inn.com* *20 rooms* *Free Breakfast.*

Shopping

Village Peddler

SOUVENIRS | FAMILY | This shop has a "chocolatorium," where you can learn all about cocoa. It sells fudge and other candies and stocks a large collection of teddy bears, one of whom is giant and made of chocolate. ✉ *261 Old Mill Rd., East Arlington* ☎ *802/375–6037* 🌐 *www.villagepeddlervt.com.*

Manchester

9 miles northeast of Arlington.

Well-to-do Manchester has been a popular summer retreat since the mid-19th century, when city dwellers traveled north to take in the cool, clean air at the base of 3,840-foot Mt. Equinox. Manchester Village's tree-shaded marble sidewalks and stately old homes—Main Street here could hardly be more picture-perfect—reflect the luxurious resort lifestyle of more than a century ago. A mile north on Route 7A, Manchester Center is the commercial twin to Colonial Manchester Village; it's also where you'll find the town's famed upscale factory outlets doing business in attractive faux-Colonial shops.

Manchester Village houses the world headquarters of Orvis, the outdoor-goods brand that was founded here in the 19th century and has greatly influenced the town ever since. The complex includes a fly-fishing school featuring lessons given in its casting ponds and the Battenkill River.

GETTING HERE AND AROUND

Manchester is the main town for the ski resorts of Stratton (a half-hour drive on Route 30) and Bromley (15 minutes to the northeast on Route 11). It's 15 minutes north of Arlington along scenic Route 7A.

ESSENTIALS

VISITOR INFORMATION Green Mountain National Forest Visitor Center. ✉ *2538 Depot St., Manchester* ☎ *802/362–2307* 🌐 *www.fs.usda.gov/main/gmfl.* **Manchester Visitor Center.** ✉ *4826 Main St., Manchester* ☎ 🌐 *www.manchestervermont.com.*

Sights

American Museum of Fly Fishing

OTHER MUSEUM | This museum houses the world's largest collection of angling art and angling-related objects—more than 1,500 rods, 800 reels, 30,000 flies, including the tackle of Winslow Homer, Babe Ruth, Jimmy Carter, and other notables. Every August, vendors sell antique equipment at the museum's fly-fishing festival. You can also practice your casting out back. ✉ *4070 Main St., Manchester* ☎ *802/362–3300* 🌐 *www.amff.org* *$5* *Closed Mon.-Wed.*

★ Hildene

GARDEN | FAMILY | A twofold treat, the summer home of Abraham Lincoln's son Robert provides insight into the lives of the Lincoln family, as well as an introduction to the lavish Manchester life of the early 1900s. In 1905, Robert built a 24-room Georgian Revival mansion where he and his descendants lived until 1975. It's the centerpiece of a beautifully preserved 412-acre estate and holds many of the family's prized possessions, including one of three surviving stovepipe hats owned by Abraham and a Lincoln Bible. When the 1,000-pipe Aeolian organ is played, the music reverberates as though from the mansion's very bones.

Rising from a 10-acre meadow, Hildene Farm is magnificent. The agriculture center is built in a traditional style—post-and-beam construction of timber felled and milled on the estate, and you can watch goat cheese being made.

The highlight, though, may be the elaborate formal gardens, where a thousand

The formal gardens and mansion at Robert Todd Lincoln's Hildene are a far cry from his father's log cabin.

peonies bloom every June. There is also a teaching greenhouse, restored 1903 Pullman car, a 600-foot floating boardwalk across the Battenkill wetlands, and more than 12 miles of walking trails. When conditions permit, you can cross-country ski and snowshoe on the property. ✉ *1005 Hildene Rd., at Rte. 7A, Manchester* ☎ *802/362–1788, 800/578–1788* 🌐 *www.hildene.org* 🎟 *$23.*

★ Southern Vermont Arts Center

ARTS CENTER | At the end of a long, winding driveway, this center has a permanent collection of more than 800 19th- and 20th-century American artworks and presents temporary exhibitions. The original building, a Georgian mansion set on 100 acres, contains 12 galleries with works by more than 600 artists, many from Vermont. The center also hosts concerts, performances, and film screenings. In summer and fall, the views from the café at lunchtime are magnificent. ✉ *930 SVAC Dr., West Rd., Manchester* ☎ *802/362–1405* 🌐 *www.svac.org* 🎟 *$10* ⏲ *Closed Mon. Nov.–May.*

Restaurants

The Crooked Ram

$ | **WINE BAR** | Originally a tiny bottle shop when it opened doors in 2017, the Crooked Ram has since transformed into a cozy beer-and-wine bar with an excellent restaurant and spacious summertime backyard serving wood-fired pizzas. It's now a destination for hyperlocal drafts, seasonal small plates, and brimming Vermont cheese boards, plus a thoughtful stock of unique ciders and natural wines to-go. **Known for:** drafts of local craft beer in stemmed beer glasses; award-winning Vermont cheeses and charcuterie; seasonal patio seating. [$] *Average main: $15* ✉ *4026 Main St., Manchester* ☎ *802/231–1315* 🌐 *thecrookedramvt.com* ⏲ *Closed Mon.-Wed.*

Mistral's at Toll Gate

$$$$ | **FRENCH** | This classic French restaurant is tucked in a grotto on the climb to Bromley Mountain. The two dining rooms are perched over the Bromley Brook, and at night a small waterfall is magically illuminated—ask for a window table. **Known for:** chateaubriand béarnaise; crispy sweetbreads Dijonnaise; wine list. *Average main: $36* ✉ *10 Toll Gate Rd., off Rte. 11/30, Manchester* ☎ *802/362–1779* 🌐 *www.mistralsattollgate.com* 🕙 *Closed Mon.-Wed. No lunch.*

★ Moonwink

$ | BURMESE | May and Wes Stannard opened this counter-service spot in 2018, spotlighting May's native Burmese cooking in Wes's childhood hometown. In one of the best stops for Burmese fare on the East Coast, you'll find vibrant noodle bowls like *Nan Gyi Thoke* (thick round rice noodles with chicken curry), fermented tea leaf salad, and "Burma Bowls" with sprouted peas and chicken curry. **Known for:** oh no kuo swel (creamy coconut broth with vegetables or chicken served over egg noodles); la phat thok (Moonwink's take on the Burmese fermented tea leaf salad); mo hinga (a special fish stew with noodles served on Friday and Saturday only). *Average main: $13* ✉ *4479 Main St., Manchester* ☎ *802/768–8671.*

★ Mystic Cafe & Wine Bar

$$ | ECLECTIC | This spacious, brand-new, Euro-chic restaurant is earning plenty of local praise for its gussied-up takes on international cuisines with a Vermont-farmhouse accent. That means plenty of kale, butternut squash, sweet potato, and cheddar in the salads, sandwiches, and tapas-style shared plates. **Known for:** paella with Israeli couscous; French toast; wine list. *Average main: $20* ✉ *4928 Main St., Manchester Center* ☎ *802/768–8086* 🌐 *www.mysticcafeandwinebar.com* 🕙 *Closed Sun. and Mon.*

The Reluctant Panther Inn & Restaurant

$$$$ | AMERICAN | The dining room at this luxurious inn is a large, modern space where rich woods and high ceilings meld into a kind of "nouveau Vermont" aesthetic. The contemporary American cuisine emphasizes farm-to-table ingredients and has earned the restaurant "Gold Barn" honors from the Vermont Fresh Network. **Known for:** wine list; chef of the year award by the Vermont Chamber of Commerce; lobster-and-Brie fondue. *Average main: $37* ✉ *39 West Rd., Manchester* ☎ *800/822–2331, 802/362–2568* 🌐 *www.reluctantpanther.com* 🕙 *Closed Sun. and Mon.*

★ The Silver Fork at the Old Library

$$$ | ECLECTIC | This intimate, elegant bistro is owned by husband-and-wife team Mark and Melody French, who spent years in Puerto Rico absorbing the flavors of the island that are reflected in the eclectic international menu. After nine years in their original space on Main Street, in 2020 the couple moved their restaurant into the newly renovated, 123-year-old Skinner Library, fashioning a bartop from the 1897 wooden shelving. **Known for:** shrimp mofongo (with mashed plantains); wine and cocktail list; special occasions. *Average main: $30* ✉ *48 West Rd., Manchester* ☎ *802/768–8444* 🌐 *www.thesilverforkvt.com* 🕙 *Closed Sun. and Mon. No lunch.*

Ye Olde Tavern

$$$ | AMERICAN | This circa-1790 Colonial inn dishes up Yankee favorites along with plenty of New England charm, made all the more intimate by the candlelight. To learn more about the colorful history of the building, simply ask the manager, who makes a regular appearance at tables. **Known for:** cheddar-and-ale onion soup; traditional pot roast; 1790 Taproom Ale (custom brew by Long Trail). *Average main: $26* ✉ *5183 Main St., Manchester* ☎ *802/362–0611* 🌐 *www.yeoldetavern.net.*

Coffee and Quick Bites

★ Willoughby's Depot Eatery

$ | BAKERY | FAMILY | Home of the World Famous Mrs. Murphy's Donuts, this beloved shop turns out fresh doughnuts daily from its small, white-clapboard storefront. Old-fashioned doughnuts come hot from the fryer in the wee hours of the morning, so arrive early for the best selection of flavors like cinnamon, maple cream, and cakey cider doughnuts loaded with warming spices. **Known for:** cinnamon raised; cider cake; sugar-dusted crullers. $ *Average main: $3 ✉ 374 Depot St., Manchester ☎ 802/362–1874 🌐 www.willoughbysdepoteatery.com.*

Hotels

Barnstead Inn

$$ | **B&B/INN** | This boutique inn has created its own little oasis, taking 1830s farmhouse lodging to the next level by pairing New England charm with luxury amenities. **Pros:** modern amenities; walking distance to the downtown area; soaking tubs and special touches in the rooms. **Cons:** no pet friendly rooms; not a class country inn in terms of decor; no children under 12 (thought some might find this a "pro"). $ *Rooms from: $299 ✉ 349 Bonnet St., Manchester 🌐 www.barnsteadinn.com 23 rooms Free Breakfast.*

Equinox

$$$ | **RESORT** | In Manchester Village, nearly all life revolves around the historic Equinox Inn, whose fame and service have carved it into the Mt. Rushmore of accommodation in Vermont. **Pros:** on-site spa, fitness center, and pool; excellent steak house on-site; newly redesigned 18 hole golf course, tennis courts, extensive network of walking trails and close proximity to several major ski mountains. **Cons:** somewhat corporate feel; lines at reception can make checking in and out take long; lots of weddings can sometimes overcrowd. $ *Rooms from: $391 ✉ 3567 Main St., Manchester ☎ 802/362–4700, 866/837–4219 🌐 www.equinoxresort.com 147 rooms No Meals.*

Inn at Manchester

$$ | **B&B/INN** | Located between the Taconic and Green Mountains just a short distance from Manchester's main strip, the Inn at Manchester has a variety of comfortable rooms, all slightly different from the next. **Pros:** free, homemade breakfast; pub on-site; pool and fireplaces. **Cons:** no-frill rooms; the decor could be consider dated and old school; 15 minutes' walk to the village center. $ *Rooms from: $200 ✉ 3967 Main St., Manchester ☎ 802/362–1793 🌐 innatmanchester.com 21 rooms Free Breakfast.*

Taconic Hotel

$$$ | **HOTEL** | Vermont's only Kimpton, which opened in 2015, attempts to walk the fine line between its corporate boutique design and a Vermont flavor—the latter of which is distilled, quite literally, in The Copper Grouse, the hotel's on-site enclave of seasonal plates and craft cocktails. **Pros:** locally handmade walking sticks from Manchester Woodcraft in rooms; no additional fee for pets; the house restaurant, the Copper Grouse, does a good turn on American bistro cuisine, cocktails included. **Cons:** not very Vermonty experience; only chain's rewards members get free high-speed Internet/Wi-Fi; tiny pool. $ *Rooms from: $339 ✉ 3835 Main St., Manchester ☎ 802/362–0147 🌐 www.taconichotel.com 87 rooms No Meals.*

Nightlife

Falcon Bar

LIVE MUSIC | This sophisticated bar has live music on weekends. In summer, don't miss the wonderful outdoor deck. In winter, the place to be is around the giant Vermont slate firepit. ✉ *Equinox Resort, 3567 Main St., Manchester ☎ 800/362–4747 🌐 www.equinoxresort.com.*

Union Underground
BARS | One of Manchester's hot spots, this part underground, part aboveground pub and restaurant offers lots of space, a sleek green-marble bar, craft beer, a pool table, and tasty classics with all the fixings. ✉ *4928 Main St., Manchester Center* ☎ *802/367–3951.*

 Shopping

ART AND ANTIQUES

Long Ago & Far Away
ANTIQUES & COLLECTIBLES | This store specializes in fine Indigenous artwork, including Inuit stone sculpture. ✉ *Green Mountain Village Shops, 4963 Main St., Manchester* ☎ *802/362–3435* 🌐 *www.longagoandfaraway.com.*

Manchester Woodcraft
CRAFTS | The millions of trees in the Green Mountains make Vermont a wood-carver's dreamscape. The saws, planes, and scrapers of the woodshop here turn out a range of handsome household goods, plus a wide selection of pieces and parts for DIY fans. ✉ *175 Depot St., Manchester Center* ☎ *802/362–5770* 🌐 *www.manchesterwoodcraft.com.*

Tilting at Windmills Gallery
ANTIQUES & COLLECTIBLES | This large gallery displays the paintings and sculptures of nationally known artists. ✉ *24 Highland Ave., Manchester Center* ☎ *802/362–3022* 🌐 *www.tilting.com.*

BOOKS

Northshire Bookstore
BOOKS | FAMILY | The heart of Manchester Center, this bookstore is adored by visitors and residents alike for its ambience, selection, and service. Up the iron staircase is a second floor dedicated to children's books, toys, and clothes. ✉ *4869 Main St., Manchester* ☎ *802/362–2200, 800/437–3700* 🌐 *www.northshire.com.*

CLOTHING

Manchester Designer Outlets
SHOPPING CENTER | This is the most upscale collection of stores in northern New England—and every store is a discount outlet. The architecture reflects the surrounding homes, so the place looks a bit like a Colonial village. The long list of famous-brand clothiers here includes Kate Spade, Yves Delorme, Michael Kors, Ann Taylor, Tumi, BCBG, Armani, Coach, Polo Ralph Lauren, Brooks Brothers, and Theory. ✉ *97 Depot St., Manchester* ☎ *802/362–3736, 800/955–7467* 🌐 *www.manchesterdesigneroutlets.com.*

Orvis Flagship Store
OTHER SPECIALTY STORE | The lodgelike Orvis store carries the company's latest clothing, fly-fishing gear, and pet supplies—there's even a trout pond. At this required shopping destination for many visitors—the Orvis name is pure Manchester—there are demonstrations of how fly rods are constructed and tested. You can attend fly-fishing school across the street. ✉ *4180 Main St., Manchester* ☎ *802/362–3750* 🌐 *www.orvis.com.*

 Activities

BIKING

Battenkill Bicycles
BIKING | This shop rents, sells, and repairs bikes and provides maps and route suggestions. ✉ *99 Bonnet St., Manchester* ☎ *802/362–2734* 🌐 *battenkillbicycles.com.*

FISHING

Trico Unlimited
FISHING | Teaching the art and science of fly-fishing, Trico Unlimited offers lessons for all different age groups and experience levels. They are an Orvis Endorsed Fly-Fishing Guide operator. ✉ *Manchester* ☎ *802/379–2005* 🌐 *www.tricounlimited.com.*

HIKING

There are bountiful hiking trails in the Green Mountain National Forest. Shorter hikes begin at the Equinox Resort, which owns about 1,000 acres of forest and has a great trail system open to the public.

Equinox Preserve

HIKING & WALKING | A multitude of well-groomed walking trails for all abilities thread the 914 acres on the slopes of Mt. Equinox, including a trail to the summit. ✉ *Multiple trailheads, End of West Union St., Manchester* ☎ *802/366–1400 Equinox Preservation Trust* 🌐 *www.equinoxpreservationtrust.org.*

Long Trail

HIKING & WALKING | One of the most popular segments of Vermont's Long Trail leads to the top of Bromley Mountain. The strenuous 5.4-mile round-trip takes about four hours. ✉ *Rte. 11/30, Manchester* 🌐 *www.greenmountainclub.org.*

Lye Brook Falls

HIKING & WALKING | This 4.6-mile hike starts off Glen Road and ends at Vermont's most impressive cataract, Lye Brook Falls. The moderately strenuous journey takes four hours. ✉ *Off Glen Rd., south from E. Manchester Rd. just east of U.S. 7, Manchester* 🌐 *www.greenmountainclub.org.*

Mountain Goat

HIKING & WALKING | Stop here for hiking, cross-country-skiing, and snowshoeing equipment (some of which is available to rent), as well as a good selection of warm clothing. ✉ *4886 Main St., Manchester* ☎ *802/362–5159* 🌐 *www.mountaingoat.com.*

SPAS

Spa at Equinox

SPAS | Some of Vermont's best spa treatments are found behind the mahogany doors and beadboard wainscoting of the Equinox Spa and are well worth the splurge. At one end are an indoor pool and outdoor hot tub; at the other end are the treatment rooms. The signature 100-minute Spirit of Vermont combines Reiki, reflexology, and massage, and will leave you feeling like a whole, complete person. The locker rooms feature steam rooms and saunas. Day passes are available for all ages. ✉ *Equinox Resort, 3567 Rte. 7A, Manchester* ☎ *802/362–4700, 800/362–4747* 🌐 *www.equinoxresort.com.*

Dorset

7 miles north of Manchester.

Lying at the foot of many mountains and with a village green surrounded by white clapboard homes and inns, Dorset has a solid claim to the title of Vermont's most picture-perfect town. Dorset has just 2,000 residents, but two of the state's best and oldest general stores.

The country's first commercial marble quarry opened here in 1785. Dozens more opened, providing the marble for the main research branch of the New York Public Library and many 5th Avenue mansions, among other notable landmarks, as well as the sidewalks here and in Manchester. A remarkable private home made entirely of marble can be seen on Dorset West Road, a beautiful residential road west of the town green. The marble Dorset Church on the green has two Tiffany stained-glass windows.

★ Dorset Quarry

BODY OF WATER | FAMILY | On hot summer days the sight of dozens of families jumping, swimming, and basking in the sun around this massive 60-foot-deep swimming hole makes it one of the most wholesome and picturesque recreational spots in the region. First mined in 1785, the stone from the country's oldest commercial marble quarry was used to build the main branch of the New York Public Library and the Montreal Museum of Fine Arts. ✉ *Rte. 30, Dorset* ☎ 🎫 *Free.*

Emerald Lake State Park

STATE/PROVINCIAL PARK | This park has a well-marked nature trail, a small beach, boat rentals, and a snack bar.

✉ 65 Emerald Lake La., East Dorset ☎ 802/362–1655 🌐 www.vtstateparks.com/emerald.html 🎟 $5 ⏲ Facilities closed mid-Oct.–mid-May.

Merck Forest & Farmland Center

FARM/RANCH | FAMILY | This 3,162-acre educational center has 30 miles of nature trails for hiking, cross-country skiing, snowshoeing, horseback riding, and rustic camping. You can visit the 62-acre farm, which grows organic fruit and vegetables (sold at the visitor center), and check out the horses, sheep, pigs, and chickens while you're there—you're even welcome to help out with the chores. *✉ 3270 Rte. 315, Rupert ☎ 802/394–7836 🌐 www.merckforest.org 🎟 Free.*

Restaurants

The Dorset Inn

$$$ | AMERICAN | Built in 1796, this inn has been continuously operating ever since, and the comfortable tavern and formal dining room serve a Colonial-influenced bistro menu. A member of the Vermont Fresh Network, the restaurant benefits greatly from its strong connections with local farmers. **Known for:** wine list; Vermont's oldest continually operating inn; whiskey and bourbon menu. *$ Average main: $27 ✉ Dorset Green, 8 Church St., Dorset ☎ 802/867–5500 🌐 www.dorsetinn.com ⏲ No lunch.*

Hotels

Barrows House

$$ | HOTEL | This renovated 19th-century manse, once the residence of the town's pastor, incorporates a modern boutique aesthetic into the traditional-style inn, especially in the attached gastropub, which features a long, polished metal bar and backlighted marble. **Pros:** good bar and restaurant; chintz-free decor; large gardens. **Cons:** rooms can become drafty in cold weather; robes only in luxury suites; no coffee or tea in rooms. *$ Rooms from: $275 ✉ 3156 Rte. 30, Dorset ☎ 802/867–4455 🌐 www.barrowshouse.com 🛏 27 rooms 🍽 Free Breakfast.*

Squire House Bed & Breakfast

$$ | B&B/INN | On a wonderfully quiet road, this inn, built in 1918, has guest rooms that combine modern comforts and antique fixtures. **Pros:** big estate feels like your own; wood-burning fireplace in two rooms; crème brûlée French toast at breakfast. **Cons:** basic bathrooms; two-night minimum required for peak periods; one-night reservation costs additional $60 fee in some periods. *$ Rooms from: $210 ✉ 3395 Dorset West Rd., Dorset ☎ 802/867–0281 🌐 www.squirehouse.com 🛏 4 rooms 🍽 Free Breakfast.*

Performing Arts

Dorset Players

THEATER | The prestigious summer theater troupe presents the annual Dorset Theater Festival. Plays are staged in a wonderful converted pre-Revolutionary War barn. *✉ Dorset Playhouse, 104 Cheney Rd., Dorset ☎ 802/867–5570 🌐 www.dorsetplayers.org.*

Shopping

Dorset Union Store

GENERAL STORE | Dating to 1816, this 200-year-old general store is the oldest continuously operating country store in Vermont. Under the reins of co-owners Cindy Laudenslager and Gretchen Schmidt, it has great prepared dinners, a full deli, delicious homemade baked goods, and a big wine selection. It also sells interesting gifts, and houses its own soft-serve ice-cream machine. *✉ Dorset Green, 31 Church St., Dorset ☎ 802/867–4400 🌐 www.dorsetunionstore.com.*

Stratton

26 miles southeast of Dorset.

Stratton is really Stratton Mountain Resort, a mountaintop ski resort with a self-contained "town center" of shops, restaurants, and lodgings clustered at the base of the slopes. When the snow melts, golf, tennis, and a host of other summer activities are big attractions, but the ski village remains quiet.

GETTING HERE AND AROUND

From Manchester or U.S. 7, follow Route 11/30 east until they split. Route 11 continues past Bromley ski mountain, and Route 30 turns south 10 minutes toward Bondville, the town at the base of the mountain. At the junction of Routes 30 and 100 is the village of Jamaica, with its own cluster of inns and restaurants on the eastern side of the mountain.

Restaurants

J.J. Hapgood General Store and Eatery

$ | **AMERICAN** | **FAMILY** | You won't find a better meal at any other general store in the state. This is really more of a classic American restaurant, serving farm-to-table breakfast, lunch, and dinner, than a place to pick up the essentials, but like any good general store, it's a friendly and relaxed gathering spot for locals. **Known for:** buttermilk biscuits; outdoor patio; wood-fired pizzas. *Average main: $12* ✉ *305 Main St., Peru* ☎ *802/824–4800* 🌐 *www.jjhapgood.com* 🕓 *No dinner Mon. and Tues.*

Hotels

Long Trail House

$$ | **APARTMENT** | Directly across the street from the ski village, this condo complex is one of the closest to the slopes. **Pros:** across the street from ski lift; views of the mountain; outdoor heated pool and hot tub. **Cons:** 4:30 check-in later than most in Vermont; two-night stay required on weekends; busy tourist center in season. *Rooms from: $230* ✉ *759–787 Stratton Mountain Access Rd., Stratton* ☎ *802/297–4000, 800/787–2886* 🌐 *www.stratton.com* *145 rooms* *No Meals.*

★ **Three Mountain Inn**

$$ | **B&B/INN** | A 1780s tavern, this romantic inn in downtown Jamaica feels authentically Colonial, from the wide-plank paneling to the low ceilings. **Pros:** romantic setting; well-kept rooms; enchanting dinners alongside wood-burning fireplaces. **Cons:** 15-minute drive to skiing; two-night reservations requested for weekends and peak foliage; deposit equal to 50% of the reserved stay required. *Rooms from: $234* ✉ *30 Depot St., Jamaica* *10 miles northeast of Stratton* ☎ *802/874–4140* 🌐 *www.threemountaininn.com* *10 rooms* *Free Breakfast.*

Nightlife

Mulligans

PUBS | Popular Mulligans hosts bands and DJs in the downstairs Green Door Pub on weekends. Upstairs, cozy up beside the fireplace with ribs, steak, and traditional fish-and-chips, or opt for tempura plates and sushi bowls from Mulligans' newest in-house offshoot, Snowfish Sushi. ✉ *Village Sq., Stratton Mountain, Stratton* ☎ *802/297–9293* 🌐 *www.mulligansstratton.com.*

Activities

SKIING

Bromley Mountain Resort

SKIING & SNOWBOARDING | **FAMILY** | About 20 minutes from Stratton, Bromley is a favorite with families thanks to a child-care center for kids ages six weeks–six years and programs for ages 2½ to 17. The trails are evenly split among beginner, intermediate, and advanced, with nothing too challenging. Beginning skiers and snowboarders have expanded access to terrain-based training in the dedicated Learning Zone, and everyone can unwind in the base lodge and "village." An added bonus: trails face south, making for glorious spring skiing and warm winter days. **Facilities:** 47 trails; 300 acres; 1,334-foot vertical drop; 9 lifts. ✉ *3984 Rte. 11, Peru* ☎ *802/824–5522, 866/856–2201 for snow conditions* 🌐 *www.bromley.com* 🎟 *Lift ticket: $96.*

Stratton Mountain

SKIING & SNOWBOARDING | About 25 minutes from Manchester, and featuring an entire faux Swiss village at its base, Stratton Mountain draws families and young professionals. Beginners will find more than 40% of the mountain accessible to them, but that doesn't mean there aren't some great steeps for the experts. The resort prides itself on its immaculate grooming and excellent cruising on all trails. An on-site day-care center takes children ages six weeks–five years for indoor activities and outdoor excursions. Children also love careening down one of four groomed lift-serviced lanes at the resort's Coca Cola Tube Park. Stratton has 11 miles of cross-country skiing, and in summer there are 15 outdoor clay tennis courts, 27 holes of golf, and hiking trails accessed by a gondola. The sports complex (open year-round) has a 75-foot indoor saltwater pool, sauna, indoor tennis courts, and a fitness center. **Facilities:** 97 trails; 670 acres; 2,003-foot vertical drop; 11 lifts. ✉ *5 Village Lodge Rd., Bondville* ☎ *802/297–4211 for snow conditions, 800/787–2886* 🌐 *www.stratton.com* 🎟 *Lift ticket: $180.*

Weston

17 miles north of Stratton.

Best known as the home of the Vermont Country Store, Weston was one of the first Vermont towns to discover its own intrinsic loveliness—and marketability. With its summer theater, classic town green with Victorian bandstand, and an assortment of shops, the little village really lives up to its vaunted image.

 Performing Arts

Weston Playhouse

THEATER | The oldest professional theater in Vermont produces plays, musicals, and other works. The season runs mid-June–late October. ✉ *703 Main St., off Rte. 100, Weston* ☎ *802/824–5288* 🌐 *www.westonplayhouse.org.*

 Shopping

The Vermont Country Store

GENERAL STORE | This store opened in 1946 and is still run by the Orton family, though it has become something of an empire, with a large catalog and online business. One room is set aside for Vermont Common Crackers and bins of fudge and copious candy. In others you'll find nearly forgotten items such as Lilac Vegetol aftershave, as well as practical items like sturdy outdoor clothing. Nostalgia-evoking implements dangle from the rafters. The associated Mildred's Grill restaurant next door serves casual meals and, if you can't get enough, there's a second store on Route 103 in Rockingham. ✉ *657 Main St., Weston* ☎ *802/824–3184* 🌐 *www.vermontcountrystore.com.*

Ludlow

9 miles northeast of Weston.

Ludlow, once a largely nondescript industrial town, is a budding hub of inns, restaurants, and cafés beside Okemo, one of Vermont's largest and most popular ski resorts.

GETTING HERE AND AROUND

Routes 100 and 103 join in northern Ludlow, separating about 2 miles south in the small downtown, where Route 103 becomes Main Street.

Restaurants

★ The Downtown Grocery

$$$ | **BISTRO** | There's a cozy romance to this oasis of seasonal and local cooking, with its corner seats, tea lights, intimate bar, and chalkboard menu. It was the area's first farm-to-table restaurant when co-owners Abby and Rogan Lechthaler opened doors in 2010, and it has continued to be a mainstay thanks to excellent hospitality, warm-spirited creativity, and nightly-changing specials. **Known for:** seasonal cocktails; small-producer-focused wine list; schedule changes month-to-month with limited seating. *Average main: $30 ✉ 41 Depot St., Ludlow ☎ 802/228–7566 🌐 thedowntowngrocery.com ⏲ Closed Tues.-Thurs. and Sunday.*

Goodman's American Pie

$ | **PIZZA** | **FAMILY** | This place has the best wood-fired pizza in town. It also has character to spare: sit in chairs from old ski lifts and step up to the counter fashioned from a vintage VW bus to design your pie from 29 ingredients. **Known for:** arcade games and pool table in the back; pizza by the slice; outdoor deck. *Average main: $17 ✉ 5 Lamere Sq., Ludlow ☎ 802/228–4271 🌐 www.goodmansamericanpie.com.*

★ The Hidden Kitchen at The Inn at Weathersfield

$$$ | **FRENCH FUSION** | So many Vermont restaurants claim the farm-to-table, local-sourcing, organic approach to cooking, but the chef at the Inn at Weathersfield is more passionate and rigorous than most, with more than 75% of ingredients coming from within a 25-mile radius in season. Enjoy the exquisite French-influenced regional dishes inside the inn itself, on its back patio, or in the separate "Hidden Kitchen" at the back of the property, where monthly cooking workshops and tastings take place. **Known for:** wine list; charcuterie and cheese boards; atmospheric inside and out. *Average main: $28 ✉ 1342 Rte. 106, Perkinsville ✣ 15 miles east of Ludlow ☎ 802/263–9217 🌐 www.weathersfieldinn.com.*

Mojo Cafe

$ | **FUSION** | In 2014, Jodi and John Seward opened this funky, casual watering hole fusing Mexican and Cajun cooking. Tacos, burritos, bowls, and po' boys frequently feature Vermont meats and produce, while craft beers and specialty cocktails continue to highlight the state's bounty in local beer and spirits. **Known for:** limited seating and no reservations; alligator and andouille gumbo; funky burritos like the "Betty," with tequila-citrus tofu and avocado sauce. *Average main: $10 ✉ 106 Main St., Ludlow ☎ 802/228–6656.*

Coffee and Quick Bites

★ Green Mountain Sugar House

$ | **ICE CREAM** | **FAMILY** | This red-roofed sugarhouse on the edge of Lake Rescue has one of the best maple creemees in the state of Vermont. Locals Ann and Doug Rose have owned the sugaring house since 1985, and almost four decades later continue to uphold their destination-worthy reputation for award-winning maple syrup. **Known for:** Vermont maple creemees; award-winning maple syrup; maple brittle and fudge. *Average main: $5 ✉ 820 Rte. 100 N, Ludlow ☎ 800/643–9338 🌐 www.gmsh.com.*

Hotels

Inn at Water's Edge

$ | **B&B/INN** | Former Long Islanders Bruce and Tina Verdrager converted their old ski house and barns into this comfortably refined haven, perfect for those who want to ski but not stay in town. **Pros:** bucolic setting on a lakefront, with swimming access; two canoes for guest use; golf and spa packages are available. **Cons:** ordinary rooms; lots of flowered

Vermont Artisanal Cheese

Vermont is the artisanal cheese capital of the country, with several dozen creameries open to the public churning out hundreds of different cheeses. Many creameries are "farmstead" operations, meaning that the animals whose milk is made into cheese are kept on-site. If you eat enough cheese during your time in the state, you may be able to differentiate between the many types of milk (cow, goat, sheep, or even water buffalo) and make associations between the geography and climate of where you are and the taste of the local cheeses.

This is one of the reasons that taking a walk around a dairy is a great idea: you can see the process in action, from grazing to aging to eating. The **Vermont Cheese Trail map**, which you can view or download on the website of the Vermont Cheese Council (☎ 866/261–8595; 🌐 www.vtcheese.com), has a comprehensive list of dairies, many of which you can visit. Though hours are given for some, it's generally recommended that you still call ahead.

At the **Vermont Cheesemakers Festival** (☎ 802/261–8595; 🌐 www.vtcheesefest.com), which takes place in July or August in Shelburne, cheesemakers gather to sell their various cheeses. Beer and wine are served to wash it all down.

wallpaper and upholstery; no sights within walking distance. *Rooms from: $175 ✉ 45 Kingdom Rd., Ludlow ✣ 5 miles north of Ludlow ☎ 802/228–8143, 888/706–9736 🌐 www.innatwatersedge.com 11 rooms Free Breakfast.*

★ Inn at Weathersfield

$$ | **B&B/INN** | Set far back from the road, this 1792 home built by a Revolutionary War veteran is a world unto itself, and an Eden-esque one at that, with flowering gardens, croaking frog pond, and extensive forest on its 21 acres. **Pros:** dynamite restaurant and tavern; ideal for weddings; monthly cooking classes. **Cons:** 15-mile drive from the Okemo slopes; no sights within walking distance; no coffee or tea in rooms. *Rooms from: $219 ✉ 1342 Rte. 106, Perkinsville ☎ 802/263–9217 🌐 www.weathersfieldinn.com ⏲ Closed 1st 2 wks in Nov. 12 rooms Free Breakfast.*

Activities

SKIING

Okemo Mountain Resort

SKIING & SNOWBOARDING | **FAMILY** | Family fun is the focus of southern Vermont's highest vertical ski resort, which has dozens of beginner trails, some wide intermediate runs, terrain parks throughout, a tubing facility, a nursery, an ice rink, indoor basketball and tennis courts, and a children's pool with slides. There's even a Kids' Night Out child-care program on Saturday evening during the regular season, so parents can have date nights. The Okemo Valley Nordic Center has miles of cross-country and snowshoeing trails. Summer diversions include golfing, mountain biking, and activities and rides in the Adventure Zone. The newer Jackson Gore base features the latest (and fanciest) venues the resort has to offer. **Facilities:** 121 trails; 667 acres; 2,200-foot vertical drop; 20 lifts. *✉ 77 Okemo Ridge Rd., Ludlow ☎ 802/228–1600 resort services, 802/228–5222 for snow* *conditions, 800/786–5366 🌐 www.okemo.com 🎫 Lift ticket: $155.*

Grafton

20 miles south of Ludlow.

Out-of-the-way Grafton is as much a historical museum as a town. During its heyday, citizens grazed 10,000 sheep and spun their wool into sturdy yarn for locally woven fabric. As the wool market declined, so did Grafton. In 1963 the Windham Foundation—Vermont's second-largest private foundation—commenced the town's rehabilitation. The Old Tavern (now called the Grafton Inn) was preserved, along with many other commercial and residential structures.

GETTING HERE AND AROUND

Routes 11, 35, and 103 intersect in Grafton.

Historical Society Museum

HISTORY MUSEUM | This endearingly cluttered museum documents the town's history with photographs, soapstone displays, quilts, musical instruments, furniture, tools, and other artifacts. *✉ 147 Main St., Grafton ☎ 802/843–2584 🌐 www.graftonhistoricalsociety.com 🎫 $5 🕒 Closed Tues. and Wed. Memorial Day–Columbus Day, and Tues., Wed., and weekends Columbus Day–Memorial Day.*

Phelps Barn Pub at The Grafton Village Inn

$$ | **BURGER** | This wood-clad restaurant with a second-floor loft, hanging tea lights, and Vermont-inspired pub fare was originally a carriage house for the guests' horses at The Grafton Village Inn. Today, it's a beautiful and rustic spot for eating local, from crispy skinned local duck breast to seasonal vegetable risotto to a Vermont beef burger capped with Grafton cheddar cheese. **Known for:** rustic interiors with a sense of history; the Phelps burger with local beef and Grafton cheddar; local ingredients as a member of the Vermont Fresh Network. *💲 Average main: $24 ✉ 92 Main St., Grafton ☎ 802/843–2248 🌐 www.graftoninnvermont.com 🕒 Closed Sun. and Mon.*

MKT: Grafton

$ | **CAFÉ** | **FAMILY** | When the 19th-century Grafton Village Store shuttered 174 years after opening, locals June Lupiani and Alexandra Hartman decided to revive the abandoned building and give it new life. Their modern, newly renovated general store opened doors in 2015, and quickly became a meeting spot for locals and travelers seeking groceries, deli sandwiches, prepared foods, and homemade pastries. **Known for:** scratch-made pastries; local groceries; deli sandwiches and salads. *💲 Average main: $10 ✉ 162 Main St., Grafton ☎ 802/843–2255.*

The Grafton Inn

$ | **B&B/INN** | This 1801 classic encourages you to linger on its wraparound porches, in its authentically Colonial common rooms, or with a book by the fire in its old-fashioned library, but those who want to get outside can access the nearby Grafton Ponds Outdoor Center and its 2,000 acres of trails, forests, and fields. **Pros:** handsome historic building; seasonal swim pond; game room with pool table and Ping-Pong; two dining options—the Old Tavern and Phelps Barn Pub—serve American fare. **Cons:** lots of flowered upholstery and wallpaper; resort fee; no tea or coffee in rooms. *💲 Rooms from: $189 ✉ 92 Main St., Grafton ☎ 802/234–8718, 800/843–1801 🌐 www.graftoninnvermont.com 🛏 45 rooms 🍽 Free Breakfast.*

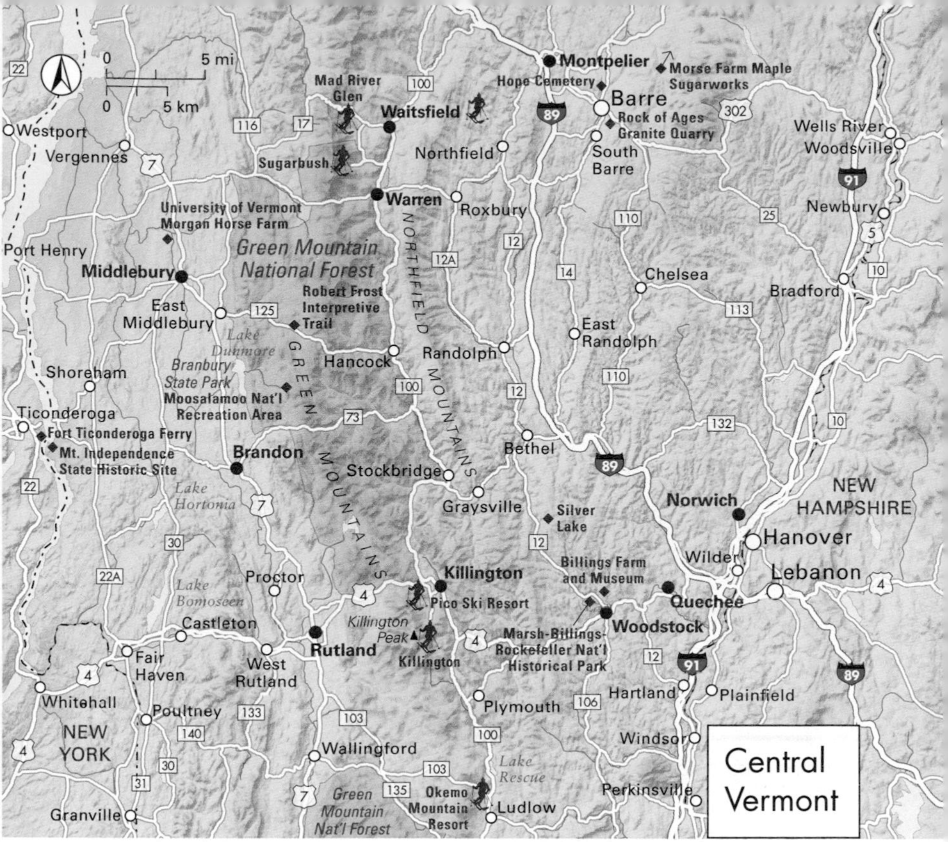

Norwich

6 miles north of White River Junction.

On the bank of the Connecticut River, Norwich is graced with beautifully maintained 18th- and 19th-century homes set about a handsome green. Norwich is the Vermont sister town to sophisticated Hanover, New Hampshire (home of Dartmouth College), across the river.

GETTING HERE AND AROUND

Most attractions are off Interstate 91; the town sits a mile to the west.

Sights

★ Montshire Museum of Science

SCIENCE MUSEUM | FAMILY | Numerous hands-on exhibits at this 100-acre science museum explore nature and technology. Kids can make giant bubbles, watch marine life swim in aquariums, construct working hot air balloons, and explore a maze of outdoor trails by the river. Adults will happily join the fun. An ideal destination for a rainy day, this is one of the finest museums in New England. ✉ *1 Montshire Rd., Norwich* ☎ *802/649–2200* 🌐 *www.montshire.org* 🎫 *$18.*

Coffee and Quick Bites

King Arthur Flour Baker's Store

$ | BAKERY | The café at King Arthur Flour is a fine spot for both the pit-stop sandwich and the leisurely pastry and latte. The adjacent shop and market area is a must-see for those who love bread; the shelves are stocked with all the ingredients and tools in the company's Baker's Catalogue, including flours, mixes, and local jams, and syrups. **Known for:** croissants, cookies, and brownies; freshly baked loaves of bread; goods to-go, such as local butter, housemade granola, and cheesy crackers. *$ Average main: $12 ✉ 105 U.S. 5 S, Norwich ☎ 802/649–3361 🌐 www.kingarthurflour.com.*

Activities

Lake Morey Ice Skating Trail

ICE SKATING | For the most fun you can have on skates, head to America's longest ice-skating trail. From January to March, the frozen lake is groomed for ice-skating, providing a magical 4½-mile route amid forested hillsides. Bring your own skates or rent them at the Lake Morey Resort, which maintains the trail. *✉ 1 Clubhouse Rd., Fairlee ☎ 800/423–1211 🌐 www.lakemoreyresort.com.*

Quechee

11 miles southwest of Norwich, 6 miles west of White River Junction.

A historic mill town, Quechee sits just upriver from its namesake gorge, an impressive 165-foot-deep canyon cut by the Ottauquechee River. Most people view the gorge from U.S. 4. To escape the crowds, hike along the gorge or scramble down one of several trails to the river.

Sights

★ Simon Pearce

FACTORY | FAMILY | A restored woolen mill by a waterfall holds Quechee's main attraction: this marvelous glass-blowing factory, store, and restaurant. Water power still drives the factory's furnace. Take a free self-guided tour of the downstairs factory floor, and see the amazing glassblowers at work. The store sells beautifully crafted contemporary glass and ceramic tableware. An excellent, sophisticated restaurant with outstanding views of the falls uses Simon Pearce glassware and is justifiably popular. *✉ The Mill, 1760 Quechee Main St., Quechee ☎ 802/295–2711 🌐 www.simonpearce.com.*

Vermont Institute of Natural Science Nature Center

COLLEGE | FAMILY | Next to Quechee Gorge, this science center has 17 raptor exhibits, including bald eagles, peregrine falcons, and owls. All caged birds were found injured and are unable to survive in the wild. In summer, experience "Raptors Up Close," a 30-minute live bird program that happens three times a day. *✉ 149 Natures Way, Quechee ☎ 802/359–5000 🌐 www.vinsweb.org 🎫 $18.*

Restaurants

★ The Mill at Simon Pearce

$$$ | AMERICAN | Sparkling glassware from the studio downstairs, exposed brick, flickering candles, and large windows overlooking the falls of the roaring Ottauquechee River create an ideal setting for contemporary American cuisine—the food alone is worth the pilgrimage. The wine cellar holds several hundred labels. **Known for:** romantic atmosphere; Simon Pearce glassware and pottery; complimentary house-made potato chips. *$ Average main: $28 ✉ 1760 Main St., Quechee ☎ 802/295–1470 🌐 www.simonpearce.com.*

Hotels

Quechee Inn at Marshland Farm

$$ | B&B/INN | Each room in this handsomely restored 1793 country home has Queen Anne–style furnishings and period antiques. **Pros:** home of Colonel Joseph Marsh, Vermont's first lieutenant governor; spacious grounds; fresh baked cookies every afternoon. **Cons:** some bathrooms are dated; fills up with weddings; lots of flowered upholstery and wallpaper. *$ Rooms from: $287 ✉ 1119 Main St., Quechee ☎ 802/295–3133, 800/235–3133 🌐 www.quecheeinn.com 🛏 25 rooms 🍴 Free Breakfast.*

Simon Pearce is a glassblowing factory, store, and restaurant; the factory's furnace is still powered by hydroelectricity from Quechee Falls.

Woodstock

4 miles west of Quechee.

Woodstock is a Currier & Ives print come to life. Well-maintained Federal-style houses surround the tree-lined village green, across the street from a covered bridge. The town owes much of its pristine appearance to the Rockefeller family's interest in historic preservation and land conservation and to native George Perkins Marsh, a congressman, diplomat, and conservationist who wrote the pioneering book *Man and Nature* (1864) about humanity's use and abuse of the land. Only busy U.S. 4 mars the tableau.

ESSENTIALS

VISITOR INFORMATION Woodstock Vermont Area Chamber of Commerce. ✉ *Woodstock* ☎ *802/457–3555, 888/496–6378* 🌐 *www.woodstockvt.com.*

Sights

Billings Farm and Museum

FARM/RANCH | FAMILY | Founded by Frederick H. Billings in 1871, this is one of the oldest operating dairy farms in the country. In addition to watching the herds of Jersey cows, horses, and other farm animals at work and play, you can tour the restored 1890 farmhouse, and in the adjacent barns learn about 19th-century farming and domestic life. The biggest takeaway, however, is a renewed belief in sustainable agriculture and stewardship of the land. Pick up some raw-milk cheddar while you're here. ✉ *69 Old River Rd., Woodstock* ✣ *½ mile north of Woodstock* ☎ *802/457–2355* 🌐 *www.billingsfarm.org* 🎟 *$17.*

Marsh-Billings-Rockefeller National Historical Park

HISTORIC HOME | Vermont's only national park is the nation's first to focus on conserving natural resources. The pristine 555-acre spread includes the mansion, gardens, and carriage roads of Frederick H. Billings (1823–90), a financier and the president of the Northern Pacific Railway. The entire property was the gift of Laurance S. Rockefeller (1910–2004), who lived here with his wife, Mary (Billings's granddaughter). You can learn more at the visitor center, tour the residential complex with a guide every hour on the hour, and explore the 20 miles of trails and old carriage roads that climb Mt. Tom. ✉ *54 Elm St., Woodstock* ☎ *802/457–3368* 🌐 *www.nps.gov/mabi* 🎫 *Tour $9.*

Silver Lake

BODY OF WATER | Vermont lakes don't get more picturesque than this gem across the street from the Barnard General Store. Plus, it's open for swimming, boating, fishing, and camping. ✉ *20 State Park Beach Rd., Barnard* ☎ *802/234–9451* 🌐 *www.vtstateparks.com/silver.html.*

Restaurants

Angkor Wat Restaurant

$$ | **CAMBODIAN** | Chef Chy Tuckerman was raised in Cambodia, Thailand, Oregon, and New Hampshire until moving to Woodstock in 1997 to continue learning the art of baking at local Mountain Creamery. A decade later, he opened his sunny, BYOB restaurant just off Route 4, where he fuses the Cambodian and Thai cooking of his heritage into mouthwatering dishes like ginger chicken stir fry, Khmer curry soup, and traditional luk lok made with beef from nearby Cloudland Farm. **Known for:** cozy atmosphere and BYOB dining; house-made desserts; dishes fusing traditional Khmer and Thai cooking. $ *Average main: $18* ✉ *61 Pleasant St., Woodstock* ☎ *802/457–9029* 🌐 *www.angkorwatvt.com* ⏲ *Closed Mon.*

Barnard Inn Restaurant and Max's Tavern

$$$$ | **AMERICAN** | The dining room in this 1796 brick farmhouse exudes 18th-century charm, but the food is decidedly 21st century. Former San Francisco restaurant chef-owner Will Dodson creates inventive three- and four-course prix-fixe menus with international flavors, or more casual versions at Max's Tavern, also on-site. **Known for:** device-free restaurant; popular for weddings; pond and perennial gardens. $ *Average main: $60* ✉ *5518 Rte. 12, 8 miles north of Woodstock, Barnard* ☎ *802/234–9961* 🌐 *www.barnardinn.com* ⏲ *Closed Sun. and Mon. No lunch.*

Cloudland Farm

$$$$ | **AMERICAN** | With the table literally on the farm, this restaurant delivers a unique farm-to-table experience that makes it worth the short drive from Woodstock. All ingredients for the seasonal prix-fixe menus come fresh from the farm or local growers, especially Cloudland's own pork, beef, chicken, and turkey. **Known for:** large fireplace in dining room; homemade carrot cake with red wine caramel and carrot jam; bring your own wine or beer. $ *Average main: $45* ✉ *1101 Cloudland Rd., North Pomfret* ☎ *802/457–2599* 🌐 *www.cloudlandfarm.com* ⏲ *No lunch Fri. and Sat.*

★ **Mountain Creamery**

$ | **AMERICAN** | **FAMILY** | This locally beloved diner in the town center sources most of its ingredients from their own farm in Killington. "Mile High Apple Pie," ice cream made with local dairy, and daily blue plate specials are only a handful of reasons Mountain Creamery is a Woodstock mainstay. **Known for:** homemade ice cream made with local dairy; farm-sourced diner fare; blue plate specials. $ *Average main: $12* ✉ *33 Central St., Woodstock* ☎ *802/457–1715* 🌐 *www.mountaincreameryvt.com.*

The Prince and the Pauper

$$ | **FRENCH** | Modern French and American fare with a Vermont accent is the focus of this candlelit Colonial restaurant off the town green. Three-course prix-fixe meals cost $53, but a less expensive bistro menu is available in the lounge. **Known for:** artwork for sale; complimentary cinema tickets; wine list. $ *Average main: $24* ✉ *24 Elm St., Woodstock* ☎ *802/457–1818* 🌐 *www.princeandpauper.com* ⏲ *Closed Sun. and Mon.*

Ransom Tavern

$$$ | **ITALIAN** | Arrive early for a seat at the wraparound bar and a perfectly made negroni. The wood-fired, Neapolitan-style pizzas are excellent, as is the inventive cocktail list and the plentiful supply of local beers on draft. **Known for:** wood-fired pizza; craft cocktail and local drafts; farm-fresh ingredients. *Average main: $30 ✉ Kedron Valley Inn, 4778 South Rd., South Woodstock ☎ 802/457–1473 🌐 www.kedronvalleyinn.com ⏲ Closed Mon. and Tues.*

★ **Worthy Kitchen**

$ | **AMERICAN** | **FAMILY** | One of Woodstock's liveliest and most popular places to eat, this upscale pub and bistro remains buzzing through most evenings. The chalkboard on the wall lists the hearty menu of American comfort classics given farm-to-table twists, and the craft beer selection is excellent. **Known for:** beer list; social hot spot; burgers with Wagyu beef patties. *Average main: $14 ✉ 442 Woodstock Rd., Woodstock ☎ 802/457–7281 🌐 www.worthyvermont.com ⏲ No lunch weekdays.*

Coffee and Quick Bites

Mont Vert Cafe

$ | **CAFÉ** | This charming two-story café in the center of Woodstock sources most of its ingredients in state. It's the perfect stop for a Vermont maple latte with local dairy, produce-laden salads, and wraps or egg sandwiches worthy of a long line. **Known for:** espresso drinks; breakfast sandwiches; seasonal specials. *Average main: $12 ✉ 28 Central St., Woodstock ☎ 802/457–7143 🌐 www.monvertcafe.com ⏲ Closed Thurs.*

Village Butcher

This emporium of Vermont edibles has great sandwiches, cheeses, local beers, and delicious baked goods—perfect for a picnic or for lunch on the go. **Known for:** great sandwiches; on-site butcher; daily sides and salads. *Average main: $ ✉ 18 Elm St., Woodstock ☎ 802/457–2756 🌐 www.villagebutchervt.com ⏲ Closed Sun.–Mon. No dinner.*

Hotels

★ **The Fan House Bed and Breakfast**

$$ | **B&B/INN** | This charming inn dating to 1840 is as authentic as it gets in Vermont. **Pros:** 300-plus-thread-count linens and down comforters; walking distance to Silver Lake and general store; library nook. **Cons:** no major sights in walking distance; on busy main road; set back and difficult to see from road. *Rooms from: $200 ✉ 6297 Rte. 12 N, Woodstock ☎ 802/234–6704 🌐 www.thefanhouse.com ▭ No credit cards ⏲ Closed Apr. 3 rooms Free Breakfast.*

506 On the River

$ | **HOTEL** | **FAMILY** | Behind a somewhat bland prefab exterior lies an eclectic boutique experience, thanks in large part to the virtual curiosity cabinet of exotic (or faux exotic) knickknacks stuffed throughout the premises, brought by the Africa-based owners. **Pros:** impressive cocktail menu in bar; patio dining with view of river; lots of activities and space for families. **Cons:** 5 miles west of Woodstock; child-friendly means lots of children; a bit buggy. *Rooms from: $199 ✉ 1653 W. Woodstock Rd., Burlington ☎ 802/457–5000 🌐 www.ontheriverwoodstock.com 45 rooms Free Breakfast.*

Kedron Valley Inn

$ | **B&B/INN** | You're likely to fall in love at first sight with the main 1828 three-story brick building here, the centerpiece of this 15-acre retreat, but wait until you see the spring-fed pond, which has a white sand beach with toys for kids. **Pros:** on-site restaurant with a great wine list; historic facade with modern interiors and amenities; next door to South Woodstock Country Store. **Cons:** 5 miles south of Woodstock; limited cell service; no sights within walking distance. *Rooms from:*

The upscale Woodstock area is known as Vermont's horse country.

$199 ✉ 4778 South Rd., South Woodstock ☎ 802/457–1473, 800/836–1193 🌐 www.kedronvalleyinn.com ⏲ Closed Apr. 🛏 16 rooms 🍴 Free Breakfast.

The Shire Riverview Motel

$ | HOTEL | Many rooms in this immaculate motel have decks, and most have fabulous views of Ottauquechee River, which runs right along the building. **Pros:** within walking distance of Woodstock's green and shops; sweeping river views; discounted access to Woodstock Recreation Center pool and fitness center. **Cons:** basic rooms; unexciting exterior; not all rooms have river views. *$ Rooms from: $198 ✉ 46 Pleasant St., Woodstock ☎ 802/457–2211 🌐 shirewoodstock.com 🛏 42 rooms 🍴 No Meals.*

★ Twin Farms

$$$$ | RESORT | Let's just get it out there: Twin Farms is the best lodging in Vermont, and the most expensive, but it's worth it. **Pros:** luxury fit for A-list Hollywood stars, including Oprah Winfrey and Tom Cruise; Japanese furo in woods; on-site spa. **Cons:** steep prices; no children allowed; minimum stays during peak periods and many weekends. *$ Rooms from: $1,900 ✉ 452 Royalton Tpke., Barnard ☎ 802/234–9999 🌐 www.twinfarms.com 🛏 20 rooms 🍴 All-Inclusive.*

★ The Woodstock Inn and Resort

$$$ | RESORT | FAMILY | A night at the Woodstock Inn, one of Vermont's premier accommodations, is an experience in itself, with a location on Woodstock's gorgeous green that's hard to beat. **Pros:** historic property; perfect central location; one of the best spas in Vermont. **Cons:** posh ambience not for everyone; slightly slick and corporate; very expensive for Vermont. *$ Rooms from: $339 ✉ 14 The Green, Woodstock ☎ 802/332–6853, 888/338–2745 🌐 www.woodstockinn.com 🛏 142 rooms 🍴 No Meals.*

Shopping

ART GALLERIES

Gallery on the Green

ART GALLERIES | This corner gallery in one of Woodstock's oldest buildings showcases paintings by New England artists depicting regional landscapes. ✉ *1 The Green, Woodstock* ☎ *802/457–4956* 🌐 *www.galleryonthegreen.com.*

CRAFTS

Andrew Pearce Bowls

CRAFTS | Son of Simon Pearce, Andrew is making a name in his own right with his expertly and elegantly carved wood bowls, cutting boards, furniture, and artwork. Visitors can watch the carvers at work through windows into the production room. ✉ *59 Woodstock Rd., Taftsville* ☎ *802/735–1884* 🌐 *www.andrewpearcebowls.com.*

Collective

CRAFTS | This funky and attractive shop sells local jewelry, glass, pottery, and clothing from numerous local artisans. ✉ *47 Central St., Woodstock* ☎ *802/457–1298* 🌐 *www.collective-theartofcraft.com.*

★ Farmhouse Pottery

CERAMICS | More and more of James and Zoe Zilian's "studio pottery" is showing up in luxury establishments around the country, even earning the Oprah seal of approval. A visit to the home shop just west of Woodstock shows why, with a rustic but elegant range of stoneware pitchers, enamel jars, linen oven mitts, and beehive salt cellars. Visitors can watch the potters in action through large windows into the production room. ✉ *1837 W. Woodstock Rd., Woodstock* ☎ *802/457–7486* 🌐 *www.farmhousepottery.com.*

FOOD

Sugarbush Farm

MARKET | FAMILY | Take the Taftsville Covered Bridge to this farm, where you can learn how maple sugar is made and sample as much maple syrup as you'd like. The farm also makes excellent cheeses. ✉ *591 Sugarbush Farm Rd., off U.S. 4, Woodstock* ☎ *802/457–1757, 800/281–1757* 🌐 *www.sugarbushfarm.com.*

Woodstock Farmers' Market

MARKET | FAMILY | The indoor market is a year-round buffet of local produce, fresh fish, and excellent sandwiches and pastries. The hot lunch and dinner embrace classic American comfort food. ✉ *979 Woodstock Rd., aka U.S. 4, Woodstock* ☎ *802/457–3658* 🌐 *www.woodstockfarmersmarket.com.*

Activities

GOLF

Woodstock Inn and Resort Golf Club

GOLF | Robert Trent Jones Sr. designed the resort's challenging course. ✉ *76 South St., Woodstock* ☎ *802/457–6674, 888/338–2745* 🌐 *www.woodstockinn.com/golf-club* 🎟 *Non-Peak (Mon.–Thurs.) $115, Peak (Fri.–Sun.) $155* ⛳ *18 holes, 6001 yards, par 70.*

SKIING

Tubbs Snowshoes & Fischer Nordic Adventure Center

SKIING & SNOWBOARDING | The Woodstock Inn's Nordic complex has nearly 25 miles of picturesque groomed cross-country ski trails around Mt. Tom and Mt. Peg. Equipment and lessons are available. ✉ *76 South St., Woodstock* ☎ *802/457–6674* 🌐 *www.woodstockinn.com* 🎟 *Trail pass: $35.*

SPAS

The Bridge House Spa at Twin Farms

SPAS | A visit to Twin Farms is a trip to another world, and a spa treatment here completes the getaway. The spa at the luxury lodging expounds a philosophy of wellness that goes beyond the realm of massages and skin treatments. Employing an organic product line by Vermont-based Tata Harper and Lunaroma, the spa offers facials, polishes, aromatherapy, massages, and mud wraps that administer a heavenly reboot to your skin and muscles. ✉ *Twin Farms, 452 Royalton Tpke., Barnard* ☎ *802/234–9999* 🌐 *www.twinfarms.com.*

Spa at the Woodstock Inn and Resort
SPAS | A mesmerizing, 10,000-square-foot, nature-inspired facility, this LEED-certified spa is a world unto itself, with 10 treatment rooms, ultratranquil relaxation area, eucalyptus steam room, and a sophisticated shop stocked with designer bath products. Elegant, minimalist design accentuates the beautiful setting: natural light pours into sparkling dressing rooms and the firelit Great Room, and an outdoor meditation courtyard has a hot tub and a Scandinavian-style sauna. The mood is serene, the treatments varied: start with the 80-minute Himalayan Salt Stone Massage. ✉ *Woodstock Inn and Resort, 14 The Green, Woodstock* ☎ *802/457–6697, 888/338–2745* 🌐 *www.woodstockinn.com/spa.*

Killington

20 miles northwest of Woodstock.

With only a gas station, a post office, a motel, and a few shops at the intersection of U.S. 4 and Route 100, it doesn't quite feel like the East's largest ski resort is nearby. The village of Killington has suffered from unfortunate strip development along the access road to the ski resort, but the 360-degree views atop Killington Peak, accessible via the resort's gondola, make it worth the drive.

Coffee and Quick Bites

Liquid Art Coffeehouse & Eatery
$ | **CAFÉ** | This cerulean blue A-frame is a mountainside gem for morning baked goods, award-winning chilli, and specialty drinks like the Mounds latte (espresso, steamed milk, coconut, and chocolate syrup). It also doubles as a local art gallery, so you can peruse the work of Vermont artists over a pick-me-up. **Known for:** specialty lattes; cozy corner tables and free Wi-Fi; award-winning vegetarian chilli. *Average main: $6* ✉ *37 Miller Brook Rd., Killington* ☎ *802/422–2787* 🌐 *www.liquidartvt.com* *Closed Tues. and Wed.*

Hotels

Birch Ridge Inn
$ | **B&B/INN** | A slate-covered carriageway about a mile from the Killington ski resort leads to this popular off-mountain stay, a former executive retreat in two renovated A-frames. **Pros:** variety of quirky designs; five-minute drive to the slopes; near Killington nightlife. **Cons:** restaurant closed Sunday and Monday; outdated and tired style; no coffee or tea in rooms. *Rooms from: $139* ✉ *37 Butler Rd., Killington* ☎ *802/422–4293, 800/435–8566* 🌐 *www.birchridge.com* *Closed May* *10 rooms* *Free Breakfast.*

The Mountain Top Inn & Resort
$$$ | **RESORT** | **FAMILY** | This four-season resort hosts everything from cross-country skiing and snowshoeing on 37 miles of trails in the winter to horseback riding, tennis, and swimming and boating in the 740-acre lake throughout the rest of the year. **Pros:** family-friendly vibe; three suites have fireplaces; views of mountains and lake from some rooms. **Cons:** fees for activities can add up; tea/coffeemakers only in suites; limited to no cell service. *Rooms from: $325* ✉ *195 Mountain Top Rd., Chittenden* ☎ *802/483–2311* 🌐 *www.mountaintopinn.com* *59 rooms* *No Meals.*

Nightlife

McGrath's Irish Pub
PUBS | On Friday and Saturday, listen to live Irish music and sip Guinness draft at the Inn at Long Trail's pub. ✉ *709 U.S. 4, Killington* ☎ *802/755–7181* 🌐 *www.innatlongtrail.com.*

Pickle Barrel Night Club

DANCE CLUBS | During ski season, this club has live music on Friday and Saturday. After 8, the crowd moves downstairs for dancing, sometimes to big-name bands. ✉ *1741 Killington Rd., Killington* ☎ *802/422–3035* 🌐 *www.picklebarrelnightclub.com.*

Activities

BIKING

True Wheels Bike Shop

BIKING | Part of the Basin Sports complex, this shop rents bicycles and has information about local routes. ✉ *2886 Killington Rd., Killington* ☎ *802/422–3234, 877/487–9972* 🌐 *www.basinski.com/true-wheels-bike-shop.*

FISHING

Gifford Woods State Park

FISHING | This state park's Kent Pond is a terrific fishing spot. ✉ *34 Gifford Woods Rd., Killington* ✣ *½ mile north of U.S. 4* ☎ *802/775–5354* 🌐 *www.vtstateparks.com/gifford.html* 🎫 *$5* ⏲ *Facilities closed late Oct.–mid-May.*

GOLF

Killington Golf Course

GOLF | At its namesake resort, the course has a challenging layout. ✉ *4763 Killington Rd., Killington* ☎ *802/422–6700* 🌐 *www.killington.com/summer/golf_course* 🎫 *$27 for 9 holes and $47 for 18 holes, weekdays; $37 for 9 holes and $52 for 18 holes, weekends* ⛳ *18 holes, 6186 yards, par 72* ⏲ *Closed mid-Oct.–mid-May.*

HIKING

Deer Leap Trail

HIKING & WALKING | This 3-mile round-trip hike begins near the Inn at Long Trail and leads to a great view overlooking Sherburne Gap and Pico Peak. ✉ *Trailhead off U.S. 4, just east of Inn at Long Trail, Rutland.*

SKIING

★ Killington

SKIING & SNOWBOARDING | **FAMILY** | "Mega-mountain" aptly describes Killington. Thanks to its extensive snowmaking capacity, the resort typically opens in early November, and the lifts often run into late April or early May. Skiing includes everything from Outer Limits, the East's steepest and longest mogul trail, to the 6½-mile Great Eastern. The 18-foot Superpipe is one of the best rated in the East. There are also acres of glades. Après-ski activities are plentiful, and Killington ticket holders can also ski Pico Mountain—a shuttle connects the two areas. Summer activities at Killington–Pico include mountain biking, hiking, and golf. **Facilities:** 155 trails; 1,509 acres; 3,050-foot vertical drop; 21 lifts.

■ TIP→ Park at the base of the Skyeship Gondola to avoid the more crowded access road. ✉ *4763 Killington Rd., Killington* ☎ *802/422–3261 for snow conditions, 800/734–9435* 🌐 *www.killington.com* 🎫 *Lift ticket: $165.*

Pico

SKIING & SNOWBOARDING | When weekend hordes descend upon Killington, locals head to Pico. One of Killington's "seven peaks," Pico is physically separated from its parent resort. Trails range from elevator-shaft steep to challenging intermediate runs near the summit. Easier terrain can be found near the bottom of the mountain's nearly 2,000-foot vertical drop, and the learning slope is separated from the upper mountain, so hotshots won't bomb through it. The lower express quad can get crowded, but the upper one rarely has a line. **Facilities:** 57 trails; 468 acres; 1,967-foot vertical drop; 7 lifts. ✉ *73 Alpine Dr., Mendon* ☎ *802/422–1330, 802/422–1200 for snow conditions* 🌐 *www.picomountain.com* 🎫 *Lift ticket: $97.*

SNOWMOBILE TOURS

Snowmobile Vermont

SNOW SPORTS | Blazing down forest trails on a snowmobile is one way Vermonters embrace the winter landscapes. Rentals are available through Snowmobile Vermont at several locations, including Killington and Okemo. Both have hour-long guided tours across groomed ski trails ($99). If you're feeling more adventurous, take the two-hour backcountry tour through 25 miles of Calvin Coolidge State Forest ($159). ✉ *170 Rte. 100, Bridgewater Corners* ☎ *802/422–2121* 🌐 *www.snowmobilevermont.com.*

Rutland

15 miles southwest of Killington, 32 miles south of Middlebury.

The strip malls and seemingly endless row of traffic lights on and around U.S. 7 in Rutland are very un-Vermont. Two blocks west, however, stand the mansions of marble magnates. In Rutland you can grab a bite and see some interesting marble, and Depot Park hosts the county farmers' market Saturday 9–2. This isn't a place to spend too much time sightseeing, though.

ESSENTIALS

VISITOR INFORMATION Rutland Region Chamber of Commerce. ✉ *Rutland* ☎ *802/773–2747, 800/756–8880* 🌐 *www.rutlandvermont.com.*

Sights

Wilson Castle

HISTORIC HOME | Completed in 1867, this 32-room mansion was built over the course of eight years by a Vermonter who married a British aristocrat. Within the opulent setting are 84 stained-glass windows (one inset with 32 Australian opals), hand-painted Italian frescoes, and 13 fireplaces. The place is magnificently furnished with European and Asian objets d'art. October evenings bring haunted castle tours. ✉ *2708 West St., Proctor* ☎ *802/773–3284* 🌐 *www.wilsoncastle.com* 🎫 *$12.*

Restaurants

Roots

$$ | MODERN AMERICAN | Since opening in 2011, chef-owner Donald Billings has created a locavore restaurant driven by ingredients made within miles of the dining room. Humanely raised livestock and Vermont-grown produce is the inspiration behind menu favorites like laden cheese boards, braised pork belly, and homemade Parker House rolls served warm with Vermont butter. **Known for:** Vermont beers and spirits; frequently changing locavore menu; special Prime Rib Thursday. 💲 *Average main: $24* ✉ *55 Washington St., Rutland* ☎ *802/747–7414* 🌐 *www.rootsrutland.com* 🕑 *Closed Sun. and Mon.*

Coffee and Quick Bites

★ Jones' Donuts

$ | BAKERY | Since 1923, Jones' has been a destination for doughnuts and baked goods made fresh each day in the earliest hours of the morning. Fill a box with cinnamon rolls, pie squares, apple turnovers, and some of the best doughnuts in the state. **Known for:** maple glazed doughnuts; crullers; sticky buns. 💲 *Average main: $2* ✉ *23 West St., Rutland* ☎ *802/773–7810* 🕑 *Closed Mon. and Tues.*

Activities

BOATING

Woodard Marine

BOATING | Rent pontoon boats, speedboats, standup paddleboards, and kayaks at the Lake Bomoseen Marina. ✉ *145 Creek Rd., off Rte. 4A, Castleton, Rutland* ☎ *802/265–3690* 🌐 *www.woodardmarine.com.*

Brandon

15 miles northwest of Rutland.

Thanks to an active group of artists, tiny Brandon is making a name for itself. In 2003 the Brandon Artists Guild, led by American folk artist Warren Kimble, auctioned off 40 life-size fiberglass pigs painted by local artists. The "Really Really Pig Show" raised money for the guild, and has since brought small-town fame to this community through its annual shows. Brandon is also home to the Basin Bluegrass Festival, held in July.

ESSENTIALS

VISITOR INFORMATION Brandon Visitor Center. ✉ *4 Grove St., Brandon* ☎ *802/247–6401* 🌐 *www.brandon.org.*

Sights

Brandon Artists Guild

ART GALLERY | The guild exhibits and sells affordable paintings, sculpture, and pottery by more than 30 local member artists. ✉ *7 Center St., Brandon* ☎ *802/247–4956* 🌐 *brandonartistsguild.org* 🎟 *Free* ⏲ *Closed Mon. Dec.–Apr.*

Brandon Museum at the Stephen A. Douglas Birthplace

HISTORY MUSEUM | The famous statesman was born in this house in 1813. He left 20 years later to establish himself as a lawyer, becoming a three-time U.S. senator and arguing more cases before the U.S. Supreme Court than anyone else. This museum recounts the early Douglas years, early town history, and the antislavery movement in Vermont, the first state to abolish slavery. ✉ *4 Grove St., at U.S. 7, Brandon* ☎ *802/247–6401* 🌐 *www.brandon.org* 🎟 *Free* ⏲ *Closed Sun. and mid-Oct.–mid-May.*

Foley Brothers Brewery

BREWERY | Though this is a bare bones tasting room—no food, no tours, just glass pours and growlers—we argue that it has great charm, unique Vermont personality, and some of the best beer in the state. There is space to sit outside in the summer months in a nearby field with beautiful views, and the brewery's golden retriever is locally beloved. ✉ *79 Stone Mill Dam Rd., Brandon* ☎ *802/465–8413* 🌐 *foleybrothersbrewing.com* ⏲ *Closed Mon. and Tues., and Sun. Jan.–May.*

Moosalamoo National Recreation Area

NATURE PRESERVE | Covering nearly 16,000 acres of the Green Mountain National Forest, this area northeast of Brandon attracts hikers, mountain bikers, and cross-country skiers who enjoy the 70-plus miles of trails through wondrous terrain. If there is anywhere to stop and smell the flowers in Vermont, this is it. ✉ *Off Rtes. 53 and 73, Brandon* 🌐 *www.moosalamoo.org.*

Mt. Independence State Historic Site

HISTORIC SIGHT | Mt. Independence is one of the nation's most revered Revolutionary War sites, documenting the efforts to defend New York, New England, and the battle for American liberty. This key defensive position gained its name between 1776 and 1777, when the barely dried ink of the Declaration of Independence was read to United States soldiers assembled on the rugged peninsula east of Lake Champlain. Annual events include guided nature and history hikes on the site's 6 miles of hiking trails; historical lectures; archaeological investigations; a "Soldiers Atop the Mount" living history weekend; and a yearly reading of the Declaration of Independence. ✉ *497 Mt. Independence Rd., Orwell* ☎ *802/948–2000* 🌐 *historicsites.vermont.gov/mount-independence.*

Red Clover Ale

BREWERY | Red Clover Ale opened in Brandon's tiny town center under the reigns of two brothers and a brother-in-law. The family trio focuses on creative ales alongside skilled representations of the classics, like their pitch-perfect pilsners and stouts. Their ongoing IPA series is as special as the birds they're named after, like American Redstart and Yellow Warbler. Excellent pop-up food vendors are occasionally found on-site—otherwise, a corkboard near the entrance is covered in local takeout menus for perusing to one's liking. *43 Center St., Brandon* *802/465–8412* *www.redcloverale.com* *Closed Mon.–Wed.*

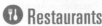

Restaurants

Café Provence

$$ | **CAFÉ** | Robert Barral, the former executive chef of the New England Culinary Institute, graces Brandon with this informal eatery one story above the main street. Flowered seat cushions, dried-flower window valences, and other hints of Barral's Provençal birthplace abound, as do his eclectic, farm-fresh dishes. **Known for:** Sunday brunch; thin tomato pie; seafood stew. *Average main: $23* *11 Center St., Brandon* *802/247–9997* *www.cafeprovencevt.com* *Closed Mon. and Tues.*

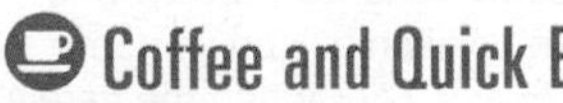

Coffee and Quick Bites

Gourmet Provence Bakery

$ | **BAKERY** | Next door to Café Provence, this French bakery offers coffee, pastries (yes, there are croissants and eclairs), prepared food, and specialty goods during the day. There's also a modest wine shop featuring plenty of old-world bottles. **Known for:** coffee and espresso drinks; homemade pastries; wine shop and artisanal goods. *Average main: $8* *37 Center St., Brandon* *802/247–3002* *cafeprovencevt.com* *Closed Mon.*

Hotels

★ Blueberry Hill Inn

$$ | **B&B/INN** | In the Green Mountain National Forest, 5½ miles off a mountain pass on a dirt road, you'll find this secluded inn with lush gardens and a pond with a wood-fired sauna on its bank; there's lots to do if you're into nature: biking, hiking, and cross-country skiing on 43 miles of trails. **Pros:** skis and snowshoes to rent in winter; the restaurant prepares a Vermont-infused, four-course prix-fixe menu most nights; homemade cookies. **Cons:** fills up with wedding parties; no cell phone service; no coffee or tea in rooms. *Rooms from: $269* *1245 Goshen–Ripton Rd., Goshen* *802/247–6735* *www.blueberryhillinn.com* *12 rooms* *Free Breakfast.*

The Lilac Inn

$ | **B&B/INN** | The best B&B in town has cheery, comfortable guest rooms in a central setting half a block from the heart of Brandon. **Pros:** many rooms have king beds; within walking distance of town; garden gazebo for relaxation. **Cons:** busy in summer with weddings; quaint but tepid traditional design; no coffee or tea in rooms. *Rooms from: $169* *53 Park St., Brandon* *802/247–5463, 800/221–0720* *www.lilacinn.com* *9 rooms* *Free Breakfast.*

Activities

GOLF

Neshobe Golf Club

GOLF | This bent-grass course has terrific views of the Green Mountains. Several local inns offer golfing packages. *224 Town Farm Rd., Brandon* *802/247–3611* *neshobe.com* *$25 for 9 holes, $44 for 18 holes* *18 holes, 6341 yards, par 72.*

HIKING

Branbury State Park

HIKING & WALKING | A large turnout on Route 53 marks the trailhead for a moderate hike to the Falls of Lana, a highlight of this park on the shores of Lake Dunmore near the Moosalamoo National Recreation Area. *3570 Lake Dunmore Rd., Brandon* *www.vtstateparks.com/branbury.html* *$5* *Facilities closed late Oct.–late May.*

Mt. Horrid

HIKING & WALKING | For great views from a vertigo-inducing cliff, hike up the Long Trail to Mt. Horrid. The steep, hour-long hike starts at the top of Brandon Gap. ✉ *Trailhead at Brandon Gap Rte. 73 parking lot, about 8 miles east of Brandon, Brandon* 🌐 *www.fs.usda.gov/main/gmfl.*

Trails at Mt. Independence State Historic Site

HIKING & WALKING | West of Brandon, four trails—two short ones of less than a mile each and two longer ones—lead to some abandoned Revolutionary War fortifications. ✉ *497 Mt. Independence Rd., just west of Orwell, Orwell* ✣ *Parking lot is at top of hill* ☎ *802/948–2000* 🌐 *historicsites.vermont.gov/mount-independence* 🎫 *$5* ⏲ *Closed mid-Oct.–late May.*

Middlebury

17 miles north of Brandon, 34 miles south of Burlington.

In the late 1800s Middlebury was the largest Vermont community west of the Green Mountains, an industrial center of river-powered wool and grain mills. This is Robert Frost country: Vermont's late poet laureate spent 23 summers at a farm east of Middlebury. Still a cultural and economic hub amid the Champlain Valley's serene pastoral patchwork—and the home of top-notch Middlebury College—the town and rolling countryside invite a day of exploration.

Sights

Edgewater Gallery

ART GALLERY | This gallery sits alongside picturesque Otter Creek, and the paintings, jewelry, ceramics, and pieces of furniture inside are just as arresting. Exhibitions in the bright, airy space change regularly, demonstrating the owner's ambition to be more gallery than shop, though all pieces are for sale. A second gallery is across the creek in the Battell Building. ✉ *1 Mill St., Middlebury* ☎ *802/458–0098* 🌐 *edgewatergallery.co* 🎫 *Free.*

Middlebury Tasting Trail

Among Vermont's craft beer, cider, spirits, and wine explosion, the Middlebury area stands out, with a large cluster of producers with welcoming tasting rooms. Seven, all within a 10-mile radius of the city, have banded together to create the Middlebury Tasting Trail. Find full details at 🌐 *www.middtastingtrail.com.*

Fort Ticonderoga Ferry

TRANSPORTATION | Established in 1759, the Fort Ti cable ferry crosses Lake Champlain between Shoreham and Fort Ticonderoga, New York, at one of the oldest ferry crossings in North America. The trip takes seven minutes. ✉ *4831 Rte. 74 W, Shoreham* ☎ *802/897–7999* 🌐 *www.forttiferry.com* 🎫 *Cars $12, bicycles $5, pedestrians $4* ⏲ *Closed Nov.–Apr.*

Lincoln Peak Vineyard

WINERY | Named "Winery of the Year" at the International Cold Climate Wine Competition in 2016, this vineyard —now owned by nearby Shelburne Vineyard— is enjoying the fruits of its labor, with an increase in traffic to its tasting room and shop. Enjoy the Frontenac, La Crescent, and Marquette varieties from both vineyards on the postcard-pretty porch overlooking a small pond. ✉ *142 River Rd., Middlebury* ☎ *802/388–7368* 🌐 *www.lincolnpeakvineyard.com* ⏲ *Closed Mon. and Tues. late Oct.–Dec.; Mon.–Thurs. Jan.–late May.*

Middlebury College

COLLEGE | Founded in 1800, this college was conceived as a more godly alternative to the worldly University of Vermont, though it has no religious affiliation today. The postmodern architecture of the **Mahaney Center for the Arts,** which offers music, theater, and dance performances throughout the year, stands in provocative contrast to the early-19th-century stone buildings in the middle of town. ✉ *131 College St., Middlebury* ☎ *802/443–5000* 🌐 *www.middlebury.edu.*

Robert Frost Interpretive Trail

TRAIL | Plaques along this easy 1.2-mile wooded trail bear quotations from Frost's poems. A picnic area is across the road from the trailhead. ✉ *Trailhead on Rte. 125, 10 miles east of downtown, Middlebury* 🌐 *www.fs.usda.gov/main/gmfl.*

University of Vermont Morgan Horse Farm

FARM/RANCH | **FAMILY** | The Morgan horse, Vermont's official state animal, has an even temper, high stamina, and slightly truncated legs in proportion to its body. This farm, about 2½ miles west of Middlebury, is a breeding and training center where in summer you can tour the stables and paddocks. ✉ *74 Battell Dr., off Morgan Horse Farm Rd., Weybridge* ☎ *802/388–2011* 🌐 *www.uvm.edu/morgan* 🎟 *$8* 🕒 *Closed late Oct.–Apr.*

Vermont Folklife Center

ARTS CENTER | The redbrick center's exhibits include photography, antiques, folk paintings, manuscripts, and other artifacts and contemporary works that examine various facets of Vermont life. ✉ *88 Main St., Middlebury* ☎ *802/388–4964* 🌐 *www.vermontfolklifecenter.org* 🎟 *Donations accepted* 🕒 *Closed Sun. and Mon.*

Woodchuck Cider House

BREWERY | This cidery has come a long way since its beginnings in a two-car garage in Proctorsville in 1991, transforming into this $34 million complex that divides its space between a pub, gift shop, and factory. A self-guided tour, with informational signs, includes a look through large windows onto the production floor. ✉ *1321 Exchange St., Middlebury* ☎ *802/385–3656* 🌐 *www.woodchuck.com* 🕒 *Closed Mon. and Tues.*

Restaurants

Minifactory

$ | **CAFÉ** | Also the home of award-winning jam company V Smiley Preserves, this all-day café serves house-made pastries, biscuit sandwiches, huge salads, creative vegetable dishes and savory yogurt with crispy lentils and poached eggs. On weekends, oysters and cocktails start in the afternoon; dinner features rich soups and roast chicken with tomato jam. **Known for:** bright, spacious seating area with big windows for people watching; well-stocked grab-and-go fridge and pantry ingredients; jammy waffle (waffle with buttered nuts, syrup, and black raspberry whip). 💲 *Average main: $16* ✉ *16 Main St., Bristol* ☎ *802/453–3280* 🌐 *vermontminifactory.com* 🕒 *No dinner Sun.–Thurs.*

The Tillerman

$$$ | **PIZZA** | New owners have transformed the longtime Inn at Baldwin Creek and Mary's Restaurant, giving the 1790s farmhouse a chic update from head to toe. Pizza isn't the only thing that comes out of the new wood-fired oven; locally sourced roasted vegetables and smokey meatballs complement the fire-kissed pies. **Known for:** thoughtful drink list, including nonalcoholic options; cozy dining rooms; fresh herbs and vegetables from the kitchen garden. 💲 *Average main: $25* ✉ *1868 N 116 Rd., Bristol* ☎ *802/643–2237* 🌐 *www.thetillermanvt.com* 🕒 *Closed Sun.–Tues. No lunch.*

Coffee and Quick Bites

★ Haymaker Bun Co.

$ | **BAKERY** | This sunlit café and bakery overlooking Otter Creek houses some of the best coffee and pastries in the state thanks to chef-owner Caroline Corrente, who honed her skills at pastry school in France before zeroing in on a love for brioche dough. Corrente's specialty sweet and savory buns change daily based on what is available locally—many ingredients are found within a few miles of Haymaker's doors. **Known for:** sweet and savory brioche buns; locally roasted Brio coffee and espresso; patio seating and riverside views. *Average main: $6 7 Bakery La., Middlebury 802/989–7026 www.haymakerbuns.com Closed Sun.*

Royal Oak Coffee

$ | **CAFÉ** | After a decade of fine-tuning their skills and tastebuds in the coffee industry, Royal Oak co-owners Alessandra and Matthew Delia-Lobo opened their own café on Seymour Street, an easy pit stop along the Middlebury Tasting Trail. The menu, featuring Vermont-based beans from Vivid Coffee Roasters, is known for shaken ice maple lattes in the summer and frothy cardamom-vanilla lattes in the winter (a seasonal special that, say the Delia-Lobos, now never leaves the menu due to popularity). **Known for:** specialty lattes using scratch-made syrups; cold brew; Gibralters, hot and iced. *Average main: $5 30 Seymour St., Middlebury 802/349–1609 www.royaloakcoffee.com.*

Stone Leaf Teahouse

$ | **CAFÉ** | Partially hidden in Middlebury's historic Marble Works district, this oasis of tea is known for made-to-order spiced chai, house-roasted oolong, and loose leaf teas imported from small farmers in China, India, Nepal, Japan, and Taiwan. **Known for:** specialty teaware sold on-site; oolong roasted in-house; seasonal herbal tea blends. *Average main: $5 Marble Works, 111 Maple St., Middlebury 802/458–0460 www.stoneleaftea.com.*

Hotels

Inn on the Green

$$ | **B&B/INN** | Listed on the National Register of Historic Places, this 1803 inn and its carriage house sit in the center of bucolic Middlebury near the college campus; the inn offers a delicious breakfast, bicycles you are free to use, and Adirondack chairs that are perfect for enjoying the grounds and views. **Pros:** ideal, central location; complimentary continental "breakfast-in-bed"; Aveda hair and skin-care products. **Cons:** some rooms small and close together; typical country-inn design; no coffee or tea in rooms. *Rooms from: $285 71 S. Pleasant St., Middlebury 802/388–7512, 888/244–7512 www.innonthegreen.com 11 rooms Free Breakfast.*

★ Swift House Inn

$$ | **B&B/INN** | The 1814 Georgian mansion channels a classic New England style into three buildings on 4 acres of lawns and gardens. **Pros:** attractive, spacious, well-kept rooms; complimentary day pass to Middlebury Fitness Club; some rooms have private decks; on-site restaurant, Jessica's, is one of the best fine-dining options in town. **Cons:** not quite in the heart of town; weak Wi-Fi in some areas; somewhat typical country-inn design. *Rooms from: $245 25 Stewart La., Middlebury 866/388–9925 www.swifthouseinn.com 20 rooms Free Breakfast.*

Nightlife

Two Brothers Tavern

PUBS | Head to this watering hole for pub food a cut above the usual, plus local microbrews on tap in the sports-friendly bar. Look closely at the dollar bills pasted to the ceiling. There's even a marriage proposal up there, along with the answer. Food is served until at least midnight. *86 Main St., Middlebury 802/388–0002 www.twobrotherstavern.com.*

Waitsfield and Warren

32 miles northeast (Waitsfield) and 25 miles east (Warren) of Middlebury.

Skiers first discovered the high peaks overlooking the pastoral Mad River Valley in the 1940s. Today, this valley and its two towns, Waitsfield and Warren, attract the hip, the adventurous, and the low-key. Warren in particular is tiny and adorable, with a general store popular with tour buses. The gently carved ridges cradling the valley and the swell of pastures and fields lining the river seem to keep notions of ski-resort sprawl at bay. With a map from the Sugarbush Chamber of Commerce you can investigate back roads off Route 100 that have exhilarating valley views.

ESSENTIALS

VISITOR INFORMATION Mad River Valley Visitor Information Center. ✉ *44 Bridge St., Waitsfield* ☎ *802/496–3409* 🌐 *www.madrivervalley.com.*

Restaurants

★ American Flatbread Waitsfield

$$ | PIZZA | The organically grown flour and vegetables—and the wood-fired clay ovens that unite them—take the pizza here to another level. In summer, you can dine outside around fire pits in the beautiful valley. **Known for:** maple–fennel sausage pie; homemade fruit crisp with Mountain Creamery ice cream; Big Red Barn art gallery on-site. *$ Average main: $18* ✉ *46 Lareau Rd., off Rte. 100, Waitsfield* ☎ *802/496–8856* 🌐 *www.americanflatbread.com* ⏲ *Closed Mon.–Wed. No lunch.*

The Mad Taco

$ | MEXICAN | Mexican cuisine rooted in Vermont ingredients makes this a go-to stop for locals and travelers alike—particularly those who just ascended the rugged incline of nearby Camel's Hump, one of the state's highest peaks. Chef-owner Joey Nagy and Georgia Von Trapp, his partner, source much of their local haul from their own Marble Hill Farm, fueling delicious cooking from carnitas and al pastor to fresh house-made salsa and slow-roasted yams in the outside smoker. **Known for:** tacos with local All Souls tortillas; Cubano sandwich with smoked Vermont meat; house-made margaritas and local craft beer. *$ Average main: $12* ✉ *5101 Main St., Waitsfield* ☎ *802/496–3832* 🌐 *www.themadtaco.com.*

★ Peasant

$$$ | EUROPEAN | The menu may be short in this small, rustic-chic space serving French- and Italian-influenced country fare, but the tastiness is immense, with some of the best pasta dishes in the state. Additional warmth is added by its "peasant family" operation, too, with dad in the kitchen, mom decorating the scene, and daughter running the front of house. **Known for:** unique "Peasant's Prunes" dessert; Vermont pork Bolognese with penne and Asiago; craft cocktail and wine list. *$ Average main: $26* ✉ *40 Bridge St., Waitsfield* ☎ *802/496–6856* 🌐 *www.peasantvt.com* ⏲ *Closed Mon.-Wed. No lunch.*

Pitcher Inn Dining Room and Tracks

$$$ | AMERICAN | Claiming two aesthetics and one menu, this dining experience offers a posh and pretty upstairs dining room with classic white tablecloths or a stony, subterranean "Tracks," with billiards and shuffleboard on the side. Dishes cover upscale versions of regional classics, with a few international flavors, too. **Known for:** cocktail list with Vermont spirits; duck breast; artisanal cheese board with onion chutney. *$ Average main: $30* ✉ *275 Main St., Warren* ☎ *802/496–6350* 🌐 *www.pitcherinn.com.*

Coffee and Quick Bites

Canteen Creemee Company

$ | AMERICAN | FAMILY | Stop by the takeout window of this new-wave snack shack for fried chicken, griddled burgers, and kimchi-stuffed grilled cheese. Stay for the homemade creemees, Vermont's answer to soft-serve ice cream; state classics like maple are always on offer, as are seasonal specials like ginger, cinnamon, lemon, and fresh blueberry. **Known for:** creemees and sundaes; fried chicken, griddled burgers, and hot dogs; limited winter hours. *Average main: $8* *5123 Main St., Waitsfield* *802/496–6003* *www.canteencreemee.com* *Closed Mon.–Fri.*

Hotels

★ The Inn at Round Barn Farm

$$ | B&B/INN | A Shaker-style round barn—one of only five in Vermont—is the centerpiece of this eminently charming B&B set among the hills of the Mad River Valley with resident ducks, squirrels, chipmunks, and songbirds that make it feel like a Disney movie. **Pros:** miles of walking and snowshoe trails; game room with billiard table and board games; gorgeous gardens with lily ponds. **Cons:** no a/c in common areas; fills up for wedding parties; no sights within walking distance. *Rooms from: $219* *1661 E. Warren Rd., Waitsfield* *802/496–2276* *www.theroundbarn.com* *12 rooms* *Free Breakfast.*

Mad River Barn

$ | B&B/INN | This supposed former bunk house for the Civilian Conservation Corps in the 1930s is now one of the Mad River Valley's chicest accommodations, thanks to extensive renovations in 2013 that transformed it into a rustic farmhouse with an edge of industrial. **Pros:** multiple-sized rooms, sleeping up to six people; game room includes shuffleboard, air hockey, foosball, and more; several family suites, with bunkbeds. **Cons:** first-floor rooms can suffer noise; lots of weddings in summer can keep it busy and booked; no TVs in rooms. *Rooms from: $145* *2849 Mill Brook Rd., Waitsfield* *802/496–3310, 800/631–0466* *www.madriverbarn.com* *18 rooms* *Free Breakfast.*

★ The Pitcher Inn

$$$$ | B&B/INN | One of Vermont's three Relais & Châteaux properties, the unique Pitcher Inn has it all including a supremely romantic restaurant and bubbling brook running alongside. **Pros:** exceptional and fun design; across from Warren General Store; complimentary hybrid bikes and access to the Sugarbush Health and Racquet Club. **Cons:** two-night minimum stay on many weekends in peak period; limited to no cell phone service; restaurant closed on Tuesday. *Rooms from: $500* *275 Main St., Warren* *802/496–6350* *www.pitcherinn.com* *11 rooms* *Free Breakfast.*

Shopping

All Things Bright and Beautiful

ANTIQUES & COLLECTIBLES | This eccentric Victorian house is filled to the rafters with stuffed animals of all shapes, sizes, and colors, as well as folk art, European glass, and Christmas ornaments. *27 Bridge St., Waitsfield* *802/496–3997.*

The Warren Store

GENERAL STORE | This general store has everything you'd hope to find in tiny but sophisticated Vermont: a nice selection of local beer and wine, cheeses, baked goods, strong coffee, and delicious sandwiches and prepared foods. In summer, grab a quick lunch on the small deck by the water; in winter, warm up at the wood stove. Warm, woolly clothing and accessories can be found upstairs. *284 Main St., Warren* *802/496–3864* *www.warrenstore.com.*

Activities

GOLF

Sugarbush Resort Golf Club

GOLF | Great views and challenging play are the hallmarks of this mountain course designed by Robert Trent Jones Sr. *Sugarbush, 1840 Sugarbush Access Rd., Warren* *802/583–6725* *www.sugarbush.com* *$115 for 18 holes, weekdays; $130 for 18 holes, weekends* *18 holes, 6464 yards, par 70.*

MULTISPORT OUTFITTER

Clearwater Sports

ADVENTURE TOURS | **FAMILY** | This outfitter rents canoes and kayaks, and leads guided river trips in warmer months. When the weather turns cold, it offers snowshoeing and backcountry skiing tours. ✉ *4147 Main St., Waitsfield* ☎ *802/496–2708* 🌐 *www.clearwatersports.com.*

SKIING

Blueberry Lake Cross Country and Snowshoeing Center

SKIING & SNOWBOARDING | This ski area has 18 miles of trails through thickly wooded glades. ✉ *424 Plunkton Rd., East Warren* ☎ *802/496–6687* 🌐 *www.blueberrylakeskivt.com* 🎫 *Daily Pass Trail Fees: $22.*

Mad River Glen

SKIING & SNOWBOARDING | A pristine alpine experience, Mad River attracts rugged individualists looking for less polished terrain. The area was developed in the late 1940s and has changed relatively little since then. It remains one of only three resorts in the country that ban snowboarding, and it's one of only two in North America that still has a single-chair lift. Mad River is steep, with slopes that follow the mountain's fall lines. The terrain changes constantly on the interconnected trails of mostly natural snow (expert trails are never groomed). Telemark skiing and snowshoeing are also popular. **Facilities:** 53 trails; 115 acres; 2,037-foot vertical drop; 5 lifts. ✉ *62 Mad River Resort Rd., off Rte. 17, Waitsfield* ☎ *802/496–3551* 🌐 *www.madriverglen.com* 🎫 *Lift ticket: $99.*

Sugarbush

SKIING & SNOWBOARDING | **FAMILY** | A true skier's mountain, Sugarbush has plenty of steep, natural snow glades and fall-line drops. Not as rough around the edges as Mad River Glen, the resort has an extensive computer-controlled system for snowmaking and many groomed trails between its two mountain complexes. This is a great choice for intermediate skiers, who will find top-to-bottom runs all over the resort; there are fewer options for beginners. Programs for kids include the enjoyable Sugarbear Forest, a terrain garden full of fun bumps and jumps. At the base of the mountain are condominiums, restaurants, shops, bars, and a health-and-racquet club. **Facilities:** 111 trails; 484 acres; 2,600-foot vertical drop; 16 lifts. ✉ *102 Forest Dr., Warren* ✣ *From Rte. 17, take German Flats Rd. south; from Rte. 100, take Sugarbush Access Rd. west* ☎ *802/583–6300, 800/537–8427* 🌐 *www.sugarbush.com* 🎫 *Lift ticket: $189.*

Montpelier

38 miles southeast of Burlington, 115 miles north of Brattleboro.

With only about 8,000 residents, little Montpelier is the country's smallest capital city, but it has a youthful energy and a quirky spirit that's earned it the local nickname "Montpeculiar." The quaint, historic downtown area bustles by day with thousands of state and city workers walking to meetings and business lunches. The nightlife can't match Burlington's, but several bars, theaters, and cinemas provide ample entertainment. The city is also a springboard for exploring the great outdoors of Central Vermont.

GETTING HERE AND AROUND

Vermont's capital city is easily accessible from Interstate 89, taking about 45 minutes from Burlington by car through the heart of the Green Mountains. It's also on the main Boston–Montreal bus route. Downtown is flat and easily walkable, but exploring the surrounding hills requires a modest level of fitness as well as a solid pair of shoes or boots, especially during the winter.

Did You Know?

Vermont actually means "Green Mountains" (in French). The Long Trail, the Appalachian Trail, and many other hiking routes crisscross the namesake peaks, which are part of the Appalachian Mountain chain.

Sights

★ Hope Cemetery

CEMETERY | Montpelier's regional rival, Barre, the "Granite Capital of the World," may lack the polish and pedigree of the state capital, but it's home to this gorgeous cemetery filled with superbly crafted tombstones by master stonecutters. A few embrace the avant-garde, while others take defined shapes like a race car, a biplane, and a soccer ball. ✉ *201 Maple Ave., Barre* ☎ *802/476–6245.*

Hubbard Park

STATE/PROVINCIAL PARK | Rising behind the Vermont State House and stretching 196 acres, this heavily forested park offers locals (and their happy, leash-free dogs) miles of pretty trails and wildlife to enjoy. On its highest peak is a romantic stone tower that looks out to 360-degree views of the surrounding mountains. ✉ *400 Parkway St., Montpelier* ☎ *802/223–7335 Montpelier Parks department* 🌐 *www.montpelier-vt.org* 🎫 *Free.*

★ Morse Farm Maple Sugarworks

FACTORY | **FAMILY** | With eight generations of sugaring, the Morses may be the oldest maple family in existence, so you're sure to find an authentic experience at their farm. Burr Morse—a local legend—heads up the operation now, along with his son Tom. More than 5,000 trees produce the sap used for syrup (you can sample all the grades), candy, cream, and sugar—all sold in the gift shop. Grab a maple creemee (soft-serve ice cream), take a seat on a swing, and stay awhile. Surrounding trails offer pleasant strolls in summer and prime cross-country skiing in winter. ✉ *1168 County Rd., Montpelier* ☎ *800/242–2740* 🌐 *www.morsefarm.com* 🎫 *Free.*

Rock of Ages Granite Quarry

NATURE SIGHT | Attractions here range from the awe-inspiring (the quarry resembles the Grand Canyon in miniature) to the mildly ghoulish (you can consult a directory of tombstone dealers throughout the country) to the whimsical (an outdoor granite bowling alley). At the crafts center, skilled artisans sculpt monuments and blast stone, while at the quarries themselves, workers who clearly earn their pay cut 25-ton blocks of stone from the sheer 475-foot walls. (You may recognize these walls from a chase scene in the 2009 *Star Trek* movie.) ✉ *558 Graniteville Rd., off I–89, Graniteville* ☎ *802/476–3119, 866/748–6877* 🌐 *www.rockofages.com* 🎫 *Guided tours $7* ⏲ *Closed Sun. and mid-Oct.–mid-May.*

Vermont History Museum

HISTORY MUSEUM | The collection here, begun in 1838, focuses on all things Vermont—from a catamount (the now-extinct local cougar) to Ethan Allen's shoe buckles. The museum store stocks fine books, prints, and gifts. A second location in Barre, the Vermont History Center, has rotating exhibits with notable photographs and artifacts. ✉ *109 State St., Montpelier* ☎ *802/828–2291* 🌐 *www.vermonthistory.org* 🎫 *$7* ⏲ *Closed Sun. and Mon.*

Vermont State House

GOVERNMENT BUILDING | The regal capitol building surrounded by forest is emblematic of this proudly rural state. With a gleaming dome and columns of Barre granite measuring 6 feet in diameter, the State House is home to the country's oldest legislative chambers still in their original condition. Interior paintings and exhibits depict much of Vermont's sterling Civil War record. A self-guided tour, available year-round, takes you through the governor's office and the house and senate chambers. Free guided tours run from late June to October. ✉ *115 State St., Montpelier* ☎ *802/828–2228* 🌐 *statehouse.vermont.gov* 🎫 *Donations accepted* ⏲ *Closed Sun.; also Sat. Nov.–June.*

Restaurants

Oakes & Evelyn

$$$$ | **AMERICAN** | Vermont may be landlocked, but regionally sourced seafood fills the menu at this upscale farm-to-table restaurant in the state capital; the raw bar—think Cape Cod oysters and cold-smoked scallop crudo—is a particular draw. Large plates include prime strip loin with bone marrow and black-truffle raclette with local ricotta ravioletto. **Known for:** luxurious ingredients; creative cocktails, including multiple Bloody Mary options at brunch; bao buns with spiced crispy local mushrooms. *Average main: $38* *52 State St., Montpelier* *802/347–9100* *www.oakesandevelyn.com* *Closed Mon.–Tues. No lunch.*

Pearl Street Pizza

$$ | **PIZZA** | The handmade Italian brick oven is the centerpiece of this hot new pizza spot, which shares a former department store building with AR Market and the curing facility for Vermont Salumi. The team cranks out perfectly blistered Neapolitan-style pizzas and thick grandma pies, with classic and weekly special toppings that range from fire-roasted mushrooms to roast pork and miso drizzle. **Known for:** Tom Cat Tiramisu made with local barrel-aged gin; housemade pasta of the week; local mozzarella and real San Marzano tomatoes. *Average main: $24* *159 N. Main St., Barre* *802/622–8600* *pearlstpizza.com* *Closed Sun.–Tues.*

Sarducci's

$$ | **ITALIAN** | **FAMILY** | Montpelier's most popular restaurant draws its crowd less for the classic American Italian dishes than the conviviality, charm, and sizeable portions, not to mention the picturesque Winooski River flowing directly alongside the windows. The pizza comes fresh from wood-fired ovens, while the rest of the menu features your favorite pennes, Alfredos, and raviolis, with pleasing tweaks on the old formulas. **Known for:** date night; large gluten-free menu; local favorite. *Average main: $18* *3 Main St., Montpelier* *802/223–0229* *www.sarduccis.com* *No lunch Sun.*

The Skinny Pancake

$ | **CAFÉ** | This dine-in crêperie makes a great stop for breakfast, lunch, or an easy dinner. The signature crepes go sweet and savory and are filled with fruit, vegetables, and meat from more than a dozen Vermont farms. **Known for:** inventive hot chocolate recipes; Locavore's Dream crepe with chicken, cran-apple chutney, spinach, and blue cheese; Pooh Bear crepe with cinnamon sugar and local honey. *Average main: $9* *89 Main St., Montpelier* *802/262–2253* *www.skinnypancake.com.*

★ Three Penny Taproom

$ | **ECLECTIC** | This celebrated taproom remains one of the state's best, thanks in large part to its ability to acquire beers few others in the region can. The vibe feels straight out of an artsy neighborhood in Brussels, but with the earthiness of Vermont. **Known for:** darn good burger; top happy-hour hangout in town; premier Vermont and hard-to-get brews. *Average main: $15* *108 Main St., Montpelier* *802/223–8277* *www.threepennytaproom.com.*

★ Wilaiwan's Kitchen

$ | **THAI** | In 2012, co-owners Wilaiwan Phonjan-Azarian and Timothy Azarian traded their locally adored street cart for a brick-and-mortar location offering some of the best Thai food in the state, if not on the East Coast. Most of the menu reflects the Laotian influence of Phonjan-Azarian's upbringing in northeast Thailand, and Vermont ingredients from eggs to chiles inspire dishes that change weekly. **Known for:** weekly changing menus featuring local ingredients; noodle specials, like khao soy and gwit diow, with homemade chili pastes; sunny interiors covered with artwork. *Average main: $10* *34 State St., Montpelier* *802/613–3587* *wilaiwanskitchen.com* *Closed Sun.*

Coffee and Quick Bites

Bohemian Bakery

$ | **BAKERY** | The original Bohemian Bakery began in 2010 as a Sunday-only pop-up in the home of co-owners Annie Bakst and Robert Hunt; it quickly became a weekly haunt for expertly made French pastries. The couple now roasts coffee beans in small batches and fills daily orders of rotating favorites, like buttery kougin-amman and croissants, custard-filled Danishes, and tall slices of cornmeal cake in their shop. **Known for:** seasonal tarts with fresh fruit and pastry cream; croissants of all kinds; coffee roasted in-house. *Average main: $8* *83 Main St., Montpelier* *802/461–8119* *www.bohemianbakeryvt.com* *Closed Mon. and Tues.*

★ Red Hen Baking Co.

$ | **CAFÉ** | If you're a devotee of artisanal bakeries, it'd be a mistake not to trek the 7-plus miles from Montpelier (15 from Stowe) to have lunch, pick up freshly baked bread, or sample a sweet treat at what many consider Vermont's best bakery. Red Hen supplies bread to some of the state's premier restaurants, including Hen of the Wood, and has varied offerings every day. **Known for:** breads and pastries; local hangout; soups and sandwiches. *Average main: $8* *961 U.S. 2, Suite B, Middlesex* *802/223–5200* *www.redhenbaking.com* *No dinner.*

Hotels

Capitol Plaza Hotel

$ | **HOTEL** | Montpelier's only major hotel benefits much from the State House across the street, hosting many of its visiting politicians, lobbyists, and business makers, not to mention tourists seeking a certain quality of accommodation. **Pros:** easy walking distance to all local sights, including bike path; small fitness center; the resident steak house, J. Morgans, serves probably the best cuts in town. **Cons:** somewhat bland design; slight corporate feel; street-facing room may suffer street and bell-tower noise. *Rooms from: $192* *100 State St., Montpelier* *802/223–5252, 800/274–5252* *www.capitolplaza.com* *65 rooms* *No Meals.*

Inn at Montpelier

$$ | **B&B/INN** | The capital's most charming lodging option, this lovingly tended inn dating to 1830 has rooms filled with antique four-poster beds and Windsor chairs—all have private (if small) baths. **Pros:** beautiful home; relaxed central setting means you can walk everywhere in town; amazing porch. **Cons:** some rooms are small; somewhat bland, traditional design; no tea or coffee in rooms. *Rooms from: $200* *147 Main St., Montpelier* *802/223–2727* *www.innatmontpelier.com* *19 rooms* *Free Breakfast.*

Shopping

AroMed

OTHER SPECIALTY STORE | Although just a small storefront in downtown Montpelier, this shop counts customers as far away as Hawaii, thanks to owner Lauren Andrew's masterful concoctions of lotions, oils, and aromatics. Her CBD- (cannabidiol-) infused versions are particularly popular. *8 State St., Montpelier* *802/505–1405* *www.aromedofvt.com.*

Artisans Hand

CRAFTS | For more than 30 years, this craft gallery has been celebrating and supporting Vermont's craft community. The store sells jewelry, textiles, sculptures, and paintings by many local artists. *89 Main St., Montpelier* *802/229–9492* *www.artisanshand.com.*

Bear Pond Books

BOOKS | FAMILY | Old-fashioned village bookstores don't get more cute and quaint than this, and locals work hard to keep it that way by actively embracing the printed word. A community hangout, the nearly 50-year-old shop hosts numerous readings by authors, workshops, and book clubs, as well as a significant section of Vermont writers. ✉ *77 Main St., Montpelier* ☎ *892/229–0774* 🌐 *www.bearpondbooks.com.*

Vermont Creamery

FOOD | A leader in the artisanal cheese movement, this creamery invites aficionados to visit its 4,000-square-foot production facility, where goat cheeses such as Bonne Bouche—a perfectly balanced, cloudlike cheese—are made on weekdays. The creamery is in Websterville, southwest of Montpelier. ✉ *20 Pitman Rd., Websterville* ☎ *802/479–9371, 800/884–6287* 🌐 *www.vermontcreamery.com.*

Stowe

22 miles northwest of Montpelier, 36 miles east of Burlington.

Long before skiing came to Stowe in the 1930s, the rolling hills and valleys beneath Vermont's highest peak, 4,395-foot Mt. Mansfield, attracted summer tourists looking for a reprieve from city heat. Most stayed at one of two inns in the village of Stowe. When skiing made the town a winter destination, visitors outnumbered hotel beds, so locals took them in. This spirit of hospitality continues, and many of these homes are now country inns. The village itself is tiny—just a few blocks of shops and restaurants clustered around a picture-perfect white church with a lofty steeple—but it serves as the anchor for Mountain Road, which leads north past restaurants, lodges, and shops on its way to Stowe's fabled slopes. The road to Stowe also passes through Waterbury, which is rapidly regenerating thanks to a thriving arts and dining scene.

ESSENTIALS

VISITOR INFORMATION Stowe Area Association. ✉ *Stowe* ☎ *800/467–8693* 🌐 *www.gostowe.com.*

Sights

★ Alchemist Brewery

BREWERY | The brewery that launched a beer revolution in Vermont with its "Heady Topper" now welcomes guests to its shop and tasting room (known here as the Beer Cafe). Intense demand still keeps stocks of beer for sale limited. Tours ($25) of the brewery last about 30 minutes and include a commemorative tasting glass and a can of beer; it's best to reserve in advance. ✉ *100 Cottage Club Rd., Stowe* ☎ *802/882–8165* 🌐 *www.alchemistbeer.com.*

★ Ben & Jerry's Factory

OTHER ATTRACTION | **FAMILY** | The closest thing you'll get to a Willy Wonka experience in Vermont, the 30-minute tours at the famous brand's factory are unabashedly corny and only skim the surface of the behind-the-scenes goings-on, but this flaw is almost forgiven when the samples are dished out. To see the machines at work, visit on a weekday (but call ahead to confirm if they will indeed be in operation). Another highlight is the "Flavor Graveyard," where flavors of yore are given tribute with tombstones inscribed with humorous poetry. Free, family-friendly outdoor movies also play through summer on Friday. ✉ *1281 Waterbury-Stowe Rd., Waterbury* ☎ *802/882–2047* 🌐 *www.benjerry.com* 🎟 *Tours $6.*

★ Cold Hollow Cider Mill

FARM/RANCH | **FAMILY** | You can watch apples pressed into possibly the world's best cider at this working mill and sample it right from the tank. Its store sells all the apple butter, jams and jellies, and Vermont-made handicrafts you could want, plus the legendary 75¢ cider doughnuts. Kids love watching the "doughnut robot"

Northern Vermont
QUÉBEC
NEW YORK
NEW HAMPSHIRE
Rouses Point
Champlain
Alburg
Missisquoi National Wildlife Refuge
Swanton
Highgate Center
Enosburg Falls
Richford
North Troy
Jay
Jay Peak
Montgomery
Lake Memphremagog
Newport
Derby Line
Norton
Beecher Falls
Colebrook
Lake Carmi
Seymour Lake
Island Pond
Orleans
Lowell
Westmore
Lake Willoughby
North Stratford
Chazy
St. Anne's Shrine
Alburgh Dunes State Park
Lake Champlain Islands
North Hero
Saint Albans
COLD HOLLOW MOUNTAINS
Albany
Bread and Puppet Museum
Hill Farmstead Brewery
Maidstone Lake
West Burke
Hyde Log Cabin
Grand Isle
Grand Isle State Park
Plattsburgh
South Hero
Fairfax
Milton
Cambridge
Jeffersonville
Hyde Park
Greensboro
Caspian Lake
Groveton
Guildhall
Burke Mountain
East Burke
Snow Farm Vineyard and Winery
Allenholm Farm
Lake Champlain
Smugglers' Notch Resort
Morrisville
Wolcott
Lyndonville
Lyndon
Port Kent
Ethan Allen Homestead Museum
Stowe Mountain Resort
Jericho
Hardwick
0
10 mi
0
10 km
Burlington
see detail map
Winooski
Essex Junction
South Burlington
Stowe
Danville
Concord
Willsboro Point
Shelburne Farms
Shelburne
Bolton Valley
Richmond
GREEN MOUNTAINS
Peacham
St. Johnsbury
Whitefield
Shelburne Museum
Shelburne Vineyard
Ben & Jerry's Factory
Molly's Falls Pond
Clemmons Family Farm
Vermont Teddy Bear Company
Waterbury
Morse Farm Maple Sugarworks
Marshfield
Barnet
Essex
Mount Philo State Park
Plainfield
Lake Groton
MONTPELIER
Lisbon
Barre
South Barre
Waitsfield
Northfield
Wells River
Woodsville
Westport
Vergennes
15
223
133
2
78
9
87
7
89
36
104
105
108
242
100
111
114
3
102
5
5A
16
15
128
12
14
116
17
22
302
91
93

in action. The tasting room is open daily with numerous ciders on tap. ✉ *3600 Waterbury–Stowe Rd., Waterbury Center* ✣ *3 miles north of I–89* ☎ *800/327–7537* 🌐 *www.coldhollow.com.*

Vermont Ski and Snowboard Museum

HISTORY MUSEUM | The state's skiing and snowboarding history is documented here. Exhibits cover subjects such as the 10th Mountain Division of World War II, the national ski patrol, Winter Olympians, and the evolution of equipment. An early World Cup trophy is on loan, and one of the most memorable mobiles you'll ever see, made from a gondola and ski-lift chairs, hangs from the ceiling. One recent exhibit, Slope Style, focused on ski fashion from 1930 to 2014. ✉ *1 S. Main St., Stowe* ☎ *802/253–9911* 🌐 *www.vtssm.com* 🎫 *$5* ⏲ *Closed Mon.-Wed.*

 Restaurants

Cork

$$ | **INTERNATIONAL** | Pursuing a mission that "the best wines are grown, not made," this natural wine bar meticu lously curates an inventory of organic, biodynamic, no-additive, unfiltered, and wild-fermented vintages, either for sale in the small retail section in the front, or complementing upscale bistro dishes and boards in the classy dining room. **Known for:** mostly old-world wines, with some local labels; lots of charcuterie and shareable appetizers; in the heart of Stowe village. $ *Average main: $23* ✉ *35 School St., Stowe* ☎ *802/760–6143* 🌐 *www.corkvt.com* ⏲ *Closed Tues. and Wed.*

Doc Ponds

$$ | **AMERICAN** | A gastropub from the folks behind the Hen of the Wood restaurant, this place has one of the best beer lists in the state. The food is excellent and the ski-lodge vibe is perfect for lunch or dinner, families or romantic two-top or solo bar seats. **Known for:** lengthy local beer list; pub fare with Vermont ingredients; log cabin atmosphere with après-ski coziness. $ *Average main: $22* ✉ *294 Mountain Rd., Stowe* ☎ *802/760–6066* 🌐 *www.docponds.com.*

Harrison's Restaurant

$$ | **AMERICAN** | A lively locals' scene, booths by the fireplace, and creative American cuisine paired with well-chosen wines and regional brews make this place perfect for couples and families alike. The inviting bar is a good spot to dine alone or to chat with a regular. **Known for:** peanut-butter pie; wine and cocktail list; wood fireplace. $ *Average main: $23* ✉ *25 Main St., Stowe* ☎ *802/253–7773* 🌐 *www.harrisonsstowe.com* ⏲ *No lunch.*

★ Hen of the Wood

$$$ | **ECLECTIC** | Ask Vermont's great chefs where they go for a tremendous meal, and Hen of the Wood inevitably tops the list, thanks to its sophisticated, almost artful, dishes that showcase an abundance of local produce, meat, and cheese. The utterly romantic candlelit setting is riveting: a converted 1835 gristmill beside a waterfall. **Known for:** special occasions and dates; outstanding cooking; wine and cocktail list. $ *Average main: $28* ✉ *92 Stowe St., Waterbury* ☎ *802/244–7300* 🌐 *www.henofthewood.com* ⏲ *Closed Sun. and Mon. No lunch.*

Idletyme Brewing Company

$$$ | **AMERICAN** | In prime position on the mountain road and the Stowe Recreation Path, this brewpub's Bavarian-style lagers and Vermont IPAs are only available on-site. A solid menu of pub food, a large outdoor patio, vegetable garden, and a rich, rustic, chic design, make it a popular stop. **Known for:** "brew-ski" beer flights; ample space for large groups; outdoor Biergarten. $ *Average main: $26* ✉ *1859 Mountain Rd., Stowe* ☎ *802/253–4765* 🌐 *www.idletymebrewing.com.*

Michael's on the Hill
$$$ | **EUROPEAN** | Swiss-born chef Michael Kloeti trained in Europe and New York City before opening this establishment in a 19th-century farmhouse outside Stowe. The seasonal three-course prix-fixe menus ($45 and $67) blend European cuisine with farm-to-table earthiness, exemplified by dishes such as spice-roasted duck breast and venison *navarin* (ragout). **Known for:** homemade potato gnocchi; wine list; views of Green Mountains and sunsets. *Average main: $34 ✉ 4182 Stowe-Waterbury Rd., 6 miles south of Stowe, Waterbury Center ☎ 802/244–7476 🌐 www.michaelsonthehill.com ⏲ Closed Tues. No lunch.*

★ **Prohibition Pig**
$ | **AMERICAN** | This restaurant and brewery in downtown Waterbury is always packed for a reason: fabulous craft beers, sandwiches, salads, and North Carolina–style barbecue served in an airy and friendly bar and dining room. If you just want a quick bite and a draft, belly up to the tasting-room bar at the brewery in the back, or pop across the street to the Craft Beer Cellar, one of the state's best beer stores. **Known for:** duck-fat fries; "craft" mac and cheese; one of the state's best draft lists and liquor collections. *Average main: $15 ✉ 23 S. Main St., Waterbury ☎ 802/244–4120 🌐 www.prohibitionpig.com ⏲ Closed Tues. and Wed.*

von Trapp Brewery & Bierhall
$$ | **AUSTRIAN** | In 2016, the Von Trapp family finally realized its long-held dream of opening a brewery making Austrian-style lagers on the grounds, and what a brewery it is. Built of thick, massive Vermont wood beams, the cavernous chalet-style space houses a rustic-chic restaurant and bar alongside the beer-making facilities serving Germanic classics, with plenty of beer to wash it down. **Known for:** Bavarian pretzels with beer-cheese dip; chicken schnitzel; Sachertorte and apple strudel. *Average main: $20 ✉ 1333 Luce Hill Rd., Stowe ☎ 802/253–5750 🌐 www.vontrappbrewing.com.*

Zen Barn
$$ | **ECLECTIC** | What's more Vermont than the name "Zen Barn," especially when it includes its own yoga studio in a former hayloft? Add to that an expansive, rustic-chic interior with local art and a stage for live music, an outdoor patio looking out to green fields and mountains, and a menu of eclectic, farm-to-table fare, and the local experience is complete. **Known for:** CBD cocktails; ramen soup; live performances. *Average main: $18 ✉ 179 Guptil Rd., Waterbury ☎ 802/244–8134 🌐 www.zenbarnvt.com.*

Coffee and Quick Bites

PK Coffee
$ | **CAFÉ** | The inviting atmosphere of this neighborhood joint is increased by the beans they use—North Carolina–based roasters Counter Culture Coffee, known for its coffee education and sustainable sourcing. Milk comes from Sweet Rowen Farmstead, and rotating breakfast sandwiches and baked goods, like buttermilk banana bread, are made in-house. **Known for:** maple lattes; expertly made espresso and drip coffee; baked goods and breakfast sandwiches. *Average main: $5 ✉ 1940 Mountain Rd., Stowe ☎ 802/760–6151 🌐 pkcoffee.com.*

Hotels

Field Guide Lodge
$ | **HOTEL** | This boutique enterprise just north of Stowe village is a whimsically stylish alternative to the town's staid resorts and cadre of inns stuck in ski-chalet mold. **Pros:** waffle kimono robes; seasonal heated pool and hot tub; Trail Suite, with a loft bedroom and view of Stowe's iconic white church. **Cons:** unique style not for everyone; no elevator; no coffee/tea in rooms. *Rooms from: $110 ✉ 433*

Continued on page 462

LET IT SNOW

WINTER ACTIVITIES IN VERMONT

SKIING AND SNOWBOARDING IN VERMONT

Less than 5 miles from the Canadian border, Jay Peak is Vermont's northernmost ski resort.

Ever since America's first ski tow opened in a farmer's pasture near Woodstock in January 1934, skiers have headed en masse to Vermont in winter. Today, 19 alpine and 30 nordic ski areas range in size and are spread across the state, from Mount Snow in the south to Jay Peak near the Canadian border. The snow-making equipment has also become more comprehensive over the years, with more than 80% of the trails in the state using man-made snow. Here are some of the best ski areas by various categories:

GREAT FOR KIDS **Smugglers' Notch, Okemo,** and **Bromley Mountain** all offer terrific kids' programs, with classes organized by age categories and by skill level. Kids as young as 3 (4 at some ski areas) can start learning. Child care, with activities like stories, singing, and arts and crafts, are available for those too young to ski; some ski areas, like Smuggler's Notch, offer babysitting with no minimum age daytime and evening.

BEST FOR BEGINNERS Beginner terrain makes up nearly half of the mountain at **Stratton**, where options include private and group lessons for first-timers. Also good are small but family-friendly **Bolton Valley** and **Bromley Mountains,** which both designate a third of their slopes for beginners.

EXPERT TERRAIN The slopes at **Jay Peak** and massive **Killington** are most notable for their steepness and pockets of glades. About 40% of the runs at these two resorts are advanced or expert. Due to its far north location, Jay Peak tends to get the most snow, making it ideal for powder days. Another favorite with advanced skiers is Central Vermont's **Mad River Glen,** where many slopes are ungroomed (natural) and the motto is "Ski it if you can." In addition, **Sugarbush, Stowe,** and **Smugglers' Notch** are all revered for their challenging untamed side country.

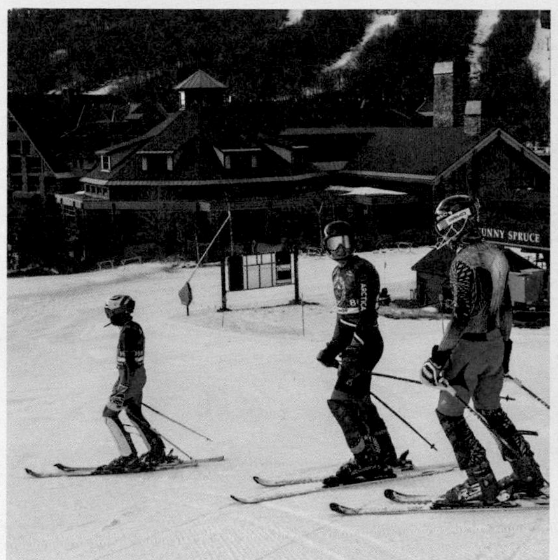

Mount Mansfield is better known as Stowe.

Stratton Mountain clocktower

NIGHT SKIING Come late afternoon, **Bolton Valley** is hopping. That's because it's the only location in Vermont for night skiing. Ski and ride under the lights from 4 until 8 Wednesday through Saturday, followed by a later après-ski scene.

APRÈS-SKI The social scenes at **Killington, Sugarbush,** and **Stowe** are the most noteworthy (and crowded). Stop by Stowe's Doc Ponds for one of the best beer lists around. For live music, try Castlerock Pub in Sugarbush or the Matterhorn Bar in Stowe.

SNOWBOARDING Boarders (and some skiers) will love the latest features for freestyle tricks in Vermont. **Stratton** has four terrain parks for all abilities, one of which features a boarder cross course. **Mount Snow's** Carinthia Peak is an all-terrain park–dedicated mountain, the only of its kind in New England. Head to **Killington** for Burton Stash, another beautiful all-natural features terrain park. **Okemo** has a superpipe and eight terrain parks and a gladed park with all-natural features. Note that snowboarding is not allowed at skiing cooperative **Mad River Glen.**

CROSS-COUNTRY To experience the best of cross-country skiing in the state, simply follow the Catamount Trail, a 300-mile nordic route from southern Vermont to Canada. **The Trapp Family Lodge** in Stowe has 37 miles of groomed cross-country trails and 62 miles of back-country trails. Another top option is **The Mountain Top Inn & Resort,** just outside of Killington. Its Nordic Ski and Snowshoe Center provides instruction for newcomers, along with hot drinks and lunches when it is time to take a break and warm up.

TELEMARK Ungroomed snow and tree skiing are a natural fit with free-heel skiing at **Mad River Glen. Bromley** and **Jay Peak** also have telemark rentals and instruction.

MOUNTAIN-RESORT TRIP PLANNER

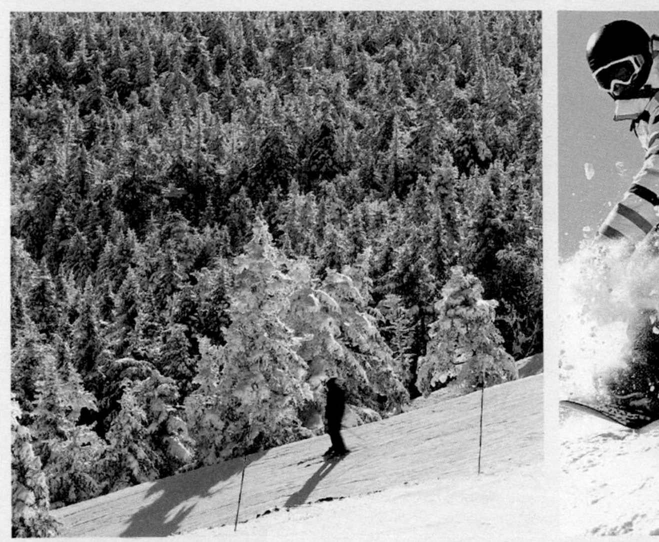

TIMING

Snow Season. Winter sports time is typically from Thanksgiving through April, weather permitting. Holidays are the most crowded.

March Madness. Most of the season's snow tends to come in March, so that's the time to go if you want to ski on fresh, nature-made powder. To increase your odds, choose a ski area in the northern part of the state.

Summer Scene. During summertime, many ski resorts reinvent themselves as prime destinations for golfers, zipline and canopy tours, mountain bikers, and weddings. Other summer visitors come to the mountains to enjoy hiking trails, climbing walls, aquatic centers, chairlift and horseback rides, or a variety of festivals.

Avoid Long Lift Lines. Try to hit the slopes early—many lifts start at 8 or 9 am, with ticket windows opening a half-hour earlier. Then take a mid-morning break as lines start to get longer and head out again when others come in for lunch.

SAVINGS TIPS

Choose a Condo. Especially if you're planning to stay for a week, save money on food by opting for a condominum unit with a kitchen. You can shop at the supermarket and cook breakfast and dinner.

Rent Smart. Consider ski rental options in the villages rather than those at the mountain. Renting right at the ski area may be more convenient, but it may also cost more.

Discount Lift Tickets. Online tickets are often the least expensive; multi-day discounts and and ski-and-stay packages will also lower your costs. Good for those who can plan ahead, early-bird tickets often go on sale before the ski season even starts.

Hit the Peaks Off-peak. In order to secure the best deals at the most competitive rates, avoid booking during school holidays. President's Week in February is the busiest, because that's when Northeastern schools have their spring break.

Top left, Killington's six mountains make up the largest ski area in Vermont. Top right, Stratton has a Snowboard-cross course.

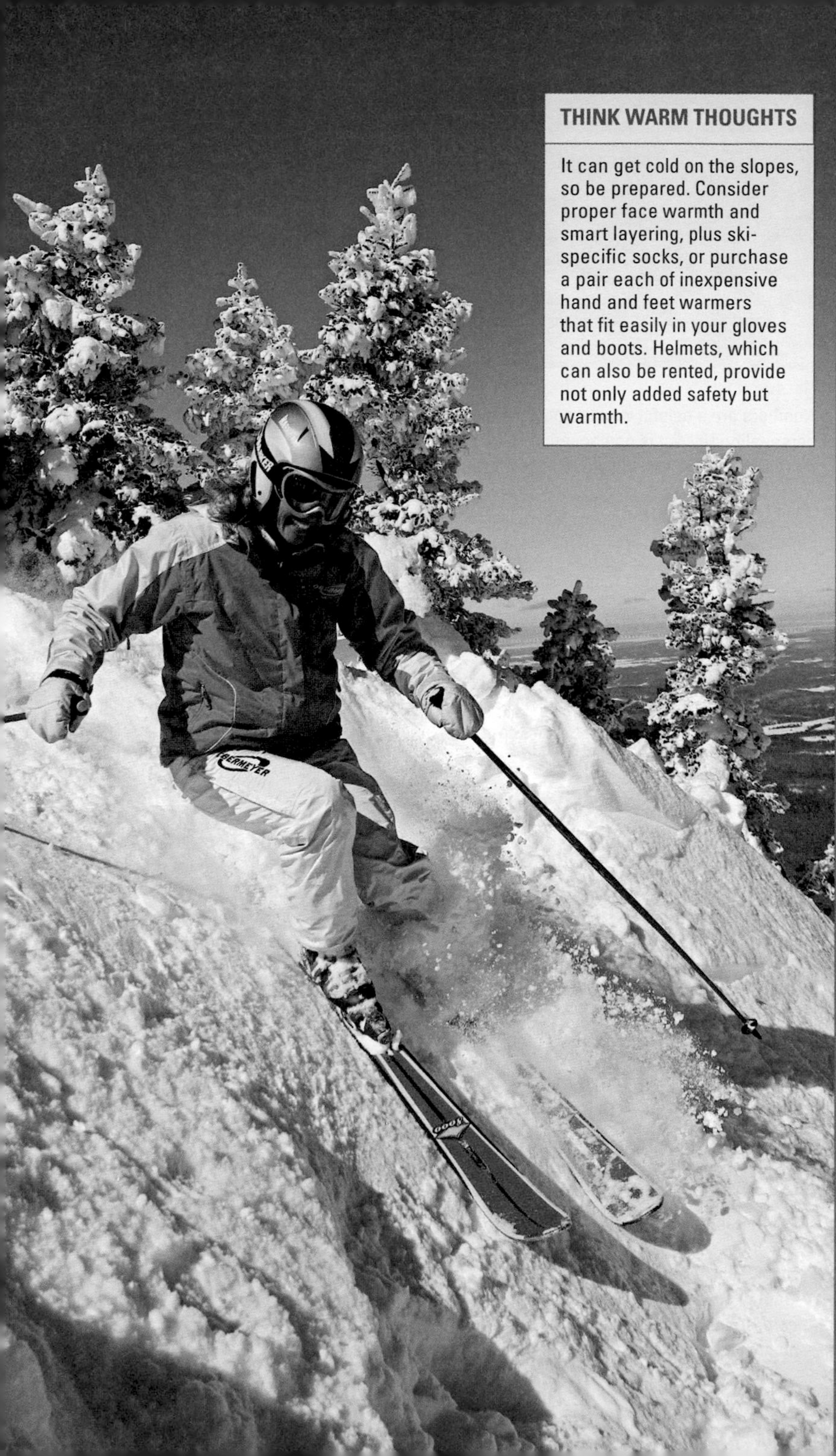

THINK WARM THOUGHTS

It can get cold on the slopes, so be prepared. Consider proper face warmth and smart layering, plus ski-specific socks, or purchase a pair each of inexpensive hand and feet warmers that fit easily in your gloves and boots. Helmets, which can also be rented, provide not only added safety but warmth.

VERMONT SKI AREAS BY THE NUMBERS

Okemo's wide slopes attract snowbirds to Ludlow in Central Vermont.

Numbers are a helpful way to compare mountains, but remember that each resort has a distinct personality. This list is composed of ski areas in Vermont with at least 100 skiable acres. For more information, see individual resort listings.

SKI AREA	Vertical Drop	Skiable Acres	# of Trails & Lifts	Terrain Type ●	■	◆/◆◆	Snowboarding Options
Bolton Valley	1704	300	70/6	36%	37%	27%	Terrain Park
Bromley Mountain	1334	178	47/9	30%	36%	34%	Terrain Park
Burke Mountain	2011	270	50/6	10%	44%	46%	Terrain Park
Jay Peak Resort	2153	385	78/22	22%	39%	41%	Terrain Park
Killington Resort	3050	1509	155/21	17%	40%	43%	Terrain Park, Halfpipe
Mad River Glen	2037	115	52/5	30%	30%	40%	Snowboarding Not Allowed
Magic Mountain	1500	205	50/6	26%	30%	44%	Terrain Park
Mount Snow Resort	1700	588	80/20	14%	73%	13%	Terrain Park, Halfpipe
Okemo	2200	655	120/19	31%	38%	31%	Terrain Park, Superpipe, TerrainCross Park
Pico Mountain	1967	468	58/7	18%	46%	36%	Triple Slope, Terrain Park
Smugglers' Notch Resort	2610	311	78/8	19%	50%	31%	Terrain Park
Stowe Mountain Resort	2160	485	116/13	16%	59%	25%	Terrain Park
Stratton Mountain Resort	2003	670	99/11	40%	30%	25%	Terrain Park, Halfpipe, SnowboardCross Course
Sugarbush Resort	2600	578	111/16	20%	45%	30%	Terrain Park
Suicide Six	650	100	24/3	30%	40%	30%	Terrain Park

CONTACT THE EXPERTS

Ski Vermont (☎ *802/223-2439* 🌐 *www.skivermont.com*), a non-profit association in Montpelier, Vermont, and **Vermont Department of Tourism** (🌐 *www.vermontvacation.com*) are great resources for travelers planning a wintertime trip to Vermont.

KNOW YOUR SIGNS

On trail maps and the mountains, trails are rated and marked:

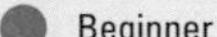

● Beginner  Advanced

■ Intermediate  Expert

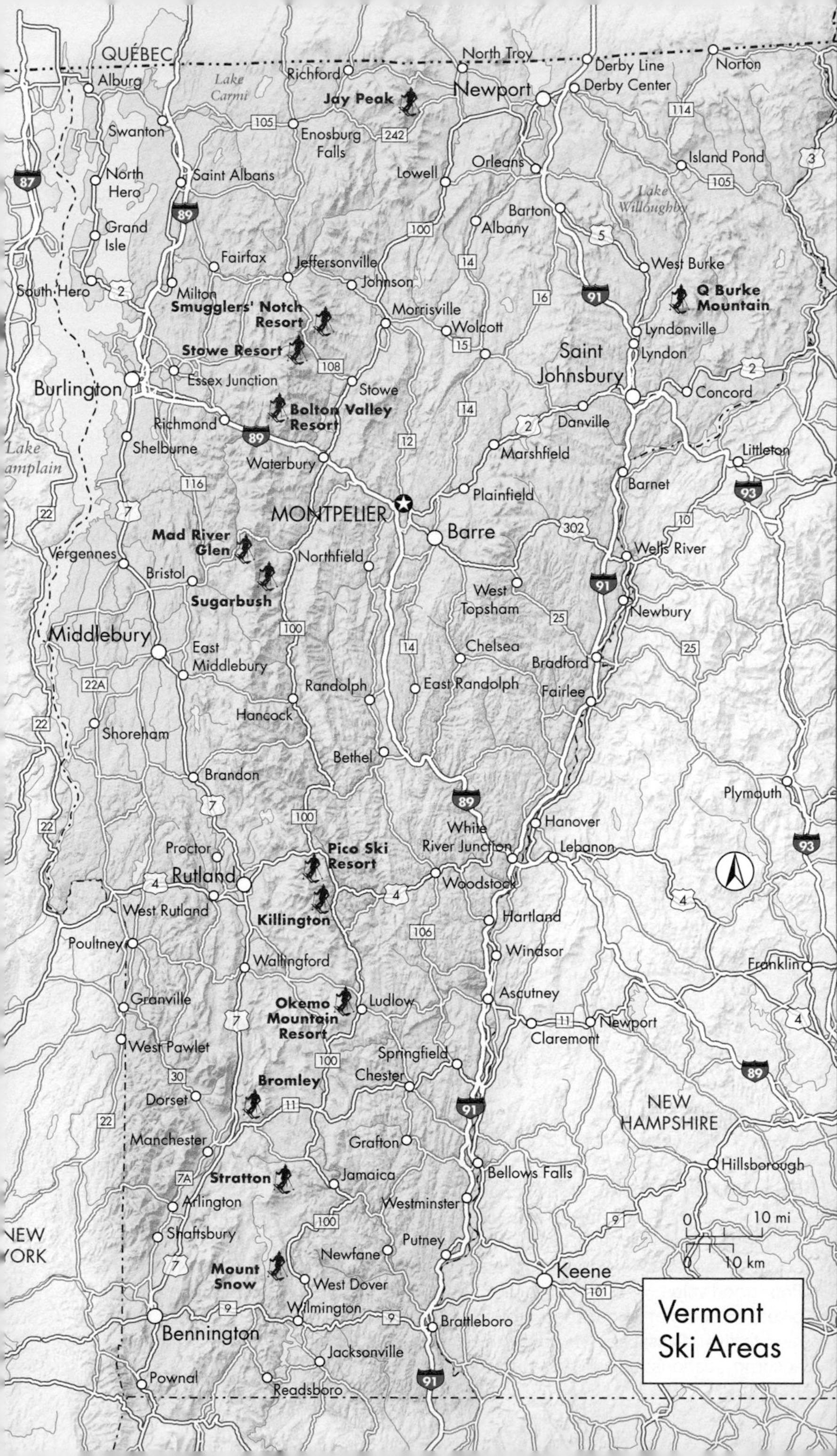

Vermont Ski Areas

QUÉBEC
NEW YORK
NEW HAMPSHIRE
Lake Carmi
Lake Willoughby
Lake Champlain

Jay Peak
Q Burke Mountain
Smugglers' Notch Resort
Stowe Resort
Bolton Valley Resort
Mad River Glen
Sugarbush
Pico Ski Resort
Killington
Okemo Mountain Resort
Bromley
Stratton
Mount Snow

Alburg
Richford
North Troy
Newport
Derby Line
Derby Center
Norton
Swanton
Enosburg Falls
Island Pond
North Hero
Saint Albans
Lowell
Orleans
Grand Isle
Barton
Albany
Fairfax
Jeffersonville
Johnson
West Burke
South Hero
Milton
Morrisville
Wolcott
Lyndonville
Lyndon
Saint Johnsbury
Concord
Burlington
Essex Junction
Stowe
Richmond
Danville
Shelburne
Waterbury
Marshfield
Littleton
Plainfield
Barnet
MONTPELIER
Barre
Wells River
Vergennes
Northfield
Bristol
West Topsham
Newbury
Middlebury
East Middlebury
Chelsea
Bradford
Randolph
East Randolph
Fairlee
Hancock
Shoreham
Bethel
Brandon
Plymouth
Hanover
White River Junction
Lebanon
Proctor
Rutland
Woodstock
West Rutland
Hartland
Poultney
Windsor
Wallingford
Franklin
Granville
Ludlow
Ascutney
Newport
Claremont
West Pawlet
Springfield
Chester
Dorset
Manchester
Grafton
Bellows Falls
Hillsborough
Jamaica
Arlington
Westminster
Shaftsbury
Putney
Newfane
Keene
West Dover
Wilmington
Bennington
Brattleboro
Jacksonville
Pownal
Readsboro

87
89
2
105
242
100
14
16
5
91
114
3
15
108
12
2
116
7
22
302
10
93
25
22A
4
106
11
30
7A
9
101

0 — 10 mi
0 — 10 km

Mountain Rd., Stowe ☎ 802/253–8088 🌐 https://www.larkhotels.com/hotels/field-guide-lodge ⇨ 30 rooms 🍽 Free Breakfast.

Green Mountain Inn

$ | **B&B/INN** | Smack-dab in the center of Stowe Village, this classic redbrick inn has been welcoming guests since 1833; rooms in the main building and the annex feel like a country inn, while the newer buildings refine with added luxury and space. **Pros:** easy walking distance to entire village and main sights; luxury rooms include large Jacuzzis; 300-thread-count Egyptian cotton bedding and Frette bathrobes. **Cons:** farther from skiing than other area hotels; road noise in front of building; no tea in rooms. [$] *Rooms from: $169 ✉ 18 Main St., Stowe ☎ 802/253–7301, 800/253–7302 🌐 www.greenmountaininn.com ⇨ 104 rooms 🍽 No Meals.*

Stone Hill Inn

$$$ | **B&B/INN** | A contemporary, romance-inducing bed-and-breakfast where classical music plays in the hallways, Stone Hill has guest rooms with two-sink vanities and two-person whirlpools in front of double-sided fireplaces. **Pros:** perennial gardens with stream; complimentary toboggan and snowshoes; Gilchrist & Soames bathroom amenities. **Cons:** possibly depressing for single people; two-night minimum on weekends and in peak period; no children allowed. [$] *Rooms from: $309 ✉ 89 Houston Farm Rd., Stowe ☎ 802/253–6282 🌐 www.stonehillinn.com ⇨ 9 rooms 🍽 Free Breakfast.*

Stowe Motel & Snowdrift

$ | **HOTEL** | **FAMILY** | The accommodations at this family-owned motel on 14 acres range from studios with small kitchenettes and modern two-bedroom suites warmed by their own fireplaces to rental houses that can sleep 10 or more people. **Pros:** good value for cost; complimentary bikes; 16 acres of landscaped grounds next to river. **Cons:** basic motel-style accommodations; design and furnishings could use an update; occasional road noise. [$] *Rooms from: $149 ✉ 2043 Mountain Rd., Stowe ☎ 802/253–7629, 800/829–7629 🌐 www.stowemotel.com ⇨ 62 rooms 🍽 Free Breakfast.*

★ Spruce Peak

$$ | **RESORT** | At the base of Mount Mansfield and Spruce Peak, this lodge would be king of the hill for its location alone, but a stay here also affords many perks including dining outposts like Tipsy Trout and Alpine Hall and rustic-meets-contemporary accommodations that run the gamut from studios and four-bedroom penthouse units to modern slopeside condos. **Pros:** mountain views; lots of children's activities; many shops supply all needs. **Cons:** somewhat sterile feel; no separate kids' pool; expensive breakfast. [$] *Rooms from: $269 ✉ 7412 Mountain Rd., Stowe ☎ 802/253–3560, 888/478–6938 reservations 🌐 www.sprucepeak.com ⇨ 300 rooms 🍽 No Meals.*

Stoweflake Mountain Resort and Spa

$ | **RESORT** | With one of the largest spas in the area, Stoweflake lets you enjoy an herb-and-flower labyrinth, a fitness center reached via a covered bridge, and a hydrotherapy waterfall that cascades into a hot tub. **Pros:** walking distances to many restaurants; wide range of rooms; across the street from the recreation path. **Cons:** mazelike layout can make rooms a bit hard to find; uninspired room design; no tea in rooms. [$] *Rooms from: $198 ✉ 1746 Mountain Rd., Stowe ☎ 800/253–2232 🌐 www.stoweflake.com ⇨ 180 rooms 🍽 No Meals.*

Sun & Ski Inn and Suites

$ | **HOTEL** | Not many hotels can boast having a bowling alley, but this part-new, part-renovated inn can top even that, adding an 18-hole minigolf course, an indoor pool, and small fitness center. **Pros:** close to the slopes; the family-friendly restaurant is open daily for lunch and dinner; tea/coffeemakers in rooms. **Cons:** not very Vermonty; family friendly can mean lots of children; often two-night minimum stay. *Rooms from: $189* *1613 Mountain Rd., Stowe* *802/253–7159, 800/448–5223* *www.sunandskiinn.com* *39 rooms* *Free Breakfast.*

★ Topnotch Resort

$$$ | RESORT | FAMILY | On 120 acres overlooking Mt. Mansfield, this posh property has a contemporary look, excellent dining options, and one of the best spas in Vermont, which combine to create a world unto itself. **Pros:** ski shuttle will take you directly to the slopes; complimentary tea and cookies every afternoon; American bistro cuisine at the intimate Flannel or tuned-up bar bites at the Roost, the lively lobby bar. **Cons:** boutique style may not be for everyone; no tea in rooms; room rates fluctuate wildly. *Rooms from: $350* *4000 Mountain Rd., Stowe* *800/451–8686, 802/253–8585* *www.topnotchresort.com* *91 rooms* *No Meals.*

★ Trapp Family Lodge

$$ | RESORT | FAMILY | Built by the Von Trapp family (of *The Sound of Music* fame), this Tyrolean lodge is surrounded by some of the best mountain views in Vermont and abundant romantic ambience, making it a favorite for weddings. **Pros:** alive with the sound of music; excellent beer brewed on-site; concert series and festivals in warm weather. **Cons:** some sections appear tired and in need of updating; overrun by tourists, especially on weekends; if not an active person, you'll miss half the amenities. *Rooms from: $225* *700 Trapp Hill Rd., Stowe* *802/253–8511, 800/826–7000* *www.trappfamily.com* *214 rooms* *No Meals.*

Performing Arts

The Current

ARTS CENTERS | Above the local library, Stowe's premier art center hosts impressive rotating exhibitions of contemporary and local art throughout the year, as well as film screenings. It also provides art education to adults and children alike through workshops, lectures, events, and courses. *90 Pond St., Stowe* *802/253–8358* *www.helenday.com.*

Spruce Peak Performing Arts Center

CONCERTS | Part of the Spruce Peak complex, this state-of-the-art space hosts theater, music, and dance performances. *122 Hourglass Dr., Stowe* *802/760–4634* *www.sprucepeakarts.org.*

Shopping

CRAFTS

Jeremy Ayers Pottery

CERAMICS | One of Vermont's most skilled and distinctive potters welcomes visitors to his shop and studio in downtown Waterbury. Keep an eye out for his Waterbury Breakfast Club, which adds food trucks and artists every other Sunday, June–September. A few apartments are also available to rent in the guesthouse; the on-site venue space, 18 Elm, is open for dinner parties and special occasion events. *18 Elm St., Waterbury* *802/363–3592* *www.jeremyayerspottery.com.*

FOOD

Cabot Cheese Annex Store

FOOD | In addition to shelves of Vermont-made jams, mustards, crackers, and maple products, the store features a long central table with samples of a dozen Cabot cheeses. *2657 Waterbury–Stowe Rd., 2½ miles north of I–89, Stowe* *802/244–6334* *www.cabotcheese.coop.*

Activities

CANOEING AND KAYAKING

Umiak Outdoor Outfitters

CANOEING & ROWING | This full-service outfitter rents canoes and kayaks, organizes tours, and sells equipment. It has seasonal outposts at the Waterbury Reservoir and at North Beach in Burlington. *849 S. Main St., Stowe* *802/253–2317* *www.umiak.com.*

FISHING

The Fly Rod Shop

FISHING | This shop provides a guide service, offers introductory classes, and rents tackle and other equipment. ✉ *2703 Waterbury Rd., 1½ miles south of Stowe, Stowe* ☎ *802/253–7346* 🌐 *www.flyrodshop.com.*

HIKING

Moss Glen Falls

HIKING & WALKING | Four miles outside of town, this short hike leads to a stupendous 125-foot waterfall that makes a great way to cool down in summer. ✉ *615 Moss Glen Falls Rd., Stowe* ☎ *888/409–7579 Vermont State Parks* 🌐 *www.vtstateparks.com.*

Mt. Mansfield

HIKING & WALKING | Ascending Mt. Mansfield, Vermont's highest mountain, makes for a challenging day hike. Trails lead from Mountain Road to the summit, where they meet the north–south Long Trail. Views encompass New Hampshire's White Mountains, New York's Adirondacks, and southern Québec. The Green Mountain Club publishes a trail guide. ✉ *Trailheads along Mountain Rd., Stowe* ☎ *802/244-7037* 🌐 *www.greenmountainclub.org.*

★ Stowe Recreation Path

HIKING & WALKING | An immaculately maintained, paved recreation path begins behind the Community Church in town and meanders about 5 miles along the river valley, with many entry points along the way. Whether you're on foot, skis, bike, or in-line skates, it's a tranquil spot to enjoy the outdoors. In autumn, there's a corn maze, and at least four shops along the path rent bikes. ✉ *Stowe* 🌐 *www.stowerec.org.*

ICE-SKATING SKIING

Stowe Mountain Resort

SKIING & SNOWBOARDING | The name of the village is Stowe, and the name of the mountain is Mt. Mansfield—but to generations of skiers, it's all just plain "Stowe." The area's mystique attracts as many serious skiers as social ones. Stowe is a giant among Eastern ski mountains with intimidating expert runs, but its symmetrical shape allows skiers of all abilities to enjoy long, satisfying runs from the summit. Improved snowmaking capacity, new lifts, and free shuttle buses that gather skiers along Mountain Road have made it all much more convenient. Yet the traditions remain, like the Winter Carnival in January and the Sugar Slalom in April, to name two. Spruce Peak, where you'll find the Adventure Center and the Mountain Lodge, is separate from the main mountain; the peak has a teaching hill and offers a pleasant experience for intermediates and beginners. In the summer, there's a TreeTop Adventure course and an awe-inspiring zipline that extends from the top of the gondola to the bottom in three breathtaking runs. **Facilities:** 116 trails; 485 acres; 2,160-foot vertical drop; 13 lifts. ✉ *5781 Mountain Rd., Stowe* ☎ *802/253–3000, 802/253–3600 for snow conditions* 🌐 *www.stowe.com* 🎫 *Lift ticket: $199.*

SPAS

Spa and Wellness Center at Spruce Peak

SPAS | This 21,000-square-foot facility has 18 private treatment rooms, a fitness center, and a year-round outdoor pool and hot tub. In addition to the usual array of facials, scrubs, and massages for adults, the spa offers a separate program for kids. ✉ *Spruce Peak, 7412 Mountain Rd., Stowe* ☎ *802/760–4782* 🌐 *www.sprucepeak.com.*

Spa at Stoweflake

SPAS | One of the largest spas in New England, the Spa at Stoweflake features a massaging hydrotherapeutic waterfall, a Hungarian mineral pool, 30 treatment rooms, and more than 150 treatments like the Bingham Falls Renewal, named after a local waterfall. This treatment begins with a body scrub and a Vichy shower, followed by an aromatherapy oil massage. The spacious men's and women's sanctuaries have saunas, steam rooms, and whirlpool tubs. ✉ *Stoweflake Mountain Resort and Spa, 1746 Mountain Rd., Stowe* ☎ *802/760–1083* 🌐 *www.stoweflake.com.*

Spa at Topnotch

SPAS | Calm pervades the Spa at Topnotch, with its birchwood doors, natural light, and cool colors. Signature treatments include the Mt. Mansfield Saucha, a three-stage herbal body treatment, and the Little River Stone Massage, which uses the resort's own wood-spice oil. There's even Rover Reiki (really) for your canine friend. Locker areas are spacious, with saunas, steam rooms, and whirlpool tubs. The indoor pool has lots of natural light. Daily classes in tai chi, yoga, and Pilates are offered in the nearby fitness center. ✉ *Topnotch Resort and Spa, 4000 Mountain Rd., Stowe* ☎ *802/253–6463* 🌐 *www.topnotchresort.com.*

Jeffersonville

18 miles north of Stowe.

Jeffersonville is just over Smugglers' Notch from Stowe but miles away in feeling and attitude. In summer, you can drive over the notch road as it curves precipitously around boulders that have fallen from the cliffs above, then pass open meadows and old farmhouses and sugar shacks on the way down to town. Below the notch, Smugglers' Notch Ski Resort is the hub of activity year-round. Downtown Jeffersonville, once home to an artists' colony, is quiet but has excellent dining and nice art galleries.

GETTING HERE AND AROUND

Like most places in Vermont, a car is essential to explore this area. From Burlington, it's about a 45-minute drive along Route 15. Or you can cruise north on Route 108 from Stowe for 30 minutes; however, the road is closed for much of the winter.

Stella14 Wines

WINERY | Master Sommelier David Keck moved home to Vermont in 2020 and started making wine with grapes from one of the state's oldest vineyards at Boyden Valley Winery. Now, Stella14's full lineup — from effervescent, lively pet-nats to intense, serious Frontenac Noir — is poured by the glass in the cozy tasting room or out on its large back patio and lawn. Wines from other Vermont producers such as La Garagista Farm + Winery, Ellison Estate Vineyard, and Iapetus are available for side-by-side tasting, too. ✉ *105 Main St., Jeffersonville* ☎ *832/431–1301* 🌐 *www.stella14wines.com* ⏲ *Closed Sun.–Wed.*

Coffee and Quick Bites

Burger Barn

$ | **AMERICAN** | **FAMILY** | Local grass-fed burgers and handcut fries are the name of the game at this bright-green food truck. Try one of Burger Barn's more inventive offshoots, like the Nutty Goat: goat cheese, maple crushed walnuts, caramelized onions, bacon and mayo. **Known for:** grass-fed burgers; food truck atmosphere and outside dining; cash only. 💲 *Average main: $8* ✉ *4968 Rte. 15, Jeffersonville* ☎ *802/730–3441* 💳 *No credit cards.*

★ Smugglers' Notch Resort

$$$ | **RESORT** | **FAMILY** | With five giant water parks for summer fun and just about every winter activity imaginable, including the new 26,000-square-foot indoor "FunZone 2.0," this resort is ideal for families; nightly rates include lift tickets, lessons, and all resort amenities. **Pros:** great place for families to learn to ski; views of several mountains; shuttles to the slopes. **Cons:** not a romantic getaway for couples; extra cost for daily cleaning; very busy during peak season.

$ *Rooms from: $322* ✉ *4323 Rte. 108 S, Jeffersonville* ☎ *802/332–6841, 800/419–4615* 🌐 *www.smuggs.com* *600 condominiums* *No Meals.*

Shopping

ANTIQUES

Route 15 between Jeffersonville and Johnson is dubbed the "antiques highway."

Buggy Man

ANTIQUES & COLLECTIBLES | This store sells all sorts of collectibles, including horse-drawn vehicles. ✉ *853 Rte. 15, 7 miles east of Jeffersonville, Johnson* ☎ *802/635–2110.*

CLOTHING

★ **Johnson Woolen Mills**

SHOPPING CENTER | This factory store has great deals on woolen blankets, household goods, and the famous Johnson outerwear. ✉ *51 Lower Main St. E, 9 miles east of Jeffersonville, Johnson* ☎ *802/635–2271* 🌐 *www.johnsonwoolenmills.com.*

Activities

KAYAKING

Vermont Canoe and Kayak

KAYAKING | This outfitter rents canoes and kayaks for use on the Lamoille River, and leads guided canoe trips to Boyden Valley Winery. ✉ *4805 Rte. 15, behind the Family Table, Jeffersonville* ☎ *802/644–8336* 🌐 *vtcanoeandkayak.com* *Closed mid-Sept.–late May.*

TOURS

Northern Vermont Llama Co.

SPECIAL-INTEREST TOURS | These llamas carry everything, including snacks and lunches, for half-day treks along the trails of Smugglers' Notch. Reservations are essential. ✉ *766 Lapland Rd., Waterville* ☎ *802/644–2257* 🌐 *www.northernvermontllamaco.com* *$60* *Closed early Sept.–late May.*

SKIING

Smugglers' Notch

SKIING & SNOWBOARDING | FAMILY | The "granddaddy of all family resorts," Smugglers' Notch (or "Smuggs") receives consistent praise for its family programs. Its children's ski school is one of the best in the country—possibly *the* best—and there are challenges for skiers of all levels, spread over three separate areas. There's ice-skating, tubing, seven terrain parks, Nordic skiing, snowshoe trails, and a snowboarding area for kids ages 2½–6. Summer brings waterslides, treetop courses, ziplines, and crafts workshops—in other words, something for everyone. **Facilities:** 78 trails; 300 acres; 2,610-foot vertical drop; 8 lifts. ✉ *4323 Rte. 108 S, Jeffersonville* ☎ *802/332–6854, 800/419–4615* 🌐 *www.smuggs.com* *Lift ticket: $85.*

Burlington

31 miles southwest of Jeffersonville, 76 miles south of Montréal, 349 miles north of New York City, 223 miles northwest of Boston.

As you drive along Main Street toward downtown Burlington, it's easy to see why this three-college city is often called one of the most livable small cities in the United States. Downtown Burlington is filled with hip restaurants and bars, art galleries, and vinyl-record shops. At the heart is the Church Street Marketplace, a bustling pedestrian mall with trendy shops, crafts vendors, street performers, and sidewalk cafés. To the west, Lake Champlain shimmers beneath the towering Adirondacks on the New York shore and provides the best sunsets in the state. The revitalized Burlington waterfront teems with outdoors enthusiasts who bike or stroll along its recreation path, picnic on the grass, and ply the waters in sailboats and motor craft in summer.

To the north, the eclectic enclave of Winooski, a newly refurbished former mill town, houses its own cadre of interesting bars, cafés, shops, and eateries.

Sights

★ Burlington Farmers Market

MARKET | Burlington's Saturday farmers' market is an absolute must-see when visiting in summer or fall. Set up in a spacious lot in the city's South End, the market is jam-packed with local farmers selling a colorful array of organic produce, flowers, baked goods, maple syrup, meats, cheeses, and prepared foods. Local artisans also sell their wares, and there's live music. ✉ *345 Pine St., Burlington* ☎ *802/310–5172* 🌐 *www.burlingtonfarmersmarket.org* 🎫 *Free.*

★ Church Street Marketplace

MARKET | **FAMILY** | For nearly 40 years, this pedestrian-only thoroughfare has served as Burlington's center of commerce, dining, and entertainment, with boutiques, cafés, restaurants, and street vendors the focus by day, and a lively bar and music scene at night. On sunny days, there are few better places to be in Burlington. ✉ *2 Church St., Burlington* ☎ *802/863–1648* 🌐 *www.churchstmarketplace.com.*

ECHO Leahy Center for Lake Champlain

SCIENCE MUSEUM | **FAMILY** | Kids and adults can explore the geology and ecology of the Lake Champlain region through the center's more than 100 interactive exhibits, including the newest additions at the Action Lab. The lab's 3D Water Projection Sandbox manages to make learning about watersheds exciting. You can also get an up-close look at 70 species of indigenous animals, or immerse digitally in the natural world at the 3D theater, which presents science and nature films every day. ✉ *1 College St., Burlington* ☎ *802/864–1848* 🌐 *www.echovermont.org* 🎫 *$18.*

Ethan Allen Homestead Museum

HISTORY MUSEUM | When Vermont hero Ethan Allen retired from his Revolutionary activities, he purchased 350 acres along the Winooski River and built this modest cabin in 1787. The original structure is a real slice of 18th-century life, including such frontier hallmarks as saw-cut boards and an open hearth for cooking. The kitchen garden resembles the one the Allens would have had. There's also a visitor center and miles of biking and hiking trails. In warmer months, climb Ethan Allen Tower at the south end of neighboring Ethan Allen Park for stupendous views of Lake Champlain and the Green Mountains.

■ TIP→ Don't forget mosquito repellent. ✉ *1 Ethan Allen Homestead, off Rte. 127, Burlington* ☎ *802/865–4556* 🌐 *www.ethanallenhomestead.org* 🎫 *$15* ⏲ *Closed Nov.–Apr.*

★ Foam Brewers

BREWERY | Co-founder and acclaimed brewer Todd Haire spent 13 years at Magic Hat Brewing and another two years at Switchback before opening his own Burlington operation alongside fellow co-founders Bobby Grim, Sam Keane, Jon Farmer, and Dani Casey in 2016. Since then, Foam has gained international praise, including a spot as one of the world's 10 best new breweries—bestowed by BeerAdvocate—the year they opened. Snack boards and food truck pit-stops compliment their sought-after drafts, also available at the attached sister restaurant, Deep City. An outdoor patio faces the stunning views of the Lake Champlain Waterfront. ✉ *112 Lake St., Burlington* ☎ *802/399–2511* 🌐 *www.foambrewers.com.*

Green Mountain Audubon Nature Center

SCIENCE MUSEUM | **FAMILY** | This is a wonderful place to discover Vermont's outdoor wonders. The center's 255 acres of diverse habitats are a sanctuary for all things wild, and the 5 miles of trails provide an opportunity to explore the

Burlington
TO NORTH BEACH
KEY
Sights
Restaurants
Quick Bites
Hotels
Lake Champlain
Burlington Bay
North Street
Allen St.
Peru Street
Monroe St.
Pearl Street
Cherry Street
Bank St
College Street
Main Street
King St.
Maple St.
Adams St.
Spruce Street
Cliff Street
Bayview St.
Marble Ave.
Howard St.
Catherine Street
Locust Street
Lakeside Avenue
Cherry Lane
Hoover St.
Sears Lane
Clymer St.
Flynn Avenue
Proctor Avenue
Henry St.
Loomis St.
Brookes Ave.
Pearl St.
Buell Street
Grant St.
Drew St.
Blodgett St.
Pitkin St.
North Avenue
Park Street
North Champlain St.
Murray St.
Elmwood Avenue
Clarke St.
North Winooski Ave.
North Union Street
School St.
Green St.
Booth St.
North Willard Street
Hungerford Terrace
Lake Street
Battery St.
South Champlain St.
Pine St.
Saint Paul St.
Church St.
South Winooski Ave.
South Union St.
South Willard Street
Saint Paul St.
Hayward St.
Pine Street
Locust Terrace
Charlotte Street
Caroline Street
South Union Street
S. Willard St.
Central Ave.
Conger Ave.
Alder Lane
Linden Terrace
Shelburne Street
Crescent Road
Briggs Street
Foster Street
Richardson St.
Wells Street
Orchard Rd.
A
B
C
D
E
F
1
2
3
4
5
6
7
8
9

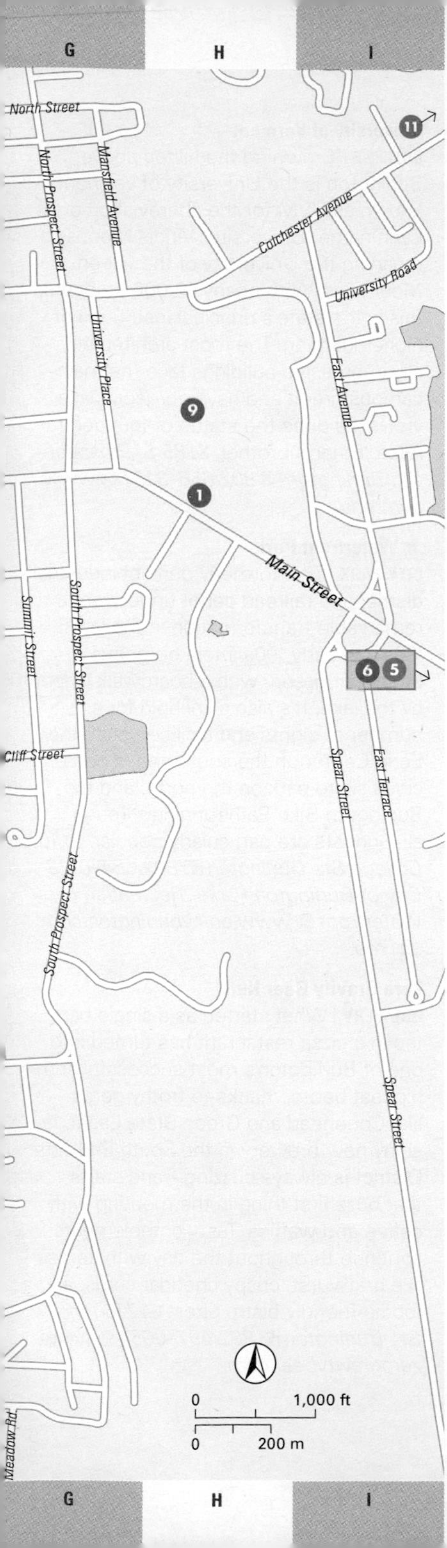

G H I

North Street
North Prospect Street
Mansfield Avenue
Colchester Avenue
University Road
University Place
East Avenue
Main Street
Summit Street
South Prospect Street
Cliff Street
Spear Street
East Terrace
Meadow Rd.
0 1,000 ft
0 200 m

G H I

Sights

1 Burlington Farmers Market........ H3
2 Church Street Marketplace............. E3
3 ECHO Leahy Center for Lake Champlain.......... C3
4 Ethan Allen Homestead Museum C1
5 Foam Brewers C2
6 Green Mountain Audubon Nature Center............ I4
7 Pine Street.............. D7
8 Switchback Brewing Co. C9
9 University of Vermont................. H3
10 Waterfront Park.......... C2
11 Zero Gravity Beer Hall................ D8

Restaurants

1 A Single Pebble......... D3
2 American Flatbread Burlington D3
3 Burlington Beer Company C8
4 Farmhouse Tap and Grill D3
5 Guild Tavern I4
6 Hen of the Wood Burlington D3
7 Honey Road E3
8 Istanbul Kebab House... E3
9 Leunig's Bistro and Cafe D3
10 May Day D1
11 Onion City Chicken & Oyster I1
12 Pizzeria Verita.......... D3
13 Restaurant Poco........ D3
14 Trattoria Delia D3
15 Zabby and Elf's Stone Soup E3

Quick Bites

1 Burlington Bay Market & Cafe C3
2 Kestrel Coffee Roasters D4
3 Onyx Tonics............. D3
4 Shy Guy Gelato........... E6
5 Speeder & Earl's Coffee................... D5

Hotels

1 Courtyard Burlington Harbor C2
2 Hilton Garden Inn....... D3
3 Hotel Vermont........... D2
4 The Lang House on Main Street............... F3
5 Made INN Vermont..... F4

workings of differing natural communities. Events include bird-monitoring walks, wildflower rambles, nature workshops, and educational activities for children and adults. ✉ *255 Sherman Hollow Rd., 18 miles southeast of Burlington, Huntington* ☎ *802/434–3068* 🌐 *vt.audubon.org* 🎫 *Donations accepted.*

Pine Street

NEIGHBORHOOD | A once-abandoned relic of the Industrial Revolution, Pine Street is the heartbeat of Burlington's recently revamped South End Arts District, an enclave of bars, restaurants, breweries, art galleries, and eateries. Start at the intersection of Pine and Maple Street and begin walking south to find a treasure trove of all things art, music, food, and drink. Dedalus Wine Market & Bar has one of the most expansive selections of natural wine on the East Coast. Myers Bagels has been turning out wood-fired, Montréal-style bagels for over twenty years. The S.P.A.C.E Gallery and Conant Metal & Light attract artists from within state borders and far beyond, and the popular restaurant and performance venue ArtsRiot hosts weekly food truck celebrations in the warmer months. Make sure to stop by The Soda Plant, a small business incubator with over thirty local artisans, artists, and makers inside a newly refurbished 19th-century industrial soda factory, including nationally acclaimed Brio Coffeeworks. ✉ *Pine St., between Maple and Flynn, Burlington.*

Switchback Brewing Co.

BREWERY | Switchback may not get as much press as other more famous craft Vermont beers, but it's a solid, respected brew that's well worth exploring at the brewery and taproom in Burlington's buzzing South End. In addition to super-fresh beer right from the tap and a short but savory menu of bar bites, the space hosts regular events and live music throughout the year. ✉ *160 Flynn Ave., Burlington* ☎ *802/651–4114* 🌐 *www.switchbackvt.com.*

University of Vermont

COLLEGE | Crowning the hilltop above Burlington is the University of Vermont, known as UVM for the abbreviation of its Latin name, Universitas Viridis Montis, meaning the University of the Green Mountains. With nearly 12,000 students, this is the state's principal institution of higher learning. The most architecturally impressive buildings face the main campus green and have gorgeous lake views, as does the statue of founder Ira Allen, Ethan's brother. ✉ *85 S. Prospect St., Burlington* ☎ *802/656–3131* 🌐 *www.uvm.edu.*

★ Waterfront Park

CITY PARK | This formerly derelict industrial district and railroad depot underwent a remarkable transformation in the late '80s and early '90s into a gorgeous stretch of green, with a boardwalk lapped by the lake. It's also a linchpin for a number of sights and facilities, with the Echo Center on the south end, a bodacious skate park on the north, and the Burlington Bike Path running through it all. Sunsets are particularly popular. ✉ *10 College St., Burlington* ☎ *802/864–0123 City of Burlington Parks, Recreation & Waterfront* 🌐 *www.enjoyburlington.com* 🎫 *Free.*

Zero Gravity Beer Hall

BREWERY | What started as a single bar tap in a pizza restaurant has turned into one of Burlington's most successful and hippest beers, thanks to frothy gems like Conehead and Green State Lager. Its shiny new brewery in the South End Arts District is always buzzing—and starts that buzz first thing in the morning with coffee and waffles. Tasty complements continue throughout the day with items like bratwurst, crispy cheddar curds, and foodie-friendly bistro bites. ✉ *716 Pine St., Burlington* ☎ *802/497–0054* 🌐 *www.zerogravitybeer.com.*

Beaches

North Beach

BEACH | FAMILY | Along Burlington's "new" North End a long line of beaches stretches to the Winooski River delta, beginning with North Beach, which has a grassy picnic area, a snack bar, and boat rentals. Neighboring Leddy Park offers a more secluded beach. **Amenities:** food and drink; lifeguards; parking (fee); showers; toilets. **Best for:** partiers; swimming; walking; windsurfing. ✉ *North Beach Park, 52 Institute Rd., off North Ave., Burlington* ☎ *802/865–7247* 🌐 *www.enjoyburlington.com/venue/north-beach* *Parking $8 (May–Oct.).*

Restaurants

American Flatbread Burlington

$$ | PIZZA | Seating is first-come, first-served at this popular pizza spot, and the wood-fired clay dome ovens pump out delicious and amusingly named pies like "Dancing Heart" (garlic oil, Italian grana padano cheese, toasted sesame seeds) and "Power to the People" (chicken, buffalo sauce, carrots, mozzarella, and blue cheese dressing) in full view of the tables. Fresh salads topped with locally made cheese are also popular. **Known for:** beers brewed on-site; spacious outdoor seating area; many ingredients sourced from farm 2 miles away. $ *Average main: $18* ✉ *115 St. Paul St., Burlington* ☎ *802/861–2999* 🌐 *www.americanflatbread.com.*

Burlington Beer Company

$$ | AMERICAN | For craft beer and inventive pub food, head to this spacious taproom in a historic factory building where the world-renowned Lumière brothers produced films in the early 1900s. Pair your pint of Strawberry Whale Cake (strawberry cream ale) or Vaulted Blue (IPA with notes of candied citrus peel and ripe peaches) with smoked trout dip and loaded birria fries, or opt for hearty sandwiches such as shaved steak or the mushroom Philly. **Known for:** lively, spacious atmosphere filled with natural light; pub food and apps to split; seasonal and classic craft beers. $ *Average main: $20* ✉ *180 Flynn Ave., Burlington* ☎ *802/863–2337* 🌐 *www.burlingtonbeercompany.com.*

Farmhouse Tap and Grill

$$ | AMERICAN | The line out the door on a typical weekend night should tell you a lot about the local esteem for this farm-to-table restaurant. Serving only local beef, cheese, and produce in a classy but laid-back style, Farmhouse Tap and Grill provides one of the finest meals in the area. **Known for:** local cheese and charcuterie plates; downstairs taproom or the outdoor beer garden; raw bar. $ *Average main: $20* ✉ *160 Bank St., Burlington* ☎ *802/859–0888* 🌐 *www.farmhousetg.com.*

Guild Tavern

$$$ | STEAKHOUSE | Some of Vermont's best steak—all meat is sourced from local farms, dry-aged a minimum of 21 days, and cooked to absolute perfection—can be found roasting over hardwood coals in this tavern's open kitchens. The space itself is also a treat, with antique chicken feeders serving as light fixtures and a soapstone-topped bar in the center. **Known for:** steak for two combo; poutine with hand-cut fries; extensive cocktail list. $ *Average main: $25* ✉ *1633 Williston Rd., Burlington* ☎ *802/497–1207* 🌐 *www.guildtavern.com* ⏲ *No lunch.*

★ Hen of the Wood Burlington

$$$ | MODERN AMERICAN | The Burlington branch of Hen of the Wood offers a slicker, more urban vibe than its original Waterbury location but serves the same inventive yet down-to-earth cuisine that sets diners' hearts aflutter and tongues wagging. Indeed, many consider this the best restaurant in Vermont, so drop your finger anywhere on the menu and you won't go wrong. **Known for:** mushroom toast; dollar oysters every night 4–5 pm; perfect date night spot. $ *Average* *main: $30* ✉ *55 Cherry St., Burlington* ☎ *802/540–0534* 🌐 *www.henofthewood.com* 🕓 *No lunch.*

★ Honey Road
$$$$ | **MEDITERRANEAN** | This Church Street restaurant has garnered multiple James Beard Foundation nominations, launching it into a golden age under the helm of co-owners Allison Gibson and chef Cara Chigazola Tobin. Serving arguably the best dinner in Burlington, high expectations are satisfied thanks to creative takes on eastern Mediterranean cuisine, including a selection of sensational mezes. **Known for:** daily Honey Time happy hour with $1 chicken wings; muhammara (hot pepper) dip with house-made pita; the cutting edge of local cuisine. 💲 *Average main: $45* ✉ *156 Church St., Burlington* ☎ *802/497–2145* 🌐 *www.honeyroadrestaurant.com* 🕓 *No lunch.*

Istanbul Kebab House
$$ | **TURKISH** | **FAMILY** | The classics of Turkish cuisine are served with surprising authenticity and maximum deliciousness thanks to the culinary talents of its Istanbul-raised owners, plus locally sourced produce and meats. The open terrace upstairs offers the only rooftop dining in Burlington. **Known for:** Turkish casseroles (güveç) baked in earthenware bowls; best kebabs in Burlington, if not Vermont; lavash bread made to order. 💲 *Average main: $19* ✉ *175 Church St., Burlington* ☎ *802/857–5091* 🌐 *www.istanbulkebabhousevt.com* 🕓 *Closed Mon.*

Leunig's Bistro and Cafe
$$$ | **CAFÉ** | This popular café delivers alfresco bistro cuisine with a distinct French flavor, plus a friendly European-style bar and live jazz. Favorite entrées include salade niçoise, *soupe au pistou* (vegetable and white bean soup with Asiago and pesto), and beef bourguignon. **Known for:** crème brûlée; Sunday brunch; outdoor seating on Church Street. 💲 *Average main: $28* ✉ *115 Church St., Burlington* ☎ *802/863–3759* 🌐 *www.leunigsbistro.com* 🕓 *Closed Mon. and Sun.*

May Day
$$ | **AMERICAN** | Local industry pros Mojo Hancy-Davis and Matthew Peterson launched this cozy neighborhood spot with a menu that ranges from nostalgic favorites—like a beef patty melt on rye—to delicately plated vegetable dishes, such as delicata squash with Bayley Hazen blue cheese custard and whey-braised tomatoes. Go lowbrow for drinks with a Narragansett lager, or highbrow with a bottle of grower Champagne. **Known for:** simple yet delectable desserts; adventurous natural wine list; bustling industry night on Mondays. 💲 *Average main: $22* ✉ *258 N. Winooski Ave., Burlington* ☎ *802/540–9240* 🌐 *www.maydayvt.com* 🕓 *Closed Tues.–Thurs. No lunch.*

Onion City Chicken & Oyster
$$ | **AMERICAN** | Laura Wade and Aaron Josinsky's new casual spot serves up fried chicken in various forms — from honey-butter wings to whole birds. Comfort-food sides include collard greens that you can add housemade bacon to, a whole grilled onion, fluffy beignets filled with cheddar, and yes, there are oysters (options change daily). **Known for:** sophisticated but fun atmosphere; lobster roll and hot dog baskets; well-made classic cocktails. 💲 *Average main: $20* ✉ *3 E. Allen St., Winooski* ☎ *802/540–8489* 🌐 *www.mlcvt.com* 🕓 *Closed Mon.–Wed. No lunch.*

Pizzeria Verita
$$$ | **ITALIAN** | "The truth is in the dough" is the long-standing motto of Burlington's destination for expert Neopolitan pies. The bubbled, chewy crusts are flame-kissed by live fire, and Italian-inspired ingredients are sourced mostly from local farmers like the house-made mozzarella that graces classic pies like the beautifully simple Margherita. **Known for:** excellent cocktails, especially the house negroni; wood-fired Neopolitan pizza; farm-sourced

ingredients. $ *Average main: $30* ✉ *156 St. Paul St., Burlington* ☎ *802/489–5644* 🌐 *www.pizzeriaverita.com.*

Restaurant Poco

$$ | **AMERICAN** | Owners Stefano Cicirello and Susie Ely parked what was originally Dolce VT food truck in a hip space that looks straight out of Brooklyn. The menu of shared plates changes regularly but leans global, with dishes such as Kung Pao cauliflower served alongside pork Milanese and a very good burger. **Known for:** cozy atmosphere; small plates to share; walk-in only. $ *Average main: $18* ✉ *55 Main St., Burlington* ☎ *802/497-2587* 🌐 *www.restaurantpoco.com* ⏲ *Closed Sun.–Tues. No lunch.*

A Single Pebble

$$ | **CHINESE** | "Gather, discover, and connect" is the slogan and theme at this intimate Chinese restaurant on the first floor of a residential row house. Traditional Cantonese- and Sichuan-style dishes are served family style, and the "mock eel" was given two chopsticks up on the Food Network's *The Best Thing I Ever Ate*. **Known for:** many vegetarian options; fire-blistered green beans wok-tossed with flecks of pork; chef's tasting menu. $ *Average main: $22* ✉ *133 Bank St., Burlington* ☎ *802/865–5200* 🌐 *www.asinglepebble.com* ⏲ *Closed Sun.*

Trattoria Delia

$$$ | **ITALIAN** | If you didn't make that trip to Umbria this year, the next best thing is this Italian country eatery around the corner from City Hall Park. The secret to the ambience goes well beyond the high-quality, handmade pasta dishes to the supercozy woody interior, a transplanted sugarhouse from New Hampshire. **Known for:** excellent wine list; wood-grilled prosciutto-wrapped Vermont rabbit; primo Italian desserts. $ *Average main: $27* ✉ *152 St. Paul St., Burlington* ☎ *802/864–5253* 🌐 *www.trattoriadelia.com* ⏲ *No lunch.*

Zabby and Elf's Stone Soup

$ | **AMERICAN** | The open front, woody interior, and community spirit make Stone Soup a downtown favorite for lunch, especially on warm days. The small but robust salad bar is the centerpiece, with excellent hot and cold dishes—a perfect complement to the wonderful soups and fresh sandwiches. **Known for:** vegetarian dishes; gluten-free baked goods; New York Jewish-style cooking. $ *Average main: $13* ✉ *211 College St., Burlington* ☎ *802/862–7616* 🌐 *www.stonesoupvt.com* ⏲ *Closed Sun. and Mon.*

Coffee and Quick Bites

Burlington Bay Market & Cafe

$ | **AMERICAN** | This may be a local hub for grabbing a quick sandwich or a case of beer, but its true fame stands with its seasonal creemee window. During the warmer months, lines snake around the corner for the café's beloved soft serve, particularly the house specialty: twisted black raspberry and maple ice cream in a cone, extra sprinkles. **Known for:** maple and black raspberry creemees; grocery staples and necessities; sandwiches, burgers, and hot dogs. $ *Average main: $5* ✉ *125 Battery St., Burlington* ☎ *802/864–0110* 🌐 *www.burlingtonbay-cafe.com.*

Kestrel Coffee Roasters

$ | **CAFÉ** | Two alumni of Blue Hill at Stone Barns, one of the country's most lauded restaurants, moved to Burlington in 2017 to realize their dreams of opening a coffee shop together. The duo focus on meticulously sourced beans roasted fresh in-house, scratch-made baked goods, and a frequently changing menu of farm-sourced sandwiches. **Known for:** small-batch roasted coffee beans; homemade baked goods; maple lattes. $ *Average main: $5* ✉ *47 Maple St., Burlington* ☎ *802/391–0081* 🌐 *www.kestrelcoffees.com* ⏲ *Closed Sun.*

Onyx Tonics
$ | **CAFÉ** | This coffee-tasting bar would satisfy the staunchest coffee aficionado, with its rotating menu of specialty drinks designed to highlight the texture and flavor profile of distinct beans and roasters; so it's not surprising that co-founder Jason Gonzales won a top 10 spot in the 2013 World Cup Tasting Championship (the coffee Olympics). If a coffee education is what you want with your morning cup, Onyx Tonics offers it—thankfully with a friendly and inviting atmosphere—as baristas have been known to warn against adding milk to a certain drip coffee, because it would raise the acidity of the brew and alter its delicate flavor. **Known for:** coffee-tasting bar; the VT Big Easy, coffee and chicory mixed with milk and maple syrup; featured espresso and drip coffee beans. *Average main: $6* *126 College St., Burlington* *802/777–2583* *onyxtonics.com.*

Shy Guy Gelato
$ | **ITALIAN** | Some of the best gelato outside of Italy is found on St. Paul Street. Co-owner Paul Sansone was inspired by his Italian heritage to work abroad as an apprentice to some of Southern Italy's most notable gelato masters; he returned to Vermont years later to open his own scoop shop alongside one of Burlington's longtime farm-to-table restaurant owners, Tim Elliot. **Known for:** small-batch gelato and sorbet made with local ingredients; fior di latte (fresh mozzarella) gelato; vegan-friendly sorbets. *Average main: $5* *198 St. Paul St., Burlington* *802/355–2320* *shyguygelato.com* *Closed Mon.–Wed.*

Speeder & Earl's Coffee
$ | **CAFÉ** | This family-owned coffee roaster has been turning out small-batch beans and blends since 1993, making it a well-loved local watering-hole for almost three decades. This quirky, funky café is a prime old-school spot to pick up a bag of beans or mull over the morning paper with a cup of Maple French Roast. **Known for:** small-batch coffee blends; house-roasted beans; quirky vibes in a sunny café space. *Average main: $4* *412 Pine St., Burlington* *802/658–6016* *speederandearls.com.*

Hotels

Courtyard Burlington Harbor
$$$ | **HOTEL** | A block from the lake and a five-minute walk from the heart of town, this attractive chain hotel has a pretty bar and lobby area with couches around a fireplace. **Pros:** right in downtown; some of the best lake views in town; across the street from park and lake. **Cons:** lacks local charm; a bit corporate in ambience; fee for self-parking. *Rooms from: $329* *25 Cherry St., Burlington* *802/864–4700* *www.marriott.com* *161 rooms* *No Meals.*

Hilton Garden Inn
$$$ | **HOTEL** | One of Burlington's newest hotels, this more playful edition of the Hilton family sits on an ideal location halfway between downtown and the lakefront, putting both in easy walking reach. **Pros:** some rooms have views of the lake; Vermont Comedy Club in the same building; well above average restaurant. **Cons:** uninspired design in rooms; surrounded by busy streets with traffic; small pool. *Rooms from: $309* *101 Main St., Burlington* *802/951–0099* *www.hiltongardeninn3.hilton.com* *139 rooms* *No Meals.*

★ Hotel Vermont
$$$ | **HOTEL** | Since opening in 2013, the Hotel Vermont has held the hospitality crown for style and cool, which is showcased in the almost magically spacious lobby, with its crackling wood fire, walls of smoky black Vermont granite, reclaimed oak floors, and local artwork. **Pros:** Juniper restaurant serves excellent cocktails; gorgeous rooms; unbelievable service. **Cons:** luxury doesn't come cheap; view of the lake often blocked by other buildings; additional fee for breakfast and

Burlington's Church Street is an open-air mall with restaurants, shops, festivals, and street performers.

self-parking. *Rooms from: $309* ✉ *41 Cherry St., Burlington* ☎ *802/651–0080* 🌐 *www.hotelvt.com* *125 rooms* *No Meals.*

The Lang House on Main Street
$$ | **B&B/INN** | Within walking distance of downtown in the historic hill section of town, this grand 1881 Victorian home charms completely with its period furnishings, fine woodwork, plaster detailing, stained-glass windows, and sunlit dining area. **Pros:** family-friendly vibe; interesting location; fantastic breakfast. **Cons:** no elevator; on a busy street; old-fashioned design not for everyone. *Rooms from: $219* ✉ *360 Main St., Burlington* ☎ *802/652–2500, 877/919–9799* 🌐 *www.langhouse.com* *11 rooms* *Free Breakfast.*

★ **Made INN Vermont**
$$ | **B&B/INN** | Few accommodations in Vermont find a dynamic balance between the traditional inn and trendy boutique spirit, but this eminently charming and quirky 1881 house topped with a cute cupola has done it. **Pros:** excellent location between the University of Vermont and Champlain College; vivacious and involved innkeeper; hot tub out back. **Cons:** bathrooms are private, but not en suite; rooms are modest in size; higher cost than most other inns in town. *Rooms from: $259* ✉ *204 S. Willard St., Burlington* ☎ *802/399–2788* 🌐 *www.madeinnvermont.com* *4 rooms* *Free Breakfast.*

Nightlife

Citizen Cider
BREWPUBS | The tiny parking lot out front gets jammed after 5 pm, as the spacious "tasting room" of this hard-cider maker fills with exuberant young, hip professionals and students. Sample cider straight or in a dozen or so cocktails. There's a full bistro menu, too. ✉ *316 Pine St., Suite 114, Burlington* ☎ *802/497–1987* 🌐 *www.citizencider.com.*

Higher Ground

LIVE MUSIC | When you feel like shaking it up to live music, come to Higher Ground—it gets the lion's share of local and national musicians. ✉ *1214 Williston Rd., South Burlington* ☎ *802/652–0777* 🌐 *www.highergroundmusic.com.*

Mule Bar

BREWPUBS | This Winooski watering hole pours some of the best craft brews from around the state and is a must for aficionados. Outdoor seating and above-average bar bites seal the deal for its young and hip clientele. ✉ *38 Main St., Winooski* ☎ *802/399–2020* 🌐 *www.mulebarvt.com.*

Nectar's

LIVE MUSIC | Jam band Phish got its start at Nectar's, which is always jumping to the sounds of local bands, stand-up comics, and live-band karaoke and never charges a cover. Don't leave without a helping of the bar's famous fries and gravy. ✉ *188 Main St., Burlington* ☎ *802/658–4771* 🌐 *www.liveatnectars.com.*

Radio Bean

LIVE MUSIC | For some true local flavor, head to this funky place for nightly live music, an artsy vibe, and a cocktail. Performances happen every day, but Tuesday night is arguably the most fun, as the Honkey Tonk band blazes through covers of Gram Parsons, Wilco, and the like. ✉ *8 N. Winooski Ave., Burlington* ☎ *802/660–9346* 🌐 *www.radiobean.com.*

Performing Arts

★ Flynn Center for the Performing Arts

CONCERTS | It's a pleasure to see any show inside this grandiose art deco gem. In addition to being home to Vermont's largest musical theater company, it hosts the Vermont Symphony Orchestra, as well as big-name acts like Neko Case and Elvis Costello. The adjacent Flynn Space is a coveted spot for more offbeat, experimental performances. ✉ *153 Main St., Burlington* ☎ *802/863–5966* 🌐 *www.flynncenter.org.*

Shopping

With each passing year, Burlington's industrial South End attracts ever greater numbers of artists and craftspeople, who set up studios, shops, and galleries in former factories and warehouses along Pine Street. The district's annual "Art Hop" in September is the city's largest arts celebration—and a roaring good time.

FOOD

Lake Champlain Chocolates

OTHER SPECIALTY STORE | This chocolatier makes sensational truffles, caramels, candies, fudge, and hot chocolate. The chocolates are all-natural, made in Vermont, and make a great edible souvenir. Factory tours are available. A retail branch is also on Church Street. ✉ *750 Pine St., Burlington* ☎ *802/864–1807 Pine St., 802/862–5185 Church St., 800/465–5909* 🌐 *www.lakechamplainchocolates.com.*

NU Chocolat

FOOD | This European-style chocolate boutique combines Swiss-trained chocolatier, premier Belgian equipment, a minimalist's eye for detail, and a family-owned mentality. Owners Laura and Kevin Toohey and their children, co-founders Rowan and Virginia Toohey, spotlight their chocolate craftsmanship with delights like cocoa-dusted almonds, chocolate-covered candied orange peel, and uniquely beautiful seasonal truffles. ✉ *180 Battery St., Burlington* ☎ *802/540–8378* 🌐 *www.nuchocolat.com.*

SPORTING GOODS

Burton

SPORTING GOODS | The folks who started this quintessential Vermont company also helped start snowboarding. The flagship store sells equipment and clothing; a second retail branch is in downtown Burlington, on 162 College Street. ✉ *80 Industrial Pkwy., Burlington*

☎ 802/660–3200, 802/333–0400 College St. 🌐 www.burton.com.

 Activities

BIKING

★ Burlington Bike Path

BIKING | FAMILY | Anyone who's put the rubber to the road on the 7½-mile Burlington Bike Path and its almost equally long northern extension on the Island Line Trail sings its praises. Along the way there are endless postcard views of Lake Champlain and the Adirondack Mountains. The northern end of the trail is slightly more rugged and windswept, so dress accordingly. ✉ *Burlington* ☎ *802/864–0123* 🌐 *enjoyburlington.com/place/burlington-greenway.*

Ski Rack

BIKING | Burlington's one-stop shop for winter sports equipment, the Ski Rack also rents bikes and sells running gear throughout the year. ✉ *85 Main St., Burlington* ☎ *802/658–3313, 800/882–4530* 🌐 *www.skirack.com.*

BOATING

Burlington Community Boathouse

BOATING | This boathouse administers the city's marina as well as a summertime watering hole called Splash, one of the best places to watch the sun set over the lake. ✉ *Burlington Harbor, College St., Burlington* ☎ *802/865–3377* 🌐 *enjoyburlington.com.*

Community Sailing Center

BOATING | FAMILY | Burlington's shiny new 22,000-square-foot Community Sailing Center has 150 watercraft to rent including kayaks, sailboats, and standup paddleboards for as little as $15 an hour. Private instruction and family lessons are available, as are floating yoga classes. ✉ *505 Lake St., Burlington* ☎ *802/864–2499* 🌐 *www.communitysailingcenter.org* ⏲ *Closed mid-Oct.–mid-May.*

Lake Champlain Shoreline Cruises

BOATING | FAMILY | The trilevel *Spirit of Ethan Allen III,* a 363-passenger vessel, offers narrated cruises, theme dinners, and sunset sails with breathtaking Adirondacks and Green Mountains views. The standard 1½-hour cruise runs four times a day; sunset cruises leave at 6:30 pm on Friday and Saturday. ✉ *Burlington Boat House, 1 College St., Burlington* ☎ *802/862–8300* 🌐 *www.soea.com.*

True North Kayak Tours

CANOEING & ROWING | This company conducts two- and five-hour guided kayak tours of Lake Champlain that include talks about the region's natural history and customized lessons. ✉ *25 Nash Pl., Burlington* ☎ *802/238–7695* 🌐 *www.vermontkayak.com.*

SKIING

Bolton Valley Resort

SKIING & SNOWBOARDING | FAMILY | The closest ski resort to Burlington, about 25 miles away, Bolton Valley is a family favorite. In addition to downhill trails—more than half rated for intermediate and beginner skiers—Bolton offers 62 miles of cross-country and snowshoe trails, night skiing, and a sports center. **Facilities:** 71 trails; 300 acres; 1,704-foot vertical drop; 5 lifts. ✉ *4302 Bolton Valley Access Rd., north off U.S. 2, Bolton* ☎ *802/434–3444, 877/926–5866* 🌐 *www.boltonvalley.com* 🎫 *Lift ticket: $89.*

Shelburne

5 miles south of Burlington.

A few miles south of Burlington, the Champlain Valley gives way to fertile farmland, affording views of the rugged Adirondacks across the lake. In the middle of this farmland is the village of Shelburne, chartered in the mid-18th century and partly a bedroom community for Burlington. Shelburne Farms and the Shelburne Museum are worth at least a few hours of exploring, as are Shelburne

Vermont's African American Heritage Trail 

The Vermont African American Heritage Trail (vtafricanamericanheritage.net) helps share the link between Vermont, the first state constitution to outlaw slavery, and African American residents who have lived here since the Revolutionary War. There are 22 sights throughout the state, including seven museums: Ferrisburgh's **Rokeby Museum & the Underground Railroad**; Middlebury's **Vermont Folklife Center**; the **Brandon Museum**; Manchester's **Hildene, The Lincoln Family Home**; the **Grafton History Museum**; Windsor's **Old Constitution House State Historic Site**; and Brownington's **Old Stone House Museum and Brownington Village.** The 148-acre **Clemmons Family Farm** in Charlotte, another stop along the heritage trail, celebrates the history, culture, arts and sciences of the African American diaspora via programs like on-site artist residencies, theater performances, literary events, and guided tours through the verdant property and its six historic buildings.

Orchards in fall, when you can pick your own apples and drink fresh cider while admiring breathtaking views of the lake and mountains beyond.

Just south of Shelburne is the beautiful, rural town of Charlotte. Expect to find open farmstands, rolling pastures and grazing cows along these serpentine roads, many of which offer hidden gems like u-pick berries and seasonal barbecues on the farm.

GETTING HERE AND AROUND

Shelburne is south of Burlington after the town of South Burlington, which is notable for its very un-Vermont traffic congestion and a commercial and fast food–laden stretch of U.S. 7. It's easy to confuse Shelburne Farms (2 miles west of town on the lake) with Shelburne Museum, which is right on U.S. 7 just south of town, but you'll want to make time for both.

Sights

★ Clemmons Family Farm

FARM/RANCH | Founded in 1962 by Jackson and Lydia Clemmons, this 148-acre farm is one of a handful of Black-owned arts and culture nonprofit organizations in the state, and one of the 22 landmarks on Vermont's African American Heritage Trail. Along with acres of lush farmland, forest, meadows and ponds, six historic buildings offer space for artist residencies, art exhibits, creative studios, retreats, small performances, and community events celebrating the African diaspora. The Storytelling Room in the Barn House is a community hub for arts, sciences and culture programs, including featured exhibits and speakers' series. *2213–2122 Greenbush Rd., Charlotte* *765/560–5445* *www.clemmonsfamilyfarm.org.*

Fiddlehead Brewing Company

BREWERY | There isn't much to the tasting room here, but there doesn't need to be: Fiddlehead only occasionally cans its celebrated beer, making this the best place outside of a restaurant to sample it on tap (and for free). Decide which one you like best and buy a growler to go—or, better yet, take it to Folino's Pizza next door, where the pies are mighty fine. *6305 Shelburne Rd., Shelburne* *802/399–2994* *www.fiddleheadbrewing.com* *Free.*

Mount Philo State Park

STATE/PROVINCIAL PARK | FAMILY | For many Vermont kids, this is their first hike, thanks to the relatively easy, gently rising, paved road that snakes around the sides to the top, where fabulous views of the lake and landscape await. If less inclined to walk, feel free to drive. ✉ *5425 Mt. Philo Rd., Charlotte* ☎ *802/425–2390* 🌐 *www.vtstateparks.com/philo.html* 🎫 *$5.*

★ Shelburne Farms

COLLEGE | FAMILY | Founded in the 1880s as a private estate for two very rich New Yorkers, this 1,400-acre farm is much more than an exquisite landscape: it's an educational and cultural resource center with a working dairy farm, an award-winning cheese producer, an organic market garden, and a bakery whose aroma of fresh bread and pastries is an olfactory treat. It's a brilliant place for parents to expose their kids to the dignity of farmwork and the joys of compassionate animal husbandry—indeed, children and adults alike will get a kick out of hunting for eggs in the oversize coop, milking a cow, and watching the chicken parade. There are several activities and tours daily, and a lunch cart serves up fresh-from-the-farm soups, salads, and sandwiches. Frederick Law Olmsted, the co-creator of New York City's Central Park, designed the magnificent grounds overlooking Lake Champlain; walk to Lone Tree Hill for a splendid view. If you fall in love with the scenery, arrange a romantic dinner at the lakefront mansion, or spend the night. ✉ *1611 Harbor Rd., west of U.S. 7, Shelburne* ☎ *802/985–8686* 🌐 *www.shelburnefarms.org.*

★ Shelburne Museum

HISTORY MUSEUM | FAMILY | You can trace much of New England's history simply by wandering through the 45 acres and 39 buildings of this museum. Some 25 buildings were relocated here, including an old-fashioned jail, an 1871 lighthouse, and a 220-foot steamboat, the *Ticonderoga*. The outstanding 150,000-object collection of art, design, and Americana consists of antique furniture, fine and folk art, quilts, trade signs, and weather vanes; there are also more than 200 carriages and sleighs. The Pizzagalli Center for Art and Education is open year-round with changing exhibitions and programs for kids and adults. ✉ *6000 Shelburne Rd., Shelburne* ☎ *802/985–3346* 🌐 *www.shelburnemuseum.org* 🎫 *$25* 🕓 *Call for hrs, which vary by season and museum.*

Shelburne Vineyard

WINERY | From U.S. 7, you'll see rows and rows of organically grown vines. Visit the attractive tasting room and learn how wine is made. Also available on-site is a Shelburne Vineyard collaboration called Iaepetus, a natural wine label from notable biodynamic winemaker Ethan Joseph. ✉ *6308 Shelburne Rd., Shelburne* ☎ *802/985–8222* 🌐 *www.shelburnevineyard.com* 🎫 *Tasting $7, tour free.*

Vermont Teddy Bear Company

FACTORY | FAMILY | On the 30-minute tour of this fun-filled factory you'll hear more puns than you ever thought possible, while learning how a few homemade bears sold from a cart on Church Street turned into a multimillion-dollar business. Patrons and children can relax, eat, and play under a large canvas tent in summer, or wander the beautiful 57-acre property. ✉ *6655 Shelburne Rd., Shelburne* ☎ *802/985–3001* 🌐 *www.vermontteddybear.com* 🎫 *Tour $5.*

Restaurants

Philo Ridge Farm & Market

$$$$ | AMERICAN | A leader in regenerative agriculture, two of the 400 acres of this diversified farm are dedicated to organic vegetable, flower, herb, and fruit production, which is then channeled into the market's sandwiches, salads, prepared foods, and pantry goods.

Farm-raised poultry, lamb, grass-fed beef, and heritage pork are the stars of the kitchen's elegant prix-fixe dinner menu, which changes seasonally. **Known for:** farm-raised ingredients; spectacular views; outstanding house-made buns with cultured butter. *Average main: $79* *2766 Mt. Philo Rd., Charlotte* *802/539—2912* *philoridgefarm.com* *Closed Sun.–Tues.*

Rustic Roots

$$ | AMERICAN | Scuffed wood floors and chunky country tables bring the "rustic" at this converted farmhouse—but not too much. An intimate bar and maroon walls adorned with woodcrafts and art add a touch of elegance, and the French-inspired food is carefully prepared. **Known for:** coffee-maple sausage; pastrami on rye; Bloody Marys. *Average main: $21* *195 Falls Rd., Shelburne* *802/985–9511* *www.rusticrootsvt.com* *Closed Mon. and Tues. No dinner Wed., Thurs., and Sun.*

Coffee and Quick Bites

Vermont Cookie Love

$ | BAKERY | The "Love Shack" on the side of VT Route 7 is known to have one of the best maple creemees in the state due to its use of Vermont maple syrup and high-butterfat dairy from Kingdom Creamery of Vermont. There are also coffee, vanilla, and chocolate creemees on offer, along with local Wilcox hard ice cream and house-made cookies made daily on-site. **Known for:** homemade cookies; maple and coffee soft serve; crushed cookie crumbles for topping cones and sundaes. *Average main: $4* *6915 Rte. 7, Ferrisburgh* *802/425–8181* *www.vermontcookielove.com* *Creemee window closed Nov.–Mar.*

Hotels

Heart of the Village Inn

$ | B&B/INN | Each of the elegantly furnished rooms at this B&B in an 1886 Queen Anne Victorian provides coziness and tastefully integrated modern conveniences. **Pros:** easy walk to shops and restaurants; elegant historical building; hypoallergenic bedding and memory foam mattresses. **Cons:** near to but not within Shelburne Farms; no room service; no children under 12. *Rooms from: $189* *5347 Shelburne Rd., Shelburne* *802/985–9060* *www.heartofthevillage.com* *9 rooms* *Free Breakfast.*

★ The Inn at Shelburne Farms

$ | B&B/INN | It's hard not to feel like an aristocrat at this exquisite turn-of-the-20th-century Tudor-style inn, perched at the edge of Lake Champlain—even Teddy Roosevelt stayed here. **Pros:** stately lakefront setting in a historic mansion; endless activities; proposal-worthy restaurant. **Cons:** lowest-priced rooms have shared baths; closed in winter; no air-conditioning. *Rooms from: $170* *1611 Harbor Rd., Shelburne* *802/985–8498* *www.shelburnefarms.org* *Closed mid-Oct.–mid-May* *28 rooms* *No Meals.*

★ Mt. Philo Inn

$$$ | B&B/INN | Practically on the slopes of Mt. Philo State Park in Charlotte, the 1896 inn offers gorgeous views of Lake Champlain from its outdoor porches and an ideal blend of historical and contemporary boutique decor. **Pros:** walking trail goes directly to Mt. Philo State Park; lots of local stonework incorporated; complimentary breakfast basket includes all the fixings. **Cons:** not walking distance to any sights; rooms too big for just one guest; you cook breakfast yourself. *Rooms from: $320* *27 Inn Rd., Charlotte* *802/425–3335* *www.mtphiloinn.com* *4 suites* *No Meals.*

Shopping

The Flying Pig Bookstore

BOOKS | It should come as no surprise that this bookstore is notable for its whimsy and carefully curated children's section: one of the owners is a stand-up comedian, and the other is a picture-book author. *5247*

At the Shelburne Museum, the restored 220-foot Ticonderoga steamboat is the last existing walking beam side-wheel passenger steamer.

Shelburne Rd., Shelburne ☎ *802/985–3999* ⊕ *www.flyingpigbooks.com.*

The Shelburne Country Store

GENERAL STORE | As you enter this store, you'll feel as though you've stepped back in time. Walk past the potbelly stove and take in the aroma emanating from the fudge neatly piled behind huge antique glass cases, alongside a vast selection of penny candies and chocolates. There are creemees, of course, but here the specialties are candles, weather vanes, glassware, and local foods. ✉ *29 Falls Rd., off U.S. 7, Shelburne* ☎ *802/985–3657, 800/660–3657* ⊕ *www.shelburnecountrystore.com.*

Lake Champlain Islands

Lake Champlain stretches more than 100 miles south from the Canadian border and forms the northern part of the boundary between New York and Vermont. Within it is an elongated archipelago comprising several islands—Isle La Motte, North Hero, Grand Isle, and South Hero—and the Alburgh Peninsula. Enjoying a temperate climate, the islands hold several apple orchards and are a center of water recreation in summer and ice fishing in winter. A scenic drive through the islands on U.S. 2 begins at Interstate 89 and travels north to Alburgh Center; Route 78 takes you back to the mainland.

ESSENTIALS

VISITOR INFORMATION Lake Champlain Islands Chamber of Commerce. ✉ *North Hero* ☎ *802/372–8400, 800/262–5226* ⊕ *www.champlainislands.com.* **Lake Champlain Regional Chamber of Commerce.** ✉ *Burlington* ☎ *802/863–3489, 877/686–5253* ⊕ *www.vermont.org.*

Sights

Alburgh Dunes State Park

STATE/PROVINCIAL PARK | This park has one of the longest sandy beaches on Lake Champlain and some fine examples of rare flora and fauna along the hiking trails. The wetlands are also an important area for wildlife refuge, providing a safe habitat for breeding, feeding, and nesting for surrounding animals like deer and wild turkey. ✉ *151 Coon Point Rd., off U.S. 2, Alburgh* ☎ *802/796–4170* 🌐 *www.vtstateparks.com/alburgh.html* 🎫 *$5.*

★ Allenholm Farm

FARM/RANCH | The pick-your-own apples at this farm are amazingly tasty—if you're here at harvest time, don't miss out. The farm also has a petting area with donkeys, miniature horses, sheep, goats, and other animals. At the store, you can buy cheeses, dried fruit, homemade pies, and maple creemees. ✉ *111 South St., South Hero* ☎ *802/372–5566* 🌐 *www.allenholm.com* 🎫 *Free.*

Grand Isle State Park

STATE/PROVINCIAL PARK | You'll find hiking trails, boat rentals, and shore fishing at Grand Isle. ✉ *36 E. Shore S, off U.S. 2, Grand Isle* ☎ *802/372–4300* 🌐 *www.vtstateparks.com/grandisle.html* 🎫 *$5.*

Hyde Log Cabin

HISTORIC HOME | Built in 1783, this log cabin on South Hero is often cited as the country's oldest surviving specimen. It's now home to the Grand Isle Historical Society. ✉ *228 U.S. 2, Grand Isle* ☎ *802/828–3051* 🎫 *$3* ⏲ *Closed weekdays mid-Oct.–May.*

Missisquoi National Wildlife Refuge

WILDLIFE REFUGE | On the mainland east of the Alburgh Peninsula, the refuge consists of 6,729 acres of federally protected wetlands, meadows, and woods. It's a beautiful area for bird-watching, canoeing, and walking nature trails. ✉ *29 Tabor Rd., 36 miles north of Burlington, Swanton* ☎ *802/868–4781* 🌐 *www.fws.gov/refuge/missisquoi.*

North Hero State Park

STATE/PROVINCIAL PARK | The 399-acre North Hero has a swimming beach and nature trails. It's open to rowboats, kayaks, and canoes. ✉ *3803 Lakeview Dr., North Hero* ☎ *802/372–8727* 🌐 *www.vtstateparks.com/northhero.html* 🎫 *$5.*

Snow Farm Vineyard and Winery

WINERY | Vermont's first vineyard was started here in 1996; today, the winery specializes in nontraditional botanical hybrid grapes designed to take advantage of the island's microclimate, similar to that of Burgundy, France. Take a self-guided tour and sip some samples in the tasting room—dessert wines are the strong suit. On Thursday evening, late May–September, you can picnic and enjoy the free concerts on the lawn. ✉ *190 W. Shore Rd., South Hero* ☎ *802/372–9463* 🌐 *www.snowfarm.com* 🎫 *Free* ⏲ *Closed late Dec.–Apr.*

Sand Bar State Park

STATE/PROVINCIAL PARK | One of Vermont's best swimming beaches is at Sand Bar State Park, along with a snack bar, a changing room, and boat rentals. ✉ *1215 U.S. 2, South Hero* ☎ *802/893–2825* 🌐 *vtstateparks.com/sandbar.html* 🎫 *$5.*

St. Anne's Shrine

HISTORIC SIGHT | This spot marks the site where, in 1665, French soldiers and Jesuits put ashore and built a fort, creating Vermont's first European settlement. Vermont's first Roman Catholic Mass was celebrated here on July 26, 1666. ✉ *92 St. Anne's Rd., Isle La Motte* ☎ *802/928–3362* 🌐 *www.saintannesshrine.org* 🎫 *Free.*

Restaurants

Blue Paddle Bistro

$$ | AMERICAN | This cozy, white clapboard house with an indicative blue awning has been a community staple for 17 years. Co-owner Mandy Hotchkiss and chef-owner Phoebe Bright share a decades-spanning friendship; today, their ongoing collaboration manifests in the bistro's seasonal menu and hand-written, daily changing nightly specials inspired by farm-sourced ingredients. **Known for:** Sunday brunch; crab cakes with mango chutney; plenty of Vermont-grown vegetables. 💲 *Average main: $24* ✉ *316*

U.S. Rte. 2, South Hero ☎ *802/372–4814* 🌐 *www.bluepaddlebistro.com.*

Kraemer & Kin

$ | **AMERICAN** | This family-owned microbrewery started in a Grand Isle garage in 2020. Now, it occupies the basement of the clubhouse at Alburg Golf Links, an 18-hole course with stunning views of Lake Champlain. **Known for:** creative small-batch beers brewed on site; local takes on classic clubhouse bites; golf course on the lake. 💲 *Average main: $12* ✉ *230 Rt.129, Alburgh* ☎ *802/796–3586* 🌐 *kraemerandkin.com* ⏲ *Closed Mon.–Wed.*

Hotels

Ruthcliffe Lodge & Restaurant

$ | **HOTEL** | If you're looking for an inexpensive summer destination—to take in the scenery, canoe the lake, or go biking—this will do quite nicely as the lodge is on the rarely visited Isle La Motte. **Pros:** inexpensive rates; high-quality restaurant; laid-back vibe. **Cons:** two-night minimum stays on weekends and holiday periods; quite remote; simple, bland design. 💲 *Rooms from: $142* ✉ *1002 Quarry Rd., Isle La Motte* ☎ *802/928–3200* 🌐 *www.ruthcliffe.com* ⏲ *Closed mid-Oct.–mid-May* *7 rooms* 🍽 *Free Breakfast.*

Activities

Apple Island Resort

BOATING | The resort's marina rents pontoon boats, rowboats, canoes, kayaks, and pedal boats. ✉ *71 U.S. 2, South Hero* ☎ *802/372–3922* 🌐 *www.appleislandresort.com.*

Hero's Welcome

BOATING | This general store rents bikes, canoes, kayaks, and paddleboards; come winter, they switch to ice skates, cross-country skis, and snowshoes. ✉ *3537 U.S. 2, North Hero* ☎ *802/372–4161* 🌐 *www.heroswelcome.com.*

Montgomery and Jay

51 miles northeast of Burlington.

Montgomery is a small village near the Jay Peak ski resort and the Canadian border. Amid the surrounding countryside are seven covered bridges.

GETTING HERE AND AROUND

Montgomery lies at the junction of Routes 58, 118, and 242. From Burlington, take Interstate 89 north to Routes 105 and 118 east. Route 242 connects Montgomery and, to the northeast, the Jay Peak Resort.

Sights

Lake Memphremagog

BODY OF WATER | Vermont's second-largest body of water, Lake Memphremagog extends 33 miles north from Newport into Canada. Prouty Beach in Newport has tennis courts, boat rentals, and a 9-hole disc-golf course. Watch the sunset from the deck of the East Side Restaurant, which serves excellent burgers and prime rib. ✉ *242 Prouty Beach Rd., Newport* ☎ *802/334–6345* 🌐 *www.newportrecreation.org.*

Coffee and Quick Bites

Miso Hungry

$ | **JAPANESE** | At the base of mammoth Jay Peak sits a wood-shingled food truck cooking arguably the best ramen in the state. Owners Momoko and Jordan Antonucci met as rafting guides in Japan, and spent three winters in Hokkaido gravitating towards the steaming bowls of noodles made at après-ski ramen trucks parked mountainside. **Known for:** spicy miso ramen; seasonal onigiri; authentic Japanese cooking made with Vermont-sourced ingredients. 💲 *Average main: $13* ✉ *830 Jay Peak Rd., Jay* ☎ *518/605–4474* 🌐 *www.misohungryramen.com.*

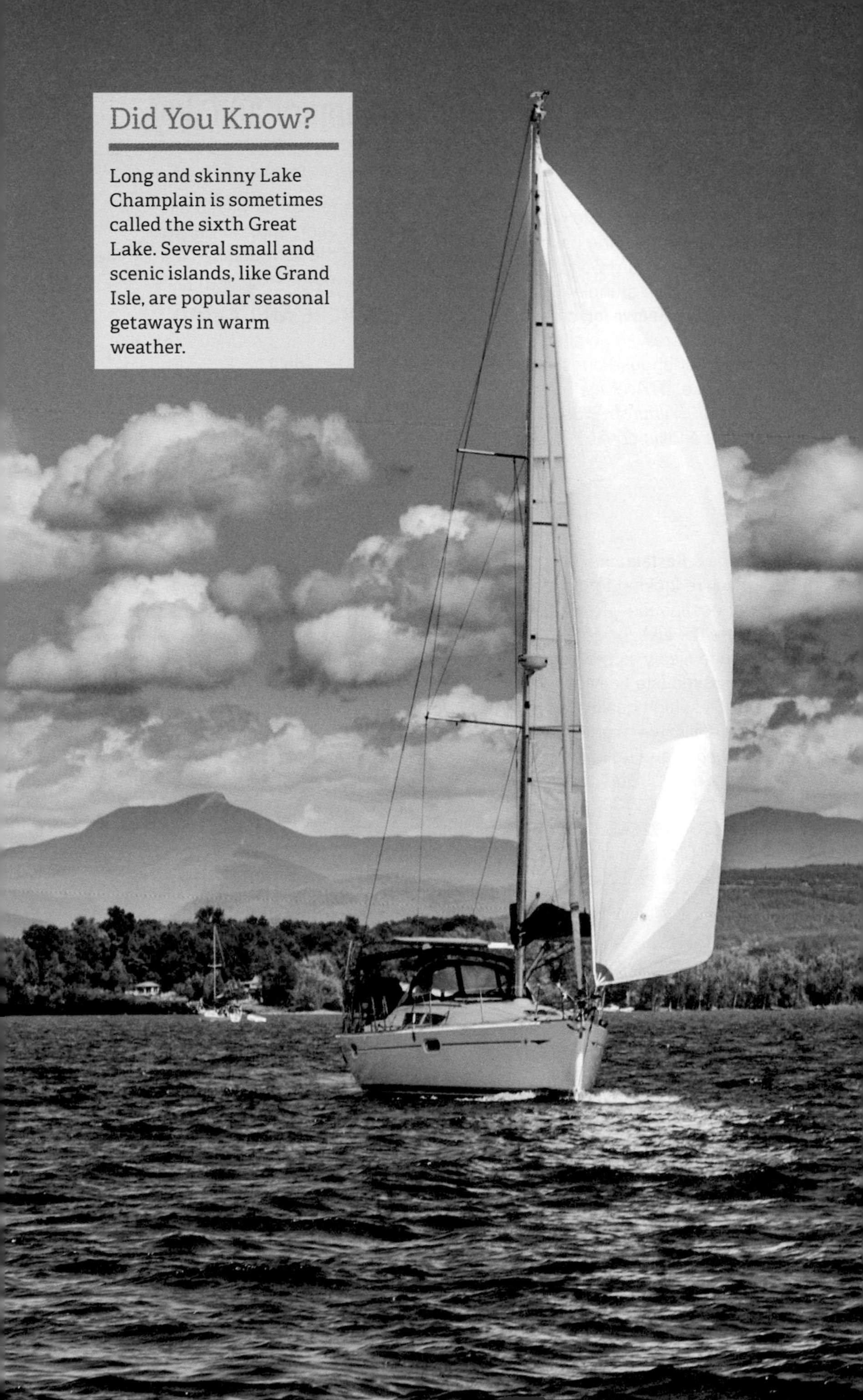

Did You Know?

Long and skinny Lake Champlain is sometimes called the sixth Great Lake. Several small and scenic islands, like Grand Isle, are popular seasonal getaways in warm weather.

Hotels

★ The INN

$ | **B&B/INN** | This smart chalet-style lodge comes with tons of character. **Pros:** Trout River views from back rooms; within walking distance of shops and supplies; smart, individually designed rooms. **Cons:** noise from bar can seep into nearby rooms; two-night minimum stay; outside food and alcohol not allowed. *Rooms from: $169 241 Main St., Montgomery 802/326–4391 www.theinn.us 11 rooms Free Breakfast.*

Jay Peak Resort

$$ | **HOTEL** | **FAMILY** | Accommodations at Jay Peak include standard hotel rooms, suites, condominiums, town houses, and cottage and clubhouse suites. **Pros:** slopes never far away; 60,000-square-foot indoor water park; kids 14 and under stay and eat free and complimentary childcare is provided. **Cons:** can get noisy; not very intimate; service can be lackluster. *Rooms from: $239 830 Jay Peak Rd., Montgomery 802/988–2611 www.jaypeakresort.com 515 units Free Breakfast.*

Phineas Swann Bed & Breakfast Inn

$ | **B&B/INN** | The top-hatted bulldog on the sign of this 1880 farmhouse isn't just a mascot: it reflects the hotel's welcoming attitude to pet owners. **Pros:** walking distance from shops and supplies; lots of dogs; each room has different design. **Cons:** decor is a tad old-fashioned; dog theme (and actual dogs) not for everyone; no outside alcohol allowed. *Rooms from: $199 195 Main St., Montgomery 802/326–4306 www.phineasswann.com 9 rooms Free Breakfast.*

Activities

ICE-SKATING

Ice Haus Arena

HOCKEY | **FAMILY** | The sprawling arena contains a professional-size hockey rink and seating for 400 spectators. You can practice your stick handling, and the rink is open to the public for skating several times a week. There are tournaments throughout the year. *830 Jay Peak Rd., Jay 802/988–2727 www.jaypeakresort.com $6.*

SKIING

Hazen's Notch Association

SKIING & SNOWBOARDING | Delightfully remote at any time of the year, this center has 40 miles of marked and groomed trails and rents equipment and snowshoes. *1423 Hazen's Notch Rd., Montgomery 802/326–4799 www.hazensnotch.org.*

Jay Peak

SKIING & SNOWBOARDING | Sticking up out of the flat farmland, Jay Peak averages 349 inches of snow per year—more than any other Vermont ski area—and it's renowned for its glade skiing and powder. There are two interconnected mountains, the highest reaching nearly 4,000 feet. The smaller mountain has straight-fall-line, expert terrain that eases mid-mountain into an intermediate pitch. Beginners should stay near the bottom on trails off the Metro quad lift. There are also five terrain parks, snowshoeing, telemark skiing, and a state-of-the art ice arena for hockey, figure skating, and curling. The Pump House, an indoor water park with pools and slides, is open year-round. **Facilities:** 78 trails; 385 acres; 2,153-foot vertical drop; 9 lifts. *830 Jay Peak Rd., Jay 802/988–2611 www.jaypeakresort.com Lift ticket: $99.*

Lake Willoughby

30 miles southeast of Montgomery (summer route; 50 miles by winter route), 28 miles northeast of Greensboro.

The jewel of the Northeast Kingdom is clear, deep, and chilly Lake Willoughby, edged by sheer cliffs and surrounded by state forest. The only town on its shores is tiny Westmore, which has a beach and a few shops that cater to campers and seasonal residents.

Sights

Bread and Puppet Museum

OTHER MUSEUM | FAMILY | This ramshackle barn houses a surrealistic collection of props used by the world-renowned Bread and Puppet Theater. The troupe has been performing social and political commentary with the towering (they're supported by people on stilts) and eerily expressive puppets for more than 50 years. In July and August, there are performances on Saturday night and Sunday afternoon, with museum tours before Sunday shows. ✉ *753 Heights Rd., 1 mile east of Rte. 16, Glover* ☎ *802/525–3031* 🌐 *www.breadandpuppet.org* 🎟 *Donations accepted* 🕒 *Closed Nov.–May.*

Lake Willoughby

BODY OF WATER | The cliffs of Mt. Pisgah and Mt. Hor drop to the edge of Lake Willoughby on opposite shores, giving this beautiful, deep, glacially carved lake a striking resemblance to a Norwegian fjord. The trails to the top of Mt. Pisgah reward hikers with glorious views. Take note: the beach on the southern end is Vermont's most famous nude beach. ✉ *Westmore.*

Greensboro

27 miles southwest of Lake Willoughby.

Tucked along the southern shore of Caspian Lake, Greensboro has been a summer resort for literati, academics, and old-money types for more than a century. Yet it exudes an unpretentious, genteel character—most of the people running about on errands seem to know each other. The town beach is right off the main street.

Sights

★ Hill Farmstead Brewery

BREWERY | It is difficult to quantify owner and master brewer Shaun Hill's contribution to the international explosion of craft beer. Hill Farmstead has won Best Brewery in the World six times in the past decade, and it's a key player in Vermont tourism, where beer contributes as much to the state economy as skiing and hiking. Since opening in 2010, Hill's eighth generation family farmstead off a rural mountain pass, miles from cell service, has drawn millions of local and international travelers pilgrimaging for a coveted pint and a growler to-go. A beautiful bar is surrounded by acres of woods and lawnspace, and a small lake sits at the bottom of a sloping field—a nice spot for pondering over a pint. ✉ *403 Hill Rd., Greensboro* ☎ *802/533–7450* 🌐 *hillfarmstead.com.*

Shopping

The Willey's Store

GENERAL STORE | This is a classic general store of the "if-we-don't-have-it-you-don't-need-it" kind. It's also the spot where locals in the know can snag hard-to-find Vermont gems like Jasper Hill Farm cheeses and bottles of Hill Farmstead beer. ✉ *7 Breezy Ave., Greensboro* ☎ *802/533–2621.*

Chapter 10

NEW HAMPSHIRE

Updated by
Andrew Collins

Sights ★★★★★ | Restaurants ★★★☆☆ | Hotels ★★★★☆ | Shopping ★★★★☆ | Nightlife ★★★☆☆

WELCOME TO NEW HAMPSHIRE

TOP REASONS TO GO

★ **The White Mountains:** Offering spectacular hiking and skiing, these dramatic peaks and notches are unforgettable.

★ **Lake Winnipesaukee:** Beaches, arcades, boat cruises, and classic summer camps fuel a whole season of family fun.

★ **Fall Foliage:** Head to the Kancamagus Highway or drive through the Monadnock mountain towns for absolutely stunning scenery.

★ **Portsmouth:** An hour's drive from Boston, this small, upbeat American city abounds with colorful Colonial architecture, trendy dining, and easy access to New Hampshire's only stretch of the Atlantic coastline.

★ **Pristine Towns:** Peterborough, Walpole, Tamworth, Center Sandwich, Bethlehem, and Jackson are among the most charming small villages in New England.

1 **Portsmouth.** Colonial homes meet hip dining.

2 **Rye.** Sweeping beaches and lavish oceanfront homes.

3 **Exeter.** Café culture and a famous prep school.

4 **Durham.** Home of the University of NH.

5 **Wolfeboro.** The U.S.'s oldest summer resort.

6 **Laconia and Weirs Beach.** Lake Winnipesaukee's hub of family fun.

7 **Meredith.** A bustling marina and mills converted to hotels.

8 **Plymouth.** A lively college town and gateway to the White Mountains.

9 **Holderness.** Base camp for Squam and Little Squam lakes.

10 **Center Sandwich.** Lake Winnipesaukee's quiet, scenic side.

11 **Tamworth.** Tranquility and Mt. Chocorua views.

12 **North Conway.** Outlet shops and family-friendly amusements.

13 **Jackson.** A storybook White Mountains town.

14 **Mt. Washington.** Highest peak in the northeastern United States.

15 **Bartlett.** A scenic ski and hiking hub.

16 **Bretton Woods.** Cog railway and a grand resort.

17 **Bethlehem.** An artsy alpine hamlet.

18 **Littleton.** A scenic river town with a lively Main Street.

19 **Franconia.** One of the White Mountains' favorite recreation hubs.

20 **Lincoln and North Woodstock.** Ski resorts and kitschy family spots.

21 **Waterville Valley.** A four-season resort and recreation village.

22 **New London.** Charming gateway to Lake Sunapee.

23 **Newbury and Lake Sunapee.** Skiing, boating, and the nation's oldest crafts fair.

24 **Hanover.** Home to Dartmouth College.

25 **Cornish.** Covered bridges and the Saint-Gaudens estate.

26 **Walpole.** A pretty village green and Connecticut River views.

27 **Keene.** A classic Main Street and views of Mt. Monadnock.

28 **Peterborough.** The inspiration for Thornton Wilder's *Our Town.*

29 **Milford.** A bustling river town near myriad appealing attractions.

30 **Manchester.** The Granite State's largest city.

31 **Concord.** The small but lively state capital.

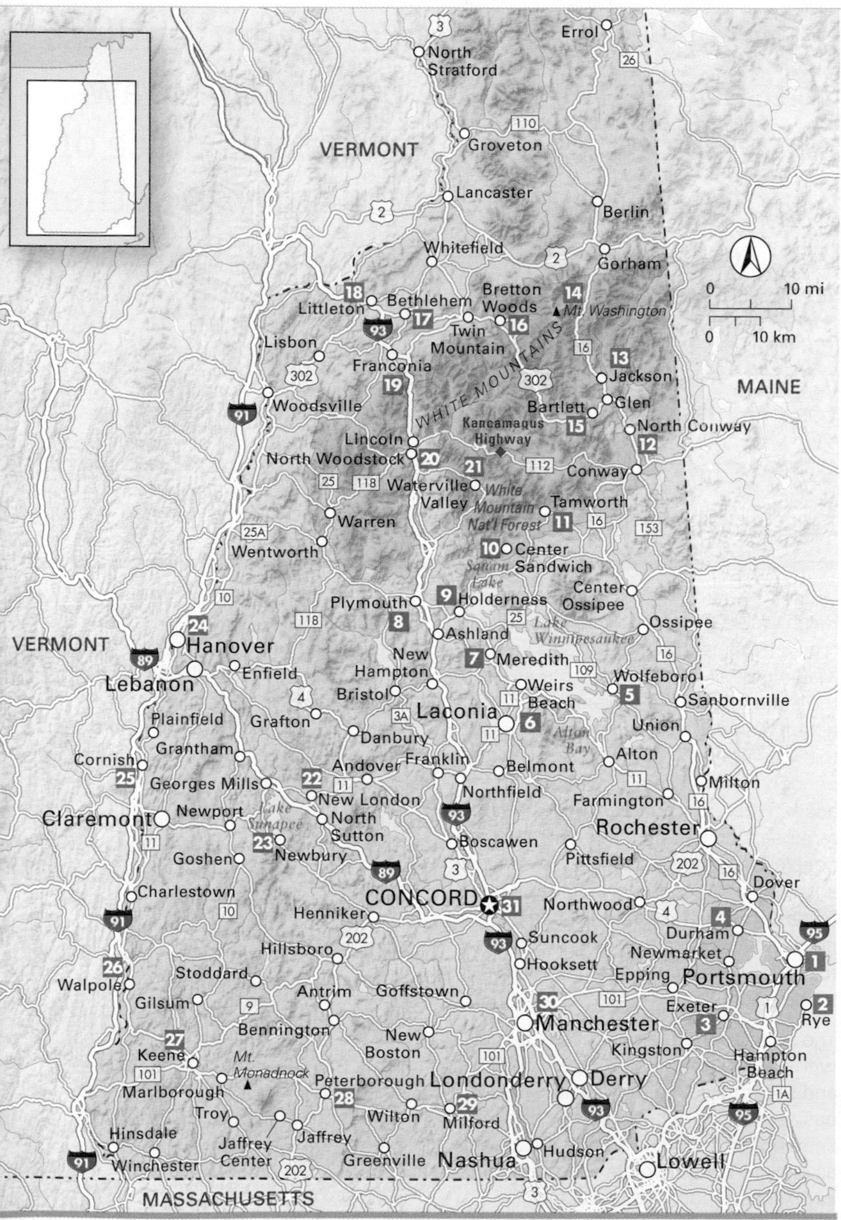
VERMONT
MAINE
MASSACHUSETTS
WHITE MOUNTAINS
Mt. Washington
Kancamagus Highway
White Mountain Nat'l Forest
Lake Winnipesaukee
Lake Sunapee
Mt. Monadnock
CONCORD
Manchester
Nashua
Portsmouth
Hanover
Lebanon
Laconia
Rochester
Dover
Concord
Keene
Claremont
Derry
Londonderry
Lowell
0 10 mi
0 10 km

New Hampshire's precipitous terrain, clear air, and sparkling lakes attract trailblazers, artists, and countless tourists. A varied geography and endless outdoor activities are part of the draw, but visitors also appreciate this place of beauty, history, and hospitality. Whether you're seeking adventure or just want to laze on the porch swing of a century-old inn, you'll find ample ways to engage with this rugged, diverse state that stretches from the sea to the Northeast's highest mountain peaks.

Ralph Waldo Emerson, Henry David Thoreau, Nathaniel Hawthorne, and Louisa May Alcott all visited and wrote about the state, sparking a fervent literary tradition. It also has a strong political history: this was the first colony to declare independence from Great Britain, the first to adopt a state constitution, and the first to require its constitution be referred to the people for approval. Politically, it remains a fiercely independent swing state that holds some of the earliest election primaries in the country and that's known for both its libertarian and progressive tendencies.

The state's varied terrain makes it popular with everyone from hard-core climbers and skiers to young families looking for easy access to nature. You can hike, ski, snowboard, snowshoe, and fish, as well as explore on snowmobiles, sailboats, kayaks, and mountain bikes. New Hampshirites have no objection to others enjoying the beauty here as long as they leave a few dollars behind: it's the only state in the union with neither sales nor income taxes, so tourism brings in much-needed revenue (and tourists can enjoy tax-free shopping).

With a few communities consistently rated among the most livable in the nation, New Hampshire has grown a bit faster than most other northeastern states over the past two decades. The state is gradually developing two distinct personalities: one characterized by rapid urbanization in the southeast and the other by quiet village life in the west and north. Although newcomers have brought change, the free-spirited sensibility of the Granite State remains intact, as does its natural splendor.

MAJOR REGIONS

The **Seacoast,** New Hampshire's 18-mile stretch of coastline, packs in plenty of gorgeous scenery and lively diversions. The northern portion of the shoreline, from the charmingly historic regional hub, **Portsmouth**, south through the affluent town of **Rye**, is especially pristine and free from the honky-tonk excess of the southern section (around Hampton Beach and Seabrook). From Rye, you can branch inland to the prep-school town of **Exeter**, and then cut north through **Durham** (home to the University of New Hampshire). From here it's a short drive to the Lakes Region.

Throughout central New Hampshire, you'll encounter lakes and more lakes in the aptly named **Lakes Region.** The largest, Lake Winnipesaukee, has 180 miles of coastline and attracts all sorts of water-sports enthusiasts to the towns of **Wolfeboro**, **Laconia** (with its bustling **Weirs Beach** section), and **Meredith**. You'll find smaller and more secluded lakes with enchanting bed-and-breakfasts in **Holderness**, which adjoins famously scenic Squam Lake. **Plymouth**, **Center Sandwich**, and **Tamworth** are great bases to explore the surrounding lakes and as well as the southern reaches of the White Mountains.

Skiing, snowshoeing, and snowboarding in the winter; hiking, biking, and riding scenic railways in the summer: the Whites, as locals call **The White Mountains,** have plenty of natural wonders. **Mt. Washington**, the tallest mountain in the Northeast, can be conquered by trail, train, or car; other towns with strong railroad ties include up-and-coming **Littleton** and touristy **North Conway**. **Lincoln** and **North Woodstock** and **Waterville Valley** are lively resort areas, and **Bethlehem**, **Jackson**, and **Franconia** are stunning alpine jewels. **Bretton Woods** and **Bartlett** are great skiing and hiking towns.

Quiet villages proliferate in the **Lake Sunapee** region; the lake itself is a wonderful place to swim, fish, or enjoy a cruise. **Hanover**, home to Dartmouth College (founded 1769), retains that true New England college-town feel, with ivy-draped buildings and cobblestone walkways. The charming town of **New London** is one of the area's main hubs, while **Newbury**, on the edge of Mt. Sunapee State Park, is a popular base for outdoor recreation. **Cornish**, once the haunt of J. D. Salinger, is where you'll find Cornish-Windsor Bridge, the country's second-longest covered bridge.

New and old coexist in **the Monadnocks and Merrimack Valley,** the state's southwestern and south-central regions, respectively. Here high-tech firms have helped reshape the cities of **Manchester** and **Concord** while small towns in the hills surrounding Mt. Monadnock, southern New Hampshire's largest peak, like **Keene** and **Peterborough**, celebrate tradition and history. **Walpole** has one of the state's loveliest town greens.

Planning

Getting Here and Around

Although New Hampshire is a small state, roads curve around lakes and mountains, making distances sometimes much longer than they appear on a map. You can get a taste of the coast, lake, and mountain areas in three to five days; eight days will give you time to make a more complete loop.

AIR

Manchester-Boston Regional Airport, the state's largest, has nonstop service from more than a dozen U.S. cities. The drive from Boston's Logan Airport to most places in New Hampshire takes one to three hours; the same is true for Bradley International Airport, outside Hartford, Connecticut.

CAR

In this generally rural state with limited public transportation, a car is definitely the easiest and most practical way to get around. Interstate 93 stretches from Boston to Littleton and on into neighboring Vermont. Interstate 89 will get you from Concord to Hanover en route to Burlington, Vermont. And Interstate 95 (a toll road) passes through New Hampshire's short coastal region on the way from Boston to Maine. Throughout the state, quiet and winding backcountry lanes can take a little longer but reward travelers with gorgeous scenery.

The speed limit on interstate and limited-access highways is usually 65 to 70 mph. On state and U.S. routes, speed limits vary considerably, from 25 mph to 55 mph, so watch signs carefully. The website of the **New Hampshire Department of Transportation** (🌐 www.nhtmc.com) has up-to-the-minute information about traffic and road conditions.

TRAIN

Amtrak's *Downeaster* passenger rain operates between Boston and Portland, Maine, with New Hampshire stops in Exeter, Durham, and Dover.

Hotels

In the mid-19th century, wealthy Bostonians retreated to imposing New Hampshire country homes in the summer. Grand hotels were built across the state, especially in the White Mountains, which at that time competed with Saratoga Springs, Newport, and Bar Harbor to draw the nation's elite vacationers. A handful of these hotel-resorts survive, and many of those country houses have since been converted into romantic inns. You'll also find quite a few well-kept motor lodges and cottage compounds, particularly in the White Mountains and Lakes regions. In ski areas, expect the usual ski condos and lodges, but most slopes are also within a short drive of a country inn or two. In the Merrimack River valley, as well as along major highways, chain hotels and motels predominate. The state is rife with campgrounds, especially in the White Mountains.

Hotel reviews have been shortened. For full information, visit Fodors.com.

Restaurants

With a dining scene that's still dominated by old-fashioned hotels, lively pubs, laid-back seafood shacks, and unfussy diners, delis, and pizza parlors, New Hampshire is still generally a bit more traditional than its neighboring states, but the times are definitely changing. You'll find a growing array of contemporary, locavore-driven bistros, international restaurants, third-wave coffee roasters, mixology-minded cocktail bars, and artisanal craft breweries around the state—especially in Portsmouth and Manchester, but also in an increasing number of smaller communities, such as Bethlehem, Exeter, Jackson, Keene, New London, and Walpole. In quite a few smaller hamlets, the best restaurant in town is often inside the historic inn. Reservations are seldom required, and dress is casual.

Restaurant reviews have been shortened. For full information, visit Fodors.com.

What It Costs in U.S. Dollars

$	$$	$$$	$$$$
RESTAURANTS			
under $18	$18–$24	$25–$35	over $35
HOTELS			
under $150	$150–$225	$226–$300	over $300

Outdoor Activities

Skiing: Ski areas abound in New Hampshire, among them Bretton Woods, Mt. Sunapee, Waterville Valley, and Cannon Mountain. For cross-country skiing, nothing beats Gunstock Mountain Resort, with 32 miles of trails, also open for snowshoeing. Or visit Franconia Village, which has 40 miles of cross-country trails.

Biking: Many ski resorts in the White Mountains offer mountain biking, providing chairlift rides to the mountaintop and trails for all skill levels at the bottom. Some of the state's most scenic road biking is along the Kancamagus Highway and around Lake Sunapee.

Hiking: New Hampshire is a fantastic state for trekking, whether you're up for an arduous hike in the White Mountains or along the Appalachian Trail, or you'd rather something a bit less taxing, maybe around the shore of Lake Sunapee or Lake Winnipesaukee, or in one of the dozens of beautiful state parks, such as Crawford Notch, Franconia Notch, and Mt. Monadnock.

Shopping

One of five U.S. states without a sales tax, New Hampshire is famously popular with bargain hunters. From outlet shopping centers to state-run liquor stores to bustling downtowns packed with independent boutiques, you'll find great deals in every corner of the state.

Visitor Information

CONTACTS Lakes Region Tourism Association. ✉ *Tilton* ☎ *603/286–8008* 🌐 *www.lakesregion.org.* **Lake Sunapee Region Chamber of Commerce.** ✉ *New London* ☎ *603/526–6575* 🌐 *www.lakesunapeeregionchamber.com.* **Ski New Hampshire.** ☎ *603/745–9396* 🌐 *www.skinh.com.* **Visit New Hampshire.** ✉ *Concord* ☎ *603/271–2665* 🌐 *www.visitnh.gov.* **White Mountains Visitors Center.** ✉ *North Woodstock* ☎ *603/745–8720* 🌐 *www.visitwhitemountains.com.* **Chamber Collaborative of Greater Portsmouth.** ✉ *Portsmouth* ☎ *603/610–5510* 🌐 *www.goportsmouthnh.com.*

When to Go

Summer and fall are the most popular and expensive times to visit New Hampshire. Fans of boating, swimming, and hiking flock to the state's many lakes as well as the short section of coastline starting around Memorial Day and continuing through mid-September. After that, for the next few weeks, the state is a magnet for fans of fall foliage. Winter is popular for skiers and other winter-sports enthusiasts, especially in the White Mountains, but outside of ski areas, many businesses and attractions close or have shorter hours from late fall until May or June. Spring's unpredictable weather—along with April's mud and late May's black flies—tends to deter visitors. Still, the season has its joys, not the least of which is the appearance, mid-May–early June, of the state flower, the purple lilac, soon followed by the blooming of colorful rhododendrons and fields of lupine.

Portsmouth

47 miles east of Concord, 50 miles south of Portland, Maine, 56 miles north of Boston.

A small but lively Colonial port across the river from Kittery, Maine, upscale Portsmouth buzzes with hip restaurants, swank cocktails bars, contemporary art galleries and boutiques, and acclaimed cultural venues that host nationally recognized speakers and performers—the action is focused largely around downtown's Market Square. Settled in 1623 as Strawbery Banke, Portsmouth grew into a prosperous port before the Revolutionary War, during which it harbored many Tory sympathizers. These days, this city of 22,000 has many grand residences from the 18th to the early 20th centuries, many of them preserved within or near the engaging Strawbery Banke Museum. For a scenic drive or bike ride, follow Rte. 1B east from downtown across the Piscataqua River, following it around leafy New Castle Island—where you'll pass Fort Constitution and the grand, historic Wentworth by the Sea Hotel.

GETTING HERE AND AROUND

Both Interstate 95 and U.S. 1 connect Portsmouth with the rest of coastal New England, while U.S. 4 and Route 101 are the easiest ways to get here from inland New Hampshire. Downtown Portsmouth is walkable, though you'll need a car for attractions farther afield.

BOAT TOURS

Gundalow Company

BOAT TOURS | FAMILY | Sail the Piscataqua River in a flat-bottom gundalow (a type of barge) built at Strawbery Banke. Help the crew set sail, steer the vessel, and trawl for plankton while learning about the region's history from an onboard educator. Passengers are welcome to bring food and beverages. Afternoon and evening sails are offered. ✉ *60 Marcy St., Portsmouth* ☎ *603/433–9505* 🌐 *www.gundalow.org* 🎟 *From $18* 🕑 *Closed mid-Oct.–late May.*

Portsmouth Harbor Cruises

BOAT TOURS | Tours of Portsmouth Harbor and the Isles of Shoals, inland-river foliage trips, and sunset and wine cruises are all in this company's repertoire. ✉ *64 Ceres St., Portsmouth* ☎ *603/436–8084, 800/776–0915* 🌐 *www.portsmouthharbor.com* 🎟 *From $21* 🕑 *Closed Nov.–early May.*

WALKING TOURS

★ Discover Portsmouth

WALKING TOURS | FAMILY | The Portsmouth Historical Society operates this combination visitor center–museum, where you can pick up maps, get the scoop on what's happening while you're in town, and view cultural and historical exhibits. Here you can also learn about self-guided historical tours and sign up for guided ones. ✉ *10 Middle St., Portsmouth* ☎ *603/436–8433* 🌐 *www.portsmouthhistory.org* 🎟 *Tours from $20* 🕑 *No tours Nov.–Apr.*

★ Portsmouth Black Heritage Trail

WALKING TOURS | FAMILY | Important local sites in African American history can be seen on the 75-minute guided Sankofa Tour. Included are the African Burying Ground and historic homes of local slave traders and abolitionists. Tours, which begin at the Old Meeting House, are conducted on Saturday afternoon throughout the summer. ✉ *222 Court St., Portsmouth* ☎ *603/570–8469* 🌐 *www.blackheritagetrailnh.org* 🎟 *$20* 🕑 *No tours Nov.–Apr.*

Portsmouth Eats

WALKING TOURS | On White Table, Best of Portsmouth, and Sweet and Savory walking tours—mostly on weekends—you get to taste the culinary delights of four or five establishments in New Hampshire's coastal city. ☎ *603/571–3287* 🌐 *www.portsmouth-eats.com* 🎟 *From $45.*

VISITOR INFORMATION

Chamber Collaborative of Greater Portsmouth

✉ *Portsmouth* ☎ *603/610–5510* 🌐 *www.portsmouthchamber.org.*

Sights

Albacore Park

MILITARY SIGHT | Built in Portsmouth in 1953, the USS *Albacore* is the centerpiece of Albacore Park. You can board this prototype submarine, which served as a floating laboratory to test an innovative hull design, dive brakes, and sonar systems for the Navy. The visitor center exhibits *Albacore* artifacts, and the nearby Memorial Garden is dedicated to those who have lost their lives in submarine service. ✉ *600 Market St., Portsmouth* ☎ *603/436–3680* 🌐 *www.ussalbacore.org* 🎟 *$9* 🕒 *Closed Tues.*

Great Bay Estuarine National Research Reserve

NATURE PRESERVE | **FAMILY** | Just inland from Portsmouth is one of southeastern New Hampshire's most precious assets. In this 10,235 acres of open and tidal waters, you can spot blue herons, ospreys, and snowy egrets, particularly during the spring and fall migrations. The Great Bay Discovery Center has indoor and outdoor exhibits, a library and bookshop, and a 1,700-foot boardwalk, as well as other trails, which wind through mudflats and upland forest. ✉ *89 Depot Rd., Greenland* ☎ *603/778–0015* 🌐 *www.greatbay.org* 🎟 *Free* 🕒 *Discovery Center closed Sun. and Mon. and Nov.–Apr.*

Isles of Shoals

ISLAND | **FAMILY** | Four of the nine small, rocky Isles of Shoals belong to New Hampshire (the other five belong to Maine), many of them still known by the earthy names—Hog and Smuttynose, to cite but two—17th-century fishermen bestowed on them. A history of piracy, murder, and ghosts suffuses the archipelago, long populated by an independent lot who, according to one writer, hadn't the sense to winter on the mainland. Celia Thaxter, a native islander, romanticized these islands with her poetry in *Among the Isles of Shoals* (1873). In the late 19th century, Appledore Island became an offshore retreat for Thaxter's coterie of writers, musicians, and artists. Star Island contains a small museum, the Rutledge Marine Lab, with interactive family exhibits. From May to early October you can take a narrated history cruise of the Isles of Shoals and walking tours of Star Island with Isles of Shoals Steamship Company. ✉ *Barker Wharf, 315 Market St., Portsmouth* ☎ *800/441–4620, 603/431–5500* 🌐 *www.islesofshoals.com* 🎟 *Cruises from $41* 🕒 *No cruises mid-Oct.–Apr.*

John Paul Jones House

HISTORIC HOME | **FAMILY** | Revolutionary War hero John Paul Jones lived at this boardinghouse while he supervised construction of the USS *America* for the Continental Navy. The 1758 hip-roof building displays furniture, costumes, glass, guns, portraits, and documents from the late 18th century. The collection's specialty is textiles, among them some extraordinary early-19th-century embroidery samplers. ✉ *43 Middle St., Portsmouth* ☎ *603/436–8420* 🌐 *www.portsmouthhistory.org* 🎟 *$10* 🕒 *Closed mid-Oct.–late May.*

★ Moffatt-Ladd House and Garden

HISTORIC HOME | The period interior of this striking 1763 mansion tells the story of Portsmouth's merchant class through portraits, letters, and furnishings. The Colonial Revival garden includes a horse chestnut tree planted by General William Whipple when he returned home after signing the Declaration of Independence in 1776. ✉ *154 Market St., Portsmouth* ☎ *603/436–8221* 🌐 *www.moffattladd.org* 🎟 *$10; garden only $2* 🕒 *Closed mid-Oct.–May.*

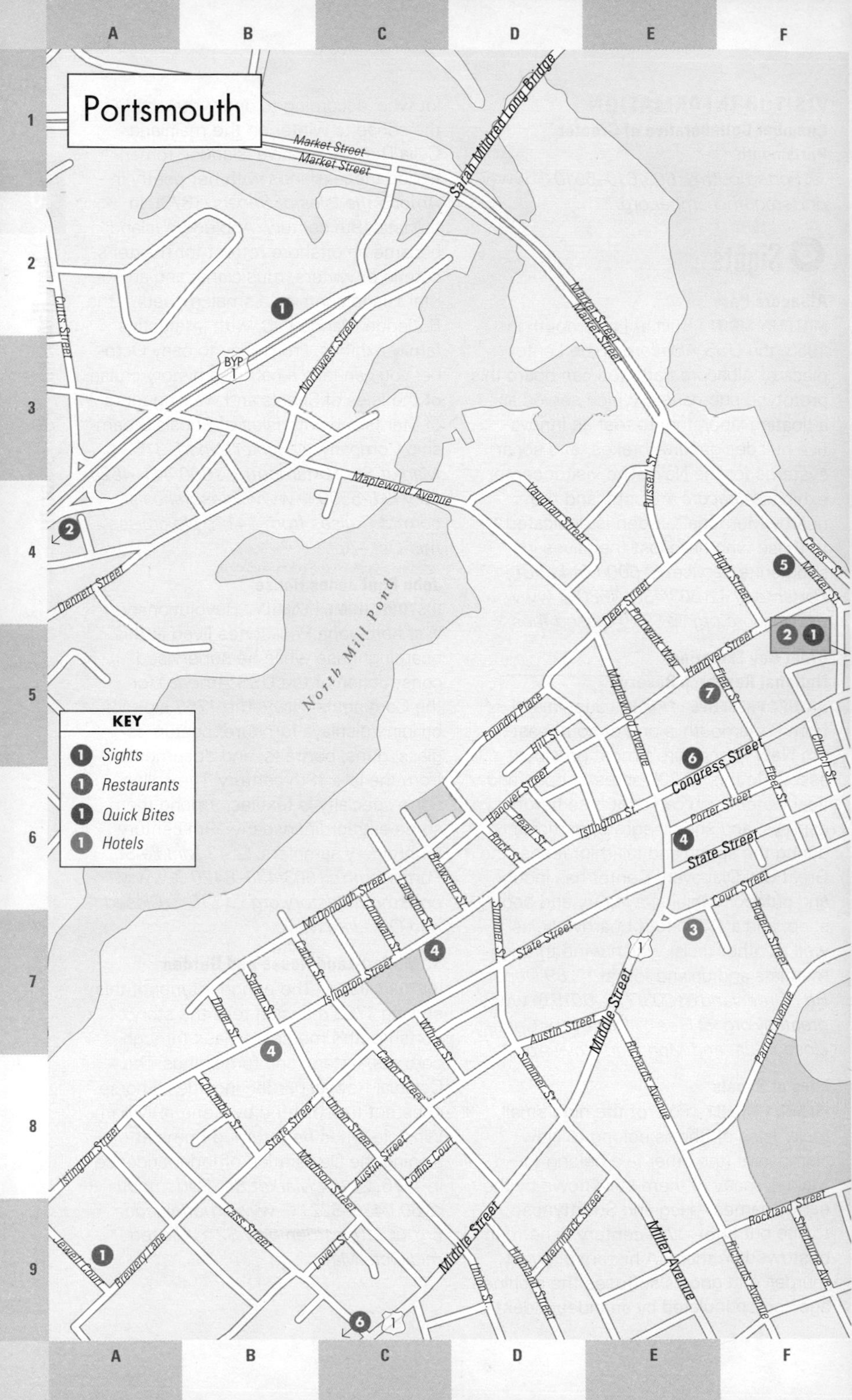

Portsmouth
KEY
Sights
Restaurants
Quick Bites
Hotels
Market Street
Sarah Mildred Long Bridge
Cutts Street
Northwest Street
Maplewood Avenue
Vaughan Street
Russell St.
Dennett Street
North Mill Pond
Deer Street
Portwalk Way
High Street
Ceres St.
Market St.
Hanover Street
Fleet St.
Foundry Place
Hill St.
Congress Street
Church St.
Islington St.
Pearl St.
Rock St.
Porter Street
State Street
Court Street
Rogers Street
McDonough Street
Langdon St.
Brewster St.
Cornwall St.
Summer St.
Cabot St.
Salem St.
Islington Street
Dover St.
Middle Street
Austin Street
Winter St.
Cabot Street
Parrott Avenue
Richards Avenue
Columbia St.
State Street
Union Street
Madison Street
Austin Street
Coffins Court
Cass Street
Jewell Court
Brewery Lane
Lovell St.
Union St.
Highland Street
Merrimack Street
Miller Avenue
Rockland Street
Sherburne Ave.

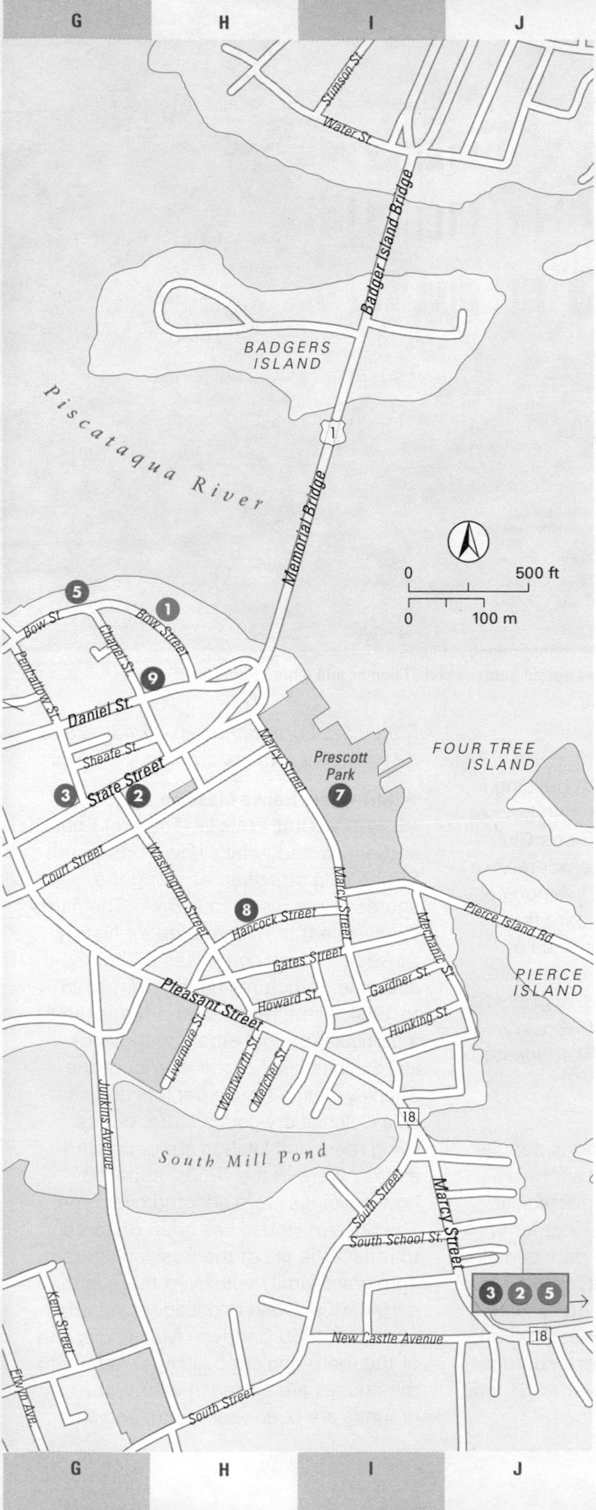

Sights

1 Albacore Park...................... **B2**
2 Great Bay Estuarine National Research Reserve................ **A4**
3 Isles of Shoals **J9**
4 John Paul Jones House............ **E6**
5 Moffatt-Ladd House and Garden................. **F4**
6 Museum of New Art (MONA)..... **E5**
7 Prescott Park........................ **I5**
8 Strawbery Banke Museum....... **H6**
9 Warner House **H5**

Restaurants

1 Botanica **A9**
2 Cava................................ **G5**
3 Cure **G5**
4 Lexie's Joint **C7**
5 Surf Restaurant...................... **G4**
6 Vida Cantina.......................... **C9**
7 The Wilder............................ **E5**

Quick Bites

1 Elephantine Bakery................ **G5**
2 Red Rover Creamery **G5**

Hotels

1 Ale House Inn....................... **H4**
2 Great Island Inn..................... **J9**
3 Hotel Portsmouth **E7**
4 Martin Hill Inn **B7**
5 Wentworth by the Sea **J9**

Strawbery Banke Museum includes period gardens and 37 homes and other structures.

Museum of New Art (MONA)

ART MUSEUM | Set in the same handsomely restored 1905 YMCA building in downtown Portsmouth that also houses acclaimed Jimmy's Jazz & Blues Club, this 6,800-square-foot contemporary art museum opened in 2021. A non-collecting institution, MONA hosts three exhibits each year, with the focus on emerging artists and often large-scale, site-specific works. ✉ *135 Congress St., Portsmouth* ☎ *603/450–1011* 🌐 *www.monaportsmouth.org* 🎫 *$10 suggested donation* ⏲ *Closed Mon.*

Prescott Park

CITY PARK | **FAMILY** | Picnicking is popular at this 3½-acre waterfront park near Strawbery Banke, whose spectacular garden with fountains is perfect for whiling away an afternoon. The park contains Point of Graves, Portsmouth's oldest burial ground, and two 17th-century warehouses. The summerlong Prescott Park Arts Festival features concerts, outdoor movies, and food-related events. ✉ *105 Marcy St., Portsmouth* ☎ *603/436–2848* 🌐 *www.prescottpark.org.*

★ Strawbery Banke Museum

MUSEUM VILLAGE | **FAMILY** | The first English settlers named what's now Portsmouth for the wild strawberries along the shores of the Piscataqua River. The name survives in this 10-acre outdoor history museum, which comprises 37 homes and other structures dating from 1695 to 1954, some restored and furnished to a particular period, others with historical exhibits. Half of the interior of the Shapley-Drisco House depicts its use as a Colonial dry-goods store, but its living room and kitchen are decorated as they were in the 1950s, showing how buildings were adapted over time. The Shapiro House has been restored to reflect the life of the Russian-Jewish immigrant family who lived there in the early 1900s. Done in decadent Victorian style, the 1860 Goodwin Mansion is one of the more opulent buildings. Although the houses are closed in winter, the grounds are open year-round, and an outdoor skating rink operates December–early March. ✉ *14 Hancock St., Portsmouth* ☎ *603/433–1100* 🌐 *www.strawberybanke.org* 🎟 *$19.50* ⏲ *Homes closed Nov.–Apr. except for guided tours on Nov. weekends.*

Warner House

HISTORIC HOME | The highlight of this circa-1716 gem is the curious folk-art murals lining the hall staircase, which may be the oldest-known murals in the United States still gracing their original structure. The house, a notable example of brick Georgian architecture, contains original art, furnishings, and extraordinary examples of area craftsmanship. The west-wall lightning rod is believed to have been installed in 1762 under the supervision of Benjamin Franklin. ✉ *150 Daniel St., Portsmouth* ☎ *603/436–5909* 🌐 *www.warnerhouse.org* 🎟 *$10* ⏲ *Closed mid-Oct.–late May and Mon.–Wed.*

Restaurants

★ Botanica

$$$ | MODERN FRENCH | This swanky spot in a gorgeous old brick brewery building in Portsmouth's up-and-coming West End is a magnet for fans of artisan gin, which figures in about a dozen intriguing cocktails, but the exquisite French-accented cuisine appeals to all. Highlights from the seasonal menu include classic steak frites with brandy jus, and grilled monkfish in a squash bisque with corn and lobster. **Known for:** imaginative gin-centric cocktails; attractive side patio; chocolate soufflé. $ *Average main: $30* ✉ *110 Brewery La., Portsmouth* ☎ *603/373–0979* 🌐 *www.botanicanh.com* ⏲ *Closed Sun.–Mon. No lunch.*

★ Cava

$$$ | TAPAS | Having a meal at this sophisticated little wine and tapas bar down a tiny alley near the downtown riverfront can feel like going to a special dinner party. It has a small exhibition kitchen and bar, and just a handful of tables and chairs, where guests can enjoy a selection of stellar bocadillos, tapas, and pintxos—from piquillo peppers with goat cheese and artichokes to char-grilled baby octopus—plus a few larger plates, such as paella. **Known for:** a superb wine list; authentic Spanish tapas; churros with hot chocolate. $ *Average main: $26* ✉ *10 Commercial Alley, Portsmouth* ☎ *603/319–1575* 🌐 *www.cavatapasandwinebar.com* ⏲ *Closed Mon. and Tues. No lunch.*

★ Cure

$$$ | MODERN AMERICAN | As its name hints, this buzzy neighborhood bistro in a lively dining room with redbrick walls, beam ceilings, and hardwood floors specializes in cured, brined, and slow-cooked meats, which you can sample through beautifully presented charcuterie boards, smoked ribs, and slow-roasted Moroccan lamb shank. But take heart if you're less disposed toward red meat—you'll find plenty of creative seafood and veggie dishes on the menu, including gooey lobster mac and cheese. **Known for:** locally sourced ingredients; well-chosen wine list; lively but romantic dining room. $ *Average main: $29* ✉ *189 State St., Portsmouth* ☎ *603/427–8258* 🌐 *www.curerestaurantportsmouth.com* ⏲ *No lunch.*

Lexie's Joint

$ | BURGER | FAMILY | What began as a humble downtown burger joint has blossomed into a regional mini empire, thanks to the high-quality ingredients, upbeat service, and groovy "peace, love, and burgers"–themed decor. The burgers are reasonably priced and topped with all sorts of goodies, but there are also hot dogs and a few sandwiches, plus plenty of addictive sides. **Known for:** milk shakes with Shain's of Maine homemade ice cream; fried pickles with chipotle aioli; the farmhouse burger, with cheddar, bacon, avocado, and fried egg. $ *Average main: $9* ✉ *212 Islington St., Portsmouth* ☎ *603/815–4181* 🌐 *www.peaceloveburgers.com.*

Surf Restaurant

$$$ | **SEAFOOD** | Whether you eat inside the conversation-filled, high-ceilinged dining room or out on the breezy deck, you'll be treated to expansive views of Old Harbour and the Piscataqua River—an apt setting for consistently fresh and tasty seafood. The menu branches into several directions, including lobster rolls, shrimp-pork ramen, sushi, and Tuscan-style shrimp with marinara sauce, but manages everything well, and there's a well-curated wine and cocktail selection to complement your choice. **Known for:** raw-bar specialties; water views; creative sushi rolls. *Average main: $29* *99 Bow St., Portsmouth* *603/334–9855* *www.surfseafood.com* *Closed Mon. and Tues. No lunch Wed. and Thurs.*

Vida Cantina

$$ | **MODERN MEXICAN** | In a state sorely lacking in notable Latin restaurants, this airy contemporary space south of downtown stands out for the ambitious modern Mexican cuisine of chef-owner and James Beard award–nominated chef David Vargas. Several kinds of street-food-style tacos are offered, including barbacoa and pork belly, along with a tangy goat cheese version of queso fundido and sous vide short rib with pistachio salsa macha. **Known for:** adobo shrimp mole; interesting sides, like blue cornbread and shishito peppers; boozy weekend brunches. *Average main: $21* *2456 Lafayette Rd., Portsmouth* *603/501–0648* *www.vidacantinanh.com.*

The Wilder

$$$ | **MODERN AMERICAN** | Have a seat at the bar or at one of the banquette seats along the wall at this convivial, upscale gastropub with offbeat artwork and a diverse crowd. The kitchen serves up well-executed takes on comfort classics like Nashville-style hot chicken sandwiches with maple-cayenne sauce; poutine smothered in roasted-bone gravy and glazed pork belly; and braised beef short rib with mushroom-onion jam and crispy shallots. **Known for:** late-night dining; lively and friendly bar scene; fun weekend brunch. *Average main: $25* *174 Fleet St., Portsmouth* *603/319–6878* *www.wilderportsmouth.com* *No lunch weekdays.*

Coffee and Quick Bites

★ Elephantine Bakery

$ | **BAKERY** | Master bakers Sherif and Nadine Farag run this cozy, conversation-filled bakery and cafe that's known for its meticulously crafted Middle Eastern and French pastries, sandwiches, and breakfast dishes. Start the day with poached eggs *cilbir* (over garlic labneh with aleppo butter, parsley gremolata, and toasted sourdough), and make every effort to save room for a slice of cardamom-rosewater cake or a brown-butter brownie. **Known for:** perfectly poured espresso drinks; Egyptian bread pudding with coconut milk; outdoor seating on a redbrick sidewalk. *Average main: $14* *10 Commercial Alley, Portsmouth* *603/319–6189* *www.elephantinebakery.com* *No dinner.*

★ Red Rover Creamery

$ | **ICE CREAM** | **FAMILY** | This tiny parlor in historic downtown produces ice cream in big, bold flavors—think black currant tea–caramel, brown sugar–nectarine, and classic cookies-and-cream. They also bake dense and chewy cookies in interesting flavors, which you can enjoy on their own or in an ice-cream sandwich. **Known for:** fresh-baked cookies; decadent ice-cream sandwiches; steps from Strawbery Banke Museum. *Average main: $6* *150 State St., Portsmouth* *603/427–8172* *www.redrovercreamery.com* *Closed Mon. and Tues.*

Hotels

Ale House Inn

$$ | **B&B/INN** | Each of the stylish rooms in this urbane inn occupying a converted Victorian redbrick brewery on the historic riverfront has plenty of handy amenities,

such as wine glasses with corkscrews, iPod docks, and plush robes, and the modern bathrooms have handsome Italian tilework. **Pros:** welcome beers from local breweries upon arrival; free parking; bicycles for local jaunts. **Cons:** no breakfast; several steps to enter hotel; rooms are a bit compact. *Rooms from: $195 121 Bow St., Portsmouth 603/431–7760 www.larkhotels.com 10 rooms No Meals.*

Great Island Inn

$$$ | **B&B/INN** | From downtown Portsmouth, it's a picturesque 2-mile drive or bike ride along the Piscataqua River to this urbane inn set inside an 1820s home that's been given a nautical-chic redesign, all of its six apartment-style studios equipped with well-stocked kitchens, washers and dryers, and light-filled living spaces. **Pros:** smart, contemporary decor; free parking if you book through the inn's website; pretty setting on historic New Castle Island. **Cons:** housekeeping services aren't offered; not directly on the water; a little far to walk to dining and shopping. *Rooms from: $280 3 Walbach St., New Castle 603/436–2778 www.greatislandinn.com 6 rooms No Meals.*

Hotel Portsmouth

$$ | **HOTEL** | This downtown Victorian mansion built in 1881 by a sea captain is now a 32-room boutique hotel with elegantly updated furnishings, plush bed linens, and such modern conveniences as iPad docks, fast Wi-Fi, and flat-screen TVs. **Pros:** close to Market Square; free parking; lounge serving wine, beer, and small bites. **Cons:** thin walls result in occasional noise; some rooms have bland views; two-night minimum during busy times. *Rooms from: $220 40 Court St., Portsmouth 603/433–1200 www.larkhotels.com 32 rooms Free Breakfast.*

Martin Hill Inn

$$ | **B&B/INN** | The quiet rooms in this yellow 1815 house surrounded by flower-filled gardens are furnished with antiques and decorated with fine period antiques; a generous full breakfast is served each morning, featuring lemon-ricotta pancakes or other delectable treats. **Pros:** refrigerators in rooms; excellent breakfast; off-street parking. **Cons:** a little outside the downtown core on busy street; breakfast is served at a communal table; no children under 12. *Rooms from: $220 404 Islington St., Portsmouth 603/436–2287 www.martinhillinn.com 7 rooms Free Breakfast.*

★ Wentworth by the Sea

$$$$ | **RESORT** | Nearly demolished in the 1980s, one of coastal New England's most elegant Victorian grand resorts—where the likes of Harry Truman and Gloria Swanson once vacationed—has been meticulously restored and now ranks among the cushiest golf, boating, and spa getaways in New Hampshire. **Pros:** amenities include an expansive full-service spa, heated indoor pool, and an outstanding golf course; marina with charters for harbor cruises and deep-sea fishing; excellent food in main restaurant and casual waterfront bistro. **Cons:** 10- to 15-minute drive from downtown Portsmouth; steep rates in summer and fall; large property lacks intimacy. *Rooms from: $365 588 Wentworth Rd., New Castle 603/422–7322, 866/384–0709 www.marriott.com 161 rooms No Meals.*

BARS AND BREWPUBS

★ Earth Eagle Brewings

BREWPUBS | This bustling gastropub produces unusual, boldly flavorful ales in the Belgian style, some using distinctive botanicals—lemongrass, ginger root—rather than hops. The food is terrific, there's an airy outdoor beer garden, and musicians perform many evenings. *175 High St., Portsmouth 603/502–2244 www.eartheaglebrewings.com.*

Four of the nine rocky Isles of Shoals belong to New Hampshire; the other five belong to Maine.

Portsmouth Book & Bar

BARS | Combine an old-school indie bookstore with a funky café–cocktail bar, set it inside a restored 1817 customhouse, and you've got this endearing hangout that's popular with everyone from college students to artists to tourists. Live music, comedy, and readings are offered, too. ✉ *40 Pleasant St., Portsmouth* ☎ *603/427–9197* 🌐 *www.bookandbar.com.*

MUSIC CLUBS

★ Jimmy's Jazz & Blue Club

LIVE MUSIC | Downtown's early 1900s YMCA building has been converted into this gorgeous, high-ceilinged music venue with brick walls, color artwork, and a snug mezzanine. An impressive lineup of jazz and blues bands perform here, and full dinner service from a Southern-accented menu is available before each show. ✉ *135 Congress St., Portsmouth* ☎ *888/603–5299* 🌐 *www.jimmysoncongress.com.*

Performing Arts

★ Music Hall

CONCERTS | Beloved for its acoustics, the 895-seat hall built in 1878 presents top-drawer music concerts, from pop to classical, along with dance and theater. The more intimate Music Hall Lounge, around the corner, presents performances by noted musicians, authors, and comedians and serves light food and drinks. ✉ *28 Chestnut St., Portsmouth* ☎ *603/436–2400* 🌐 *www.themusichall.org.*

Seacoast Repertory Theatre

THEATER | Here you'll find a year-round schedule of musicals, classic dramas, and works by up-and-coming playwrights, as well as everything from a youth theater to drag cabaret nights. ✉ *125 Bow St., Portsmouth* ☎ *603/433–4472* 🌐 *www.seacoastrep.org.*

 Shopping

The historic city center, especially around Market Square, abounds with gift and clothing boutiques, book and gourmet food shops, and crafts stores and art galleries.

Byrne & Carlson

CHOCOLATE | Watch elegant cream truffles and luscious chocolates being made in the European tradition at this small artisanal shop. ✉ *121 State St., Portsmouth* ☎ *207/439–0096* 🌐 *www.byrneandcarlson.com.*

New Hampshire Art Association

ART GALLERIES | Since 1940, this venerable local arts organization has served as an incubator of local painters, sculptors, and other talented creatives. Works by the association's more than 300 juried members appear on the walls of this lively downtown gallery. NHAA also organizes other shows throughout the state—check the website for the latest schedule. ✉ *136 State St., Portsmouth* ☎ *603/431–4230* 🌐 *www.nhartassociation.org.*

Off Piste

SOUVENIRS | Look to this quirky emporium for offbeat gifts and household goods—everything from painted buoy birdhouses to irreverent books, games, and mugs. ✉ *37 Congress St., Portsmouth* ☎ *603/319–6910.*

Portsmouth Farmers' Market

MARKET | **FAMILY** | One of the best and longest-running farmers' markets in the state showcases seasonal produce along with regional treats such as maple syrup and artisanal cheeses. There's live music, too. It's held Saturday morning, May–early November. ✉ *City Hall parking lot, 1 Junkens Ave., Portsmouth* ☎ *888/600–0128* 🌐 *www.seacoasteatlocal.org.*

Rye

8 miles south of Portsmouth.

In 1623 the English established a settlement at Odiorne Point in what is now the minimally developed and picturesque town of Rye, making it the birthplace of New Hampshire. Top draws include a lovely state park, beaches, and the views from Route 1A, which is prettiest if you follow it south, passing the group of late-19th- and early-20th-century mansions known as Millionaires' Row. Strict town laws prohibit commercial development in Rye, creating a dramatic contrast with its frenetic neighbor, Hampton Beach.

GETTING HERE AND AROUND

Interstate 95 and U.S. 1, just west of town, provide easy access, but Rye shows its best face from coastal Route 1A.

 Sights

★ Fuller Gardens

GARDEN | Arthur Shurtleff, a noted landscape architect from Boston, designed this late-1920s estate garden in the Colonial Revival style. In a gracious seaside residential neighborhood a couple of miles south of Jenness Beach, this peaceful little botanical gem encompasses 1,700 rosebushes, hosta and Japanese gardens, and a tropical conservatory. ✉ *10 Willow Ave., North Hampton* ☎ *603/964–5414* 🌐 *www.fullergardens.org* 🎫 *$9* 🕒 *Closed mid-Oct.–early May.*

★ Odiorne Point State Park

STATE/PROVINCIAL PARK | **FAMILY** | These 135 acres of protected seaside land are where David Thompson established New Hampshire's first permanent English settlement. Several signed nature trails provide vistas of the nearby Isles of Shoals and interpret the park's military history. The rocky shore's tidal pools shelter crabs, periwinkles, and sea anemones. The park's **Seacoast Science Center** hosts exhibits on the area's natural history. Its tidal-pool touch tank and 1,000-gallon Gulf of Maine deepwater aquarium are popular with kids. ✉ *570 Ocean Blvd., Rye* ☎ *603/436–8043* 🌐 *www.seacoastsciencecenter.org* *Park $4, Science Center $10* ⏲ *Closed Tues.*

Beaches

Jenness State Beach

BEACH | FAMILY | Good for swimming and sunbathing, this long, sandy beach is a favorite among locals who enjoy its light crowds and nice waves for bodysurfing. Wide and shallow, Jenness Beach is a great place for kids to run and build sand castles. **Amenities:** lifeguards; parking (fee); showers; toilets. **Best for:** surfing; swimming; walking. ✉ *2280 Ocean Blvd., Rye* ☎ *603/227–8722* 🌐 *www.nhstateparks.org* *Parking $2/hr Apr.–Sept., $1/hr Oct.*

★ Wallis Sands State Beach

BEACH | FAMILY | This family-friendly swimmers' beach has bright white sand, a picnic area, a store, and beautiful views of the Isles of Shoals. **Amenities:** food and drink; lifeguards; parking (fee); showers; toilets. **Best for:** swimming; walking. ✉ *1050 Ocean Blvd., Rye* ☎ *603/436–9404* 🌐 *www.nhstateparks.org* *$15 per car (late May–mid-Sept.).*

Restaurants

The Carriage House

$$$ | SEAFOOD | Across from Jenness Beach, this elegant cottage serves innovative dishes with an emphasis on local seafood, from raw bar specialties like scallop crudo and littleneck clams on the half shell to roasted cod and tarragon lobster salad. A first-rate hanger steak and lamb stew with eggplant and fry bread round out the menu. **Known for:** classic daily blue-plate specials; breezy, refreshing cocktails; cozy upstairs tavern with ocean views. $ *Average main: $31* ✉ *2263 Ocean Blvd., Rye* ☎ *603/964–8251* 🌐 *www.carriagehouserye.com* ⏲ *Closed Sun. and Mon. No lunch.*

Hotels

★ Rye Motor Inn

$$$$ | MOTEL | This chicly remade mid-century motel, comprising 12 spacious apartment-style suites with kitchens and retro-cool decor, enjoys direct beach access along a mostly undeveloped and gorgeous stretch of Atlantic coastline between Odiorne Point and Wallis Sands Beach. **Pros:** all units have fully equipped kitchens; directly across the road from the beach; adults (21 and over) only. **Cons:** adults (21 and over) only; rooms themselves don't actually overlook the ocean; two-night minimum stay on weekends. $ *Rooms from: $349* ✉ *741 Ocean Blvd., Rye* ☎ *603/436–2778* 🌐 *www.ryemotorinn.com* *12 rooms* *No Meals.*

Nightlife

★ Throwback Brewery

BREWPUBS | FAMILY | After a day of fun at the beach, head a few miles inland to this working farm on 12 acres and its sustainable brewery that crafts first-rate ales using as much local ingredients as possible—some of the hops are grown on-site. On sunny days, sample Throwback's beers in the tented beer garden, and any time of year, you can sip and dine on farm-to-table pub fare, from cheese plates to Korean beef bowls. You can also buy seasonal produce at the farmstand. ✉ *7 Hobbs Rd., North Hampton* ☎ *603/379–2317* 🌐 *www.throwbackbrewery.com.*

Activities

Granite State Whale Watch

WILDLIFE-WATCHING | FAMILY | This respected outfitter conducts naturalist-led whale-watching tours aboard the 100-passenger *Granite State*, along with excursions around the Isles of Shoals and to Star Island. ✉ *Rye Harbor*

New Hampshire Coast

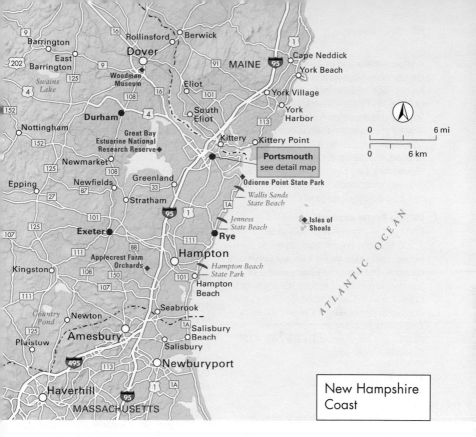

State Marina, 1870 Ocean Blvd., Rye ☎ *603/964–5545, 800/964–5545* 🌐 *www.granitestatewhalewatch.com* 🎫 *$46* ⏲ *Closed mid-Oct.–mid-May.*

Exeter

11 miles west of Rye.

During the Revolutionary War, Exeter served as the state capital, and it was here amid intense patriotic fervor that the first state constitution and the first Colonial Declaration of Independence from Great Britain were put to paper. These days this dapper river town shares more in appearance and personality with Boston's blue-blooded satellite communities than the rest of New Hampshire. Cheerful cafés, coffeehouses, and boutiques with artisanal wares fill the bustling town center.

GETTING HERE AND AROUND

Amtrak's *Downeaster* stops here between Boston and Portland, Maine. By car, Route 101 provides access from the east and west.

ESSENTIALS

VISITOR INFORMATION Exeter Area Chamber of Commerce. ✉ *Exeter* ☎ *603/772–2411* 🌐 *www.exeterarea.org.*

Sights

American Independence Museum

HISTORY MUSEUM | Guided tours of this museum that celebrates the nation's birth focus on the family who lived here during the Revolutionary War. Among 3,000 artifacts, see drafts of the U.S. Constitution and the first Purple Heart, as well as letters and documents written by George Washington and the household furnishings of John Taylor Gilman, one of New Hampshire's early governors. In July, the museum hosts the two-week American Independence Festival, and occasional architectural tours are offered, too. *Ladd-Gilman House, 1 Governor's La., Exeter 603/772–2622 www.independencemuseum.org $8 Closed Sun.–Tues. and Dec.–Apr.*

Phillips Exeter Academy

COLLEGE | The grounds of this elite 1,100-student prep school, open to the public, resemble an Ivy League university campus. The school's library is one of the masterworks of modernist architect Louis I. Kahn. The Lamont Gallery, in the Frederick R. Mayer Art Center, mounts free contemporary art exhibitions. *20 Main St., Exeter 603/772–4311 www.exeter.edu.*

Restaurants

★ Il Cornicello

$$$ | ITALIAN | At this intimate, romantic downtown restaurant overlooking the Exeter River, artfully prepared dishes like gemelli with chestnut mushrooms and smoked ham in a leek-taleggio-mustard sauce, and classic shrimp linguine with a garlicky scampi sauce take center stage. There's also a long and impressively curated list of Italian wines. **Known for:** lovely views of the downtown riverfront; seasonally inspired antipasti; fresh, hand-cut pasta. *Average main: $27 11 Water St., Exeter 603/580–4604 www.ilcornicello.com Closed Sun.–Tues. No lunch.*

★ Otis

$$$$ | MODERN AMERICAN | This romantic, urbane restaurant set inside the early-19th-century Inn by the Bandstand offers exceptional five-course tasting menus featuring farm-to-table fare that changes often to reflect what's in season. Typical offering include sea scallops with orange and fennel, and lamb with Brussels sprouts, shallots, and a sherry sauce, and everything is always plated beautifully. **Known for:** market-fresh, seasonal ingredients; views of charming village center; sticky toffee pudding with a bourbon caramel sauce. *Average main: $70 Inn by the Bandstand, 4 Front St., Exeter 603/580–1705 www.otisrestaurant.com Closed Sun.–Wed. No lunch.*

Coffee and Quick Bites

Laney & Lu

$ | CAFÉ | FAMILY | This snug counter service café is a handy option for organic coffees, blended tea elixirs, and creative smoothies and bowls—the blueberry-basil with banana, avocado, spinach, and almond milk is a standout. Or tuck into a salad of locally sourced fruit, veggies, and greens, or try one of the hearty but healthy salads made on locally baked sourdough. **Known for:** artisan toasts with different toppings; fresh smoothies; a great kids' menu. *Average main: $13 26 Water St., Exeter 603/580–4952 www.laneyandlu.com No dinner.*

Hotels

★ Inn by the Bandstand

$$$$ | B&B/INN | This gorgeously appointed luxury B&B in the heart of downtown Exeter exudes character and comfort, with individually themed rooms furnished with fine antiques, Oriental rugs, and cushy bedding. **Pros:** steps from downtown shopping and dining; exceptional dining in Otis and Ambrose restaurants; fabulous breakfasts. **Cons:** minimum stay on busy weekends; in a busy part of downtown; steep rates. *Rooms from: $329 6 Front St., Exeter 603/772–6352 www.innbythebandstand.com 8 rooms Free Breakfast.*

Shopping

Applecrest Farm Orchards

FOOD | FAMILY | At this 250-acre farm, pick apples and berries or buy freshly baked fruit pies and cookies and outstanding homemade ice cream. A café serves ice cream. Fall brings cider pressing, hayrides, pumpkins, and music on weekends. Author John Irving's experiences working here as a teen inspired *The Cider House Rules.* ✉ *133 Exeter Rd., Hampton Falls* ☎ *603/926–3721* 🌐 *www.applecrest.com.*

★ Exeter Fine Crafts

CRAFTS | This acclaimed nonprofit cooperative formed in 1966 features creations by more than 300 of Northern New England's top pottery, painting, jewelry, textile, glassware, and other artisans. ✉ *61 Water St., Exeter* ☎ *603/778–8282* 🌐 *www.exeterfinecrafts.com.*

Durham

12 miles north of Exeter, 11 miles west of Portsmouth.

A lively college town settled in 1635, Durham became a maritime hub in the 19th century thanks to its easy access to Great Bay via the Oyster River. With the University of New Hampshire anchoring its town center, it's a good hub for exploring two other nearby riverfront communities with thriving historic downtowns, Dover and Newmarket.

GETTING HERE AND AROUND

You can reach Durham on Route 108 from the north or south and on U.S. 4 from Portsmouth or Concord. The *Downeaster* Amtrak train stops here.

Sights

★ Bedrock Gardens

GARDEN | FAMILY | It's easy to lose yourself for a couple of hours, or longer if you pack a picnic lunch, as you wander along the peaceful trails and through the astoundingly gorgeous flower beds of this 30-acre former farm that's now a thriving public garden dotted with hundreds of sculptures and art installations. Features range from formal parterre and spiral gardens to more whimsical and impressionistic plantings. ✉ *19 High Rd., Lee* ☎ *603/659–2993* 🌐 *www.bedrockgardens.org* 🎫 *$15* 🕒 *Closed mid-Oct.–mid-May.*

Children's Museum of New Hampshire

CHILDREN'S MUSEUM | FAMILY | The state's best and largest museum for kiddos is set inside a LEED-certified 1920s armory with big windows overlooking downtown Dover's Cocheco River. In this bright and colorful space, well-designed interactive exhibits on submarines, river ecosystems, dinosaurs, and music are geared to kids up to around age 12, and storytelling sessions are offered regularly. ✉ *6 Washington St., Dover* ☎ *603/742–2002* 🌐 *www.childrens-museum.org* 🎫 *$12.50* 🕒 *Closed Mon.*

★ Woodman Museum

HISTORY MUSEUM | FAMILY | This campus of four impressive, historic museums consists of the 1675 Damm Garrison House, the 1813 Hale House (home to abolitionist Senator John P. Hale from 1840 to 1873), the 1818 Woodman House, and the 1825 Keefe House, which contains the excellent Thom Hindle Gallery. Exhibits focus on Early American cooking utensils, clothing, furniture, and Native American artifacts, as well as natural history and New Hampshire's involvement in the Civil War. ✉ *182 Central Ave., Dover* ☎ *603/742–1038* 🌐 *www.*

woodmanmuseum.org $15 Closed Mon. and Tues. and Dec.–Mar.

Restaurants

Hop + Grind

$ | **BURGER** | Students and faculty from UNH, whose campus is just a few blocks away, congregate over mammoth burgers with flavorful, original sides (kimchi, fries topped with cilantro-pickled peppers or black-garlic-truffle aioli) and other creative takes on gastropub fare. This is a hot spot for craft-beer aficionados, who appreciate the long list of options, including a rotating cache of rare and seasonal selections. **Known for:** impressive local beer selection; fun and lively student crowd; malted milk shakes with unusual flavors. *Average main: $11 Madbury Commons, 17 Madbury Rd., Durham 603/397–5564 www.hopandgrind.com.*

Savannah Kitchen

$$ | **SOUTHERN** | Located inside a restored mill building on the Lamprey River in the historic village of Newmarket, this festive tavern and bar with boldly colored walls and timber-beam ceilings specializes in flavorful—if decadent—regional Southern dishes like classic shrimp and grits, braised pork shoulder with Creole spices and red gravy, and grilled New Orleans–style oysters. It's also a fun spot for cocktails and conversation. **Known for:** $1 oysters on the half shell at happy hour; colorful drinks served in tiki-style tumblers; warm blueberry-peach bread pudding. *Average main: $19 55 Main St., Newmarket 603/292–5158 www.savannahkitchennewmarket.com No lunch.*

★ Stages at One Washington

$$$$ | **MODERN AMERICAN** | Offering stunning, reservation-only prix-fixe dinners featuring 8 to 10 small courses, this intimate open-kitchen space occupies the third floor of a converted redbrick mill building in Dover. The daily menu is based on what the talented culinary team here has sourced from farms and fishing boats—perhaps cured monkfish with green pea dashi and ramps, or lobster mushrooms with coffee, razor clams, and hazelnuts. **Known for:** artfully presented food; lavish multicourse dinners; optional wine pairings. *Average main: $150 1 Washington St., Dover 603/842–4077 www.stages-dining.com Closed Sun.–Tues. No lunch.*

Hotels

Three Chimneys Inn

$$ | **B&B/INN** | Since 1649, this stately yellow house has graced a hill overlooking the Oyster River; it now offers attractive rooms filled with period antiques and reproductions in the main house and a 1795 barn. **Pros:** charming, historic ambience; free parking and continental breakfast; reasonable rates. **Cons:** a long walk (or short drive) into town; restaurant is uneven in quality; books up on fall and spring weekends. *Rooms from: $179 17 Newmarket Rd., Durham 603/868–7800, 888/399–9777 www.threechimneysinn.com 23 rooms Free Breakfast.*

Nightlife

Garrison City Beerworks

BREWPUBS | In a stylish light-filled storefront space in downtown Dover with a large redbrick side patio, sip some of the state's most inventive craft beers, from saisons to stouts. Globally inspired street tacos (Korean beef, Nashville chicken) are offered too. *455 Central Ave., Dover 603/343–4231 www.garrisoncity-beerworks.com.*

★ Stone Church

LIVE MUSIC | This cool music club and pub in beautifully restored 1835 former Methodist church on a hilly bluff in

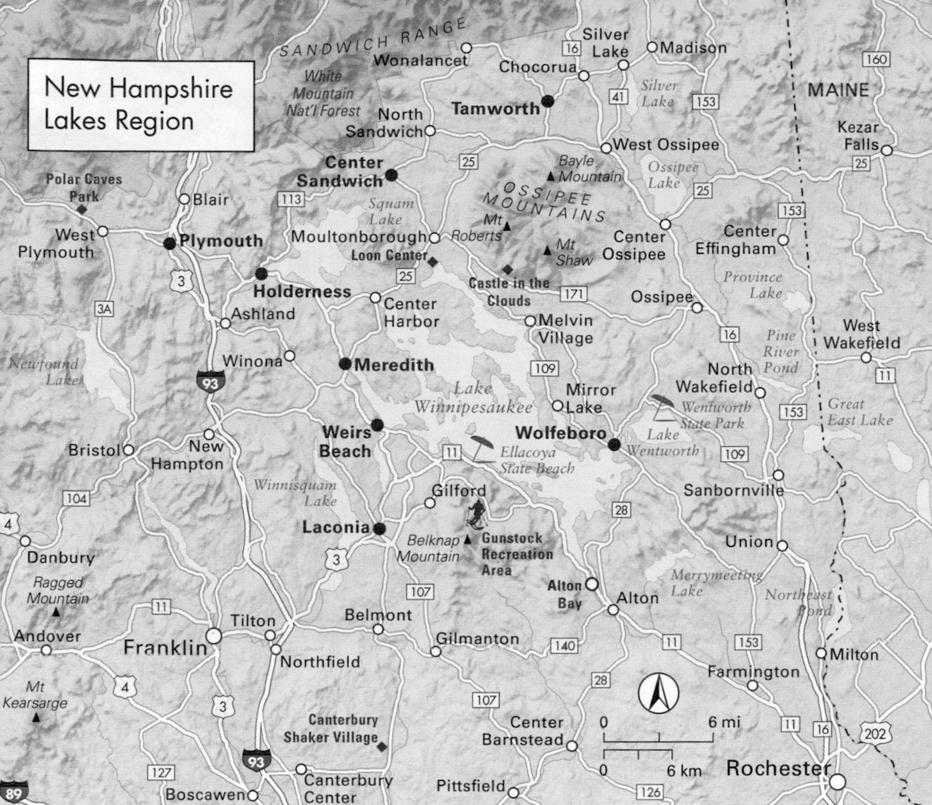

historic Newmarket presents first-rate rock, reggae, folk, jazz, and blues. ✉ *5 Granite St., Newmarket* ☎ *603/659–7700* 🌐 *www.stonechurchrocks.com.*

Shopping

★ Emery Farm

FOOD | FAMILY | In the same family since 1655, Emery Farm sells berries and produce in summer, pumpkins in fall, and Christmas trees in winter. The farm shop carries breads, pies, and local crafts, and a café serves sandwiches, ice cream, cider doughnuts, and other light fare. Enjoy pumpkin-patch hayrides in autumn and visit the petting barn May–October. ✉ *147 Piscataqua Rd., Durham* ☎ *603/742–8495* 🌐 *www.emeryfarm.com.*

Wolfeboro

40 miles northwest of Durham, 40 miles northeast of Concord.

Quietly upscale and decidedly preppy Wolfeboro has been a vacation getaway since Royal Governor John Wentworth built a home on the shore of Lake Winnipesaukee in 1768—hence its reputation as the country's oldest summer resort. Its waterfront downtown bursts with tony boutiques and eateries, while smaller Lake Wentworth—a few miles east—offers a quieter vibe. The century-old, white clapboard buildings of Brewster Academy prep school bracket the town's southern end.

With 240 miles of shoreline, Lake Winnipesaukee has something for everyone.

GETTING HERE AND AROUND

Route 28 connects Wolfeboro with the rest of Lake Winnipesaukee. Be prepared for lots of traffic in the summer.

ESSENTIALS

VISITOR INFORMATION Wolfeboro Area Chamber of Commerce. ✉ *Wolfeboro* ☎ *603/569–2200* 🌐 *www.wolfeborochamber.com.*

Sights

Alton Bay

TOWN | FAMILY | Two mountain ridges frame picturesque Alton Bay, which is the name of both a narrow 4-mile inlet and village at the southern tip of Lake Winnipesaukee, near Wolfeboro. Cruise boats dock here, and small float planes buzz just over the bay, sometimes flying in formation. There's a boardwalk, mini golf, a public beach, and a Victorian-style bandstand, and a few basic but fun short-order eateries near the waterfront, such as Pop's Clam Shell and Stillwells Ice Cream. ✉ *Rte. 11 at Rte. 28A, Alton Bay.*

★ New Hampshire Boat Museum

OTHER MUSEUM | FAMILY | Set in a 1950s quonset hut–style former dance hall near Lake Wentworth, this small but fascinating museum and boat-building center celebrates New Hampshire's maritime legacy with displays of vintage wooden boats, models, antique engines, racing photography, trophies, and vintage marina signs. You can also attend workshops on boat building and restoration, take sailing lessons, and go on 45-minute narrated rides on Lake Winnipesaukee in the *Millie B.*, reproduction 1928 triple-cockpit Hacker-Craft. ✉ *399 Center St., Wolfeboro* ☎ *603/569–4554* 🌐 *www.nhbm.org* 🎟 *$9, boat tours $40* ⏲ *Closed mid-Oct.–late May.*

Wright Museum

HISTORY MUSEUM | Uniforms, vehicles, and other artifacts at this museum illustrate the contributions of those on the home front to the U.S. World War II effort. ✉ *77 Center St., Wolfeboro* ☎ *603/569–1212* 🌐 *www.wrightmuseum.org* 🎟 *$14* ⏲ *Closed Nov.–Apr.*

Beaches

Wentworth State Park

BEACH | FAMILY | Away from the hustle and bustle of Wolfeboro on pretty little Lake Wentworth, this simple park features a quiet beach with good fishing, picnic tables and grills, and ball fields. **Amenities:** parking (no fee); showers; toilets. **Best for:** swimming; walking. *297 Governor Wentworth Hwy., Wolfeboro 603/569–3699 www.nhstateparks.org $4.*

Restaurants

East of Suez

$$ | ASIAN | In a countrified lodge on the south side of town, this friendly restaurant serves creative Asian cuisine, with an emphasis on Philippine fare, such as *lumpia* (pork-and-shrimp spring rolls with a sweet-and-sour fruit sauce) and *pancit canton* (panfried egg noodles with sautéed shrimp and pork and Asian vegetables with a sweet oyster sauce). You can also sample Thai red curries, Japanese tempura, and Korean-style flank steak. **Known for:** BYOB policy; banana tempura with coconut ice cream; plenty of vegan options. *Average main: $24 775 S. Main St., Wolfeboro 603/569–1648 www.eastofsuez.com Closed Mon. and early Sept.–late May. No lunch.*

★ Pavilion

$$$ | MODERN AMERICAN | Guests of the Pickering House hotel had become so enamored of the inn's occasional dinners and other food events that the owners opened this full-time restaurant in the Victorian house next door. Showcasing creative American fare sourced locally and seasonally as much as possible, the kitchen serves an oft-changing menu that might feature pan-roasted duck breast with garlic-roasted radicchio and roasted figs, and mussels in a green curry–coconut broth with lime and cilantro. **Known for:** elegant early-19th-century building; exceptional wine list; creative seasonal fruit desserts and house-made ice creams. *Average main: $33 126 S. Main St., Wolfeboro 603/393–0851 www.pavilionwolfeboro.com Closed Mon. and Tues. No lunch.*

Hotels

Lake Wentworth Inn

$ | MOTEL | This attractively renovated vintage motor lodge, just a five-minute walk from Lake Wentworth and Albee Beach, has been brightened up with an inviting midcentury cottage look and such family-friendly features as a game room and guest library. **Pros:** pool, game room, and library; short walk to beach; clean and very affordable. **Cons:** no breakfast; not directly on the water; a short drive from downtown. *Rooms from: $149 427 Center St., Wolfeboro 603/569–1700 www.lakewentworthinn.com 43 rooms No Meals.*

★ Pickering House

$$$$ | B&B/INN | Following an extensive renovation by amiable innkeepers Peter and Patty Cook, this striking yellow 1813 Federal mansion ranks among New Hampshire's most luxurious small inns. **Pros:** ultracushy rooms; the adjacent restaurant, Pavilion, is superb; in-town location. **Cons:** on busy street; among the highest rates in the state; not suitable for children. *Rooms from: $610 116 S. Main St., Wolfeboro 603/569–6948 www.pickeringhousewolfeboro.com 10 rooms Free Breakfast.*

Nightlife

Lone Wolfe Brewing

BREWPUBS | Sample raspberry sours and the heady Dippah Double IPA in the cheerful taproom of this downtown brewhouse that also serves tasty pub fare and presents live music many weekends inside or in the outdoor beer garden. *36 Mill St., Wolfeboro 603/515–1099 www.thelonewolfe.com.*

Shopping

Black's Paper Store

SOUVENIRS | Browse regionally made soaps, chocolates, maple products, pottery, candles, lotions, potions, yarns, toys, and gifts at this vast old-fashioned emporium that dates back to the 1860s. ✉ *8 S. Main St., Wolfeboro* ☎ *603/569–4444* 🌐 *www.blacksgiftsnh.com.*

The Country Bookseller

BOOKS | **FAMILY** | You'll find an excellent regional-history section and plenty of children's titles at this independent bookstore, where you can do a little reading in the small café. ✉ *23A N. Main St., Wolfeboro* ☎ *603/569–6030* 🌐 *www.thecountrybookseller.com.*

Yum Yum Shop

FOOD | Picking up freshly baked breads, pastries, cookies, ice cream, and other sweets here has been a tradition since 1948. ✉ *16 N. Main St., Wolfeboro* ☎ *603/569–1919* 🌐 *www.yumyumshop.com.*

Activities

HIKING

Abenaki Tower

HIKING & WALKING | **FAMILY** | A quarter-mile hike to this 100 foot post-and-beam tower north of town, followed by a climb to the top, rewards you with views of Lake Winnipesaukee and the Ossipee mountain range. It's particularly photogenic at sunset. ✉ *Rte. 109, Tuftonboro.*

Blue Job Mountain

HIKING & WALKING | A wildflower-strewn 3.3-mile loop trail reaches the summit of Blue Job Mountain, 25 miles south of Wolfeboro, where a 1913 fire tower provides a panoramic view of the Atlantic Ocean, White Mountains, and even Boston on a clear day. ✉ *First Crown Point Rd., Strafford.*

★ Mt. Major

HIKING & WALKING | About 5 miles north of Alton Bay, a rugged 3-mile trail up a series of granite cliffs leads to this dramatic summit. At the top you'll find a four-sided stone shelter built in 1925, but the real reward is the spectacular view of Lake Winnipesaukee. ✉ *Rte. 11, Alton Bay.*

Laconia and Weirs Beach

25 miles west of Wolfeboro, 27 miles north of Concord.

The arrival of the railroad in 1848 turned the sleepy hamlet of Laconia into the Lakes Region's chief manufacturing hub—downtown's 1823 Belknap Mill still stands as a monument to this legacy. At the north end of town, Weirs Beach is a hub of summertime arcade activity, with souvenir shops, fireworks, the Bank of NH outdoor concert pavilion, and legions of kids. Cruise boats also depart from here, and the refurbished Winnipesaukee Pier has family-oriented restaurants and other amusements. In June, bikers from around the world arrive for Laconia Motorcycle Week.

GETTING HERE AND AROUND

Laconia offers easy access from Interstate 93 in Tilton, where you'll find a clutch of outlet shops, and to both Winnisquam and Winnipesaukee lakes, via U.S. 3 or Route 11.

Sights

★ Canterbury Shaker Village

MUSEUM VILLAGE | **FAMILY** | Established in 1792, this community 15 miles south of Laconia flourished in the 1800s and practiced equality of the sexes and races, common ownership, celibacy, and pacifism. The last member of the religious community passed away in 1992. Shakers invented such household items as the clothespin and the flat broom and were known for the simplicity and integrity of their designs. Engaging

View simple yet functional furniture, architecture, and crafts at Canterbury Shaker Village.

guided tours—you can also explore on your own—pass through some of the 694-acre property's nearly 30 restored buildings, many of them with original furnishings. Crafts demonstrations take place daily. An excellent shop sells handcrafted wares. *288 Shaker Rd., Canterbury 603/783–9511 www.shakers.org Grounds free, guided tours $25 Closed Dec.–Apr.*

Funspot

AMUSEMENT PARK/CARNIVAL | FAMILY | The mothership of Lake Winnipesaukee's family-oriented amusement parks, Funspot's more than 600 video games make it the world's largest arcade—there's even an arcade museum. You can also work your way through an indoor minigolf course and 20 lanes of bowling. Rates vary depending on the activity. *579 Endicott St. N, Weirs Beach 603/366–4377 www.funspotnh.com.*

★ MS Mount Washington

MARINA/PIER | FAMILY | The 230-foot M/S *Mount Washington* offers 2½-hour scenic cruises of Lake Winnipesaukee, departing Weirs Beach with stops at Wolfeboro, Alton Bay, Center Harbor, and Meredith depending on the day. Sunset cruises include live music and a buffet dinner. The same company operates the *Sophie C.* ($42), which has been the area's floating post office for more than a century. The boat departs from Weirs Beach with mail and passengers, passing through parts of the lake not accessible to larger ships. The *Winnipesaukee Spirit* ($30) offers summer cocktail cruises on Meredith Bay. *211 Lakeside Ave., Weirs Beach 603/366–5531 www.cruisenh.com From $42 Closed mid-Oct.–mid-May.*

Winnipesaukee Scenic Railroad

TRAIN/TRAIN STATION | FAMILY | You can board this scenic railroad's restored cars at Weirs Beach or Meredith for one- or two-hour rides along the shoreline. Special excursions include fall foliage and the Santa train. *211 Lakeside Ave., Weirs Beach 603/745–2135 www.hoborr.com From $22.*

Beaches

Ellacoya State Park

BEACH | FAMILY | Families enjoy this secluded 600-foot sandy beach and park on the southwestern shore of Lake Winnipesaukee. Ellacoya, with views of the Sandwich and Ossipee mountains, has a shallow beach that's safe for small children, sheltered picnic tables, and a small campground. **Amenities:** parking (fee); toilets. **Best for:** solitude; swimming. *266 Scenic Rd., Gilford 603/293–7821 www.nhstateparks.org $5 mid-May–late Sept.*

Restaurants

Local Eatery

$$$ | MODERN AMERICAN | Proof that impressive dining in the Lakes Region isn't always near the water, this elegant restaurant is set beneath the soaring ceiling of downtown Laconia's historic train depot. Favoring local ingredients, the kitchen turns out inventive renditions of classic American dishes, like scallops and grits with a sweet corn butter sauce, and coffee-rubbed pork tenderloin. **Known for:** artisan butter boards with roasted garlic and focaccia; inviting patio; apple tart tatin with caramel sauce. *Average main: $30 21 Veterans Sq., Laconia 603/527–8007 www.laconialocaleatery.com Closed Sun. and Mon. No lunch.*

Hotels

★ Lake House at Ferry Point

$$ | B&B/INN | This gracious red Victorian farmhouse, built as a summer getaway for the Pillsbury family of baking fame, has a peaceful setting on Lake Winnisquam. **Pros:** hearty full breakfast included; free use of kayaks; private dock and a small beach. **Cons:** not within walking distance of dining or shopping; may be a little quiet for some families; two-night minimum many weekends. *Rooms from: $215 100 Lower Bay Rd., Sanbornton 603/637–1758 www.newhampshire-inn.com 9 rooms Free Breakfast.*

Lake Opechee Inn & Spa

$$$ | HOTEL | Slightly removed from, but within a short drive of, the crowds of Weirs Beach, this boutique spa hotel set in a converted mill is a great place to chill out, enjoy a shiatsu massage or cranberry facial, and savor dinner and cocktails on a patio overlooking the lake. **Pros:** views of Lake Opechee; appealing spa and restaurant; many rooms have balconies, gas fireplaces, and jetted tubs. **Cons:** indoor pool is small; in a busy part of Laconia; 10-minute drive to Winnipesaukee. *Rooms from: $244 62 Doris Day Ct., Laconia 603/524–0111 www.opecheeinn.com 34 rooms Free Breakfast.*

Activities

SKIING

Gunstock Mountain Resort

SKIING & SNOWBOARDING | FAMILY | This ski resort with a 2,267-foot summit and ample snowmaking capacity offers plenty of beginner terrain along with snow-tubing and a 22-acre terrain park. Nearly half of the trails offer night skiing, and you'll find 14 miles of cross-country and snowshoeing runs. In summer the Adventure Park offers a fantastic zipline system—the longest run at 3,981 feet—an aerial obstacle course, a 4,100-foot mountainside roller coaster (also open in winter), and scenic chairlift rides that access great hiking (the Ridge Trail is especially scenic). There's also mountain biking, a wetlands boardwalk, e-bike tours, kayak rentals, and a stocked fishing pond. **Facilities:** 49 trails; 227 acres; 1,340-foot vertical drop; 7 lifts. *719 Cherry Valley Rd., Gilford 603/293–4341 www.gunstock.com Lift ticket: $100.*

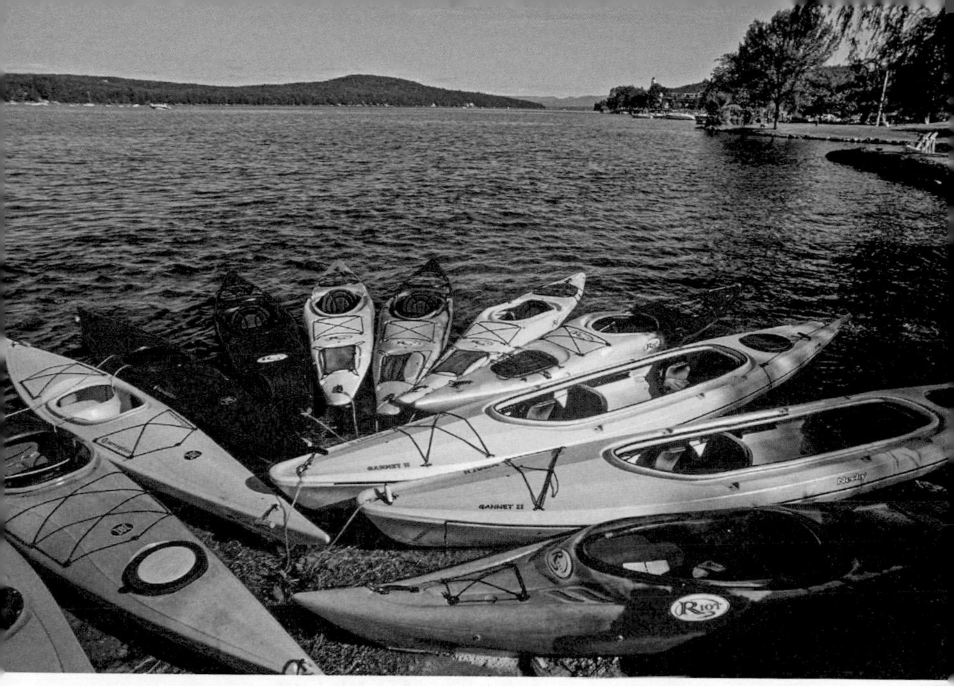

What's your vessel of choice for exploring New Hampshire's Lakes Region: kayak, canoe, powerboat, or sailboat?

Meredith

11 miles north of Laconia.

For many years a workaday mill town with relatively little touristic appeal, Meredith has become a popular summer getaway thanks largely to the transformation of several historic buildings into Mill Falls, now a cluster of hotels, restaurants, and shops overlooking Lake Winnipesaukee. Take a stroll down Main Street, which is dotted with boutiques and antiques stores, and along the lakefront, where you'll find a bustling marina, sculpture walk, and some lively dockside restaurants.

GETTING HERE AND AROUND

You can reach Meredith from Interstate 93 via Route 104, or from points south on U.S. 3 (beware the heavy weekend traffic). In town, it's easy to get around on foot.

ESSENTIALS

VISITOR INFORMATION Meredith Area Chamber of Commerce. ✉ *Meredith* ☎ *603/279–6121* 🌐 *www.meredithareachamber.com.*

Sights

Hermit Woods Winery

WINERY | Stop by this contemporary downtown winery to sample the light and fruity wines and hard ciders, made with local blueberries, apples, cranberries, and honeys as well as imported grapes. Tours, which include a barrel tasting, are available, and you can order cheese, charcuterie, and other treats from the deli to enjoy while sipping outside on the deck. On weekend evenings, there's live piano in the Loft lounge. ✉ *72 Main St., Meredith* ☎ *603/253–7968* 🌐 *www.hermitwoods.com.*

Meredith Sculpture Walk

PUBLIC ART | **FAMILY** | Throughout town, especially in parks beside the lake and at the gardens at Mill Falls Marketplace, you'll see colorful contemporary artworks. They're part of the Annual Meredith Sculpture walk, a year-round juried event featuring 33 distinctive pieces by renowned sculptors. Each June, a new collection of sculptures is installed. For a detailed look, take a free guided tour, offered at 10 am daily, mid-July and early September. ✉ *Meredith* 🌐 *www.meredithsculpturewalk.org.*

Restaurants

Canoe

$$ | MODERN AMERICAN | Just up the road in Center Harbor, this boathouse-inspired bistro sits high above Lake Winnipesaukee and has seating in both a quieter dining room and a convivial bar with an open kitchen. It's known for seafood, including wood-fired, bacon-wrapped scallops and a creamy, entrée-size haddock chowder topped with herbs and crushed Ritz Crackers. **Known for:** fun people-watching at the bar; great wine and beer selection; salted-caramel brownie sundaes. *$ Average main: $25* ✉ *232 Whittier Hwy., Center Harbor* ☎ *603/253–4762* 🌐 *www.canoecenterharbor.com* ⏲ *Closed Wed. No lunch weekdays.*

Lakehouse Grille

$$$ | AMERICAN | With big windows overlooking the lake and timber posts and ceiling beams, this popular restaurant inside the Church Landing at Mill Falls hotel captures the rustic ambience of an old-fashioned camp dining room. Feast on classic American favorites with interesting twists, such as eggs Benedict topped with Maine lobster in the morning, and char-grilled steaks, chops, and seafood in the evening. **Known for:** blueberry pie with lemon ice cream; water views; Sunday jazz brunch. *$ Average main: $32* ✉ *Church Landing, 281 Daniel Webster Hwy., Meredith* ☎ *603/279–5221* 🌐 *www.thecman.com.*

Hotels

Mill Falls at the Lake

$$$ | HOTEL | Choose from four lodgings at this rambling resort: relaxing Church Landing and Bay Point are both on the shore of Lake Winnipesaukee; convivial Mill Falls—with a pool—and Chase House are across the street, next to a 19th-century mill that houses shops and restaurants. **Pros:** activity center with boat rentals and lake cruises; many dining options; spa with heated indoor-outdoor pool. **Cons:** rooms with water views are expensive; some properties aren't directly on the lake; somewhat impersonal, corporate feel. *$ Rooms from: $239* ✉ *312 Daniel Webster Hwy., Meredith* ☎ *603/279–7006, 844/745–2931* 🌐 *www.millfalls.com* *188 rooms* *No Meals.*

Nightlife

Twin Barns Brewing

BEER GARDENS | Serving a roster of well-crafted ales along with tasty comfort food (flatbread pizzas, burgers), this beer-centric compound occupies a handsome 1850s restored barn with a large tented beer garden. ✉ *194 Daniel Webster Hwy., Meredith* ☎ *603/279–0876* 🌐 *www.twinbarnsbrewing.com.*

Performing Arts

Interlakes Summer Theatre

THEATER | During its 10-week season of summer stock, this striking 420-seat theater presents classic Broadway musicals like *42nd Street, Evita,* and *West Side Story.* ✉ *1 Laker La., Meredith* ☎ *603/707–6035* 🌐 *www.interlakestheatre.com.*

★ Winnipesaukee Playhouse

THEATER | Since this critically lauded theater opened in a rustic yet state-of-the-art red-barn-style venue in 2013, it's become one of the top performing arts centers in the region, presenting well-known Broadway shows and original dramas and comedies year-round. ✉ *33 Footlight Circle, Meredith* ☎ *603/279–0333* 🌐 *www.winnipesaukeeplayhouse.org.*

Shopping

Annalee Dolls

TOYS | FAMILY | Everyone from young kids to ardent collectors makes the pilgrimage to the showroom of this internationally renowned shop that's been hand-crafting whimsical dolls since 1934. Annalee's expressive mice are a top draw, but holiday figurines are also highly popular. ✉ *339 Daniel Webster Hwy., Meredith* ☎ *800/433–6557* 🌐 *www.annalee.com.*

★ League of New Hampshire Craftsmen

CRAFTS | This eclectic gallery offers wares by more than 250 artisans working in everything from stained glass and ceramics to wrought iron and mixed media. Prices are surprisingly reasonable for many items, and there are additional branches in Center Sandwich, Concord, Hookset, Littleton, Nashua, and North Conway. ✉ *279 Daniel Webster Hwy., Meredith* ☎ *603/279–7920* 🌐 *www.meredith.nhcrafts.org.*

Activities

BOATING

Home to a popular marina, Meredith is also near the quaint village of Center Harbor, another boating hub in the middle of three bays at the north end of Lake Winnipesaukee.

★ EKAL

WATER SPORTS | At the lakefront activity center at Mill Falls, you can rent standup paddleboards, kayaks, canoes, aqua cycles, and bicycles, and book excursions on a restored 1931 Chris Craft runabout. ✉ *285 Daniel Webster Hwy. (U.S. 3), Meredith* ☎ *603/677–8646* 🌐 *www.ekalactivitycenter.com.*

GOLF

Waukewan Golf Club

GOLF | This beautiful, well-groomed course with undulating fairways and several challenging blind shots has been a local favorite since the late '50s. ✉ *166 Waukewan Rd., Center Harbor* ☎ *603/279–6661* 🌐 *www.waukewangolfclub.com* 🎫 *$34* ⛳ *18 holes, 5828 yards, par 72.*

Plymouth

16 miles northwest of Meredith, 22 miles south of North Woodstock.

Home to Plymouth State University, whose small but attractive campus clings to a steep hill looming over an attractive, bustling downtown, Plymouth acts as a bridge between White Mountains and the Lakes Region; it's especially convenient for visiting 4,000-acre Newfound Lake, one of the state's deepest and purest bodies of water, as well as Squam Lake. It's also close to some great hiking to the west, including 3,121-foot Mt. Cardigan, in nearby Alexandria, and Big and Little Sugarloaf peaks, the trailhead for which is reached along West Shore Road, near the entrance to Wellington State Park.

GETTING HERE AND AROUND

Plymouth is just off Interstate 93.

Sights

Polar Caves Park

CAVE | FAMILY | From the attractive log cabin–style main lodge, an easy trail leads to nine granite caves that formed some 50,000 years ago, during the last ice age. This family-friendly attraction begun in 1922 also contains a small petting zoo with a herd of adorable fallow deer. ✉ *705 Rte. 25, Rumney* ☎ *603/536–1888* 🌐 *www.polarcaves.com* 🎫 *$27* ⏲ *Closed mid-Oct.–mid-May.*

★ **Wellington State Park**

STATE/PROVINCIAL PARK | FAMILY | At this picturesque 220-acre park on the west shore of glorious Newfound Lake, about 12 miles from Plymouth, you'll find the largest freshwater beach in the state park system. Enjoy the picnic and fishing areas, numerous hiking trails, and boat launch. ✉ *614 W. Shore Rd., Bristol* ☎ *603/744–2197* 🌐 *www.nhstateparks.org* 🎟 *$5 mid-May–mid-Sept.*

Restaurants

★ **Benton's Sugar Shack**

$ | AMERICAN | FAMILY | A legit contender in New Hampshire's fierce battle for the best pancake house, this rustic timber-frame roadhouse is run by a family who've been producing maple syrup for five generations. Open only on weekends, Benton's serves stacks of pancakes in several flavors, including strawberry shortcake, Mounds Bar, and Grandma's apple cinnamon. **Known for:** sides of maple kielbasa and baked beans; "design your own" pancakes with custom fillings; raspberry-stuffed French toast. $ *Average main: $9* ✉ *2010 Rte. 175, Thornton* ☎ *603/726–3867* 🌐 *www.bentonssugarshack.com* ⏲ *Closed Mon.–Wed. No dinner.*

Covered Bridge Farm Table

$$ | MODERN AMERICAN | With tall windows as well as a large deck overlooking the historic Blair Covered Bridge and the Pemigewasset River, this rustic restaurant serves an eclectic mix of Asian, Mediterranean, and American dishes and is a favorite place to refuel after hiking in the White Mountains or boating on Squam Lake. Good bets include wild-caught salmon with a ginger-scallion vinaigrette and butter chicken with garam masala, ginger, and jasmine rice. **Known for:** apple-cider-donut ice cream sandwiches; diverse, international menu; expansive riverfront deck. $ *Average main: $23* ✉ *57 Blair Rd., Campton* ☎ *603/238–9115* 🌐 *www.farmtablenh.com* ⏲ *Closed Sun. and Tues.*

★ **Little Red Schoolhouse**

$$ | AMERICAN | FAMILY | Lobster-roll aficionados flock to this funky converted schoolhouse with screened-in and outdoor seating high on a bluff above the Pemigewasset River. Start with a cup of lobster bisque or clam chowder before digging into a traditional (lightly dressed, with mayo) or hot-buttered lobster roll—both come on a warm, buttered brioche roll, best enjoyed with a side of garlic fries. **Known for:** pretty river and forest views; good craft beer selection; homemade ice-cream sandwiches. $ *Average main: $22* ✉ *1994 Daniel Webster Hwy., Campton* ☎ *603/726–6142* 🌐 *www.littleredschoolhousenh.com* ⏲ *Closed mid-Oct.–mid-May.*

Six Burner Bistro

$$$ | MODERN AMERICAN | In this charming red Victorian house on Plymouth's bustling Main Street, with some seats on the front veranda and others set in a warren of cozy rooms with art on the walls, this casually elegant spot offers tasty American and international fare. Consider Szechuan-style salmon ramen, and blackened grilled chicken with honeydew-melon salsa and tzatziki sauce. **Known for:** sourcing from local farms; well-selected wine and beer list; creative salad options with myriad protein add-ons. $ *Average main: $28* ✉ *13 S. Main St., Plymouth* ☎ *603/536–9099* 🌐 *www.sixburnerbistro.com* ⏲ *Closed Sun.–Tues.*

Hotels

Common Man Inn & Spa

$$ | HOTEL | This contemporary hotel with country lodge–inspired furnishings, just off I–93 a little north of downtown, contains warmly appointed rooms in a variety of configurations; some have whirlpool tubs and fireplaces, and a few have cozy sleeping lofts. **Pros:** pets are welcome; relaxing spa; convenient to White Mountains and Lakes Region. **Cons:** often booked up with weddings; small pool; 15-minute walk from downtown. $ *Rooms from: $159* ✉ *231 Main St., Plymouth* ☎ *603/536–2200, 866/843–2626* 🌐 *www.thecmaninnplymouth.com* *38 rooms* *Free Breakfast.*

 Performing Arts

★ Flying Monkey

CONCERTS | Set in downtown Plymouth's brightly restored 1920s movie house, this cinema and performing arts center presents dinner theater and other live comedy and music shows, plus retro movies. A balcony bar serves wine and beer. ✉ *39 Main St., Plymouth* ☎ *603/536–2551* 🌐 *www.flyingmonkeynh.com.*

Holderness

7 miles southeast of Plymouth, 8 miles northwest of Meredith.

This peaceful village straddles two of the state's most scenic lakes, Squam and Little Squam, both of which have been spared from excessive development but do offer some memorable inns that are perfect for a tranquil getaway. *On Golden Pond,* starring Katharine Hepburn and Henry Fonda, was filmed on Squam, whose beauty attracts nature lovers.

GETTING HERE AND AROUND

Holderness is easy to reach from Interstate 93 and U.S. 3.

 Sights

★ Squam Lakes Natural Science Center

NATURE PRESERVE | FAMILY | This 230-acre property includes a ¾-mile nature trail that passes by trailside live-animal exhibits of black bears, bobcats, otters, fishers, mountain lions, red foxes, and raptors. A pontoon boat cruise offers the best way to tour the waterfront—naturalists talk about native fauna, from bald eagles to loons; dinner and sunset options are available. Kids' programs teach about insects and wilderness survival skills. The center also operates nearby 1-acre Kirkwood Gardens and maintains three short hiking trails, all of which you can access for free. ✉ *23 Science Center Rd., Holderness* ☎ *603/968–7194* 🌐 *www.nhnature.org* *Trail $22, lake cruise $27* *Live-animal exhibits closed Nov.–Apr.*

 Restaurants

Walter's Basin

$$$ | AMERICAN | A former bowling alley in the heart of Holderness makes an unlikely but charming setting for meals overlooking Little Squam Lake—local boaters dock right beneath the dining room. Among the specialties on the seafood-intensive menu are shellfish paella, and sea scallops with a creamy bacon-corn-poblano succotash, while sandwiches and salads are among the lighter options. **Known for:** dockside setting; live music some summer evenings; fried whole-belly clams. $ *Average main: $26* ✉ *859 U.S. 3, Holderness* ☎ *603/968–4412* 🌐 *www.waltersbasin.com.*

 Hotels

Cottage Place on Squam

$$ | MOTEL | This sweet, old-fashioned compound of cottages and suites on Little Squam Lake is a terrific find—and value—for families, as nearly all units have partial or full kitchens, and many can comfortably sleep up to five guests (there's also a six-bedroom lodge that groups can rent entirely). **Pros:** reasonably priced; lots of on-site activities, from kayaking to shuffleboard; well-curated shop has fun one-of-a-kind gifts. **Cons:** the retro ambience isn't at all fancy; family popularity might be a turnoff if seeking peace and quiet; no restaurant. $ *Rooms from: $159* ✉ *1132 U.S. 3, Holderness* ☎ *603/968–7116* 🌐 *www.cottageplaceonsquam.com* *15 rooms* *No Meals.*

★ Inn on Golden Pond

$$$$ | B&B/INN | The hospitable innkeepers at this comfortable and informal B&B a short distance from Squam Lake make every possible effort to accommodate their guests—many of whom are repeat clients—from providing them with hiking trail maps to using rhubarb grown on property to make the jam served during the delicious country breakfasts. **Pros:** 50-acre property with woodland and lake views; comfortable indoor and outdoor common spaces; generous full breakfast. **Cons:** not directly on the lake; a bit pricey; can't accommodate pets. *Rooms from: $315* ✉ *1080 U.S. 3, Holderness* ☎ *603/968–7269* *www.innongoldenpond.com* *8 rooms* *Free Breakfast.*

Manor on Golden Pond

$$$ | B&B/INN | A name like this is a lot to live up to, but the Manor generally succeeds: it's one of the region's most atmospheric inns, situated on a slight rise overlooking Squam Lake, with 15 acres of lawns, towering pines, and hardwood trees; a grand restaurant serving lavish modern European fare; and a small but well-outfitted spa. **Pros:** fireplaces and Jacuzzis in many rooms; gracious common spaces; afternoon high tea is served in the library. **Cons:** the top-tier suites are quite expensive; furnishings could stand a little refreshing; not suitable for younger kids. *Rooms from: $245* ✉ *31 Manor Rd., off Shepard Hill Rd., Holderness* ☎ *603/968–3348, 800/545–2141* *www.manorongoldenpond.com* *24 suites* *Free Breakfast.*

Activities

★ Squam Lakes Association

BOATING | FAMILY | You can rent kayaks and canoes, reserve campsites, enroll kids in education programs, and learn about local wildlife watching, fishing, and hiking opportunities at this nonprofit organization that's been focused on lake conservation since it formed in 1904. ✉ *534 U.S. 3, Holderness* ☎ *603/968–7336* *www.squamlakes.org.*

West Rattlesnake Mountain

HIKING & WALKING | The nearly 500-foot elevation gain of this moderately strenuous but fairly short 2.3-mile loop trail to the top of West Rattlesnake Mountain will get your heart pounding, but the panoramic views over Squam Lake are a satisfying reward. ✉ *Rte. 113, Holderness.*

Center Sandwich

12 miles northeast of Holderness.

With Squam Lake to the west, Lake Winnipesaukee to the south, and the Sandwich Mountains to the north, Center Sandwich offers one of the prettiest settings in the Lakes Region. So appealing are the town and its views that John Greenleaf Whittier used the Bearcamp River as the inspiration for his poem "Sunset on the Bearcamp." The town attracts artisans—crafts shops abound among its clutch of charming 18th- and 19th-century buildings.

GETTING HERE AND AROUND

You reach this rural town from Holderness via Route 113 and Meredith—by way of Center Harbor and Moultonborough—by Routes 25 and 109.

Sights

★ Castle in the Clouds

CASTLE/PALACE | Resembling a fairy-tale castle, this grand 1914 mountaintop estate is anchored by an elaborate mansion with 16 rooms, 8 bathrooms, and doors made of lead. Owner Thomas Gustave Plant spent $7 million—the bulk of his fortune—on this project and died penniless in 1941. Tours include the mansion and the Castle Springs water facility on this high Ossipee Mountain Range property overlooking Lake Winnipesaukee. Hiking (and cross-country skiing in winter) and pony and horse rides are also offered, along with lakeview terrace jazz dinners many summer evenings at the Carriage House restaurant, which is also open for lunch when mansion tours are offered. ✉ *455 Old Mountain Rd., Moultonborough* ☎ *603/476–5900* 🌐 *www.castleintheclouds.org* 🎟 *$20* ⏲ *Closed late Oct.–late May.*

Loon Center

WILDLIFE REFUGE | FAMILY | Recognizable for its eerie calls and striking black-and-white coloring, the loon resides on many New Hampshire lakes but is threatened by the gradual loss of its habitat. Two trails wind from the modern visitor center through this 200-acre lakeside wildlife sanctuary, which has made great progress in helping to restore the state's loon population, which currently stands at around 550; vantage points on the Loon Nest Trail overlook the spot resident loons sometimes occupy in late spring and summer. ✉ *183 Lee's Mills Rd., Moultonborough* ☎ *603/476–5666* 🌐 *www.loon.org* 🎟 *Free* ⏲ *Closed Sun.–Wed. in late-Oct.–Apr.*

Restaurants

Corner House Inn

$$ | AMERICAN | In a converted barn adorned with paintings by local artists, this rustic tavern in an 1840s building in charming Center Sandwich village dishes up classic American fare. Salads made with local greens and a maple vinaigrette are a house specialty, but don't overlook the mac and cheese with house-made sauce and steak tips–and–lobster surf and turf. **Known for:** inviting art-filled dining room; tender steaks and prime rib; good list of reasonably priced wines. 💲 *Average main: $23* ✉ *22 Main St., Center Sandwich* ☎ *603/476–3060* 🌐 *www.nhcornerhouse.com* ⏲ *Closed Sun.–Tues. No lunch.*

Coffee and Quick Bites

Sandwich Creamery

$ | CAFÉ | FAMILY | This artisan dairy is located inside a converted general store that now carries gifts and foods from a few other local vendors, which you pick out from shelves and refrigerator cases and pay for yourself with cash or Venmo (the shop is unstaffed). The creamery sells delicious farmstead-made cheddar cheese as well as ice cream and ice cream sandwiches in about two-dozen flavors, including cinnamon, blueberry, and ginger. **Known for:** PB&J ice cream sandwiches; artisan cheddar cheeses; fresh-baked breads and other foods from local purveyors. 💲 *Average main: $4* ✉ *22 Main St., Center Sandwich* ☎ *603/284–6675* 🌐 *www.facebook.com/thesandwichcreamery* ⏲ *Closed Mon. and Tues.*

Shopping

Old Country Store and Museum

GENERAL STORE | A quirky spot to pick up maple syrup, aged cheeses, jams, molasses, penny candy, and other treats, this rambling shop dates to 1781 and also contains antique farm and forging equipment and other artifacts. ✉ *1011 Whittier Hwy., Moultonborough* ☎ *603/476–5750* 🌐 *www.nhcountrystore.com.*

Activities

BOATING

Wild Meadow Canoes & Kayaks

BOATING | Canoes and kayaks at this shop at the north tip of Lake Winnipesaukee, near the Center Harbor town line. ✉ *6 Whittier Hwy., Moultonborough* ☎ *603/253–7536* 🌐 *www.wildmeadowcanoes.com.*

HIKING

Red Hill

HIKING & WALKING | FAMILY | This 2,030-foot mountain really does turn red in autumn. At the top of the moderately steep 1.7-mile Fire Tower Trail, you can climb a fire tower for 360-degree views of Lake Winnipesaukee and Squam Lake, as well as the White Mountains beyond. To make a loop, return via the Cabin Trail. At the parking area, a small snack bar (open mostly on weekends) dispenses organic coffee, ice cream, and other treats. ✉ *Red Hill Rd., 2 miles west of Rte. 25, Moultonborough.*

Tamworth

13 miles east of Center Sandwich.

President Grover Cleveland summered in what remains a place of almost unreal quaintness: Tamworth is equally photogenic in verdant summer, during the fall foliage season, or under a blanket of winter snow. Cleveland's son, Francis, returned and founded the acclaimed Barnstormers Theatre in 1931. One of America's first summer theaters, it continues to this day. Tamworth has a clutch of villages within its borders, and six historic churches. In the hamlet of Chocorua, the view through the birches of Chocorua Lake has been so often photographed that you may experience déjà vu. Rising above the lake is Mt. Chocorua (3,490 feet), which has many good hiking trails.

GETTING HERE AND AROUND

Tamworth's main village, at the junction of Routes 113 and 113A, is tiny and can be strolled.

Sights

Remick Country Doctor Museum and Farm

FARM/RANCH | **FAMILY** | For 99 years (1894–1993) Dr. Edwin Crafts Remick and his father provided medical services to the Tamworth area and operated a family farm. These two houses now comprise a farm museum, with the second floor of the house kept as it was when Remick passed away, providing a glimpse into the life of a country doctor. The still-working farm features special activities, such as maple-syrup making, and has hiking trails and picnicking areas. ✉ *58 Cleveland Hill Rd., Tamworth* ☎ *603/323–7591* 🌐 *www.remickmuseum.org* 🎫 *Pay as you wish* 🕒 *Museum closed Sat.–Tues. in Nov.–Apr.*

★ Tamworth Distilling & Mercantile

DISTILLERY | Using a 250-gallon copper still constructed in Kentucky, this artisanal distillery set in a stately barn just a short stroll from famed Barnstormers Theatre produces exceptional craft spirits, including Chocorua Straight Rye, Von Humboldt's Turmeric Cordial, Tamworth Garden Spruce Gin, and several flavorful cordials. If you're lucky, your stop will include a chance to sample Eau de Musc, a limited-release whiskey infused with an oil extracted from the castor glands of beavers. ✉ *15 Cleveland Hill Rd., Tamworth* ☎ *603/323–7196* 🌐 *www.tamworthdistilling.com* 🕒 *Closed Mon.–Tues.*

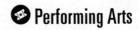

Performing Arts

★ Barnstormers Theatre

THEATER | Founded in 1931, this highly respected theater company presents dramas and comedies June–August. ✉ *104 Main St., Tamworth* ☎ *603/323–8500* 🌐 *www.barnstormerstheatre.org.*

Activities

White Lake State Park

HIKING & WALKING | The 72-acre stand of native pitch pine here is a National Natural Landmark. The park has a picnic area and a sandy beach, trails you can hike, trout you can fish for, and canoes you can rent. ✉ *94 State Park Rd., Tamworth* ☎ *603/323–7350* 🌐 *www.nhstateparks.org* 🎫 *$5 late May–mid-Oct.*

North Conway

20 miles north of Tamworth, 42 miles east North Woodstock, 62 miles northwest of Portland, Maine.

Before the arrival of the popular Settlers Green outlet stores, this town drew visitors for its inspiring scenery, ski resorts, and access to White Mountain National Forest. Today, however, the feeling of natural splendor is gone. Shopping is the big sport, and businesses line Route 16 for several miles. You'll get a close look at them as traffic often slows to a crawl. It's a bit of a food desert, too, with plenty of options but few of them notable.

GETTING HERE AND AROUND

Route 16 bisects town but can be clogged with traffic. Take the scenic West Side Road from Conway to Intervale, or even on to Bartlett if you're headed farther north, to circumvent the traffic and take in splendid views.

ESSENTIALS

VISITOR INFORMATION Mt. Washington Valley Chamber of Commerce. ✉ *North Conway* ☎ *877/948–6867* 🌐 *www.visitmwv.com.*

Sights

Conway Scenic Railroad

TRAIN/TRAIN STATION | FAMILY | Departing from historic North Conway Station, the railroad operates various trips aboard vintage trains. The Notch Train to Crawford Depot or to Fabyan Station travels through rugged territory yielding wonderful views, which are best enjoyed from the premium-class Upper Dome cars. The shorter Conway Valley Train offers glimpses of Mt. Washington during a 55-minute round-trip journey to Conway or a 1¾-hour excursion to Bartlett. The 1874 station displays lanterns, old tickets and timetables, and other artifacts. Reserve early during foliage season. Some rides include box lunches or full dinners. ✉ *38 Norcross Cir., North Conway* ☎ *603/356–5251* 🌐 *www.conwayscenic.com* 🎫 *From $21* 🕓 *Closed Dec.–Mar.*

Echo Lake State Park

STATE/PROVINCIAL PARK | FAMILY | You don't have to be a rock climber to enjoy the views from the 700-foot White Horse and Cathedral ledges, which you can reach via a 1.7-mile road. From the top, you'll see the entire valley, including Echo Lake, which offers fishing, swimming, boating, and, on quiet days, an excellent opportunity to shout for echoes. ✉ *68 Echo Lake Rd., Conway* ☎ *603/356–2672* 🌐 *www.nhstateparks.org* 🎫 *$4 early May–Oct.*

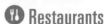

Restaurants

Muddy Moose

$ | AMERICAN | FAMILY | This playfully themed lodge-style restaurant buzzes with the sound of happy kids, but everyone seems to enjoy the rustic trappings, which include a huge stone fireplace, moose-antler chandeliers, and mounted animals. The comfort food here is reliably good, from barbecue rack of ribs to peppercorn-mushroom burgers, and there's a good selection of local beers. **Known for:** half-pound burgers with plenty of toppings; extensive kids offerings; Paradise four-layer chocolate cake. [$] *Average main: $17* ✉ *2344 White Mountain Hwy., North Conway* ☎ *603/356–7696* 🌐 *www.muddymoose.com.*

Table + Tonic Farm Cafe

$ | MODERN AMERICAN | The green-thumb-savvy proprietors of the popular and adjacent Local Grocer natural foods market operate this hip farm-to-table café. In this sleek, solar-powered establishment you can feast on fresh baked goods, organic-egg dishes, leafy salads, healthy sandwiches, and smoothies and espresso drinks. **Known for:** healthy breakfast and lunch fare; good selection of local beers and craft cocktails; attractive side patio overlooking a leafy garden. [$] *Average main: $11* ✉ *3358 White Mountain Hwy.,*

The White Mountains
CANADA
QUÉBEC
VERMONT
MAINE
Highlands
Gorham
Mt. Madison
Mt. Adams
Mt. Jefferson
Mt. Clay
Mt. Washington Auto Road
Mount Washington Cog Railway
Mt. Washington State Park
Fabyan
Observatory
Pinkham Notch
Bretton Woods
Mt. Washington
Crawford Notch
WHITE MOUNTAINS
Jackson
Crawford Notch State Park
Story Land
Glen
Bartlett
Echo Lake State Park
North Conway
0 4mi
0 4 km
First Connecticut Lake
Pittsburg
Lake Francis
Aziscobos Lake
Beecher Falls
Wilsons Mills
The Great North Woods
Colebrook
Dixville Notch
Errol
Lake Willoughby
North Stratford
Umbagog Lake
Upton
0 8mi
0 8 km
West Burke
Maidstone Lake
Groveton
West Milan
Milan
Guildhall
White Mountain Nat'l Forest
Lyndonville
Lyndon
Lancaster
Berlin
Weeks State Park
Jefferson
Gilead
Concord
See Detail Above
Danville
Saint Johnsbury
Whitefield
Mount Adams
Littleton
Bethlehem
Twin Mountain
Barnet
The Rocks Estate
Franconia
Wildcat Mountain
North Chatham
Lisbon
Old Man of the Mountain
Franconia Notch State Park
Wells River
Cannon Mt.
Woodsville
Flume Gorge
White Mountain National Forest
Cranmore Mountain
Whale's Tale Waterpark
Lost River Gorge & Boulder Caves
Loon Mountain
Attitash Ski Resort
Newbury
Bear Notch Rd.
Fryeburg
White Mountain Nat'l Forest
Lincoln
North Woodstock
Kancamagus Hwy.
Conway
Bradford
Waterville Valley
Mount Chocurua
Conway Lake
TO HANOVER
TO CONCORD
TO SNOWVILLE, EAST MADISON
257
2
16
3
102
26
105
5
114
110
91
113
93
116
302
112
10
25
49
118
153

North Conway ☎ 603/356–6068 🌐 www.tableandtonic.com ⏲ Closed Tues. and Wed. No dinner.

Hotels

The Buttonwood Inn
$$$ | **B&B/INN** | A tranquil oasis in a busy resort area, the Buttonwood sits on Mt. Surprise, 2 miles northeast of North Conway village—close enough to access area dining and shopping, but far away from noise and crowds of downtown. **Pros:** delicious breakfasts; year-round outdoor hot tub and fire pit; 6 acres of peaceful grounds. **Cons:** too secluded for some; swimming pool is seasonal; some rooms have private baths down the hall. *Rooms from: $238 ✉ 64 Mt. Surprise Rd., North Conway ☎ 603/356–2625 🌐 www.buttonwoodinn.com 10 rooms Free Breakfast.*

Cranmore Inn
$$ | **B&B/INN** | **FAMILY** | Just a block from the restaurants, shops, and attractions along Route 16 in North Conway, this rambling structure built in 1863 offers a nice range of upscale accommodations with modern furnishings, from two-bedroom apartments with kitchens and balconies to cozier standard rooms. **Pros:** very friendly and kind innkeepers; short walk from local dining and attractions; a wide range of room sizes and configurations. **Cons:** no elevator; in a town that can get very crowded in high season; some noise from street traffic. *Rooms from: $174 ✉ 80 Kearsarge Rd., North Conway ☎ 603/356–5502 🌐 www.cranmoreinn.com 20 rooms Free Breakfast.*

Huttopia White Mountains
$ | **RESORT** | **FAMILY** | Convenience to the Kancamagus Highway and the Lakes Region are among the draws of this 50-acre glamping (cabins and canvas tents) compound on a pristine mountain lake and offering a wealth of amenities, including a food truck, pool, beach, yoga classes, and recreational activities. Kayak and paddleboard rentals are available. Some units overlook the lake. **Pros:** plenty to keep kids and families entertained; high-quality bedding and cooking equipment; good range of accommodation types and styles. **Cons:** at some sites you can hear cars from the road; lively, family-oriented vibe may not suit everyone; units can be hard to heat on cool spring and fall nights. *Rooms from: $112 ✉ Pine Knoll Rd., Albany ☎ 844/488–8674, 603/447–3131 🌐 www.canada-usa.huttopia.com ⏲ Closed mid-Oct.–mid-May 97 units No Meals.*

Inn at Crystal Lake
$$ | **B&B/INN** | In the quaint village of Eaton Center, about 10 miles south of North Conway, this stately 1884 Greek Revival inn contains finely appointed rooms with dramatic themes, each filled with a mix of curious and whimsical art and collectibles from the innkeepers' travels. **Pros:** short walk to the lake; convivial pub with good food; good base for White Mountains, Lakes Region, and Maine's Stone Mountain Arts Center. **Cons:** secluded area; few dining options nearby; may feel a bit old-fashioned for some. *Rooms from: $169 ✉ 2356 Eaton Rd., Eaton Center ☎ 603/447–2120 🌐 www.innatcrystallake.com 11 rooms Free Breakfast.*

Purity Spring Resort
$$ | **RESORT** | **FAMILY** | Set on the pine-shaded shore of a rippling outdoor lake and adjacent to the slopes of King Pine Ski Area, this inviting boutique resort is a year-round destination for family-friendly recreation. Amenities are extensive and include lawn games, an indoor pool, free use of kayaks and canoes, and a restaurant with traditional but reliably good food. Accommodations come in a variety of shapes and sizes, and many have kitchens. This is a great option for a family getaway or reunion. **Pros:** wide range of accommodations (some that are perfect for large families); scenic

lakefront setting; lots of recreational activities. **Cons:** lots of very active families; resort fee; remote location with few dining options nearby. *Rooms from: $159* *1256 Eaton Rd. Madison* *603/367-8896, 800/373-3754* *www.purityspring.com* *67 units* *No Meals.*

★ Snowvillage Inn

$$ | B&B/INN | The finest room in this pastoral inn's main gambrel-roof house (built in 1916) has 12 windows that look out over the Presidential Range, and many guest rooms—some in a carriage house and a new outbuilding—have fireplaces. **Pros:** spectacular views; use of snowshoes and 10 acres of trails; delicious full breakfasts. **Cons:** off the beaten path; no TVs in rooms; not many dining options nearby. *Rooms from: $179* *136 Stewart Rd., Eaton Center* *603/447-2818* *www.snowvillageinn.com* *17 rooms* *Free Breakfast.*

Nightlife

Delaney's Hole in the Wall

PUBS | This legendary après-ski tavern has a real fondness for ski history, displaying early photos of local ski areas, old signs and placards, and odd bits of lift equipment. Enjoy watching games on TV in the sports-bar area and noshing on comforting pub fare. *2966 White Mountain Hwy., North Conway* *603/356-7776* *www.delaneys.com.*

★ Tuckerman Brewing Co.

BEER GARDENS | Offering live music on weekends, seating inside as well as—during the warmer months—in a huge tented beer garden, light snacks, and some of the freshest and tastiest beer in the state, this venerable craft brewery on the edge of downtown Conway is a fun place to relax after a hike or mingle with friends. *66 Hobbs St., Conway* *603/447-5400* *www.tuckermanbrewing.com.*

Shopping

More than 120 factory outlets—including L.L. Bean, J. Crew, New Balance, Columbia, Talbots, Polo, Nike, Banana Republic, and American Eagle—line Route 16.

Handcrafters Barn

CRAFTS | The work of 150 area artists and artisans are sold in this attractive red-clapboard building. *2473 White Mountain Hwy., North Conway* *603/356-8996* *www.handcraftersbarn.com.*

Activities

SKIING

Cranmore Mountain Resort

SKIING & SNOWBOARDING | FAMILY | This fun-to-ski area has been a favorite with families since it opened in 1938. Most runs are naturally formed intermediates that weave in and out of glades. Beginners have several slopes and routes from the summit; experts must be content with a few short, steep pitches. Snowboarders can explore five different terrain parks. A mountain coaster, a tubing park, a giant swing, and a zipline provide additional entertainment, and there's night skiing on Saturdays and holidays. **Facilities:** 56 trails; 170 acres; 1,200-foot vertical drop; 8 lifts. *1 Skimobile Rd., North Conway* *800/786-6754* *www.cranmore.com* *Lift ticket: $94.*

Mt. Washington Valley Ski Touring and Snowshoe Foundation

SKIING & SNOWBOARDING | Nearly 30 miles of groomed cross-country trails weave through the North Conway countryside, maintained by this foundation. Membership to the Mt. Washington Valley Ski Touring Club, available by the day or year, is required. Equipment rentals are available. *279 Rte. 16/U.S. 302, Intervale* *603/356-9920* *www.mwvskitouring.org.*

Jackson

9 miles north of North Conway.

Just off Route 16 via a red covered bridge, photogenic Jackson retains its storybook New England character. Art and antiques shopping, tennis, golf, fishing, and hiking to waterfalls are among the draws, as well as a high concentration of upscale country inns. When the snow falls, Jackson becomes the state's cross-country skiing capital, and there are also four downhill ski areas nearby—hotels and inns provide ski shuttles.

ESSENTIALS

Jackson is on Route 16, just north of the junction with U.S. 302.

VISITOR INFORMATION Jackson Area Chamber of Commerce. ☎ *603/383–9356* 🌐 *www.jacksonnh.com.*

Sights

Story Land

AMUSEMENT PARK/CARNIVAL | FAMILY | This theme park with life-size storybook and nursery-rhyme characters is geared to kids (ages 2–12). The two-dozen rides include a flumer, a river raft, and the Roar-O-Saurus and Polar Coaster roller coasters. Play areas and magic shows provide additional entertainment. There's also the Living Shores Aquarium, which offers 32,000-square-feet of mostly interactive, touch-friendly pools and exhibits. ✉ *850 Rte. 16, Glen* ☎ *603/383–4186* 🌐 *www.storylandnh.com* 🎟 *$55, aquarium $25.*

Restaurants

★ Thompson House Eatery

$$$ | MODERN AMERICAN | The domain of celebrated chef-owner Jeff Fournier, who's cooked at some of Boston's most acclaimed restaurants, this exceptional eatery is set inside a chicly restored farmhouse in the village of Jackson. Ethereal highlights from the oft-changing menu include seared Maine bluefin tuna with a leek-fennel emulsion and brown sugar–and–chili-roasted delicata squash, and a superb cheese board with raspberry-hibiscus jam, nuts, and local honey. **Known for:** elegant and historic farmhouse setting; on-site shop with gourmet goods to go; seasonally flavored house-made ice creams. $ *Average main: $34* ✉ *193 Main St., Jackson* ☎ *603/383–9341* 🌐 *www.thethompsonhouseeatery.com* ⏲ *Closed Mon. and Tues. No lunch.*

Hotels

Inn at Ellis River

$$ | B&B/INN | Most of the rooms—which are all outfitted with armchairs and ottomans and floral-print duvet covers and featherbeds—in this unabashedly romantic 1893 inn on the Ellis River have fireplaces, and some also have balconies with Adirondack chairs and whirlpool tubs. **Pros:** pretty riverside location; abundantly charming; multicourse breakfasts and afternoon refreshments included. **Cons:** some rooms up steep stairs; not suitable for kids under 12; the least expensive rooms are quite compact. $ *Rooms from: $179* ✉ *17 Harriman Rd., Jackson* ☎ *603/383–9339, 800/233–8309* 🌐 *www.innatellisriver.com* *21 rooms* *Free Breakfast.*

Inn at Jackson

$ | B&B/INN | This homey yet distinctive B&B—designed in 1902 by famed architect Stanford White for the Baldwin family of piano fame—is reasonably priced, charmingly furnished, and in the heart of the village. **Pros:** great value considering its many charms; peaceful setting; wonderful breakfasts. **Cons:** top-floor rooms lack fireplaces; rooms could use some updating; a bit frilly for some tastes. $ *Rooms from: $149* ✉ *Thorn Hill Rd. and Main St., Jackson* ☎ *603/383–4321, 800/289–8600* 🌐 *www.innatjackson.com* *14 rooms* *Free Breakfast.*

★ The Inn at Thorn Hill & Spa

$$$ | **B&B/INN** | With a large reception room and sweeping staircase, a deck overlooking the rolling hills around the village, and a common area with a wet bar and a cozy fireplace, this lovely inn—modeled after an 1891 Victorian designed by Stanford White—is breathtaking throughout. **Pros:** superb restaurant; soothing full spa; exceptional full breakfasts. **Cons:** rigid peak-season cancellation policy; not suitable for kids; carriage house and cottages are less sumptuous. *Rooms from: $259* *42 Thorn Hill Rd., Jackson* *603/383–4242* *www.innatthornhill.com* *22 rooms* *No Meals.*

Wentworth

$$ | **B&B/INN** | **FAMILY** | Thoughtful renovations have given new life and elegance to the guest rooms at this baronial 1869 Victorian, whose amenities include a full spa, a first-rate restaurant, and access to a terrific golf course and cross-country ski trails. **Pros:** discounts at neighboring Wentworth Golf Club; interesting architecture; very good farm-to-table restaurant. **Cons:** some rooms up steep stairs; two-night minimum many weekends; at a somewhat busy intersection. *Rooms from: $189* *1 Carter Notch Rd., Jackson* *603/383–9700, 800/637–0013* *www.thewentworth.com* *61 rooms* *Free Breakfast.*

Activities

CROSS-COUNTRY SKIING

★ Jackson Ski Touring Foundation

SKIING & SNOWBOARDING | **FAMILY** | This acclaimed cross-country ski operation has an attentive staff and 90 miles of groomed trails for skiing, skate skiing, and snowshoeing. The varied terrain offers something for all abilities—lessons and rentals are offered, too. Trails wind through covered bridges and into the picturesque village of Jackson, where you can warm up in cozy trailside restaurants. *153 Main St., Jackson* *603/383–9355* *www.jacksonxc.org.*

ICE-SKATING

Nestlenook Farm

ICE SKATING | **FAMILY** | This picturesque farm maintains an outdoor ice-skating rink with rentals, music, and a bonfire as well as offering snowshoeing and sleigh rides. *66 Dinsmore Rd., Jackson* *603/383–7101* *www.nestlenookfarmsleighrides.com.*

Mt. Washington

12 miles north of Jackson, 39 miles east of Bretton Woods.

At 6,288 feet, Mt. Washington is the tallest peak in the northeastern United States. The world's highest winds, 231 mph, were recorded here in 1934. You can take a guided van tour, a drive, or a hike to the summit. A number of trails circle the mountain and access the other peaks in the Presidential Range, but all of them are fairly strenuous and best attempted only if you're somewhat experienced and quite fit. It gets cold up here: even in the summer, you'll want a jacket.

GETTING HERE AND AROUND

Mt. Washington Auto Road climbs west from Route 16, about 2 miles north of Wildcat Mountain ski resort and 8 miles south of Gorham.

Sights

★ Mt. Washington Auto Road

MOUNTAIN | **FAMILY** | The drive to the top of this imposing summit is truly memorable. Your route: the narrow, curving Mt. Washington Auto Road, which climbs 4,600 feet in about 7 miles. Drivers can download an app with a narrated tour and receive a bumper sticker that reads, "This car climbed Mt. Washington." The narration is fascinating, and the views are breathtaking. Once at the top, check out **Extreme Mount Washington,** an interactive museum dedicated to science and weather. If you're nervous about heights or the condition of your car, book a guided van tour or a ride up the cog railway in Bretton Woods. ✉ *1 Mt. Washington Auto Rd., Gorham* ☎ *603/466–3988* 🌐 *www.mt-washington.com* *Car and driver $39–$45; guided bus tour from $45–$51* ⏲ *Closed late Oct.–early May.*

Restaurants

Big Day Brewing

$ | **AMERICAN** | You certainly don't have to be a beer lover to appreciate this airy, modern brewpub that serves exceptionally good pub fare like fries topped with house-made curry aioli, roasted–sweet potato tacos, and farm-raised-beef burgers with bacon and barbecue sauce—the kind of sustenance that warms the soul after a day of White Mountains hiking. But Big Day does produce some of the region's best brews, including European-style classics like a golden Munich Dunkel and a citrusy Hefeweizen. **Known for:** churros house-made strawberry compote; spacious, pet-friendly beer garden; distinctive, well-crafted beers. $ *Average main: $15* ✉ *20 Glen Rd., Gorham* ☎ *603/915–9006* 🌐 *www.bigdaybrewing.com* ⏲ *Closed Mon.–Tues. No lunch Wed.–Thurs.*

Nonna's Kitchen

$$ | **ITALIAN** | **FAMILY** | Set in a vintage barber shop in downtown Gorham—8 miles north of the Mt. Washington Auto Road—this homey restaurant is a tribute to the owners' Italian grandmothers. Indeed, the menu reads like a roll call of favorites from the best restaurants in Boston's or New Haven's Little Italy neighborhoods—classic antipasto, feathery gnocchi with pesto, eggplant parmigiana, veal piccata, and linguine with clams and red sauce. **Known for:** friendly service; cod puttanesca; fresh handmade pastas, cooked to order. $ *Average main: $20* ✉ *19 Exchange St., Gorham* ☎ *603/915–9203* 🌐 *www.nonnasgorham.com* ⏲ *Closed Mon. and Tues. No lunch.*

Hotels

★ Glen House Hotel

$$$ | **HOTEL** | The latest of four Glen House hotels that have stood on this site at the base of the Mt. Washington Auto Road since 1852, this upscale three-story retreat opened in 2018 in a Shaker-inspired building whose soaring windows, a yellow clapboard exterior, and simple lines hark back to its predecessors. **Pros:** easy access to Mt. Washington activities; beautifully designed; excellent on-site restaurant. **Cons:** remote area; may be a bit shiny and new for some tastes; limited dining options in the area. $ *Rooms from: $284* ✉ *979 Rte. 16, Gorham* ☎ *603/466–3420* 🌐 *www.theglenhouse.com* *68 rooms* *Free Breakfast.*

Activities

All trails to Mt. Washington's peak are demanding and require a considerable investment of time and effort. Perhaps the most famous is the **Tuckerman Ravine Trail,** the path used by extreme skiers who risk life and limb to fly down the face of the steep ravine. The hike to the top can easily take six–nine hours round-trip. However you get to the top, because the weather here is so erratic, it's critical to check weather conditions, to be prepared, and to keep in mind that Mt. Washington's summit is much colder than the base.

CROSS-COUNTRY SKIING

★ Great Glen Trails Outdoor Center

SKIING & SNOWBOARDING | **FAMILY** | Featuring a dramatic 28-mile network of both mild and wild cross-country ski and mountain-biking trails at the foot of Mt. Washington, Great Glen provides access to more than 1,100 acres of backcountry. You can also book to the summit via SnowCoach, a nine-passenger van refitted with triangular snowmobile-like treads. You have the option of skiing or snowshoeing down or just enjoying the magnificent winter view. There's

The highest peak in New England, Mt. Washington rewards those who drive or hike to the top with spectacular views.

also a huge ski and sports shop, a food court, and a climbing wall. In summer you can also rent kayaks and book excellent paddling, rafting, and float trips along the Androscoggin River. ✉ *1 Mt. Washington Auto Rd., at Rte. 16, Gorham* ☎ *603/466–3988* 🌐 *www.greatglentrails.com* 🎫 *SnowCoach tours $65.*

HIKING

Pinkham Notch

HIKING & WALKING | On Mt. Washington's eastern slopes, scenic Pinkham Notch encompasses several ravines, including famous Tuckerman. The Appalachian Mountain Club operates a visitor center that provides trail information. Guided hikes leave from here, and outdoor skills workshops are offered. On-site are an outdoors shop, a lodge with basic overnight accommodations, and a dining hall. Not all the trails ascend Mt. Washington or are necessarily strenuous. Good bets for shorter, moderate hikes include Glen Ellis Falls and Crystal Cascade, which both lead to scenic waterfalls. ✉ *AMC Pinkham Notch Visitor Center, 361 Rte. 16, Gorham* ☎ *603/466–2727* 🌐 *www.outdoors.org.*

SKIING

Wildcat Mountain

SKIING & SNOWBOARDING | Glade skiers love Wildcat's 80 acres of tree skiing. Runs include some stunning double–black diamond trails; experts can really zip down the Lynx. Beginners, as long as they can hold a wedge, should check out the 2½-mile-long Polecat, which offers excellent views of the Presidential Range. The trails are classic New England—narrow and winding—and the vistas are stunning. For an adrenaline rush, there's a terrain park. In summer you can dart to the top on the four-passenger gondola, hike the many trails, and fish in the crystal clear streams. **Facilities:** 48 trails; 225 acres; 2,112-foot vertical drop; 5 lifts. ✉ *Rte. 16, Gorham* ☎ *603/466–3326* 🌐 *www.skiwildcat.com* 🎫 *$115.*

Bartlett

19 miles south of Mt. Washington, 9 miles northwest of North Conway.

With Bear Mountain to its south, Mt. Parker to its north, Mt. Cardigan to its west, and the Saco River to its east, Bartlett—incorporated in 1790—has an unforgettable setting. Lovely Bear Notch Road (closed in winter) has the only midpoint access to the Kancamagus Highway. There isn't much town to speak of: the dining options listed here are actually nearby in Glen. It's best known for the Attitash Ski Resort.

GETTING HERE AND AROUND

U.S. 302 passes through Bartlett from Bretton Woods and west from Glen.

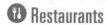

Restaurants

White Mountain Cider Co.

$$$ | **MODERN AMERICAN** | Set in a historic cider mill near the Saco River, this rustic yet elegant bistro and adjacent gourmet market and deli presses fresh cider in the fall—it's served with traditional homemade cider doughnuts. But it's also a terrific farm-to-table restaurant, featuring a seasonal menu of eclectic, contemporary dishes. **Known for:** flavorful sandwiches and soups in the adjacent market; creative cocktails; friendly, knowledgeable service. *Average main: $32* *207 U.S. 302, Glen* *603/383–9061* *www.ciderconh.com* *Closed Tues. No lunch in restaurant.*

Hotels

★ Alpine Garden Camping Village

$$ | **RESORT** | This relatively cozy glamping compound nestled in a serene wooded property in the heart of the White Mountains consists of charming cabins, a couple of campers, and a pair of luxurious, beautifully designed tree houses. There's reliable Wi-Fi, and each of the individually decorated units have climate-control, record players, and minibars stocked with wine and cider. **Pros:** peaceful, wooded setting; on-site winery and tasting room; heated pool. **Cons:** there's a small charge for linens; no pets; not a great fit for kids. *Rooms from: $165* *125 U.S. 302, Bartlett* *603/374–5154* *www.alpinegardenglamping.com* *Closed mid-Apr.–Nov.* *11 units* *No Meals.*

★ Bernerhof Inn

$$ | **B&B/INN** | Skiers, hikers, and adventurers who favor a luxurious, intimate lodging over a bustling condo resort adore this grand Victorian inn operated with eco-friendly practices and furnished with a mix of fine antiques and period reproductions. **Pros:** excellent on-site cooking school; exudes old-world charm; small but wonderfully relaxing spa. **Cons:** guests under 21 not permitted; some rooms receive a little road noise. *Rooms from: $189* *342 U.S. 302, Glen* *603/383–4200* *www.bernerhof-inn.com* *12 rooms* *Free Breakfast.*

Golden Apple Inn

$ | **MOTEL** | **FAMILY** | This small, attractively updated, and economical motel is an easy drive from the Mt. Washington Auto Road, skiing at Attitash Mountain Resort, and the inviting villages of Jackson and North Conway. **Pros:** well-tended gardens and grounds with a pool, playground, and barbecue grill; superb value; excellent base for skiing and hiking. **Cons:** on a somewhat busy road; no breakfast or restaurant; simple decor. *Rooms from: $109* *322 U.S. 302, Glen* *603/383–9680* *www.goldenappleinn.com* *17 rooms* *No Meals.*

Grand Summit Hotel at Attitash

$$ | **RESORT** | **FAMILY** | All of the pleasantly furnished rooms at this ski-in, ski-out condo-style resort at the base of Bear Peak have kitchenettes, and many have private balconies with splendid views. **Pros:** appealing slope-side setting; ski-package deals; kitchenettes in rooms. **Cons:** generally bland decor; could use some sprucing up; restaurants are a bit

meh. $ *Rooms from: $159* ✉ *104 Grand Summit Rd., Bartlett* ☎ *603/374–6700* 🌐 *www.grandsummitattitash.com* *143 rooms* *No Meals.*

Nightlife

Red Parka Pub

PUBS | This homey pub decorated with license plates and ski memorabilia has been an institution, especially during winter ski season, since the early 1970s, providing a fun and festive venue for après-ski or-hike socializing. Beer is served in Mason jars, the kitchen serves up juicy steaks and comfort fare, and there's live music many evenings. ✉ *3 Station St., Glen* ☎ *603/383–4344* 🌐 *www.redparkapub.com.*

Activities

SKIING

Attitash Ski Resort

SKIING & SNOWBOARDING | **FAMILY** | With one of New Hampshire's higher vertical drops, Attitash Mountain has dozens of trails to explore, and there are more on the adjacent Attitash Bear Peak. You'll find traditional New England ski runs and challenging terrain alongside wide-open cruisers that suit all skill levels. There are acres of glades, plus a progressive freestyle terrain park. The Attitash Adventure Center offers rentals, lessons, and children's programs. **Facilities:** 68 trails; 311 acres; 1,750-foot vertical drop; 9 lifts. ✉ *775 U.S. 302, Bartlett* ☎ *800/223–7669* 🌐 *www.attitash.com* *Lift ticket: $115.*

Bretton Woods

21 miles northwest of Bartlett.

In the early 1900s private railcars brought the elite from New York and Philadelphia to the Mount Washington Hotel, the jewel of the White Mountains. A visit to this property, which was the site of the 1944 United Nations conference that created the International Monetary Fund and the International Bank for Reconstruction and Development (and the birth of many conspiracy theories), is not to be missed. This rural area—there's no real town per se—is also known for the cog railway to the summit of Mt. Washington, Bretton Woods ski resort, and unparalleled hiking at Crawford Notch State Park.

GETTING HERE AND AROUND

Bretton Woods is in the heart of the White Mountains on U.S. 302. A free shuttle makes it easy to get around the resort's many venues.

Sights

★ Crawford Notch State Park

STATE/PROVINCIAL PARK | **FAMILY** | Scenic U.S. 302 winds southeast of Bretton Woods through the steep, wooded mountains on either side of spectacular Crawford Notch. At this 5,775-acre state park, you can picnic and hike to Arethusa Falls, the longest drop in New England, or to the Silver and Flume cascades—they're among more than a dozen outstanding trails. Roadside photo ops abound, and amenities include an Adirondack-style visitor center, gift shop, snack bar, and fishing pond. ✉ *1464 U.S. 302, Hart's Location* ☎ *603/374–2272* 🌐 *www.nhstateparks.org.*

★ Mount Washington Cog Railway

TRAIN/TRAIN STATION | **FAMILY** | In 1858, Sylvester Marsh petitioned the state legislature for permission to build a steam railway up Mt. Washington. One politico retorted that Marsh would have better luck building a railroad to the moon, but 11 years later the Mount Washington Cog Railway chugged its way up to the summit along a 3-mile track on the mountain's west side. Today it's a beloved attraction—a thrill in either direction. A small museum has exhibits about the cog rail, and a casual restaurant offers great views of the trains beginning their ascent. The full trip on these eco-friendly, biodiesel trains takes three hours including an hour at the summit. In winter, the railway runs shorter and less-expensive trips to the Waumbek Station (elevation 3,900 feet), which still offers impressive vistas of the snow-covered countryside. *3168 Base Station Rd., Bretton Woods 603/278–5404, 800/922–8825 www.thecog.com Summit from $72, Waumbek Station from $41.*

Hotels

★ The Notchland Inn

$$$ | B&B/INN | Built in 1862 by Sam Bemis, America's grandfather of landscape photography, the gracious granite manor house exudes mountain charm and is popular with Crawford Notch hikers who favor luxury. **Pros:** set amid soaring mountains; marvelous house and common rooms; outstanding breakfasts and dinners. **Cons:** very isolated; fills up well in advance on summer and fall weekends; not ideal for young kids. *Rooms from: $295 2 Morey Rd., Hart's Location 603/374–6131, 800/866–6131 www.notchland.com 15 rooms Free Breakfast.*

★ Omni Mount Washington Hotel

$$$$ | RESORT | FAMILY | The two most memorable sights in the White Mountains might just be Mt. Washington and this dramatic 1902 resort with a 900-foot veranda, glimmering public rooms, astonishing views of the Presidential Range, and dozens of recreational activities like tubing, sleigh rides, horseback riding, and fly-fishing. **Pros:** incomparable setting and ambience; loads of amenities and dining options; free shuttle to skiing and activities. **Cons:** lots of kids running around the property; a drive from nearest decent-size town; rates soar on summer–fall weekends. *Rooms from: $386 310 Mt. Washington Hotel Rd., Bretton Woods 603/278–1000, 888/444–6664 www.mountwashingtonresort.com 269 rooms No Meals.*

Activities

SKIING

★ Bretton Woods

SKIING & SNOWBOARDING | FAMILY | New Hampshire's largest ski area is also one of the country's best family ski resorts. The views of Mt. Washington alone are worth the visit, and the scenery is especially beautiful from the two-story restaurant at the dramatically contemporary Rosewood Lodge, which sits at 3,000 feet in elevation and is reached via the all-glass eight-passenger Skyway Gondola. The resort has something for everyone, from extensive kids' programs and lessons to some seriously steep pitches near the top of the 1,500-foot vertical. And the 35 glades will keep experts busy, while snowboarders enjoy the three terrain parks. The Nordic trail system has 62 miles of cross-country ski tracks. Both night skiing and snowboarding are available on weekends and holidays. There's also the year-round Canopy Tour, with nine ziplines, two sky bridges, and three rappelling stations. **Facilities:** 63 trails; 464 acres, 1,500-foot vertical drop; 10 lifts. *99 Ski Area Rd., Bretton Woods 603/278–3320 www.brettonwoods.com Lift ticket: $104.*

HIKING

Sugarloaf Trail

HIKING & WALKING | A relatively easy hike offering impressive views of Mt. Washington and the Presidential Range, this 3.4-mile round-trip hike starts near a tributary of the Ammonoosuc River, a 10-minute drive west of Bretton Woods. The trail runs alongside the river for a short way before ascending the somewhat steep eastern slope of Sugarloaf Mountain (the total elevation gain is about 1,050 feet). At the top of the ridge, you can cut across to both the North and South Sugarloaf summits; if you're short on time, choose the southern summit, which offers the most impressive panoramas. *Zealand Rd. Twin Mountain 1 miles south of US 302.*

Bethlehem

14 miles west of Bretton Woods.

In the days before antihistamines, hay-fever sufferers came by the trainload to this enchanting village whose crisp air has a blissfully low pollen count. Today this progressive, artsy hamlet with fewer than 1,000 residents is notable for its art deco Colonial Theatre (which presents indie films and concerts), distinctive galleries and cafés, and stately Victorian and Colonial homes, many of which line the village's immensely picturesque Main Street, a highly enjoyable locale for a stroll.

GETTING HERE AND AROUND

U.S. 302 and Route 142 intersect in the heart of this small village center that's easy to explore on foot.

Sights

The Rocks Estate

NATURE PRESERVE | FAMILY | The estate of John Jacob Glessner (1843–1936), one of the founders of International Harvester, now serves as a 1,400-acre conservation and education center. The property is named for the many surface boulders on the estate when Glessner bought it—some were used to erect the rambling rock walls that flanks the estate's striking shingle-style restored buildings. The Rocks presents natural-history programs and has self-guided tours and hiking trails with excellent views of the Presidential Range. Come winter, cross-country ski trails and a select-your-own-Christmas-tree farm open up. In early spring, you can watch how maple syrup is made. Note that the property's trails have been closed during an extensive restoration project but are expected to reopen in summer 2023. ✉ *4 Christmas La., Bethlehem* ☎ *603/444–6228* 🌐 *www.forestsociety.org/the-rocks.*

Restaurants

★ Cold Mountain Cafe

$$ | ECLECTIC | Adjacent to the Marketplace at WREN, this homey art-filled storefront eatery and wine bar is one of the area's social focal points, with a welcoming staff and a thoughtful, international menu. Pork tacos, Indian lamb stew, and heirloom tomato caprese salads are a few of the best dishes, but save room for the flourless chocolate torte with strawberry-balsamic coulis. **Known for:** friendly, upbeat crowd and staff; bounteous salads; intriguing cocktail list. $ *Average main: $22* ✉ *2015 Main St., Bethlehem* ☎ *603/869–2500* 🌐 *www.coldmountaincafe.com* 🕒 *Closed Sun.*

Coffee and Quick Bites

Maia Papaya

$ | CAFÉ | Pause during your stroll through inviting Bethlehem for breakfast, lunch, smoothies, lattes, or homemade chai tea at this quirky organic café that specializes in vegetarian fare and made-from-scratch baked goods (try not to pass up one of the justly renowned scones). On cool mornings, warm up with a hearty breakfast burrito; terrific lunchtime options include the artichoke melt panini or the bountiful green salad. **Known for:** plenty of gluten-free and vegetarian options; fruit-filled oat bars; organic oatmeal with local maple syrup. $ *Average main: $9* ✉ *2161 Main St., Bethlehem* ☎ *603/869–9900* 🌐 *www.themaiapapaya.com* 🕒 *Closed Tues. No dinner.*

★ Super Secret Ice Cream

$ | ICE CREAM | FAMILY | It may have the word "secret" in its name, but this artisan ice-cream shop with a walk-up window and deck as well as a spacious indoor seating area has a devoted following—let's just say the cat's out of the bag. This is some of the richest and delicious ice cream in the state, and there's always a great lineup of unusual flavors, such as Thai tea, roasted cherry chip, honeycomb, and strawberry buttermilk. **Known for:** unusual flavors; the milk and many ingredients are sourced locally; sunny patio seating. *Average main: $6* *2213 Main St., Bethlehem* *www.supersecreticecream.com* *Closed Mon.–Tues.*

 Hotels

★ Adair Country Inn and Restaurant
$$$ | B&B/INN | An air of yesteryear refinement suffuses Adair, a three-story Georgian Revival home that attorney Frank Hogan built as a wedding present for his daughter in 1927—her hats adorn the place, as do books and old photos from the era. **Pros:** a superb, romantic restaurant; rates include a memorable breakfast and afternoon tea; cross-country skiing and hiking trails. **Cons:** not within walking distance of town; sometimes books up with weddings; closed for a month each fall and spring. *Rooms from: $279* *80 Guider La., Bethlehem* *603/444–2600, 888/444–2600* *www.adairinn.com* *Closed mid-Nov. and Apr.* *11 rooms* *Free Breakfast.*

 Nightlife

★ Rek-Lis Brewing Company
BEER GARDENS | After a day of hiking or skiing, grab a seat inside this cozy tavern or out on one of the expansive decks and savor the outstanding house-made beers along with guest taps from other notable breweries. There's great pub food, too, and a popular Sunday brunch. *2085 Main St., Bethlehem* *603/991–2357* *www.reklisbrewing.com.*

 Shopping

★ Marketplace at WREN
ART GALLERIES | WREN (the Women's Rural Entrepreneurial Network) has been a vital force in little Bethlehem's steady growth into a center of more than 100 artists, craftspersons, and other business owners. At WREN's headquarters, there's an outstanding gallery that presents monthly juried exhibits and a retail gift boutique, Local Works, featuring crafts, foods, books, and one-of-a-kind gifts. *2011 Main St., Bethlehem* *603/869–9736* *www.wrenworks.org.*

Littleton

5 miles west of Bethlehem.

One of northern New Hampshire's largest towns (this isn't saying much, mind you) sits on a granite shelf along the Ammonoosuc River, whose swift current and drop of 235 feet enabled the community to flourish as a mill center in its early days. The railroad came through later, and Littleton grew into the region's commercial hub. Long merely a place to stock up than a real destination, it's reinvented itself in recent decades, and lively Main Street now abounds with intriguing shops and eateries set inside tidy 19th- and early-20th-century buildings you might expect to see in an old Jimmy Stewart movie.

GETTING HERE AND AROUND

Littleton sits just off Interstate 93, and its downtown is easily explored on foot.

ESSENTIALS

VISITOR INFORMATION Littleton Area Chamber of Commerce. *Littleton* *603/444–6561* *www.littletonareachamber.com.*

★ Schilling Beer Taproom
$ | PIZZA | With a storybook setting in a converted 18th-century mill on the Ammonoosuc River, this craft brewpub offers tasty wood-fired pizzas, bratwurst sandwiches, house-baked soft pretzels, and other fare that pairs well with its distinctive European ales. The pie topped with prosciutto, pears, chèvre,

mozzarella, and beer-caramelized onions is a favorite, best enjoyed with a farmhouse-style saison. **Known for:** seating overlooking the river; beer tastings; great pizzas. *Average main: $14* *18 Mill St., Littleton* *603/444–4800* *www.schillingbeer.com.*

Taste the Thai & Sushi House

$$ | THAI | This friendly, laid-back Asian restaurant excels with just about everything it offers, from creative sushi rolls and sashimi (try the salmon topped with house-made truffle sauce) to well-seasoned (or fiery hot, on request) curries to boba teas. House specialties include the sweet-and-tangy shrimp pineapple curry, ginger stir-fried salmon, and basil crispy duck. **Known for:** quite possibly the most authentic Thai food in New Hampshire; Thai tea shaved ice; colorful cocktails. *Average main: $19* *406 Union St., Littleton* *603/575–5488* *www.tastethethaiandsushihouse.com* *Closed Wed.*

★ Tim-Bir Alley

$$$$ | MODERN AMERICAN | In this terrific contemporary downtown restaurant, you can sample some of the tastiest farm-to-table fare in the White Mountains. The menu changes frequently and uses regional American ingredients in creative ways—try country pâté with venison and pistachio, followed by crispy maple-glazed duck breast with smashed carrots and bok choy. **Known for:** stylish yet unpretentious; local artisan cheese plates; beautifully plated desserts. *Average main: $36* *7 Main St., Littleton* *603/444–6142* *www.timbiralleyrestaurant.com* *No credit cards* *Closed Mon. and Tues. No lunch.*

Coffee and Quick Bites

★ Crumb Bum

$ | CAFÉ | Stop by this cute cake shop to stock up on creative, and utterly delectable, baked goods, such as grapefruit-rosemary-cardamom short bread cookies, maple cinnamon rolls, and macarons in a variety of flavors, and egg-bacon-cheese breakfast sandwiches constructed on ethereal duck-fat biscuits. Fine coffees are available, too. **Known for:** great baked goods; duck-fat angel biscuit breakfast sandwich; vegan options. *Average main: $5* *97 Main St., Littleton* *603/575–1773* *www.crumbbumbakery.com* *Closed Tues.–Wed.*

The Inkwell

$ | CAFÉ | Drop by this hip café with two downtown Littleton locations, both of them with ample indoor and outdoor seating, for a light bite, to relax with a book, or sip one of the well-crafted fair-trade coffee or organic loose-leaf tea drinks. Several kinds of toast with tasty toppings (ricotta and lemon honey; cheddar, ham, and egg) are available at breakfast, along with myriad scones, cookies, and gluten-free pastries. **Known for:** creative panini sandwiches for lunch; lots of outdoor seating; iced and hot coffees with local maple syrup. *Average main: $8* *24 Beacon St,, Littleton* *603/575–5335* *www.inkwellnh.com* *Closed Sun. No dinner.*

Hotels

Mountain View Grand Resort & Spa

$$ | RESORT | FAMILY | Casual elegance and stunning views of the White Mountains define this stately yellow wedding cake of a hotel that dates to 1865 and sprawls over 1,700 acres that include a working farm and a well-maintained golf course. **Pros:** full-service spa; dozens of activities; babysitting service and summer camp. **Cons:** breakfast not included in rates; not too many dining options nearby; sometimes fills up with corporate meetings and retreats. *Rooms from: $219* *101 Mountain View Rd., Whitefield* *855/837–2100* *www.mountainviewgrand.com* *144 rooms* *No Meals.*

Thayers Inn

$ | **HOTEL** | This former grande dame with a distinguished roster of past guests—including Ulysses S. Grant, Henry Ford, and PT Barnum—offers quirky and fun budget accommodations and a great location in one of the liveliest little downtowns in the White Mountains. **Pros:** some rooms have kitchenettes; fascinating building filled with memorabilia and exhibits; on lively and festive Main Street. **Cons:** no elevator; functional decor; tiny bathrooms. *Rooms from: $129* *111 Main St., Littleton* *603/444–6469* *www.thayersinn.com* *34 rooms* *Free Breakfast.*

Chutters

CANDY | **FAMILY** | Boasting the world's longest candy counter, at 112 feet, this kid- and adult-approved century-plus-old candy shop with satellite locations in Lincoln, Loon Mountain Resort, and Bretton Woods carries just about every variety of sweet treat you could imagine. *43 Main St, Littleton* *603/444–5787* *www.chutters.com.*

★ Just L Modern Antiques

ANTIQUES & COLLECTIBLES | Fans of mid-century furnishings, from low-slung modern sofas and sleek Danish coffee tables to both fashionable and kitschy housewares, vintage paintings, and kitchen items flock to this enormous two-floor emporium set along Littleton's increasingly hip Main Street. *35 Main St., Littleton* *603/259–3125* *www.facebook.com/midmodliving.*

Little Village Toy and Book Stop

TOYS | **FAMILY** | Maps, history books, unusual children's toys and many adult fiction and nonfiction titles fill this cheerful shop, the lower level of which contains a branch of the venerable League of New Hampshire Craftsmen's gallery. *81B Main St., Littleton* *603/444–4869* *www.littlevillagetoy.com.*

Pentimento

SOUVENIRS | This eclectic shop, packed into a Victorian house a few steps from the historic Opera House, is a great place to find unusual jewelry, candles, fashion eyewear, and handmade cards. *34 Union St., Littleton* *603/444–7797* *www.facebook.com/pentimentonh.*

Franconia

7 miles south of Littleton.

Travelers have long passed through spectacular Franconia Notch, and in the late 18th century this town just to the north evolved just to serve them. It and the region's jagged rock formations and heavy coat of evergreens stirred the imaginations of Washington Irving, Henry Wadsworth Longfellow, and Nathaniel Hawthorne, who penned a short story about the iconic—though now crumbled—cliff known as the Old Man of the Mountain. Tiny downtown consists of a handful of businesses and the remains of the interesting old 1840s Besaw Iron Furnace. Drive west 4 miles to visit Sugar Hill, a village of about 500 people that's famous for its spectacular sunsets and views of Franconia Ridge, best seen from Sunset Hill, where a row of grand hotels and mansions once stood.

GETTING HERE AND AROUND

Franconia is right off Interstate 93.

ESSENTIALS

VISITOR INFORMATION Franconia Notch Chamber of Commerce. *Franconia* *603/823–2000* *www.franconianotch.org.*

★ Franconia Notch State Park

STATE/PROVINCIAL PARK | **FAMILY** | Traversed by the Appalachian Trail and a stretch of Interstate 93 that narrows for 8 miles to become Franconia Notch Parkway, this stunning 6,692-acre state park feels as awesome as a national park and offers dozens of diversions, including myriad hiking trails, summer swimming at **Echo Lake Beach,** and winter downhill skiing at **Cannon Mountain,** whose 4,080-foot summit observation deck you can explore on the **Aerial Tramway,** an 80-passenger cable car. One of the top park draws, the dramatic, narrow 800-foot-long **Flume Gorge** is reached from a modern visitor center via a picturesque 2-mile loop hike along wooden boardwalks and stairways. The park was long famous as the site of the **Old Man of the Mountain,** an iconic profile high on a granite cliff that crumbled unexpectedly in 2003. Overlooking Profile Lake, at the small Old Man of the Mountain Park, you can walk the short but pretty paved trail to view the mountain face through steel rods that seem literally to put the beloved visage back on the mountain. You can see related photographs and memorabilia in a small museum, and also visit the **New England Ski Museum** (which has a second location in North Conway) to learn how skiing was popularized as a sport in New England, through artifacts, clothing, and equipment, as well as Bode Miller's five Olympic medals. ✉ *260 Tramway Dr., Franconia* ☎ *603/823–8800* 🌐 *www.nhstateparks.org* 🎟 *Aerial Tramway $28, Echo Lake parking $4, Flume Gorge $18, museums free.*

The Frost Place

HISTORIC HOME | Robert Frost's year-round home from 1915 to 1920, this modest homestead on a peaceful unpaved road is surrounded by well-tended gardens and offers stunning mountain views. The place is imbued with the spirit of his work—two rooms contain memorabilia and signed editions of his books. Poetry readings are scheduled some summer evenings. Out back, you can follow short trails marked with lines from his poetry. The grounds are always open and beautiful for a stroll. ✉ *158 Ridge Rd., Franconia* ☎ *603/823–5510* 🌐 *www.frostplace.org* 🎟 *$5* ⏲ *Closed mid-Oct.–Apr.*

Restaurants

★ Polly's Pancake Parlor

$ | AMERICAN | FAMILY | In the Dexter family for generations, Polly's has been serving up pancakes and waffles (from its own original recipe, with several batter options available, including cornmeal and gingerbread) since the 1930s—the current space dates to 2015 but retains the original country charm. Try the smoked bacon and ham, eggs Benedict, sandwiches on homemade bread, delicious baked beans, and such tempting desserts as raspberry pie. **Known for:** gift shop with maple products; gingerbread pancakes with blueberries and walnuts; pretty hilltop setting. 💲 *Average main: $14* ✉ *672 Rte. 117, Franconia* ☎ *603/823–5575* 🌐 *www.pollyspancakeparlor.com* ⏲ *Closed Wed. No dinner.*

Hotels

Franconia Inn

$ | RESORT | FAMILY | At this 107-acre family-friendly resort anchored by an affordable three-story inn with unfussy country furnishings, you can play tennis on four clay courts, soak in the outdoor heated pool or hot tub, hop on a mountain bike, or soar in a glider, and cross-country ski on 40 miles of groomed trails. **Pros:** tons of family oriented activities; outdoor heated pool; peaceful setting with mountain views. **Cons:** a bit remote; historic hotel with some quirks; popularity with families can make it a little noisy. 💲 *Rooms from: $135* ✉ *1172 Easton Rd., Franconia* ☎ *603/823–5542, 800/473–5299* 🌐 *www.franconiainn.com* ⏲ *Closed Apr.–mid-May* 🛏 *34 rooms* 🍽 *No Meals.*

Sunset Hill House

$$ | HOTEL | It's all about the view at this striking Victorian inn set high on a ridge in tiny Sugar Hill, its 70 acres holding lovely gardens, a seasonal outdoor pool, and a great little golf course. **Pros:** mesmerizing views; excellent 9-hole golf course; unusually good restaurant with outdoor dining. **Cons:** slightly remote setting; not a great option for kids; some bathrooms are shower-only. *$ Rooms from: $160 ✉ 231 Sunset Hill Rd., Sugar Hill ☎ 603/823–7244 ⊕ www.thesunsethillhouse.com ⇨ 28 rooms 🍽 Free Breakfast.*

★ Sugar Hill Inn

$$$ | B&B/INN | Although this upscale inn surrounded by neatly manicured gardens dates to 1789, it has a decidedly current vibe, from its sumptuous rooms with such modern perks as whirlpool tubs, gas fireplaces, and Bose sound systems, to the superb prix-fixe restaurant serving sublime contemporary American fare. **Pros:** many rooms have private decks; dining packages available; gorgeous countryside setting. **Cons:** somewhat remote; books up well ahead on weekends; not a good fit for kids. *$ Rooms from: $239 ✉ 116 Sugar Hill Rd. (Rte. 117), Sugar Hill ☎ 603/823–4100 ⊕ www.sugarhillinn.com ⇨ 15 rooms 🍽 Free Breakfast.*

Shopping

★ Harman's Cheese & Country Store

GENERAL STORE | It's worth a slight but pretty detour over the hill from Franconia to visit this rambling old village store and dairy that turns out legendarily rich, sharp aged cheddar, which is also available smoked and in port-and-cognac spreads. The venerable red-clapboard shop carries plenty of other foodie-pleasing products. *✉ 1400 Rte. 117, Sugar Hill ☎ 603/823–8000 ⊕ www.harmanscheese.com.*

Activities

SKIING

Cannon Mountain

SKIING & SNOWBOARDING | FAMILY | Serviced by the first aerial tramway in North America, which was built in 1938, this classic New England ski resort inside Franconia Notch State Park offers terrain that runs the gamut from steep pitches off the peak to gentle blue cruisers. Beginners may want to head over to the separate Tuckerbrook family area, which offers 13 trails and four lifts. Adventurous types will want to try out the Mittersill area, which has 86 acres of lift-accessed "side country" trails and glades where the snow is au naturel. **Facilities:** 97 trails; 285 acres; 2,180-foot vertical drop; 10 lifts. *✉ 260 Tramway Dr., Franconia ☎ 603/823–8800 ⊕ www.cannonmt.com 🎟 Lift ticket: $99.*

Lincoln and North Woodstock

17 miles south of Franconia, 42 miles west of North Conway, 64 miles north of Concord.

These neighboring towns at the White Mountains' southwestern corner are the western gateway to the famed Kancamagus Highway. They form a lively resort base camp, especially for metro Boston families who get here via the easy two-hour drive straight up Interstate 93. Although the town itself isn't much of an attraction, myriad festivals and activities keep Lincoln swarming with visitors year-round.

Tiny North Woodstock maintains a more inviting village feel and is close to some easy, scenic, family-friendly hikes, such as Georgiana Falls and the slightly more ambitious Indian Head Trail.

GETTING HERE AND AROUND

Accessed from Interstate 93, Lincoln and North Woodstock are connected by Route 112—it's a short 1-mile drive between the two.

ESSENTIALS

VISITOR INFORMATION Western White Mountains Chamber of Commerce. *✉ North Woodstock ☎ 603/745–6621 ⊕ www.westernwhitemtns.com.*

TOURS

Pemi Valley Moose Tours

WILDLIFE-WATCHING | FAMILY | If you're eager to see a mighty moose, embark on a moose-watching bus tour into the northernmost White Mountains. The 3- to 3½-hour trips depart at 8:30 pm May to late September for the best wildlife-sighting opportunities. ✉ *136 Main St., Lincoln* ☎ *603/745–2744* 🌐 *www.moosetoursnh.com* 🎫 *$45.*

Sights

Hobo Railroad

TRAIN/TRAIN STATION | FAMILY | Restored vintage train cars take you on 80-minute excursions along the scenic banks of the Pemigewassett River. A Santa Express runs late November–mid-December. ✉ *64 Railroad St., Lincoln* ☎ *603/745–2135* 🌐 *www.hoborr.com* 🎫 *$20* ⏲ *Closed mid-Dec.–Apr.*

★ Kancamagus Highway

SCENIC DRIVE | FAMILY | In 1937, two old local roads were connected from Lincoln to Conway to create this remarkable 34.5-mile national designated scenic byway through a breathtaking swath of the White Mountains. This section of Route 112 known as the Kancamagus—often called simply "the Kanc"—contains no businesses or billboards and is punctuated by overlooks, picnic areas, and memorable hiking trailheads. These include **Lincoln Woods,** an easy 6-mile round-trip trek along a railroad bed that departs from the Lincoln Woods Visitor Center, crosses a dramatic suspension bridge over the Pemigewasset River, and ends at a swimming hole formed by dramatic Franconia Falls. There's also **Sabbaday Falls,** a short ½-mile stroll to a multilevel cascade that plunges through two potholes and a flume. For a slightly harder but less crowded trek, take the 3.5-mile **Boulder Loop Trail,** which rises precipitously some 1,000 feet from the banks of the Swift River to a granite-crowned summit with mountain views. The road's highest point, at 2,855 feet, crosses the flank of Mt. Kancamagus, near Lincoln—a great place to view the fiery displays of foliage each autumn. On-site in lots and overlooks costs $5. ☎ *603/536–6100* 🌐 *www.fs.usda.gov/whitemountain.*

★ Lost River Gorge & Boulder Caves

NATURE SIGHT | FAMILY | Parents can enjoy the looks of wonder on their kids' faces as they negotiate wooden boardwalks and stairs leading through a granite gorge formed by the roaring waters of the Lost River. One of the 10 caves they can explore is called the Lemon Squeezer (and it's a tight fit). Visitors can also pan for gems and search for fossils and walk through a fascinating giant man-made birdhouse, venture across a suspension bridge, and climb up into a big tree house. The park offers lantern tours on weekend evenings. ✉ *1712 Lost River Rd., North Woodstock* ☎ *603/745–8720* 🌐 *www.lostrivergorge.com* 🎫 *$22* ⏲ *Closed mid-Oct.–Apr.*

Seven Birches Winery

WINERY | With a tasting room at Lincoln's RiverWalk resort and steps away in a bright and modern wine bar with a big patio, this respected winery offers its classic European-varietal dry wines and sweeter fruit wines by the glass or flight, along with a selection of snacks. ✉ *22 S. Mountain Dr., Lincoln* ☎ *603/745–7550* 🌐 *www.sevenbirches.com.*

Whale's Tale Waterpark

WATER PARK | FAMILY | You can float on an inner tube along a gentle river, plunge down one of five waterslides, hang five on the Akua surf simulator, or bodysurf in the large wave pool at Whale's Tale. There's plenty here for toddlers and small children, too. ✉ *481 Daniel Webster Hwy. (U.S. 3), Lincoln* ☎ *603/745–8810* 🌐 *www.whalestalewaterpark.net* 🎫 *From $44* ⏲ *Closed early Oct.–Apr.*

Continued on page 550

HIKING THE APPALACHIAN TRAIL

Tucked inside the nation's most densely populated corridor, a simple footpath in the wilderness stretches more than 2,200 miles, from Georgia to Maine. The Appalachian Trail passes through some of New England's most spectacular regions, and daytrippers can experience the area's beauty on a multitude of accessible, rewarding hikes.

Running along the spine of the Appalachian Mountains, the trail was fully blazed in 1937 and designed to connect anyone and everyone with nature. Within a day's drive of two-thirds of the U.S. population, it draws an estimated three million people every year. Through-hikers complete the whole trail in one daunting six-month season, but all ages and abilities can find renewal and perspective here in just a few hours. One-third of the AT passes through New England, and it's safe to say that the farther north you go, the harder the trail gets. New Hampshire and Maine challenge experienced hikers with windy, cold, and isolated peaks.

Top, hiking in New Hampshire's White Mountains. Above, autumn view of Profile Lake, Pemigewasset, NH.

ON THE TRAIL

New England's prime hiking season is in late summer and early fall, when the blaze of foliage viewed from a high peak is unparalleled. Popular trails see high crowds; if you seek solitude, try hiking at sunrise, a peaceful time that's good for wildlife viewing. You'll have to curb your enthusiasm in spring and early summer to avoid mud season in late April and black flies in May and June.

With the right gear, attitude, and preparation, winter can also offer fine opportunities for hiking, snowshoeing, and cross-country skiing.

FOLLOW THE TRAIL

Most hiking trails are marked with blazes, blocks of colored paint on a tree or rock. The AT, and only the AT, is marked by vertical, rectangular 2-by 6-inch white blazes. Two blazes mark route changes; turn in the direction of the top blaze. At higher elevations, you might also see cairns, small piles of rocks carefully placed by trail rangers to show the way when a blaze might be obscured by snow or fog.

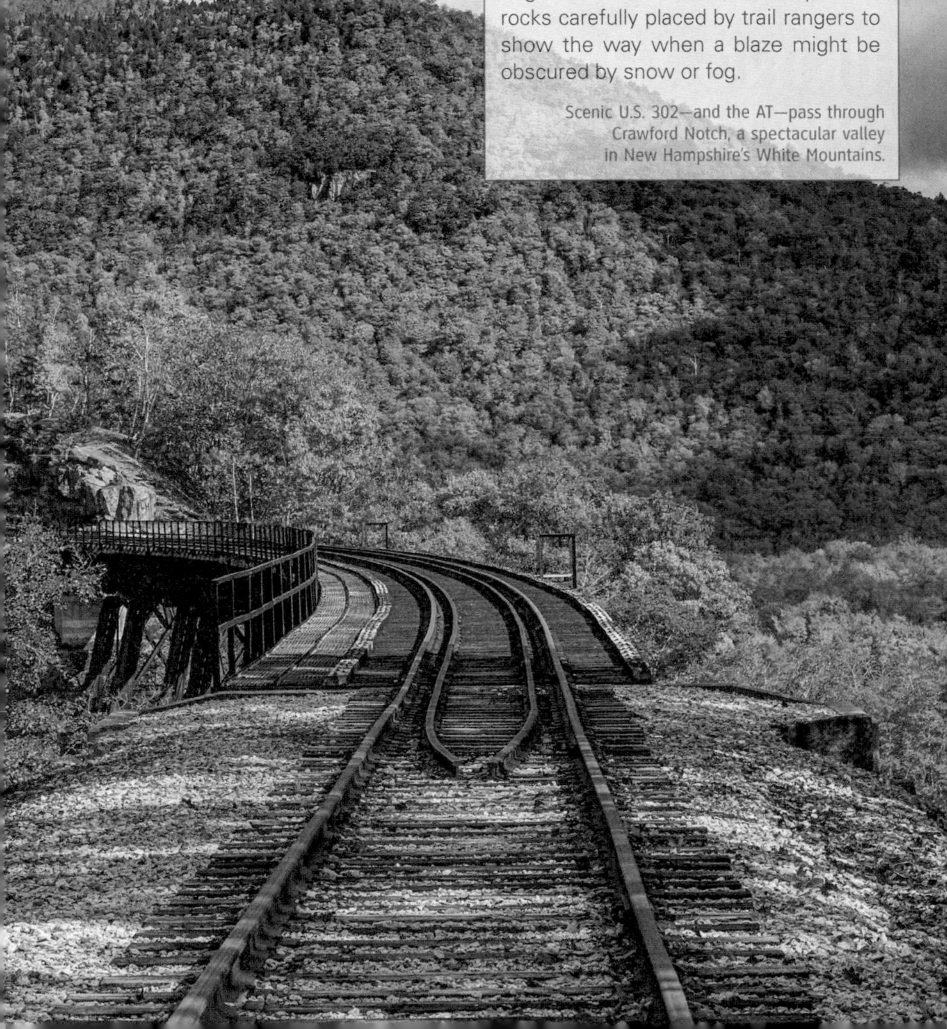

Scenic U.S. 302—and the AT—pass through Crawford Notch, a spectacular valley in New Hampshire's White Mountains.

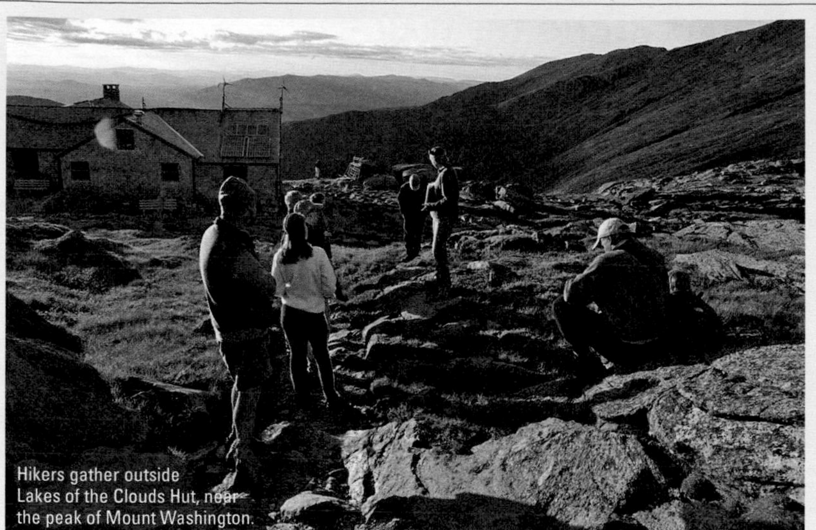
Hikers gather outside Lakes of the Clouds Hut, near the peak of Mount Washington.

TRIP TIPS

WHAT TO WEAR: For clothes, layer with a breathable fabric like polypropylene, starting with a shirt, a fleece, and a wind- or water-resistant shell. Bring gloves, a hat, and a change of socks.

WHAT TO BRING: Carry plenty of water and lightweight high-energy food. Don't forget sunscreen and insect repellent. Bring a map and compass. Just in case: a basic first-aid kit, a flashlight or headlamp, whistle, multi-tool, and matches.

PLAN AHEAD: In your car, leave a change of clothing, especially dry socks and shoes, as well as extra water and food.

PLAY IT SAFE: Tell someone your hiking plan and take a hiking partner. Carry a rescue card with emergency contact information and allergy details.

BE PREPARED: Plan your route and check the weather forecast in advance.

REMEMBER YOUR BEGINNINGS: Look back at the trail especially at the trailhead and at tricky junctions. If you've got a digital camera, photograph trail maps posted at the trailhead or natural landmarks to help you find your way.

WHERE TO STAY

Day hikers looking to extend the adventure can also make the experience as hard or as soft as they choose. Through-hikers combine camping with overnight stays in primitive shelters, mountain huts, comfortable lodges, and resorts just off the trail.

Rustic cabins and lean-tos provide basic shelter in Maine's Baxter State Park. In Maine and New Hampshire, the Appalachian Mountain Club runs four-season lodges as well as a network of mountain huts for backcountry hikers. A hiker code of camaraderie and conviviality prevails in these huts. Experience a night and you might just find yourself dreaming of a through-hike.

FOR MORE INFORMATION

Appalachian Trail Conservancy
(🌐 *www.appalachiantrail.org*)

Appalachian National Scenic Trail
(🌐 *www.nps.gov/appa*)

Appalachian Mountain Club
(🌐 *www.outdoors.org*)

ANIMALS ALONG THE TRAIL

❶ Black bear

Black bears are the most common—and smallest—bear in North America. Clever and adaptable, these adroit mammals will eat whatever they can (though they are primarily vegetarian, favoring berries, grasses, roots, blossoms, and nuts). Not naturally aggressive, black bears usually make themselves scarce when they hear hikers. The largest New England populations are in New Hampshire and Maine.

❷ Moose

Spotting a moose in the wild is unforgettable: their massive size and serene gaze are truly humbling. Treasure the moment, then slowly back away. At more than six feet tall, weighing 750 to 1,200 pounds, a moose is not to be trifled with, particularly during rutting and calving seasons (fall and spring, respectively). Dusk and dawn are the best times to spot the iconic animal; you're most likely to see one in Maine, especially in and around ponds.

⚠ Black flies

Especially fierce in May and June, these pesky flies can upset the tranquility of a hike in the woods as they swarm your face and bite your neck. To ward them off, cover any exposed skin and wear light colors. You'll get some relief on a mountain peak; cold weather and high winds also keep them at bay.

❸ Bald eagles

Countless bird species can be seen and heard along the AT, but what could be more exciting than to catch a glimpse of our national bird as it bounces back from near extinction? Now it's not uncommon to see the majestic bald eagle with its tremendous wing span, white head feathers, and curved yellow beak. The white head and tail distinguish the bald from the golden eagle, a bit less rare but just as thrilling to see. Most of New England's bald eagles are in Maine, but they are now present—albeit in small numbers—in all six states.

WILDFLOWERS ALONG THE TRAIL

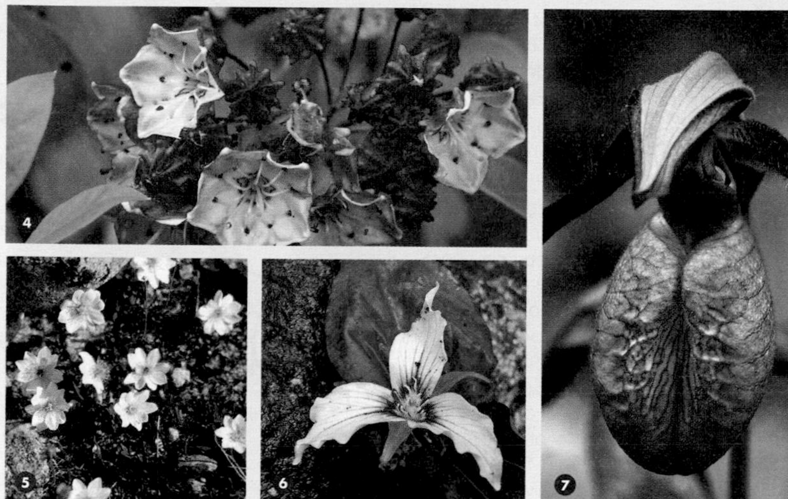

❹ Mountain laurel

The clusters of pink and white blooms of the mountain laurel look like bursts of fireworks. Up close, each one has the delicate detail of a lady's parasol. Blooms vary in color, from pure white to darker pink, and have different amounts of red markings. Connecticut's state flower, mountain laurel flourishes in rocky woods, blooming in May and June. Look for the shrub in southern New England; it's rare along the Appalachian trail in Vermont and Maine.

❺ Mountain avens

A member of the rose family, these showy yellow flowers abound in New Hampshire's White Mountains. You can't miss the large buttercup-like blooms on long green stems when they are in bloom from June through August. So common here, yet extremely rare: the only other place in the whole world where you can find mountain avens is on an island off the coast of Nova Scotia.

❻ Painted trillium

You might smell a trillium before you see it; these flowers have an unpleasant odor that may attract the flies that pollinate it. To identify this impressive flower, look for sets of three: three large pointed blue-green leaves, three sepals (small leaves beneath the petals), and three white petals with a brilliant magenta center. It can take four or five years for a trillium to produce one flower, which blooms in May and June in wet woodlands.

❼ Pink lady slippers

These delicate orchids can grow from 6 to 15 inches high and favor specific wet wooded areas in dappled sunlight. The slender stalk rises from a pair of green leaves, then bends a graceful neck to suspend the paper-thin pale pink closed flower. The slow-growing plant needs help from fungus and bees to survive and can live to be 20 years old. New Hampshire's state wildflower, the pink lady slipper blooms in June throughout New England.

● = Somewhat Common ● = Rare

CHOOSE YOUR DAY HIKE

MAINE

GULF HAGAS, Greenville

Difficult, 8-plus miles round-trip, 6–7 hours

This National Natural Landmark in the North Maine Woods is a spectacular sight for the adventurous day hiker. It involves a long drive on logging roads east from Greenville (see Inland Maine section) to a remote spot and a slippery, sometimes treacherous 8-mile hike around the rim of what's been dubbed Maine's Grand Canyon. Swimming in one of the sparkling pools under a 30-foot-high waterfall and admiring the views of cliffs, cascades, gorges, and chasms in this slate canyon, otherwise unthinkable in New England, will take your breath away.

TABLE ROCK, Bethel

Medium, 2.7 miles round-trip, 2 hours

Maine's Mahoosuc Range is thought to be one of the most difficult stretches of the entire AT, but north of Bethel at Grafton Notch State Park, day hikes range from easy walks in to cascading waterfalls to strenuous climbs up Old Speck's craggy peak. The Table Rock trail offers interesting sights—great views of the notch from the immense slab of granite that gives this trail its name, as well as one of the state's largest system of slab caves—narrow with tall openings unlike underground caves.

NEW HAMPSHIRE

ZEALAND TRAIL, Bretton Woods

Easy, 5.6 miles round-trip, 3.5–4 hours

New Hampshire's Presidential range gets so much attention and traffic that sometimes the equally spectacular Pemigewasset Wilderness, just to its west, gets overlooked. Follow U.S. 302 to the trailhead on Zealand Rd. near Bretton Woods. For an easy day hike to one of the Appalachian Mountain Club's excellent overnight huts, take the mostly flat Zealand Trail over bridges and past a beaver swamp to Zealand Pond. The last tenth of a mile is a steep ascent to the mountain retreat, where you might spot an AT through-hiker taking a well-deserved rest. (Most north-bound through-hikers reach this section around July or August.) In winter, you can get here by a lovely cross-country ski trip.

TRAIL NAMES

For through-hikers, doing the AT can be a life-altering experience. One of the trail's most respected traditions is taking an alter ego: a trail name. Lightning Bolt: fast hiker. Pine Knot: tough as one. Blubearee: because a bear got all her food on her very first night on the trail.

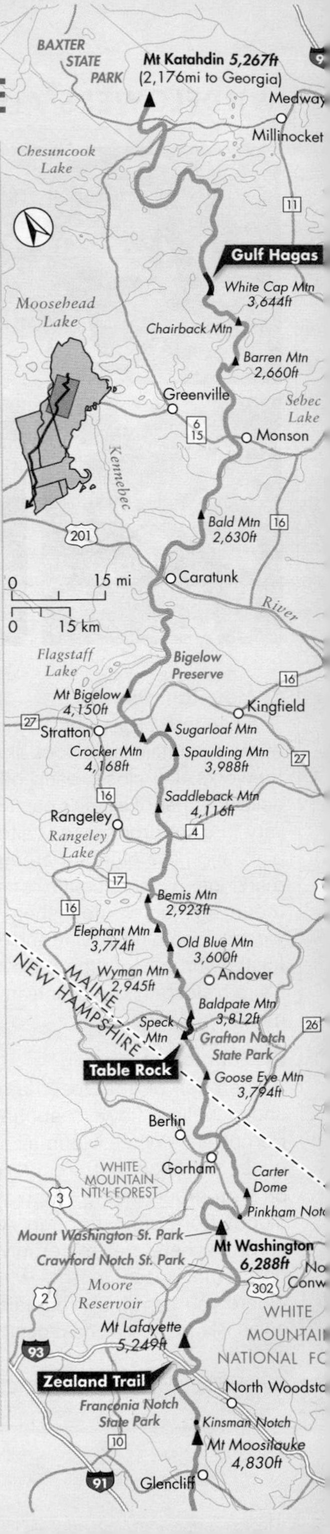

VERMONT

HARMON HILL, Bennington

Medium to difficult, 3.3 miles round-trip, 3–4 hours

This rugged hike in the Green Mountains goes south along the AT where it coincides with the Long Trail, Vermont's century-old "footpath in the wilderness." From the trailhead on Route 9 just east of Bennington, the first half mile or so is strenuous, with some rock and log staircases and hairpins. The payback is the sweeping view from the top; you'll see Mount Anthony, Bennington and its iconic war monument, and the rolling green hills of the Taconics to the west.

STRATTON MOUNTAIN, Stratton

Difficult, 6.6 miles round-trip, 5–6 hours

A steep and steady climb from the trailhead on Stratton Arlington Rd. (west of the village of Stratton) up the 3,936-foot-high Stratton Mountain follows the AT and Long Trail through mixed forests. It's said that this peak is where Benton MacKaye conceived of the idea for the Appalachian Trail in 1921. An observation tower at the summit gives you a great 360-degree view of the Green Mountains. From July to October, you can park at Stratton resort and ride the gondola up (or down) and follow the .75-mile Fire Tower Trail to the southern true peak.

MASSACHUSETTS

MOUNT GREYLOCK, North Adams

Easy to difficult, 2 miles round-trip, less than 1 hour

There are many ways to experience Massachusetts's highest peak. From North Adams, follow Route 2 to the Notch Rd. trailheads. For a warm-up, try the Rounds Rock trail (Easy, 0.7 mi) for some spectacular views. Or drive up the 8-mile-long summit road and hike down the Robinson's Point trail (Difficult, 0.8 miles) for the best view of the Hopper, a glacial cirque that's home to an old-growth red spruce forest. At the summit, the impressive **Bascom Lodge**, built in the 1930s by the Civilian Conservation Corps, provides delicious meals and overnight stays (🌐 www.bascomlodge.net).

CONNECTICUT

LION'S HEAD, Salisbury

Medium, 4.6 miles round-trip, 3.5–4 hours

The AT's 52 miles in Connecticut take hikers up some modest mountains, including Lion's Head in Salisbury. From the trailhead on Route 41, follow the white blazes of the AT for two easy miles, then take the blue-blazed Lion's Head Trail for a short, steep push over open ledges to the 1,738-foot summit with its commanding views of pastoral southern New England. Try this in summer when the mountain laurels—Connecticut's state flower—are in bloom.

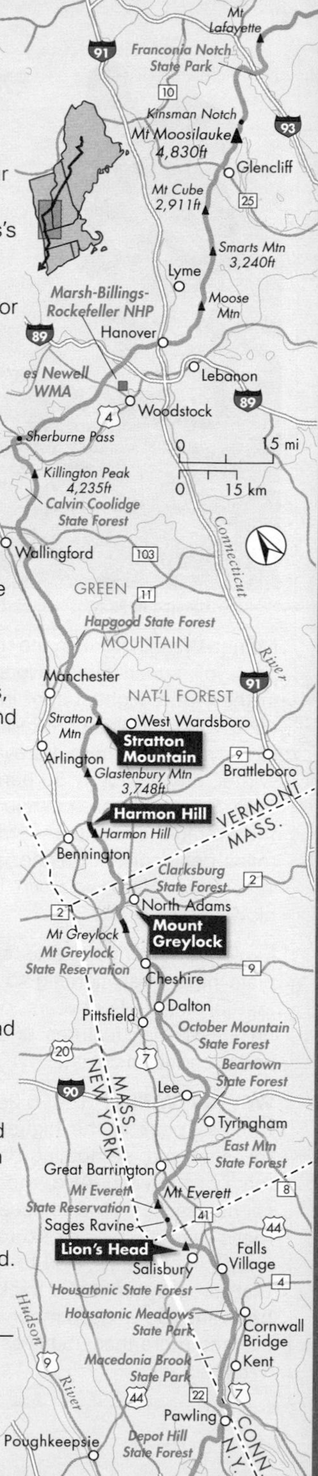

EXPERIENCE MOUNT WASHINGTON

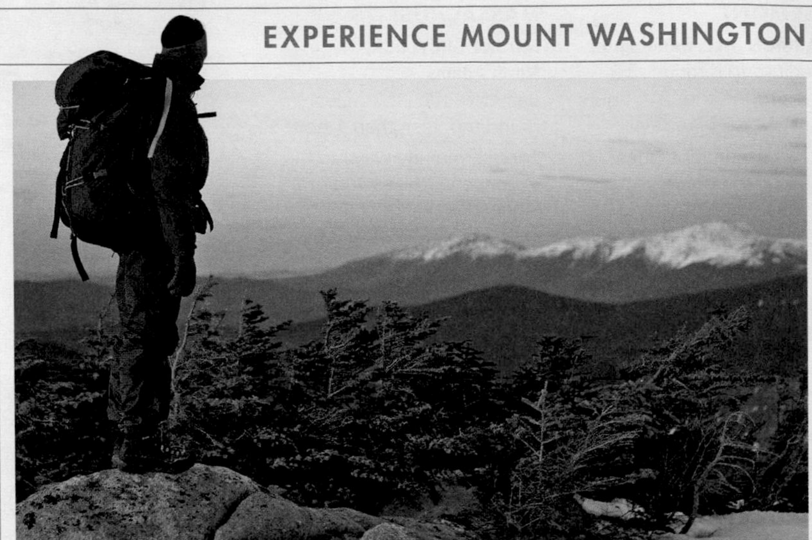

Looking at Mt. Washington from Mt. Bond in the Pemigewasset Wilderness Area, New Hampshire.

Mount Washington is the Northeast's peak of superlatives: worst weather in the world, highest spot in the northeast, windiest place on Earth. It snows in the summer, there are avalanches in winter, and it's foggy 60 percent of the time. Strong 35-mile-per-hour winds are the average, and extreme winds of 100 miles per hour with higher gusts blow year-round. Here, you can literally get blown away.

Explorers, scientists, artists, and botanists have been coming to the mountain for hundreds of years, drawn by its unique geologic features, unusual plants, and exceptional climate.

WHY SO WINDY? The 6,288-foot-high treeless peak is the highest point for miles around, so nothing dampens the force of the wind. Also, the sharp vertical rise causes wind to accelerate. Dramatic changes in air pressure also cause strong, high winds. Add to that the fact that three major storm tracks converge here, and you've got a mountain that has claimed more than 150 lives in the past 175 years.

GOING UP THE MOUNTAIN

An ascent up Mount Washington is for experienced hikers who are prepared for severe, unpredictable weather. Even in summer, cold, wet, foggy, windy conditions prevail. The most popular route to the top is on the eastern face up the Tuckerman Ravine Trail. But countless trails offer plenty of moderate day hikes, like the Alpine Garden Trail, as an alternative to a summit attempt. Start at the Pinkham Notch Visitor Center on Route 16 to review your options.

BACKPACKING ON THE MOUNTAIN

Lakes of the Clouds Hut perches 5,050 feet up the southern shoulder, providing bunkrooms and meals in summer; reservations are required. On the eastern face, the **Hermit Lake Shelter Area** has shelters and tent platforms; to camp here you'll need a first-come, first-served permit from the Visitors Center. Both are operated by the **AMC** (☎ *603/466-2727*; 🌐 *www.outdoors.org*).

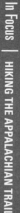

NON-HIKING ALTERNATIVES

In the summer, the **Auto Road** (☎ *603/466-3988* 🌐 *www.mt-washington.com*) and the **Cog Railway** (☎ *800/922-8825* 🌐 *www.thecog.com*) present alternate ways up the mountain; both give you a real sense of the mountain's grandeur. In winter, a **Snow-Coach** (☎ *603/466–3988* 🌐 *www.mt-washington.com*) hauls visitors 4.5 miles up the Auto Road with an option to cross-country ski, telemark, snowshoe, or ride the coach back down.

Restaurants

Woodstock Inn Brewery

$$ | **AMERICAN** | This big and festive brewpub inside a late-1800s train station is decorated with old maps, historic photographs, and other fun curiosities. The kitchen turns out reliably good pub fare—pizza, burgers, steaks, seafood—and filling breakfasts, and the brewery produces nearly 20 different varieties of exceptionally good beers. **Known for:** game room and kids' menu; brewery tours; inviting indoor and outdoor seating. *Average main: $21 ✉ 135 Main St., North Woodstock ☎ 603/745–3951 🌐 www.woodstockinnnh.com.*

Coffee and Quick Bites

The Moon Bakery & Cafe

$ | **CAFÉ** | A must for delicious sustenance and potent lattes before hitting the slopes or hiking along the Kancamagus Highway, this homey café offers ample indoor seating in exposed-brick-wall nooks or outside on the sidewalk. Popular items include ham and cheddar sandwiches with maple mustard, avocado-egg breakfast sandwiches, and matcha green tea smoothies. **Known for:** fresh smoothies; hefty sandwiches on house-baked bread; trail mix cookies. *Average main: $11 ✉ 28 S. Mountain Dr., Lincoln ☎ 603/745–5013 🌐 www.facebook.com/themoonlincoln ⏲ Closed Tues. No dinner.*

Hotels

Indian Head Resort

$ | **RESORT** | **FAMILY** | This early-20th-century resort, identified by its 100-foot-tall observation tower and its lovely setting overlooking Shadow Lake, offers inexpensive and spacious rooms, making it a good choice for families on a budget. **Pros:** near kid-friendly attractions; fun, old-school personality; a free ski shuttle to Cannon or Loon Mountain. **Cons:** some rooms overlook parking lot; on busy road 5 miles north of Woodstock; shows wear in places. *Rooms from: $139 ✉ 664 Daniel Webster Hwy. (U.S. 3) ☎ 603/745–8000, 800/343–8000 🌐 www.indianheadresort.com 148 rooms Free Breakfast.*

★ Lumen Nature Retreat

$ | **RESORT** | With easy access to the many recreational activities of Waterville and Woodstock, this 20-acre glamping hideaway offers downright plush accommodations in stylish safari tents and A-frame cabins, all with premium linens, cooking utensils, and battery chargers. **Pros:** units are well-stocked for cooking and campfires; all units have patios and smokeless firepits; spotless accommodations with plush bedding. **Cons:** no camp store or reception area; two-night minimum stay on weekends; some noise from Interstate 93. *Rooms from: $109 ✉ 11 Sugar Plum La., North Woodstock ☎ 603/764–7244 🌐 www.stayatlumen.com ⏲ Closed Nov.–Apr. 15 units.*

Mountain Club on Loon

$$ | **RESORT** | **FAMILY** | With a diverse range of accommodations, including large family suites, and many units with full kitchens, this functional if pretty standard condo-style lodge provides convenient ski-in, ski-out accommodations on Loon Mountain. **Pros:** within walking distance of the lifts; full-service spa; easy proximity to great hiking. **Cons:** very busy on winter weekends; decor is a bit perfunctory; not within walking distance of town. *Rooms from: $171 ✉ 90 Loon Mountain Rd., Lincoln ☎ 603/745–2244, 800/229–7829 🌐 www.mtnclub.com 235 rooms No Meals.*

Shopping

Fadden's General Store

GENERAL STORE | The Fadden family, who have been making maple syrup for several generations, operates this inviting general store, sugarhouse, and maple museum that dates to 1896. Come in to buy syrup, souvenirs, and gourmet treats, or for a self-guided tour of the operations. ✉ *109 Main St., North Woodstock* ☎ *603/745–8371* 🌐 *www.nhmaplesyrup.com.*

Activities

HIKING

Mt. Moosilauke

HIKING & WALKING | One of the most rewarding, though heavily trafficked, summits in the White Mountains, 4,802-foot Mt. Moosilauke soars high to the west of the Pemigewasset Valley and can be approached via a few routes, including the Appalachian Trail and from Route 112 near Lost River Gorge. The most enjoyable trek is via the 7-mile South Peak Loop. It begins near Route 118 at the 1930s Moosilauke Ravine Lodge, which is operated by Dartmouth College and offers basic overnight accommodations. However you ascend to the treeless peak, you'll enjoy sweeping views of the Presidential Range, Lake Winnipesaukee, and even the Adirondacks. ✉ *Ravine Rd., North Woodstock.*

SKIING

Loon Mountain

SKIING & SNOWBOARDING | **FAMILY** | Wide, straight, and consistent intermediate ski trails prevail at this modern resort on the Pemigewasset River. The most advanced runs are grouped on the North Peak, with beginner trails set apart. There's snow tubing on the lower slopes, and eight terrain parks suitable for all ability levels. A base lodge offers dining and lounges. You'll also find 13 miles of cross-country trails, an outdoor ice-skating rink, snowshoeing and snowshoeing tours. During the summer months, popular resort activities include disc golf, ziplining, mountain-biking, e-bikes, a rock-climbing wall, and exploring glacially carved caves. **Facilities:** 61 trails; 370 acres; 2,100-foot vertical drop; 11 lifts. ✉ *90 Loon Mountain Rd., Lincoln* ☎ *603/745–8111* 🌐 *www.loonmtn.com* 🎫 *Lift ticket: $116.*

Waterville Valley

25 miles southeast of North Lincoln.

Although visitors have been exploring this dramatic alpine landscape since 1835, and the first ski trails were installed on 3,997-foot Mt. Tecumseh in the 1930s, Watervalley Valley didn't become a major destination until a group of developers led by Olympic skier Tom Corcoran built a full-service ski area here in 1966. That led to a planned resort with several hotels and condominiums, a town square with shops and restaurants, a golf course, and other amenities. Today it's a terrific family-friendly winter-sports destination, but there's also plenty to do in warmer months, including great hiking and mountain-biking. Rates at the resort hotels come with passes that include cross-country ski and bike rentals, access to the well-equipped White Mountain Athletic Club, and other perks—it's a remarkable value.

GETTING HERE AND AROUND

You get here from Interstate 93 in Campton, via Route 49, which runs alongside the Mad River and dead-ends at the Town Square. Free shuttle buses whisk guests from hotels to the ski area. In summer, you can also get here by way of unpaved Tripoli Road, a bumpy but beautiful route through White Mountain National Forest that accesses some amazing campgrounds and hikes, such as Mt. Osceola and Mt. Tecumseh. It leads out to Interstate 93 in Woodstock.

Restaurants

Coyote Grill

$$ | **AMERICAN** | **FAMILY** | On the second floor of the White Mountain Athletic Club, Waterville Valley's best restaurant is a rambling space with big windows offering up grand views of the White Mountains. The food is hearty and well-prepared, just what you need after a day of hiking or skiing. **Known for:** mountain views; lighter fare served downstairs by the pool; Oreo-crusted white-chocolate cheesecake. *Average main: $22* ✉ *98 Valley Rd., Waterville Valley* ☎ *603/236–4919* 🌐 *www.wildcoyotegrill.com* ⏲ *Closed Mon. and Tues. No lunch.*

Hotels

Golden Eagle Lodge

$$ | **HOTEL** | **FAMILY** | Waterville Valley's premier condominium resort, its steep roof punctuated by dozens of gabled dormers, recalls the grand hotels of an earlier era. **Pros:** steps from Town Square; units all have kitchens and lots of elbow room; sweeping mountain views. **Cons:** decor is a little dated; no a/c in many units; lots of kids and families create a sometimes hectic pace. *Rooms from: $179* ✉ *28 Packard's Rd., Waterville Valley* ☎ *603/236–4600* 🌐 *www.goldeneaglelodge.com* *139 condos* *No Meals.*

Valley Inn

$ | **HOTEL** | **FAMILY** | One of the region's better values, the Valley Inn offers few frills, but when you factor in the free activities pass and the quiet but convenient location, it's an excellent option. **Pros:** very reasonable rates; largest units have kitchens and can sleep six; peaceful setting. **Cons:** a few minutes' walk to Town Square; cookie-cutter decor; very basic breakfast. *Rooms from: $119* ✉ *17 Tecumseh Rd., Waterville Valley* ☎ *603/236–8425, 800/343–0969* 🌐 *www.valleyinn.com* *48 rooms* *Free Breakfast.*

Activities

HIKING

★ Welch-Dickey Trail

HIKING & WALKING | This at times steep but gorgeous 4½-mile loop hike ascends a wooded hillside before climbing above the sheer granite faces of 2,605-foot Welch and 2,734-foot Dickey mountains. There are higher climbs in the White Mountains, but this trail offers incredible views in every direction. Parking costs $5. ✉ *Orris Rd., Waterville Valley.*

SKIING

Waterville Valley Resort

SKIING & SNOWBOARDING | **FAMILY** | This family-friendly ski area has hosted many World Cup races, so advanced skiers can look forward to a challenge. About two-thirds of the 50 trails are intermediate: straight down the fall line, wide, and agreeably long. About 20 acres of tree-skiing and six terrain parks add heart-pounding stimulus, and full snowmaking coverage ensures good skiing even when nature doesn't cooperate. The resort also offers 46 miles of groomed cross-country trails. **Facilities:** 50 trails; 220 acres; 2,020-foot vertical drop; 11 lifts. ✉ *1 Ski Area Rd., Waterville Valley* ☎ *603/236–8311, 800/468–2553* 🌐 *www.waterville.com* *Lift ticket: $112.*

New London

60 miles southwest of Waterville Valley, 33 miles west of Laconia, 40 miles northwest of Concord.

The progressive and quaint town of New London is anchored by the campus of Colby-Sawyer College (1837) and makes a good base for exploring Lake Sunapee. You'll find an engaging array of eateries and boutiques in town.

GETTING HERE AND AROUND

New London is just off Interstate 89.

Sights

★ Mt. Kearsarge

MOUNTAIN | There are two main ways to access this dramatic 2,937-foot granite peak east of Lake Sunapee. Approach it through **Winslow State Park,** which is closer to New London, by driving to the picnic area and hiking a 1.8-mile loop

trail to the top. Or, more popularly, drive the 3½-mile scenic auto route through **Rollins State Park,** which snakes up the mountain's southern slope and leads to a ½-mile summit trail. However you get there, the views from the top are astounding. The park road at Rollins State Park closes at 5 pm nightly and from mid-November to late May, but from Winslow State Park you can hike Mt. Kearsarge any time of day or night, year-round. Rollins State Park is accessed from the cute Colonial village of Warner, which is worth a quick stroll. ✉ *Rollins State Park, 1066 Kearsarge Mountain Rd., Warner* ✣ *20.3 miles south of New London via I-89* ☎ *603/456–3808* 🌐 *www.nhstateparks.org* 🎫 *$4.*

Mt. Kearsarge Indian Museum

INDIGENOUS SIGHT | Learn about not only the Native tribes of New England but also indigenous culture throughout the rest of the United States at this terrific museum set on a 12½-acre tract of meadows and forest on the road to Rollins State Park and Mt. Kearsarge. Exhibits are organized by region and feature ancient dugout birch canoes, headdresses and jewelry, basketry, textiles, pottery, musical instruments, and wood carvings, and docents are happy to provide free guided tours. Outside, you can stroll through Medicine Woods to discover the many kinds of plants used by Native communities for food, healing, and tools, and around a small arboretum with local flora. ✉ *18 Highlawn Rd., Warner* ✣ *16.4 miles south of New London via I-89 South* ☎ *603/456–2600* 🌐 *www.indianmuseum.org* 🎫 *$11* ⏲ *Closed Dec.–Apr. and weekdays in Nov.*

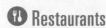

Restaurants

★ Oak & Grain

$$$$ | MODERN AMERICAN | The refined yet relaxed restaurant in the historic Inn at Pleasant Lake makes a splendid destination for a special occasion dinner, or simply to savor a delicious brunch in the window-lined dining room or out on the patio—both areas have views of the lake in the near distance. The kitchen here turns out artfully plated contemporary fare, such as grilled octopus with Spanish chorizo and a smoked-paprika vinaigrette, and sea scallops with a ginger-citrus chimichurri. **Known for:** pretty lake views; knowledgeable, friendly service; locally sourced meats and seafood. *$ Average main: $37 ✉ Inn at Pleasant Lake., 853 Pleasant St., New London ☎ 603/873–4833 🌐 innatpleasantlake.com ⏲ Closed Mon. and Tues. No lunch.*

Peter Christian's Tavern

$$ | MODERN AMERICAN | Exposed beams, wooden tables, a smattering of antiques, and half shutters on the windows make the amiable Peter Christian's a cool summer oasis and a warm winter haven. From shepherd's pie to seafood and grits with lobster butter, the flavorful comfort fare relies heavily on seasonal ingredients. **Known for:** outstanding seafood chowder; well-curated craft-beer and wine selection; dog-friendly patio. *$ Average main: $22 ✉ 195 N. Main St., New London ☎ 603/526–2964 🌐 www.peterchristiansnh.com.*

Coffee and Quick Bites

Blue Loon Bakery

$ | BAKERY | Have a seat in this cheerful bakery's sunny seating nooks or out on the back patio, while you savor an egg-cheddar croissant, house-made granola, a Brie-fig-apple baguette, or one of the delectable pastries or cakes. Favorite treats include maple-pumpkin pie, seasonal fruit tarts, raspberry scones, and praline sticky buns. **Known for:** savory artisan breads; fresh-baked pies; picnic supplies for nearby hiking and beach adventures. *$ Average main: $9 ✉ 12 Lovering La., New London ☎ 603/526–2892 🌐 www.blueloonbakery.com ⏲ Closed Mon. and Tues. No dinner.*

Hotels

★ Follansbee Inn

$$ | B&B/INN | FAMILY | Built in 1840, this rambling country inn on the shore of Kezar Lake is the kind of place that almost instantly turns strangers into fast friends. **Pros:** relaxed lakefront setting with 3-mile walking trail; free use of canoes, kayaks, sailboats, rowboats, and bicycles; excellent breakfast. **Cons:** not all rooms have lake views; Wi-Fi can be spotty in places; no restaurants within walking distance. *$ Rooms from: $165 ✉ 2 Keyser St., North Sutton ✣ 5½ miles south of New London via Rte. 114 South ☎ 603/927–4221 🌐 www.follansbeeinn.com 17 rooms 🍽 Free Breakfast.*

★ Inn at Pleasant Lake

$$$ | B&B/INN | Overlooking the shore of Pleasant Lake, and offering views of majestic Mt. Kearsarge in the distance, and just a short drive from downtown New London, this beautifully appointed 1790s inn has spacious, bright rooms filled with fine country antiques and high-end bedding. **Pros:** adjacent to lakefront and a small beach; tennis courts; rates includes an outstanding full breakfast and afternoon tea. **Cons:** not within walking distance of town; not a good fit for kids; minimum stay at busy times. *$ Rooms from: $229 ✉ 853 Pleasant St., New London ☎ 603/526–6271, 800/626–4907 🌐 innatpleasantlake.com 10 rooms 🍽 Free Breakfast.*

Nightlife

Flying Goose Brew Pub

BREWPUBS | Offering a regular menu of about a dozen handcrafted beers, including a much lauded black IPA and a heady barley wine as well as a few seasonal varieties—made with hops grown on-site—this pub, and solar-powered brewery is a hit with beer connoisseurs. The kitchen serves juicy ribs, paper-thin onion rings, excellent burgers, and other tasty victuals. ✉ *40 Andover Rd., New London* ☎ *603/526–6899* 🌐 *www.flying-goose.com.*

Performing Arts

New London Barn Playhouse
THEATER | FAMILY | Broadway-style musicals and children's plays are presented here every summer in New Hampshire's oldest continuously operating theater. ✉ *84 Main St., New London* ☎ *603/526–6710* 🌐 *www.nlbarn.org.*

Newbury and Lake Sunapee

8 miles southwest of New London.

In the west-central part of the state, the towns around prestigious Dartmouth College and rippling Lake Sunapee vary from sleepy, old-fashioned outposts that haven't changed much in decades to bustling, sophisticated towns filled with cafés, art galleries, and boutiques. Newbury lies at the southern edge of 6-square-mile Lake Sunapee, one of the highest—and cleanest—lakes in the state, and a wonderful destination for boating, swimming, and fishing. Mt. Sunapee State Park has a picturesque beach on the lake as well as a mountain section that rises to an elevation of nearly 3,000 feet and offers some of the best skiing in southern New Hampshire. The popular League of New Hampshire Craftsmen's Fair, the oldest crafts fair in the nation, is held here in early August.

GETTING HERE AND AROUND

From Interstate 89, Route 103A leads here via the eastern shore of Lake Sunapee.

For a great drive, follow the Lake Sunapee Scenic and Cultural Byway, which runs about 25 miles from Georges Mills (a bit west of New London) down into Warner, tracing much of the Lake Sunapee shoreline.

Sights

★ John Hay Estate at the Fells
GARDEN | The former home of the statesman who served as private secretary to Abraham Lincoln and U.S. Secretary of State to Presidents William McKinley and Theodore Roosevelt, built the 22-room Fells on Lake Sunapee as a summer home in 1890. House tours offer a glimpse of late Victorian life on a New Hampshire estate. The grounds, a gardener's delight, include a 100-foot-long perennial garden and a rock garden with a brook flowing through it. Miles of hiking trails can also be accessed from its 83½ acres. ✉ *456 Rte. 103A, Newbury* ☎ *603/763–4789* 🌐 *www.thefells.org* *$10 when house open, $8 when house closed* *House closed Mon. and Tues. and mid-Oct.–late May.*

★ Sunapee Harbor
TOWN | On the west side of Lake Sunapee, this old-fashioned summer resort community has a large marina, a few restaurants and shops on the water, a tidy village green with a gazebo, and a small museum. ✉ *Main St. at Lake Ave., Sunapee.*

Beaches

Mt. Sunapee State Park Beach
BEACH | FAMILY | A great family spot, this beach adjoining a 4,085-acre mountain park has picnic areas, fishing, and a bathhouse, plus access to great hiking trails. You can also rent canoes and kayaks, and there's a campground. **Amenities:**

lifeguards; parking (fee); showers; toilets. **Best for:** swimming; walking. ✉ *86 Beach Access Rd., Sunapee* ☎ *603/763–5561* 🌐 *www.nhstateparks.org* 🎫 *$5 mid-May–mid-Oct.*

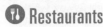

Restaurants

Suna

$$ | **MODERN AMERICAN** | On a wooded country road just up the hill from Lake Sunapee, this lively little bar and bistro is great for a romantic meal or a relaxed bite after a day on the water or the mountain. The eclectic menu features a mix of classic American and Continental dishes with creative touches. **Known for:** excellent craft cocktails; lively après-ski scene; sublime desserts. $ *Average main: $22* ✉ *6 Brook Rd., Sunapee* ☎ *603/843–8998* 🌐 *www.sunarestaurant-nh.com* ⏲ *Closed Mon. No lunch.*

Wildwood Smokehouse

$$ | **BARBECUE** | The hulking metal smoker outside this Old West–inspired tavern with high pressed-tin ceilings, chandeliers, and red Victorian wallpaper hints at the delicious barbecue served inside. Plates heaped with ribs, beef brisket, pulled chicken, and smoked bratwurst reveal the considerable skill of Wildwood's pit master, and plenty of tasty sides are offered, too, from mac and cheese to dirty rice. **Known for:** pecan pie; "hog wings" (pork shanks in barbecue sauce); popular early evening happy hour. $ *Average main: $19* ✉ *45 Main St., Sunapee* ☎ *603/763–1178* 🌐 *www.wildwoodsmokehousesunapee.com* ⏲ *Closed Sun. and Mon. No lunch.*

Coffee and Quick Bites

Sanctuary Dairy Farm Ice Cream

$ | **ICE CREAM** | **FAMILY** | Enjoy a scoop or two of rich homemade ice cream at this 10th-generation dairy farm a couple of miles from Lake Sunapee. Interesting flavors like hazelnut, lemon cookie, and maple pecan keep regulars coming back for more, but the barnyard with adorable goats, bunnies, and other critters is almost as big a draw. **Known for:** unusual ice-cream flavors; seating in picturesque pasture; cute barnyard animals to feed. $ *Average main: $5* ✉ *209 Rte. 103, Sunapee* ☎ *603/863–8940* 🌐 *www.icecreamkidbeck.com* ⏲ *shop closed mid-Oct.–late May.*

Hotels

Sunapee Harbor Cottages

$$$ | **HOTEL** | **FAMILY** | This cozy compound of six charming, eco-friendly cottages—each sleeping five–eight people and with small but well-equipped kitchens—is a stone's throw from Sunapee Harbor and an easy drive from winter skiing at nearby Mt. Sunapee. **Pros:** ideal for families or friends traveling together; free beach passes; pet-friendly. **Cons:** no maid service; limited clothes storage; cottage porches overlook one another. $ *Rooms from: $265* ✉ *4 Lake Ave., Sunapee Harbor* ☎ *603/763–5052* 🌐 *www.sunapeeharborcottages.com* *6 cottages* 🍽 *No Meals.*

Shopping

Wild Goose Country Store

SOUVENIRS | On the harbor in Sunapee, this old-fashioned general store carries teddy bears, penny candy, pottery, and other engaging odds and ends. ✉ *77 Main St., Sunapee* ☎ *603/763–5516.*

Activities

BOAT TOURS

Sunapee Cruises

ENTERTAINMENT CRUISE | This company operates narrated afternoon and dinner cruises of Lake Sunapee from June to mid-October. Ninety-minute afternoon cruises on the *M/V Mt. Sunapee* focus on Lake Sunapee's history and the mountain scenery. A buffet dinner is included on the two-hour sunset cruises aboard the *M/V Kearsarge*, a vintage-style steamship.

⌂ *Town Dock, 81 Main St., Sunapee Harbor* ☎ *603/938–6465* 🌐 *www.sunapee-cruises.com* 🎟 *From $24.*

HIKING

Monadnock-Sunapee Greenway Trail

HIKING & WALKING | This 50-mile trail starts in Newbury at Mt. Sunapee and snakes through verdant forests and the handsome village greens of Washington and Nelson and over jagged granite peaks south to Mt. Monadnock. One of the most enjoyable ways to access this trail is to hike the 2.3-mile (one-way) Andrew Brook Trail up to the granite ledges above Lake Solitude, where you'll cross with it. ⌂ *Andrew Brook Trailhead, Mountain Rd., Newbury* 🌐 *www.msgtc.org.*

SKIING

Mt. Sunapee

SKIING & SNOWBOARDING | **FAMILY** | This family-friendly resort is one of New England's best-kept secrets. The owners have spent millions upgrading their snow machines and grooming equipment and turning this into a four-season resort. Mt. Sunapee offers 67 trails and slopes for all abilities. There are four terrain parks and nine glade trails. In summer, the adventure park features a canopy zipline tour, an aerial challenge course, an 18-hole disc-golf course, miniature golf, and numerous hiking trails. **Facilities:** 67 trails; 233 acres; 1,510-foot vertical drop; 9 lifts. ⌂ *1398 Rte. 103, Newbury* ☎ *603/763–3500* 🌐 *www.mountsunapee.com* 🎟 *Lift ticket: $114.*

Hanover

30 miles northwest of New London, 60 miles southwest of Littleton, 20 miles east of Woodstock, Vermont.

Eleazar Wheelock founded Hanover's Dartmouth College in 1769 to educate the Abenaki "and other youth." When he arrived, the town consisted of about 20 families. Over time the college and the town grew symbiotically, with Dartmouth eventually becoming the northernmost Ivy League school. Hanover is still synonymous with Dartmouth, but it's also a respected medical and cultural center. Mostly independent shops fill the town's commercial district, which blends almost imperceptibly with Dartmouth's campus. Hanover and West Lebanon, with Woodstock, Quechee, Norwich, and White River Junction across the Connecticut River in Vermont, form an appealing two-state vacation destination.

GETTING HERE AND AROUND

Lebanon Municipal Airport is served by Cape Air from Boston and White Plains, New York. By car, there's easy access from Interstates 91 and 89.

ESSENTIALS

AIRPORT Lebanon Municipal Airport. ⌂ *5 Airpark Rd., West Lebanon* ☎ *603/298–8878* 🌐 *www.flyleb.com.*

VISITOR INFORMATION Upper Valley Business Alliance. ⌂ *Lebanon* ☎ *603/448–1203* 🌐 *www.uppervalleybusinessalliance.com.*

Sights

Dartmouth College

COLLEGE | The poet Robert Frost spent part of a brooding freshman semester at this Ivy League school before giving up college altogether, but the school counts politician Nelson Rockefeller, actor Mindy Kaling, TV producer Shonda Rhimes, and author Theodor ("Dr.") Seuss Geisel among its many illustrious grads. The buildings clustered around the picturesque green, which is lovely for strolling, include the **Baker Memorial Library,** which houses such literary treasures as 17th-century editions of William Shakespeare's works. The library is also well-known for Mexican artist José Clemente Orozco's 3,000-square-foot murals that depict the story of civilization in the Americas. Free campus tours are available. ⌂ *N. Main and Wentworth Sts., Hanover* ☎ *603/646–1110* 🌐 *www.dartmouth.edu.*

Enfield Shaker Museum

MUSEUM VILLAGE | In 1782, two Shaker brothers from Mt. Lebanon, New York, arrived on the still-beautiful shores of Lake Mascoma. Eventually, they formed Enfield, the ninth of 18 Shaker communities in the United States, and relocated to the lake's southern shore, where they erected more than 200 buildings. The Enfield Shaker Museum preserves the legacy of these Shakers, who numbered 330 members at the village's peak. By 1923, interest in the society had waned, and the last 10 members joined the Canterbury community, south of Laconia. A self-guided walking tour takes you through 13 of the remaining buildings, among them an 1849 stone mill. Demonstrations of Shaker crafts techniques also take place, and overnight accommodations are available in the community's stately six-story Great Stone Dwelling. ⊠ *447 Rte. 4A, Enfield* ✥ *12 miles southeast of Hanover* ☎ *603/632–4346* 🌐 *www.shakermuseum.org* 🎟 *$14* ⏲ *Closed Mon.–Wed., Nov.–mid-May, and weekdays mid-May–June.*

★ Hood Museum of Art

ART MUSEUM | Dartmouth's excellent art museum owns Picasso's *Guitar on a Table,* silver by Paul Revere, a set of Assyrian reliefs from the 9th century BC, along with other noteworthy examples of African, Peruvian, Oceanic, Asian, European, and American art. The range of contemporary works—including pieces by John Sloan, William Glackens, Mark Rothko, Fernand Léger, and Joan Miró—is particularly notable. Rivaling the collection is the museum's architecture: a series of austere, copper-roof, redbrick buildings arranged around a courtyard. The museum galleries received an ambitious renovation and expansion in 2019 that added five new galleries and a striking new entrance designed by the husband-and-wife architectural team of Tod Williams and Billie Tsien (known for the Barnes Foundation in Philadelphia and New York's downtown Whitney Museum). ⊠ *Wheelock St., Hanover* ☎ *603/646–2808* 🌐 *hoodmuseum.dartmouth.edu* ⏲ *Closed Sun.–Tues.*

Hopkins Center for the Arts

ARTS CENTER | If the towering arcade at the entrance to the center appears familiar, it's probably because it resembles the project that architect Wallace K. Harrison completed just after designing it: New York City's Metropolitan Opera House at Lincoln Center. The complex includes a 900-seat theater for concerts and film screenings, a 480-seat theater for plays, and a black-box theater for new plays. This is the home of the Dartmouth Symphony Orchestra and several other performance groups. ⊠ *2 E. Wheelock St., Hanover* ☎ *603/646–2422* 🌐 *hop.dartmouth.edu.*

Restaurants

★ Ariana's

$$$ | **MODERN AMERICAN** | With its stone fireplace, cathedral ceiling, and rustic-elegant barnlike interior, this inviting restaurant in the venerable Lyme Inn turns out farm-fresh modern American fare with international influences. Try the blackened scallops with an orange-chili-butter sauce or sliced-duck salad with shaved fennel and a ginger dressing, before moving on to herb-crusted swordfish with a saffron-sherry butter sauce. **Known for:** five-course prix-fixe chef dinners; a well-curated wine list; peaceful setting in a historic hamlet. 💲 *Average main: $29* ⊠ *1 Market St., Lyme* ✥ *10.8 miles north of Hanover via Rte. 10* ☎ *603/353-4405* 🌐 *www.arianasrestaurant.com* ⏲ *Closed Sun.–Tues.*

Base Camp

$$ | **NEPALESE** | This inviting restaurant in the lower level of a downtown retail-dining complex serves authentic, prepared-to-order Nepalese cuisine. Start with an order of momos (steamed dumplings) bursting with buffalo, paneer-and-spinach, wild boar, or several other

A Lovely Drive Through the Upper Valley 

From Hanover, make the beautiful 60-mile drive up Route 10 to Littleton for a stunningly scenic tour of the upper Connecticut River and lower Ammonoosuc river valleys. You'll have views of Vermont's Green Mountains from many points. The road passes through groves of evergreens, over leafy ridges, and through delightful hamlets abundant with fine Georgian- and Federal-style mansions. Grab gourmet picnic provisions at the historic general stores in Lyme or Bath, view several covered bridges on nearby side roads, and, stop by pastoral family farms, like Hatchland Farm's Dairy Delites, for ice cream and Collins Farm for its corn maze. There are numerous spots for a picnic, including little-visited Bedell Bridge State Park in Haverhill, which overlooks the Connecticut River.

fillings, and then try one of the easily shared *tarkari* (tomato-based) curries or chilies, offered with an extensive variety of meats and vegetables, from goat and duck to sweet potato and mushroom. **Known for:** everything can be prepared from mild to very spicy; plenty of meatless options; helpful, friendly staff. *$ Average main: $22 ✉ 3 Lebanon St., Hanover ☎ 603/643–2007 🌐 www.basecampcafenh.com.*

Latham House Tavern

$$ | **AMERICAN** | This convivial, easygoing gastropub in historic Lyme's rambling Dowd's Country Inn—which also has pleasant guest accommodations—features an impressive list of New England craft beers as well as an enticing selection of reasonably priced comfort fare. Favorites include the half-pound house burger topped with bacon and a beer–smoked gouda fondue, and the confit-pork poutine with a chipotle-cider barbecue sauce. **Known for:** elevated pub fare; interesting list of beers on tap; warmly lighted dining room with beam ceiling. *$ Average main: $20 ✉ 9 Main St., Lyme ✢ 10.7 miles north of Hanover via Rte. 10 ☎ 603/795–9995 🌐 www.lathamhousetavern.com ⏲ Closed Tues.*

Murphy's On the Green

$$ | **AMERICAN** | Students, visiting alums, and locals regularly descend on this wildly popular pub, which has walls lined with shelves of old books. The varied menu features burgers and salads as well as meat loaf, lobster mac and cheese, and vegetarian dishes like crispy-tofu pad Thai and house-smoked tofu street tacos. **Known for:** sourcing ingredients from local farms; good people-watching; extensive beer list. *$ Average main: $20 ✉ 5 Main St., Hanover ☎ 603/643–7777 🌐 www.murphysonthegreen.com ⏲ No lunch Mon.–Wed.*

Coffee and Quick Bites

Lou's Restaurant

$ | **AMERICAN** | **FAMILY** | A Hanover tradition since 1947, this diner-cum-café-cum-bakery serves possibly the best breakfast in the valley, with favorites that include blueberry-cranberry buttermilk pancakes, and corned beef brisket hash with free-range poached eggs. Or just grab a seat at the old-fashioned soda fountain for a juicy burger and an ice-cream sundae. **Known for:** colorful mix of locals and Dartmouth folks; fresh-baked pastries and brownies; breakfast served all day. *$ Average main: $15 ✉ 30 S. Main St.,*

The Cornish–Windsor Bridge is the second-longest covered bridge in the United States.

Hanover ☎ *603/643–3321* 🌐 *www.lousrestaurant.com* ⏲ *No dinner.*

Hotels

Hanover Inn

$$$ | **HOTEL** | A sprawling Georgian-style brick structure rising six white-trimmed stories above the gracious Dartmouth Green contains this chichi boutique hotel and is also home to the acclaimed farm-to-table restaurant, Pine. **Pros:** overlooks campus green in center of town; excellent restaurant and bar; well-equipped fitness center. **Cons:** in a busy area; pricey during busy times; books up way in advance many weekends. $ *Rooms from: $265* ✉ *2 E. Wheelock St., Hanover* ☎ *603/643–4300* 🌐 *www.hanoverinn.com* *108 rooms* 🍽 *No Meals.*

★ **Lyme Inn**

$$$ | **B&B/INN** | With an enchanted setting on the elliptical village common in Colonial Lyme, this four-story inn that began life as a stagecoach stop in the early 1800s offers an elegant, tranquil respite from the crowds of Hanover and offers meals in an esteemed restaurant. **Pros:** quiet setting; rates include a tasty but light breakfast; good base for exploring Hanover as well as Norwich and Woodstock, Vermont. **Cons:** can book up well in advance at busy times; a 15-minute drive to Hanover; minimum-night stays during some periods. $ *Rooms from: $239* ✉ *1 Market St., Lyme* ✣ *10.8 miles north of Hanover via Rte. 10* ☎ *603/795-4824* 🌐 *www.thelymeinn.com* *14 rooms* 🍽 *Free Breakfast.*

Six South St Hotel

$$$ | **HOTEL** | With its bold black and red color scheme and angular light fixtures and furnishings, this redbrick boutique hotel just off Hanover's bustling Main Street is a perfect roost for visiting Dartmouth and its museums. **Pros:** hip contemporary design; great little bistro and bar; downtown location steps from campus. **Cons:** expensive parking; breakfast buffet costs extra; busy in-town setting. $ *Rooms from: $239* ✉ *6 South*

St., Hanover ☎ 603/643–0600 🌐 *www.sixsouth.com* 🛏 *63 rooms* 🍴 *No Meals.*

Ledyard Canoe Club

BOATING | On the banks of the Connecticut River, this outfitter rents canoes, kayaks, and standup paddleboards by the hour, as well as rustic cabins. ✉ *9 Boathouse Rd., Hanover* ☎ *603/643–6709* 🌐 *www.ledyardcanoeclub.org.*

Cornish

22 miles south of Hanover.

Today Cornish is best known for its covered bridges and for having been the home of the late reclusive author J. D. Salinger, but at the turn of the 20th century the village was acclaimed as the home of the country's then-most-popular novelist, Winston Churchill (no relation to the British prime minister). His novel *Richard Carvel* sold more than a million copies. Churchill was such a celebrity that he hosted President Theodore Roosevelt in 1902. At that time Cornish was an artistic enclave: painter Maxfield Parrish lived and worked here, and sculptor Augustus Saint-Gaudens set up his studio here, where he created the heroic bronzes for which he is known.

GETTING HERE AND AROUND

About 5 miles west of town off Route 12A, the Cornish–Windsor Bridge crosses the Connecticut River, leading to Interstate 91 in Vermont.

Cornish-Windsor Bridge

BRIDGE | This 460-foot bridge, 1½ miles south of the Saint-Gaudens National Historic Site, connects New Hampshire to Vermont across the Connecticut River. Erected in 1866, it is the longest covered wooden bridge in the United States. The notice on the bridge reads, "Walk your horses or pay two dollar fine." ✉ *Bridge St., Cornish.*

★ Saint-Gaudens National Historic Site

HISTORIC HOME | On a bluff in rural Cornish with views of Vermont's stately Mt. Ascutney, this pastoral property celebrates the life and artistry of Augustus Saint-Gaudens, a leading 19th-century sculptor with renowned works on Boston Common, Manhattan's Central Park, and Chicago's Lincoln Park. In summer you can tour his house (with original furnishings), studio, and galleries, and year-round it's a pleasure to explore the 150 gorgeous acres of lawns, gardens, and woodlands dotted with casts of his works and laced with 2½ miles of hiking trails. Concerts are held Sunday from late June through August. ✉ *139 Saint-Gaudens Rd., Cornish* ☎ *603/675–2175* 🌐 *www.nps.gov/saga* 🎫 *$10* 🕒 *Buildings closed Nov.–late May.*

Common Man Inn

$ | **HOTEL** | New Hampshire's distinctive Common Man hotel and restaurant group runs this quirky boutique hotel fashioned out of a striking 19th-century redbrick mill on downtown Claremont's Sugar River; the on-site restaurant serves hearty pub fare and has great water views. **Pros:** distinctive, historic architecture; deck and hot tub overlooking river; good location for exploring both sides of Connecticut River. **Cons:** 12 miles from Cornish; in a quiet town with few attractions; not many good dining options in area. 💲 *Rooms from: $129* ✉ *21 Water St., Claremont* ☎ *603/542–6171* 🌐 *www.thecmaninnclaremont.com* 🛏 *30 rooms* 🍴 *Free Breakfast.*

Walpole

33 miles south of Cornish.

Walpole possesses one of the state's prettiest town greens. Bordered by Elm and Washington streets, it's surrounded by homes dating to the 1790s, when the townsfolk constructed a canal around the Great Falls of the Connecticut River, bringing commerce and wealth to the area. This upscale little town now has 4,000 inhabitants. Walpole is also home to Florentine Films, documentarian Ken Burns's production company.

■ TIP→ Charlestown, which boasts one of the state's largest historic districts, with about 60 homes—all handsome examples of Federal, Greek Revival, and Gothic Revival architecture (and 10 built before 1800), is just down the road from Walpole.

GETTING HERE AND AROUND

Walpole is a short jaunt up Route 12 from Keene, and is just across the Connecticut River from Bellows Falls, Vermont.

Sights

Fort at No. 4

MILITARY SIGHT | FAMILY | In 1747, this timber fort overlooking the Connecticut River, 15 miles north of Walpole, served as an outpost on the periphery of Colonial civilization. That year fewer than 50 militiamen at the fort withstood an attack by 400 French soldiers, ensuring that northern New England remained under British rule. Today, costumed interpreters at this living-history museum cook dinner over an open hearth and demonstrate weaving, gardening, and candle making. The museum also holds reenactments of militia musters and the battles of the French and Indian War. *267 Springfield Rd. (Rte. 11), Charlestown* *13.3 miles north of Walpole via Hwy 12* *603/826–5700* *www.fortat4.org* *$10* *Closed Mon. and Tues. and Nov.–Apr.*

Restaurants

★ Hungry Diner

$ | MODERN AMERICAN | FAMILY | A departure from the old-school greasy-spoon diners that proliferate in New England, this contemporary space with a white-tile and light-wood interior and a big, inviting outdoor seating area serves delicious, eclectic comfort fare that relies heavily on seasonal, local ingredients, including pasture-raised meats. Think Korean barbecue tacos with house-made kimchi and pickled carrots, or the buttermilk-fried chicken sandwich with a tangy secret sauce and dill pickles. **Known for:** superb craft beer, wine, and cocktail program; mac and cheese with bacon; milk shakes and soft-serve ice cream. *Average main: $17* *9 Edwards La., Walpole* *603/756–3444* *www.hungrydinerwalpole.com* *Closed Tues.*

The Restaurant at Burdick's

$$$ | MODERN AMERICAN | Famous artisanal chocolatier and Walpole resident Larry Burdick, who sells his hand-filled, hand-cut chocolates to top restaurants around the country, founded this acclaimed restaurant next door to his shop in Walpole's charming little downtown. With the easygoing sophistication of a Parisian café and incredibly rich desserts, the restaurant features a French-inspired international menu that utilizes fresh, often local, ingredients and changes daily. **Known for:** noteworthy wine list; adjacent gourmet grocery with delicious picnic supplies; decadent desserts featuring house-made chocolates and pastries. *Average main: $27* *47 Main St., Walpole* *603/756–9058* *www.47mainwalpole.com* *Closed Sun. and Mon.*

Coffee and Quick Bites

★ Walpole Creamery

$ | CAFÉ | FAMILY | Arguably the state's best purveyor of artisanal, small-batch ice cream, this unassuming parlor in Walpole always features a long list of both regular and seasonal flavors, such as Fijan ginger, fresh peach, wild blueberry, and mint dark-chocolate-chip. Thick, rich, and using only all-natural ingredients, this luscious ice cream is also sold in many of the region's restaurants, farmstands, and groceries. **Known for:** using many local, seasonal ingredients; sandwiches and light lunch fare in the parlor; brownie sundaes. *Average main: $5 532 Main St., Walpole 603/445–5700 www.walpolecreamery.com.*

Keene

17 miles southeast of Walpole, 20 miles northeast of Brattleboro, Vermont.

Keene, the largest city in southwestern New Hampshire (population 23,000), has one of the prettiest and widest main streets in the state, with several engaging boutiques and cafés—you can spend a fun few hours strolling along it. Home to Keene State College, the city feels both youthful and lively, with its funky crafts stores and eclectic entertainment, like the Monadnock International Film Festival, held in late September.

GETTING HERE AND AROUND

Routes 9 and 101 pass through Keene, connecting it with Brattleboro, Vermont and Peterborough.

ESSENTIALS

VISITOR INFORMATION Greater Keene and Peterborough Chamber of Commerce. *Keene 603/352–1303 www.keene-chamber.com.*

Sights

Madame Sherri Forest

NATURE SIGHT | FAMILY | The focal point of this rugged 513-acre tract of deciduous forest in West Chesterfield are the stone chimney, grand staircase, and foundation of a chateau-style summer house owned by Parisian-born socialite and theatrical costume designer Madame Antoinette Sherri (the house burned down in 1963, and she died shortly after). A short woodland path from the parking area accesses the ruins, which are still fascinating despite a partial collapse of the staircase following heavy rains in 2021. Two fairly easy but hilly trails offer longer hikes through the surrounding forest, including the 3-mile round-trip trek up Wantastiquet Mountain, which offers clear views up and down the Connecticut River and across to Vermont. Trails also lead into the adjacent Wantastiquet State Forest, and there's more great hiking nearby in Pisgah State Park. *Gulf and Egypt Rds., West Chesterfield 23.1 miles south of Walpole via I-91 N 603/224–9945 www.forestsociety.org.*

Stonewall Farm

FARM/RANCH | FAMILY | At this picturesque nonprofit early-1800s farm and educational center, you can stop by to pick up produce and goods raised on-site (including delicious Frisky Cow Gelato) and procured from other artisanal producers in the area. Leave time to explore the grounds, dairy and small-animal barns, gardens, and chicken coops—a wide range of education tours are offered, plus seasonal hay and sleigh rides. There's also a maple sugaring house and small farm tool museum, and the property is traversed by hiking trails and accesses the 20-mile Cheshire Rail Trail, which stretches from Walpole through Keene and down to the Massachusetts border. *242 Chesterfield Rd., Keene 603/357–7278 www.stonewallfarm.org.*

Restaurants

★ Luca's Mediterranean Café

$$ | MEDITERRANEAN | A deceptively simple storefront bistro with sidewalk tables overlooking Keene's graceful town square, Luca's dazzles with epicurean creations influenced by Italy, France, Greece, Spain, and North Africa. There's always an extensive selection of small plates, such as almond-crusted fried mozzarella and roasted Brussels sprouts with bacon and pomegranate-infused honey, plus handmade pastas and complexly flavored grills and stews. **Known for:** fresh, creative pastas; affable but knowledgeable service; great wine list. *Average main: $22 ✉ 10 Central Sq., Keene ☎ 603/358–3335 🌐 www.lucascafe.com ⏲ Closed Sun.*

Machina Kitchen & Art Bar
$$ | **ECLECTIC** | This farm-to-table restaurant in downtown Keene is a vital force in the community, offering not only stellar, sustainably sourced food and craft cocktails but also an art gallery with rotating exhibits and occasional live music performances. The menu changes often but always features a mix of classics and unexpected adventures like the salt cod croquettes with preserved-lemon remoulade, fried frog legs with mango-habanero salsa, or Korean-spiced-brisket bulgogi bowls with fresh pears and sesame. **Known for:** interesting cocktails and mocktails; friendly, creative-spirited crowd; occasional prix-fixe dinners with cocktail pairings. *Average main: $20 ✉ 9 Court St., Keene ☎ 603/903–0011 🌐 www.machinaarts.org ⏲ Closed Sun. No lunch weekdays.*

Hotels

★ Chesterfield Inn
$$ | **B&B/INN** | Fine antiques and Colonial-style fabrics adorn the spacious guest quarters in this opulent yet unpretentious country inn nestled on a 10-acre farmstead a couple of miles from the Connecticut River. **Pros:** beautifully tended gardens; kids and pets are welcome; excellent full breakfast included. **Cons:** restaurant closed on Sunday; two-night minimum at busy times; 20-minute drive from Keene. *Rooms from: $194 ✉ 20 Cross Rd., off Rte. 9, West Chesterfield ✣ 14 miles west of Keene via Rte. 9 ☎ 603/256–3211 🌐 www.chesterfieldinn.com ➡ 15 rooms 🍽 Free Breakfast.*

Fairfield Inn and Suites Keene Downtown
$$ | **HOTEL** | It's unusual to find a midrange chain property set in a historic building on a picturesque downtown Main Street, but this well-kept hotel—inside the restored early 1900s Goodnow department store—is a rarity with its reasonably priced rooms, exposed-brick walls, 12-foot ceilings, and modern furnishings. **Pros:** the bilevel loft suites have two bathrooms; good fitness room; steps from great dining and shopping. **Cons:** bustling downtown center can be a little noisy; complimentary breakfast is pretty basic; historic building with quirky layout. *Rooms from: $175 ✉ 30 Main St., Keene ☎ 603/357–7070 🌐 www.fairfieldinnkeene.com ➡ 40 rooms 🍽 Free Breakfast.*

The Inn at East Hill Farm
$$$ | **RESORT** | **FAMILY** | For those with kids who like animals, East Hill Farm is heaven: a family resort with daylong children's programs on a 160-acre farm overlooking Mt. Monadnock that include milking cows; collecting eggs; feeding the sheep, donkeys, cows, rabbits, horses, chickens, goats, and ducks; horseback and pony rides; hiking and hay rides in summer; and sledding and sleigh rides in winter. **Pros:** family-friendly; farm fun and activities galore; beautiful setting. **Cons:** very remote location; noisy dining room; not an ideal choice for adults seeking a romantic retreat. *Rooms from: $334 ✉ 460 Monadnock St., Troy ✣ 11 miles southeast of Keene ☎ 603/242–6495, 800/242–6495 🌐 www.east-hill-farm.com ➡ 65 rooms 🍽 All-Inclusive.*

Riverside Hotel
$$ | **HOTEL** | With a boat dock and dazzling views of the Connecticut River, this simple but nicely kept three-story hotel is perfect for price-conscious travelers exploring the southwestern Monadnocks as well as nearby Brattleboro, Vermont. **Pros:** stunning river views; just a hop across river from Brattleboro; reasonable rates. **Cons:** decor is pleasant but

not especially distinctive; noise travels between rooms; pretty basic breakfast. *Rooms from: $170 20 Riverside Dr., West Chesterfield 603/256–4200 www.riversidehotelnh.com 34 rooms Free Breakfast.*

Nightlife

Branch and Blade Brewing

BEER GARDENS | Don't be put off by the location inside a small industrial park—this convivial taproom offers seating at picnic tables with wooden-keg tables, a big outdoor seating area where you can nosh on tasty pub fare, and, most importantly, great beer, including a tart Gose and potent triple IPA. *17 Bradco St., Keene 603/354–3478 www.babbrewing.com.*

Performing Arts

Colonial Theatre

CONCERTS | This beautifully renovated 1924 vaudeville theater presents comedy, music, and dance performances as well as occasional indie film screenings. *95 Main St., Keene 603/352–2033 www.thecolonial.org.*

Shopping

Hannah Grimes Marketplace

CRAFTS | The pottery, kitchenware, soaps, greeting cards, toys, and specialty foods of more than 250 artisans are on display in this colorful downtown gallery. *42 Main St., Keene 603/352–6862 www.hannahgrimesmarketplace.com.*

Peterborough

20 miles east of Keene.

Thornton Wilder's play *Our Town* was based on Peterborough, which was the first in the region to be incorporated (1760) and remains a commercial and cultural hub, drawing big crowds for its theater and concerts in summer. Downtown's charming Depot Square district abounds with distinctive boutiques, galleries, and restaurants. At Putnam Park on Grove Street, stand on the bridge and watch the roiling waters of the Nubanusit River.

GETTING HERE AND AROUND

Walkable downtown Peterborough is easily reached via Route 101 and U.S. 202.

ESSENTIALS

VISITOR INFORMATION Monadnock Travel Council. *Peterborough www.monadnocktravel.com.*

Sights

Cathedral of the Pines

NATURE SIGHT | This 236-acre outdoor memorial pays tribute to Americans who have sacrificed their lives in service to their country. There's an inspiring view of Mt. Monadnock and Mt. Kearsarge from the Altar of the Nation, which is composed of rock from every U.S. state and territory. All faiths are welcome, and you can hear organ music some afternoons. The Memorial Bell Tower, built in 1967 with a carillon of bells from around the world, is built of native stone. Norman Rockwell designed the bronze tablets over the four arches. Flower gardens, an indoor chapel, and a museum of military memorabilia share the hilltop, and several trails lace the property, leading to tranquil peaceful areas. *10 Hale Hill Rd., Rindge 603/899–3300 www.cathedralofthepines.org.*

Mariposa Museum

ART MUSEUM | **FAMILY** | You can play instruments or try on costumes from around the world and indulge your cultural curiosity at this nonprofit museum dedicated to hands-on exploration of international folk art. The three-floor museum is housed inside a historic Baptist church, across from the Universalist church in the heart of town. The museum hosts workshops and presentations on dance and arts and crafts. *26 Main St., Peterborough*

Charming Peterborough was the inspiration for the fictional Grover's Corners in Thornton Wilder's play, Our Town.

603/924–4555 www.mariposamuseum.org $8 Closed Mon. and Tues.

Monadnock State Park

STATE/PROVINCIAL PARK | Said to be America's most-climbed mountain—more than 400 people sometimes crowd its bald peak—Monadnock rises to 3,165 feet, and on clear days you can see the Boston skyline. When the parking lots are full, rangers close the park, so it's prudent to make a reservation online or get a very early morning start, especially during fall foliage. Five trailheads branch out into more than two dozen trails of varying difficulty (though all rigorous) that wend their way to the top. Allow three–five hours for any round-trip hike. The visitor center has free maps as well as exhibits documenting the mountain's history. In winter, you can cross-country ski along roughly 12 miles of groomed trails on the lower elevations. Pets are not permitted in the park. *116 Poole Rd., off Rte. 124 7½ miles west of Peterborough 603/532–8862 www.nhstateparks.org $15 parking.*

Restaurants

Coopershill Public House

$$ | **IRISH** | Choose a sidewalk table overlooking bustling Depot Square or a table inside the conversation-filled dining room at this lively gastropub adjacent to Peterborough's popular independent cinema and steps from Mariposa Museum. The specialty here is rare whiskies, and there's also a nice selection of wines, craft beers, and other drinks, but don't overlook the consistently excellent Irish-influenced pub fare, including Guinness stew, mushroom-and-kale flatbread, bangers and mash, and terrific burgers. **Known for:** superb whiskey selection; ingredients sourced from New England farms; pecan bread pudding. *Average main: $18 6 School St., Peterborough 603/371–9036 www.coopershillpublichouse.com.*

Pearl Restaurant & Oyster Bar

$$ | **ASIAN FUSION** | Despite its prosaic setting in a shopping center a little south of Peterborough's historic downtown, this sleek, contemporary Asian bistro and oyster bar is quite welcoming once inside. Several types of fresh oysters are always available, along with such diverse offerings as ahi tuna poke, Hanoi-style pork spring rolls, Korean barbecue pork, and coconut-veggie rice bowls. **Known for:** creative fusion fare; superb wine list; oysters on the half shell. *Average main: $22 ✉ 1 Jaffrey Rd., Peterborough ☎ 603/924–5225 ⊕ www.pearl-peterborough.com ⊙ Closed Sun. No lunch.*

Hotels

Benjamin Prescott Inn

$ | **B&B/INN** | Thanks to the dairy farm surrounding this 1853 Colonial house—with its stenciling and wide pine floors—you'll feel as though you're miles out in the country rather than just 10 minutes from Peterborough and even closer to the cute downtown of Jaffrey. **Pros:** reasonably priced; relaxing, scenic grounds; delicious breakfast included. **Cons:** minimum-night stays at busy times; not within walking distance of town; not suitable for young children. *Rooms from: $135 ✉ 433 Turnpike Rd., Jaffrey Center ✣ 8 miles southeast of Peterborough ☎ 603/532–6637 ⊕ www.benjaminprescottinn.com 10 rooms Free Breakfast.*

Birchwood Inn

$ | **B&B/INN** | Overlooking the village green of tiny, quiet Temple, this affordable and friendly B&B built in 1775 once hosted Henry David Thoreau. **Pros:** friendly, old-fashioned tavern; quite affordable; good base for exploring Peterborough and Milford areas. **Cons:** secluded small town; quirky place with just three rooms; not suited for kids. *Rooms from: $139 ✉ 340 Rte. 45, Temple ✣ 7.3 miles east of Peterborough via Rte. 101 ☎ 603/878–3285 ⊕ www.thebirchwoodinn.com 3 rooms Free Breakfast.*

Jack Daniels Inn

$ | **MOTEL** | **FAMILY** | This clean, bright, and handsomely decorated 17-room motor inn just a half-mile north of downtown Peterborough is a terrific find with large, affordable rooms furnished with attractive reproduction antiques. **Pros:** great value; one of the only lodgings in Peterborough; continental breakfast included. **Cons:** unfancy motel-style rooms; some street noise; a 10-minute walk from downtown. *Rooms from: $134 ✉ 80 Concord St. (U.S. 202), Peterborough ☎ 603/924–7548 ⊕ www.jackdanielsinn.com 17 rooms Free Breakfast.*

Nightlife

Post & Beam Brewing

BREWPUBS | Serving boldly flavored saisons, grisettes, and other fine, mostly old-world-style ales and lagers as well as soft pretzels with hummus, chili, and other tasty edibles, this terrific brewery in downtown Peterborough has a beautiful setting inside the stately 1837 G.A.R. (Grand Army of the Republic) meeting hall. *✉ 40 Grove St., Peterborough ☎ 603/784–5361 ⊕ www.postandbeambrewery.com.*

Performing Arts

Monadnock Music

CONCERTS | From early summer through late autumn, Monadnock Music sponsors a series of solo recitals, chamber music concerts, and orchestra and opera performances by renowned musicians. Events take place throughout the area, and some of the offerings are free. *✉ Peterborough ☎ 603/852–4345 ⊕ www.monadnockmusic.org.*

Peterborough Folk Music Society

CONCERTS | The Music Society presents folk concerts by artists such as John Gorka, Red Molly, and Cheryl Wheeler at the Peterborough Players Theatre and Bass Hall at Monadnock Center.

⊠ *Peterborough* ☎ *603/827–2905* 🌐 *www.pfmsconcerts.org.*

★ **Peterborough Players**

THEATER | FAMILY | This first-rate summer (mid-June–mid-September) theater troupe has been performing since 1933, these days presenting seven main-stage productions in a converted 18th-century barn throughout the summer. The Players also present children's shows in July and August. ⊠ *55 Hadley Rd., Peterborough* ☎ *603/924–7585* 🌐 *www.peterborough-players.org* ⏲ *Closed mid-Sept.–late June.*

★ **Harrisville Designs**

FABRICS | Hand-spun and hand-dyed yarn, as well as looms, felt, knitting yarn, and instruction books, are sold at this famous shop that occupies a striking redbrick, water-powered mill in the heart of a Monadnock village that's been famous for textiles since 1794. The shop also conducts classes in knitting, spinning, and weaving.

■ **TIP→ Across the street, the inviting Harrisville General Store—open since 1838—serves tasty salads and sandwiches using locally sourced ingredients.** ⊠ *4 Mills Alley, Harrisville* ↕ *10 miles northwest of Peterborough* ☎ *800/338–9415* 🌐 *www.harrisville.com.*

Milford

18 miles east of Peterborough.

A once thriving mill town in the Souhegan River Valley, between the eastern peaks of the Monadnocks and the state's busy Nashua–Manchester corridor, Milford has a lively downtown centered around a leafy oval green and a growing crop of notable restaurants and bars. The town is a good base for exploring several interesting area attractions, from the neatly preserved Colonial historic district of neighboring Amherst to the twisting back country roads that lead to offbeat shops, eateries, and scenic hikes in Brookline, Mason, and Wilton. Although Milford lacks hotels, nearby Nashua has about a dozen chain properties in every price range.

GETTING HERE AND AROUND

Routes 101 and 114 cross in Milford, providing easy access to Manchester to the northeast and Peterborough to the west.

Andres Institute of Art

ART MUSEUM | More than 80 contemporary sculptures, reached by 11 hiking trails, dot this 140-acre former ski hill. Established in 1996 by local engineer Paul Andres and sculptor John Weidman, it's the largest outdoor sculpture park in New England. Exploring this tranquil site, you'll discover these abstract works set amid leafy woodlands and occasional garden clearings. Some trails are open to mountain bikers in summer and snowmobilers in winter. ⊠ *98 Rte. 13, Brookline* ↕ *8 miles south of Milford* ☎ *603/673–8441* 🌐 *www.andresinstitute.org.*

LaBelle Winery

WINERY | Set on a leafy hilltop midway between Milford and Manchester, this contemporary winery with high ceilings and tall windows contains a tasting room, a bistro serving excellent lunch and dinner fare, an art gallery with rotating exhibits, and a spacious dog-friendly terrace. ⊠ *345 Rte. 101, Milford* ☎ *603/672–9898* 🌐 *www.labellewinery.com.*

★ **Pickity Place**

HISTORIC HOME | The winding 10-mile drive through Russell-Abbott State Forest is part of the fun of visiting this enchanted—and secluded—1786 red clapboard cottage on which artist Elizabeth Orton Jones based her illustrations in *Little Red Riding Hood* in the 1940s. Surrounded by fragrant, organic herb and flower gardens (you can buy seeds and plants in the nursery in back), the house today contains a sweet gift shop that sells dried herbal blends and other gourmet products, a small museum with Little Red Riding Hood memorabilia, and a wonderful little restaurant that serves five-course lunches featuring herbs and produce grown on-site. ✉ *248 Nutting Hill Rd., Mason* ✣ *9.4 miles southwest of Milford via Mason Rd.* ☎ *603/878–1151* 🌐 *www.pickityplace.com.*

Restaurants

★ Greenleaf

$$$ | MODERN AMERICAN | Set in an arresting redbrick Victorian bank building with soaring windows and a private dining room inside an old vault, Greenleaf is worth the trip for absolutely sublime modern American fare. Consider cast-iron New York strip steak with sweet potato and black garlic, or poached lobster tossed with angel hair pasta with tomatoes and mustard greens. James Beard–nominated chef Chris Viaud also runs the acclaimed Haitian Creole restaurant, Ansanm, around the corner. **Known for:** superb cocktail program; food sourced from local purveyors; inventive, delicious desserts. $ *Average main: $33* ✉ *54 Nashua St., Milford* ☎ 🌐 *www.greenleafmilford.com* ⏲ *Closed Sun. and Mon. No lunch.*

Parker's Maple Barn

$ | AMERICAN | FAMILY | At this rustic establishment begun in the late 1960s on a country lane in Mason, the word "maple" appears no fewer than 15 times on the menu, accenting everything from the maple-infused coffee to maple-glazed ribs to maple milk shakes. Naturally, pancakes—available with wild blueberries, chocolate chips, or pumpkin seasoning—are the big draw, but don't overlook the savory fare, including corned-beef-hash omelets and waffle breakfast sandwiches. **Known for:** Belgian waffles with maple ice cream; maple chicken sausage; maple milk shakes and root beer floats. $ *Average main: $11* ✉ *1316 Brookline Rd., Mason* ✣ *10.3 miles southwest of Milford via Rte. 13* ☎ *603/878–2308* 🌐 *www.parkersmaplebarn.com* ⏲ *Closed Tues. and Wed. No dinner.*

Shopping

★ Frye's Measure Mill

CRAFTS | Since 1858, this picturesque sawmill on a tranquil a pond has been a destination in rural Wilton. Since the 1960s, it's produced and sold classic Shaker-style maple-wood boxes, but the shop here also sells all sorts of beautiful folk art pieces, from hand-blown glass to finely forged ironware. Tours of the mill and its old print shop are also available. ✉ *12 Frye Mill Rd., Wilton* ✣ *7.6 miles west of Milford via Rte. 101A/Elm St.* ☎ *603/654–6581* 🌐 *www.fryesmill.com.*

Manchester

17 miles northeast of Milford, 45 miles west of Portsmouth, 53 miles north of Boston.

With 117,000 residents, New Hampshire's largest city grew up around the Amoskeag Falls on the Merrimack River, which drove small textile mills through the 1700s. By 1828 Boston investors had bought the rights to the Merrimack's water power and built the Amoskeag Mills, which became a testament to New England's manufacturing capabilities. In 1906 the mills employed 17,000 people and churned out more than 4 million yards of cloth weekly. When this vast enterprise closed in 1936, the town was devastated. Today Manchester is the state's most prominent business center, but many of the old mill buildings have been converted into condos, restaurants, museums, and office space, and the downtown dining, nightlife, and arts scenes have flourished in recent years.

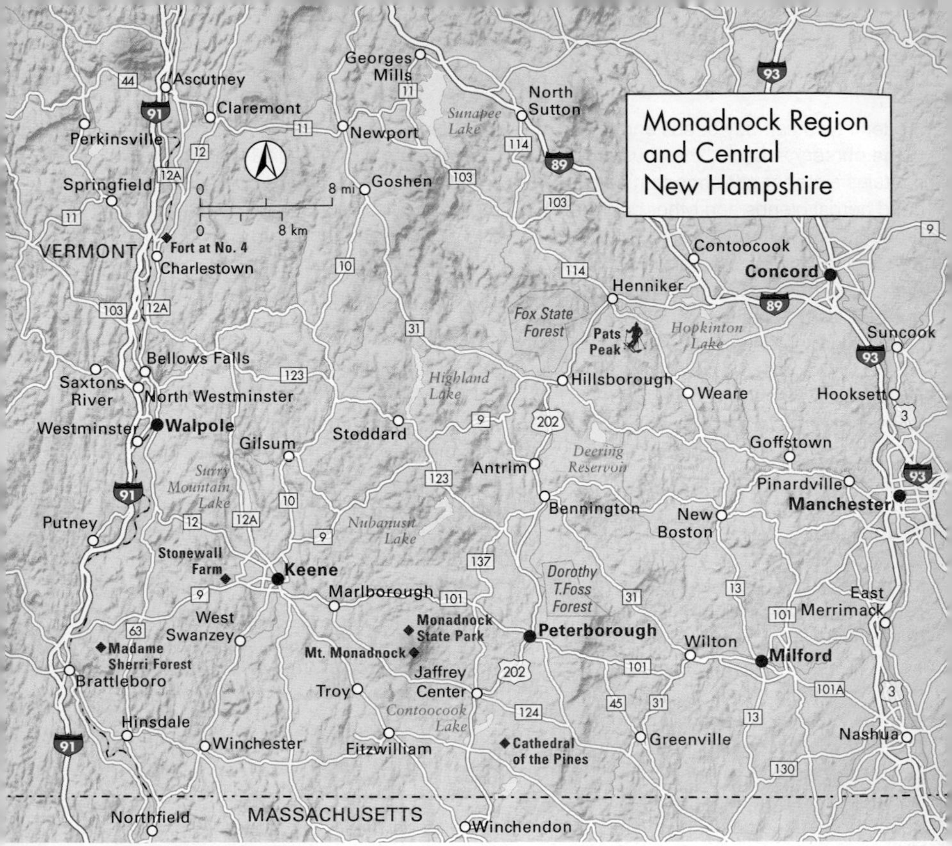

Monadnock Region and Central New Hampshire

GETTING HERE AND AROUND

The state's largest airport, Manchester-Boston Regional Airport, is a modern, cost-effective, and hassle-free alternative to Boston's Logan Airport, with nonstop service from about a dozen cities. Public transit is limited here—a car is the best way for visitors to get around.

ESSENTIALS

AIRPORT Manchester-Boston Regional Airport. ✉ *1 Airport Rd., Manchester* ☎ *603/624–6539* 🌐 *www.flymanchester.com.*

VISITOR INFORMATION Greater Manchester Chamber of Commerce. ✉ *Manchester* ☎ *603/792–4100* 🌐 *www.manchester-chamber.org.*

Sights

★ Currier Museum of Art

ART MUSEUM | The Currier maintains an astounding permanent collection of works by European and American masters, among them Claude Monet, Edward Hopper, Winslow Homer, John Marin, Andrew Wyeth, and Childe Hassam, and it presents changing exhibits of contemporary art. The museum also arranges guided tours of the nearby Zimmerman House. Completed in 1950, it's New England's only Frank Lloyd Wright–designed residence open to the public. Wright called this sparse, utterly functional living space "Usonian," a term he used to describe several dozen similar homes based on his vision of distinctly American architecture. ✉ *150 Ash St., Manchester* ☎ *603/669–6144* 🌐 *www.currier.org* 🎟 *$15; $35 for Zimmerman House.*

Millyard Museum

OTHER ATTRACTION | FAMILY | In one of the most architecturally striking Amoskeag Mills buildings, state-of-the-art exhibits depict the region's history from when Native Americans lived here and fished the Merrimack River to when the machines of Amoskeag Mills wove cloth. The museum also offers lectures and walking tours, and has a child-oriented Discovery Gallery. There's a very good book and gift shop, too. *200 Bedford St., Manchester* *603/622–7531* *www.manchesterhistoric.org* *$10* *Closed Sun. and Mon.*

SEE Science Center

SCIENCE MUSEUM | FAMILY | The world's largest permanent LEGO installation at minifigure scale, depicting Amoskeag Millyard and Manchester as they looked a century ago, is the star attraction at this hands-on science lab and children's museum. The mind-blowing exhibit, covering 2,000 square feet, is made up of about 3 million LEGO bricks. It conveys the massive size and importance of the mills, which ran a mile on each side of the Merrimack. The museum also contains touch-friendly interactive exhibits and offers daily science demonstrations. *Amoskeag Millyard, 200 Bedford St., Manchester* *603/669–0400* *www.see-sciencecenter.org* *$10.*

Restaurants

Cotton

$$ | MODERN AMERICAN | Mod lighting and furnishings lend this restaurant inside an old Amoskeag Mills building a swanky atmosphere, although on warm days you may want to have a seat on the patio, set in an arbor. The farm-to-table-inspired comfort food changes regularly but has featured pan-seared crab cakes, grilled Atlantic salmon with sweet corn and gnocchi, and Delmonico steak with a choice of sauces. **Known for:** well-prepared comfort food; creative mixed drinks; handsome converted-warehouse setting. *Average main: $23* *75 Arms St., Manchester* *603/622–5488* *www.cottonfood.com* *Closed Sun. and Mon. No lunch.*

Red Arrow Diner

$ | AMERICAN | One of New England's most celebrated diners, this bustling downtown greasy spoon has been catering to students, artists, and most famously U.S. Presidential candidates since 1922. This colorful restaurant, open around the clock, is a friendly place with fresh daily specials as well as such classics as kielbasa-and-cheese omelets and triple-bun Dinahmoe burgers. **Known for:** filling breakfasts; colorful people-watching; house-brewed root beer and cream soda. *Average main: $11* *61 Lowell St., Manchester* *603/626–1118* *www.redarrowdiner.com.*

Coffee and Quick Bites

Restoration Cafe

$ | CAFÉ | Set on the ground floor of a vintage redbrick apartment building on the east side of downtown, this hip café and gathering spot excels both with drinks—everything from nitro cold brews to creative smoothies—and healthy, well-crafted food. At breakfast, consider the egg-cheddar-chive brioche sandwich, while tandoori bowls and rare-seared tuna sandwiches, along with craft cocktails and beers, are popular in the afternoon and for brunch. **Known for:** healthy smoothies; sleek industrial vibe; cheerful outdoor patio. *Average main: $10* *235 Hanover St., Manchester* *603/518–7260* *www.restorationcafenh.com* *Closed Mon. No dinner.*

Hotels

★ Ash Street Inn

$$ | B&B/INN | Each of the five rooms in this striking sage-green 1885 B&B near the Currier Museum of Art and a few blocks from Elm Street dining is painted a different color, and all have soft bathrobes, flat-screen satellite TVs, and beds topped with Egyptian cotton linens. **Pros:** stylishly decorated rooms; excellent full breakfast included; free off-street parking. **Cons:** pricey for Manchester; not a great choice for children; urban setting isn't for those seeking quiet. *Rooms from: $219* ✉ *118 Ash St., Manchester* ☎ *603/668–9908* 🌐 *www.ashstreetinn.com* *5 rooms* *Free Breakfast.*

★ Bedford Village Inn
$$$ | RESORT | A few miles southwest of Manchester, this upscale complex consisting of an 1810 Federal inn and a bigger, contemporary boutique hotel is all about luxury and pampering, with Italian marble bathrooms, whirlpool tubs, sumptuous linens, four-poster beds, and Molton Brown bath products in the rooms. **Pros:** ultraposh accommodations and amenities; gorgeous gardens and grounds; outstanding food and beverage. **Cons:** in a suburb outside Manchester; breakfast not included in rates; often booked with weddings on weekends. *Rooms from: $278* ✉ *2 Olde Bedford Way, Bedford* ☎ *603/472–2001, 800/852–1166* 🌐 *www.bedfordvillageinn.com* *64 rooms* *No Meals.*

Crown Tavern
BARS | Set in a stunningly restored downtown theater with a huge adjacent outdoor patio, the Crown is a splendid venue for dining, but it's the natty bar—with noteworthy craft-cocktail list, exposed-brick walls, and tile floor—that's especially alluring. If you are hungry, try the thick-cut truffle fries or Nashville hot chicken sandwich. ✉ *99 Hanover St., Manchester* ☎ *603/218–3132* 🌐 *www.thecrownonhanover.com.*

815
BARS | A scene-y crowd mixes and mingles at this dimly lighted Prohibition Era–inspired, speakeasy-style cocktail bar with plush arm chairs and sofas and Oriental rugs, and an impressive list of both innovative and classic cocktails, plus unusual local and international beers. ✉ *825 Elm St., Manchester* ☎ *603/782–8086* 🌐 *www.815nh.com.*

The Palace Theatre
CONCERTS | This 1914 former vaudeville house presents musicals and plays, comedy, and concerts throughout the year. ✉ *80 Hanover St., Manchester* ☎ *603/668–5588* 🌐 *www.palacetheatre.org.*

★ Dancing Lion Chocolate
CHOCOLATE | This acclaimed confectioner produces edible works of art in the form of strikingly designed chocolate bars like the WhiteSand with juniper, cardamom, and white chocolate, and the earthy Silk Flowers bar colored and flavored with peppercorns, chrysanthemums, and marigolds. Other specialties include bonbons and Mayan drinking chocolate, which you can sip in the adjacent café. ✉ *917 Elm St., Manchester* ☎ *603/625–4043* 🌐 *www.dancinglion.us.*

Concord

20 miles north of Manchester, 47 miles west of Portsmouth.

New Hampshire's capital (population 42,000) is a small and somewhat quiet city that tends to state business and little else. With that said, downtown has seen a steady influx of new restaurants and bars. Stop in town to get a glimpse of New Hampshire's State House, which is crowned by a gleaming, eagle-topped gold dome.

GETTING HERE AND AROUND

Interstate 93 bisects Concord north–south and is intersected by Interstate 89 and U.S. 202, which becomes Interstate 393 near the city line. Main Street near the State House is walkable, but a car is the best way to explore farther afield.

ESSENTIALS

VISITOR INFORMATION Greater Concord Chamber of Commerce. ✉ *Concord* ☎ *603/224–2508* 🌐 *www.concordnhchamber.com.*

Sights

McAuliffe-Shepard Discovery Center
SCIENCE MUSEUM | FAMILY | New England's only air-and-space center offers a full day of activities focused mostly on the heavens. See yourself in infrared light, learn about lunar spacecraft, examine a replica of the Mercury-Redstone rocket, or experience what it's like to travel in space—you can even try your hand at being a television weather announcer. There's also a café. ✉ *2 Institute Dr., Concord* ☎ *603/271–7827* 🌐 *www.starhop.com* 🎫 *$12* ⏲ *Closed Mon.–Thurs. in Sept.–May.*

New Hampshire Historical Society
HISTORY MUSEUM | Steps from the state capitol, this museum is a great place to learn about the Concord coach, a popular mode of transportation before railroads. The Discovering New Hampshire exhibit delves into a number of facets of the state's heritage, from politics to commerce. Rotating shows might include locally made quilts or historical portraits of residents. ✉ *30 Park St., Concord* ☎ *603/228–6688* 🌐 *www.nhhistory.org* 🎫 *$7* ⏲ *Closed Sun.–Wed.*

★ State House
GOVERNMENT BUILDING | The gilded-dome state house, built in 1819, is the nation's oldest capitol building in which the legislature still uses the original chambers. From January through June, you can watch the two branches in action. The Senate has 24 members, and the House house has 400—a ratio of 1 representative per 3,500 residents (a world record). The visitor center coordinates guided and self-guided tours, bookable online or on-site, and displays history exhibits and paraphernalia from presidential primaries. ✉ *Visitor center, 107 N. Main St., Concord* ☎ *603/271–2154* 🌐 *www.gencourt.state.nh.us* 🎫 *Free* ⏲ *No tours on weekends.*

Restaurants

Barley House
$$ | **AMERICAN** | A lively, old-fashioned tavern with Irish overtones, the Barley House is steps from the state capitol and typically buzzes with a mix of politicos, businesspeople, and tourists. The melting pot of a menu includes chorizo-topped pizzas, burgers smothered with a peppercorn-whiskey sauce, chicken potpies, beer-braised bratwurst, and Mediterranean chicken salad—all reliably prepared. **Known for:** live Irish music some nights; great beer selection; hefty, delicious burgers. 💲 *Average main: $20* ✉ *132 N. Main St., Concord* ☎ *603/228–6363* 🌐 *www.thebarleyhouse.com* ⏲ *Closed Wed.*

★ Revival
$$$ | **MODERN AMERICAN** | In this handsome, high-ceilinged redbrick building on a downtown side street, foodies and revelers congregate for some of the most creative and accomplished regional American cuisine in the Merrimack Valley. Highlights, in addition to an impressive selection of whiskies and cognacs, might include an artful platter of charcuterie and New England artisanal cheeses, hearty beef and veal Bolognese with mushroom tagliatelle, and seared salmon with pancetta and olive tapenade, but the menu changes regularly. **Known for:**

ingredients sourced from local farms; see-and-be-seen vibe; decadent desserts. *Average main: $26 11 Depot St., Concord 603/715–5723 www.revivalkitchennh.com Closed Sun. and Mon. No lunch.*

Hotels

The Centennial

$$ | **HOTEL** | Concord's most distinctive and romantic hotel occupies an imposing brick-and-stone building constructed in 1892 for widows of Civil War veterans, but the interior has been given a head-to-toe makeover: boutique furnishings and contemporary art immediately set the tone in the lobby; pillow-top beds sport luxurious linens and down pillows; and bathrooms have stone floors, granite countertops, and stand-alone showers. **Pros:** elegant redesign of historic structure; attractive residential setting; great bar and restaurant. **Cons:** not within walking distance of downtown dining; rooms facing road can get a little road noise; breakfast costs extra. *Rooms from: $179 96 Pleasant St., Concord 603/227–9000 www.thecentennialhotel.com 32 rooms No Meals.*

★ Hotel Concord

$$$ | **HOTEL** | This sleek, stunning contemporary boutique hotel lies within a short stroll of the city's top arts venues and eateries; the airy and light-filled rooms, many with balconies, have hardwood floors, distinctive artwork, big windows, and are outfitted with Amazon Echo devices, huge HD TVs, and spacious marble baths. **Pros:** inexpensive parking; hip, cosmopolitan design; lots to see and do within walking distance. **Cons:** on a busy street; some may find the in-room high-tech gadgets a little challenging; books up when statehouse is in session. *Rooms from: $239 11 S. Main St., Concord 603/504–3500 www.hotelconcordnh.com 38 rooms Free Breakfast.*

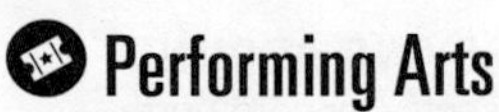

Performing Arts

★ Capitol Center for the Arts

ARTS CENTERS | The Egyptian-motif artwork, part of the original 1927 decor, has been restored in this historic 1,304-seat venue that now hosts touring Broadway shows, dance companies, and musical acts. A few blocks away (at 16 S. Main Street), the organization also operates **Bank of NH Stage**, a restored historic movie house that presents music, comedy, and other notable shows. *44 S. Main St., Concord 603/225–1111 www.ccanh.com.*

Chapter 11

INLAND MAINE

Updated by
Mary Ruoff

Sights ★★★★☆ | Restaurants ★★★☆☆ | Hotels ★★★☆☆ | Shopping ★★☆☆☆ | Nightlife ★★☆☆☆

WELCOME TO INLAND MAINE

TOP REASONS TO GO

★ **Baxter State Park:** Mt. Katahdin, the state's highest peak, stands sentry over Baxter's forestland in its "natural wild state."

★ **Moosehead Lake:** Surrounded by mountains, Maine's largest lake—dotted with islands and chiseled with inlets and coves—retains the rugged beauty that so captivated author Henry David Thoreau in the mid-1800s.

★ **Water Sports:** It's easy to get out on the water on scheduled cruises on large inland lakes; guided or self-guided boating, canoeing, and kayaking trips; and white-water rafting excursions on several rivers.

★ **Winter Pastimes:** Downhill skiing, snowmobiling, snowshoeing, cross-country skiing, fat-tire biking, and ice fishing are all popular winter sports. You can even go dogsledding!

★ **Foliage Drives:** Maine's best fall foliage is inland, where hardwoods outnumber spruce, fir, and pine trees in many areas.

Though Maine is well known for its miles of craggy coastline, the inland part of the state is surprisingly vast and far less populated. Not one hour's drive from the bays and ocean, huge swaths of forestland are punctuated by lakes (sometimes called ponds, despite their size). Summer camps, ski areas, and small villages populate the mountainous western part of the state, which stretches north along the New Hampshire border to Québec. In the remote North Woods, wilderness areas beckon outdoors lovers. You can take a drive (go slow!) down a "moose alley" in both regions.

1 Sebago Lake Area. Less than 20 miles northwest of Portland, the Sebago Lake area bustles with activity in summer.

2 Bridgton. Bridgton is a classic New England town with many nearby lakes to explore.

3 Bethel. In the valley of the Androscoggin River, Bethel is home to Sunday River, one of Maine's major ski resorts.

4 Rangeley. Rangeley, along its namesake lake, anchors a lake-dotted region with long stretches of pine, beech, spruce, and sky.

5 Kingfield. Just north of Kingfield is Sugarloaf ski resort, Maine's other big ski resort, which has plenty to offer year-round.

6 Greenville. The woodsy town, on Moosehead Lake, Maine's largest, is a great base for day trips.

7 Millinocket. The gateway to the premier wilderness destinations of Baxter State Park and the Allagash Wilderness Waterway.

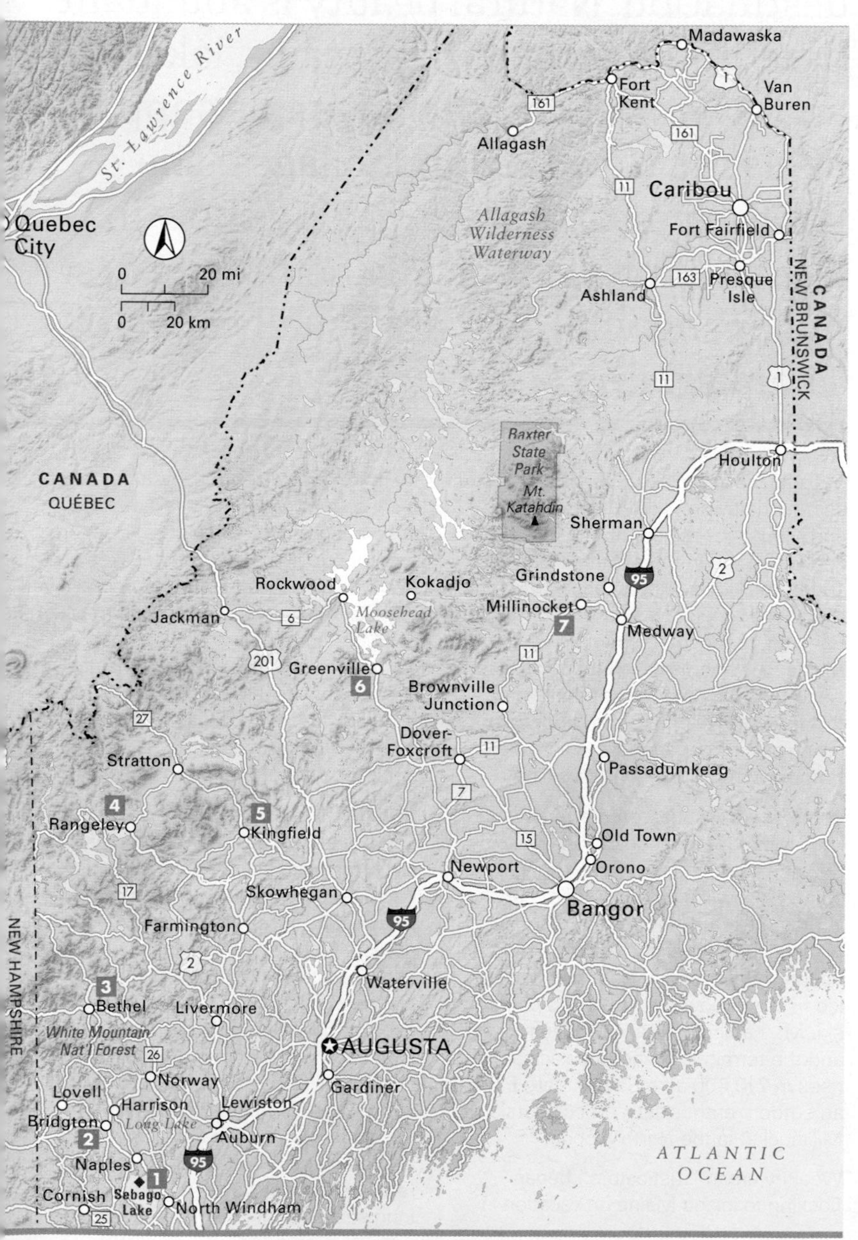
St. Lawrence River
Quebec City
0
20 mi
0
20 km
CANADA
QUÉBEC
Madawaska
Fort Kent
Van Buren
Allagash
Caribou
Allagash Wilderness Waterway
Fort Fairfield
Ashland
Presque Isle
CANADA
NEW BRUNSWICK
Baxter State Park
Mt. Katahdin
Houlton
Sherman
Grindstone
Rockwood
Kokadjo
Millinocket
Medway
Jackman
Moosehead Lake
Greenville
Brownville Junction
Dover-Foxcroft
Passadumkeag
Stratton
Rangeley
Kingfield
Old Town
Orono
Newport
Bangor
Skowhegan
Farmington
Waterville
Bethel
Livermore
White Mountain Nat'l Forest
AUGUSTA
Norway
Gardiner
Lovell
Harrison
Lewiston
Bridgton
Long Lake
Auburn
Naples
Cornish
Sebago Lake
North Windham
ATLANTIC OCEAN
NEW HAMPSHIRE
1
2
3
4
5
6
7

Unlike the state's higher-profile coastline, inland Maine is a four-season destination. Natural beauty is abundant here, in the form of mountains, lakes, and rivers, and there's an ample supply of classic New England villages. The large ski resorts start making snow in late autumn, so typically before the first major snowfall, and are usually open by Thanksgiving.

Sebago and Long lakes, north of Portland and the gateway to the Western Lakes and Mountains region, hum with boaters and watercraft in the summer. Bridgton and Bethel ooze quintessential New England charm and draw skiers come winter. Rangeley, a mountain town in western Maine, has been a haven for anglers since the 19th century, but these days this lake-strewn area is also known for hiking and winter sports and activities, from snowmobiling to alpine skiing.

In the North Woods, remote forestland lines most of Moosehead Lake, New England's largest lake within a single state. Greenville, at its southern end, is the hub in this neck of the woods. Visitors come to enjoy the lake, explore nearby wilderness locales, snowmobile, ice fish, and downhill and cross-country ski. Mt. Katahdin, Maine's highest peak and the terminus of the Appalachian Trail, rises in 210,000-acre Baxter State Park, an outdoor enthusiast's mecca outside Millinocket in the North Woods.

Wealthy urban "rusticators" began flocking to inland Maine on vacation in the mid-1800s. Their legacy, and that of the locals who catered to them, lives on at sporting camps still found—albeit in smaller numbers—on remote lakes and rivers, in displays at small but impressive regional museums, and through Maine's unique system of licensed outdoor guides. Known as Registered Maine Guides, these well-qualified practitioners lead such excursions as kayaking, white-water rafting, hiking, fishing, hunting, canoeing, or moose spotting.

MAJOR REGIONS

The sparsely populated **Western Lakes and Mountains** region stretches north and west, bordered by New Hampshire and Québec. Each season offers different outdoor highlights: you can choose from snow sports, hiking, mountain biking, leaf peeping, fishing, swimming, and paddling. The **Sebago Lake Area** bustles with activity in summer. **Bridgton** is a classic New England town, as is **Bethel**, in the valley of the Androscoggin River. Sunday River, a major ski resort nearby, also offers summer activities. The more remote **Rangeley** Lakes region contains long stretches of pine, beech, spruce, and sky, and classic inns. Just north of **Kingfield** is Sugarloaf ski resort, Maine's other big ski resort, which has plenty to offer year-round.

Much of the **North Woods** is best experienced by canoeing or kayaking, fishing, hiking, snowshoeing, cross-country skiing, or snowmobiling. The woodsy town of **Greenville**, on Moosehead Lake, is a great base for day trips, including excursions into Maine's 100 Mile Wilderness. **Millinocket** is the gateway to Baxter State Park, Allagash Wilderness Waterway, and Katahdin Woods and Waters National Monument, all premier wilderness destinations open for public recreation.

Planning

Visitors to inland Maine often spend their entire vacation in the region. That's certainly true of those who come to ski at a resort, fish at a remote sporting camp, or just relax at a lakeside cabin. Resort towns offer scenic cruises, intriguing small museums, and nearby hiking but are also hubs for exploring farther afield. Visitors may head out early for white-water rafting, to recreate in a renowned wilderness area, or day trip among the lake towns closer to Portland. The farther inland you go, the farther between destinations. Lodgings and rentals often have minimum stays during peak times.

Getting Here and Around

AIR

Two primary airports serve Maine: Portland International Jetport (PWM) and Bangor International (BGR). Portland is closer to the Western Lakes and Mountains area; Bangor is more convenient to the North Woods. Offering charter as well as scenic flights, regional flying services pick visitors up at major airports and transport them to remote locales.

CAR

Because Maine is large and rural, a car is essential. U.S. 2 is the major east–west thoroughfare in Western Maine, winding from Bangor to New Hampshire. Interstate 95 is a departure point for many visitors to inland Maine, especially the North Woods. The highway heads inland at Brunswick and becomes a toll road (the Maine Turnpike) from the New Hampshire border to Augusta. Because of the hilly terrain and abundant lakes and rivers, inland Maine can get curvy. Traffic rarely gets heavy, though highways often pass right through instead of around the larger towns, which can slow your trip a bit.

In Maine's North Woods, private logging roads are often open to the public (sometimes by permit and fee). When driving these roads, always give lumber-company trucks the right-of-way; loggers must drive in the middle of the road and often can't move over or slow down for cars. Be sure to have a full tank of gas before heading onto private roads in the region.

Activities

People visit inland Maine year-round, coming to hike, bike, camp, fish, canoe, kayak, white-water raft, downhill and cross-country ski, snowshoe, and snowmobile.

BIKING

Bicycle Coalition of Maine

BIKING | The coalition provides information about biking in the state. ☎ *207/623–4511* 🌐 *www.bikemaine.org*.

FISHING

Maine Department of Inland Fisheries and Wildlife

FISHING | You can buy hunting and fishing licenses online through this state agency, which has a wealth of information about where and how to enjoy these outdoor activities in Maine. ☎ *207/287–8000* 🌐 *www.maine.gov/ifw*.

GUIDE SERVICES

Maine Professional Guides Association
The association can help you find a state-licensed guide to lead a fishing, hunting, hiking, kayaking, canoeing, white-water rafting, snowshoeing, birding, or wildlife-watching trip. 🌐 *www.maineguides.org.*

HIKING

Maine Appalachian Trail Club
HIKING & WALKING | The club publishes seven Appalachian Trail maps ($8 per map for nonmembers, $6.40 for members), all of which are bound together in its Maine trail guide ($34.95 for nonmembers, $27.96 for members). Maps are also available (free and for purchase) via a free app (*see the website for details*). The organization's interactive online map has information on everything from side trails to communities along the AT in Maine. 🌐 *www.matc.org.*

Maine Trail Finder
HIKING & WALKING | The website has trail descriptions, photos, user comments, directions, and interactive maps for trails to hike, walk, mountain bike, paddle, snowshoe, and cross-county ski. 🌐 *www.mainetrailfinder.com.*

SKIING

Ski Maine Association
SURFING | For alpine and cross-country skiing information. ☎ *207/773–7669* 🌐 *www.skimaine.com.*

SNOWMOBILING

Maine Snowmobile Association
SNOW SPORTS | The website has contacts and links for about 10,000 miles of local and regional trails and an excellent statewide map of the approximately 4,000-mile Interconnected Trail System (ITS). ☎ *207/622–6983* 🌐 *www.mainesnowmobileassociation.com.*

WHITE-WATER RAFTING

Raft Maine Association
WHITE-WATER RAFTING | An association of four white-water rafting outfitters, the website has information on the companies and Maine's three major white-water rafting rivers—the Kennebec, the Dead, and the West Branch of the Penobscot, which together make Maine New England's premier destination for white-water rafting. The Kennebec and Dead rivers converge at The Forks in Western Maine, while the West Branch of the Penobscot flows near Millinocket in the North Woods.

■ TIP→ Family-friendly rafting trips are available. 🌐 *www.raftmaine.com.*

Hotels

Well-run inns, bed-and-breakfasts, and motels can be found throughout inland Maine, including some more sophisticated lodgings. During high season, or seasons, you may be required to stay two nights minimum. At places near ski resorts, you'll find peak-season rates in winter as well as at the height of summer and the fall foliage peak. Both hotel rooms and condo units are among the options at the two largest ski resorts, Sunday River and Sugarloaf. Greenville has the largest selection of lodgings in the North Woods region, with elaborate and homey accommodations alike. Lakeside sporting camps are popular around Rangeley and the North Woods; many have cozy cabins heated with wood stoves and provide three hearty meals a day (lunch is packed to go), perhaps featuring fish you caught. Conservation organizations also operate wilderness retreats.

Hotel reviews have been shortened. For full reviews visit Fodors.com.

Maine Campground Owners Association
The association's helpful membership directory is available by mail and on its website, which also has an interactive map. Many campgrounds have RV spaces and cabin rentals. ☎ *207/782–5874* 🌐 *www.campmaine.com.*

Maine Sporting Camp Association
Representing 45 camps, the association's goal is to "preserve the sporting camp's uniqueness" in Maine. Visit the website to search for camps by activity, meal plan, season of operation, and even the fish in local waters. ☎ *207/888–3931* 🌐 *www.mainesportingcamps.com.*

Maine State Parks Campground Reservations Service
You can get information about and make reservations for 12 state park campgrounds through this service. Note: reservations for Baxter State Park, which is administered separately, are not handled by the service. ☎ *207/624–9950, 800/332–1501 in Maine* 🌐 *www.campwithme.com.*

What It Costs in U.S. Dollars

	$	$$	$$$	$$$$
RESTAURANTS	under $18	$18–$24	$25–$35	over $35
HOTELS	under $200	$200–$299	$300–$399	over $399

Restaurants

Fear not, lobster lovers: this succulent, emblematic Maine food is on the menu at many inland restaurants, from fancier establishments to roadside places. Dishes containing lobster are more common than boiled lobster dinners; look for daily specials. Shrimp, scallops, and other seafood are also menu mainstays, and you may find bison burgers or steaks from a nearby farm. Organic growers and natural foods producers are found throughout the state and often sell their products to nearby restaurants. Pumpkins, blackberries, apples, and strawberries make their way into homemade desserts, as do Maine's famed blueberries. Many lakeside resorts and sporting camps have a reputation for good food—some of the latter will even cook the fish you catch.

Restaurant reviews have been shortened. For full reviews visit Fodors.com.

Visitor Information

The more than 2 million acres overseen by the Maine Bureau of Parks and Lands encompass 33 state parks, 15 historic sites, three scenic waterways, and about 300 miles of multiuse trails (popular with ATV riders and snowmobilers). Its free public lands—approximately 600,000 acres—are wilderness areas managed for recreation, wildlife preservation, and timbering. Some are in remote areas accessible only by logging roads; others are relatively close to town centers; and some have trails, outhouses, and primitive campsites.

CONTACTS Maine Office of Tourism. ☎ *888/624–6345* 🌐 *www.visitmaine.com.* **Maine Tourism Association.** 🌐 *www.mainetourism.com.* **Maine Bureau of Parks and Lands.** ☎ *207/287–3821* 🌐 *www.parksandlands.com.*

When to Go

As a rule, inland Maine's most popular hiking trails and lakeside beaches get busier when the weather gets warmer, but if splendid isolation is what you crave, you can still find it. In summertime, lodging rates rise with the temperature and traffic picks up—though rarely jams, outside of a few spots. Inland Maine gets hotter than the coast in July and August; lakes and higher elevations are naturally cooler. Of course the weather also makes it a beautiful time of year to visit. September is a good bet: temperatures are more moderate, and the crowds thinner. Western Maine is the state's premier destination for leaf peepers—hardwoods are more abundant inland. Peak foliage season runs late September–mid-October.

Maine's largest ski resorts typically start making snow for the trails before the first large snowfall and are open by Thanksgiving. As the weather has warmed in recent years, winters here have started later and ended sooner. In northerly and mountain destinations, snowmobiling and cross-country skiing are unlikely to be in full swing before mid-January. Early spring snowmelt ushers in mud season, which leads to black fly season mid-May–mid-June. The flies are especially pesky in the woods but less bothersome in town. Spring is prime time for canoeing and fishing.

Sebago Lake Area

20 miles northwest of Portland.

Seasonal and year-round dwellings, from simple camps to sprawling showplaces, line the shores of sprawling Sebago Lake and fingerlike Long Lake. Both are popular with water-sports enthusiasts, as is Brandy Pond and other bodies of water in the area. Several rivers flow into Sebago Lake—Maine's second largest—linking nearby lakes and ponds to form a 43-mile waterway. Naples, on the causeway separating Long Lake from Brandy Pond, pulses with activity in the summer, when the area swells with seasonal residents and weekend visitors. Open-air cafés overflow with patrons, boats buzz along the water, and families parade along the sidewalk edging Long Lake. On clear days the view includes snowcapped Mt. Washington. The nonextant Cumberland and Oxford Canal was part of a water route from Long Lake to Portland in the mid-1800s. At Sebago Lake State Park, the one remaining canal lock operates on the Songo River, which connects Brandy Pond and Sebago Lake.

GETTING HERE AND AROUND

Sebago Lake, gateway to Maine's Western Lakes and Mountains, is less than 20 miles from Portland on U.S. 302.

VACATION RENTALS

CONTACTS Krainin Real Estate. ✉ *1539 Roosevelt Tr., Raymond* ☎ *207/655–5189 for vacation rentals* 🌐 *www.krainin.com.*

VISITOR INFORMATION

CONTACTS Sebago Lakes Region Chamber of Commerce. ✉ *909 Roosevelt Tr., Suite A, Windham* ☎ *207/892–8265* 🌐 *www.sebagolakeschamber.com.*

Sights

Sabbathday Lake Shaker Village

MUSEUM VILLAGE | FAMILY | Established in the late 18th century, this is the last active Shaker community in the world. The farmstead's many structures include the 1794 Meetinghouse; the 1839 Ministry's Shop, where the elders and eldresses lived until the early 1900s; and the 1821 Sister's Shop, where household goods and candies were made. Visitors can take self-guided exterior building tours; check out free exhibits in the 1850 Boys' Shop, about Shaker childhood, and the 1816 Granary, on the community's history and evolution; and walk the gardens and grounds. The Shaker Store sells community-produced foods and goods as well as handicrafts by area artisans and has an antique shop whose offerings may include "fancy goods" made here years ago for sale to tourists. Check the website for events, including workshops. ✉ *707 Shaker Rd., New Gloucester* ☎ *207/926–4597* 🌐 *www.maineshakers.com* 🎟 *Free* 🕒 *Closed mid-Oct.–late May and Sun. late May–mid-Oct.*

Sebago Lake State Park

This 1,400-acre expanse on the north shore of Sebago Lake is a great spot for swimming, boating, and fishing for both salmon and togue (lake trout). Its 250-site campground is the largest at any Maine state park. Bicycling along the park's roads is a popular pastime in warm weather, as is hiking. Come winter, the park offers 5½ miles of groomed cross-country trails and 6 miles of ungroomed trails, also used for snowshoeing. On the park's edge, Songo Lock State Historic Site, an operational lock along the twisting, narrow Songo River and a remnant of a 19th-century canal system, is a pleasant—and free—picnic area. You can also fish off the handicapped-accessible pier and launch a kayak or canoe. ⊠ *11 Park Access Rd., Casco* ☎ *207/693–6231* 🌐 *www.maine.gov/sebagolake* 🎫 *Nonresident $8, Maine resident $6.*

Hotels

Lakeview Inn

$ | **B&B/INN** | Built in 1906 as a hotel annex, the four-story inn has 16 rooms and suites—all on the upper floors—and a wide, inviting front porch that overlooks gardens and offers an angled view of Long Lake beyond Naples' main thoroughfare. **Pros:** cornhole outside, pool table inside; convenience center has kitchenette (no stove top) with courtesy coffee and tea; several deluxe larger rooms and family-friendly suites. **Cons:** third-floor rooms but no elevator; stairs a bit steep; "comfy" rooms are smallish. $ *Rooms from: $189* ⊠ *15 Lake House Rd., Naples* ☎ *207/693–9099* 🌐 *www.lakeviewinnmaine.com* *16 rooms* 🍽 *Free Breakfast.*

Activities

Sebago and Long lakes are popular areas for sailing, fishing, and motorboating. As U.S. 302 cuts through the center of Naples, you'll find rental craft for fishing or cruising at the causeway.

TOURS

Songo River Queen II

BOAT TOURS | **FAMILY** | Departing from the Naples causeway, the *Songo River Queen II,* a 93-foot stern-wheeler, takes passengers on scheduled cruises on Long Lake and also offers private charters. The narration is awash in local history and fun facts about noteworthy dwellings along the shore, including a former home of horror writer and Mainer Stephen King. There's a bar and snack bar on board. Check the website for themed evening cruises with live music, offered most weekends. ⊠ *841 Roosevelt Tr., Naples* ☎ *207/693–6861* 🌐 *www.songoriverqueen.net* 🎫 *From $35.*

WATER SPORTS

Dingley's Wharf

WATER SPORTS | **FAMILY** | Smack in the middle of the Naples causeway on Long Lake, Dingley's offers lots of choices for getting out on the water. Wakeboarding, waterskiing, wake surfing, knee boarding, and tube riding excursions with a certified instructor include lessons. If you have your own boat, you can rent equipment for these activities. Dingley's rental options include Jet Skis, aqua trikes, kayaks, canoes, and standup paddleboards. Need to make a bigger splash? Rent a pontoon boat or Boston Whaler. ⊠ *851 Roosevelt Tr., Naples* ✣ *On Naples causeway* ☎ *207/693–5253* 🌐 *www.dingleyswharf.com.*

Bridgton

8 miles north of Naples, 30 miles south of Bethel.

Downtown Bridgton is a great place to spend the day, with restaurants, a movie theater, museums, a nice mix of shops and galleries, and a handful of parks. Steps from the action, a covered pedestrian bridge leads to 66-acre Pondicherry Park, a nature preserve with wooded trails and two streams. Highland Beach is off the north end of Main Street, across from an inviting small park. On hot summer days, kids dive off the dock as mountains lounge on the horizon. Come winter, skiers head to Pleasant

Western Lakes and Mountains
The Forks
Moxie Pond
Monson
Stratton
Bingham
Outdoor Heritage Museum
Wilhelm Reich Museum
Sugarloaf
Oquossoc
Rangeley
Kingfield
Wilsons Mills
Rangeley Lake State Park
Saddleback Mountain
Solon
New Portland
Height of Land
Phillips
New Vineyard
Skowhegan
Weld
Farmington
Andover
Grafton Notch State Park
Mexico
Wilton
Waterville
Rumford
Dixfield
Hanover
Newry
Chisholm
Livermore Falls
Sunday River
Bethel
Locke Mills
Bryant Pond
Mt. Abram Ski and Ride
Livermore
White Mountain National Forest
Greenwood
Buckfield
AUGUSTA
South Paris
Turner
Norway
Center Lovell
Waterford
Greene
Mechanic Falls
Lovell
Harrison
Lewiston
Auburn
Bridgton
Fryeburg
Pleasant Mountain
Long Lake
Casco
Newcastle
Sebago Lake Area
Sabbathday Lake Shaker Village
South Casco
Brunswick
Brownfield
Sebago Lake State Park
Bath
Hiram
Sabago Lake
Raymond
Freeport
Boothbay
Kezar Falls
Georgetown
Yarmouth
Standish
Falmouth
Gorham
Portland
Casco Bay
ATLANTIC OCEAN
NEW HAMPSHIRE
0 10 mi
0 10 km

Mountain (formerly Shawnee Peak) and cross-country ski at Bridgton's ridgetop golf course. The town is the hub for a region strewn with lakes and large ponds popular for boating, fishing, and swimming; the surrounding countryside is a good choice for leaf peepers and hikers. Harrison is a few miles north at the end of Long Lake. Beyond here, Waterford's villages evoke Old New England. In fall, head west to Fryeburg, home to Fryeburg Fair (🌐 www.fryeburgfair.org), Maine's largest agricultural fair. North of the New Hampshire border town, Center Lovell draws boaters to Kezar Lake (author and Mainer Stephen King summers here) and hikers to Mount Sabattus.

GETTING HERE AND AROUND

From Portland, U.S. 302 runs northwest to Bridgton along the east side of Sebago Lake and the west side of Long Lake, then continues west 15 miles to Fryeburg, where Route 5 continues north to Center Lovell. Route 117 skirts the west side of Long Lake en route to Harrison, north of Bridgton. Both Route 37 (in North Bridgton) and Route 35 (in Harrison) depart Route 117 for Waterford.

VISITOR INFORMATION

CONTACTS Greater Bridgton Lakes Region Chamber of Commerce. ✉ *257 Main St., Suite 1, Bridgton* ☎ *207/647–3472* 🌐 *www.gblrcc.org.*

Sights

★ Rufus Porter Museum of Art and Ingenuity

ART MUSEUM | FAMILY | Local youth Rufus Porter became a leading folk artist in the early 1800s, painting landscape and harbor murals on the walls of New England homes, like this museum's barn red Cape Cod–style Nathan Church House, which bears unsigned murals by Porter (or one of his apprentices). In 2016, the late-18th-century structure was moved to the museum's downtown setting, where an eye-catching circa-1830s former residence on Main Street has exhibits about Porter, who was also an "ahead of his time" inventor, writer, and founder of *Scientific American* magazine. Early issues are on display, as are models of some of his inventions and his miniature portraits. A video about this ingenious man is shown. Both buildings have changing exhibits, and the museum's excellent gift shop has books about Porter. ✉ *121 Main St., Bridgton* ☎ *207/647–2828* 🌐 *www.rufusportermuseum.org* 🎫 *$8* 🕒 *Closed mid-Oct.–mid-June and Sun.–Tues. mid-June–mid-Oct.*

Beaches

With many lakes in the Bridgton area, it's not surprising the town has three public beaches. Two have playgrounds and a dock: the crown jewel, Highland Beach, at the end of Highland Lake at the edge of downtown on Highland Road, and Woods Pond Beach off Route 117. Salmon Point Beach, part of the town-owned campground of the same name, has fewer amenities but is on one of the area's premier bodies of water, Long Lake.

Restaurants

Standard Gastropub

$ | AMERICAN | FAMILY | Like the facade, a cooler wall—stocked with hundreds of beers from around Maine and the world, sold to diners and to go—attests to Gastropub's gas station past (it even served gas initially). Craft brews, many hard to find, accompany snazzy, farm-to-table takes on American classic and foreign-inspired comfort foods. **Known for:** smash burgers (local grass-fed beef) with house sauce and twice-fried fries; chili mayo–smothered smoked street corn and street corn dip and chips (at least one is always on the menu); Sunday brunch. 💲 *Average main: $15* ✉ *233 Main St., Bridgton* ☎ *207/647–4100* 🌐 *www.standardgastropub.com* 🕒 *Closed Tues.*

Hotels

★ Bear Mountain Inn + Barn

$$ | **B&B/INN** | Aside Bear Pond in South Waterford, this 1800s 25-acre homestead inn features country chic decor with plaid accents and handsome baths (some with tub and shower); most accommodations—nine guest rooms and family-friendly suites, plus the snuggly cottage and post-and-beam apartment—have lake views and a fireplace (or wood stove). **Pros:** small beach and docks for swimming, boating, and fishing on Bear Pond, and courtesy canoes, kayaks, standup paddleboards, and row boats to use on the lake-like body of water; hot tub, hammocks, picnic areas, and 1-mile riverside trail; woodsy yet luxurious suite-like Mountain Ash has a fireplace, two-person Jacuzzi tub (plus walk-in shower), wet bar, armchairs, king bed, built-in daybed, and private deck. **Cons:** no shops and restaurants in immediate vicinity; some third-floor rooms but no elevator; typically fully booked on weekends for weddings spring through fall. *Rooms from: $225 ✉ 364 Waterford Rd., Waterford ☎ 866/450–4253, 207/583–4404 www.bearmtninn.com Closed mid-Nov.–late Dec. and Apr. 9 rooms, 1 cabin, 1 apartment Free Breakfast.*

★ Noble House Inn

$$ | **B&B/INN** | Just beyond downtown, state Senator Winburn Staples (1855–1939) built this stately 1903 home above Highland Lake on large grounds that include a pine grove; guests enjoy luxury comforts and a relaxing atmosphere where they can kick back on the wraparound porch, in an Adirondack chair by one of the fire pits, or in the living room or den (both have fireplaces)—perhaps with a drink from the intimate guests-only bar. **Pros:** distinctive suites have king or queen beds and queen sleeper sofas, one has an electric fireplace, and two guest rooms can be joined as a family suite; courtesy canoes and kayaks for Highland Lake; enjoy a massage (fee, by appointment) in your room or the inn's massage suite. **Cons:** limited lake views; during the warm season, some weekends are fully booked for weddings; third-floor suite but no elevator. *Rooms from: $225 ✉ 81 Highland Rd., Bridgton ☎ 207/647–3733 www.noblehouseinn.com 8 rooms Free Breakfast.*

Activities

SKIING

Pleasant Mountain

SKIING & SNOWBOARDING | **FAMILY** | Just a few miles from Bridgton, Pleasant Mountain (formerly Shawnee Peak) appeals to families and those who enjoy nighttime skiing—nearly half the trails are lighted except most Sundays. The ski area got its original name back in 2022 after its sale to Boyne Resorts, owner of Maine's largest ski resorts, Sugarloaf and Sunday River. Opened in the 1930s and Maine's first ski area to add a lift, Pleasant Mountain's three terrain parks and glade areas offer alternatives to downhill runs. A great room looks up at the slopes in the main base lodge, which has a cafeteria and a pub restaurant with an expansive deck; the smaller East Lodge anchors some of the more challenging terrain and has an eatery. Summer visitors can hike and pick blueberries. For a rustic stay, the ski area offers a slope-side mountaintop yurt (sleeps four) and cabin (sleeps six) year-round via Airbnb; guests hike up or, in winter, can opt for the chairlift. **Facilities:** 42 trails; 239 acres; 1,300-foot vertical drop; 6 lifts. *✉ 119 Mountain Rd., off U.S. 302, Bridgton ☎ 207/647–8444 www.pleasantmountain.com Lift ticket: $89.*

Shopping

Whether you are a browser or a shopper, downtown Bridgton beckons. Main Street often looks and feels like a Norman Rockwell painting, and it's here that you'll find mostly year-round shops selling books, antiques, gifts, art, handcrafts, chocolates, souvenirs, T-shirts, and clothing, anchored by a branch of Renys (www.renys.com), the state's friendly, spic-and-span outlet department store chain, aka "A Maine Adventure."

Firefly Boutique

WOMEN'S CLOTHING | Picture windows line the walls of this welcoming corner boutique that sells unique women's attire from the "USA and beyond" including cashmere and cashmere-feel print shawls, leggings in fun prints, and lively dresses for evenings out as well as running about. In business since 2009, Firefly is also known for jewelry: more than 30 of its jewelry and clothing lines are American-made. Several of the former are by Maine artisans. ✉ *103 Main St., Bridgton* ☎ *207/647–3672* *www.fireflyshopmaine.com.*

Gallery 302

ART GALLERIES | Creative shop windows showcase an individual artist on a rotating biweekly basis, inviting passers-by into Bridgton Art Guild's wide-open tin-ceilinged gallery in a former hardware store. Eclectic and fun—definitely not stuffy—the gallery opened in 2003 and represents more than 40 local and regional artists working in various media. Artists' displays have their bio and photograph. Don't miss the back-corner gift shop with cards, small prints, and the like. Along with hosting wine and cheese receptions and community events, the guild holds classes and workshops—many for a day or half day, so consider signing up. ✉ *112 Main St., Bridgton* ☎ *207/647–2787* *www.gallery302.com.*

Bethel

27 miles north of Bridgton, 66 miles south of Rangeley.

Bethel is pure New England: a town with white clapboard houses, a large green, white-steeple churches, and a mountain vista at the end of every street. Gould Academy, a college prep school founded in 1836, anchors the east side of downtown. On Main Street, the world class Maine Mineral & Gem Museum honors the region's storied mining history—and has a moon rock collection that rocks. In winter, Bethel is ski country. Sunday River, one of Maine's big ski resorts, is only a few miles north in Newry, while family-friendly Mt. Abram is east of town. On the third weekend in July, Bethel Area Summerfest includes a parade, fireworks, and live music. Whatever the season, folks hit Bethel Village Trails on the edge of the village, and the 978-acre Bethel Community Forest a few miles from the town center. Under the tutelage of nonprofit Inland Woods + Trails (www.woodsandtrails.org), the locales welcome hikers, mountain bikers, fat-tire cyclists, snowshoers, and cross-country skiers.

GETTING HERE AND AROUND

From the south, both Routes 35 and 5 lead to Bethel, overlapping several miles south of town. Route 5 from Bethel to Fryeburg is especially pretty come fall, with long stretches of overhanging trees and glimpses of Kezar Lake as the road passes through tiny Center Lovell. If you're coming to Bethel from the west on U.S. 2, you'll pass White Mountain National Forest.

VACATION RENTALS

CONTACTS Four Seasons Realty & Rentals. ✉ *303 Mayville Rd., Bethel* ☎ *207/824–3776* *www.fourseasonsrealtymaine.com.*

VISITOR INFORMATION

CONTACTS Bethel Area Chamber of Commerce. ✉ *8 Station Pl., off Cross St., Bethel* ☎ *207/824–2282, 800/442–5826* 🌐 *www.bethelmaine.com.*

Sights

Artist's Bridge

SCENIC DRIVE | FAMILY | The most painted and photographed of Maine's nine covered bridges can be found on a detour from Newry. Head south on U.S. 2 and then northwest on Sunday River Road (stay to the right at "Y" intersections). Trails flow alongside Sunday River from the pedestrian-only bridge, which is a popular swimming spot. ✉ *Sunday River Rd., 4 miles northwest of U.S. 2, Newry.*

Grafton Notch State Park

STATE/PROVINCIAL PARK | FAMILY | Grafton Notch Scenic Byway along Route 26 runs through Grafton Notch, a favorite destination for viewing fall foliage that stretches along the Bear River Valley 14 miles north of Bethel. It's an easy walk from roadside parking areas to the distinctive Screw Auger Falls, which drops through a gorge, creating pools; Mother Walker Falls; and Moose Cave. Trailhead parking and the nicely shaded Spruce Meadow picnic area are also right along the road. Table Rock Loop Trail (2.4 miles round-trip) rewards hikers with views of the mountainous terrain. More challenging is the 7.6-mile round-trip trek along the Appalachian Trail to the viewing platform atop 4,180-foot Old Speck Mountain, one of the state's highest peaks. The Appalachian Trail also traverses the 31,764-acre Mahoosuc Public Land—its two tracts sandwich the park—whose trails offer stunning, if strenuous, backcountry hiking (there are backcountry campsites). In winter, a popular snowmobile trail follows the river through the park. ✉ *1941 Bear River Rd., Newry* ☎ *207/824–2912 mid-May–mid-Oct. only, 207/624–6080* 🌐 *www.maine.gov/graftonnotch* 🎫 *Nonresidents $4, Maine residents $3.*

★ Maine Mineral & Gem Museum

SCIENCE MUSEUM | FAMILY | Moon rocks, Maine mineralogy, and western Maine's mineral and gem mining legacy converge at this interactive 15,000-square-foot museum—unexpected in a town of Bethel's size. Opened in 2019 and founded by philanthropists, the handsome structure (two Main Street buildings were joined) is surrounded by garden beds with large rocks, some resembling modern sculpture and all placarded with interesting facts about their origins, etc. Inside, 19 exhibits are spread about four galleries on two floors. Kids love the simulated mining blast, part of an exhibit on gem discoveries and mica and feldspar mining in the Bethel area. When the "Space Rocks" gallery darkens, a 3D film beams about, making it look as if a meteorite shower has blown up the walls, revealing Bethel. The windowless space displays more moon meteorites than the world's other natural history museums combined. This museum's collection includes the biggest chunk of Mars on earth, weighing 32 pounds; 6,000 meteorites from the moon, Mars, and the asteroid belt; and nearly 38,000 mineral specimens, some 15,000 of them Maine-mined. A replica of a shuttered Maine mineral store, once a tourist hot spot, showcases prized specimens. In the "Hall of Gems" (and the gift shop!), Maine's famed pink and "watermelon" tourmaline and other gems bedazzle. ✉ *99 Main St., Bethel* ☎ *207/824–3036* 🌐 *www.mainemineralmuseum.org* 🎫 *$15* 🕒 *Closed Tues.*

Museums of the Bethel Historical Society

HISTORY MUSEUM | Across from the Village Common, the society's campus comprises two buildings: the 1821 O'Neil Robinson House and the 1813 Dr. Moses Mason House, both on the National Register of Historic Places. The O'Neil Robinson House has well-done exhibits about the region's history and a Maine Ski and Snowmobile Museum display. One parlor room serves as a gift shop with a nice book selection. The Moses Mason House has nine period rooms, and the front hall and stairway are decorated with Rufus Porter School folk art murals. The barn gallery has changing exhibits. In town when the museum is closed? Touch base as it does open by appointment.

■ **TIP→ Head out back to check out the Sunday River snow roller, pulled by a team of horses back in the day, and a giant Mt. Zircon Moon Tide Spring "Ginger Champagne" soda bottle lunch stand, a 1920s promotion for a defunct western Maine spring and soda water company.** *✉ 10 Broad St., Bethel ☎ 207/824–2908 🌐 www.bethelhistorical.org 🎟 By donation ⏲ O'Neil Robinson closed mid Oct.–late May, Sun. and Mon. July and Aug., and Sat.–Mon. June and Sept.; Moses Mason closed Sept.–June and Sun.–Wed. July and Aug.*

White Mountain National Forest

FOREST | FAMILY | This forest straddles New Hampshire and Maine, with the highest peaks on the New Hampshire side. The Maine section, though smaller, has magnificent rugged terrain. Hikers can enjoy everything from hour-long nature loops to a day hike up Speckled Mountain. The mountain is part of the 14,000-acre Caribou-Speckled Mountain Wilderness Area, one of several in the forest, but the only one entirely contained within Maine. The most popular Maine access to the national forest is via Route 113, which runs south from its terminus at U.S. 2 in Gilead, 10 miles from downtown Bethel. Most of the highway is the Pequawket Trail Maine Scenic Byway, and the section through the forest is spectacular come fall. This stretch is closed in winter but is used by snowmobilers and cross-country skiers. Two of the forest's campgrounds are in Maine; backcountry camping is allowed. *✉ Rte. 113, off U.S. 2, Gilead ☎ 603/466–2713 🌐 www.fs.usda.gov/whitemountain 🎟 From $5 per car.*

Restaurants

Cho Sun

$$$ | KOREAN | Offering sushi and more, dishes here are deeply rooted in Korea and Maine: the chef's Korean mother owns the restaurant, which she founded in 2002, and spices for the kimchi are grown at the family's local homestead. On summer nights, dining on the wide front porch—lit by torches and candles and right above the sidewalk on Main Street in downtown Bethel—is delightful, but the lively storm-blue dining rooms are also inviting, and perfect for a post-ski meal. **Known for:** dolsot bibimbop (a dish of steamed rice and veggies) served in a hot stone pot with tofu, beef, chicken, shrimp, or calamari to mix in at your table; seasonal satellite restaurant, Cho Sun Sushi and Noodle Bar (has a full bar) at Sunday River ski resort; Sunday karaoke night in the cabin-like bar at the back of the main restaurant. *$ Average main: $25 ✉ 141 Main St., Bethel ☎ 207/824–7370 🌐 www.chosun207.com ⏲ No lunch. Closed Mon. and Tues.*

Coffee and Quick Bites

Good Food Store

$ | AMERICAN | FAMILY | A cheery red door welcomes customers to this hip, cozy grocery, opened in 1994 and selling specialty, organic, and Maine-produced foods and goods, from sodas to local poultry. Friendly staff will help you select from the specials-friendly takeout menu and the great to-go beer and wine selection, or suggest grocery items for a picnic or dinner at your lodging. **Known for:** pumpkin whoopie pies; "heat and eat" meals; outdoor Smokin' Good BBQ. *$ Average main: $8 ✉ 212 Mayville Rd., Bethel ☎ 207/824–3754 🌐 www.goodfoodbethel.com ⏲ Smokin' Good BBQ closed mid-Apr.–mid-May and mid-Oct.–mid-Nov.*

One of the Rangeley Lakes, Mooselookmeguntic is said to mean "portage to the moose feeding place" in the Abenaki language.

Hotels

Holidae House Bed & Breakfast
$ | **B&B/INN** | Welcoming hospitality keeps guests returning year after year to this charming, affordable, light blue downtown B&B, where innkeepers are at the ready with day-trip tips (or to kindly help guests as needed), and eight guest rooms occupy two floors of the antiques-filled home, which was originally built for a lumber executive in 1906. **Pros:** military and first responder discounts and walk-in rates; fresh-baked treats in afternoon; blow-up mattresses available. **Cons:** nice porch and a brick patio out front but otherwise no yard; no mountain views; no king beds. *Rooms from: $160* *85 Main St., Bethel* *207/824–3400* *www.holidaehouse.com* *8 rooms* *Free Breakfast.*

Activities

CANOEING AND KAYAKING

Bethel Outdoor Adventure and Campground
CANOEING & ROWING | **FAMILY** | On the Androscoggin River, this outfitter rents canoes, kayaks, tubes, and standup paddleboards, with and without shuttle service, and has a campground. There's also an open-air facility where you can sluice for precious and semiprecious gems and minerals (the Bethel region has a long history of mining for them). All Bethel Outdoor Adventure activities get customers a free trek on the Burma Bridge, which leads to a walking trail on the company's private, wild river island. This outfitter also sells state fishing licenses. *121 Mayville Rd., Bethel* *207/824–4224* *www.betheloutdoor-adventure.com.*

Whoopie Pies

When a bill aiming to make the whoopie pie Maine's official dessert was debated in state legislature, some lawmakers countered that the blueberry pie (made with Maine wild blueberries, of course) should have the honor. The blueberry pie won out, but what might have erupted into civil war instead ended civilly, with whoopie pies designated the official state "treat." Spend a few days anywhere in Maine and you'll soon know what a sweet, and popular, treat they are.

The name is misleading: it's a "pie" only in the sense of a having a filling between two "crusts"—namely, a thick layer of sugary frosting sandwiched between two saucers of rich cake, usually chocolate. It may have acquired its distinctive moniker from the jubilant "yelp" farmers emitted after discovering it in their lunch-boxes. The whoopie pie is said to have Pennsylvania Dutch roots, but many Mainers insist that it originated here. Typically, the filling is made with butter or shortening; some recipes add Marshmallow Fluff. Many bakers have indulged the temptation to experiment with flavors and ingredients, particularly in the filling but also in the cake, offering pumpkin, raspberry, oatmeal cream, red velvet, peanut butter, and more.

DOGSLEDDING

Mahoosuc Guide Service

ADVENTURE TOURS | This acclaimed guide company leads day and multiday dog-sledding trips in the Umbagog National Wildlife Refuge on the Maine–New Hampshire border. The outfitter also offers overnight dogsledding, fly fishing, and canoe excursions inside and outside Maine. One of the multiday canoe trips is an immersion in the ways of the Penobscot Nation, a Maine Native American tribe. Mahoosuc has lodging that's good for groups. ✉ *1513 Bear River Rd., Newry* ☎ *207/824–2073* 🌐 *www.mahoosuc.com* 🎫 *Dogsledding trips from $450 per person.*

SKIING

Carter's Cross-Country Ski Center

SKIING & SNOWBOARDING | **FAMILY** | Mountain views await at this acclaimed cross-country ski center, which offers 34 miles of trails for all levels of skiers. Skis, snowshoes, and sleds to pull children are all available for rent, as are fat-tire bikes. Both bike and ski lessons are offered. Carter's also rents three rustic ski-in cabins (available off-season except for April–mid-May) and has a ski shop. ✉ *786 Intervale Rd., Bethel* ☎ *207/824–3880 Bethel location* 🌐 *www.cartersxcski.com* 🎫 *$22.*

Mt. Abram Ski & Ride

SKIING & SNOWBOARDING | **FAMILY** | Family-friendly and affordable, Mt. Abram is open Thursday–Sunday during ski season. It allows off-trail "boundary-to-boundary" skiing, has two terrain parks, and welcomes uphill snowshoers and skiers ($5 day pass). Westside, the popular lift-served beginner area, has its own base lodge. The main lodge is home to Loose Boots Lounge, which occasionally features live music. Mountain biking is big here during the warm months: Mt. Abram offers rentals and lessons and trails are lift-served. **Facilities:** 44 trails; 650 acres; 1,150-foot vertical drop; 5 lifts. ✉ *308 Howe Hill Rd., off Rte. 26, Greenwood* ☎ *207/875–5000* 🌐 *www.mtabram.com* 🎫 *Lift ticket: $35.*

★ Sunday River

SKIING & SNOWBOARDING | FAMILY | Once-sleepy Sunday River has evolved into a sprawling resort that attracts skiers from around the world. Stretching for 3 miles, it encompasses eight trail-connected peaks and six terrain parks. Off-trail "boundary-to-boundary" skiing is allowed, and there's night skiing (well, "twilight" as it's from 3–6:30) on select Fridays and Saturdays and some holidays. Fireworks light the skies at the main South Ridge base lodge, one of three at the resort, for some holidays and special events. Sunday River has several lodging choices, including condos and two slope-side hotels: the family-friendly Grand Summit, at one of the mountain bases, and the more upscale Jordan Grand, near a summit at the resort's western end. (It's really up there, several miles by vehicle from the base areas, but during ski season a shuttle serves the resort, or you can ski over for lunch.)

■ TIP→ At both slope-side hotels, the outdoor heated pool and hot tub are open year-round.

From the less costly Snow Cap Inn, it's a short walk to the slopes. Come summer, the resort offers archery, kayaking, and standup paddleboarding lessons and guided kayak tours, and at the main South Ridge Base Lodge, chairlift rides to North Peak. Many visitors opt to hike down, or hit a trail up top, before riding down. Perhaps take in a chairlift ride after a game of golf: Sunday River Golf Club is acclaimed for its wide-open mountain and valley views and challenging elevation changes.

■ TIP→ Don't golf? Grab a drink or a bite at the clubhouse and hit those views—there's a building-length deck and a soaring Palladian window framed by polished wood walls.

Facilities: 139 trails; 884 acres; 2,340-foot vertical drop; 19 lifts. ✉ *15 S. Ridge Rd.* ☎ *207/824–3000, 207/824–5200 for snow conditions, 800/543–2754 for reservations* 🌐 *www.sundayriver.com* 🎫 *Lift ticket: $122.*

Rangeley

66 miles north of Bethel.

With 100-plus lakes and ponds linked by rivers and streams, the vastly forested Rangeley region has a rough, wilderness feel and has long attracted winter-sports enthusiasts, hikers, and anglers—it's been hailed for centuries as a "fly-fishing mecca." The four-season resort town of Rangeley stretches along the north side of its namesake lake. Right behind Main Street, Lakeside Park ("Town Park" to locals) has a large swimming area, a playground, picnic shelters, and a boat launch. Come winter, Saddleback Mountain ski resort lures downhill skiers, many of them families. Other winter activities in these parts include cross-country skiing, snowshoeing, fat-tire biking, snowmobiling, and pond skating. In late January, the Rangeley Snowmobile Snodeo offers thrilling snowmobile acrobatics, fireworks, a parade, and a cook-off for which area restaurants enter their chilies and chowders. Seven miles west on Route 4, tucked at the east end of Rangeley Lake near Mooselookmeguntic Lake, tiny Oquossoc is another hub for outdoor activities and dining. At the main crossroads, the Outdoor Heritage Museum beckons visitors; nearby Bald Mountain is a family-friendly day hike. South of the hamlet on Route 17 is the western gateway to the region, Height of Land—a must-see overlook with distant views stretching to mountains on the New Hampshire border.

GETTING HERE AND AROUND

To reach Rangeley on a scenic drive through Western Maine, take Route 17 north from U.S. 2 in Mexico past Height of Land to Route 4 in Oquossoc, then head east into town. Much of the drive is the Rangeley Lakes National Scenic Byway. From Rangeley, Route 16 continues east to Sugarloaf ski resort and Kingfield.

VACATION RENTALS

CONTACTS Morton & Furbish Vacation Rentals. ✉ *2478 Main St., Rangeley* ☎ *888/218–4882* 🌐 *www.rangeleyrentals.com.*

VISITOR INFORMATION

CONTACTS Rangeley Lakes Chamber of Commerce. ✉ *6 Park Rd., Rangeley* ☎ *207/864–5571* 🌐 *www.rangeleymaine.com.*

Sights

★ Height of Land

SCENIC DRIVE | FAMILY | Height of Land is the highlight of Rangeley Lakes National Scenic Byway, with unforgettable views of mountains and lakes. One of Maine's best overlooks, it hugs Route 17 atop Spruce Mountain several miles south of Rangeley's Oquossoc village. On a clear day, you can look west to mountains on the New Hampshire border. There's off-road parking, interpretive panels, stone seating, and a short path to the Appalachian Trail. Rangeley Lake unfolds at a nearby overlook on the opposite side of the road. ✉ *Rte. 17, Rangeley.*

★ Moose Alley

OTHER ATTRACTION | FAMILY | Bowling is just one reason families, couples, locals, and visitors head here for a night out, or indoor fun on a rainy—or sunny!—day. There's arcade games, billiards, foosball, cornhole, shuffleboard, darts, air hockey, and dancing and live music (check the website for details), plus ten bowling lanes. Moose Alley's Spirit Bar Grill & Cafe serves breakfast, lunch, and dinner. Folks also stop here for ice cream or baked goods, espresso or bubble tea, settling in upfront at the soda fountain-style and curvy lounge seating. Images of fish, moose, loons, and Rangeley Lake are smattered on the dance floor and antler chandeliers provide a mellow glow, but the woodsy decor is modern, stylish, and hip, not overdone. The cool curved bar in the center is faced to resemble river stones, as are pillars inside and out. There's table seating, couches, and around the firepit, roomy armchairs (put your feet on the surround but not your food, as the sign reminds!). Order at the counter: your meal or snack is delivered to your table, bar seat, lane, or game spot. The pub fare is delish (try the chipotle sweet potato fries), and food is served until close. ✉ *2809 Main St., Rangeley* ☎ *207/864–9955* 🌐 *www.moosealley.me* ⏲ *Closed Wed.*

★ Outdoor Heritage Museum

HISTORY MUSEUM | FAMILY | Spruce railings and siding on the museum's facade replicate a local taxidermy shop from about 1900. Inside, there's an authentic log sporting camp from the same period, when grand hotels and full-service sporting lodges drew well-to-do rusticators to Rangeley for long stays. One of the big draws is the exhibit on local flytier Carrie Stevens, whose famed streamer flies increased the region's fly-fishing fame in the 1920s. The many diverse exhibits include displays on U.S. presidents Dwight D. Eisenhower and Herbert Hoover fishing in Rangeley; vintage watercraft; Native American birch-bark canoes and artifacts; art of the region; and gleaming fish mounts of world-record-size brook trout. With free exhibits out front, this is a popular stop even when closed—don't miss the 12,000-year-old Native American meat cache. ✉ *8 Rumford Rd., Oquossoc* ☎ *207/864–3091* 🌐 *www.outdoorheritagemuseum.org* 🎟 *$8* ⏲ *Closed Nov.–Apr., closed Mon. May.–Oct. and also Tues. May, June, Sept., and Oct.*

Rangeley Lake State Park

STATE/PROVINCIAL PARK | FAMILY | On the south shore of Rangeley Lake, this 869-acre park has superb lakeside scenery, swimming, picnic tables, a playground, a boat ramp, a few short trails, and a campground. In the off-season, visitors can park outside the gate and walk-in. ✉ *1 State Park Rd., Rangeley* ✥ *Turn on S. Shore Rd. from Rte. 17 or Rte. 4* ☎ *207/864–3858 May–mid-Oct. only, 207/624–6080 regional state parks office (off-season contact)* 🌐 *www.maine.gov/rangeleylake* 🎫 *Nonresident $6, Maine resident $4* ⏲ *Closed Oct.–Apr.*

Wilhelm Reich Museum

SCIENCE MUSEUM | FAMILY | The museum showcases the life and work of Austrian physician, scientist, and writer Wilhelm Reich (1897–1957), who believed that all living matter and the atmosphere contain a force called orgone energy. The hilltop Orgone Energy Observatory exhibits biographical materials, inventions, and equipment used in his experiments, whose results were disputed by the Food and Drug Administration and other government agencies. Stone faces the exterior of the boxy 1949 structure, which is listed on the National Register of Historic Places. A mid-century gem inside and out, Reich's second-floor study, library, and laboratory look as they did in his day, with original sleek modern furniture. The observatory deck has magnificent countryside views. In July and August, the museum presents engaging nature programs; trails lace the largely forested 175-acre property, known as Orgonon, which has a waterside vacation rental cottage. Reich's tomb sits next to one of his inventions, a cloud accumulator. ✉ *19 Orgonon Cir., off Rte. 4, Rangeley* ☎ *207/864–3443* 🌐 *wilhelmreichmuseum.org* 🎫 *Museum $10, grounds free* ⏲ *Museum closed Oct.–June, Sun.–Tues. in July and Aug. and Sun.–Fri. in Sept. Private tours May–Oct. by appt.*

Restaurants

Loon Lodge

$$$ | AMERICAN | Built as a summer home, this rustically elegant 1909 log lodge alongside Rangeley Lake on Rangeley village's outskirts has been a restaurant and inn for much of its life; lovely lake views float beyond midcentury picture windows in dining spaces that were part of a porch. Locally sourced seasonal fine dining thrives with updated classics such as Moroccan-spiced rack of lamb with English mint and Indian curry spices, ginger-crusted tuna with Asian slaw, and desserts like skillet du jour. **Known for:** six original guestrooms with gleaming wood walls on the second floor, two modern ones on the lower level, and four in a separate building; the restaurant menu is available at Pickford Pub, where folks grab a drink while waiting for a table in the dining rooms, often heading down to the lakefront lawn or the dock below that; specials are big on less pricey comfort foods, as is the winter menu. 💲 *Average main: $35* ✉ *16 Pickford Rd., Rangeley* ☎ *207/864–5666* 🌐 *www.loonlodgeme.com* ⏲ *No lunch. Closed late Oct.–late Nov. and Mon. late Nov.–late Oct., also Tues. early April–mid-May (inn open year-round).*

Coffee and Quick Bites

Pine Tree Frosty

$ | FAST FOOD | FAMILY | A summertime visit to Rangeley isn't complete without a stop at this cash-only snack bar—in business since 1964—for ice cream and simple meals like burgers and fries. Both hard and soft ice cream are served, as are sundaes, milk shakes, flurries, and banana splits. **Known for:** Maine-made Gifford's hard ice cream; lobster rolls; waterside Adirondack chairs and picnic tables. 💲 *Average main: $7* ✉ *2459 Main St., Rangeley* 🌐 *facebook.com/pinetreefrosty* 💳 *No credit cards* ⏲ *Closed early Sept.–late May.*

Hotels

The Rangeley Inn

$ | HOTEL | FAMILY | Painted eggshell blue, this historic downtown hotel was built around 1900 for wealthy urbanites on vacation—from the wide covered front porch, you step into a grand lobby with polished pine wainscoting, statement oversized cushioned red chairs, and a brick fireplace. **Pros:** warms the dinner-only tavern in winter, and the elegant original dining room is a breakfast-only restaurant; on Hayley Pond, paddle a courtesy canoe or kayak or take a guided kayak photography trip (fee); nice variety of suites (largest sleeps six). **Cons:** no elevator; not on Rangeley Lake; a couple minutes walk from lodge to main inn. *Rooms from: $195 ✉ 2443 Main St., Rangeley ☎ 207/864–3341 🌐 www.therangeleyinn.com ⏲ Closed mid-Nov.–early Dec. and mid-April–mid-May 42 rooms No Meals.*

Activities

Rangeley and Mooselookmeguntic lakes are good for canoeing, kayaking, sailing, fishing, and motorboating. For paddlers, options abound whether you're a novice or an expert. Lake fishing for landlocked salmon and the region's famed brook trout is at its best in May, June, and September. The area's rivers and streams are especially popular with fly-fishers, who enjoy the sport May–October. Ice fishing shacks dot Rangeley Lake come winter.

Saddleback Mountain ski resort and Rangeley Lakes Trails Center offer mountain biking; trails are groomed in winter for fat-tire biking as well as cross-country skiing and snowshoeing.

GOLF

Mingo Springs Golf Course

GOLF | FAMILY | This popular course is known for its mountain and water views. The course is short but challenging, with very angled drives. The front nine holes are the hilliest; the back nine holes the longest. You can also take in the views and spot wildlife on the Mingo Springs Trail & Bird Walk, an easy 3-mile loop trail through the woods along the course. *✉ 43 Country Club Rd., Rangeley ☎ 207/864–5021 🌐 www.mingosprings.com $23 for 9 holes, $34 for 18 holes 18 holes, 6024 yards, par 71.*

HIKING

Hiking options in the Rangeley Lakes region include 39 miles of trails and access roads on Rangeley Lakes Heritage Trust's 16,250 acres of conserved lands, which also welcome many other types of outdoor recreation. Trail maps and information are available at the organization's website (🌐 www.rlht.org) and its downtown Rangeley office (✉ 2424 Main Street).

MULTISPORT OUTFITTERS

Ecopelagicon Rangeley Adventure Co.

KAYAKING | FAMILY | Off Main Street on Hayley Pond, this outfitter and retailer has an easy, affordable way to get you on the water: rent a kayak, canoe, standup paddleboard, or paddle boat by the hour ($10–$18) and head out back to the pond. Or rent one (paddle boats excepted) for a half-, full-, or multiday trip and paddle where you please; shuttle service is offered to locales on the Northern Forest Canoe Trail and the Appalachian Trail. Come winter you can rent snowshoes ($15 adults, $10 kids). In business since 1993, this welcoming "nature store" sells outdoor recreation gear galore, books and guides, and a slew of gifts, many Maine-themed. Shoppers linger at the back window to gaze at Saddleback Mountain and ducks and loons on the pond. *✉ 7 Pond St., Rangeley ☎ 207/864–2771 🌐 www.rangeleyadventureco.com.*

★ **River's Edge Sports**

BOATING | FAMILY | Hugging Route 4 in Oquossoc and resembling a sporting lodge, this is a convenient stop for gear galore and great way to get out on the water. Rent a kayak, canoe, or standup paddleboard for the day or week. If you'd like you can put in at the dock out back on Rangeley Lake, near the outflow into Rangeley River. This outfitter will also deliver, and pick up, your rental craft (fee). River's Edge sells Maine fishing licenses, and owner Gerry White, a Registered Maine Guide, leads fishing trips on Rangeley and Mooselookmeguntic lakes. Other guided trips are offered, too. Along with camping, fishing, hunting, and hiking gear, the 8,000-some-item store stocks souvenirs, apparel—from jackets to Rangeley and Oqussoc hoodies and tees—and gifts, many Maine-made. Don't miss the bins of colorful flies for fishing and the mounted wildlife: the "indoor zoo" has salmon, bobcats, bears, moose, and more. River's Edge's website has detailed information to help you enjoy the great outdoors in Rangeley. Gerry and his wife, Sally, happily share tips in person, too. ✉ *38 Carry Rd. (Rte. 4), Rangeley* ☎ *207/864–5582* 🌐 *www.riversedgesports.com* 🎫 *Rentals from $30.*

SEAPLANES

★ Acadian Seaplanes

AIR EXCURSIONS | In addition to 15-, 30- and 75-minute scenic flights high above the mountains by seaplane, this operator offers enticing "fly-in" excursions: travel by seaplane to wilderness locales to dine at a sporting camp or go white-water rafting on the remote Rapid River. The 1¼-hour "Mountain Explorer" scenic flight splash lands on a remote pond. Yes, seaplane passengers spot moose from the air. Acadian also provides charter service, including between the Rangeley area and Boston, New York, Portland, Bangor, and other places in Maine. ✉ *2640 Main St., Rangeley* ☎ *207/864–5307* 🌐 *www.acadianseaplanes.com* 🎫 *From $99.*

SKIING

Rangeley Lakes Trails Center

LOCAL SPORTS | **FAMILY** | A largely wooded, 34-mile trail network stretches along lower Saddleback Mountain and leads to Saddleback Lake. In winter, trails are groomed (double- and single-track) for cross-country skiing, back country skiing, snowshoeing, and fat-tire biking. A yurt lodge has ski, snowshoe, and fat-tire rentals and a snack bar known for tasty soups. Call ahead for ski, snowshoe, and fat-tire tours and cross-country lessons. In warmer weather, the trails are popular with mountain bikers, hikers, and runners. ✉ *524 Saddleback Mountain Rd., Dallas* ☎ *207/864–4309 winter only* 🌐 *www.rangeleylakestrailscenter.org* 🎫 *From $12.*

Saddleback Mountain

SKIING & SNOWBOARDING | **FAMILY** | Maine's third largest ski area has a high-speed quad lift, and the beginner ski area is one of New England's best, partly because it is below the base lodge. At the other end of the spectrum, it's black diamonds only all the way down at Kennebago Steeps!, touted as the East's largest steep-skiing area. Saddleback also has extensive glade areas, two terrain parks, and lots of natural snow. A fieldstone fireplace keeps things warm in the post-and-beam base lodge, which has a cafe and an upper-level pub (open most of the year) where diners savor mountain views with a hand-tossed pizza or smash burger. Or grab a bite between runs in the mid-mountain lodge (to open in early 2023). On-mountain lodging choices include ski-in, ski-out homes and trailside condos. Come summer the resort offers hiking and mountain biking, including rentals (lift-served mountain biking is to start in 2023), and guided kayak, canoe, standup paddleboard, and birding trips. **Facilities:** 68 trails; 600 acres; 2,000-foot vertical drop; 6 lifts. ✉ *976 Saddleback Mountain Rd., Dallas* ☎ *207/864–5671, 866/918–2225* 🌐 *www.saddlebackmaine.com.*

SNOWMOBILING

More than 100 miles of maintained trails link lakes and towns to wilderness camps in the Rangeley area.

Rangeley Snowmobile Rentals

SNOW SPORTS | Rangeley is one of Maine's top snowmobiling destinations, but you don't need to bring a sled: you can rent one here (one seat or two) for two hours, half a day, or a full day. ✉ *11 Swains Rd., Rangeley* ☎ *207/491–6625* 🌐 *www.rangeleysnowmobiles.com.*

Kingfield

38 miles east of Rangeley.

Dotted with white clapboard churches, and in the shadows of Mt. Abraham ("Mt. Abram" to locals) and Sugarloaf Mountain, home to the eponymous ski resort, Kingfield is "real" New England. The pretty Carrabassett River slices the village and flows over a dam downtown, creating a great swimming spot below the Route 16 bridge. Small pullouts mark swimming holes along Route 27 as it flows north along the rock-strewn river through Carrabassett Valley (also the name of the neighboring town) to the resort. On the other side of the waterway, the 6.6.-mile Narrow Gauge Pathway rail-trail wends through the narrow, steep-walled valley. The path was first cleared in the late 1800s for a narrower-than-standard railway that transported timber and tourists. Today it's part of an extensive and growing mountain biking network and one of many activities along the 47-mile State Route 27 Maine Scenic Byway from Kingfield to the remote Canadian border crossing at Coburn Gorge. Fantastic backcountry recreation awaits in the northern half of the drive around Eustis and Stratton. Near these small recreation hubs, the state's 36,000-acre Bigelow Preserve takes in the entire Bigelow Range and borders 20,000-acre Flagstaff Lake.

GETTING HERE AND AROUND

From Rangeley it's 37 miles to Kingfield, traveling south on Route 4 to Phillips, and from there, north on Route 142. Or head over from Rangeley on Route 16 via Stratton, where the road joins State Route 27 Maine Scenic Byway and continues south to Kingfield. This route is just 5 miles longer, and you can link the two for a scenic loop or fall foliage drive.

VISITOR INFORMATION

CONTACTS Franklin County Chamber of Commerce. ✉ *615 Wilton Rd., Farmington* ☎ *207/778–4215* 🌐 *www.franklincounty-maine.org.*

Sights

Stanley Museum

HISTORY MUSEUM | Original Stanley Steamer cars built by twin brothers Francis and Freelan Stanley—Kingfield's most famous natives—are the main draw at this museum inside a 1903 Georgian-style former school. Also well worth the stop here are exhibits about the glass-negative photography business the identical twins sold to Eastman Kodak, and the well-composed photographs, taken by their sister, Chansonetta Stanley Emmons, of everyday country life at the turn of the 20th century. ✉ *40 School St., Kingfield* ☎ *207/265–2729* 🌐 *www.stanleymuseum.org* 🎫 *$8* 🕒 *Closed Jan.–Feb., Sat.–Mon. Mar.–May and Nov. and Dec., and Mon. June–Oct.*

Coffee and Quick Bites

Orange Cat Cafe

$ | **AMERICAN** | **FAMILY** | Just past downtown en route to Sugarloaf, this café serves breakfast items (bagels with a choice of spreads, burrito and sandwich with or without meat), flavor-filled lunch fare (wraps, sandwiches, salads), and scrumptious baked goods; local and organic ingredients are kitchen staples, even the salsa is made right here, and the coffee is great. In a landmark

Federal-style former residence known as the "Brick Castle," it's presently drive-through only, but there's colorful seating on the large front lawn. **Known for:** turmeric-flavored coconut Golden Milk; Vegetarian's Revenge wrap with hummus; huge chocolate chip cookies. 💲 *Average main: $10* ✉ *329 Main St., Kingfield* ☎ *207/265–2860* 🌐 *www.orangecatcafe.com.*

Activities

BIKING

Carrabassett Valley and environs has emerged as a prime mountain biking destination, with Carrabassett Valley Trails offering a network of 80-plus miles of trails for all abilities. Signed, well-maintained trails link with the 6.6-mile Narrow Gauge Pathway (nonmotorized) aside the Carrabassett River. Several trailheads with kiosks are in the valley along or near Route 27. Come winter, some trails are groomed for cross-country skiing and fat-tire biking. Maps, trail conditions and closures, and suggested loops are available at the Carrabassett Region of the New England Mountain Bike Association website (www.carrabassettnemba.org). Area businesses distribute its large printed maps, and you can rent mountain bikes in-season and get maps and trail advice at a couple of valley spots. Freeman Ridge Bike Park south of Kingfield town center has single-track trails with berms, jumps, etc. (🌐 www.freemanridgebike.com; $12 day pass). North of Carrabassett Valley in the Eustis-Stratton area, mountain biking trails offer a rugged wilderness ride.

Allspeed Cyclery

BIKING | FAMILY | Portland-based Allspeed Cyclery rents mountain bikes from late May through early October at its satellite operation at Sugarloaf's Outdoor Center, where there is a trailhead. Adult rentals are $109 per day, and there are less expensive options for kids; the rate drops if you rent for multiple days. The locale is also a bike repair shop and sells items from tires and tubes to helmets and apparel, but not bikes. ✉ *3001 Outdoor Center Rd., Carrabassett Valley* ✣ *Off Route 27* ☎ *207/779–3951* 🌐 *www.allspeed.com.*

Carrabassett Valley Bike

BIKING | A local mountain biking enthusiast runs this rental, repair, and sales outfit from late spring through early fall at Happy Tunes! Ski Service Center, where he works come winter. Rentals are $50 for a full day and $35 half day. ✉ *1106 Valley Crossing, Carrabassett Valley* ✣ *Just off Rte. 27 next to Tufulio's Restaurant* ☎ *207/235–6019* 🌐 *www.facebook.com/CarrabassettValleyBike.*

SKIING

Sugarloaf

SKIING & SNOWBOARDING | FAMILY | An eye-catching setting, abundant natural snow, and the only above-the-tree-line lift-service skiing in the East have made Sugarloaf one of Maine's best-known ski resorts. Glade areas, six terrain parks—including a border-cross track—amp up the skiing options, as do ski bike rentals and ungroomed Sidecountry on Burnt Mountain and Brackett Basin. Snowshoers and uphill skiers (fee, regardless of what's on your feet) can attack this terrain as well as "the Loaf." Cat Skiing is offered on Burnt Mountain: hop a snowcat ride to the top and ski down (fee; slots fill fast). Along with hundreds of slope-side condos and rental homes with ski-in, ski-out access, the resort has two slope-side hotels: Sugarloaf Mountain Hotel is in the ski village, as are shops and restaurants; smaller, more affordable Sugarloaf Inn is a bit down the mountain. Just off Route 27 below the mountain, the Outdoor Center has an NHL-size ice rink; is the gateway to a 56-mile network of groomed trails for cross-country skiing, snowshoeing, and fat-tire biking; and rents equipment for all these activities.

■ TIP→ After skiing or other winter fun, unwind on-mountain at the Sports & Fitness

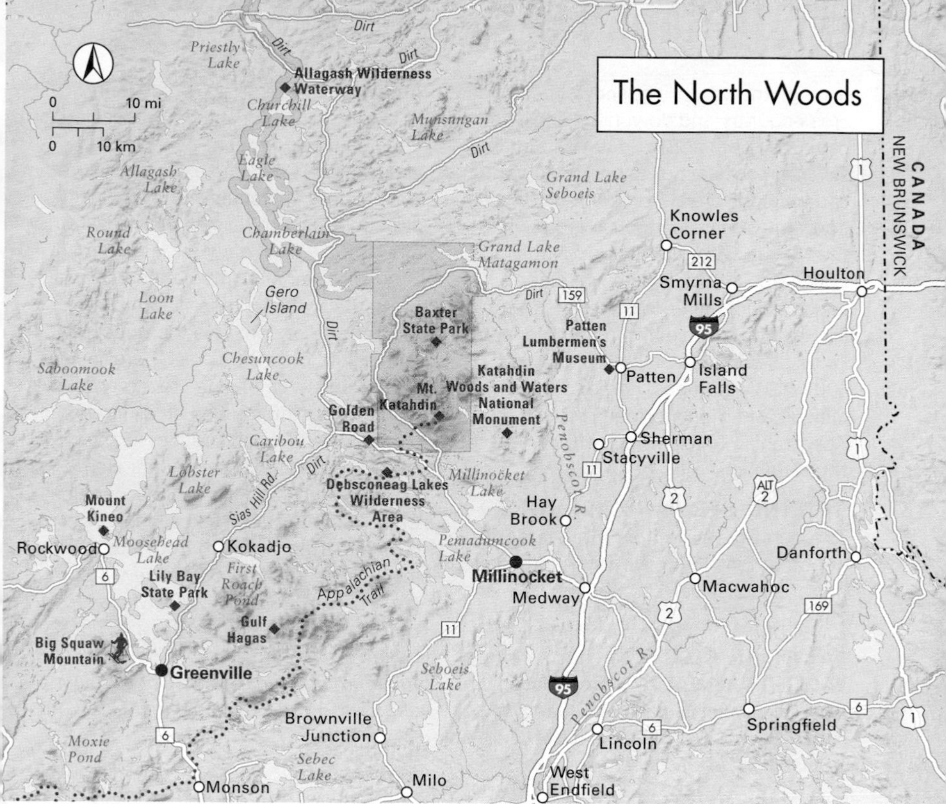

Center (fee), which includes a pool, sauna, hot tubs, steam rooms, and by-appointment massages (fee).

Once at Sugarloaf, you'll find a car unnecessary—a shuttle connects all operations during the season. In summer you can mountain bike, hike, or zipline; take a scenic lift ride or rent a Onewheel, kayak, or standup paddleboard; or play golf, either disc golf or a round on what many consider Maine's best golf course. Designed by Robert Trent Jones Jr., it's known for challenging elevation changes.

Facilities: 162 trails (includes glades); 1,240 acres; 2,820-foot vertical drop; 14 lifts. ✉ *5092 Sugarloaf Access Rd., Carrabassett Valley* ☎ *207/237–2000, 800/843–5623 for reservations* 🌐 *www.sugarloaf.com* 🎫 *Lift ticket: $129.*

Greenville

155 miles northeast of Portland, 70 miles northwest of Bangor.

Greenville, tucked at the southern end of island-dotted, mostly forest-lined Moosehead Lake, has the best selection of shops, restaurants, and inns in the North Woods region. In the mid-1800s, Henry David Thoreau departed from here on two of his three famous trips into Maine's wilderness, led by Penobscot guides Chief Joseph Attean and Joseph Polis. The region encompassing the lake—at 75,000 acres, Maine's largest and the largest entirely within New England—is an outdoors lover's paradise. In summer, boating, fishing, kayaking, canoeing, and hiking are popular on Moosehead Lake. Come winter, folks head to the Greenville area for ice fishing, snowmobiling, snowshoeing, and cross-country and downhill skiing—you can enjoy both at Big Squaw Mountain ski area northeast of town. Restaurants and lodgings are also clustered 20 miles north of Greenville in Rockwood, where the Moose River flows through the village and—across from Mt. Kineo's majestic cliff face—into the lake. There's also a gaggle in hip hiking hub Monson, 14 miles south of Greenville. Maine's 100 Mile Wilderness, home to the most difficult and most northerly stretch of the Appalachian Trail, stretches from here to Mt. Katahdin.

GETTING HERE AND AROUND

To reach Greenville from Interstate 95, get off at Exit 157 in Newport and head north, successively, on Routes 7, 23, and 15.

VACATION RENTALS

VACATION RENTALS Vacasa (Moosehead Lake Cabin Rentals). ✉ *Greenville* ☎ *207/695–4300, 855/861–5757* 🌐 *www.vacasa.com/usa/Moosehead-Lake.*

VISITOR INFORMATION

CONTACTS Destination Moosehead Lake. ✉ *480 Moosehead Lake Rd., Greenville* ☎ *207/695–2702* 🌐 *www.destinationmooseheadlake.com.*

Sights

The busy Moosehead Historical Society has several museums in Greenville. Two are in a former church in the small downtown and several more are about a mile east of there at the society's campus in the town's Greenville Junction section.

★ Moosehead Cultural Heritage Center and Moosehead Lake Aviation Museum

HISTORY MUSEUM | FAMILY | At East Cove in downtown Greenville, a former church houses two of five Moosehead Historical Society museums. The center exhibits Native American artifacts and items from the Moosehead Lake region dating from 9,000 BC. Displays about Native American residents spotlight Henry Perley, a guide and author who gained fame as a performer in Wild West shows and movies. Changing exhibits explore local history and culture. The adjoining aviation museum reveals the impact of aviation—from early bush pilots to Greenville's annual International Seaplane Fly-In the weekend after Labor Day—in this remote region. One room focuses on the Air Force B-52 crash here in 1963 that killed seven of nine crew members (you can get information on hiking to the debris-littered crash site, now a memorial). Outside, sculptures honor Henry David Thoreau and his Penobscot guides, Chief Joseph Attean and Joseph Polis, who departed with him from Greenville for Maine's wilds. ✉ *6 Lakeview St., Greenville* ☎ *207/695–2909 Moosehead Historical Society office* 🌐 *www.mooseheadhistory.org* 💵 *$3 (includes both museums)* 🕒 *Closed mid-Oct.–late June and Sun.–Wed. late June–mid-Oct.*

Gulf Hagas

NATURE SIGHT | Called the "Grand Canyon of the East" and part of the Appalachian Trail Corridor, this National Natural Landmark has chasms, cliffs, four major waterfalls, pools, exotic flora, and intriguing rock formations. The West Branch of the Pleasant River flows through the 3-mile, slate-walled gorge east of Greenville in a remote, privately owned commercial forest, KI Jo-Mary, which allows access via gravel logging roads (always yield to trucks). A fee (cash or check only) is charged from late spring to late fall at forest checkpoints, where you can get trail maps and hiking information.

From either parking area you can hike to one of the showcase falls and mostly avoid the difficult rim trail. A good choice for families with young children: start at Head of Gulf parking area for a 3½-mile round-trip hike to Stair Falls on the gorge's western end. From the Gulf Hagas parking area, it's a 3-mile round-trip hike to spectacular Screw Auger Falls on the gulf's eastern end. Gulf hikers who start from this parking area must ford the Pleasant River—usually easily done in summer, but dangerous in high water—and pass through the Hermitage, a stand of old pines and hemlock. A loop route that follows the rim and the less difficult Pleasant River Tote Trail is an 8- to 9-mile trek; there are shorter loops as well. Slippery rocks and rugged terrain make for challenging progress along the rim trail. ✉ *Greenville* ⊕ *From Greenville, travel 11 miles east via Pleasant St., which becomes Katahdin Iron Works Rd., to Hedgehog checkpoint. Follow signs to parking areas: Head of Gulf, 2½ miles; Gulf Hagas, 6½ miles* 🌐 *www.northmainewoods.org.*

Lily Bay State Park

STATE/PROVINCIAL PARK | FAMILY | Nine miles northeast of Greenville on Moosehead Lake, this 925-acre park has good lakefront swimming, a 2-mile walking trail with water views, two boat-launching ramps, a playground, and two campgrounds with a total of 90 sites. In winter, the entrance road is plowed to access the groomed cross-country ski trails and the lake for ice fishing and snowmobiling. ✉ *13 Myrle's Way, Greenville* ⊕ *Turn onto State Park Rd. from Lily Bay Rd.* ☎ *207/695–2700* 🌐 *www.maine.gov/lilybay* 🎫 *Nonresident $6, Maine resident $4.*

★ Moosehead Historical Society Museums

HISTORY MUSEUM | FAMILY | Anchoring the society's campus in Greenville Junction is the Eveleth-Crafts-Sheridan Historical House, a large 1890s home that's changed little since the last resident of a prominent Greenville family lived here. Each year there's a new changing exhibit within the period rooms. The original kitchen, state of the art back in the day, is a highlight of the guided tours; cooks will also savor the museum's collection of old utensils and kitchen items in a basement gallery. You can even check out the attic. In the home's carriage house the Moosehead Lumbermen's Museum has exhibits about the region's logging history. A highlight here is a 30-foot bateau used on log drives until the 1960s. Upstairs next to the society's office, a display about hotels on Mt. Kineo, where wealthy Americans flocked to vacation in the rusticator era, is a visitor favorite. In the barn, the Moosehead Outdoor Heritage Museum's covers subjects like Maine Warden Service flight rescues and wildlife—there are bobcat, moose, and caribou mounts. Outside is a sunken garden. ✉ *444 Pritham Ave., Greenville Junction* ☎ *207/695–2909* 🌐 *www.mooseheadhistory.org* 🎫 *$7.50 (includes guided tours of all three museums)* ⏲ *Closed mid-Oct.–late June and Sat.–Tues. late June–mid-Oct. (Lumbermen's Museum open year-round Tues.-Fri., $3 off-season).*

Mount Kineo

MOUNTAIN | FAMILY | Accessible primarily by steamship, Kineo House was a thriving upscale summer resort that sits below its namesake's 700-foot cliff on an islandlike, 1,200-acre peninsula jutting into Moosehead Lake. The last of three successive hotels with this name was built in 1884 and became America's largest inland waterfront hotel. It was torn down in 1938, but Kineo remains an outstanding day trip. Trails to the summit of the spectacular landmark, now part of Mount Kineo State Park, lead to a fire tower that rewards with a 360-degree sweep of Maine's largest lake and rugged mountains. Hikers scramble on the challenging Indian Trail, but it also has amazing views. All hikes begin on the Carriage Trail, a flat, shore-hugging remnant of the halcyon hotel days. You can play a round on the 9-hole Mount Kineo Golf Course, one of New England's oldest. There is no road access, but you can take a 15-minute boat trip to Mount Kineo from Rockwood on the golf course's seasonal shuttle (fee). Historic summer "cottages" line the greens near the small clubhouse, which has a snack bar and welcomes hikers. ✉ *Kineo Dock, Village Rd., Rockwood* ☎ *207/534–9012 for golf course and shuttle, 207/941–4014 for park regional office* 🌐 *www.maine.gov/mountkineo* 🎫 *Nonresident $4, Maine resident $3.*

Coffee and Quick Bites

Harris Drug Store and Dairy Bar

$ | **AMERICAN** | **FAMILY** | Inside this tidy, well-stocked downtown drug store you can twist on a red stool at the well-kept 1960s-era soda fountain while enjoying a sundae or scoop of ice cream. Hot and cold drinks are also served. **Known for:** soda fountain milk shakes served in traditional glasses; owned by the Harris family since 1896 (not the original locale); soft and hard serve at the seasonal Dairy Bar next door. $ *Average main: $5* ✉ *10 Pritham Ave., Greenville* ☎ *207/695–2921* 🌐 *facebook.com/harrisdrugstore* ⏲ *Dairy Bar closed mid-Sept.–mid-May.*

★ Appalachian Mountain Club Maine Wilderness Lodges

$$$ | **RESORT** | **FAMILY** | In Maine's 100-Mile Wilderness, the Appalachian Mountain Club's 100,000-plus acres includes three historic sporting-camp retreats, each with a woodsy main lodge with a fireplace, sitting area with games and books, and long tables where meals (included in rates) are served family-style. **Pros:** courtesy canoes (some on outlying ponds), kayaks, and standup paddleboards (no boards at Little Lyford); Little Lyford and Gorman Chairback are near Gulf Hagas; Medawisla has some self-service cabins (otherwise lodge rates include meals). **Cons:** winter access only by cross-country skiing, snowshoeing, hiking, or snowmobile transport (fee) at Little Lyford and Gorman Chairback, but gear is transported for you; no waterfront cabins at Little Lyford; no courtesy bikes. $ *Rooms from: $300* ✉ *North Woods outside Greenville, Greenville* ☎ *603/466–2727 reservations* 🌐 *www.outdoors.org/lodging/mainelodges* ⏲ *Gorman Chairback and Medawisla closed early March–late June and mid-Oct.–mid-Jan.; Little Lyford closed early March–mid-May and mid-Oct.–mid-Jan.* 🛏 *Gorman Chairback: 12 cabins, 1 bunkhouse (sleeps 10); Little Lyford: 10 cabins, 1 bunkhouse (sleeps 14); Medawisla, 9 cabins, 2 bunkhouses (each sleeps 16)* 🍴 *All-Inclusive.*

★ Blair Hill Inn & Restaurant

$$$$ | **B&B/INN** | Beautiful gardens, high stone walls, and a hilltop location with marvelous views over Moosehead Lake distinguish this 1891 country estate, one of New England's top inns, with spacious elegant rooms and baths (many have oversize tubs and showers) and a fine dining restaurant. **Pros:** free concierge plans outdoor excursions; two two-room suites nice for families; amenities range from snacks, hiking guides, and beach towels to a fitness center, hillside hot tub, and flat or bubbly artesian well water. **Cons:** when open, the dinner-only restaurant uses most of the inside common space; not on Moosehead Lake; no elevator to three third-floor guestrooms. $ *Rooms from: $529* ✉ *351 Lily Bay Rd., Greenville* ☎ *207/695–0224* 🌐 *www.blairhill.com* ⏲ *Closed Nov.–mid-Dec. and Apr.–mid-May* 🛏 *10 rooms* 🍴 *Free Breakfast.*

BOATING

Capt. Rogers Pontoon Rental

BOATING | Operated by a captain with decades of experience on local waters, the business rents swim ladder-equipped pontoon boats (8–13 passengers) for full-day excursions and overnight trips on 40-mile-long Moosehead Lake. The Rockwood business is on the Moose River just a mile from where it enters the lake across from Mount Kineo, Moosehead's famed landmark. Boat rentals start at $275 per day. You can also rent a tube (with rope for towing) for $35 per day. ✉ *9 Maynard Rd., Rockwood* ✣ *At Moose River Bridge* ☎ *207/233–3820* 🌐 *www.captrogerspontoonrental.com.*

MULTISPORT OUTFITTERS

Northwoods Outfitters

WATER SPORTS | You can rent canoes, kayaks, standup paddleboards, camping and fishing equipment, UTVs and ATVs, comfort and mountain bikes, snowmobiles, snowshoes, cross-country skis, and winter clothing here. Northwoods also guides a host of outdoor trips (some multiday), including open-water and ice fishing, waterfall hikes, photography, snowmobiling, and moose-watching (by land or water); operates a shuttle to remote areas; and offers recreation packages with area lodging establishments. At the base in downtown Greenville, you can pick up sporting goods, souvenirs, and clothing; get trail advice; and kick back in the Hard Drive Café. ✉ *5 Lily Bay Rd., Greenville* ☎ *207/695–3288, 866/223–1380* 🌐 *www.maineoutfitter.com.*

SKIING

Big Squaw Mountain

SKIING & SNOWBOARDING | **FAMILY** | A local nonprofit was formed in 2013 to reopen the lower portion of Big Moose Mountain (the resort uses Moose Mountain's old name) after it closed for a few years, and the ski area now operates Friday through Sunday, on holidays, and during school vacation weeks. The summit chairlift, unused since 2004, and the shuttered hotel loom trailside like something out of a Stephen King novel (he is a Mainer, remember), but the mostly intermediate trails on the lower mountain are plenty high enough to wow skiers with views up and down Moosehead Lake, Maine's largest. On a clear day, Mt. Katahdin, the state's highest peak, accents the mountainous horizon. The terrain, cheap prices, a surface lift for beginners, and the spacious, retro-fun chalet lodge draw families. The resort also has free trails for cross-country skiing, snowshoeing, and fat-tire biking. **Facilities:** 28 trails; 58 acres; 660-foot vertical drop; 2 lifts. ✉ *447 Ski Resort Rd., Greenville Junction* ☎ *207/695–2400* 🌐 *www.skibigsquaw.com* 🎫 *Lift ticket: $40.*

TOURS

Currier's Flying Service

AIR EXCURSIONS | You can take sightseeing flights, either a tour or a custom trip, in vintage seaplanes over the Moosehead Lake region from ice-out until mid-October. ✉ *447 Pritham Ave., Greenville Junction* ☎ *207/695–2778* 🌐 *www.curriersflyingservice.com* 🎫 *From $70.*

Katahdin Cruises & Moosehead Marine Museum

BOAT TOURS | The Moosehead Marine Museum runs 2-, 3- and 5-hour afternoon trips on Moosehead Lake aboard the *Katahdin,* a 115-foot 1914 steamship converted to diesel. Cruisers learn about the rich logging and tourism history of Maine's largest lake and environs on the narrated excursions. (The longer one skirts Mt. Kineo's cliffs.) Also called the *Kate,* this ship carried resort guests to Mt. Kineo until 1938; the logging industry then used it until 1975. The boat and the free shoreside museum have displays about the steamships that transported people and cargo on Moosehead Lake for a century starting in the 1830s. ✉ *12 Lily Bay Rd., Greenville* ☎ *207/695–2716* 🌐 *www.katahdincruises.com* 🎫 *From $40.*

Millinocket

67 miles north of Bangor, 88 miles northwest of Greenville.

Millinocket, a former paper-mill town with a population of about 4,000, is the gateway to "forever wild" Baxter State Park and a jumping-off point for Maine's North Woods. The town is the place to stock up on supplies, fill your gas tank, grab a meal, and nab a motel room (and hit the shower!) before heading into or upon returning from the wilderness. On the east side of Baxter, President Obama created the Katahdin Woods and Waters National Monument in 2016. Numerous rafting and canoeing outfitters and guides are based in the region. Katahdin Woods & Waters Scenic Byway, much of which flows along Route 11, links the region's conserved lands and scattered towns.

GETTING HERE AND AROUND

From Interstate 95, take Route 157 (Exit 244) west to Millinocket. From here follow signs to Baxter State Park (Millinocket Lake Road becomes Baxter Park State Road), 18 miles from town.

VISITOR INFORMATION

CONTACTS Katahdin Chamber of Commerce. ✉ *1029 Central St., Millinocket* ☎ *207/723–4443* 🌐 *www.katahdinmaine.com.*

Sights

Allagash Wilderness Waterway

BODY OF WATER | A spectacular 92-mile corridor of lakes, ponds, streams, and rivers, the waterway park cuts through vast commercial forests, beginning near the northwestern corner of Baxter State Park and running north to the town of Allagash, 10 miles from the Canadian border. From May to mid-October, the Allagash is prime canoeing and camping country. The Maine Bureau of Parks and Lands has campsites along the waterway, most not accessible by vehicle. The complete 92-mile course, part of the 740-mile Northern Forest Canoe Trail, which runs from New York to Maine, requires 7–10 days to canoe. Novices may want to hire a guide, as there are many areas with strong rapids. A good outfitter can help plan your route and provide equipment and transportation. ✉ *Millinocket* ☎ *207/941–4014 for regional parks bureau office* 🌐 *www.maine.gov/allagash.*

★ Baxter State Park

STATE/PROVINCIAL PARK | FAMILY | A gift from Governor Percival Baxter, this is the jewel in the crown of northern Maine: a 210,000-acre wilderness area that surrounds Mt. Katahdin, Maine's highest mountain and the terminus of the Appalachian Trail. Every year, the 5,267-foot Katahdin draws thousands of hikers to make the daylong summit, rewarding them with stunning views of forests, mountains, and lakes. There are three parking-lot trailheads for Katahdin. *If you're not an expert hiker, skip the hair-raising Knife Edge Trail.*

■ TIP→ Reserve a day-use parking space at the trailheads June 1–October 15.

The crowds climbing Katahdin can be formidable on clear summer days and fall weekends, so if it's solitude you crave, head for one of the many other park mountains accessible from the extensive trail network, including 11 peaks exceeding an elevation of 3,000 feet. The Brothers and Doubletop Mountain are challenging daylong hikes; the Owl takes about six hours; and South Turner can be climbed in a morning—its summit has a great view across the valley. A trek around Daicey Pond, or from the pond to Big and Little Niagara Falls, are good options for families with young kids. Another option if you only have a couple of hours is renting a canoe at Daicey or Togue Pond (bring cash for this honor system); many of the park's ponds, including some of the most remote ones, have rental canoes. Roads are unpaved, narrow, winding, and not plowed in winter; there are no pay phones, gas stations, or stores; and cell phone service is unreliable. Dogs are not allowed. Camping is primitive and reservations are required; there are 10 campgrounds plus backcountry sites.

■ TIP→ The park has a visitor center at its southern entrance, but you can get information and make parking and camping reservations at park headquarters in Millinocket

There are amazing views from the top of the 5,267-foot-tall Mt. Katahdin.

(64 Balsam Drive). ✉ *Baxter State Park Rd.* ⊕ *Togue Pond Gate (southern entrance) is 18 miles northwest of Millinocket; follow signs from Rte. 157. Matagamon Gate (northern entrance) is 27 miles west of Patten; follow signs from Rte. 159.* ☎ *207/723–5140* 🌐 *www.baxterstateparkauthority.com* 🎫 *$16 per vehicle; Maine residents free* ⏱ *Mt. Katahdin trails are closed and park access is limited in Nov. and Apr.–mid-May.*

Debsconeag Lakes Wilderness Area

NATURE PRESERVE | Bordering the south side of the Golden Road below Baxter State Park, the Nature Conservancy's 46,271-acre Debsconeag Lakes Wilderness Area is renowned for its rare ice cave, old forests, abundant pristine ponds, and views of Mt. Katahdin—they are mesmerizing along a challenging 5-mile circuit hike that includes the Rainbow Loop Trail. The access road for the Ice Cave Trail (2 miles round-trip) and Hurd Pond is 17 miles northwest of Millinocket, just west of the Golden Road's Abol Bridge. The kiosk at this entrance has information about the preserve, including a large map. Nearby the Appalachian Trail exits the conservancy land, crossing the bridge en route to Baxter. Hugging the curving, scenic West Branch of the Penobscot River and revealing Katahdin, the first few miles of the 5-mile dirt access road deserve a drive even if you aren't stopping to recreate. Before hiking, paddling, fishing, or camping in the remote preserve (no fees or reservations required), visit the conservancy's website for directions, maps, and other information. ✉ *Golden Rd., Millinocket* 🌐 *www.nature.org/maine.*

Golden Road

SCENIC DRIVE | Near Baxter State Park, a roughly 20-mile no-fee stretch of this private east–west logging road—named for the huge sum a paper company paid to build it, according to one story—offers access to Maine's wilderness without venturing too far in. Though paved, it's rutty and bumpy; yield (keep right!) to logging trucks. From Millinocket follow signs for Baxter State Park from

Route 157; eight miles from the railroad overpass at the edge of town there's a crossover from Millinocket Lake Road to the Golden Road. This is where the drive begins. North Woods Trading Post is here, across from Ambajejus Lake on the Millinocket Lake Road side of the crossover. Stop not just for gas, coffee, a bite, or to shop but to pick up the free handout highlighting stops along the drive, with mileage—you'll need it, since ponds for moose spotting aren't signed and hiking spots that are can be easy to miss. At the end of the drive, drive or walk across Ripogenus Dam, just off the Golden Road between Ripogenus lake and gorge. Below the dam is the best spot (marked on the handout) for watching white-water rafters.

■ **TIP→ Take photos of Baxter's Mt. Katahdin from the footbridge alongside Abol Bridge: this view is famous.** ✉ *Golden Rd., Millinocket.*

Katahdin Woods and Waters National Monument

NATIONAL PARK | Two rivers flow and streams and ponds abound at this 87,500-acre North Woods preserve, created east of Baxter State Park in 2016 and home to moose, bald eagles, salmon, and bobcats. There's no visitor center, but you can get information from late May to mid-October at the staffed welcome center in Patten at the Patten Lumbermen's Museum (61 Shin Pond Road). Access and park roads are gravel; sanitary facilities are limited; and there is no water, food, fuel, or reliable cell service. In the monument's southern portion, 17-mile Katahdin Loop Road has scenic views of Baxter's Mt. Katahdin and trailheads to short hikes and Barnard Mountain, a 4-mile round-trip that links with the International Appalachian Trail. There are mountain biking options as bike-designated routes link with the loop road (biking is allowed on park roads). In the northern section, visitors hike, mountain bike, cross-country ski (some groomed trails), and snowshoe along and near the waterfall-dotted East Branch of the Penobscot River. Folks paddle and fish on the river and other monument waters. ✉ *Patten* ✥ *Southern entrance: From Rte. 11 in Stacyville, head west on gravel Swift Brook Rd. (use caution when turning; it's about 12 miles to Katahdin Loop Dr.). Northern entrance: from Pattern turn on Rte. 159 (becomes Grand Lake Rd.); it's about 30 miles to entrance (take 2nd left after crossing the East Branch of the Penobscot River).* ☎ *207/456–6001* 🌐 *www.nps.gov/kaww.*

Patten Lumbermen's Museum

HISTORY MUSEUM | **FAMILY** | Two reproduction 1800s logging camps are among the 10 buildings filled with exhibits depicting the history of logging in Maine. They include sawmill and towboat models, dioramas of logging scenes, horse-drawn sleds, and a steam-powered log hauler. Exhibits also highlight local artists and history as well as logging-related topics. The museum is a welcome center for nearby Katahdin Woods and Waters National Monument. ✉ *61 Shin Pond Rd., Patten* ☎ *207/528–2650* 🌐 *www.lumbermensmuseum.org* 🎫 *$12* 🕒 *Closed mid-Oct.–mid-May; Mon.–Thurs. late May–June; and Mon. (except holidays) July–early Oct.*

Penobscot River Trails

TRAIL | **FAMILY** | A New York philanthropist was so taken with the Mt. Katahdin region he spurred creation of 16 miles of free public recreation trails along the East Branch of the Penobscot River, conveniently off Route 11. Opened in 2019, the "crusher dust" paths are akin to the famed carriage trails at coastal Maine's Acadia National Park. The trails are used for mountain biking and walking and, after the snow flies, groomed for cross-country skiing. Folks also snowshoe and fat-tire bike here in winter. You can chill after a workout or eat your lunch in the woodsy chic visitor center. Come winter, wood stoves heat up two warming huts—one offers an outstanding view of Mt. Katahdin—along the trails. Courtesy (donation requested) bikes, snowshoes, and cross-country skis are available, as are strollers. Paddlers head to the hand-carry boat launch. ✉ *2540 Grindstone Rd., Stacyville* 🌐 *www.penobscotrivertrails.org.*

Restaurants

River Drivers Restaurant

$$ | **AMERICAN** | **FAMILY** | At the deservedly popular restaurant at the New England Outdoor Center resort—serving lunch and dinner, and breakfast too in winter and summer—wood for the trim, wainscoting, bar, and floors was milled from old logs salvaged from local waters, and diners enjoy views of Mt. Katahdin from beyond rows of windows or the patio. Many dishes feature local ingredients; for dinner, entrees join offerings like sandwiches, tacos, and fish and chips. **Known for:** dining as Katahdin anchors the sunset across Millinocket Lake; crab cake appetizer with remoulade sauce; sister restaurant Knife Edge Brewing has a wood-fired pizzeria. $ *Average main: $21* ✉ *30 Twin Pines Rd., Millinocket* ✢ *7 miles from the railroad overpass at the edge of Millinocket, en route to Baxter State Park, turn right on Black Cat Road, drive approximately 1 mile, NEOC entrance on left* ☎ *207/723–8475* 🌐 *www.neoc.com.*

Coffee and Quick Bites

North Woods Trading Post

$ | **AMERICAN** | **FAMILY** | Yummy, freshly prepared to-go fare includes pizza, breakfast and regular sandwiches, and house-made baked goods at this cabin-style "last stop" for gear, supplies, and gas before Baxter State Park. Quality Maine-made gifts and souvenirs, Baxter and Mt. Katahdin art and attire, and Maine- and park-theme books are tastefully arrayed; gear basics, packaged wine and beer, and grocery essentials are also sold. **Known for:** provides area information, as do placards at rest area next door; co-owned by a former Baxter ranger; across from Ambajejus Lake at a crossover to the Golden Road. $ *Average main: $12* ✉ *1605 Baxter State Park Rd., Millinocket* ☎ *207/723–4326* 🌐 *www.northwoodstradingpostme.com* ⏲ *Closed late Oct.–early May.*

Hotels

Libby Camps

$$$$ | **RESORT** | **FAMILY** | Run by a fifth-generation Libby family member, this sporting camp on Millinocket Lake draws fishing and hunting enthusiasts as well as folks who want to unplug and relax in nature; well-kept log cabins have handmade quilts, wood stoves, gas lamps, modern baths, and coolers with lake-cut ice. **Pros:** courtesy kayaks, canoes, and motorboats and pistols for shooting skeet and sporting clays (lessons and ammunition, fee); fishing, hunting, and paddling guides, fly-casting equipment and lessons, and seaplane trips to remote ponds with stashed canoes and Baxter State Park (fees); dreamy hiking trail from camp edges Millinocket Lake en route to a wooden dam. **Cons:** 20 miles on private gravel roads into camp; 4x4 vehicle recommended if driving to fishing and hiking locales beyond camp; Wi-Fi only in the lodge (though for most guests that's a pro). $ *Rooms from: $600* ✉ *Millinocket* ✢ *Off Oxbow Rd. (private logging road, fee) on Millinocket Lake (Maine has two) north of Baxter State Park* ☎ *207/435–8274* 🌐 *www.libbycamps.com* ⏲ *Closed late Nov.–mid-Jan. and mid-Mar.–mid-May* 🛏 *9 cabins* 🍽 *All-Inclusive.*

★ New England Outdoor Center

$$$ | **RESORT** | **FAMILY** | Just 8 miles from Baxter State Park, Mt. Katahdin rises across Millinocket Lake from this 1,400-acre four-season great outdoors resort, with older renovated log cabins—and a

few newer ones— scattered beneath tall pines on a grassy nub of land jutting into Millinocket Lake. **Pros:** kayaks and canoes to use on the lake; resort trails for cross-country skiing, snowshoeing, mountain and fat-tire biking, and hiking link with nearby trails; two restaurants: River Drivers, with a wonderful Katahdin view, and more casual Knife Edge Brewing. **Cons:** no or limited water views from newer cabins near the cove; no lodge with common space for relaxing; only six smaller cabins (sleep four–six). *Rooms from: $300* ✉ *30 Twin Pines Rd., Millinocket* ✣ *7 miles from the railroad overpass at the edge of Millinocket, en route to Baxter State Park, turn right on Black Cat Road, drive approximately 1 mile, NEOC entrance on left* ☎ *800/766–7238, 207/723–5438* 🌐 *www.neoc.com.*

MULTISPORT OUTFITTERS

Katahdin Outfitters

BOATING | This company provides trip planning, gear, and shuttles for overnight canoe and kayak expeditions on the Allagash River, the West Branch of the Penobscot River, and the St. John River. ✉ *360 Bates St., Millinocket* ☎ *207/723–5700* 🌐 *www.katahdinoutfitters.com* *Call for prices.*

★ New England Outdoor Center (*NEOC*)

ADVENTURE TOURS | **FAMILY** | A major player in North Woods tourism and conveniently located between Millinocket and Baxter State Park, NEOC offers a full slate of guided excursions: fishing, hiking, canoeing, and kayaking; white-water rafting on the West Branch of the Penobscot River; photography, moose- and wildlife-spotting; and snowmobiling and ice fishing. It also rents canoes, kayaks, standup paddleboards, snowmobiles (attire, too), fat-tire bikes, cross-country skis, and snowshoes and offers cross-country skiing and paddling lessons. The onsite Knife Edge Brewing (open daily for lunch and dinner and breakfast too in winter and summer), has wood-fired pizzas, salads, and sandwiches, along with house and other craft brews. Nonguests can use showers (fee) after hiking or camping at Baxter. ✉ *30 Twin Pines Rd., Millinocket* ✣ *6.3 miles from railroad overpass at the edge of Millinocket en route to Baxter State Park, turn right on Katahdin View Drive (across from Duck Cove Road) and drive about a mile.* ☎ *207/723–5438, 800/766–7238* 🌐 *www.neoc.com.*

SEAPLANES

Katahdin Air Service

AIR EXCURSIONS | In addition to operating ½- and 1-hour scenic flights over the Katahdin area, this seaplane operator offers fly-in excursions to backcountry locales to picnic at a pond beach, dine at a sporting camp, or moose-watch and bask in nature. Or take a one-way trip to a remote spot to begin a hiking or canoe trip. Katahdin Air also provides charter service, including to and from Maine airports and the region's small towns and remote locales and sporting camps. ✉ *1888 Golden Rd., Millinocket* ☎ *207/723–8378* 🌐 *www.katahdinair.com* *From $135.*

WHITE-WATER RAFTING

North Country Rivers

WHITE-WATER RAFTING | North Country Rivers's base for white-water rafting trips on the West Branch of the Penobscot River is at Big Moose Inn, Cabins & Campground, on Millinocket Lake south of Baxter State Park. The businesses team up on lodging packages. (In Western Maine, the outfitter runs white-water rafting trips on the Dead and Kennebec rivers in The Forks and has a resort south of there in Bingham.) ✉ *102A Baxter State Park Rd., Millinocket* ☎ *800/348–8871* 🌐 *www.northcountryrivers.com.*

Chapter 12

THE MAINE COAST

Updated by
Alexandra Hall, Annie Quigley,
Christine Burns Rudalevige,
Mary Ruoff, Mimi Steadman

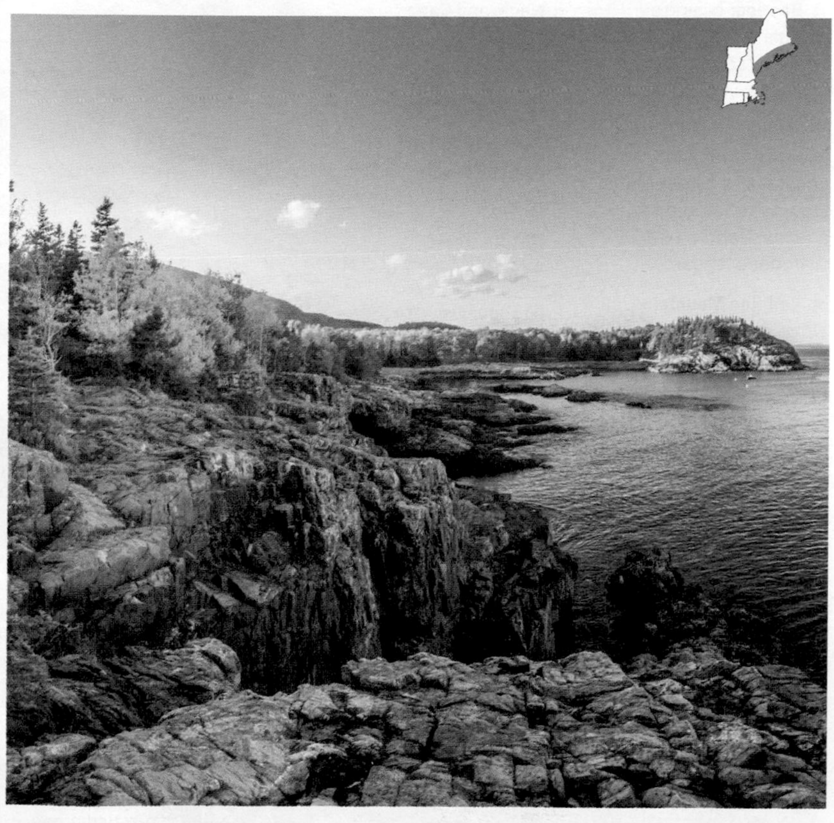

Sights	Restaurants	Hotels	Shopping	Nightlife
★★★★☆	★★★★☆	★★★★★	★★★☆☆	★★★☆☆

WELCOME TO THE MAINE COAST

TOP REASONS TO GO

★ **Lobster and Wild Maine Blueberries:** It's not a Maine vacation unless you don a bib and dig into a steamed lobster with drawn butter, and finish with a wild blueberry pie for dessert.

★ **Boating:** Maine's coastline was made for boaters, so make sure you get out on the water.

★ **Hiking the Bold Coast:** Miles of unspoiled coastal and forest paths Down East make for a hiker's (and a bird-watcher's) dream.

★ **Cadillac Mountain:** Drive a winding 3½ miles to the 1,530-foot summit in Acadia National Park for the sunrise.

★ **Dining in Portland:** With more than 250 restaurants and counting, Forest City is a foodie haven with one of the highest per capita restaurant densities in the United States.

1. **Kittery.**
2. **The Yorks and Cape Neddick.**
3. **Ogunquit.**
4. **Wells.**
5. **Kennebunk, Kennebunkport, and Cape Porpoise.**
6. **Biddeford.**
7. **Scarborough, Prout's Neck, and Cape Elizabeth.**
8. **Portland.**
9. **Casco Bay Islands.**
10. **Freeport.**
11. **Brunswick.**
12. **Bath.**
13. **Wiscasset.**
14. **Boothbay.**
15. **Damariscotta.**
16. **Monhegan Island.**
17. **Rockland.**
18. **Rockport.**
19. **Camden.**
20. **Belfast.**
21. **Bucksport.**
22. **Blue Hill.**
23. **Deer Isle.**
24. **Bar Harbor.**
25. **Bass Harbor.**
26. **Schoodic Peninsula.**
27. **Lubec.**
28. **Campobello Island, Canada.**
29. **Eastport.**

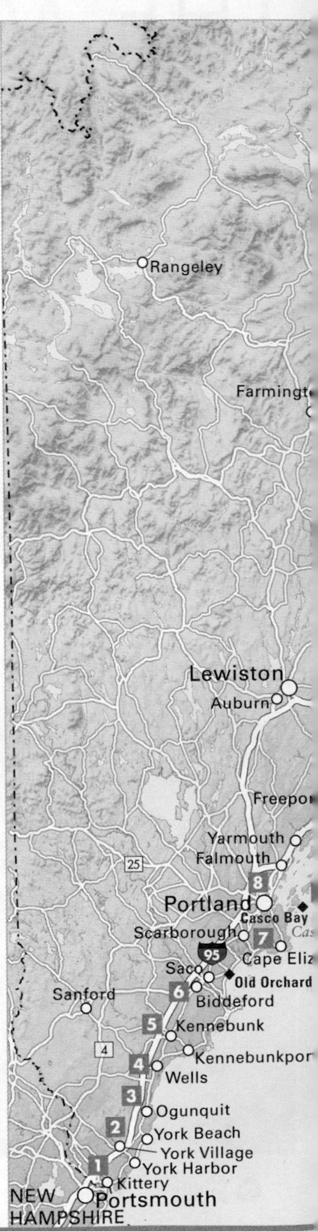

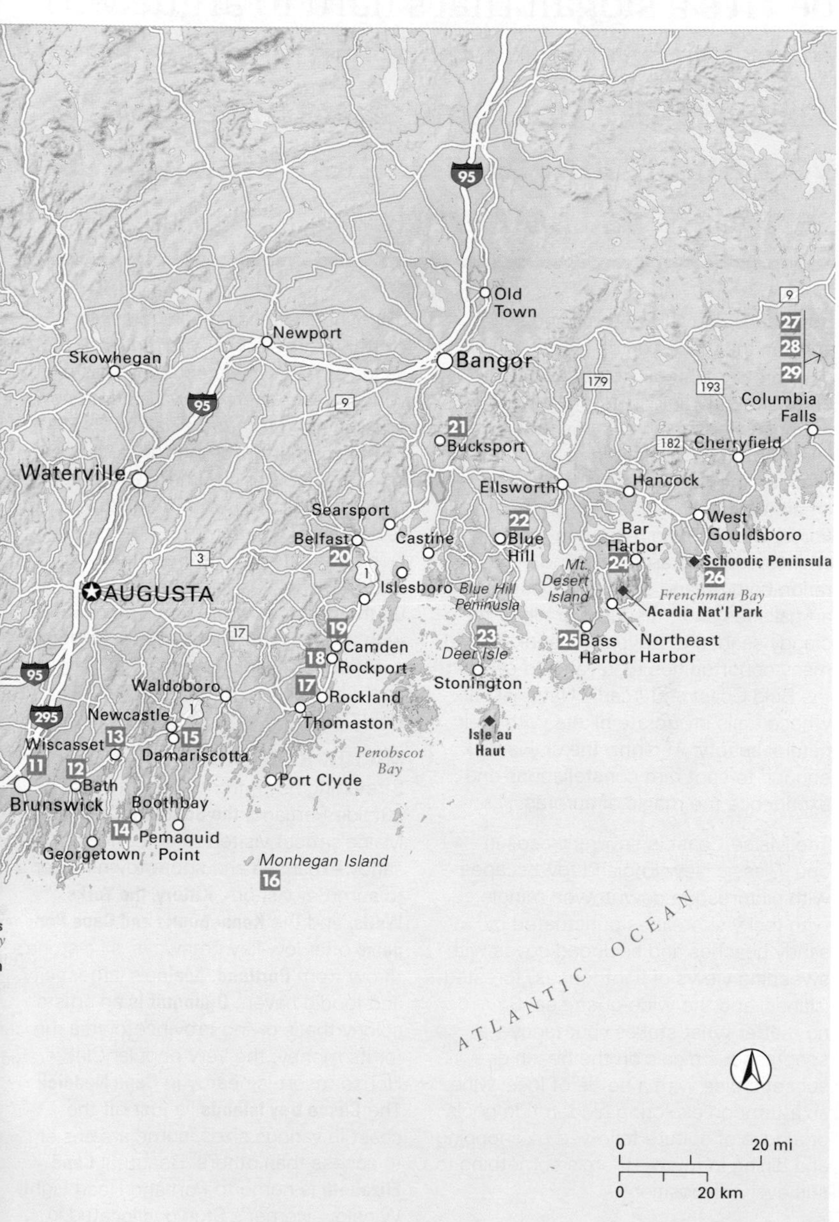

Old Town
Bangor
Newport
Skowhegan
Waterville
AUGUSTA
Bucksport
Ellsworth
Hancock
Columbia Falls
Cherryfield
West Gouldsboro
Bar Harbor
Schoodic Peninsula
Frenchman Bay
Acadia Nat'l Park
Mt. Desert Island
Northeast Harbor
Bass Harbor
Searsport
Belfast
Castine
Blue Hill
Islesboro
Blue Hill Peninsula
Deer Isle
Stonington
Isle au Haut
Camden
Rockport
Rockland
Thomaston
Penobscot Bay
Port Clyde
Waldoboro
Newcastle
Damariscotta
Wiscasset
Bath
Brunswick
Boothbay
Pemaquid Point
Georgetown
Monhegan Island
ATLANTIC OCEAN
0
20 mi
0
20 km

As you drive across the border into Maine, a sign reads, "The way life should be." It's a slogan that's hard to argue with once you've spent some time in the Pine Tree State. Here, time stays in step with you, and Mainers take their play just as seriously as their work.

Romantics thrill at the wind and salt spray in their faces on a historic windjammer. Birders fill their notebooks to the brim with new field notes. Families love the unspoiled beaches and sheltered inlets dotting the shoreline—not to mention the numerous homemade-ice-cream stands. Foodies revel in greater Portland's booming restaurant scene, while artists and art lovers find inspiration both on and off the canvas amid art galleries and museums or along the craggy seaboard. Adventure-seekers find many opportunities to kayak and cycle at the Bold Coast and Acadia National Park, whose trails invigorate hikers with their natural beauty. At night, the sky is dark enough to spot rare constellations and experience the magic of auroras.

The Maine Coast is several places in one. Classic New England townscapes with picturesque downtowns mingle with rocky shorelines punctuated by sandy beaches and secluded coves with sweeping views of lighthouses, forested islands, and the wide-open sea. So, no matter what strikes your fancy—a spontaneous picnic on the beach or a sunset cruise with a bottle of local wine, an afternoon exploring hidden tide pools or a dose of culture followed by shopping and dining in town—there's something to suit every disposition.

Counting all its nooks, crannies, and crags, Maine's coast would stretch thousands of miles if you could pull it straight, which means there's always some new, undiscovered territory awaiting you. Stretching north from Kittery to just outside Portland, the Southern Coast is the most popular area, with many top-notch restaurants, museums, and wineries. Don't let that stop you from heading farther Down East (Maine-speak for "way up the coast"), where you'll be rewarded with the majestic mountains and rugged coastline of Acadia National Park, as well as the unspoiled, dramatic scenery of the Bold Coast.

MAJOR REGIONS

Stretching north from Kittery to just outside Portland, **the Southern Coast** is Maine's most visited region; miles of sandy expanses and shore towns cater to summer visitors. **Kittery, the Yorks, Wells,** and the **Kennebunks and Cape Porpoise** offer low-key getaways, all a stone's throw from **Portland**, Maine's largest city and foodie haven. **Ogunquit** is an artists' colony that's giving Provincetown a run for its money; the very popular Cliff House resort is nearby in **Cape Neddick**. The **Casco Bay Islands** lie just off the coast in various sizes, some are easier to access than others. Beautiful **Cape Elizabeth** is home to Portland Head Light; Winslow Homer's Studio is located in nearby **Scarborough,** which is also home to the tiny hamlet of **Prout's Neck**.

North of Portland, **the Mid-Coast Region** has a craggy coastline that winds its way around pastoral peninsulas. Its villages boast maritime museums, innovative restaurants, antique shops, and beautiful architecture. **Freeport** is home to the headquarters of L.L. Bean and a lovely harbor. **Brunswick**, while a bigger, more commercial city, has rows of historic brick and clapboard homes and is home to Bowdoin College. **Bath** is known for its maritime heritage. On the **Wiscasset** waterfront, you can choose from a variety of seafood shacks competing for the best lobster rolls. **Damariscotta**, too, is worth a stop for its good seafood restaurants, and you'd be hard-pressed to find better-tasting oysters than those from the Damariscotta River. **Boothbay** is one of the Mid-Coast's quaintest towns, and it's where you'll find the Coastal Maine Botanical Gardens. It's also one of three towns from which you can take a ferry to **Monhegan Island**, which seems to be inhabited exclusively by painters at their easels, intent on capturing the windswept cliffs and weathered homes with colorful gardens. **Pemaquid Point** sits at the tip of the Pemaquid Peninsula, while the sleepy town of **Port Clyde** and neighboring **Tenants Harbor** sit on the St. George Peninsula.

Penobscot Bay covers an estimated 1,070 square miles and is home to more than 1,800 islands. Its dramatic natural scenery highlights its picture-perfect coastal towns, which include **Belfast, Rockport,** and **Camden**. **Rockland** gets lots of attention thanks to a trio of attractions: the renowned Farnsworth Art Museum, the popular summer Lobster Festival, and the lively North Atlantic Blues Festival. **Bucksport** has the stunning Penobscot Narrows Bridge and the Fort Knox historic site.

The large **Blue Hill Peninsula** juts south into Penobscot Bay. Painters, photographers, sculptors, and other artists are drawn to the peninsula; you can find more than 20 galleries on **Deer Isle** and at least half as many on the mainland. Not far from the mainland are the islands of Little Deer Isle and Deer Isle. **Blue Hill** and Castine are the area's primary business hubs. Isle Au Haut is only accessible by mail boat, but worth the effort.

Millions come to enjoy Acadia National Park and the region around it. **Ellsworth** is the gateway town for Mount Desert Island. **Bar Harbor** is fun to explore, with its many gift shops and restaurants, while **Bass Harbor** offers quieter retreats.

The "real Maine," as some call the region known as **Down East,** unfurls in thousands of acres of wild blueberry barrens, congestion-free coastlines, vast wilderness preserves, and a tangible sense of rugged endurance. The landscape of **Schoodic Peninsula's** craggy coastline, towering evergreens, and views over Frenchman Bay are breathtaking year-round. Towns on the peninsula include Grindstone Neck, Winter Harbor, and Gouldsboro; the peninsula's southern tip is home to the Schoodic section of Acadia National Park. **Lubec** is a frequent destination for outdoor enthusiasts; a popular excursion is New Brunswick's **Campobello Island**, which has the Roosevelt Campobello International Park. **Eastport** is connected to the mainland by a granite causeway; it was once one of the nation's busiest seaports.

Planning

You could easily spend a lifetime's worth of vacations along the Maine Coast and never truly see it all. But if you are determined to travel the coast end-to-end, allot at least two weeks at a comfortable pace. Count on longer transit time getting from place to place in summer, as traffic along U.S. 1 can be agonizing in high season, especially in the areas around Wiscasset and Acadia National Park.

Getting Here and Around

AIR

Maine has two international airports, Portland International Jetport and Bangor International Airport, near the coast. Manchester–Boston Regional Airport in New Hampshire is about 45 minutes away from the southern end of the Maine coastline. Boston's Logan Airport is the only major international airport in the region; it's about 90 minutes south of the Maine's border with New Hampshire.

BUS

The seasonal Shoreline Explorer trolleys link southern Maine's beach towns from the Yorks to the Kennebunks, allowing travel in this region without a car.

Concord Coach Lines has express service between Portland and Boston's Logan Airport and South Station. Concord operates out of the Portland Transportation Center (⊠ *100 Thompson's Point Road*).

CONTACTS Shoreline Explorer. 🌐 *www.shorelineexplorer.com/*.

CAR

Once you're here, the best way to experience the craggy Maine Coast, with its scenic and winding country roads, is in a car. There are miles and miles of roads far from the larger towns that have no bus service, and you won't want to miss the chance to discover your own favorite ocean vista while on a scenic drive. From the New Hampshire border through Portland to Brunswick, you can greatly cut down on travel time by following the dull but efficient interstates, I–95 and I–295; note that from York to Augusta, I–95 is a toll road.

TRAIN

Amtrak offers regional service from Boston to Portland via its *Downeaster* line, which originates at Boston's North Station and makes six stops in Maine: Wells, Saco, Old Orchard Beach (seasonal), Portland, Freeport, and Brunswick.

When to Go

Maine's dramatic coastline and pure natural beauty welcome visitors year-round, but note that many smaller museums and attractions are open only in high season (Memorial Day–mid-October), as are many waterside attractions and eateries.

Summer begins in earnest on July 4, and you'll find that many smaller inns, bed-and-breakfasts, and hotels from Kittery on up to Bar Harbor are booked a month or two in advance for dates through August. That's also the case come fall, when the fiery foliage draws leaf peepers. After Halloween, hotel rates drop significantly until ski season begins around Thanksgiving. B&Bs that stay open year-round but are not near ski slopes will often rent rooms at far lower prices than in summer.

In spring, the fourth Sunday in March is designated as Maine Maple Sunday, and farms throughout the state open their doors to visitors not only to watch sap turn into golden syrup but to sample the sweet results.

Activities

No visit to the Maine Coast is complete without some outdoor activity—on two wheels, two feet, holding two paddles, or pulling a bag full of clubs.

If your adventures find you swimming in the ocean or floating close to its surface on a kayak, be on the lookout for sharks. Their populations have rebounded in recent years following conservation and regulatory efforts. In the summer of 2020, off Bailey

Driving in Coastal Maine

	Miles	Time
Boston–Portland	112	2 hours
Kittery–Portland	50	50 minutes
Portland–Freeport	18	20 minutes
Portland–Camden	80	2 hours
Portland–Bar Harbor	175	3 hours 20 minutes

Island, a swimming woman was killed by a great white shark in Maine's first recorded shark fatality; authorities surmised her wet suit caused her to appear to be a seal, a favored prey of sharks.

BIKING

Both the Bicycle Coalition of Maine and Explore Maine by Bike are excellent resources for trail maps and other riding information.

CONTACTS Bicycle Coalition of Maine. ✉ *34 Diamond St., Portland* ☎ *207/623–4511* 🌐 *www.bikemaine.org.*

HIKING

Exploring the Maine Coast on foot is a quick way to acclimate yourself to the relaxed pace of life here—and sometimes the only way to access some of the best coastal spots. Many privately owned lands are accessible to hikers, especially Down East. Inquire at a local establishment about hikes that may not appear on a map.

KAYAKING

Nothing gets you literally off the beaten path like plying the saltwaters in a graceful sea kayak.

CONTACTS Maine Association of Sea Kayak Guides and Instructors. ☎ 🌐 *maskgi.org.* **Maine Island Trail Association.** ✉ *100 Kensington St., 2nd fl., Portland* ☎ *207/761–8225* 🌐 *www.mita.org.*

Hotels

Beachfront and roadside motels, historic-home B&Bs and inns, as well as a handful of newer boutique hotels, make up the majority of lodging along the Maine Coast. There are a few larger luxury resorts, such as the Samoset Resort in Rockport or the Bar Harbor Inn in Bar Harbor, but most accommodations are simple, comfortable, and relatively inexpensive. You will find some chain hotels in larger cities and towns, including major tourist destinations like Portland, Freeport, and Bar Harbor. Many properties close during the off-season (mid-October–mid-May); those that stay open year-round often drop their rates dramatically after high season. (It is often possible to negotiate a nightly rate with smaller establishments during low season.) There is a 9% state hospitality tax on all room rates.

Hotel reviews have been shortened. For full reviews visit Fodors.com.

What It Costs in U.S. Dollars

$	$$	$$$	$$$$
RESTAURANTS			
under $18	$18–$24	$25–$35	over $35
HOTELS			
under $200	$200–$299	$300–$399	over $399

Restaurants

Many breakfast spots along the coast open as early as 6 am to serve the working crowd, and as early as 4 am for fishermen. Lunch generally runs 11–2:30; dinner is usually served 5–9. Only in larger cities will you find full dinners offered much later than 9, although in larger towns you can usually find a bar or bistro with a limited menu available late into the evening.

Many restaurants in Maine are closed Monday. Resort areas make an exception to this in high season, but these eateries often shut down altogether in the off-season.

Unless otherwise noted in reviews, restaurants are open daily for lunch and dinner.

Credit cards are generally accepted at restaurants throughout Maine, even in more modest establishments, but it's still a good idea to have cash on hand wherever you go, just in case.

The one signature meal on the Maine Coast is, of course, the lobster dinner. It typically includes a whole steamed lobster with drawn butter for dipping, a clam or seafood chowder, corn on the cob, coleslaw, and a bib. Lobster prices vary from day to day, but generally a full lobster dinner should cost around $25–$30, or about $18–$20 without all the extras.

Restaurant reviews have been shortened. For full reviews visit Fodors.com.

Visitor Information

CONTACTS DownEast and Acadia Regional Tourism. ✉ *7 Ames Way, Machias* ☎ *207/255–0983, 888/665–3278* 🌐 *www.downeastacadia.com.* **Maine Lobster Marketing Collaborative.** ✉ *2 Union St., Suite 204, Portland* ☎ *207/541–9310* 🌐 *www.lobsterfrommaine.com.* **Southern Midcoast Maine Chamber.** ✉ *Brunswick* ☎ *207/725–8797* 🌐 *www.midcoastmaine.com.* **State of Maine Visitor Information Center.** ✉ *Hallowell* ☎ *800/767–8709* 🌐 *www.mainetourism.com.*

Kittery

60 miles north of Boston, 4 miles north of Portsmouth, New Hampshire.

Known as the "Gateway to Maine," Kittery has become primarily a major shopping destination thanks to its massive complex of factory outlets. Flanking both sides of U.S. 1 are more than 120 stores, which attract serious shoppers year-round. But Kittery has more to offer than just retail therapy: head east on Route 103 to the area around Kittery Point to experience the great outdoors.

Here you'll find hiking and biking trails, as well as fantastic views of Portsmouth, New Hampshire, Whaleback Light, and, in the distance, Isles of Shoals. The isles and the light, along with two others, can be seen from two forts near this winding stretch of Route 103: Fort McClary State Historic Site (closed to vehicles off-season) and Fort Foster, a town park (with vehicle access to parking lots in the off-season, except in the case of ice or snow).

The Kittery Visitor Information Center is an excellent place to get information for mapping out your tour of Maine (and for a quick photo op with Smokey the Bear). Sometimes local organizations are on hand selling delicious homemade goodies for the road.

GETTING HERE AND AROUND

Three bridges—on U.S. 1, U.S. 1 Bypass, and Interstate 95—cross the Piscataqua River from Portsmouth, New Hampshire, to Kittery. Interstate 95 has three Kittery exits. Route 103 is a scenic coastal drive through Kittery Point to York.

VISITOR INFORMATION

CONTACTS Kittery Visitor Information Center. ✉ *U.S. 1 and I–95, at Maine mile marker 3.5 on I–95 northbound, Kittery* ☎ *207/439–1319* 🌐 *www.mainetourism.com.*

Restaurants

Chauncey Creek Lobster Pier

$$ | **SEAFOOD** | **FAMILY** | From the road you can barely see the red roof hovering below the trees, but chances are you can see the line of cars parked at this popular outdoor restaurant that has been serving up fresh lobster for more

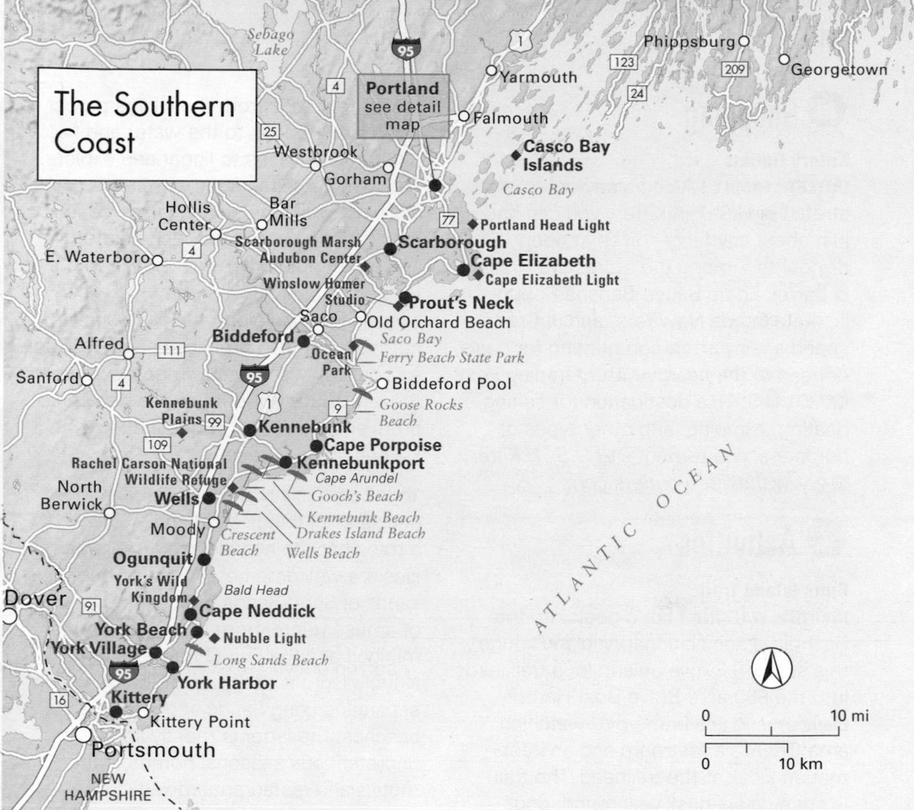

than 70 years. Brightly colored picnic tables fill the deck, and enclosed eating areas sit atop the high banks of the tidal river, beside a working pier, which delivers fresh seafood straight to your plate. **Known for:** classic lobster dinners; BYOB; ocean-to-plate. *Average main: $25 16 Chauncey Creek Rd., Kittery 207/439–1030 www.chaunceycreek.com Closed Mon. post-Labor Day–Columbus Day. Closed post-Columbus Day–Mother's Day.*

Coffee and Quick Bites

Bob's Clam Hut

$$ | SEAFOOD | FAMILY | With fresh (never frozen) shellfish and a cheery, old-school vibe, Bob's also serves up scrumptious, homemade sauces to smother over golden fried clams, alongside some of the creamiest New England clam chowders around. **Known for:** retro-coastal decor; a classic stop since 1956; tangy Moxie barbecue sauce. *Average main: $16 315 U.S. 1, Kittery 207/439–4233 www.bobsclamhut.com.*

★ Lil's

$ | CAFÉ | This Kittery Foreside café is named for the woman who worked the register at nearby Bob's Clam Hut for two decades, but you'll find no shellfish here—just excellent pastries and breads, made on-site daily. Don't miss the top-notch old-fashioned crullers, and duck into the vault in back—filled with vintage records—while you're at it. **Known for:** chill spot to refuel between explorations; lots of parking; a variety of excellent house-made crullers. *Average main: $6 7 Wallingford Sq., Unit 106, Kittery 207/703–2800 lilscafe.com No dinner.*

Shopping

Kittery Outlets

OUTLET | FAMILY | Along a several-mile stretch of U.S. 1 in Kittery you can find just about anything—often at deep discounts. Among the stores are Crate & Barrel, Eddie Bauer, Banana Republic, Kate Spade New York, and J. Crew; spend a rainy afternoon hunting for deals, or head to the nearby Kittery Trading Post (✉ 301 U.S. 1), a destination for fishing, boating, camping, and other types of outdoor accoutrements. ✉ *U.S. 1, Kittery* 🌐 *www.thekitteryoutlets.com.*

Activities

Cutts Island Trail

HIKING & WALKING | For a peek into the Rachel Carson National Wildlife Refuge, this scenic 1.8-mile upland loop trail leads into the 800-acre Brave Boat Harbor Division and is a prime bird-watching area. There's a restroom and an information kiosk at the trailhead. The trail is open dawn–dusk year-round; dogs are not allowed. ✉ *Seapoint Rd., Kittery* ☏ *207/646–9226* 🌐 *www.fws.gov/refuge/rachel-carson/visit-us.*

The Yorks and Cape Neddick

8 miles north of Kittery via I–95, U.S. 1, and U.S. 1A.

Spending an afternoon in York Village is like going back in time—and you really only need a couple of hours here to roam the historic streets of this pint-size but worthwhile town. One of the first permanent settlements in Maine, the village museums detail its rich history. York is also home to the flagship store of Stonewall Kitchen, one of Maine's signature gourmet-food purveyors; the store has a café, too. There's also a cluster of vibrant contemporary-art galleries.

A short distance from the village proper, York Harbor opens to the water and offers many places to linger and explore. The harbor itself is busy with boats of all kinds, while the sandy harbor beach is good for swimming. Much quieter and more formal than York Beach to the north, this area has a somewhat exclusive air. Perched along the cliffs on the north side of the harbor are huge "cottages" built by wealthy summer residents in the late 1800s, when the area became a premier seaside resort destination with several grand hotels.

York Beach is a real family destination, devoid of all things staid and stuffy, and a throwback to nostalgic summers past: kids are welcome here. Just beyond the sands of Short Sands Beach are a host of amusements, from bowling to indoor minigolf and the Fun-O-Rama arcade. Nubble Light is at the tip of the peninsula separating Long Sands and Short Sands beaches. The latter is mostly lined with unpretentious seasonal homes, with motels and restaurants mixed in.

Cape Neddick is 1 mile north of York Beach via U.S. 1A. It's still one of the less developed of York's areas, and there's no distinct village hub, though it's become something of an elevated destination, with acclaimed restaurants and trendy lodgings popping up. Cape Neddick Harbor is at its southern end, beyond York Beach village.

GETTING HERE AND AROUND

York is Exit 7 off I–95; follow signs to U.S. 1, the modern commercial strip. From here, U.S. 1A will take you to the village center and on to York Harbor and York Beach before looping back up to U.S. 1 in Cape Neddick. After passing through York Village to York Harbor (originally called Lower Town), U.S. 1A winds around and heads north to York Beach's village center, a 4-mile trip.

It's a scenic 6 miles to York Beach via the loop road, U.S. 1A, from its southern intersection with U.S. 1. Although 2 miles longer, it's generally faster to continue north on U.S. 1A to Cape Neddick and then U.S. 1A south to the village center, home to Short Sands Beach. Here U.S. 1A is known as Ocean Avenue as it heads north from York Harbor along Long Sands Beach en route to York Beach village and Short Sands Beach.

You can get from beach to beach on a series of residential streets that wind around Nubble Point between these beaches. Also, from late June through Labor Day, the bright-red vehicles of the York Trolley Company link Short Sands Beach in York Beach village with nearby Long Sands Beach, running along U.S. 1A, making a number of stops. Maps can be picked up throughout York; fares are $2 one-way, $4 round-trip, cash only (payable to driver upon boarding). You can also connect with a shuttle service to Ogunquit.

TRANSPORTATION York Trolley Co.. ✉ *York* ☎ *207/363–9600* 🌐 *www.yorktrolley.com.*

VISITOR INFORMATION

CONTACTS Greater York Region Chamber of Commerce. ✉ *1 Stonewall La., off U.S. 1, York* ☎ *207/363–4422* 🌐 *www.gatewaytomaine.org.*

Sights

Cliff Walk and Fisherman's Walk

TRAIL | Two walking trails begin near Harbor Beach. Starting in a small nearby park, the Cliff Walk ascends its granite namesake and passes the summer "cottages" at the harbor entrance. There are some steps, but, as signs caution, tread carefully because of erosion. Fisherman's Walk, on the other hand, is an easy stroll. Starting across Stage Neck Road from the beach, it passes waterfront businesses, historic homes, and rocky harbor beaches on the way to York's beloved Wiggly Bridge. This pedestrian suspension bridge alongside Route 103 (there is minimal parking here) leads to Steedman Woods, a public preserve with a shaded loop trail along the York River estuary's ambling waters. You can also enter the preserve near the George Marshall Store in York Village. ✉ *Stage Neck Rd., off U.S. 1A, York.*

Old York Historical Society

HISTORY MUSEUM | FAMILY | Nine historic 18th- and 19th-century buildings, clustered on York Street and along Lindsay Road and the York River, highlight York's rich history, which dates from the early colonial period. Start your visit at the museum's visitor center in the Remick Barn at the corner of U.S. 1A and Lindsay Road. The Old Gaol (established 1656) was once the King's Prison for the Province of Maine; step inside for a look inside its dungeons, cells, and jailer's quarters. The 1731 Elizabeth Perkins House reflects the Victorian style of its last occupants, the prominent Perkins family. ✉ *Old York Museum Center, 3 Lindsay Rd., York Village* ☎ *207/363–1756* 🌐 *www.oldyork.org* 🎫 *$10* ⏲ *Closed Nov.–Memorial Day.*

★ Nubble Light

LIGHTHOUSE | On a small island just off the tip of Cape Neddick, Nubble Light is one of the most photographed lighthouses on the globe. Direct access is prohibited, but the small Sohier Park right across from the light has parking, historical placards, benches, and a seasonal information center that shares the 1879 light's history. ✉ *11 Sohier Park Rd., York* ☎ *207/363–3569 May 1–mid-Oct.* 🌐 *www.nubblelight.org.*

Sayward-Wheeler House

HISTORIC HOME | FAMILY | Built in 1718, this waterfront home was remodeled in the 1760s by Jonathan Sayward, a local merchant who had prospered in the West Indies trade. By 1860, his descendants had opened the house to the public to share the story of their Colonial ancestors. Accessible only by guided tour (first and third Saturday, June through mid-October, 11–4 with the last tour at 3), the house reveals the decor of a prosperous New England family and the stories of the free and enslaved people who lived here at the outset of the Revolutionary War. The parlor—considered one of the country's best-preserved Colonial interiors, with a tall clock and mahogany Chippendale-style chairs—looks pretty much as it did when Sayward lived here. ✉ *9 Barrell La. Ext., York Harbor* ☎ *207/384–2454* 🌐 *www.historicnewengland.org/property/sayward-wheeler-house* 🎫 *$10* ⏲ *Closed mid-Oct.–June.*

Beaches

Long Sands Beach

BEACH | FAMILY | In the peak of summer, each day sees thousands of visitors along this swath of white sand, which stretches for more than a mile. They come to sunbathe, surf (in designated areas), play volleyball, and explore tide pools. You can rent umbrellas and rafts here, but you'll have to walk to nearby restaurants for a bite to eat. Dogs are allowed (however, between late May and late September, only before 8 am and after 6:30 pm). **Amenities:** lifeguards (seasonal); parking (fee); toilets. **Best for:** surfing; swimming; walking. ✉ *189 Long Beach Ave., Rte. 1A, York Beach.*

Restaurants

Dockside Restaurant

$$ | SEAFOOD | On an islandlike peninsula overlooking York Harbor, this restaurant has plenty of seafood on the menu. Floor-to-ceiling windows in the stepped modern dining space transport diners to the water beyond—every seat has a water view. **Known for:** "drunken" lobster (lobster and seared scallops in an Irish-whiskey cream); decadent seafood chowder and lobster bisque; lively, dockside vibe with spectacular views. 💲 *Average main: $25* ✉ *22 Harris Island Rd., off Rte. 103, York Harbor* ☎ *207/363–2722* 🌐 *www.dockside-restaurant.com* ⏲ *Closed Tues. in summer and late Oct.–mid-May.*

The Goldenrod

$$ | AMERICAN | FAMILY | People line the windows to watch Goldenrod Kisses being made the same way they have since 1896—and thousands of pounds are made every year at this York Beach classic. Aside from the famous taffy (there's penny candy, too), this eatery is family-oriented, very reasonably priced, and a great place to get homemade ice cream from the old-fashioned soda fountain. **Known for:** laid-back, kid-friendly atmosphere; breakfast served all day; classic American fare, like burgers, hot dogs, and baked dinners. 💲 *Average main: $10* ✉ *2 Railroad Ave., York Beach* ☎ *207/363–2621* 🌐 *www.thegoldenrod.com* ⏲ *Closed mid-Oct.–mid-May.*

Coffee and Quick Bites

Flo's Steamed Hot Dogs

$ | AMERICAN | Yes, it seems crazy to highlight a hot-dog stand, but this is no ordinary place—who would guess that a hot dog could make it into *Saveur* and *Gourmet* magazines? There is something grand about this shabby, red-shingle shack, where the classic dog has mayo and a special sauce—consisting of, among other things, onions and molasses (you can buy a bottle to take home, and you'll want to). **Known for:** family-owned and-operated; in business since 1959; lines out the door (but efficient service means waits aren't that long). 💲 *Average main: $3* ✉ *1359 U.S. 1, Cape Neddick* ☎ *No phone* 🌐 *www.floshotdogs.com* 💳 *No credit cards* ⏲ *Closed Wed. No dinner.*

Hotels

★ Cliff House

$$$ | HOTEL | FAMILY | At this luxurious hotel overlooking the Atlantic Ocean, you can watch the white crests smash the craggy bluffs below while nestled in a hooded flannel robe on your balcony. **Pros:** the views; rooms have private terraces;

plenty of activities to keep everyone busy. **Cons:** no in-room coffee setups (only one communal coffee station per floor to help reduce waste); meals not included; central location means a drive to the nearest town centers. *$ Rooms from: $600 ✉ 591 Shore Rd., Cape Neddick ☎ 207/361–1000 🌐 www.cliffhousemaine.com 226 rooms 🍽 No Meals.*

★ Stage Neck Inn

$$ | RESORT | FAMILY | A family-run operation that is now in the competent hands of the second generation, this resort hotel takes full advantage of its gorgeous harborside location, with Adirondack chairs, chaise longues, and a fire pit on the surrounding lawns; water views from most guest rooms; and floor-to-ceiling windows in the common spaces. **Pros:** elaborate breakfast buffet with scrumptious baked goods; poolside service and snack bar in season; rooms have balconies or deck areas and most have water views. **Cons:** spa is on the small side; some rooms have only partial water views; rooms with two beds have doubles rather than queens. *$ Rooms from: $300 ✉ 8 Stage Neck Rd., off U.S. 1A, York Harbor ☎ 800/340–1130, 207/363–3850 🌐 www.stageneck.com ⏲ Closed 1st 2 wks in Jan. 60 rooms 🍽 Free Breakfast.*

York Harbor Inn

$ | B&B/INN | A mid-17th-century fishing cabin with dark timbers and a fieldstone fireplace forms the heart of this historic inn, which now includes several neighboring buildings. **Pros:** many rooms have harbor views; close to beaches, scenic walking trails; kid-friendly. **Cons:** rooms vary greatly in style, size, and appeal; no ocean views at the Chapman Cottage; only Harbor Crest Inn is pet-friendly. *$ Rooms from: $199 ✉ 480 York St., York Harbor ☎ 207/363–5119 🌐 www.yorkharborinn.com 65 rooms 🍽 Free Breakfast.*

Shopping

Stonewall Kitchen

FOOD | FAMILY | You've probably seen Stonewall Kitchen's jars of chutneys, jams, jellies, salsas, and sauces in specialty stores back home. This complex houses the expansive flagship store, which has a viewing area of the bottling process. Sample all the mustards, salsas, and dressings you can stand, or have lunch at the café, then meander through the stunning gardens to the Stonewall Home Company Store, offering candles, hand lotions, and essentials for the garden and home. *✉ 2 Stonewall La., off U.S. 1, York ☎ 207/351–2712 🌐 www.stonewallkitchen.com.*

Activities

Shearwater Charters

FISHING | Shearwater offers light-tackle and fly-fishing charters in the York River and along the shoreline from Kittery to Ogunquit. Bait-fishing trips are also available. Departures are from Town Dock #2 in York Harbor; just note that trips are capped at three people. *✉ Town Dock #2, 20 Harris Island Rd., York ☎ 207/363–5324 🌐 www.mainestripers.net.*

Ogunquit

7 miles north of the Yorks via U.S. 1.

A resort village since the late 19th century, Ogunquit made a name for itself as an artists' colony. Today it has become a mini Provincetown, with a population that swells in summer, boutique shops and galleries, and many inns and small clubs that cater to an LGBTQ+ clientele.

Nightlife in Ogunquit revolves around the precincts of Ogunquit Square and Perkins Cove, where people stroll, often enjoying an after-dinner ice-cream cone or espresso. For a scenic drive, take Shore Road from downtown to the 175-foot Bald

Ogunquit's Perkins Cove is a pleasant place to admire the boats (and wonder at the origin of their names).

Head Cliff; you'll be treated to views up and down the coast. On a stormy day the surf can be quite wild here.

GETTING HERE AND AROUND

Parking in the village and at the beach is costly and limited, so leave your car at the hotel or in a public parking space and hop the trolley. It costs $5 per trip and runs Memorial Day weekend–Columbus Day, with weekend-only service during the last few weeks, after Labor Day. From Perkins Cove, the trolley runs through town along Shore Road and then down to Ogunquit Beach; it also stops along U.S. 1.

TRANSPORTATION Shoreline Explorer. ☎ *800/965–5762* 🌐 *www.shorelineexplorer.com.*

VISITOR INFORMATION

CONTACTS Ogunquit Chamber of Commerce. ✉ *36 Main St., Ogunquit* ☎ *207/646–1279* 🌐 *www.ogunquit.org.*

Sights

Marginal Way

PROMENADE | FAMILY | This mile-plus-long, paved footpath hugs the shore of a rocky promontory just beyond Ogunquit's downtown. Thirty-nine benches along the easygoing path allow you to appreciate the open sea vistas. Expect heavy foot traffic, even in the off-season—which is the only time of the year that dogs are allowed. ✉ *Perkins Cove Rd., Ogunquit* 🌐 *www.marginalwayfund.org.*

★ Ogunquit Museum of American Art

ART MUSEUM | FAMILY | Ogunquit has long been an important site for artists, and this stellar museum—the only one in Maine focused solely on American art—continues that legacy. The collection includes 3,000 early modern and contemporary paintings, sculptures, drawings, and more, including works with ties to Ogunquit's once-famous artist colony. The main gallery offers sweeping views of Perkins Cove. Leave time to stroll around the 3-acre seaside sculpture park in good weather. ✉ *543 Shore Rd., Ogunquit* ☎ *207/646–4909* 🌐 *ogunquitmuseum.org* 🎫 *$12* ⏲ *Closed Nov. 1–Apr. 30.*

Perkins Cove

OTHER ATTRACTION | FAMILY | This neck of land off Shore Road in the lower part of Ogunquit village has a jumble of sea-weathered fish houses and buildings that were part of an art school. These have largely been transformed by the tide of tourism into shops and restaurants, including the classic Barnacle Billy's seafood spot. When you've had your fill of browsing, stroll out along the mile-long Marginal Way. ✉ *Perkins Cove Rd., off Shore Rd., Ogunquit.*

 Beaches

Ogunquit Beach

BEACH | FAMILY | Perfect for just about every beach fan—sunbathers to beachcombers and bodysurfers—this 3-mile-long, sandy beach is located between the Atlantic Ocean and the Ogunquit River. Beach chairs and umbrellas are available for rent seasonally. Dogs are welcome from September through March. **Amenities**: food and drink; lifeguards; parking (fee); toilets. **Best For:** sunset; swimming; walking. ✉ *Ogunquit* ✣ *End of Ocean Ave.* 🌐 *www.ogunquit.org/our-beaches* 🎫 *Parking $35 a day (mid-Apr.–Oct.).*

 Restaurants

Barnacle Billy's

$$$ | SEAFOOD | Overlooking Perkins Cove, Barnacle Billy's has been serving up fresh, local seafood since 1961. Place your order at the counter before settling into a table on the deck to await delivery of your clam chowder, fried clams, broiled scallops, or lobster roll. **Known for:** lobster rolls and chowder; takeout counter and ice cream; deck seating overlooking Perkins Cove. $ *Average main: $38* ✉ *50–70 Perkins Cove Rd., Ogunquit* ☎ *207/646–5575* 🌐 *www.barnbilly.com* ⏲ *Closed late Oct.–late Apr.*

The Lobster Shack

$$ | SEAFOOD | A fixture since 1947 in Ogunquit's bustling Perkins Cove, this cozy, weathered-shingle lobster pound is just across from the oft-photographed footbridge. Choose from a ¼- to a whopping 1-pound lobster roll, or try the delicious roll with hand-picked Maine crab meat. **Known for:** Maine beers on tap; lobsters rolls; chowder. $ *Average main: $26* ✉ *110 Perkins Cove Rd., Ogunquit* ☎ *207/646–2941* 🌐 *www.lobster-shack.com.*

★ Northern Union

$$ | CONTEMPORARY | From the moment you walk into Northern Union you know you're going to be in very good hands. A genuine, welcoming staff and laid-back yet elegant design scheme put you in the mood for a slow, very memorable dinner of seasonally inspired small plates like braised pork belly or duck confit and rotating entrées like seared scallops and lobster fettuccine—all available with spot-on wine pairings that you won't find anywhere else in the area. **Known for:** almost everything is made in-house; dishes that can easily be shared; a terrific selection of cured meats and cheese boards with a local, seasonal bent. $ *Average main: $27* ✉ *261 Shore Rd., Ogunquit* ☎ *207/216–9639* 🌐 *www.northern-union.me* ⏲ *No lunch.*

 Performing Arts

Ogunquit Playhouse

THEATER | FAMILY | Over its nearly century-long history, this classic summer theater has brought some the country's best talent to its stage. The stately green-and-white building feels like a relic from an old-time summer resort, and with an average of five productions each season, the Playhouse offers a good reason to take a break from the beach and spend an evening indoors. ✉ *10 Main St., Ogunquit* ☎ *207/646–5511* 🌐 *www.ogunquitplayhouse.org* 🎫 *Show tickets: from $47* ⏲ *Closed Nov.–May.*

Wells

6 miles north of Ogunquit via U.S. 1.

Lacking any kind of discernible village center, Wells could be easily overlooked as nothing more than a commercial stretch of U.S. 1 between Ogunquit and the Kennebunks. But look more closely: this is a place where people come to enjoy some of the best beaches on the coast. Until 1980 the town of Wells incorporated Ogunquit, and today this family-oriented beach community has 7 miles of densely populated shoreline, along with nature preserves, where you can explore salt marshes and tidal pools.

GETTING HERE AND AROUND

Amtrak's *Downeaster* train stops at Wells Transportation Center, but from there, this town is best explored by car. U.S. 1 is the main thoroughfare, with antiques stores, shops, and diners lining both sides. Venture down the roads that branch off U.S. 1 to the east (and the coast), like Mile Road, which has spots to eat and drink and leads to Wells Beach. Just north, where U.S. 1 intersects with Route 9, is the Rachel Carson National Wildlife Refuge.

VISITOR INFORMATION

CONTACTS Wells Chamber of Commerce. ✉ *136 Post Rd., Wells* ✥ *At intersection of Post Rd. (U.S. 1) and Kimballs La.* ☎ *207/646–2451* 🌐 *www.wellschamber.org.*

Sights

Rachel Carson National Wildlife Refuge

WILDLIFE REFUGE | FAMILY | At the headquarters of the Rachel Carson National Wildlife Refuge, which has 11 divisions from Kittery to Cape Elizabeth, is the Carson Trail, a 1-mile loop. The trail traverses a salt marsh and a white-pine forest where migrating birds and waterfowl of many varieties are regularly spotted, and it borders Branch Brook and the Merriland River. ✉ *321 Port Rd., Wells* ☎ *207/646–9226* 🌐 *www.fws.gov/refuge/rachel_carson.*

Beaches

Crescent Beach

BEACH | FAMILY | Lined with summer homes, this sandy strand is busy in the summer, but the beach and the water are surprisingly clean, considering all the traffic. The swimming's good, and beachgoers can also explore tidal pools and look for seals on the sea rocks nearby. **Amenities:** lifeguards; parking (fee); toilets. **Best for:** swimming. ✉ *Webhannet Dr., south of Mile Rd., Wells.*

Wells Beach

BEACH | FAMILY | The northern end of a 2-mile stretch of golden sand, Wells Beach is popular with families and surfers, who line up in the swells and suit up on the boardwalk near the arcade and snack shop. The beach's northern tip is a bit quieter, with a long rock jetty perfect for strolling. **Amenities:** food and drink; lifeguards; parking (fee); toilets. **Best for:** surfing; walking. ✉ *Atlantic Ave., north of Mile Rd., Wells.*

Restaurants

★ Batson River Fish Camp

$$ | AMERICAN | This outpost of the popular Batson River brewing and distilling company channels the feel of a trendy lakeside camp (think vintage thermoses and prize catches mounted on the walls) all year round. The menu includes standout cocktails, well-done bar fare, and beers brewed on-site, just behind Fish Camp. **Known for:** limited-edition brews; throwback camp decor; fun spot for a well-made cocktail after a day at the beach. $ *Average main: $20* ✉ *73 Mile Rd., Wells* ☎ *207/360–7255* 🌐 *batsonriver.com/wells-maine* ⏲ *Closed Wed. No lunch.*

Billy's Chowder House
$$ | **SEAFOOD** | **FAMILY** | Locals and vacationers head to this roadside seafood restaurant and bar in the midst of a salt marsh en route to Wells Beach. The menu features classic seafood dishes like lobster rolls and chowders, but there are plenty of nonseafood choices, too. **Known for:** views of the Rachel Carson National Wildlife Refuge; generous lobster rolls; one of the oldest waterfront restaurants in Wells. *Average main: $24 216 Mile Rd., Wells 207/646–7558 www.billyschowderhouse.com Closed mid-Dec.–mid-Jan.*

★ Bitter End
$$ | **SEAFOOD** | Pete and Kate Morency, the duo originally behind the ever-popular Pier 77 and the Ramp Bar and Grill in Kennebunkport, are also the masterminds behind this seafood spot, where Mediterranean and American classics are given brilliant, contemporary twists. The fabulous decor consists of an unlikely marriage of old-school American sports memorabilia and something that might be described as shabby ballroom chic—crystal chandeliers hang above old leather boxing gloves, and shiny trophies (including a 1961 Miss Universe cup) and black-and-white photos of sports icons line the bar. **Known for:** cuisine fusion and a rotating menu; outdoor seating area with firepit; superbly curated bevy of liquors. *Average main: $24 2118 Post Rd., Wells 207/360–0904 www.bitterend.me Closed Tues.*

Maine Diner
$$ | **AMERICAN** | One look at the 1953 exterior, and you'll start craving diner food, but be prepared to get a little more than you bargained for: after all, how many greasy spoons make an award-winning lobster pie? There's plenty of fried seafood in addition to the usual diner fare, and breakfast is served all day. **Known for:** classic diner fare; wild Maine blueberry pie; sources a lot of produce from its very own vegetable garden. *Average main: $15 2265 Post Rd., Wells 207/646–4441 www.mainediner.com No dinner. Closed Wed. and at least 2 wks in Jan.*

Coffee and Quick Bites

Congdon's Doughnuts
$ | **AMERICAN** | **FAMILY** | These superior doughnuts have been made by members of the same family since 1945 and at the same location since 1955. Congdon's has about 40 different varieties, some seasonal, though the plain variety really gives you an idea of just how good these doughnuts are: it's the biggest seller, along with the honey dipped and black raspberry jelly. **Known for:** perfect spot to start a rainy day; Congdon's After Dark features food trucks and live music nightly in summer; outrageously good, classic doughnuts. *Average main: $3 1090 Post Rd., Wells 207/646–4219 www.congdons.com No dinner. Closed Wed. in season and Mon.–Wed. off-season; check website for details.*

Hotels

Haven by the Sea
$$ | **B&B/INN** | Once the summer mission of St. Martha's Church in Kennebunkport, this exquisite inn, just a block from the beach, has retained many details from its former life, including cathedral ceilings and stained-glass windows. **Pros:** rotating breakfasts that cater to dietary restrictions without compromising taste; nightly happy hour with complimentary appetizers and sherry, port, and brandy; beach towels and beach chairs available. **Cons:** not an in-town location; distant ocean views; $50 cancellation fee no matter how far in advance. *Rooms from: $260 59 Church St., Wells 207/646–4194 www.havenbythesea.com 9 rooms Free Breakfast.*

Kennebunk, Kennebunkport, and Cape Porpoise

6 miles north of Wells via Rte. 9.

The town centers of Kennebunk and Kennebunkport are separated by 5 miles and two rivers, but, what are probably best described as the Hamptons of the Pine Tree State are united by a common history and laid-back seaside vibe. Kennebunkport has been a resort area since the 19th century, and its most recent residents have made it even more famous: the dynastic Bush family is often in residence on its immense estate, which sits dramatically out on Walker's Point on Cape Arundel. Newer homes have sprung up alongside the old, and a great way to take them all in is with a slow drive out Ocean Avenue along the cape.

Sometimes bypassed on the way to its sister town, Kennebunk has its own appeal. Once a major shipbuilding center, Kennebunk today retains the feel of a classic New England small town, with an inviting shopping district, steepled churches, and fine examples of 18th- and 19th-century brick and clapboard homes. There are also plenty of natural spaces for walking, swimming, birding, and biking, and the area's major beaches are along its shores.

Just north of Kennebunkport is the fishing village of Cape Porpoise, with a working lobster pier, spectacular views of the harbor and lighthouse, and excellent restaurants.

GETTING HERE AND AROUND

Kennebunk's main downtown sits along U.S. 1, extending west from the Mousam River. The Lower Village is along routes 9 and 35, 4 miles down Route 35 from downtown, and the way between is lined on both sides by mansions, making it a spectacular drive.

To reach the beaches of Kennebunk, continue straight (the road becomes Beach Avenue) at the intersection with Route 9. If you turn left instead, Route 9 will take you across the Kennebunk River, into Kennebunkport's touristy downtown, called Dock Square (or sometimes just "the Port"). Here you'll find the most activity (and crowds) in the Kennebunks, thanks to restaurants, shops, galleries, and boats that offer cruises.

The Intown Trolley runs narrated jaunts in season, passing Kennebunk's beaches and Lower Village as well as neighboring Kennebunkport's scenery and sights. The main stop is at 21 Ocean Avenue in Kennebunkport, around the corner from Dock Square.

TRANSPORTATION Intown Trolley. ✉ *Kennebunkport* ☏ *207/967–3686* 🌐 *www.intowntrolley.com.*

WALKING TOURS

To take a little walking tour of Kennebunk's most notable structures, begin at the Federal-style Brick Store Museum at 117 Main Street. Head south on Main Street (turn left out of the museum) to see several extraordinary 18th- and early-19th-century homes, including the **Lexington Elms** at No. 99 (1799), the **Horace Porter House** at No. 92 (1848), and the **Benjamin Brown House** at No. 85 (1788).

When you've had your fill of historic homes, head back up toward the museum, pass the 1773 **First Parish Unitarian Church** (its Asher Benjamin–style steeple contains an original Paul Revere bell), and turn right onto **Summer Street.** This street is an architectural showcase, revealing an array of styles from Colonial to Federal. Walking past these grand beauties will give you a real sense of the economic prowess and glamour of the long-gone shipbuilding industry.

At noon on Thursday and Saturday from June through October (or by appointment off-season), the museum offers a guided architectural walking tour of Summer

Street. You can also purchase a $4.95 map that marks historic buildings or a $15.95 guidebook, *Windows on the Past.*

For a dramatic walk along Kennebunkport's rocky coastline and beneath the views of Ocean Avenue's grand mansions, head out on the **Parson's Way Shore Walk,** a paved 4.8-mile round-trip. Begin at Dock Square and follow Ocean Avenue along the river, passing the Colony Hotel and St. Ann's Church, all the way to Walker's Point. Simply turn back from here.

VISITOR INFORMATION

CONTACTS Kennebunk-Kennebunkport Chamber of Commerce. ✉ *16 Water St., Kennebunk* ☎ *207/967–0857* 🌐 *www.gokennebunks.com.*

Sights

Brick Store Museum

HISTORY MUSEUM | FAMILY | The cornerstone of this block-long preservation of early-19th-century commercial and residential buildings is William Lord's Brick Store. Built as a dry-goods store in 1825 in the Federal style, the building has an openwork balustrade across the roofline, granite lintels over the windows, and paired chimneys. Exhibits chronicle the Kennebunk area's history, art, and culture for kids and adults alike. In addition, museum staffers lead walking tours of Kennebunk's National Historic District (at noon on Thursday and Saturday from June through October) and of the town's beaches (at 11 on Saturday from July through September). ✉ *117 Main St., Kennebunk* ☎ *207/985–4802* 🌐 *www.brickstoremuseum.org* 🎫 *$5* 🕒 *Closed Mon.*

★ Dock Square

PLAZA/SQUARE | Restaurants, art galleries, clothing boutiques, and other shops—both trendy and touristy—line this bustling square and nearby streets and alleys. Walk onto the drawbridge to admire the tidal Kennebunk River; cross to the other side and you are in the Lower Village of neighboring Kennebunk. ✉ *Dock Sq., Kennebunkport.*

Seashore Trolley Museum

OTHER MUSEUM | FAMILY | This fun, visitor-favorite museum is an homage to transport from years past. Get an up-close look at trolleys from major metropolitan areas worldwide—from Boston to Budapest, New York to Nagasaki, and San Francisco to Sydney—beautifully restored and displayed (and, sometimes, operational). Best of all, you can take a nearly 4-mile ride on the tracks of the former Atlantic Shore Line Railway, with a stop along the way at the museum restoration shop, where trolleys are transformed from junk into gems. The outdoor museum is self-guided. ✉ *195 Log Cabin Rd., Kennebunkport* ☎ *207/967–2800* 🌐 *www.trolleymuseum.org* 🎫 *$13* 🕒 *Closed weekdays in May and Mon. and Tues. June 1–Oct. 31. Closed Nov.–Apr. except 1st 2 weekends in Dec.*

Beaches

Kennebunk Beach

BEACH | FAMILY | Kennebunk Beach has three distinct stretches, one after another, along Beach Avenue, which is lined with cottages and old Victorians. The southernmost **Mother's Beach** is popular with families. Rock outcroppings lessen the waves, and a playground and tidal pools keep kids busy. This is followed by the stony **Middle Beach.** The most northerly, and the closest to downtown Kennebunkport, is **Gooch's Beach,** the main swimming beach. **Amenities:** lifeguards; parking (fee); toilets. **Best for:** walking; swimming. ✉ *Beach Ave., south of Rte. 9, Kennebunk.*

★ Goose Rocks Beach

BEACH | FAMILY | Three-mile-long Goose Rocks, a 10-minute drive north of Kennebunkport, has a good long stretch of smooth sand and plenty of shallow pools for exploring. It's a favorite of families with small children. Pick up a $25 daily parking permit at one of two kiosks along the beach: one outside of Goose Rocks Beach General Store at 3 Dyke Road and the other at the Proctor Avenue beach path. Dogs are allowed (on a leash), but only before 9 and after 5 during the summer season. There is one porta potty behind the General Store, but otherwise no facilities are available at the beach. **Amenities:** parking (fee). **Best for:** walking; swimming. ✉ *Dyke Rd., off Rte. 9, Kennebunkport* 🌐 *www.kennebunkportme.gov.*

Restaurants

★ The Clam Shack

$$ | **SEAFOOD** | **FAMILY** | For more than a half century, this shack has been known for speedy service and great takeout fare, like its traditional boiled lobster dinners and lobster rolls on freshly baked buns. Eat at one of several wooden picnic tables that overlook the Kennebunk River. **Known for:** clam chowder; lobster rolls and fried clams; ships lobster nationally. $ *Average main: $17* ✉ *2 Western Ave., Kennebunk* ☎ *207/967–3321* 🌐 *www.theclamshack.net.*

★ Earth at Hidden Pond

$$$ | **FUSION** | Each and every meal feels like a special occasion at his splurge-worthy place, which offers thoughtful attention to flavor and texture and uses the freshest locally sourced ingredients. The seasonally inspired menu is always in flux, but you can be sure that even hard-core foodies will be delighted with this culinary experience. **Known for:** wood-fire surf-and-turf dishes; ingredients culled from its own garden; private dining sheds and cabanas for special occasions and groups. $ *Average main: $38* ✉ *354 Goose Rocks Rd., Kennebunkport* ☎ *207/967–6550* 🌐 *hiddenpondmaine.com/earth.*

★ Old Vines Wine Bar

$$ | **MODERN AMERICAN** | Housed in a historic barn, this wine bar and its front patio get busy in summer, and for good reason: artisan cocktails and flavorful small plates are expertly made, and, as the name suggests, the wine list is stellar. Except for a six-week break in midwinter, it's open year-round and cozy on cold nights, too. **Known for:** regular entertainment by Maine musicians; wine list featuring small vineyards and unique varietals; lively Yard Bar open outdoors in summer. $ *Average main: $24* ✉ *173 Port Rd., Kennebunk* ☎ *207/967–2310* 🌐 *oldvineswinebar.com* ⏲ *No lunch. Closed for 6 wks in Feb. and Mar.*

★ Pier 77 Restaurant

$$ | **AMERICAN** | Here, phenomenal views share center stage with a sophisticated menu that emphasizes seafood. The ground-level restaurant's large windows overlook Cape Porpoise harbor, ensuring that every seat has a view of the water; tucked around the corner, the tiny but funky and fun Ramp Bar & Grill pays homage to a really good burger, fried seafood, and other pub-style classics; and, up a flight of stairs, Ramp Up offers crow's-nest harbor views and a place to wait for your table when lines to get in are long. **Known for:** live music in summer; great spot for cocktails on the water while watching boats and sea life pass by; a packed house almost every meal in the summer (reservations highly recommended). $ *Average main: $25* ✉ *77 Pier Rd., Cape Porpoise* ☎ *207/967–8500* 🌐 *www.pier77restaurant.com.*

★ The Tides Beach Club Restaurant

$$$ | **SEAFOOD** | Maritime accents and a crisp color palette help to make this unfussy, beachside restaurant a good place to relax and enjoy a prebeach bite or a post-beach sit-down meal. The menu features lighter seafood fare and salads alongside heartier options, such as lobster rangoons, crispy fried-chicken

Maine's rocky coastline stretches for about 3,400 miles, including Kennebunkport.

sandwiches, and burgers. **Known for:** no dress code—think beach-hair-don't-care chic; delicious craft cocktails; exceptional service that isn't cloying. *Average main: $35 930 Kings Hwy., Kennebunkport 207/967–3757 tidesbeachclubmaine.com/food.*

Coffee and Quick Bites

Dock Square Coffee House

$ | **AMERICAN** | European-style coffee drinks, tea, pastries, smoothies, and other seasonal snacks are on the menu at this small café built over a tidal river in the midst of Dock Square. The coffee is sourced from Portland-based and nationally recognized Coffee By Design, one of the state's best. **Known for:** locally sourced coffee, pastries and breakfast sandwiches; quiet place to sit amid the bustle of Dock Square; central location. *Average main: $5 18 Dock Sq., Kennebunkport 207/967–4422 www.docksquarecoffeehouse.biz Closed Jan.–Mar.*

Hotels

★ Hidden Pond

$$$$ | **RESORT** | Tucked away on 60 wooded acres near Goose Rocks Beach, this resort enclave has hiking trails, two pools, a sumptuous spa, a phenomenal restaurant, a working farm and a variety of lodging options—from luxurious one-bedroom bungalows and two-bedroom cottages to rustic-chic lodges with interconnected suites and studios. **Pros:** use of beach facilities at nearby Tides Beach Club and free beach shuttle and beach-cruiser bikes; lots of on-site activities for adults and children; guests can cut fresh flowers and harvest vegetables from the property's many gardens. **Cons:** steep prices; away from the center of town; no dogs allowed. *Rooms from: $1050 354 Goose Rocks Rd., Kennebunkport 207/967–9050 hiddenpondmaine.com Closed Nov.–Apr. 46 units No Meals.*

★ Kennebunkport Captains Collection

$$ | **B&B/INN** | The four historic inns and houses in this Lark Hotels collection were painstakingly restored in 2020 and 2021, and each was given its own sumptuous, traditional-meets-modern twists. **Pros:** complimentary bikes; easy walk into town; fireplaces in the guest rooms. **Cons:** the nontraditional resort layout may not be everyone's ideal; no pool; no elevators (as these are historic homes). *$ Rooms from: $349 ✉ 6 Pleasant St., Kennebunkport ☎ 207/967–3141 ⊕ www.larkhotels.com/hotels/kennebunkport-captains-collection ⇰ 45 rooms 🍽 Free Breakfast.*

The Nonantum Resort

$$$ | **RESORT** | **FAMILY** | Hands down the most family-friendly resort in the Kennebunks, this place is a dream for parents who want to have a quality family vacation without stress. **Pros:** comfortable beds from local Portland Mattress Makers; seasonal, Maine-centric childrens' activities; friendly, service-oriented staff. **Cons:** wedding events add to bustle; heavy visitor traffic; no indoor pool. *$ Rooms from: $449 ✉ 95 Ocean Ave., Kennebunkport ☎ 207/967–4050 ⊕ nonantumresort.com ⏲ Closed mid-Dec.–late Apr. ⇰ 109 rooms 🍽 Free Breakfast.*

★ Sandy Pines Campground

$ | **RESORT** | The "glamping" (glamorous camping) tents, camp cottages, and A-frame hideaway huts on wheels at Sandy Pines Campground deliver every bit as much comfort and luxury as a fine hotel (with a few caveats, including communal bathing areas), but give you a chance to get up close and personal with nature. **Pros:** the glamping areas of Sandy Pines are quiet zones; nightly bonfires under the stars without roughing it; all lodgings equipped with outdoor sitting area, picnic table, and fire ring. **Cons:** expect all that comes with being in nature; glamping options are not pet-friendly; three-night minimum stay (seasonal). *$ Rooms from: $109 ✉ 277 Mills Rd., Kennebunkport ☎ 207/967–2483 ⊕ sandypinescamping.com ⏲ Closed mid-Oct.–mid-May ⇰ 60 units 🍽 No Meals.*

The Wanderer Cottages

$$ | **MOTEL** | This cluster of tidy, well-appointed cottages opened in summer 2022 in a quiet area that's still a stone's throw from beaches and Dock Square. **Pros:** serene, nicely landscaped setting; heated saltwater pool; private, spacious-feeling cottages, some with sitting areas. **Cons:** no food or bar on-site; no kids allowed; 1.5 miles from Dock Square and 1.2 miles from Parson's Beach. *$ Rooms from: $349 ✉ 195 Sea Rd., Kennebunk ☎ 207/849–7400 ⊕ wanderercottages.com ⇰ 17 cottages 🍽 Free Breakfast.*

Shopping

★ Daytrip Society

SOUVENIRS | **FAMILY** | The impossibly hip and well-selected array of goods at this modern-design shop makes it an excellent place for both window-shopping and finding gifts for just about anyone on your list (including yourself). A refreshing departure from the rest of the somewhat stodgy gift shops in the village, this boutique is chock-full of eye candy, most of which is also functional. There are many locally sourced and contemporary products, from hats and jewelry to novelty books, home decor, and outdoor adventure essentials. Check out Daytrip Jr., its equally hip children's store around the corner. *✉ 4 Dock Sq., Kennebunkport ☎ 207/967–4440 ⊕ www.daytripsociety.com.*

★ Farm + Table

HOUSEWARES | This delightful shop is housed in a bright-red Maine barn filled with household items both useful and pleasing to the eye. Browse the collection of ceramics, linens, kitchen essentials, and more by small-batch makers, and pick up a few artisan treats, too. *✉ 8 Langsford Rd., Cape Porpoise ☎ 207/604–8029 ⊕ www.farmtablekennebunkport.com.*

Port Canvas

HANDBAGS | Since 1968, Port Canvas has been hand-crafting sporty, customizable canvas totes and duffels perfect for lugging your souvenirs home. Other products range from raincoats to keychains. Each stitcher puts their initials inside the bag ensuring authenticity and quality. ✉ *39 Limerick Rd., Kennebunkport* ☎ *207/985–9767* 🌐 *www.portcanvas.com* ⏲ *Closed Fri.–Sun.*

Activities

Rugosa Lobster Tours

BOATING | FAMILY | Lobster-trap hauling trips aboard the *Rugosa* in the scenic waters off the Kennebunks run daily, from Memorial Day through Columbus Day. ✉ *Nonantum Resort, 95 Ocean Ave., Kennebunkport* ☎ *207/468–4095* 🌐 *www.rugosalobstertours.com* 🎫 *$49 per person for a group tour.*

★ The Pineapple Ketch

SAILING | FAMILY | One terrific way to get out on the water and see some marine life is aboard a classic 38-foot, Downeaster ketch steered by a knowledgeable captain and crew. Tours last 90 minutes, and soft drinks are provided. You'll have to bring your own snacks, as well as wine, beer, or cocktails, which are especially good to have on hand during the sunset cruises. ✉ *95 Ocean Ave., Kennebunkport* ☎ *207/888–3445* 🌐 *pineappleketch.com* 🎫 *From $55 per person* ⏲ *Closed mid-Oct.–late May.*

Biddeford

11 miles north of Kennebunkport, 18 miles south of Portland.

Biddeford is waking from a deep sleep, having devolved into something of a ghost town for a good deal of the past half century. Chefs and small-business owners who have relocated from Portland are giving Biddeford's beautiful old-mill-town architecture a new lease on life. Developers have taken note as well, revamping many historic buildings, including the imposing 233,000-square-foot Lincoln Mill. Today, Biddeford is filled with art galleries and quirky boutiques, a distillery, an art school, and top-notch restaurants.

GETTING HERE AND AROUND

From I–95, get off at Exit 32 and follow Alfred Street to Biddeford's downtown. U.S. 1 also runs right through town. Amtrak's *Downeaster* train stops at Saco; the train station is just steps from Biddeford's mill buildings, breweries, and restaurants.

VISITOR INFORMATION

CONTACTS Biddeford-Saco Chamber of Commerce. ✉ *28 Water St., Biddeford* ☎ *207/282–1567* 🌐 *www.biddefordsaco-chamber.org.*

Restaurants

★ Elda

$$$$ | MODERN AMERICAN | Award-winning chef Bowman Brown is behind this restaurant, situated in an old mill building—transformed with exquisite, Scandinavian-style decor—and offering just two tasting-menu seatings (at 5 and 8:30) a night. This is one of Maine's most highly regarded and splurge-worthy dining experiences, featuring meticulously prepared, seasonally inspired dishes, but if your budget is tight, note that the first-floor Jackrabbit Cafe serves small plates and pastries for a fraction of the tasting-menu price. **Known for:** unhurried, indulgent dining (meals often last three hours); focus on locally sourced ingredients; impeccable, modern-meets-original design, with an old vault serving as bar. $ *Average main: $160* ✉ *14 Main St., 2nd fl., Biddeford* ☎ *207/602–0359* 🌐 *www.eldamaine.com* ⏲ *No lunch. Closed Sun.–Tues. and for 2-wk break in spring.*

★ Goldthwaite's Pool Lobster

$$ | **SEAFOOD** | **FAMILY** | This classic spot has been a go-to in the seaside hamlet of Biddeford Pool for over 100 years. Now part general store, part takeout spot, it's a one-stop-shop for sunscreen, wine and beer, and locally made pies; the kitchen offers a bevy of Maine classics (including lobster dinners and fresh lobster rolls), sometimes with a twist (like haddock tacos with ginger-cucumber salsa or a blueberry cream cheese tart for dessert). **Known for:** award-winning clam chowder; decadent desserts made in-house; reasonable prices with million-dollar views. *Average main: $22 ✉ 3 Lester B. Orcutt Blvd., Biddeford ☎ 207/284–5000 🌐 poollobster.com ⏲ General store closed mid-Sept.–mid-May; restaurant closed Labor Day–early June.*

★ Palace Diner

$$ | **AMERICAN** | Everything about this diner, set in an old-fashioned train car just off Main Street, is retro except the food. Hop on a stool at the counter (that's all there is), enjoy the Motown tunes, and tuck into one of the deluxe sandwiches for breakfast or lunch. **Known for:** diner food that's anything but standard; delicious fried-chicken sandwich with cabbage slaw and French fries; fantastic collaboration with local chefs from regional restaurants. *Average main: $12 ✉ 18 Franklin St., Biddeford ☎ 207/284–0015 🌐 www.palacedinerme.com No credit cards ⏲ No dinner.*

Hotels

★ The Lincoln Hotel

$$ | **HOTEL** | A far cry from Maine's coastal bed-and-breakfasts and quaint inns, this hotel in the massive, revitalized Lincoln Mill has a distinctly urban feel. **Pros:** cool base for exploring Biddeford's many watering holes; gas fireplaces in every room; soaring ceilings and huge windows with city views. **Cons:** not close to beaches or outdoor activities; no room service (only grab-and-go food in the lobby); trendy vibe might not appeal to some. *Rooms from: $299 ✉ 17 Lincoln St., Biddeford ☎ 207/815–3977 🌐 www.lincolnhotelmaine.com 33 rooms No Meals.*

Scarborough, Prout's Neck, and Cape Elizabeth

Scarborough and Prout's Neck: 10 miles northeast of Biddeford. Cape Elizabeth: 10 miles southeast of Scarborough, 8 miles southeast of Portland.

Among the noteworthy attractions in the affluent Portland bedroom community of Cape Elizabeth are the famed Portland Head Light and the Cape Elizabeth Light, the subject of a well-known Edward Hopper painting.

Speaking of famous artists, Winslow Homer painted many of his famous oceanscapes from a tiny studio on the rocky peninsula known as Prout's Neck, a now-exclusive gated community 7 miles south of Cape Elizabeth. The studio is open to tours only through the Portland Museum of Art. The only other way to access Prouts Neck is by parking outside the gates and walking along a popular cliff trail.

GETTING HERE AND AROUND

The somewhat rural landscapes of Scarborough, the hamlet of Prout's Neck, and Cape Elizabeth are best explored by car. From Route 1 North, Routes 207 and 77 travel along the coast; most of the state parks, preserves, and vistas are along this route. From Portland, take the Casco Bay Bridge and continue onto Route 77 South.

Sights

Cape Elizabeth Light

LIGHTHOUSE | **FAMILY** | This was the site of twin lighthouses erected in 1828—and locals still call it Two Lights—but one of the lighthouses was dismantled in 1924 and converted into a private residence.

Old Orchard Beach

Located between Kennebunkport and Portland, Old Orchard Beach was a classic, upscale, place-to-be-seen resort area in the late 19th century, when the railroad brought wealthy families looking for entertainment and the benefits of fresh sea air. During the 1940s and '50s, the pier had a dance hall where stars of the time performed. Although the luster has dulled and Old Orchard is now a little tacky (though pleasantly so) these days, it remains a good place for seaside entertainments.

The center of the action is a 7-mile strip of sand beach that's accompanied by Palace Playland, New England's only boardwalk amusement park (think Coney Island or Seaside Heights). Fire claimed the end of the pier—at one time it jutted out nearly 1,800 feet into the sea—but rides, miniature golf, midway games, and souvenir stands still line both sides. Despite the peak-season crowds and fried-food odors, the atmosphere is captivating; the town even sponsors a fireworks display every Thursday night in the summer. Places to stay range from cheap motels to cottage colonies to full-service seasonal hotels. You won't find free parking, but there are ample lots. Amtrak has a seasonal stop here, too.

For even more family fun, Saco's Funtown Splashtown USA is just 10 minutes from the Old Orchard Beach Pier. Kids of all ages can cool off and play for hours amid the thrill adventures, kiddie rides, waterslides, and play pools.

The other half still operates, and you can get a great photo of it from the end of Two Lights Road (note that it's not quite visible from the nearby Two Lights State Park). The lighthouse itself is closed to the public, but you can explore the tidal pools at its base, looking for small, edible snails known as periwinkles, or just "wrinkles," as they're sometimes referred to in Maine. Picnic tables are also available. ✉ *At end of Two Lights Rd., across from The Lobster Shack at Two Lights (225 Two Lights Rd.), Cape Elizabeth.*

★ Portland Head Light

LIGHTHOUSE | **FAMILY** | Familiar to many from photographs and the Edward Hopper painting *Portland Head-Light* (1927), this lighthouse was commissioned by George Washington in 1790. The towering, white-stone structure stands over the keeper's quarters, a white home with a blazing red roof, today the Museum at Portland Head Light. The lighthouse is in 90-acre Fort Williams Park, a sprawling green space with walking paths, picnic facilities, a beach and—you guessed it—a cool old fort. ✉ *1000 Shore Rd., Cape Elizabeth* ☎ *207/799–2661* 🌐 *www.portlandheadlight.com* 🎫 *Museum $2* ⏲ *Museum closed mid-Oct.–late May.*

★ Winslow Homer Studio

HISTORIC HOME | **FAMILY** | The great American landscape painter created many of his best-known works in this seaside home between 1883 until his death in 1910. It's easy to see how this rocky, jagged peninsula might have been inspiring. The only way to get a look is on a tour with the Portland Museum of Art, which leads 2½-hour strolls through the historic property. ✉ *5 Winslow Homer Rd., Scarborough* ☎ *207/775–6148* 🌐 *www.portlandmuseum.org* 🎫 *$65* ⏲ *Closed Nov.–Apr.*

Restaurants

★ Bite Into Maine

$$ | SEAFOOD | FAMILY | Hands down Maine's best lobster roll is found at this food truck that overlooks the idyllic Portland Head Light in Cape Elizabeth. Traditional rolls smothered in ungodly amounts of drawn butter are delicious, but you've also got the option to get out of the lobster comfort zone with rolls featuring flavors like wasabi, curry, and chipotle. **Known for:** quick and informal spot for a bite; unbeatable view over the ocean; always fresh lobster. *Average main: $24 1000 Shore Rd., Cape Elizabeth 207/289–6142 www.biteintomaine.com Closed mid-Nov.–mid-Apr.*

★ The Lobster Shack at Two Lights

$$ | SEAFOOD | FAMILY | A classic spot since the 1920s, you can't beat the location—right on the water, below the lighthouse pair that gives Two Lights State Park its name—and the food's not bad either. Enjoy fresh lobster whole or piled into a hot-dog bun with a dollop of mayo, or opt for the delicious chowder, fried clams, or fish-and-chips. **Known for:** picnic tables with unparalleled views; family-friendly environment; mini-homemade blueberry pies. *Average main: $25 225 Two Lights Rd., Cape Elizabeth 207/799–1677 www.lobstershacktwolights.com Closed late Oct.–late Mar.*

★ Shade Eatery at Higgins Beach Inn

$$ | SEAFOOD | FAMILY | This charming neighborhood restaurant and bar just steps from the beach serves up generous, deeply satisfying dishes filled with locally sourced ingredients. Seafood plays a big role in the menu, with lobster rolls brimming with fresh meat; fish tacos stuffed with cilantro, lime crema, and coleslaw; a seafood chowder; and a lobster tostada. **Known for:** family-friendly environment; three-season-porch dining; casual and perfect for a postbeach bite. *Average main: $24 Higgins Beach Inn, 36 Ocean Ave., Scarborough 207/883–1479 www.higginsbeachinn.com/dining Breakfast daily and dinner Wed.–Sun. mid-May–mid-Oct. Lunch daily Memorial Day–Labor Day.*

Hotels

★ Higgins Beach Inn

$$ | B&B/INN | FAMILY | Decidedly "new Maine," this lovingly renovated 1892 inn with a laid-back, summer-casual kind of nonchalance is just steps from the surfer's paradise that is Higgins Beach. **Pros:** very family-friendly; exceptionally efficient and warm service; small touches (beach towels, sparkling-water dispenser) that make a difference. **Cons:** no pets allowed; a short walk to the beach; limited common areas. *Rooms from: $269 34 Ocean Ave., Scarborough 207/883–6684 www.higginsbeachinn.com Closed Oct.–Apr. 23 rooms Free Breakfast.*

★ Inn by the Sea

$$$$ | B&B/INN | With a location on stunning Crescent Beach, some of the state's most gracious service, and a top-notch restaurant that delights at every meal, you might never want to leave the aptly named Inn by the Sea. **Pros:** amenities like a spa and an outdoor pool with water views; hands down the most dog-friendly accommodations in Maine; direct access to Crescent Beach with chic beach chairs, towels, and umbrellas on hand. **Cons:** a little removed from Portland's food scene; not for the budget-minded; minimum stays in the high season. *Rooms from: $719 40 Bowery Beach Rd., Cape Elizabeth 207/799–3134 www.innbythesea.com 62 rooms No Meals.*

Portland

28 miles from Kennebunk via I–95 and I–295; 122 miles from Boston via I-95.

Maine's largest city may be considered small by national standards—its population is just 66,000—but its character, spirit, and appeal make it feel much larger. It's well worth at least a day or two of exploration, even if all you do is spend the entire time eating and drinking at the many phenomenal restaurants, bakeries and specialty dessert shops, craft cocktail bars, and microbreweries scattered across the city.

Portland's burgeoning Arts District centers on a revitalized Congress Street, which runs the length of the peninsular city from alongside the Western Promenade in the southwest to the Eastern Promenade on Munjoy Hill in the northeast. Washington Street, home to some of the city's newest and most exciting restaurants, runs through the East End and Munjoy Hill. Congress Street is peppered with interesting shops, eclectic restaurants, and excellent museums.

Just beyond the Arts District is the West End, an area of extensive architectural wealth. Predominantly residential, it's filled with stunning examples of the city's emphasis on preserving this past. Water tours of the harbor and excursions to the Casco Bay islands depart from the piers of Commercial Street.

GETTING HERE AND AROUND

If you're flying, the Portland International Jetport is about a 20-minute drive from Old Port. It offers direct flights to many domestic destinations; airlines include American, United, Delta, Elite Airways, Frontier, JetBlue, Southwest, and Sun Country.

If you're driving, take Interstate 95 to Interstate 295 to get to the Portland Peninsula and downtown. Commercial Street runs along the harbor, Fore Street is one block up in the heart of the Old Port, and the Arts District stretches along diagonal Congress Street. Munjoy Hill is on the eastern end of the peninsula and the West End on the opposite side.

Alternatively, there is Amtrak (via the Downeaster train) and bus (Concord Coach Lines) service from Boston.

Portland is wonderfully walkable, but there are taxis and ride-shares available. To get to many islands in Casco Bay, hop aboard a waterfront ferry or taxi.

TOURS

Casco Bay Lines

BOATING | FAMILY | Casco Bay Lines operates ferry service to the seven bay islands with year-round populations. Summer offerings include music cruises, lighthouse excursions, and a trip to Bailey Island with a stopover for lunch. Round-trip fees range from $7.70 to $11.55, depending on which island you're visiting.

Peaks Island is the only island to allow cars to be transported by ferry, and those car reservations are often tough to get during the busy summer months. On most islands, bikes and/or golf carts are available for rent close to the ferry terminal. You can bring along your own bike on the ferry for $6.50 per adult and $3.25 per child. ✉ *Maine State Pier, 56 Commercial St., The Old Port and the Waterfront* ☎ *207/774–7871* 🌐 *www.cascobaylines.com.*

Lucky Catch Cruises

BOATING | FAMILY | Set sail in a real lobster boat: This company gives you the genuine experience, which includes hauling traps and the chance to purchase the catch. ✉ *Long Wharf, 170 Commercial St., The Old Port and the Waterfront* ☎ *207/761–0941* 🌐 *www.luckycatch.com* 🎫 *From $25* 🕑 *Closed Nov.–Apr.*

Maine Foodie Tours

SPECIAL-INTEREST TOURS | Learn about Portland's culinary history and sample such local delights as lobster tacos,

Portland's busy harbor is full of working boats, pleasure craft, and ferries headed to the Casco Bay Islands.

organic cheese, and the famous Maine whoopie pie. The culinary walking tours include stops at fishmongers, bakeries, and cheese shops that provide products to Portland's famed restaurants. From summer into early fall, you can also take a chocolate tour, a bike-and-brewery tour, or a trolley tour with a stop at a microbrewery. Tours begin at various locales in the Old Port. ✉ *320 Fore St., Portland* ☎ *207/233–7485* 🌐 *www.mainefoodietours.com* 🎫 *From $29.*

Odyssey Whale Watch

BOATING | **FAMILY** | From mid-May to mid-October, Odyssey Whale Watch leads whale-watching and deep-sea-fishing excursions. ✉ *Long Wharf, 170 Commercial St., The Old Port and the Waterfront* ☎ *207/775–0727* 🌐 *www.odysseywhalewatch.com* 🎫 *From $29* ⏲ *Closed Nov.–Apr.*

★ Portland Schooner Co.

BOATING | **FAMILY** | May through October this company and its efficient crew offers daily two-hour windjammer cruises aboard the beautiful vintage schooners, *The Bagheera, Timberwind,* and *Wendameen.* The sunsets alone are worth the sail, but breezes on a hot summer day and views of the islands put the experience over the top. You can also arrange private charters. ✉ *Maine State Pier, 56 Commercial St., The Old Port and the Waterfront* ☎ *207/766–2500* 🌐 *www.portlandschooner.com* 🎫 *Prices vary according to time of sails* ⏲ *Closed Nov.–Apr.*

Portland Discovery Land and Sea Tours

BUS TOURS | **FAMILY** | These informative trolley tours detail the city's historical and architectural highlights, Memorial Day–October. It's one of the best ways to tour the harbor and Casco Bay, including an up-close look at several lighthouses. Options include combining a city tour with a bay or lighthouse cruise. ✉ *Long Wharf, 170 Commercial St., Portland* ☎ *207/774–0808* 🌐 *www.portlanddiscovery.com* 🎫 *From $23* ☞ *Closed Nov.–Apr.*

Portland Fire Engine Co. Tours

SPECIAL-INTEREST TOURS | FAMILY | See Portland on a vintage Fire Engine on these narrated, 50-minute tours that highlight the city's lighthouses, civil war forts, and historical buildings, and architecture. Tours leave from the waterfront and circle through the city, passing everything from the Maine State Pier and East End Beach to Longfellow Square, Portland Museum of Art, and Monument Square. ✉ *180 Commercial St., Old Port, Portland* ☎ *207/252–6358* 🌐 *portlandfiretours.com* 🎫 *From $30* ⏲ *Closed Nov.–May.*

VISITOR INFORMATION

CONTACTS Downtown Portland. ✉ *549 Congress St., Portland* ☎ *207/772–6828* 🌐 *www.portlandmaine.com.* **Greater Portland Convention and Visitors Bureau.** ✉ *14 Ocean Gateway Pier, Portland* ☎ *207/772–4994* 🌐 *www.visitportland.com.*

The Old Port and the Waterfront

A major international port and a working harbor since the early 17th century, Portland's Old Port and the Waterfront bridge the gap between the city's historic commercial activities and those of today. It is home to fishing boats docked alongside whale-watching charters, luxury yachts, cruise ships, and oil tankers from around the globe. Commercial Street parallels the water and is lined with brick buildings and warehouses that were built following the Great Fire of 1866. In the 19th century, candle makers and sail stitchers plied their trades here; today specialty shops, art galleries, and restaurants have taken up residence.

Cannabis in Vacationland

Though Maine voters approved legalizing the recreational use and sales of marijuana in November 2016, various delays prevented retail shops from opening until October 2020. Since then a deluge of outlets has opened in the Greater Portland area, and although availability has expanded statewide, Portland is by far the place to find the most retail options.

Sights

Harbor Fish Market

STORE/MALL | A Portland favorite since 1968, this freshest-of-the-fresh seafood market ships lobsters and other Maine delectables almost anywhere in the country. A bright-red facade on a working wharf opens into a bustling space with bubbling lobster tanks and fish, clams, and other shellfish on ice; employees are as skilled with a fillet knife as sushi chefs. There is also a small retail store. ✉ *9 Custom House Wharf, The Old Port and the Waterfront* ☎ *207/775–0251* 🌐 *www.harborfish.com* 🎫 *Free.*

Restaurants

Flatbread

$$ | PIZZA | FAMILY | Families, students, and bohemian types gather at this popular New England chain flatbread-pizza place where two massive wood-fire ovens are the heart of the soaring, warehouselike space. Waits can be long on weekends and in summer, but you can call a half-hour ahead to put your name on the list, or grab a drink from the bar and wait outside with a view of the harbor. **Known for:** unfussy, kid-friendly atmosphere;

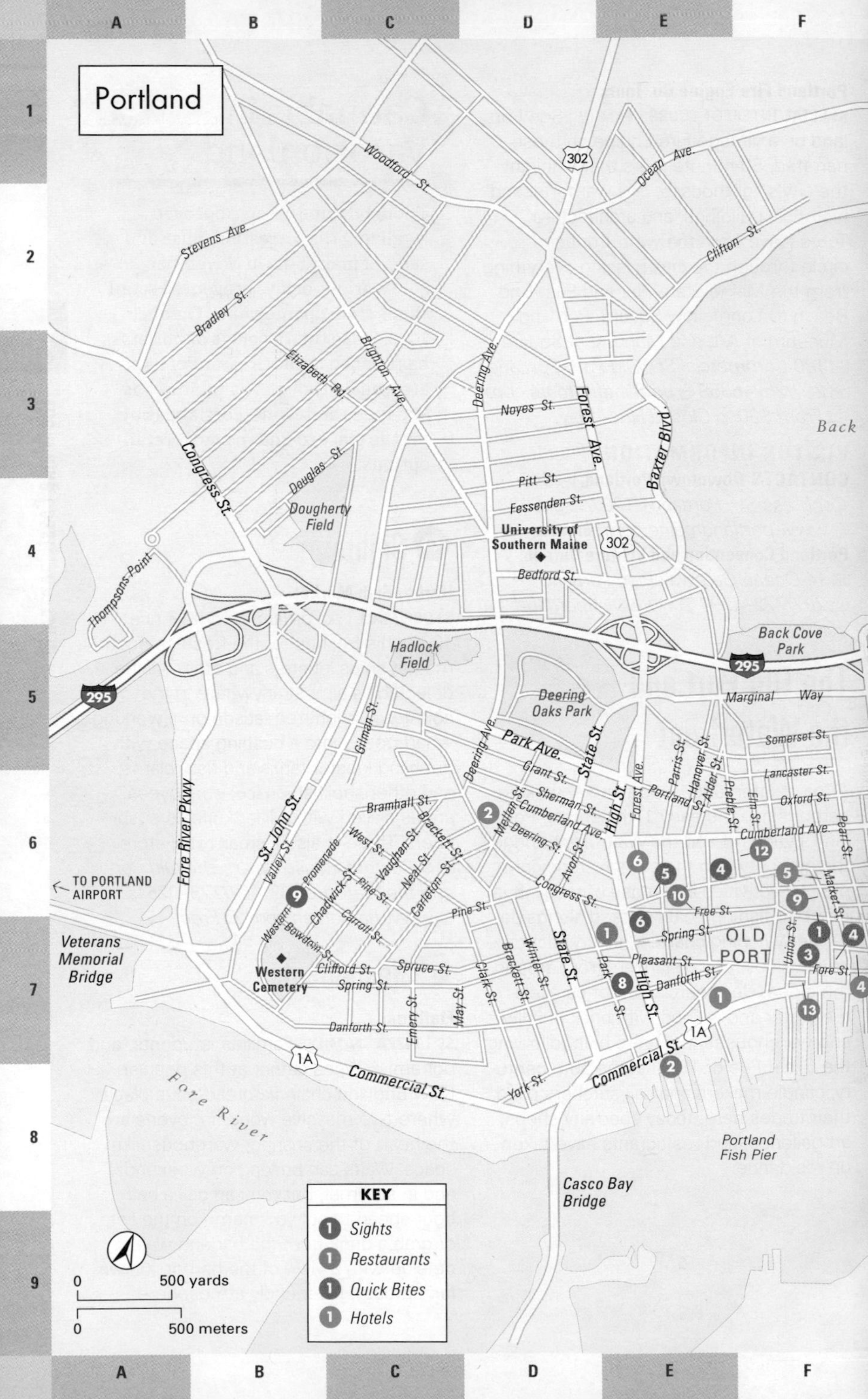

Portland
A
B
C
D
E
F
1
2
3
4
5
6
7
8
9
Woodford St.
302
Ocean Ave.
Stevens Ave.
Clifton St.
Bradley St.
Elizabeth Rd.
Brighton Ave.
Deering Ave.
Noyes St.
Forest Ave.
Baxter Blvd.
Back
Congress St.
Douglas St.
Pitt St.
Fessenden St.
Dougherty Field
University of Southern Maine
302
Thompsons Point
Bedford St.
Hadlock Field
Back Cove Park
295
295
Deering Oaks Park
Marginal Way
Gilman St.
Deering Ave.
Park Ave.
State St.
Somerset St.
Parris St.
Hanover St.
Alder St.
Lancaster St.
Forest Ave.
Grant St.
High St.
Portland St.
Preble St.
Oxford St.
Fore River Pkwy
St. John St.
Bramhall St.
Brackett St.
Sherman St.
Elm St.
Cumberland Ave.
Melien St.
Cumberland Ave.
Pearl St.
Deering St.
West St.
Vaughan St.
Promenade
Valley St.
Neal St.
Avon St.
Carleton St.
Market St.
TO PORTLAND AIRPORT
Chadwick St.
Pine St.
Congress St.
Free St.
Western
Pine St.
Carroll St.
Bowdoin St.
Spring St.
OLD PORT
Union St.
Veterans Memorial Bridge
Winter St.
State St.
Park St.
Pleasant St.
Fore St.
Brackett St.
Clifford St.
Spruce St.
Clark St.
Danforth St.
Western Cemetery
Spring St.
High St.
Emery St.
May St.
Danforth St.
1A
1A
Commercial St.
Commercial St.
York St.
Fore River
Portland Fish Pier
Casco Bay Bridge
KEY
Sights
Restaurants
Quick Bites
Hotels
0
500 yards
0
500 meters

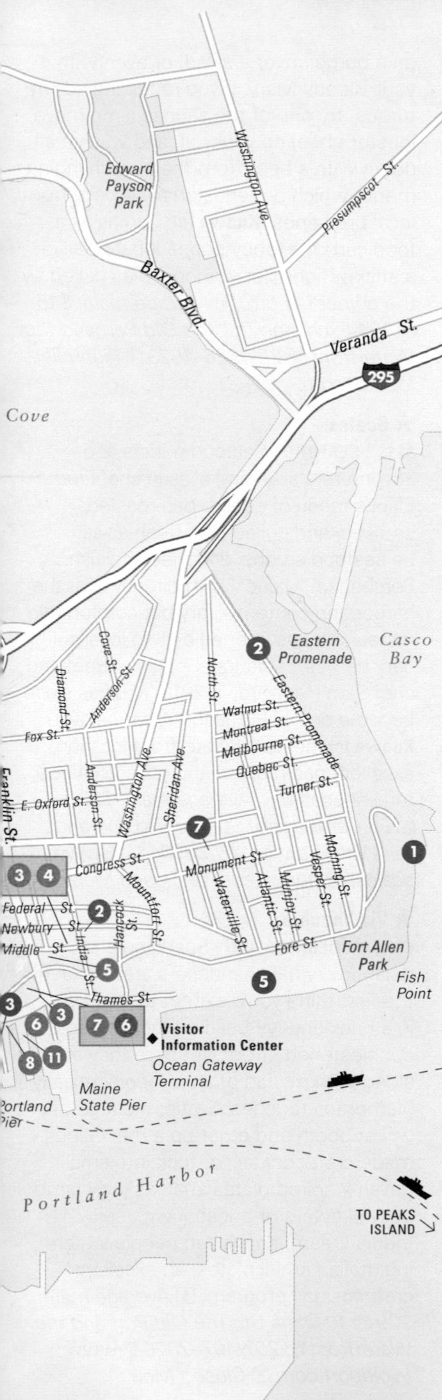

Sights

1 East End Beach I6
2 Eastern Promenade H5
3 Harbor Fish Market G7
4 Maine Historical Society and Longfellow House E6
5 Maine Narrow Gauge Railroad Museum H7
6 Portland Museum of Art E7
7 Portland Observatory H6
8 Victoria Mansion E7
9 Western Promenade B6

Restaurants

1 BaoBao Dumpling House E7
2 Becky's Diner E8
3 Duckfat G7
4 East Ender G7
5 Eventide Oyster Co. G7
6 Flatbread G7
7 Fore Street G7
8 Gilbert's Chowder House G7
9 Highroller Lobster Co. ... F6
10 Leeward E6
11 Scales G7
12 Slab Sicilian Street Food F6
13 Via Vecchia F7

Quick Bites

1 Bard Coffee F6
2 Coffee by Design G6
3 Gelato Fiasco F7
4 The Holy Donut F7
5 Speckled Ax Wood Roasted Coffee E6
6 Standard Baking Co G7

Hotels

1 Canopy by Hilton Portland Waterfront E7
2 The Francis D6
3 Hilton Garden Inn Portland Downtown Waterfront G7
4 The Portland Regency Hotel and Spa F7
5 The Press Hotel F6
6 The Westin Portland Harborview E6

outdoor dining on a deck that overlooks the working waterfront; dogs allowed on outside deck. *Average main: $18* ✉ *72 Commercial St., The Old Port and the Waterfront* ☎ *207/772–8777* 🌐 *www.flatbreadcompany.com.*

★ Fore Street

$$$ | **MODERN AMERICAN** | One of Maine's most legendary chefs, Sam Hayward, opened this much-lauded restaurant in a renovated warehouse on the edge of the Old Port in 1996; today every copper-top table in the main dining room has a view of the enormous brick oven and soapstone hearth that anchor the open kitchen. The menu changes daily to reflect the freshest ingredients from Maine's farms and waters, as well as the tremendous creativity of the staff. **Known for:** turnspit roasted meats; handmade charcuterie; last-minute planners take heart: a third of the tables are reserved for walk-ins. *Average main: $30* ✉ *288 Fore St., The Old Port and the Waterfront* ☎ *207/775–2717* 🌐 *www.forestreet.biz* ⏲ *No lunch.*

Gilbert's Chowder House

$$ | **SEAFOOD** | **FAMILY** | This is the real deal, as quintessential as old-school Maine dining can be. Clam rakes and nautical charts hang from the walls of this unpretentious waterfront diner, and the flavors come from the depths of the North Atlantic, prepared and presented simply: fried scallops, haddock, clams and extraordinary clam cakes, and fish, clam, and seafood chowders (corn, too). **Known for:** family-friendly environment; classic lobster rolls, served on toasted hot-dog buns bursting with claw and tail meat; an ice-cream parlor to round out your meal; chalkboard daily specials. *Average main: $19* ✉ *92 Commercial St., The Old Port and the Waterfront* ☎ *207/871–5636* 🌐 *www.gilbertschowderhouse.com.*

Highroller Lobster Co.

$$ | **SEAFOOD** | **FAMILY** | Opened in early 2018, this high-energy spot serves lobster numerous ways—in a roll, on a stick, on a burger, over a salad, or even with your Bloody Mary. If you're feeling adventurous, try one of the sauces (lime mayo, lobster ghee) on your roll, and wash it all down with a beer from the ever-changing menu, which depends on availability from local breweries. **Known for:** origins as a food cart; the lobby pop (a lobster tail on a stick); Highroller whoopie pies baked by the owner's mom. *Average main: $15* ✉ *104 Exchange St., The Old Port and the Waterfront* ☎ *207/536–1623* 🌐 *highrollerlobster.com.*

★ Scales

$$$$ | **SEAFOOD** | Seafood purists and adventurers alike find bliss in chef Fred Elliot's menu of superb pan-roasted, smoked, and grilled fish; fresh-as-can-be seafood crudos; and fried shellfish. Perched on Maine Wharf directly over the harbor, the contemporary-but-comfortable restaurant was opened by two local culinary heroes, restaurateur Dana Street and chef Sam Hayward, in 2016, and has since become one of Portland's most beloved. **Known for:** beautiful waterfront location; excellent pan-roasted and grilled seafood; fun bar scene. *Average main: $39* ✉ *68 Commercial St., The Old Port and the Waterfront* ☎ *207/8050444* 🌐 *www.scalesrestaurant.com* ⏲ *Closed Mon.*

★ Via Vecchia

$$$ | **MODERN ITALIAN** | Sparkling and gigantic crystal chandeliers aren't exactly the first thing you'd expect to greet you in a brick-and-ivy building tucked into a cobblestoned street, yet here they are—along with myriad other unapologetically glamorous touches. Settle into a green velvet booth and order up a meticulously made craft cocktail, or tuck into small Italian-inspired plates such as juicy lamb belly skewers or bucatini with spicy 'nduja cream. **Known for:** people-watching; Italian small plates; an excellent craft cocktail program. *Average main: $29* ✉ *10 Dana St., The Old Port and the Waterfront* ☎ *207/407–7070* 🌐 *www.vvoldport.com* ⏲ *Closed Mon.*

Coffee and Quick Bites

Bard Coffee

$ | **CAFÉ** | The beans sourcing this shop's delicious brew are bought from a handful of small growers—you can read their bios on the website—and roasted in-house. Enjoy your brew hot, cold, or iced with a locally made baked good. **Known for:** close relationships with sources; passionate, knowledgeable baristas; bulk coffee and tea. *Average main: $5* *185 Middle St., The Old Port and the Waterfront* *207/899–4788* *www.bardcoffee.com.*

★ Gelato Fiasco

$ | **CAFÉ** | **FAMILY** | Proper Italian gelato and *sorbetto* here come in traditional flavors as well as more offbeat varieties like torched marshmallow s'more, mascarpone pistachio caramel, and mint brownie cookie. There are new flavors every day, along with espresso and other hot drinks. **Known for:** you can try every single flavor before deciding on what you'll get; long lines out the door in the summer; multigenerational bonding spot. *Average main: $5* *425 Fore St., The Old Port and the Waterfront* *207/699–4314* *www.gelatofiasco.com.*

The Holy Donut

$ | **CAFÉ** | **FAMILY** | Don't pass up a chance to try these sweet and savory, all-natural, Maine potato-based doughnuts glazed in flavors such as dark chocolate–sea salt, maple, pomegranate, triple berry, and chai, or stuffed with delicious fillings like bacon and cheddar, or ricotta. There are always new inventions, too, such as salted chocolate caramel and key lime pie. **Known for:** long lines, but worth the wait; shop closes for the day once all the doughnuts are sold; vegan and gluten-free options are available. *Average main: $5* *177 Commercial St., The Old Port and the Waterfront* *207/331–5655* *www.theholydonut.com.*

★ Standard Baking Co.

$ | **BAKERY** | **FAMILY** | You'd be hard-pressed to find a more pitch-perfect bakery in the Pine Tree State, but you'll have to pop by early (or put in an order in advance) to get your mitts on these delectable baked goods. The perfectly airy croissants, crusty baguettes, beguiling tarts, dainty Madeleines, and creative breads incorporate locally sourced grains and are nothing short of revelations. **Known for:** good selection of locally roasted coffees; amazing galettes and brioches; creative scones. *Average main: $3* *75 Commercial St., The Old Port and the Waterfront* *207/772–5519* *www.standardbakingco.com.*

Hotels

Hilton Garden Inn Portland Downtown Waterfront

$$$ | **HOTEL** | This bright, clean, and modern hotel is a perfect base for exploring on foot the adjacent Old Port and nearby East End, and it's only a walk across the street to catch a ferry to the Casco Bay islands. **Pros:** heated saltwater lap pool; central location for exploring; some rooms with harbor view. **Cons:** no pets; no self-parking; some rooms face neighboring businesses. *Rooms from: $379* *65 Commercial St., The Old Port and the Waterfront* *207/780–0780* *www.hilton.com/en/hilton-garden-inn* *120 rooms* *No Meals.*

The Portland Regency Hotel and Spa

$$ | **HOTEL** | Not part of a chain despite the "Regency" name, this brick building in the center of the Old Port served as Portland's armory in the late 19th century. **Pros:** easy walk to sites; pet-friendly ($75 nonrefundable cleaning fee); full-service spa with lounges, saunas, steam rooms, hot tub, and an array of luxurious treatments. **Cons:** no pool; busy downtown location; not all rooms have noteworthy views. *Rooms from: $300* *20 Milk St., The Old Port and the Waterfront* *207/774–4200, 800/727–3436* *www.*

theregency.com 95 rooms No Meals.

★ The Press Hotel

$$$ | **HOTEL** | **FAMILY** | In a former newspaper building, this boutique hotel is part of Marriott's Autograph Collection; the hotel feels both broadly cosmopolitan and distinctly Maine. **Pros:** Frette bed linens and Maine-made Cuddledown comforters and bed throws; sparkling-clean rooms with a modern-design feel; art gallery and excellent public spaces with tasteful furnishings. **Cons:** right next to the fire department; valet parking can be expensive; some rooms have underwhelming views. *Rooms from: $375* *119 Exchange St., The Old Port and the Waterfront* *877/890–5641* *www.thepresshotel.com* *110 rooms* *No Meals.*

Nightlife

Gritty McDuff's Portland Brew Pub

BREWPUBS | Maine's original brewpub serves fine ales, British pub fare, and seafood dishes. There are between six and eight rotating ales on tap, and there's always a seasonal offering. *396 Fore St., The Old Port and the Waterfront* *207/772–2739* *www.grittys.com.*

★ Portland Hunt and Alpine Club

BARS | Scandinavian-inspired dishes and serious craft cocktails drive this hip locale that also offers excellent charcuterie and seafood boards. If it's free, grab a seat in the intimate alpine-style hut, off to the side of the main room. And don't miss the excellent happy hour, weekdays 1–6. *75 Market St., The Old Port and the Waterfront* *207/747–4754* *www.huntandalpineclub.com.*

Shopping

Abacus Gallery

ANTIQUES & COLLECTIBLES | This appealing crafts gallery has gift items in glass, wood, and textiles, as well as fine modern jewelry. *44 Exchange St., The Old Port and the Waterfront* *207/772–4880* *www.abacusgallery.com.*

Lisa Marie's Made in Maine

SOUVENIRS | Here you'll find an excellent selection of locally sourced items from soaps and candles to dish towels, pottery, and jewelry, all made in the great state of Maine. *35 Exchange St., The Old Port and the Waterfront* *207/828–1515* *www.lisamariesmadeinmaine.com.*

★ Sea Bags

OTHER SPECIALTY STORE | The brand's flagship location displays totes in every shape and size made from recycled sailcloth and decorated with bright, graphic patterns. Check out the display that shows you exactly how a sail is used to create all the different bags and accessories. The factory store, located just a few blocks away on the Custom House Wharf, is where the bags are actually sewn; you can find some factory sales as well. *123 Commercial St., The Old Port and the Waterfront* *207/835–0096* *www.seabags.com.*

★ Sherman's Maine Coast Book Shops

BOOKS | Open since 1886, Sherman's is Maine's oldest bookstore chain. The Portland store has an impressive stock of well-selected books interspersed with excellent gift choices, such as stationery, candles, and holiday decor, as well as a fun array of toys. It's a good place to spend a cold or rainy day perusing the selection. *49 Exchange St., The Old Port and the Waterfront* *207/773–4100* *www.shermans.com.*

Activities

Casco Bay Lines

BOATING | **FAMILY** | Casco Bay Lines operates ferry service to the seven bay islands with year-round populations. Summer offerings include music cruises, lighthouse excursions, and a trip to Bailey Island with a stopover for lunch. Round-trip fees range from $7.70 to $11.55, depending on which island you're visiting.

Peaks Island is the only island to allow cars to be transported by ferry, and those car reservations are often tough to get during the busy summer months. On most islands, bikes and/or golf carts are available for rent close to the ferry terminal. You can bring along your own bike on the ferry for $6.50 per adult and $3.25 per child. ✉ *Maine State Pier, 56 Commercial St., The Old Port and the Waterfront* ☎ *207/774–7871* 🌐 *www.cascobaylines.com.*

Lucky Catch Cruises

BOATING | FAMILY | Set sail in a real lobster boat: This company gives you the genuine experience, which includes hauling traps and the chance to purchase the catch. ✉ *Long Wharf, 170 Commercial St., The Old Port and the Waterfront* ☎ *207/761–0941* 🌐 *www.luckycatch.com* 🎟 *From $25* ⏲ *Closed Nov.–Apr.*

Odyssey Whale Watch

BOATING | FAMILY | From mid-May to mid-October, Odyssey Whale Watch leads whale-watching and deep-sea-fishing excursions. ✉ *Long Wharf, 170 Commercial St., The Old Port and the Waterfront* ☎ *207/775–0727* 🌐 *www.odysseywhalewatch.com* 🎟 *From $29* ⏲ *Closed Nov.–Apr.*

★ **Portland Schooner Co.**

BOATING | FAMILY | May through October this company and its efficient crew offers daily two-hour windjammer cruises aboard the beautiful vintage schooners, *The Bagheera, Timberwind,* and *Wendameen.* The sunsets alone are worth the sail, but breezes on a hot summer day and views of the islands put the experience over the top. You can also arrange private charters. ✉ *Maine State Pier, 56 Commercial St., The Old Port and the Waterfront* ☎ *207/766–2500* 🌐 *www.portlandschooner.com* 🎟 *Prices vary according to time of sails* ⏲ *Closed Nov.–Apr.*

East End, Munjoy Hill, and Washington Ave.

These three sections of town are often referred to independently, but they also overlap in large parts; Washington Avenue runs through both areas, and Munjoy Hill is part of the East End. The latter includes the Eastern Promenade, East End Beach, and the Portland Observatory. Meanwhile, Washington Avenue has become one of the most concentrated areas of fantastic food in all Maine. From authentic Thai fixings and ultrafresh oysters to creative barbecue and locally made kombucha, it's all here.

Sights

East End Beach

BEACH | FAMILY | Portland's only public beach, it's set at the bottom of the hill of the Eastern Promenade. Its panoramic views of Casco Bay make it a popular summer spot, as do amenities like convenient parking, picnic tables, and a boat launch. **Amenities:** food and drink; parking (fee); toilets; water sports. **Best for:** sunrise; sunsets; swimming; walking. ✉ *Cutter St., East End.*

Eastern Promenade

PROMENADE | FAMILY | Between the city's two promenades, this one, often overlooked by tourists, has by far the best view. Gracious Victorian homes, many now converted to condos and apartments, border one side of the street. On the other is 68 acres of hillside parkland that includes Ft. Allen Park and, at the base of the hill, the Eastern Prom Trail and tiny East End Beach and boat launch. On a sunny day the Eastern Prom is a lovely spot for picnicking, snacking (there are always a few top-notch food trucks), and people-watching. ✉ *Washington Ave. to Fore St., East End.*

Maine Narrow Gauge Railroad Museum

TRAIN/TRAIN STATION | FAMILY | Whether you're crazy about old trains or just want to see the sights from a different perspective, the railroad museum has an extensive collection of locomotives and rail coaches, and offers scenic tours on narrow-gauge railcars. The 3-mile jaunts run on the hour, at 10, 11, noon, 1, 2, and 3 every day in the operating season. Rides take you along Casco Bay, at the foot of the Eastern Promenade. The operating season caps off with a fall harvest ride (complete with cider), and during the Christmas season there are special Polar Express rides, based on the popular children's book. ✉ *58 Fore St., East End* ☎ *207/828–0814* 🌐 *www.mainenarrowgauge.org* 🎫 *Museum $5, train rides $12* ⏲ *Closed Nov.–Apr.*

Portland Observatory

OBSERVATORY | FAMILY | This octagonal observatory on Munjoy Hill was built in 1807 by Captain Lemuel Moody, a retired sea captain, as a maritime signal tower. Moody used a telescope to identify incoming ships, and flags to signal to merchants where to unload their cargo. Held in place by 122 tons of ballast, it's the last remaining historic maritime signal station in the country. The guided tour leads all the way to the dome, where you can step out on the deck and take in views of Portland, the islands, and inland toward the White Mountains. ✉ *138 Congress St., East End* ☎ *207/774–5561* 🌐 *www.portlandlandmarks.org* 🎫 *$10* ⏲ *Closed mid-Oct.–late May.*

Restaurants

★ Duckfat

$$ | MODERN AMERICAN | FAMILY | Even in midafternoon, this small, casual, and cool panini-and-more shop in the Old Port is packed. The focus here is everyday farm-to-table fare: the signature Belgian fries are made with Maine potatoes cooked, yes, in duck fat and served in paper cones, and standards include meat loaf and the BGT (bacon, goat cheese, tomato). **Known for:** decadent poutine with duck-fat gravy; hopping atmosphere—waits for a table can be long; thick milk shakes prepared with local gelato by Gelato Fiasco. $ *Average main: $12* ✉ *43 Middle St., East End* ☎ *207/774–8080* 🌐 *www.duckfat.com* ⏲ *Closed Wed.*

★ East Ender

$$$ | AMERICAN | FAMILY | The emphasis at this cozy neighborhood restaurant is on the superb food rather than the atmosphere, which isn't surprising, given that the owners formerly served their tasty, no-fuss fare from a truck. Lunch and dinner feature locally sourced, sustainable ingredients in dishes that reflect the seasons. **Known for:** mouthwatering house-smoked bacon; crispy, thrice-cooked fries; brunch cocktails that incorporate ingredients from local distilleries and house-made cordials. $ *Average main: $24* ✉ *47 Middle St., East End* ☎ *207/879–7669* 🌐 *www.eastenderportland.com* ⏲ *Closed Sun. and Mon.*

★ Eventide Oyster Co.

$$ | SEAFOOD | Not only does Eventide have fresh, tasty oysters from all over Maine and New England, artfully prepared with novel accoutrements like kimchi, ginger ices, and cucumber-champagne mignonette, it also serves delicious crudos and ceviches with unique ingredients like blood orange and chili miso. The menu constantly changes, depending on what's in season. **Known for:** brown-butter lobster rolls; a decent selection of alternatives for nonseafood lovers; teaming up with other local restaurants for special cook-offs and menus. $ *Average main: $15* ✉ *86 Middle St., East End* ☎ *207/774–8538* 🌐 *www.eventideoysterco.com.*

Coffee and Quick Bites

★ Coffee By Design
$ | CAFÉ | Housed in a former bakery building, this small and local coffeehouse company pours specialty coffee employing unusually high standards for environmental and economic sustainability. Flavor-wise, the sturdy coffee is brewed from beans they roast themselves, which have become a staple in many locals' home kitchens. **Known for:** among Portland's original artisanal coffee roasters; community commitment; three locations citywide. *Average main: $6* ✉ *67 India St., East End* ☎ *207/780–6767* 🌐 *www.coffeebydesign.com.*

The Arts District

This district starts at the top of Exchange Street, near the upper end of the Old Port, and extends west past the Portland Museum of Art. Congress Street is the district's central artery. Much of Portland's economic heart is here, including several large banking and law firms. It's also where Maine College of Art and the Portland Public Library make their homes. Art galleries, specialty stores, and a score of restaurants line Congress Street. Parking is tricky; two-hour meters dot the sidewalks, but there are several nearby parking garages.

★ Maine Historical Society and Longfellow House
HISTORIC HOME | The boyhood home of the famous American poet was the first brick house in Portland and the oldest building on the peninsula. It's particularly interesting, because most of the furnishings, including the young Longfellow's writing desk, are original. Wallpaper, window coverings, and a vibrant painted carpet are period reproductions. Built in 1785, the large dwelling (a third floor was added in 1815) sits back from the street and has a small portico over its entrance and four chimneys surmounting the roof. It's part of the Maine Historical Society, which includes an adjacent research library and a museum with exhibits about Maine life. After your guided tour, stay for a picnic in the Longfellow Garden; it's open to the public during museum hours. ✉ *489 Congress St., Arts District* ☎ *207/774–1822* 🌐 *www.mainehistory.org* *House and museum $15, gardens free* *Closed Nov.–Apr.*

★ Portland Museum of Art
ART MUSEUM | Maine's largest public art institution's collection includes fine seascapes and landscapes by Winslow Homer, John Marin, Andrew Wyeth, Edward Hopper, Marsden Hartley, and other American painters. Homer's *Weatherbeaten*, a quintessential Maine Coast image, is here, and the museum owns and displays, on a rotating basis, 16 more of his paintings, plus more than 400 of his illustrations (and it offers tours of the Winslow Homer Studio in nearby Prouts Neck). The museum has works by Monet and Picasso, as well as Degas, Renoir, and Chagall. I.M. Pei's colleague Henry Cobb designed the strikingly modern Charles Shipman Payson building. ✉ *7 Congress Sq., Arts District* ☎ *207/775–6148* 🌐 *www.portlandmuseum.org* *$18 (free Fri. 4–8 pm)* *Closed Mon. and Tues.*

Victoria Mansion
HISTORIC HOME | Built between 1858 and 1860, this Italianate mansion is widely regarded as the most sumptuously ornamented dwelling of its period remaining in the country. Architect Henry Austin designed the house for hotelier Ruggles Morse and his wife, Olive. The interior design—everything from the plasterwork to the furniture (much of it original)—is the only surviving commission of New York designer Gustave Herter. Behind the elegant brownstone exterior of this National Historic Landmark are colorful frescoed walls and ceilings,

ornate marble mantelpieces, gilded gas chandeliers, a magnificent 6-foot-by-25-foot stained-glass ceiling window, and a freestanding mahogany staircase. A guided tour runs about 45 minutes and covers all the architectural highlights. Victorian era–themed gifts and art are sold in the museum shop, and the museum often has special theme events. *109 Danforth St., Arts District* *207/772–4841* *www.victoriamansion.org* *$18* *Closed Nov.–Apr.*

Restaurants

★ Leeward

$$$ | ITALIAN | With nods from critics far and wide, one of the state's most celebrated restaurants is also one of its newest. This high-ceilinged, Italian-centric restaurant comes from husband and wife team Jake and Raquel Stevens who turn out exquisite handmade pasta like the spaghettini Nero laced with squid, serrano chile, pork brood, white wine, and bread crumbs—a revelation of flavors both strong and soothing. **Known for:** thoughtfully chosen wine list; delicious handmade pastas; happening bar scene on weekend nights. *Average main: $25* *85 Free St., Arts District* *207/8088623* *www.leewardmaine.com* *Closed Sun. and Mon. No lunch.*

Coffee and Quick Bites

Speckled Ax Wood Roasted Coffee

$ | CAFÉ | The Speckled Ax serves up a seriously delicious coffee, whether cold brewed or piping hot with frothy milk. The secret to the richness of the beans is the painstaking roasting process, using a vintage Italian Petroncini roaster fired with local hardwood—ask to take a peek at that contraption while you wait for your drink. **Known for:** pastries and other baked goods; local gathering space; a hip vibe. *Average main: $4* *567 Congress St., Arts District* *207/660–3333* *www.speckledax.com.*

Hotels

The Westin Portland Harborview

$$ | HOTEL | This imposing structure was New England's largest hotel, the Eastland, when built in 1927 and is a well-known part of the Portland skyline. **Pros:** the views from the rooftop bar and lounge; pet friendly; on-site laundry. **Cons:** rooms with city views cost more; not all rooms have harbor views; often bustling with event attendees. *Rooms from: $254* *157 High St., Arts District* *207/775–5411* *www.marriott.com* *289 rooms* *No Meals.*

Shopping

Renys Department Store

DEPARTMENT STORE | With its emphasis on high-value merchandise—from Timberland shoes and Carhartt jackets to locally made products like Maine Chefs Wild Blueberry Jam, Raye's Mustard, and bamboo cutting boards made into a map of Maine—this third-generation family-run Maine-centric department has been serving Mainers since 1949. There are 17 stores around the state, but this location is an excellent place to pick up clever souvenirs, a sweater for chilly nights, gifts for folks back home, or just a home accessory to reinforce your love of the Pine Tree State. *540 Congress St., Arts District* *207/553–9061* *www.renys.com.*

The West End

A leisurely walk through Portland's West End, beginning at the top of the Arts District, offers a real treat to historic architecture buffs. Elaborate building began in the mid-1800s, encouraged by both a robust economy and Portland's devastating fire of 1866, which leveled nearly one-third of the city. The neighborhood, on the National Register of Historic Places, reveals an extraordinary display of architectural splendor, from High

Victorian Gothic to lush Italianate, Queen Anne, and Colonial Revival.

Sights

Western Promenade

PROMENADE | FAMILY | Developed beginning in 1836 and landscaped by the Olmsted Brothers, this 18-acre park is one Portland's oldest preserved spaces. It offers wonderful sunset views in spots, as well as a network of wooded trails, places to sit and people-watch, and paths that pass by the neighborhood's historic homes.

A good place to start is at the head of the Western Promenade, which has benches and a nice view. From the Old Port, take Danforth Street all the way up to Vaughn Street; take a right on Vaughn and then an immediate left onto Western Promenade. Pass by the Western Cemetery, Portland's second official burial ground, laid out in 1829—inside is the ancestral plot of poet Henry Wadsworth Longfellow—and look for street parking. ✉ *Danforth St. to Bramhall St., West End.*

Restaurants

BaoBao Dumpling House

$$ | ASIAN | FAMILY | In a historic town house with traditional Asian decor (a 30-foot copper dragon watches over diners) in Portland's quaint West End, this dumpling house serves deeply satisfying Asian-inspired comfort food in an intimate setting. Start with the house-made Asian slaw, then move to dumplings filled with tried-and-trues such as pork and cabbage or something less traditional, like beef bulgogi or shrimp and bacon. **Known for:** dishes integrating local, seasonal ingredients; tap takeovers by local brewmasters; dishes other than the namesake dumplings. [$] *Average main: $12* ✉ *133 Spring St., at Park St., West End* ☎ *207/772–8400* 🌐 *www.baobaodumplinghouse.com* ⏲ *Closed Mon. and Tues.*

Becky's Diner

$$ | DINER | FAMILY | You won't find a more local or unfussy place—or one more abuzz with conversation at 4 am—than this waterfront institution way down on the end of Commercial Street. The food is cheap, generous in proportion, and has that satisfying, old-time-diner quality. **Known for:** classic Maine diner food featuring many seafood dishes; very lively atmosphere commingling locals and visitors; parking is easy—a rarity in Portland. [$] *Average main: $14* ✉ *390 Commercial St., West End* ☎ *207/773–7070* 🌐 *www.beckysdiner.com.*

★ Slab Sicilian Street Food

$$ | PIZZA | FAMILY | Let the fact that this incredibly popular outfit doesn't even bother to call its signature foodstuff "pizza" (but instead, "Sicilian street food") be your first hint that the pie here is a different animal altogether. And while there are perfectly good sandwiches on offer, almost everyone's here for the pillowy, chewy, old world–style pizza, by turns smothered in mushrooms or meats, freshly chopped herbs, or graced with a dollop of blue cheese dip. **Known for:** excellent thick- and thin-crust pizzas; dough and pizza fixings to make at home; good sandwiches. [$] *Average main: $14* ✉ *25 Preble St., West End* ☎ *207/245–3088* 🌐 *www.slabportland.com* ⏲ *Closed Tues. and Wed.*

Hotels

Canopy by Hilton Portland Waterfront

$$$$ | HOTEL | FAMILY | One of the newest additions to Portland's hotel landscape, there's a soft contemporary feel throughout the property—abstract carpets, plenty of warm lighting, textured headboards, compact tables, and multimedia artwork give guest rooms a nice mix of sleekness and coziness. **Pros:** pet-friendly room available; two good on-site restaurants; well-equipped fitness center. **Cons:** a short walk from Old Port; no self-parking available; valet parking is $38. [$] *Rooms* from: $460 ✉ 9 Center St., West End ☎ 207/791–5000 🌐 www.hilton.com 🛏 135 rooms 🍽 No Meals.

★ The Francis
$$$ | **HOTEL** | In the beautifully restored Mellen E. Bolster House, this charming boutique hotel has a mid-century-modern vibe that seamlessly compliments the building's immaculately preserved historical design elements. **Pros:** bars in rooms; smart spa on second floor; guest rooms feature custom-built furniture. **Cons:** only 15 rooms; some rooms not accessible by elevator; no bathtubs. $ *Rooms from: $300* ✉ *747 Congress St., West End* ☎ *207/772–7485* 🌐 *www.thefrancismaine.com* 🛏 *15 rooms* 🍽 *No Meals.*

Nightlife

Luna Rooftop Bar
COCKTAIL LOUNGES | Sophisticated and blessed with stunning views of the city and waterfront, Luna has plenty to recommend as a spot to grab drinks before or after an evening stroll around the city. Perched atop the Canopy by Hilton Portland Waterfront, its talented bar staff pour creative cocktails and the kitchen turns out enough filling small plates to snack on or make a dinner out of. (The eclectic menu spotlights petite lobster rolls; tuna tataki; Korean BBQ beef sliders; and desserts like ricotta lavender fritters.) ✉ *Canopy Portland Waterfront, 285 Commercial St., West End* ☎ *207/791–0011* 🌐 *lunarooftopbarmaine.com.*

Casco Bay Islands

The islands of Casco Bay are also known as the Calendar Islands, because an early explorer mistakenly thought there was one for each day of the year (in reality there are only 140 or so). These islands range from ledges visible only at low tide to populous Peaks Island, a suburb of Portland. Some are uninhabited; others support year-round communities, as well as stores and restaurants. Ft. Gorges commands Hog Island Ledge, and Eagle Island is the site of Arctic explorer Admiral Robert Peary's home.

The brightly painted ferries of Casco Bay Lines are the islands' lifeline. There is service to the most populated ones, including: Bailey Island, Chebeague Island, Cliff Island, Great Diamond / Little Diamond, Long Island, and Peaks Island.

There is little in the way of overnight lodging on the islands—the population swells during the warmer months due to summer residents—and there are few restaurants or organized attractions other than the natural beauty of the islands themselves. Meandering about by bike or on foot is a good way to explore on a day trip.

GETTING HERE AND AROUND

Casco Bay Lines provides year-round ferry service from Portland to the following islands in Casco Bay: Little Diamond and Great Diamond; Chebeague; Bailey; Cliff; Peaks; and Long Islands. Boats leave from the terminal in Old Port, and schedules vary according to season—ferries leave more often in summer, less so in fall and spring, and only several times per day in the winter. Islands also have different schedules; Peaks Island, the closest to Portland and the most populated, has the most frequent ferries. On-island transportation should be planned for. Peaks Island is the only one allowing cars to be transported by ferry, and if your aim is to do that, plan in advance, as ferries fill up fast in the summer. On most of the islands, you can rent a bike or a golf cart as soon as you get off the ferry terminal. You can also bring your own bike on the ferry to all islands; rates are $6.50 per adult bike and $3.25 per child's bike. Pets can tag along, too, for an additional $4.10 round-trip.

Specialty cruises are offered (also with differing schedules and prices according to season) passing by various islands, depending on the theme. There's a

Moonlight Run, Sunset Run, Sunrise Run, and the popular Mailboat Run, which lets passengers join as the working ferry delivers real mail to Little Diamond, Great Diamond, Long, Cliff, and Chebeague Islands.

CONTACTS Casco Bay Lines. ✉ *56 Commercial St., Portland* ☎ *207/774–7871* 🌐 *www.cascobaylines.com.*

Sights

Chebeague Island

ISLAND | FAMILY | About 5 miles long and 1½ miles wide, Chebeague (pronounced shah-big) has a year-round population of about 390, which more than quadruples in the summer season. Originally used as a fishing ground by Abenaki Indigenous people, the island later became a place known for stone slooping—those workers who carried ballast and granite for 19th-century ships, to be used in grand buildings. The island has a number of impressive Greek Revival homes built by them. There are a couple of small beaches, but most visitors come to spend time at The Chebeague Island Inn, where there's golf and tennis to play, and a very good restaurant open for lunch, dinner, or just drinks. ✉ *Great Chebeague Island* ☎ *207/846–3148* 🌐 *www.townofchebeagueisland.org.*

Cliff Island

ISLAND | FAMILY | Little wonder that the farthest island from Portland served by ferry service is also the most secluded and natural. Roads are unpaved, and most of the woods and beaches here are conservation land. Food isn't always easy to find here; there is but one store, and hours can be limited, so bring a lunch if you're looking to picnic. If a beach is on your agenda, head toward Stone Beach for great views of the nearby islands. ✉ *Cliff Island.*

Great Diamond Island and Little Diamond

ISLAND | FAMILY | Though most of Great Diamond is closed to the public, the Inn at Diamond Cove welcomes visitors and offers plenty to do. Housed in what was once Fort McKinley, a United States Army coastal defense fort built in the late 1800s and retired in the 1940s, it's a combination resort, with several eateries as well as private residences. Guests can play tennis and indoor basketball, lounge at the pool, or use the complimentary bikes. Visitors often take the ferry just for the day, or for dinner at the property's fine dining establishment, Diamond's Edge. The area is car-free, so if you're not staying at the Inn, be prepared to explore on foot or bring your own bike.Meanwhile, Little Diamond can be accessed on foot at low tide via Lamson Cove, and is filled with private residences, many of which can be rented during the summer months. ✉ *Great Diamond Island.*

Long Island

ISLAND | FAMILY | Three miles long and one-mile wide, Long Island lives up to its name in shape, and is home to 200 year-round residents (many of whom work in the fishing industry) and 1,000 summer dwellers. There are a few lovely beaches here, including South Beach, Andrews Beach, and Fowler Beach. A few country stores and a bakery can supply you with vittles for a picnic. Bike rentals are not available, so bring your own over on the ferry or rent a golf cart close to the ferry landing when you arrive. ✉ *Long Island* 🌐 *townoflongisland.us/wp/.*

Peaks Island

ISLAND | FAMILY | Nearest to Portland (only a 15-minute ferry ride away), this is the most developed of the Calendar Islands, but it still allows you to experience the relaxed pace of island life. Explore an art gallery or an old fort, and meander along the alternately rocky and sandy shore on foot, or rent a kayak, bike, or golf cart once off the ferry. A number of spots are open for both lunch and dinner.

The Fifth Maine Museum, a small museum with Civil War artifacts, open only in summer, is maintained in the building of the 5th Maine Regiment. (*$8;* *207/766–3330,* *www.fifthmainemuseum.org*). When the Civil War broke out in 1861, Maine was asked to raise a single regiment to fight, but the state came up with several (the number eventually totaled 40), and sent the 5th Maine Regiment into the war's first bat tle, at Bull Run. The museum also offers guidebooks for a two-hour self-guided tour of the World War II Peaks Island Reservation. *Peaks Island* *peaksisland.info.*

Freeport

6 miles northeast of Yarmouth.

Boston may be called Beantown, but Freeport could easily lay claim to the moniker: L.L. Bean put the town on visitors' radar. The company's flagship store and impressive campus dominate Main Street, and a plethora of outlets and specialty stores edge both the main drag and nearby streets. But those who visit Freeport only to shop are missing out.

Lovely old clapboard houses line the town's shady backstreets, and, a few miles away, South Freeport's pretty harbor sits on the Harraseeket River. In addition, the area's nature preserves have miles of walking trails.

GETTING HERE AND AROUND

Interstate 295 has three Freeport exits and passes by on the edge of the downtown area. U.S. 1 is Main Street here. Note that parking in Freeport is free. The Amtrak *Downeaster* stops in the heart of town, and the Metro Breez bus travels between Portland and Freeport several times every day except Sunday.

CONTACTS Metro Breez Buses. *Portland* *207/774–0351* *gpmetro.org.*

VISITOR INFORMATION

CONTACTS Visit Freeport. *115 Main St., Freeport* *207/865–1212* *www.visitfreeport.com.*

Sights

Freeport Historical Society

HISTORY MUSEUM | FAMILY | Pick up a village walking map and delve into Freeport's rich past through the exhibits at the Freeport Historical Society, located in Harrington House, a hybrid Federal- and Greek Revival-style home built in the 1830s. It's a good idea to call ahead to make sure it's open. The historical society also offers walking tours a few times a month in the summer. *45 Main St., Freeport* *207/865–3170* *www.freeporthistoricalsociety.org* *Closed Sat.–Mon.*

★ L.L. Bean

STORE/MALL | FAMILY | Founded in 1912 after its namesake invented the iconic hunting boot, L.L. Bean began as a mail-order merchandiser with a creaky old retail store. Today, the giant flagship store attracts more than 3 million visitors annually. Open 365 days a year, 24 hours a day, it is the anchor in the heart of Freeport's outlet-shopping district. You can still find the original hunting boots, along with cotton and wool sweaters; outerwear of all kinds; casual clothing, boots, and shoes for men, women, and kids; and camping equipment. Nearby are the company's home furnishings store and its bike, boat, and ski store. Don't miss the chance to snap a photo with the 16½-foot-tall statue of its signature rubber boot outside the main entrance, or visit its discount outlet, across the street in the Freeport Village Station mall. *95 Main St., Freeport* *877/755–2326* *www.llbean.com.*

Pettengill Farm

FARM/RANCH | **FAMILY** | The grounds of the Freeport Historical Society's saltwater Pettengill Farm—140 beautifully tended acres along an estuary of the Harraseeket River—are open to the public. It's about a 15-minute walk from the parking area down a farm road to the circa-1800 saltbox farmhouse, which is open by appointment. Little has changed since it was built, and it has rare etchings (called sgraffiti) of ships and sea monsters on three bedroom walls. ✉ *31 Pettengill Rd., Freeport* ☎ *207/865–3170* 🌐 *www.freeporthistoricalsociety.org* 🎫 *Free (donations appreciated).*

Restaurants

Harraseeket Lunch and Lobster Co.

$$ | **SEAFOOD** | **FAMILY** | Take a break from Main Street's bustle and drive 3 scenic miles to South Freeport, where this popular, bare-bones, counter-service place sits beside the town landing and serves up seafood baskets and lobster dinners. Save room for strawberry shortcake, blueberry crisp, bread pudding, whoopie pies, or another of the homemade desserts. **Known for:** great seafood; harbor views; picnic table dining inside or out. $ *Average main: $18* ✉ *36 S. Main St., South Freeport* ☎ *207/865–3535, 207/865–4888* 🌐 *www.harraseeketlunchandlobster.com* 💳 *No credit cards* ⏲ *Closed mid-Oct.–May.*

Maine Beer Company
$$ | PIZZA | FAMILY | Of the half dozen breweries in Freeport, the Maine Beer Company is a standout. Its beer is well crafted, as are its salads, charcuterie, and wood-fired pizzas, and you can dine indoors or out. **Known for:** delicious IPAs; beautiful bilevel space; community-spirited owners. *Average main: $20* *525 U.S. 1, Freeport* *207/221–5711* *www.mainebeercompany.com.*

Coffee and Quick Bites

★ Met Coffee House
$ | CAFÉ | Sit at a table to enjoy a bagel, croissant, Belgian waffles, or quiche at breakfast or a cold or toasted sandwich or flatbread at lunch. At any time of the day, sink into a comfy chair or sofa to indulge in a great cup of regular coffee, an "artistic" latte (try the Heath Bar version), or one of 15 specialty hot chocolates, including almond joy and peppermint. **Known for:** 16 smoothie choices; relaxed atmosphere; decorated with art that's for sale. *Average main: $13* *48 Main St., Freeport* *207/869–5809* *www.metropolitancoffeehouse.com.*

Hotels

★ Harraseeket Inn
$ | HOTEL | FAMILY | The welcome is warm at this inn, where gas fireplaces glow in the lobby, and guest rooms—about half of them in a historic wing—have serene color schemes and reproduction Federal-style furnishings. **Pros:** generous breakfast buffet; amenities include an indoor pool and a gym; easy walk to shopping district. **Cons:** rooms in newer wings lack historic charm; not all rooms have a garden view; fireplaces only in select rooms. *Rooms from: $179* *162 Main St., Freeport* *207/865–9377, 800/342–6423* *www.harraseeketinn.com* *84 rooms* *Free Breakfast.*

Performing Arts

L.L. Bean Summer Concert Series
CONCERTS | FAMILY | Throughout the summer, L.L. Bean hosts free activities, including concerts, at the L.L. Bean Discovery Park, part of the company's large campus. It's set back from Main Street, along a side street that runs between the company's flagship and home furnishings stores. Additional offerings include family movie nights and wellness classes. *18 Morse St., Freeport* *877/755–2326* *www.llbean.com* *Free* *Bring chairs.*

Activities

★ L.L. Bean Outdoor Discovery Programs
GROUP EXERCISE | FAMILY | It shouldn't come as a surprise that one of the world's largest outdoor outfitters also provides instructional adventures to go with its products. L.L. Bean's year-round Outdoor Discovery Programs include courses in canoeing, biking, kayaking, fly-fishing, snowshoeing, cross-country skiing, and other outdoor sports. Some last for only a few hours, while others are multiday experiences. Special offerings include women's-only adventures and team-building programs. *11 Desert Rd., Freeport* *888/552–3261* *www.llbean.com.*

Shopping

You really do need a strategy to shop smartly in Freeport, where Maine retailers and major brands—including Levi's, Dooney & Bourke, J.Crew, Under Armour, Vineyard Vines, and Ralph Loren—are all represented. Visit Freeport's guide (complete with coupons) to area offerings lists hundreds of stores on Main Street, Bow Street, and elsewhere. It's available at the visitor information center and other places in town.

Brunswick

10 miles north of Freeport.

Lovely brick or clapboard buildings are the highlight of Brunswick's Federal Street Historic District, which includes Federal Street, Park Row, and the stately campus of Bowdoin College. From the intersection of Pleasant and Maine streets, in the center of town, you can walk in any direction and discover an array of restaurants, bookstores, boutiques, and jewelers. Bowdoin's campus is home to several museums, and the college's performing-arts events are open to the public.

GETTING HERE AND AROUND

From I–295, take the Coastal Connector to U.S. 1 in Brunswick. The Concord Coach Lines bus that runs along the coast stops at the Brunswick Visitor Center, which is next to the train tracks and has a self-service ticket kiosk for Amtrak's *Downeaster* train. Brunswick Link buses can shuttle you around town and to Brunswick Landing and Cook's Corner every day (between 6:45 am and 6:30 pm) except Sunday.

CONTACTS Brunswick Link. ☎ *207/721–9600* 🌐 *brunswicklink.org.*

VISITOR INFORMATION

CONTACTS Brunswick Visitor Center. ✉ *16 Station Ave., Brunswick* ☎ *207/721–0999* 🌐 *brunswickdowntown.org.*

Sights

★ Bowdoin College Museum of Art

ART MUSEUM | FAMILY | This small museum housed in a stately building on Bowdoin's main quad features one of the oldest permanent collections of art in the United States. The more than 20,000 objects include paintings, sculpture, decorative arts, and works on paper. They range from Ancient, European, Asian, and Indigenous works to modern and contemporary art. The museum often mounts well-curated, rotating exhibitions and has programs for getting children excited about art. ✉ *245 Maine St., Brunswick* ☎ *207/725–3275* 🌐 *www.bowdoin.edu/art-museum* 🎫 *Free* 🕒 *Closed Mon.*

Restaurants

★ 555 North

$$$ | AMERICAN | Set within the gracious Federal hotel, 555 North is the rebirth of chef-owner Steve Corry's popular Portland restaurant, which closed in 2019 after an 18-year run. Diners will find the same exceptionally creative, seasonal approach to food as well as a sophisticated but relaxed atmosphere. **Known for:** imaginative menu; prominent, accomplished chef; attentive and polished service. 💲 *Average main: $30* ✉ *The Federal, 10 Water St., Brunswick* ☎ *207/481–4535* 🌐 *555-north.com* 🕒 *Closed Tues. and Wed.*

Coffee and Quick Bites

Little Dog Coffee Shop

$ | MODERN AMERICAN | FAMILY | The coffee is freshly roasted and richly flavorful, the baked goods are straight from the oven, and the atmosphere is chill. Have a muffin or croissant, select from several toasties with imaginative fillings, or try the delicious avocado toast on homemade wheat bread. **Known for:** exhibits of local art; excellent light bites; grab-and-go burritos. 💲 *Average main: $10* ✉ *87 Maine St., Freeport* ☎ *207/721–9500* 🌐 *www.littledogcoffeeshop.com.*

Hotels

★ The Federal

$$ | HOTEL | With a large modern wing attached to a historic Federal house, this refined hotel offers an airy, contemporary atmosphere blended with period-appropriate warmth. **Pros:** excellent on-site restaurant; personalized welcome; sophisticated decor. **Cons:** 20-minute walk to

Bowdoin College campus; a bit tricky to find; no elevator to third floor in Federal House. $ *Rooms from: $287* ✉ *10 Water St., Brunswick* ☎ *207/481–4066* 🌐 *www.thefederalmaine.com* 🛏 *30 rooms* 🍴 *No Meals.*

Bath

18 miles northeast of Harpswell Neck.

Bath's tradition of shipbuilding dates from 1607 with the construction of the pinnace *Virginia*, the first oceangoing ship built by Europeans in the Americas. (A full-size replica of the small sailing vessel was launched in June 2022.) It was a very lucrative industry, as evidenced by the historic district's architecture, including the 1820 Federal-style home at 360 Front Street; the 1810 Greek Revival, white-clapboard mansion at 969 Washington Street; and the raspberry-color Victorian gem at 1009 Washington Street. All three operate as inns.

In 1890, the venerable Bath Iron Works (BIW as it's known locally) completed its first passenger ship. During World War II, the company was capable of launching a new ship every 17 days. Today, BIW is one of the state's largest employers, with about 6,800 workers building destroyers for the U.S. Navy. (It's a good idea to avoid U.S. 1 on weekdays 3:15–4:30 pm, when a major shift change takes place.)

The must-see Maine Maritime Museum highlights shipbuilding history in Bath and elsewhere along the Maine Coast. It also offers tours to the perimeter of BIW's grounds (due to security concerns, it's a restricted property). Also, be sure to look up at City Hall, on Front Street: the bell in its tower was cast by Paul Revere in 1805.

Dangling to seaward of Woolwich, just east of Bath, Georgetown Island is connected to the mainland via a series of bridges. The island's exceptional beauty makes it well worth a detour. Along miles of corrugated shoreline, you'll find a few charming seafood eateries, old-fashioned lodging, and the natural jewel that is Reid State Park.

GETTING HERE AND AROUND

U.S. 1 passes through downtown and across the Kennebec River at Bath. Downtown is on the north side of the highway along the river. The Maine Maritime Museum is on the south side of the highway. Concord Coach Lines bus service that runs along the coast stops in Bath.

VISITOR INFORMATION

CONTACTS Bath Regional Information Center. ✉ *15 Commercial St., Bath* ☎ *207/443–1513* 🌐 *visitbath.com.*

Sights

★ Maine Maritime Museum

HISTORY MUSEUM | FAMILY | No trip to Bath is complete without visiting the cluster of preserved 19th- and early 20th-century buildings that were once part of the historic Percy & Small Shipyard. Plan to spend at least half a day exploring them and the adjacent modern museum. Indeed, there's so much to see that admission tickets are good for two days.

During hour-long shipyard tours, you'll learn how massive wooden ships were built, and you might see shipwrights and blacksmiths at work. One of the vintage buildings houses a fascinating, 6,000-square-foot lobstering exhibit. In the main building ship models, paintings, photographs, and artifacts showcase maritime history. The grounds also contain a gift shop and bookstore; a seasonal café; and a huge, modern sculpture representing the 450-foot-long, six-masted schooner *Wyoming*, built right here and one of the longest wooden vessels ever launched.

From late May through late October, daily nature and lighthouse cruises, ranging from 30 minutes to three hours, are offered aboard the motor vessel *Merrymeeting,* which travels along the scenic

Kennebec River. The museum also has guided tours of Bath Iron Works (June–mid-October). ✉ *243 Washington St., Bath* ☎ *207/443–1316* 🌐 *www.mainemaritimemuseum.org* 🎟 *$18, good for 2 days within 7-day period.*

★ Popham Beach State Park

BEACH | **FAMILY** | At the tip of the Phippsburg Peninsula, Popham Beach State Park faces the open Atlantic between the mouths of the Kennebec and Morse rivers. At low tide, you can walk several miles of tidal flats and also out to small Fox Island, where you can explore tide pools or fish off the ledges (pay attention to the incoming tide unless you want to swim back). Shifting sand and beach and sea dynamics have led to dramatic erosion here, and, in recent years, the sea has taken a big bite out of the beach. There are picnic tables, plus a bathhouse, showers, and toilets. About a mile from the beach, the road ends at the Civil War–era Fort Popham State Historic Site, an unfinished semicircular granite fort overlooking the sea. The site of the Popham Colony, an early 1600s English settlement, is also nearby. Enjoy beach views and some fresh seafood at nearby Spinney's Restaurant. ✉ *10 Perkins Farm La., off Rte. 209, Bath* ☎ *207/389–1335* 🌐 *www.maine.gov/pophambeach* 🎟 *$8.*

★ Reid State Park

BEACH | **FAMILY** | On Georgetown Island, this park's jewel is a gorgeous, unspoiled, mile-long beach framed by sand dunes; there's a second, ½-mile beach as well. Climb to the top of rocky Griffith Head to take in sea views that stretch to lighthouses on Seguin Island, Hendricks Head, and The Cuckolds. If you're swimming, be aware of the possibility of an undertow. Walking along the beach or following one of the hiking trails are popular pastimes as well. During a storm, this is a great place to observe the ferocity of the waves crashing onto the shore. In summer, parking lots fill by 11 am on weekends and holidays. ✉ *375 Seguinland Rd., Georgetown* ☎ *207/371–2303* 🎟 *$8* ⏲ *Closed sunset to 9 am.*

Restaurants

★ Bath Brewing Company

$$ | **MODERN AMERICAN** | You'll feel right at home in this intimate modern pub, offering casual dining on two floors plus an upper outdoor deck. The beer ranges from IPAs to stouts and sours. **Known for:** surprising pub food; welcoming modern pub in the heart of downtown; tasty craft beers. [$] *Average main: $20* ✉ *141 Front St., Bath* ☎ *207/389–6039* 🌐 *www.bathbrewing.com* ⏲ *Closed Mon. and Tues.*

★ Five Islands Lobster Company

$$ | **SEAFOOD** | Drive to the end of Route 127 and relax in the breezes off Sheepscot Bay in the tiny fishing village of Five Islands, not too far from Reid State Park. This award-winning lobster shack overlooks at least islands from its perch atop the working wharf, and you can watch lobstermen unload their traps onto the dock while you feast on fresh lobster rolls or a full lobster dinner and sample Maine-made ice cream. **Known for:** BYOB; authentic Maine setting with gorgeous scenery; excellent lobster rolls. [$] *Average main: $24* ✉ *1447 5 Islands Rd., Georgetown* ☎ *207/371–2990* 🌐 *www.fiveislandslobster.com* ⏲ *Closed Wed. in summer; closed weekdays spring and fall; closed early May–early Oct.*

Coffee and Quick Bites

Café Crème

$ | **BAKERY** | **FAMILY** | Located in the heart of downtown, this café with its own on-site bakery draws visitors and locals alike for delicious coffee paired with made-that-day goods served with a smile. The cinnamon roll with maple bacon is a savory Maine take on a classic

Continued on page 663

MAINE'S LIGHTHOUSES

GUARDIANS OF THE COAST

Perched high on rocky ledges, on the tips of wayward islands, and sometimes seemingly on the ocean itself are the more than five dozen lighthouses standing watch along Maine's craggy and ship-busting coastline.

Marshall Point Light

LIGHTING THE WAY: A BIT OF HISTORY

Portland Head Light

Most lighthouses were built in the first half of the 19th century to protect vessels from running aground at night or when the shoreline was shrouded in fog. Along with the mournful siren of the foghorn and maritime lore, these practical structures have come to symbolize Maine throughout the world.

SHIPWRECKS AND SAFETY

These alluring sentinels of the eastern seaboard today have more form than function, but that certainly was not always the case. Safety was a strong motivating factor in the erection of the lighthouses. Commerce also played a critical role. For example, in 1791 Portland Head Light was completed, partially as a response to local merchants' concerns about the rocky entrance to Portland Harbor and the varying depths of the shipping channel. In 1789, the federal government created the U.S. Lighthouse Establishment (later the U.S. Lighthouse Service) to manage them. In 1939 the U.S. Coast Guard took on the job.

Maine's lighthouses were built in a much-needed locations, but the points and islands upon which they sat were prone to storm damage. Along with poor construction, this meant that over the years many lighthouses had to be rebuilt or replaced.

LIGHTHOUSES TODAY

In modern times, many of the structures still serve a purpose. Technological advances, such as GPS and radar, are mainly used to navigate through the choppy waters, but a lighthouse or its foghorns are helpful secondary aids, and sometimes the only ones used by recreational boaters. The numerous channel-marking buoys still in existence also are testament to the old tried-and-true methods.

Of the 66 lighthouses along this far northeastern state, 57 are still working, alerting ships (and even small aircraft) of the shoreline's rocky edge. Government agencies, historic preservation organizations, and mostly private individuals own the decomissioned lights.

KEEPERS OF THE LIGHT

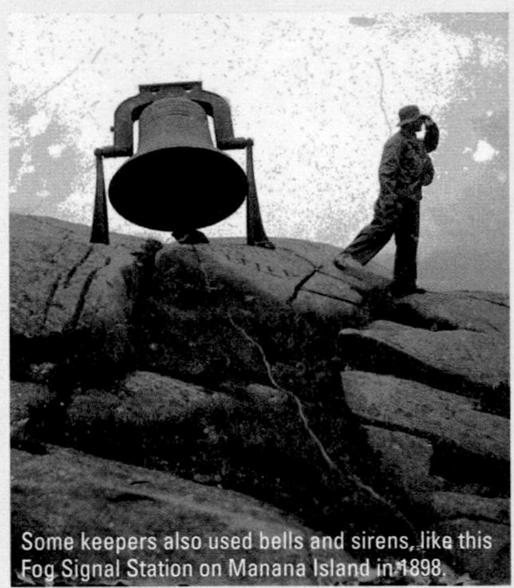
Some keepers also used bells and sirens, like this Fog Signal Station on Manana Island in 1898.

Pemaquid Point's fourth-order Fresnel lens

LIFE OF A LIGHTKEEPER

One thing that has changed with the modern era is the disappearance of the lighthouse keeper. In the early 20th century, lighthouses began the conversion from oil-based lighting to electricity. A few decades later, the U.S. Coast Guard switched to automation, phasing out the need for an on-site keeper.

While the keepers of tradition were no longer needed, the traditions of these stalwart, 24/7 employees live on through museum exhibits and retellings of Maine's maritime history, legends, and lore. The tales of a lighthouse keeper's life are the stuff romance novels are made of: adventure, rugged but lonely men, and a beautiful setting along an unpredictable coastline.

The lighthouse keepers of yesterday probably didn't see their own lives so romantically. Their daily narrative was one of hard work and, in some cases, exceptional solitude. A keeper's primary job was to ensure that the lamp was illuminated all day, every day. This meant that oil (whale or coal oil and later kerosene) had to be carried about and wicks trimmed on a regular basis. When fog shrouded the coast, they sounded the solemn horn to pierce through the damp darkness that hid their light. Their quarters were generally small and often attached to the light tower itself. The remote locations of the lights added to the isolation a keeper felt, especially before the advent of radio and telephone, let alone the Internet. Though some brought families with them, the keepers tended to be men who lived alone.

THE LIGHTS 101

Over the years, Fresnel (fray-NELL) lenses were developed in different shapes and sizes so that ship captains could distinguish one lighthouse from another. Invented by Frenchman Augustin Fresnel in the early 19th century, the lens design allows for a greater transmission of light perfectly suited for lighthouse use. Knowing which lighthouse they were near helped captains know which danger was present, such as a submerged ledge or shallow channel. Some lights, such as those at Seguin Island Light, are fixed and don't flash. Other lights are colored red.

DID YOU KNOW?

A lighthouse's personality shines through its flash pattern. For example, Bass Harbor Light (pictured) is on for three seconds, off for one second. Some lights, such as Seguin Island Light, are fixed and don't flash.

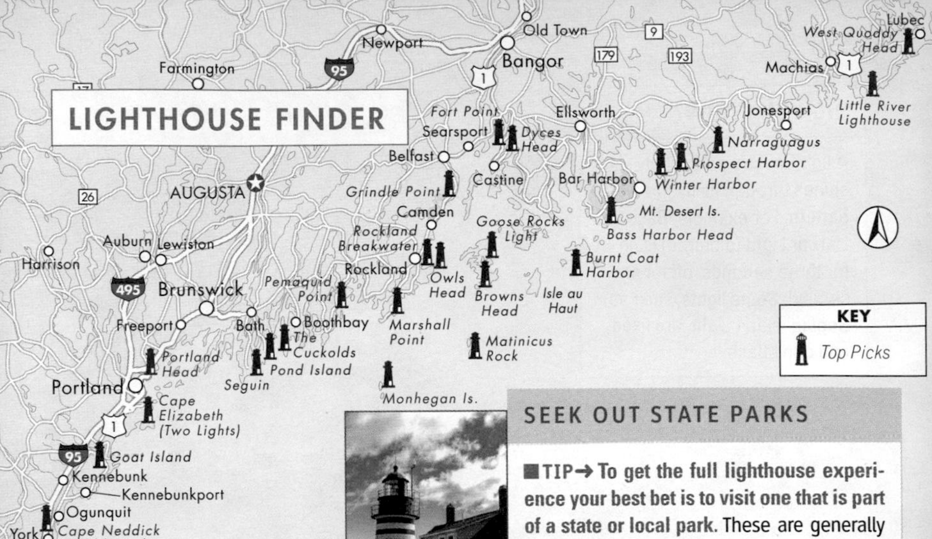

West Quoddy Head

SEEK OUT STATE PARKS

■ **TIP→ To get the full lighthouse experience your best bet is to visit one that is part of a state or local park.** These are generally well kept and tend to allow up-close approach, though typically only outside. While you're at the parks you can picnic or stroll on the trails. Wildlife is often abundant in and near the water; you might spot sea birds and even whales in certain locations (try West Quoddy Head, Portland Head, or Two Lights).

VISITING MAINE'S LIGHTHOUSES

As you travel along the Maine Coast, you won't see lighthouses by watching your odometer—there were no rules about the spacing of lighthouses. The decision as to where to place a lighthouse was a balance between a region's geography and its commercial prosperity and maritime traffic.

Lighthouses dot the shore from as far south as York to the country's eastern most tip at Lubec. Accessibility varies according to location and other factors. A handful are so remote as to be outright impossible to reach (except perhaps by kayaking and rock climbing). Some don't allow visitors according to Coast Guard policies, though you can enjoy them through the zoom lens of a camera. Others you can walk right up to and, occasionally, even climb to the top. Lighthouse enthusiasts and preservation groups restore and maintain many of them. All told, approximately 30 lighthouses allow some sort of public access.

MUSEUMS, TOURS, AND MORE

Most keeper's quarters are closed to the public, but some of the homes have been converted to museums, full of intriguing exhibits on lighthouses, the famous Fresnel lenses used in them, and artifacts of Maine maritime life in general. Talk to the librarians at the **Maine Maritime Museum** in Bath (🌐 *www.mainemaritimemuseum.org*) or sign up for one of the museum's daily lighthouse cruises to pass by up to ten on the Lighthouse Lovers Cruise. In Rockland, the **Maine Lighthouse Museum** (🌐 *www.mainelighthousemuseum.org*) has the country's largest display of Fresnel lenses. The museum also displays keepers' memorabilia, foghorns, brassware, and more. Maine Open Lighthouse Day is the second Saturday after Labor Day; you can tour and even climb about two dozen lights usually closed to the public.

For more information, check out the lighthouse page at Maine's official tourism site: 🌐 *visitmaine.com*.

SLEEPING LIGHT: STAYING OVERNIGHT

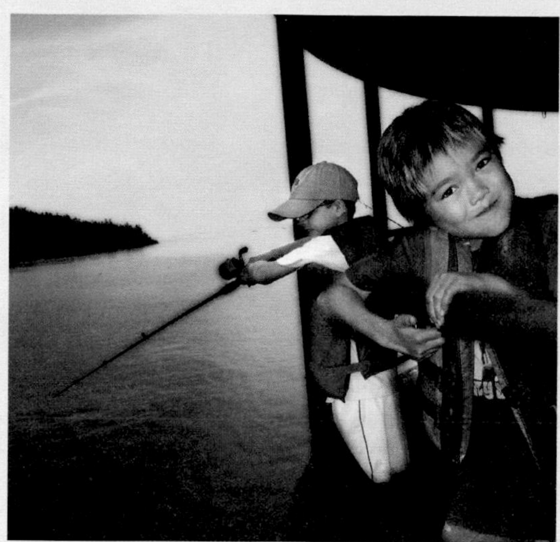

Goose Rocks, where you can play lighthouse keeper for a week.

Want to stay overnight in a lighthouse? There are several options to do so. ■ **TIP→ Book lighthouse lodgings as far in advance as possible, up to one year ahead.**

Our top pick is **Pemaquid Point Light** *(L. Dewey Chase Rentals ☎ 207/677–2100 🌐 newharborrentals.com)* because it has one of the most dramatic settings on the Maine coast. Two miles south of **New Harbor**, the second floor of the lighthouse keeper's house is rented out on a weekly basis early May through mid-November to support upkeep of the grounds. When you aren't enjoying the interior, head outdoors: the covered front porch has a rocking-chair view of the ocean. The one-bedroom, one-bath rental sleeps up to a family of four.

Situated smack dab in the middle of a major maritime thoroughfare between two Penobscot Bay islands, **Goose Rocks Light** (*☎ 203/400–9565 🌐 www.beaconpreservation.org*) offers lodging for the adventuresome—the 51-foot "spark plug" lighthouse is completely surrounded bywater. Getting there requires a ferry ride from Rockland to nearby **North Haven**, a 5- to 10-minute ride by motorboat, and then a climb up an iron-rung ladder from the pitching boat—all based on high tide and winds, of course. There's room for up to six people. It's a bit more cushy experience than it was for the original keepers: there's a flat-screen TV with DVD player and a selection of music and videos for entertainment. In addition, a hammock hangs on the small deck that encircles the operational light; it's a great place from which to watch the majestic windjammers and the fishing fleet pass by.

Little River Lighthouse (*☎ 877/276–4682 🌐 www.littleriverlight.org*), along the far northeastern reaches of the coast in **Cutler**, has three rooms available for rent from mid-June to September. You're responsible for food and beverages, linens, towels, and other personal items (don't forget the bug spray), but kitchen and other basics are provided. The lighthouse volunteers with Friends of Little River Lighthouse will provide a boat ride to the island upon which the lighthouse sits.

TOP LIGHTHOUSES TO VISIT

BASS HARBOR HEAD LIGHT

Familiar to many as the subject of countless photographs is Bass Harbor Head Light, at the southern end of **Mount Desert Island.** It is within Acadia National Park and 17 miles from the town of Bar Harbor. The station grounds are open year-round.

CAPE ELIZABETH LIGHT

Two Lights State Park is so-named because it's next to two lighthouses. Both of these **Cape Elizabeth** structures were built in 1828. The western light was closed in 1924 and eventually converted into a private residence; the eastern light, Cape Elizabeth Light, still projects its automated cylinder of light. The grounds surrounding the building and the lighthouse itself are closed to the public, but the structure is easily viewed and photographed from nearby at the end of Two Lights Road.

CAPE NEDDICK LIGHT

More commonly known as Nubble Light for the smallish offshore expanse of rock it rests upon, Cape Neddick Light sits a few hundred feet off a rock point in **York Beach.** With such a precarious location, its grounds are inaccessible to visitors, but close enough to be exceptionally photogenic, especially during the Christmas season.

MONHEGAN ISLAND LIGHT

Only the adventuresome and the artistic see this light, because **Monhegan Island** is accessible by an approximately one-hour ferry ride. To reach the lighthouse, you have an additional half-mile walk uphill from the ferry dock. The former keeper's quarters is home to the Monhegan Museum, which has exhibits about the island. The tower itself is closed to the public.

PORTLAND HEAD LIGHT

One of Maine's most photographed lighthouses (and its oldest), the famous Portland Head Light was completed in January 1791. At the edge of Fort Williams Park, in **Cape Elizabeth**, the towering white stone lighthouse stands 101 feet above the sea. The Coast Guard operates it and it is not open for tours. However the adjacent keeper's dwelling is now a museum.

WEST QUODDY HEAD LIGHT

Originally built in 1808 by mandate of President Thomas Jefferson, West Quoddy Head Light sits in **Lubec** on the easternmost tip of land in the mainland United States. The 49-foot-high lighthouse with distinctive red and white stripes, is part of Quoddy Head State Park.

Cape Neddick

Portland Head

West Quoddy Head

sweet treat. **Known for:** sweet and savory stuffed croissants; creative coffee drinks; friendly staff. Ⓢ *Average main: $7* ✉ *56 Front St., at Centre St., Bath* ☎ *207/443–6454* 🌐 *www.cafecremebath.com.*

 Hotels

Sebasco Harbor Resort
$$$$ | **RESORT** | **FAMILY** | This nearly century-old resort on 450 water-side acres at the western side of the Phippsburg Peninsula is a good choice for both couples and families. **Pros:** very good on-site restaurant; children's activities and an array of lawn games; golf course, tennis courts, and heated saltwater pool. **Cons:** no sandy beach; heavy traffic and large number of rooms can diminish quality and service; golf fee not included in stay. Ⓢ *Rooms from: $420* ✉ *29 Kenyon Rd., off Sebasco Rd., Phippsburg* ☎ *866/389–2072, 207/389–1161* 🌐 *www.sebasco.com* ⏲ *Closed late Oct.–mid-May* *89 rooms* *No Meals.*

Wiscasset

10 miles north of Bath.

Settled in 1663, Wiscasset sits on the bank of the Sheepscot River. It bills itself as "Maine's Prettiest Village," and it's easy to see why: it has graceful churches, old cemeteries, and elegant sea captains' homes (many converted into antiques shops and galleries).

This is where everyone wants to stop for a lobster roll. Red's Eats gets all the publicity—and the resulting long, long lines—for its positively overflowing rolls. At Sprague's, just across the street, the quality is just as high, and although they don't stuff the rolls with quite as much lobster, you do pay a few dollars less.

GETTING HERE AND AROUND

U.S. 1 becomes Wiscasset's Main Street. Traffic often slows to a crawl in summer, as everyone traveling along the coast here must funnel onto a two-lane bridge across the Sheepscot River. The speed limit is reduced in town, and there are several stop lights, both of which further slow things down. There's no parking on Main Street in front of the shops, but there are several free nearby lots to either side of the main drag. The Concord Coach Lines bus that goes along the coast stops in Wiscasset.

Restaurants

★ **Red's Eats**
$$$ | **SEAFOOD** | **FAMILY** | The customers lined up beside this little red shack at the bottom of Wiscasset's Main Street, just before the bridge across the Sheepscot River, have come from far and wide for one of the Maine Coast's best lobster rolls—namely, a perfectly buttered and griddled split-top roll that's absolutely, positively stuffed with fresh, sweet meat and served with melted butter and mayo on the side. Devotees swear that the wait (up to two hours!) is worth it, and it helps that staffers hand out ice water, popsicles, umbrellas to protect from rain or hot sun, and even dog biscuits for the pups. **Known for:** more than a whole lobster goes into each roll; the unholy "Puff Dog," a hot dog loaded with bacon and cheese and deep-fried; long lines in summer, especially on weekends. Ⓢ *Average main: $25* ✉ *41 Water St., Wiscasset* ✣ *Corner of U.S. 1* ☎ *207/882–6128* 🌐 *www.redseatsmaine.com* *No credit cards* ⏲ *Closed late-Oct.–mid-Apr.*

★ **Water Street Kitchen and Bar**
$$$ | **MEDITERRANEAN** | Step into this welcoming, airy space, and settle at a table with a view of the Sheepscot River to enjoy local seafood, meats, and produce. Many of the pastas, paellas, and risottos have a Mediterranean flavor; other dishes showcase the chef's creative approach to modern American cuisine. **Known for:** eclectic menu; raw bar; pleasant atmosphere. Ⓢ *Average main: $25* ✉ *15 Water*

St., Wiscasset ☎ *207/687–8076* 🌐 *www.waterstreetkitchen.com.*

Coffee and Quick Bites

Treats

$ | **AMERICAN** | What started as a candy shop over 30 years ago has grown into a Wiscasset staple featuring baked goods, coffee, wine, craft beer, cheese, and more. All of the "treats"—scones, cookies, croissants, muffins, cakes, sweet buns, babka, coffee cake—are baked right here every day. **Known for:** scones made from owner's nana's recipe; a morning gathering spot for locals; locally sourced ingredients. *Average main: $5* ✉ *80 Main St., Wiscasset* ☎ *207/882–6192* 🌐 *www.treatsofmaine.com* *Closed Mon.*

Boothbay

11 miles south of Wiscasset.

The shoreline of the Boothbay Peninsula is a craggy stretch of inlets where pleasure craft of all sizes and types bob alongside lobster boats and sightseeing vessels. Boothbay Harbor is something of a smaller version of Bar Harbor: touristy, but friendly and fun, with pretty, winding streets and lots to explore. Commercial Street, Wharf Street, Townsend Avenue, and the By-Way are lined with shops and ice-cream parlors.

Be sure to take in the coast and islands from the water aboard one of many sightseeing cruises. One of the biggest draws here is the stunning Coastal Maine Botanical Gardens, a short drive north in the town of Boothbay. Its more than 300 acres encompass spectacular plantings and natural landscapes, walking trails, and a delightful children's garden.

GETTING HERE AND AROUND

Soon after crossing the Sheepscot River bridge just east of Wiscasset, turn right onto Route 27 and follow it to Boothbay and all the way into the heart of Boothbay Harbor, just 2 miles farther south. For some incredible scenery, take Route 96 off Route 27 out to Ocean Point in East Boothbay.

Note that, in season, a daily boat to Monhegan Island leaves from a dock on Boothbay Harbor's Commercial Street.

VISITOR INFORMATION

CONTACTS Boothbay Harbor Region Chamber of Commerce. ✉ *192 Townsend Ave., Boothbay* ☎ *207/633–2353* 🌐 *www.boothbayharbor.com.*

Sights

★ **Coastal Maine Botanical Gardens**

GARDEN | **FAMILY** | Reserve your admission tickets in advance online (required), and set aside a couple of hours to explore New England's largest botanical garden, where, depending on the time of year, you can stroll amid the lupines, rhododendrons, or roses. Regardless of the season, you'll encounter the site's biggest (literally and figuratively) draws: the five gigantic and utterly irresistible trolls constructed by Danish artist Thomas Danbo using scrap wood and other found materials that are placed in wooded areas throughout the 323-acre grounds.

The children's garden is a wonderland of stone sculptures, rope bridges, small teahouse-like structures with grass roofs, and even a hedge maze. Children and adults alike adore the separate woodland fairy area. The Garden of the Five Senses lets you experience flora through much more than just sight. Inside the main building are a café, grab-and-go market, shop, and resource library. During the holiday season, the gardens mount a dazzling, nighttime Gardens Aglow show, with 650,000 LED bulbs lighting up the darkness.

Comfortable walking shoes are a must, but, if you'd prefer not to walk everywhere, there's free shuttle service to several key locales. In addition, free, hour-long, docent-led tours of the central gardens leave from the visitor center at 11 each day from May through October. There's also a one-hour golf cart tour ($10; free on Wednesday). ✉ *132 Botanical Gardens Dr., off Rte. 27, Boothbay* ☎ *207/633–8000* 🌐 *www.mainegardens.org* 🎫 *$22* ⏲ *Closed late Oct.–May 1, except for holiday season Gardens Aglow extravaganza* ✍ *Reservations required.*

Restaurants

★ The Deck Bar & Grill

$$ | **AMERICAN** | Located at Linekin Bay Resort, this casual, mostly outdoor restaurant offers a serene waterside setting coupled with fresh lobster rolls, haddock BLTs, mussels, crab cakes, crudo yellowfin tuna, fish tacos, and clams linguine. There are plenty of meat, gluten-free, and vegan options, too. **Known for:** stunning view down Linekin Bay; a wonderful escape from the bustle; live music on weekends. 💲 *Average main: $20* ✉ *Linekin Bay Resort, 92 Wall Point Rd., Boothbay Harbor* ☎ *207/633–2494* 🌐 *www.linekinbayresort.com/dining* ⏲ *Closed mid-Oct.–mid May.*

★ Shannon's Unshelled

$ | **SEAFOOD** | **FAMILY** | The namesake of this shack first got the idea to set up shop when her father posed the simple question: "Where can you buy a quick lobster roll in Boothbay Harbor?" Unable to answer, Shannon's Unshelled was born, and the shack is now beloved for its grilled, buttered buns stuffed with whole lobsters and served with a side of garlicky, sea-salted, drawn butter. **Known for:** fried seafood features gluten-free batter; seaweed salads; trap-to-table lobster. 💲 *Average main: $16* ✉ *23 Granary Way, Boothbay Harbor* ☎ *207/350–7313* 🌐 *www.shannonsunshelled.biz* ⏲ *Closed Sun. and Wed.*

Coffee and Quick Bites

★ Downeast Ice Cream Factory

$ | **ICE CREAM** | **FAMILY** | Stop in at this cute little house next to the boardwalk and order an ice-cream cone to enjoy at a nearby picnic table or as you stroll along the waterfront. You'll probably want to make it a two-scooper, so you can try at least two of the many flavors, all made right here in Boothbay Harbor. **Known for:** more than 50 flavors; super-premium ice cream; vegan sorbets. 💲 *Average main: $6* ✉ *1 By-Way, Boothbay Harbor* ☎ *207/315–6670* 🌐 *www.downeasticecreamfactory.com* ⏲ *Closed Nov.–mid-May.*

Hotels

Spruce Point Inn

$$$ | **RESORT** | **FAMILY** | Since 1892, this refined seaside resort has welcomed guests, including members of the Kennedy family, to its own sea-lapped point at the eastern side of the outer harbor. **Pros:** two on-site restaurants; private boat tour of harbor; lots of included amenities and activities. **Cons:** a few private residences close to premises; no elevators; some of the more-historic buildings have quirks. 💲 *Rooms from: $300* ✉ *88 Grandview Ave., Boothbay Harbor* ☎ *207/633–4152, 800/553–0289* 🌐 *www.sprucepointinn.com* ⏲ *Closed mid-Oct.–mid-May* 🛏 *63 rooms* 🍽 *No Meals.*

★ Topside Inn

$$$$ | **B&B/INN** | Dating from 1865 and once the home of a wealthy sea captain, this grand, hilltop inn has an immense lawn dotted with Adirondack chairs, a wraparound porch, and a fireside lounge with a stylish bar. **Pros:** knockout harbor views; exceptional breakfasts; walking distance to downtown. **Cons:** two-person maximum per room; books up quickly in summer; steep, short walk back up the hill from town. 💲 *Rooms from: $550* ✉ *60 McKown St., Boothbay Harbor* ☎ *207/633–5404* 🌐 *www.topsideinn.*

com ⊙ Closed late Oct.–early May ⇐ 22 rooms ¶ Free Breakfast.

Damariscotta

18 miles northeast of Boothbay Harbor.

Near the head of the Damariscotta River, and flanked by the Boothbay and Pemaquid peninsulas, this vibrant little town has a bevy of shops, many tucked into 150-year-old brick buildings in the three-block long National Historic District. This is also the place to slurp your fill of freshly plucked oysters.

Indigenous peoples summered on these shores millennia ago, leaving behind huge, still-visible, oyster-shell middens. By the late 1800s, the shellfish had disappeared. A century later, aquaculture programs spawned new enterprises, and today some of the country's most prized oysters come from the clear, clean Damariscotta River. Some say this is the Napa Valley of oyster growing.

Damariscotta is also the commercial hub of an eponymous region made up of several communities along the rocky coast. The closest is Newcastle, just a stroll across the bridge. It was settled in the early 1600s and later had shipyards and mills. The oldest Catholic church in New England, St. Patrick's, is here, and it still rings its original Paul Revere bell. South of Damariscotta on the Pemaquid Peninsula are the towns of Bristol, South Bristol, Round Pond, New Harbor, and Pemaquid Point.

Thousands descend on Damariscotta every October over Indigenous Peoples Day/Columbus Day Weekend for the zany Pumpkinfest, whose events include pumpkin-boat races on the harbor—yes, people actually race around in giant, tubby, tippy, paddle- and outboard-powered pumpkins.

GETTING HERE AND AROUND

From Boothbay Harbor follow Route 27 north to U.S. 1. Turn off U.S. 1 onto business U.S. 1, which runs through the village of Damariscotta.

At the northern end of downtown, Routes 129 and 130 lead south from business U.S. 1. In a few miles, 129 turns off to South Bristol and Christmas Cove. Route 130 continues down to Bristol, New Harbor, and Pemaquid. From there, you can take Route 32 north up through New Harbor, Round Pond, and Bremen, returning to U.S. 1 in Waldoboro.

The Concord Coach Lines bus that travels the coast stops in Damariscotta daily.

VISITOR INFORMATION

CONTACTS Damariscotta Region Chamber of Commerce. *✉ 67–A Main St., Damariscotta ☎ 207/563–8340 ⊕ www.damariscottaregion.com.*

 Restaurants

King Eider's Pub and Restaurant
$$$$ | AMERICAN | FAMILY | At this restaurant in an adorable building just off Main Street, the acclaimed crab cakes and the oysters fresh from the Damariscotta River are good bets, but so are the steak-and-ale pie, seafood stew, and fish-and-chips (made with fresh haddock that's sautéed rather than fried). With exposed-brick walls and low, wood-beamed ceilings hung with pottery beer mugs, the downstairs is a snug place to enjoy a Maine craft ale. **Known for:** live music in the pub; cozy atmosphere; extensive whiskey collection. *$ Average main: $36 ✉ 2 Elm St., Damariscotta ✣ Just off Main St. ☎ 207/563–6008 ⊕ www.kingeiderspub.com.*

Newcastle Publick House
$$ | AMERICAN | FAMILY | In a large, historic, handsomely renovated brick building, Newcastle Publick House serves delicious comfort food in a pleasant dining room and welcoming bar. Specialties include

Maine is the largest lobster-producing state in the United States.

fresh oysters prepared several ways, a selection of burgers, and one of the best French onion soups around. **Known for:** stacked burgers; cozy, old-school atmosphere; desserts and breads made by nearby Oysterhead Pizza Co.. *Average main: $20* *52 Main St., Newcastle* *207/563–3434* *www.newcastlepublickhouse.com* *Closed Mon.*

Coffee and Quick Bites

Barn Door Baking Company Cafe

$ | **BAKERY** | **FAMILY** | Connected to Sherman's Maine Coast Book Shop through an arched doorway, this little café turns out excellent coffee and hot and cold coffee drinks, plus fresh-from-the-oven sweet and savory baked items. It's hard to choose among the scones, slices of cake and pie, sinful cookies, cupcakes, and old-fashioned dessert bars. **Known for:** daily selection of irresistible baked goodies; good place to chill and catch up on email; friendly service. *Average main: $5* *162 Main St., Damariscotta* *207/563–3662* *www.barndoorbakingcompany.com.*

S. Fernald's Country Store

$ | **SANDWICHES** | **FAMILY** | Settle into the couch or sit at a table for breakfast and try the Eggs Bigelow (two eggs in a hole, bacon, cheddar, and locally baked sourdough) or grab a sandwich, wrap, or sub for lunch. The biggest challenge is deciding among the many breads and filling choices on the extensive menu. **Known for:** a local favorite; penny candy, toys, and other nostalgic items; great for picnic provisions. *Average main: $10* *50 Main St., Damariscotta* *207/563–8484* *www.sfernalds.com* *Closed Sun. and Mon.*

Hotels

★ Newcastle Inn

$$ | **B&B/INN** | **FAMILY** | A riverside location, tasteful decor, and lots of common areas (inside and out) make this an especially relaxing country inn. **Pros:** guests can order beer or wine; suites have sitting areas; water views from many rooms. **Cons:** flights of stairs to rooms on upper floors; not all rooms have water views;

some rooms lack ample sitting areas. *$ Rooms from: $250 ⊠ 60 River Rd., Newcastle ☎ 207/563–5685 🌐 www.newcastleinn.com 🛏 13 rooms 🍴 Free Breakfast.*

Monhegan Island

East of Pemaquid Peninsula, about 10 miles offshore.

If you like the idea of a slow-paced vacation on a remote island, Monhegan is for you. What's more, if you're also an artist or an art aficionado, you might never want to leave: there's a reason this has been a haven for artists for over a century.

To get here you'll need to take a ferry. A tiny hamlet greets you at the harbor. There are no paved roads. It doesn't take long to grasp that Monhegan is the place where simple and artful living is the order of the day.

The island was known to Basque, Portuguese, and Breton fishermen well before Columbus discovered America. English fishermen spent summers catching cod here in the 1600s. About a century ago, Monhegan was discovered by some of America's finest painters—Rockwell Kent, Robert Henri, A.J. Hammond, and Edward Hopper among them—who sailed out to paint its open meadows, savage cliffs, wild ocean views, and fishermen's shacks.

In summer, the tiny village and its dirt lanes buzz with day trippers who've come to hike the island's trails, visit a few shops and artists' studios, lunch in a handful of eateries, and enjoy the unspoiled remoteness. The island has 17 miles of trails, and serenity awaits at the lighthouse atop the hill overlooking the harbor and at the high cliffs of White Head, Black Head, and Burnt Head. From these rugged headlands, you can gaze across the ocean, where the next landfall is Spain.

GETTING HERE AND AROUND

Excursion vessels transport passengers between three mainland harbors and Monhegan. The boat trip is almost as exhilarating as exploring the island itself. Be on the lookout for seals, porpoises, and perhaps even small whales. Note that visitors are not allowed to bring cars to the island, so be prepared to wander on foot.

The Port Clyde boat landing is home to Monhegan Boat Line's *Elizabeth Ann* and the *Laura B.* There are three round-trips daily mid-June through mid October, one trip daily in late fall and early spring, and three trips weekly in the winter. In season, Hardy Boat offers daily trips between New Harbor and Monhegan, while Balmy Days Cruises makes crossings from Boothbay Harbor. All three companies also offer a variety of regional sightseeing cruises.

CONTACTS Balmy Days Cruises. *⊠ 42 Commercial St., Pier 8, Boothbay Harbor ☎ 207/633–2284 🌐 www.balmydayscruises.com.* **Hardy Boat Cruises.** *⊠ 129 State Rte. 32, New Harbor ☎ 207/677–2026 🌐 hardyboat.com.* **Monhegan Boat Line.** *⊠ 880 Port Clyde Rd., Port Clyde ☎ 207/372–8848 🌐 www.monheganboat.com.*

Sights

★ Monhegan Brewing Company

BREWERY | There's something to be said for enjoying a cold beer after a long hike. You can slake your thirst at a seasonal tap "room" (seating is actually outdoors beneath umbrellas and tents) of this tiny brewery owned by a local lobstering family. Options could include Crow's Nest IPA, Balmy Days Citra Kölsch, or Mad Cow Milk Stout. There might also be icy cold root beer, and you can get lunch to go at the on-site Bait Bag food trailer. *⊠ 1 Boody La., Monhegan ☎ 297/596–0011 🌐 monheganbrewing.com 🕒 Closed mid-Oct.–late May.*

Monhegan Island Light

LIGHTHOUSE | FAMILY | Getting a close-up look at this squat stone lighthouse, which was automated in 1959, requires a ½-mile, slightly steep uphill walk from the island's ferry dock. The tower is open sporadically throughout the summer for short tours. In the former keeper's quarters, the small Monhegan Museum of Art & History provides a peek into island life past and present. It also exhibits works by artists with a connection to this special place. ✉ *Lighthouse Hill Rd., ½ mile east of dock, Monhegan* ☎ *207/596–7003* 🌐 *monheganmuseum.org* 🎫 *$10 (museum)* ⏲ *Closed Oct.–late June.*

Restaurants

★ **Fish House Market**

$$ | SEAFOOD | Although everything served at this seafood shack and market beside Fish Beach is delicious and simply prepared, the crab roll—a large, split-top roll buttered and griddled and stuffed with fresh, sweet, mayo-tossed crabmeat—may just be the best on the Maine coast. Order at the window, carry your tray to a picnic table inches from the water, and lap up the view of lobster boats in the harbor. **Known for:** BYOB; outstanding fish chowder; lovely waterside location. 💲 *Average main: $18* ✉ *98 Fish Beach La., Monhegan* ☎ *207/594–8368* 🌐 *www.facebook.com/fishhousemonhegan* ⏲ *Closed late Sept.–late May.*

Coffee and Quick Bites

The Barnacle

$ | AMERICAN | On the wharf a few steps from the boat landing, The Barnacle serves espresso and a selection of coffees from Monhegan Coffee Roasters along with baked goods such as scones and brownies, and ice cream. For lunch, choose from prepared sandwiches, chowders, and salads, which you can eat at a picnic table or take with you. **Known for:** a place to wait for the ferry; eat outdoors or grab-and-go; locally roasted coffee. 💲 *Average main: $15* ✉ *Monhegan Boat Landing, wharf, Monhegan* ☎ *207/596–0371* 🌐 *www.islandinnmonhegan.com/the-barnacle* ⏲ *Closed mid-Oct.–late May.*

Rockland

25 miles north of Damariscotta via U.S. 1.

This town is considered the gateway to Penobscot Bay and is the first stop on U.S. 1 offering a glimpse of the often-sparkling and island-dotted blue bay. Though previously considered by visitors to be a place to pass through on the way to places like Camden, Rockland now gets lots of attention on its own. This is thanks to a great selection of small but excellent restaurants; a terrific Main Street lineup of shops and galleries; the renowned Farnsworth Art Museum and the Center for Maine Contemporary Art; and several popular summer festivals. Despite all of these developments, Rockland continues to be a fishing port and the commercial hub of this coastal area.

The best place to view Rockland's windjammers as they sail in and out of the harbor is the mile-long granite breakwater that protects Rockland Harbor. To get there, from U.S. 1, head east on Waldo Avenue and then right on Samoset Road; follow this short road to its end.

GETTING HERE AND AROUND

U.S. 1 runs along Main Street here. It is one way (headed north) as it goes through downtown. U.S. 1A curves through the residential neighborhood just west of the business district, offering a southbound route as well as a faster route if you are just passing through in either direction.

The Concord Coach Lines bus that runs along the coast stops in Rockland.

Ferries to the islands of Vinalhaven, North Haven, and Matinicus leave from the ferry terminal at the northern end of Main Street.

VISITOR INFORMATION

CONTACTS Penobscot Bay Area Chamber of Commerce. ✉ *Rockland* ☎ *207/596–0376, 800/562–2529* 🌐 *www.camdenrockland.com.*

WHEN TO GO

Late summer is an ideal time to visit Rockland—if you don't mind the crowds. The Maine Lobster Festival highlights the calendar in August. September is a beautiful month, with bright, clear skies and cooling breezes. In addition, it may be easier than it is at the height of summer to book a reservation at the many popular restaurants.

March is a dreary month. The skies are often gray, and it isn't too late in the season for snow. Some restaurants and shops that close in winter may not yet be open. But if you enjoy solitude, this is a great time for walking the shore, watching the waves, and searching for intriguing finds brought ashore by winter storms.

FESTIVALS AND EVENTS

Maine Lobster Festival

FESTIVALS | FAMILY | Rockland's annual Maine Lobster Festival, held in early August, is the region's largest annual event. About 10 tons of lobsters are steamed in a huge lobster cooker—you have to see it to believe it. The festival, held in Harbor Park, includes a parade, live entertainment, food booths, and, of course, the crowning of the Maine Sea Goddess. ✉ *Harbor Park, Main St., south of U.S. 1, Rockland* ☎ *800/576–7512* 🌐 *www.mainelobsterfestival.com.*

North Atlantic Blues Festival

FESTIVALS | FAMILY | About a dozen well-known musicians gather for the North Atlantic Blues Festival, a two-day affair held the first or second full weekend after July 4. The show officially takes place at the public landing on Rockland Harbor Park, but it also includes a "club crawl" through downtown Rockland on Saturday night. Admission to the festival is $45 at the gate, $75 for a weekend pass. ✉ *Public Landing, 275 Main St., Rockland* ☎ *207/596–6055* 🌐 *www.northatlanticbluesfestival.com.*

Sights

★ Center for Maine Contemporary Art

ART MUSEUM | The impressive Center for Maine Contemporary Art sprang from a 50-year legacy that originated in makeshift exhibitions in barns and a potato-barrel storage loft before settling into a small, antique fire house in Rockport. Since 2016, this striking, light-filled building designed by Toshiko Mori has allowed the museum to showcase modern works by accomplished artists with a Maine connection in a space that befits the quality of the art. Expect envelope-pushing, changing exhibitions and public programs. Visitors are invited to drop into the museum's ArtLab to gain greater insight into current exhibitions by trying their own hand at making art inspired by the works on display. ArtLab is open weekends in summer; daily the rest of the year. ✉ *21 Winter St., Rockland* ☎ *207/701–5005* 🌐 *cmcanow.org* 🎫 *$8.*

★ Farnsworth Art Museum

ART MUSEUM | FAMILY | One of the most highly regarded small museums in the country, the Farnsworth's collection is largely devoted to works by three generations of the famous Wyeth family, who have spent summers on the Maine Coast for a century. N.C. Wyeth was an accomplished illustrator whose works were featured in many turn-of-the-20th-century adventure books; his son Andrew was one of the country's best-known and-loved painters; and Andrew's son Jamie is an accomplished painter in his own right. Galleries in the main building always display some of Andrew Wyeth's works, such as *The Patriot, Witchcraft,* and *Turkey Pond.* Across the street, the Wyeth Center, in a former church, exhibits art by Andrew's father and son. The museum's collection also includes works by such lauded, Maine-connected artists as Fitz Henry Lane, George Bellows, Winslow Homer, Edward Hopper, Louise Nevelson, and Rockwell Kent. Changing exhibits are shown in the Jamien Morehouse Wing.

Just across the garden from the museum, the Farnsworth Homestead, the handsome, circa-1850 Greek Revival home of the museum's original benefactor, retains its original lavish Victorian furnishings and is open late June–mid-October.

In Cushing, a village on the St. George River about 10 miles south of Thomaston (a half-hour drive from Rockland), the museum operates the Olson House. The large, weathered-shingle structure was the home of Christina Olson and her brother, Alvarez, who were good friends of Andrew Wyeth. He depicted them and their home in numerous works, including his famous painting *Christina's World*. It is open spring through fall. ✉ *16 Museum St., Rockland* ☎ *207/596–6457* 🌐 *www.farnsworthmuseum.org* 🎟 *$15* 🕒 *Closed Tues. Nov.–Dec.; closed Mon. and Tues. Jan.–May; Wyeth Center closed Jan.–May.*

Maine Lighthouse Museum
HISTORY MUSEUM | FAMILY | The lighthouse museum has more than 25 Fresnel lighthouse lenses, as well as what's said to be the nation's largest collection of lighthouse and life-saving artifacts, and Coast Guard memorabilia. Permanent exhibits spotlight topics like lighthouse heroines—women who manned the lights when the keepers couldn't—and lightships. ✉ *1 Park Dr., Rockland* ☎ *207/594–3301* 🌐 *www.mainelighthousemuseum.org* 🎟 *$10.*

Restaurants

Claws
$$$ | SEAFOOD | FAMILY | Set right beside the road at the northern end of town, this lobster shack gets consistently enthusiastic reviews—many say the overstuffed lobster roll is one of the best. The large menu includes all the usual suspects plus a great selection of "snacky things" and entrées, and even a taco bar—butter-poached lobster tacos, anyone? **Known for:** wild Maine blueberry shortcake; lobster rolls stuffed with a pound of meat; award-winning lobster bisque. 💲 *Average main: $25* ✉ *743 Main St., Rockland* ☎ *207/596–5600* 🌐 *www.clawsrocklandmaine.com.*

★ **In Good Company**
$$$ | MODERN AMERICAN | As the name suggests, this is an excellent spot to slow down and catch up with good friends over a bottle of wine while savoring small, internationally flavored plates or a full meal. The creative blend of textures and flavors that comes out of the kitchen is exceptional. **Known for:** outside dining in summer; excellent wine pairings; pared-down aesthetic with a focus on the food. 💲 *Average main: $30* ✉ *415 Maine St., Rockland* ☎ *207/593–9110* 🌐 *www.ingoodcompanymaine.com.*

★ **Primo**
$$$$ | MEDITERRANEAN | Chef Melissa Kelly has twice won the James Beard Best Chef: Northeast, and she and her world-class restaurant have been written up in such magazines as *Gourmet, Bon Appétit,* and *O*. Named for the chef-owner's Italian grandfather, Primo serves masterfully prepared pasta, fresh seafood, and local meats. **Known for:** housemade pasta; fresh Maine ingredients with Mediterranean influences; consistently excellent; $1 oysters every Sunday. 💲 *Average main: $38* ✉ *2 N. Main St., Rockland* ☎ *207/596–0770* 🌐 *www.primorestaurant.com* 🕒 *Closed Tues.*

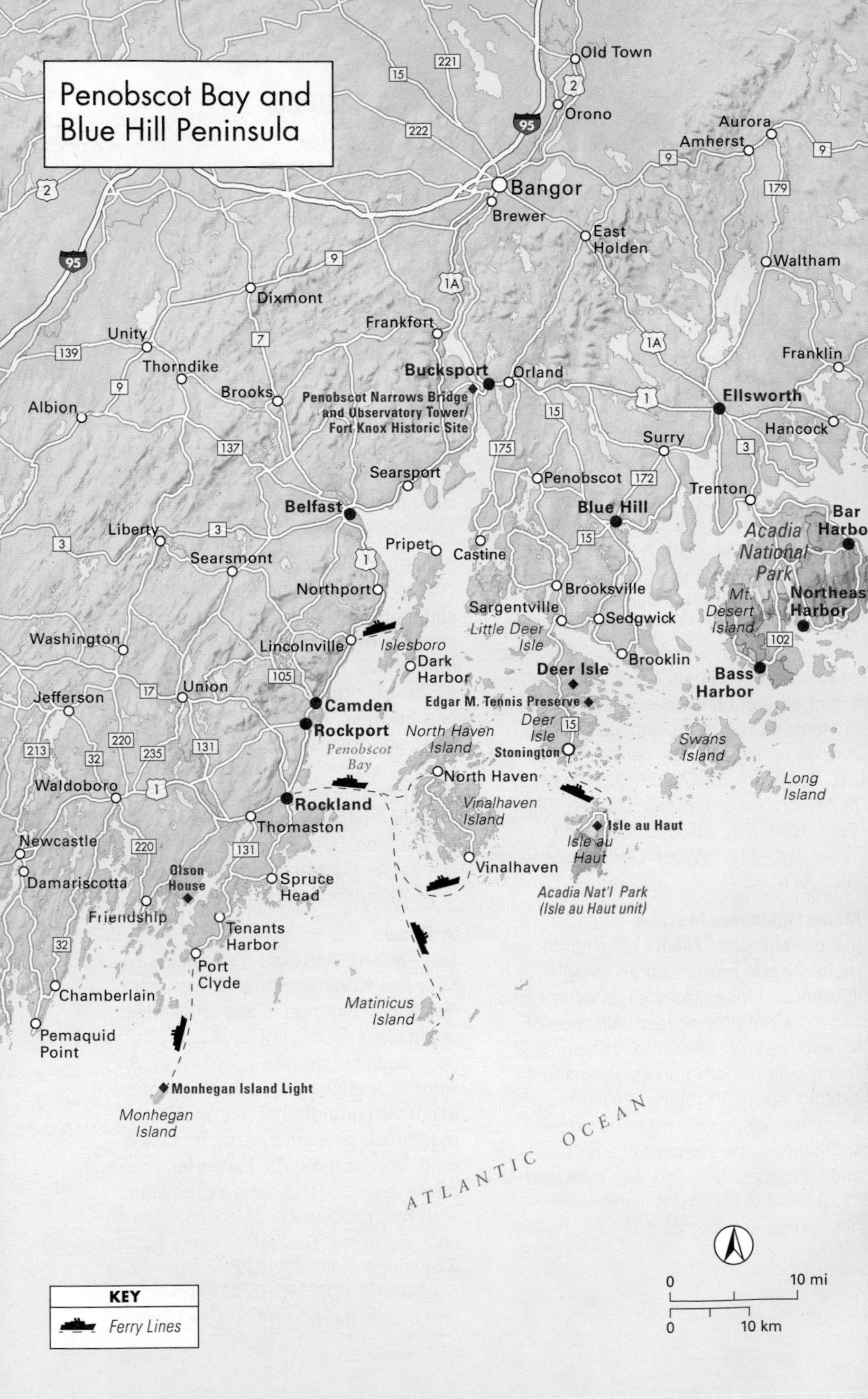
Penobscot Bay and Blue Hill Peninsula
Old Town
Orono
Aurora
Amherst
Bangor
Brewer
East Holden
Waltham
Dixmont
Frankfort
Unity
Thorndike
Brooks
Albion
Bucksport
Orland
Penobscot Narrows Bridge and Observatory Tower/ Fort Knox Historic Site
Franklin
Ellsworth
Hancock
Surry
Searsport
Penobscot
Trenton
Belfast
Blue Hill
Bar Harbor
Acadia National Park
Liberty
Searsmont
Pripet
Castine
Northport
Brooksville
Mt. Desert Island
Northeast Harbor
Sargentville
Sedgwick
Little Deer Isle
Washington
Lincolnville
Islesboro
Dark Harbor
Brooklin
Deer Isle
Bass Harbor
Union
Jefferson
Camden
Edgar M. Tennis Preserve
Rockport
North Haven Island
Deer Isle
Stonington
Swans Island
Penobscot Bay
North Haven
Long Island
Waldoboro
Rockland
Vinalhaven Island
Thomaston
Isle au Haut
Newcastle
Damariscotta
Olson House
Spruce Head
Vinalhaven
Acadia Nat'l Park (Isle au Haut unit)
Friendship
Tenants Harbor
Port Clyde
Chamberlain
Matinicus Island
Pemaquid Point
Monhegan Island Light
Monhegan Island
ATLANTIC OCEAN
0
10 mi
0
10 km
KEY
Ferry Lines

Windjammer Excursions

Nothing defines the Penobscot Bay area better than its fleet of historic windjammers, and a sailing trip on one of these beauties, whether for just a few hours or a few days, is an unforgettable experience. Originally designed to carry cargo and built along the East Coast in the 19th and early 20th centuries, the wooden-hulled vessels once plied coastal waters in such trades as lumbering, granite, fishing, and oystering. Members of today's windjammer fleet range from as small as 46 feet, accommodating six passengers (plus a couple of crew members), to more than 130 feet, carrying 30 passengers.

In the past few years, nearly all of the windjammers have been passed on to new, young captain-owners who bring fresh energy as well as solid qualifications to their stewardship of these beloved tall ships.

On a windjammer excursion, passengers are welcome to participate in on-board tasks, be it helping to hoist a sail or taking a turn at the wheel. Exceptional meals help keep them fueled for the effort.

During the Camden Windjammer Festival (🌐 www.facebook.com/WindjammerFestival), held Labor Day weekend, crowds gather to watch the region's fleet sail into the harbor, and most boats are open for tours. The schooner-crew talent show later in the weekend is a bit more irreverent than the majestic arrival ceremony.

A windjammer cruise gives you a chance to soak up Maine's dramatic coast from the water. Overnight cruises can run anywhere from two to eight days; day trips—usually just a couple of hours long—feature a tour of the harbor and some lighthouse and wildlife sightseeing. Prices depend on trip length; overnight cruises include all meals. Trips leave from Camden, Rockland, and Rockport. You can find information on the fleets by visiting the individual vessels' websites or by contacting the Penobscot Bay Regional Chamber of Commerce (🌐 camdenrockland.com), the Maine Windjammer Association (🌐 www.mainewindjammercruises.com), or Maine Windjammer Cruises (🌐 www.sailmainecoast.com).

Rockland Café

$ | **DINER** | **FAMILY** | Famous for the size of its breakfasts—don't pass up the lobster or fish-cake Benedict—Rockland Café has been a local favorite for decades. The large menu includes plenty of lunch and dinner choices from the excellent clam, fish, and seafood chowder to fried haddock, clams, shrimp, and scallops or lobster, clam, shrimp, and scallop rolls. **Known for:** lots of traditional seafood dishes; classic liver and onions; lively place where locals come to catch up. *$ Average main: $12 ✉ 441 Main St., Rockland ☎ 207/596–7556 🌐 www.rocklandcafe.com.*

Coffee and Quick Bites

★ Atlantic Baking Company

$ | **AMERICAN** | **FAMILY** | Classic European and American breads such as batards, baguettes, ciabatta, focaccia, sourdough boules, and rolls come out of French ovens every morning at this popular little spot. The cases are also filled with just-baked croissants, scones, muffins, cookies, and more. **Known for:** French macarons; apricot pistachio oat cookies; classic sourdough. *$ Average main: $5 ✉ 351 Main St., Rockland ☎ 207/596–0505 🌐 atlanticbakingco.com ⏲ Closed Sun.*

Hotels

Berry Manor Inn

$$$ | B&B/INN | Originally the residence of Rockland merchant Charles H. Berry, this 1898 shingle-style B&B sits in Rockland's National Historic District. **Pros:** guest pantry stocked with drinks, sweets, and treats—there's always pie; 10-minute walk to downtown and the harbor; some rooms can be combined to create two-room suites. **Cons:** view limited to gardens; somewhat fussy decor consistent with Victorian-era property; not pet-friendly. *Rooms from: $350 ✉ 81 Talbot Ave., Rockland ☎ 207/596–7696, 800/774–5692 ⊕ www.berrymanorinn.com ⇨ 18 rooms ¦◎¦ Free Breakfast.*

★ 250 Main Hotel

$$$$ | HOTEL | Finely crafted by local shipwrights, this jazzy little boutique hotel is filled with stylish and colorful mid-century-modern design. **Pros:** heated bathroom floors; complimentary afternoon wine-and-cheese hour; walk to shops and restaurants. **Cons:** no pool; some noise from the street and from the harbor in the morning; parking (free) is across the street and down the hill. *Rooms from: $450 ✉ 250 Main St., Rockland ☎ 207/594–5994 ⊕ 250mainhotel.com ⇨ 26 rooms ¦◎¦ Free Breakfast.*

Activities

Schooner Heritage

SAILING | FAMILY | Designed and built specifically for passengers, the 95-foot *Heritage* carries up to 30 guests. Both captains are musicians and enjoy playing their guitars for guests in the evening. Trips range from three to six nights in length, and children aged 10 and up are welcome. *✉ North End Shipyard, 11 Front St., Rockland ☎ 207/594–8007, 800/648–4544 ⊕ www.schoonerheritage.com ▭ From $780 ⏲ Closed Oct.–early June.*

Schooner J. & E. Riggin

SAILING | FAMILY | The schooner *J. & E. Riggin,* originally an oyster dredger, offers multiday sailing cruises that thoroughly immerse passengers in traditional life under sail. Measuring 120 feet overall, the *Riggin* carries up to 24 overnight guests plus six crew. The experience is highlighted by three daily meals, plus snacks, all prepared using locally sourced seafood, vegetables, and other ingredients. *✉ Windjammer Wharf, 3 Captain Spear Dr., Rockland ☎ 207/594–1875, 800/869–0604 ⊕ www.mainewindjammer.com ▭ From $615 ⏲ Closed early Oct.–late May.*

★ Schooner Ladona

SAILING | Unlike her windjammer sisters, which were built to work hard, the schooner *Ladona* began her career as a private racing yacht, though she was later called into duty during World War II. Built in 1922 (rebuilt in 1971), and restored from bow to stern before joining the windjammer fleet a few years ago, this graceful schooner takes guests on cruises of three to seven nights. The on-board experience recalls *Ladona*'s past as a private yacht, with greater comfort and luxury, as well as more elegant dining, than the other members of the windjammer fleet. All trips include breakfast, lunch, and dinner, as well as a selection of fine wines and beers every evening. One trip features daily wine tastings led by an experienced wine professional. *✉ 40 Tillson Ave., Rockland ☎ 800/999–7352, 207/594–4723 ⊕ www.schoonerladona.com ▭ From $1108 ⏲ Closed mid-Oct.–early June.*

Rockport

4 miles north of Rockland via U.S. 1.

Heading north on U.S. 1 from Rockland, you enter Rockport before you reach the tourist mecca of Camden. Hugging the harbor, Rockport Village is a short drive off U.S. 1. It's home to a handful of very good small restaurants.

Originally called Goose River, Rockport was part of Camden until 1891. The cutting and burning of limestone was once a major industry in this area. The stone was cut in nearby quarries and then burned in hot kilns; the resulting lime powder was used to create mortar. Some of the kilns can still be seen down on the harbor.

If you drive from Rockport to Camden on Union Street, you'll pass under the Camden-Rockport Arch at the town line. It has appeared in a number of movies, including *Peyton Place* and *In the Bedroom*.

GETTING HERE AND AROUND

Rockport is off U.S. 1 between Rockland and Camden. Turn on Pascal Avenue to get to the village center.

The Concord Coach Lines bus that runs along the coast makes a stop near Rockport village on Route 1 just over the town line in Camden.

Restaurants

★ 18 Central Oyster Bar and Grill

$$$ | SEAFOOD | 18 Central Oyster Bar and Grill produces excellent, creative dishes in a cozy spot high above Rockport's working harbor. Seasonally inspired, locally harvested seafood plus dishes with a hint of Southern comfort make up the backbone of the menu—think fried green tomatoes with local peekytoe crab, chili oil, and microgreens, or crispy fried chicken accompanied by collards and heirloom grits. **Known for:** evenly paced, well-balanced dinners transition gracefully from one course to the next; lively atmosphere encouraged by botanically infused cocktails; packed as soon as the door opens for dinner. *$ Average main: $30 ✉ 18 Central St., Rockport ☎ 207/466–9055 🌐 www.18central.com ⏲ Closed Tues.–Thurs. ☞ Reservations strongly advised; credit card required to secure reservations for more than 4; max party size 8 people.*

Nina June

$$$ | MEDITERRANEAN | FAMILY | This lovely trattoria is known for its cheery harbor-view setting and frequently changing menus where locally sourced ingredients shine. Highly regarded chef-owner Sara Jenkins's fresh but authentic takes on Mediterranean-spanning dishes use seafood harvested along Maine's rocky coast, including local oysters, and everything from the pasta to the pickled veggies is made in-house; the presentation of each dish makes for sheer eye candy. **Known for:** weekly five-course prix-fixe menu plus a small à la carte café menu; craft cocktails; harbor views, especially from outdoor deck; cooking classes with Sara Jenkins and guest chefs. *$ Average main: $26 ✉ 24 Central St., Rockport ☎ 207/236–8880 🌐 www.ninajunerestaurant.com ⏲ Closed Sun.–Tues. No lunch.*

Hotels

Samoset Resort

$$$$ | RESORT | FAMILY | Located on the Rockland-Rockport town line along the edge of Penobscot Bay and the eastern side of Rockland harbor, this 230-acre resort offers luxurious rooms, suites, and cottages, all with a private balcony or patio and an ocean or garden view. **Pros:** sweeping ocean views; choice of restaurants on-site; a beautiful resort that seems to meet every need. **Cons:** not for those who prefer quiet, intimate lodging; not within easy walking distance of downtown Rockland or Camden; no beach. *$ Rooms from: $400 ✉ 220 Warrenton St., off Rte. 1, Rockport ☎ 207/594–2511 🌐 www.samosetresort.com ⏲ Closed weeknights Dec.–Apr. 🛏 178 rooms 🍽 Free Breakfast ☞ Daily $40 resort fee; 2 dogs under 30 lbs. permitted ($75 per night per dog).*

Schooner Heron

SAILING | FAMILY | Docked in the Rockport Marine Park, the lovely 65-foot, Alden-designed schooner takes passengers sailing on Penobscot Bay three times a day, weather permitting. She was built and is operated by a very experienced, qualified, and licensed couple who sail their schooner to the Caribbean every winter. In Maine from June through early October, they offer an Educational Eco Sail, a happy-hour sunset sail, and private morning charters. While underway, they share their knowledge of local maritime history, sea life, and lobstering. ✉ *Rockport Marine Park, Rockport* ☎ *207/236–8605* 🌐 *www.sailheron.com* ⏲ *Closed late Oct.–June.*

Camden

8 miles north of Rockland.

Known as the Jewel of the Maine Coast, Camden is one of the region's most popular spots. The town's compact size makes it perfect for exploring on foot: shops, restaurants, and galleries line Main Street, as well as the side streets and alleys around the harbor. But be sure to include Camden's residential area on your tour. It is quite charming and filled with lovely period houses from the time when Federal, Greek Revival, and Victorian architectural styles were the rage among the wealthy; many of them are now B&Bs. The Chamber of Commerce, on the Public Landing, can provide you with a walking map.

Rising on the north side of town are the Camden Hills. Drive or hike to the summit of Mt. Battie, in Camden Hills State Park, to enjoy panoramic views of the town, harbor, and island-dotted bay. This perch is where Pulitzer-winning poet Edna St. Vincent Millay penned "Renascence," describing the view in the lines: All I could see from where I stood /Was three long mountains and a wood; / I turned and looked another way, / And saw three islands in a bay."

Camden's not only famous for its geography, but also for its fleet of windjammers—originals from the age of sailing as well as replicas—with their romantic histories and great billowing sails. If possible, sign up for a cruise, whether for a couple of hours or as much as a week.

GETTING HERE AND AROUND

U.S. 1 runs right through the middle of Camden. If you're driving from farther south on U.S. 1 and would like to bypass Thomaston and Rockland on your way to Camden, turn left off onto Route 90 in Warren and rejoin Route 1 at the other end of Route 90 in Rockport.

U.S. 1 has lots of names as it runs through Maine. Within Camden's town limits, it begins at the southern end of town as Elm Street, changes to Main Street in the downtown area, and then becomes High Street.

The Concord Coach Lines bus that drives the coastal route stops on Route 1 in Camden, just south of town.

VISITOR INFORMATION

CONTACTS Penobscot Bay Regional Chamber of Commerce. ✉ *Visitor Center, 2 Public Landing, Camden* ☎ *207/236–4404, 800/562–2529* 🌐 *www.camdenrockland.com.*

WHEN TO GO

From June to September, the town is crowded with visitors, but that doesn't detract from its charm. Just make reservations for lodging and restaurants well in advance and be prepared for busy traffic on the town's Main Street. This is also the best time to book a windjammer excursion.

FESTIVALS AND EVENTS

Camden Shakespeare Festival

THEATER | FAMILY | Every year, a professional troupe of actors presents a midsummer festival of Shakespeare plays beside the harbor. Held in Camden's beautiful amphitheater, the performances strive to engage audiences of all ages, including children. The festival is presented in association with the Camden Public Library. ✉ *Box 1206, Camden* ☎ *207/464–0008* 🌐 *camdenshakespeare.org* 🎫 *$28* ⏲ *Closed Aug.–June.*

★ Camden Windjammer Festival

FESTIVALS | FAMILY | One of the biggest and most colorful events of the year is the Camden Windjammer Festival, which takes place over Labor Day weekend. The harbor is packed with historic vessels, there are lots of good eats, and visitors can tour the magnificent ships. ✉ *Camden* ☎ *207/236–3438* 🌐 *www.facebook.com/WindjammerFestival/.*

Restaurants

★ Natalie's Restaurant

$$$$ | MODERN AMERICAN | Located in the stylish and elegant Camden Harbour Inn, this fine-dining restaurant serves imaginative, beautifully plated creations starring local seafood, meats, and other seasonal ingredients like vegetables and herbs from the property's garden. Probably the most sophisticated dining spot in Camden, Natalie's is the creation of Dutch owners Raymond Brunyanszki and Oscar Verest, who have brought in talented chefs to create splurge-worthy dishes that are served by a polished waitstaff. **Known for:** phenomenal service with true attention to detail; signature five-course lobster tasting menu; grand views of the Camden Hills, harbor, and bay. $ *Average main: $38* ✉ *Camden Harbour Inn, 83 Bay View St., Camden* ☎ *866/658–1542, 207/236–7008* 🌐 *www.nataliesrestaurant.com* ⏲ *Closed Sun. Nov.–May. No lunch.*

The Waterfront

$$ | AMERICAN | Come to this long-standing local favorite for a ringside seat on Camden Harbor; the best view, when the weather cooperates, is from the deck. The menu features fresh local seafood, but there are also beef and chicken entrées and salads. **Known for:** great salad choices; harborside dining, including outdoor deck; solid menu that never disappoints. $ *Average main: $20* ✉ *48 Bay View St., Camden* ☎ *207/236–3747* 🌐 *www.waterfrontcamden.com* ⏲ *Closed Tues.* ☞ *No groups larger than 8 people.*

Coffee and Quick Bites

Harbor Dogs

$ | SEAFOOD | FAMILY | A summertime fixture for five decades, the Harbor Dogs shack on the town landing is the perfect place to grab lunch to enjoy at a nearby bench beside the harbor or before or after a cruise. Hot dog toppings include southwestern, Asian, and Chicago, and there are also lobster and crab rolls, fish tacos, haddock Reubens, and fried-seafood platters. **Known for:** lengthy hot-dog menu; watching the sightseeing boats and sailboats coming and going; delicious takeout to enjoy on a harborfront bench. $ *Average main: $15* ✉ *1 Public Landing, Camden* ☎ *207/230–9638* 🌐 *www.harbordogs.com* ⏲ *Closed Wed. and Thurs. and mid-Oct.–mid-May. No dinner.*

★ Owl and Turtle Bookshop and Café

$ | CAFE | FAMILY | This pint-size but well-stocked independent bookstore with a tiny café has been serving Camden for more than 50 years. The full menu of coffee drinks is based on locally roasted beans and includes a selection of homemade baked goods. **Known for:** locally roasted coffee beans; homemade baked goods; independent bookstore. $ *Average main: $5* ✉ *33 Bay View St., Camden* ☎ *207/230–7335* 🌐 *www.owlandturtle.com* ⏲ *Closed Sun. and Mon.*

Zoot Coffee

$ | **CAFÉ** | Locals and visitors alike are drawn to this community gathering spot by the irresistible aroma of freshly roasted coffee; it's a great spot to visit with friends or open your tablet to do some work. There's a wide selection of hot and cold coffee drinks, chai variations, and hot chocolate, as well as Italian ices and to-go choices that include porridge, yogurt, toast, soup, quiche, grilled cheese, pie, and even beans on toast! **Known for:** well-prepared coffee drinks; relaxed atmosphere; simple breakfast and lunch choices. *Average main: $5 5 Elm St., Camden 207/236–9858 www.facebook.com/ZootCoffee No dinner.*

Hotels

Hartstone Inn & Hideaway

$$$ | **B&B/INN** | Inside this circa-1835 mansard-roofed Victorian home at the southern edge of Camden's downtown area is a plush, sophisticated retreat and a culinary destination. **Pros:** pet-friendly; extravagant breakfasts; some private entrances. **Cons:** not on water; no wheelchair access; not all rooms have fireplaces. *Rooms from: $300 41 Elm St., Camden 207/236–4259 www.hartstoneinn.com Restaurant closed Mon. and Tues. 22 rooms Free Breakfast.*

Lord Camden Inn

$$ | **HOTEL** | **FAMILY** | If you want to be in the midst of the shops and not far from the harbor, this handsome Main Street brick building with bright blue-and-white awnings is the perfect choice. **Pros:** buffet breakfast with hot entrées; all rooms have mini-refrigerators and microwaves; most rooms have balconies. **Cons:** Main Street noise can drift up into front rooms; no on-site restaurant; $15/night parking unless room is booked directly with hotel. *Rooms from: $299 24 Main St., Camden 207/236–4325, 800/336–4325 www.lordcamdeninn.com 36 rooms Free Breakfast.*

★ The Norumbega

$$$$ | **B&B/INN** | With a commanding position overlooking the bay just north of downtown Camden, this impressive, turreted "castle" exudes Old World grandeur. **Pros:** eye-popping architecture; beautiful views of both the ocean and the sloping, waterside lawn; elegant rooms and suites. **Cons:** stairs to climb; a short drive from the center of town; no pets. *Rooms from: $450 63 High St., Camden 207/236–4646 www.norumbegainn.com 11 rooms Free Breakfast.*

Activities

★ Mary Day

SAILING | **FAMILY** | Sailing for more than 50 years, the *Mary Day* was the first schooner in Maine built specifically for vacation excursions. Accommodating up to 28 guests and seven crew, she is continually maintained and upgraded. Cruise lengths range from one night to six nights. *Camden Harbor, Atlantic Ave., Camden 800/992–2218 www.schoonermaryday.com From $450 Closed Nov.–mid-June.*

Olad

SAILING | Captain Aaron Lincoln skippers two-hour sailing trips aboard the 57-foot *Olad* and the smaller *Owl*. Out on Penobscot Bay, passengers spot lighthouses, coastal mansions, seals, and the occasional red-footed puffin cousins known as guillemots. Either boat can also be chartered for longer trips. *Camden Harbor, 1 Bay View Landing, Camden 207/236–2323 www.maineschooners.com $55 Closed Oct.–June 1 BYOB and snacks.*

Shopping

★ Swans Island Company

CRAFTS | For luxurious handcrafted blankets, throws, pillows, wraps, and scarves, look no further. All products are made in Maine using natural, heirloom-quality yarns. The expert craftsmanship explains the hefty price tag. ✉ *2 Bayview St., Camden* ☎ *207/706–7926* 🌐 *swansislandcompany.com.*

★ Hearth and Harrow

HOUSEWARES | Featuring tea towels, napkins, the softest T-shirts, and other textiles hand-printed in Rockport with delightful animals and other nature themes, this inviting shop also stocks home goods, glassware, cards, cooking and gardening books, and plants. ✉ *20 Main St., Camden* ☎ *207/252–9675* 🌐 *www.hearthandharrow.com.*

Belfast

13 miles north of Lincolnville via U.S. 1.

Along with several other Maine communities, Belfast is a strong contender for being named the state's prettiest town. Old-fashioned street lamps set the streets aglow at night and there are handsome ship captain's mansions and a tantalizing selection of shops, galleries, and restaurants all along Main and adjacent streets as well as a lively arts scene. Take the time to stroll down one side of Main Street all the way to the harbor, and then back up the other side. Within a few blocks, you can enjoy not only fresh local seafood, but also a taste of Thai, Lao, Japanese, Italian, and Jamaican cuisines. It's a delightful place to spend a day or two.

■ TIP→ As you walk around town, you will see a number of cream-color signs labeled THE MUSEUM IN THE STREETS. Be sure to read them. The signs present all sorts of interesting facts and factoids about the history of Belfast.

GETTING HERE AND AROUND

As it traces the coast, U.S. 1 runs through Belfast, though the center of town is a short drive off the highway. If you're traveling Interstate 95, take U.S. 3 East in Augusta to get here. The highways meet in Belfast, heading north. Concord Coach Lines' coastal bus stops in Belfast.

VISITOR INFORMATION

The information center has a large array of magazines, guidebooks, maps, and brochures that cover the entire Mid-Coast. It also can provide you with a free walking-tour brochure that describes the various handsome, historic buildings.

CONTACTS Belfast Area Chamber of Commerce. ✉ *Belfast* ☎ *207/338–5900* 🌐 *www.belfastmaine.org.*

Sights

Belfast is infused with a decidedly artistic atmosphere, thanks in part to its having been a magnet for artists, artisans, and back-to-the-landers in the late 20th century. Today, the streets are lined with eclectic and sophisticated boutiques as well as a surprising array of restaurants. And, there's still evidence of the wealth of the mid-1800s, as High Street and the residential area above it are lined with the Greek Revival and Federal-style mansions of business tycoons, shipbuilders, and ship captains. Indeed, the town has one of the best showcases of Greek Revival homes in the state. Don't miss the privately owned "White House," an especially imposing mansion that stands where High and Church streets merge, several blocks south of downtown. Built in 1840, it's named for James P. White, its original owner; while it also used to be painted white, it's actually more cream-colored these days.

Islesboro

If you would like to visit a Penobscot Bay island but don't have much time, Islesboro (🌐 *townofislesboro.com*) is a pleasant choice, as it's only a 20-minute ferry ride from Lincolnville Beach on the mainland. But do plan accordingly as the ferry terminal on Islesboro is miles from the heart of the island, so you'll need wheels—a car or a bike—to explore the 14-mile-long island that includes the tiny village of Dark Harbor. ■ **TIP→ If you plan on simply walking, you won't have time before boarding the return ferry to see much other than a country road and the museum at the lighthouse (the ferry landing is right beside it)—if the museum is open.**

Round-trip ferry passage for a driver and one passenger plus car is $42. When you add a reservation for your car—optional but strongly recommended in-season to ensure space on the ferry for your car—the total comes to $82.

The drive along Islesboro's main road from one end of the island to the other is lovely, though, and a number of nature preserves offer hiking trails that wend through woodlands to bold shores. Most visitor-oriented businesses are open seasonally (Memorial Day to Labor Day) including the Dark Harbor Shop, which sells sandwiches and ice cream. You can also buy picnic supplies at two stores: the Island Market, on the main road a short distance from the road to the ferry terminal; and Durkee's General Store (✉ *867 Main Rd.*), 5 miles farther north. There are no full-service restaurants on the island. Next to the ferry terminal is the Grindle Point Lighthouse; the Sailor's Memorial Museum is in the keeper's house (open on summer weekends).

The Islesboro Ferry (🌐 *www.maine.gov/mdot/ferry/islesboro*), operated by the Maine State Ferry Service, makes nine daily round trips from Lincolnville April through October and seven daily trips November through March. Try to head out on one of the early ferries so you have enough time to drive around and get back without missing the last ferry. There are *no* public lodging accommodations on the island.

Restaurants

Darby's Restaurant and Pub

$$ | **AMERICAN** | **FAMILY** | With pressed-tin ceilings, this charming, old-fashioned restaurant and bar—it's been such since 1865—is a perennial local favorite with a welcoming community feel to it. Pad Thai, chicken chili salad with cashews, a Buddha bowl, and a few Mexican-flavored items are signature dishes, but the menu also serves hearty, scratch-made soups, sandwiches on homemade bread, and classic fish-and-chips. **Known for:** excellent happy hour; gluten-free menu choices; homemade breads. $ *Average main: $18* ✉ *155 High St., Belfast* ☎ *207/338–2339* 🌐 *www.darbys-restaurant.com* ⏲ *Closed Sun.*

★ Young's Lobster Pound

$$$ | **SEAFOOD** | **FAMILY** | Right on the water's edge, across the harbor from downtown Belfast, this corrugated-steel building looks more like a fish cannery than a restaurant, but it's one of the best places for an authentic Maine lobster dinner, known here as the "shore dinner." Lobster rolls, surf-and-turf dinners, steamed clams, steak tips, and hot dogs

are popular, too. As this is a real-deal lobster pound, with absolutely no frills, lobstermen tie up at the dock to unload their catch. **Known for:** "shore dinner": clam chowder or lobster stew, steamed clams or mussels, a 1½-pound boiled lobster, corn on the cob, and chips; family-friendly environment; BYOB. *Average main: $30 ✉ 2 Fairview St., off U.S. 1, Belfast ☎ 207/338–1160 🌐 www.youngslobsters.com 🕒 Takeout only Jan.–Mar.*

Coffee and Quick Bites

Must Be Nice Lobster

$$ | **SEAFOOD** | Not only does Sadie Samuels captain her own lobster boat, the *Must Be Nice*, but she also transforms her haul into lobster rolls that she sells—along with crab rolls, fries, hot dogs, and burgers—from a lunch wagon parked at the bottom of Main Street, just up from the harbor. There are outdoor tables plus indoor seating alongside a small shop of items Samuels crafts herself. **Known for:** made by a local lobsterwoman; award-winning lobster rolls; mini lobster rolls at half the price of the full-size rolls. *Average main: $18 ✉ 2 Cross St., Belfast ☎ 207/218–1431 🌐 www.mustbenicelobster.com 🕒 Closed Mon.*

★ The Scone Goddess

$ | **BAKERY** | **FAMILY** | In a petite gray Cape (look for the mini red-and-white-striped lighthouse beside it), the Scone Goddess makes what are almost certainly the best scones you've ever tasted. Tender and a little crumbly—they bear no resemblance to those stone-hard lumps so often passed off as scones—flavors, which change daily, include ginger lemon, wild Maine blueberry lemon, raspberry cream, and bacon cheddar. **Known for:** unusual flavors; lattes and other beverages; easy-to-mix-and-bake mixes. *Average main: $4 ✉ 1390 Atlantic Hwy., Northport ⊕ 3 miles from downtown Belfast ☎ 207/323–0249 🌐 www.thesconegoddess.com 🕒 Closed Sun. and Mon.*

Bucksport

9 miles north of Searsport via U.S. 1.

Bucksport experienced a bumpy time following the closing a few years ago of a large paper mill that was a major employer. Happily, it is now experiencing a renaissance with new restaurants and shops popping up along Main Street. Just across from town, the stunning and graceful Penobscot Narrows Bridge and Observatory (the world's tallest public bridge observatory) stands taller than the Statue of Liberty. Take the time to ascend via elevator to the bridge-top observatory for sweeping views of land and sea. Fort Knox, Maine's largest historic fort, also overlooks the town from across the Penobscot River. Stroll the paved, garden-bordered riverfront walkway that edges Bucksport's downtown to take in magnificent vistas of both the imposing fort and the bridge.

GETTING HERE AND AROUND

Driving north on Route 1, pass over the spectacular Penobscot Narrows Bridge onto small Verona Island. Then cross a second bridge to Bucksport. Turn left to head down Main Street.

Sights

Fort Knox Historic Site

HISTORIC SIGHT | **FAMILY** | Next to the Penobscot Narrows Bridge is Fort Knox, Maine's largest historic fort. It was built of granite on the west bank of the Penobscot River between 1844 and 1869 when, despite a treaty with Britain settling boundary disputes, invasion was still a concern—after all, the British controlled this region during both the Revolutionary War and the War of 1812. The fort never saw any real action, but it was used for troop training and as a garrison during the Civil War and the Spanish-American War. Ghost hunters have reported a range of paranormal activities here. Visitors are welcome to explore the many rooms and passageways. Guided tours are given between 11 and 3 when volunteers are available. ✉ *740 Ft. Knox Rd., Prospect* ☏ *207/469–6553* 🌐 *www.fortknoxmaine.com* 🎫 *Fort $7; fort and observatory $9* ⏲ *Fort closed Nov.–Apr.*

★ Penobscot Narrows Bridge and Observatory Tower

VIEWPOINT | FAMILY | An "engineering marvel" is how experts describe this beautiful, cable-stayed, 2,120-foot-long Penobscot Narrows Bridge, which is taller than the Statue of Liberty. As one approaches, the bridge appears in the distance like the towers of a fairy-tale castle. The observatory, perched near the top of a 437-foot-tall tower and accessed by an elevator, is the tallest public bridge observatory in the world. Don't miss it—the panoramic views, which take in the hilly countryside and the Penobscot River as it widens into Penobscot Bay, are breathtaking. ✉ *711 Ft. Knox Rd., off U.S. 1, Prospect* ☏ *207/469–6553* 🌐 *www.maine.gov/mdot/pnbo* 🎫 *Fort and observatory $9* ⏲ *Closed Nov.–May.*

Restaurants

★ Friar's Brewhouse Taproom

$ | AMERICAN | FAMILY | You probably wouldn't expect to find an eatery run by Franciscan friars in this little town, but you'll be glad you did. Dressed in long brown habits, your hosts happily serve excellent European-style beers brewed in their nearby mountainside friary, which pair well with sandwiches on freshly baked baguettes, or hearty entrées that blend Maine and French Canadian flavors like family-recipe meat loaf, from-scratch soups, pâté, and fresh local fish dishes. **Known for:** fresh-baked breads; thoughtfully prepared dishes; warm and welcoming friars. $ *Average main: $15* ✉ *84A Main St., Bucksport* ☏ *207/702–9156* 🌐 *www.facebook.com/friarbrew.hotmail/* ⏲ *Closed Sun. and Mon.*

Blue Hill

20 miles east of Castine; 20.6 miles south of Bucksport

Nestled snugly between Blue Hill Mountain and Blue Hill Bay, the village of Blue Hill sits right beside Blue Hill Harbor. About 30 miles from Acadia National Park, the village is a good laid-back base for exploring the Mount Desert Island area, though summertime traffic can significantly increase out-and-back travel times.

Originally known for its granite quarries, copper mines, and shipbuilding, today Blue Hill has galleries, boutiques, and a modest but varied dining scene that offers everything from good coffee at Bucklyn's to fine dining at Arborvine. Tucked near the harbor, a charming little park explodes with sound on Monday nights in summer, when a renowned steel-drum band gives free concerts.

GETTING HERE AND AROUND

From Castine, take Route 166 to 166A. Turn right onto Route 199 North, and follow it to Route 175 South. Turn left onto Route 177 East, which takes you right into town.

From Bucksport, take Route 15 south into town.

Coffee and Quick Bites

★ Bucklyn Coffee

$ | CAFÉ | This tiny, friendly shop serves big, flavorful coffee and interesting sweet and savory pastries. **Known for:** great place for a morning or early afternoon pick-me-up; Maine-roasted beans; coffee served anyway you like it. $ *Average main: $9* ✉ *103 Main St., Blue Hill* ☏ *917/971–3246* 🌐 *bucklyncoffee.square.site* ⏲ *Closed Sun.*

★ The Co-Op Cafe
$ | **AMERICAN** | **FAMILY** | Housed in the Blue Hill Co-Op Community Market, this is a prime place for soups, sandwiches, and pastries. The bread selection alone is worth a stop. **Known for:** eat in or takeout; gluten-free and vegan options; great salad and hot-entrée bars. $ *Average main: $11* ✉ *70 South St., Blue Hill* ☎ *207/374–2165* 🌐 *www.bluehill.coop/the-coop-cafe.*

Hotels

Blue Hill Inn
$$$ | **B&B/INN** | At this Federal-style inn, which was built as a home in 1835 and expanded into a lodging in the 1850s, wide-plank, pumpkin-pine floors perfectly complement the mix of antiques that fill the parlor, library, and guest rooms, several of which have working fireplaces, clawfoot tubs, and flower-garden views. **Pros:** plenty of charm; modern suites with kitchens in separate building; excellent service. **Cons:** narrow stairs; thin walls; only some rooms available in winter. $ *Rooms from: $315* ✉ *40 Union St., Blue Hill* ☎ *207/374–2844* 🌐 *www.bluehillinn.com* *13 rooms* *Free Breakfast.*

Under Canvas
$$$$ | **RESORT** | **FAMILY** | Amid 100 acres on Union River Bay, this glamping property has luxury tents with king-size beds, bathrooms, organic toiletries, wood stoves, and other creature comforts. **Pros:** breathtaking coast and Cadillac Mountain views; good base for Acadia National Park visits; lots of on-site amenities and activities. **Cons:** it still feels like camping; pricey rates and food and activities cost extra; some might find 10 pm quiet time restricting. $ *Rooms from: $620* ✉ *702 Surry Rd., Surry* ☎ *888/496–1148* 🌐 *www.undercanvas.com/camps/acadia* ⏲ *Closed mid-Oct.–mid-May* *63 tents* *No Meals.*

Shopping

★ Blue Hill Wine Shop
WINE/SPIRITS | In a restored barn and Cape-style house, one of Blue Hill's earliest residences, this shop carries more than 3,000 carefully selected wines, as well as cheeses, breads, groceries, local and imported beer, cider, cooking ingredients, and coffees and teas. ✉ *138 Main St., Blue Hill* ☎ *207/374–2161* 🌐 *www.bluehillwineshop.com* ⏲ *Closed Sun.*

★ Handworks Gallery
CRAFTS | Set in what was once a department store, this gallery sells fine art; contemporary fabric, metal, wood, glass, and ceramic decorative items and housewares; and jewelry and accessories. Everything is handcrafted by a diverse group of established and emerging Maine artists. ✉ *48 Main St., Blue Hill* ☎ *207/374–5613* 🌐 *handworksgallery.org* ⏲ *Closed Sun.* ☞ *Limited hrs Jan.–Apr.*

Deer Isle

16 miles south of Blue Hill.

Reachable by a bridge, the thick woods of Deer Isle and Little Deer Isle give way to tidal coves at almost every turn. Stacks of lobster traps populate the backyards of shingled houses, and dirt roads lead to secluded summer cottages.

The village of Deer Isle is nestled between Northwest Harbor and Mill Pond. While it's only got one of each, it's got a great coffee shop, a lovely inn with a beer garden, an art gallery, and a quirky shop with all Maine-made books, toys, and crafts.

GETTING HERE AND AROUND

From Sedgwick, Route 15 crosses a 1930s suspension bridge onto Little Deer Isle and continues on to the larger Deer Isle.

From Blue Hill, follow Route 175 south to Route 172 through Sedgwick and then follow the directions above.

VISITOR INFORMATION

CONTACTS Deer Isle–Stonington Chamber of Commerce. ✉ *114 Little Deer Isle Rd., Deer Isle* ☎ *207/348–6124* 🌐 *www.deer-isle.com.* **Isle au Haut Boat Services.** ✉ *37 Seabreeze Ave., Stonington* ☎ *207/367–5193* 🌐 *isleauhaut.com.*

Sights

Edgar M. Tennis Preserve

NATURE PRESERVE | While enjoying miles of woodland and shore trails at the Edgar M. Tennis Preserve, you can look for hawks, eagles, and ospreys, and wander among old apple trees, fields of wildflowers, and ocean-polished rocks. ✉ *Tennis Rd., off Sunshine Rd., Deer Isle* ☎ *207/348–2455* 🌐 *www.islandheritagetrust.org* *Free.*

Stonington

TOWN | A charming seaside town with only 1,000 year-round residents, Stonington sits at the southern end of Route 15, which has helped retain its unspoiled small-town flavor. This picturesque working waterfront, where boats arrive overflowing with the day's catch, is Maine's largest lobster port. It's also a tranquil tourist destination with boutiques and galleries lining Main Street that cater mostly to out-of-towners.

Stonington includes the villages of Burnt Cove, Oceanville, Green Head, and Clam City. It also serves as the gateway to Isle au Haut, which is home to a remote section of Acadia National Park. ✉ *Stonington.*

Restaurants

★ Aragosta at Goose Cove

$$$$ | **CONTEMPORARY** | Executive chef and proprietor Devin Finigan has created magic in this location with endless views of East Penobscot Bay and food that speaks to the prowess of this region's fishermen and farmers. Whether you're experiencing the chef's tasting menu—think scallops with sorrel and whey; Wagyu with ramps and new potato; and rhubarb with lemon and shortbread—Sunday a-la-carte brunch (seasonal), or a summer happy hour, you're in for a high-quality treat. **Known for:** seasonal tasting menu; delicious hand-crafted cocktails; locally sourced ingredients that dictate the menu. *Average main: $150* ✉ *300 Goose Cove Rd., Deer Isle* ☎ *207/348–6900* 🌐 *aragostamaine.com* *Closed Nov. and Dec. No lunch Mon.–Sat.*

★ 44 North Coffee

$ | **BAKERY** | This place offers amazing (and equitably sourced) coffee and invites you to take a minute to have a conversation while you wait for your slow-pour brew to flow through a colorful, custom-built wooden drip bar. Grab a pastry supplied by a variety of local bakers—if there are any left when you arrive. **Known for:** no Wi-Fi; pastries from Brooksville's Tinder Hearth Bakery; great coffee. *Average main: $15* ✉ *7 Main St., Deer Isle* ☎ *207/348–5208* 🌐 *44northcoffee.com* *Closed Sun.*

Hotels

★ Aragosta

$$$$ | **RESORT** | Nestled among spruces, moss-covered rocks, and the Barred Island Nature Preserve, Aragosta is one of Maine's most tranquil oceanfront complexes. **Pros:** excellent on-site restaurant; postcard-perfect location; cottages are dog-friendly. **Cons:** a car is a must; Wi-Fi is only available in the restaurant; suites are not dog-friendly. *Rooms from: $500* ✉ *300 Goose Cove Rd., Deer Isle* ☎ *207/348–6900* 🌐 *aragostamaine.com* *Closed mid-Oct.–mid-May* *9 cottages, 3 suites* *Free Breakfast.*

Activities

★ Isle au Haut Boat Services

BOATING | FAMILY | To get to and from Isle au Haut, the mail boat operated by this company is your best bet, with four trips a day Monday through Saturday and two trips on Sunday in summer. Parking is available at the Stonington ferry terminal and at several lots in town that are within walking distance. This company also offers regular puffin and lighthouse tours and private charters to Camden and Mt. Desert Island. ✉ *27 Seabreeze Ave., Stonington* ☎ *207/367–5193* 🌐 *www.isleauhaut.com* 🎫 *Mail boat: $20 each way. Tours: $80.*

Ellsworth Area

140 miles northeast of Portland, 28 miles south of Bangor.

Ellsworth is the main gateway to Acadia National Park making it a good spot for refueling—literally and figuratively. With two supermarkets, several good restaurants, and a range of shops, the city has nearly everything you need. Big box stores are along Route 3 and there's a nice downtown area on Main Street with unique shops set in attractive brick buildings. From here you continue through to Trenton, where there are souvenir shops, roadside eateries, and less expensive lodgings before crossing onto Mount Desert Island. **■ TIP→ Folks stay in Ellsworth and Trenton for the less expensive lodging.**

GETTING HERE AND AROUND

Ellsworth is the eye of the storm through which all vehicles traveling to Mount Desert Island must pass. As such, the few short miles of U.S. 1 that pass through the city can be gnarled with traffic in summer.

VISITOR INFORMATION

CONTACTS Ellsworth Area Chamber of Commerce. ✉ *151 High St., Ellsworth* ☎ *207/667–5584* 🌐 *www.ellsworthchamber.org.*

Restaurants

Airline Brewing Company

$ | BURGER | With red cushioned seating and wood walls around the bar, this cozy-as-can-be brew pub (the brewery itself is inland) right on Main Street has a decor and menu that reflects its British ownership. Several of the dozen or so beers served are hand-pulled, and food options include steak and ale pie and bangers and mash. **Known for:** being a community gathering place; warm beer cheese appetizers; "signature toasties" (yes, British for toasted sandwiches). 💲 *Average main: $13* ✉ *173 Main St., Ellsworth* ☎ *207/412–0045* 🌐 *www.abcmaine.beer/.*

Fogtown Brewing Company

$ | PIZZA | FAMILY | Though tucked back on an Ellsworth residential street, folks find this hip brewpub—yes, the brewery is right here—with a large, inviting beer garden, housed on the lower level of an old brick warehouse. The simple menu includes hotdogs and bratwurst, and pizza cooked in the outdoor oven. **Known for:** live music; seasonal pizza toppings; community gathering spot. 💲 *Average main: $15* ✉ *25 Pine St., Ellsworth* ☎ *207/370–0845* 🌐 *www.fogtownbrewing.com* ⏲ *No lunch Closed Mon. from late May–mid-Oct. and Mon.–Wed. from mid-Oct.–late May.*

Shopping

John Edwards Market

FOOD | With a selection of organic and natural foods, and soup, sandwiches, salads, baked goods, and coffee to go, John Edwards Market is a pleasant option whether you're packing a picnic or stocking the kitchenette at your rental.

Downstairs, a wine cellar and an art gallery showcase work by area artists. Wine tastings are on the first Friday of the month 5–7 pm. ✉ *158 Main St., Ellsworth* ☎ *207/667–9377* 🌐 *www.johnedwards-market.com.*

Bar Harbor

20 miles from Ellsworth via Route 3.

A resort town since the 19th century, Bar Harbor is the artistic, culinary, and social center of Mount Desert Island, providing visitors to nearby Acadia National Park with lodging, shops, and restaurants. Around the turn of the last century, the town was a premier summer haven for the very rich because of its cool breezes and stunning interplay of mountains and sea. Many of their lavish mansions in and near town burned down in the Great Fire of 1947. The business district—centered around Main, Mount Desert, Cottage, and West streets—was spared. You can stroll past mansions that survived the fire on the shore path and West Street, a national historic district.

Bar Harbor has a few excellent museums and numerous greens and parks. Some were the sites of grand hotels like Agamont Park overlooking the harbor, and the Village Green, a gathering spot with a piano (that anyone can play) under the gazebo. Spring through fall, scenic cruises and whale-watching trips come and go from the town pier, boats cluster in the harbor, and visitors linger on the many sidewalk benches. At low tide, folks walk to Bar Island.

GETTING HERE AND AROUND

Route 3 leads to Bar Harbor. Acadia National Park's Hulls Cove Visitor Center is off the highway three miles before downtown, near the oceanside hamlet of Hulls Cove. The Cadillac Mountain entrance for Acadia's Park Loop Road (two-way section) is on Route 233 just west of downtown. Continuing on Route 233 to its terminus at Route 198, turn left for Northeast Harbor or right to reach Route 102, which loops the western side of Mount Desert Island. A few miles from downtown Bar Harbor on Route 3 is an entrance for Acadia's Sieur de Monts section and the loop road (one-way section). A more scenic and only slightly longer route to Northeast Harbor is via Route 3. Tiny Otter Creek is about midway along the drive, which has hilly forested sections and ocean views in Seal Harbor and Northeast Harbor.

VISITOR INFORMATION

CONTACTS Bar Harbor Chamber of Commerce. ✉ *2 Cottage St., Bar Harbor* ☎ *207/288–5103* 🌐 *www.visitbarharbor.com.*

Sights

★ Abbe Museum

HISTORY MUSEUM | FAMILY | This important museum dedicated to Maine's Indigenous tribes—collectively known as the Wabanaki—is the state's only Smithsonian-affiliated facility and one of the few places in Maine to experience Native culture as interpreted by Native peoples themselves. Spanning 12,000 years, the "core" exhibit, People of the First Light, features items such as birch bark canoes, basketry, and bone tools as well as photos and interactive displays. Changing exhibits often showcase contemporary Native American art. A birchbark canoe made at the Abbe anchors the free Orientation Gallery beside the gift shop at the entrance. Check the website for events, from basket weaving and boatbuilding demonstrations to author talks and family-friendly pop-up rainy days activities.

Opened in 1928, the Abbe's Acadia National Park location at Sieur de Monts is its original home. Longtime exhibits in the small eight-sided building include artifacts from early digs on Mount Desert Island and dioramas of Native American

Long ramps on Maine's many docks make it easier to access boats at either high or low tide.

life here before European settlement. ✉ *26 Mount Desert St., Bar Harbor* ☎ *207/288–3519* 🌐 *www.abbemuseum.org* 🎟 *$10* ⏲ *Closed Nov.–early May; Fri. and Sat. mid-May–Oct.*

★ La Rochelle Mansion and Museum
HISTORY MUSEUM | Stepping into the large foyer of this 1903 brick chateau, your view flows through glass doors on the opposite side, then across the piazza and flat lawn to a serene coastal expanse. A business partner of J.P. Morgan, George Bowdoin, and his wife, Julia, built this 13,000-square-foot, 41-room mansion near downtown Bar Harbor as their seasonal residence. Unlike many of the area's summer "cottages" of the nation's elite, it was spared from the Great Fire of 1947. In 2020, La Rochelle became Bar Harbor Historical Society's museum and the town's only Gilded Age mansion open to the public. While the Bowdoins' story weaves through displays, each room has themed exhibits on local history: in the foyer, baskets the Wabanaki made to sell to tourists; the dining room, grand hotels of yesteryear; the master bedroom, old maps (one shows where the fire raged); a guest room, the town's famous visitors; and so on. Under the elegant wishbone staircase, a "flower room" with a curved wall spotlights the famous landscape artist who created the long-gone sunken garden. In the servants' quarters on the third floor, their story is shared—don't miss the hallway callbox. ✉ *127 West St., Bar Harbor* ☎ *207/288–0000* 🌐 *www.barharborhistorical.org* 🎟 *$15* ⏲ *Closed Nov.–late May.*

Restaurants

Atlantic Brewing Co. Midtown
$ | **AMERICAN** | **FAMILY** | Glass walls let you see this busy craft brewery spot in action even before you enter, but look up or head up—there's rooftop seating with great Bar Harbor views. After ordering a flight or glass of beer, choose from a food menu offering soups, sandwiches, salads, and lobster and crab rolls. ✉
Known for: jumbo pretzel with cheese and mustard made with an English Brown

Ale; Old Soaker natural blueberry soda and root beer for the kids; also selling beer to go. *Average main: $16* *52 Cottage St., Bar Harbor* *207/288–2326* *www.atlanticbrewing.com.*

Jeannie's Great Maine Breakfast
$ | **AMERICAN** | **FAMILY** | After enjoying the sunrise atop Acadia National Park's Cadillac Mountain, snuggle into a wooden booth or grab a table at this homey, yellow-walled eatery that opens at 6 am to catch the crowds who flock to the spectacle. Signature items include homemade oatmeal bread, stuffed French toast, and the Great Maine Breakfast, with three eggs, meat, pancakes, and vegetarian baked beans—the tradition here is to eat leftovers from Saturday night's bean supper on Sunday morning. **Known for:** gluten-free and vegan options; strawberry rhubarb fruit spread; serving breakfast through lunch (closes 1 pm). *Average main: $13* *15 Cottage St., Bar Harbor* *207/288–4166* *www.jeanniesbreakfast.com* *Closed mid-Oct.–early May and Tues. early May–mid-Oct. No dinner.*

★ Side Street Cafe
$ | **AMERICAN** | **FAMILY** | On a side street near the Village Green, this place (and its sister arm, The Annex) hops on busy summer evenings as folks line up for its comfort food like fish tacos and burgers. Outdoor and indoor dining spaces, one anchored by a horseshoe bar, flow together and exposed brick, and a cork wall and ceiling, add warmth to the welcoming, modern, family-friendly vibe; friendly dogs are allowed outside. **Known for:** handcrafted cocktails and live music nightly in The Annex; "signature" mac-and-cheese including lobster and meatball as well as "create-your-own"; margaritas. *Average main: $14* *49 Rodick St., Bar Harbor* *207/801–2591* *www.sidestreetbarharbor.com* *Main restaurant: closed late Oct.–early Apr.; The Annex: no lunch, closed mid-Oct.–late May.*

Coffee and Quick Bites

★ Burning Tree
$ | **AMERICAN** | An early standout in Maine's farm-to-table movement, this acclaimed establishment not far from Bar Harbor in tiny Otter Creek sells to-go foods—prepared (including breakfast pastries) and ready-to-cook, all made on-site and largely featuring ingredients from the owners' extensive gardens. The retail side has a small gardenside outdoor eating area and also sells small-scale wines (natural, organic, and biodynamic) as well as ciders. **Known for:** crab cakes with jalapenos; inventive seasonal items like pickled plums; nice selection of vegetarian offerings. *Average main: $10* *69 Otter Creek Dr., Otter Creek* *5 miles from Bar Harbor, 7 miles from Northeast Harbor* *207/288–9331* *www.theburningtreerestaurant.com* *Closed late Oct.–late May; closed Tues. late May–late Oct.*

Downeast Deli & Boxed Lunch Co.
$ | **AMERICAN** | Don't be fooled by this tiny takeout-only joint's no-frills storefront: many praise its lobster rolls as the best around. On summer mornings, the line often stretches around the corner by 10 am as folks come to get lobster rolls as well as wraps, sandwiches, salads, and slices of blueberry pie for outings to Acadia National Park and elsewhere around Mount Desert Island. **Known for:** taking orders the night before; several lobster roll options, including just plain "naked"; selling a few breakfast items, too. *Average main: $13* *65 Main St., Bar Harbor* *207/288–1001* *www.downeastdeli.com* *Closed late Oct.–early May.*

Mount Desert Island Ice Cream
$ | **ICE CREAM** | Madagascar Vanilla Bean has specks from beans scraped from vanilla pods—just one example of the prep work that goes into creating these heralded artisanal ice creams (and a few sorbets), made at a nearby production

facility with as many local ingredients as possible. The shop's double doors open like a huge window, welcoming passersby right in; grab a seat or head across the street to the Village Green to savor every bite. **Known for:** unique rotating flavors like Bay of Figs; locations in Portland, Maine; Washington, D.C.; and Japan; ice cream on menus at area restaurants. *$ Average main: $5 ✉ 7 Firefly La., Bar Harbor ☎ 207/801–4007 🌐 www.mdiic.com ⏱ Closed late Oct.–early Apr.*

Hotels

Bar Harbor Grand Hotel
$$$ | **HOTEL** | **FAMILY** | Taking one of the well-appointed, modern rooms in this 2011 replica of Bar Harbor's famed Rodick House hotel puts you a stone's throw from the town's lively restaurants, cafés, and gift shops, and though it's a short walk to the waterfront, you can relax here with a dip in the hotel's heated pool or Jacuzzi. **Pros:** "extended stay" suites with kitchenettes; standard rooms have a king or two queens; courtesy full breakfast includes local pastries. **Cons:** summer street noise in front-facing rooms; no restaurant or bar on-site; not on or in sight of the ocean. *$ Rooms from: $389 ✉ 269 Main St., Bar Harbor ☎ 207/288–5226, 888/766–2599 🌐 www.barharborgrand.com ⏱ Closed mid-Nov.–early Apr. 72 rooms 🍽 Free Breakfast.*

★ Salt Cottages
$$$$ | **MOTEL** | **FAMILY** | Renovated into a chic family-friendly resort in 2022, these 1940s-era roadside cottages surround a green that sweeps uphill across Route 3 from Hulls Cove beach just 3 miles from Bar Harbor—Acadia is even closer. **Pros:** stylish lodge where you can relax by the fireplace and go to Picnic, a takeout restaurant serving breakfast, lunch, and dinner; kids 12 and under stay free in cabins with adults; resort amenities include heated pool, hot tubs, bocce, lawn games, "game shed," and courtesy s'mores for the firepit. **Cons:** cabins aren't stocked with utensils or dishes; no courtesy coffee in the lodge (but provided for cottage coffeemakers); limited or no water views from inside most cabins. *$ Rooms from: $480 ✉ 20 Rte. 3, Hulls Cove ☎ 207/288–9918 🌐 www.saltcottagesbarharbor.com ⏱ Closed Nov.–mid-May 31 cottages 🍽 No Meals.*

★ Terramor Outdoor Resort
$$$$ | **RESORT** | **FAMILY** | Luckily for visitors to Acadia National Park, Kampgrounds of America transformed one of its traditional campgrounds into its first glampground in 2020; anchoring 64 tents (all with floors, beds, private fire rings, and hotel-like amenities) on well-shaded, well-spaced sites is an impressive lodge with a high sloped wood ceiling and restaurant (eat in or get items to go), bar, fireplaces, chic chairs and couches, and decks. **Pros:** activities galore, including yoga, stargazing, concerts, and lobster bakes; big fancy grill sites (fee; all you need is provided including food); covered sitting area by swank pool and hot tub. **Cons:** no "en tent" baths in four tents remaining from KOA campground (but baths are private and the price is right); not on the water; road noise at some sites. *$ Rooms from: $400 ✉ 1453 Rte. 102, Bar Harbor ☎ 207/288–7500 🌐 terramoroutdoorresort.com ⏱ Closed mid-Oct.–mid-May 64 units 🍽 Free Breakfast.*

★ West Street Hotel
$$$$ | **RESORT** | With only 85 mostly water-view rooms and suites, attention to detail comes naturally here, and the panoramic views from the fabulous adults-only infinity pool on the rooftop deck are hands down the best in town. **Pros:** each floor is equipped with guest pantries filled with snacks and goodies; one of Maine's most tastefully decorated boutique hotels; many rooms and suites have balconies. **Cons:** $35 daily resort fee; chilly Maine weather can limit use of resort amenities; near but not on the water. *$ Rooms from: $700 ✉ 50 West*

St., Bar Harbor ☎ 207/288–0825 ⊕ www.opalcollection.com/west-street ⊙ Closed from late Oct.–early May 🛏 85 rooms 🍽 No Meals.

BIKING

Bar Harbor Bicycle Shop

BIKING | FAMILY | Rent bikes for a half day, full day, or week at the Bar Harbor Bicycle Shop. The selection includes hybrid and Class 1 e-bikes as well as tag-alongs, child trailers, and car racks. ✉ *141 Cottage St., Bar Harbor* ☎ *207/288–3886* ⊕ *www.barharborbike.com.*

BOATING

Coastal Kayaking Tours

GUIDED TOURS | FAMILY | This outfitter has been leading trips in the scenic waters off Mount Desert Island since 1982. Trips are limited to no more than 12 people. The season is mid-May–mid-October. ✉ *48 Cottage St., Bar Harbor* ☎ *207/288–9605* ⊕ *www.acadiafun.com.*

★ Downeast Windjammer Cruises

BOAT TOURS | FAMILY | Cruises among the islands of Frenchman Bay are offered on the 151-foot four-masted schooner *Margaret Todd* and 58½-foot two-masted *Bailey Louise Todd,* both with distinctive red sails, as well as 72-foot, two-masted Schooner *Joshua,* with traditional white sails. Trips run morning, afternoon, and at sunset for 1½ to 2 hours, except in the fall when sunset cruises are a bit shorter than usual. Whatever the season, these evening excursions feature live folk music. The tour operator often offers longer specialty cruises and does fishing and sailing charters. ✉ *Bar Harbor Inn pier, 7 Newport Dr., Bar Harbor* ☎ *207/288–4585* ⊕ *www.downeastwindjammer.com* 🎫 *From $44 per person* ⊙ *Closed mid-Oct.–mid-May.*

WHALE-WATCHING

Bar Harbor Whale Watch Co.

BOAT TOURS | FAMILY | This company has six boats, one of them a 130-foot jet-propelled double-hulled catamaran with spacious decks. There are lighthouse and puffin-watching, lobstering and seal-watching, whale-watching, nature, and sunset cruises. The Somes Sound trip takes in four lighthouses; one to Acadia National Park's Baker Island is led by a park ranger. ✉ *1 West St., Bar Harbor* ☎ *207/288–2386, 888/942–5374* ⊕ *www.barharborwhales.com* 🎫 *From $43.*

Shopping

Cadillac Mountain Sports

SPORTING GOODS | One of the best sporting-goods stores in the state, Cadillac Mountain Sports has developed a following of locals and visitors alike. Here you'll find top-quality climbing, hiking, boating, paddling, and camping equipment, and in winter you can rent cross-country skis, ice skates, and snowshoes. ✉ *26 Cottage St., Bar Harbor* ☎ *207/288–4532* ⊕ *www.cadillacsports.com.*

Island Artisans

ART GALLERIES | Works by more than 100 Maine artisans are sold here, including basketry, pottery, fiber work, embossed paper, wood bowls and objects, and jewelry. ✉ *99 Main St., Bar Harbor* ☎ *207/288–4214* ⊕ *www.islandartisans.com* ⊙ *Closed Jan.–Apr.*

Northeast Harbor

12 miles south of Bar Harbor via Rtes. 3 and 198.

A summer community for some of the nation's wealthiest families, Northeast Harbor on the eastern side of the entrance to Somes Sound has one of the best harbors on the Maine coast. Filled with yachts and powerboats, you can catch a cruise or hop the year-round ferry to the Cranberry Isles.

The small downtown—two blocks from the harbor on Sea Street—is nicely clustered with shops, galleries, and eateries. The village's extensive trail network (maintained by a village improvement association) provides access to Acadia National Park's Lower Hadlock Pond (you can hike around the pond or connect with other trails). Most of the Land & Garden Preserve, which stretches from Northeast Harbor to Seal Harbor, was formerly part of John D. Rockefeller Jr.'s summer estate; the preserve encompasses the world-renowned Asticou Azalea Garden, Thuya Garden, and the Abby Aldrich Rockefeller Garden.

GETTING HERE AND AROUND

After crossing onto Mount Desert Island, it's 11 miles via Route 198 to Northeast Harbor. Be sure to slowly cruise Sargeant Drive during your stay—about 4 miles long and well-shaded with a few small pullovers, this narrow scenic drive edges the fjord-like deep sound between its terminuses in the village center and at Route 198.

From Northeast Harbor, Route 3 travels eastward to Seal Harbor, affording lovely ocean views. Here, Acadia National Park's Stanley Brook Road (closed off-season; about 2 miles long) connects to Park Loop Road where it becomes two-way near Jordan Pond. Continuing to Bar Harbor from Seal Harbor, Route 3 passes through Otter Creek and by lovely forested Acadia slopes. The 11½-mile route to Bar Harbor from Northeast Harbor via Route 198/Route 3 and Route 233 is only a few minutes faster and a half-mile shorter than the Route 3 way. Both routes pass through sections of Acadia.

VISITOR INFORMATION

CONTACTS Town of Mount Desert Chamber of Commerce. ✉ *41 Harbor Dr., Northeast Harbor* ☎ *207/276–5040* 🌐 *mtdesertchamber.org.*

Sights

Land & Garden Preserve manages and cares for 1,400 acres in Northeast Harbor and Seal Harbor that encompasses the Abby Aldrich Rockefeller Garden, Asticou Azalea Garden, Little Long Pond Natural Lands, and Thuya Garden.

Parking areas at the Preserve's gardens are small and fill quickly at peak times; you may have to return later in the day. Thuya Garden also has a parking area below the garden on Route 3, from which you can ascend to the garden on a trail with granite stairs. In lieu of a day hike, consider walking up to Thuya and Asticou Azalea gardens from the village at the end of Route 198. It's about 2 miles from there to Asticou at the corner of Route 198/Route 3. Take the sidewalk all the way or hit the preserve's Asticou Stream Trail for the last leg. It's a 15-minute walk along Route 3 between Asticou and Thuya. You can also hike between them on a route that includes a side road and a bit of the sidewalk near Asticou (see the preserve map online or at parking area kiosks).

Abby Aldrich Rockefeller Garden

GARDEN | The Abby Aldrich Rockefeller Garden is the creation of its namesake and famed landscape designer Beatrix Farrand. An ever-present Narnia vibe begins on the drive up through the woods to the hilltop locale: leaf blowers keep the large mossy granite rocks free of leaves and needles, to magical effect. Even before entering on the Spirit Path, lined with Korean funerary statues, the garden's earthy pink high wall is entrancing as it resembles walls in Beijing's Forbidden City. The English-style main border garden has many colorful annuals; one side is more shaded so bed heights vary, adding whimsy to the symmetrical space. In smaller garden spaces nearby, you can rest on a bench, step through a pagoda, look out on Little Long Pond, and contemplate more Eastern sculptures, from seated Buddhas to guardian animals. An easy forest trail leads to the large terrace—with commanding extended ocean views—that fronted The Eyrie, the Rockefellers' massive summer "cottage," until it was torn down in 1962. ✉ *Lawn & Garden Preserve, Seal Harbor* 🌐 *www.gardenpreserve.org/abby-aldrich-rockefeller-garden* 🎫 *$15* ⏲ *Closed early Sept.–early July* ✍ *Reservations only.*

Asticou Azalea Garden

GARDEN | With many varieties of rhododendrons and azaleas, the Japanese-style garden is spectacular from late May to mid-June as the pink, white, and blue flowers not only bloom but reflect in a stream-fed pond. Whatever the season there's plenty to admire, especially in fall when the many native plants brighten the landscape. You can contemplate on a bench along the winding paths as intended, perhaps by the white sand garden—raked to evoke moving water. Created with azaleas from famed landscape designer Beatrix Farrand's Bar Harbor garden, Asticou was designed by Charles Savage, a self-educated garden designer who managed his family's nearby Asticou Inn. ✉ *Land & Garden Preserve, 3 Sound Dr., on corner of Rte. 3 and Rte. 198, Northeast Harbor* ☎ *207/276–3699* 🌐 *www.gardenpreserve.org/asticou-azalea-garden* 🎫 *$5 suggested donation* ⏲ *Closed Nov.–early May.*

Little Long Pond Natural Lands

NATURE PRESERVE | The Land & Garden preserve expanded greatly in 2015 when David Rockefeller, son of Acadia National Park founder John D. Rockefeller Jr., donated about 1,000 acres of largely forested land in Seal Harbor to the conversation group. The property includes 17 acres of meadows; 12 acres of marsh; a bog and streams; carriage roads and trails, some connecting with Acadia's trails; stone staircases on the Richard Trail, steep in sections, similar to those in Acadia; and a pond you can hike around and swim in (at designated areas). Upon David Rockefeller's death in 2017, the preserve was gifted the old estate's formal garden, the Abby Aldrich Rockefeller Garden.

Two of several preserve parking areas on Route 3 are for Little Long Pond Natural Lands. The one beside the pond across from Bracy Cove is small, so consider using the parking area west of here, where a 0.4-mile trail leads to the cove and pond. ✉ *Lawn & Garden Preserve, Rte. 3 Seal Harbor* 🌐 *www.gardenpreserve.org/little-long-pond.*

Thuya Garden

GARDEN | Hidden atop a hill above Route 3, this garden is part of what was once the summer home of Boston landscape designer and engineer Joseph Henry Curtis. Today the site is a peaceful and elegant spot to take in formal perennial gardens. Designed by Charles Savage and named for the property's majestic white cedars, Thuja occidentalis, the garden is filled with colorful blooms throughout summer. Walk the immaculately groomed grass paths or enjoy the view from a well-placed bench. You'll find delphiniums, daylilies, dahlias, heliotrope, snapdragons, and other types of vegetation. You can take a look at the sitting room in the Curtis home, which has a large collection of books compiled by Savage. Check the website for docent-led tours of the "lodge" as it's known. ✉ *Land & Garden Preserve, 15 Thuya Dr., Northeast Harbor* ☎ *207/276–5130* 🌐 *www. gardenpreserve.org* 🎫 *$5 suggested donation* ⏲ *Closed mid-Oct.–mid-June.*

Restaurants

★ Abel's Lobster

$$$ | **SEAFOOD** | **FAMILY** | Located on a nub jutting into Somes Sound a few miles from Northeast Harbor, this place hums on summer nights as adults grab a drink from the outside bar, kids and dogs romp, and folks angle to watch lobsters cook in an open-air kitchen before eating at tables about the sloping lawn; the window-lined mid-century wood-walled dining room has views from every table. There are separate menus for each dining space though there is some overlap including the wood-fired boiled lobster, a lobster roll, fried clams, and the 9-ounce house burger. **Known for:** outside bar-type table curves above the shore; largely locally sourced menu; house-made cornbread. *Average main: $33* *13 Abels Lane, Mount Desert, Somesville* *207/276–8221* *www.abelslobster-mdi.com* *Closed mid-Oct.-mid-May and Sun. and Mon. from mid-May–mid-Oct.*

Asticou Inn

$$$ | **AMERICAN** | **FAMILY** | Overlooking the water out back and practically hugging Route 3 out the front, this 1883 four-story gray-shingled restaurant and inn can't be missed nor is the opportunity to dine here and savor the spectacular view of picturesque Northeast Harbor, especially from the large deck fronting the classic old New England dining room. The menu offers a handful of entrées, including filet mignon, and lighter fare like fish tacos. **Known for:** popovers with strawberry jam; award-winning seafood chowder; lodging choices outside the main inn include funky six-sided 1960s cottages nick-named "spaceships." *Average main: $33* *15 Peabody Rd., Northeast Harbor* *207/276–3344* *www.asticou.com* *Closed Tues. and early Oct.–mid May.*

Bass Harbor

9 miles south of Somesville via Rtes. 102 and 102A.

Tucked below Southwest Harbor at the bottom of Mount Desert Island, this small lobstering village doesn't bustle with seasonal tourists like larger island villages, but it does have a few restaurants. It's also the departure point for the ferry to Frenchboro and Swans Island.

Two miles south of Bass Harbor and part of Acadia National Park, Bass Harbor Head Light is the most popular attraction on the island's "quiet side" and one of the most photographed lighthouses in Maine. Acadia's Ship Harbor and Wonderland trails, both easy and under 1½ miles, are also nearby.

GETTING HERE AND AROUND

Bass Harbor is 2.7 miles from Southwest Harbor via Route 102 and Route 102A (Seawall Road), but many visitors travel between them on the 7-mile-long scenic route that loops below Route 102 on a coastal swath bordered by the ocean and both harbors: Southwest on the north and Bass on the west. The road provides access to several popular Acadia National Park attractions.

ESSENTIALS

CONTACTS Southwest Harbor & Tremont Chamber of Commerce. *329 Main St., Southwest Harbor* *207/244–9264* *www.acadiachamber.com.*

Sights

Burnt Coat Harbor Lighthouse and Swans Island

LIGHTHOUSE | **FAMILY** | Swans Island is a picturesque 6-mile ferry ride from Bass Harbor at the bottom of Mount Desert Island. There are numerous outdoor activities, like hiking, swimming, fishing, and biking, but the 35-foot-tall white Burnt Coat Harbor Lighthouse on the south shore is not to be missed. Both the light and the keeper's house, which has history exhibits, an art gallery, bathrooms, and a small gift shop, are open from late June to early September. An apartment upstairs can be rented on a weekly basis from June through October. Aside from vacation rentals, there's only one lodging, the five-room Harbor Watch Inn (*www.harborwatchinnswansisland.com*). The Island Market & Supply (*www.tims-swans-island.com*) is a great place to get picnic supplies or other general store needs. ✉ *Swans Island, Bass Harbor* 🌐 *www.burntcoatharborlight.com.*

Restaurants

Thurston's Lobster Pound

$$ | **SEAFOOD** | **FAMILY** | Right on Bass Harbor, Thurston's is easy to spot because of the bright yellow awnings covering much of its outdoor-only seating. You can order everything from a grilled-cheese crab sandwich, haddock chowder, or hamburger to a boiled lobster served with clams or mussels. **Known for:** selling fresh cooked or uncooked lobsters to go—it's also a lobster wholesaler; lobster fresh off the boat sold in three size ranges; good place to watch sunsets. $ *Average main: $20* ✉ *9 Thurston Rd., Bernard* ☎ *207/244–7600* 🌐 *www.thurstonforlobster.com* ⏲ *Closed mid-Oct.–late spring; closed Sun. and Mon. late spring–mid-Oct.*

Schoodic Peninsula

25 miles east of Ellsworth via U.S. 1 and Rte. 186.

Acadia National Park's only mainland section sits at the bottom of Schoodic Peninsula, extending to its very tip. As at the park over on Mount Desert Island, visitors to the Schoodic District hike, bike, camp, and savor spectacular views. Crowds are smaller, though they are increasing, and it's here that you'll find Winter Harbor and Gouldsboro.

On the peninsula's western side, Winter Harbor's small but sweet downtown is en route to Grindstone Neck. Granite steps lead to rocky shorefront on tucked-away street ends in the wealthy summer community, which gives an inkling of Bar Harbor before a 1947 fire destroyed many mansions there. Surrounding Winter Harbor, Gouldsboro is also a proud lobstering and fishing community, sprinkled with coastal villages. Guarded by its namesake light, Prospect Harbor stretches along Route 186. Tiny Wonsqueak and Birch harbors flash after you exit Acadia. On the peninsula's most easterly shore, Corea is tucked away from it all on a small roundish harbor, the open ocean beyond.

GETTING HERE AND AROUND

Route 186 loops Schoodic Peninsula, intersecting with the U.S. Route 1 twice.

A seasonal passenger ferry travels Frenchman Bay between Bar Harbor and Winter Harbor, where visitors can connect with the seasonal free Island Explorer bus service to Acadia National Park's Schoodic District and nearby villages . Route 195 runs down the middle of the peninsula from U.S. 1 to Prospect Harbor and continues east to Corea, where it ends.

VISITOR INFORMATION

CONTACTS Schoodic Chamber of Commerce. ✉ *Winter Harbor* 🌐 *schoodicchamber.com.*

Sights

For more information on the Schoodic District area of Acadia National Park, see the Acadia National Park chapter.

Restaurants

Lunch on the Wharf

$$ | **SEAFOOD** | **FAMILY** | A fisherman's wife owns this popular establishment, which buys lobster right off the boat and has covered tables spread about a deck atop a wharf. As stunning as the setting is, folks also come for the excellent food, including boiled lobster with sides; there are plenty of non-seafood choices, too, including pulled pork. **Known for:** BYOB; lobster rolls; whoopie pies. $ *Average main: $18* ✉ *13 Gibbs La., Corea, Gouldsboro* ☎ *207/276–5262* 🌐 *www.corealunch.com.*

Did You Know?

A far cry from the bloated berries at most grocery stores, Maine's small, flavor-packed wild blueberries are a must in-season, late July–early September. Try a handful fresh, in pancakes, or a pie.

Wild for Blueberries

Native only to northern New England, Atlantic Canada, and Quebec, wild blueberries have long been a favorite food and a key ingredient in cultural and economic life Down East. Maine's crop averages 85 million pounds annually, accounting for virtually all U.S. production and one-fourth of North America's. Washington County yields about 75% of Maine's crop, which is why the state's largest wild blueberry processors are here: Jasper Wyman & Son in Milbridge and the predecessor of what is now Cherryfield Foods in Cherryfield were founded shortly after the Civil War, during which Maine blueberries were shipped to Union soldiers.

Wild blueberries, which bear fruit every other year, thrive in the region's cold climate and sandy, acidic soil. Undulating blueberry barrens stretch for miles in Deblois and Cherryfield (the "Blueberry Capital of the World") and are scattered throughout Washington County. Look for tufts among low-lying plants along roadways. In spring, the fields shimmer as the small-leaf plants turn myriad shades of mauve, honey orange, and lemon yellow. White flowers appear in June. Fall transforms the barrens into a sea of otherworldly red.

Amid Cherryfield's barrens, a plaque on a boulder lauds the late J. Burleigh Crane for helping advance an industry that's not as wild as it used to be. Fields are irrigated, honeybees have been brought in to supplement native pollinators, and rocks and boulders are removed to literally "level" the field. In the past, barrens were typically burned to rid plants of disease and insects, reducing the need for pesticides to improve yield. Native Americans, who are still active in the industry, taught European settlers the practice, now used mostly by organic growers.

Most of the barrens in and around Cherryfield are owned by large blueberry processors. At least 90% of Maine's crop is harvested with machinery. That requires moving boulders, so the rest continues to be harvested by hand with blueberry rakes, which resemble large forks and pull the berries off their stems. Years ago, year-round residents did this work; today, it's mostly seasonal migrant workers.

Blueberries get their dark color from anthocyanins, which act as an antioxidant. Wild blueberries have more of these antiaging, anticancer compounds than their cultivated cousins; they're also smaller and more flavorful, and therefore mainly used in packaged foods, many of the frozen variety. Just 1% of the state's crop (some 500,000 pints) is consumed fresh, most of it in Maine. Look for fresh berries (usually starting in late July and lasting until early September) at roadside stands, farmers' markets, and supermarkets.

Find farm stores, stands, and markets statewide selling blueberries and blueberry jams and syrups at 🌐 *www.realmaine.com*, a Maine Department of Agriculture, Conservation and Forestry site that promotes Maine foods. Wild blueberries are the state's official berry and pies made with them are its official dessert.

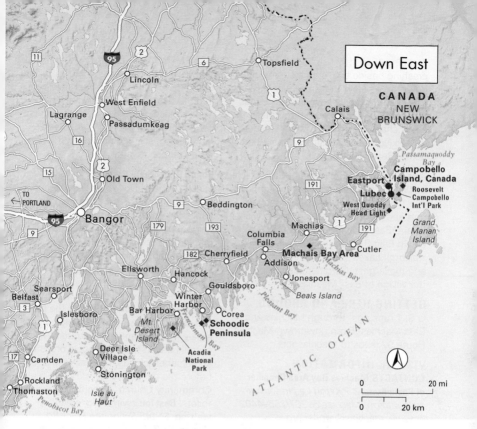

Hotels

★ Acadia Oceanside Meadows Inn

$ | B&B/INN | FAMILY | A must for nature lovers, this lodging sits on a 200-acre preserve dotted with woods, streams, salt marshes, and ponds, with spacious guest rooms in two historic buildings overlooking a private white sand beach (rare for these parts); it's also home to Oceanside Meadows Innstitute for the Arts and Sciences, which holds lectures, musical performances, art exhibits, and other events in the restored barn. **Pros:** separate guest kitchen and picnic area with a grill; sea captain's home has three two-room suites that are ideal for families; laminated pamphlets with daily itineraries for exploring Schoodic Peninsula and beyond are available for guest use and purchase. **Cons:** beach is across the road; some dated baths; some third floor rooms. *Rooms from: $199* *202 Corea Rd., Prospect Harbor* *207/963–5557* *gomaine.com* *Closed mid-Oct.–late May* *15 rooms* *Free Breakfast.*

Machias Bay Area

20 miles northeast of Jonesport.

The Machias area—Machiasport, East Machias, and Machias (Washington County's seat)—was the site of the Revolutionary War's first naval battle. Despite being outnumbered and out-armed, a small group of Machias men under the leadership of Jeremiah O'Brien captured the armed British schooner *Margaretta*. That battle, fought on June 12, 1775, is known as the "Lexington of the Sea." "Machias" is a Native American word meaning "bad little falls," for those falls crashing beside U.S. 1 as it curves into downtown below the University of Maine campus. If you only have a few minutes to watch the water churn through the rocky channel from the viewing platform or walking bridge at the small park here, do so. Better yet, picnic.

A few miles on, the village of East Machias flanks its namesake river, which flows into the Machias River above Machiasport and Machias Bay. Also linking Machias and East Machias is the multi-use Down East Sunrise Trail (🌐 *www.sunrise-trail.org*). Lakes streak the countryside, and the largest, Gardiner Lake, is outside the village of East Machias.

GETTING HERE AND AROUND

U.S. 1 runs right through Machias and East Machias. From downtown Machias, Route 92 leads to Machiasport.

VISITOR INFORMATION

CONTACTS Machias Bay Area Chamber of Commerce. ✉ *2 Kilton La., in former train station, Machias* ☎ *207/255–4402* 🌐 *www.machiaschamber.org.*

Beaches

★ Jasper Beach

BEACH | FAMILY | Sea-polished stones fascinate with glistening tones—many reddish but also heather, bluish, and creamy white—at this mesmerizing rock beach; removing stones from the beach is illegal. Banked in unusual geologic fashion, you must walk up and over a rock dune to get to the beach. When you do, you know you have arrived at a special place. Stones graduate from gravel at the shore to palm-size further back. Reddish volcanic rhyolite stones were mistaken for jasper, hence the name. Stretching a half mile across the end the rectangular-ish Howard Cove, bedrock at both ends deems this a pocket beach, but it's not your typical small one. A saltmarsh and fresh and saltwater lagoons intrigue visitors, and there are sea caves in the bedrock (be careful if you tread that way—the rocks are slippery). Tucked between the hamlets of Bucks Harbor and Starboard, Jasper Beach has long been a place of respite for folks in these parts. **Amenities:** parking (free). **Best for:** walking; solitude. ✉ *Jasper Beach, Machiasport.*

Roque Bluffs State Park

BEACH | FAMILY | Down East's rock- and fir-bound shores give way to the 274-acre park's half-mile crescent-shaped sand and pebble beach: one with any sand is a rarity in the region, and expansive ocean views enhance this one's beauty. Just beyond the beach you'll find a freshwater pond that's ideal for swimming and kayaking—rent flatwater kayaks here—and stocked for fishing. The park has changing areas (no showers), picnic area with grills, and a playground. Miles of trails traverse woods, apple orchards, and blueberry fields. The trailhead is just before the park entrance at Roque Bluffs Community Church. **Amenities:** parking; toilets. **Best for:** swimming; solitude, walking. ✉ *145 Schoppee Point Rd., Roque Bluffs, Machias* ✣ *Follow signs from U.S. 1 in Jonesboro or Machias* ☎ *207/255–3475* 🌐 *www.maine.gov/dacf/park* 🎫 *$4 Maine residents, $6 nonresidents.*

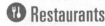

Restaurants

Helen's Restaurant

$$ | AMERICAN | FAMILY | In business for many years, the look here is updated and fresh, as the family-run establishment was rebuilt after a fire in 2014; it serves lunch and dinner, with entrées as well as burgers, sandwiches, salads, and the like. While the menu is big on seafood, don't expect only fried: try choices like charbroiled salmon topped with a maple glaze made with mustard, maple syrup, and blueberry jam, all Maine-made. **Known for:** fish-and-chips; lunch or dinner on the riverside deck come summer; Maine wild blueberry pie. 💲 *Average main: $20*

✉ 111 Main St., Machias ☎ 207/255–8423 🌐 www.helensrestaurantmachias.com ⏲ Closed Sun. and Mon.

Lubec Area

28 miles northeast of Machias via U.S. 1 and Rte. 189.

Lubec is one of the first places in the United States to see the sunrise and a popular destination for outdoors enthusiasts. The Bold Coast of high cliffs between here and the quaint fishing hamlet Cutler offers some of the best coastal hiking in the Eastern United States, with sweeping views and rocky beaches. But there are trails throughout the area, not just on the high Bold Coast, and many aren't especially difficult. Along with government parks and lands, many conservation groups have preserves in and near Lubec. Birding is renowned as many migratory seabirds head this way; mudflats, marshes, and headlands offer diverse habitats for observing birds.

Lubec is a good base for visiting New Brunswick's Campobello Island across the bridge from downtown—the only one to the island, so don't forget your passport! The village itself is perched at the end of a neck, so you can often see water in three directions. While there are some rundown buildings in and around the small downtown, there's also a small cluster of restaurants, inns, shops, and lively murals that reveal the spirit of this remote, peaceful, and beautiful place.

GETTING HERE AND AROUND

From U.S. 1 in Whiting, Route 189 runs 11 miles to Lubec. To travel here on a slightly longer scenic route through the seaside hamlet of Cutler, take Route 191 from U.S. 1 in East Machias to Route 189 in West Lubec. From Lubec to Eastport, it's 3 miles by boat but 38 miles by the circuitous northerly land route. In summer, a water taxi links the towns, as does a seasonal ferry.

Sights

West Quoddy Head Light/Quoddy Head State Park

STATE/PROVINCIAL PARK | FAMILY | Candy cane–stripe West Quoddy Head Light marks the easternmost point of land in the United States. One of Maine's most famous lighthouses, it guards Lubec Channel as it flows into much wider Atlantic waters that also demarcate Canada and the United States. Authorized by President Thomas Jefferson, the first light here was built in 1808. West Quoddy, just inside the park entrance, was constructed in 1858. You can't climb the tower, but the former lightkeeper's house is a seasonal museum; there are displays about the lighthouse and its former keepers, works by local artists, and a gift shop. Plan for more than a lighthouse visit at this enticing 541-acre Bold Coast park. Whales are often sighted offshore, the birding is world-famous, and there's a seaside picnic area. Visitors beachcomb, walk, or hike several miles of trails; a 2-mile trail along the cliffs yields magnificent views of Canada's cliff-clad Grand Manan Island, while the 1-mile roundtrip Bog Trail reveals arctic and subarctic plants rarely found south of Canada. Leading to a lookout with views of Lubec across the channel, the western leg of the 1-mile Coast Guard Trail is wheelchair accessible. In the off-season, visitors can park outside the gate and walk in. ✉ *973 S. Lubec Rd., Lubec* ☎ *207/733–0911* 🌐 *www.maine.gov/dacf/parks* 🎫 *$4* ⏲ *Closed mid-Oct.–mid-May.*

Restaurants

Water Street Tavern & Inn

$$$ | SEAFOOD | FAMILY | Perched on the water in a shingled building downtown, this popular restaurant serves some of the sweetest scallops you'll ever eat; *moqueca* (a Brazilian seafood stew); and filet mignon for those so inclined. It's also a great place to grab a glass of wine or a beer at the bar or a cup of coffee while gazing out at the water. **Known for:** laid-back, friendly atmosphere; specialty house-baked cake changes daily; also three guest rooms and a cozy suite. *Average main: $25* ✉ *12 Water St., Lubec* ☎ *207/733–0122* 🌐 *www.waterstavernandinn.com* ⏲ *No lunch; closed late Oct.–late Apr.*

Hotels

★ **Peacock House**

$ | **B&B/INN** | Five generations of the Peacock family lived in this 1860 sea captain's home in the middle of the village before it was converted to an inn in 1989; with a large foyer, living room with fireplace, and cozy library, the white-clapboard house has plenty of places where you can relax—there's even a sunroom that opens to a deck and gardens. **Pros:** guests welcome to play the instruments in the living room; four suites, including two on the first floor with sitting rooms and a primo open-plan one upstairs; innkeepers direct guests to area's tucked-away spots. **Cons:** not on the water; no self-check-in; one bedroom has slanted ceiling. *Rooms from: $175* ✉ *27 Summer St., Lubec* ☎ *207/733–2403, 888/305–0036* 🌐 *www.peacockhouse.com* *7 rooms* *Free Breakfast.*

Campobello Island, Canada

Across the international bridge from downtown Lubec.

A popular excursion from Lubec, New Brunswick's Campobello Island has two small fishing villages, Welshpool and Wilson's Beach, but Roosevelt International Park, the former summer home of Franklin and Eleanor Roosevelt, is the big draw. If you have the time, you can take a whale-watching excursion, explore the large provincial park, or check out two lighthouses: Mulholland Point across from Lubec and East Quoddy just off the opposite end of the island. There are a few places to stay or grab a bite scattered around the lowkey island.

GETTING HERE AND AROUND

The only land route is the bridge from Lubec, but in summer a car ferry shuttles passengers from Campobello Island to Deer Island, where you can continue to the Canadian mainland on the free government ferry.

After coming across the bridge from Lubec, Route 774 runs from one end of the island to the other, taking you through the two villages and to Roosevelt Campobello International Park.

VISITOR INFORMATION

Campobello Island is part of New Brunswick, Canada, so U.S. Citizens will need their passports to get here.

CONTACTS Visit Campobello Island. ✉ *Campobello* 🌐 *www.visitcampobello.com.*

Sights

East Quoddy Lighthouse (*Head Harbour Lighthouse*)

LIGHTHOUSE | **FAMILY** | Get an update on the tides before heading here if you want to walk out to the lighthouse (also known as Head Harbour Lighthouse) as you can only do so at low tide, via the ladders there—be careful on the wet rocks. On a tiny island off the eastern end of Campobello, this distinctive lighthouse is marked with a large red cross and is accessible only at and around low tide, but it's worth a look no matter the sea level. You may spot whales in the island-dotted waters off the small park on the rock-clad headland across from the light. Seasonal tours of the light may be offered. ✉ *East end of Rte. 774, Campobello.*

★ **Roosevelt Campobello International Park**
HISTORIC HOME | FAMILY | President Franklin D. Roosevelt and his family spent summers at this estate, which is now an international park with neatly manicured lawns that stretch out to the beach. Guided tours of the 34-room Roosevelt Cottage run every 15 minutes. Presented to Eleanor and Franklin as a wedding gift, the wicker-filled structure looks essentially as it did when the family was in residence. A visitor center has displays about the Roosevelts and Canadian-American relations. In the neighboring Wells-Shober Cottage, Eleanor's Tea is held at 11 am (10 am EST) and 3 pm (2 pm EST) daily. A joint project of the American and Canadian governments, this park is crisscrossed with interesting hiking trails. Groomed dirt roads attract bikers. Eagle Hill Bog has a wooden walkway and signs identifying rare plants. ✉ *459 Rte. 774, Welshpool* ☎ *506/752–2922, 877/851–6663* 🌐 *www.fdr.net* 🎫 *Free* ⏲ *Roosevelt Cottage closed late Oct.–late May* ☞ *Islands are on Atlantic Time, which is an hour later than Eastern Standard Time.*

Eastport

38 miles northeast of Lubec via Rte. 189, U.S. 1, and Rte. 190.

Occupying Moose Island on Cobscook and Passamaquoddy bays, a causeway links Eastport to the mainland. "Island City" has wonderful island views, and downtown looks across Friar Roads (part of Passamaquoddy Bay) to Canada's Campobello Island. The water is so deep that whales are often spotted off the large municipal pier (a.k.a. the Breakwater), where you can eye fishing boats and freighters. Among the highest in the world, tides fluctuate as much as 28 feet—thus the ladders and steep gangways for accessing boats. Old Sow, the Western Hemisphere's largest whirlpool, is offshore.

Smuggling with British-controlled Canada thrived here in the early 1800s and sardine-canning at the century's end. Fishing, aquaculture, and a marine terminal are part of today's economy, as is tourism. Art galleries and interesting shops fill storefronts in the largely brick downtown; folks amble on a waterfront walkway with an amphitheater and sculptures. One with a granite-carved fish is on the Maine Sculpture Trail; there's also a tall, jolly fisherman and Nerida, a sweet bronze-cast mermaid. Known for artsy flair with a quirky twist, Eastport drops a sardine on New Year's Eve, plus a maple leaf for the Canadians. In September, buccaneers from Eastport and Lubec battle during the pirate festival.

GETTING HERE AND AROUND

From U.S. 1, Route 190 leads to Eastport, the only road to the city. Before the causeway over, it passes through Sipayik (Pleasant Point) Passamaquoddy reservation. Continue on Washington Street to the water. In the summer, you can take a water taxi from here to Lubec—a few miles by boat but about 40 miles by land. There's also a seasonal ferry service.

VISITOR INFORMATION

CONTACTS Eastport Area Chamber of Commerce. ✉ *141 Water St., in Port Authority lobby, Eastport* ☎ *207/853–4644* 🌐 *www.eastportchamber.net.*

National Historic Waterfront District
NEIGHBORHOOD | Anchoring downtown Eastport, this waterfront district extends from the Customs House down Water Street to Bank Square and the Peavey Memorial Library. Spanning such architectural styles as Federal, Victorian, Queen Anne, and Greek Revival, the district was largely built in the 19th century. A cannon sits on the lawn at the Romanesque Revival library, one of the many interesting structures. Benches are beside an iron drinking

trough-turned-fountain in front of a bank-turned-museum, the Tides Institute & Museum of Art. ✉ *Eastport.*

Coffee and Quick Bites

Bocephus

$ | **AMERICAN** | Modern takes on sandwich fare and salads at this convenient takeout at the north end of downtown are so beautifully prepared that you almost hate to take a bite. One popular offering is the Bocephus Banh Mi (slow-cooked, Vietnamese-style pork loin served on a baguette with lightly pickled veggies, lettuce, cilantro, maple mayo, and house fish sauce for dipping). **Known for:** lobster sandwich on a brioche bun; local craft brews and wine from small-scale producers; crab sandwiches on a brioche bun. *Average main: $16* ✉ *104 Water St., Eastport* ☎ *207/853–0600* *www.facebook.com/biteintobocephus* *Closed late Oct.–mid-June and Sun. and Thurs. from mid-Sept.–late Oct.*

Dastardly Dick's Wicked Good Coffee

$ | **CAFÉ** | **FAMILY** | The coffee isn't the only thing that's wicked good at this local café; homemade pastries, rich soups, and tasty sandwiches are all prepared daily, and the hot chocolate and chai are worth writing home about. There are nice murals on the walls, too. **Known for:** local gathering spot; daily soup specials; wicked good baked goods. *Average main: $6* ✉ *62 Water St., Eastport* ☎ *207/853–2090* *No lunch Sat. Closed Sun. and Mon. May–mid-Sept and Sat.–Mon. mid-Sept.–May.*

Hotels

The Kilby House Inn B&B

$ | **B&B/INN** | In this 1887 Queen Anne residence built by seaman Herbert Kilby, creamy white walls offset fine antique furnishings, for a brightening effect that evokes an old-fashioned summer home, especially as sea breezes blow through the large windows on a summer day; a carriage house can be booked for an extended stay. **Pros:** master bedroom has four-poster bed; rates adjusted for single occupancy; innkeeper goes all out to help guests plan outings, often to hidden gems beyond Eastport. **Cons:** carriage house only available weekly or longer; some small bathrooms; not on the water. *Rooms from: $130* ✉ *122 Water St., Eastport* ☎ *207/214–6455, 207/853–0989* *www.kilbyhouseinn.com* *4 rooms* *Free Breakfast.*

Chapter 13

ACADIA NATIONAL PARK

Updated by Mary Ruoff

Camping ★★★★☆

Hotels ★★★★☆

Activities ★★★★★

Scenery ★★★★★

Crowds ★★★★☆

WELCOME TO ACADIA NATIONAL PARK

TOP REASONS TO GO

★ **Looping the park:** Get oriented along the 27-mile Park Loop Road, leaving plenty of time to stop at acclaimed locales like Sand Beach, Thunder Hole, and Otter Point.

★ **Unique roadways:** Acadia's 45 miles of crushed-stone carriage roads built and gifted by a famed philanthropic family can be enjoyed via two feet, two wheels, or horse-drawn carriage.

★ **A choice of flavors:** Many of the park's most popular attractions are on the east side of Mount Desert Island, including Park Loop Road, the carriage roads, and Cadillac Mountain. But Acadia's grand seascapes, forested lakes, and hiking trails also await on the "quiet" west side.

★ **Powerful popovers.** At the park's only restaurant, Jordan Pond House, gigantic popovers filled with strawberry jam have delighted visitors for more than 100 years.

★ **The parting sea:** Low tide exposes a land bridge between Bar Harbor and Bar Island—and an Acadia hike unlike any other.

Acadia National Park sprawls on both sides of Mount Desert Island.

1 East Side of Mount Desert Island. The busiest and largest part of Acadia National Park is near the amenities hub of Bar Harbor and home to many of its best-known attractions, including the carriage roads, Park Loop Road, Jordan Pond House, Cadillac Mountain, and Sieur de Monts. Hulls Cove Visitor Center is off Route 3, 3 miles from downtown Bar Harbor.

2 West Side of Mount Desert Island. Acadia also offers stunning scenery and great recreational opportunities on the island's "quiet side," where Southwest Harbor is a lower-key tourist hub and Bass Harbor lower yet. You can swim at the park's popular Echo Lake Beach, visit iconic Bass Harbor Head Light, and hike to the landmark Beech Mountain fire lookout tower.

3 Schoodic District. Visitors enjoy grand seascapes with a more secluded feel at the park's only mainland section at the bottom of this peninsula across Frenchman Bay from the east side of Mount Desert. Highlights include a loop road, bike paths, hiking trails, and the Schoodic Institute, an educational facility on the grounds of a former Navy base.

4 Isle au Haut. Acadia occupies half of this island out in the ocean 15 miles southwest of Mount Desert. It's accessible by ferry from Stonington on Deer Isle, itself reachable by bridge from the mainland west of Mount Desert. There's a small primitive campground, gravel roads for mountain biking, and hiking trails. Island amenities are meager.

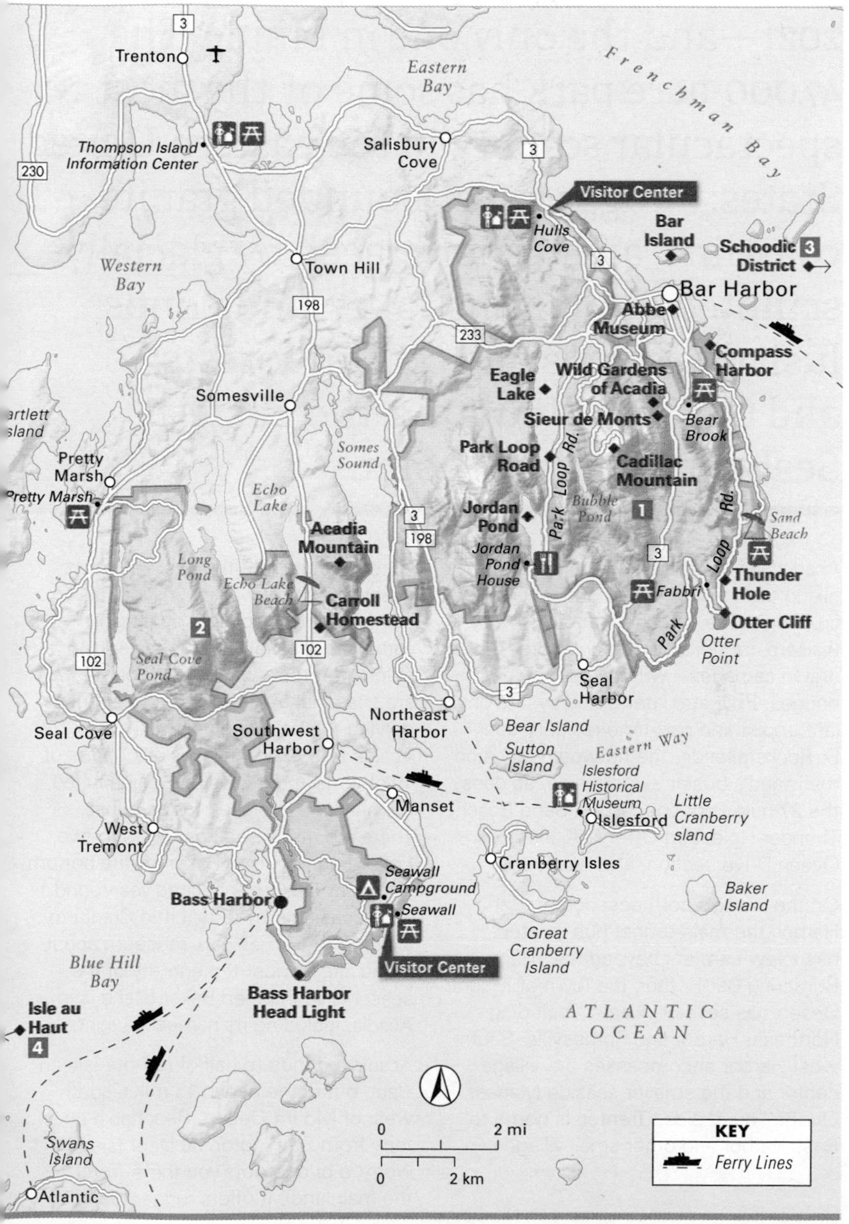
3
Trenton
Eastern Bay
Frenchman Bay
Thompson Island Information Center
230
Salisbury Cove
3
Visitor Center
Hulls Cove
Bar Island
Schoodic District 3
Western Bay
Town Hill
3
Bar Harbor
198
Abbe Museum
233
Compass Harbor
Eagle Lake
Wild Gardens of Acadia
Somesville
Sieur de Monts
Bear Brook
Bartlett Island
Pretty Marsh
Pretty Marsh
Somes Sound
Park Loop Road
Park Loop Rd.
Cadillac Mountain
Echo Lake
Jordan Pond
Bubble Pond
1
Rd.
Sand Beach
Acadia Mountain
3
198
Jordan Pond House
3
Loop
Thunder Hole
Long Pond
Echo Lake Beach
Carroll Homestead
Fabbri
Otter Cliff
2
Park
Otter Point
102
Seal Cove Pond
102
Seal Harbor
3
Northeast Harbor
Bear Island
Seal Cove
Southwest Harbor
Sutton Island
Eastern Way
Islesford Historical Museum
Manset
Little Cranberry Island
Islesford
West Tremont
Cranberry Isles
Seawall Campground
Bass Harbor
Seawall
Baker Island
Great Cranberry Island
Visitor Center
Blue Hill Bay
Bass Harbor Head Light
Isle au Haut 4
ATLANTIC OCEAN
0
2 mi
0
2 km
KEY
Ferry Lines
Swans Island
Atlantic

Mostly on Mount Desert Island, Acadia is among the nation's most popular national parks—4.07 million visits in 2021—and the only one in Maine. The 47,000-acre park has some of the most spectacular scenery in the eastern United States: a rugged surf-pounded granite coastline; an interior graced by glacially sculpted mountains, lakes, and ponds; lush deciduous and conifer forests; and Cadillac Mountain, the Eastern Seaboard's highest point.

Acadia has more than 150 miles of hiking trails and 45 miles of finely crafted crushed-stone carriage roads—used by walkers, runners, bikers, and horse-drawn carriages—with elegant stone bridges. Built and later gifted by late philanthropist and part-time resident John D. Rockefeller Jr., the network wends on the island's busier eastern side, as does the 27-mile Park Loop Road. Sand Beach, Thunder Hole, and Otter Cliff, along its Ocean Drive section, are must-sees.

On the island's northeast corner, Bar Harbor, the main tourist hub located, has a few hamlets beyond the village. Bordering Bar Harbor, the Town of Mount Desert has several villages, including Northeast Harbor and Somesville. Southwest Harbor encompasses the village center and the smaller seaside Manset. On the "quiet side," Trenton is home to Bass Harbor and other small villages.

To truly appreciate the park you must experience it by walking, hiking, biking, rock climbing, paddling, boating, or carriage ride. Making that easier, and helping protect Acadia's environment, are seasonal free Island Explorer buses serving the park and nearby towns. Acadia also encompasses all or parts of 19 other islands. Most are uninhabited, but only one is closed to the public. There are ranger-led boat tours to two, Little Cranberry and Baker off the bottom of Mount Desert. Inhabited year-round and accessible by ferry, Little Cranberry is home to a small park museum about island life. Almost the entirety of the seasonally inhabited Baker Island is in Acadia, including its namesake light.

Acadia extends to half of remote Isle au Haut, out in the ocean 15 miles southwest of Mount Desert. Reachable by ferry from Stonington on Deer Isle (don't worry, a bridge gets you there from the mainland), it offers rugged trails,

AVERAGE HIGH/LOW TEMPERATURES					
Jan.	Feb.	Mar.	Apr.	May	June
32/17	34/19	40/27	50/36	59/44	67/52
July	Aug.	Sept.	Oct.	Nov.	Dec.
73/57	72/57	65/51	56/43	46/34	37/24

primitive camping, and unpaved roads. On the Schoodic Peninsula east of Mount Desert, Acadia's only mainland district has bike paths, hiking, camping, ranger programs, and a loop drive all its own, with views of Mount Desert—Maine's largest island.

Planning

When to Go

During the summer season, days are usually warm and nights cool—bring a jacket. July tops the charts with a comfortable average daily high of 73°F. But there are hot and humid spells, more so in recent years. Peak visitation is late spring through October. July and August are the busiest months, but September—when the heat and humidity of summer begin to taper off—is one of the most enjoyable, and also busy. The foliage season in the first few weeks of October bustles, too. While Memorial Day and Labor Day mark the traditional beginning and end of high season, nowadays many seasonal establishments stay open through Indigenous Peoples Day/ Columbus Day and some longer.

Consider coming in mid-spring when temperatures start to rise but crowds haven't yet formed. Be sure to check for seasonal closures due to ice, snow, or mud on Acadia's carriage roads, unpaved roads, and trails. For hardy souls, winter can be a wonderful time to visit. While many dining and lodging facilities are hibernating, you can still find good options. Just know that from December through mid-April, paved park roads are closed to vehicles except for two short sections of Park Loop Road. For unpaved roads, it's mid-November to mid-May. When enough snow flies, folks head to the park to snowshoe and cross-country ski—many carriage roads are groomed. Snowmobilers take to Park Loop Road, drive up Cadillac Mountain, and hit unpaved roads.

Regardless of when you decide to go, it's best to book your accommodations in advance, especially if you have a particular type of lodging in mind or will be visiting on a holiday weekend. Visitors are advised not to travel to the Acadia area in peak season without a reservation.

Getting Here and Around

AIR

Bangor International Airport (BGR) in Bangor is the closest major airport to Acadia National Park. The driving distance from Bangor to Mount Desert Island is approximately 50 miles. Car rentals, taxi, bus, and shuttle service are available.

Farther south, Portland International Airport (PWM) is approximately three hours to the Mount Desert Island area. Renting a car is your best bet for getting to Acadia National Park from here.

The small regional Hancock County–Bar Harbor Airport (BHB) is in Trenton just minutes from the causeway to Mount Desert Island. Cape Air/JetBlue have flights to and from Boston's Logan International Airport (BOS). Car rentals and taxi service are available, and the airport is a stop for the free seasonal Island

Explorer buses that serve Acadia and nearby towns.

CONTACTS Bangor–Bar Harbor Express Shuttle. ✉ *Bangor* ☎ *207/944–8429* 🌐 *www.bangorbarharborexpressshuttle.com.* **Bangor International Airport.** *(BGR)* ✉ *287 Godfrey Blvd., Bangor* ☎ *207/992–4600* 🌐 *www.flybangor.com.* **Hancock County–Bar Harbor Airport.** *(BHB)* ✉ *143 Caruso Dr., Trenton* ☎ *207/667–7329* 🌐 *www.bhbairport.com.*

BUS

Operating seasonally, Island Explorer buses serve Acadia and communities throughout Mount Desert Island as well as neighboring Trenton. Though touted as free, donations are requested to support the service. Island Explorer also serves the mainland district of Acadia and nearby villages, including Winter Harbor, on the Schoodic Peninsula. You can get to the park's Schoodic District from the seasonal Bar Harbor–Winter Harbor Ferry via an Island Explorer bus.

Bus service starts in late May on the Schoodic Peninsula and late June in the Mount Desert area and runs through Indigenous Peoples Day/Columbus Day. A reduced fall schedule starts in late August. Island Explorer's designated stops include many campgrounds and hotels. The buses also pick up and drop off passengers anywhere along the route where it's safe to stop.

Buses have bike racks, but they only hold four or six bicycles. During the peak summer season, the Island Explorer Bicycle Express takes bikes and passengers by van from downtown Bar Harbor to Acadia's Eagle Lake Carriage Road. These vans can take tag-along bikes and small children's bikes but not tandem, fat-tire, or electric bikes; Island Explorer buses can't transport any specialty bikes.

CONTACTS Island Explorer. ✉ *Acadia National Park* ☎ *207/667–5796* 🌐 *www.exploreacadia.com.*

CAR

Route 3 leads to Mount Desert Island and Bar Harbor from Ellsworth and circles the eastern part of the island. Route 102 is the major road on the west side. Acadia National Park's Hulls Cove Visitor Center is off Route 3, 3 miles from downtown Bar Harbor. Acadia's main thoroughfare, 27-mile Park Loop Road, is accessible from the visitor center as well as park entrances (Cadillac Mountain) near downtown Bar Harbor on Route 233, south of Bar Harbor proper on Route 3 (Sieur de Monts), and in Seal Harbor on Route 3 (Stanley Brook Road). Much of the road is one-way.

Shaped like an upside-down "U" (some liken it to a pair of lobster claws), Mount Desert is relatively easy to navigate, though it may take longer than expected to reach some points. Somes Sound, a fjard (less steep-sided than a fjord) that runs up the middle of Mount Desert Island, requires drivers at the ends of the "U" to travel quite a distance to get to a town that is close as the crow flies. Beyond the geographical barriers, summer traffic can slow your progress and make finding a parking space, especially in Bar Harbor or Acadia, difficult to nearly impossible. Avoid the problem by hopping on one of the seasonal free Island Explorer buses that serve the park and nearby towns.

Park Essentials

ACCESSIBILITY

Many Acadia National Park sights and amenities are at least partly accessible to those with accessibility challenges. Island Explorer buses (but not all bus stops), park visitor and information centers, and many picnic areas and camping sites are wheelchair accessible. Accessibility varies for scenic overlooks, trails, and carriage roads. Echo Lake Beach has wheelchair-accessible changing rooms; stairs to the water prevent wheelchair access at Sand Beach. The Sieur de Monts area of the park has a Nature Center with exhibits and an information desk at wheelchair height; a trailhead for the mostly wheelchair-accessible 1.5-mile Jesup Path and Hemlock Path Loop; a level if narrow path through Wild Gardens of Acadia; and a wheelchair-accessible water fountain and water bottle-filling station. Check the park website for information on accessibility.

PARK FEES AND PERMITS

A National Parks pass is required to enter Acadia year-round; display it on your dashboard when parking at trailheads or parking areas. An annual national park's pass ($80) and the Acadia weekly pass ($30 per vehicle) can be purchased online at 🌐 *www.Recreation.gov.*

Within the park, passes can be purchased at the Hulls Cove Visitor Center, the Sand Beach Entrance Station on Park Loop Road, and park campgrounds (except Isle au Haut). Automated fee machines in the Hulls Cove Visitor Center parking lot pavilion and at Acadia's mainland Schoodic District (inside the gatehouse at the entrance to Schoodic Institute) sell Acadia's weekly pass. Third-party sellers like local chambers of commerce and park concessionaires also sell Acadia weekly passes.

The park is free on Martin Luther King Jr. Day (third Monday in January); Great American Outdoors Day (August 4); first Monday of National Park Week in mid-April; National Public Lands Day (fourth Saturday in September); and Veterans Day, November 11.

PARK HOURS

The park is open 24 hours a day year-round, but paved roads within the park on Mount Desert Island close December–mid-April except for two small sections of Park Look Road: Ocean Drive and the section providing access to Jordan Pond. Unpaved roads are closed from mid-November–mid-May. Paved roads are open year-round at Acadia's mainland section on Schoodic Peninsula.

CELL PHONE RECEPTION

Depending on your cell phone carrier, you may not always be able to rely on your cell phone while visiting Mount Desert Island.

Hotels

Lodging is not available within Acadia National Park. Bar Harbor has the greatest variety and number of lodging facilities, but they are also found in other Mount Desert Island towns and villages. Northeast Harbor and Southwest Harbor having the largest concentration outside Bar Harbor. With short notice in high season the Ellsworth area might be your best bet. Visiting the Acadia area in peak season without a reservation is not advised.

Restaurants

The Jordan Pond House Restaurant is the only dining option within the park, serving lunch, tea, and dinner late May to late October; it also has a takeout place. There are a number of restaurants serving a variety of cuisines in Bar Harbor, while smaller coastal communities typically have at least one or two small eateries. Northeast Harbor and Southwest Harbor have the largest concentration outside the main tourist hub of Bar Harbor.

PRICES

Restaurant prices in the reviews are the average cost of a main course at dinner, or if dinner is not served, at lunch. Restaurant reviews have been shortened. For full information, visit Fodors.com.

What It Costs In U.S. Dollars			
$	$$	$$$	$$$$
RESTAURANTS			
under $18	$18–$24	$25–$35	over $35

Visitor Information

Mount Desert Chamber of Commerce isn't an island-wide chamber; it serves the Town of Mount Desert (Northeast Harbor, Somesville, and a few other villages). The two other island chambers are Bar Harbor Chamber of Commerce and Southwest Harbor & Tremont Chamber of Commerce.

CONTACTS Acadia National Park. ✉ *Acadia National Park* ☎ *207/288–3338* 🌐 *www.nps.gov/acad.* **Bar Harbor Chamber of Commerce.** ✉ *2 Cottage St., Bar Harbor* ☎ *207/288–5103* 🌐 *www.visitbarharbor.com.* **Mount Desert Chamber of Commerce.** ✉ *41 Harbor Dr., Northeast Harbor* ☎ *207/276–5040* 🌐 *www.mtdesertchamber.org.* **Southwest Harbor & Tremont Chamber of Commerce.** ✉ *329 Main St., Southwest Harbor* ☎ *207/244–9264* 🌐 *www.acadiachamber.com.* **Thompson Island Information Center.** ✉ *1319 Bar Harbor Rd., Bar Harbor* ☎ *207/288–3338* 🌐 *www.nps.gov/acad/planyourvisit/hours.htm.*

East Side of Mount Desert Island

10 miles south of Ellsworth via Rte. 3.

Many of Acadia National Park's best-loved features, including all of its carriage roads, Sand Beach, and Cadillac Mountain, are on this side of Mount Desert Island. So, too, is Bar Harbor, the island's largest town and your best bet for finding lodging and dining.

Sights

BEACHES

Sand Beach

BEACH | FAMILY | At this 290-yard-long pocket beach, hugged by picturesque rocky outcroppings, the combination of crashing waves and chilly water (normal range is 50–60°F) keeps most people on the beach. You'll find some swimmers at the height of summer, when lifeguards may be on duty, but the rest of the year this is a place for strolling and snapping photos. In fact, when the official swimming season (mid-June to early September) ends, more activities are allowed, from fishing and surfing to dog walking and boat launching/landing. **Amenities:** parking; toilets. **Best for:** solitude; sunrise; walking. ✉ *Ocean Dr. section of Park Loop Rd., Acadia National Park* ☎ *207/288–3338* 🌐 *nps.gov/acad.*

GEOLOGICAL FORMATIONS

Thunder Hole

CAVE | When conditions are just so at this popular visitor attraction, the force of pounding surf being squeezed into a narrow slot of cliffside pink granite causes a boom that sounds like thunder and often sends ocean spray up to 40 feet into the air—soaking observers standing nearby behind safety railings. Time your visit within an hour or two of high tide for the best chance to observe the phenomenon; at low tide, take the stairway down to a viewing platform for a peak at the water-carved walls of the tiny inlet. ✉ *Ocean Dr. section of Park Loop Rd., Acadia National Park* ✣ *About 1 mile south of Sand Beach* ☎ *207/288–3338* 🌐 *nps.gov/acad.*

SCENIC DRIVES

★ Park Loop Road

SCENIC DRIVE | FAMILY | This 27-mile road provides a perfect introduction to the park. You can drive it in an hour, but allow at least half a day, so that you can explore the many sites along the way, including Thunder Hole, Sand Beach, and Otter

Cliff. The route is also served by the free Island Explorer buses. Traffic is one-way from near the Route 233 entrance to the Stanley Brook Road entrance south of the Jordan Pond House. The 2-mile section known as Ocean Drive is open year-round, as is a small section that provides access to Jordan Pond from Seal Harbor. ✉ *Acadia National Park* ☎ *207/288–3338* 🌐 *nps.gov/acad.*

SCENIC STOPS

Bar Island

ISLAND | FAMILY | Offering one of Acadia National Park's more unique experiences, Bar Island is only accessible by foot and during a three-hour window when low tide exposes a ½-mile gravel bar connecting Bar Island to Bar Harbor. The entire Bar Island trail offers an easy 1.9-mile round-trip hike; once on the island you can enjoy views of Bar Harbor and Frenchman Bay. Make sure to check the tide charts before setting out, because once covered by rising tidal waters it'll be another nine hours before the land bridge is once again exposed. ✉ *Bar Harbor* ✣ *Access via West St. then Bridge St.* ☎ *207/288–3338* 🌐 *nps.gov/acad.*

★ Cadillac Mountain

MOUNTAIN | FAMILY | One of Acadia's premier attractions, 1,530-foot Cadillac Mountain is the Eastern Seaboard's tallest mountain. Stunning panoramic views sweep across bays, islands, and mountains on and off Mount Desert Island. You can see Bar Harbor below on the northeast side and Eagle Lake to the west. Low-lying vegetation like pitch pine and wild blueberry plants accent granite slabs in the "subalpine-like" environment. There's a paved summit loop trail and several hiking trails up Cadillac, named for a Frenchman who explored here in the late 1600s and later founded Detroit. From mid-May–mid-October, a vehicle reservation (done through 🌐 www.recreation.gov) is needed to drive to the summit. Sunrise slots are in high demand, as this is one of the first places in the country to see first light, not to mention the perfect spot to watch the sunset or stargaze in the spring and fall—Bar Harbor's light ordinance helps with that. ✉ *Cadillac Summit Rd., Acadia National Park* ☎ *207/288–3338* 🌐 *www.nps.gov/acad* 💵 *$6 per car in addition to park entrance fee (via www.recreation.gov)* ⏲ *Access road closes at 10 pm in season and Dec.–mid-Apr.*

Compass Harbor

TRAIL | FAMILY | Just beyond Bar Harbor proper, this easy 0.8-mile round-trip trail through woods to the shore passes through land that belonged to George B. Dorr—Acadia National Park's first superintendent and a key player in its creation. Views extend to Ironbound Island across Frenchman Bay, and you can check out remnants of Dorr's estate, including the manor house's foundation, remains of a saltwater pool, stone steps to the ocean, and old gardens and apple trees. *Easy.* ✉ *399 Main St., trailhead parking, Bar Harbor* ☎ *207/288–3338* 🌐 *nps.gov/acad.*

Eagle Lake

MARINA/PIER | Located just east of Acadia National Park headquarters, 436-acre Eagle Lake is the largest freshwater lake on Mountain Desert Island. Swimming is not allowed, but kayaking, canoeing, boating, and fishing are, and the encircling 6.1-mile carriage road invites walkers and cyclists. ✉ *Rte. 233, Bar Harbor* ✣ *½ mile east of Acadia National Park headquarters* ☎ *207/288–3338* 🌐 *nps.gov/acad.*

★ Jordan Pond

BODY OF WATER | FAMILY | Soak up the mountain scenery, listen for the call of loons, and watch for cliff-nesting peregrine falcons along the 3.3-mile trail around this 187-acre tarn—a mountain lake formed by retreating glaciers—on Park Loop Road's two-way portion. Several carriage roads converge here, one marked by a fanciful gatehouse, one of two on the road network. Visitors kayak and canoe on the deep water (no swimming) and gaze down on Great Pond after hiking up nearby mountains. A popular choice is The Bubbles, with twin peaks whose distinct shape makes up for what they lack in size. They rise across the water from Jordan Pond House Restaurant, where folks come for popovers served with strawberry jam and tea, hoping for a table on the expansive lawn—a tradition started in the 1890s in the original Jordan Pond House, which burned in 1979. The rebuild has a two-story gift shop and, on the upper level, an observation deck and Carriage Road Carry Out, with to-go items like sandwiches and salads—or try the popover sundae. Parking lots here fill fast in high season; consider biking or taking the free Island Explorer bus. ✉ *2928 Park Loop Rd. Seal Harbor* ☎ *207/288–3338* 🌐 *nps.gov/acad.*

Otter Cliff

NATURE SIGHT | Looming 110 feet above the crashing surf of the North Atlantic, Otter Cliff is the terminus of the popular Ocean Path walking trail, which starts 2 miles north at the Sand Beach parking lot. Don't fret if you're not up for the walk: you can still enjoy the view from the overlook just beyond the cliff, where you can often watch rock climbers on the cliff face. Nearby on the shore are thousands of round boulders of various sizes that have been smoothed into shape by many thousands of years of wave action. ✉ *Park Loop Rd., Bar Harbor* ✣ *About ¾ mile south of Thunder Hole on Park Loop Rd.* ☎ *207/288–3338* 🌐 *nps.gov/acad.*

★ Sieur de Monts

NATURE SIGHT | FAMILY | The seasonal ranger-staffed Nature Center is the first major stop along the Park Loop Road. There are exhibits about the park's conservation efforts, as well as a park information center. The area is known as the "Heart of Acadia," which memorializes George Dorr, Acadia National Park's first superintendent, and includes walking trails, Sieur de Monts Spring, Wild Gardens of Acadia, and Abbe Museum (its main location is in downtown Bar Harbor), which honors the area's Native American heritage. ✉ *Park Loop Rd., Bar Harbor* ✣ *Also accessible from Rte. 3* ☎ *207/288–3338* 🌐 *nps.gov/acad* ⏲ *Nature Center closed mid-Oct.–mid-May.*

The Early Bird Gets the Sun

Many people believe the top of Cadillac Mountain is the first place in the United States to see the sunrise. It is, though only from early October to early March. To experience first light atop Cadillac's granite summit, plan to get up *very* early. A timed reservation ($6 per car in addition to the park entrance fee via 🌐 *www.recreation.gov*) is required to drive up the mountain from mid-May through mid-October; sunrise slots are especially popular.

TRAILS

Cadillac Mountain North Ridge Trail

TRAIL | The mostly exposed 4.4-mile round-trip summit hike rewards with expansive views of Bar Harbor, Frenchman Bay, and the Schoodic Peninsula for much of the way. The trail is worth undertaking at either sunrise or sunset (or both!). Parking can be limited, especially in high season, so park officials recommend taking the Island Explorer bus for access via a 0.1-mile section of the Kebo Brook Trail. *Moderate.* ✉ *Park Loop Rd., Bar Harbor* ✣ *Trailhead: Access is via Park Loop Rd. near where one-way travel to Sand Beach starts* ☎ *207/288–3338* 🌐 *nps.gov/acad.*

★ Ocean Path Trail

TRAIL | This easily accessible 4.4-mile round-trip trail runs parallel to the Ocean Drive section of the Park Loop Road from Sand Beach to Otter Point. It has some of the best scenery in Maine: cliffs and boulders of pink granite at the ocean's edge, twisted branches of dwarf jack pines, and ocean views that stretch to the horizon. Be sure to save time to stop at Thunder Hole, named for the sound the waves make as they thrash through a narrow opening in the granite cliffs, into a sea cave, and whoosh up and out. It's roughly halfway between Sand Beach and Otter Cliff, with steps leading down to the water to watch the wave action close up. Use caution as you descend (access may be limited due to storms), and also if you venture onto the outer cliffs along this walk. *Easy.* ✉ *Ocean Dr. section of Park Loop Rd., Acadia National Park* ✥ *Trailhead: Upper parking lot of Sand Beach* ☎ *207/288–3338* 🌐 *nps.gov/acad.*

VISITOR CENTERS

Hulls Cove Visitor Center

VISITOR CENTER | **FAMILY** | This is a great spot to get your bearings. A large 3D relief map of Mount Desert Island gives you the lay of the land, and there are free park and carriage road maps. The gift shop sells hiking maps, guidebooks, and a CD for a self-driving park tour and is well-stocked with books about Acadia. Ranger-led programs include guided hikes and other interpretive events, and there are Junior Ranger programs for kids, family-friendly campfire talks at campground amphitheaters (open to all visitors), and night sky talks at Sand Beach. ✉ *25 Visitor Center Rd., Bar Harbor* ☎ *207/288–3338* 🌐 *www.nps.gov/acad.*

Restaurants

Jordan Pond House Restaurant

$$ | **AMERICAN** | The only dining option within Acadia serves lunch, tea, and dinner as well as to-go items like sandwiches and salads. Most folks come for tea and popovers with strawberry jam on the lawn—a tradition started in the 1890s in the original Jordan Pond House—but the menu also includes chowders and entrees like a lobster dinner or the fresh catch of the day. **Known for:** popover sundae; lawn seating; popovers and strawberry jam. $ *Average main: $20* ✉ *2928 Park Loop Rd., Acadia National Park* ☎ *207/276–3610* 🌐 *jordanpondhouse.com* ⏲ *Closed Nov.–late May.*

West Side of Mount Desert Island

8 miles east of Bar Harbor via Rte. 233 and Rte. 3.

On Acadia National Park's "quiet side" west of Somes Sounds, there's plenty to explore including Echo Lake Beach, which is the park's swimming beach with the warmest water, and Bass Harbor Head Light. Popular hiking trails adorn Acadia and Beech mountains.

Sights

BEACHES

Echo Lake Beach

BEACH | **FAMILY** | A quiet lake surrounded by woods in the shadow of Beech Mountain, Echo Lake is one of Acadia's few swimming beaches. The water is considerably warmer, if muckier, than nearby ocean beaches, and dogs are allowed in the off-season. The surrounding trail network skirts the lake and ascends the mountain. A boat ramp is north of here along Route 102 at Ikes Point. **Amenities:** lifeguards (at times); parking; toilets. **Best for:** sunset;

swimming; solitude. ✉ *Echo Lake Beach Rd., off Rte. 102 between Somesville and Southwest Harbor, Acadia National Park* ☎ *207/288–3338* 🌐 *nps.gov/acad.*

HISTORIC SIGHTS

★ Bass Harbor Head Light

LIGHTHOUSE | FAMILY | Built in 1858, this is one of Maine's most photographed lighthouses; it's been a part of Acadia National Park since 2020. Now automated, it marks the entrance to Bass Harbor and Blue Hill Bay at the island's southernmost point nearly 2 miles below Bass Harbor village. You can't go inside, but a walkway brings you to a seaside viewing area with placards about its history. The small parking lot typically fills for sunset viewing in high season and parking isn't allowed on the entrance road or on Route 102A. The free Island Explorer bus doesn't serve the lighthouse. ✉ *116 Lighthouse Rd., off Rte. 102A, Bass Harbor* ☎ *207/288–3338* 🌐 *www.nps.gov/acad* 🎫 *A National Parks pass is required.*

Carroll Homestead

FARM/RANCH | FAMILY | For almost 100 years beginning in the early 1800s, three generations of the Carroll family homesteaded at this small-scale farm that was donated to the park in 1982. A few miles north of the village of Southwest Harbor, the weathered farmhouse still stands and is occasionally opened for ranger-led tours during the summer; check the park website for details. ✉ *Acadia National Park* ✣ *Turn off Rte. 102* ☎ *207/288–3338* 🌐 *nps.gov/acad.*

TRAILS

Beech Mountain

TRAIL | FAMILY | A unique payoff awaits on this 1.2-mile round-trip hike: a fire lookout tower where you can enjoy views of Somes Sound, Echo Lake, Acadia Mountain, and beyond from its platform. The forested and rocky trail is popular with sunset seekers, who are reminded to carry appropriate clothing and headlamps for the descent. *Moderate.* ✉ *Beech Hill Rd., Southwest Harbor* ✣ *Trailhead: 4 miles south of Somesville on Beech Hill Rd. off Rte. 102* ☎ *207/288–3338* 🌐 *nps.gov/acad.*

Ship Harbor Trail

TRAIL | FAMILY | Popular with families and birders, this 1.3-mile figure-8 trail loops through woods and follows a sheltered cove where you may spot great blue herons feeding in the mudflats during low tide. *Easy* ✉ *Rte. 102A, Acadia National Park* ✣ *Trailhead: 1.2 miles west of Seawall picnic area on Rte. 102A* ☎ *207/288–3338* 🌐 *nps.gov/acad.*

★ St. Sauveur and Acadia Mountain Loop

TRAIL | If you're up for a challenge, this is one of the area's best hikes. The 3.9-mile round-trip loop summits both St. Sauveur and Acadia mountains. Ascents and descents are steep and strenuous, but the views of Somes Sound and beyond are grand. The hike begins at the Acadia Mountain trailhead. For a shorter excursion, follow the fire road that connects with the Acadia Mountain Trail section of the loop. *Difficult.* ✉ *Rte. 102, Mount Desert* ✣ *Trailhead (Acadia Mountain): Rte. 102 just after Ikes Pt. on Echo Lake (opposite side of road)* ☎ *207/288–3338* 🌐 *www.nps.gov/acad.*

VISITOR CENTER

Seawall Ranger Station

VISITOR CENTER | This small information center is located at the park's Seawall Campground along Route 102A near the island's southernmost point. Stop here for park information and to purchase park passes. ✉ *664 Seawall Rd., Southwest Harbor* ✣ *Off Rte. 102A* ☎ *207/288–3338* 🌐 *www.nps.gov/acad* 🕒 *Closed mid-Oct.–mid-May.*

Schoodic District

25 miles east of Ellsworth via U.S. 1 and Rte. 186.

Acadia National Park's 3,900-acre Schoodic District sits at the bottom of Schoodic Peninsula, east of Mount Desert Island and mostly in Winter Harbor. The landscape of craggy coastline, towering evergreens, and views over Frenchman Bay is breathtaking—and less crowded than over at the park on Mount Desert. A scenic loop road spurs to Schoodic Point, the experiential pinnacle. Schoodic Head, the literal one, also has spectacular views—of ocean as well as forested peninsula. Biking is popular on the loop road and 8.3 miles of wide, interconnected packed-gravel bike paths (*no Class 2 or Class 3 e-bikes*). Also used by walkers, they were added in 2015 along with the campground and additional hiking trails. Ranging from easy coastal treks to difficult ascents, most trails are part of a network that links with the bike path system, which has some challenging climbs. The Schoodic District has education programs for visitors, including Junior Ranger activities for the kiddos. A seasonal passenger ferry links Bar Harbor and Winter Harbor, where it connects with free seasonal Island Explorer buses serving the park and peninsular villages (*see the Getting Here and Around section of the Chapter Planner for more information*).

Sights

HISTORIC SIGHTS

Schoodic Institute

COLLEGE | FAMILY | Formerly apartments and offices for the U.S. Navy base that operated here for decades, this massive 1934 French Eclectic-style structure is on the National Registry of Historic Places. Today, the building is known as Rockefeller Hall, and its home to the Schoodic Institute, which is home base for many ranger-led programs and family-friendly activities at the park's Schoodic District, including public programs of its own (*some have fees and require overnight stays; check the institute's website for more information*); it's the largest facility of its kind at a national park. The Rockefeller Welcome Center is on the first floor. ✉ *1 Atterbury Circle, Winter Harbor* ☎ *207/288–1310* 🌐 *www.schoodicinstitute.org.*

SCENIC DRIVES

Schoodic Loop Road

SCENIC DRIVE | FAMILY | Less than a mile from the entrance to Schoodic Woods Campground and Ranger Station, and just beyond Frazer Point Picnic Area, the only road into the park becomes one-way and continues for about 6 miles to the park exit (no RVs are allowed on the road after the campground entrance). Edging the coast and sprinkled with pullouts, the first few miles yield views of Grindstone Neck, Winter Harbor, Winter Harbor Lighthouse, and, across the water, Cadillac Mountain. After a few miles, a two-way spur, Arey Cove Road, passes Schoodic Institute en route to Schoodic Point. Here, huge slabs of pink granite lie jumbled along the shore, thrashed unmercifully by the crashing surf, and jack pines cling to life amid the rocks. Continuing on the loop road, stop at Blueberry Hill parking area to look out on near-shore islands. The Anvil and Alder trailheads are near here. From the park exit, continue two miles to Route 186 in Birch Harbor. There's a biking path trailhead with parking at the exit and another one about midway to Route 186, both on your left. ✉ *Schoodic Loop Rd., Winter Harbor* ☎ *207/288–3338* 🌐 *nps.gov/acad.*

SCENIC STOPS

Blueberry Hill

SCENIC DRIVE | About a half mile beyond the Schoodic Point spur on the scenic one-way loop drive, this spot looks out on nearby Little Moose and Schoodic islands and the ocean beyond. It's also where to

Did You Know?

The Somesville Bridge, found on the West Side of Mount Desert Island, is a popular stop for a photo op.

park if you're planning to hike a loop consisting of the Alder and Anvil trails across the road from the parking lot. ✉ *Schoodic Loop Rd., Winter Harbor* ✣ *About 1 mile east of Schoodic Point* ☎ *207/288–3338* 🌐 *nps.gov/acad.*

★ Schoodic Point

NATURE SIGHT | FAMILY | Massed granite ledges meet crashing waves at Schoodic Peninsula's tip, off the loop road at the end of Arey Cove Road. Dark basalt rock slices through pink granite, to dramatic effect. Look east for a close view of Little Moose Island; a bit farther away to the west is a sidelong view of Mount Desert Island; and to the south, an inspiring open ocean view. There are bathrooms and a good-size parking area. ✉ *Arey Cove Rd., Winter Harbor* ☎ *207/288–3338* 🌐 *nps.gov/acad.*

TRAILS

Alder and Anvil Trails

TRAIL | Popular with birders, the Alder trail heads inland, passing fruit trees and alder bushes on an easy 1.2-mile out-and-back hike, but many hit the grassy path as part of a near-loop with the challenging 1.1-mile Anvil Trail, since trailheads for both are near the Blueberry Hill parking area on the loop road (you must cross the road to get to them). Steep and heavily rooted in sections as it climbs Schoodic Head, Anvil requires lots of rock climbing but rewards with wonderful water and island views from the rock knob overlook (side trail) for which it's named. After connecting with Schoodic Head Trail from Alder or Anvil, it's not far to the top of Schoodic Head, where expansive views of the surrounding seascape and landscape await. ✉ *Schoodic Loop Rd., Winter Harbor* ✣ *Beyond turn for Schoodic Point* ☎ *207/288–3338* 🌐 *nps.gov/acad.*

Schoodic Head Ascents

TRAIL | FAMILY | You can drive up or walk up to the 440-foot summit —the highest point in these Acadia lands—along a narrow 1-mile gravel road. It's unmarked, so watch for it 2½ miles from the start of the one-way portion of Schoodic Loop Road. Prefer an actual hiking trail? You've got options: plot your course for an easier or longer way up, or down. Starting at Schoodic Woods Campground, Buck Cove Mountain Trail—Schoodic's longest at 3.2 miles—summits its namesake before climbing Schoodic Head's north face. On the southeastern side, the challenging 1.1-mile Anvil trail links with 0.6-mile Schoodic Head Trail to the summit, as does the easy 0.6-mile Alder Trail. Trailheads for both are along the loop drive near the Blueberry Hill parking area; hikers often combine them. A bit farther is a terminus for the ½-mile East Trail; this challenging, steep climb up Schoodic Head's east face connects, near the summit, with Schoodic Head Trail. Regardless of your route, on a clear day atop Schoodic Head, spectacular views flow across the forested peninsula and island-dotted Frenchman Bay to Cadillac Mountain. ✉ *Schoodic Loop Rd.* ☎ *207/288–3338* 🌐 *nps.gov/acad.*

VISITOR CENTERS

Rockefeller Welcome Center

VISITOR CENTER | FAMILY | This impressive 1934 structure resembles a mansion but was built as housing for personnel at the U.S. Navy base that operated on Schoodic Peninsula for decades. Now part of Schoodic Institute, an Acadia-affiliated research and education nonprofit, the first floor houses a seasonal park welcome center. You can get information, watch a video about Schoodic, and check out kid-friendly exhibits about this neck of Acadia and the navy base. There's a small gift shop area. An automated fee machine inside the gatehouse at the complex's entrance sells Acadia weekly park passes. ✉ *1 Atterbury Circle, Winter Harbor* ✣ *Off Arey Cove Rd.* ☎ *207/288–3338* 🌐 *nps.gov/acad.*

Schoodic Woods Ranger Station

VISITOR CENTER | FAMILY | Built with materials from the surrounding region and opened in 2015 along with the campground here, this striking post-and-beam structure serves double duty as campground host and information center—Acadia passes and Federal Lands passes are sold. Inside, a large Schoodic District relief map centers the room, which has a gift shop area and exhibits, some hands-on, about the park. Comfy chairs flank a fireplace, inviting visitors to relax, pamphlet in hand, after chatting with a ranger or park volunteer. Outside, the setting is village-like, with walkways and handsome signage for bike paths that converge here, a stop for the free Island Explorer buses, and restrooms in a cabin-like building. Trailheads for 3.2-mile Buck Cove Mountain and 1.5-mile Lower Harbor trails are nearby. A campground amphitheater hosts ranger programs for park visitors and campers. ✉ *54 Farview Dr., Winter Harbor* ✥ *Off Schoodic Loop Rd.* ☎ *207/288–3338* 🌐 *nps.gov/acad* ⏲ *Closed late Oct.–mid-May.*

Isle Au Haut

6 miles south of Stonington via ferry.

French explorer Samuel D. Champlain discovered Isle au Haut—or "High Island"—in 1604, but native populations left heaps of oyster shells here prior to his arrival. The only ferry is a passenger-only "mail boat" out of Stonington, but the 45-minute journey is well worth the effort. Acadia National Park covers about half of the island, with miles of rugged trails, and the boat will drop visitors off in the park at Duck Harbor in peak season. The park ranger station (restroom) is a quarter mile from the Town Landing, and from there it's about 4 miles to Duck Harbor. To get there, hit the trail or walk (or bike) the unpaved road, a slightly longer but faster route. Isle au Haut has a small general store and a gift shop but no restaurants or inns, though there are vacation rentals. There's one main road: partly paved and partly unpaved, it circles the island and goes through the park.

Book a Carriage Ride

Riding down one of the park's scenic carriage roads in a horse-drawn carriage is a classic way to experience Acadia. Carriages of Acadia (🌐 *www.acadiahorses.com,* ☎ *877/276–3622*) offers rides out of Wildwood Stables in the park from late May to mid-October. Reservations are strongly recommended and can only be made by phone. There is a wheelchair-accessible carriage as well as a step stool to assist with boarding.

Sights

SCENIC STOPS

Duck Harbor

MARINA/PIER | Acadia National Park's most primitive (and therefore secluded) campground is here, as is a dock for the passenger-only ferry that serves Isle au Haut from Stonington. Duck Harbor (there's a composting toilet) is the best jumping off point for the 18 miles of trails in the park, which lead through woods and to rocky shoreline, marshes, bogs, and a freshwater lake. Note that the ferry only stops at Duck Harbor from early June through early October. Off-season or if you miss the boat, you'll be hoofing it about 4 miles to the Isle au Haut Town Landing. Bring your bike or kayak for an extra fee or rent a bike from the ferry service. *Note: Kayaks and bikes are dropped off and picked up at the Town Landing only, not at Duck Harbor.* ✉ *Duck Harbor, Isle Au Haut* ☎ *207/288–3338* 🌐 *nps.gov/acad.*

Western Head

TRAIL | Located at the southern tip of remote Isle au Haut, Western Head is accessible by foot or bicycle from the Town Landing. There are no amenities, so be sure to pack plenty of water and snacks.

Western Head Trail is most often hiked as a loop that includes Western Head Road and Cliff Trail (*bicycles are not allowed on trails*). Starting from Duck Harbor (*the ferry doesn't drop bikes off here, only at the Town Landing*) on the unpaved road, it's approximately 4 miles round-trip. Once off the wooded road, the trail alternates between forest and volcanic rock clifftop, with opportunities to go off-course and explore the rocky shoreline. Dramatic coastal cliff views are your reward for visiting perhaps the most remote corner of Acadia National Park. ✉ *Isle Au Haut* ☎ *207/288–3338* 🌐 *nps.gov/acad.*

Activities

The best way to see Acadia National Park is to get out of your vehicle and explore on foot or by bicycle or boat. There are 45 miles of carriage roads that are perfect for walking and biking in the warmer months and for cross-country skiing and snowshoeing in winter. There are more than 150 miles of trails for hiking; numerous ponds and lakes for canoeing, kayaking, standup paddle boarding, fishing, and boating; a handful of beaches for swimming; and steep cliffs for rock climbing.

BIKING

Exploring Acadia National Park on a bike can be heavenly, and there are a variety of surfaces from paved to gravel, inland to seaside; always check ahead of time for trail closures. A park pass is required to ride anywhere within park boundaries; be sure to carry your pass or leave it in view in your parked car. On carriage roads, bicyclists must yield to everyone, including horses, and not exceed 20 mph; in winter, bikes are not permitted on carriage roads groomed for cross-country skiing. Bikes are allowed on carriage roads; biking Park Loop Road during peak season is discouraged as it's narrow, often congested, and lacks shoulders. Cyclists must ride with the flow of traffic where the road is one-way. Seasonal Island Explorer buses that have four or six bike racks operate between Bar Harbor and Eagle Lake carriage road. Pick up a free carriage road map at the park's Hulls Cove Visitor Center or Nature Center, or download it from the website.

BIRD-WATCHING

Acadia National Park is for the birds—much to the enjoyment of birders of a feather from all corners. Famed ornithologist and avian illustrator Roger Tory Peterson is known to have deemed Mount Desert Island as "the warbler capital of the world." More than 20 species of the energetic and colorful songbirds breed here, while 300-plus bird species have been "encountered in or around the park," according to the National Park Service. The park's website outlines a dozen areas rich in birdwatching opportunities. Come fall, park rangers lead hawk watches from the summit of Cadillac Mountain, counting hundreds and even thousands of migrating raptors. In addition to its namesake tours, Bar Harbor Whale Watch Co. offers cruises that seek out the comically colorful seabird known as the puffin.

EDUCATIONAL PROGRAMS

The National Park Service offers a variety of ranger-led programming and tours, including the popular Junior Ranger Program for kids and, unique to Acadia National Park, citizen science opportunities at the Schoodic Institute, based at the mainland section on Schoodic Peninsula. Two ranger-led boat tours depart from Mount Desert Island. Out of Northeast Harbor, Islesford Historic and Scenic Cruise travels Somes Sounds and stops at Islesford on Little Cranberry Island to tour the park's Islesford Historic Museum. Departing from Bar Harbor, Baker Island Cruise follows the shoreline en route to Baker Island nine miles away. Passengers explore the island and check out its namesake light and an old homestead. Virtually all of Baker Island, including the lighthouse, is part of

Acadia. Baker Island doesn't have a year-round population and like Little Cranberry is part of the Cranberry Isles. *Visit the park website for more information.*

FLIGHTSEEING

Viewing the Acadia National Park region from above is a great way to get your bearings for your on-the-ground (and on-the-water) explorations, and perhaps the easiest way to wrap your arms around the sheer variety of scenery and attractions.

★ Scenic Flights of Acadia

AIR EXCURSIONS | For $144 per person, Scenic Flights of Acadia offers a 35-minute tour around the shoreline of Mount Desert Island, plus three other tours and fall foliage trips that fly over some of the island but head inland for the best color. Trips are out of Hancock County–Bar Harbor Airport. You can make reservations online or by phone; in Bar Harbor tickets are sold at Acadia Stand Up Paddle Boarding (*200 Main Street*). ✉ *1044 Bar Harbor Rd., Rte. 3, Trenton* ☎ *207/667–6527* 🌐 *www.scenicflightsofacadia.com.*

HIKING

Acadia National Park maintains more than 150 miles of hiking trails. Generally rocky and rooted, many are steep and require scrambling: most visitors find hiking here harder than expected. Even trails that aren't that difficult may take longer than you think. But there is a range of options, from easier strolls around lakes and mostly level paths to rigorous treks with climbs up rock faces and scrambles along cliffs. Whatever you have in mind, park rangers can help you plan hikes and walks that fit your abilities and time frame. Although trails are concentrated on the east side of the island, where they often connect with the park's carriage roads, the west side has plenty of scenic ones, too. For those wishing for a longer trek, try hiking up Cadillac Mountain or Dorr Mountain; Parkman, Sargeant, and Penobscot mountains are also good options. Most hiking is done mid-May–mid-November. In winter, cross-country skiing and snowshoeing replace hiking, assuming enough snow flies. Melting snow and ice can create precarious conditions in early to mid-spring.

■ TIP→ Every so often folks die in Acadia National Park, from falling off trails or cliffs or being swept out to sea. The rocky shore can be gravelly and slippery—so watch your step. In springtime, conditions may seem fine for hiking until you get on a trail where shade has kept ice and snow intact or mud lingers from snowmelt.

MULTISPORT OUTFITTERS

Name just about any popular sporting activity—kayaking, cycling, rock climbing, cross-country skiing, and snowshoeing, to say nothing of hiking—and chances are you can do it at Acadia National Park. Cadillac Mountain Sports (🌐 *www.cadillacsports.com*), with locations in Bar Harbor and Ellsworth, sells what you need to do all of them, and their staff will be happy to answer your questions and offer advice for where to go to exert yourself.

SWIMMING

The park has three swimming beaches. Sand Beach on Park Loop Road and Echo Lake Beach off Route 102 are the largest and most popular, with changing rooms and sometimes lifeguards on duty. Neither are found at Lake Wood, but its small, secluded beach is near Hulls Cove Visitor Center (the access road to the beach doesn't open until June 1).

Index

A

B

G

H

P

Q

R

S

T

U

V

W

Photo Credits

Front Cover: Pat & Chuck Blackley/ Alamy Stock Photo [**Description:** Basin Harbor Club, View of Lake Champlain and the Adirondack Mountains, Vergennes, Vermont, USA]. **Back cover, from left to right:** Sean Pavone/ iStockPhoto. SeanPavonePhoto/ iStockPhoto. Sean Pavone/ iStockPhoto. **Spine:** Patrick Perry/ iStockPhoto. **Interior, from left to right:** Kirkikis/iStockphoto (1). LorenzattoPhotos/iStockphoto (2-3). DonLand/iStockphoto (5). **Chapter 1: Experience New Egland:** Doug Lemke/Shutterstock (8-9). James Kirkikis/Shutterstock (10-11). Tanya Bird/Shutterstock (11). Vermont Elm/Shutterstock (11). QualityHD/Shutterstock (12). Oleg_P/Shutterstock (12). Courtesy of NH Tourism Board (12). Julie Czyzewski/ Shutterstock (12). Flashbacknyc/Shutterstock (13). Courtesy of Connecticut Office of Tourism (13). Eric Full/Shutterstock (14). Calvin Henderson/Shutterstock (14). Cfarmer/Dreamstime (14). Albert Pego/Shutterstock (14). Don Land/Shutterstock (15). Jejim/Shutterstock (15). Christian Delbert/Shutterstock (15). Courtesy of Mohegan Sun (15). TJ Muzeni Photography (16). Sepavo/ Dreamstime (16). Wangkun Jia/Shutterstock (17). Courtesy of Maine Office of Tourism (18). Andreas Juergensmeier/Shutterstock (18). Sara Kendall/Shutterstock (18). Cindy Creighton/Shutterstock (18). Jon Bilous/Shutterstock (19). Jiawangkun/Shutterstock (19). Mathew Trogner/ Allagash Brewing Company (22). Jimmy Emerson/Flickr (22). Kindra Clineff (22). Molly Eyres/Flickr (22). LS First Light LH (22). Mia & Steve Mestdagh/Flickr (23). Courtesy of Floís Clam Shack (23). Dan Cutrona/Courtesy of Arnoldís Lobster and Clam Bar (23). Bonmi Pan/Flickr (23). Lillian Moy (23). Agnes Kantaruk/Shutterstock (24). PunkbarbyO/Shutterstock (24). Bogdanhoda/Dreamstime (24). TravnikovStudio/ Shutterstock (24). Bhofack2/Dreamstime (24). Alexander Sviridov/Shutterstock (25). Viivien/Shutterstock (25). Dennis W Donohue/ Shutterstock (25). E.J.Johnson Photography/Shutterstock (25). Daniel Rossi Limpi/Shutterstock (25). Snehit/Shutterstock (26). Fitr/ Dreamstime (26). James Kirkikis/Shutterstock (26). John Santoro/Shutterstock (26). Leo W Kowal/Shutterstock (26). Kate Sfeir/Shutterstock (27). Albert Pego/Shutterstock (27). American Spirit/Dreamstime (27). Adam Nixon Photography/ Shutterstock (27). E.J. Johnson Photography/Shutterstock (27). Tony Baldasaro/Shutterstock (28). Enfi/Shutterstock (28). Marthas Vineyard Chamber of Commerce (28). Eric Cote/Shutterstock (29). Lucky-photographer/Shutterstock (29). Lucky-photographer/ Shutterstock (30). James Kirkikis/Shutterstock (30). Courtesy of Maine Maritime Museum (30). Jiawangkun/Shutterstock (30). Andy Duback Photography (30). TJ Muzeni Photography (31). Julie Grant/Shuttestock (31). F11photo/Shutterstock (31). Zack Frank/Shutterstock (31). Alexander Sviridov/Shutterstock (31). SamaraHeisz5/ Shutterstock (32). Xiaolin Zhang/ Shutterstock (32). Joseph Sohm/Shutterstock (32). Songquan Deng/Shutterstock (33). Ricky Batista/ Shutterstock (33). **Chapter 3: Best Fall Foliage Drives and Road Trips:** Aivoges/Dreamstime (65). Rabbit75_ist/ iStockPhoto (66-67). Michał Krakowiak/iStockphoto (69). Liliboas/iStockphoto (69). Adventure_Photo/iStockphoto (69). Steffen Foerster Photography/Shutterstock (69). magdasmith/iStockphoto (69). Michał Krakowiak/iStockphoto (69). Denis Jr. Tangney/pixels (70). Kevin Davidson/iStockphoto (70). Kindra Clineff Photography (71). DonLand/iStockphoto (72). Don land/Dreamstime (73). Denis Jr. Tangney/iStockphoto (74). Denis Jr. Tangney/ iStockphoto (75). Romiana Lee/Shutterstock (76). Joe Tabacca/Shutterstock (77). Kindra Clineff/Rhode Island (78). Public Domain (79). Sharan Singh/iStockphoto (80). Leesniderphotoimages/Dreamstime (81). Denis Tangney Jr./iStockphoto (82). Jill_InspiredByDesign/iStockphoto (83). Dr Pospisil/Shutterstock (84). The Wilhelm Reich Infant Trust (85). Luckydoor/Dreamstime (86). **Chapter 4: Boston and Environs:** Sepavo/ Dreamstime (87). F11photo/Dreamstime (107). Mbastos/Dreamstime (115). Janniswerner/iStockphoto (124). Ken Sawyer/ Peabody Essex Museum (135). **Chapter 5: Cape Cod, Martha's Vineyard and Nantucket:** Lunamarina/Dreamstime (141). Denis Jr. Tangney/ iStockphoto (144). Kenneth Wiedemann/iStockphoto (145). Kindra Clineff Photography/Coast Guard Beach, Eastham, Cape Cod, Massachusetts (145). Kindra Clineff/Cape Cod Museum of Natural History (159). Massachusetts Office Of Travel & Tourism/Flickr (165). Guido Caroti/Audubon Wellfleet Bay Wildlife Sanctuary (181). Lhalvorsen/Dreamstime (205). Kindra Clineff Photography/Nantucket, Steps Beach (209). **Chapter 6: The Berkshires and Western Massachusetts:** Denis Tangney Jr./iStockphoto (215). Sterling and Francine Clark Art Institute, Williamstown, Massachusetts (225). Denis Jr. Tangney/iStockphoto (230) Sandrafoyt/Dreamstime (249). Kindra Clineff

Photo Credits

Photography_Deerfield VillageMassachusetts (256). **Chapter 7: Connecticut:** Sean Pavone/Shutterstock (259). Alex Nason/Norwalk Maritime Aquarium (272). Sean Pavone/Shutterstock (289). Kindra Clineff Photography/Connecticut River Tidelands (308). Sphraner/Dreamstime (313). **Chapter 8: Rhode Island:** JJM Photography/Shutterstock (321). Luckyphotographer/Dreamstime (337). Hotcore (360). Discovernewport (360-361). Carolyn M Carpenter/Shutterstock (360). The Preservation Society of Newport County/Nemanett (360). The Preservation Society of Newport County (362). Library of Congress (362). Kindra Clineff (363). Library of Congress Prints and Photographs Division (363). Public domain (363). Science History Images/Alamy Stock Photo (363). Frymire Archive/Alamy (363). The Preservation Society of Newport County (364). Sergio Orsanigo (365). The Preservation Society of Newport County (365). Travel Bug/Shutterstock (365). Public Domain (373). Lee Snider Photo Images/Dreamstime (375). Cumnonchai/ Shutterstock (378). Matthew Huang/iStockphoto (385). Tupungato/Shutterstock (387). **Chapter 9: Vermont:** Sean Pavone/iStockphoto (399). Alizada Studios/Shutterstock (411). Vtphotos/Dreamstime (418). Simon Pearce (431). DaleBHalbur/iStockphoto (434). Jonathan A. Mauer/Shutterstock (447). Don Landwehrle/Shutterstock (455). Skye Chalmers Photography (456). FashionStock.com/ Shutterstock (457). Hubert Schriebl (457). Marcio Silva/iStockphoto (450). Hubert Schriebl (458). Smugglers Notch Resort/Ski Vermont (459). Okemo Mountain Resort (460). Sean Pavone/iStockphoto (475). Sean Pavone/shutterstock (481). Meg M/ Shutterstock (484). **Chapter 10: New Hampshire:** Sepavo/Dreamstime (487). Edella/ Dreamstime (498). Denis Tangney Jr/iStockphoto (502). Denis Tangney Jr./iStockphoto (510). Zack Frank/Shutterstock (513). Kindra Clineff/Lake Winnipesaukee (515). Appalachianviews/ Dreamstime (530). Liz Van Steenburgh/Shutterstock (541). Blacklist Mauer/Dreamstime (541). Jim Lozouski/Shutterstock (542). REI/Mike Kautz, Courtesy of AMC (543). Nialat/Shutterstock (544). RestonImages/Shutterstock (544). Nialat/Shutterstock (544). Jadimages/Shutterstock (545). Rebvt/Shutterstock (545). Ansgar Walk/wikipedia (545). J. Carmichael/wikipedia (545). Matty Symons/Shutterstock (547). Danita Delimont/Alamy (548). MRicart_Photography/ Shutterstock (549). Jet Lowe/Wikimedia Commons (560). George Carmichael (566). **Chapter 11: Inland Maine:** E.J.Johnson Photography/Shutterstock (575). Mountinez/ iStockphoto (590). Kazela/Shutterstock (605). **Chapter 12: The Maine Coast:** Visit Maine (609). Kirkikisphoto/Dreamstime (622). Lewis Directed Films/Shutterstock (629). James Mattil/Shutterstock (636). Flashbacknyc/Shutterstock (656). Sean Pavone/Shutterstock (657). Maine State Museum (658). Allan Wood Photography/Shutterstock (658). Paul D. Lemke/iStockphoto (659). Bill Florence/Shutterstock (660). Robert Campbell (661). Casey Jordan (661). Dave Johnston (661). Paul Dionne/iStockphoto (662). Doug Lemke/Shutterstock (662). Imel9000/iStockphoto (662). Spwidoff/Shutterstock (667). Kindra Clineff/Desert Island,Southwest Harbor (687). Kindra Clineff Photography/Down East,Jonesport,Wild Blueberry Harvest (695). **Chapter 13: Acadia National Park:** Try Media/iStockphoto (703). f11photo/Shutterstock (716). **About Our Writers:** All photos are courtesy of the writers.

*Every effort has been made to trace the copyright holders, and we apologize in advance for any accidental errors. We would be happy to apply the corrections in the following edition of this publication.

Notes

Fodor's NEW ENGLAND

Publisher: Stephen Horowitz, *General Manager*

Editorial: Douglas Stallings, *Editorial Director;* Jill Fergus, Amanda Sadlowski, *Senior Editors;* Brian Eschrich, Alexis Kelly, *Editors;* Angelique Kennedy-Chavannes, *Assistant Editor*

Design: Tina Malaney, *Director of Design and Production;* Jessica Gonzalez, *Senior Designer;* Erin Caceres, *Graphic Design Associate*

Production: Jennifer DePrima, *Editorial Production Manager;* Elyse Rozelle, *Senior Production Editor;* Monica White, *Production Editor*

Maps: Rebecca Baer, *Senior Map Editor*; Mark Stroud (Moon Street Cartography) and David Lindroth, *Cartographers*

Photography: Viviane Teles, *Senior Photo Editor;* Namrata Aggarwal, Neha Gupta, Payal Gupta, Ashok Kumar, *Photo Editors;* Eddie Aldrete, *Photo Production Intern;* Kadeem McPherson, *Photo Production Associate Intern*

Business and Operations: Chuck Hoover, *Chief Marketing Officer;* Robert Ames, *Group General Manager*

Public Relations and Marketing: Joe Ewaskiw, *Senior Director of Communications and Public Relations*

Fodors.com: Jeremy Tarr, *Editorial Director;* Rachael Levitt, *Managing Editor*

Technology: Jon Atkinson, *Director of Technology;* Rudresh Teotia, *Associate Director of Technology;* Alison Lieu, *Project Manager*

Writers: Diane Bair, Jordan Barry, Andrew Collins, Bob Curley, Cheryl Fenton, Alexandra Hall, Leigh Harrington, Lindsey Hollenbaugh, Jessica Kelly, Kim Foley MacKinnon, Annie Quigley, Christine Burns Rudalevige, Mary Ruoff, Mimi Steadman, Jane E. Zarem

Editor: Alexis Kelly

Production Editor: Jennifer DePrima

35th Edition

ISBN 978-1-64097-580-4

ISSN 0192-3412

SPECIAL SALES
This book is available at special discounts for bulk purchases for sales promotions or premiums. For more information, e-mail SpecialMarkets@fodors.com.

PRINTED IN THE UNITED STATES OF AMERICA

10 9 8 7 6 5 4 3 2 1

About Our Writers

Diane Bair is an award-winning travel journalist whose work has appeared in national magazines, online, and in major daily newspapers, including frequent stories for *The Boston Globe.* She's also co-authored (with Pamela Wright) more than two dozen books on travel, outdoor recreation, and wildlife-watching. Seeing all of the inhabited Caribbean islands is a life goal and she's getting close to reaching it. She updated the Cape Cod, Martha's Vineyard, and Nantucket chapter. Follow her on Instagram @dianebairtravel.

Jordan Barry is a food writer for *Seven Days,* an alt-weekly newspaper based in Burlington, Vermont. She previously produced podcasts for Heritage Radio Network and Food52, and researched language development in the American cider industry as part of a master's degree in food studies at New York University. Barry grew up in Norman Rockwell's Arlington and now lives in Vergennes, Vermont's smallest city. You can follow her @jordankbarry. She updated the Vermont chapter.

Former Fodor's staff editor **Andrew Collins** is based in Mexico City, but spends much of his time in a small village in New Hampshire's Lake Sunapee region. A long-time contributor to more than 200 Fodor's guidebooks, he's also written for dozens of mainstream and LGBTQ publications including *Travel + Leisure, New Mexico Magazine, AAA Living,* and *The Advocate.* In addition, Collins teaches travel writing and food writing for New York City's Gotham Writers Workshop. Follow him on Instagram @TravelAndrew or at 🌐 AndrewsTraveling.com. He updated the Experience and Travel Smart chapters.

Bob Curley is a Rhode Island-based freelance writer and editor with more than 20 years of experience covering his home state as well as writing about travel to the Caribbean and other international and U.S. destinations. The author of three travel guidebooks, Bob also writes about a variety of other topics including healthcare, architecture and interior design, snow sports, and sailing. He updated the Rhode Island chapter.

Lindsey Hollenbaugh is a managing editor of content engagement for *The Berkshire Eagle.* A native of upstate New York, she has a journalism degree from Ithaca College and has also worked at the Albany *Times Union* and *The Post-Star.* She lives in Pittsfield, Massachusetts, with her husband and son, where they enjoy spending summers on The Lawn at Tanglewood and hiking the many trails in the area in the fall. Find her on Twitter @Lhollenbaugh. She updated the Berkshires and Western Massachusetts chapter.

Jessica Kelly is a food and travel journalist and photographer living in New York. Her work has appeared in *Condé Nast Traveler, Global Traveler, Elite Traveler, Insider, Wine Enthusiast, Kitchn, AAA World Magazine, Cosmopolitan, Food 52, Eater, Food & Wine,* Thrillist, *Bon Appétit,* Matador Network, *Hemispheres*, Lonely Planet, and more. You can follow her @Adventures.Are.Waiting. She updated parts of the Vermont chapter.

About Our Writers

Freelance writer and former newspaper reporter **Mary Ruoff** has written travel articles about her adopted state for the *Portland Press Herald* and other publications. During her career, she's covered many other subjects too, including shoe retailing, veterans, and locally grown foods. A St. Louis native, Mary has several journalism awards and a bachelor of journalism from Missouri School of Journalism. Her go-to Mainer is her husband, Michael Hodsdon, a mariner and grandson of a Down East fisherman. They live in Belfast. She updated Inland Maine, Acadia National Park, and parts of Maine Coast.

Jane E. Zarem, a Connecticut native, is a regular contributor to Fodor's travel publications. She has covered regional areas for *Fodor's New England* and several islands for Fodor's Caribbean coverage; she also authored *Fodor's InFocus Barbados and Saint Lucia*. In the past, she contributed to *Fodor's USA*, *Fodor's Cape Cod & the Islands*, *Fodor's Bahamas*, and various Fodor's guides focused on adventure vacations, healthy escapes, and weekend travel. Jane updated the Connecticut chapter.

The Boston chapter was updated by **Cheryl Fenton, Kim Foley MacKinnon,** and **Leigh Harrington.**

The Maine Coast chapter was updated by **Andrew Collins, Alexandra Hall, Annie Quigley, Christine Burns Rudalevige, Mary Ruoff,** and **Mimi Steadman.**